D1789454

Greek Waters Pilot

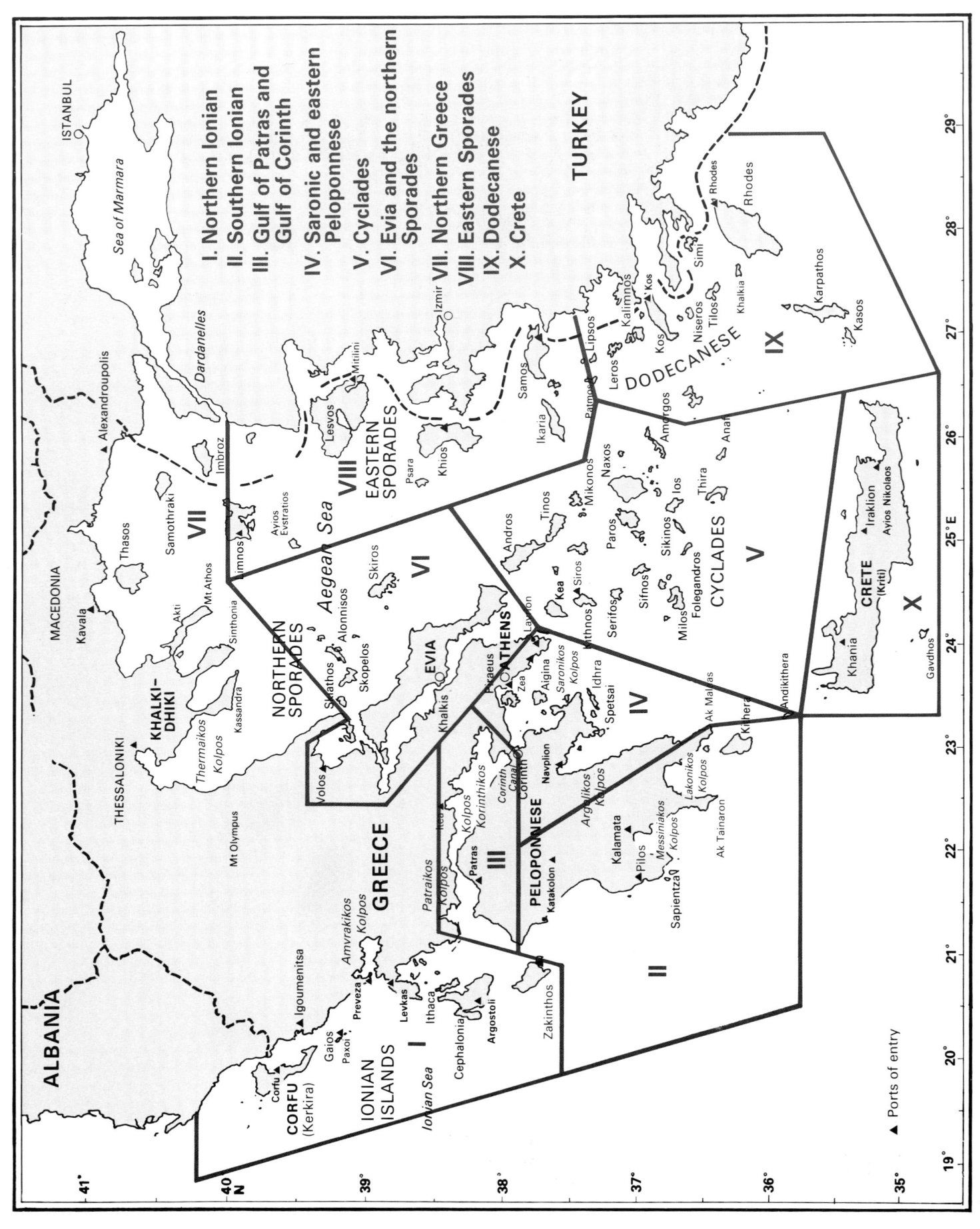

I. Northern Ionian
II. Southern Ionian
III. Gulf of Patras and Gulf of Corinth
IV. Saronic and eastern Peloponnese
V. Cyclades
VI. Evia and the northern Sporades
VII. Northern Greece
VIII. Eastern Sporades
IX. Dodecanese
X. Crete

▲ Ports of entry

Greek Waters Pilot

A yachtsman's guide to the coasts and islands of Greece

ROD HEIKELL

Imray Laurie Norie & Wilson Ltd
St Ives Cambridgeshire England

Published by
Imray, Laurie, Norie & Wilson Ltd
Wych House, St Ives, Huntingdon, Cambridgeshire, PE17 4BT,
England ☎+44 (0)1480 462114 *Fax* +44(0)1480 496109
1994

All rights reserved. No part of this publication may be reproduced,
transmitted or used in any form by any means – graphic, electronic or
mechanical, including photocopying, recording, taping or information
storage and retrieval systems or otherwise – without the prior
permission of the Publishers.

© Rod Heikell 1992
1st edition 1982, Revised reprint 1983
2nd edition 1985
3rd edition 1987
4th edition 1990
5th edition 1992
6th edition 1994
This work has been corrected to September 1994.

A catalogue record for this book is available from the British Library.

ISBN 0 85288 280 7

CAUTION
While every care has been taken to ensure accuracy, neither the
Publishers nor the Author will hold themselves responsible for errors,
omissions or alterations in this publication. They will at all times be
grateful to receive information which tends to the improvement of the
work.

CORRECTIONAL SUPPLEMENTS
Imray pilot books are amended at intervals by the issue of
correctional supplements. Supplements, if available, are
supplied free of charge with the books when they are
purchased. Further supplements are available from the
publishers. The following should be quoted:

1. Name of book
2. Date of edition (above)
3. Date of last supplement (if applicable)
4. Name and address to which supplement should be
   sent on a stamped addressed A4 envelope.

Printed in Great Britain at The Bath Press, Avon

Contents

Prefaces

I didn't sit down one day to conceive of and write this book. Like many books and like Topsy 'it just growed' over a number of years until it emerged the conglomerate collection of information you see now. To organise the information for the harbour plans from my muddled filing system was easier than I imagined but to write the text required a real effort of willpower. Over one winter and between the geographical extremes of Corfu and Pin Mill in Suffolk I laboured over the text and managed to establish the framework for the book. In the spring of 1980 I devoted myself full-time to the task. I packed up the embryo text and took it down to Greece where I spent a year sailing and writing.

The first harbour plans were drawn while I was a flotilla skipper in the Saronic Gulf. Tired of describing a particular harbour approach, one morning I resolved to sit down and draw up a set of harbour plans for the area and have them photocopied. This put me into a fever over the next month, sounding harbours and pacing off breakwaters until I had drawn all the harbours visited. The company I worked for was impressed and suggested I draw up plans for the other areas they operated in. Since that time the local Greeks have been mystified by this crazy yachtsman who persists in fishing in their harbours with no hooks on his line and an extra large sinker...

One of my enduring problems over and above the actual harbour plans has been somehow to convey my impressions, feelings, love – if you like – of modern Greece. I say modern Greece because if you come here expecting to find the cradle of western civilization lying like an open book waiting to be read then you come on a false journey. You have to dig beneath modern Greece for that. After so many hundreds of years of invasion – the Turks, Franks, Venetians, Slavs, Romans – after such cultural bombardment, the Greeks could not remain the nation they were more than 2000 years ago. And yet for all that Greece remains somehow quintessentially Greek. You can see it in that quality of light that silences the artist. You can see the remains of a perfect form and siting of architecture. You can see it in the modern meeting place, the coffee shop, where everything from a new brand of cigarettes to the relative merits of government is being passionately argued. Beneath the surface the ancients are still there.

I first sailed into Greece in *Roulette*, a twenty-foot, hard chine plywood boat that had brought me safely from England in little over six months. At the time I never planned to stay long but the sailing was good, it was cheap, and I found a little work with a charter company to top up the money bank. Before long, six months had passed and it was winter. I sailed my yacht back to Levkas and laid her up determined to find some way of sailing and earning a living in Greece. As it turned out it was less difficult than I had anticipated. I found a job skippering a flotilla fleet around the Saronic Gulf and began drawing my first harbour plans for that company. In the winter I sailed *Roulette* for the last time before selling her to buy another boat. This was a modern twenty-eight foot glass fibre sloop I named *Fiddlers Green* after that rather bawdy vision of heaven sailors of old knew of, where jugs of ales grow on trees and women are comely and free. I sailed *Fiddlers Green* down to Greece in a very cold winter in time to skipper another flotilla fleet for the season around the Ionian.

About this time the idea of writing a cruising guide on Greece using my harbour plans as the backbone of the book began to emerge. Was I really qualified? Certainly there were others who had spent longer than I cruising around Greece. I got out my folio of plans and with some surprise I found I had covered a good two thirds of the harbours. Many of these I had visited either while skippering or while delivering boats around Greece. I suspect I made up my mind then to write the book and to take a year off to visit those harbours I hadn't been to and to revisit some I only dimly recollected.

In March 1980 I left Corfu and sailed down the western coast of the Peloponnese to Crete and thence to the Dodecanese where I left *Fiddlers Green* and went back to the Ionian to deliver a friend's yacht, *Supermac*, to Kos. En route I dawdled around the Cyclades exploring harbours and anchorages there. For some time we sailed together around Turkey and the Dodecanese before I sailed *Supermac* back to Levkas and returned to *Fiddlers Green*. Continuing up the coast of Turkey I explored the eastern Sporades, northern Greece and the northern Sporades. By December I was on Evia and it was time to get back to Levkas in time for Christmas with friends. The groundwork was done and the task of organising the new information remained.

Now the book is finished and I hope that the following will not only assist you to discover the coasts and islands, harbours and anchorages, but will also pass on my impressions of Greece. Greece is changing and yet it has never changed. Henry Miller got it just right when he visited Greece forty years ago:

'Somehow, almost as if He were nodding, Greece still remains under the protection of the Creator. Men may go about their puny, ineffectual bedevilment, even in Greece, but God's magic is still at work and, no matter what the

race of man may do or try to do, Greece is still a sacred precinct – and my belief is it will remain so until the end of time.'
Henry Miller *The Colossus of Maroussi*

Rod Heikell
London
1981

Acknowledgements
Much of the information in this edition is from my own wandering around Greece in *Tetra*, but as always there are thankfully others out there keeping an eye on what is going on in Greek waters. To those of you who contributed information my thanks. In particular my thanks to Joe Charlton in Levkas for the loan of his *Norfos* and to Robyn for shelter; to Alan Wilkinson for his peripatic gleanings and patient editing; to Michael Manton of S.Y. *Amber Witch*; to Julian Blatchley in the lightning quick *Van de Stadt*; to Graham and Katrina Sewell of S.Y. *Songline*; to Nigel Patten for information and climbing to the top of the highest parts of Greece to take photographs; Rear Admiral D C Jenkin; R K Sapey; Claude Mauge, accomplished wine taster for the area; Michael Bell; G Beets; Barry Nielson; and to Jill, Jo, and Debbie in the drawing office at Imrays. As always Willie Wilson organised everything into the book you hold in your hands. The errors (and I try to keep them to the mimimum) are mine.
Rod Heikell
Homps, France 1994

Also by Rod Heikell
Imray Mediterranean Almanac (Editor)
Mediterranean France and Corsica - A sea guide
Italian Waters Pilot
Turkish Waters & Cyprus Pilot
Mediterranean Cruising Handbook
The Danube - A river guide
The Turquoise Coast of Turkey NET
Ionian Tetra Publications Ltd
Mediterranean Sailing A & C Black Ltd
Saronic Tetra Publications Ltd.

Author's note A large number of photocopies of my books circulate around the eastern Mediterranean. For those of you sitting and reading a photocopy of this book, I suggest you reflect on the fact that you forfeit your own moral basis for objecting to any theft from yourself and your boat. You have after all stolen something from me and my publishers, both in a moral and legal sense, so when you have something stolen, think about how it feels. To those of you who buy the book, my thanks.
RJH

Introduction

Yacht and equipment

Engines

A reliable engine is necessary for motoring through the inevitable calms a yacht will encounter. On other occasions a powerful engine will be required to motor against the strong winds and short steep seas of the Mediterranean to get into harbour. A petrol engine, whether inboard or outboard, can be dangerous in the Mediterranean where the high temperatures cause petrol to vaporize easily and the risk of an explosion and fire is a constant risk.

Ventilation

Most British-built yachts have inadequate ventilation for the hot Mediterranean. Extra skylights and vents and additional insulation can help solve the problem. An air scoop to funnel air down the front hatch is an excellent investment and will repay its modest cost tenfold. Make your own or buy one of the commercially produced scoops on the market.

Shaded and cool. Permanent bimini over the cockpit and a wind scoop to keep things cool down below.

Refrigerator

A refrigerator is considered by many to be a necessity in the Mediterranean. If it is going to draw power from your batteries it may be necessary to install an additional battery and revise your charging methods – a refrigerator is estimated to use around 50–60% of the total power consumption on yachts. The heat absorption and thermoelectric types do not work well in the high ambient temperatures in the Mediterranean. The type having a compressor working off the batteries (high current drain) or off the engine (expensive to purchase and install) with a holding plate work the best. As a general rule most refrigerators do not have adequate insulation – 10 cm/4 inches should be the minimum. Get the top opening type so the cold air does not fall out every time the refrigerator is opened.

Ice

Large blocks of ice or ice cubes can be bought in many places. Many fishing boats use ice either to supplement their own refrigeration systems or as the sole means of keeping the catch cold on smaller boats. In most harbours there is an ice factory which supplies the fishing boats and it is usually a simple matter to locate the 'ice-man' or the local supplier. Some of the ice contains chemicals to keep it solid longer and is unsuitable for consumption in drinks. In some of the larger harbours used regularly by yachts ice cubes, suitable for those all-important cold drinks, can be found.

Using ice, whether in blocks or in cubes, is the cheapest way of keeping food cool and at the height of summer helps out refrigeration systems which are usually struggling to keep things cold.

Shower

A shower is useful inside a yacht, but in the Mediterranean it is perhaps more useful if it can be used outside on deck or in the cockpit to wash off after swimming in the sea. Larger water tanks or even a separate water tank may be required. A cheap alternative is a pressurised garden spray unit. Replace the spray head with a shower rose, pump it up, and you have a portable and economical shower unit. The sun-shower, basically a black plastic bag with a shower rose attached that you haul up on a halyard, works well – but beware of the water getting too hot.

Anchors

Preference for different anchors varies with the individual but the following information may be useful for coping with the different types of bottom found near Greek coasts. Often the bottom will be hard sand covered with thick weed and some anchors have difficulty penetrating the weed and digging in. It is common practice to go astern once the anchor is down to ensure it bites. Otherwise the anchor could be caught on weed or just be sitting on the bottom until a puff of wind blows you astern and the anchor drags.

Bruce A good main anchor. It holds well, even on a short scope, and is good over a range of different holding ground. Some people have reported difficulties getting the Bruce to dig through thick weed. It will sometimes collect a clump of weed and must be raised to clear it.

CQR A good main anchor. Holds well in mud and sand though it will sometimes pull through soft mud. In weed it will often pick up a clump on the point and must be raised to clear it.

Delta A new anchor similar to the CQR, but with no moving parts. Its one-piece construction makes it strong and it has been designed to turn itself over to a holding position however it lands.

Danforth Good for getting through weed, but like the CQR picks up weed easily. My favourite for a kedge.

Fortress A new Danforth lookalike, but constructed of aluminium and therefore very light. This anchor defies the long-held notion that an anchor must be heavy to hold and in my experience works well with the advantage that it is easy to lay from a dinghy.

Fisherman Excellent for getting through weed but doesn't have the holding power of the plough types. However it will hold on rocky bottoms, in thick weed, and on very soft bottoms where other anchors don't get through. A good alternative to the Danforth for a kedge.

Grapnel types The folding grapnel anchors which can be bought in England are useless except on a rocky bottom. A few yachtsmen swear by the large grapnels used by the Greeks but I have never found them to be very good.

Berthing lines

It is useful to have two stout lines made up for the stern lines when mooring stern-to. A short loop of chain on the end of the line which can be dropped over a bollard (or unfastened with a carbine clip or shackle to go through a mooring loop) will reduce chafe on the line. However care is needed not to brain bystanders or anyone helping you to berth when throwing the lines ashore. The line should be fairly heavy as the surges which can develop in some harbours with gale force winds can be greater than those encountered in many other cruising grounds.

Gas

In most of the larger towns *Camping Gaz* can be obtained, but it may be difficult to find in the islands where stocks of full canisters can run down and not be replenished for weeks. If a yacht is fitted with Calor Gas type bottles an adaptor can be bought in Greece to take Greek gas bottles. As elsewhere the common practice is to change the old empty bottle for a full new one. If staying for an extended period

and if a lot of gas is used for a refrigerator, hot water, heating and cooking, then it is worth changing over to Greek gas which is comparatively cheap. There are gas filling stations at Gouvia, Preveza, Kalamata, Piraeus, Kalamata and Iraklion.

Paraffin

It is getting more and more difficult to find paraffin as the ubiquitous bottled gas takes over. It is normally sold by one dealer in a village or town and his shop can be anything from a general grocery shop to a bulk wine dealer. Ask for *petroleon katharon*. Methylated spirit is easily obtained in grocery shops.

Yacht spares

Much yacht equipment is now available in Greece or can be ordered now that Greece is part of the EU. On the whole the cost of equipment is only marginally more than in many of the other EU countries. Any equipment shipped or mailed to Greece is subject to Greek VAT. Locally produced goods can often be used instead of imported goods – especially paint, adhesives, sealants, bronze and stainless steel gear like cleats and fairleads, batteries, cordage – and small engineering works are good at making boat bits and pieces.

Antifouling

A yacht bottom fouls more quickly in the warm waters of the Mediterranean than it would in more northerly waters. Consequently a more potent antifouling must be used. Eroding antifoulings such as International *Micron*, Blake's, and Hempel's *Blue* work well as long as your boat is moving and not sitting still at anchor or berthed for long periods when the build up of weed and coral worm overcomes the antifouling's ability to erode itself and rubbing down just takes the antifouling off. Hard scrubbable antifoulings like Blake's tin-free *Tiger*, Hempel's *Hard Racing* and Veneziani *Hard Antifouling* work well and although they tend to foul more quickly than eroding antifoulings, they can be satisfactorily rubbed down without removing all the antifouling. Local antifouling of the soft type (*TransOcean* is popular and works well) is widely available, cheap, and effective – you cannot of course rub it down through the season, but generally for an eight-month sailing season and four months on the hard I find it copes well with fouling just beginning in the eighth month. If you haul every winter then in terms of cost effectiveness the local soft antifouling is difficult to beat – working out at around one third the cost or less of more sophisticated antifoulings.

Gang planks (passerelles)

They can be an elaborate affair or simply a plank. Make sure the halyard supporting the end is beefy enough and comes off a substantial mast – I've seen a few mizzens with an unnatural curve to them.

Awnings

A good sun awning is a necessary piece of boat equipment in the Mediterranean. Much of your time will be spent in the cockpit and the awning should be designed to be a comfortable height above the cockpit seats and ideally should have side curtains for when the sun is low in the evening. Make the awning from dark coloured canvas as light coloured materials cause an uncomfortable glare and nylon or Terylene materials flap and crack in the slightest breeze.

A permanent awning rigged over the cockpit along the lines of the Bimini hood common in the Caribbean keeps you cool not only in harbour, but when sailing or motoring as well.

Navigation

A yacht will require no more navigation equipment than would be used around the English coast and in all probability will use less in practice. Apart from a steering compass, hand-bearing compass, and a log, little else is required.

A radio direction finder is useful but the RDF beacons should not be relied upon. Most of the beacons are for aircraft and the frequencies and the hours of operation can change without warning.

A depth-sounder is useful although after a while when you have become adept at judging depths in the clear water (it is not uncommon to see the bottom at 7–10 metres) it will be redundant except in murky water or at night. However remember it takes a little time to become adept at judging the depth visually. As a general rule deep blue is 15 metres plus, turquoise is 10 metres, green is 5 metres, and brown is rock just below the water. Colours vary with the type of bottom and in places fine silt in the water reduces visibility.

A VHF radio is useful for talking to other yachts, but in my and others' experience it has been difficult, if not impossible, to elicit a reply from Hellas Radio. Perhaps more useful would be a ham radio; these are now very compact and do not drain batteries to the extent the old sets did. I know of one businessman on a yacht in Greece who calls up on his ham set once a week to make sure his small business is still ticking over and supplying him with the income to carry on cruising.

Electronic navigation aids

The new breed of electronic navigation equipment has revolutionized position finding, but some care is needed if you are using it in Greece.

Loran C Although the technology is dated compared to satellite position-finding systems, nonetheless good accuracy can be obtained throughout most of the Mediterranean with a little care. In the SE Mediterranean you are on the limits of signal reception and around the SE Aegean there is a hole in the coverage covering the sea area around Kos, Rhodes, and the E tip of Crete. It has to be one of the cheapest electronic position-finding systems (excepting RDF) for the Mediterranean with receivers costing from £300 in the lower range.

Accuracy varies, but is normally within 0·1 mile to 0·5 mile when the relevant offsets are included. The latitude is usually within 0·1 mile with the longitude giving the maximum error. Like RDF or any radio signals, care is needed at dawn and dusk when the signals can be refracted and inaccurate fixes result.

Transit (Satnav) Good satellite passes will give you an accuracy in the Mediterranean comparable to that obtained elsewhere. Accuracy appears to be within 200–500 metres with good satellite fixes. The life of the transit satellites appears to extend some time into the late 1990s.

GPS (Navstar) This new satellite position-finding system is now up and running after some initial hiccups. The cost of receivers is plummeting all the time with bottom end receivers costing around £400 at the time of writing. With an accuracy of around 100 metres in its degraded form, GPS provides the most accurate position-finding system going. However this very accuracy can at times be a positive danger (see below).

Chart plotters A number of yachts are fitting chart plotters which when interfaced to an electronic position-finding system show a yacht's position on a chart. The problem with chart plotters is the difficulty of storing the charts; they require a large memory, and so in practice small-scale charts are scanned and then blown up on the screen to get a larger scale. Consequently much information normally on a large-scale chart will not be displayed on a blown-up small-scale chart. In addition the problems outlined below are exacerbated on electronic charts where an electronically derived 'real' position is displayed on a cartographically inaccurate chart.

Radar Now radar is more compact and more economical with your amps, it can be used as a useful navigation tool. Its great value is in reproducing a map of what is, rather than a latitude and longitude that you then plot on an (inaccurate) chart.

A caution Most of the charts for Greece were surveyed in the 19th century using celestial fixes and basic triangulation techniques. Subsequent observations have shown considerable errors, in some cases up to 1½ minutes of longitude. While you may know your latitude and longitude to within 100–200 metres, the chart you are plotting it on may contain errors of up to 1½ miles though normally less. The practice of including the datum point for a chart and an offset to be used with electronic position-finding equipment only confuses a very complicated picture because the old charts have varying inaccuracies over the area they cover. For instance one cape may be out by ½ a mile whereas another cape on the same chart may be out by 1½ miles. The solution to the problem lies in the hands of the relevant hydrographic authorities who could use satellite-derived photographs to resurvey the areas and produce new charts – however this seems unlikely to happen in the near future and so we are left with what amounts to basically 19th-century charts patched up here and there as best the hydrographic departments are able. The problem is further complicated because the old 19th-century 'fathoms' charts are being metricated and so look like new surveys – even when the attribution is to a Greek survey, the basis for the chart will still have been the original Admiralty 19th-century survey.

It hardly needs to be stated that you should exercise great caution in the vicinity of land or hazards to navigation – eyeball navigation rules OK.

Fuel

Where fuel is shown in the pilotage notes as being close to or on the quay I am referring in most cases to diesel fuel. In some cases petrol will also be available, but usually you will have to go to a petrol station in the town to obtain it.

Duty-free fuel can be obtained in some places although the hassle involved means it is only worthwhile doing so for reasonably large amounts. Duty-free fuel is approximately half the price of fuel obtained at normal pump prices. The fuel supplier will usually only supply 300 or more litres at duty-free prices and even then will moan at the paperwork involved. To obtain duty-free fuel you must take a slip from the bank (showing you have changed foreign currency into drachmae) to customs who will issue you with a 'pink slip'. The fuel supplier is then contacted, customs approve the purchase and annotate the 'pink slip' for the cost of the duty-free fuel, and you get the fuel. EU yachts require a transit log to obtain duty-free fuel. There are numerous pitfalls along the way including customs denying the existence of a 'pink slip', the supplier refusing outright to supply duty-free fuel, and the supplier getting onto his buddy in customs to stall the whole process. Some ports are better than others for the ease with which duty-free fuel can be obtained and the procedure does require persistence.

Water

The English quarrel about the respective merits of different beers, the French about wines, and the Greeks about water. Water is important above all else in Greece and to abuse it is to insult it. In many of the islands and some mainland areas water is in short supply. Towards the end of the summer is the most critical period and at this time some places which normally have water will turn off public supply points.

In most harbours a local is appointed as the 'water-man' who controls the water and charges for it. The charges for water are normally fixed by the local

Facilities for grubby sailors in Vasiliki on Levkas.

council, but usually vary according to what the 'water-man' thinks he can get. Ask beforehand and if the charge seems excessive, haggle a bit. In some harbours a local entrepreneur will truck water in and in this case there is no fixed charge and the cost will inevitably be higher because of the costs of operating a tanker service. A length of hosepipe (about 25 metres) with a selection of connectors is useful for refilling the water tanks.

The water is nearly always safe to drink except where a sign states otherwise or in a few places I have mentioned. To any water of doubtful quality add the requisite number of proprietary water-purifying tablets (such as *Puritabs*) or a little bleach solution or potassium permanganate.

It is now possible to buy bottled water all over Greece though I don't encourage it. It is an affectation encouraged by the bottling companies that does not reflect upon the quality of most of the tap water available. Enough thoroughly obnoxious plastic mineral water bottles already litter the seas and shores of Greece and as far as I am concerned the practice of drinking bottled mineral water should be actively discouraged.

The recent mild and dry winters in Europe have meant that summer water supplies in the Mediterranean have been steadily eroded. At one point in the summer of 1990 Athens had only two days' supply of water left in the reservoirs and in 1991 water rationing was again imposed. Though many optimistically pin their hopes on a mini-climatic aberration that will right itself in a few years, evidence for the 'greenhouse effect' continues to accumulate and if this is so then water poverty in the Mediterranean will become a fact of life. Already I see yachtsmen, both local and foreign, surreptitiously washing their boats down when there is a ban on this activity, and they have only themselves to blame if they are denied water altogether. In recent years small communities have denied yachtsmen water because the precious stuff is in short supply and yachtsmen have abused it. It is an insult to wash your boat down when the supplies in a small village may not last the summer and just because you are paying for it, don't assume you can abuse it. I can see the day when reverse osmosis water makers become a common piece of equipment on board cruising yachts.

Hauling out

All over Greece there are local boat yards which haul out *caïques* on a sledge and runners. A yacht can be hauled out in this fashion and although it is primitive, I do not know of any yacht which has been badly damaged by the method. There are travel-hoists at Salamis, Perama, Gaidhouromandra (Olympic), Leros and Rhodes. A number of yards also use hydraulic trailers to haul yachts. No doubt as yacht facilities are improved there will be additional travel-hoists introduced, but in my experience the old method is just as safe and somewhat cheaper. Shop around for a hauling-out price as they vary considerably.

Popular places for hauling out are as follows: Corfu, Levkas, Nidri, Katakolon, Patras, Kalamaki, Lavrion (Gaidhouromandra), Aigina, Spetsai, Porto Kheli, Volos, Leros, Rhodes and Iraklion.

Berthing

In all harbours you will normally go stern-to or bows-to the quay with an anchor laid out from the quay or mole. Going stern-to or bows-to rather than alongside prevents vermin and insects, particularly cockroaches, coming on board and avoids damage to a yacht from wash or surge in the harbour. Even if there is room to go alongside it is nearly always better to go stern or bows-to.

Hauling the old fashioned way on a sledge and runners – it looks primitive but it works just as well as more modern methods. Levkas.

It takes some skill to go stern-to, especially if there is a strong crosswind and a narrow gap to fit into between other yachts. Always have plenty of fenders out and when close to the quay warp the yacht into place rather than using the engine. For yachts up to 10–13 metres long it is easier to go bows-to as a yacht can more easily be manoeuvred into a berth when going forward. If ballasting extends a short distance underwater (as it often does) then damage to the rudder is avoided by going bows-to. Moreover there is a gain in privacy as people on the quay cannot see into the cockpit or into the cabin.

There are few laid moorings in Greece and where there are, these will nearly always be a line tailed from the mooring to the quay or a small buoy. However fishermen often have laid moorings with a line tailed to the quay and this will almost always be a floating line which can easily get caught around the rudder and propeller of a yacht berthing amongst or near to fishing boat berths.

Sails

Under the hot Mediterranean sun a yacht's sails suffer from ultra-violet degradation faster than in more northerly climes. It is a good policy to cover the mainsail and bag any headsails whenever they are not in use. If you have a roller-reefing headsail then have a sacrificial strip on the luff and foot to protect the sail when it is furled. Roller-reefing headsails are now more common than hanked-on headsails and speak volumes for the practicality and reliability of the system.

Garbage

The steady increase in man-made disposables found in the oceans and seas of the world is saddening. Around the seas of Greece the amount of rubbish, particularly plastic, has steadily increased. Locals are partly to blame for this – in many Greek villages you will see garbage thrown into the sea – but shore-based tourists and sadly some yachtsmen are also to blame. No one on a yacht has any excuse for polluting somebody else's waters and anybody who does so should not be there. In most harbours there are containers for garbage and it is here and not in the sea that it belongs.

Rescue services

There are no lifeboat services like those offered by the RNLI in England. All the harbours with port police have a police boat of some description. In the larger harbours these are powerful all-weather craft which will answer a coastal distress call. Coast radio stations monitor VHF Ch 16 or 2182kHz for distress calls.

Greek *caïques*.

usually have a sideline changing money. Banks are open from 0800–1300 Monday–Friday. Getting money sent to Greece from outside the country is a tedious and prolonged affair – expect it to take literally weeks longer than you anticipate.

Public holidays
January 1 New Year's Day
January 6 Epiphany
March 25 Independence Day
May 1 Labour Day
August 15 Assumption Day
October 16 St Dimitrius' Day (Salonika)
October 28 *Ochi* ('no') Day
December 25 Christmas Day
December 26 St Stephen's Day
Moveable
First day of Lent
Good Friday
Easter Monday
Ascension

Insurance
A comprehensive insurance policy for the eastern Mediterranean is not excessively expensive, but shop around the various companies to get the best deal. Most policies do not cover you after 30°E but since this covers all Greek waters there is no problem here.

Documents
Passports for all the crew are required, but no special visas are necessary for most foreign nationals. Check with the relevant consulate if you have an unusual passport. For the yacht the RYA Small Ship's Register papers or full Part 1 Registration papers (the *Blue Book*) are both acceptable. A certificate of competency for the skipper may be asked for in some harbours. The RYA Helmsman's or Yachtmaster's Certificate are acceptable.

General information

Tourist offices
In the cities and larger towns there are tourist offices which can often provide useful maps and pamphlets relevant to the local area.

Banks
Eurocheques, Postcheques, major credit cards (*Visa* and *Access*), major debit cards (American Express) and travellers' cheques are accepted in the cities, larger towns and popular tourist spots. Many places have ATS (Automatic Teller Service or 'hole in the wall machines' to you and me) which work well with major credit cards. In general there are few places of any size where you cannot change money either in a bank, post office, or at a tourist agent who will

Laundry
In most places there will be someone who takes in laundry. Often a laundry will be associated with a dry-cleaner. The charge is usually per item so it doesn't pay to have your 'smalls' laundered this way. There are few self-service laundromats in Greece. Prices vary considerably, and are usually comparatively high, so ascertain the cost first.

Security
By and large Greece is an honest country, but in the cities and larger resorts crime is on the increase. Take all sensible precautions. In general the harbours around Athens and Rhodes have a bad reputation for theft.

Drugs
There are very strict penalties for the importation of drugs (hashish, cocaine, etc.) in Greece and by all accounts the prisons are primitive and harsh places. Your yacht can be confiscated if drugs are found on board so play it safe and avoid them and anyone associated with them. A momentary 'high' is hardly worth the loss of your yacht and a stiff jail sentence.

Health
Medical facilities vary from good in the cities to average in the villages. Dental treatment is good in the cities, but almost nonexistent in out-of-the-way spots. Fees vary from moderate to high. There are reciprocal agreements with the other EC countries.

Medicines
Specially-prescribed drugs should be bought in sufficient quantities in England before departure. Most drugs and medical requisites are freely available over the counter in Greece (including the pill, wide-spectrum antibiotics, antibiotic powder etc.) although they may be under unfamiliar brand names.

Mail

The postal system is reliable and efficient for letters, but packages take a long time to be distributed. A private address is preferable to *Poste Restante*.

Telephone

All towns and most villages have an overseas telephone exchange (OTE) where international calls can be made. However even the smallest village will have a metered telephone in a hotel, shop, taverna, or commonly in a *periptero* (the kiosks that sell everything from cigarettes to sweets), though charges will be slightly more (in hotels considerably more) than in the OTE. Many travel agents also operate a fax service. Now new equipment has been installed the communication services in Greece are considerably improved and direct dialling to other countries is normally fairly quick although delays occur at peak periods when a lot of business calls are made.

Spinning wool in Ay Marina, Zakinthos.

Yithion. Fish and chips and chicken-in-a-basket.

Provisioning

In all but the smallest villages you will have few problems obtaining the basic provisions. In the larger towns and popular tourist resorts there is now a wide range of imported goods available and even in small villages you will find the ubiquitous fare that some tourists feel they cannot do without. Why some people should feel an overwhelming need for Heinz baked beans or spaghetti hoops in Greece is beyond me, but they are there.

Fresh fruit and vegetables are seasonal although now Greece is an EU member there is a better selection over a longer period and of course prices have gone up.

Shopping hours are 0800–1300 and 1630–2000, although shopkeepers will stay open through the siesta period or later at night if there are enough customers to warrant it. Shops often close on Monday afternoon and sometimes on Wednesday afternoon as well.

Meat Is usually not hung for long, if at all, and is invariably butchered in a peculiarly eastern Mediterranean fashion so that none of the normal cuts of meat can be recognised. Lamb and beef are the most expensive and pork and chicken the cheapest. Meat is reasonably priced though of inferior quality and cut compared to that in other European countries.

7

Swordfish. Spetsai.

Fish Is expensive. Large fish such as red snapper and grouper are very expensive and the prices of prawns and lobsters are considerable – certainly comparable to or higher than in Italy and France.

Fruit and vegetables Are reasonably priced and usually fresh. In the smaller centres fruit and vegetables are seasonal. All fresh produce should be washed.

Staples Can be obtained in even the smaller villages. Many items (sugar, rice, legumes, beans etc.) are often sold loose. Both loose and packaged items may contain weevils.

Cheese Imported cheeses such as Dutch Edam and Gruyere are widely available and not too costly. Local hard cheeses such as *Kaseri* are good and *Feta*, a soft sheep's cheese, is available everywhere and is good value.

Canned foods Local canned goods are excellent and cheap, but there is not a wide variety. Canned tomatoes and fruit are good value. Canned meat is usually imported and is expensive.

Bread Greek bread straight out of the oven in the morning is delicious, but it doesn't keep well. Small milk loaves called *tsoureki* keep better and toast well even when stale should you stay an extra day or two where supplies are not available. In some places brown or rye bread can be obtained and this also keeps better than your average white loaf.

Coffee and tea Most popular brands of instant coffee are commonly available although it costs more than in some of the other European countries. Good filter coffee is also widely available and is not too expensive. Local coffee is ground very fine and tends to clog filters and percolators. Local tea bags make an insipid cup of tea, imported tea bags are more expensive and can be difficult to find sometimes. Some of the loose tea packed locally is cheap and good.

Wines, beers and spirits Bottled wines are numerous and vary from excellent to terrible. Local wine can often be bought cheaply from the barrel, but taste it first. The ubiquitous retsina is an acquired taste. Wine is on the whole cheap. Local beer is quite palatable and cheap. Local spirits, ouzo (akin to Pernod) and brandy (sweetish) are excellent value, especially when bought in bulk. Imported spirits are expensive.

Recommended Greek yoghurt is the best in the world. If you like soft cheese, *feta* is good value. Tinned fruit. Ouzo and local brandy.

Formalities

Greece as part of the European Union (EU) comes under EU legislation regarding the implementation of the Single Market Agreement. From the 1st of January 1993 the Single Market Agreement for the EU states that customs borders between member countries were removed and goods could be imported from one EU country to another free of hindrance. This agreement effectively removed temporary importation agreements previously in operation for pleasure craft. Prior to this date it was possible to purchase a yacht without paying VAT and keep it in another EU country under the temporary importation agreements. The new agreement which came into force in 1993 exempted pleasure craft on which VAT had not been paid and which were built before the 1st January 1985 (or on which the VAT was negligible) and which were in an EU country at midnight on the 31st December 1992, from VAT payment.

Which means that if you have a boat built after 1st January 1985 and on which VAT has not been paid and in an EU country on the 1st January 1993 then you are liable for VAT payment.

The following points will hopefully clarify what is a murky area despite the terms of the EU Single Market Agreement.

1. The following countries come under the Single Market Agreement: United Kingdom, Ireland, Denmark, Holland, Germany, Luxembourg, Belgium, France, Spain, Portugal, Italy, and Greece.

   The Channel Islands, Gibraltar, Malta and Cyprus do not come under the agreement. Any future additions to the EU(Finland, Norway, Sweden and Austria will be next) will automatically come under the Single Market Agreement.

2. Under the Single Market Agreement it should be possible to move a yacht on which VAT has been paid or which is VAT exempt without involving customs in import and export regulations. However you are still subject to other customs regulations in force in a country (e.g. carrying banned drugs or unauthorised firearms on board is illegal in most countries) and all countries will carry out random customs enquiries.

3. VAT can be paid in the EU country in which a boat is based or in the EU country of registration. In practice boats have moved from one country to another to pay VAT, usually to take advantage of a lower VAT rate or valuation by customs.

4. Evidence of VAT payment or exemption from VAT must be obtained unless you want to be liable for VAT payment. In the UK customs introduced a simple method of paying VAT or acquiring proof of exemption with the SAD (Single Administrative Document) form. In Greece customs have been slow to implement the rule on VAT and at the time of publication reports were mixed over the situation. To my knowledge there is as yet no procedure to pay VAT due on a boat in Greece.

Customs (*Telenion*)

Greece as part of the EU comes under EU legislation regarding the payment of VAT. Proof of payment or exemption from payment should be carried. Yachts from other EU countries which have paid VAT can keep their boats in Greece without any further restrictions. Non-EU boats should report to customs at the first Port of Entry. Here you will be issued with a Transit Log which is valid for 6 months renewable for another 6 months before you must leave Greece for a non-EU country.

Entry formalities

EU yachts on which VAT has been paid or which are exempt can enter Greece from another EU country without formalities in principal although in practice the rule is being interpretted somewhat haphazardly. Transit Logs are optional for EU yachts at most ports In many ways they are useful as you have something to show the port police in out-of-the-way ports where they may not be conversant with EU procedure. Personally I recommend you obtain one.

A Greek courtesy ensign should be flown.

Non-EU yachts should fly a 'Q' flag and a Greek courtesy ensign and make their first port of call at one of the designated Ports of Entry. Here a Transit Log will be issued on which is listed an inventory of dutiable goods and crew members.

A Transit Log is issued for 6 months renewable for another 6 months. The old Law 438 tax relating to boats staying more than one year in Greek waters ($US15 per foot per year) has been abolished for EU flag boats. However given the haphazard situation in Greece this may not be everywhere understood. The relevant parts of Law 438 relating to chartering in Greece are still in place as part of the national regulations (see over in the section on Chartering) and EU flag yachts still cannot charter in Greece.

Further information on the situation can be obtained from the Royal Yachting Association, RYA House, Romsey Road, Eastleigh, Hampshire, SO5 4YA, United Kingdom ☎ (01703) 629 962 *Fax* (01703) 629 924

Other EU laws for yachts

Small craft licences At the time of publication there was no clear EU directive on small craft licenses and it appeared to be up to individual countries to determine agreement on what license or certificate corresponded with what. At the present time the RYA Helmsman's Certificate of Competence or Yachtmaster's Certificate are accepted in Greece. In the future it is to be expected that there will be some harmonisation of small craft licences for EU countries.

Recreational craft directive A directive governing the construction and equipping of recreational craft. It will not to be applied retrospectively, but will be applied to second hand craft bought outside the EU and imported into an EU country. Not yet implemented and thought to be due in May 1998.

Harbour dues

When I first came to Greece there were no harbour fees except in the marinas. In subsequent years a modest charge was made and in 1990 a revised scale of harbour dues was introduced. At present charges are made only haphazardly in harbours depending on the inclination of the port police.

The formula is a little complicated and goes something like this. Length (in metres, but see below) x 10·5 Dx (though this figure will undoubtedly change in the future) plus tonnage x 2·336 Dx. Thus for a 10 metre/5 ton yacht the daily charge would be around 117 Dx. However a few port police were calculating the figure using the length of the boat in feet which of course gives a larger figure, around 353 Dx for the example above, which is still not excessive at around a pound on current exchange rates. Given that not all harbours, especially small ones, are bothering to charge at all for short stays, there should be no grumbles about this.

Charges are of course made in marinas, although since there are only a few marinas in Greece this doesn't come up very often. In some marinas payment was being demanded in foreign currency although under EU regulations this is illegal.

Port police

The port police offices are generally on the waterfront. They can be easily recognised by the crossed anchors next to the sign saying port police (*Limenario*) and the very large Greek flag flying from the building. The port police handle most of your papers and you can also have your mail sent to them. They will sometimes be able to supply you with a weather forecast although weather forecasts leave a lot to be desired in Greece. On one occasion in Crete I asked the port police for a weather forecast whereupon one of them strode across to the window, threw it open and looked out, before turning to me to state in a stentorian tone that it was OK for me to go, the weather was good!

An interesting point is that the port police can keep yachts in harbour if the weather forecast predicts winds of over Force 6. Often they will not bother. Should they make such a ruling the skipper of a yacht can sign a form which states in effect that he has been warned and any misfortune due to bad weather is entirely his own fault.

In my dealings with the port police I have invariably found them to be courteous and helpful, although business may be conducted with that typical Greek disdain for time that the English sometimes find so infuriating. Occasionally the yachtsman will come across an official who is rude and difficult, but this does not characterise officialdom in Greece – that, after all, is a disease to be found wherever officialdom exists.

Port police.

PORTS OF ENTRY LISTED ALPHABETICALLY

Ayios Nikolaos	(Crete)
Alexandroupolis	(Northern Greece)
Argostoli	(Cephalonia)
Ermoupolis	(Siros)
Gaios (Paxoi)	(Ionian)
Iraklion	(Crete)
Itea	(Korinthiakos Kolpos)
Kalamata	(Peloponnese)
Katakolon	(Peloponnese)
Kavala	(Northern Greece)
Kerkira (Corfu)	(Ionian)
Khania	(Crete)
Khios	(Eastern Sporades)
Kos	(Dodecanese)
Lavrion	(Saronic Gulf)
Levkas	(Ionian)
Mirina	(Limnos)
Mitilini	(Lesvos)
Navplion	(Argolikos Kolpos)
Patras	(Patraikos Kolpos)
Pilos	(Western Peloponnese)
Pithagorion	(Samos)
Preveza	(Ionian)
Rhodes	(Rhodes)
Thessaloniki	(Northern Greece)
Volos	(Northern Greece)
Vouliagmeni Marina	(Saronikos Kolpos)
Zakinthos	(Ionian)
Zea Marina	(Saronikos Kolpos)

Other laws relevant to the yachtsman

There are a number of laws which while not specifically maritime law, nonetheless are of special relevance to the yachtsman.

The first of these is to do with extended stays in Greece. Normally when entering Greece non EC passport holders are allowed to stay three months without a visa (two months for some passport holders including the USA) and after that period is up, an extension for a further three months' stay must be applied for. However when you enter on a yacht you can stay indefinitely provided you remain with the yacht. A problem arises if you enter on a yacht and depart by some other means. I photocopy my transit log and present that when departing other than by yacht.

The second law of possible interest concerns the acquisition and export of antiquities. Greece loses valuable and irreplaceable antiquities every year and some of these are smuggled out of the country on yachts. Any antiquities found in Greece must be surrendered to the state. Any yacht with antiquities on board is liable to be impounded and confiscated and I know of several instances when this has occurred. This law also applies to antiquities and works of art which have been sold to you so it would pay to find out if an article can be exported before you exchange any money.

The last law of relevance is that forbidding the use of compressed air tanks for underwater fishing. You may use a spear gun with a snorkel and mask but not with compressed air tanks. Such apparatus may be used for pleasure or filming except in areas where there may be antiquities on the seabed. These prohibited areas are so extensive that the National Tourist Board of Greece finds it easier to list those areas where compressed air tanks can be used for pleasure and filming. These are:

Kassandra promontory (Khalkidhiki peninsula)
All along a 500-metre belt of sea stretching out from the eastern shore of the promontory from the village of Polihrono to Ak Glarokavos.

Sinthonia promontory (Khalkidhiki peninsula)
All along a similar belt of the eastern shore of the promontory from Ak Armenistis to Ak Dhrepanon.

Athos promontory (Khalkidhiki peninsula)
a. Along a 500-metre belt from the shore in Ormos Provlaka from Pirgos Oranoupolis to Xerxes Canal.
b. Along the northern shore of Nisis Ammouliani from Ak Trigona to Ak Kokkino, within a 300-metre belt running parallel with the shore.

Mikonos
Within a 500-metre belt around the island's shores, save for the stretch from Ak Ayios Yeoryios to Ak Alogomandra.

Kerkira (Corfu)
a. Within a 500-metre belt around the island's shores from Ak Rodha to Ak Dhrastis.
b. Within a similar belt of sea from Palaiokastrita to Ak Arkoudila, with the exception of the waters surrounding Nisidhes Langoudhia.
c. Within a similar 500-metre belt of sea from Ak Koundhouri to Ak Agni, with the exception of the waters surrounding the islands of Vidho and Lazaretto.

Paxoi
Within a 500-metre belt of sea round the island's shores except for the area of Voutsi.

Levkas
a. Within the usual 500-metre belt along the island's western shores from Yiropetra to Ak Dhoukaton.
b. Within a similar 500-metre belt along the island's eastern shore from the point on the beach in line with the village of Katouna as far as the eastern entrance to Ormos Rouda, but not within the bay itself nor around the island of Madhouri.
c. Within a 500-metre belt of sea all round the island of Meganisi.

Cephalonia
a. Within a 500-metre belt along the island's shores, except for Dhiavlos Ithaca from the level of Fiskardho to Ormos Andisami and Ormos Sami to Ay Eufimia.
b. Also excluded are the stretches of coast from Ak Kapri to Ak Mounda, the waters round the Variani islets and the coast from Ak Ortholithia to Ak Atheras.

Zakinthos
All around the island's shore, along a 500-metre belt.

Obviously it would pay to check with the local port police since any of these areas can be designated 'out of bounds' if the Archaeological Service suspect there are antiquities on the seabed.

Chartering

Sometimes when I am talking about sailing in Greece, particularly to newcomers, I realise it sounds as if I have spent a lifetime sailing here. I suppose nearly 20 years is a lifetime for some of you. Yet in that time there have been quite substantial changes for the yachtsman. Just prior to my arrival in *Roulette*, Law 438 was passed by the Legislature and this law effectively stopped foreign-registered yachts from chartering. Many charter boats left Greece. Their place has largely been filled by bare boat and flotilla charter, all under the Greek flag, but most owned and organised by English and German companies.

Flotilla chartering involves a group of boats, usually ten to twelve, sailing in company around a more or less planned route. In this way someone with only a little experience can skipper his own boat, but remain confident that help is at hand should anything go wrong. If anything does go wrong there is a lead boat constantly with the group and on board are a skipper, a hostess and an engineer who can sort out any problems you have.

Most bare boat and skippered chartering is out of Piraeus and these boats usually head for the Saronic Islands or for the Cyclades. Like flotilla charter, a bare boat charter is usually for two weeks. The yachts do not range any great distance, especially in the *meltemi* season when they must bash into the eye of the wind to get back to Piraeus. Bare boat charter has grown at the same pace as flotilla charter, but because the boats are generally alone and localized in one area their effect has not been as dramatic as that of flotilla charter.

It seems to be a commonplace dream among impoverished yachtsmen arriving in Greece that they will quickly replenish their coffers by chartering – until they learn of the regulations governing charter. It's Law 438 again. If your yacht is to be chartered in Greek waters then it must be registered in Greece. To obtain a Greek flag you will need to acquire the services of a Greek agent to whom you will sign away 51 per cent of your yacht or yachts. After being measured, checked for safety equipment and entered on the maritime register you will be issued with a wad of certificates and you can then raise your Greek flag. You still have not finished with the paperwork. For every charter party you must fill out a charter agreement detailing the duration of the charter, the number and nationality of the charterers, the cost of the charter and so on. The cost of the charter is detailed because you are required to have a certain proportion of the charter fee paid in Greece. The amount of paperwork is prodigious and the charter agreement may be checked at any port.

If your yacht exceeds a certain length (about 15 metres I believe) then you must employ a Greek captain and crew. This was the reason for so many foreign-registered yachts leaving Greece when Law 438 was passed. A couple or a family using their yacht and home to make a living by chartering it in

Flotilla sailing in the Saronic.

the summer months could not afford to have it Greek registered or to engage a Greek captain and crew to do their job. To charter outside these regulations is to run the risk of having your yacht impounded.

For more detailed information on the whys and wherefores of chartering I suggest you get in touch with the National Tourist Board of Greece. On a more practical level you would do better to talk to someone in the charter game in Greece. A number of English and German companies will put your boat under the Greek flag and charter it, paying you a percentage of the returns as well as allowing you the use of your boat in the off-season and for a limited period (usually two weeks) in the season. Just be sure you choose a reputable company or your beautiful new yacht may be a wreck by the end of a season of bare boat charter.

Food and wine
Compiled by Bridgit Marsh

Greece is not a country for the gourmet. Eating out is as much a part of life in Greece as in other Mediterranean countries, but the food is not the sophisticated fare found in Italy or France or the carefully prepared food of the Levant. Not that the Greeks don't eat well – they do. The food is invariably fresh, simply cooked, and appetizing, but the choice will often be limited, the food sometimes served cold or lukewarm, and the garnishing meagre. In the larger towns and cities a wider choice will be found on the menu than in the smaller islands and villages.

One of the things which will be most noticeable is the seasonality of the food. Although most fruits and vegetables are available in Greece they may only be available during the ripening season. Apricots for instance ripen in early June and will only be in the shops for two to three weeks. This can be quite surprising to the visitor who is used to being able to buy fruit over an extended season. The seasonality of ingredients leads to a variation in the dishes served in the tavernas. This of course applies with special significance to the small village tavernas where only those foods in season will be served whereas places with access to better markets will be able to serve such things as *moussaka* (normally only served when aubergines are in season) most of the year round.

Now that increasing numbers of tourists arrive in the summer the bigger tourist areas have to import considerable amounts of foodstuffs for the bulging taverna tables. Often your *kalamari* will come frozen from Californian waters, your lamb will come frozen from New Zealand, your *feta* was probably manufactured in Denmark, and even the aubergines in your *moussaka* may have come from Spain. Only in the smaller, more out-of-the-way places will you get locally grown produce tossed into the salad and grilled over the charcoal.

A taverna generally prepares its dishes for the day in the morning and these will be cooked in time for the midday meal when they will be served hot. These oven dishes will stand on a hot plate or by the oven for the rest of the day and by evening will be luke-warm at best. You will find that it is better in Greece to eat the baked dishes such as *moussaka*, stuffed vegetables, or *pastitsio*, at midday and in the evening order something grilled or fried which will be served hot. In recent years the introduction of the convenient microwave has meant food can now be warmed quickly for the evening meal, but this is really stale midday food warmed over and not that appetizing.

Do not expect food to be rushed steaming hot to your table as the Greeks are not used to eating their food piping hot and do not always understand our continued repetition of the word *zeste* (hot) whenever we are ordering in a taverna. In the more touristy spots food arrives hotter than it used to, but this is the exception rather than the rule.

When you first go into a taverna do not be confused by the menu. It will probably (if there is one, that is) have printed on it a large variety of food and drink. Some of the items will have prices beside them. These are the ones available that day and the menu should be dated at the top. There will be two prices on the menu, the one on the right proportionately more than the one on the left. The first is the price without service and the second the price with service, but as food always comes with service, you pay the higher price on the right. This means a service charge is included in your bill and consequently a tip is not required.

A word of advice: do not order your food all at once or your main course, side orders and starters will arrive at the table at the same time. Eating is done slowly and leisurely in Greece and it is quite alright to occupy a table all night.

The menu
You can start with appetizers. Common appetizers are: *tzatziki* (yoghurt flavoured with grated cucumber and garlic); *taramasalata* (cod roe ground into a paste); aubergine salad; *merithes*, small fried fishes (eaten whole, head and all); *kalamaris* (fried baby squid); peas or green beans in a tomato sauce; and invariably a Greek salad consisting of some or all of the following – tomatoes, onions, green peppers, olives, cucumber, *feta* (sheep's cheese) dressed in oil and oregano.

This can be followed with soup or a vegetable dish: fish, tripe or bean soups are common; vegetables are often stuffed and you will find tomatoes, green peppers and aubergines stuffed with a rice and cheese mixture as well as *dolmades* (stuffed vine leaves often cooked in a tomato sauce mixture). Garlic is a favourite seasoning and is used frequently and liberally. Lemon is probably the second most popular seasoning and you will find it by the side of most of your dishes and in the cooking of everything from egg and lemon soup to the flavouring of rice pudding.

The main course will probably be a choice of the following: grilled chops (beef, pork or lamb); grilled fish depending on what the local fishermen have caught; *souvlaki* (pieces of pork or beef on a skewer grilled over charcoal); kebabs which are a bigger version of *souvlaki*, usually with pieces of tomato and onion between the meat; lamb baked in a pastry case; a beef stew (*stifado*) or beef cooked in a garlic sauce (*sofrito*); *moussaka* (Greek shepherd's pie); *pastitsio* (lamb or beef in pasta); barbecued chicken, lamb or beef; spaghetti with a variety of sauces ranging from terrible to passable; meatballs; and probably a variety of leftover baked dishes from the midday meal.

In the larger towns choice will be good and there may be specialities depending on the skill and whims of the cook, but in the smaller islands and villages you must get used to a more limited choice. Chips are served with everything and although delicious when hot (they are usually home-made and not the instant packaged 'French fries'), are not at all appealing when cold.

It is usual to finish a meal with fresh fruit, but occasionally some form of sweet may be offered such as *crème caramel* or ice cream. Cakes, pastries and sweets are more often eaten in a 'cake shop'. Here you will find *baklava* (pastry filled with walnuts and steeped in honey); *loukamathes* (fritters coated in honey); *kadaifi* (nuts and honey in shredded pastry); and the best yoghurt in the world which can be eaten plain or mixed with honey and fruit.

Wines

Wine has been made and drunk in Greece for centuries and in ancient times was carried to most parts of the known world. It is thought the wine was stored in amphoras and pine resin poured on top to seal them – from this ancient practice it is believed we get the retsina wines which are artificially produced today.

You either like or hate retsina. Do not be put off by the bottled varieties which are much inferior to retsina from the barrel. Retsina is made locally all over Greece and often a café or taverna will be famous not only for its food or company, but also for its retsina.

Locally produced wines, resinated and unresinated, are available in bulk in most places and are served in tavernas by the litre. They vary a great deal, can be quite palatable, and if awful at least have the merit of being cheap. Do not try to carry them for any distance as they do not usually travel or keep.

Bottled wines vary a great deal from the ordinary to some excellent wines such as *Robola* or *Achaia Claus Château* (numbered bottles). The following are generally of a consistent quality: *Demestica* – red or white; *Robola* – red or white; *Manzavino* – rosé; *Atlantis* – white; *St Helena* – white; *Robola* – red; *Cambas* – white; *Limnos* – red; *Samena* – white; *Porto Carras* – red and white; *Agrilos* – red; *Apellis* – red; *Nikteri* – white; *CAIR* – champagne from Rhodes.

Beer is also made in Greece and the common *Heninger* and *Amstel* beers are cheap and palatable.

Besides wine and beer there are several other drinks deserving a mention. Firstly, ouzo which qualifies as the national tipple of Greece. It is similar to French *pastis* and may be drunk with or without water. Greek cognac or brandy is another popular drink and makes a refreshing long drink mixed with Coca-Cola and ice. *Metaxa* and *Botrys* are two of the better known brands. Ouzo and brandy can be bought in bulk from the barrel and are very cheap and not at all inferior when purchased like this. Take along a bottle to a *cava* or wine shop (or in the smaller villages the local grocer or café) and you will be able to get a litre or more of either ouzo or brandy for very little.

Miscellaneous

There are a few sundry items not often found on the menu but nonetheless an important part of Greek life. First, in the *galaktopolia* or dairies you will find fresh yoghurt made from cow or sheep milk. The dairy will also probably stock the variety made in Athens and strained so that you believe you are eating not yoghurt, but tasty whipped cream. These shops also have *feta* (a soft cheese made from sheep's milk), local honey and eggs.

In some of the cafés you will see a long homemade sausage cooking on the spit. Made from lamb's offal and cooked with garlic and herbs, it is called *kokoretsi* and is delicious. At every bus station or ferry terminal you will find a kiosk where pork or beef *souvlaki* are soused in lemon juice and herbs and cooked on the spot as a snack. You may also find the Greek hamburger which is pitta bread (unleavened) filled with a *souvlaki*, tomato, onion and a dollop of yoghurt. The kiosk will probably also have cheese pies (*tiropitta*) or spinach pies (*spinakopitta*).

Kali oretsi – bon appetit!

Marine life

The marine life in the Mediterranean is at first disappointing to the yachtsman used to life around the English coast. It is not as prolific or as diverse as you might imagine; there are fewer seabirds, good eating fish are scarce and difficult to catch and in places the sea bottom can be quite bereft of interest compared with, say, the Red Sea or the west coast of France.

There are a number of reasons for the relative paucity of marine life. The first is the non-tidal nature of the sea which means there is not the inter-tidal zone in which a varied and rich amount of life can live and contribute to the whole marine ecosystem. The second is the fact that the Mediterranean has been fished far longer and more intensively than any other sea area. Particularly devastating was the use of dynamite after the First World War and this practice continues to the present day despite the fact that it carries heavy penalties and some considerable risk. In almost any village you will see a man without a hand or an arm lost when he miscalculated on the fuse.

Although the marine life is initially disappointing the yachtsman is in a unique position to discover and explore the life in the eastern Mediterranean. Dolphins, whales, turtles, flying fish, tuna, swordfish and sunfish will be seen in many places and, with a mask and a snorkel, the warm waters invite exploration.

Whales and dolphins (cetaceans)

Dolphins sadly are becoming less common in Greek waters than they were even a few years ago. You will still see dolphins and occasionally a school of dolphins will come up to a yacht and play around it. At night the phosphorescence created by dolphins around a yacht is something marvellous to behold. The numbers of dolphins have decreased for several reasons. Food stocks, normally mackerel and tuna, have decreased. Drift netting, common in Italy and unfortunately recently resumed there, catches dolphins as well as swordfish and tuna. Estimates of the numbers killed in this manner vary, but are thought to be in the thousands rather than hundreds. Lastly pollution in the form of heavy metals, PCBs and other carcinogenic compounds, and spills of toxic chemicals, have caused a form of 'flu' similar to that which killed many seals around British coasts. I can only suggest you support any of those groups fighting for the continued survival of this magnificent mammal which has never harmed humans and, anecdotal trivia aside, is known actively to have aided humans in distress in the water. Renew your subscription to Greenpeace, Friends of the Earth, or the Environmental Investigation Agency.

In antiquity the dolphin was mentioned and often depicted in mosaics. Aristotle and Pliny mentioned it as a friend of man and Herodotus tells of the poet Arion of Lesvos who was thrown overboard by mutinous sailors and rescued by a music-loving dolphin. The modern Greek fisherman is not so fond of the dolphin as his ancestors were, believing it to rob him of fish and there are stories (though I cannot vouch for any of them) that the friendly animals have been killed by fishermen.

Cetaceans are divided into toothed and non-toothed whales. In the eastern Mediterranean most of the cetaceans seen belong to the toothed whales, which are fish-eaters and so possess teeth to grip their prey. To this class belong the porpoise, dolphin, pilot whale and killer whale. The common dolphin (*Delphinus delphis*) will often be seen. Less common are the larger bottle-nosed dolphin (*Tursiops truncatus*) and the common porpoise (*Phocoena phocoena*). The pilot whale (*Globicephala melaena*) is fairly common and grows up to 8·5 metres long. The bottle-nosed whale (*Hyperoodon ampullatus*), Risso's dolphin (*Grampus griseus*) and the killer whale (*Orcinus orca*) have been reported in the eastern Mediterranean.

Monk seals

The Mediterranean monk seal, *Monachus monachus*, is numbered amongst the twelve most endangered animals in the world and is the rarest species of seal left. It is specific to the warm waters of the Mediterranean although small numbers are found on the Atlantic coast of Morocco. There are estimated to be only 500 to 800 of these animals left with approximately half the population in Greece.

One of the big problems is the encroachment of tourism into the habitat occupied by the seals. Illegal spear-fishing using subaqua equipment is eroding the food supply – visitors have been cited as the chief culprits and there have been several convictions, but the blame does not lie solely here. Small powerboats and inflatables with powerful outboards exploit quiet places and the coastal caves where these retiring animals live. Those on the water and the land can help by keeping away from coastal caves and rocky coastlines and at all times should avoid making too much noise – the seals are easily frightened. Any illegal fishing whether by subaqua divers or dynamiting should be reported to the port police or any other authority.

Good eating fish

Although Greece is fished out to some extent, there are still sufficient good eating fish remaining. If you despair of catching any then treat yourself in a taverna. The fish is mostly grilled and arrives without a sauce or other trimmings. Particularly good eating are the following:

Tuna (Tonnos) Frequents northern waters in the summer and travels south to the Mediterranean in winter. The white flesh is a little oily but delicious.

Swordfish (Xsifia) As above and just as delicious.

Grouper (Sfiritha) Prefers sandy or rocky bottoms and you may be lucky enough to get one in the less populated areas. Pleasant white flesh.

Red mullet (Barbouni) Tasty white flesh but full of small bones.

Bream (Fagri, Sinagritha) Tasty and not too bony.

Whitebait (Merithes) Often served as a starter, the little fish are cooked and eaten whole.

Octopus (Octopothi) Sometimes a bit tough but always tasty. Pickled octopus is delicious.

Squid (Kalamari) Normally deep-fried. Delicious.

Prawns (Garides) Often expensive and not always fresh. Buy them off a fishing boat and cook them yourself for the best results.

Crayfish (Astakos) Just as delicious as lobster. Normally boiled or grilled.

Greek fishing methods

When a fishing boat is sighted a good look-out must be kept for floats and lines in the water. Some of the fishing methods could be dangerous to a yacht if it is not understood what is going on. The following methods are used:

1. Trawling either singly or in pairs.
2. Purse seine netting, in Greek *grigia*, in which a large *caïque*, a smaller net-*caïque* and two to four small *caïques* or light-floats are used. The smaller *caïques* and/or light floats are set adrift with powerful gas or arc lamps to attract fish to the surface. The large *caïque* and its helper then lay the net in a semicircle around the fish and haul them in. Large catches of mackerel and sardines are made. The gas lamps are conspicuous from a long distance off.
3. Netting off the land. A long rope is run out to a net and then to a *caïque* which circles to enclose any fish. Particularly dangerous to a yacht as the rope is generally just under the water between the *caïque* and the shore.
4. A set net in a bay or near the shore. Usually weighted to be below the surface although sometimes a surface net is laid.
5. *Lampera*. A gas lamp on a *caïque* is used to attract fish which are speared or hooked. Often used for octopus.
6. Long-lining from a *caïque*: the lines are attached to a float which is allowed to drift.

Fish farms

With Greece's entry into the EU grants were made available for all sorts of enterprises. One of these was for the establishment of fish farms and in recent years they have proliferated everywhere. Unfortunately for the yachtsman the requirements for a fish farm are much the same as those for a good anchorage – shelter from strong winds and reasonable depths to anchor the farm in. Consequently a number of coves and bays formerly frequented only by yachtsmen and fishing boats have now sprouted fish farms which may obstruct much of the cove or bay.

In most places the operators of the fish farm are content to allow yachts to use the anchorage if there is room, but in some places the operators have expressed disapproval and actively chased yachts out of anchorages. In Port Pandelimon in the Ionian the fish farm operator has produced official bits of paper claiming to have the approval of the authorities to use the bay. The legality of this is somewhat dubious since it is impossible to own anything below the high-water mark; even the late Onassis and Niarchos did not own that section of the beach or the sea bed below the high-water mark on their private islands (much to their consternation), so unless legislation has been passed exempting fish farms, it may be illegal. Certainly town councils in the vicinity of some fish farms have had them removed and others have denied operators permission to set up.

For the yachtsmen it is largely a matter of putting up with fish farm operators until the grants run out. I appreciate that fish farms are a possible solution to the natural poverty in fish in the eastern Mediterranean, but such a programme needs to be carefully administered and the operators properly trained. I know some of the operators and they have received none or little training at all. Some fish farms are already going out of business after the grant has run out and there seems to be a bit of a short-term racket going on using EU money. Personally I do not like the 'muddy' taste of farmed fish and I am sceptical of the ability of many of the operators (in any country where fish farming goes on) to handle safely and measure accurately the restricted chemicals necessary to eliminate disease amongst fish farmed in close quarters. I suggest that you enquire where the fish in a restaurant has come from and if it is farmed give it a miss.

Note Fish farms must be moved at regular intervals because of the build-up of detritus and fish-poo under the farm. Consequently the location of fish farms on the plans may vary from that shown and should be interpreted as a general guide to the vicinity of a fish farm, not a precise position.

Pollution

Being a closed sea it was inevitable that as the population around the shores grew, so pollution in the Mediterranean increased. The less densely-populated eastern Mediterranean is comparatively less polluted than the western half, but around the heavily-populated Saronic Gulf and Thessaloniki Gulf there is some pollution. Around Athens it has been estimated there is more than 50% of Greece's industry and the air and water quality suffers badly because of this. Down by the Ionian Islands there is also some hydrocarbon pollution from the numerous oil-tankers cleaning out their tanks after leaving the Adriatic.

Up until recently nothing was being done about the increasing pollution in the Mediterranean, but in 1975 the United Nations Environment Programme decided to get together the culturally and politically diverse countries around the Mediterranean and work out a programme to clean up the sea. In 1980 all the countries (except Albania) agreed to a ten billion dollar plan to go ahead. Some progress has been made since then, but much remains to be done and it may be that the political will to do something has weakened and that it is up to environmental pressure groups to force the pace of the clean-up programme.

Part of the antipollution plan will probably affect yachtsmen in the future. No thinking yachtsman should ever dump garbage in the sea – especially plastic. In harbour, regulations already exist by which a yachtsman can be fined up to 10,000 drachmae for pumping out a toilet or dumping waste oil overboard, although these regulations are not rigidly enforced. All charter boats must now be fitted with holding tanks and these should be used when in harbour and pumped out only when well out to sea. It is likely that in the future antipollution measures affecting the yachtsman will be introduced and this is only right. The yachtsman may curse the extra cost, but must acknowledge the necessity of such regulations when so much of the Mediterranean, and for that matter the other seas and oceans of the world, is threatened by pollution of one sort or another.

Dangerous marine animals

In the Mediterranean there are no more dangerous marine animals than you would encounter off the English coast, but the warm sea temperatures mean that you are in the water more often and therefore more likely to encounter these animals.

Sharks Probably the greatest fear of a swimmer, yet in all probability the least to be feared. Films such as *Jaws* and *Blue Water, White Death* have produced a phobia amongst swimmers that is out of all proportion to the menace. After many years of sailing around the eastern Mediterranean I have positively identified a shark in the water on only three occasions. Fishermen occasionally bring in sharks from the deep water – usually the mackerel shark or sand shark. I have not been able to establish one fatality from a shark attack in Greece and so far as I know the total recorded number of fatalities for the Mediterranean is six.

Moray eels Of the family Muraenidae, these eels are quite common in the eastern Mediterranean and are often caught by fishermen. They inhabit holes and crevices in rocks and can bite and tear if molested. Usually they will retire and are not aggressive unless wounded or sorely provoked.

Octopus Are very shy and do not attack. They have much more to fear from man than man from them.

Stingrays The European stingray (*Dasytatis pastinaca*) is common in the Mediterranean. It inhabits shallow waters, partially burying itself in the sand. If it is trodden on accidentally it will lash out with its tail and bury a spine in the offending foot. Venom is injected which produces severe local pain, sweating, vomiting and rapid heart beat, but rarely death. Soak the foot in very hot water and seek medical help.

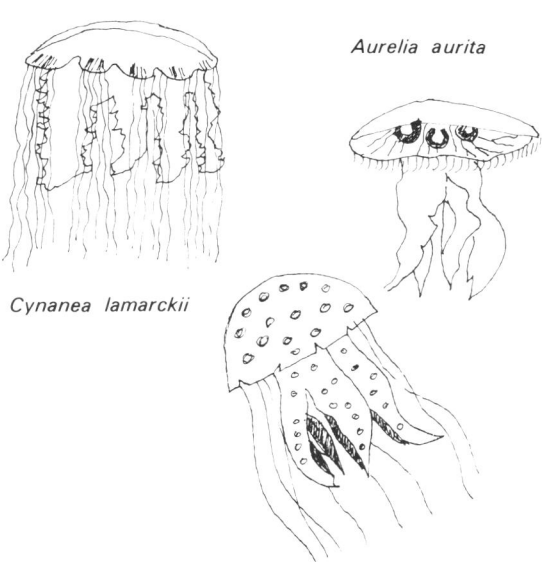

Apparently innocuous catch, but the largest fish is a weever and even when dead the dorsal spines can inject a neuro-toxin when handled which causes severe pain and occasionally death.

Weeverfish Members of the family Trachinidae. The two most common are the great weever (*Trachinus draco*) and lesser weever (*Trachinus vipera*). The dorsal and opercular fins contain venom spines. When disturbed or annoyed the Weever will erect its dorsal fin and attack. The venom injected produces instant pain which spreads to other parts of the body and is very painful. The victim may lose consciousness and death sometimes occurs. There are no known antidotes. Bathe the wound in hot water and seek medical help as soon as possible.

Note When walking in the water where stingrays or weevers are thought to be, wear sand-shoes and shuffle the feet along the bottom. Do not handle dead weevers or stingrays.

Jellyfish Of all the animals described, the ones you are most likely to encounter are jellyfish. At certain times of the year and in certain places there will be considerable numbers of jellyfish in the water. All jellyfish sting, for this is the way they immobilize their prey, but some species have more powerful stings than others and consequently deserve greater respect.

Aurelia aurita The common jellyfish. It is a transparent dome-shaped body with four purple-violet crescents grouped around the centre. Transparent or light violet mouth arms hang below. Up to 25cm in diameter. A light contact with the stings is something like a nettle, but prolonged contact can hurt.

Pelagia noctiluca A mushroom-shaped jellyfish up to 10cm in diameter. It is easily identified, being light brown-yellow in colour and covered in 'warts'. It has long trailing tentacles and can inflict severe and painful stings.

Cyanea lamarckii A blue-violet saucer-shaped jellyfish up to 30cm across. It can be identified by the frilly mass of mouth arms underneath. It has long tentacles which can inflict severe and painful stings. There is a brown variety (*Cyanea capillata*) which can grow up to 50cm in diameter.

Charybdea marsupialis Mediterranean sea-wasp. A transparent, yellow-red box-shaped 'umbrella' up to 6cm high. Rarely seen but can inflict severe and painful stings.

Physalia physalis Portuguese man-o-war. Has a large conspicuous float (pneumatophore) above water growing to 30cm long and 10cm wide. Below it stream very long tentacles. Rarely seen but can inflict dangerous stings.

Rhizostoma pulmo Dome-shaped blue-white jellyfish up to 90cm in diameter. Its mouth arms are fused in a grey-green 'cauliflower' mass below the body. It has no long tentacles and is not known as a vicious stinger.

There are no known antidotes to jellyfish stings, but there are a number of ways of obtaining relief. Diluted ammonium hydroxide, sodium bicarbonate, olive oil, sugar and ethyl alcohol have been used. A tip which I have not tried but which sounds promising is to use meat tenderizer which apparently breaks down the protein base of the venom. Gloves should be worn when hauling up an anchor in jellyfish-infested water as the tentacles, especially those of *Pelagia*, can stick to the anchor chain.

Bristleworms In some locations numbers of bristleworms, probably of the family Nereidae, will be found. They are black and may grow up to 25cm long. The *setae* can produce a mild irritation similar to a stinging nettle if touched.

Sea urchins In some places on rocky coasts large colonies of sea urchins (*Paracentrotus lividus* and *Arbacia lixula*) will be found. While they do not have a venom apparatus, the spines penetrate and break off when the urchin is trodden on and are very painful. Care must be taken not to get a secondary infection.

History

Sailing in Greece

When you think of Greece you think of the sea and the islands. The bowl of the Aegean Sea is dotted with islands, hundreds of islands with comparatively small distances between them so that navigation is a matter of looking for the next island and heading in that direction. In this way it is possible to island-hop from one side of the Aegean to the other. Add to this seascape a regular summer wind blowing steadily from a northerly direction and you have the ideal climate for the evolution of sailing craft and associated skills. For this reason the development of sailing craft occurred relatively early on in this part of the world and until the introduction of petrol and diesel motors, sail was the principal method of moving people and goods.

In this setting it would be surprising if the indigenous folklore and mythology were not concerned with the sea and ships. Homer wrote the first great epic of sailors and shipwrecks in the *Odyssey*. The saga of Jason and the Argonauts in pursuit of the Golden Fleece added another classic to classical bedtime reading. In this atmosphere of sailing craft and adventure it is surprising that there are so few records of sailing for pleasure. Pausanias records that in Ermioni during the festival of Dionysus 'they hold a musical contest in his honour and offer prizes for a diving competition and boat race.' There is some difficulty with the translation of the word for boat race and it may mean a swimming race, so even this brief mention of boating for pleasure is suspect.

Not until the Roman occupation of Greece do we find a concrete reference to sailing for pleasure in the poems of Catullus. Catullus is little known today, but in his time instigated something of a revolution in poetic style. A contemporary of Cicero, he moved in high government circles and is believed to have entertained Caesar several times. In addition to his literary credits, Catullus had a small sailing boat constructed for his own pleasure and in this craft he achieved some notable passages. After visiting his brother in the Troad he sailed across the Aegean and up the Adriatic to the river Po. He sailed up the Po as far as he could and then hauled the boat out and transported it overland to Lake Garda. Catullus retired to a villa on the shores of Lake Garda, spending his last years writing poetry and sailing with friends around the lake.

Not until the 19th and 20th centuries do we know that pleasure craft again sailed around the Greek islands, although during the interim there must have been such craft around. In the late 19th and early 20th centuries gentlemen and their yachts cruised around the Mediterranean, often combining their sailing with shooting expeditions or amateur archaeology. In those days a yacht meant a small ship by today's standards. Some of them still survive – marvellous creations of the boatbuilder's art which

Caïque building the traditional way – Spetsai.

would cost a small fortune to duplicate today and must cost the same to maintain. Some are available for charter, but not by the impecunious.

Until thirty years ago Greece was relatively unknown to the cruising man. A few yachts cruised around the islands simply for the fun of it and a few took charter parties around the islands. To read an account of sailing in Greek waters written then is much like reading an account today of sailing in the Pacific – it all seemed a long way away and somehow exotic. Today, the improved design of small yachts has made the long passages possible and it is now commonplace to see yachtsmen in all manner and size of craft sailing in Greece.

The voyage of the Heroes

In 1984 author Tim Severin set out from Volos (ancient Iolcos) to trace the path sailed by Jason and the Argonauts in their search for the Golden Fleece. The craft sailed by Tim Severin and his crew was a twenty-oared scouting galley, a replica of the sort of craft that would have been around in Homeric times. The galley crossed the northern Aegean in May and passed through the Dardanelles to arrive in Istanbul in June. From here it passed through the Bosphorus to the Black Sea and voyaged along its north coast to the mouth of the Rhion in Soviet Georgia, the Land of the Golden Fleece.

In 1985 the same craft investigated the wanderings of Odysseus in the Mediterranean on his way home from the Trojan War. This is the first time a practical experiment to trace the routes of these two early voyages has been carried out and Severin came to some unorthodox conclusions about the voyage of Odysseus. Formerly it was assumed Odysseus was blown around the Mediterranean to such diverse places as Libya, Tunisia, Gibraltar, Malta and Italy, but according to Severin Odysseus took the prudent and logical route home to Ithaca, and all of the places mentioned in Homer's *Odyssey* can be identified in Greece. For instance the one-eyed Cyclops historians assumed to have lived in Sicily can be identified with tales of triamates in Crete. It is a startling hypothesis that anyone sailing in Greek waters will find fascinating. I leave it up to you to determine which holds up best: Severin's hypothesis or the more conventional interpretation of the voyage of Odysseus.

The vessel for the voyage of the heroes, a replica of a Homeric scouting galley, was built in Spetsai according to ancient techniques using mortice and tenon joints to join the planks of Samos pine. The galley is 16 metres (54ft) LOA, 2·85 metres (9ft 4ins) beam, and 0·30 metres (1ft) draught. It carries a square sail of approximately 300 sq. ft. and is steered with twin steering oars over the stern. The crew was a polyglot lot that at one time or other contained Greeks, Turks, Russians, a Bulgarian, a Syrian, an Australian, Americans and Norwegians as well as English and Irish members.

General

Most people, like myself, arrive in Greece without the benefit of a classical education. Homer, Herodotus, Thucydides, Plato, Aristotle, Pausanias, Livy, Pliny and Catullus are all names we may have heard of. Some of their works we may even have read, but do not know in the way that schoolboys of old did. The glories of Greece, the might of Rome, the splendour of Byzantium, the atrocities of the Saracens and Turks, the romantic passions of Byron and other Philhellenes, these we know of only superficially. In Greece my outstanding difficulty was to put the places inhabited by the ancients, the monuments, castles and forts, into some sort of historical order. The following brief history will sort out some of that chaos, but for detail and for scholarly wrangling over precise dates and alternative explanations the reader must turn elsewhere.

Pre-Cycladic times

Little is known of early Neolithic life in the Aegean. Man lived on a number of Aegean islands and must somehow have travelled between them to get there in the first place. Milos was of considerable importance because of the obsidian (volcanic glass) found there which was used to make knives, razors, spears and so on.

Cycladic civilisation

By about 4000 BC Neolithic colonists were living on Crete and the Cyclades. Mostly a farming and fishing community, it flourished and artwork in stone, clay, obsidian and later metal has been discovered. The civilisation produced a distinctive form of geometric sculpture which has been found on the Greek mainland and in Asia Minor as well as in graves in the Cyclades. Some of the statuettes are of harp players and the civilisation has been nicknamed

'harpist' after these. From widespread distribution of the geometric statuettes it is believed that sailing craft regularly plied across the Aegean and even as far as France and Spain.

Minoan civilisation
(2000 BC–1450 BC)

Around 2000 BC new peoples bringing with them the advances of the Bronze Age filtered into the Aegean from the Balkans and Turkey. They brought not only the art of working in bronze, but also the Mesopotamian pottery wheel and the eastern Mother Goddess. The Minoan empire based on Crete and Thira expanded and flourished until it was the dominant civilisation in the eastern Mediterranean.

It was a remarkably advanced and peaceful culture. Knossus on Crete was not a fort but a palace which was both beautiful and functional; the Minoan art form worked into frescoes, pottery, and jewellery was both intricate and graceful and compares with any modern pottery and jewellery; and the Minoan fleet traded all round the Mediterranean and established order and peace under the aegis of the Mother Goddess. The civilisation ended abruptly, probably with the cataclysmic eruption of Thira round 1450 BC – one of the biggest eruptions known to have occurred on the Earth. The tidal waves, earthquakes and ash destroyed the Minoan civilisation overnight.

Mycenaeans, Dorians and Phoenicians
(1500 BC–1100 BC)

With the demise of the Minoans, the Mycenaeans based at Mycenae on the Peloponnese became the power to be reckoned with in the Aegean. These are the Aecheans of Homeric fame and were dominant from 1300 BC–1100 BC. The Mycenaeans were supplanted by the Dorians who invaded from the north and brought with them the Iron Age. For some two centuries between 1100 BC and 900 BC Greece lay in the grip of an era which is known now as the Greek 'Dark Age'. In this period writing and painting disappeared. The Dorians settled around the eastern Sporades and Dodecanese, while the Phoenicians from the southern shores of the Mediterranean took control of the sea-routes. By 800 BC a distinct language was emerging from the chaos of the 'Dark Age'.

Greek civilisation
(800 BC–27 BC)

What we know as the Classical and Hellenic periods began about 800 BC and lasted until the Romans arrived. This era saw the birth of the city-state (*polis*) and for this period there was never a united Greece, more a collection of city-states – some of which were more powerful and existed in alliance with others. Colonies were established all around the Mediterranean and Black Sea.

Homer, Sappho, Alcaeus, and Archilochus belong to the early Greek period. Around 500 BC the first threat to the Greeks came from the east when the Persians invaded and captured Naxos. Nine years later they were back and the famous battles of

Marathon and Salamis were fought. The latter destroyed the Persian fleet and turned the Persian threat. Athens, the most powerful city-state, formed the Delian league based around the island of Delos to which all other city-states contributed and so Athens, through the league, controlled Greece.

At various times some of the city-states fell out with Athens, but not until the Peloponnesian War (431–404 BC) was Athens really threatened. Sparta was the eventual winner though its influence was not as great as Athens' had been. The islands on the eastern seaboard, Rhodes, Kos, Khios and Lesvos, became powers unto themselves. In 330 BC, Philip II of Macedon conquered most of Greece and later his remarkable son, Alexander the Great, completed the job. Greece continued to prosper, but the country was gradually coming under Roman domination.

The Romans
(27 BC–330 AD)

By 27 BC Greece was part of the Roman Empire. For nearly four centuries Rome controlled Greece, but for the most part had little cultural influence on it. Greek remained the official language and most cities were allowed to remain autonomous. Little by little Christianity filtered into Greece and merged with the ancient rituals and beliefs. The crunch came with the conversion of the Emperor Constantine to Christianity and the beginning of the Byzantine period.

Byzantium
(330 AD–1204 AD)

The foundation of Constantinople and the rise of Christianity marks the rise of the first Christian Empire. In 6 AD numerous tribes from the north, the Slavs, Avars, Huns and Bulgars, raided Greece, although the forces of Byzantium afforded protection to many cities. Nonetheless many islands were depopulated and towns contracted in size. Later the Saracens were active in the Aegean and some islands were to become completely deserted. The Saracens completely occupied Crete for some time (810–961 AD). The Emperor Nicephorus regained control of some of the islands, but the power of the Byzantine Empire was waning. The churches, particularly the mosaics and frescoes within, are the most enduring monument of Byzantium.

The Franks and Venetians
(1204–1550)

In 1204 the Fourth Crusade sacked Constantinople and the Byzantine Empire was divided up between Venice and numerous other Italian adventurers. In the eastern Sporades, the Gattelusis and Giustianinis, on Naxos, Marco Sanudo, and in the Peloponnese, Villehardouin, were the most notable duchies established. On Rhodes, the Knights of St. John established a castle stronghold which they lost to the Turks in 1522. During this period the Venetians established castles and forts at the principal ports along the Aegean trade routes. Many of these strongholds were held well into the Turkish occupation of Greece.

The Turkish occupation
(1460–1830)

In 1453 the Turks took Constantinople and ended the rule of Byzantium. By the end of the 16th century most of Greece was under Turkish rule. The Turkish occupation was partly one of oppression and neglect although the horrors of Turkish rule have often been exaggerated. In the 17th century the Venetians regained some possessions in the west and English adventurers travelled around Greece collecting the antiquities which can now be seen in British museums. Few remains of the Turkish occupation are to be seen today as after the War of Independence most of the minarets and mosques were torn down except in Crete and the eastern Sporades.

The war of independence
(1822–1830)

In 1822 the Turks massacred 25,000 people on Khios and so aroused Greek passions that many parts of Greece revolted against their Turkish masters. Hydra and Spetsai greatly aided the war effort by committing their fleets to the cause and the war was won when the combined English, Russian and French fleets bottled up the Turkish fleet in Navarino and destroyed it.

The twentieth century

The newly born republic got off to a shaky start and after a series of assassinations the West put a Bavarian prince on the throne. He proved unpopular and was replaced by George I from Denmark who proved to be acceptable. Greece gradually acquired more territory, Thessaly and the Epirus in 1881, and the northern Aegean islands after the Balkan Wars in 1913. The Greeks fought on the allied side in the First World War and with the defeat of the Turks on

The *caïque*. The traditional cargo carrier of Greece.

the Axis side embarked on a disastrous campaign to acquire territory in Asia Minor. When the Greeks were finally driven out the Turkish population remaining in Greece was exchanged for Greeks in Turkey.

Greece fought on the allied side in the Second World War and obtained the Dodecanese at the end of the war. Greece had attempted to remain neutral at the onset of the war, but when Mussolini proposed a coalition with the then Prime Minister of Greece, Metaxa, he declined it with a curt telegram which simply read *Ochi* (No). British, New Zealand and Australian troops fought in Greece, but the Germans overwhelmed them and occupied it until 1944.

After the war a bloody civil war split the country until 1947 when a series of conservative governments ruled until the notorious junta of the Colonels in 1967 ushered in seven years of autocratic and repressive rule. Democracy returned in 1974 with Karamanlis. The first socialist government, PASOK, under Papandreou, was elected in 1981. In 1986 Greece joined the European Union.

Climate and weather

I will make only some general comments here as at the beginning of each chapter there is a detailed description of the weather patterns for a particular area.

Wind strength

All wind strengths are described as a force on the Beaufort Scale.

Winds

In the summer months the winds in the Ionian and Aegean are predominantly from the north. In the Aegean the constancy of the northerly winds in the summer has been noted from ancient times when they were called the *etesians* from *etos* (annual). Today they are commonly called by the Turkish name – the *meltemi*. This wind begins blowing in June and early July, reaches full strength in July and August, and dies off at the end of September and early October. In the northern Aegean the *meltemi*

LOCAL NAMES FOR THE WINDS:
Vorias, Boreas, Tramonata: *North Winds*
Vorias Anatolikos, Gregorio, Grego: *NE Winds*
Anatolikos, Levante, Ageliotes: *East Winds*
Notios Anatolikos, Sirocco, Souroko, Euros: *SE Winds*
Notios, Ostra: *South Winds*
Notios Ditikos, Garbis: *SW Winds*
Pounente, Ditikos, Zephyros: *West Winds*
Vorias Ditikos, Maistro, Schiron: *NW Winds*
Etesians, Meltemi: *Northerly Winds*

Greece - Prevailing summer winds

blows from the NE, in the middle Aegean from the north, and in the southern Aegean from the NW–WNW: in effect the wind describes an arc from the NE through to NW from the northern Aegean to the southern Aegean. In strength it varies from Force 4 to Force 7–8. The *meltemi* blows less strongly in the north and south than into the central Aegean.

The *meltemi* is a consequence of a pressure gradient between a low-pressure area over Pakistan (the Asian monsoon low) which extends its influence as far as the eastern Mediterranean and the high-pressure area over the Azores which affects the western Mediterranean. The pressure gradient between these two stable pressure areas produces the constant northerlies in the summer.

In the winter the pressure gradients over the eastern Mediterranean are not pronounced at all and the winds are not from any constant direction. An almost equal proportion of northerly and southerly winds can be expected. Gales in the winter result from small depressions moving in an easterly direction, either southeastward towards Cyprus or northeastward to the Black Sea. Although these depressions are usually of small dimensions they can give rise to violent winds. In the winter of 1979–80 one such storm was recorded at Force 10–11 and in Corfu a yacht was blown off its cradle in an exposed yard. The depressions can develop rapidly and are often difficult to track as they move rapidly and then stop before moving off rapidly again. Depressions often linger in the Ionian Sea and the southern Aegean.

The Tower of Winds

If you wander around Plaka, the old quarter of Athens, you will come across the Tower of Winds standing just outside the site of the Roman market place. Built in the first century BC by the Macedonian astronomer, Andronikos of Kyrrhos, the octagonal tower is remarkable for a number of reasons. On each of the eight marble sides there is a relief of a winged figure representing the wind that blows from that direction. Originally the tower was capped by a revolving bronze Triton holding a wand which pointed to the prevailing wind.

It was also a clock-tower. Beneath the figures of the winds are eight sundials. Within the tower a water clock registered the hours, fed by a reservoir on the south side of the roof.

But what is most remarkable is that each of the eight sides of the tower faces the cardinal and half-cardinal points of the compass, although the compass in its most rudimentary form was not introduced from the east until over a thousand years later. Moreover the figures depicting the wind fly around the tower in an anticlockwise direction which is the direction in which any cyclonic system entering the Mediterranean also revolves, with the winds of a depression following the same pattern and sequence as that shown on the tower.

The figures

North: *Boreas*, the violent and cold north wind, represented by a bearded old man wrapped in a thick mantle with the folds being plucked by the wind.

Northeast: *Kaikias*, a cold bitter wind represented by a man holding a vessel from which olives are being scattered, representing the valuable olive crop being destroyed by this wind.

East: *Apeliotes*, a handsome young man, carries flowers and fruit, depicting the mild and kindly nature of the wind.

Southeast: *Euros*, represented by an old man with his right arm muffled in his mantle, heralds the stormy southeast wind.

South: *Notios*, a sour-looking figure, empties an urn, implying rain and sultry weather.

Southwest: *Lips*, represented by a figure pushing the prow of a ship, signifies the wind that is unfavourable for ships leaving Athens.

West: *Zephyros*, the mild west wind, is represented by a handsome youth showering a lapful of flowers into the air.

Northwest: *Skiron*, represented by a bearded man with a vessel in his hands, is interpreted in various ways. Either he is carrying a vase denoting occasional rain showers, or a charcoal vessel with which he dries up rivers.

Fog

Fog is very rare. It has been reported in the winter and spring with the highest incidence recorded in January at the entrance to the Dardanelles (3·8 per cent) and in Saronikos Kolpos (2·6 per cent). In all my years of sailing around Greek waters in every month of the year, I have encountered fog only rarely.

Radiation fog

In some areas, especially the northern Ionian and northern Greece, there can be radiation fog in the early morning when conditions are right. The fog has normally burned off by early morning, but in exceptional circumstances may linger to midday.

Visibility

In the summer, dust particles suspended in the air may reduce visibility to as little as 2 miles, but rarely to less.

Thunderstorms

These occur most frequently in the spring and autumn and are often accompanied by a squall. They are usually of short duration and are over in one to three hours. The distribution of thunderstorms is reported to vary over the mainland and the islands: thunderstorms are more frequent over the mainland in the spring and autumn and over the islands in the winter.

Waterspouts

Waterspouts have been reported in some areas in the winter and the spring. Reliable reports of waterspouts have come mostly from the northern Ionian, especially at the entrance to Patraikos Kolpos and the channel between Cephalonia and Zakinthos.

Humidity

The relative humidity is low in the eastern Mediterranean. At 1400 local time the average value in winter is 50–75 per cent and in summer 35–55 per cent.

Sea temperature

The monthly average values vary considerably. In the winter (February) it is 10°C in the north and 16°C in the south. In the summer (August) it is 23°C in the north and 25°C in the south.

Cloud

In the summer cloud is rare. In the winter there is more cloud in the northerly regions and the Ionian than in the more southerly regions.

Swell

Although there is never the large swell encountered in the Atlantic, at times winds from the west and south can build up a large swell. The seas in the Mediterranean with any winds are much shorter, steeper and more powerful than seas around, for instance, the English Channel. Going to windward in a Force 5–6 is a very wet and uncomfortable process.

Currents

In the eastern Mediterranean there is roughly an anticlockwise current: this flows towards the north up the coast of Asia Minor and then turns to flow towards the west and southwest in the north and middle Aegean before turning to flow towards the northwest in the Ionian close to the Greek coast. The many islands and channels in Greek waters means that this flow can be diverted so that in places the current flows in a completely opposite direction to the direction of the general flow. Wherever possible I have mentioned particular currents with the description of a specific channel or sea area.

Sea levels

In most of the eastern Mediterranean the sea level is more influenced by the wind than the tide. The barometric pressure also influences the sea level. With a high barometric pressure and an offshore wind the sea level is lowered and conversely with a low barometric pressure and an onshore wind the sea level is raised.

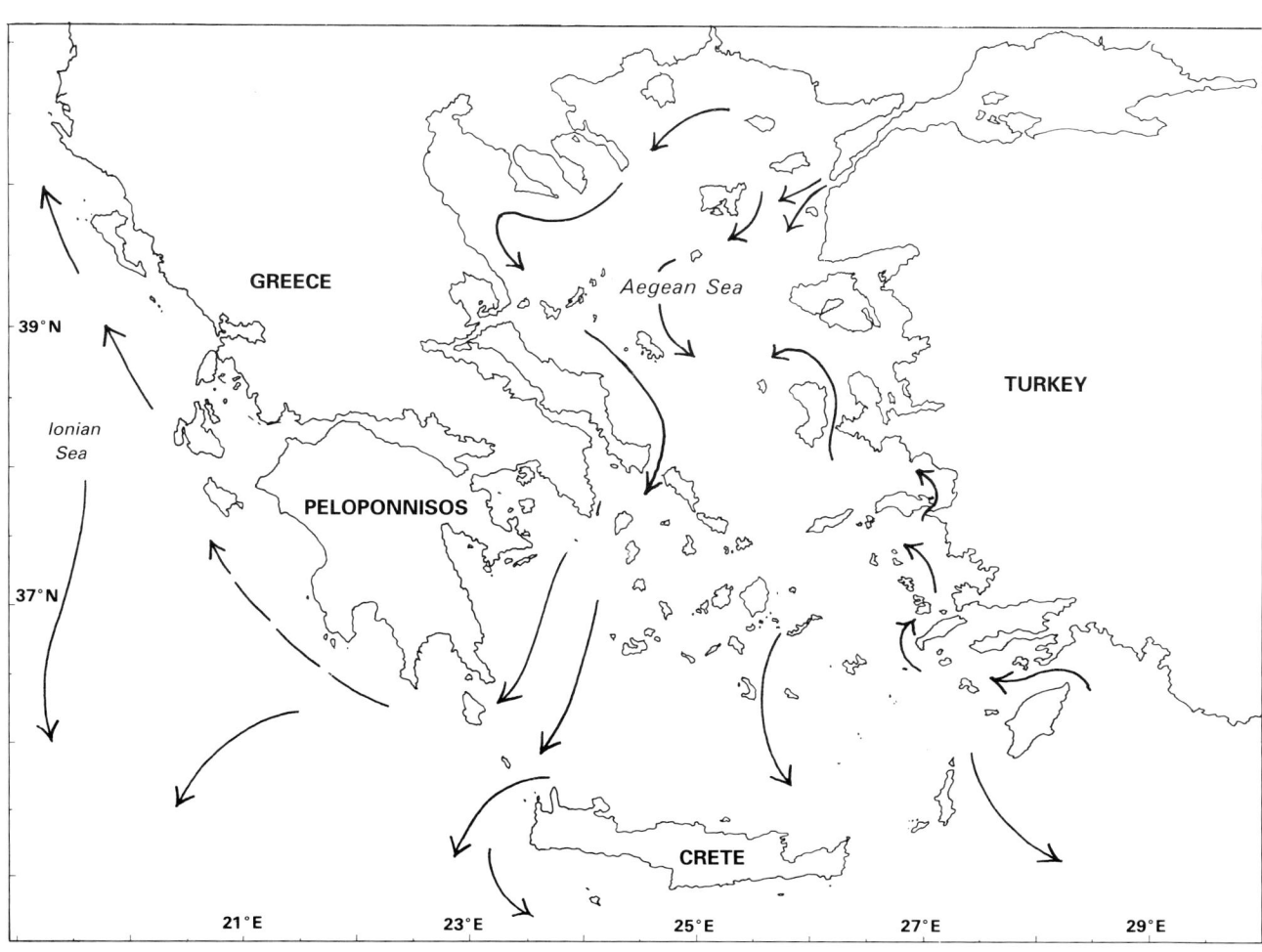

Principal surface currents in July

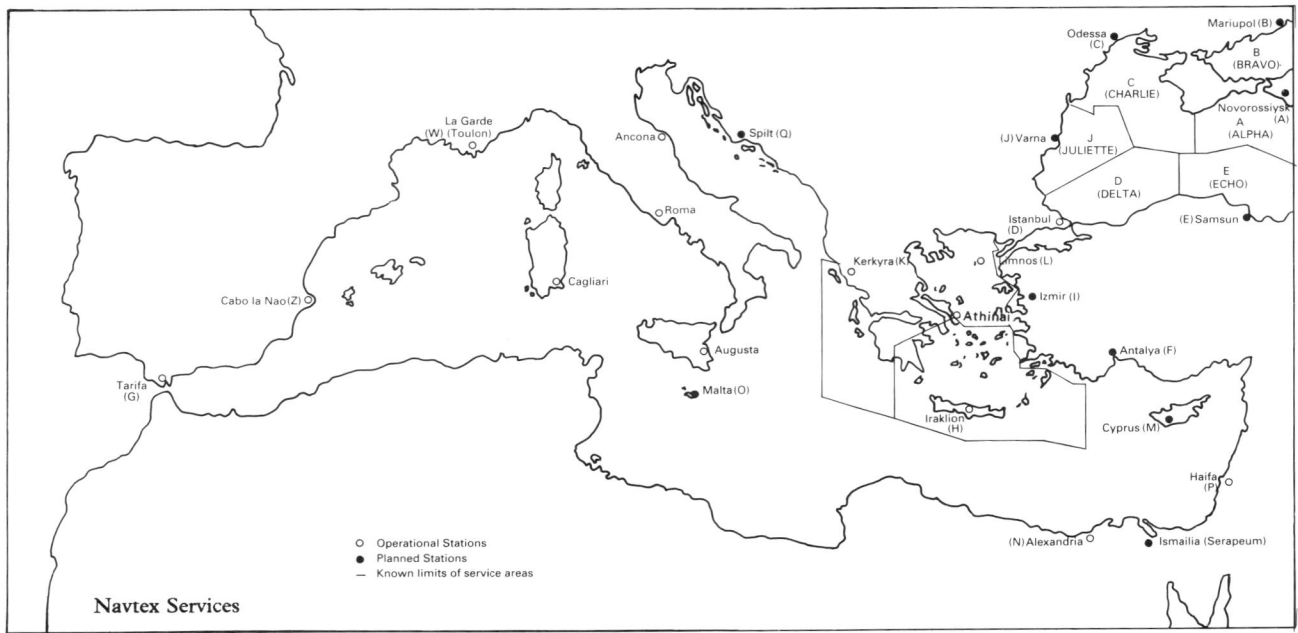

Navtex Services

Tides

The spring rise of tides varies from 10 centimetres to 0·8 metres (2·5ft). The greatest spring rise is in Pagasitikos Kolpos (Gulf of Volos) and Evvoikos Kolpos (Evia Gulf). Tidal streams are weak in Greece except in the narrow channel between Evia and the Greek mainland where at springs it may reach 7 knots at Khalkis.

Routes

The constancy of the summer wind from the north makes the planning of routes quite straightforward. In the spring a yacht should keep to the north and plan to go south and east with the summer northerlies. It can then return to the north and west

Weather forecasts

Because of the high and large landmasses to all sea areas in Greece it is extremely difficult to predict what local winds and wind strength will be. The Greek Meteorological Service does its best but nonetheless cannot give accurate forecasts for many areas. Warnings of approaching depressions will be given but again the erratic progress of these makes forecasting difficult.

Weather forecasts are transmitted on the National Programme.

Local times	Station	Frequency	Wavelength
0630 in Greek and English (winter 0650)	Athens	729kHz	412m
	Thessaloniki	1044kHz	288m
1310–1350	Corfu	1008kHz	298m
1330	Rhodes	1494kHz	200m
2145–2200	Khania	1511kHz	198m
2400	Patras	1485kHz	202m
	Volos	1485kHz	202m

In the Saronic (Argo Saronikos which is Argolida and Saronico areas) a VHF service operates 24 hours on Channel 86 giving a weather forecast for the area in Greek and English.

A maritime weather forecast is broadcast by Radio Hellas. You can get it on radio capable of receiving SSB (with a BFO switch) although it requires fine tuning. The forecast is in Greek and English on the following frequencies.

Athens	2590kHz	0703, 0933, 1503, 2103 UT
Limnos	2730kHz	0703, 0903, 1533, 2133 UT
Iraklion	2799kHz	0703, 0903, 1533, 2133 UT
Rhodes	2830kHz	0703, 0903, 1533, 2133 UT

On the National Television Channel, a weather forecast in Greek (but with synoptic charts and wind directions and forces shown on a map) is given after the news at 2130 local time. In almost any café you will find a television you can watch.

For the Ionian, Italian radio stations gives a weather forecast in Italian on the following frequencies: Radio One on 567, 657, 666, 675, 1062, 1332 kHz on Mondays 0748/2344; Tuesday to Friday 0740/2344; Saturday 0740/2352; Sunday 0748/2352. Radio Two on 846, 1035 kHz on Monday to Friday 1635; Saturday 1645; Sunday 1632.

For the eastern Mediterranean a marine weather forecast is given by Austrian short wave service (in German only) on 6150 MHz/49 metres. 0945 and 1400 local Greek time (from May 1st to Oct 1st only).

Navtex

Navtex is reported to work well in Greece although the positioning of the antenna is critical. Mount the antenna as high as possible or high land can block out reception. Navtex transmissions in Greece are in English.

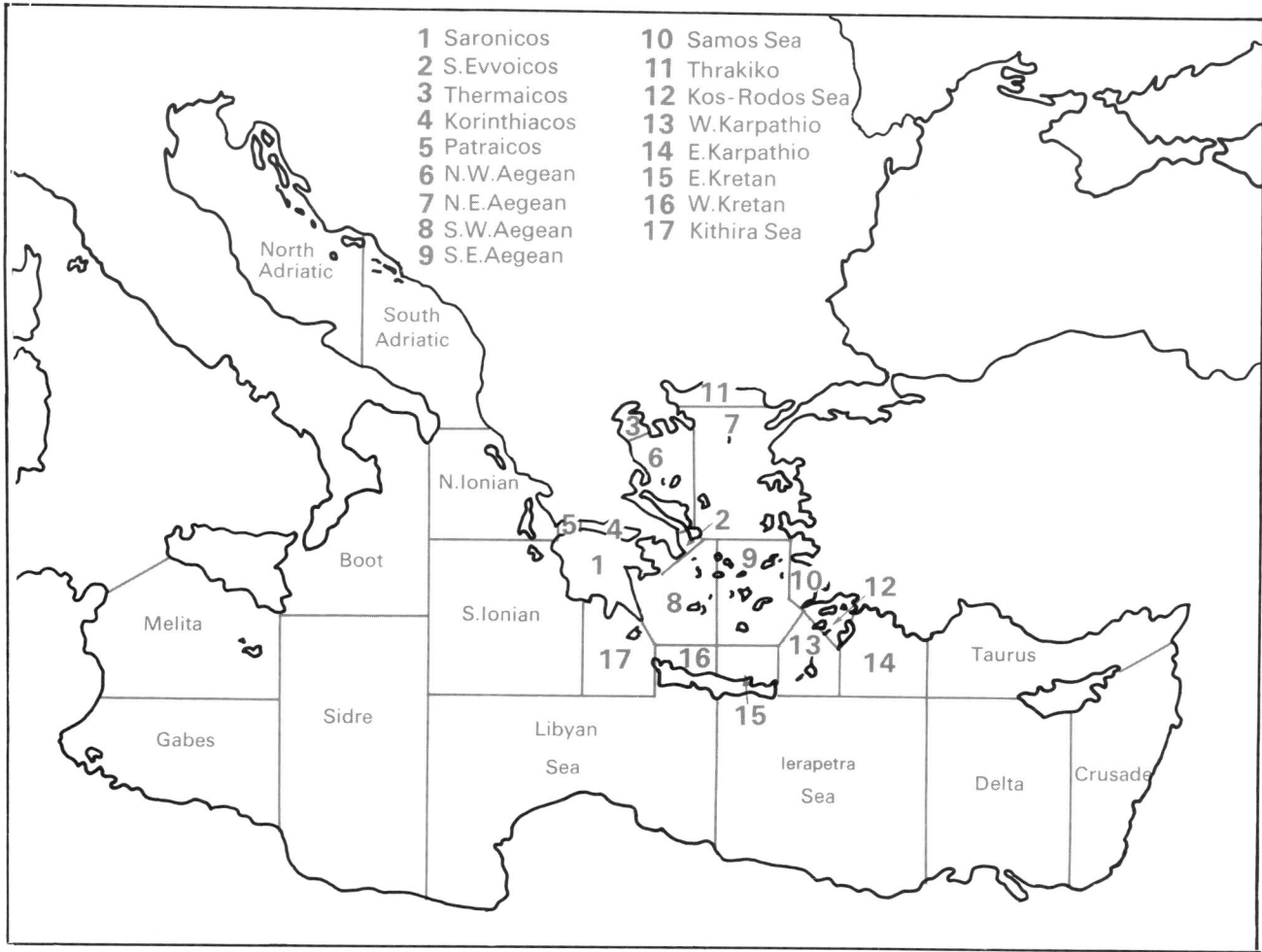

1 Saronicos	10 Samos Sea
2 S.Evvoicos	11 Thrakiko
3 Thermaicos	12 Kos-Rodos Sea
4 Korinthiacos	13 W.Karpathio
5 Patraicos	14 E.Karpathio
6 N.W.Aegean	15 E.Kretan
7 N.E.Aegean	16 W.Kretan
8 S.W.Aegean	17 Kithira Sea
9 S.E.Aegean	

Weather forecast areas and radiobeacons.

Navtex has three message priorities:

Vital   For immediate broadcast.
Important   For broadcast at the next available period.
Routine   For broadcast at the next scheduled transmission period.

The following subject indication characters are used:

A Navigational warnings.
B Meteorological warnings.
C Ice reports.
D Search and rescue information.
E Meteorological forecasts.
F Pilot service messages.
G Decca messages.
H Loran messages.
I Omega messages.
J Satnav messages.
K Other electronic navaid messages.
L Navigational warnings.
Z No messages on hand.

Local weather lore

The following is a collection of bits and pieces of local weather lore gathered at various times in various places. I vouch for none of it, but it may come in useful when planning passages or deciding on where you are going.

1. A warning sign of the *meltemi* is a long white cigar-shaped cloud over an island (particularly in the Cyclades). The cloud will normally form before the wind arrives and will remain in place when the wind is blowing. In the Ionian low dense cloud hugging the summit of the islands warns of a strong *maistro*.
2. In the summer dry decks in the early morning forecasts wind while dewy decks mean there will be little or no wind.
3. The formation of the stages of the new moon forecast whether there will be strong winds or not in the month. If the phases of the new moon form vertically or sideways (the moon 'can't hold water') then there will not be strong winds. If the phases of the moon form horizontally or from the bottom up (the moon 'can hold water') then strong winds will blow in the month.
4. In the eastern Aegean and Crete the Coptic calendar (reproduced in *Turkish Waters and Cyprus Pilot* and *Mediterranean Cruising Handbook*) showing the dates of gales and their direction and duration could prove useful.

Radiobeacons

Preveza Aero RC (38°55′N 20°46′·00E approx) PRV 353kHz 50M

Kerkira Aero RC (39°35′·20N 19°54′·63E) KEK 403kHz 25M

Amalias Aero RC (37°46′·50N 21°20′·83E) AML 367kHz 100M (only when airfield is open)

Kalamata Aero RC (37°04′·17N 22°01′·17E) KTA 348kHz 45M

Korinthos Aero RC (37°55′·77N 22°56′·18E) KOR 392kHz 50M

Aiyina Aero RC (37°46′·02N 23°25′·60E) EGN 382kHz 50M

Kavóuri Aero RC (37°48′·92N 23°45′·60E) KVR 357kHz 200M

Soúnion Aero RC (37°40′·27N 24°02′·89E) SUN 319kHz 50M

Milos Aero RC. (36°41′·90N 24°28′·37E) MLO 378kHz 25M

Thira Aero RC. (36°24′·07N 25°28′·85E) THR 307kHz 80M

Karistos Aero RC (38°00′·86N 24°24′·83E) KRS 285kHz 50M

Alexandroupolis Aero RC (40°51′·45N 25°56′·65E) ALP 351kHz 100M

Limnos (Ormos Moudhros) Aero RC (39°55′·48N 25°14′·93E) LIO 429kHz 150M

Lesvos Aero RC (39°03′·05N 26°36′·40E) LVO 397kHz 25M

Samos Aero RC (37°41′·18N 26°55′·02E) SMO 375kHz 80M

Rhodes/Paradisi Aero RC (36°25′·17N 28°07′·12E) ROS 339kHz 150M

Kos Aero RC (36°47′·70N 27°05′·50E) KOS 311kHz 25M

Karpathos Aero RC (35°25′·25N 27°09′·03E) KRC 314kHz 25M

Soudha Aero RC (35°31′·39N 24°09′·62E) SUD 409kHz 200M

Coastal radio stations

The call sign to Greek coastal radio stations on VHF and on 2182 kHz is HELLAS RADIO. The best policy to elicit a reply is to use a callsign rather than the yacht's name.

All port police stations have a VHF and listen out on Channels 8, 12, 16 and 19. The following stations are the major HELLAS RADIO installations:

Station	Call Letters	Calling	VHF	Traffic lists on
Athens	SVN	2182kHz	16	2590kHz 16,23,26 1879kHz 1829kHz
Khios	SVX	2182kHz	16	1820kHz
Iraklion	SVH	2182kHz	16	2799kHz
Corfu	SVK	2182kHz	16	2830kHz 16,23,28
Rhodes	SVR	2182kHz	16	2624kHz 16,24,27
Limnos	SVL	2182kHz	16	2730kHz 16,23,26
Corinth Canal Zone Authorities			11	

About the plans and pilotage notes

Nomenclature

The spelling of Greek names presents many problems not the least of which is the difficulty of transforming demotic Greek accurately into English. For instance the island of Evia (my spelling) may be Euboea, Evvoia, or Evoia. Even if you get the modern Greek nearly right you may find the place is normally talked of in the diminutive, so Levkas for example becomes Levkadha. To add to the confusion an alternative name from the Venetian, Turkish, French, Italian or English occupation may be the name by which a place is commonly called. For example Thira is commonly called by its Italian name of Santorini.

In this edition I have adopted the convention, in common with all hydrographic departments, of calling a place by the Greek name translated into the Latin alphabet. One interesting point here is that if the rules for transliteration are followed inflexibly, the result can at times be nonsense. Consequently I have modified the rules where I think the end result is truer to the name in Greek. For several places I have used the name commonly used and familiar to English-speaking readers, so Crete is not called Kriti, Corfu is not Kerkira and Piraeus is not Pireefs. After the familiar name I have added the alternative names and any confusing variations so the reader can sort through the different names for himself.

Abbreviations

In the pilotage notes for a harbour or anchorage all compass directions are abbreviated to the first or first and second letters in capitals as is common practice, e.g. N is north, SE is southeast, etc.

Harbour plans

The harbour plans and charts are designed to illustrate the accompanying notes which are set out in a standard format:
APPROACH/MOORING/FACILITIES/GENERAL
It is stressed that many of these plans are based on the author's sketches and therefore should only be used in conjunction with the official charts. They are not to be used for navigation.

Photographs

Most of the photographs were taken by the author. Many were taken under difficult conditions – when navigating short-handed or single-handed or under poor light conditions – and consequently the quality is not all that might be desired. There are many places where photographs are prohibited for military reasons and for the same reason aerial photographs are all but impossible to obtain.

Bearings

All bearings are in 360° notation and are true.

Magnetic variation

The magnetic variation in Greece is very small and for the normally quite short voyages made, the variation can be ignored. It varies from half a degree to two degrees, but is mostly just over one degree east.

Soundings

All soundings are in metres and are based on mean low-water springs. In the case of my own soundings there will sometimes be up to half a metre more water than the depth shown when the sea bottom is uneven, but in most cases there is for all practical purposes the depth shown.

For those used to working in fathoms and feet the use of metres may prove difficult at first and there is the danger of reading the depths in metres as the depths in fathoms. For all practical purposes one metre can be read as approximately three feet and therefore two metres is approximately equal to one fathom. Therefore as an instant check on the depths in fathoms without reference to the conversion tables in the appendix it is possible simply to divide the depth in metres by two and that will be approximately equal to the depth in fathoms: e.g. 3 metres = 1½ fathoms whereas accurately 3 metres = 1 fathom 3·8 feet.

Quick reference guide

At the beginning of each chapter there is a summary of the important information:
PORTS OF ENTRY / PROHIBITED AREAS / RADIOBEACONS/MAJOR LIGHTS. Following this there is a list of all the harbours and anchorages described in the chapter with a classification of the shelter offered, mooring, and whether fuel, water, provisions and tavernas exist. Compressing information about a harbour or anchorage into such a framework is difficult and not a little clumsy, but the list can be useful for route planning and as an instant memory aid to a harbour.

Key

Shelter
A Excellent
B Good with prevailing winds
C Reasonable shelter but uncomfortable and sometimes dangerous
O In settled weather only

Mooring
A Stern or bows-to
B Alongside
C Anchored off

Fuel
A On the quay
B In the town
O None or limited

Water
A On the quay
B In the town
O None or limited

Provisioning
A Excellent
B Most supplies can be obtained
C Meagre supplies
O None

Tavernas
A Excellent choice and range
B Several tavernas to choose from
C One or two tavernas
O None
(*Note* These ratings are nothing to do with the quality of food served in a taverna)

Plan
• Harbour plan illustrates text

Keys to symbols used on the plans

⊕ : waypoint
3 : depths in METRES
: shallow water with a depth of one metre or less
: rocks with less than 2 metres' depth over them
: rock just below or on the surface
: a shoal or reef with the least depth shown
: wreck partially above water
: eddies
: wreck
4 wk : dangerous wreck
: rock ballasting on a mole or breakwater
: above-water rocks
: cliffs
⚓ : recommended anchorage
: prohibited anchorage
⛪ : church
: chimney
: ruins
: windmill
: castle
: houses
: airport
: port police
: customs
: fish farm
: pine
: trees other than pine
: water
: fuel
: travel-hoist
YC : yacht club
i : tourist information
✉ : post office
(O.T.E. : overseas telecommunications exchange

⚡	:	electricity
▲	:	Port of entry
○	:	Radiobeacon
▣	:	oil platform
⛵	:	yachts
⛵	:	yacht harbour
⊷⚓	:	yacht berth
⟨	:	*caïques* or local boats (usually shallow or reserved)
☼	:	light and characteristics
▦	:	lighthouse
o	:	bn
⌂	:	port hand buoy
▲	:	starboard hand buoy
▲	:	mooring buoy
F	:	fixed
Fl	:	flash
Fl(2)	:	group flash
Oc	:	occulting
R	:	red
G	:	green
W	:	white
M	:	miles
s	:	sand
m	:	mud
w	:	weed
r	:	rock

Buoyage

In general buoyage is not developed or consistent in Greece. The IALA Maritime Buoyage System 'A' was introduced in 1983–4.

CARDINAL MARKS

Used to indicate the direction from the mark in which the best navigable water lies, or to draw attention to a bend, junction or fork in a channel, or to mark the end of a shoal.

LIGHTS: ALWAYS WHITE

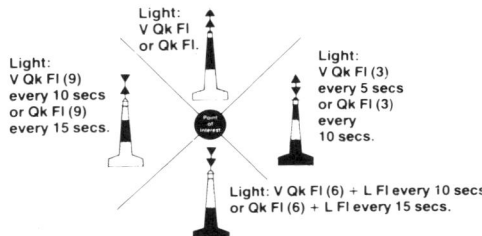

LATERAL MARKS

Used generally to mark the sides of well defined navigable channels

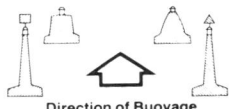

Direction of Buoyage

PORT HAND MARKS
Light: Colour — red
Rhythm — any

STARBOARD HAND MARKS
Light: Colour — Green
Rhythm — any

OTHER MARKS

ISOLATED DANGER MARKS
Use: to mark a small isolated danger with navigable water all around
Light: Colour — white
Rhythm — group flashing (2)

SAFE WATER MARKS
Use: Mid-channel or landfall
Light: Colour — white
Rhythm — isophase, occulting or 1 long flash every 10 secs.

SPECIAL MARKS   Any shape permissible
Use: of no navigational significance
Light: Colour — yellow
Rhythm — different from any white lights used on buoys

I. The Northern Ionian
Corfu (Kerkira) to Zakinthos

From the heel of Italy most yachts cross the Otranto Strait to Corfu only 70 miles away. Corfu is the first of the Heptanesoi, the seven islands of the Ionian. Proceeding south from Corfu you come to the islands of Paxoi and Andipaxoi, Levkas, Ithaca, Cephalonia and Zakinthos, and the island of Kithera. Along the eastern shores of the Ionian are Albania, mainland Greece and the Peloponnese. Some yachts cross direct from Sicily or Malta to Preveza on the mainland, Levkas, Argostoli on Cephalonia or to Zakinthos – all ports of entry in the Ionian.

The Ionian derives its name from the goddess Io. Io was a priestess of Hera and for a short time a mistress to Zeus. Inevitably there was conflict when Hera discovered Zeus was deceiving her and fearing what Hera in her wrath might do, he changed Io into a white cow. Not to be outdone Hera sent a gadfly to torment the unfortunate Io who plunged into the sea to rid herself of the stinging pest – hence the Ionian Sea.

Historically the importance of the Ionian was as a stepping-stone route from the Aegean to Italy and Sicily. Corfu has always been identified as the Homeric island home of the Phaeacians, those mythical ancient sailors who ferried Odysseus home to Ithaca. On a more substantive level Corfu was the ancient Corcyra, a colony of Corinth and the stepping stone to another important Corinthian colony – Siracusa in Sicily.

The seven islands were not united as a historical group until the 14th century when the islands appealed to Venice for protection from their tyrannical Norman and Genoese overlords. Venice seized the chance to consolidate her trade route from Venice around the Peloponnese to the Aegean and thus the seven islands became one political unit. It was this long occupation by the Venetians that gave the Ionian its Italianate qualities. Many of the old gnarled olive trees seen today were planted during the Venetian occupation so the local population could pay its taxes in olive oil. Later the French and English added their own flavour to the islands until, in 1864, the seven islands reverted to Greece.

To those of you who visualize a Greece of sun-baked rock dotted with dazzling whitewashed houses, the Ionian comes as a gentle surprise. This is not the Greece of the popular travel brochure but a shaded green country, sheltering red-tiled Latin houses – an eccentric collection of Italian and French architecture and English tastes (in Corfu the locals play cricket and you can buy currant buns and ginger beer) welded together into a whole that is indubitably Greek. Evergreen cypress, pine, elm, green fields, flowers even in the height of summer, and everywhere the dull dark sheen of the olive, characterise the lower land while higher up the slopes are covered in pine and the tenacious Mediterranean *maquis*. If the wind is in the right direction you can smell the pungent herby aroma a mile out to sea.

The green luxuriance of the islands is in direct contrast to the high eroded mountains of Albania and mainland Greece that form the eastern boundary to the Ionian. Here there is a barren backdrop to the islands that gives a taste of the topography to come. In between there are protected waters where the wind seldom blows too strongly and a multitude of little anchorages accessible only by yacht. From the inland sea bordered by Levkas, Ithaca and Cephalonia you leave the rolling almost English landscape of Zakinthos to confront the rocky slopes of the Peloponnese.

From the Ionian you can reach the Aegean by one of two routes: around the capes of the Peloponnese following the old trade route, or through the Gulf of Patras and the Gulf of Corinth to the Corinth Canal that severs mainland Greece from the Peloponnese.

Weather patterns in the North Ionian

Winds are consistent in the summer. From June to the end of September the normal wind in the northern Ionian is from the NW to WNW. Generally it arrives around noon, blows between Force 2 and 5 and dies at sunset. In the morning there may be a light E or SE wind but it rarely reaches Force 1–2. After October until April/May winds can be from the N or S though gales tend to be more from the S–SE.

In July and August a wind known as the *maistro* may blow from the NW with a little more strength than the normal NW wind. Care needs to be taken at this time of gusts off the lee side of high islands, especially in the inland sea where there can be strong gusts off Levkas, Ithaca, Cephalonia and Zakinthos. Usually when the wind is going to be strong dense white cigar-shaped clouds hug the tops of the mountains on the islands. In the evening there may be a katabatic wind off the high mainland mountains for several hours. It generally blows from a NE direction and can get up to Force 5–6.

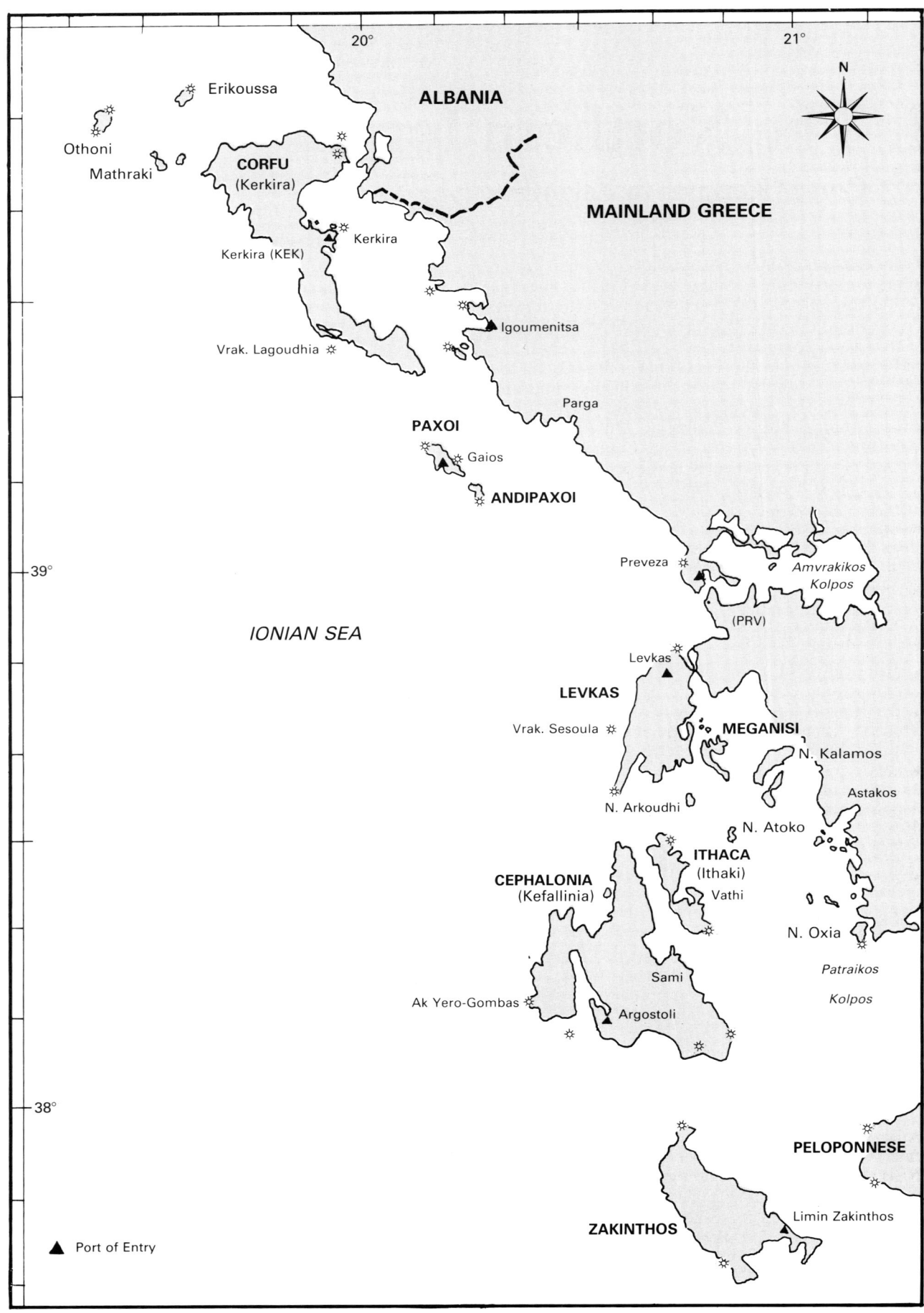

ALBANIA

Erikoussa

Othoni

Mathraki

CORFU
(Kerkira)

Kerkira

Kerkira (KEK)

MAINLAND GREECE

Vrak. Lagoudhia

Igoumenitsa

Parga

PAXOI

Gaios

ANDIPAXOI

Preveza

Amvrakikos
Kolpos

39°

IONIAN SEA

(PRV)

Levkas

LEVKAS

MEGANISI

Vrak. Sesoula

N. Kalamos

Astakos

N. Arkoudhi

N. Atoko

ITHACA
(Ithaki)

CEPHALONIA
(Kefallinia)

Vathi

N. Oxia

Sami

Patraikos
Kolpos

Ak Yero-Gombas

Argostoli

38°

PELOPONNESE

ZAKINTHOS

Limin Zakinthos

▲ Port of Entry

In summer the climate in the northern Ionian is sunny with little rain. The temperature can reach 32°C plus in July and August. In the spring and autumn there are often thunderstorms and associated squalls but these seldom last for very long. In the winter Corfu has one of the highest rainfalls in Greece. As you proceed further south and east the rainfall decreases dramatically; so too does the prolific greenery that goes with a high winter rainfall.

Data

PORTS OF ENTRY

Kerkira (Corfu)
Igoumenitsa
Preveza
Gaios (Paxoi)
Levkas
Argostoli
Zakinthos

PROHIBITED AREAS

The NE coast of Corfu and mainland coast 1M offshore from the Albanian border to Nisis Prasoudhi. Limin Vathi immediately N of Preveza.

Theoretically permission must be obtained from the navy before entering the prohibited areas around Corfu and the adjacent mainland coast, but in practice this is not normally necessary and no problems have arisen from not obtaining formal permission. Likewise Vathi near Preveza is used by yachts without permission. However it should be remembered that these areas are still classified as prohibited areas on the latest Greek charts.

MAJOR LIGHTS

Nisis Othoni NE Point (Akra Kastri) Fl.10s21M
Nisis Othoni SW Point Fl(2)6s6M
Nisis Erikoussa Akra Potamopoulo Fl(3)15s6M

Kerkira (Corfu)
Akra Aikaterini Fl.10s6M
Akra Sidhero (Citadel/Corfu town) Fl(2)6s13M
Akra Levkimmis Fl.6s6M
Vrakhoi Lagoudhia Fl(3)14s6M
Nisis Prasoudhi (Igoumenitsa) Fl(2)9s5M
Nisis Sivota Fl(3)20s11M

Nisos Paxoi
Lakka Fl(3)24s20M
Nisis Panayia Fl.WR.5s10/8M
Nisos Andipaxoi Oc.WR.6s12/9M

Akra Mitikas (Preveza) Fl.WR.3s7/5M

Nisos Levkas
Fort Santa Maura (Levkas Canal N Entrance) Fl(2)WR.12s8/5M
Nisidha Sesoula Fl.4·5s8M
Akra Dhoukaton Fl.10s24M

Nisos Kefallinia (Cephalonia)
Akra Yero-Gombas LFl(2)15s24M
Nisis Vardhianoi Fl.WR.7·5s6/3M
Nisis Kaloyeros Fl.4s8M
Nisis Pondikos Fl.3s8M
Akra Katelios Fl(2)WR.15s6/4M
Akra Kapri Fl(3)WR.9s6/4M
Limin Samis Fl.R.2s7M
Akra Fiskardho Fl.3s6M

Ithaki (Ithaka)
Akra Ay Nikolaou Fl(3)15s7M
Akra Ay Ioannis Fl.12s6M
Akra Pisaitos Fl.5s6M
Akra Oxia Fl(2)15s17M

Zakinthos (Zante)
Akra Skinari Fl.1·5s22M
Nisidhia Ay Nikolaos Fl.2s7M
Akra Krioneri Fl(2)16s6M
Akra Keri Fl(3+1)15s17M

Quick reference guide

	Shelter	Mooring	Fuel	Water	Provisioning	Tavernas	Plan
Corfu and outlying islands							
Nisis Othoni							
Ormos Fiki							
(N Bay)	C	C	O	O	O	O	
Ormos Ammou							
(S Bay)	B	C	O	B	C	C	•
Nisis Erikoussa							
(S Bay)	B	AC	O	B	C	C	•
Nisos Kerkira (Corfu I)							
*Kassiopi	C	AC	B	B	B	A	•
*Ayios Stefanos	B	C	O	B	C	B	•
*Kouloura	C	C	O	O	O	C	•
Kalami	C	C	O	O	O	C	•
Agni	C	C	O	O	O	C	•
Limin Gouvion	A	ABC	AB	B	A	A	•
Limin Kerkira							
(Corfu)	A	AB	A	A	A	A	•
Benitses	O	C	O	O	C	B	
Petriti	B	AC	O	A	C	B	
Kavos	C	A	O	O	O	O	•
Palaiokastrita	B	AC	B	B	B	A	•
Ay Yeoryiou	O	C	O	O	O	C	
Nisos Paxoi							
Lakka	B	AC	B	B	C	B	•
Longos	C	C	O	O	C	C	
Gaios	A	A	B	B	B	B	•
Mongonisi	A	AC	O	O	O	C	•
Mainland coast adjacent to Corfu							
*Pagania	A	C	O	O	O	O	•
*Sayiadha	B	A	O	A	B	B	•
Ormiskos Valtou							
(Igoumenitsa							
Creek)	A	C	O	O	O	O	•
Igoumenitsa	C	AB	B	B	B	B	•
Nisos Sivota and							
Mourtos	B	AC	B	B	B	B	•
Parga	B	AC	B	B	B	A	•
Ay Ioannou	C	C	O	O	O	O	
Ligia	B	A	O	O	C	C	
Preveza	B	AB	B	A	A	B	•
Amvrakikos Kolpos (Gulf of Amvrakia)							
Vonitsa	B	AC	B	B	B	C	•
Loutraki	C	C	O	B	C	C	
Amfilokhia	C	BC	B	B	B	C	•
Menidhion	B	AC	O	B	C	C	•
Koronisia	B	AB	O	B	C	C	

	Shelter	Mooring	Fuel	Water	Provisioning	Tavernas	Plan
Nisos Levkas and adjacent islands							
Levkas							
Levkas Town	A	AB	A	A	A	A	●
Ligia	C	C	O	B	C	C	
Nikiana	B	A	O	A	C	C	
Nidri	B	AC	B	A	B	A	●
Tranquil Bay	A	C	O	O	O	O	●
Ormos Vlikho	A	AC	B	B	C	C	●
Sivota	A	AC	O	A	C	B	●
Vasiliki	B	A	B	A	B	B	●
Nisos Meganisi							
Spartakhori	B	AC	O	B	C	C	●
Port Vathi	B	AC	O	O	C	C	●
Abelike and Kapali	B	C	O	O	O	O	●
Port Atheni	B	C	O	O	O	C	●
Nisos Ithaki (Ithaca)							
Frikes	B	A	O	B	C	C	●
Kioni	B	AC	O	O	C	C	●
Port Vathi	A	AC	B	B	B	B	●
Pera Pigadhi	B	AC	O	O	O	O	●
Ay Andreou	C	C	O	O	O	O	
Port Polis	C	C	O	O	C	C	
Nisos Kefallinia (Cephalonia)							
Argostoli	A	AB	A	A	A	B	●
Lixouri	B	A	B	B	B	C	●
Ay Kiriakis	C	A	O	O	O	C	
Assos	C	AC	O	B	C	B	●
Fiskardho	A	AC	B	A	B	A	●
Ay Eufimia	B	AC	B	A	C	B	●
Sami	C	AB	B	A	B	C	●
Poros	B	AC	B	B	B	B	●
Mainland coast adjacent to the inland sea							
Palairos (Zaverda)	B	A	B	A	B	B	●
Mitika	C	AC	B	B	C	C	●
Nisos Kalamos							
Port Kalamo	B	A	O	B	C	C	●
Port Leone	B	C	O	O	O	O	●
Episkopi	B	AB	O	O	O	O	
Nisos Kastos							
Port Kastos	B	A	O	O	C	C	●
Marathia	C	C	O	O	O	O	
Astakos	B	A	B	A	B	C	●
Port Pandelimon	A	C	O	O	O	O	●
Plati Yialos	B	C	O	O	O	O	●
Nisis Petalas	B	C	O	O	O	O	●
Nisis Oxia	C	C	O	O	O	O	
Nisos Zakinthos (Zante)							
Ay Nikolaos	B	C	O	O	O	C	●
Port Zakinthos	A	A	A	A	A	A	●
Porto Roma	O	C	O	O	O	C	
Lagana	C	AC	O	O	C	B	●
Port Kieri	C	C	O	O	O	C	
Port Vromi	C	C	O	O	O	O	

*See 'Prohibited Areas' above.

Nisoi Othoni and Erikoussa

When crossing from Italy to Corfu there are two islands, Othoni and Erikoussa, lying off the N end of Corfu island, which have useful anchorages often used by yachts to break the passage between Italy and Corfu.

NISIS OTHONI (Othonoi, Fano)
Admiralty chart no. 206
Imray-Tetra G11

Nisis Othoni is a bold precipitous island (500 metres high with a sheer cliff face on the western side), but with the normal summer haze it will often not be seen until two or three miles off. There are two anchorages, Fiki on the N and Ammou on the S. Ammou is the bay normally used in the summer with the prevailing NW–WNW winds.

ORMOS AMMOU

Approach
From the N the lighthouse on the NE corner will be seen. From the W head for the SW tip of the island – the light tower on the SW cannot be seen until closer in. The houses of the hamlet will not be seen until you open the bay.

Dangers Care needs to be taken in the approaches of Ifalos Aspri Petra, a reef lying directly in the S approach. Care also needs to be taken of underwater rocks lying off the coast on the E side of the entrance. The approach should be made from a SW direction with a lookout forward conning you in.

Mooring
Anchor in 2–10 metres where convenient without blocking the immediate approaches to the small harbour. The ferry charges in here at speed and needs all the space at the entrance to manoeuvre.

Approach to Ormos Ammou with the light structure on the SW of Othoni just visible.

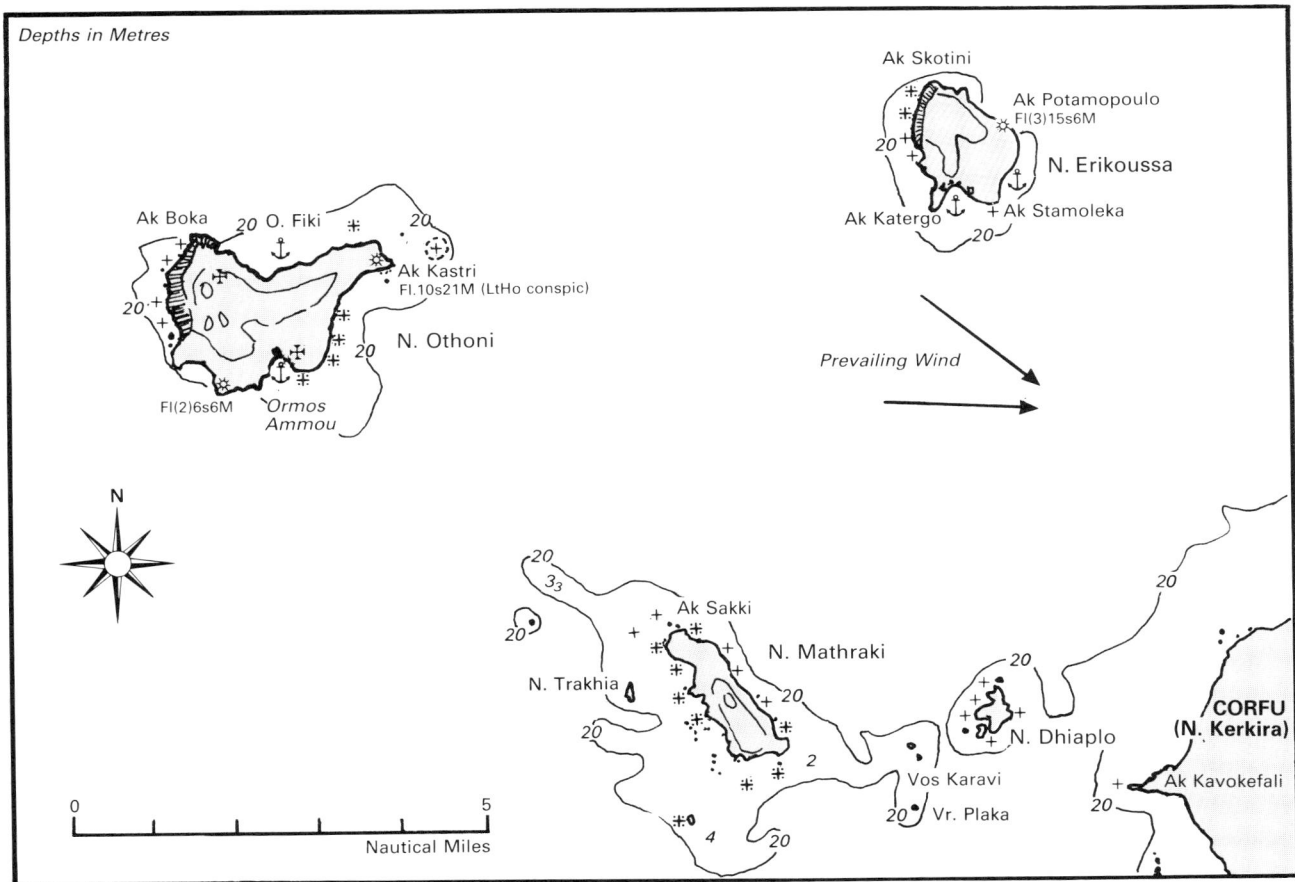

Depths in Metres

NISOI OTHONI, ERIKOUSSA AND MATHRAKI
Note: The shoals and reefs around the islands, especially N. Mathraki, are not all shown and reference should be made to a large scale chart.

The bottom is sand and weed, mostly good holding, although there are some anchor-snagging rocks closer in. It is possible to go bows-to part of the quay when the ferry is not due though care must be taken as the bottom comes up quickly off parts of the quay. Alternatively anchor and take a long line to the outside of the breakwater.

Shelter With the normal NW wind there are mild gusts out of the bay and some swell works its way around into here, but it is secure enough in settled conditions.

Facilities

Ashore there are several tavernas which often have fresh fish. Limited provisions can be obtained and even small amounts of money can be changed if you arrive from Italy without drachmae. Telephone in the local shop.

Note Yachts should not attempt to enter the small fishing harbour to the E as the entrance is rock-bound and depths in the harbour are variable.

ORMOS FIKI

The bay on the N side of the island offers a good anchorage in the event of winds from the S and SE. Care must be taken of the numerous above- and below-water rocks in the vicinity of the bay. When anchoring try to find a patch of sand for plough-type

anchors although a fisherman or grapnel can be hooked on the rocky bottom – attach a trip line. A reef extends a little way from the middle of the bay so caution is necessary close to the shore. I have used this anchorage to ride out a gale from the SE and the shelter from that quarter is excellent.

ERIKOUSSA (Merlera, Merikha)

The island lying about 7 miles due E of Othoni. It is a lower island than Othoni and like Othoni difficult to spot until 1½–2 miles off with the normal summer heat haze. The only village is on the shores of the large sandy bay on the S which affords good shelter from the prevailing NW winds.

South Bay

The approach is free from dangers except for reefs running out a short distance from Ak Katergo and Ak Stamoleka on either side of the bay. Anchor in 3–6 metres on a sandy bottom, good holding. The bottom slopes gradually to the shore. Care needs to be taken of a cable, presumably an electricity cable, lying approximately 150 metres off the shore. Good shelter from the prevailing NW winds.

On the W side of the bay there is a small harbour with mostly 1·5–2·5 metre depths off the quay though care is needed as the bottom is uneven. Care is also needed of the remains of an old jetty which obstruct part of the harbour.

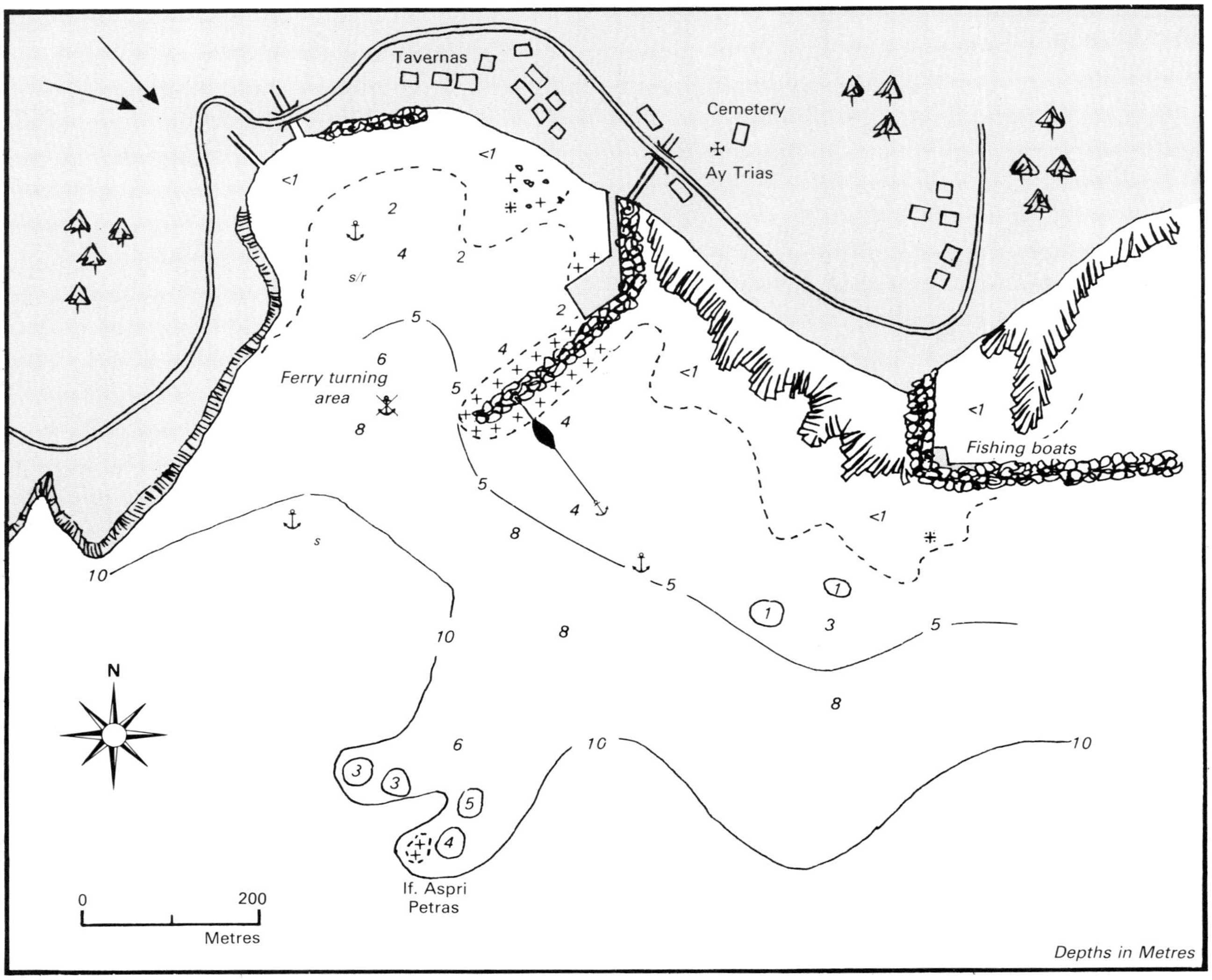

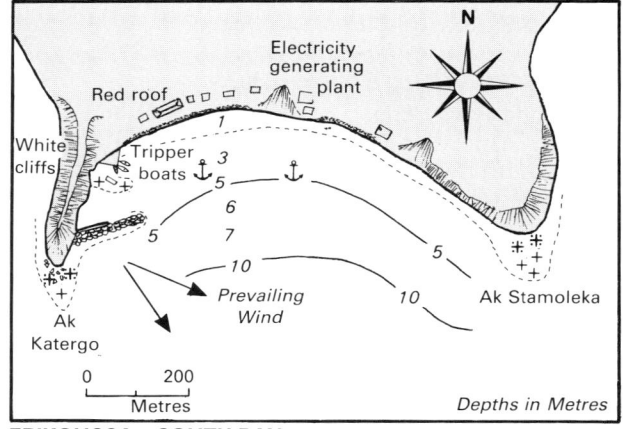

ORMOS AMMOU
39°50'·5N 19°24'·5E

ERIKOUSSA – SOUTH BAY

The anchorage in South Bay on Erikoussa.

Ashore there are several tavernas, often with excellent fresh fish, and limited provisions can be obtained. Tripper boats from Corfu run across here in the summer, but they all disappear by 1600 and the anchorage is then a peaceful one.

Note On the E side of the island there are some delightful coves and bights that a yacht can explore in calm weather or with light NW–WNW winds.

Nisos Kerkira

(Corfu Island)

Most people know little of the Ionian but there are few who have not heard of Corfu. The references to Corfu from Homer to the present day praise the island as a lush green paradise spinning a soothing spell over all who visit it. In an age of package holidays the Corfu magic is continuously battered by jets winging in bringing yet more holidaymakers – and far, far more go to Corfu than to the rest of the Ionian – so it is surprising to find there are still charming and beautiful places on the island.

Corfu lies like a plump sickle off the west coast of Albania and mainland Greece. The channel between the northern end of Corfu and Albania is just one mile across – from Corfu you can see the military outpost at Butrino quite clearly. In contrast to the bare mountains of Albania, Corfu is a luxuriant green island from Mt Pandokrator in the north sloping down to the coastal plains in the south. In the centre are broken slopes cut by green valleys and grassy fields. Seeing cows grazing on the slopes of Ayii Deka it is sometimes difficult to believe you are in Greece.

One of the spin-offs of tourism is the proliferation of guides describing the history, places-to-see and things-to-do here and so rather than attempt to condense the whole history of the island from such guides I have prepared instead a brief synoptic history. This little history also describes, somewhat more loosely, the chain of events and invasions determining the character of the other islands in the Ionian.

c.1200 BC It is surmised that Homer's Skheria, the island home of the Phaeacians, was Corfu. Palaiokastrita is thought to be the site of the castle of King Alkinoos. The Phaeacians ferried Odysseus home to Ithaca, in so doing arousing the wrath of Poseidon who turned their ship to stone. The island of Gravia off Palaiokastrita is said to be this petrified ship although some say it is the island of Pondokonisi (Mouse Island) near Kanoni.

c.734 to 434 BC Corfu is colonised by the Corinthians. Corfu, itching for independence from the mother city, called on the Athenians to aid it against the Corinthians who naturally enough asked the opposing Spartans to give them a hand in quelling Corfu. Thus Corfu was indirectly the cause of the disastrous Peloponnesian War that effectively obliterated Athens and classical Greece.

229 BC Corfu colonised by Rome.

722 AD Corfu passed to the eastern Byzantine Empire.

1080 to 1386 After a collection of Norman and Sicilian rulers, Corfu invites the Venetians to restore order. Corfu remained under Venetian rule until 1797.

1460 The body of St Spiridon is brought to the island and becomes the patron saint of Corfu. Every year there are four processions on which the body of St Spiridon is brought out: Palm Sunday, Easter Saturday, the 11th of August, to commemorate the defeat of the Turks in 1716, and the first Sunday in November to commemorate the end of a plague. Every second male in Corfu seems to be called Spiros after the patron saint.

1431, 1537, 1716 Major assaults by the Turks on Corfu.

1797 Corfu taken over by the French. The French laid out a regular street plan for Corfu and began the construction of the arcaded buildings on the esplanade in Corfu town.

1814 Corfu occupied by the British who began many public works as well as introducing ginger beer, fruit cake and cricket.

1864 Corfu ceded to Greece.

Today Corfu reflects many of these influences in its own special Corfiot architecture and culture. The eerie Medusa in the museum, the Venetian forts and galley port, the French architecture raising a second Rue de Rivoli far from Paris, cricket and cake on Sundays, Byzantine churches...yet undeniably Greek as Lawrence Durrell will tell you:

'A glance at the synoptic history of the place will do nothing to decrease the sense of being out of one's depth, submerged by too much data. But as time goes on, as sunny Greek mornings succeed each other, you will find everything sinking to the bottom of your mind's harbour, there to take up shapes and dispositions which are purely Greek and have no frame or reference to history anywhere else.'

Lawrence Durrell *The Greek Islands*

North coast of Corfu

KASSIOPI (Avlon Kassapeto)*

Approach

From the W the castle on the headland and a number of houses around Ormos Imerola will be seen. From the E the buildings of Kassiopi are readily identified. The small harbour itself will not be seen until you are right into the bay.

Mooring

A short mole extends in a W–E direction behind the head of which there are 4 metre depths shelving to less than a metre at the root of the mole. Behind the mole there is some protection from the NW wind. Alternatively anchor in the middle of the harbour.

Shelter Good behind the short mole. In the middle of the harbour it can be very uncomfortable and possibly dangerous with the prevailing NW winds. Most of the quay extending from the mole around the bay has depths of less than a metre for some distance off.

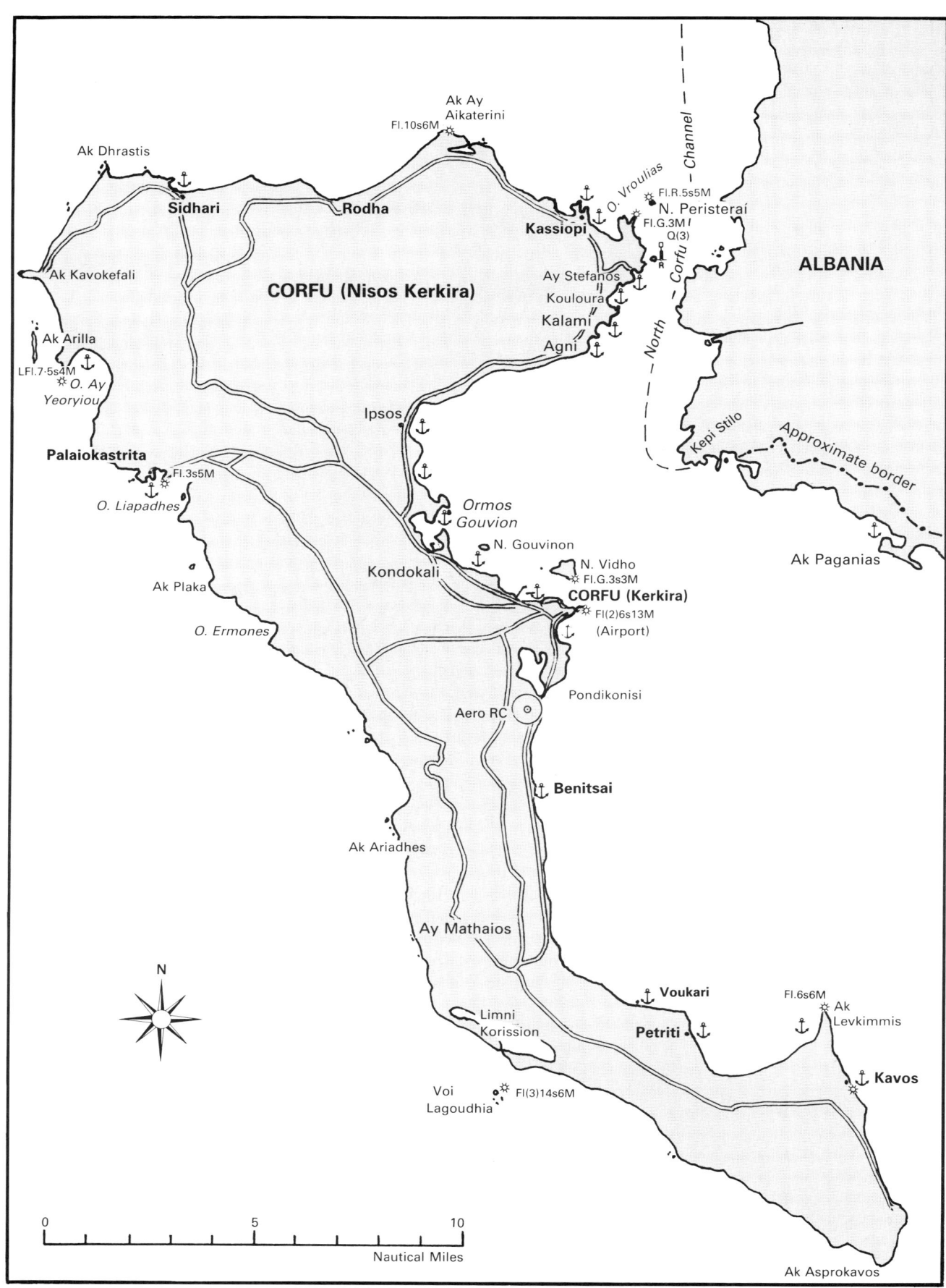

Ak Ay
Aikaterini
Fl.10s6M
Ak Dhrastis

Sidhari   **Rodha**

O. Vroulias
Fl.R.5s5M
N. Peristeraí
Fl.G.3M
Q(3)
Kassiopi

Ak Kavokefali

CORFU (Nisos Kerkira)   **ALBANIA**

Ak Arilla
Ay Stefanos
Kouloura
LFl.7·5s4M
O. Ay Yeoryiou   Kalami

Agni

Palaiokastrita
Ipsos
Kepi Stilo
Approximate border

Fl.3s5M
O. Liapadhes

Ormos Gouvion

Ak Paganias

Ak Plaka
N. Gouvinon

O. Ermones
Kondokali   N. Vidho
Fl.G.3s3M
CORFU (Kerkira)
Fl(2)6s13M
(Airport)

Pondikonisi

Aero RC

Benitsai

Ak Ariadhes

Ay Mathaios

Voukari
Fl.6s6M
Ak
Levkimmis
Limni
Korission   **Petriti**

N

Kavos

Voi
Lagoudhia   Fl(3)14s6M

0   5   10

Nautical Miles

Ak Asprokavos

NISOS KERKIRA (CORFU)

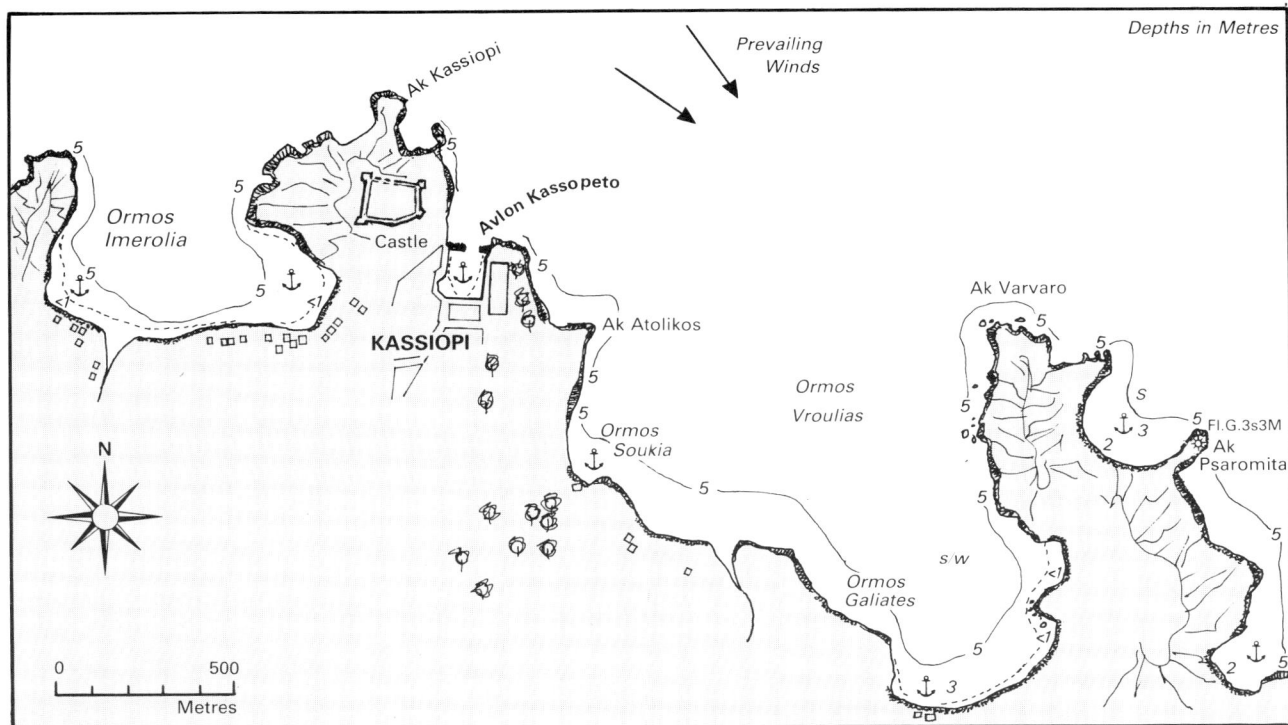

Depths in Metres

Prevailing Winds

Ak Kassiopi

Ormos Imerolia

Castle

Avlon Kassopeto

KASSIOPI

Ak Atolikos

Ormos Soukia

Ormos Vroulias

Ormos Galiates

Ak Varvaro

S

Fl.G.3s3M
Ak Psaromita

s/w

N

0   500
Metres

ORMOS IMEROLIA TO AK PSAROMITA

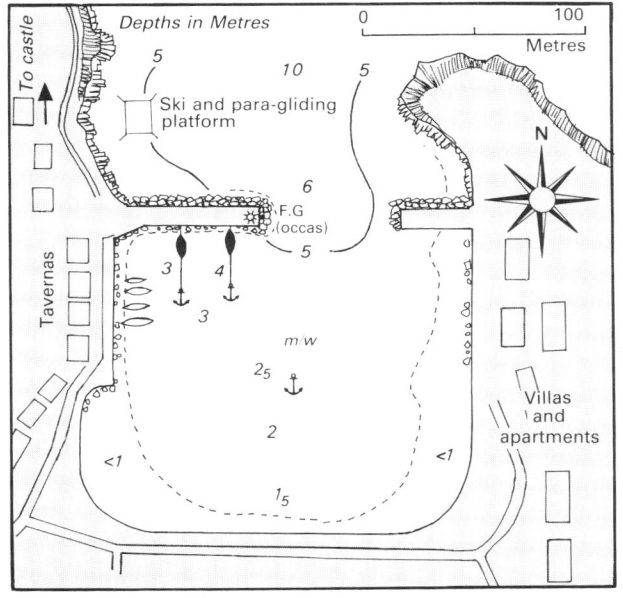

To castle

Depths in Metres

0   100
Metres

Ski and para-gliding platform

F.G (occas)

Tavernas

m/w

Villas and apartments

N

KASSIOPI (Avlon Kassopeto)
39°47'·5N 19°55'·5E

Kassiopi harbour looking SSE from near the short mole.

Facilities

Water from private sources. A fuel station in the town. Good shopping for provisions and numerous tavernas and restaurants of all types. Bank. PO. Hire scooters.

General

Kassiopi is a thriving tourist spot with numerous small hotels and self-catering apartments around the original village. In July and August it is crowded with holidaymakers, but outside high season it retains some of the charm of what was a small fishing village.

ORMOS VROULIAS

The large bay immediately E of Kassiopi. In settled weather there are several attractive anchorages on the W side and at the head of the bay. The bottom is mostly sand and weed. On the E side of Ak Varvaro there is a small cove affording reasonable shelter under Ak Psaromita.

East coast of Corfu

Northern Corfu channel (Vorion Stenon Kerkiras)

Imray-Tetra chart no. G11

From the N pass between Nisis Perasterai and Corfu and proceed with caution into the channel until the stone beacon on Ifalos Serpa is sighted. Leave the beacon well to starboard – it is not on the extremity of the reef. When you pass through the channel outside Ifalos Serpa you are less than a mile from the Albanian coast. At night the light on Nisis Peristerai (Fl.R.5s5M) is easily seen from the distance stated and once into the channel the Q(3)10s7M on the beacon at the end of Ifalos Serpa will be seen.

At present no reliable information is available on Albania. A number of yachts have stopped over in Albania, but seem to have had high level connections

Nisis Peristerai and lighthouse (at the N end of North Corfu Channel) looking ESE.

to do so. Tripper boats run from Corfu across to Butrinti and Saranda taking people on day trips. But despite the end of totalitarian rule and day trips I would not voluntarily take a yacht to Albania without authorisation. At the time of publication relations between Greece and Albania were strained and yachtsman should keep a weather eye on the utterances of politicians in the two countries. The situation will certainly change in the near future and it is expected arrangements will be made for yachts to enter Albania, but in the present confused climate exercise some care near the Albanian border.

AYIOS STEFANOS★

A small inlet immediately S of Ifalos Serpa in the North Corfu Channel. Although just below a military post no objection is normally made to anchoring here.

Proceed into the middle of the bay and anchor in 3–6 metre depths. The bottom is mud and thick weed which can be difficult to get through. Excellent shelter from the NW wind. On the S side of the bay there is a rough stone mole, but this is usually occupied by local boats.

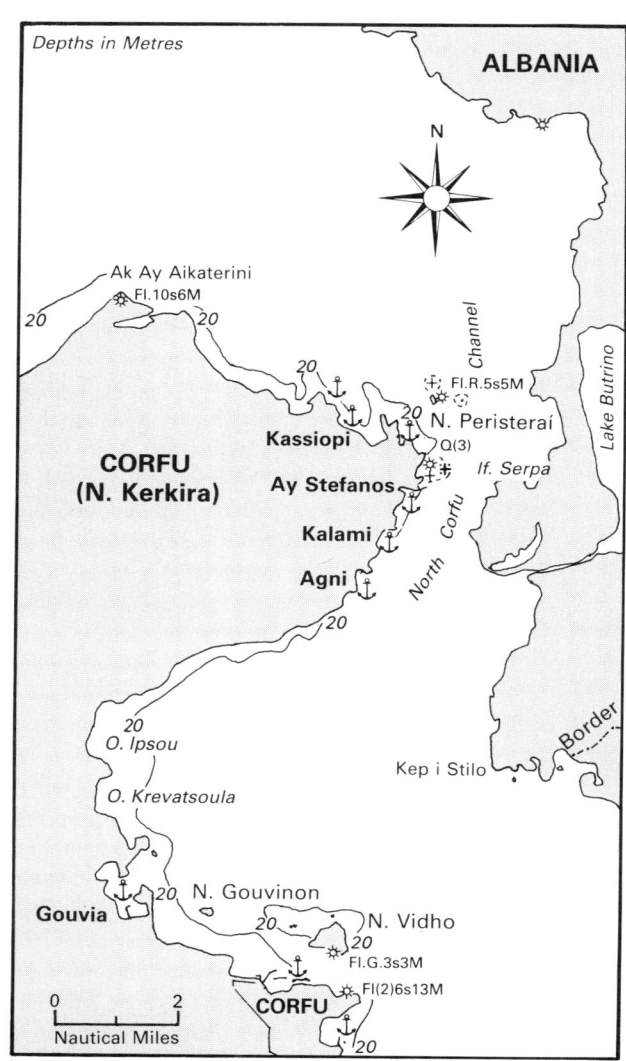

CORFU: NORTH CHANNEL

Ay Stefanos looking SE.

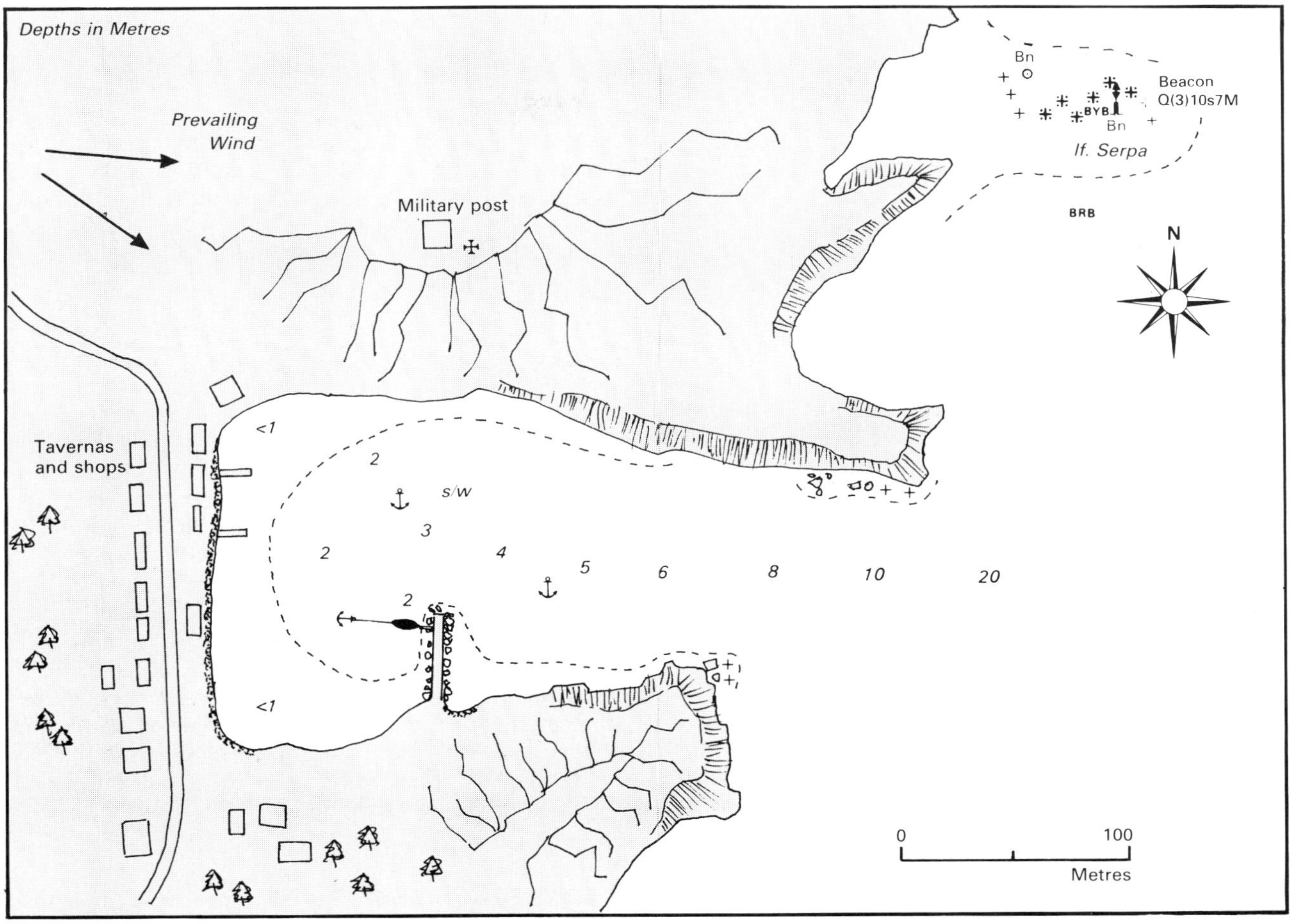

Depths in Metres

Prevailing
Wind

Military post

Tavernas
and shops

<1

2

2

3

4

5

6

8

10

20

s/w

2

2

<1

Bn
Beacon
Q(3)10s7M
BYB
Bn
If. Serpa
BRB

N

0   100
Metres

AY STEFANOS
39°46′N 19°57′E

Some provisions can be obtained and there are numerous tavernas around the shore. Although a number of holiday villas have been built here, the bay retains a calm and beauty well worth the stop for the night.

KOULOURA★

A small bay S of Ay Stefanos. There is a miniature harbour surrounded by shoal water at the SE end of the bay. A yacht drawing one metre or less can enter with care from the N. Excellent shelter inside. Alternatively anchor in 5–10 metre depths immediately W of the small harbour and take a long line ashore or anchor in the W of the bay in 8–15 metres. The bottom is covered in thick weed. Good shelter from the prevailing NW wind.

Ashore above the small harbour is a taverna which though frequently crowded for lunch is less hectic at night.

★These harbours lie within an officially prohibited area though the prohibition is disregarded in practice.

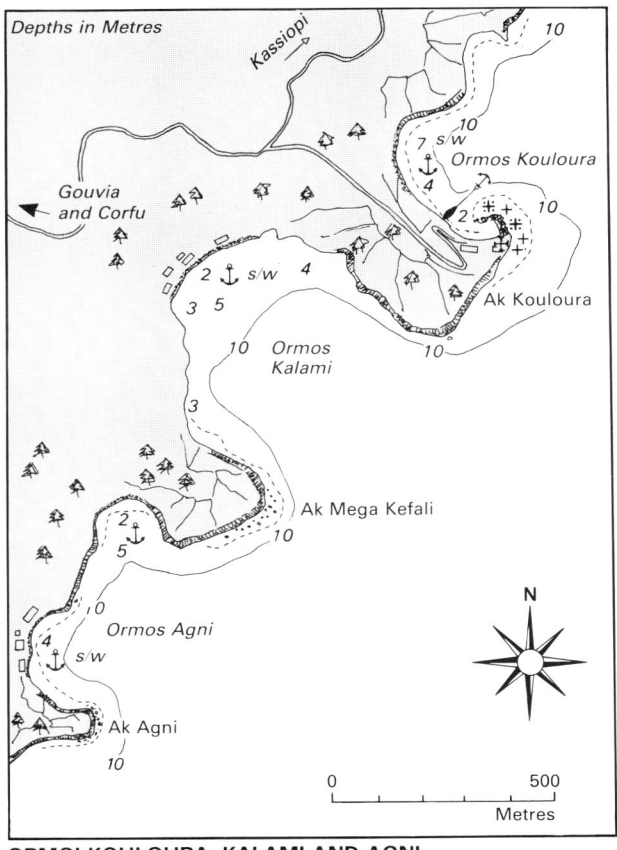

Depths in Metres

Kassiopi

10

10

7 s/w

Ormos Kouloura

4

Gouvia
and Corfu

2 s/w 4

2

10

3 5

Ak Kouloura

10 Ormos
Kalami

10

3

Ak Mega Kefali

2

5

10

0

Ormos Agni

4

s/w

Ak Agni

10

N

0   500
Metres

ORMOI KOULOURA, KALAMI AND AGNI

The miniature harbour at Kouloura looking S.

KALAMI*

Immediately S of Kouloura is Ormos Kalami. Open to the S and E, it offers good shelter from the prevailing NW wind. Anchor in 4–6 metre depths in the NW of the bay. Some provisions and tavernas ashore.

AGNI

The bay immediately S of Kalami. Anchor at the N end or at the S end. Good shelter from the NW wind although it gusts into the bay. Taverna ashore.

ORMOS GOUVION (Gouvia)
Imray-Tetra chart no. G11

The large enclosed bay NW of Corfu town with Gouvia Marina at the S end.

Approach
Conspicuous Nisis Gouvion in the S approach and Akra Kommeno and Vrakhos Foustanopidhima on the N are readily identified. Two large hotels on the N side of the entrance are conspicuous. Once up to the entrance to the bay the red and green buoys marking the channel into the bay are readily seen. Entering the bay keep to the N side of the entrance to avoid the extensive shallows on the S. A transit between the small islet off Ak Kommeno Vrakhos Foustanopidhima (joined by a footbridge to Ak Kommeno so it appears to be part of the cape) and a red house just above the loading quay will keep you clear of the shallows, though the buoys make it obvious where the channel lies.
By night There are no major lights to guide you in, but the conical buoys marking the channel are lit

Fl.G and Fl.R, range probably about one mile. The lights on the channel buoys cannot always be relied upon. The end of the marina pier is lit: 2F.R(vert)3M.

Dangers The southern half of the entrance is obstructed by a shallow mud bank. The aforementioned buoys show the channel into the bay clear of the shoal water.

Mooring
1. *Gouvia Marina* Go stern-to or bows-to where directed or wherever convenient. There are laid moorings tailed to the quay and a yacht should not use its own anchor except if the mooring is missing as some of them are. Although the marina was initially dredged to 5–6 metres, parts of it have silted to as little as 2·5 metres. Shelter in the marina varies according to where you are. The best all-round shelter is in the SW corner. The berths on the quay off the marina office are dangerous in strong NE winds. Likewise berths on the E side of the long central pier are also dangerous in strong N–NE winds.
2. *South anchorage* Anchor off to the E of the marina pier in 2–5 metres. The bottom is mud and excellent holding. Open to the slop across the bay from northerlies, but the excellent holding means this is not a problem.

Note 1. It is now prohibited to anchor in the N of Ormos Gouvia.
Note 2. Two sewerage outfall pipes are laid across the bay from the W side to the entrance. In the N bay there are reported to be only 1·8 metre depths over the rocks piled on top of the pipe.

Authorities Marina staff. A charge is made in the marina. The relevant officials for clearing into Greece and obtaining a transit log are at Corfu harbour.

Facilities
Gouvia Marina

Services Water (non-potable) on the quay. Drinking water can be delivered by mini-tanker. Electricity on the quay though it is not always working. Showers and toilet near the marina office a considerable walk away from most berths.
Fuel Can be delivered by mini-tanker.
Repairs Yachts can be craned onto the hard by a mobile crane. Alternatively there are yards between the marina and Corfu town. Mechanical, engineering, GRP and wood repairs, electrical and minor electronic repairs can be carried out. Some sail repairs possible. A long-established yacht service company is Yacht Maintenance Service. They can carry out mechanical, wood and GRP repairs and general yacht maintenance. *Gardiennage* can be arranged. Contact Brian Clarke tel/answering machine/fax (0661) 90382. Several chandlers near the marina in Kondokali.

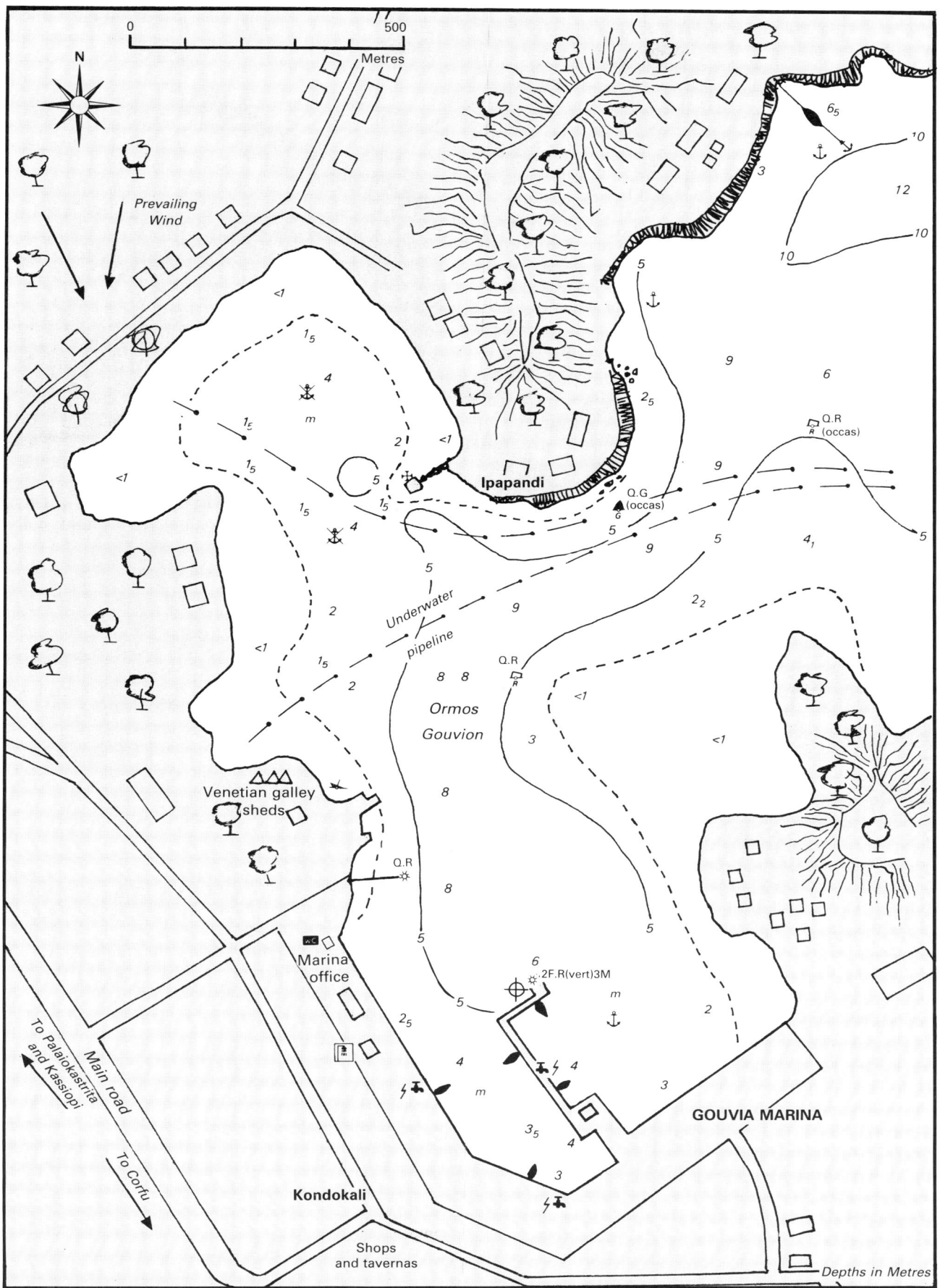

ORMOS GOUVION AND GOUVIA MARINA
39°39'N 19°51'·1E (2F.R(vert)3M)

Provisions Good shopping for all provisions nearby at Kondokali. A number of the mini-markets will deliver to the marina. Ice from an ice truck that does the rounds in the summer.

Eating out Numerous tavernas and bars in Kondokali.

Other PO. Exchange offices. Greek gas and *Camping Gaz*. Hire cars and motorbikes. Irregular bus into Corfu town. Mail can be sent to the marina: National Tourist Organisation of Greece, Marina at Gouvia, PO Box 29, Corfu, Greece. ☎ Corfu (0661) 91475

General

Kondokali was once a small fishing village, but that was long ago before hotels and self-catering apartments were built around the coast. Now it plays host to predominantly English tourists who can find all things English here – English newspapers, English breakfasts, an English pint, English Sunday lunches – but few things Greek.

The marina itself remains much as it was built more than ten years ago which is a half-finished developers' site waiting for the buildings that are rumoured to be planned for 'next year'. It is not an attractive place though the surrounding countryside outside the hotel and apartment periphery is lush and attractive. In the winter it rains...and rains, so be prepared for a damp time if wintering here.

Gouvia marina looking N along the T-pier.

LIMIN KERKIRA (Corfu Harbour)

Admiralty chart no. 2406
Imray-Tetra chart no. G11

Approach

Conspicuous From the N Nisis Vidho obscures part of the town. Nisis Vidho and the rock (Vos Navsika) nearby are conspicuous from the distance. As you near the harbour the buildings of the town will be seen. From the S the Venetian citadel on Ak Sidhero and the lighthouse atop it are clearly visible from some distance off. A red belfry in the town and the two radio masts to the W of the town are also conspicuous.

Corfu looking W from near Ak Sidhero.

Note It is safe to pass between Nisis Vidho and Vos Navsika.

By night Use the light on Ak Sidhero (Fl(2)6s13M) and closer in the lights of the harbour. The old harbour is lit at the W end (Fl.R(3s)2M and the detached breakwater is lit: Q.G.2M and Fl.R.2s2M. The end of the new breakwater has a light buoy (Fl.G) though it should not be relied upon. The red lights atop the radio masts in the town are clearly visible and the citadel is often spotlit in the summer.

Note The harbour is used by considerable numbers of ferries from Italy and smaller landing-craft-type ferries from Igoumenitsa. A yacht should give way to these ferries at all times and a good lookout should be kept for them in the approaches to the harbour.

Mooring

If you require a transit log go on the customs quay. After obtaining your transit log moor in the old harbour to the E of the customs quay. If there is a strong NW wind you can sometimes moor in the old harbour and obtain your transit log from there as the customs quay can be dangerous with the prevailing NW wind. In the summer it is best to arrive early in the morning aiming to be off the customs quay before the NW wind arrives about noon. In the old harbour the most comfortable place is alongside the outer breakwater where the NW wind will hold you off. The town quay is mostly occupied by local boats and there is rarely room on it. In any case much of the town quay has silted close to and only small yachts will be able to go bows-to.

Ak Siderho   Old harbour entrance

Approaches to Ak Sidhero and Corfu looking SE.

Shelter Good shelter in the old harbour where only southerly gales set up a surge. As mentioned the quay off the customs area is open to the prevailing NW wind which blows straight down onto it.

Authorities Customs, immigration, and port police in the customs enclosure. A transit log can be obtained here and as all the relevant authorities are grouped close together this is a comparatively easy process.

Facilities

Water On the customs quay.
Fuel On the customs quay.
Repairs There are several boatyards to the W of the town. Most mechanical repairs can be carried out (agents for most makes of engine though many of the spares will have to be delivered from Athens). Engineering including stainless steel fabrication, GRP, and wood repairs. Electrical and some electronic repairs. Chandlers nearby on the waterfront.

Provisions Good shopping for all provisions. There are several small mini-markets on the waterfront, but you are better off going into town where there is a better choice. Ice can be ordered.

Eating out A wide choice of tavernas. Those clustered around the square SE of the harbour are as good as any or wander around and find your own favourite. Numerous bars dotted about everywhere.

Other PO. OTE (open 24 hours and will change foreign banknotes). Banks and exchange offices. Greek gas and *Camping Gaz*. Hospital. Hire cars, motorbikes, bicycles. Bus service to most parts of the island. Ferry service to Brindisi, Patras and Igoumenitsa. International flights and regular internal flights to Athens.

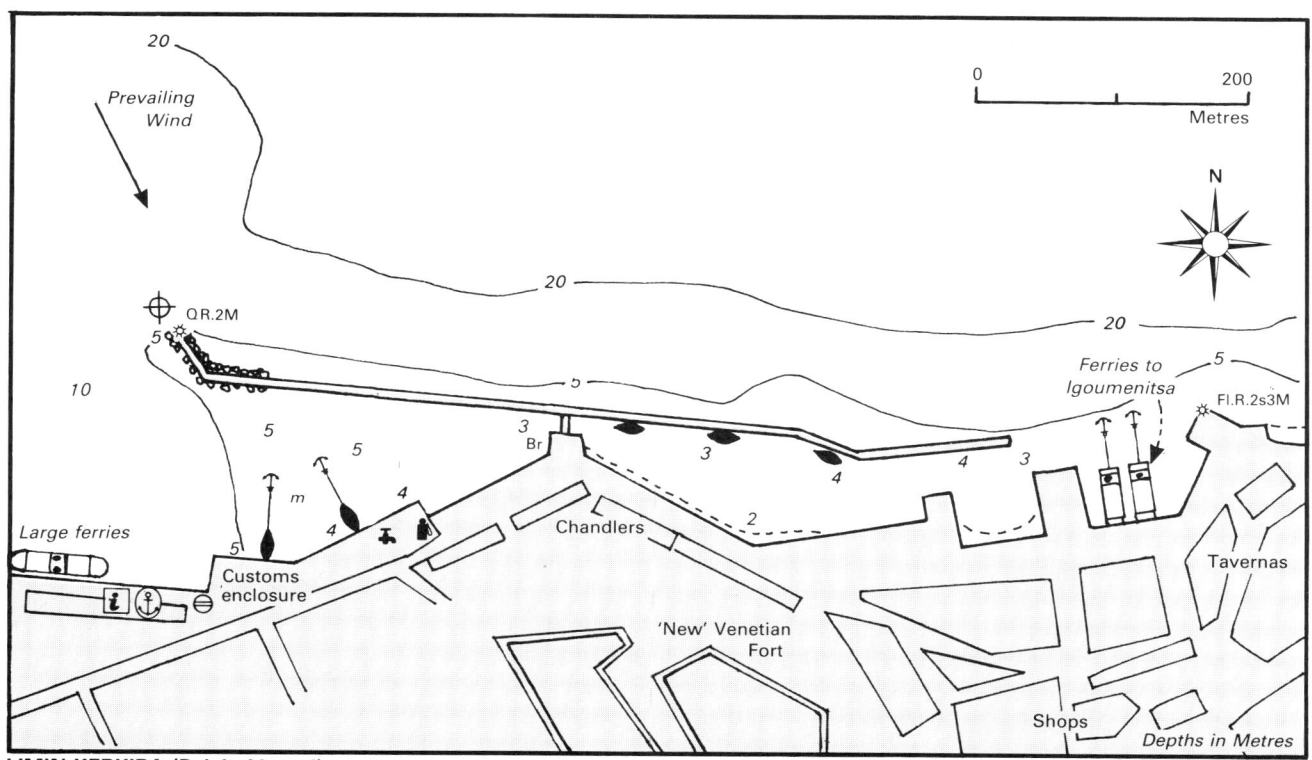

LIMIN KERKIRA (Palaio Limani)
39°37'·7N 19°55'·7E (Q.R.2M)

General

Corfu town is one of those special places that grows on you the longer you stay. Unfortunately Corfu old harbour is smelly and crowded in the summer which adversely affects your views on the town. Gouvia is too far away unless you have your own land-based transport. As well, the myriad tourists choking the narrow alleys can put you off. Nonetheless persevere until Corfu charms you. There are many things to do and see in and around Corfu, but as much as anything it is just wandering around that gives pleasure and despite the increase in 'tourist alleys' selling nondescript knick-knacks, there is still much of the old town remaining intact and alive.

BOATYARDS

Just W of the commercial docks are a number of boatyards. Yachts up to 20–25 tons can be hauled out here on a cradle and slipway and propped on hard standing. Most mechanical, engineering, GRP, and wood work can be arranged at the yards.

ORMOS GARITSAS

A yacht can anchor off on the S side of Ak Sidhero in Ormos Garitsas where there is good shelter from the prevailing NW wind. Anchor in 5–12 metres on mud, good holding.

Berthing alongside in Corfu old harbour.

Ormos Garitsas on the S side of Ak Sidhero.

NAOK YACHT CLUB

The yacht harbour on the W side of Ormos Garitsas belongs to a local yacht club. There are a limited number of berths for visiting yachts in the summer on the end of the mole decreasing further into the harbour. There are mostly 2–3 metre depths off the outer end of the mole. Go stern-to or bows-to where directed or where convenient. Good shelter from the prevailing summer wind. Showers and water at the yacht club ashore. A charge is made.

BENITSAI

An exposed anchorage 5 miles S of Corfu town. A large white hotel complex is conspicuous N of Benitsai. Anchor in 3–10 metres. The anchorage is only really tenable in calm weather as the prevailing wind funnelled between Corfu and the mainland coast blows down from the N and pushes a swell in. There is a small harbour, but it is always full of local and tripper boats. Ashore Benitsai is a booming resort full of tavernas and bars for the tourists in the hotels and apartments around the original village.

PETRITI

Approach

Seven miles SE of Benitsai and just around Ak Voukari is the bay and little fishing port of Petriti. From the N the hamlet will not be seen but an eroded escarpment just S of Ak Voukari is conspicuous. Once the bay is opened the harbour mole and houses will be seen. From the E the houses of the hamlet are easily identified.

Petriti looking NNW from the anchorage in the bay.

Dangers In the approach from the E care must be taken of the shoal water extending off the low-lying Ak Levkimmis.

Mooring

Anchor in the bay in 2–4 metres on mud, sand and weed, good holding. A mole extends in a NW–SE direction with 1·5–2·5 metre depths behind it. The harbour bottom is uneven so great care is needed, but there is usually room for two or three small yachts behind the mole which is otherwise occupied by local fishing boats.

Note A flotilla company has constructed a pier on the W side of the harbour and you may be able to berth here when the flotilla boats are not in. Water on the pier. Enquire first!

Shelter Good shelter from the prevailing NW wind although some swell creeps around into the anchorage.

Facilities

Good tavernas ashore and limited provisions can be obtained.

General

Petriti gets few visitors by land and is one of those sleepy hollows you quickly develop an affection for. It is a green place, watered by a stream, with a good sandy beach and clear water.

AK LEVKIMMIS

The low-lying cape E of Petriti. It is difficult to pick out from the distance though the light structure near the end will eventually be seen. Shoal water extends for up to half a mile E and nearly a mile N off the cape and you should keep a healthy distance off.

LEVKIMMI CANAL

Just S of Ak Levkimmi is the entrance to the canal leading to Levkimmi town (clearly visible). The entrance to the canal has silted and the depths just inside the canal are uneven – reported to be between 1–1·5 metres.

KAVOS

A new harbour just S of Levkimmi. At present it is still under construction though it is in use. The harbour has been built for ferries operating from Platarias and they use the space on the W quay. Berth where convenient clear of the ferry quay. The entrance is open to the prevailing wind and it can get uncomfortable and may be untenable with strong N winds. Strong southerlies cause a surge. At present there are no facilities.

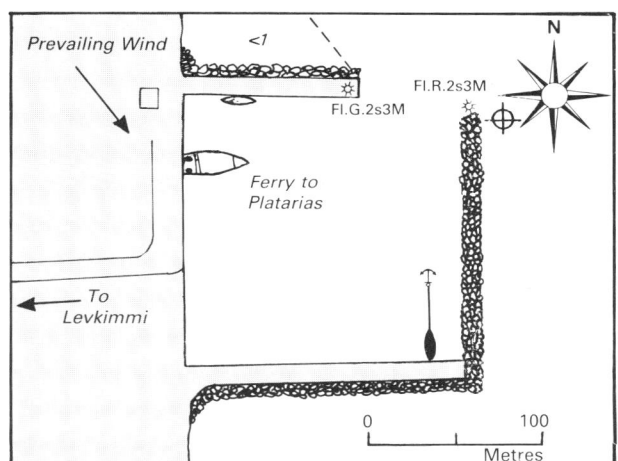

KAVOS (Skala Potamou) (Work in progress)
39°26'·2N 20°05'·3E (Fl.R.2s3M)

West coast of Corfu

AYIOS YEORYIOU (Agios Georgis)
Admiralty chart no. 206

A wide sandy bay just N of Palaiokastrita. Anchor in 4 metre depths in the N corner of the bay or off Ayios Yeoryios if it is calm. There is a taverna ashore. The swell from the prevailing WNW wind works its way around into the bay.

PALAIOKASTRITA (Limin Alipa)
Admiralty chart no. 206

Approach
Difficult by day and night.

Conspicuous The village of Lakones on the hill above Palaiokastrita is conspicuous from a distance. Nearer the coast the monastery and the large hotels around the bay are the best marks. You will not see the harbour mole until you are right into the bay.

By night Use the light on Ak Kosteri (Fl.3s5M) and the light at the end of the mole (F.R.3M). A night entrance is not recommended.

Dangers
1. Entering the harbour proper stay close to the head of the moles to avoid the rocky shoal which is easily visible (rocks awash) by day but not by night.

2. With the prevailing NW wind a heavy swell is pushed onto the coast which rebounds off causing a wicked cross sea.

Mooring
Go stern-to or bows-to the mole. The harbour is full of local boats but there is normally space somewhere. Alternatively anchor in the N bay, taking care of the

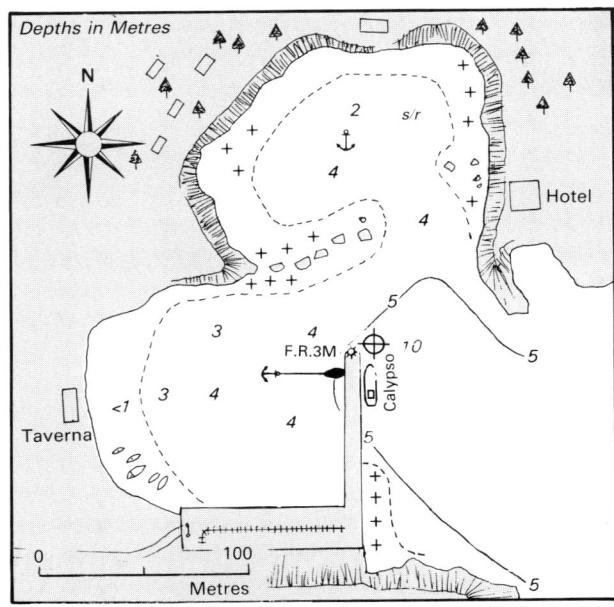

PALAEOKASTRITA (LIMIN ALIPA
39°40'·4N 19°42'·6E (F.R.3M)

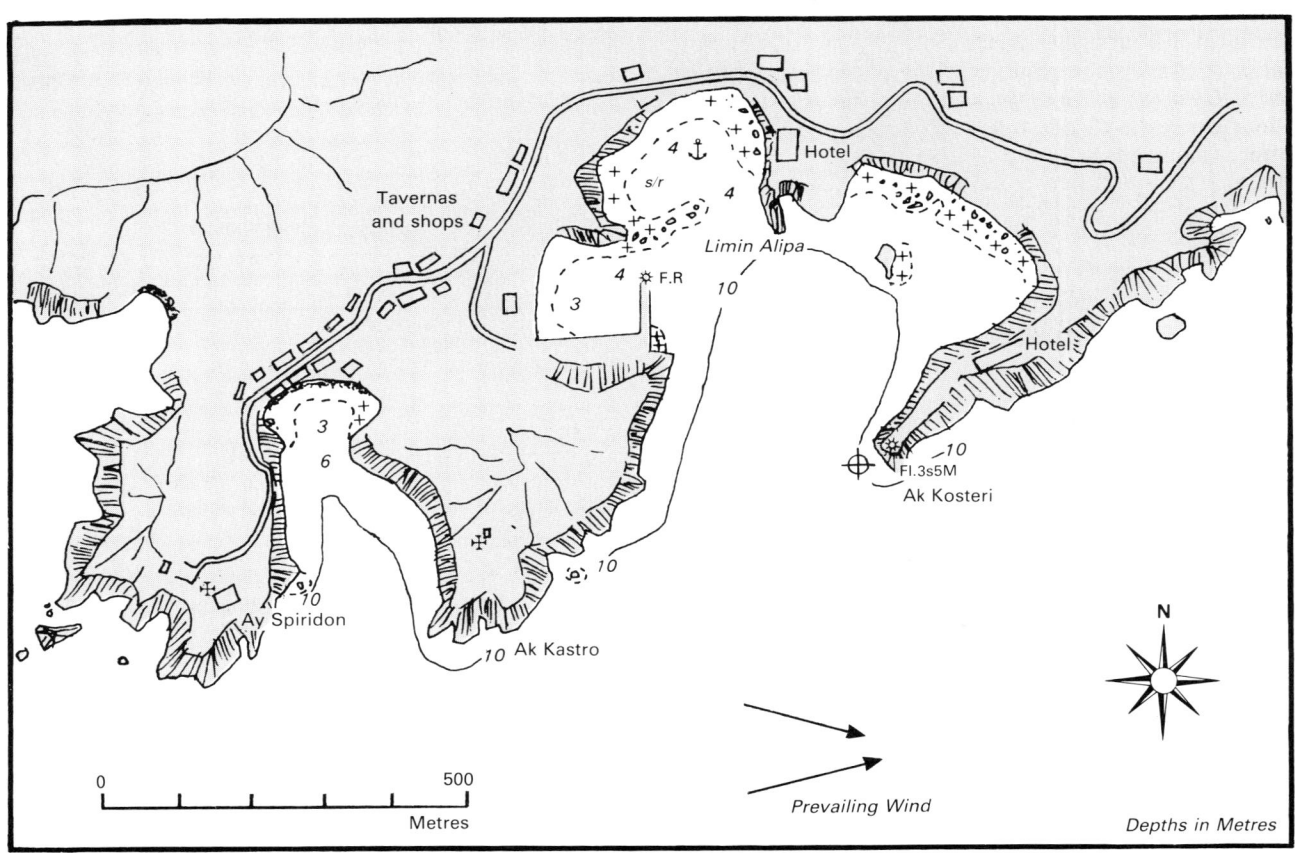

APPROACHES TO LIMIN ALIPA (PALAIOKASTRITA)
39°40'·3N 19°42'·8E (Ak Kosteri light)

Palaiokastrita harbour looking SW. Note the rocks off the N side of the entrance.

rocks near the entrance to the harbour. The bottom is sand, good holding.

Shelter Good shelter from the prevailing NW winds. The harbour is dangerous with strong southerlies when a surge develops and waves break over the mole. If strong southerlies are likely a yacht should vacate the harbour straight away.

Facilities

Water and fuel in the town. Most provisions can be found. Numerous tavernas and bars although prices can be expensive on account of the captive customers in the large hotels around the bay. Bus to Corfu.

General

In a watercolour by Edward Lear, Palaiokastrita is depicted as it was before the hotels – a beautiful bay guarded by the monastery and a few fishermen's houses. Today the giant hotels surrounding the bay considerably mar the landscape, yet the seascape and the view from the monastery are still superb. Now no more hotels are to be built – the authorities consider there are enough here – though service buildings still keep popping up every summer. By the harbour a NATO storehouse is concealed under the hill and theoretically no photographs are allowed to be taken of the NATO installation, though you can buy a postcard showing the prohibited view!

Nisoi Paxoi and Andipaxoi
(Paxos and Anti-Paxos Islands)

Seven miles south of Corfu lies Paxoi and its diminutive Andipaxoi. Five miles long and two miles wide, Paxoi until recently produced little else than olive oil for which it is famous; (Harrods apparently sells only olive oil from Paxoi). Now tourists from Corfu regularly visit the island and in recent years a large number of villas have been built. The island is also popular with flotilla companies and in the summer the harbours and anchorages are full of yachts.

It was off Paxoi that a significant historical event occurred – little remembered now but of momentous importance in ancient times. It was announced to a

pilot on a ship that the great god Pan was dead; the only god to have died in our time according to Robert Graves. The Egyptian pilot Thamus was bound for Italy when he was becalmed off Paxoi. A voice came over the water commanding him to announce that Pan was dead. Twice he disobeyed until the third command, whereupon he obeyed. Immediately a great wail of lamentation arose from the sea. It is a strange story recorded for us by Plutarch in the *Moralia* and yet when Pausanias visited Greece a century later he found Pan was still actively worshipped.

Andipaxoi, immediately south of Paxoi, is only sparsely populated. It has some attractive anchorages but none safe except in settled weather. The few inhabitants cultivate their vines and olives and are dependent on Paxoi for their needs and entertainment.

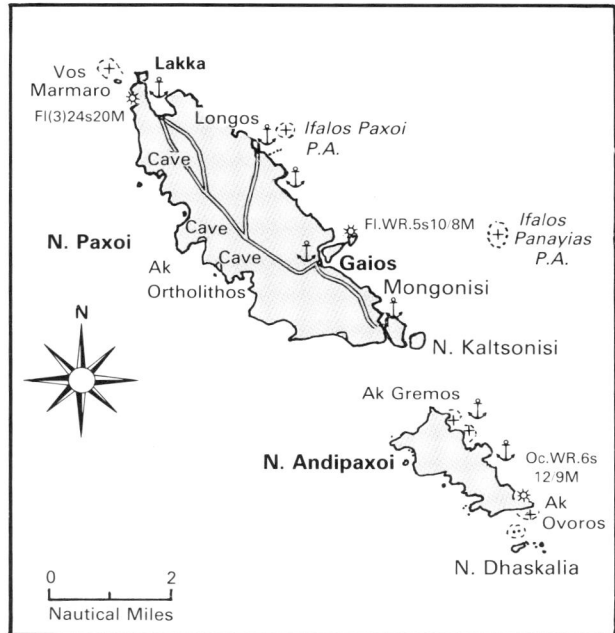

NISOI PAXOI AND ANDIPAXOI

ORMOS LAKKA

A virtually landlocked bay on the N end of Paxoi.

Approach

Conspicuous The exact location of the bay is difficult to determine from the distance. From the W the lighthouse is conspicuous. From the N and E the light structures at the entrance will be seen when you are closer in.

By night Use the main light Fl(3)24s20M and closer in the lights at the entrance: Fl.G.2s3M and Fl.R.2s3M.

Mooring

Anchor off in the bay where convenient or anchor in the NW corner with a long line ashore. There is some room on the quay for small yachts to go bows-to, but care is needed as the depths are uneven. The bottom is sand and weed, good holding.

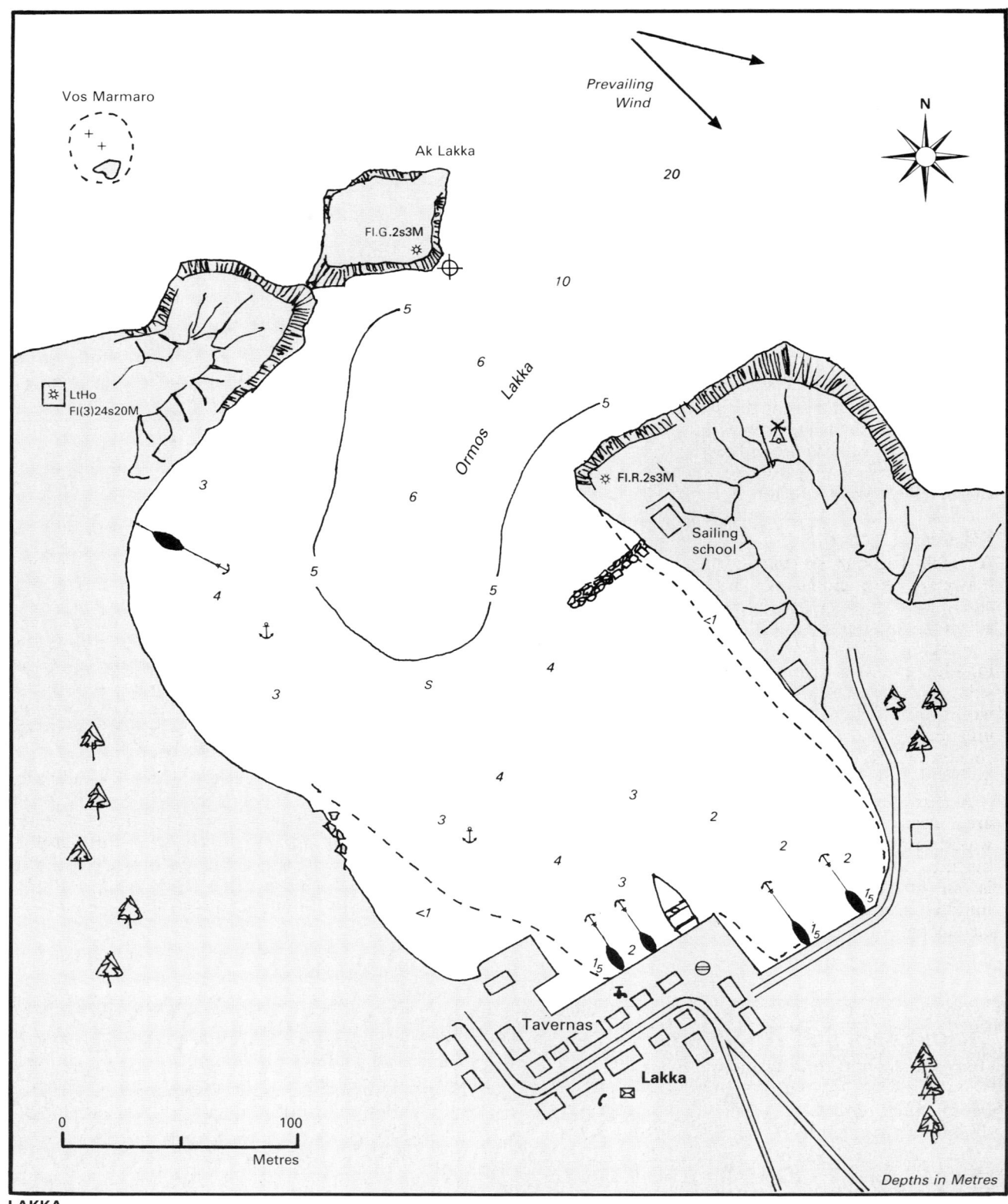

LAKKA
39°14'·4N 20°07'·8E (Fl.G.2s3M)

Shelter Good shelter from the prevailing winds. Uncomfortable and untenable in places with strong NE winds. With NE winds tuck into the E side as far as possible.

Facilities
Water Sometimes available on the quay.
Provisions Most provisions can be obtained.
Eating out Tavernas and bars.
Other PO. OTE. Ferry to Parga.

Entrance to Lakka looking SW. The lighthouse is conspicuous on the ridge behind.

General

The anchorage is picturesque under olive-clad slopes with the huddle of houses of the hamlet at the head of the bay. A sailing school operates here in the summer and between the sailing dinghies, sailboards, charter boats and tripper boats, the anchorage is a riot of colour and confusion.

LONGOS (Logos)

A small harbour on the E coast of Nisos Paxoi between Lakka and Gaios. The harbour is very small and yachts are restricted from berthing inside where all the space is reserved for local and tripper boats.

Either go stern-to the outside of the mole with a long line to it or anchor and take a long line to the N side of the bay. With the prevailing wind a swell works its way around making these berths uncomfortable. The new breakwater under construction N of the harbour does not yet provide useful berthing space.

Ashore most provisions can be obtained and there are numerous tavernas and bars around the waterfront. It is a pity there is not a comfortable berth to be had at Longos as the small fishing village is an attractive place with whitewashed houses huddled around the miniature harbour under olive-clad slopes.

IFALOS PAXOI

Approximately half a mile E of Longos there is a reef, Ifalos Paxoi, which is difficult to see even in calm weather. It is possible to pass between the reef and the island though care is needed and it is prudent to have someone up front keeping an eye out for it. Some believe the charted position is in error and it is closer to Nisos Paxoi than shown.

IFALOS PANAYIAS

A reef lying approximately 2½ miles E of Port Gaios. The reef and shoal water around it is difficult to see with the wind whipping up a chop on the water so it should be given a prudent berth. The reef lies just S of the direct route from Gaios to Parga so care is needed. Some believe it should be closer to the mainland than its charted position though I think it looks about right.

PORT GAIOS (Port Gayo, Limin Paxon, Limin Paxoi)

Admiralty chart no. 2406

Approach

Conspicuous From the N the entrance to the harbour is difficult to see. From the distance the houses and tall chimney at Longos can be seen and as you close the port the lighthouse enclosed by a whitewashed wall on Nisis Panayia marks the entrance to the N channel. From the S the lighthouse on Nisos Andipaxoi is conspicuous and closer to Gaios a number of large white villas S of the town and the lighthouse and wall on Nisis Panayia are visible before the buildings of Port Gaios itself.

By night Use the light on Andipaxoi (Oc.WR.6s12/9M) and on Nisis Panayia (Fl.WR.5s10/8M). The N entrance is lit: Fl.R.3s3M and Fl.G.3s3M and the bend in the channel Fl.R.2s3M. The N end of the quay is lit F.G.3M. The S entrance is lit: Fl.G.2s3M and F.R.2M, though the lights should not always be relied on.

Approach to Longos looking W. The chimney at the old soap factory is conspicuous.

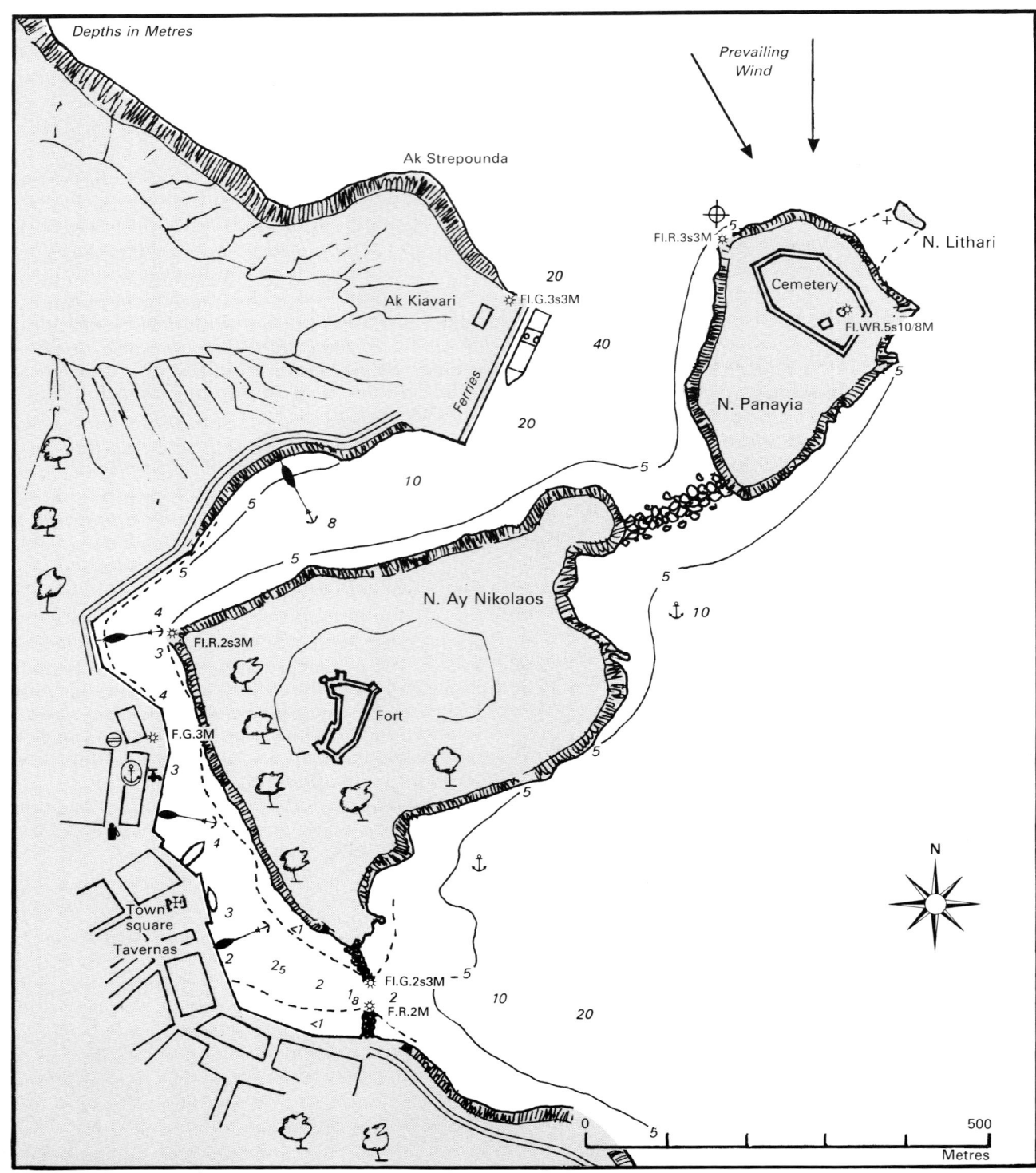

GAIOS (LIMIN PAXON)
39°12'·4N 20°11'·7E (Fl.R.3s3M)

Dangers

1. Care needs to be taken of Ifalos Panayia in the approach from the E.
2. Ferries and tripper boats are constantly churning in and out of the harbour. In the N entrance care must be taken of the blind bend in the channel where you cannot see what is coming the other way. In the S entrance there are barely 2 metre depths in the middle and no room to manoeuvre

so wait until the way is clear. On either side of the S channel it is shallow though work is under way dredging it.

Mooring

Go stern-to or bows-to the town quay leaving the ferry and tripper boat berths clear. The bottom is mud, good holding. In the summer the quay is very crowded and there may be no room. Yachts can also

Nisis Panayia and lighthouse at the N entrance to Gaios looking W.

Gaios looking SE towards the S entrance.

The S entrance to Gaios.

berth around the N channel on the N side with a long line ashore though it is quite deep here for anchoring. There may also be room in the W corner of the N channel. Large yachts can anchor under the causeway between Nisis Ay Nikolaos and Nisis Panayia.

Shelter Good shelter from the prevailing summer winds. Strong southerlies cause a surge on the town quay and a yacht may have to move to a berth in the N channel.

Note Crossed anchors are a fact of life with all the boats using Gaios and there is not a lot you can do about it except remain cool and use some muscle power in the morning when you leave.

Authorities Port police and customs.

Facilities

Water Near the quay, but it is often turned off in the summer.

Fuel Near the quay.

Provisions Most provisions can be found, though most things are brought in on the ferries and hence may be in short supply at times.

Eating out Numerous tavernas. Try those on the road out of Gaios.

Other PO. OTE. Bank. Hire motorbikes. Ferries to Patras, Parga, and Corfu.

General

Gaios is a popular choice for excursions from Corfu making it a very crowded place in the summer. Ferry boats, flotilla yachts and private yachts churn in and out choking the little harbour. If you want a berth in the height of summer be here early in the afternoon. For all this, Gaios is still an attractive town. Sitting in the cockpit of your yacht you are literally in the middle of town watching the hurly-burly of Gaios life go by. Alternatively, you can sip your ouzo in the square amidst all the activity, probably with a number of cats begging for scraps at your feet (Gaios appears to possess as many cats as tourists), and watch your yacht gently rocking in the harbour.

MONGONISI

At the S tip of Paxoi, just over a mile SE of Gaios, is the landlocked bay of Mongonisi. The entrance is difficult to determine from the distance, but closer in

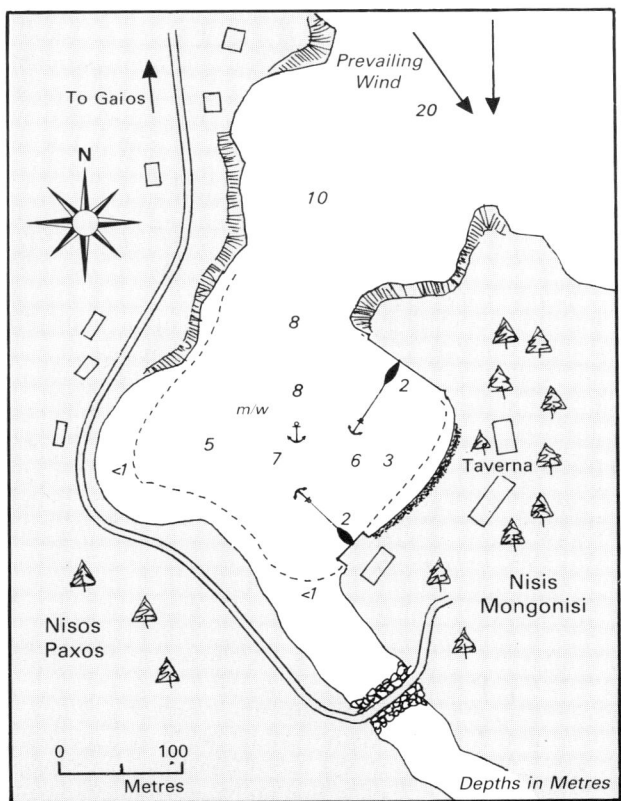

MONGONISI (ORMOS SPUZZO)
39°11′N 20°12′·5E

can be determined. Once inside go bows-to the quay on the NE side or on the S side. Alternatively anchor in the middle in 3–5 metres. The bottom is sand and weed, good holding once through the weed. Good shelter from the prevailing winds although with a strong N-NW breeze the western side of the anchorage is extremely uncomfortable. Taverna and bar ashore. Fast speedboat ferry runs to Gaios in the day.

NISOS ANDIPAXOI

There are two bays on the NE side of the island suitable for anchoring off in settled weather: care should be taken of reefs off the coast especially in the bays on the N end. When the prevailing wind gets up a swell is pushed down the coast making the anchorages uncomfortable. The bays are too exposed to be overnight anchorages.

The mainland coast from Corfu to Preveza

Opposite Corfu the Albanian-Epirote mountains rise to an impressive 1300 metres. The craggy peaks often have snow on them even in April. Proceeding south the mountain range curves inland and the coastline flattens to salt marsh around Preveza and Levkas. The much-indented coastline has some good harbours and anchorages, some of them much removed from the island tourism.

PAGANIA

Approach

From the S it is difficult to see the entrance. From the distance the road cut into the hill appears to disappear where Pagania headland obscures it. Once into the entrance to the bay the farm buildings will be seen.

Note A fish farm extends out from the W side of the bay. It is easily seen by day.

Mooring

Anchor in the SW or SE corner. The bottom is mud and weed, good holding. Good all-round shelter.

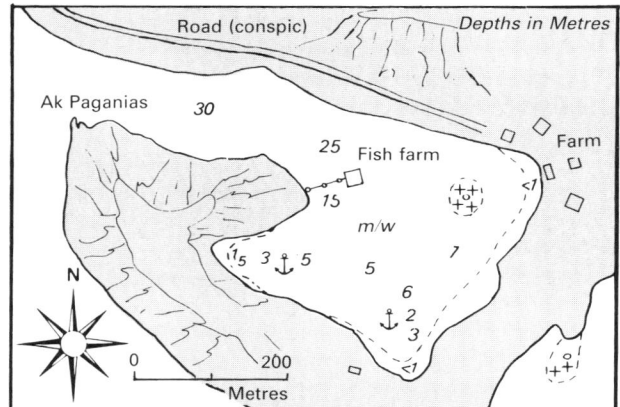

PAGANIA
39°40′N 20°06′E

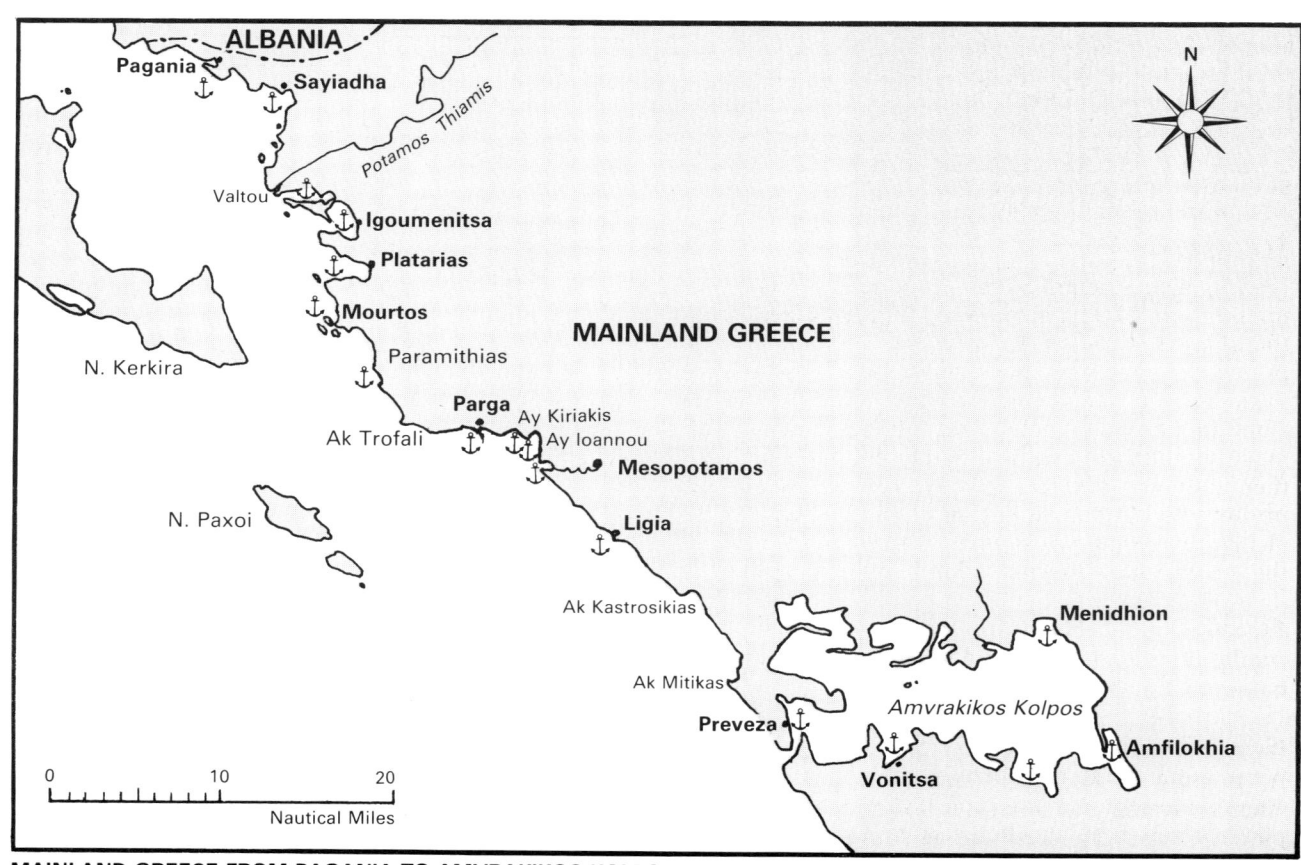

MAINLAND GREECE FROM PAGANIA TO AMVRAKIKOS KOLPOS

Facilities
You may get a few eggs from the farm, but otherwise none.

General
An idyllic spot little visited by yachts or anyone at all for that matter. The only inhabitants are the farmer and his family on the NE side of the bay. Occasionally a Greek patrol boat will turn up and may order yachts here to leave.

SAYIADHA

Approach
The buildings of the hamlet can be identified from the distance and closer in the harbour will be seen. The old entrance on the NW side has been closed off and a new entrance on the SE side opened.

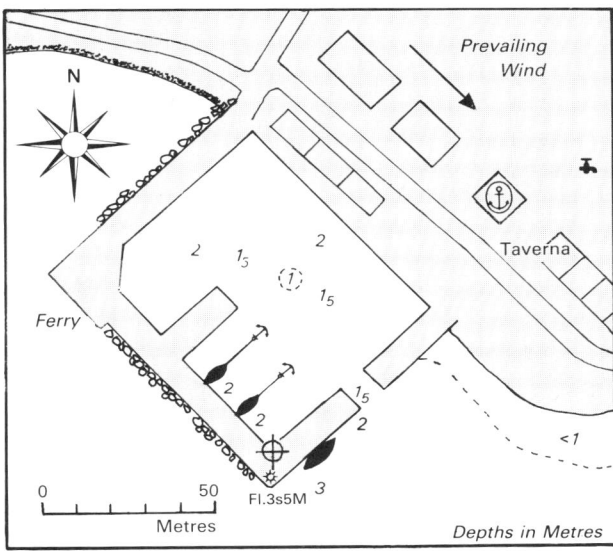

SAYIADHA
39°37'·5N 20°10'·9E (Fl.3s5M)

Mooring
Only shallow-draught yachts drawing less than 1·40 metres should attempt to enter. The new entrance on the SE side is narrow and bordered by rocks. It was probably opened by the simple Greek method of dynamiting a gap in the old wall. It is best to go alongside the outer mole as the holding is poor. Care must be taken of a shallow patch near the middle of the harbour. Shelter in the harbour is much improved with the new entrance. A yacht can also go alongside the quay just outside the entrance where there is reasonable shelter from the prevailing wind.

Facilities
Port police. Water near the quay. A grocery shop, baker, and several tavernas.

General
A friendly little village untouched by tourism. Alexi's taverna has been recommended as a good place to eat with fresh prawns and fish at good prices.

Note Pagania and Sayiadha fall within the restricted area where theoretically permission should be obtained for a visit. In practice this is not normally necessary.

ORMISKOS VALTOU (Igoumenitsa Creek)
Admiralty chart no. 2406

To the N of Nisidha Prasoudhi and the entrance to the bay of Igoumenitsa is the deserted bay known as Igoumenitsa Creek. Care must be taken of the shoals off the river mouth (Potamos Thiamis) when entering. In the third cove near the bottom of the inlet there is excellent all-round shelter in 3–8 metre depths, sand and weed. Care must be taken of shoal water extending out from the shore. Fish traps cut off the very bottom of the inlet.

Just over the neck of the inlet is a long sandy beach and there are some good walks around the area. The high land trapped in the silt of the river delta is thought to be the ancient Sivota Islands where the Corinthians and Corcyreans fought a naval battle in 433BC that eventually led to the Peloponnesian War.

IGOUMENITSA
Admiralty chart no. 2406

Approach
Conspicuous Nisidha Prasoudhi is easily identified and the town of Igoumenitsa can be seen at the head of the bay. The three pairs of buoys marking the channel into the bay stand out clearly. The approaches and entrance to the bay can usually be determined by the constant coming and going of car ferries to Corfu.

By night Use the light on Nisidha Prasoudhi (Fl(2)9s5M) and the light on the S side of the entrance (Ak Kondramourto) (Fl.3s5M). The buoys marking the channel are lit (Q.G and Q.R) and a 2F.R.5M is exhibited on the pier head at Igoumenitsa.

Ormos Valtou

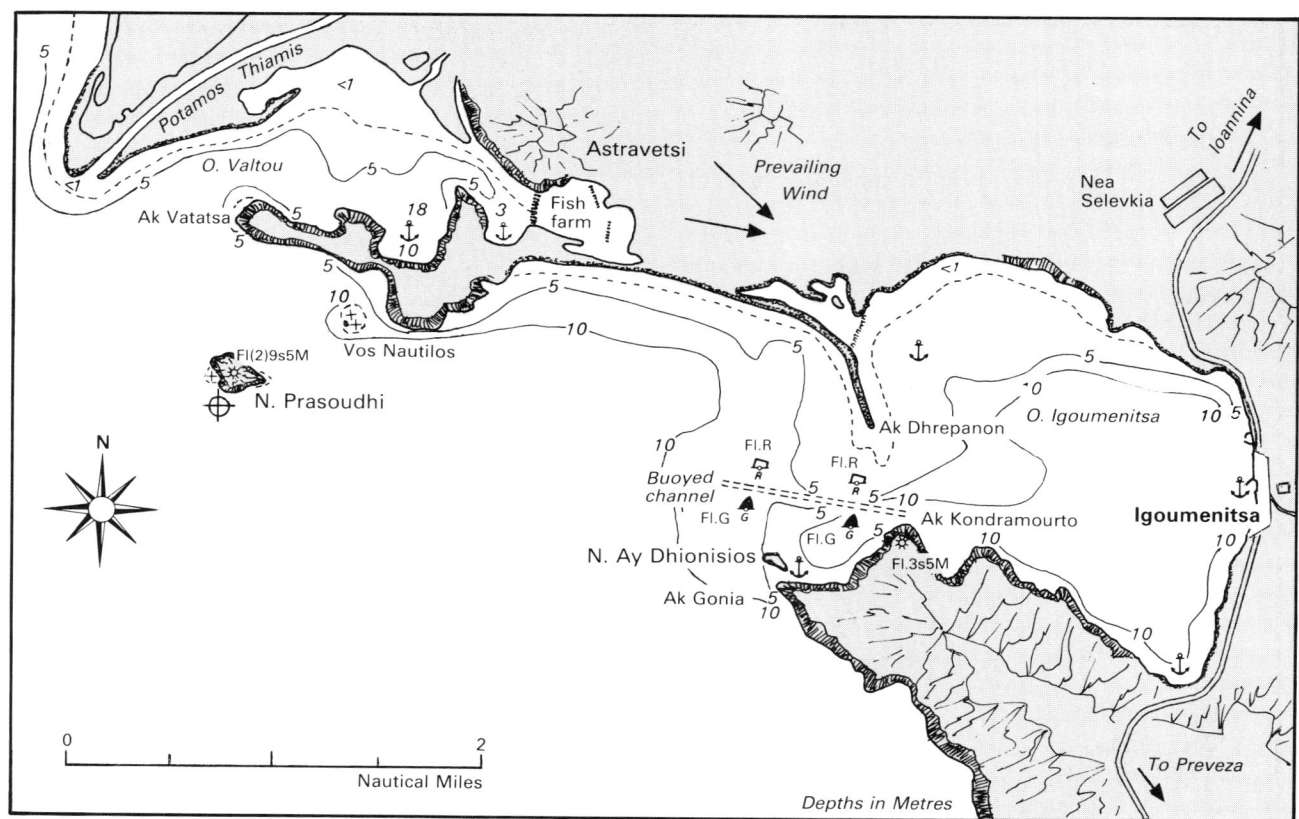

ORMOS VALTOU AND ORMOS IGOUMENITSA
39°30'·6N 20°09'·3E (N. Prasoudhi light)

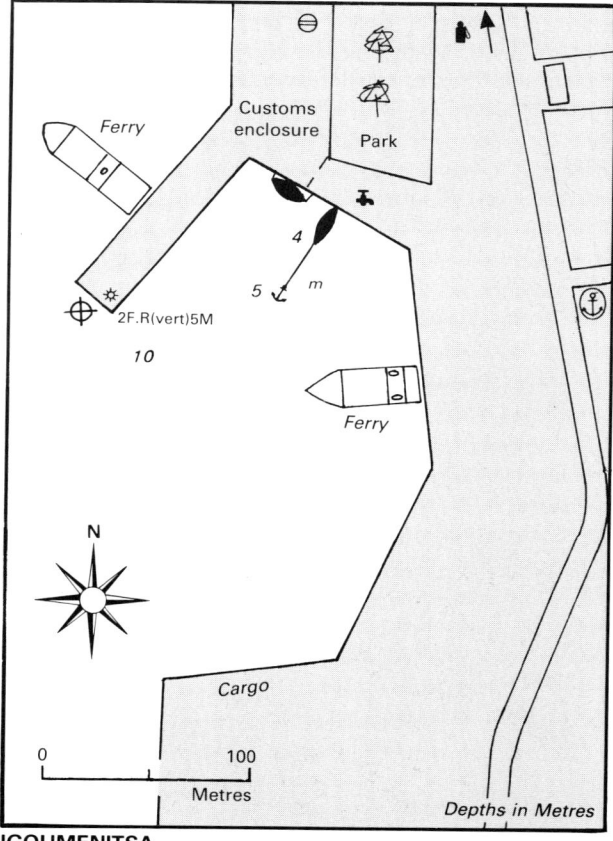

IGOUMENITSA
39°30'·1N 20°15'·7E (2F.R(vert)5M)

Mooring

Go stern-to or bows-to or alongside the quay. The bottom is mud – good holding.

Shelter Reasonable shelter although with strong NW winds it can be uncomfortable here and it may be better to anchor at the N end of the bay. There is a small fishing harbour N of the main pier but it is usually crowded and the depths are uneven (1–2 metres).

Anchorage Yachts can anchor at the N end of the bay where there is good shelter from the prevailing wind. There is also reported to be a good lee under Nisis Ay Dhionisios in attractive surroundings. In calm weather yachts anchor at the S end of Ormos Igoumenitsa.

Authorities Port police and customs. It has been reported that Igoumenitsa is a port of entry and several yachts have cleared out of here. Customs, port police and immigration are all located near the harbour.

Facilities

Water On the quay.
Fuel Near the quay.
Provisions Good shopping for provisions.
Eating out Numerous tavernas and a number of fast-food places.
Other PO. OTE. Bank. Greek gas and *Camping Gaz.* Infrequent buses to Preveza and Athens. Car ferry to Corfu. Ferries to Patras and Italy (Brindisi, Ancona and Bari).

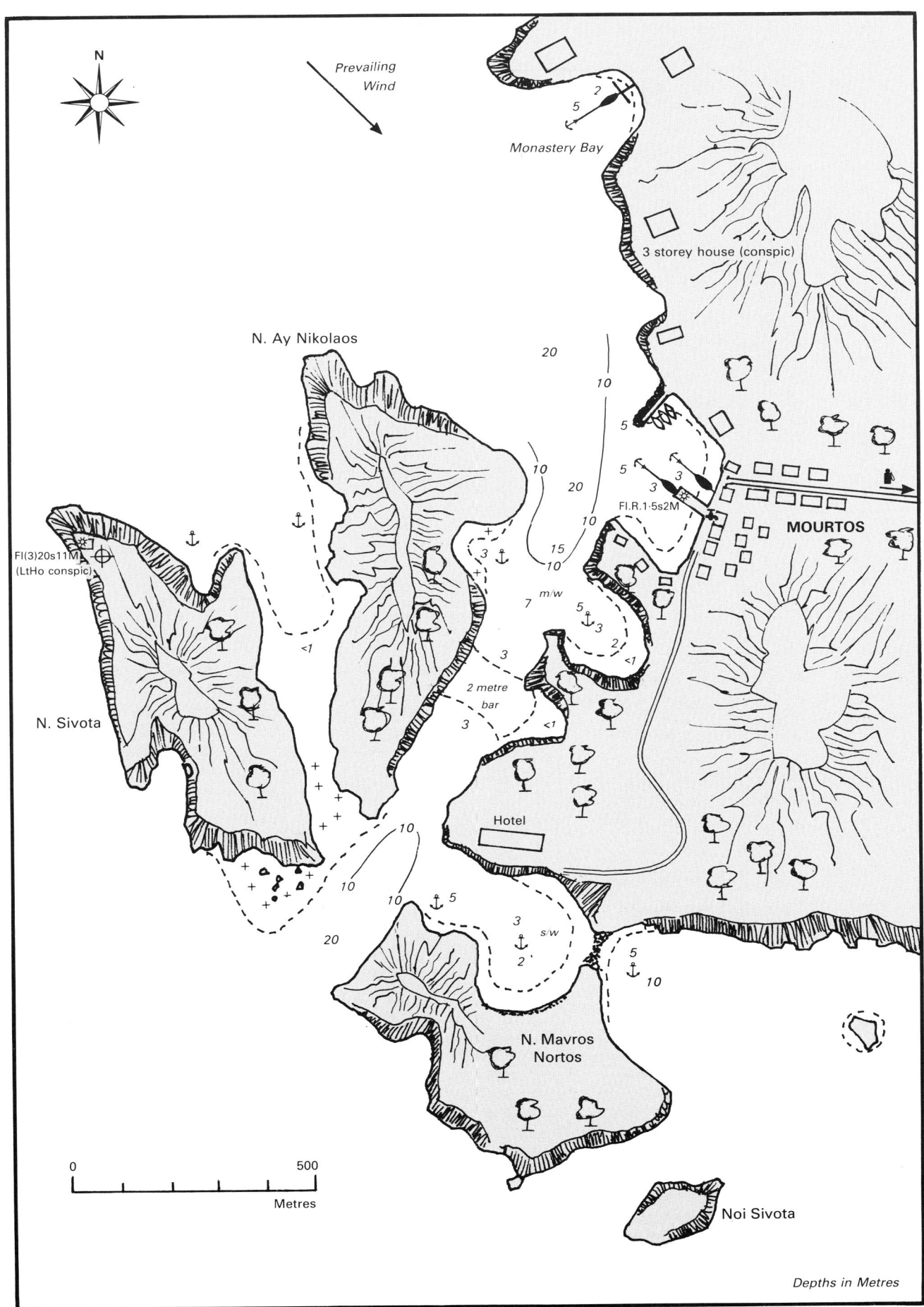

N

Prevailing Wind

Monastery Bay

3 storey house (conspic)

N. Ay Nikolaos

20

10

5

5   3

5   3 3

Fl.R.1·5s2M

10

MOURTOS

Fl(3)20s11M
(LtHo conspic)

20

10

15
10

7   m/w

5   3

2

<1

N. Sivota

3

3

2 metre
bar

3   <1

Hotel

10

10

10   5

3

s/w

2

5

20

N. Mavros
Nortos

0   500

Metres

Noi Sivota

Depths in Metres

MOURTOS AND NISOI AY NIKOLAOS, SIVOTA AND MAVROS NOROS
39°24·'4N 20°12'·6E (N. Sivota light)

Mourtos looking NE.

General

Igoumenitsa is a rather unattractive convenience ferry-terminal town, although the large bay is attractive. In 1979 an earthquake destroyed some of the buildings and 200 people lived in tents for some 6 months after the event. The town is a good place from which to organise a visit to Ioannina and Dodona.

PLATARIAS

A small ferry port at the head of Ormos Platarias. Although the ferries running to Kavos on Corfu use the harbour, there is room for yachts as well.

Once into the bay the houses of the village and the harbour are easily identified. Go stern-to or bows-to in the inner basin where there are mostly 2 metre depths. Good shelter from the prevailing wind. Water on the quay. Most provisions can be found and there are several tavernas.

Mourtos and adjacent islands

Just S of Ormos Platarias lie the Sivota islands with the village of Mourtos on the mainland nearby. There are three islands: Nisis Sivota (Sybota), Nisis Ay Nikolaos, and Nisis Mavros Notos.

Approach

Conspicuous From the N the lighthouse on Nisis Sivota and a large three-storeyed house on the mainland are conspicuous. As you close Mourtos village the houses on the hill above can be easily identified. From the S the islands are more difficult to identify, but the lighthouse on Nisis Sivota will be seen.

By night There is only the light on Nisis Sivota (Fl(3)20s11M) and a light on the pierhead at Mourtos (Fl.R.2M). A night approach is not recommended for the first time.

Dangers
1. Do not attempt to pass between Nisis Sivota and Nisis Ay Nikolaos as the channel is obstructed by the reef running across the S end.
2. The passage between the mainland and the islands has only 2 metre depths at one point (see plan).
3. From the S keep to the E to avoid the reef jutting out from Nisis Sivota. Waves break on some of the rocks of the reef.

Mooring

There are a number of possibilities.
1. Anchor in the bay off Mourtos in settled weather or go bows-to the pier. It is possible for shallow-draught boats to go bows-to the quay in places though care is needed as the bottom is uneven. The space behind the short mole is usually occupied by fishing boats. Shelter here is not the best with the prevailing NW wind which blows straight in. With moderate winds it is just tenable,

but with a strong blow from the NW it is untenable.
2. *Monastery Bay* The cove NW of Mourtos quay. Anchor and take a line to the shore or the jetty. Shelter here is better than it looks.
3. In the cove on the SE just inside the N entrance to the channel. Anchor in 3–7 metres and take a long line ashore if possible. The bottom is mud and thick weed, good holding once through the weed. This is the best place to be with good shelter and a short dinghy trip to Mourtos. The cove opposite on the NW side is mostly too shallow and has underwater rocks fringing it.
4. *Sand Bar Bay* At the S end of the channel there is a cove sheltered by Nisis Mavros Notos. Much of the cove is taken up with moorings for the sailing dinghies from the hotel on the slopes above, but there is usually room for several yachts to find somewhere to anchor. Anchor in 2–3 metres on sand. Good shelter.
5. On the E side of Nisis Mavros Notos a yacht can find reasonable shelter from the prevailing winds. Anchor in 4–10 metres on sand and weed.

Notes
1. Depths in the channel between Nisis Ay Nikolaos and the mainland decrease abruptly to a 2 metre bar before increasing quickly again.
2. There can be a S-going current in the channel with the prevailing wind.

Facilities

(Mourtos)
Water Local sources.
Fuel In the village about 600 metres away.
Provisions Some provisions can be found on the waterfront. There are better grocery shops and a bakery 600 metres away.
Eating out Good tavernas on the waterfront and up in the village.
Other PO. OTE. Bus to Igoumenitsa.

General

Mourtos village is a pleasant place in a wooded setting with friendly locals. Sand-Bar Bay is now overlooked by a monstrous concrete hotel that has not only cluttered the bay with moorings for its boats and dinghies, but also disturbs this once tranquil spot with loud music far into the night. Although called the Sivota Islands these are not thought to be the ancient Sybota Islands off which the Corinthians and Corcyraeans fought their battle in 433 BC. The ancient Sybota Islands are probably the low hills in the creek immediately N of Igoumenitsa.

PARGA
Admiralty chart no. 2406

Approach
Conspicuous From the W the fort at Kastelli in the hills NW of Parga is conspicuous and closer in the belfry on Ak Ay Spiridhonos will be seen. From the S the belfry, fort and the buildings of Parga village are conspicuous. The small white chapel on Nisidha Ay Nikolaos also stands out well.

By night The light on the fort at Parga (Fl(2)6s6M) will be seen from the S but is obscured in the approach from the W. The small harbour in Ormos Valtou is not lit.

Dangers Care needs to be taken of the reef lying approximately 100 metres off Ak Ay Spiridhonos. In calm weather it is easily spotted, but with any whitecaps it can be difficult to pick out.

Nisidha Ay Nikolaos and chapel in the southern approaches to Parga.

Mooring
Most yachts head for the small harbour on the W side of Ormos Vakltou. Go stern or bows-to. Alternatively anchor S of the mole and take a line ashore or to the old mole. The new breakwater S of the old mole provides some shelter if you are tucked right under it with a line ashore – it is likely it will be extended some time in the future to provide additional berths for yachts. Although the wharf at Parga village appears to be adequately protected a swell rolls around into here with the afternoon breeze and in southerlies it is untenable. In any case it is normally occupied by local ferries and tripper boats.

Shelter In the harbour at Ormos Valtou is good.

Facilities
At Ormos Valtou water can sometimes be obtained from the holiday camp. Taverna/bars open on the beach in the summer. For any provisions you will need to go into Parga itself where there is good shopping for provisions. Tavernas in Parga. Also: PO. OTE. Bank. Irregular bus service to Igoumenitsa. Ferry to Paxoi.

General
Parga village is a delightful place built down the steep slopes to the water's edge. It is about a twenty-minute walk around the bay from the small harbour to the village – remember to take a torch if you are returning at night. The slopes behind the bay and the village are wooded, mostly pine and olive with some deciduous trees around the foreshore.

The castle on the promontory between the two bays is of Norman origin (c.1337). Well defended to seaward and landward by the monolithic rock on which it sits, this castle has always been difficult to capture. The Venetians considered it 'the eye and ear of Corfu' and consequently the Parganiotes enjoyed special trade privileges with Venice. The notorious Ali Pasha attempted to capture the castle many times, finally succeeding in a roundabout way with the help of the English. In 1814 when the French held Parga British agents managed to persuade the Parganiotes to overthrow the garrison and hand it over to the English. After holding Parga for two years the English then sold it to Ali Pasha to

The approach to the small harbour in Ormos Valtou looking NW.

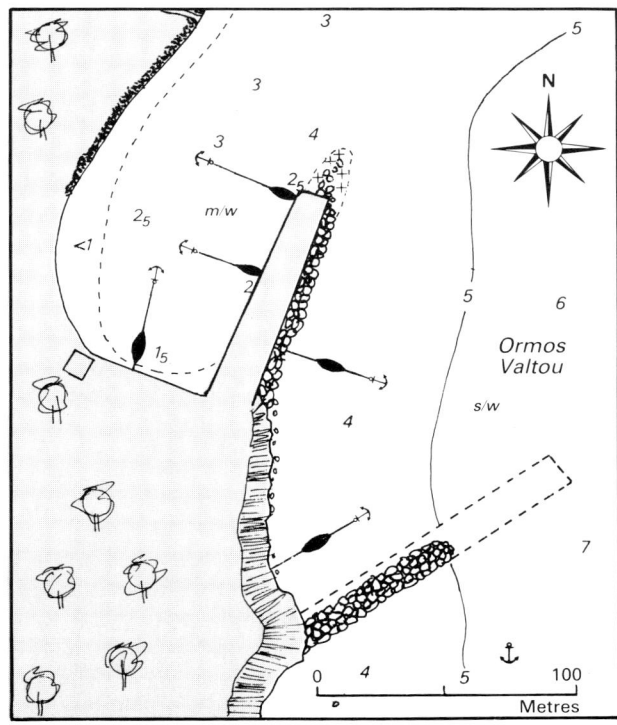

ORMOS VALTOU (PARC
39°17′N 20°23′·4E

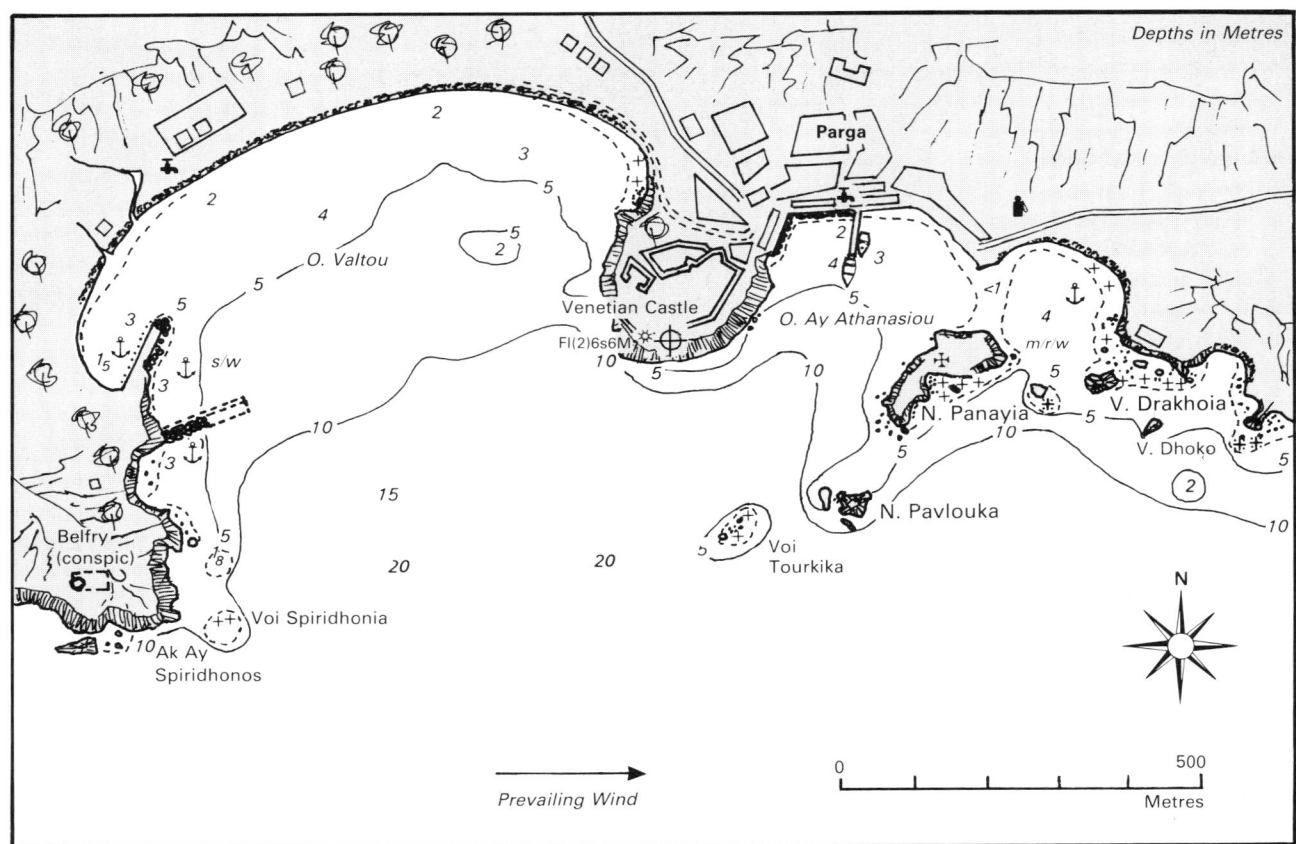

ORMOS PARGAS
39°17′N 20°23′·8E (light on the castle)

strengthen their claim with the Turks to the Ionian Islands. The inhabitants were evacuated to the islands, only returning generations later. Parga only became Greek in 1913.

ORMOS AY KIRIAKIS

A large bay a mile E of Nisidha Ay Kiriakis. A yacht can find reasonable protection from the prevailing wind in the NW corner. Anchor in 3–10 metres on sand and weed, good holding. Hotel and villas ashore and several taverna/bars open in the summer.

ORMOS AYIOU IOANNOU

Admiralty chart no. 2406

Three miles east of Parga is Ay Ioannou affording good shelter from the NW wind although some swell does work its way around into the bay. Anchor in the NW corner of the bay in 4–10 metres on mud, rock and weed, bad holding in places. The cove in the NW corner is now obstructed by a mussel farm. On the W side of the bay a freshwater spring wells up from the bottom into the sea and the murky slow whirlpool of fresh water is easily spotted.

ORMOS FANARI

Two miles south of Ioannou there is the bay of Fanari. Most of the bay has silted and a yacht will have to squeeze into the N side. Poor shelter from the prevailing wind.

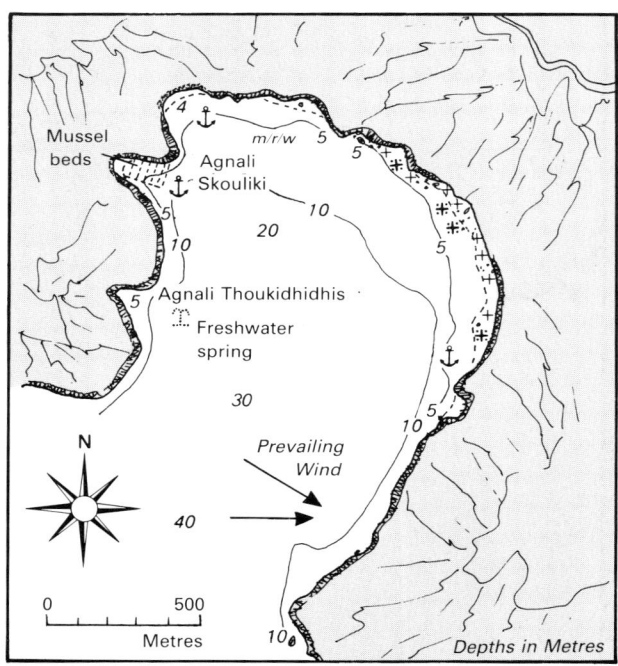

ORMOS AY IOANNOU 39°16′·2N 20°28′·2E

TWO ROCK BAY

A cove lying approximately 2 miles S of Fanari which offers surprisingly good shelter from the NW wind. Several large rocks just in the entrance identify it. A small yacht can squeeze in – depths are not great, 1·5–2 metres over a sandy bottom.

Preveza harbour looking NW.

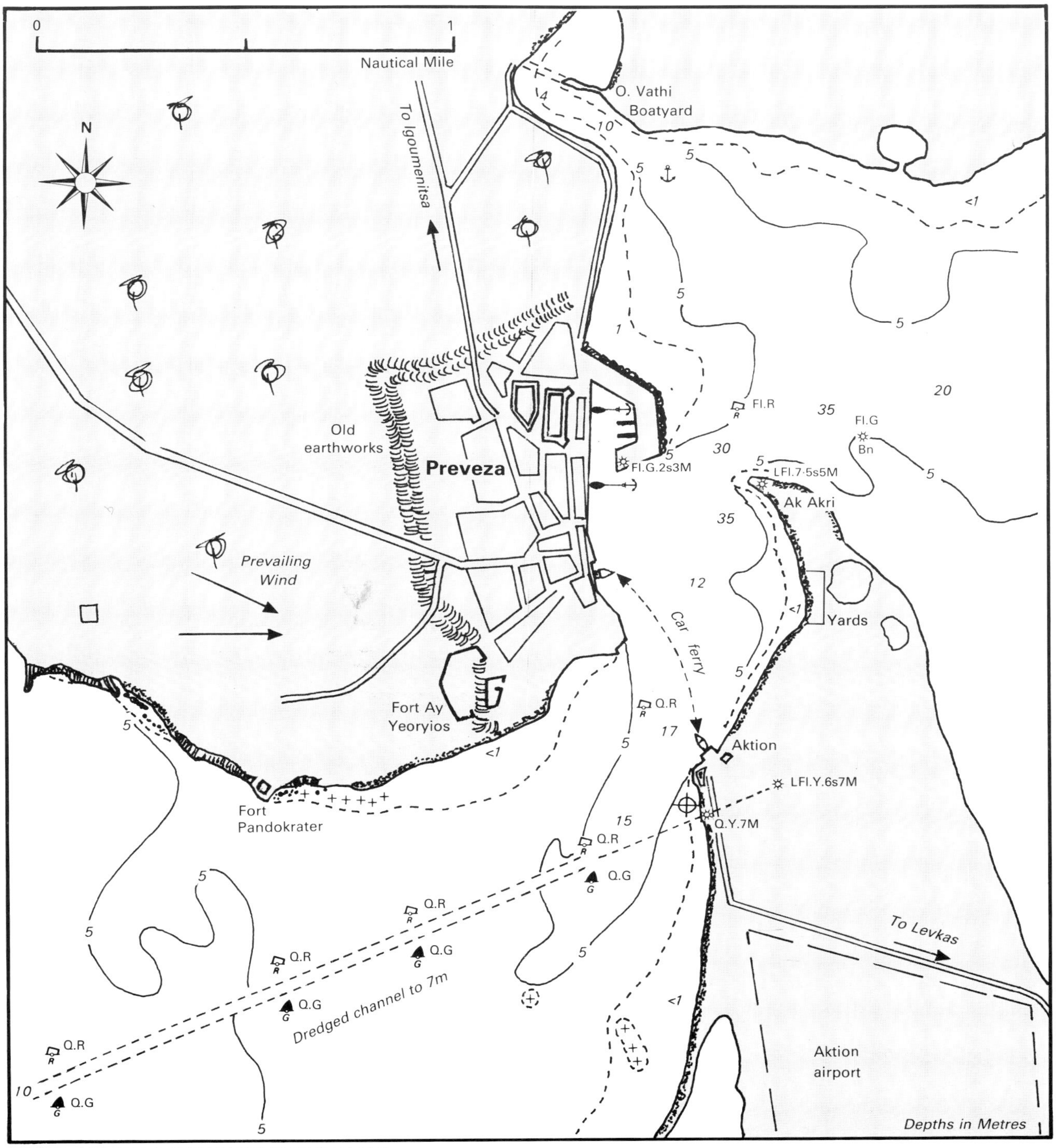

0   1

Nautical Mile

To Igoumenitsa

N

O. Vathi
Boatyard

Old
earthworks

Preveza

Prevailing
Wind

Fl.R

Fl.G

Fl.G.2s3M

LFl.7·5s5M

Ak Akri

Car ferry

Yards

Fort Ay
Yeoryios

Q.R

Aktion

Fort
Pandokrater

Q.R

LFl.Y.6s7M

Q.Y.7M

Q.R

Q.G

To Levkas

Q.R

Q.G

Dredged channel to 7m

Q.R

Aktion
airport

Q.G

Depths in Metres

STENO PREVEZA 38°56'·7N 20°45'·7E (Q.Y.7M)

LIGIA

A small harbour lying 6 miles SSE of Two Rock Bay. The harbour entrance is rock-bound and extreme care is needed in the approach. The entrance is between the reef off the breakwater and the reef just S of it. There are 1-3 metre depths inside. Small yachts can go bows-to the rough pier off the shore or anchor and take a long line to the outer breakwater. Good shelter from the prevailing wind. In the village just up the hill there are provisions and tavernas.

PREVEZA

Admiralty chart no. 2405

Approach

Conspicuous From the N and S, a low thickly-wooded hill and Fort Ay Yeoryios on the N side of the channel are conspicuous. On the S side of the channel there is Aktion Airport and planes will often be seen landing or taking off in the summer. The buoys marking the narrow channel are difficult to see from the distance. Closer in the buoys will be seen and the navigable channel is obvious.

By night Use the light on Ak Mitikas: Fl.WR.3s7/5M, the red sector covers 026°-129°. There are leading lights into the channel on 066°: Q.Y.7M and LFl.Y.6s7M. The buoys marking the channel are lit Q.G and Q.R. Ak Akri is lit LFl.7·5s5M and the end of the mole in the harbour is lit Fl.G.2s3M.

Dangers

1. A current will often be running in the buoyed channel – sometimes as much as 3 knots. The prevailing wind from the NW blowing down over the shallowing water and against the current kicks up a confused swell – uncomfortable rather than dangerous in the summer.
2. The channel is claimed to be dredged to 8 metres but is only 5–6 metres in places. Outside the channel the depths can also vary from those shown on the chart due to silting.
3. Keep an eye on the car ferries plying across the channel between Aktion and Preveza although they will usually wait for you to pass.

Mooring

Go stern-to or bows-to the W quay in the basin or alongside just outside the basin. The bottom is uneven close to the quay in the basin so care is needed. The bottom is mud and excellent holding.

Shelter Good shelter from the prevailing winds. With strong SE winds it can get uncomfortable and the best place to be is inside the S end of the mole.

Authorities A port of entry. Port police, customs and immigration. It is a bit of a walk between the various offices, but the tourist office on the waterfront is helpful and can supply a map.

Facilities

Water On the quay.

Fuel On the quay.

Repairs On Aktion just N of the ferry berth are two yards. Hauling is by hydraulic trailer although a travel hoist is planned for one of the yards. Mechanical, wood, and minor GRP repairs undertaken. Contact Preveza Marine, Atintanon 53, 48100 Preveza ☎ (0682) 24305 *Fax* (0682) 29805. In Ormos Vathi, an inlet immediately N of the harbour, there is a boatyard used to hauling yachts. Some mechanical, engineering, and GRP repairs (a factory just out of town makes small GRP boats). Hardware and limited chandlery.

Provisions Good shopping for all provisions. Ice can be ordered.

Eating out Numerous tavernas, though some are a bit ordinary. In the back streets there is a retsina taverna which does good grilled sardines and salad.

Other PO. OTE. Bank. Greek gas and *Camping Gaz*. A gas factory just out of town can fill most types of gas bottle. Buses to Igoumenitsa (limited), Levkas,

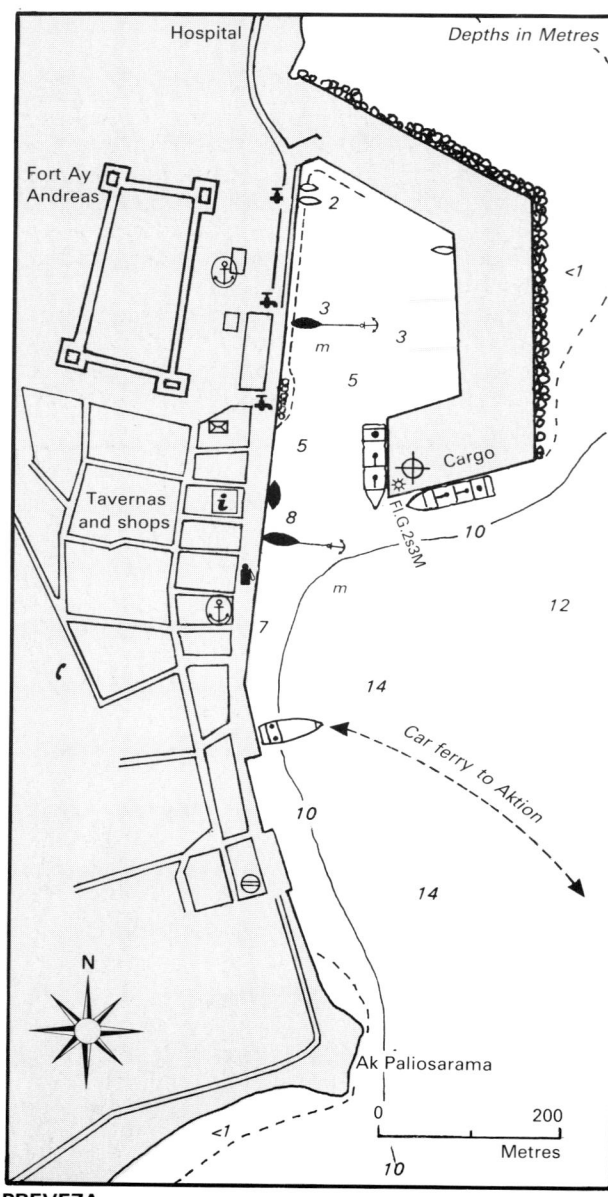

PREVEZA
38°57'·4N 20°45'·3E (Fl.G.2s3M)

and Athens. International charter flights from Aktion Airport in the summer and internal flights.

General

Preveza is a commercial port surrounded by lush orchards and market gardens. Preveza would not win many points in the scenic stakes, but it is a likable working town with interesting shops and workshops in the back streets and most people develop an affection for it after a while. About 3 miles N of the town are the ruins of Nikopolis built by Octavian to commemorate his victory over Antony in the Battle of Actium. This battle fought in the approaches to Preveza effectively determined the course of the Roman Empire. The ruins are well worth a visit: a large theatre, a villa and the city walls are well preserved and a small museum houses an interesting collection of artifacts.

Nikopolis

After the assassination of Julius Caesar in 44 BC a civil war was intermittently waged until 31 BC when Octavian's victory over Anthony decided the fate of the known world. Anthony had assembled his soldiers and ships at Actium intending to invade Italy. Octavian based his fleet at Mitikas to forestall Anthony and all through the summer the opposing fleets waited for the other to move. Eventually Anthony decided to initiate an action by moving his fleet to the mouth of the estuary. Octavian waited for the afternoon NW wind and when it arrived his swifter and more manoeuvrable galleys attacked the rival fleet. The rout of Anthony's fleet was completed when Cleopatra fled taking her Egyptian

ships – Anthony followed leaving his men and ships to be scattered by Octavian.

To commemorate the victory Octavian built Nikopolis (Victory City) on the site from which he commanded his victory. It soon grew to be the capital for the area and to populate it many of the inhabitants of the surrounding countryside were resettled here. The present walls encompass a city about one fifth of the area of the original city which boasted theatres, temples, baths and three harbours – one at Mitikas and two on the Gulf of Amvrakia. Here the Apostle Paul stayed a winter and wrote his Epistle to Titus. Towards the end of 4 AD the city was destroyed by Alaric the Goth and though rebuilt on a smaller scale, it was soon abandoned in the face of the Slavic invasion from the N.

Amvrakikos Kolpos
(Gulf of Amvrakia)

Few yachts enter the Gulf of Amvrakia yet it offers some good sailing and interesting anchorages. There are also a multitude of ancient sites dotted around the edge of the gulf: Nikopolis, erected by Octavian after his defeat of Anthony; the Venetian castle at Vonitsa built on a Byzantine original; the remains of Limnaea near Karvasaras; ancient Arta and its famous bridge up the Arakthos river.

When entering the gulf from Preveza make for the red buoy (Fl.R) keeping clear of the shallows off Ak Akri (white beacon LFl.7·5s5M). Then leave the white beacon with a green band (Fl.G.7·5s2M) and

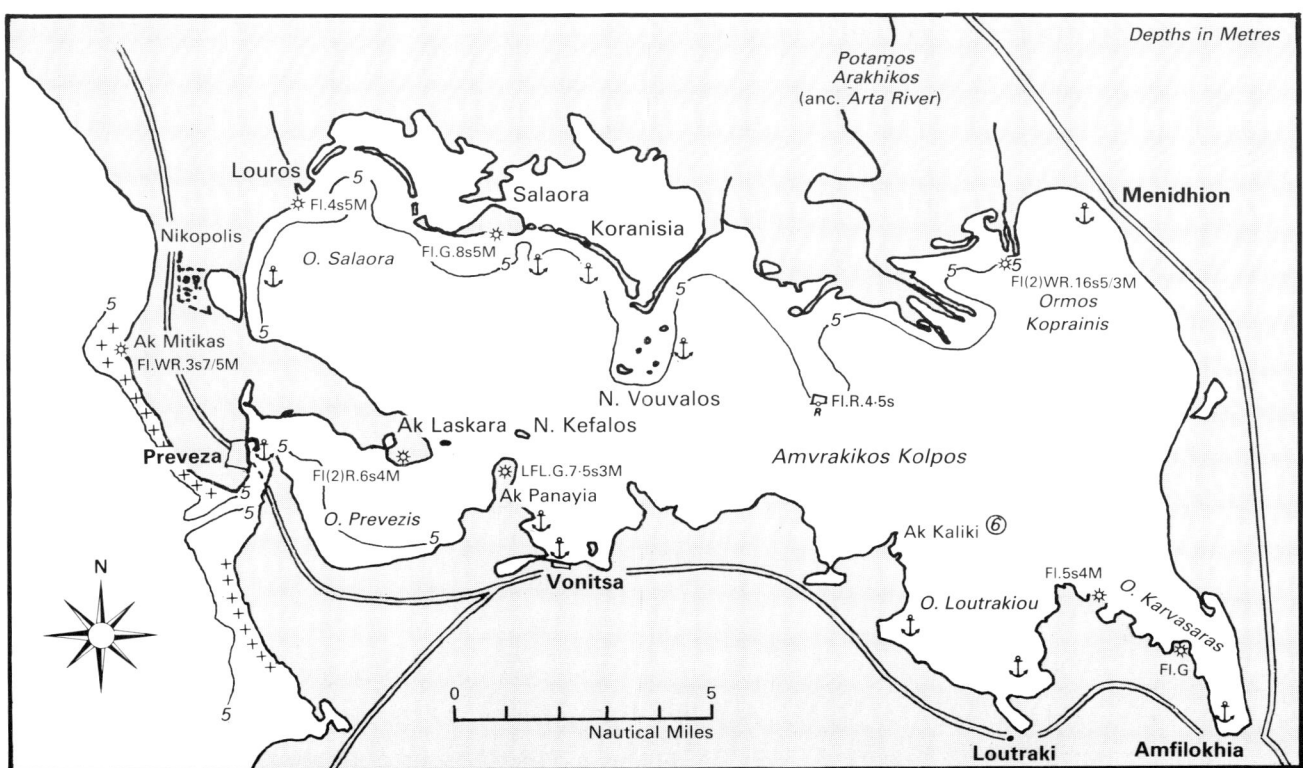

AMVRAKIKOS KOLPOS (Gulf of Amvrakia)

the green lightbuoy to starboard. Once into the gulf there are good depths except around the N coast where it has silted in places and shallows may extend further than shown on the chart.

VONITSA
Admiralty chart no. 2405

Approach
Once into Ormos Vonitsa the buildings of the town and the castle will be seen. The cove on the W side will not be seen until you are in the entrance. The detached breakwater off Vonitsa is easily identified.

Mooring
Go stern-to or bows-to off the town quay. Care is needed as the depths off the quay are irregular. Reasonable shelter from the prevailing NW wind which normally does not blow home. The new detached breakwater provides little additional shelter from the slop set up by the NW wind.

Alternatively anchor in Ay Markou, the cove on the W side of the bay. The N side of the cove is obstructed by a mussel farm and it is quite deep in here: 8–15 metres. It may be better to anchor off the shoal patch in 5 metres on the S side of the entrance.

Facilities
Water and fuel in the town. Most provisions can be obtained and there are several tavernas. PO. OTE. Bank. The bus to Athens and Levkas stops here.

General
Above the town is a large Venetian fort (built on the site of a Byzantine fort) which offers excellent views

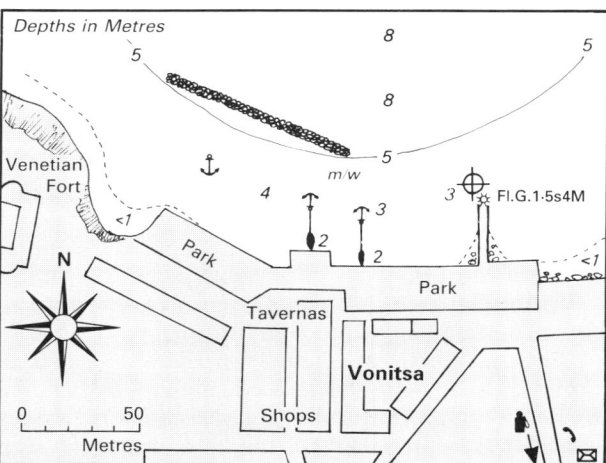

VONITSA
38°55'·3N 20°53'·2E (FI.G.4M)

out over the Gulf. According to Alexander Paradissis, Robert Guiscard died here of an epidemic along with 10,000 of his Norman troops...however, he is also supposed to have died in Fiskardho on Cephalonia.

ORMOS PALAIOMILOS
A deserted bay on the W side of Ormos Loutrakios. It is now mostly obstructed by a fish farm but it is still possible to squeeze in. Good shelter from the NW wind.

LOUTRAKI
The anchorage under the small village of the same name. Like Palaiomilos this is now obstructed by a fish farm, but you may find somewhere to squeeze into. Limited provisions and taverna in the village.

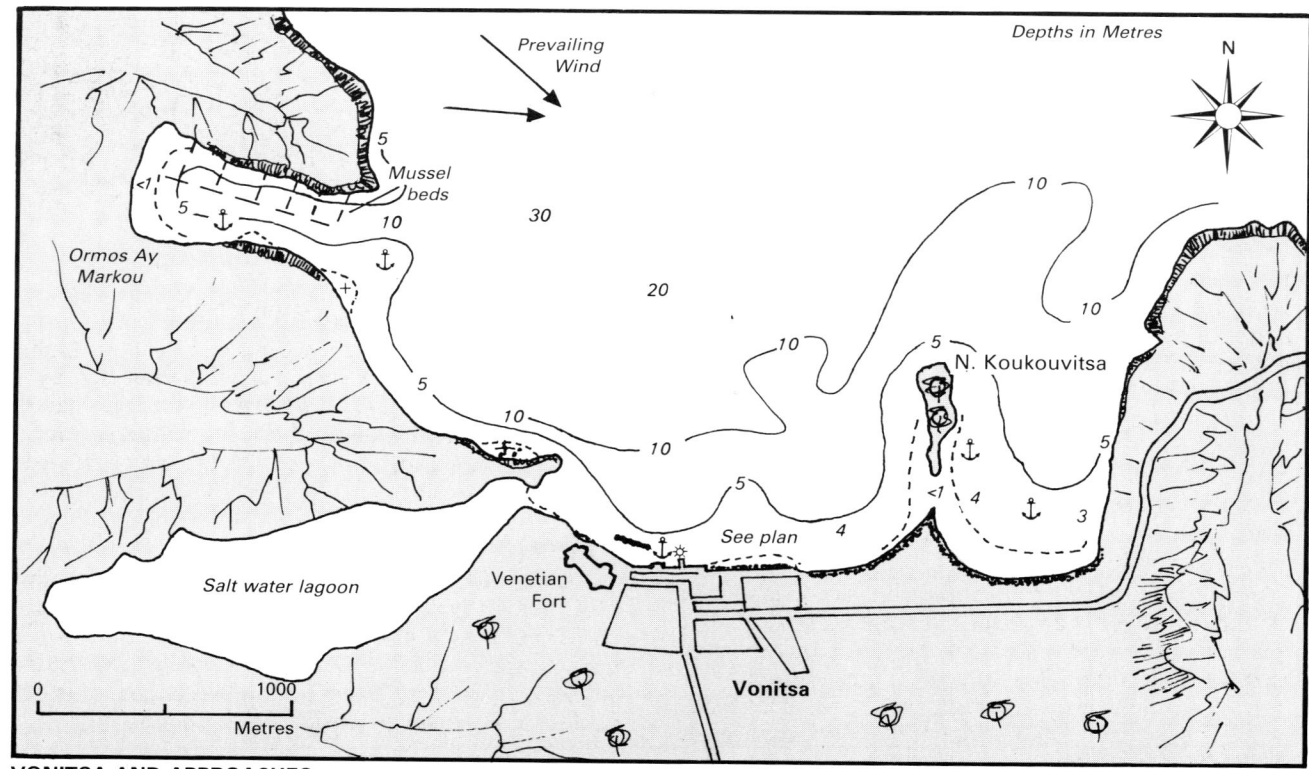

VONITSA AND APPROACHES

AMFILOKHIA (Karvasaras)

A small harbour off a village in the SE corner of the gulf. It is possible to go alongside the quay where shown with an anchor out to hold you off. However with a strong afternoon wind a considerable chop is pushed onto the quay and it is better to anchor off. It is very deep in here and you will have to anchor in 12–15 metres. The harbour is invariably uncomfortable with the prevailing wind and may become untenable.

Fuel and water in the town. Good shopping and tavernas.

Near the town are the remains of the ancient Arcanian city of Limnaea. According to H. M. Denham, in the 19th century a small volcano erupted in this bay in the early part of this century killing most of the fish in the gulf.

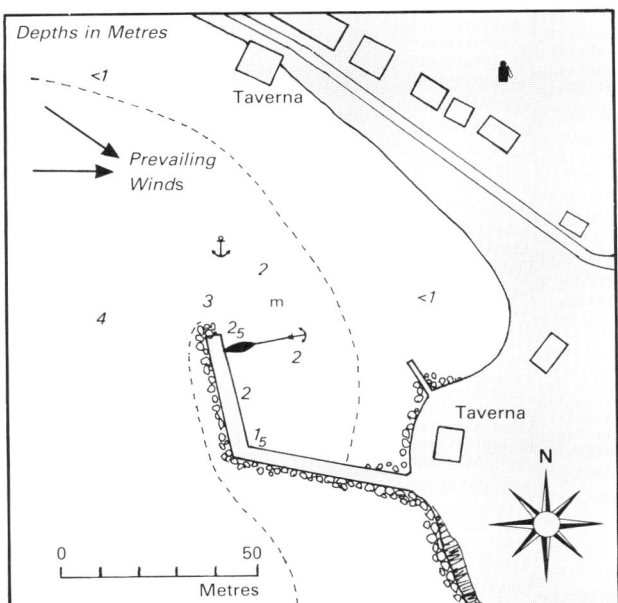

MENIDHION
39°02'N 21°08'E

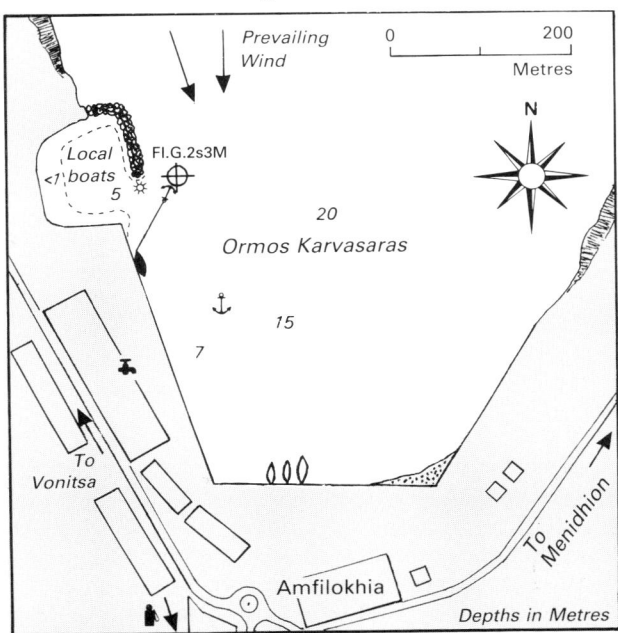

AMFILOKHIA (Ormos Karvasaras)
38°51'·1N 21°09'·8E (Fl.G.2s8M)

MENIDHION (Kopraina)

In the NE corner of the gulf in Ormos Kopraina is the small harbour of Menidhion. There is normally room for small to medium-sized yachts to go bows-to squeezed onto the end of the mole. Alternatively anchor off on a mud bottom – good holding. Good shelter from the prevailing wind.

Several tavernas ashore and limited provisions can be obtained in the village. A taxi can be hired here to visit Arta (18 Km). Little remains of ancient Arta (Ambracia) but its medieval bridge (with a delightful little museum nearby) and an eccentric Byzantine church are well worth the visit.

Note At one time it was possible to ascend the Arakhikos River near Menidhion to Arta upriver, but the construction of a hydroelectric dam on the river now so restricts the flow of water in the summer that this is virtually impossible and moreover dangerous when water is run off from the dam and levels increase very quickly.

Menidhion harbour looking E.

VOUVALOS AND ADJACENT ISLANDS

Good shelter from the prevailing wind can be found under these islets. The two islets are connected by a gravel bar and a yacht should anchor in the lagoon between. Anchor in the middle in 2-3 metres. Good shelter. At one time there used to be lots of mussels around the islets.

KORONISIA 39°00'·9N 20°54'·8E

A small fishing harbour between Salaora and Nisidhes Vouvalos. The entrance to the harbour has silted but small yachts can enter with care. Keep close to the end of the W breakwater where there are 1.5 metre depths in the entrance. Reconnoitre first if in doubt. Good shelter inside. Tavernas ashore.

Nisos Levkas, Nisos Meganisi, and adjacent islands

Levkas is an island only because of the canal which separates it from the mainland. The present canal was built just after the turn of the century by the Greek government although earlier canals were dug by the Corinthians around the 7th century BC and by Augustus during the Roman occupation. What appears to be an old canal cut can be seen running through the salt marsh just to the E of the present canal. The line of ruined stone on the W is the remains of an old Turkish/Venetian bridge.

The main town of Levkas is sited on a bend of the canal and in common with many other towns on this earthquake belt was rebuilt after the 1953 earthquake. Unlike Vathi on Ithaca or Zakinthos it was not rebuilt to a style and consequently the town is a riotous jumble of corrugated iron and brick houses leaning over narrow streets. It has its own charm despite the chaotic housing and hand-me-down appearance and is in fact a major cultural centre for the area. Every August the town council sponsors bands, folk dancing and exhibitions in the town. The local band practices for weeks before to perfect its cacophonous contributions, storekeepers decorate their shops, the police bedeck the street with flags and banners and Levkas fairly bustles with locals and visitors out to enjoy themselves.

The flat salt marsh and sand spits at the northern end of the island are in marked contrast to the steep-to limestone mountain range forming the rest of the island. Most of the population is around the S and E sides of the island which are attractively wooded in places. The large fort at the N entrance to the canal, called Santa Maura after a small chapel within its walls, was built in the Middle Ages (c.1300). Later it was used by the Turks and the Venetians. It is worth a visit to wander around the large complex, especially the small galley port adjacent to the E wall. At the S end of the canal is a fort built by the Venetians to guard the approaches to Ormos Dhrepanou.

On the SW corner of the island is a precipitous white cliff called Leukatas from which Levkas takes its name. This is the cliff presumed to be Sappho's Leap and from which Sappho of Lesvos, the famous lyric poetess of the 6th century BC, is supposed to have flung herself. After Sappho there are records of criminals being flung from the cliffs; if they succeeded in reaching the sea unharmed, they were recovered and pardoned. There is no anchorage here although the small port of Vasiliki is nearby.

The E coast of Levkas is fringed by a number of small green islands including Skorpios, the private parkland island of the late Aristotle Onassis, and Meganisi, looking like a giant tadpole on the chart and indented on its N coast with half a dozen sheltered anchorages. This area is the setting for Hammond Innes' novel *Levkas Man* which supposes that these islands are the remains of a land bridge over which primitive man crossed from Africa to Europe. Much of the factual basis of this book is derived from excavations by the German archaeologist Dorpfeldt who discovered Neolithic remains near Evgiros on the S of Levkas. Dorpfeldt also put forward the controversial theory that Levkas fulfills all the requirements for the Ithaca of Homer and indeed he uncovered Mycenaean remains near Sivota and Vasiliki. Dorpfeldt contended that during the Middle Ages the inhabitants of Levkas were driven from their homeland to the more remote Ithaca of today and so transferred their name and cultural identity to that island. However archaeological opinion still favours the present Ithaca as the original home of Odysseus.

LEVKAS CANAL
Admiralty chart no. 2405
Imray-Tetra chart no. G12, G121

Levkas canal, cut through the salt marsh between the island proper and the mainland, effectively severs it from the mainland and provides a passage for boats down the E coast of the island.

The canal has recently been widened and dredged to a minimum depth of 6 metres although some of it is deeper than this. With the prevailing wind pushing you down onto a lee shore with just the entrance to the canal to get you out of it, the first entry from the N is hair-raising. A yacht should have everything prepared, all sails down and stowed, and the anchor ready in case the engine fails, before negotiating the entrance.

Approach from the N
Approaching the island in the afternoon haze it is not easy to identify where the entrance to the canal is. At times the haze can obscure even the high mountains of the island and you may be only 3 or 4 miles off before you see it. Closer in the wine co-op factory and warehouse on the W side of the canal and Ayios Mavros fort on the E side will be seen against the flat sandbanks of Yera spit to the W and Plaka spit to the E. From the NW two windmills stand out on Yera spit and behind the buildings of Levkas town will be seen.

On rounding the protecting mole, two rusty 44 gallon drums are the buoys marking the underwater rocks and shallows on the SE side of the canal entrance, though they cannot always be relied on to be in place. A sand bar extends a short distance from the western entrance-point to the canal. Although it is periodically dredged, care must be taken as it silts up and extends rapidly in the summer with the prevailing northerlies.

Just beyond this are two chain ferries and a floating bridge with a section that can be raised. The chain ferries operate only intermittently now. When the section of the floating bridge is raised it leaves a 9 metre wide gap on the W side of the canal. For larger craft the floating bridge swivels to lie parallel to the E bank. This combination of ferries and the floating bridge makes the transit of the canal at the N end difficult. When the chain ferries and the floating

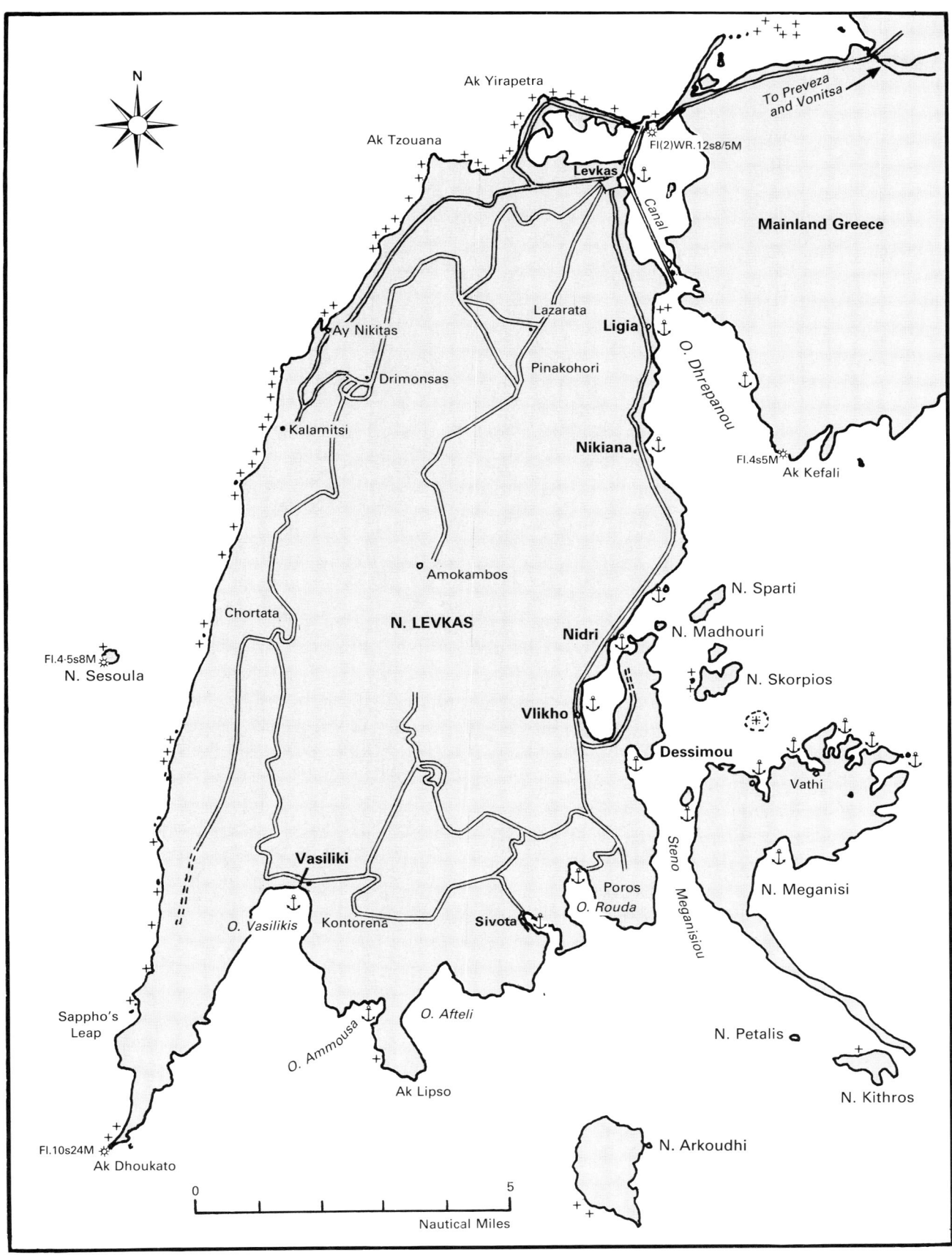

N

Ak Yirapetra

Ak Tzouana

To Preveza
and Vonitsa

Fl(2)WR.12s8/5M

Levkas

Mainland Greece

Canal

Lazarata

Ligia

Ay Nikitas

Pinakohori

O. Dhrepanou

Drimonsas

Kalamitsi

Nikiana

Fl.4s5M

Ak Kefali

Amokambos

N. Sparti

Chortata

N. LEVKAS

Nidri

N. Madhouri

Fl.4·5s8M

N. Sesoula

N. Skorpios

Vlikho

Dessimou

Vathi

Vasiliki

N. Meganisi

O. Vasilikis

Kontorena

Poros

Sivota

O. Rouda

Steno Meganisiou

Sappho's
Leap

O. Afteli

O. Ammousa

N. Petalis

Ak Lipso

N. Kithros

Fl.10s24M

Ak Dhoukato

N. Arkoudhi

0   5

Nautical Miles

NISOS LEVKAS

65

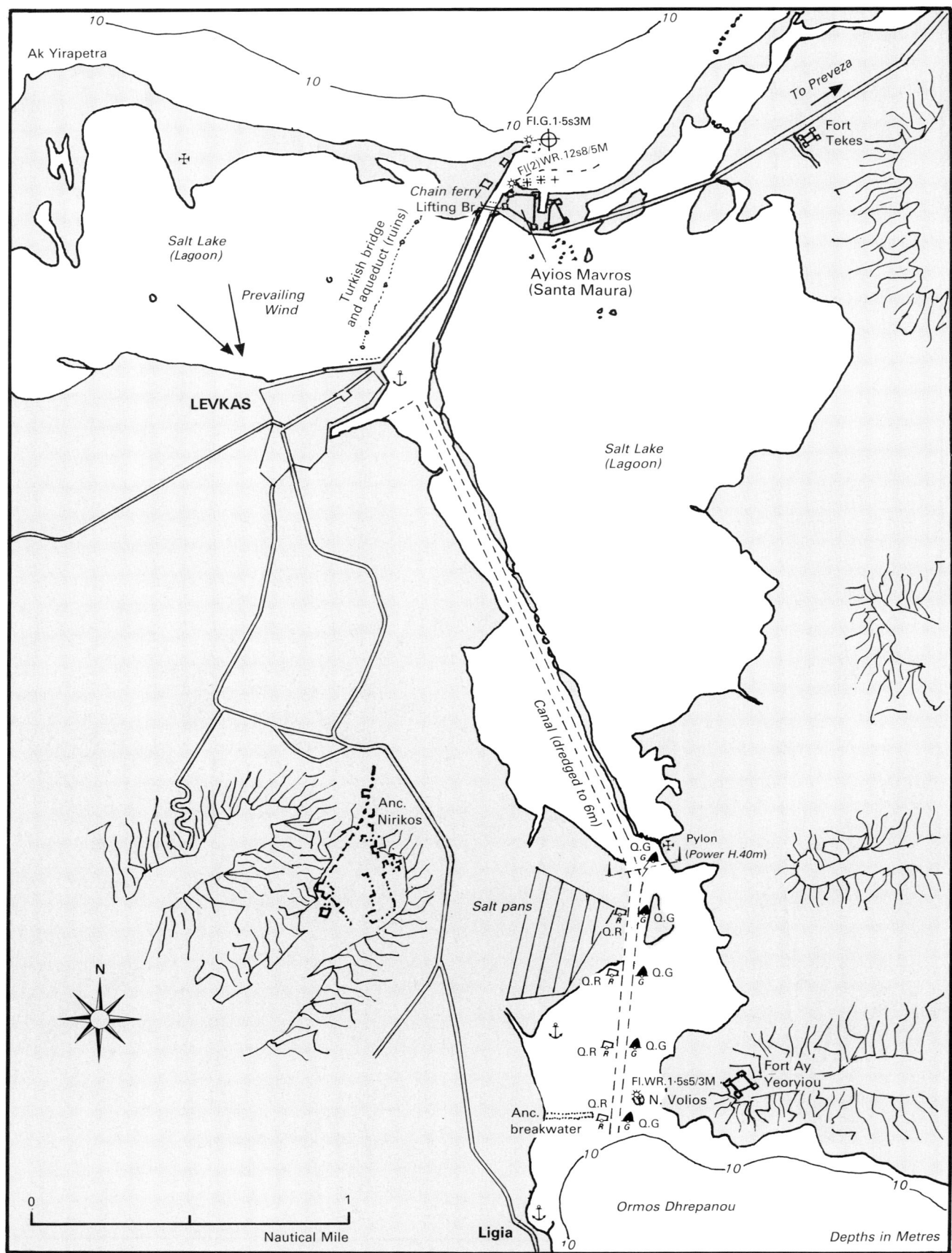

LEVKAS CANAL (Dhioriga Levkadhos)
38°50'·9N 20°43'·3E (Fl.G.1·5s3M N entrance)

Approach to the N end of the Levkas canal looking S. Ayios Mavros (Santa Maura) fort and the breakwater are easily identified.

The floating bridge (Ag Mavra) at the N end of Levkas canal looking S down the canal. For small yachts the end section of the bridge lifts up vertically. For larger vessels the whole bridge swivels to lie parallel to the bank.

bridge are ready for you to go, the signal on the E bank (two triangles, points together over a ball) is lowered and a siren sounds on the floating bridge. If that doesn't work the operator will make it plain that you are to go with much waving of the hands. The canal opens on the hour and traffic heading N from Levkas goes first followed by traffic going S. There may be a current in the canal at times, occasionally up to 1½ knots, which makes manoeuvring in the canal difficult. Levkas town is a short distance down the canal.

Approach from the S

Fort Ay Yeoryiou is conspicuous on a summit above the E side of the entrance to the canal. Closer in you will see Nisis Volios, an islet at the entrance with a light structure on it, and the first set of buoys marking the channel. The channel is then shown by pairs of buoys and beacons and in the salt marsh by poles with cones and baskets. The direction of buoyage is from Ormos Dhrepanou.

A yacht should not attempt to cut outside the buoys marking the channel: there is a reef on the E and the remains of an old breakwater on the W.

By night From the N use the light on Ayios Mavros (Santa Maura) fort (Fl(2)WR.12s8/5M, red sector covers 075°-120°) and the light on the end of the short mole sheltering the entrance to the canal (Fl.G.1·5s3M).

From the S use the Ak Kefali (Fl.4s5M), Nisis Volios (Fl.WR.8s5/3M, red sector covers 293°-335°), and the lights of the buoys and beacons marking the channel (Q.G and Q.R).

Ayios Mavros (Santa Maura) fort and lighthouse at the N end of Levkas canal looking SW.

LEVKAS TOWN

Levkas town lies a short distance down the canal at the point where the canal turns to run SE. The buildings of the town are easily seen and the location of the harbour is hard to mistake.

Mooring

Go stern-to or bows-to the town quay on the NE or S side. Care needs to be taken on the S side as the ballasting runs out underwater in places and a yacht should really go bows-to rather than stern-to. The bottom is sticky mud, good holding, although in places a bit soft so your anchor pulls through it. If

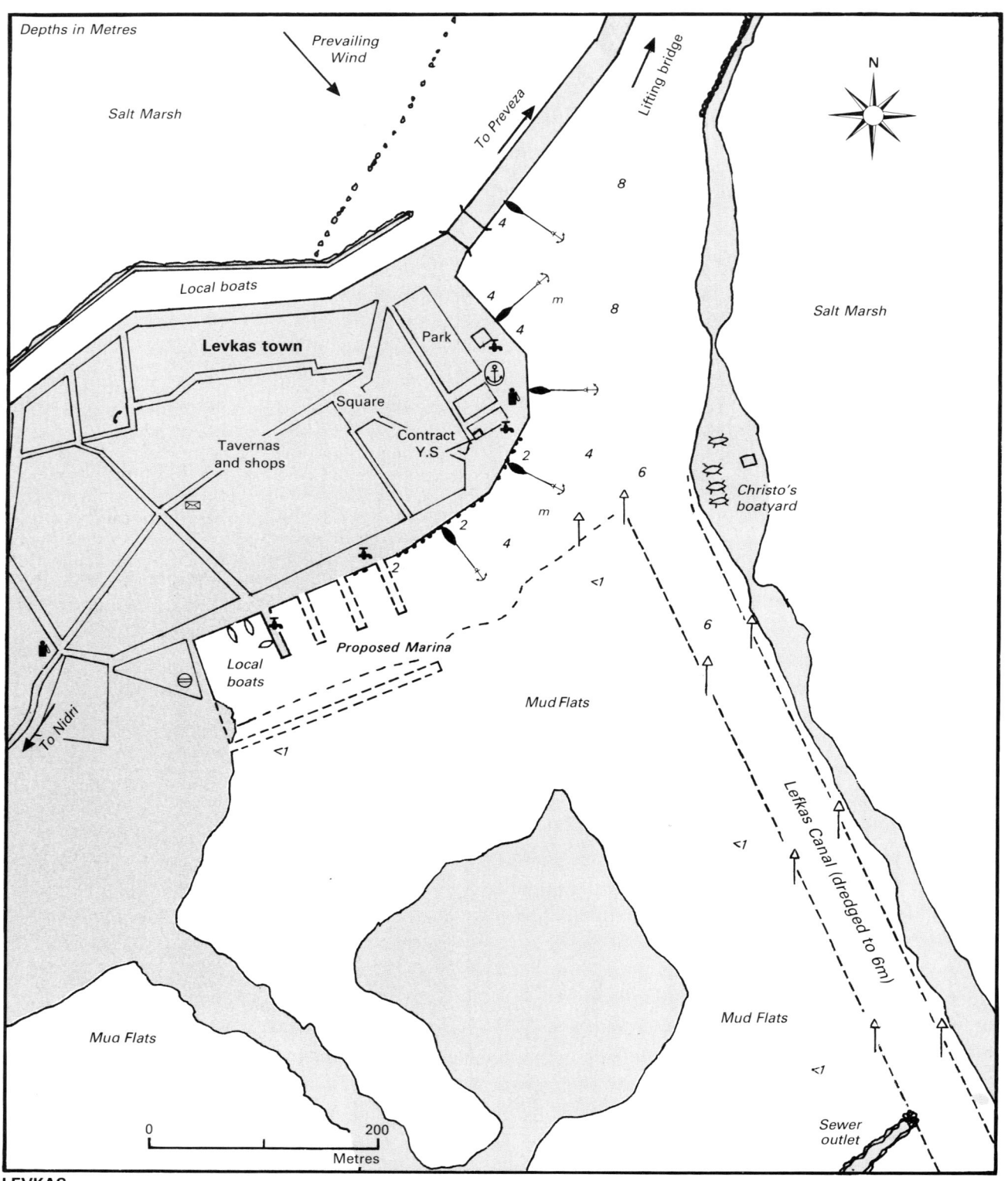

LEVKAS
38°50′·1N 20°42′·8E

Levkas town quay.

the harbour is very crowded a yacht can go stern-to or bows-to the W side of the canal just above the road bridge.

Shelter Good all-round shelter. The berths on the S side have the advantage that you are blown off the quay by the prevailing NW–W wind, but care is needed of the underwater ballasting and the wind also blows all the dust from the town across your boat. Berths on the NE quay have the prevailing wind blowing beam-on which is not normally a problem unless it is very strong or your anchor comes unstuck. Berths above the road bridge also have the prevailing wind blowing you off the quay. Southerlies set up a considerable surge for a landlocked harbour and care is needed.

Note Plans exist to build a small marina where shown on the plan of Levkas. Basically this will involve building three jetties out from the quay and installing water and electricity points. Work has been intermittent at the time of writing.

Authorities A port of entry. Customs, port police and immigration.

Note Care should be taken not to cut across the corner of the canal E of the town when arriving from the S or leaving to go S. Every summer yachts pile up on the E corner despite the poles marking it and despite the brown muddy-coloured water indicating a depth of half a metre or so.

Facilities
Services Water on the quay.
Fuel On the quay at the E corner.
Repairs A boatyard nearby. Most mechanical repairs can be carried out. Light engineering work. GRP and wood repairs. Electrical and minor electronic repairs. Some sail repairs. Chandlers. See Contract Yacht Services below.
Provisions Good shopping for all provisions. Several supermarkets near the quay and other shops in the town. A good town for restocking the larder. Levkas wine, TAOL, is palatable enough. Wine can bought from the barrel in the town. Ice from Contract Yacht Services.

Eating out Numerous tavernas in the town.
Other PO. OTE. Banks. Greek gas and *Camping Gaz*. Hire cars and motorbikes. Occasional buses around Levkas Island. Ferries to Meganisi. International and internal flights from Aktion.
Contract Yacht Services Contract Yacht Services is an English-run company that is now well established after over ten years in operation. In conjunction with the boatyard opposite they will winter your yacht and get it ready for the summer. All manner of work can be carried out: mechanical and engineering work, wood repairs and interior work, GRP work, and much else that can be arranged locally or in Piraeus. Sail repairs and life raft servicing including certification of life rafts. *Gardiennage* carried out – the company has many regulars who leave their boats in Joe's care. There is a quota on the number of yachts that can be cared for so book early. The office is close to the SE quay. Contact Joe Charlton, Petrou Filippa 3a, Levkas. ☎ and *Fax* (0645) 4490. Telex 0342 162 CYS.
Levkas Marine Services also operates a service similar to Contract Yacht Services. Office on the quay.

General
Levkas is growing into a centre for the inland sea after the devastation of the 1953 earthquake. Small tremors occasionally occur, the last in 1981 causing only a few cracks around the town houses. A small museum underneath the town library houses those relics (icons and antiquities) that have survived the earthquakes.

Ayios Mavros (Santa Maura) fort at the S end of the canal is not the only fort on Levkas, merely the most obvious. S of present-day Levkas, the remains of ancient Levkas, or Nirikos as it was called in Mycenaean times, can just be discerned. Huge walls surrounded a town that was larger than present-day Levkas. Walk along the road running along the W side of the canal or take a taxi.

Levkas town used to be the centre for cigarette smuggling to Italy. Cigarettes were brought by freighter from Belgium or Holland and then run to the Italian coast by fast motorboats. Today the trade is dying off as the Italian police get tougher and the profit margin less.

The old galley harbour at Santa Maura.

Ligia looking SE.

LIGIA

On Levkas near the southern entrance to the canal is Ligia, a small fishing harbour. A short mole has 2–5 metre depths but is normally cluttered with the resident fishing boats. The quay around from the mole is mostly too shallow although there are a few spots a small yacht can go bows-to if there is room amongst the local boats. Most yachts anchor off in 3–7 metres on mud and thick weed; make sure you get through the weed. With the afternoon breeze gusting into here it is not the most comfortable place. Ashore limited provisions are available and there are several tavernas. The local *gri-gri* fishing boats supply some of the tavernas with good fresh fish.

NIKIANA

A small harbour lying approximately 1½ miles S of Ligia. There are 2–4 metre depths along the outer half of the breakwater. Go stern-to or bows-to the mole. A number of charter boats are kept here and between the yachts and the local boats it can be difficult to find a berth. The bottom is mud, sand and weed, good holding once through the weed. Good all-round shelter.

Tavernas and some provisions ashore.

Note In the approaches to Nidri and Ormos Vlikho are three islands: Sparti, Kheloni and Madhouri. Off Nisis Sparti there is a 2 metre patch where care is needed. Between Nisis Kheloni and Levkas there are shallow patches off the islet and off the coast of Levkas – care needed.

NIDRI

Admiralty chart no. 1620

Approach

Is straightforward and there are no dangers by day. The town is obscured in the approach from the N but the islands of Sparti, Kheloni and Madhouri make location easy and the town of Nidri will be seen in the closer approaches. From the S the town will not be seen until you are around the headland opposite Nisis Madhouri. A night approach is not recommended for a first time entry.

Note Nidri is a watersports and yacht charter base and there are invariably yachts, motorboats, sailing dinghies, sailboards, water-bikes, tripper boats and ferries to watch out for.

Mooring

Go stern-to or bows-to the quay at Nidri. The quay is invariably crowded and you may have to anchor off to the S of the quay in the summer. The bottom is mud and weed, generally good holding.

Shelter The prevailing wind tends to blow down onto the quay making it uncomfortable though not usually

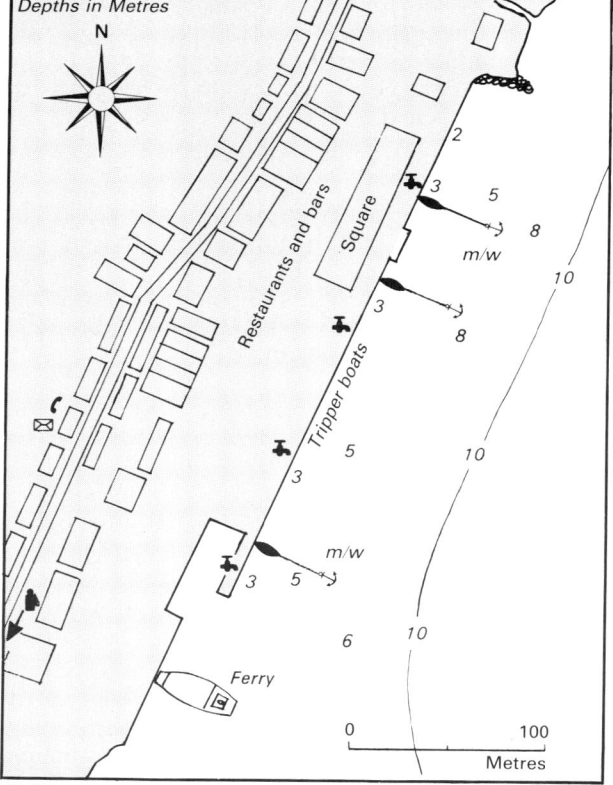

NIDRI
38°42′N 20°43′·8E

The baroque Vallaoritis villa on Nisis Moudhra.

Nidri town quay looking W.

untenable. The wake from tripper boats and local ferries is more bothersome than the chop from the wind.

Authorities Port police.

Facilities

Water On the quay
Fuel On the road to Vlikho.
Repairs A boatyard used to hauling yachts just S of the town. Some mechanical repairs. Electrical work. Sail repairs. Chandlers.
Provisions Good shopping for all provisions.
Eating out Tavernas and restaurants stretch from one end of the town to the other.
Other PO. OTE. Bank. Greek gas and *Camping Gaz*. Hire cars and motorbikes. Occasional bus to Levkas. Ferries to Meganisi.

General

Nidri is a busy little centre in the summer, something of a crossroads for private and flotilla yachts going N or S. Add in a large watersports centre and a lot of land-based accommodation and you come up with one of the busiest resorts on Levkas, though it retains much charm. The busy square by the harbour has a superb view out over the

bay and across to the islands and the mountains of the mainland opposite.

The Baroque villa on Nisis Madhouri in the approaches to Nidri belongs to the Valaoritis family, descendants of Aristoteles Valaoritis (1824–79), Greece's national poet and composer of the national hymn.

Nidri town quay.

TRANQUIL BAY

Opposite Nidri town there is the large bay called, (some time ago when the name was accurate), Tranquil Bay. It provides good all-round shelter in attractive surroundings. Anchor in 8–12 metres on soft mud and weed, good holding once your anchor is dug in. Care needs to be taken of a shallow muddy shelf extending around the S and E side of the bay – it can be difficult to see at times.

The slopes around the bay are heavily wooded, mostly with olives and cypress, and there is little habitation to intrude on the peace and quiet, only the numerous other yachts that use it. A number of yachts have wintered afloat here. It is a longish row over to Nidri town for supplies or a cold beer (an outboard helps) but water can be obtained from a tap near the chapel at the entrance to the bay.

Dorpfeldt, the archaeologist who challenged the orthodox theories about the homeland of Odysseus, claiming Levkas to be the original Ithaca of Homer, is something of a folk hero in Nidri. On the N side of the bay an obelisk has been erected to his memory just above his beautiful villa which houses a small museum. Unfortunately you need permission from the Director of Antiquities in Athens to see over it.

ORMOS VLIKHO

From Nidri and Tranquil Bay, Ormos Vlikho extends S through a bottleneck opening and opens up into an oval landlocked bay. There is good all-round shelter here 'and you can anchor in a number of

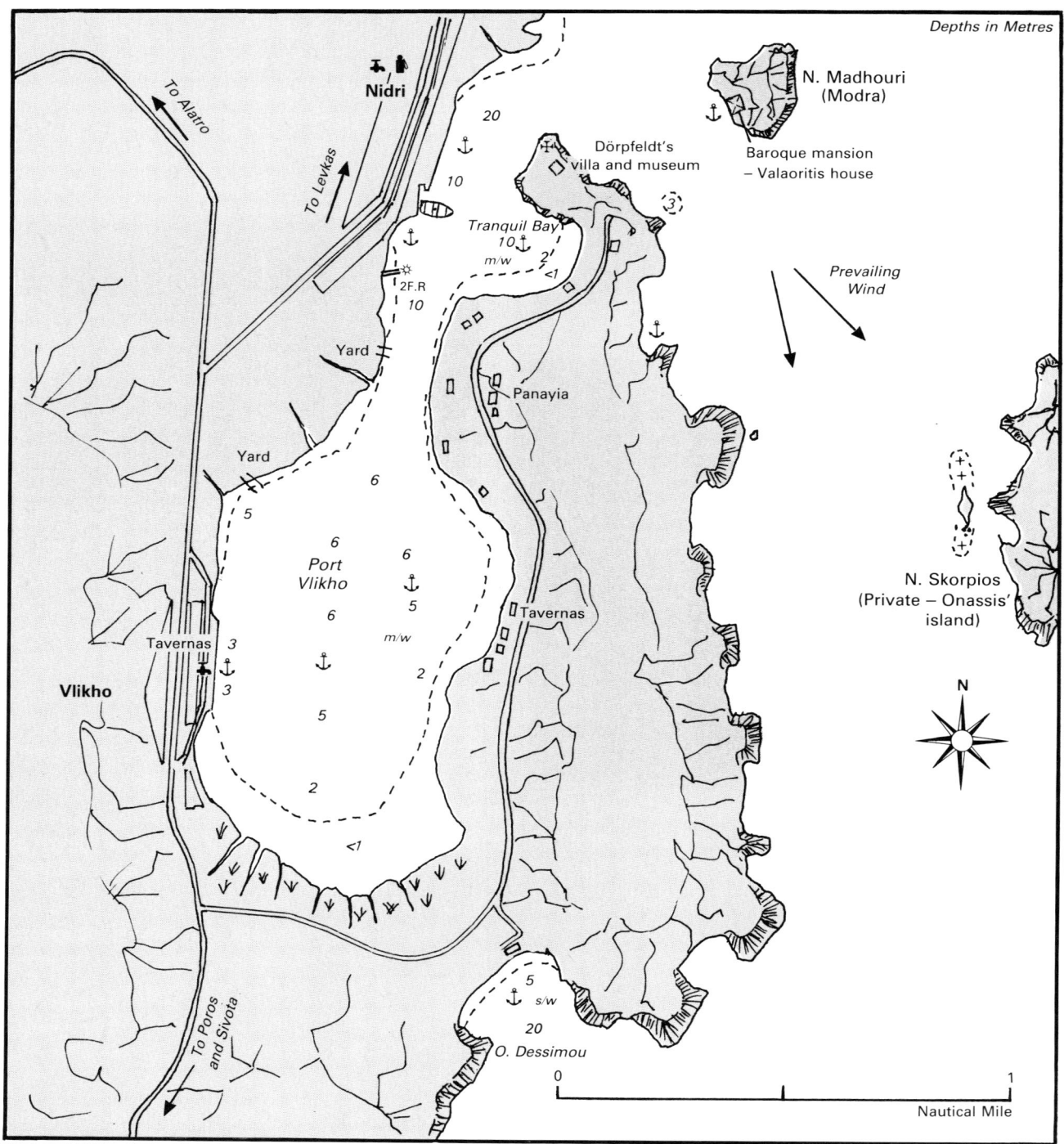

PORT VLIKHO AND APPROACHES

places. The bottom is everywhere mud and weed, good holding once through the weed.

1. On the NE side of the bay. Anchor in 5–6 metres. Good shelter from the prevailing wind which tends to gust down from the N. Good tavernas on the E side.
2. On the NW side off the boatyard. Anchor in 5–6 metres taking care of a shallow ledge off the NW corner. Good shelter.
3. Off the quay at Vlikho village. At anchor this is the most uncomfortable spot with the prevailing wind, but quite tenable with good holding on the

muddy bottom once you are through the weed. A yacht can also go stern-to or bows-to the middle section of the quay where there are 2–4 metre depths. This can be quite uncomfortable as the prevailing wind tends to push a chop onto it. In Vlikho village some provisions are available and there are several tavernas.

Vlikho is a quiet relaxed spot after Nidri where the tourists seem either to pass by or dally for only a short time. In the evening after the wind dies down a yacht can comfortably go onto the quay.

ORMOS DESSIMOU

A large bay about 1 mile S of Nisis Madhouri. It is very deep for anchoring – anchor in the N corner in 10–15 metres. Good shelter from the prevailing wind. Camping ground and taverna ashore.

ORMOS ROUDA

A large bay on the SE corner of Levkas. Anchor at the end of the bay in 5–15 metres. The prevailing wind gusts out of the bay and a swell may work its way into here. Taverna ashore.

ORMOS SIVOTA

Admiralty chart no. 1620

Approach

Entrance is easy in all weather. The entrance is difficult to make out from the distance but closer in a number of houses on the slopes on the W side of the entrance will be seen. The houses of the hamlet cannot be seen until you are around the dog-leg of the bay.

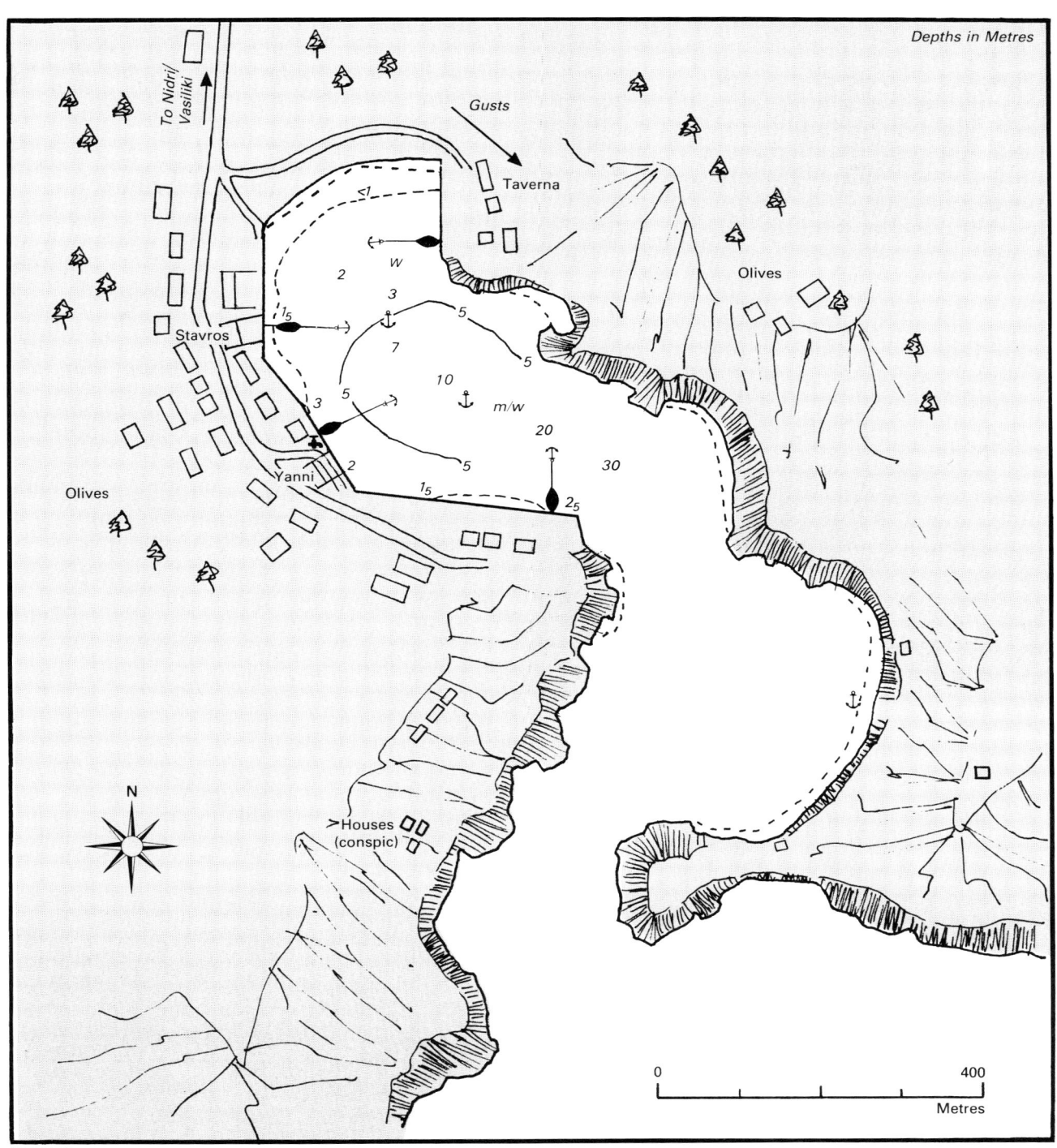

SIVOTA
38°37'·5N 20°41'E

Vlikho quay.

Sivota looking SE.

Approach to Vasiliki looking N.

Note With the prevailing wind there will sometimes be strong gusts off the high land in the vicinity of the bay.

Mooring

Anchor where convenient in 3–10 metres although when there are large numbers of yachts using the bay you will be forced to anchor further out in 10–20 metres. The bottom is mud and thick weed, good holding once through the weed though this can take some doing.

The quay along the W and S side has mostly 2–3 metre depths. If there is room go stern-to or bows-to, though it is usually crowded with charter boats. The N end of the W quay has variable depths from 1–2 metres, so investigate before charging into berth on it.

Shelter Good all-round shelter. With the prevailing wind there are gusts into the bay so make sure your anchor is well in. Yachts are wintered afloat here.

Facilities

Water on the quay at Yannis. Limited provisions. Numerous tavernas.

General

The enclosed bay with olives around the steep slopes is a picturesque place, though several new clusters of self-catering apartments threaten the character of the bay. The local community is largely engaged in accommodating the large numbers of yachts visiting the bay – on which the tavernas largely depend for their income. Yanni who runs one of the tavernas here is helpful and Stavros' taverna can also be recommended. Sivota is sometimes used to winter flotilla boats which clutter up the whole bay.

ORMOS VASILIKI

Admiralty chart no. 720
Imray-Tetra chart no. G121

Approach

Conspicuous The white lighthouse on Ak Dhoukaton is easily identified and once you are into the large bay the houses of Pondi at the W end of the beach will be seen. From the E the houses of Vasiliki village will not be seen until you are right into the bay.

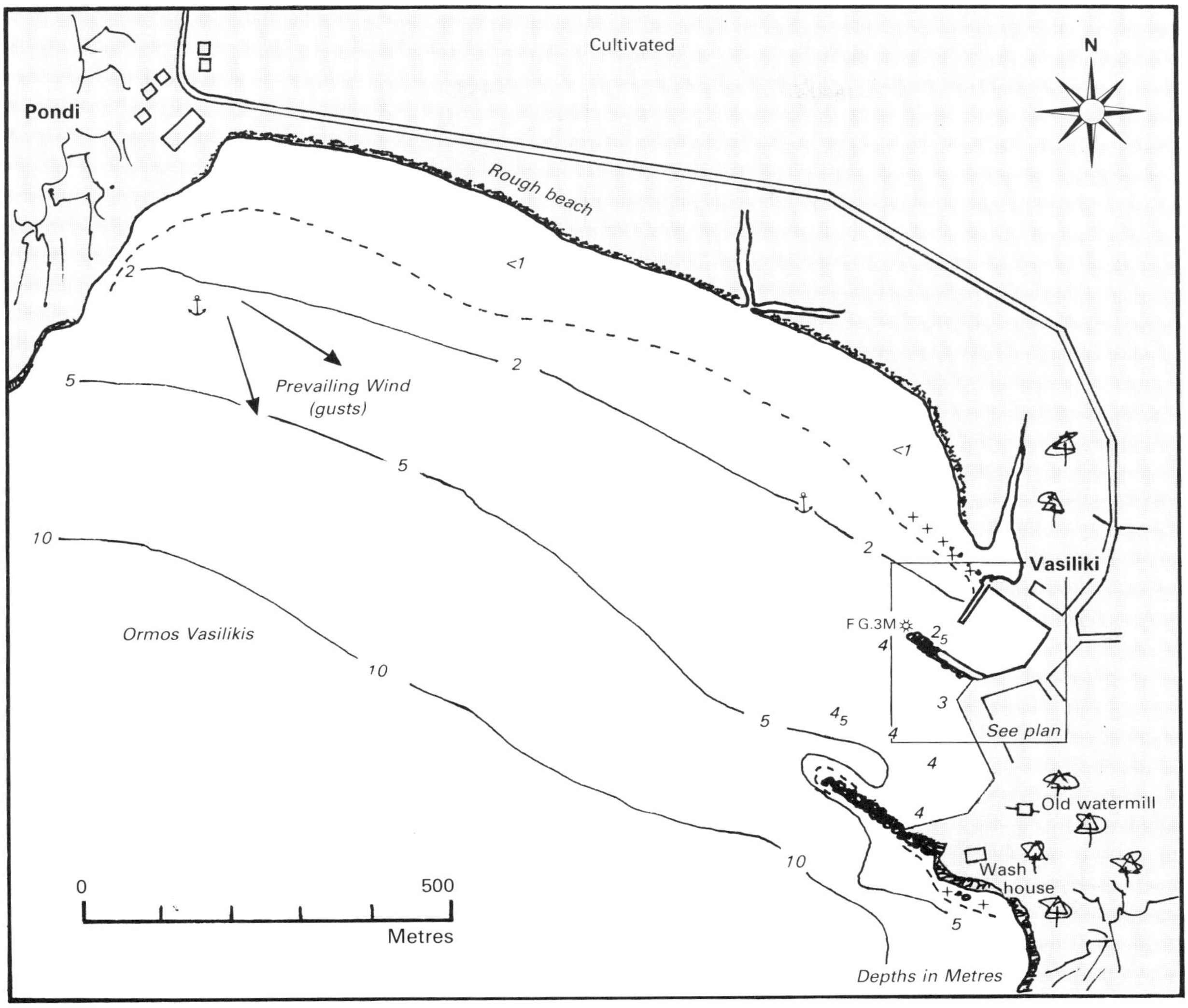

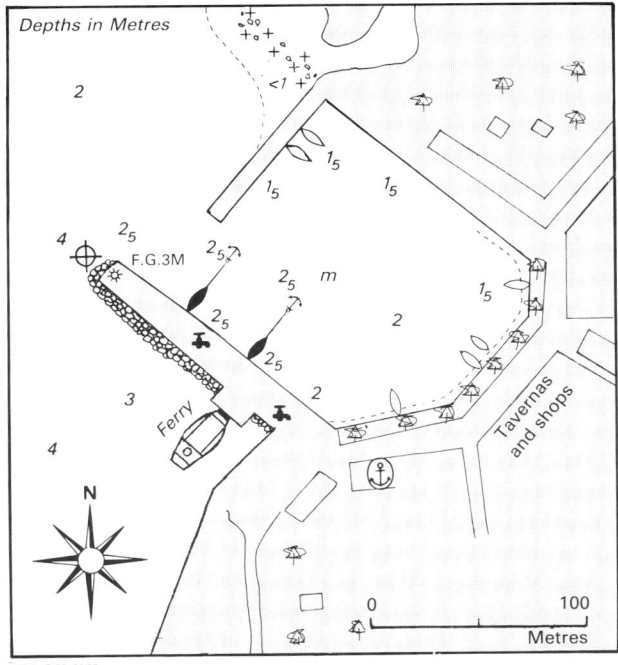

Cultivated

N

Pondi

Rough beach

<1

⚓

Prevailing Wind
(gusts)

2

5

5

<1

⚓

10

2

Vasiliki

F.G.3M ☼ 2₅

Ormos Vasilikis

4

10

3

See plan

5   4₅

4

4

Old watermill

4

10   Wash
house

5

Depths in Metres

0   500
Metres

ORMOS VASILIKIS

Depths in Metres

2

<1

1₅   1₅   1₅

4   2₅

F.G.3M

2₅

2₅   m

2₅   1₅

2

4   2₅

Ferry   2

3

4

N

Tavernas
and shops

⚓

0   100
Metres

VASILIKI
38°37'·7N 20°36'·4E (F.G.3M)

Vasiliki.

By night Care is needed in a night approach. Use the light on Ak Dhoukaton (Fl.10s24M) and the light on the end of the harbour mole (Fl.G.3M occas).

Dangers

1. Care is needed of the old outer mole running parallel to the mole enclosing the harbour.
2. With the prevailing wind there are strong gusts out of the bay.

Mooring

Go stern-to or bows-to where convenient. The bottom is mud, good holding.

Shelter Good shelter although the prevailing wind tends to blow into the harbour, bothersome rather than troublesome.

Anchorage A yacht can anchor in the bay in calm weather or light NW winds. Anchor off Pondi in 2–5 metres on sand or under the old breakwater clear of the ferry berth.

Note The harbour is prone to silting and already since my first surveys depths have decreased substantially in the harbour.

Facilities

Water On the quay. A natural spring favours this corner of Levkas and keeps the extensive plains watered. Immediately S of the town an outdoor washing house contains four tubs through which cold spring water constantly runs.

Fuel On the outskirts of the village.

Provisions Most provisions can be found.

Eating out Tavernas in the village.

Other PO. Metered telephone. Exchange office. Ferry to Fiskardho.

General

Until the arrival of watersports centres here, Vasiliki was a sleepy little agricultural and fishing village. Now it deals with the summer flock of tourists in its own homespun way without neglecting the fertile agricultural plain behind the beach. For sailboard buffs the regular strong down draughts into the bay make Vasiliki one of the top ten spots in the world for the sport – so I am told.

This is the nearest secure anchorage to the white cliffs of Sappho's leap close to Ak Dhoukaton. Here also is the site of a temple dedicated to Apollo where in antiquity panhellenic games were held to celebrate the god. Today only a few fragments and shards mark the site.

NISIS SKORPIOS AND SKORPIDHI
(Scropio Island)

Close E of Ormos Vlikho are the twin islands of Skorpios and Skorpidhi. These are the private islands of the Onassis family, originally bought by the late Aristotle Onassis. Sailing between Skorpidhi and Skorpios you used to see *Christina*, the late Onassis' motor yacht (read ship), moored to two large buoys. The whole of Skorpios has been planted as a park and requires a considerable full-time staff to maintain

it. On the SW corner there is a farm to supply fresh milk and meat, on the E side are the generating plant, warehouses and employees' houses. Unfortunately for those who buy islands to gain privacy, the very scale of the acquisition seems to attract sightseers and from Nidri a number of *caïques* run day trips around Skorpios.

You can sail around the islands, you can even anchor off the coast, but you cannot land above the high water mark. All the anchorages are on the S of Skorpios. There is a cove on the SW with a small beach house that Jackie Onassis favoured. Further E is a sandy isthmus and a yacht can anchor on either side of it. The best spot is on the E side of the isthmus off a sandy beach.

Nisos Meganisi
Admiralty chart no. 1620

This Rorschach blob of an island lies immediately E of Levkas. The strait between Meganisi and Levkas, Stenon Meganisiou, is one of the loveliest channels in the Ionian with the high precipitous slopes of Levkas on one side and the lower more gentle slopes of Meganisi fringed by a beach on the other. Winds in the channel are fickle and often you will have wind from a southerly direction at the S end and a northerly wind at the N end.

The N side of Meganisi is much indented with several natural harbours and numerous enclosed bays. Most of the bays are fringed by olive and cypress with clear blue water – a combination that makes them popular with yachts though there is always somewhere in high season and a little more solitude outside of July and August.

On the SW coast of Meganisi, on the 'tail' of the island, are a number of caves. The most famous of these, Papanicolis, is quite large and rumoured by the locals to be the hiding place of a Greek submarine during the second World War.

Further south of this cave are a number of small but deep caves which lead 60 to 70 feet in. There is some good fishing to be had around this part of the island.

IFALOS HIEROMITI

Between Nisis Skorpios and Nisos Meganisi there is a shoal patch and reef. The reef is usually marked in the summer, but this cannot be relied upon. In calm weather the shoal and reef are easily seen, but with the chop from the prevailing wind it can be difficult to see.

SPARTAKHORI (Port Spiglia)

Approach

The village of Spartakhori perched on top of a hill on the W side of the bay is easily seen from the N and W. Once you are into the bay the small harbour will be seen.

NISOS MEGANISI

Mooring

Go stern-to or bows-to the quay or short pier where possible. You will have to drop your anchor in quite deep water so ensure you have plenty of scope. Good shelter with the prevailing winds although the evening NE breeze makes some berths on the W side of the harbour uncomfortable – ensure your anchor is well in when berthing here.

Anchorage Anchor off the beach at the head of the bay. It is deep here and you will be anchoring in considerable depths.

Facilities

Water from the taverna. Limited provisions in the village. Tavernas by the harbour, at the head of the bay, and in the village. The Porto Spiglia taverna is popular with flotillas.

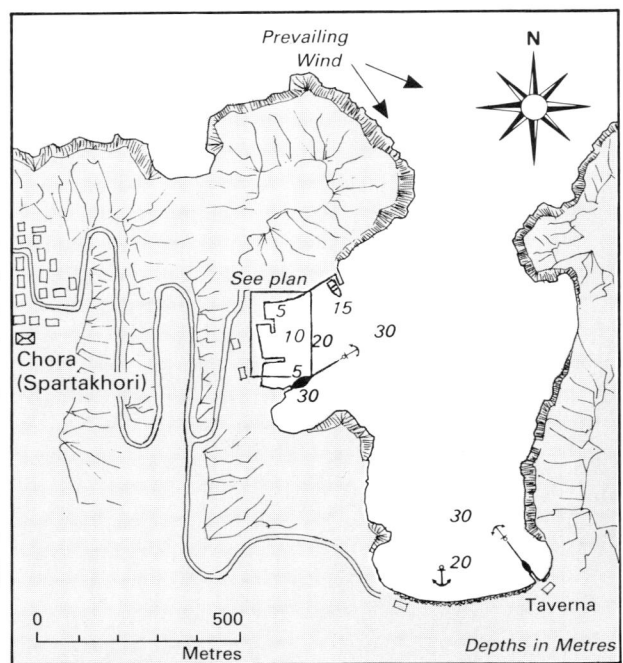

SPARTAKHORI (SPIGLIA)
38°39'·6N 20°46'·6E

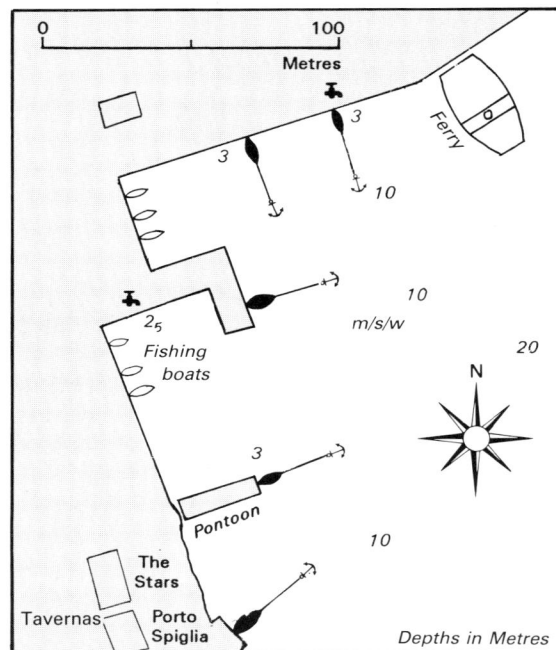

SPARTAKHORI

General

The village is reached by a winding cypress-lined road and is worth the hot walk to reach it. From a bend in the road before you get to the village you have a view over the whole of the N part of the inland sea. Even if you eat at the bottom it is well worth the steep climb up to the village for both the stupendous view and the enchanting village itself.

Spartakhori harbour looking up to the village on the hill. *Nigel Patten.*

PORT VATHI

Approach

The entrance to the bay is difficult to determine and you cannot see the houses of the hamlet until you are well into the bay itself.

Mooring

Anchor in the bay or go stern-to or bows-to in the harbour. Good shelter from the prevailing winds. A NE wind can blow in the evening making things a bit rolly, although it generally dies down after a few hours.

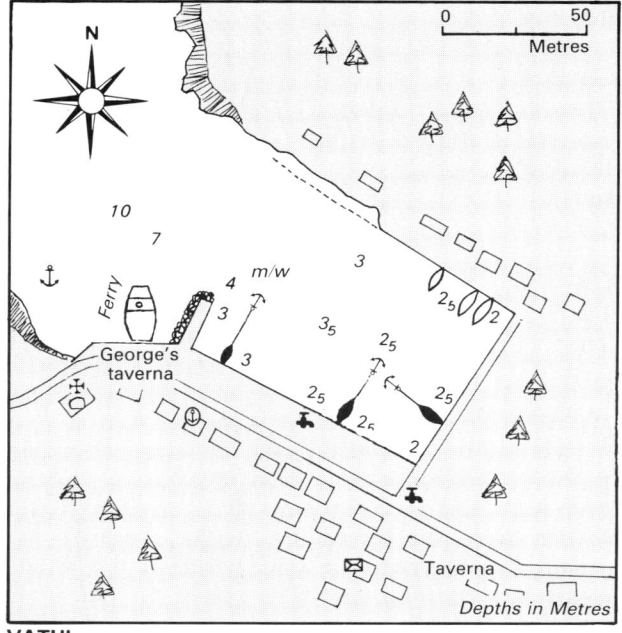

VATHI
38°39'·8N 20°48'E

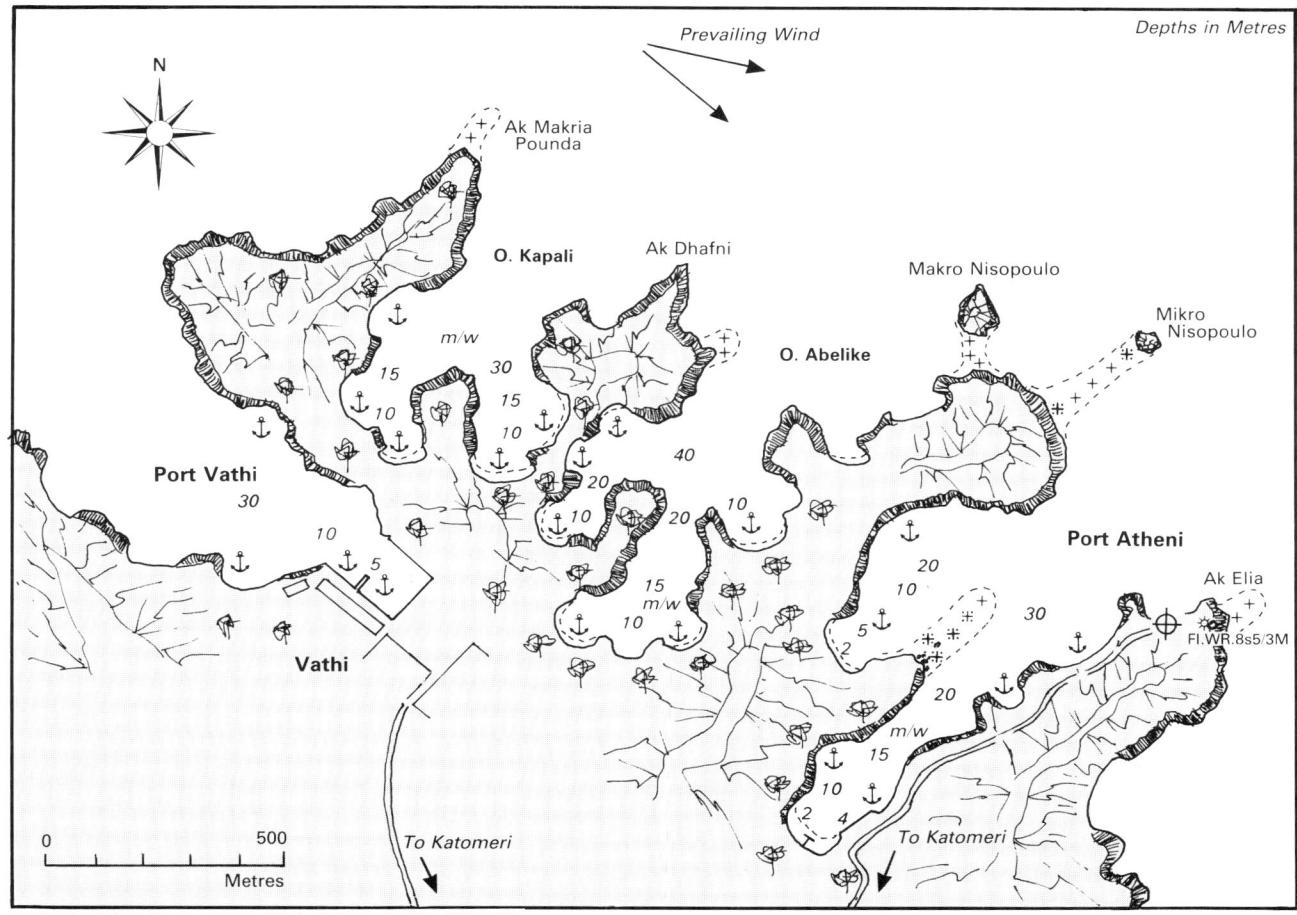

NISOS MEGANISI: PORT VATHI TO PORT ATHENI
Ak Elia light: 38°40′N 20°48′·5E

Facilities
Water close to the quay, although it is often turned off in the summer. Limited provisions and several tavernas. Georges behind the mole often has good fish.

General
The small village is the nominal capital of the island, though the dusty little place hardly acknowledges it. It is a charming place, seemingly half asleep in summer. Good walks inland through the olive groves.

ORMOS KAPALI AND ABELIKE
Two large indented bays between Vathi and Atheni. There are no dangers apart from a few reefs, easily seen, extending a short distance off the rocky coast. From the plan it is apparent there are numerous places a in which yacht can anchor.

There are considerable depths in both bays, mostly 10–15 metres until close to the coast. Anchor where convenient and take a long line ashore – there is little room in the bays to swing to an anchor. The bottom is mud and weed, good holding once through the weed.

The coves in the two bays can get crowded in the summer, but these are peaceful places for all that.

There are no facilities and nor should there be. It is about a 10-minute walk from Kapali over the saddle to Vathi.

Note In Abelike part of the bay is now buoyed off for swimmers. There have been reports here of bold rats attracted to the rubbish left by yachts on the shore. Since I and a lot of other skippers expended some energy keeping the place clean in years gone by I'd suggest that anyone visiting here do likewise. It is not a place to dump or bury rubbish.

PORT ATHENI

Approach
From the N and W the two islets of Megalo Nisopoulo and Mikro Nisopoulo are easily identified. From the E the light structure on the E side of the entrance will be seen. Pass to seaward of the two islets as a reef connects them to Meganisi.

Note There is a reef running out into the middle of the bay. Most of it is just underwater and numbers of yachts run up on it in the summer. Care needed!

Mooring
There are several places to anchor.
1. Most boats anchor on the W side of the bay with a long line ashore. Most of the bay is quite deep,

10–20 metres except at the head of the bay. The bottom is sand and weed, good holding.
2. On the E side of the bay.
3. At the head of the bay. It is quite deep until the very end. The bottom is mud, sand, and thick weed, good holding once through the weed.
4. Stern-to or bows-to the quay on the SE side at the head of the bay. There are 2–4 metre depths off the quay.

There is generally good shelter although a NE wind sometimes blows at night, it usually dies down after several hours.

Facilities

Some provisions and tavernas at Katomeri.

General

It is about 30 minutes' picturesque walk through the olive groves to the small village of Katomeri, though remember to take a torch if returning at night – there are no streetlights here.

Nisos Ithaca
(Ithaki)

According to Homer this is the island home of Odysseus. Archaeologists can dispute whether or not this is so, but Homer still provides the best description of the island:

'In Ithaca there are not wide courses, nor meadowlands at all. It is a pasture land of goats, and more pleasant in my sight than one which pastureth horses...,

Homer Odyssey

The island consists of two peninsulas connected by a narrow isthmus which is the backbone to Kolpos Aetou (Gulf of Molo). The steep-to mountains are bare and rocky, although in a few of the valleys there is a swathe of green fed by some small subterranean spring.

In common with many of the Ionian Islands, Ithaca has a strong seafaring tradition and many of the young make their living in the merchant navy. Many more have emigrated to Australia or South Africa, although a substantial number do return and it is not unusual to be greeted by an Australian *gidday sport* around the island.

The important port on the island is Port Vathi, although there are a number of other harbours and anchorages suitable for an overnight stop. One of these is Port Polis, a bay below the town of Stavros where the local school teacher looks after a small museum housing a collection of items from excavations on the supposed site of Odysseus' palace. Although the site of the palace has not been conclusively proved, a number of tripods and masks indicating later hero worship of Odysseus have been unearthed. Certainly the fact that Ithaca is on a major fault line may mean that the Homeric palace was completely buried by an earthquake, or perhaps the subject of Homer's epic lived in a comparatively modest dwelling.

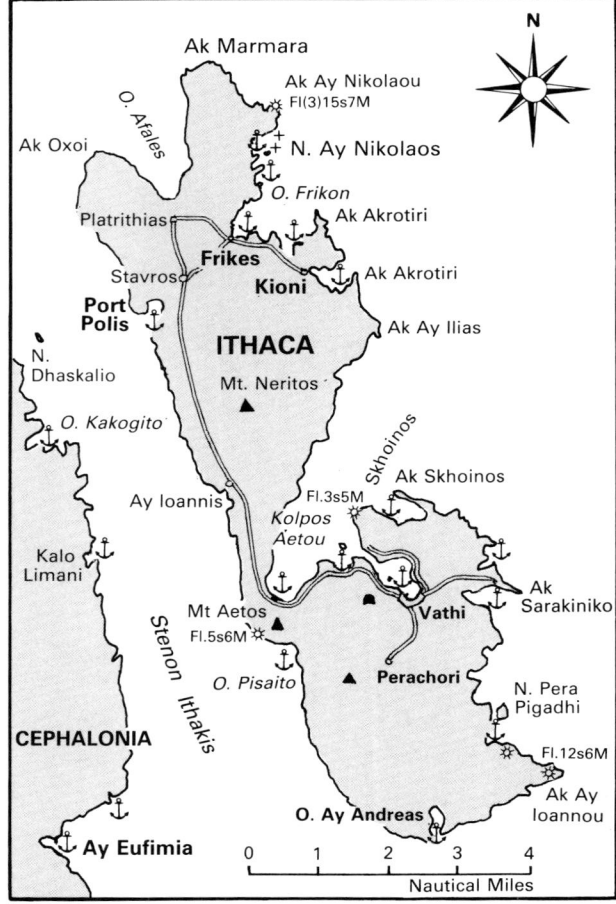

ITHACA

Ithaca and Odysseus

Despite the paucity of archaeological evidence for Ithaca as the island home of Odysseus and despite Dorpfeldt's claim that Levkas is the real Ithaca, the Ithaca of today remains the favoured archaeological choice. Consequently the places on the island mentioned in Homer have nearly all been identified on Ithaca.

Port Polis is the harbour of ancient Polis which stood on the ridge above. Just N on the summit of a hill called Pelikata are the ruins of a Bronze Age settlement which is generally accepted to be the palace of Odysseus. Some of the walls and a section of paved road are all that remain. On the N side of Port Polis there existed a cave, the Cave of the Nymphs, where archaeologists have found Mycenaean pottery and bronze relics including a number of tripods and terra cotta masks indicating later hero worship of Odysseus.

Port Frikes can be identified with the Reithron of the *Odyssey*.

Ormos Pera Pigadhi lies at the bottom of Arethusa's spring. The spring still flows today and above it is the raven's rock (*Korax*) of the *Odyssey*, still called by the same name today. Above here lies the plateau of Marathia and it is probably here that Odysseus met Eumaneus the swine herd.

On Mt Aetos, on the narrow peninsula joining the two halves of the island, are the scanty remains of what may have been a shrine or temple.

All of this is largely speculation and indeed Dorpfeldt was able to single out equally convincing sites on Levkas.

ITHACA CHANNEL (Stenon Ithakis)

Caution With the prevailing afternoon W–NW breeze there are strong gusts off the high land into the Ithaca Channel and off the E side of Ithaca. In July and August when the *maistro* is blowing these gusts can be quite severe. The most notorious spots are the S end of the Ithaca Channel, Ormos Frikon, and Kolpos Aetou (Gulf of Molo).

FRIKES

Admiralty chart no. 720
Imray-Tetra G121

Approach

A small harbour tucked into the W corner of Ormos Frikon on the NE of Ithaca. The buildings of the hamlet will not be seen until closer in, when two windmills on a bluff by the hamlet are conspicuous. Care must be taken of above- and below-water rocks around the islets under Ak Ay Nikolaou.

Note With the prevailing wind there are strong gusts out of Ormos Frikon and care is needed.

Mooring

Once into the harbour go alongside or stern-to the mole. It is preferable to be alongside rather than stern-to because of strong down-draughts into the harbour with the prevailing NW winds. Larger yachts can go stern-to the outside of the mole with a long line to it, keeping clear of the ferry berth.

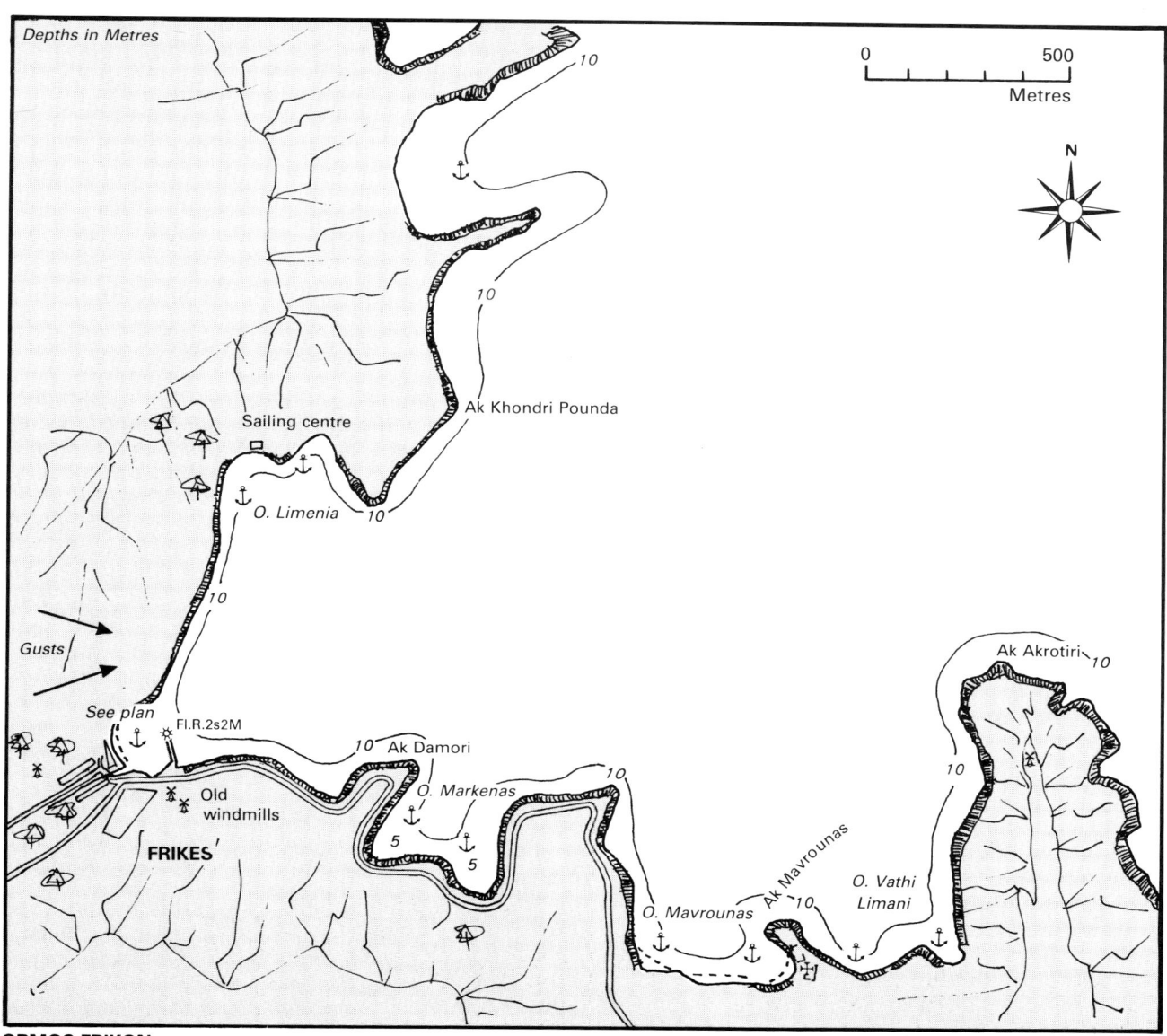

ORMOS FRIKON

Approach to Frikes looking W.

Frikes harbour looking SW.

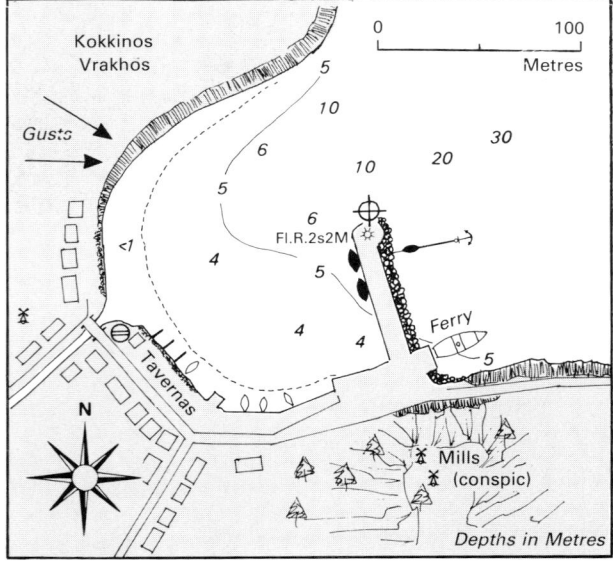

FRIKES
38°27'·6N 20°39'·9E (Fl.R.2s2M)

Facilities

Water in the village. Most provisions can be found ashore and there are a number of good tavernas. Ferries to Vasiliki and Fiskardho in the summer.

General

The village is a picture postcard place set at the bottom of a wooded ravine with a stream running down to the sea keeping everything green through the summer. A couple of windmills sit above the village on a rocky crag. Inevitably this once isolated village has begun to attract tourists, but it is still a gem and well worth a visit.

Anchorages around Ormos Frikon

In general the anchorages on the N and W side of Ormos Frikon are the best with the prevailing wind.

Port Ay Nikolaos The bay under Ak Ay Nikolaou. Good protection though there are gusts.

Khondri Pounda Reasonable shelter though some swell may work its way into here.

Limenia A two-headed bay under Ak Khondri Pounda. There is a watersports centre in the W cove. Reasonable shelter.

Damori Immediately E of Frikes. Poor shelter.

Mavrounas Calm weather anchorage.

Vathi Limani Calm weather anchorage. Ruined monastery ashore.

The bottom is mostly mud, shingle and weed, not everywhere good holding.

PORT KIONI

Admiralty chart no. 720

Approach

Is straightforward and there are no dangers from N or S. The three ruined windmills on the S point of the bay and the cluster of houses on the saddle of the hill are easily distinguished.

Mooring

Go stern-to or bows-to the quay. As the bottom shelves steeply you must drop your anchor in quite deep water, so have plenty of scope ready. Alternatively anchor off, though again, because it is so deep, you will be anchoring in 10–20 metres. The bottom is hard mud and weed, uncertain holding in places. With the prevailing wind there are strong

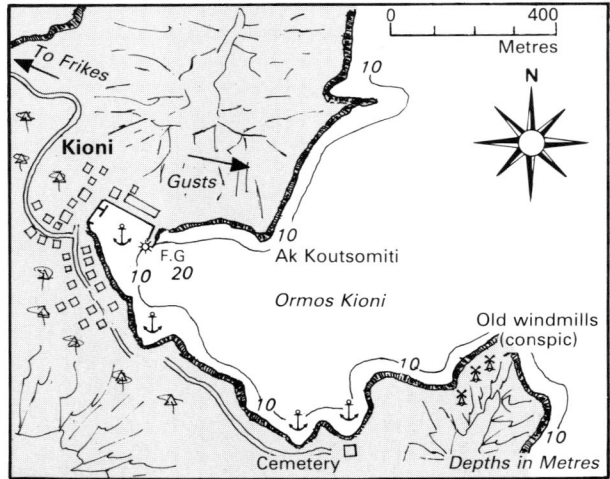

ORMOS KIONI

Kioni harbour.

Ak Ay Ilias and chapel between Kioni and Kolpos Aetou looking N.

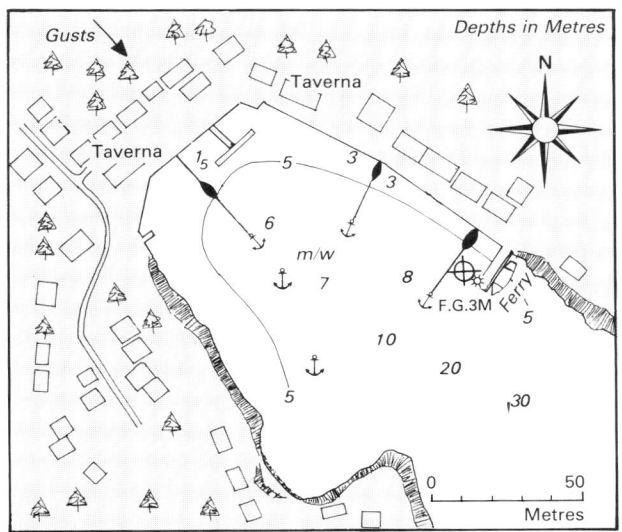

KIONI
38°27'N 20°47'·5E (F.G.3M)

Chapel and light on Ak Ay Andreou (looking NE) in the immediate approaches to Vathi on Ithaca.

gusts down into the bay, so ensure that your anchor is well in and holding.

Note In calm weather or light W winds a yacht can anchor off the cemetery in the SE, though again depths are considerable for anchoring.

Facilities

There is no water supply other than cisterns. Most provisions (baker, grocers) can be found. Several tavernas on the waterfront.

General

Kioni is an attractive huddle of whitewashed houses around the slopes at the head of the bay. If the place seems to have more houses than people, this is because a large part of the population has emigrated to Australia and the USA and many of the houses are still owned by these expatriates. In twenty years the school roll has fallen from some 600 to 20. A *caïque* runs from here to Port Vathi in the season. Pleasant walks over the saddle to a number of small coves.

VATHI (Ithaki)
Admiralty chart no. 1620
Imray-Tetra chart no. G12

Approach

Conspicuous From the N and S a belfry and the earthworks scar of the road on Mt Korini are conspicuous. Once into Kolpos Aetou (Gulf of Molo) the light structure and the chapel on Ak Ay Andreou are easily distinguished. The light structure on Nisis Katzurbo, the small island at the bottleneck entrance to Port Vathi, will also be seen.

By night Use the lights on Ak Ay Andreou (Fl.3s5M) and on Nisis Katzurbo (Fl.G.4s3M). Once into Port Vathi use the light on the small islet in the harbour (Q.G.2M).

Dangers With the prevailing wind there are severe gusts down into Kolpos Aetou.

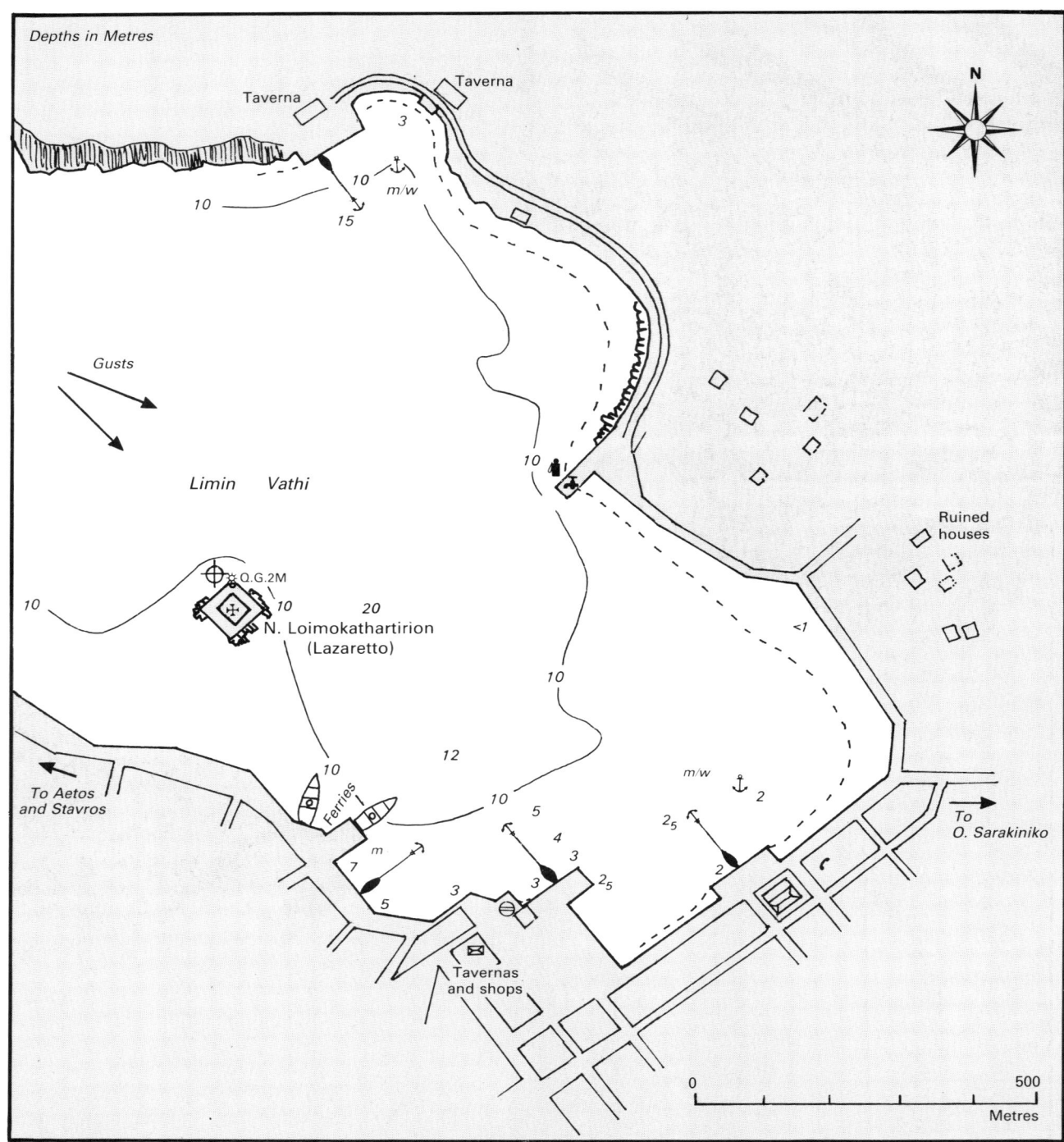

VATHI (ITHACA)
38°22'·2N 20°42'·8E (Q.G.2M)

Mooring

Go stern-to or bows-to the quay on the W under the ferry berths. Alternatively go stern-to the outside of the mole sheltering the basin. Yachts also go stern or bows-to the protruding bit of quay at the head of the bay or anchor off to the E. In the NE corner a new quay has been built and yachts can go stern or bows-to here or anchor off in the bay. The bottom is everywhere mud and thick weed, not the best holding until you get your anchor through the weed.

Shelter The prevailing wind tends to blow into the bay with some force so make sure your anchor is well in and holding. Once the breeze dies at dusk you will have no further worries. No sea enters with the wind and as long as care is taken in anchoring there is good all-round protection.

Authorities Port police and customs.

Facilities

Water Can be delivered by mini-tanker to the quay or on the fuel quay.
Fuel Fuel quay on the E side of the bay.
Repairs Limited mechanical repairs only.
Provisions Good shopping for all provisions. Black

Vathi on Ithaca looking N from near Palaiochora. *Chris Boutwood.*

SW quay at Vathi.

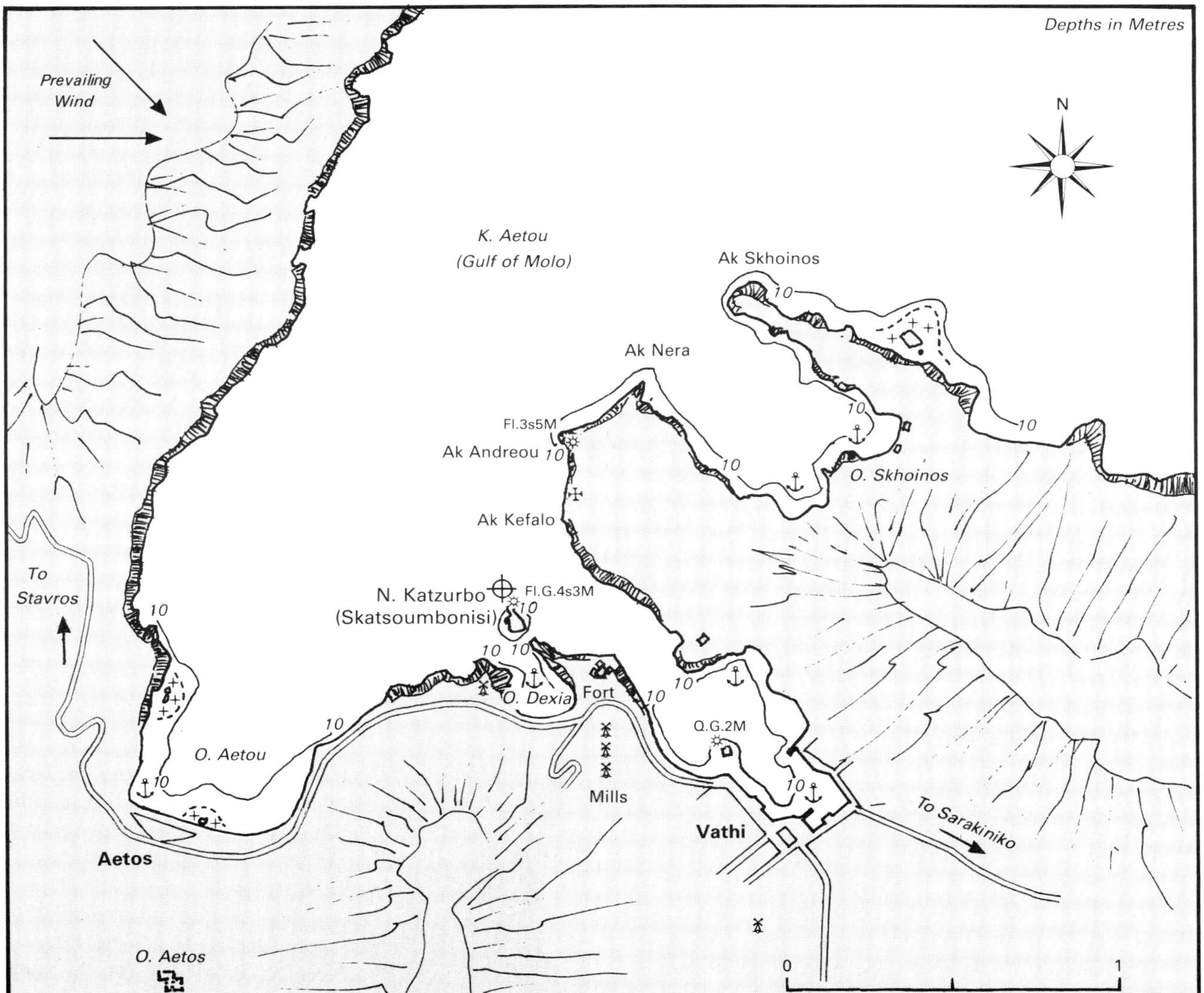

Depths in Metres

Prevailing Wind

N

K. Aetou (Gulf of Molo)

Ak Skhoinos

10

Ak Nera

Fl.3s5M

Ak Andreou *10*

10

O. Skhoinos

Ak Kefalo

To Stavros

10

N. Katzurbo (Skatsoumbonisi) Fl.G.4s3M

10

10 *10*

O. Dexia Fort

10 *10*

10

O. Aetou

Q.G.2M

Mills

10

Vathi

To Sarakiniko

Aetos

O. Aetos (anc. ruins)

0   1

Nautical Mile

KOLPOS AETOU (GULF OF MOLO)
38°22'·6N 20°42'·E (Fl.G.4s3M)

Ithaca wine, a dark sweet wine similar to *Mavro Daphne*, and a good local dry white wine, can be bought in bulk. Ice available.

Eating out Numerous tavernas in the town. There are also two tavernas in the N bay.

Other PO. OTE. Bank. Motorbike and car hire. Ferries to Patras, Corfu, Astakos, Ay Eufimia and Italy.

General

Vathi suffered severe damage in the 1953 earthquake, but although most of the town around the harbour is new, it is not an unattractive place. The port hums and bustles with *caïques* coming and going and when the Patras-Brindisi ferry arrives most of the town turns out to watch. Vathi is the best place to leave a yacht and hire a car or motorbike to explore the island – Stavros, the likely site of Odysseus' palace, is about a one hour drive. In late August there is an Ithaca theatre festival at Vathi.

Anchorages around Kolpos Aetou

Imray-Tetra chart no. G12

Ormos Aetou In calm weather you can anchor in the SW corner of the gulf. Anchor in 5–10 metres on the W. Care is needed of the reef about half way along the bay.

Ormos Dexia The bay under Nisos Katzurbo. In calm weather anchor in 5–12 metres.

Ormos Skhoinos The large bay under Ak Skhoinos. Anchor in 8–12 metres in the SE corner. Tenable in light W winds.

ORMOS SARAKINIKO

A bay on the E coast of Ithaca immediately above Ak Sarakiniko which is easily recognised by the building housing the reverse osmosis plant for the island. Anchor in 3–10 metres off the beach on sand, rock and weed. Reasonable protection from the prevailing wind which gusts down from the W. The bay is a delightful spot and in settled weather can be used as an overnight anchorage. Just over the saddle of the ridge is Vathi town, about an hour's walk.

PERA PIGADHI

Admiralty chart no. 720
Imray-Tetra chart no. G121

On the SE side of Ithaca the small islet of Pera Pigadhi lies close to the coast. It is difficult to distinguish until you are close to. South of the islet on Ithaca is Ormos Pera Pigadhi.

Anchor in Ormos Pera Pigadhi or just S of the islet. There is room for a few yachts to go alongside the small quay on the islet. There are 4 metre least depths through the channel between the islet and Ithaca that though the water is so clear, it is difficult

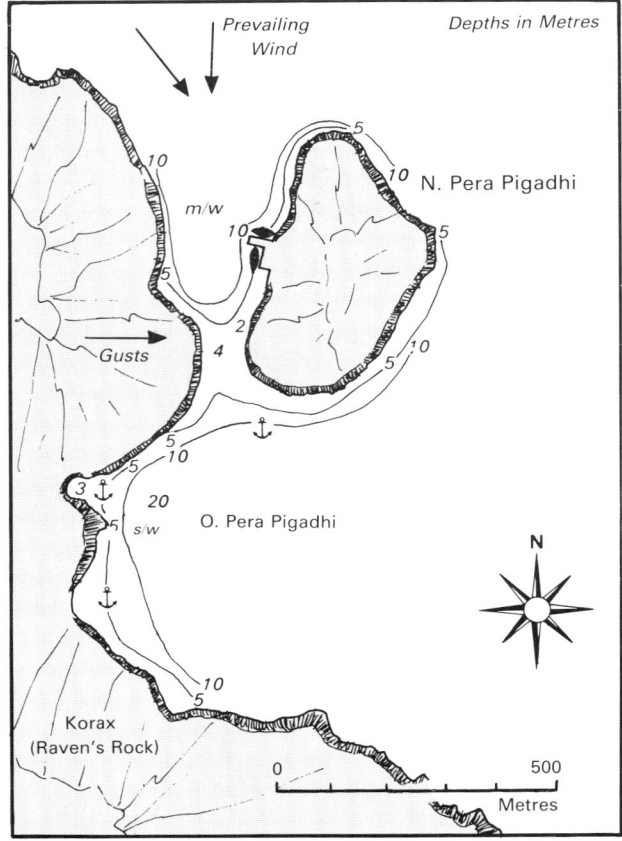

PERA PIGADHI
38°20'·2N 20°45'E

to believe you are not going to touch bottom. Outside the channel depths drop off quickly and you will usually be anchoring in 10–20 metres in the bay or S of the islet. The bottom is sand and weed, good holding.

The afternoon breeze does not get here until mid-afternoon, when, unless you are tucked right into Ormos Pera Pigadhi or securely on the quay, it may become untenable. There have been a number of reports of very big and bold rats on the island that have no hesitation in invading a yacht moored overnight on the quay. The steep-to slope above Ormos Pera Pigadhi is called Koraka, corresponding to the *korax* in the *Odyssey*.

Pera Pigadhi channel and jetty looking N.

Ak Ay Ioannis and light structure looking N.

AYIOS ANDREAS
Admiralty chart no. 720

An impressive deserted anchorage on the S of Ithaca. Anchor in 8–15 metres at the head of the bay or in the cove on the W with a long line ashore. Some swell enters with the prevailing wind pushing down the Ithaca channel, uncomfortable rather than untenable. Open to the S.

PORT POLIS
Admiralty chart no. 720

A large bay on the NW side of Ithaca. Anchor off the beach or go stern-to on the end of the small mole. The bottom shelves steeply, so you will have to anchor in 10–20 metres. With the afternoon breeze gusting down the channel between Cephalonia and Ithaca it can be uncomfortable in here, but not untenable. Southerlies blow straight into the anchorage and a yacht should go to Fiskardho.

Nisos Cephalonia
(Kefallinia)

Across the narrow sea strait from Ithaca lies Cephalonia, the largest in area of the Ionian Islands. Like Ithaca, Cephalonia is rugged and steep-to. Starting at the N end of the island a jagged mountain spine runs S to the highest mountain of the Ionian Islands, Mount Nero, standing over 1600 metres (5200ft) above sea level. Most of the slopes are bare rock, but in the valleys, particularly on the E side of the island, beautiful pine forests run down to the sea. Much of this forest is composed of a local fir tree, *Abies cephalonica*, a tall slim pine which, despite its name, grows elsewhere in Greece.

In ancient times Cephalonia formed part of the kingdom of Odysseus, and here at least archaeologists have been able to find evidence of the ancient sites mentioned in Homer. There were four important towns: Pale, Krane, Same, and Pronoi. Same or Sami (similarly Pale-Pali and Krane-Krani) was the most important town built on the heights immediately N of the small ferry port of the same name. Extensive ruins of all four towns remain, those at Krani being particularly well preserved relics of

Mycenaean occupation. The tombs here are said to be the best examples of Mycenaean tombs in Greece.

Like many of the Ionian Islands, Cephalonia has close links with Italy, and a wartime story is often told which illustrates just how strong this association can be. The Italians invaded the islands in the early days of the Second World War but failed to gain real control. In 1943 the Germans landed in Cephalonia, but the occupying Italian force, some 9000 troops of the Alpine Division, not only refused to co-operate but actually fought against them for seven days. Of the Italian force only 3000 survived, and these were brutally lined up and shot, it is said on Hitler's personal orders. Only 34 survived and, so the story goes, one of the survivors swam to Ithaca where he was sheltered by the local Greeks until he escaped. Until recently he was captain on one of the Patras-Brindisi ferries and every time he passed Ithaca gave a long toot on the ship's horn to salute his Greek friends.

Cephalonia produces some good wines though not from its Italian connection, but from local initiative and the French and surprisingly an Englishman. Although not cheap by Greek standards (in fact nearly double the price of the ubiquitous *Demestica*), the *Robola* whites and reds are excellent and for those who like a rosé, the *Manzavino* is also very good.

The earthquake belt that blights the other Ionian Islands likewise touches Cephalonia. Edward Lear, when he was touring the Ionian Islands, recorded 43 small tremors in 1863 alone. The major earthquake of 1953 effectively demolished every town on Cephalonia except Fiskardho, because, it is said, it sits on a bed of soft clay. One inhabitant of Argostoli who experienced the '53 quake described to me how the ground undulated like a three-foot swell on the sea. In some of the rebuilding of Cephalonia there is a sameness about the reinforced concrete architecture that contrasts poorly with the gentle nineteenth-century grace of Fiskardho.

ARGOSTOLI (Argostolion)
Admiralty chart no. 1557
Imray-Tetra chart no. G12

Approach
Conspicuous From the W the large lighthouse on Ak Yero Gombos is conspicuous. From the E Nisis Thionisi and a white hotel on Ak Pelagia are easily identified. Closing the low-lying Nisis Vardhianoi it is safe to pass between it and Cephalonia, but a more prudent course is to stand off leaving the island to port and then proceed up the Gulf of Argostoli. Once you are in the Gulf of Argostoli, the town of Lixouri and a Doric-style lighthouse on Ak Ay Theodhoroi are conspicuous. Rounding the green wooded slopes of Ak Ay Theodhoroi keep to the middle of the inlet that forms the harbour of Argostoli. Leave the concrete beacon to starboard – although there are three metre depths between the beacon and the docks there are shoal patches close to the docks.

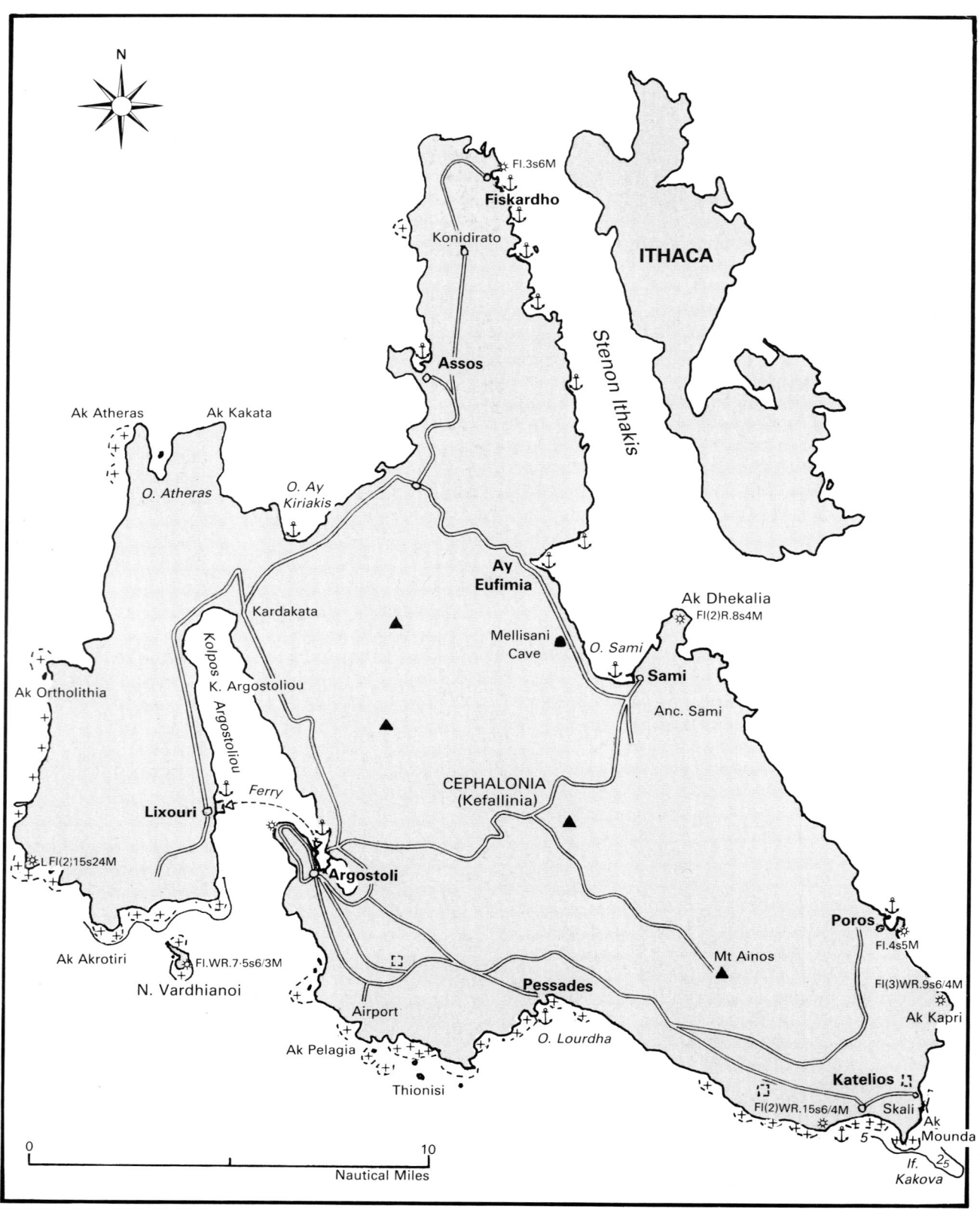

N

Fiskardho Fl.3s6M

Konidirato

ITHACA

Assos

Ak Atheras   Ak Kakata

O. Atheras

*O. Ay
Kiriakis*

Stenon Ithakis

Ak Ortholithia

Kardakata

Ay
Eufimia

Ak Dhekalia
Fl(2)R.8s4M

Mellisani
Cave   *O. Sami*

Sami

Anc. Sami

Kolpos Argostoliou

K. Argostoliou

CEPHALONIA
(Kefallinia)

Lixouri   *Ferry*

LFl(2)15s24M

Argostoli

Poros
Fl.4s5M

Mt Ainos

Ak Akrotiri

Fl.WR.7·5s6/3M

N. Vardhianoi

Fl(3)WR.9s6/4M

Ak Kapri

Pessades

Airport   *O. Lourdha*

Ak Pelagia

Thionisi

Katelios

Skali

Fl(2)WR.15s6/4M

Ak
Mounda

5

*If.
Kakova*

2·5

0   10

Nautical Miles

CEPHALONIA (KEFALLINIA)

Above. Marooned chapel east of Levkas Island. p.64
Below. Poros harbour at sunset looking across to the 'sleeping lady'. p.194

Left. Kalami anchorage on Corfu. p.40
Above. Spartakhori looking NE from the road up to the village. p.76
Below. Levkas. Karnayo boatyard in the bottleneck entrance to Vlikho proper. p.71

Top. Levkas canal looking out across the mud flats from Levkas town. p.64
Above. Octopus drying for the evening *meze*. Chopped up and grilled over charcoal it needs an ouzo to accompany it.
Right. Old fishing *caïque*. Ay Eufimia on Cephalonia. p.94

Top. Mending the nets. Itea town quay. p.163
Left. Farmer. Near Apothikai on Lesvos. p.373
Above. Fishing *caïque* near Volos. p.313

Above. Assos on Cephalonia. Not suitable with the prevailing
northwest winds but idyllic in calm weather. p.91
Below. One of the last trading *caïques* in the Ionian. Kalamos. p.100

Remains of the Roman theatre at Nikopolis near Preveza. p.61

Anchorage on the Levkas side of the Meganisi channel – be warned, it is very deep for anchoring here. p.76

The new *caïque* harbour at Erateini in the Gulf of Corinth. p.159

The abandoned monastery of Maniote towers on the north side of Porto Kayio at the bottom of the Pelonponnese. p.136

Navpaktos medieval harbour and town looking from just outside the entrance. p.155

Above. Navpaktos medieval harbour looking out towards the
entrance. p.155
Below. Inner basin of Idhra harbour. p.200

Nisis Bourtzoi looking down from the Venetian citadel above
Navplion. p.210

The monastery built into the cliffs
inland from Leonidhion. p.213

By night Use the light on Ak Yero-Gombos (LFl(2)15s24M) and closer in the light on Nisis Vardhianoi (Fl.WR.7·5s6/3M red sector covers 080°-107°). (The range of the light on Nisis Vardhianoi appears to be less than stated.) Once into the gulf use the light on Ak Ay Theodhoroi (Fl.3s5M) and the light on the beacon (Fl.G.3s3M).

Dangers Care is needed of the reef running SE from Ak Pelagia and of the reef running W from Ak Ay. Nikolaos.

Note With a fresh afternoon breeze blowing down into the approaches to Argostoli (regularly Force 5–6 in the summer) it can be hair-raising entering this dead-end inlet for the first time.

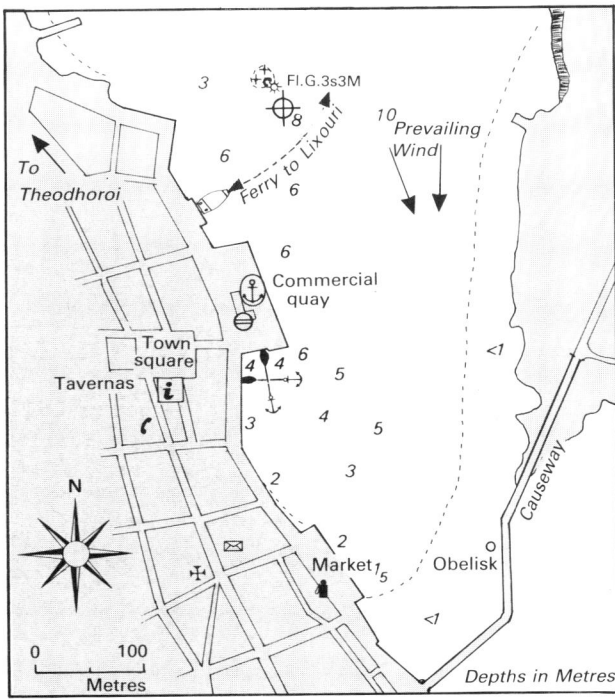

ARGOSTOLI
38°11'·2N 20°29'·5E (Fl.G.3s3M)

Mooring

Berth stern-to or bows-to the S of the ferry quay or on the N end of the W quay. If clearing into Greece go on the S side of the ferry quay within the customs enclosure. The bottom is mud, good holding.

Shelter The ferry quay provides a good lee from the prevailing wind whistling down into the inlet.

Authorities A port of entry. Port police, customs and immigration.

Anchorage If you prefer to anchor off there is a cove on the E side near the entrance to the inlet but shelter here is poor.

Note There is a small basin under construction to the N of the commercial quay.

Facilities

Water On the quay.

Fuel Can be delivered by mini-tanker.

Repairs Mechanical and engineering work can be carried out. Electrical work. According to reports good emergency repairs have been carried out here. Good hardware shops but limited chandlery available. Some boats have been hauled N of the customs quay but there is no good boatyard as such here.

Provisions Good shopping in the town for provisions. Ice can be delivered.

Eating out Numerous tavernas in the town and some awful fast-food bars.

Other PO. OTE. Banks. Greek gas and *Camping Gaz*. Hire cars, motorbikes and bicycles. Buses to most parts of Cephalonia. Regular car ferry to Lixouri. International and internal flights from the airport a short distance out of town.

General

Argostoli looks like a frontier town from the harbour – a Greek setting for a spaghetti western. Yet up until the 1953 earthquake it was an elegant town looking somewhat like a larger Fiskardho. Following the earthquake the town has largely been rebuilt of

Argostoli town quay looking W from the opposite side of the inlet.

The town quay at Argostoli looking N.

The Doric style lighthouse on Ak Ay Theodhoroi.

the ubiquitous reinforced concrete, but here and there around the town some buildings remain to give an indication of what the capital was like. There is an excellent museum in the town with exhibits from the many ancient sites around the area.

On Ak Ay Theodhoroi there is a reconstruction of the mill built by an Englishman, Stevens, in the 19th century. It is powered by the sea pouring into subterranean channels – a team of Austrian scientists, by putting a dye in the water, showed that it eventually reappears at Melissani near Sami. The flow of water is now much reduced after the 1953 earthquake. Also on the headland is the Doric-style lighthouse, which is conspicuous from seawards.

LIXOURI

Approach

Directly across the Gulf from Argostoli is Lixouri. The buildings of the town and the harbour moles are easily identified. The entrance is lit: Fl.R.3M and Fl.G.3M.

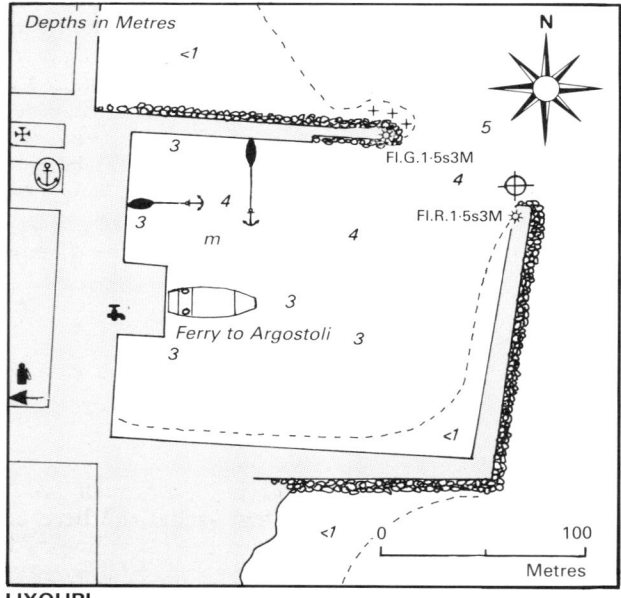

LIXOURI
38°12'·1N 20°26'·6E (Fl.R.1·5s3M)

Mooring

Berth stern-to or bows-to the N or W mole. The bottom is soft mud, poor holding until the anchor digs in. The prevailing NW wind sets up a surge in the harbour which can be most uncomfortable.

Port police and customs.

Facilities

Fuel and water near the quay. Shower on the S mole. PO. OTE. Bank. Good shopping and tavernas in the town. Regular car ferry to Argostoli.

General

Between the surge with the prevailing wind and the constant smell of sewers, few yachts visit the sister town to Argostoli. The town itself is a likable place, mostly busy with agricultural concerns and its own little cottage industries.

Ay Kiriakis looking W.

AY KIRIAKIS

A small harbour in Ormos Kiriakis is suitable only for small yachts in calm weather. The harbour is very small and partially rock-bound. There are 2–3 metre depths in the entrance and 1–3 metre depths inside. Berth under the outer breakwater with a long line to it. Depths inside the harbour are irregular so care is needed.

The little harbour is a gem with just local fishing boats and a couple of simple tavernas ashore.

PORT ASSOS

Approach

A natural harbour on the W coast 6 miles S of Ak Dafnoudhi (Vlioti). A large Venetian fort on the headland forming the W side of the harbour is not as conspicuous as it might appear on the plan, but can usually be made out from the distance. Closer in the houses of the village and the mole will be seen.

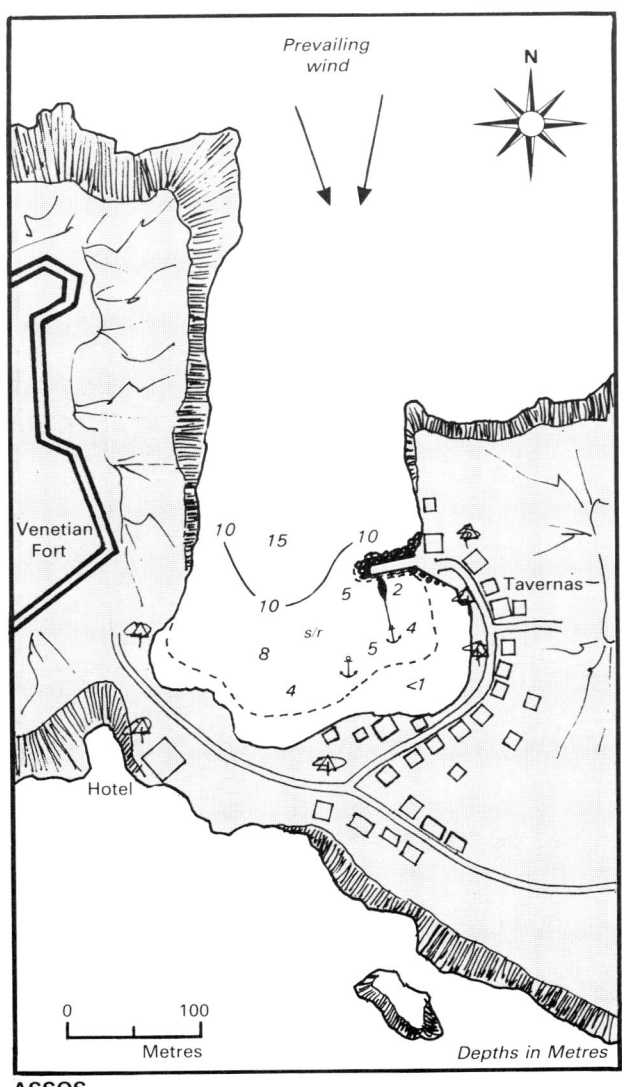

ASSOS
38°22′·8N 20°32′·2E

Assos looking N.

Mooring

Go stern-to or bows-to the mole with a long line ashore, or anchor off. The short mole and the quayed area have mostly 1·5–2 metre depths, but the ballasting extends a considerable distance underwater making it difficult to get close in. It is quite deep in the bay, some 7–10 metres mostly, coming up quickly to the quay. The bottom is mud, shingle, and weed, not everywhere good holding. With the normal NW winds a swell rolls into the harbour – uncomfortable and untenable with strong NW winds. There is no nearby shelter as the swell is just as bad on the S side of the headland and in nearby Ormos Mirto.

Facilities

Good tavernas ashore and some provisions can be found.

General

The picturesque little harbour is popular with tourists in the summer but few yachts call here on account of the poor shelter from the prevailing NW winds. The Venetian fort which enclosed a sizeable town was built in the 16th century and is well worth a wander around.

FISKARDHO (Phiscardo)
Admiralty chart no. 720
Imray-Tetra chart no. G121

Approach
Conspicuous It can be difficult to work out just where the bay is, though the general location at the N end of the Ithaca Strait is obvious. From the NE a number of new buildings in the bay immediately N of Fiskardho are conspicuous. Closer in the twin ruined towers, the large stone lighthouse and the smaller Venetian lighthouse on the N side of Ormos Fiskardho will be seen, although from the NE they can be difficult to pick out when the sun is low in the sky. The new villas and the hotel on the S side of the bay will also be seen. From the S the houses in the bay are easily discerned once past Nisis Dhaskalio which has a small chapel on it.

By night Use the light on Ak Fiskardho (Fl.3s6M) and the light on the end of the short breakwater (F.R.2M occas).

Fiskardho town quay looking SE.

Mooring
Go stern-to or bows-to on the S or W quay. Care is needed on the S quay where the ballasting protrudes underwater in places. Do not berth in the SW corner

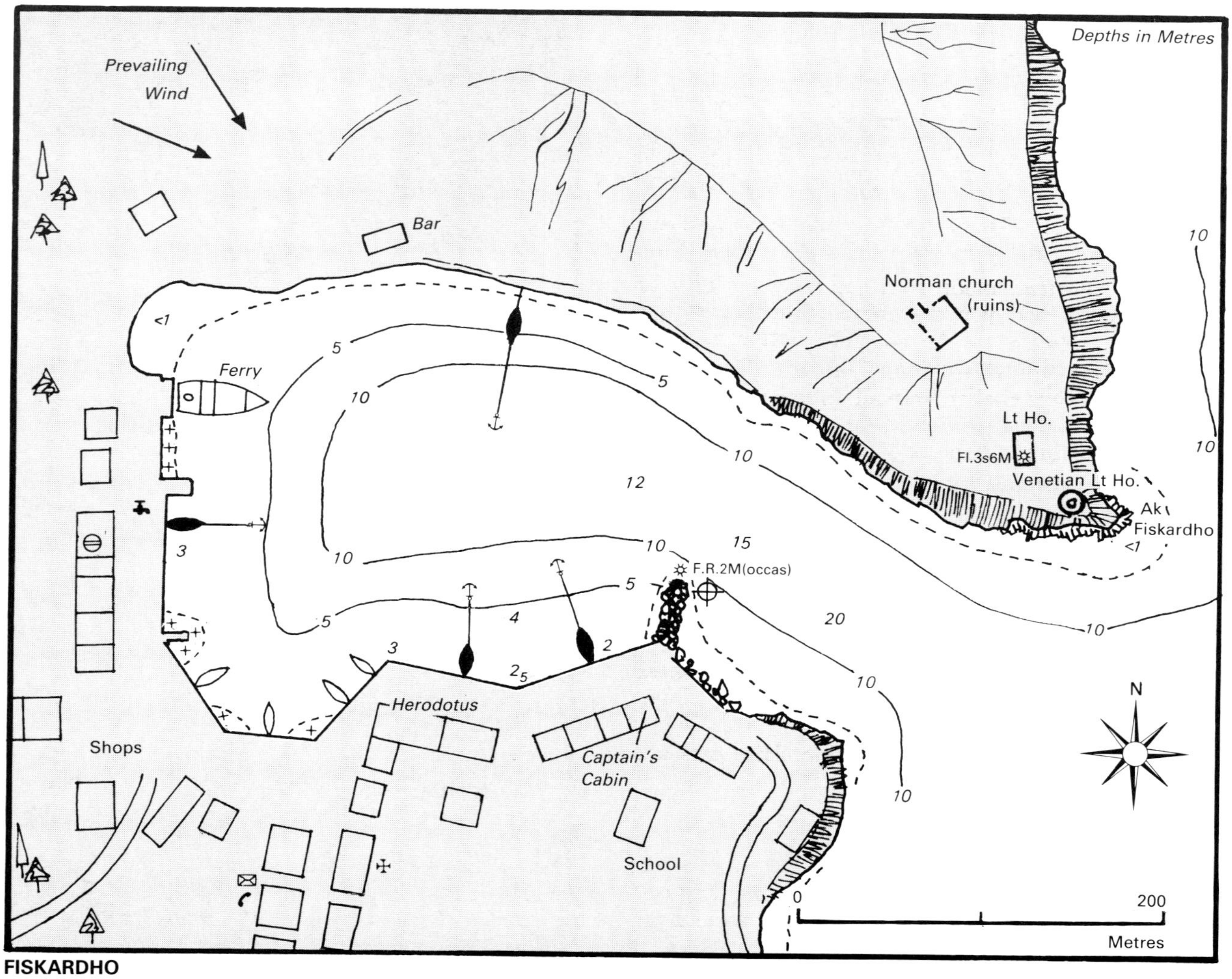

FISKARDHO
38°27'·7N 20°34'·7E (F.R.2M)

Cephalonia that escaped damage in the 1953 earthquake that devastated much of the Ionian.

The village is named after Robert Guiscard (thus Guiscardo/Phiscardo/Fiscardho), a Norman adventurer who briefly ruled these parts and who is said to have died of fever here in 1085. Unfortunately for local folk history, it is also recorded that he died in Vonitsa in the Gulf of Amvrakia – also of fever. The ruined Norman towers in the N of the bay are believed to be part of a church built in his memory.

The east coast between Fiskardho and Ayios Eufimia

On this green wooded stretch of coastline there are a number of small bays suitable for an overnight stay. Palaiokaravo, Ormos Kakogito and Kalo Limeni are

Modern lighthouse and Venetian lighthouse (looking NE) on the N side of the entrance to Ormos Fiskardho.

Fiskardho town quay. The village was virtually the only place on Cephalonia spared damage in the devastating earthquake of 1953.

where local *caïques* moor. In the summer the harbour gets crowded and you may have to anchor with a long line ashore to the N side. The bottom is sand, rocks and weed, reasonable holding.

Shelter Excellent shelter from all directions, although strong prolonged southerlies cause a surge, troublesome rather than dangerous.

Authorities Customs.

Facilities

Water On the W quay.
Fuel Can be delivered by mini-tanker.
Provisions Good shopping for all provisions.
Eating out Good tavernas and bars. Tassos in the Captain's Cabin is well known to visiting yachties and may he able to advise you on where to get things or who to ask.
Other PO. OTE. Exchange possible. Hire cars and motorbikes. Ferry to Frikes and Vasiliki.

General

Fiskardho is a popular spot for yachts, and in the season the quay is normally packed. The safe port and picturesque 19th-century houses set amid green pine groves remain pretty much original and a historical preservation order will hopefully keep them that way. This was the only place on

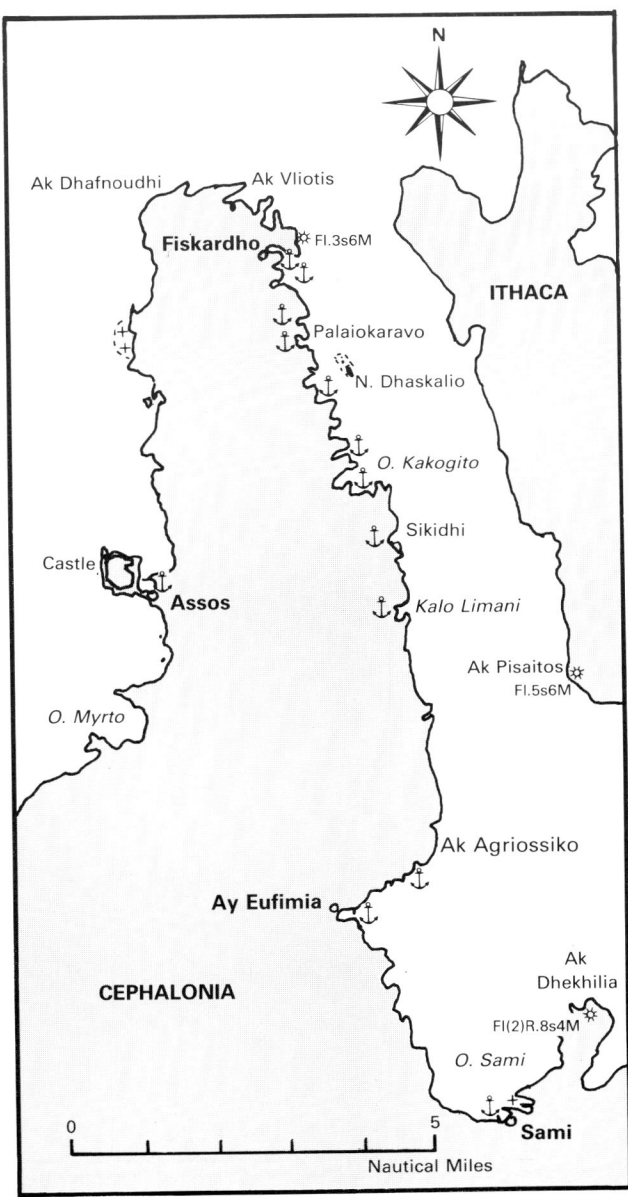

STENON ITHAKIS

all sheltered from the NW wind, although there may be gusts off the high hills above and some swell may roll into some of them. The bays are deserted except for Kalo Limini, where there are a few houses ashore. Exercise some caution when anchoring as the bottom is loose shingle in places.

AYIOS EUFIMIA (Sta Eufemia, Pilaros Cove)
Admiralty chart no. 720
Imray-Tetra chart no. G121

Approach

Conspicuous From the N you will not see the town and the mole until you round Ak Agriossiki. From the E the town is conspicuous from the S end of Ithaca and as you close the port you will see the short mole.

By night Use the light on Ak Dhekalia (Fl(2)R.8s4M) and closer in the light on the end of the mole (Q.G.2M).

Note The channel between Cephalonia and Ithaca has a reputation for being very windy but in my experience of taking a flotilla both up and down the channel for two seasons this is unfounded. Kolpos Aetou (Gulf of Molo) and Ormos Frikon are usually more windy than the Ithaca Channel. The wind does however tend to blow either up or down the channel (usually down from the N) and you will get gusts down the valleys and out of Ay Eufimia.

Mooring

Go stern-to or bows-to on the N quay where shown. Alternatively anchor off, keeping well clear of the

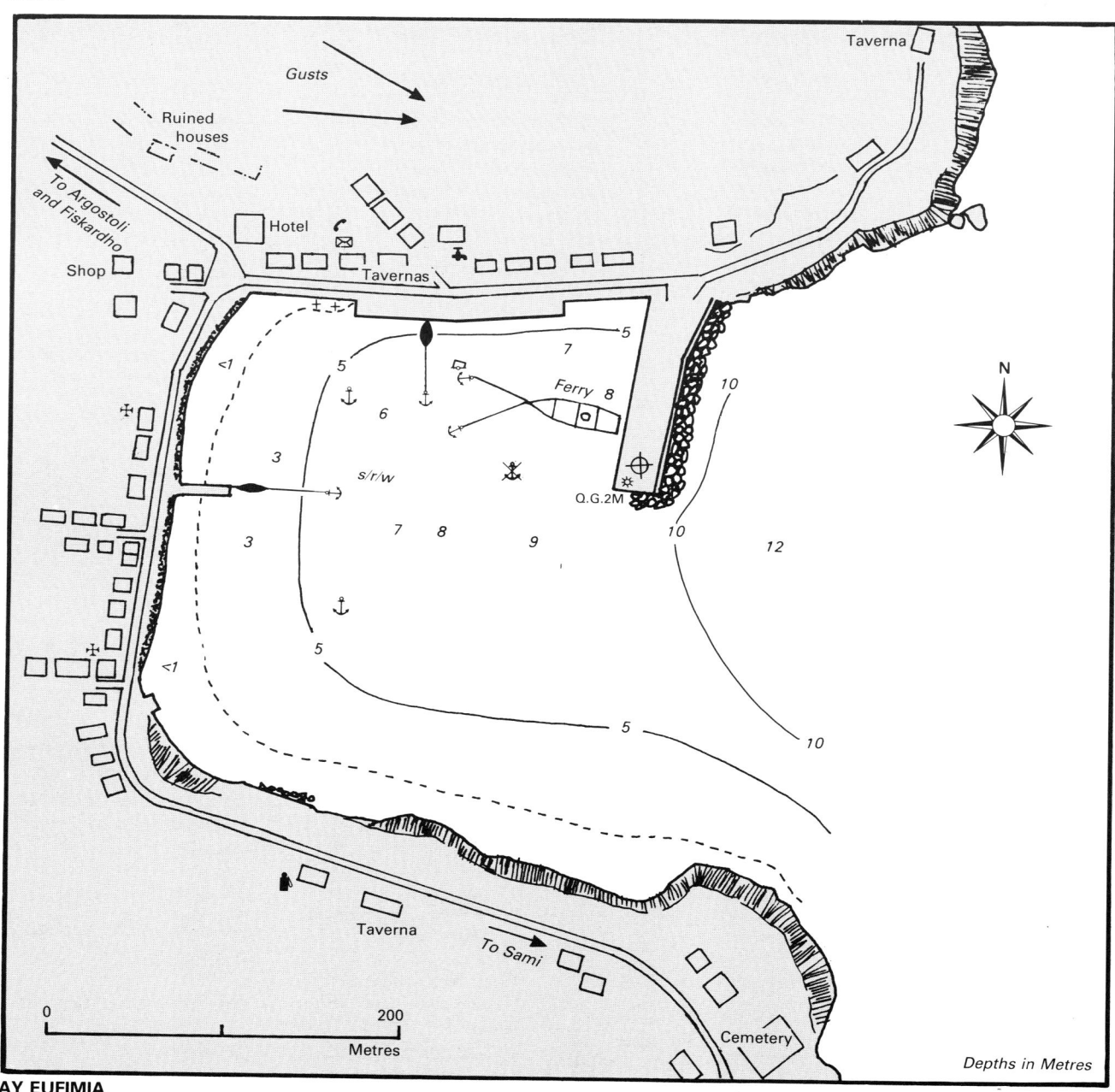

AY EUFIMIA
38°18'·2N 20°36'·1E (Q.G.2M)

Ay Eufimia looking NNW from the S entrance point.

Ay Eufimia looking E from the W pier.

area where the ferry enters and turns to berth. The bottom is sand, rocks and weed, not everywhere the best holding.

Shelter Good shelter from the prevailing wind, although it tends to gust down the valley and blow beam on, so ensure that your anchor is well in to hold you off the quay. The wind dies off in the evening. With a strong SE wind a swell enters the harbour.

Facilities

Water On the quay.
Fuel Can be delivered by mini-tanker. The fuel station is on the S side of the bay.
Provisions Most provisions can be found.
Eating out Numerous tavernas. The one around the coast from the root of the mole is worth a visit.
Other PO. OTE. Exchange. Ferry to Vathi and Astakos.

General

This used to be the main port for the east of Cephalonia, but after the 1953 earthquake it was abandoned and Sami became the major port for the area. It is a better port than Sami for visiting Lake Melissani and the Cave of Drogarati. Lake Melissani is an underground cave and lake which a boatman will row you around. It is crowded in the summer but still worth a visit, as much for the subterranean cool as for the limpid waters of the lake.

SAMI

Admiralty chart no. 720

Approach

Conspicuous From the N the double-storeyed buildings lining the quay are easily visible under the green wooded slopes. From the S the harbour will not be seen until you are around Ak Dhekalia.

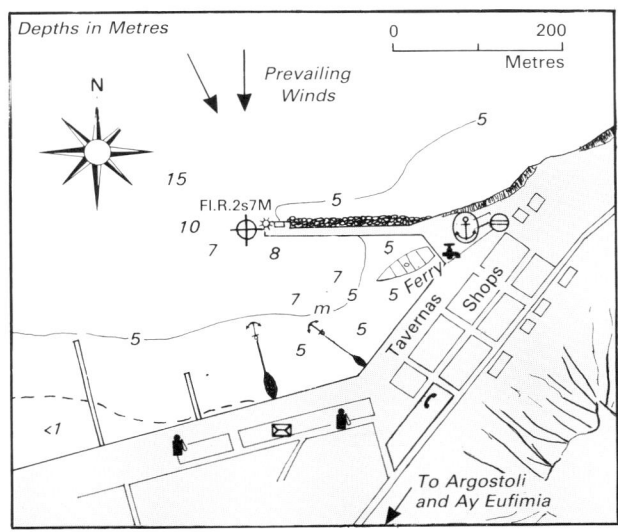

SAMI
38°15'·3N 20°38'·8E (Fl.R.2s7M)

By night Use the light on Ak Dhekalia (Fl(2)R.8s4M) and the light on the molehead ((Fl.R.2s7M).

Mooring

Go stern-to or bows-to the quay on the S side of the harbour. The bottom is mud, good holding.
Shelter Uncomfortable though tenable with the prevailing NW wind which sends a chop into here.
Authorities Port police and customs.

Facilities

Water On the quay at the root of the mole, though it can be difficult to find the man to turn it on.
Fuel Near the quay.
Provisions Good shopping for provisions near the quay.
Eating out Numerous tavernas and bars.
Other PO. OTE. Bank. Hire cars and motorbikes. Ferry to Patras.

Limin Sami looking NW from the town quay.

General

Sami was completely rebuilt after the 1953 earthquake as the ferry terminal for Cephalonia. The green wooded slopes above Sami are attractive but the town itself is mostly new, though now mellowing with the patina of a few years aging. It is an alternative to Ay Eufimia for visiting the semi-underground Lake Melissani and the Cave of Drogarati. The ruins of ancient Sami are close to the town though there is little to see.

POROS (Pronos Bay)

A small harbour tucked under Ak Pronos. At the time of writing there is considerable work going on expanding the harbour and quayed areas around the bay. Although the basic shape of the harbour seems evident, details may vary from the plan given.

Approach

Conspicuous From the N the buildings of the village will be seen and closer in the breakwater is easily identified. From the S the village and harbour will not be seen until you round Ak Pronos.

By night Use the light on Ak Kapri (Fl(3)WR.9s6/4M) and that on the end of the mole (Q.G.2M).

Dangers With the prevailing wind there can be strong gusts down the coast.

Mooring

Go stern-to or bows-to the new quay in the SW corner. The bottom is mud and weed, mostly good holding.

Shelter Uncomfortable but tenable with the prevailing wind which blows down from the N. When the wind dies down at night things become more comfortable.

Authorities Port police.

Note Yachts should keep well clear of the ferry berth. The ferry normally comes in and drops an anchor and then takes a line to one of the mooring buoys in the harbour.

Facilities

Water Near the ferry quay.

Fuel In the village.

Provisions Most provisions can be found in the village.

Eating out Taverna at the harbour (recommended) and others in the village.

Other PO. Greek gas. Buses to Argostoli. Ferry to Killini.

Poros looking N. *Graham Sewell.*

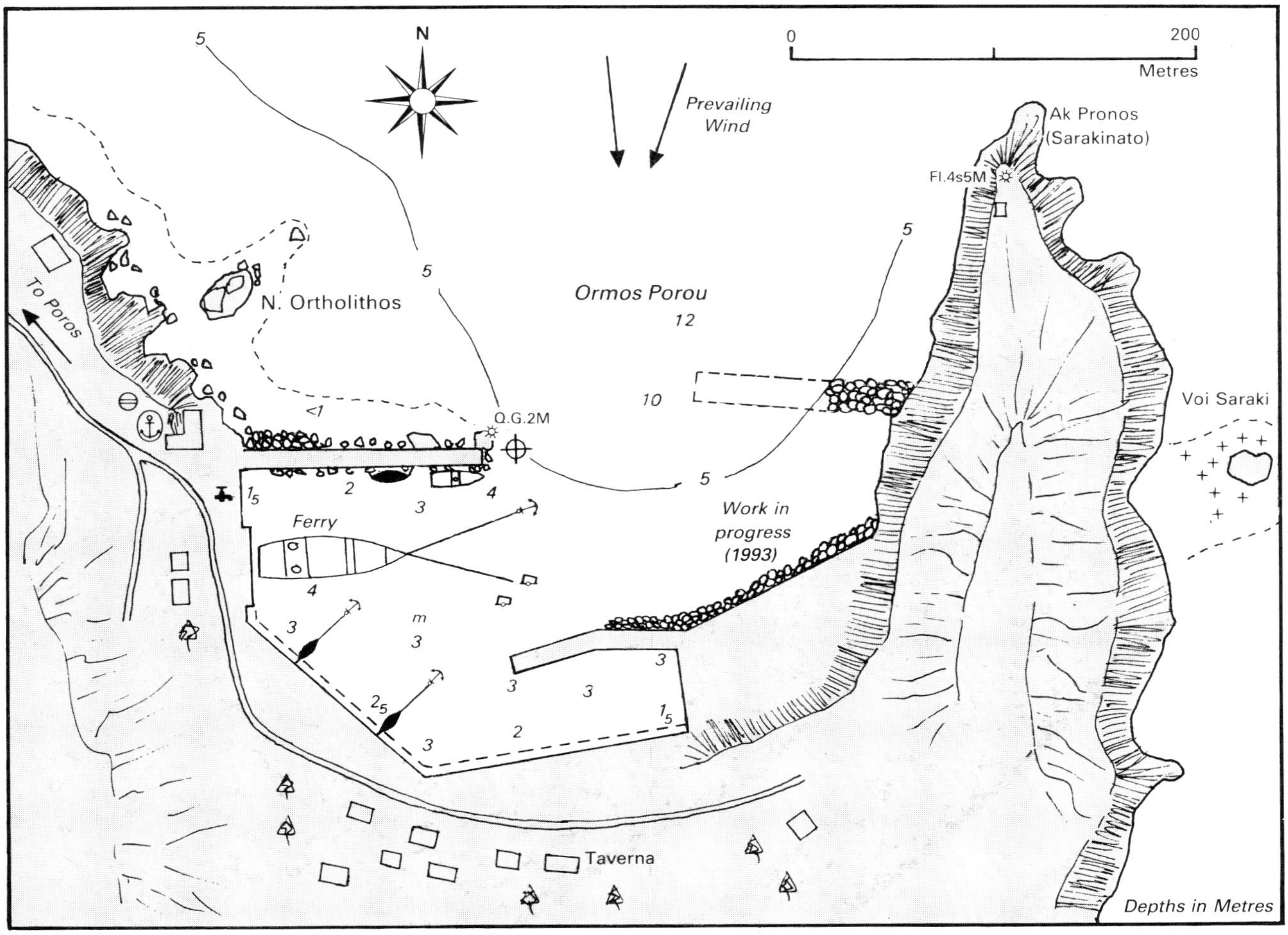

POROS
38°08'·9N 20°46'·9E (Q.G.2M)

General

The village is set in a spectacular position on a strip of flat land between a precipitous gorge and the sea. It has a modest tourist trade, though most people arriving here on the ferry from Killini hardly stop and are on the bus to Argostoli before you even notice they have arrived.

IFALOS KAKOVA

Admiralty chart no. 203 recommends the following to avoid the Kakova Shoal off the SE tip of Cephalonia: for N–S traffic Ak Kapri kept open of the W end of Nisis Atoko; for E–W traffic Ay Yioryios castle in line with Ak Koroni clears the shoal. While the marks for E–W traffic are easily located the mark of Nisis Atoko for N–W traffic is difficult to locate with the summer heat haze. Although quite large *caïques* cut across the shoal, it is wise to give it a good offing.

KATO KATELIOS

In the NW corner of the large bay under Ak Monda a yacht can find some shelter from the prevailing wind which blows from the W around the bottom of Cephalonia. A detached rough stone breakwater shelters fishing boats here but a reef obstructs the entrance and a yacht is not advised to try to enter. Anchor off the beach on the N taking care of the off-lying reefs.

Ormos Porou looking across to Ak Pronos with Ortholithos in the foreground.

PESSADES

A miniature ferry harbour connecting with Ay Nikolaos on Zakinthos. The tiny harbour and the ferry apron are tucked up in Ormos Lourtha under Ak Sosti. There may be room for a small yacht to tuck in under the end of the short breakwater.

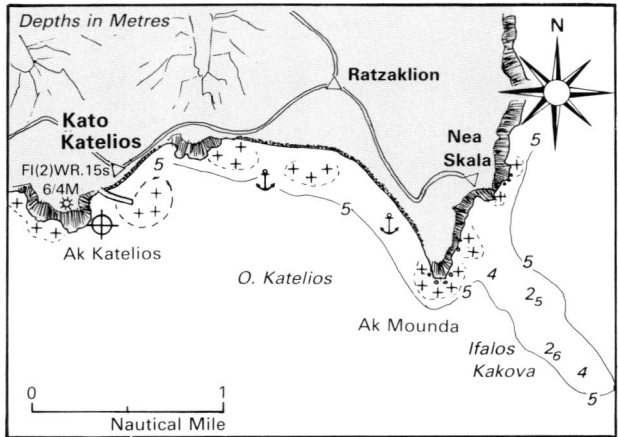

ORMOS KATELIOS
38°03'·8N 20°44'·6E (Ak Katelios light)

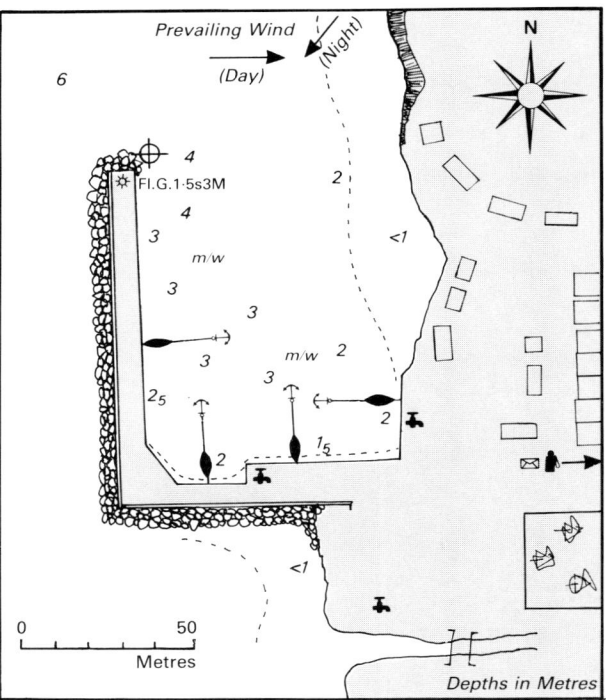

PALAIROS (ZAVERDA)
38°46'·9N 20°52'·8E (Fl.G.1·5s3M)

The mainland coast and adjacent islands to Oxia Island

Following the east boundary of the inland sea is the steep-to coast of mainland Greece. The eroded brown mountains rise straight out of the sea to some 1550 metres in places providing an impressive backdrop to the islands dotting the sea. The two principal islands near the coast and the only inhabited islands are Kalamos and Kastos. Kalamos lies like a great stranded whale in the sea with skinny Kastos alongside. Further S the Dragonera and Echinades (meaning 'sea urchin') islands lie scattered off the marshlands at the foot of the mountains. These numerous small islands are all uninhabited although sheep and goats are grazed on the larger of them. This area is little visited by yachts although it contains a number of safe anchorages and ports, possibly because it is off the yacht 'motorway' to the Gulf of Patras and the Aegean and the few towns in the area are poor in tavernas. For those yachtsmen who like remote anchorages and spectacular, if desolate, scenery, this area makes a good cruising ground.

VATHI-VALI

A small inlet on the mainland coast just S of the Levkas canal. A fish farm now obstructs most of this inlet though it is still possible to squeeze in. Good shelter except from the S.

PALAIROS (Zaverda)

Approach

The buildings of the village straggling down the hillside to the harbour are easily identified. Closer in the harbour mole will be seen. The molehead is lit: Fl.G.1·5s3M.

Mooring

Go stern-to or bows-to the quay where convenient. The harbour is used by a charter company and it can get crowded in the summer. The bottom is mud and weed, reasonable holding. Good shelter from the prevailing wind. At night a katabatic breeze may blow in from the NE, but dies down after 2–3 hours.

Facilities

Water Water on the quay.
Fuel Can be delivered.
Provisions Good shopping for provisions in the town.
Eating out Numerous tavernas. The Old Mill restaurant is a fair walk away at the top of the town, but is worth the effort.
Other PO. OTE. Irregular bus service to Vonitsa and Mitika.

General

A largely agricultural village that now adds to its income from the charter company based here. The village is attractive in a proper working way, serving the needs of the surrounding farmers, and the inhabitants are a friendly lot. Above the village the slopes of the Arkarnanika rise abruptly to 1590 metres (5167ft), barren stony slopes bereft of trees and even *maquis*.

Note Just S of Palairos a small harbour has been built under the hotel complex ashore. It is not yet known whether it will be available to yachts.

MITIKA

There is a quay on the E side of Ak Mitika, but this is only tenable in the morning calm before the afternoon breeze gets up. On the S side of Ak Mitika

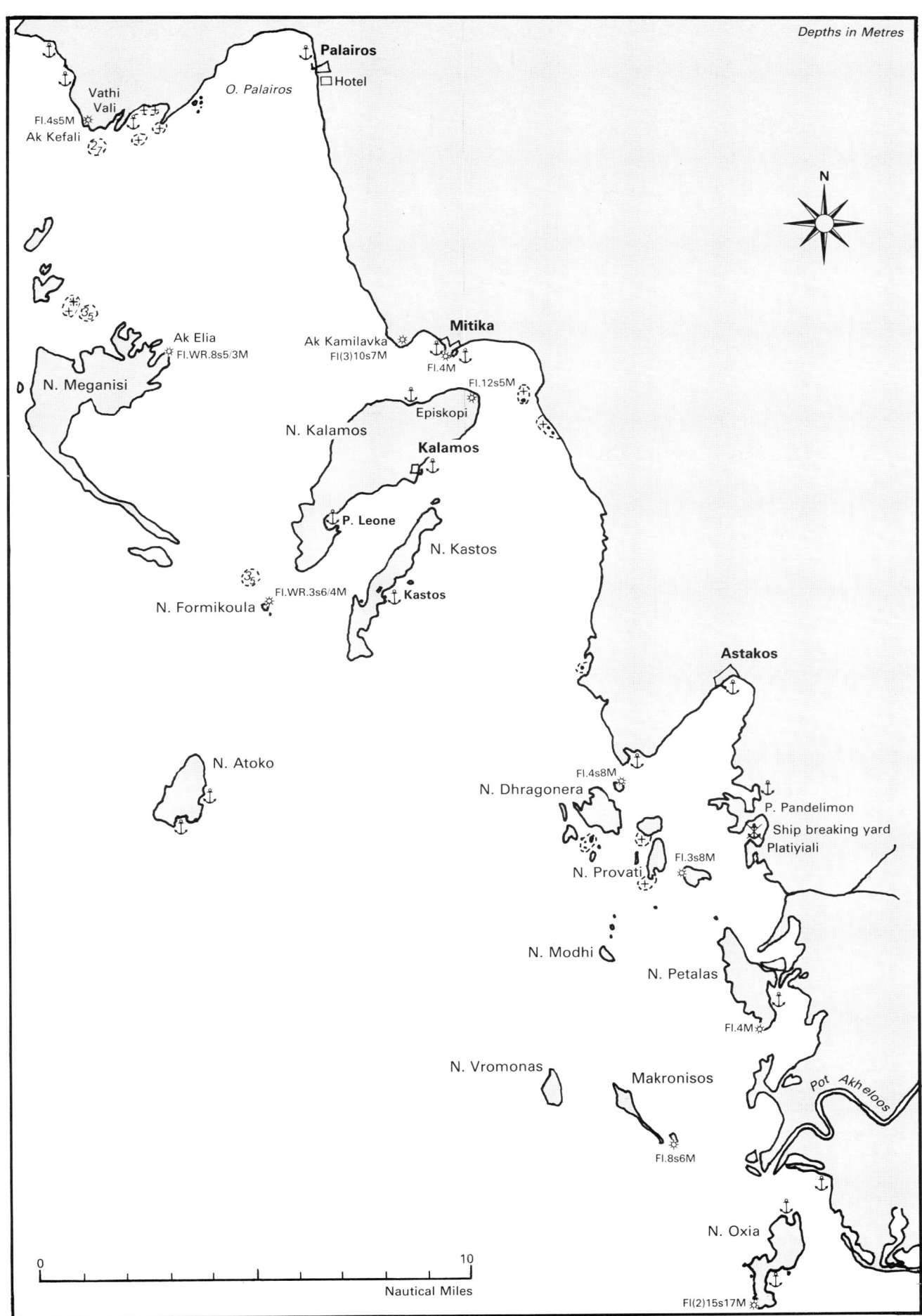

Depths in Metres

Palairos

O. Palairos

□ Hotel

Vathi
Vali
Fl.4s5M
Ak Kefali

2₇

3₅

Ak Elia
Fl.WR.8s5/3M

N. Meganisi

Mitika

Ak Kamilavka
Fl(3)10s7M
Fl.4M

Fl.12s5M

Episkopi

N. Kalamos

Kalamos

P. Leone

N. Kastos

3₅

N. Formikoula
Fl.WR.3s6/4M

Kastos

Astakos

N. Atoko

Fl.4s8M

N. Dhragonera

P. Pandelimon
Ship breaking yard
Platiyiali

N. Provati
Fl.3s8M

N. Modhi

N. Petalas

Fl.4M

N. Vromonas

Makronisos

Pot Akheloos

Fl.8s6M

N. Oxia

Fl(2)15s17M

0
10

Nautical Miles

THE MAINLAND COAST AND ADJACENT ISLANDS (Levkas to Nisis Oxia)

Mitika looking E.

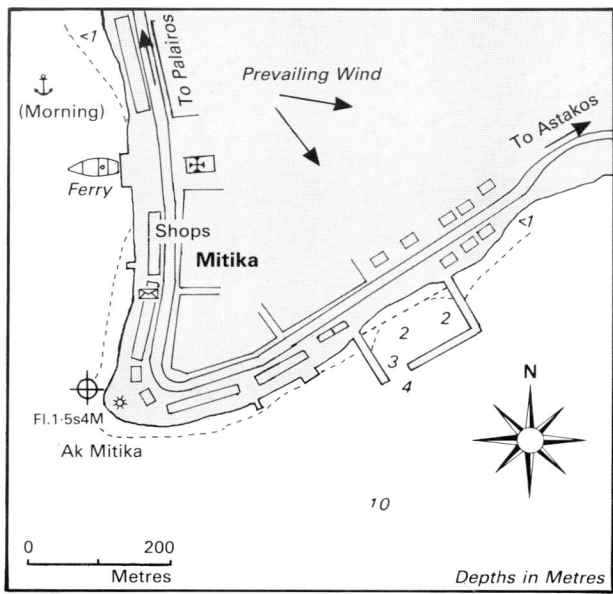

MITIKA
38°39'·7N 20°56'·9E (Akra Mitika light)

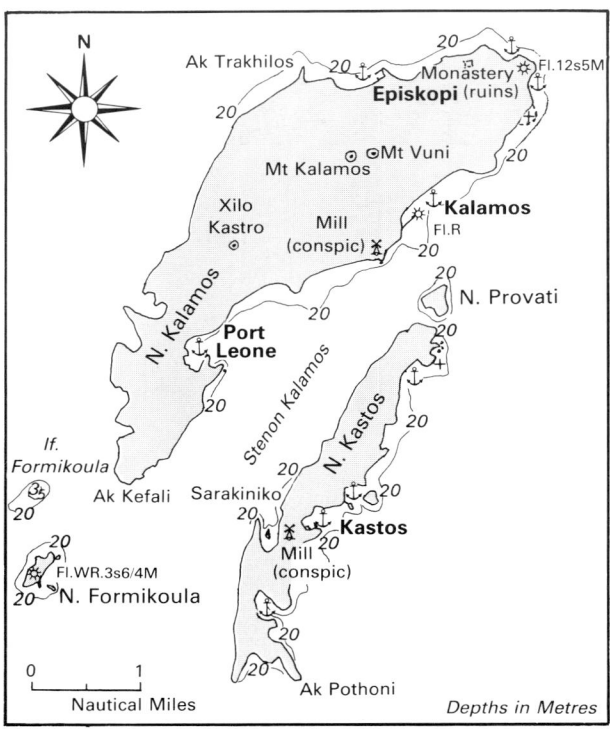

NISOI KALAMOS AND KASTOS

a new harbour has been built. There are mostly 2–3 metre depths inside shallowing to the beach. On the NE quay local fishing boats are berthed although there may be spaces available. Care is needed of numerous floating mooring lines off the quay. Alternatively anchor and take a long line to the SW side. Good shelter from the prevailing wind.

Ashore most provisions can be found and there are several tavernas and bars. *Caïque* ferries to Kalamos and Kastos.

Nisos Kalamos

PORT KALAMOS

Approach

Straightforward. From the N the houses of Kalamos village on the hill will be seen. From the S a number of old windmills, including one on a rocky outcrop before the harbour, will be seen. Care is needed in the afternoon when the prevailing wind gusts up the channel between Kalamos and Kastos.

Mooring

Go stern-to or bows-to the mole. At the head of the harbour and around the quay there are insufficient depths. The bottom is mud, sand and weed, mostly good holding. Good shelter from the prevailing wind. A strong SE wind can make the harbour uncomfortable and even dangerous if it is a prolonged blow.

Facilities

Mini-market and bakery in the village. Several tavernas. PO.

General

At Kalamos town and on the NE of the island there are cool green pine glades running down to the sea. The islanders make a living from fishing and a little agriculture and, one suspects, remittances from

Southern approaches to Kalamos harbour with the windmill on the
spit conspicuous.

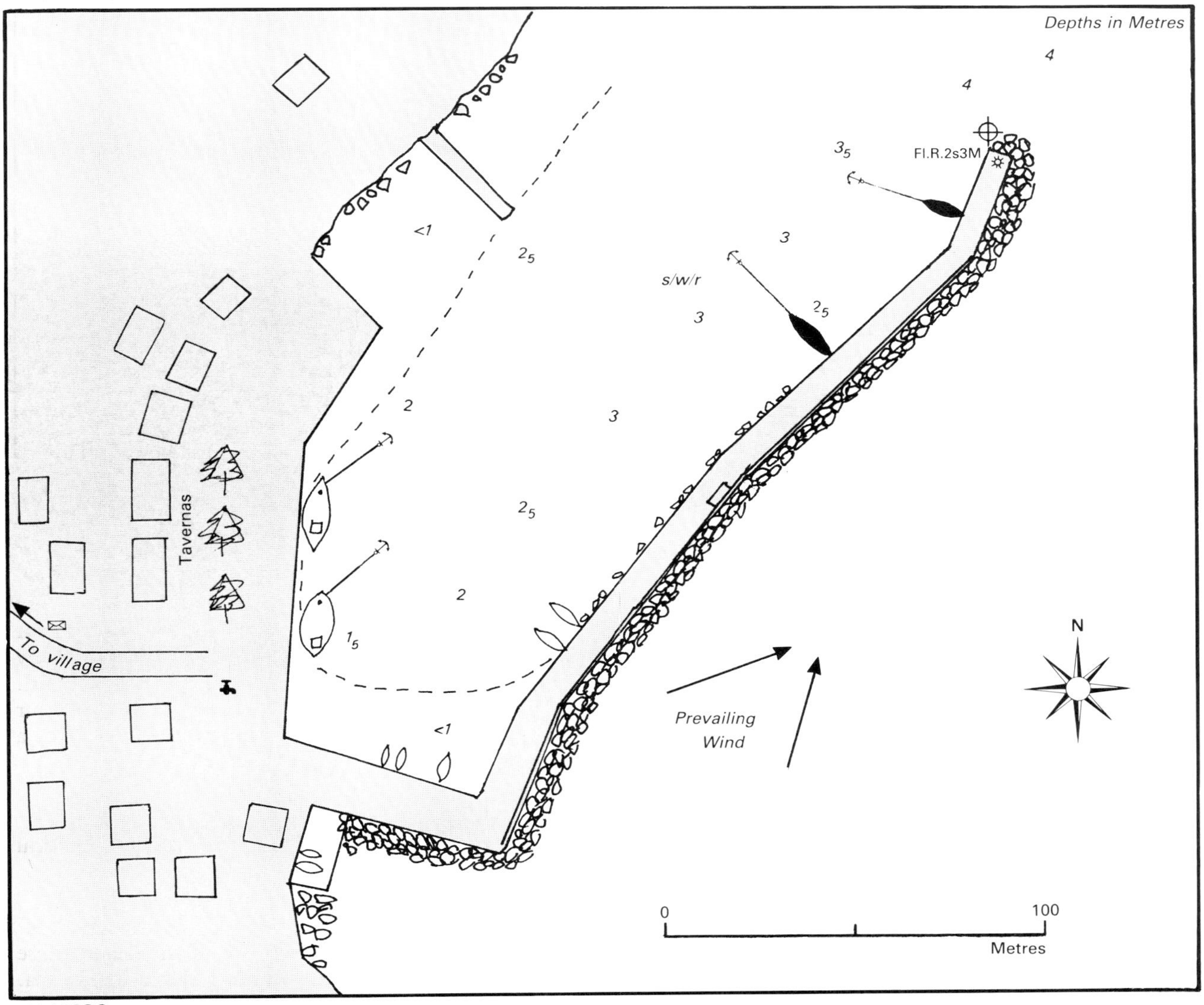

Depths in Metres

4

4

3₅   Fl.R.2s3M

<1

2₅

s/w/r   3

3

2₅

2

3

Tavernas

2₅

To village

2

1₅

<1

Prevailing
Wind

N

0   100

Metres

KALAMOS
38°37'·4N 20°56'E (Fl.R.2s3M)

Kalamos harbour looking NE.

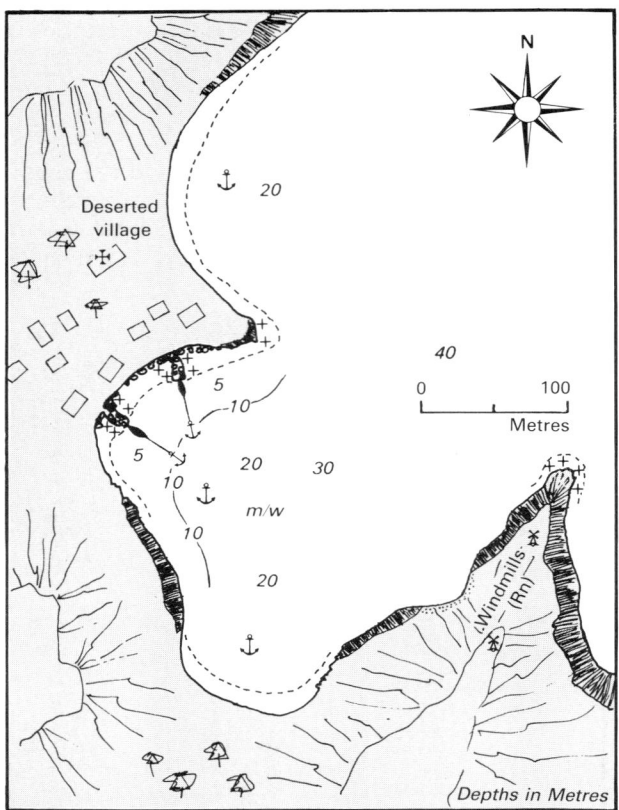

PORT LEONE
38°35'·8N 20° 54'E

abroad. Sadly the village is dying as the young move away to more lucrative jobs on the mainland and the local population is skewed to the elderly.

One of the last trading *caïques* in the Ionian. Kalamos harbour.

PORT LEONE

To the S of the island lies Port Leone, an anchorage sheltered from the prevailing winds and only open to the E. The entrance is difficult to determine from the distance though closer in two old windmills will be seen on the E side of the entrance. The bay is very deep to anchor in and you will probably be in 10–20 metre depths. A few yachts will be able to get close in to the ruined piers off the village. The bottom is sand, mud and weed, mostly good holding.

The small village has been deserted since the 1953 earthquake destroyed the local water supply and the inhabitants decided to emigrate rather than rebuild. Every Sunday three or four people from Kalamos come to clean the church and say a few prayers.

Port Leone and the deserted village.

EPISKOPI

A small harbour on the N side of Kalamos. A few small yachts can get in here though care is needed as there is little room to manoeuvre and the depths decrease from 2 metres on the outer mole to 1·5 metres in the middle and less towards the beach. No facilities.

Nisis Kastos

PORT KASTOS

Approach

From the N the flat island of Prasnoi and the houses of Kastos identify where the harbour is. From the S a mill on the headland sheltering Port Kastos will be seen, but you will not see the village until you round the headland.

Mooring

Stern-to or bows-to the outer end of the small mole, or anchor off in the bay. The bottom is mud and weed, good holding once through the weed. Shelter behind the mole is good, and anchored off you are safe enough, though the prevailing wind sends in a residual swell that sets yachts rolling.

Port Kastos looking ENE.

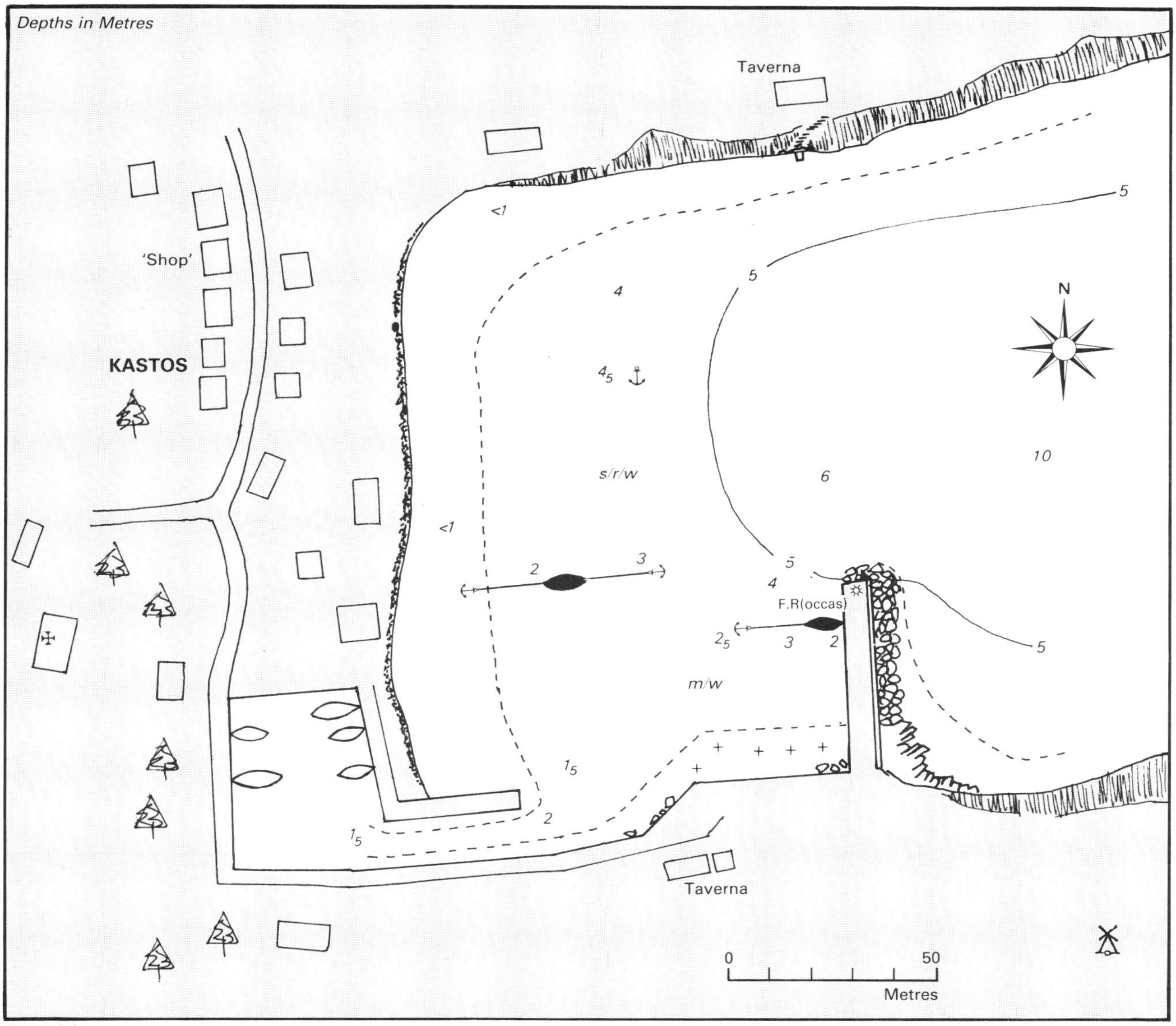

Depths in Metres

Taverna

'Shop'

KASTOS

<1

4

5

5

4_5 ⚓

s/r/w

6

10

<1

2

3

5

4

F.R(occas)

2_5 3   2

5

m/w

1_5

1_5

2

Taverna

N

0   50
Metres

KASTOS
38°34′N 20°55′·4E

Facilities

Several tavernas and a few provisions if you are lucky. Most provisions arrive from Astakos by *caïque*.

General

The population of Kastos was evacuated in 1976 because of a suspected typhoid outbreak. The islanders are gradually returning, although the population in the winter is still only 30 or so. The village and its setting are beautiful and there is good snorkelling in the waters around the island.

Anchorages around Nisis Kastos

On the W side of the island Port Sarakiniko is suitable in calm weather, but not with the prevailing wind which blows straight into it.

On the E side there are several bays and coves that can be explored, with a bay on the SE corner suitable for an overnight stop.

Nisis Atoko

Directly E of Frikes on Ithaca lies Nisis Atoko, a dome-shaped island easily identified from the distance.

There are two anchorages on the island. In calm weather or light NW winds Cliff Bay on the S side can be used, although it is very deep (10–15 metres either end) to anchor in.

On the SE side One House Bay affords better shelter and more suitable depths for anchoring and consequently is more popular. Anchor in 5–12 metres on sand, good holding. Shelter from the prevailing NW wind is good and it is possible to stay overnight in settled weather. Clear turquoise water and a solitary house ashore.

ASTAKOS (Astokos, Dragonmestre)

Approach

Conspicuous Once you are into Ormos Astakou the buildings of the small town will be seen, and closer in the harbour breakwater is easily identified. A new low breakwater has recently been built to the E of the original.

By night The end of the breakwater is lit: Fl.R.4s3M.

Mooring

Go stern-to or bows-to the N quay, leaving the ferry berth clear. Yachts may have to move off part of the quay when the hydrofoil arrives so if there is a space on the mole it may be worthwhile going there. Care is needed as rock ballasting extends out underwater in places along the mole. The bottom is mud, good holding.

Shelter Good shelter from the prevailing winds. Open to southerlies.

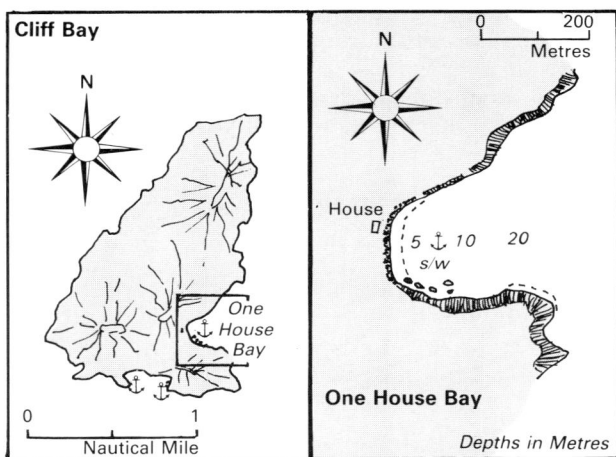

NISOS ATOKO

Nisis Atoko looking E.

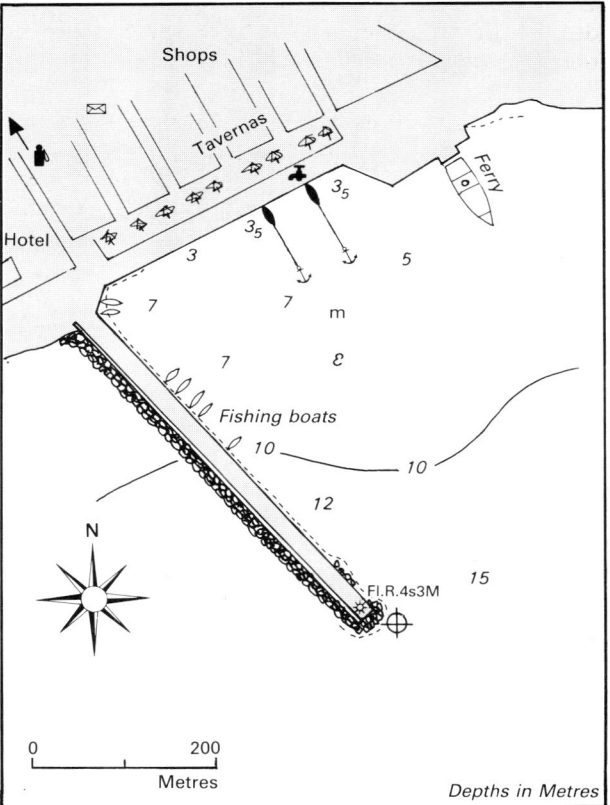

ASTAKOS
38°31'·8N 21°05'·6N (Fl.R.4s3M)

One House Bay on Atoko.

ANCHORAGES NEAR ASTAKOS

Port Marathia A deserted inlet SW of Astakos. Good shelter from the prevailing wind. Anchor near the head of the bay on mud. The new coast road running across the N of the bay rather shatters the calm and beauty of the place.

Boulder Bay A bight just before Astakos that can be recognised by the prominent boulder/rock near the shore. Anchor off the beach where convenient. Gusts with the prevailing WNW wind.

Anchorages around the Dragonera and Echinades islands

Nisis Dragonera On the SE tip of the island there is a miniature inlet that a small yacht can use. On the N side are two coves suitable in calm weather before the prevailing wind gets up.

Nisis Karlonisi Small yachts can tuck themselves into the narrow channel between Karlonisi and Provati. Care is needed of the reef running out from the W side.

PORT PANDELIMON

A double-headed inlet now partially obstructed by a fish farm. The perimeter of the two fish farms here is marked by small plastic buoys. A sign on the shore and a set of papers that will be shown to you by the resident 'caretaker' explains (in English and other languages) that the bay is for the express use of the Ionian Fisheries Company and that anchoring is only permitted with the approval of said company. There is some doubt about the legality of all this, but in practice it effectively means that you can only anchor in the E creek.

Facilities

Water On the quay.
Fuel A mini-tanker can deliver.
Repairs Caïques are hauled in a yard across the bay. Limited mechanical repairs. Chandlers.
Provisions Good shopping for provisions in the town.
Eating out Several tavernas on the waterfront and in the town.
Other PO. OTE. Banks. Ferry to Ithaca and Ay Eufimia on Cephalonia.

General

Astakos has a little tourist trade, mostly from Greeks on holiday here, but is principally a fishing and agricultural town. Astakos means 'lobster' but despite this promise the restaurants in the town never seem to have the delectable crustacean. Do the locals keep them for themselves or are there really no lobsters in the town called 'Lobster'?

Approach to Astakos looking N from just outside the breakwater.

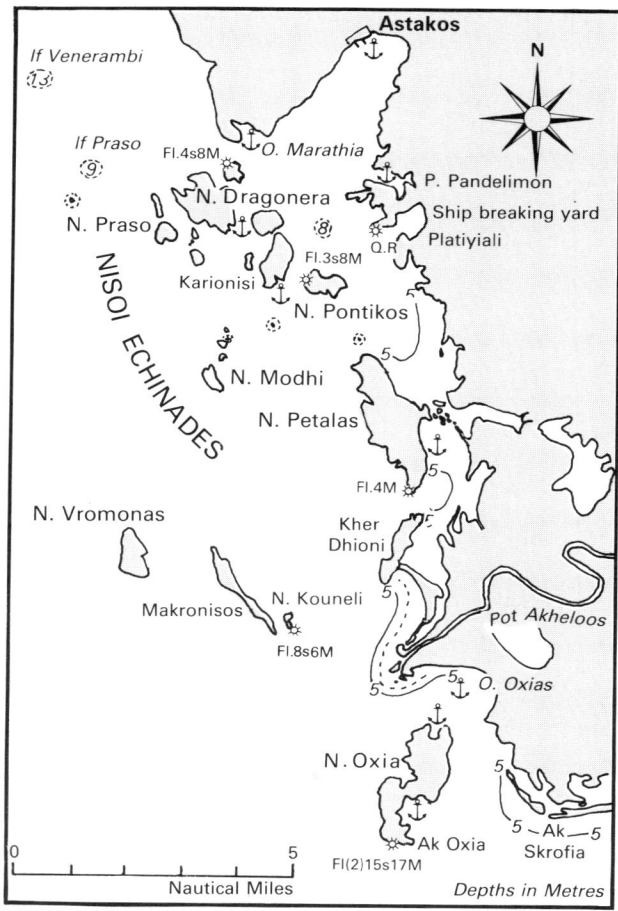

**NISOI DRAGONERA AND ECHINADES
AND ADJACENT COAST**

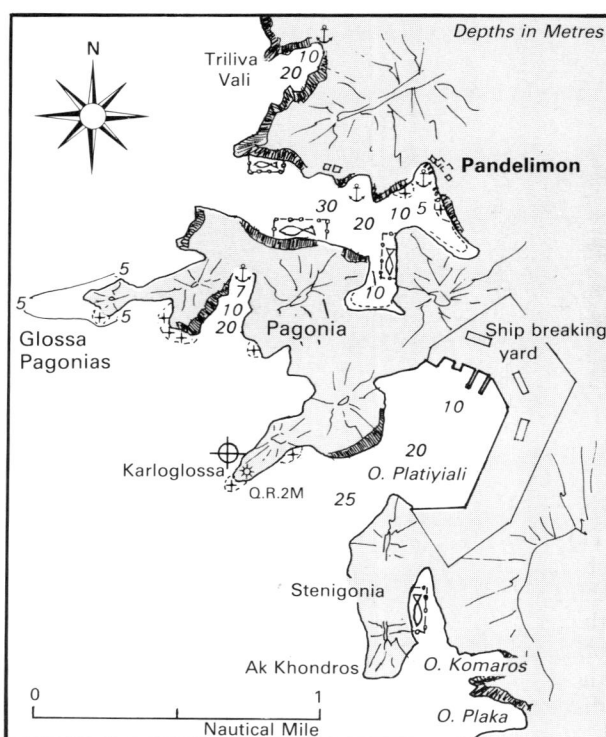

PANDELIMON AND PLATI YIALI
Karloglossa light· 38°28'·5N 21°05'·E

Anchor in the E or the S creek if you obtain permission; the latter affords the best shelter. The bottom is mud and weed, good holding once through the weed. The E creek can become uncomfortable with the chop pushed in by the prevailing wind, though rarely dangerous. In the S creek it is a good idea to take a long line ashore. No facilities unless you can get a fish or two from the fish farm.

Note The fish farms are often moved because of the debris (uneaten food and excrement) that builds up under them over time. Consequently do not rely on the buoyed off areas for the fish farms being in the exact position shown.

PLATI YIALI (Plateali)

The large bay lying immediately S of Pandelimon. For some time massive engineering work has been carried out to create huge concrete aprons and quays and the infrastructure ashore for a ship-breaking yard. Despite the massive amount of money that has been spent it seems that there may be some uncertainty over its future.

KOMAROS

A small inlet S of Platiyiali, now effectively obstructed by a fish farm.

NISIS PETALA

The large island lying close off the coast 2½ miles S of Plati Yialos. A yacht can find good shelter from the prevailing winds tucked in behind the island. Anchor behind the SE corner of the island in 2–3 metres. The bottom shelves gently towards the marshland at the N end. Shelter here is much better than it looks and the holding is good in glutinous mud.

Above the anchorage a cave is conspicuous. On one late autumn evening I spied a huge bird sitting by the cave and from a pinion feather retrieved from the cave the breeding pair of vultures here were estimated to have a wing-span of around eight feet. They are shy birds and it is unlikely you will see them through the summer when they retire to even more remote areas.

Nisis Petalas looking NE.

Nisis Oxia looking W.

POTAMOS AKHELOOS (River Achelos)

This river, the longest in Greece, empties into the sea about 3 miles S of Nisis Petala. The exact mouth of the river is difficult to identify and shoal water from the silt brought down extends at least a mile offshore. The shoal water appears to extend further than charted and care is needed to keep a safe distance off.

NISIS OXIA

The high island with a jagged ridge running down the spine at the entrance to the Gulf of Patras. Once seen its spiny outline is unmistakable. The lighthouse on the S end (Fl(2)15s17M) is conspicuous from the W and E. There are only two indifferent anchorages, both very deep.

1. *North Bay* There is now a fish farm in North Bay leaving no room to anchor.
2. *East Bay* A bay on the E side affording some shelter from the prevailing westerlies. Anchor in 15–20 metres with a long line ashore. Spectacular surroundings and utter isolation except for a few fishing boats.
3. *Ormos Oxias* Some shelter from the prevailing wind can be obtained under the spit of land formed by the river delta of the Akheloos. Anchor in 4–6 metres on mud, sand and weed.

Nisos Zakinthos

(Zante Island)

Zakinthos, the ancient name now officially readopted, is the southernmost of the Heptanesoi. (Kithera and Andikithera, although originally part of the Heptanesoi, are now administered separately.) Like a bowl holding something precious, the mountains of Zakinthos enclose the fertile central plain except where it overflows onto the sands of Laguna Beach. The Venetians called Zakinthos 'the flower of the Levant' and looking down on the plain planted with vines, mostly of the dwarf variety for currants, figs, olives, orange and lemon groves, it is easy to see why.

The first time I saw Zakinthos was in the autumn. After the baked islands of the Cyclades, the green slopes dotted with grazing cows were reminiscent of England. Yet despite English rule before Greece became independent, and English commercial interests in the currant trade, there is little apart from the green fields to remind you of England – Zakinthos is an Italianate island. Until the 1953 earthquake destroyed much of the Venetian architecture it must have appeared to be almost a cameo left behind by Venice.

'Only in Italy itself could one find this sort of baroque style, fruit of the seventeenth and eighteenth-century mind. Then in 1953 came the definitive earthquake which engulfed the whole of the Venetian past and left the shattered town to struggle to its knees once more. This it has done, in a manner of speaking; but it is like a beautiful woman whose face has been splashed with vitriol. Here and there, an arch, a pendent, a shattered remains of arcade, is all that is left of her renowned beauty.'

Lawrence Durrell *The Greek Islands*

Lawrence Durrell goes on to slate the modern town which I personally do not find so distasteful – but then I never saw the old Venetian town.

Zakinthos town overlooks a sheltered bay that has harboured naval fleets since ancient times. Anybody who wanted to move south needed Zakinthos to control the strait into the Gulf of Patras and the route south around the Peloponnese. First the Athenians, then Philip of Macedon, the Romans, Vandals, Normans, Turks, Venetians, French, Russians and finally the British held the island. While under British rule the island was a constant source of irritation to the Turks, since Greeks could easily escape to it and seek protection under the neutral Ionian flag – only to venture out again to fight the Turks on the mainland.

Twenty-five miles to the south of Zakinthos lie the remote Strophades Islands (Nisidhes Strofadhes). Administered from Zakinthos, the largest island was once a prosperous monastery until the Turks sacked it.

PORT ZAKINTHOS (Zante, Zakynthos)

Admiralty chart no. 2402
Imray-Tetra chart no. G12

Approach

Conspicuous From the N the hills dominated by Mt Skopio (520 metres) to the E of the central plain look like a separate island from the distance. As you near Ak Krioneri the hotels on the beach to the N of the cape and a tower on the hills immediately above are conspicuous. The buildings of Zakinthos are obscured until you round the cape when the N mole will be easily identified. From the S the buildings of Zakinthos stand out well against the eroded cliffs behind.

By night From the N use the lights on Ak Skinari (Fl.1·5s22M), Ay Nikolaos (Fl.2s7M) and on Ak Krioneri (Fl(2)16s6M). From the S use the lights on

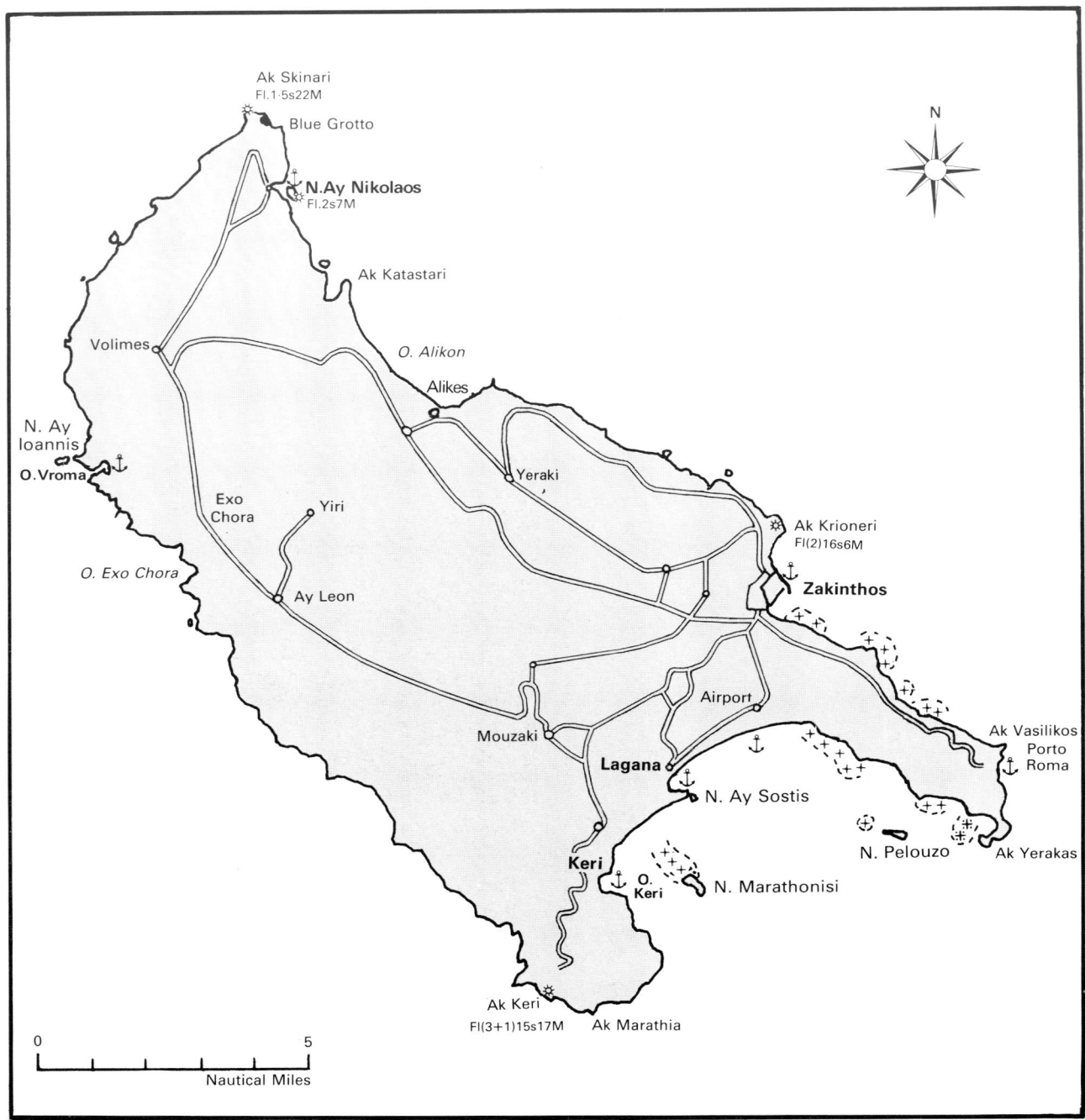

NISOS ZAKINTHOS

Ak Keri (Fl(3+1)15s17M and Ak Krioneri (Fl(2)16s6M). A constant red aerobeacon just W of the town is visible for about 5 miles and two alternate flashing red aerobeacons are also visible for about 3 miles to the W of the town. The entrance to the harbour is lit: Fl.G.1·5s3M and Fl.R.1·5s3M., though in the approach from the S the lights at the entrance are difficult to make out against the lights of the town until you are near the harbour.

Dangers

1. Care is needed of Ifalos Dhimitris, a reef and shoal water lying approximately 900 metres ESE of the harbour entrance. It has been reported that the reef has been removed and least depths here are now 6 metres and not 2 metres. Nonetheless care is counselled. It is marked by a red conical buoy.
2. Closer to the coast there is a group of unlit mooring buoys off the end of an oil pipeline.
3. A good lookout should be kept for ferries, which are constantly coming and going from the harbour.

Mooring

Moor stern-to the N mole (Ay Nikolaos) on the N side of the protruding loading quay. Keep well clear of the ferry berths on the N mole and the town quay. The bottom is mud and good holding.

Approach to Limin Zakinthos looking W.

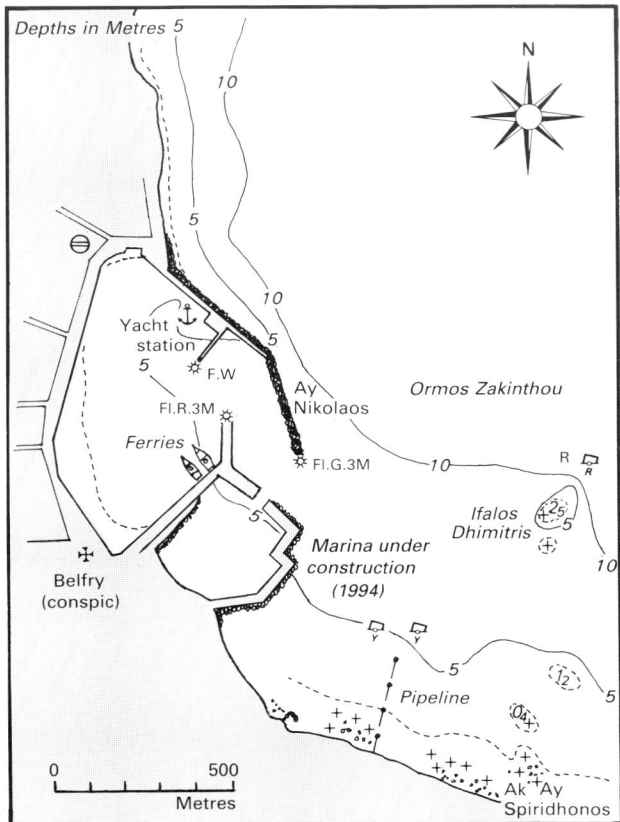

APPROACHES TO LIMIN ZAKINTHOS

Limin Zakinthos looking S from the slopes behind the town.
Neville Bulpitt.

Facilities

Water On the quay.
Fuel On the quay.
Repairs Caïques are hauled out at the root of the S mole. Some mechanical repairs. Hardware shops. Chandlers.
Provisions Good shopping for all provisions in the town.
Eating out Tavernas in the town.
Other PO. OTE. Banks. Greek gas and *Camping Gaz*. Hire cars and motorbikes. Ferries to Killini. International and internal flights.

General

Until its total destruction in the 1953 earthquake the town consisted largely of Venetian buildings. In the rebuilding of the town a Venetian aura has been retained – spacious boulevards, arcaded shops, central square and imposing public buildings. A museum in the town houses some of the relics, particularly some fine icons, recovered after the earthquake. Zakinthos is the logical spot to leave a yacht and explore the interior of the island – I suggest you head for the W side where there is some spectacular scenery, small villages, and fewer tourists.

Zakinthos Marina Under the S breakwater (Ay Dhimitrios) a new breakwater has been built enclosing what will be Zakinthos Marina. At present the rough stone breakwater has been built but no quayed areas are in place and no pontoons or jetties installed. When finished most facilities (water, electricity, showers and toilets) will be available. The new marina will provide much needed extra yacht berths and good shelter.

Shelter Good shelter from the prevailing NW wind. With strong southerlies a surge builds up in the harbour, and it may be best to anchor off to the W if possible.

Authorities A port of entry. Port police, customs and immigration.

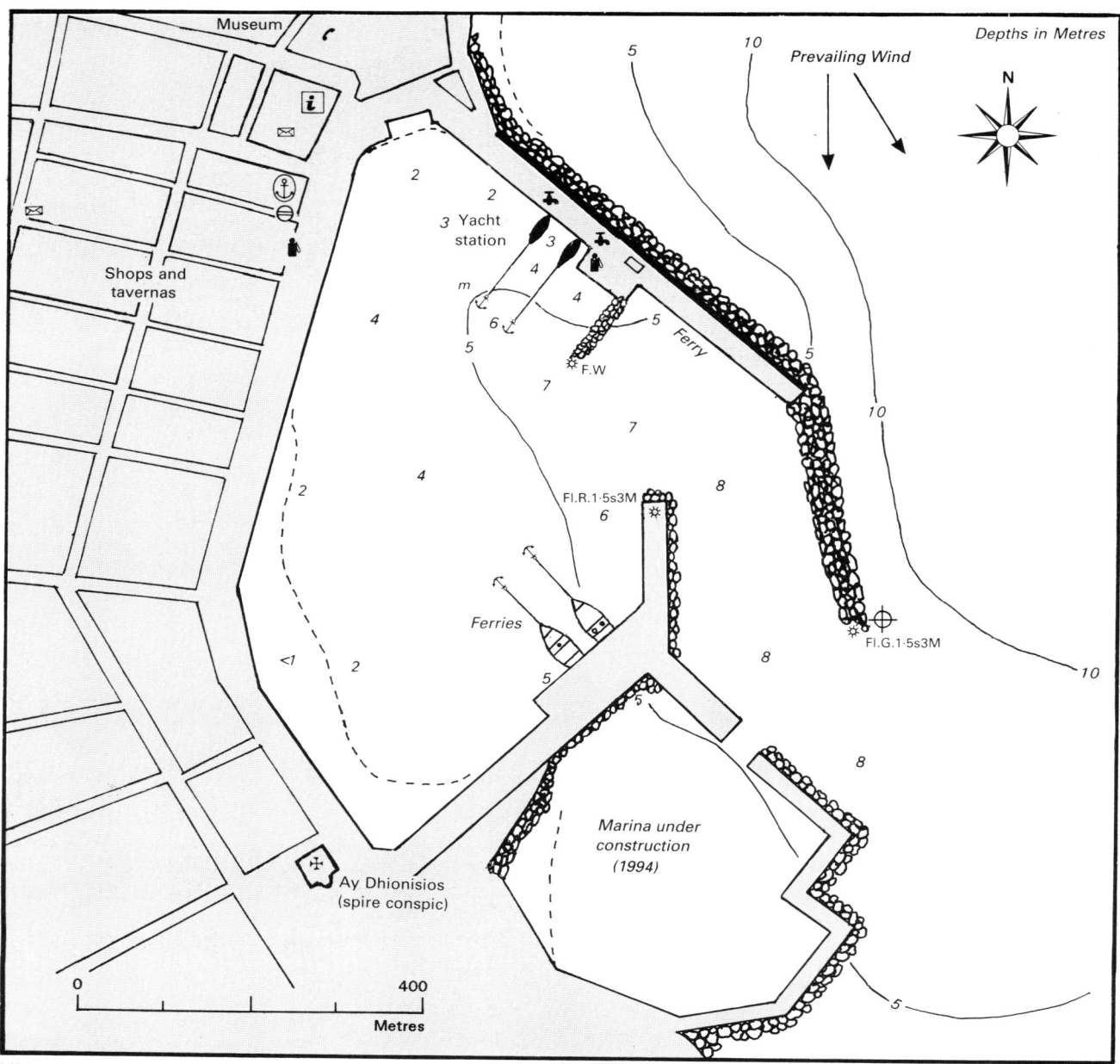

LIMIN ZAKINTHOS
37°46'·9N 20°54'·4E (Fl.G.1·5s3M)

ORMOS AY NIKOLAOS

A bay on the northern tip of Zakinthos partially sheltered by the islet of Ay Nikolaos in the entrance to the bay. Entry can be made on either side of the islet, though care is needed of the reef and shoal water extending N from the N end of the islet and S from the N entrance to the bay.

Anchor in 5–10 metres where convenient leaving the approach to the ferry ramp clear. Yachts can also anchor and take a long line to the outside of the rough stone breakwater. When the afternoon breeze gets up there are strong down-draughts into the bay so ensure your anchor is well in if staying.

Tavernas ashore. Ferry to Pessades on Cephalonia in the summer. Local *caïques* run excursions from here to caves near the northern tip of the island which are said to rival the Blue Grotto on Capri.

PORTO ROMA

A fair weather anchorage on the SE tip of the island on the E coast. Porto Roma is sheltered from the prevailing NW–W wind but a swell tends to roll into here. Taverna on the beach and several others a short walk away.

YERAKAS BAY

The bay lying immediately N of Ak Yerakas. Entry should be made on approximately 040' towards the beach. Anchor where convenient. Normally good protection from the prevailing NW wind although it will sometimes blow around the bottom of Zakinthos and into the anchorage. Tavernas ashore. The beach is a turtle breeding ground and nobody is allowed on the beach after sunset.

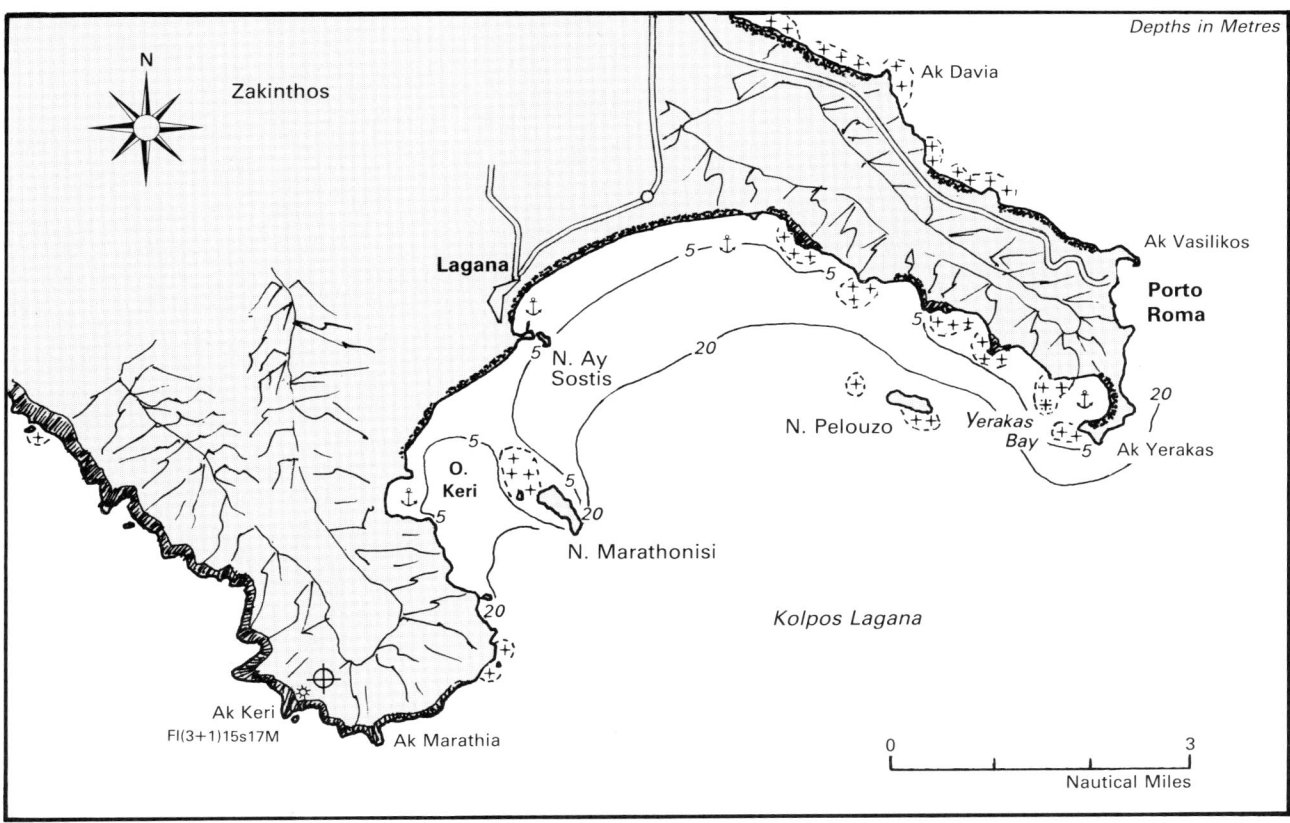

ZAKINTHOS: KOLPOS LAGANA
37°39'·4N 20°49'E (Ak Keri light)

LAGANA BEACH

In settled weather a yacht can anchor off Lagana Beach. The sandy bottom shelves gently to the shore. The anchorage is entirely open to southerlies when a heavy swell sets into the bay. The beach has been much developed for tourism recently and there are numerous tavernas and hotels along it.

The beach is a breeding area for turtles and they are now protected in the breeding season. Formerly they were caught in large numbers when they came ashore to lay their eggs in the sand.

PORT LAGANA

The fishing port for the village of Lithakia. On Admiralty chart no. 207 there is an unnamed islet (N. Ayios Sostis) at the W end of Lagana beach. A small harbour has been built out from the point behind the islet. There are 1·5–3 metre depths in the harbour but beware of large ropes stretched between the moles just under the water. The harbour is usually packed with fishing boats and local craft. Open to the SE. Taverna and worse, a disco on the beach.

ORMOS KERI (Kieri)

An anchorage on the E side of Ak Marathia and to the W of Nisis Marathonisi. Anchor in 2–4 metre depths on either side of the rough stone mole – the E side is appreciably deeper than the W side. The

ballasting on the mole extends a considerable distance underwater making it difficult to moor close to it. Excellent shelter from the NW–W wind, open to the S and E.

The famous pitch wells recorded by Herodotus still exist inland.

ORMOS VROMI

A deep inlet close to the NW corner of Zakinthos. It affords reasonable shelter from the prevailing NW–W wind although there may be gusts down into it. It is dangerous in southerlies when a swell rolls in. Anchor and take a long line ashore as there can be katabatic gusts at night off the high land. Picturesque setting although the new road takes away some of the solitude of the place. Tripper boats run here and a simple taverna opens in the summer.

II. The Southern Ionian

Zakinthos to Kithera

The images retained of the northern Ionian are seldom anything but fond memories of rolling green islands and fine sailing days. By contrast the southern Ionian is more rugged and fierce: the shores are for the most part bordered by high mountains, often still snow-capped in spring, under which there is a thin coastal plain washed down over time by the winter torrents. These mountains run irregularly from the centre of the Peloponnese into the sea in all directions although the two principal mountain ranges, the Taiyetos and the Parnon, run south ending in Cape Matapan (Ak Tainaron) and Cape Malea (Ak Maleas) respectively.

Like the mountains, the peoples of this country have been rugged and tough. It was known in ancient times as the Island of Pelops (hence Peloponnisos or Peloponnese) after Pelops, son of Tantalus. His bizarre history included being sliced up and stewed for the gods by his father (Zeus later brought him back to life) and outwitting King Oenomaus for the hand of his daughter Hippodamia in a chariot race by removing the pins from the wheels of his competitor's chariot. On a more substantive basis we know that around 2000 BC the Peloponnese was invaded by the first Greek-speaking peoples, a warrior race from whom the hero legends of Perseus and Pericles were probably derived. Later came the Mycenaeans (the Homeric Achaeans) and later still (around 850 BC) the warrior race supreme, the Spartans, emerged as a power.

Ancient Sparta occupied a spectacular site sandwiched between the Taiyetos and Parnon mountains – in a gorge in the Taiyetos the weak and deformed children considered unfit to belong to this militaristic race were left to die. Nothing much remains of ancient Sparta, but the word 'spartan' has passed into our vocabulary to describe what was a way of life.

With the decline of Sparta the peoples occupying the Mani peninsula formed themselves into the Free-Laconian League and their descendants acquired the name Maniotes. The Maniotes have been the most fierce race to people the Peloponnese – the Spartans notwithstanding. They lived in clans, and feuds within and between clans were common. Families built towers to shelter from reprisals and these strange structures still exist on the Mani peninsula. While the rest of the Peloponnese was subjugated by a succession of invaders, the Mani remained independent – both Rome and Turkey failed to defeat these fierce warriors.

Along the coastline the forts and castles at strategic points – Pilos, Methoni, Koroni, Kithera – tell of the importance of the Peloponnese as part of the trade route between the Aegean and Europe. Until the Corinth canal was cut most of the trade between east and west passed around this lonely stretch of coast. Whoever controlled this route controlled the flow of spices (especially pepper), silk, precious metals and stones, pearls, opium, perfumes – the exotic wealth of the Indian Ocean – to Europe. The Venetians and, to a lesser extent, the Turks have left the lasting monuments, but often their forts incorporate masonry from more ancient colonists. Even today a lot of the shipping traffic in the eastern Mediterranean travels down this coast rather than through the Corinth Canal.

The forbidding physical geography of the Peloponnese is perhaps the reason why comparatively few yachts cruise down this coast. Certainly the twin capes at the bottom of the Peloponnese, Matapan and Malea, have acquired a reputation as minor Cape Horns. Yet the weather is really no worse than that of many other areas of the Aegean and there are sufficient harbours and anchorages to provide refuge in the event of bad weather. Moreover you are off the tourist track and the impecunious will also save the Corinth Canal dues.

Weather patterns in the South Ionian

In the north half of the south Ionian from Katakolon to Methoni the weather pattern in the summer is very nearly identical to that of the northern Ionian: a NW wind gets up about noon and dies down in the evening. Sometimes it may be more from the W than NW and a little fresher than the Force 3–5 of the northern Ionian.

In the southern half of the south Ionian the wind is more from the W and SW and may last longer into the evening than in the northern Ionian. The wind tends to blow up into Messiniakos Kolpos and Lakonikos Kolpos although it may also gust off the W side of the gulfs. There is rarely a land breeze in the morning. Around Ak Maleas and Kithera, and sometimes in Lakonikos Kolpos, there is a NE wind which may blow all day although it rarely exceeds Force 4 – more often Force 2–3. After October and until March–April the winds are predominantly from

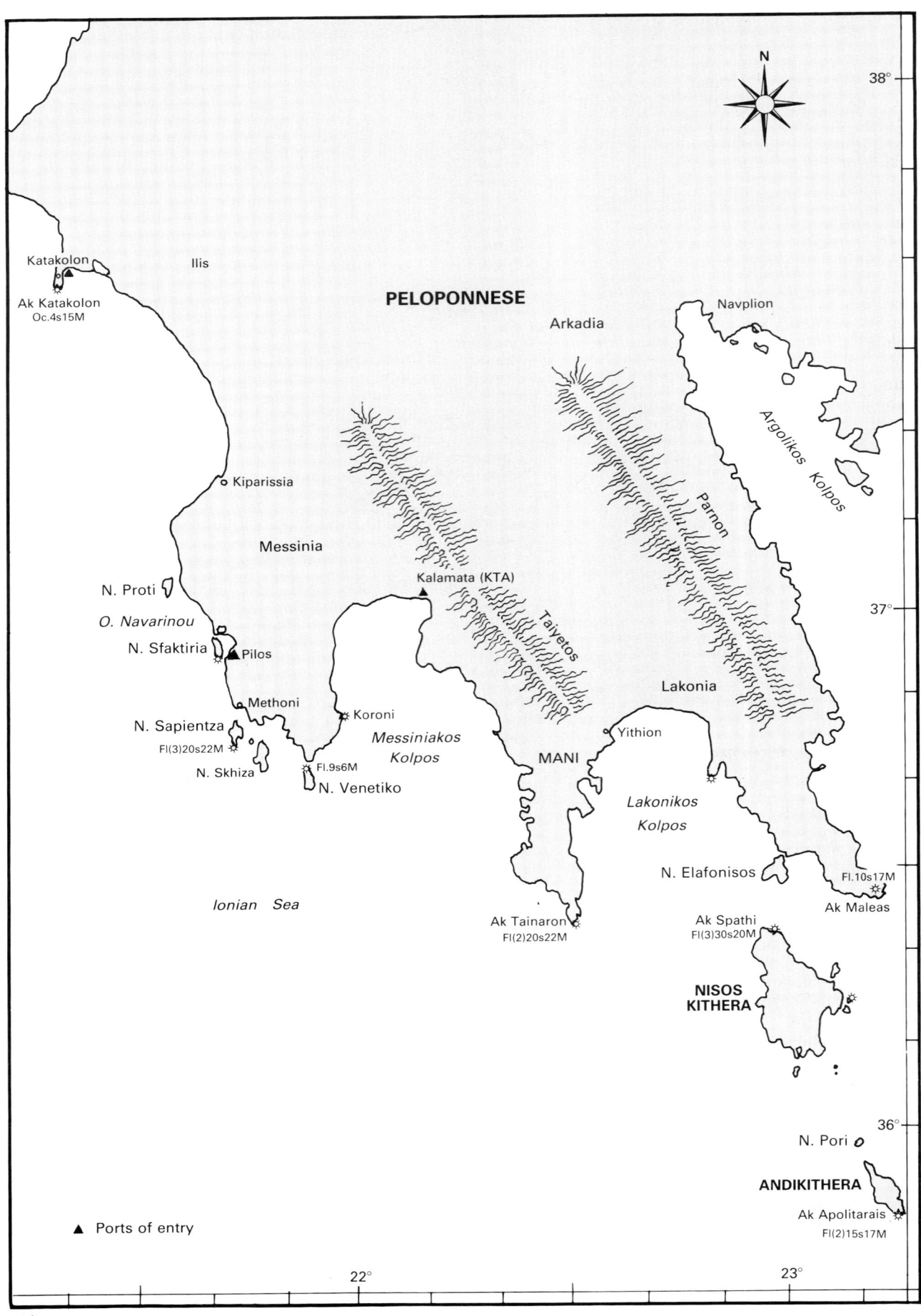

Katakolon

Ilis

PELOPONNESE

Navplion

Ak Katakolon
Oc.4s15M

Arkadia

Argolikos Kolpos

Kiparissia

Messinia

N. Proti

Kalamata (KTA)

37°

O. Navarinou

N. Sfaktiria
Pilos

Parnon

Methoni
Koroni

Taïyetos

N. Sapientza
Fl(3)20s22M

*Messiniakos
Kolpos*

Lakonia

N. Skhiza
Fl.9s6M

MANI
Yithion

N. Venetiko

*Lakonikos
Kolpos*

N. Elafonisos
Fl.10s17M

Ionian   Sea

Ak Tainaron
Fl(2)20s22M

Ak Maleas

Ak Spathi
Fl(3)30s20M

**NISOS
KITHERA**

36°
N. Pori

ANDIKITHERA

▲ Ports of entry

Ak Apolitarais
Fl(2)15s17M

22°

23°

the SE although there may be strong winds from the N associated with nearby depressions.

There are two problem areas as regards the weather in the south Ionian. The first is to do with the very high mountain ranges down which there can be severe gusts on the lee side. Gusts off the mountains are particularly severe on either side of Ak Maleas and Ak Tainaron (the gusts are coming off the Taiyetos and Parnon mountains) and off Kithera. At night there may be a katabatic wind which can be quite strong and arrive without warning.

The second problem in this area is that of the six generalised depression tracks over Greece; three of these tracks converge in the strait between Ak Maleas and Crete. Consequently the weather can deteriorate rapidly around the bottom of the Peloponnese, especially in spring and autumn. It should be borne in mind when seeking shelter in the summer that strong southerlies will often veer to strong northerlies. This is not quite so true in the spring and autumn when a strong southerly may be prolonged and followed by only a weak northerly.

In the summer there may be thunderstorms around the coast with associated squalls but these seldom last for very long. The temperatures in the summer are marginally warmer than those in the northern Ionian except on Kithera where the climate is more like that on Crete.

Data

PORTS OF ENTRY
Katakolon
Pilos
Kalamata

PROHIBITED ANCHORAGES
Nisis Skhiza is used for target practice by the air force.

MAJOR LIGHTS
Ak Katakolon Fl.4s15M
Nisis Stamfani Fl(2)15s17M
Nisis Proti Fl.1·5s6M
Nisis Pilos Fl(2)10s7M
Ak Karsi (Nisis Sapientza) Fl.3s5M
Nisis Sapientza (SW Summit) Fl(3)20s22M
Nisis Venetiko Fl.9s6M
Ak Kitries Fl(2)12s6M
Ak Tainaron (Cape Matapan) Fl(2)20s22M
Nisis Kranai (Yithion) Fl(3)18s9M
Ak Xilis Fl.3s5M
Ormos Vatika Fl.3s6M
Ak Zovolo Fl.7s8M
Ak Maleas Fl.10s17M
Ak Spathi (Kithera) Fl(3)30s20M
Vrak Antidragonera (Kithera) Fl(3)15s6M
Ak Apolitarais (Andikithera) Fl(2)15s17M

Quick reference guide

	Shelter	Mooring	Fuel	Water	Provisions	Tavernas	Plan
Katakolon to Ormos Navarinou							
Katakolon	A	A	A	A	B	B	•
Kiparissia	C	C	B	B	B	B	•
Nisis Proti	C	C	O	O	O	O	•
Ak Marathos (*Caïque* Harbour)	C	A	B	B	C	C	•
Pilos	B	AB	A	A	B	B	•
Pilot Yacht Harbour	A	AB	B	B	B	B	•
Ormos Navarinou	B	C	O	O	O	C	•
Messiniakos Kolpos (Gulf of Messinia)							
Methoni	B	AC	B	B	B	B	•
Port Longos	B	C	O	O	O	O	•
Finakunda	B	AC	O	B	C	B	•
Maratho	C	C	O	O	O	O	
Koroni	B	C	B	B	B	B	•
Petalidhion	B	C	B	B	B	B	•
Kalamata	A	A	A	A	A	A	•
Kardamila	C	C	O	O	B	B	•
Limeni	C	C	O	B	C	C	•
Diros	O	C	O	B	O	C	•
Mezapo	C	C	O	B	C	C	•
Yerolimena	O	C	O	B	C	O	
Lakonikos Kolpos (Gulf of Lakonika)							
Porto Kayio	B	AC	O	O	C	C	•
Ormos Skoutari	C	C	O	O	O	O	•
Yithion	B	AB	A	A	A	A	•
Elaia	B	AC	B	B	B	C	•
Plitra	B	A	O	B	O	C	•
Nisos Elafonisos	C	C	O	O	O	O	•
Elafonisos village	B	AC	O	B	B	C	•
Neapolis	C	AC	B	B	B	B	•
Kithera and Andikithera							
Panayia	C	AB	O	B	C	C	
Nisis Makri	C	C	O	O	O	O	
Ay Nikolaos	C	C	O	O	C	O	•
Ormos Kapsali	C	ABC	A	A	B	B	•
Ormos Potamos	O	C	B	O	C	C	•

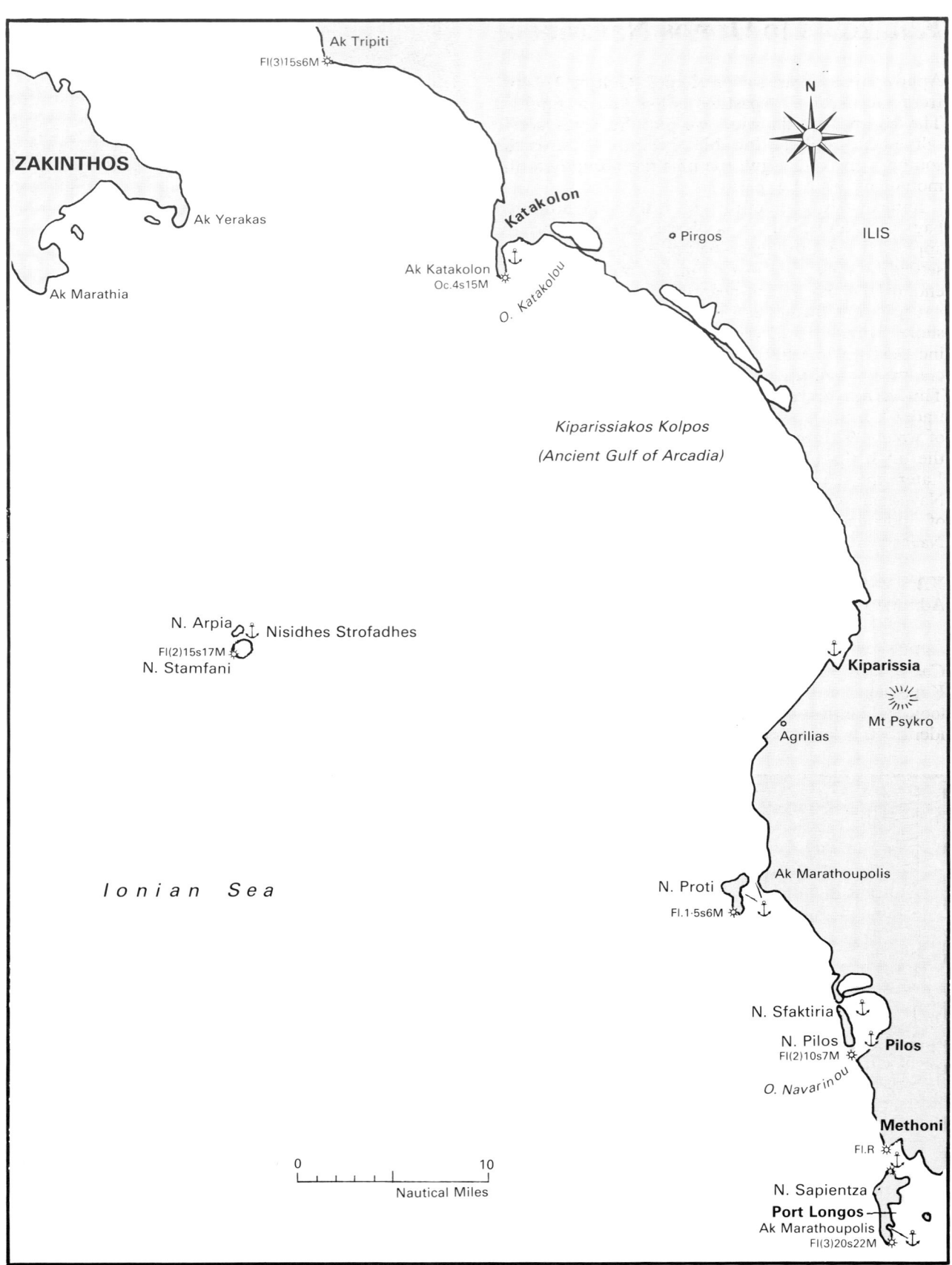

ZAKINTHOS

Ak Tripiti
Fl(3)15s6M ☼

Katakolon
⚓
Ak Katakolon
Oc.4s15M ☼

Ak Yerakas

Ak Marathia

○ Pirgos

ILIS

O. Katakolou

Kiparissiakos Kolpos
(Ancient Gulf of Arcadia)

N. Arpia ⚓ Nisidhes Strofadhes
Fl(2)15s17M ☼
N. Stamfani

Kiparissia ⚓

Mt Psykro

○ Agrilias

I o n i a n   S e a

N. Proti
Fl.1·5s6M ☼ ⚓

Ak Marathoupolis

N. Sfaktiria ⚓
N. Pilos ⚓ **Pilos**
Fl(2)10s7M ☼

O. Navarinou

Methoni
Fl.R ☼ ⚓

N. Sapientza
Port Longos
Ak Marathoupolis
Fl(3)20s22M ☼ ⚓

0   10
Nautical Miles

KATAKOLON TO METHONI

Katakolon to Ormos Navarinou

Approaching Kiparissiakos Kolpos (Gulf of Arcadia) from the north the coastline is low and featureless. The land beyond the wide sweep of the bay is largely salt marsh until the low hills behind. Towards the southern end of the gulf the hills rise abruptly to the mountains behind Kiparissia.

Immediately south of the gulf is the large protected bay of Navarinon – a large natural harbour approximately three and a half miles by two miles. In settled weather a yacht can anchor off the northern end of the bay either near the Sikia channel (not navigable) or further east on the low sandy mainland shore. From here the scene of the Sphakteria incident can be explored and easily visualized in the craggy deserted landscape. The incident described by Thucydides occurred when a group of Athenians under Demosthenes besieged a force of 400 Spartans of which 292 eventually surrendered, thus destroying the myth that Spartans always fought to the death. Later the bay was the scene of the Battle of Navarinon which effectively decided the Greek War of Independence. (See the section on the Ormos Navarinou.)

KATAKOLON (Limin Katakolou)
Admiralty chart no. 2404

Approach

Conspicuous From the N and S the lighthouse on Ak Katakolon is conspicuous. The low-lying cape looking like an aeroplane wing in cross section can be identified a long way off. From the N the harbour

Ak Katakolou and Limin Katakolon looking N.

breakwater and village will not be seen until around Ak Katakolon, but from the S the breakwater is easily identified.

By night Use the light on Ak Katakolon (Oc.4s15M) and the light on the end of the breakwater (Q.R.2M).

Dangers Care is needed off the E side of Ak Katakolon not to shave the reef and shoal water here – keep at least 700 metres off the coast.

Note The three small red conical buoys on the N side of the harbour mark the limit of the deep water channel for large ships. They are not always in place.

Mooring

Berth stern-to or bows-to the quay on either side of the central loading quay or alongside the central quay. The bottom is mud and clay, excellent holding.

Shelter Good shelter from the prevailing winds. In unsettled weather go on the S side of the central loading quay.

Authorities A port of entry: port police, customs and immigration.

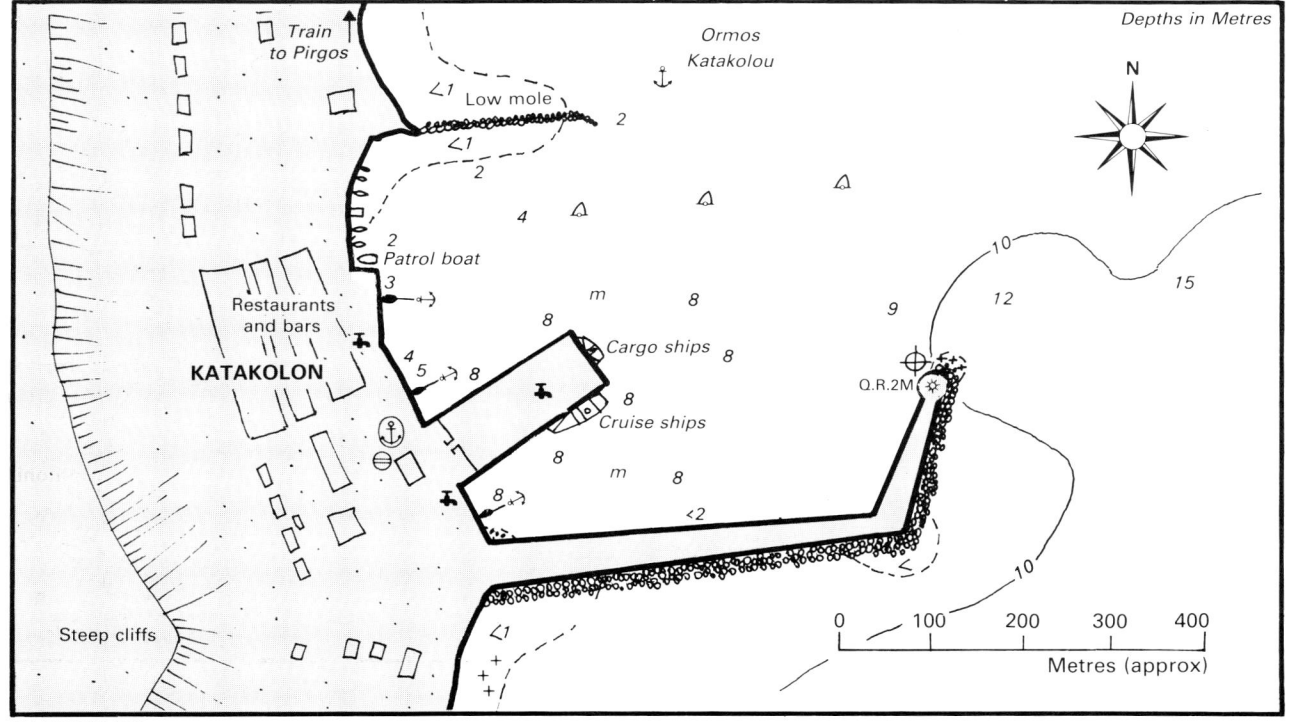

KATAKOLON
37°38'·8N 21°19'·6E (Q.R light)

The entrance to Limin Katakolon looking W.

Facilities

Water On the quay.

Fuel In the town. A mini-tanker delivers to the quay.

Repairs Ionian Yacht Services run by Yannis Kalofonos can haul yachts up to 16 tons. Larger yachts can be hauled by arrangement. He uses a crane and puts yachts onto a specially designed trailer to trundle them to the boatyard. The only disadvantage is that your mast must come down. Mechanical and engineering work can be carried out. Some GRP and general repairs. *Gardiennage.* ☎ (0621) 21353 (winter) and (0621) 21302 (summer).

Provisions Most provisions can be found in the village. Better shopping in Pirgos.

Eating out Numerous tavernas and an inordinate number of pizzerias for the size of the place.

Other PO. Telephone. Bus and train to Pirgos. Taxis. Hire motorbikes.

General

Katakolon was built in 1875 for the then thriving currant trade. Now it is used by small cargo ships and by cruise ships as a base for the visit to Olympia about 25 miles away. This is the best place to leave a yacht if you wish to visit Olympia – usually you will be accosted by a taxi driver as soon as you arrive. Alternatively hire a motorbike or take the bus or train to Pirgos and another bus on to Olympia.

KIPARISSIA (Ormos Kiparissias)
Admiralty chart no. 207

Approach

From the N the town of Kiparissia is conspicuous under the steep-to Mt Psikro (1350 metres). From the W a Disneyland castle situated on the seafront at Agrilias (about 5 miles SW of Kiparissia) is both conspicuous and incongruous.

By night There are no lights.

Dangers With strong NW–W winds there is a confused swell rebounding off the coast in the approaches. Moreover as shelter is not good in here from strong NW–W winds it is recommended you head for somewhere else.

Kiparissia harbour looking SE from the breakwater. *Neville Bulpitt.*

Mooring

Go stern or bows-to the quayed section of the breakwater or anchor off. Care is needed of numerous permanent moorings and floating lines on the surface. The bottom is hard sand with some rocks, good holding once the anchor is in though this can take some doing. Shelter from the N and W is only just adequate and with the regular NW–W wind there is a very uncomfortable surge in the harbour. With strong winds from the N the nearest shelter is in Ormos Navarinou or Methoni. With strong winds from the N or W the harbour is untenable – locals report that in the winter of 1990 a northerly gale sank every boat in the harbour – so enough said.

Facilities

Water At the taverna near the quay.

Fuel In the town about 500 metres away.

Provisions Good shopping in the town.

Eating out Tavernas on the waterfront and in the town.

Other PO. OTE. Bank. Greek gas and *Camping Gaz.* Buses to Pilos and Patras.

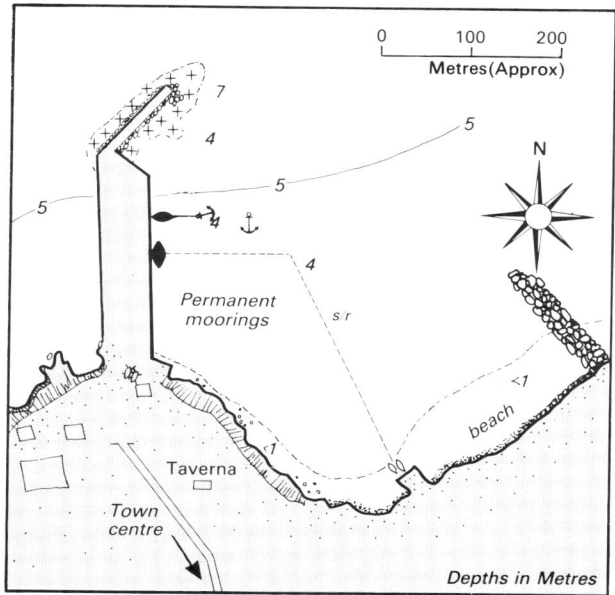

KIPARISSIA
37°15′N 21°41′E

General

Once an important harbour for nearby Messene, today only a few fishermen keep their boats here because of the poor shelter. This is a pity for yachtsmen because the town and the surrounding countryside are wonderful – as you sail along the coast you realise you are going to miss it all unless you take a chance here. A number of new hotels have been built to take advantage of the nearby sandy beaches.

Nisidhes Strofadhes

These lonely islands lie approximately 32 miles due W of Kiparissia and 26 miles due S of Ak Yerakas on Zakinthos. A light is exhibited on Nisis Stamfani: Fl(2)15s17M. On Nisis Arpia, the N island, a church is conspicuous at the N end. On Nisis Stamfani the lighthouse and the monastery are conspicuous.

The islands once supported a prosperous monastery but today there is just one monk who with the aid of a tractor looks after a flock of sheep, poultry, a vineyard, and a vegetable garden! At one time the island was plagued by rabbits but a recent visitor reported there were no rabbits but a lot of spent cartridges lying around!

Ormos Tavernas A bay on the S side of Nisis Arpia. The approach to the bay should be made from the E only – the W side of the channel between Arpia and Stamfani is obstructed by above and below water rocks. Anchor in 4–10 metres. Water from a number of wells ashore.

Ormos Prasa A bay on the S side of Nisis Stamfani. Not recommended as an anchorage as the coast is one long low sea cliff and the sea bed is littered with large boulders.

Note In unsettled weather a yacht should not remain at Nisidhes Strofadhes. The waters around the island with gales from any direction have been likened to a giant washing machine swirling around – a potent image that should have you moving as soon as bad weather brews up.

NISIS PROTI AND CHANNEL (Stenon Protis)
Admiralty chart no. 207

On the E coast of Nisis Proti there is a small bay which fishing boats sometimes use to shelter from NW winds. Depths are considerable and it is not a good anchorage. A few deserted houses ashore.

Local fishing boats also anchor on the SW side of Marathoupolis village where there is a surprisingly good lee from NW winds although some swell penetrates.

Note The light formerly on Ak Marathoupolis off the village is now on the S end of Nisis Proti: characteristic Fl.1·5s6M.

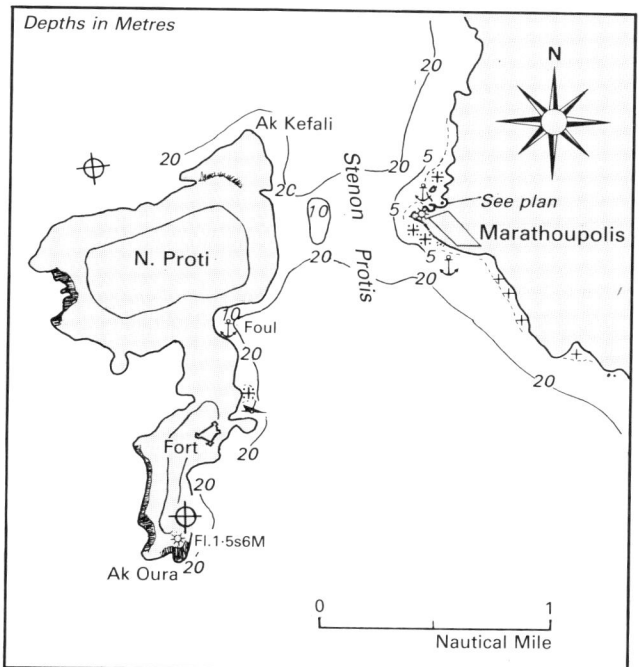

STENON PROTIS
37°02′N 21°33′E (Fl.1·5s6M)

MARATHOUPOLIS

Approach

A small *caïque* harbour on the NE corner of Proti Channel to the N of Ak Marathoupolis. Suitable for small yachts perhaps up to 10 metres. The entrance is difficult with rock-bound shallows on either side of the channel. By day enter from the N keeping an eye open for the shallows.

Marathoupolis village on the E side of the Proti channel. The small *caïque* harbour is 'around the top' of the headland.

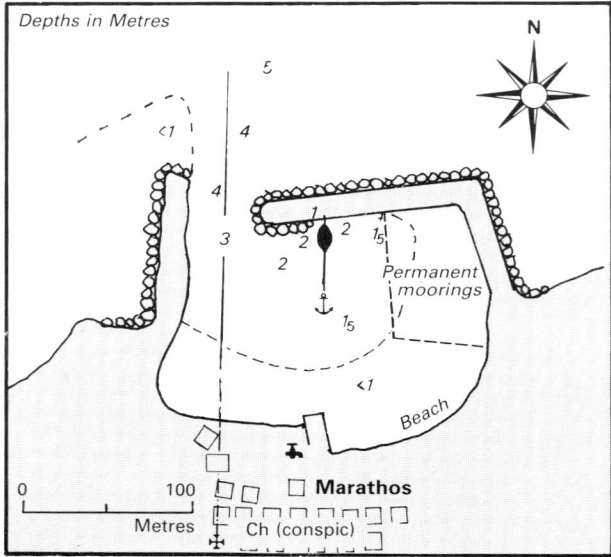

MARATHOS
37°04′N 21°34′.5E

Conspicuous A church with two blue cupolas is conspicuous and if the church is lined up with a cream house near the harbour this shows the way in.

By night There are no lights and entry at night would be dangerous.

Dangers With moderate NW winds there is a considerable swell at the entrance and care is needed. With strong NW–W winds a heavy sea builds up in the approaches and entry is not advised.

Mooring

There are 2 metre depths off the extremity of the mole running E–W on the N side of the harbour. Go bows-to tucked just inside the mole. The E side of the harbour is taken up with permanent moorings.

Shelter Reasonable shelter from moderate N-NW winds. Good shelter from S winds.

Facilities

Water in the village. Taverna and limited provisions in the village.

General

The village cannot be described as an attractive place, but it is convivial and the situation on the edge of the channel looking across to Nisis Proti is wonderful.

PILOS (Pylos, Navarino, Neokastro)
Admiralty chart no. 2404
Imray-Tetra chart no. G15

Approach

Conspicuous Nisis Sfaktiria (ancient Sphakteria) and Nisis Pilos are easily identified. Nisis Pilos has a huge natural arch through it and the lighthouse and a white memorial on it are conspicuous. Entering Ormos Navarinou the large Venetian fort with a conspicuous church on the S side of the entrance is easily identified. Once in Ormos Navarinou the small town of Pilos will be seen. The pier running out from the town is easily identified.

By night Use the light on Nisis Pilos (Fl(2)10s7M, the light on Ak Neokastron off the Venetian fort (Fl.G.3s6M) and the light on the extremity of the pier (F.G.3M). The light on Nisis Khelonisis (Fl.WR.3s4/2M) towards the N end of Ormos Navarinou may also be useful.

Dangers With moderate to strong W winds a heavy sea piles up in the approaches to Ormos Navarinou. Once inside the bay there is comparative calm although there can be strong gusts off Nisis Sfakteria.

Note Large ships use Ormos Navarinou to resupply and a good lookout should be kept for ships leaving and entering the bay. There will usually be several ships at anchor in the bay.

Mooring

Go stern or bows-to or alongside in the new 'marina' built just E of Pilos pier. The approach should be made from the N and not from the W. At the time of publication the harbour was in place but not finished off so care is needed. There are 3·3 metre depths in the entrance and mostly 2–3·5 metre depths inside. Permanent moorings tailed to the quay. It was in use in 1994 by yachts and fishing boats. Eventually additional facilities will be added.

Nisis Pilos looking W.

The Venetian fort and light structure in the immediate approaches to Pilos.

Shelter Good shelter in the 'marina'.

Authorities A port of entry: port police, customs and immigration. The authorities are housed in a building at the root of the pier.

Facilities

Water On the main pier.

Fuel In the town. A mini-tanker will deliver to the pier and may deliver to the 'marina'.

Repairs 20-ton crane at the marina. Limited mechanical repairs.

Provisions Good shopping for all provisions.

Eating out Numerous tavernas around the harbour and in the town.

Other PO. OTE. Greek gas and *Camping Gaz*. Buses to Methoni, Kalamata, and Kiparissia.

General

Pilos was largely built by the French in the 19th century after the Battle of Navarinon, the shaded square has a memorial to the three admirals who commanded the fleet which destroyed Turkish sea power – Admirals Codrington, de Rigny and von Heyden. The fort to the W of the harbour so prominent from seawards was originally built by the Venetians and added to by the Turks. It has an impressive mosque, now a church, inside the walls.

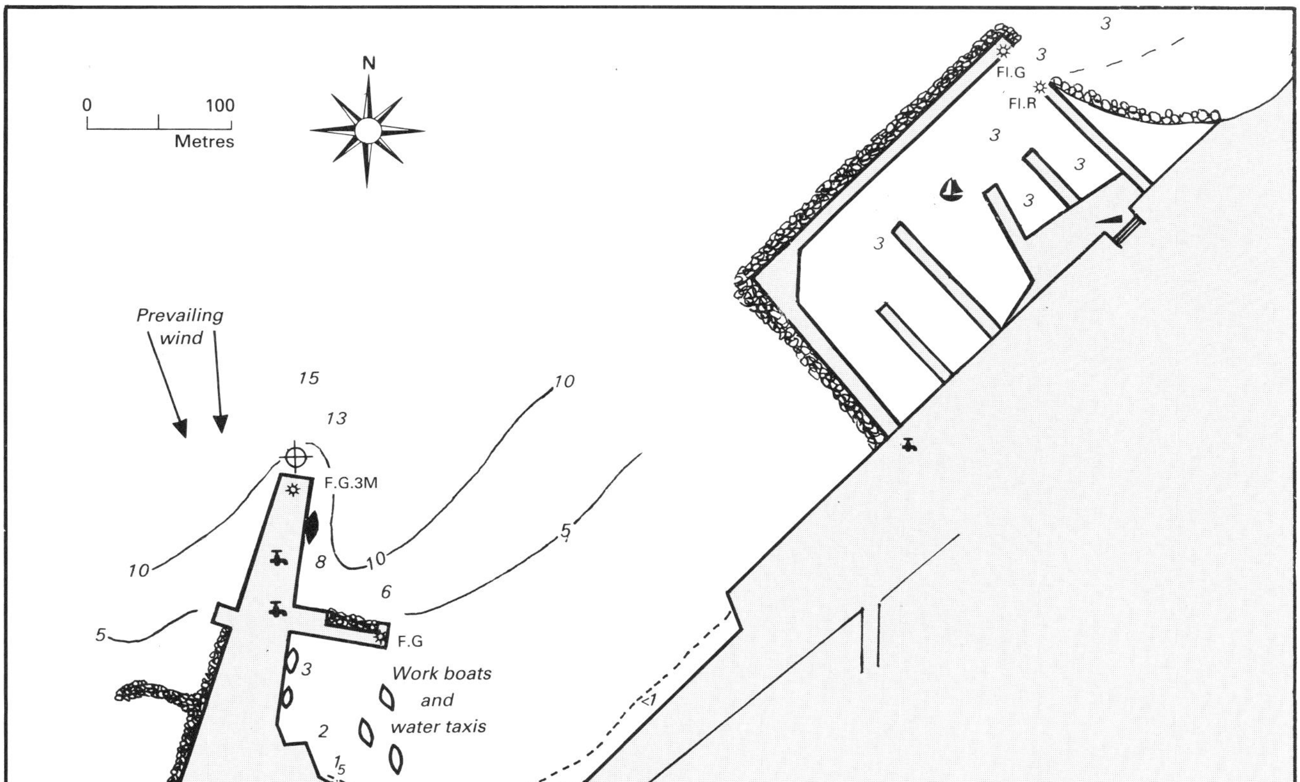

0   100
Metres

N

Prevailing wind

15

13

10

F.G.3M

10

8

10

5

6

10

5

F.G

3

Work boats and water taxis

2

1.5

<1

<1

To Castle

Tavernas and bars

Square

3

3
Fl.G
Fl.R

3

3

3

3

Note
Sketch plan of Pilos Marina to be used with caution

PILOS
36°54'·9N 21°41'·6E (F.G.3M)

The castle is open from 0930 hours.

Pilos is the place to organise a visit to Ano Englianos and ancient Pilos, the Mycenaean city believed be King Nestor's. There is in fact little to see at the site except the foundations of various buildings and the few artifacts which were not carted off to Athens.

ORMOS NAVARINOU – N END

A yacht can anchor at the N end of Ormos Navarinou where convenient. The bottom comes up quickly to the sandy beach so you will have to anchor in 8–12 metres. The bottom is sand and mud, good holding once the anchor has dug in, though this can take a bit of doing for some reason. Good shelter from the prevailing wind which blows in from between NW and N. At night after the wind has died down it can be a bit uncomfortable here with the residual swell creeping in through the entrance and up into the bay.

There are a couple of snack bars that open in the summer, but little else. If you anchor in the NW corner you can walk across to Nisos Sfaktiria. A shallow bar shuts off the northern entrance to the bay and it is possible to wade across to the island.

Pilos harbour looking NW.

The energetic may like to hike up to the summit of Ak Koryfasion where a Venetian castle can be seen from the anchorage. The castle is built on the ruins of a former Frankish castle and also on the ruins of the second Pilos built after the first at Englianos was mysteriously destroyed by fire. There is nothing to see although a cave nearby has been dubbed Nestor's Cave. If you want to visit ancient Pilos and Nestor's Palace, this is best done from Pilos or Methoni.

The Battle of Navarinon

At the very time when the Greek forces were at their lowest ebb during the War of Independence, the fortuitous naval engagement in the Bay of Navarinon changed the whole order of things and effectively won the war. On 6 July 1827, the Treaty of London between Great Britain, France and Russia provided that Greece should be autonomous but under the control of the Turks. This piece of legal chicanery was implemented so that the three powers might remain friendly to both Greece and Turkey and allowed for their fleets to guarantee the treaty. The senior admiral, Codrington, was given wide powers of discretion in the policing of the treaty.

Presented with the terms of the treaty, the Greeks agreed (they had little option) while the Turks did not. Codrington decided to enter the Bay of Navarinon where the Turko-Egyptian fleet was assembled, even though his fleet was outnumbered and outgunned (the allied fleet numbered 26 ships and 1270 guns; the Turko-Egyptian fleet numbered 89 warships and 2450 guns) and despite the fact that his country was not at war with the opposing fleet. The Turko-Egyptian fleet was anchored in a three quarter circle facing the entrance, in theory a trap in which ships sailing in would be caught by fire from all sides before they could sail out again. Codrington led his fleet in, the bands playing on the deck and the gun ports half open, and anchored in the middle of the trap. An Egyptian ship fired a shot and the battle began. 'The bloody and destructive battle was continued with unabated fury for four hours; and the scene of wreck and devastation which presented itself at its termination was such as has been seldom before witnessed', Codrington wrote in his dispatch.

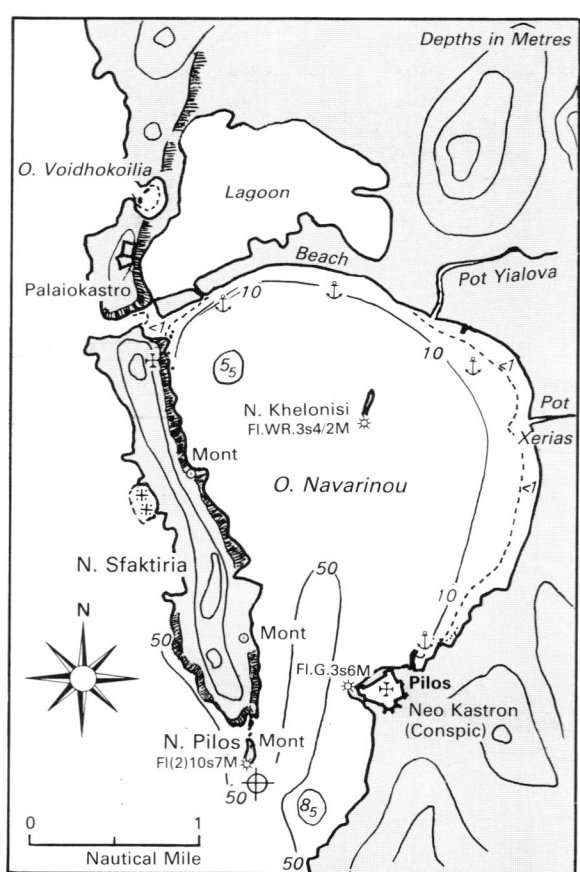

ORMOS NAVARINOU
36°54'·2N 21°40'·3E (N. Pilos light)

It was an unremitting battle fought at anchor which Codrington won, proving that European gun crews were more efficient in the heat of battle than their eastern counterparts. Codrington was not censured over this action although the English government expressed regret over it. France mopped up any remaining opposition in the Peloponnese and in the end Greece was free.

Methoni Roadstead and Messiniakos Kolpos

Five miles south of Ormos Navarinou the once important port of Methoni is tucked behind a small headland dominated by a large fort. Following the coast east for some 12 miles, the wide gulf of Messiniakos (Gulf of Messinia, Gulf of Kalamata) opens up between Nisis Venetiko and Ak Tainaron (Cape Matapan). Bordered on the west by comparatively tame mountains, the country is for the most part green and wooded down to sandy beaches. The harbours of Koroni and Petalidhion offer reasonable shelter in the summer months. At the head of the gulf lies the low marshland of the Makaria plain with the large port of Kalamata at its eastern end.

Towering above Kalamata is the Taiyetos (2307 metres high) running south to the Mani peninsula ending in Ak Tainaron. Tainaron, a.k.a Matapan, was the ancient Tenaron, the entrance to the underworld, and for all that exists around the cape it might as well be the end of the world for yachtsman and ancient alike. Tainaron is very nearly the most southerly cape of Europe; only Cape Tarifa at the entrance to the Gibraltar Strait is further south by just 14 miles.

METHONI (Modon)
Admiralty chart no. 682
Imray-Tetra chart no. G15

Approach

Conspicuous From the N and S the Venetian fort and the Turkish tower on the extremity of Ak Soukouli are conspicuous. The silhouette of the Turkish tower is unmistakable once seen. From the W and S the lighthouse on the S end of Nisis Sapientza stands out clearly. Once in the Methoni Roadstead the small harbour is easily identified.

By night Use the light on S end of Nisis Sapientza (Fl(3)20s22M), the light on Ak Karsi at the N end of Sapientza (Fl.3s5M), and the light on the end of the breakwater (Fl.R.3s3M).

Dangers

1. With westerlies a confused swell piles up between Ak Soukouli and Ak Karsi, but a short distance into the roadstead things quieten down.

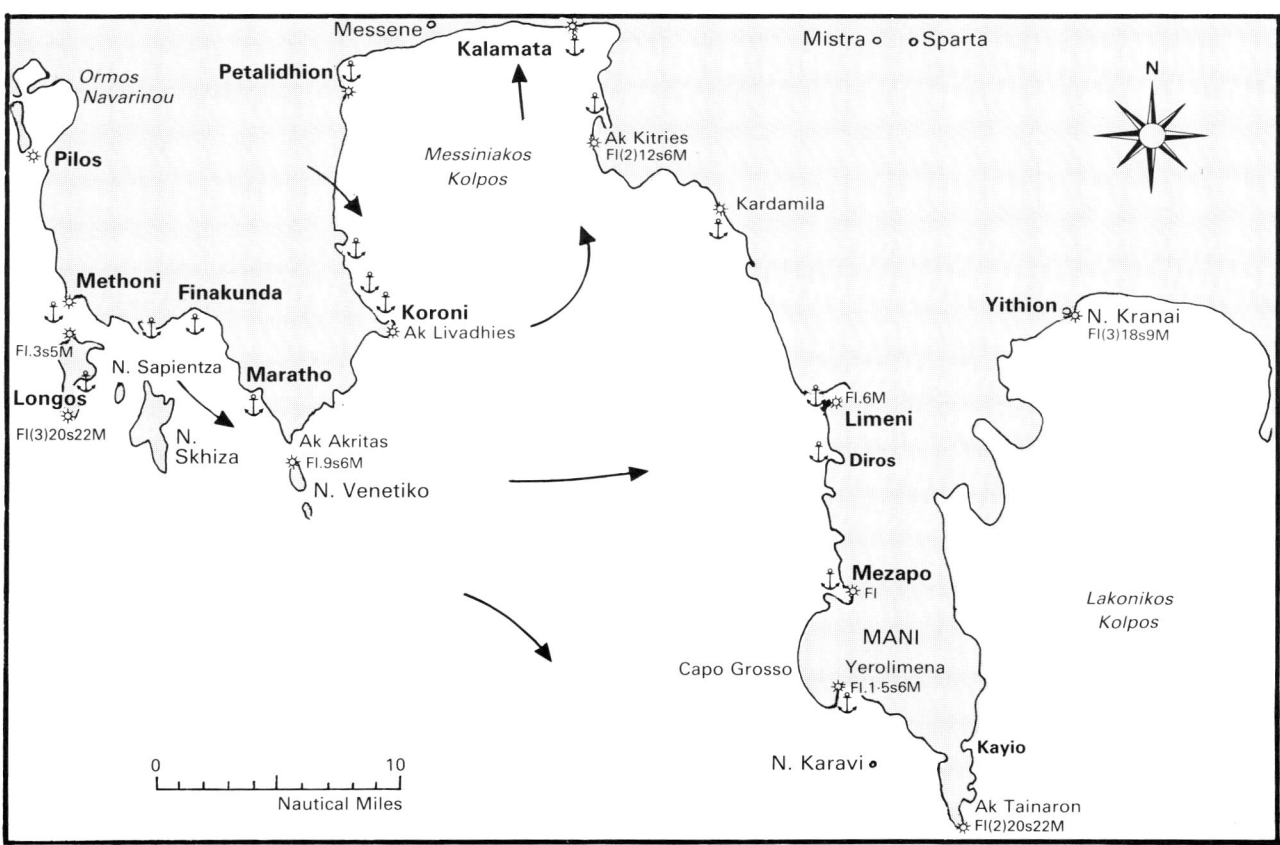

MESSINIAKOS KOLPOS (GULF OF MESSINIA) Arrows show the prevailing wind

The castle and Turkish tower at Methoni looking SW from the harbour.

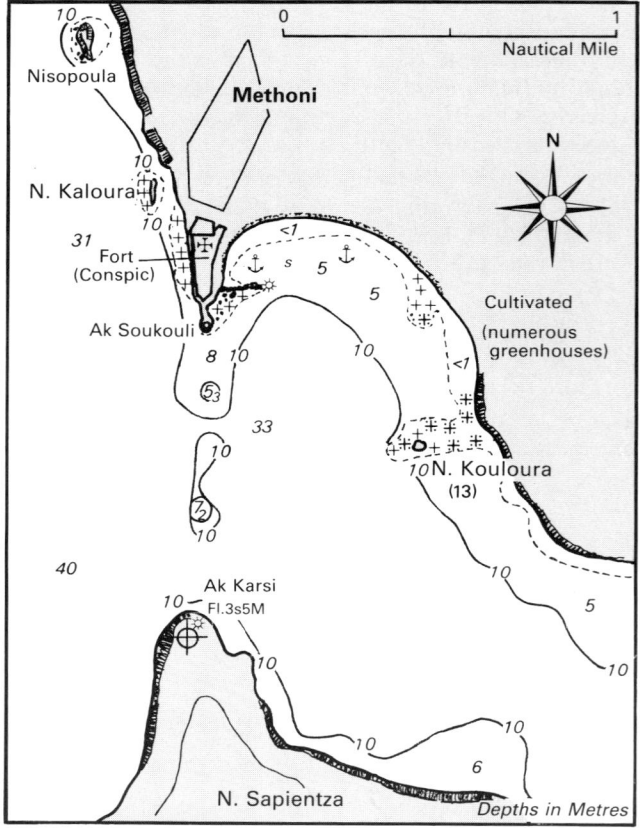

STENON METHONIS
36°47'·7N 21°42'·2E (Ak Karsi light)

2. Care should be taken of the reef running W from Nisis Kouloura – there is usually broken water around it.

3. A yacht should keep well clear of Nisis Skhiza which is used by the air force for target practice.

Mooring

Anchor off under the breakwater. The bottom is mud or sand, mostly sand N of the breakwater, good holding.

Shelter Good shelter from all but strong SE winds.

Facilities

Water At the root of the breakwater or on the beach.
Fuel In the town about 500 metres from the beach.
Repairs Limited mechanical repairs.
Provisions Good shopping in the village.
Eating out Tavernas on the beach and in the town.
Other PO. OTE. Greek gas and *Camping Gaz*. Bus to Pilos.

General

The harbour bounded by the large fort and the sandy beach is one of my favourite places on the W Peloponnese. Methoni was mentioned by Homer as being 'rich in vines'; later under the Venetians it was famous for its wine and pork. Today the hinterland is still intensively cultivated and you will often see the greenhouses flashing in the sun as you near the harbour.

The Venetian fort guarded the shipping route around the Peloponnese and Methoni along with Koroni was called 'the eye of the Republic'. Later the Turks captured it and Cervantes was a prisoner here – the tale in *Don Quixote* of the captive may relate his experiences as a Turkish prisoner. The entrance is at the NE wall and the fort is open from 1000–1600 hours.

PORT LONGOS

On the SE end of Nisis Sapientza (Sapienza Island) there is the deserted bay of Port Longos. The lighthouse is conspicuous from some distance off. A fish farm now occupies the E side of the bay, but there is still room for 3 or 4 yachts to anchor. Anchor in the N or S of the bay in 5–6 metres on a sandy bottom. Good shelter although strong easterlies send a swell in and there can be gusts off the land with the prevailing wind.

The lighthouse can be reached by a track from the bay and is now surrounded by an impressive bank of solar cells. Greece was comparatively late in modernising its lights and as a consequence was able to bypass other outmoded 'modern' methods and convert its lights (which used to be mostly powered by bottled gas) to solar power.

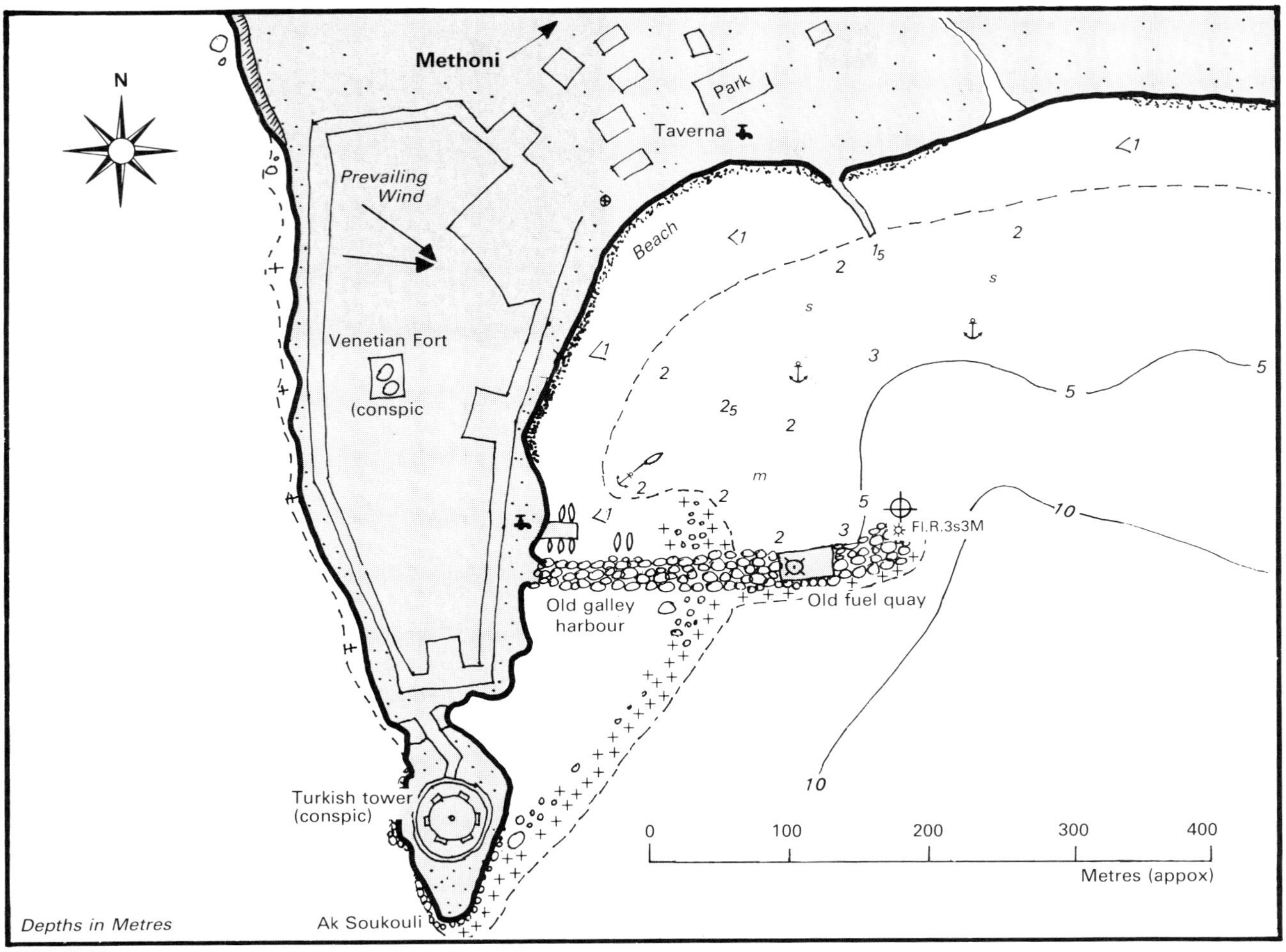

METHONI
36°48′·7N 21°42′·2E (Fl.R.3s3M)

Nisis Sapientza. Port Longos looking NNE from the lighthouse.
Note fish farm on the E side of the bay. *Neville Bulpitt*

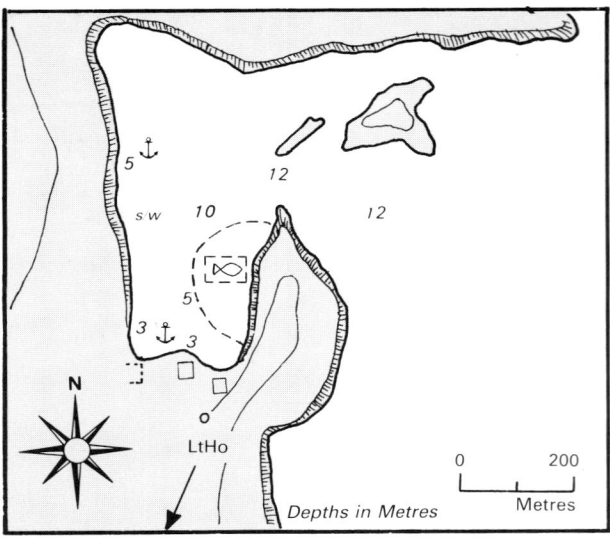

PORT LONGOS
36°45'·5N 21°42'E

NISIS SKHIZA

The S end of the island is a prohibited area. The air force use it for bombing practice and unless you happen to get a thrill out of F.111s approaching at masthead height on a bombing run, it is wise to keep well clear of the whole island. And yes, they do use real bombs and rockets.

FINAKUNDA

A small harbour in Ormos Finakunda lying approximately 5 miles E of Ak Karsi on Sapientza. Once into the large bay the village around the edge of the beach is easily identified. A church on the headland sheltering the harbour is conspicuous. The rough stone breakwater will be seen closer in. There are no lights. With the prevailing wind funnelled W there is often a considerable swell rolling across the entrance to the harbour.

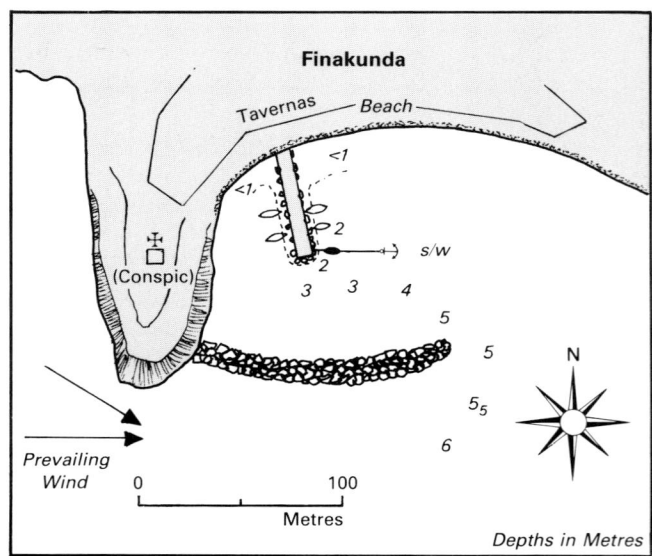

FINAKUNDA

Ak Akritas, the western entrance point to Messiniakos Kolpos, looking W.

Berth bows-to the end of the pier or anchor off under the shelter of the breakwater. Good shelter from the prevailing W winds but open to the S.

Ashore provisions are available and there are numerous tavernas. The once tranquil fishing village has been somewhat shattered by the arrival of a water sports centre, but retains a likable character. The setting is wonderful with the village huddled around the beach under a low rocky bluff and a fertile hinterland.

PORT MARATHO

A small inlet 3½ miles NW of Ak Akritas. The inlet is difficult to identify from the distance, but the beach around its head will be seen between the rocky sides to the cove. Care is needed of a group of rocks awash off the N side of the entrance. Anchor in 2–4 metres on mud and sand, good holding. Reasonable shelter from westerlies and from the N–E winds which sometimes blow out of Kolpos Messiniakos.

KORONI (Coron)
Admiralty chart no. 719

Approach

Conspicuous The fort atop the headland is conspicuous from the N and S. From the N the buildings of Koroni village under the castle are conspicuous. From the S the buildings of the town on the crown of the hill and around the bay to the S are conspicuous. From the S the harbour will not be seen until around Ak Livadhia.

By night Use the light on Ak Livadhia (Fl.1·5s4M) and the light on the end of the harbour breakwater (Fl.R.1·5s3M).

Mooring

Anchor in 2–5 metre depths on the W side of the bay – the depths come up slowly so you can usually potter in until satisfied and then anchor. The bottom is mostly mud, sand and weed, good holding. However large boulders (I mean large) litter the bottom in places and care should be taken not to snag one of these. Although there are 2 metre depths

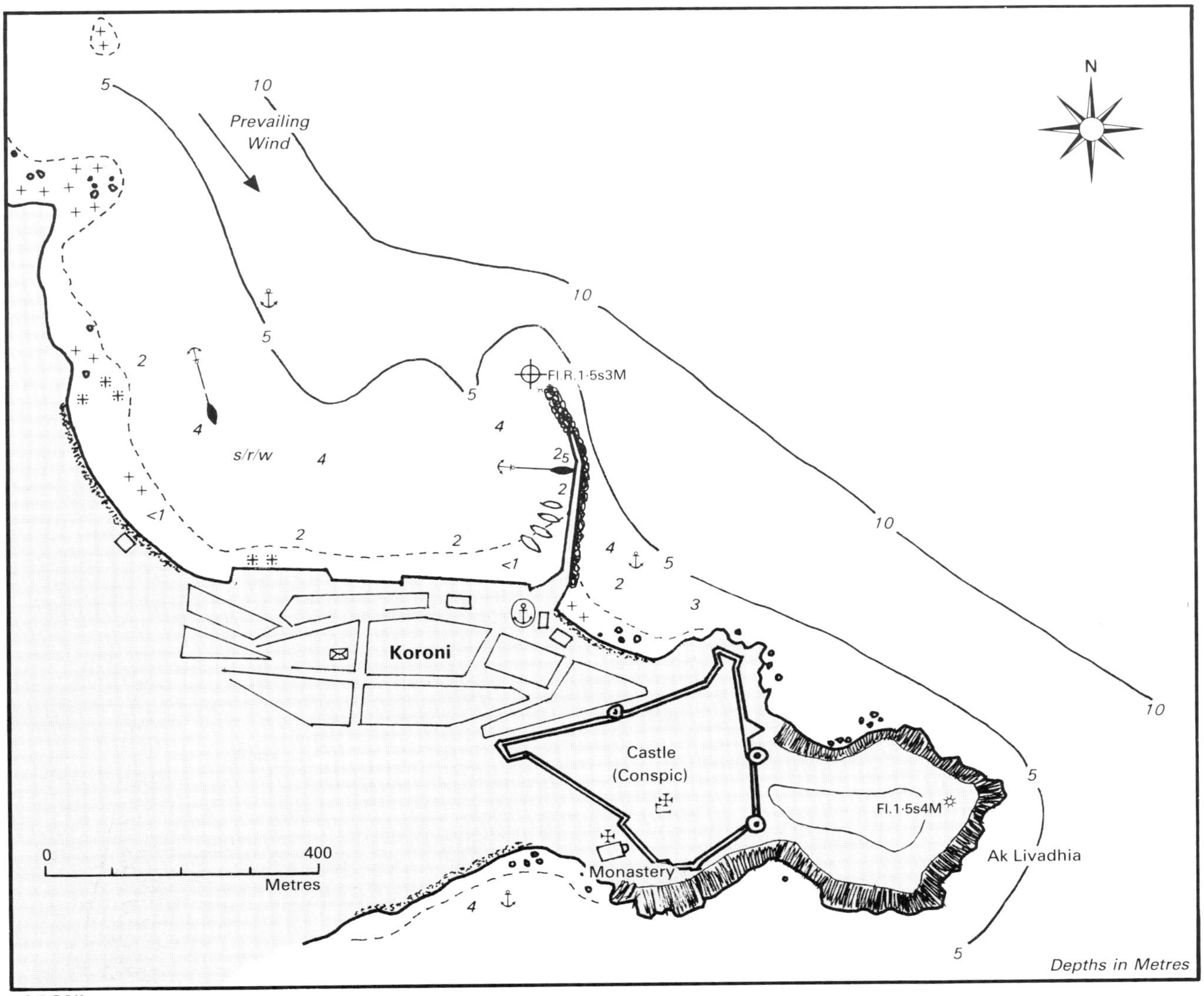

N

10
Prevailing
Wind

5

10

10

5

⊕ Fl.R.1·5s3M

s/r/w

<1

⊠ **Koroni**

⊕

Castle
(Conspic)

Fl.1·5s4M ☼

Ak Livadhia

Monastery

0 ————————— 400
Metres

Depths in Metres

KORONI
36°48′·1N 21°57′·6E (Fl.R.1·5s3M)

Koroni harbour looking from the town quay.

at the extremity of the concrete walkway on the mole where a yacht can moor bows-to this is not advised as the prevailing wind normally blows onto here and the bottom is littered with permanent moorings.

Shelter Good shelter from the prevailing wind which normally blows across the headland from the S or off the hills from the NW–W. At night a NE wind may blow which can be uncomfortable but rarely dangerous.

Alternative anchorages
1. In calm weather or light westerlies a yacht can anchor off on the E side of the harbour breakwater. This is an idyllic place under the bastions of the castle.
2. A yacht can anchor off on the S side of the headland ending in Ak Livadhies. The beach stretching around the coast from here is wonderful and popular with the locals in the summer.

Facilities

Water Not easily available. Can be delivered by tanker.
Fuel 1½km out of the village.

Koroni harbour looking NW from the Venetian castle.

Provisions Good shopping in the village.
Eating out Good tavernas around the waterfront.
Good *ouzeries*.
Other PO. OTE. Bank. Greek gas and *Camping Gaz*.
Regular bus service to Kalamata.

General

Built on the steep slopes under and partly inside the
Venetian fort, Koroni is an attractive town with some
fine old houses. The town acquired the name Korone
(corrupted to Coron) via migrants from ancient
Korone, now Petalidhion. The Venetians rightly
perceived that the headland was the ideal site for a
fort to defend their trade route around the
Peloponnese. Much of it is still largely intact and
incorporates bits of ancient masonry from nearby
Asine. The fort, entered through the massive
gateway at the eastern end of the village (follow the
road up from the harbour mole), is a wonderfully
tranquil place much overgrown and now mostly
occupied by a monastery. This fort was the other
second 'eye of the Republic' after Methoni.

The harbour front, though a bit smelly in places
from the sewerage emptying into it, is alive at night
with the locals promenading and a few tourists
stuffing themselves at the tavernas – there are several
good *ouzeries* specialising in charcoal-grilled octopus.

The castle at Koroni, the Venetians called it 'the eye of the
Republic' (Methoni was the 'other eye'), looking from the
harbour.

128

Koroni to Petalidhion

The coast between Koroni and Petalidhion is pleasantly wooded and there are a number of attractive bays with sandy beaches where a yacht can anchor in settled weather. In Homeric times this was part of ancient Messene and later was conquered by the Spartans. Many of the Messenians fled to Sicily around about this time. Their descendants captured Zancle, renaming it Messana, hence modern Messina and the Messina Strait.

PETALIDHION (Petalidi)
Admiralty chart no. 682

An attractive sheltered bay in the NW corner of the gulf. A rough mole has been built a short distance out from the sand spit in a NE direction making the bay safe from all but strong NE and E winds. A church, a white two-storeyed building, and the light structure are conspicuous. Anchor in 2–4 metre depths where convenient – good holding in sand.

Fuel and water in the town. Good shopping and tavernas. The old village on the edge of a sandy beach is attractive and well worth a visit.

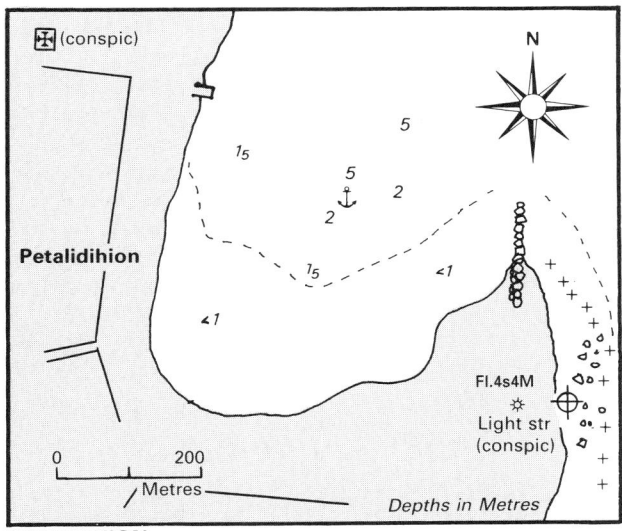

PETALIDHION
36°57′·6N 21°56′·2E (Fl.4s4M)

KALAMATA (Kalami, Kalamon)
Admiralty chart no. 2404
Imray-Tetra chart no. G15

Approach
Straightforward by day and night.
Conspicuous The cluster of buildings of the small city is conspicuous. The exact location of the harbour is difficult to see from the distance but closer in a large flour mill at the W end of the harbour and the harbour breakwater will be seen.
By night Use the light on Ak Kitries (Fl(2)12s6M) and the lights at the entrance: Fl.R.1·5s3M and Fl.G.1·5s3M. The inner jetty is lit: Q.G.1M. The lights at the entrance are difficult to make out against the loom of the lights behind, especially the bright lights of the funfair behind the harbour.

Mooring
Go alongside on the W side of the basin. The only problem with the basin is that the quay is quite high and it can be difficult to get on and off the boat.
Shelter Excellent all-round shelter.
Authorities A port of entry: port police, customs, and immigration are close to the quay in the basin.

Facilities
Water On the W quay in the basin or from a cafe on the W side of the basin.
Fuel Close to the quay. Can be delivered by mini-tanker.
Repairs There is little in the way of dedicated yacht repair facilities, but there are workshops in the city for mechanical, engineering, electrical, and basic wood repairs. Good hardware shops.
Provisions Excellent shopping for all provisions. A large supermarket close to the basin.

The entrance to Kalamata harbour looking NW.

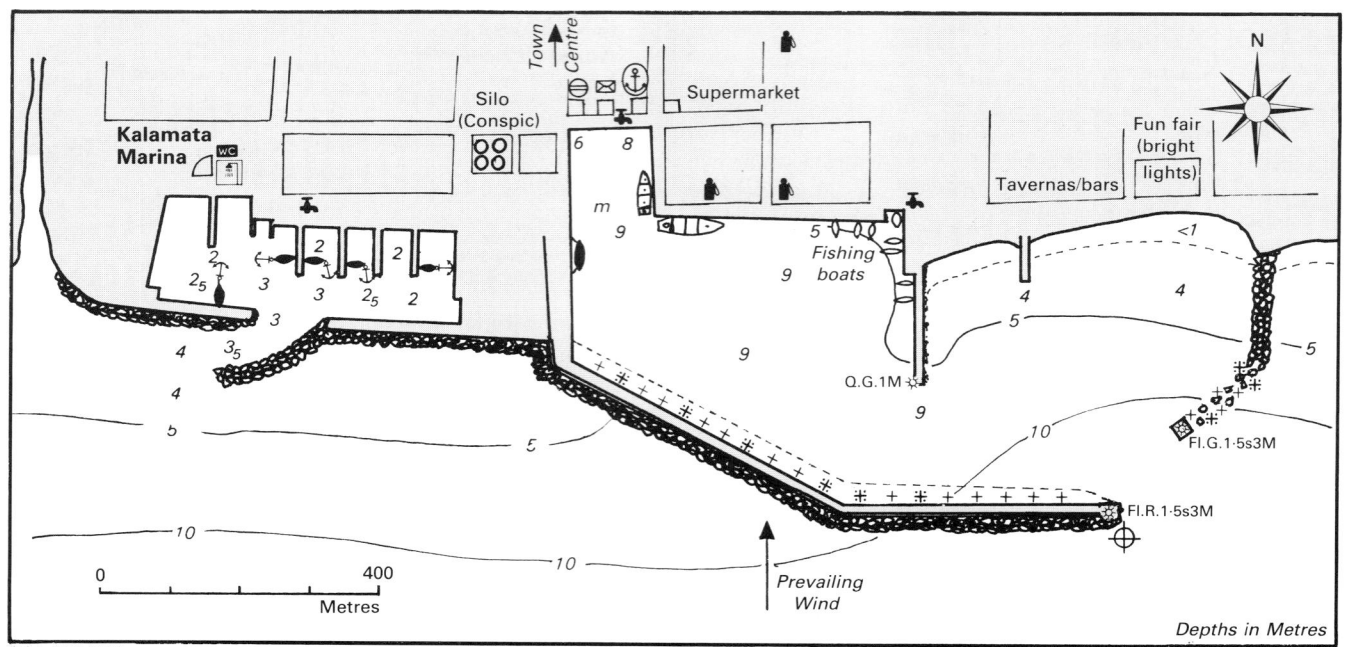

KALAMATA
37°01′·3N 22°07′·2E (Fl.R.3M)

Eating out Excellent tavernas nearby. Good fresh fish at a reasonable price is often available. Good *ouzeries* and local tavernas close to the basin.

Other PO. OTE. Banks. Greek gas and *Camping Gaz*. (from the service station E of the basin). Hire cars and motorbikes. Buses to Athens and most destinations around the Peloponnese. Internal flights and some international flights.

Note A regular bus service operates past the harbour into the centre of town – Bus No.1.

General

Kalamata was once the principal port of the Peloponnese, but now its commercial traffic is much diminished. The harbour and town are more undistinguished than unattractive. The recent earthquake here caused much damage and consequently parts of the town have an abandoned appearance while the rest is undergoing reconstruction.

There are all sorts of surprises in the town. From the basin if you walk straight up from the W corner you will come to a park you can walk through nearly into the middle of town. The park incorporates the old railway station and on the tracks around it are numerous restored locomotives and carriages from all ages – a must for railway buffs and a pleasant walk into town for the mildly curious.

Kalamata was the capital for the Franks when they controlled the area and the redoubtable Guillaume de Villehardouin (1218–1287) was born and died here – above the town are the remains of the castle he built though most of what remains is later modifications and additions from the Venetians. Modern Kalamata was built by the French in the 19th century though most of the old buildings from this period have decayed. Kalamata is the nearest safe harbour to Messene and the safest harbour for visiting Mistra although Yithion is also suitable.

Weather note

In the late summer there are frequently black clouds over the plain behind Kalamata and over the Taiyetos and the Mani. More often than not these come to nothing even though they look threatening, but on occasion there will be some rain and an associated squall. The locals in Kalamata say their summer begins in May and ends in the middle of August.

The weather over the land sometimes affects the weather further out over Messiniakos Kolpos and there may be squalls in the gulf. Normally the prevailing wind blows from the W into the bottom of the gulf and then curves to blow from the SW and finally from the S at Kalamata.

The lighthouse on Ak Kitries looking NE.

KALAMATA MARINA
Imray-Tetra chart no. G15

A new yacht marina has been built immediately W of Kalamata harbour. At the time of writing the basic structure is in place, but it remains for the ancillary facilities to be completed.

Approach
The marina lies immediately W of Kalamata harbour. The entrance is difficult to make out from the distance as the breakwaters overlap giving the impression of a solid rock wall. Closer in the entrance will be seen. There are no lights at present.

Mooring
Go alongside one of the concrete jetties where convenient. Laid moorings are to be installed at a later date and yachts will then go stern-to or bows-to. Good all-round shelter although strong southerlies could cause a surge in here.

Facilities
Water on the jetties. When complete there will be water and electricity at every berth. Toilets and showers to be installed.

General
The new marina is basically complete, but requires all the finishing touches to make it work. The timetable for completion is difficult to ascertain although the authorities maintain it will be 'next year'. It remains to be seen just when the building site is transformed into the yacht marina the locals have been promised.

ORMOS KITRIES
On the N side of Ak Kitries there is the large bay of Kitries itself. The bay provides good shelter from the prevailing southerlies and reasonable shelter from northerlies which do not normally blow home. Anchor off the beach where convenient.

Tavernas ashore. The slopes around the bay are terraced and planted in olive and citrus with villas dotted around the beach and lower slopes. It is an entrancing spot and in settled weather can be used as an overnight anchorage.

KARDAMILA
An open anchorage lying about 5 miles SSE of Ak Kitries. There is a small harbour off the village but there are barely 2 metre depths in the entrance and 1–1.5 metre depths inside. Anchor off the mole under the islet in 4–8 metres or in the bay to the S. There is nearly always some swell in here making it uncomfortable and in unsettled weather it would be untenable.

Numerous tavernas in the village and good shopping for provisions ashore. Fuel available in the village.

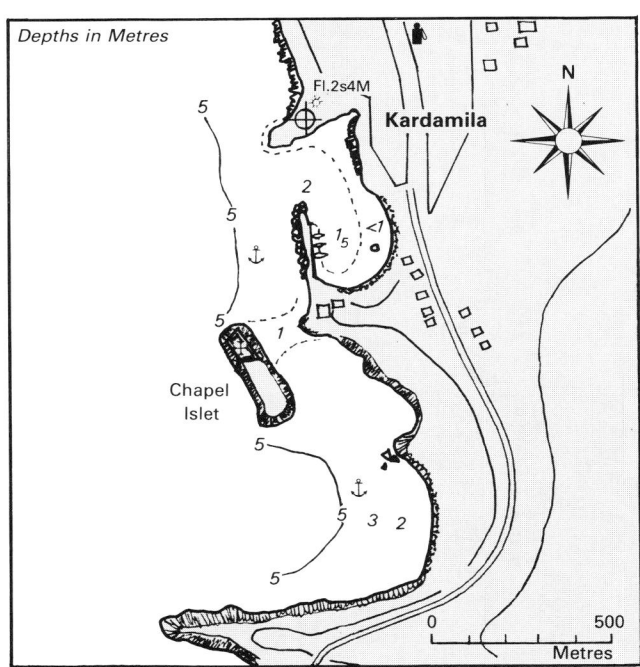

KARDAMILA
36°53'N 22°14'E (Fl.2s4M)

Kardamila looking SW from the village across the harbour to the islet.

The village is an attractive place, all creepers and tile roofs, though somewhat overrun with visitors with a professorial gait, in search of inspiration from the village's literary inhabitant (though I suspect he escapes from the summer visitors), Patrick Leigh Fermor. For wonderful writing on Greece and all sorts of esoteric information difficult to locate elsewhere, Leigh Fermor's two books on Greece, *Mani* and *Roumeli*, should go on everybody's priority list of books to read.

Approaches to Limeni looking ESE.

PORT LIMENI (Ormos Limenion)

Approach

This large bay lies 18 miles SE of Ak Kitries. The bay is difficult to identify from the distance, but once up to the entrance the ravine splitting the land at the head of it stands out well and closer in the houses around the bay will be seen. The neo-Maniote village above Limeni and the church by the light structure on the S entrance point are conspicuous.

By night The S side of the entrance is lit (Fl.1·5s6M) but a night entrance is not advised.

Mooring

Anchor on the E side of Limeni cove and take a long line ashore. It is quite deep here and you will have to drop anchor in 10–12 metres. The bottom is sand and weed with a scattering of rocks over it. In settled weather the prevailing wind tends to blow in only lightly in the summer and though it is a little uncomfortable, it is quite tenable.

An alternative anchorage is tucked into the NE corner of the bay. A short stone breakwater runs out from the coast but the small amount of space behind it is occupied by local fishing boats.

Facilities

Water from local sources ashore. Several tavernas at Limeni and around the beach at the head.

General

The large bay lies approximately halfway down the W side of the Mani peninsula, ideally placed to break the voyage between Kalamata and Porto Kayio. The fact that the bay is open to westerlies puts most people off, but for those willing to chance it, and in

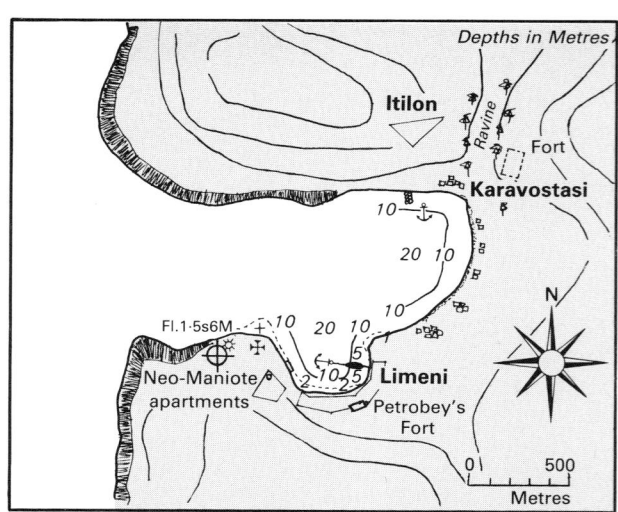

LIMENI
36°40'·6N 22°22'E (Fl.1·5s6M)

Limeni looking N.

132

the summer you will have no problems most of the time, this is a wonderful place in a magnificent setting. The small hamlet at Limeni has a little tourism in the summer, but nothing overwhelming. The tavernas serve simple but good fare with views out over the cove and the bay.

There are two architectural anomalies in the bay. The first is the Maniote village on the hillside above Limeni which is not a Maniote village but a hotel and apartment complex built in neo-Maniote style – only the large windows and the large building at the rear give it away. The second is what appears to be a reproduction of a Scottish Presbyterian church in the village which is in fact a fortress built by Petros Mavromichalis, a clan leader from Areopolis on the hilltop.

DIROS (Dyros)

A bay about 3 miles S of Limeni. The entrance is difficult to make out from the distance. A tall tower in Pirgos village N of the bay is conspicuous, but then there are a lot of towers along this stretch of coast. The shelter from the prevailing winds is poor, but in the morning calm a yacht can put in here to visit the Caves of Diros. Anchor in the NE corner or in the SE corner where a few local boats are kept on moorings. The caves and the reception buildings are housed on the SE side of the bay.

The caves are spectacular – one of those sights that stays with you a long time and which few adjectives adequately describe. The viewing of the caves is strictly controlled and it is best to go early before the coaches and cars of other sightseers arrive. The ticket booth is a short distance up the road from the caves. A guide punts and pushes a flat-bottomed boat around the subterranean passages which literally drip with stalactites – unfortunately in recent years the guides have taken to racing through the caves as quickly as possible and a protest is in order if you receive such treatment. The interconnected passages are lit for the convenience of tourists and although the tour is an extensive one, you emerge with the feeling that there are many more passages trailing off into an inky blackness than you have seen from the boat.

Although I am not a speleologist, caves have always fascinated me and I have toured and explored a good number. The Caves of Diros rank with the best of them. Between Limeni and Diros and indeed further S of Diros there are a great many caves in the cliffs and it would appear that this whole area is riddled with them. If it is too rough to anchor at Diros, go to Yithion and take a bus from there.

At Diros there is a small PO and money exchange booth, a bar, café, and taverna.

MEZAPO (Ormos Mezapos)

A large bay with the village of Mezapos in the SE corner some 10 miles S of Limeni. The vast mountainous bulk of Capo Grosso just S is difficult to miss. On the thin peninsula partially sheltering the bay (Tigani = frying pan, because of its shape) the remains of a fort will not be seen until close in. Once at the entrance to the bay the houses of Mezapo can be seen.

Anchor off the small harbour and take a long line ashore. Very small yachts may find a space in the harbour though care is needed as the bottom is uneven. The bay affords some shelter from the prevailing winds but at night a strong katabatic wind may blow in from a northerly direction making it uncomfortable and possibly untenable. Tavernas ashore and limited provisions are available.

The small fishing harbour under vertical cliffs is a spectacular spot. Mezapo for a long time had a reputation as a local pirating and smuggling village and it continues to give that impression. Tim Severin on his voyage to retrace the route of Odysseus identified the place with the harbour of the Laestrygones, the cannibal giants who threw stones down on Odysseus and his men, killing many of them and sinking all but the galley of Odysseus. Formerly Bonifacio on Corsica was identified with the harbour of the Laestrygones. Make up your own mind on the matter.

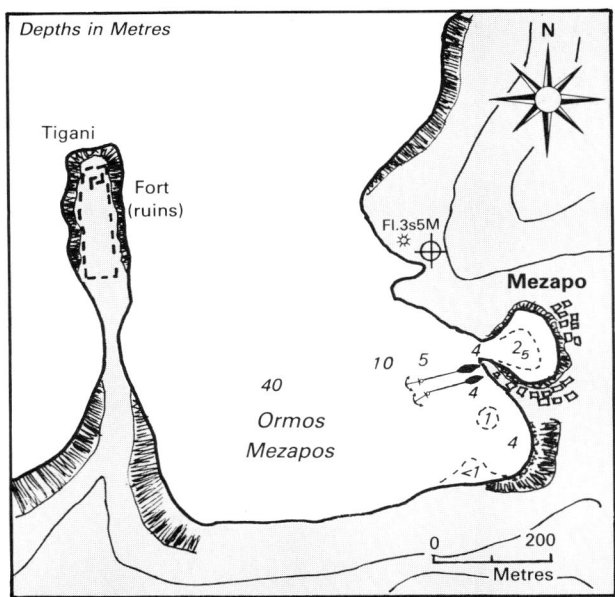

MEZAPO
36°32'·8N 22°23'·2E (Fl.3s5M)

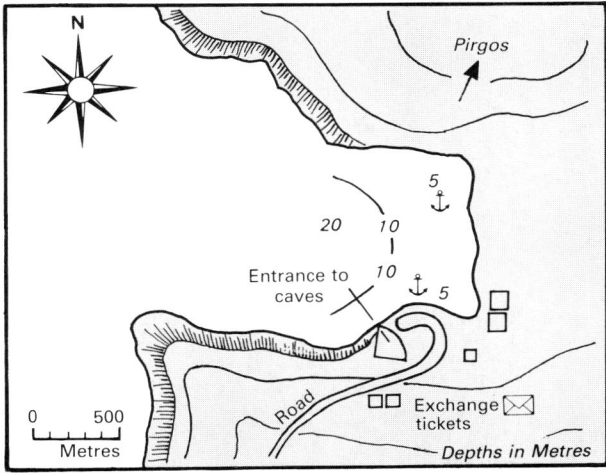

DIROS

Ak Tainaron and lighthouse looking W.

CAPO GROSSO

Immediately SW of Mezapo lies the vast bulk of Capo Grosso, a huge precipitous mass of rock that is unmistakable once seen – if any large cape should be called 'gross' it is this one. The cliffs rise sheer from the sea to 250 metres (800ft) and more, split by ravines and peppered with caves. Some of the caves have been walled up and it is said these contained the wealth of the Mezapo pirate families, but you would need to be a rock climber to get to them.

On the S side of Grosso just before Yerolimena there is a huge natural cave in the cliffs, easily identified from seawards, and this cave would be a natural choice for the ancients' entrance to Hades said to be situated at Tainaron (Matapan).

YEROLIMENA

A bay tucked in S of Capo Grosso. There is a small quay for fishing boats where two or three small yachts could berth with care. The bay is open W and S and invariably has some swell rolling into it. It should not be relied upon for shelter in any weather though it is possible to use it in calm weather. At one time this was the principal ferry port for the Mani.

Lakonikos Kolpos
(Gulf of Lakonika, Gulf of Kolokythia)

Around Ak Tainaron (Cape Matapan) lies the steep-sided and heavily indented Lakonikos Kolpos. Bordered on the west by the Taiyetos and on the east by the Parnon, it is a forbidding place although the weather at the head of the gulf is often more settled than around the southern end. On the eastern side Nisos Elafonisos must be rounded before Ak Maleas is encountered.

Now, as in ancient times, the channel between Ak Maleas and the island of Kithera is an important channel for ships leaving and entering the Aegean. The chances are you will encounter a fair number of large ships in this channel a sharp lookout must be kept.

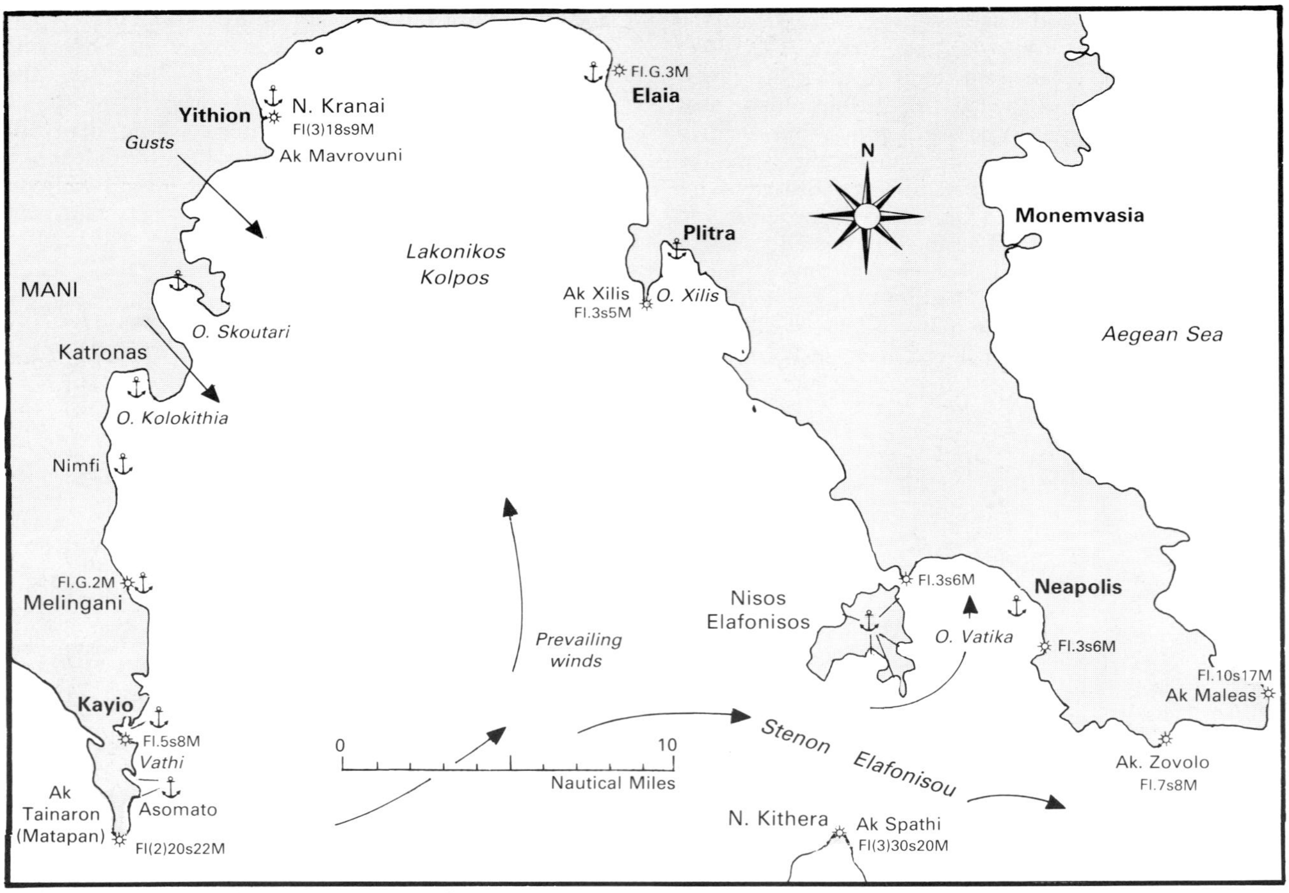

LAKONIKOS KOLPOS (GULF OF LAKONIKA)

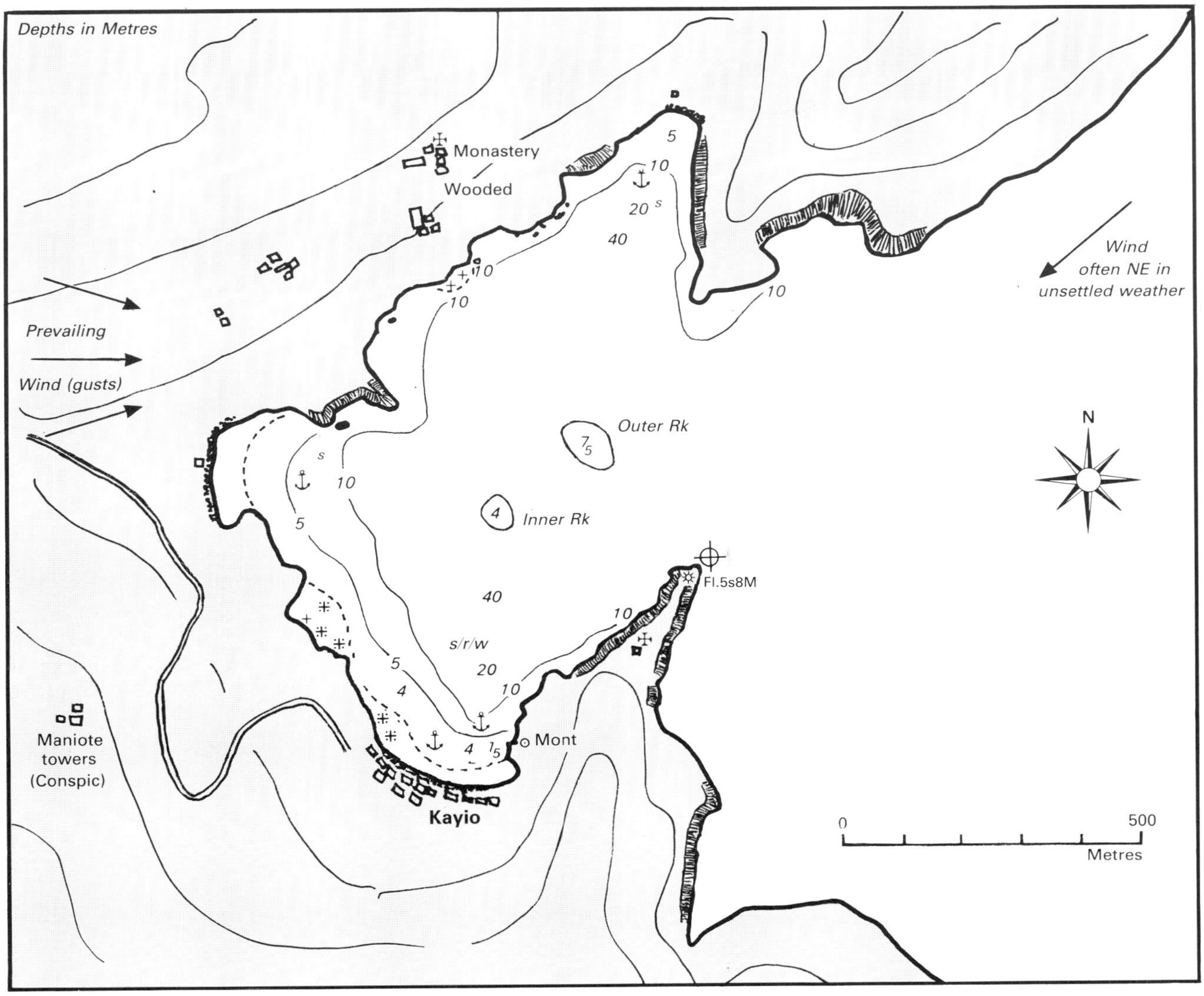

Depths in Metres

✠ Monastery
Wooded

Prevailing

Wind (gusts)

5
⚓ 10
20 ˢ
40

10

10
✠ 10
10

N

Outer Rk
7
5

⚓
s
10
4 Inner Rk
5

40

⊕
※
Fl.5s8M

✳
+ ✳
✳
✠
5

s/r/w

10

20

10

4
✳
5

Maniote
towers
(Conspic)

✳
⚓
4 5 ○ Mont

Kayio

0   500

Metres

LIMIN KAYIO
36°25′·6N 22°29′·4E (Fl.8M)

Porto Kayio looking ENE. *Nigel Patten.*

Light

Approaches to Porto Kayio looking WSW.

The lighthouse on Ak Maleas.

Ak Maleas is a mountainous headland some 780 metres high. It has a formidable reputation: mariners leaving Greece coined the saying: 'Round Malea, forget your native country': it was the *Formidatum Maleae caput* of the Roman poet Statius; and the cape where Odysseus was blown south to the land of the Lotus Eaters...

'I might have made it safely home, that time, but as I came round Malea the current took me out to sea, and from the north a fresh gale drove me on, past Kythera.'
Odyssey

Today, even with the aid of weather forecasts, it pays to treat the cape with respect.

PORTO ASOMATO AND ORMOS VATHI
Admiralty chart no. 712

These two inlets on the E side of Ak Tainaron are suitable overnight anchorages in calm weather. Both are subject to severe gusts with W–SW winds and are open to the SE whence a heavy swell rolls in. Only one mile N is the better shelter of Limin Kayio.

It was off here on 29 March 1941 that the British fleet from Alexandria surprised the Italian fleet and sank five Italian ships for the loss of only one plane. Despite this success the Axis powers soon pushed down through Greece and two months later Crete fell and British troops were hurriedly evacuated to Alexandria.

PORTO KAYIO (Kaio)

Approach
Conspicuous The Maniote towers of the two small villages on the hilltops and the ruined monastery on the NW side are conspicuous. Closer in a small church on the S entrance point and the light structure will be seen. The houses of the hamlet will not be seen until into the bay.

By night Use the light on Ak Tainaron (Fl(2)20s22M) and the light at the entrance (Fl.5s8M).

Dangers With strong westerlies there can be strong gusts out of the bay and off the high land in the approaches.

Mooring
With the normal W–SW wind anchor in 4–10 metres in the S cove of the bay. The gusts off the hills are not violent or frequent here. The holding in the S cove is not always to be relied upon. The bottom is hard sand with weed and some rocks. It is also possible to anchor and take a long line ashore to the quay in the SE corner where you are nicely tucked into the coast with good shelter from E–NE winds. Occasionally strong NE winds may blow in unsettled weather and in that case the N cove is the best place to be. Here the bottom comes up very quickly from 30 metres to the shore so there is really only space for 2 or 3 yachts to anchor in reasonable depths. The bottom here is sand and weed, good holding.

Shelter Good shelter from the prevailing W–SW winds. Good shelter in the N cove from NE winds.

Facilities
Water from local sources. Several tavernas in the summer. Fruit and vegetables from a small truck that calls at the bay.

General
The bay was called Psamathous in ancient times and Porto Quaglio by the Venetians, from which the present name probably comes – 'Quaglio' means quail and apparently great numbers of quails were caught here and salted for export. The bay was used by the Venetians, the Turks, and by various Maniote pirates of whom the most famous was Katsonis – a monument to the freedom fighter-cum-pirate stands near the quay in the SE corner.

In 1980 there were only a few families including the fishermen living in the small hamlet in the S of the bay. Since then the summer arrival of yachts on passage around the Peloponnese and numbers of camper-vans has rejuvenated the hamlet.

ORMOS MELINGANI

Five miles N of Porto Kayio is the bay of Melingani offering indifferent shelter. It is easily identified by a few houses at its head and the white light structure (Fl.G.1·5s2M) on the N side of the bay.

PORTO NIMFI (Nymphi)

Four miles N of Melingani is a narrow inlet open to the E. The village is situated on the hill above the inlet. Subject to squalls with W winds.

KOTRONAS

A village at the N end of Ormos Kolokithia. Severe squalls come down the valley with W winds.

ORMOS SKOUTARI (Scutari Bay)

Admiralty chart no. 712

The large bay between Ak Stavri and Ak Pagania. There are several anchorages around the large bay which can be used in settled weather.

Skoutari Anchor off the beach below the village or in the rocky cove by a prominent cave in the N. There can often be severe gusts down off the high land onto these anchorages.

Fisherman's Cove A cove with a beach at the head. Depending on the severity of the gusts off the land, this is an attractive anchorage open W–NW.

Storm Cove A cove immediately S of Fisherman's Cove. Reasonable shelter tucked into here.

Weather note

The severity of gusts off the land in the vicinity of Skoutari varies greatly. Sometimes there may be next to no wind at all and another time there can be severe gusts. The latter usually arrive in the afternoon and continue until dusk. If on passage between Yithion and Melingani exercise some caution or leave early in the morning. The two last mentioned coves afford good shelter from the NE winds which sometimes blow in the gulf.

Approaches to Yithion looking NNW. Note the snow on the Taiyetos behind.

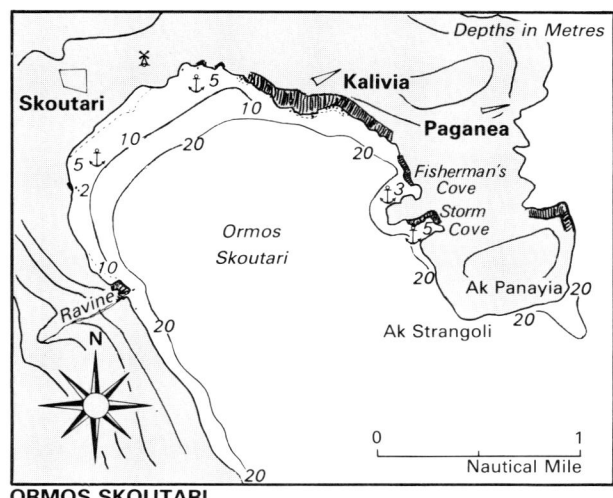

ORMOS SKOUTARI
36°39′N 22°31′E

YITHION (Githion, Gytheoin)

Approach

Conspicuous From the SE, especially if you are approaching at dusk, it is difficult to pick out just where Yithion town is. By day the village of Mavrovouni atop Ak Mavrovouni and the tall white octagonal lighthouse on Nisis Kranai are conspicuous. From the S the buildings of Yithion town are not visible until you round Ak Mavrovouni.

By night Use the light on Nisis Kranai (Fl(3)18s9M) and the light on the extremity of the mole (F.R.3M).

Dangers Care needs to be taken of gusts off the high land in the approaches.

Mooring

Go stern-to or bows-to the mole. Good depths and good holding in mud.

Shelter Good from the prevailing winds. With strong winds from the NW (not common in my experience) there may be strong gusts off the Taiyetos mountains – in this case the best place is bows-to the W quay where you will be held off the quay by the wind. Strong NE winds are reported to cause a surge.

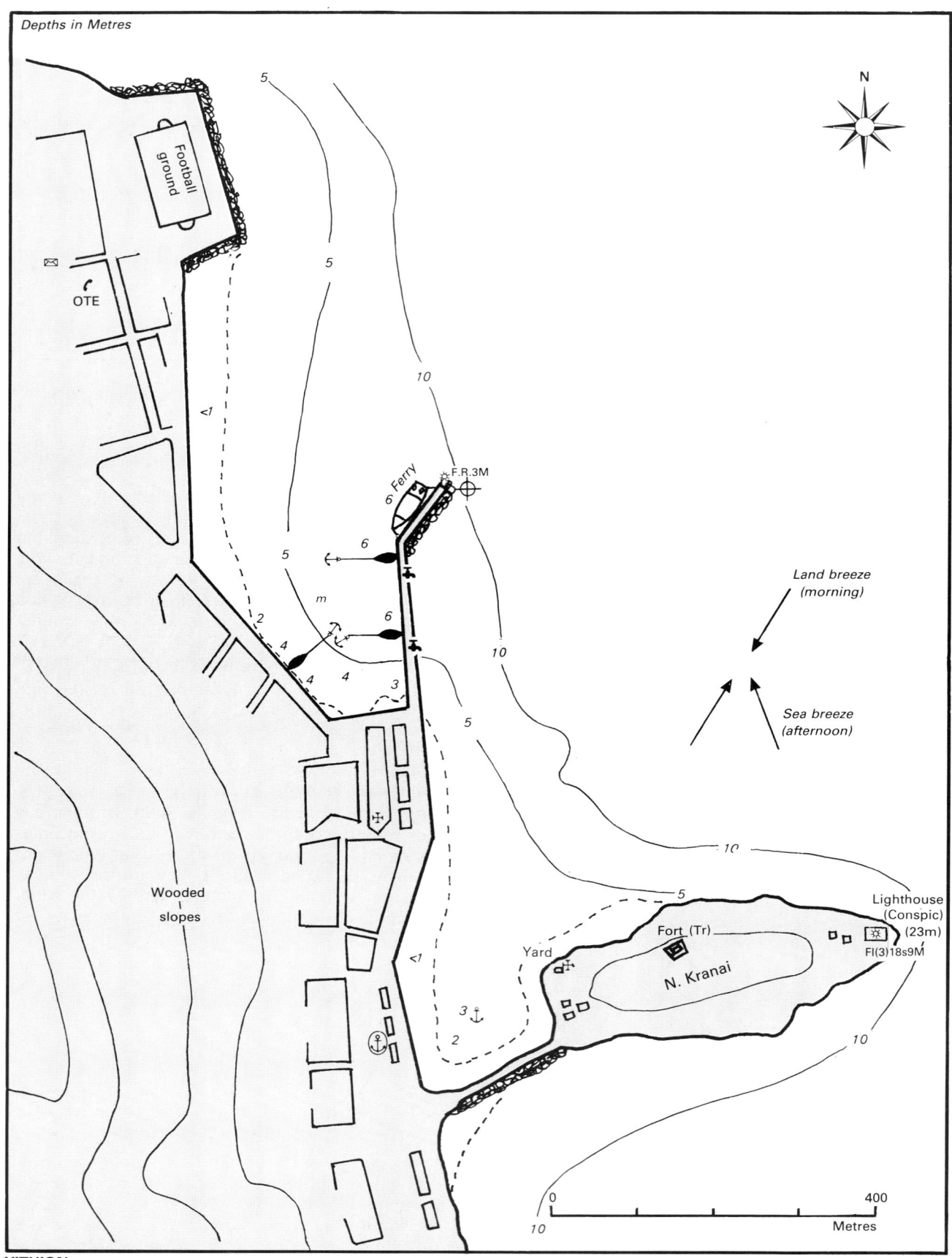

Depths in Metres

Football ground

OTE

5

5

10

Ferry

☀F.R.3M

6

6

5

m

6

2

4

4

4

3

10

10

5

Wooded
slopes

<1

5

Yard

<1

3 ⚓

2

Land breeze
(morning)

Sea breeze
(afternoon)

N. Kranai

Fort (Tr)

Lighthouse
(Conspic)
(23m)
FI(3)18s9M

N

0   400

Metres

10

YITHION
36°45′·4N 22°34′E (F.R.3M)

Authorities Port police and customs.

Note There are plans to build a mole out from the coast to the E to improve the shelter in the harbour.

Facilities

Water On the quay.

Fuel Some distance out of town. A mini-tanker may deliver. A mini-tanker can deliver.

Repairs Limited mechanical repairs.

Provisions Good shopping for all provisions close by.

Eating out Good tavernas nearby including good fish restaurants.

Other PO. OTE. Bank. Greek gas and *Camping Gaz.* Buses to Sparta and Athens. Ferry to Piraeus twice a week calling at Yerolimena, Neapolis, Monemvasia and Kithera.

General

Yithion is seldom visited by yachts yet it is an excellent base for exploring Kolpos Lakonikos and a pleasant low-key place in itself. Yithion itself has a long pedigree: claimed to have been founded by Heracles and Apollo, it has seen Mycenaean and Phoenician colonists and was the chief port of Sparta. With the decline of Sparta, Yithion became the most important town of the Free-Laconian League and later of the Maniotes. Before all this Kranai is the island mentioned by Homer in the *Iliad* where Paris and Helen spent their first night after eloping together

'...when I snatched thee first

From lovely Lacedaemon's vale, put out to sea in hollow ships,

And on Kranai lay with thee upon a couch of love'

Homer *Iliad* Book 3

The result was of course the siege of Troy and the battle of the heroes, not to mention the birth of Greek literature.

Yithion makes a good base for exploring the medieval town of Mistra – a remarkable fortified town of narrow streets crowned by a large castle. It is the completeness and size of the town in a forbidding setting that visually impresses one although here is preserved some of the finest Byzantine architecture. Mistra may be visited by taxi or bus from Yithion.

Yithion looking NE from the slopes behind the town.

ELAIA (Elea)

Across the gulf to the E of Yithion the large village of Elaia is conspicuous.

The small harbour at Elaia offers good all-round protection except from strong NW winds. Moor stern-to the inside of the mole. Water available in the town. Most provisions can be obtained. Bus to Yithion.

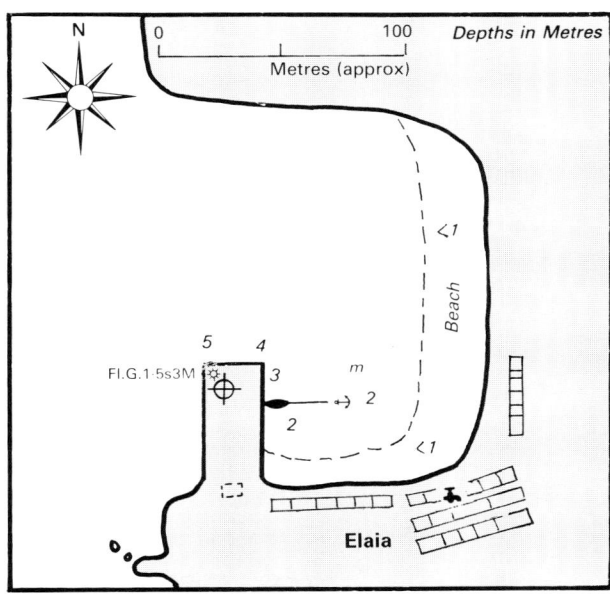

ELAIA
36°44'·6N 22°47'·8E (Fl.G.3M)

ORMOS XILIS AND PLITRA (Xyli Bay, Plythra)

Approach

Conspicuous From the W and S the steep-to craggy Ak Xilis is conspicuous. Nearing Plitra the buildings of the small village and the mole are easily identified.

By night Use the light on Ak Xilis (Fl.3s5M) and the light on the end of the mole (Q.G.3M).

Dangers Caution is called for to avoid the above and below water rocks lying approximately 30 metres N of the extremity of the mole. The rocks are marked by an iron pipe beacon. A night entry is possible, but care must be taken of the rocks N of the mole as the beacon is not lit.

Mooring

Go stern-to or bows-to the outer end of the mole. The bottom is largely rock and there are numerous permanent moorings on the bottom. Care is needed and it may be wise to use a trip-line on the anchor.

Shelter Good protection from all but strong souther-lies although the fishermen say they leave their boats here all year round. With the normal SW wind a limited swell of no consequence creeps around the end of the mole making it a bit uncomfortable.

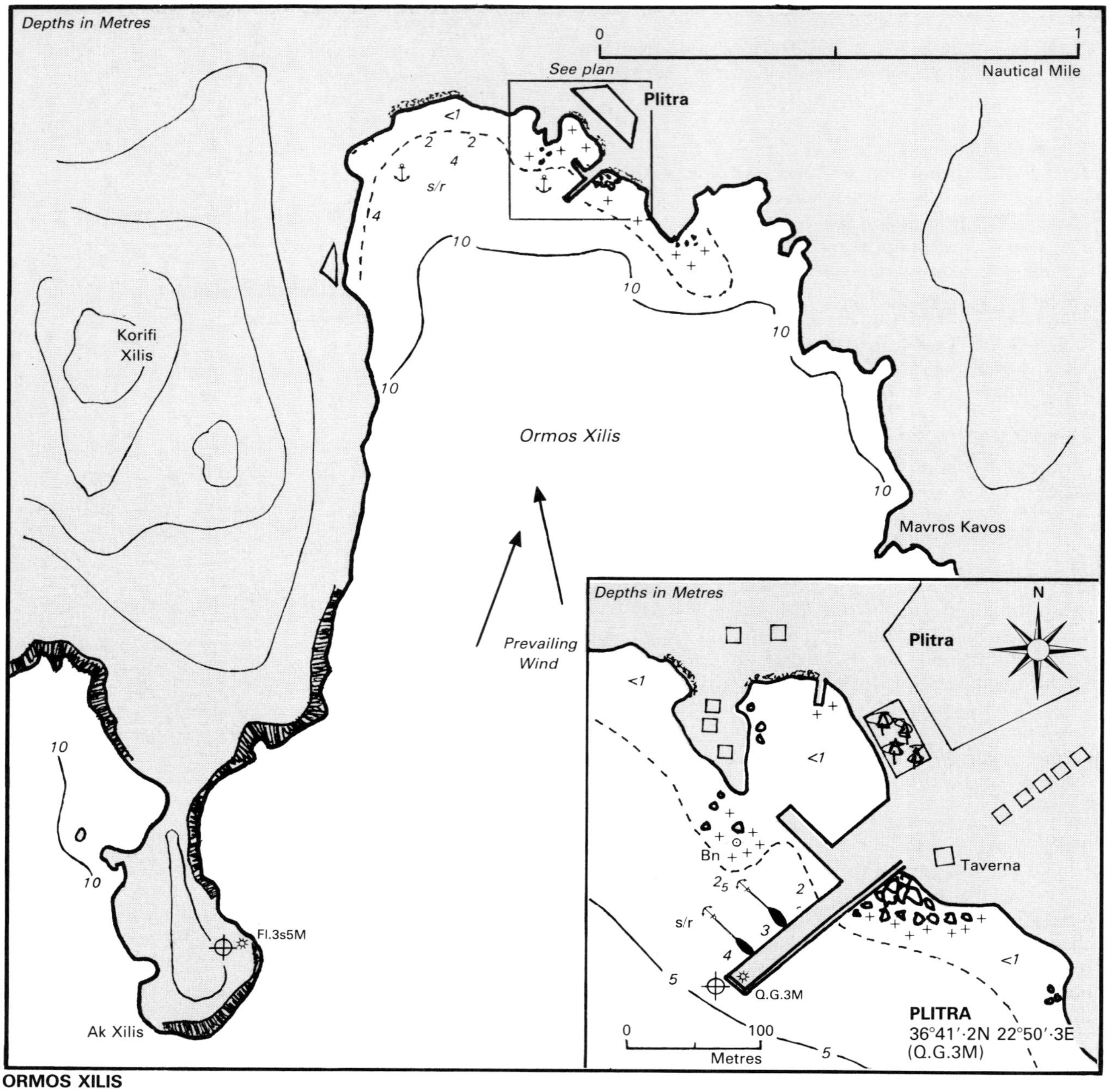

Depths in Metres

0   1

See plan

Plitra

Nautical Mile

Korifi
Xilis

Ormos Xilis

2   4   2

s/r

4

4

10

10

10

10

10

10

Mavros Kavos

*Prevailing
Wind*

10

10

Fl.3s5M

Ak Xilis

Depths in Metres

N

Plitra

<1

<1

<1

Bn

2₅

2

s/r

3

4

5

Q.G.3M

Taverna

PLITRA
36°41'·2N 22°50'·3E
(Q.G.3M)

0   100

Metres

5

ORMOS XILIS
36°39'·4N 22°49E (Fl.3s5M)

Facilities

Water from local sources only. In the summer there are several tavernas around the shore. The nearest village for supplies is 4km away.

General

Plitra is an unprepossessing village but manages to attract a few tourists to its sandy beaches in the summer. It is a pleasant sleepy little place that grows on you. Good snorkelling to be had around the coastline.

Note Some yachts use Arkhangelos in the SE corner of Ormos Xili. It is open N-NW but may be tenable with the prevailing wind which tends to curve and blow in from the W-SW into Ormos Xili.

Ormos Xilis and Plitra looking SE.

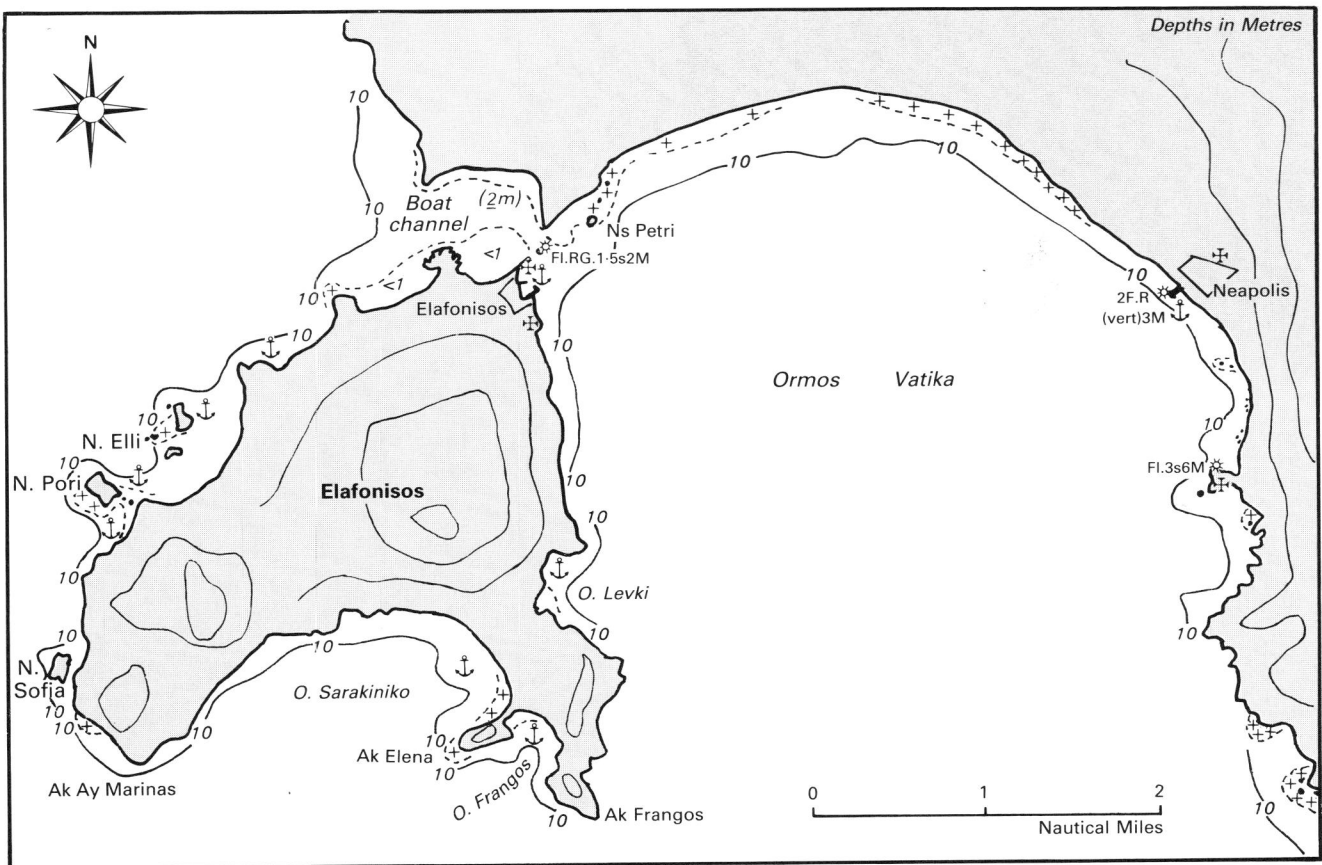

ELAFONISOS AND ORMOS VATIKA

Nisos Elafonisos and channel

Nisos Elafonisos is the island on the N side of the channel between Nisos Kithera and the Peloponnese. It is separated from the Peloponnese by a shallow boat channel that those with iron nerve can negotiate if they so desire. Elafonisos means 'deer island' although nobody, myself included, has ever seen any here. In antiquity there was a trading post here and the island was known as Onugnathos, ass's jaw, which with a little imagination the island can be seen to resemble.

There are a number of anchorages around the island and a small harbour at the village of Elafonisos on the NE corner.

Anchorages around Elafonisos
1. *W coast* On the W coast there are several anchorages in and around Nisis Pori and Nisis Elli. Anchor where convenient on sand.
2. *Ormos Sarakiniko* The large bay on the S of the island. Anchor off the beach on the E side on sand, good holding. Reasonable shelter from the day breeze depending on its strength.
3. *Ormiskos Frangos* The bay immediately E of Sarakiniko. Anchor off the beach on sand. Good shelter and suitable as an overnight anchorage in settled weather.

4. *Ormos Levki* The bay on the E side of the island. It affords good shelter from the prevailing wind. The bottom is sand and rock with good holding reported at the S end of the bay.

The attractions of all these anchorages are wonderful sandy beaches and translucent water in deserted surroundings, although camper vans somehow seem to have penetrated to Sarakiniko and Frangos in the summer.

Weather note
The normal summer breeze is from the W curving up to blow from the S in Ormos Vatika. At night a NE wind may blow and may continue to do so through the day. In unsettled weather care is needed as there can be violent winds around this area.

ELAFONISOS VILLAGE

Approach
Conspicuous From the S the church sitting out in the channel is conspicuous. The houses of the village will also be seen, but the rough stone mole of the harbour will not be seen until closer in.

By night Use the light on the E side of Ormos Vatika (Fl.3s6M) and the light on the beacon (Vrakhos Stavros: Fl.RG.1·5s4M). The harbour entrance is not lit.

The church at Elafonisos village conspicuous from seawards.

Facilities
Water tap near the fishing harbour. Most provisions can be found in the village. Tavernas and bars around the waterfront. OTE. Ferry to the mainland opposite. Ferry to Kithera.

General
The village is a ramshackle sort of place, but convivial. Greek tourists come here and camp on the mainland opposite off the magnificent beach fronted by the turquoise waters of the boat channel. At night the entertainment for the locals and tourists can reach fairly high decibel levels.

ELAFONISOS BOAT PASSAGE
Separating Elafonisos from the Peloponnese is the shallow boat channel which can be seen as the expanse of turquoise water N of Elafonisos village. Passage through the channel is possible for yachts drawing less than 2 metres in calm weather, but with any swell a yacht should go S of the island. It is essential to have someone up front conning you through and a careful eye should be kept on the depth sounder. Even so the passage requires an iron nerve and a calm day. Every feature on the bottom can be clearly identified and the depths are such that you are never out of 2–2·5 metres for nearly a mile.

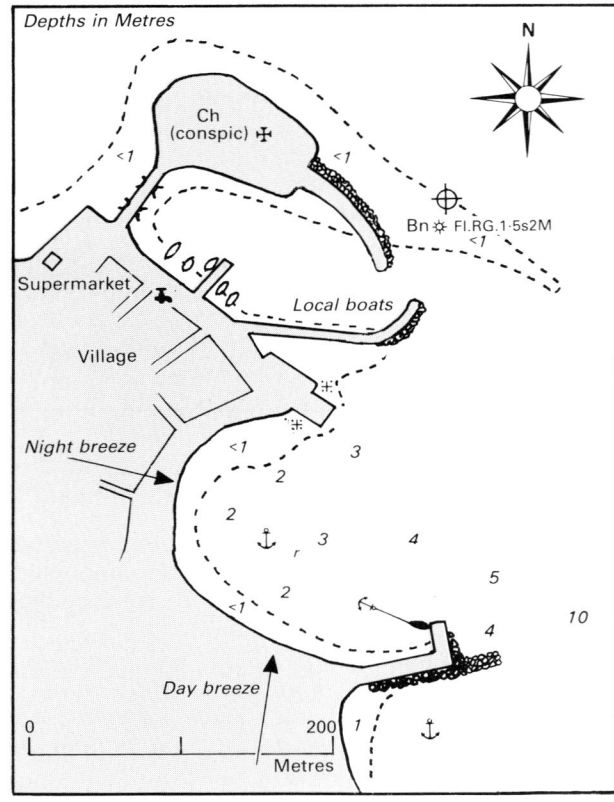

ELAFONISOS VILLAGE
36°30'·8N 22°58'·7E (Fl.RG.2M)

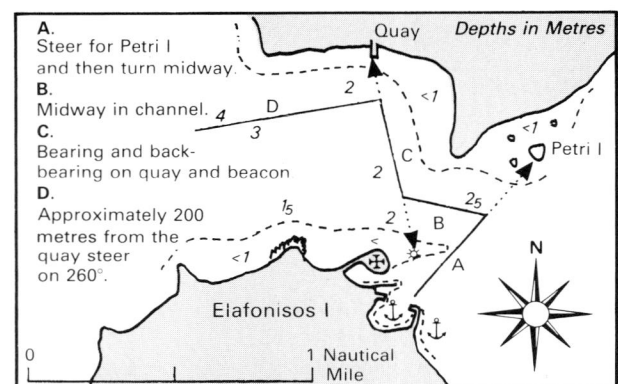

ELAFONISOS BOAT PASSAGE

Mooring
Anchor in the bay. There are a few berths on the mole under the ferry berth but it is better to anchor off. The bottom is rock covered by a minuscule amount of sand, bad holding. Snorkel over your anchor to make sure it has snagged on something and preferably use a fisherman.

Shelter Good shelter from the prevailing winds. The harbour is open E and in strong southerlies I would expect a surge in here.

Note The fishermen's harbour N of the ferry harbour is packed full of local boats.

Ak Ay Ilios, the E entrance point to Ormos Vatika, looking NW.

142

Elafonisos *caïque* harbour.

NEAPOLIS

The large town on the E side of Ormos Vatika is visible from some distance off. A large church is prominent behind the town. A jetty for the ferry extends off the waterfront and a yacht can use this in calm weather. Go alongside or stern or bows-to the NW side. The SE side is used by the ferry and fishing boats. With any swell a yacht should anchor off. With the normal summer winds which are light SW or W it is normally sheltered enough to spend the night here, though it may not be comfortable.

Water and fuel in the town. Good shopping for provisions and numerous tavernas. PO. OTE. Ferry to Piraeus.

Neapolis is an interesting place which has a little local tourism but otherwise functions as the main town for the area. Unfortunately, like Elafonisos, it suffers from high decibel levels.

Nearby the tiny fishing harbour of Neapolis is too small and shallow for a yacht. The entrance is rock-bound with around 1·7m depths in the entrance and less inside. A rock with less than 2 metres over it is reported to lie in the immediate approaches. Not recommended for yachts though very small motorboats drawing less than a metre might find some shelter inside. Extreme care needed here.

Nisos Kithera and Andikithera
(Kythera, Cerigo and Anti-Kithira, Cerigotto, Lious)

Kithera and Andikithira form an island bridge between the Peloponnese and Crete. As a convenient lee or port of refuge the islands have played an important part as stepping-stones on the ancient trade routes around the Peloponnese to the Aegean and east along Crete. Near Avelomona, a small village on the south of Kithera, a Minoan trading post (c.2000–1450 BC) has been excavated. Later the Phoenicians (the island was reputed to be rich in murex from which the Phoenicians extracted their famous purple dye), Mycenaeans, Romans and Venetians used the island.

Kithera has another claim to classical fame and it is that Aphrodite was born here, though other islands, notably Cyprus, also lay claim to the goddess. Her worship was probably introduced to this lonely rocky island by the Phoenicians and when she was later adopted by the Greeks, her birthplace was assumed to be Kithera. This seems as good a place as any to let Lawrence Durrell describe this most human of goddesses:

'Under her title Urania, she stood for pure and ideal love; as Genetrix or Nymphia, she was the protector of lawful marriage and favoured all serious unions; as Pandemos or Porne she was the patron of all prostitutes and favoured all lust and venal love. Everything to do with

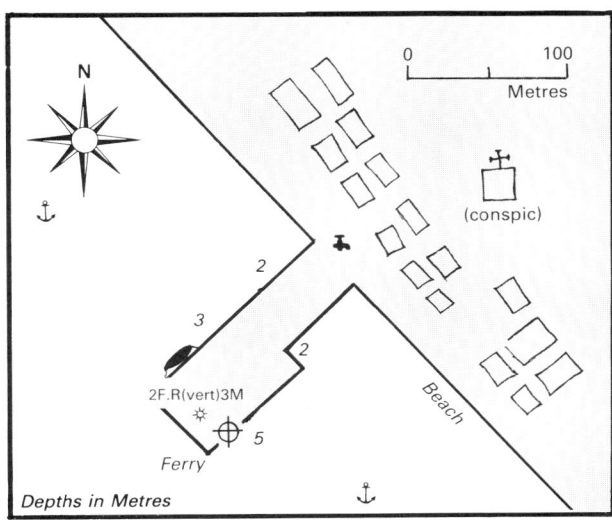

2F.R(vert)3M

Ferry

Depths in Metres

NEAPOLIS
36°30'·5N 23°03'·3E (2F.R.3M)

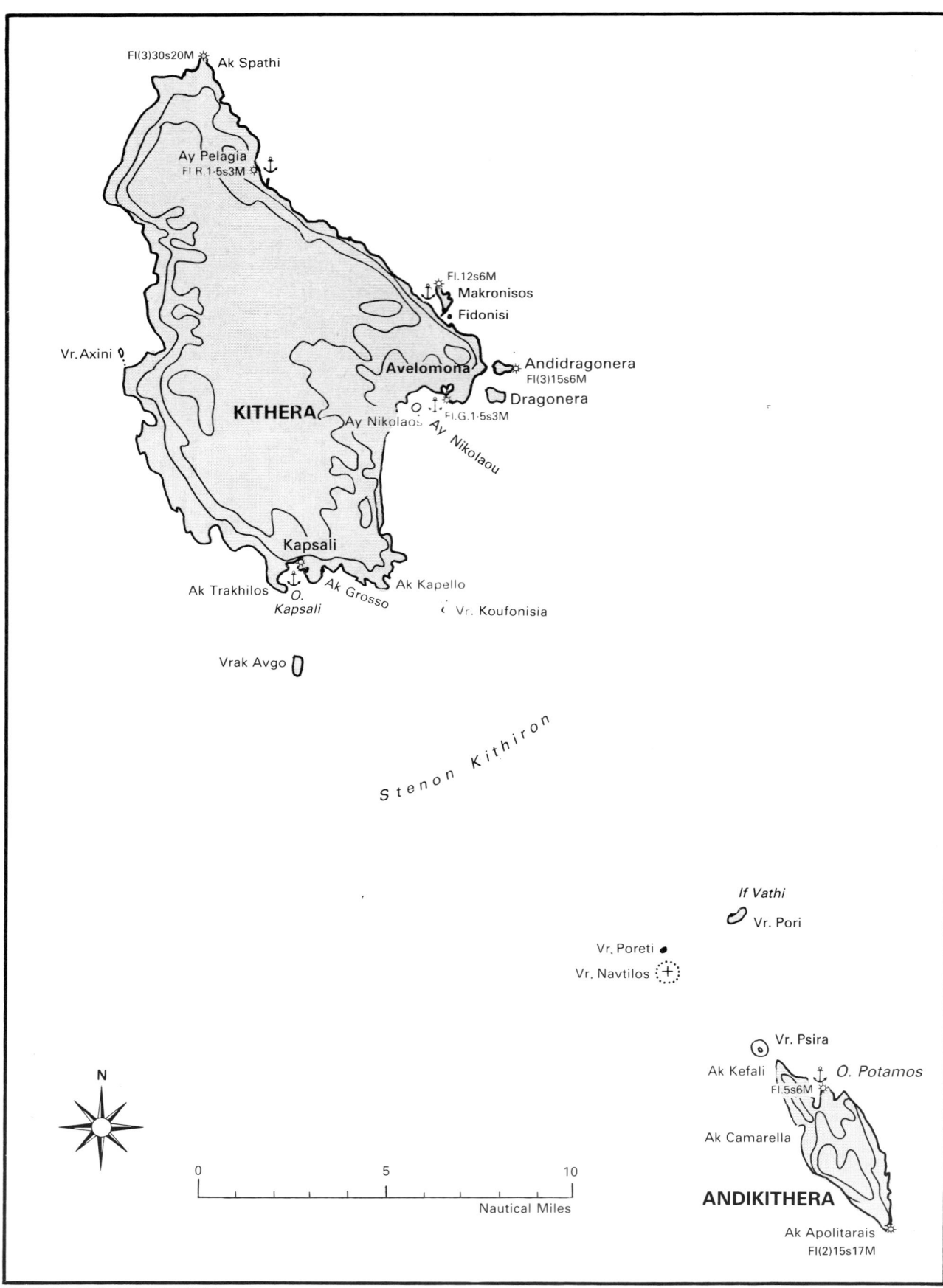

Fl(3)30s20M ☼ Ak Spathi

Ay Pelagia
Fl.R.1·5s3M ☼

Vr. Axini

Fl.12s6M
☼
Makronisos
• **Fidonisi**

Avelomona   □ ☼ **Andidragonera**
                     Fl(3)15s6M
                □ **Dragonera**
KITHERA ↻ Ay Nikolaos   Fl.G.1·5s3M
                         Ay Nikolaou

Kapsali

Ak Trakhilos   O.   Ak Kapello
              Kapsali *Ak Grosso*
                    (*Vr. Koufonisia*

Vrak Avgo 〇

S t e n o n   K i t h i r o n

If Vathi
〇 *Vr. Pori*

Vr. Poreti ●
Vr. Navtilos ⊕

◉ *Vr. Psira*

Ak Kefali ↓ *O. Potamos*
          Fl.5s6M ☼

Ak Camarella

ANDIKITHERA

Ak Apolitarais ☼
Fl(2)15s17M

N

0   5   10

Nautical Miles

KITHERA AND ANDIKITHERA

passion, from the noblest to the most degraded, came within her scope. It is her completeness, compounded of many attributes, which wins our hearts. With her loving had a comprehensiveness that accepted every human foible, good or bad.

Nor was she averse to using her powers mischievously – as when she took it into her head to light a short fuse under the chair of Zeus in Olympus, which gave him one of the worst attacks of skirt-fever ever to win a place in the Olympian version of 'The Guinness Book of Records'. Was there nothing sacred, he asked her, all lit up like a Christmas tree? Yes, she must have answered, everything is sacred, without distinction, even laughter. Especially laughter.'

Lawrence Durrell *The Greek Islands*

When the Union of the Seven Islands was declared, Kithera and Andikithera were declared to be part of the Heptanesoi despite the distance between them and the other Ionian islands. After the War of Independence the islands gradually came under the administration of Athens. Today a few tourists who enjoy quiet places visit Kithera but on the whole the island remains a comparatively untouched spot.

Eighteen miles south of Kithera lies its diminutive Andikithera (Anti-Kithera) – a pitted rocky island rising sheer from the sea and inhabited by a few hardy souls. Few yachts call here as the only harbour is unsafe in all except calm weather. Early this century a wreck of the 1st century BC was discovered near the island and a number of valuable bronze and marble statues recovered. These are now displayed in the National Museum in Athens.

PELAGIA

Four miles SE of Ak Spathi is Pelagia, the ferry port for Kithera. The small village and the mole are conspicuous. The mole, approximately 100 metres long, extends in a NE direction providing shelter from the SW–W wind. There are 4 metre depths at the head. With SW–W winds there are strong gusts down into the harbour and should the wind turn to the NE, as it often does, the harbour becomes untenable.

NISIS MAKRI (Dhiakofti Island)

Five miles SE of Panayia, Nisis Makri, connected to Kithera by a sand bar, provides good shelter from SW and W winds. The bottom is sand, excellent holding. With SW and W winds there are gusts into the bay and like Pelagia it is open to the NE. The Admiralty *Pilot* reports a wreck just N of the small island (Vrakhonisis Makronisos) to the S of Makri.

AYIOS NIKOLAOU (Avelomona)

In the NE corner of Ormos Ayios Nikolaou is the small natural harbour of Avelomonas. The harbour extends in a NE direction with 6–12 metre depths in the outer part of the cove. There is a short quay within the harbour but there are shallows and underwater rocks for some distance out and it is

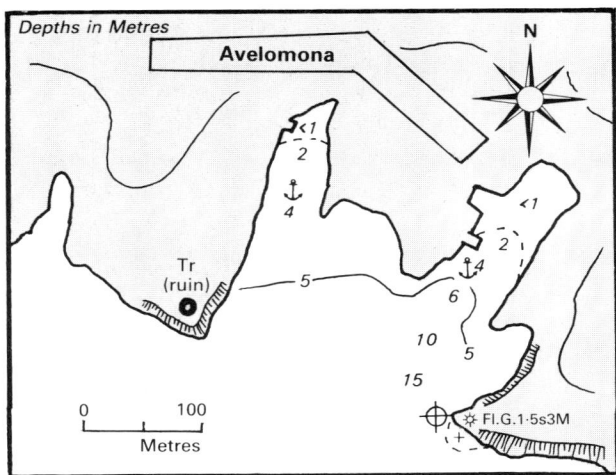

AYIOS NIKOLAOU
36°13'·2N 23°04'·8E (Fl.G.3M)

difficult to moor up to it although a line can be taken ashore. The bottom is sand and rock, poor holding. Recommended as the best small craft harbour on Kithera by the Admiralty *Pilot*, I have always experienced a considerable surge in the harbour, with NE and SW–W winds. Because of this surge and the limited room within the harbour Ormos Kapsali is a better harbour to bring up for the night.

By night Use the light on the northernmost of Vrak Andidragonera (Fl(3)15s6M) and the Fl.G.1·5s3M on the SE side of the bay.

The small village of Avelomona is not the most attractive place when compared to Kapsali. Some provisions available. Taverna.

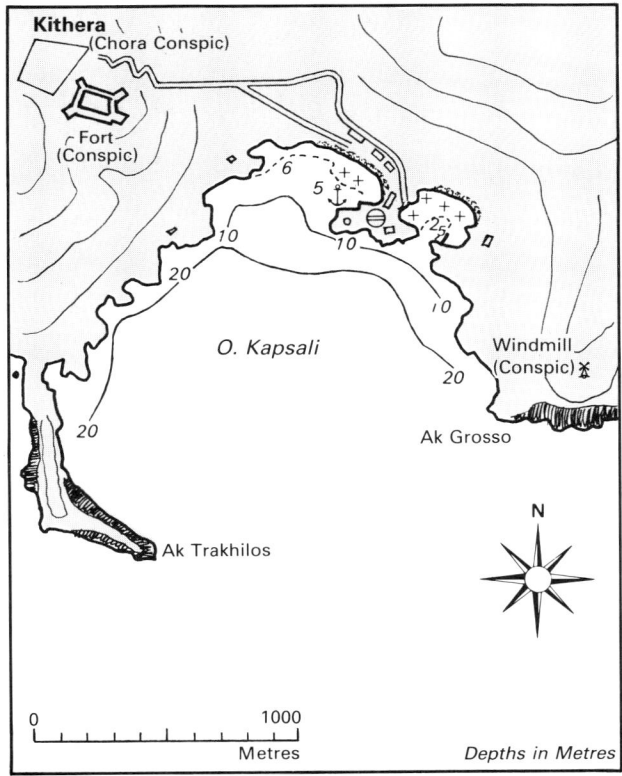

APPROACHES TO ORMOS KAPSALI

Kapsali looking ESE.

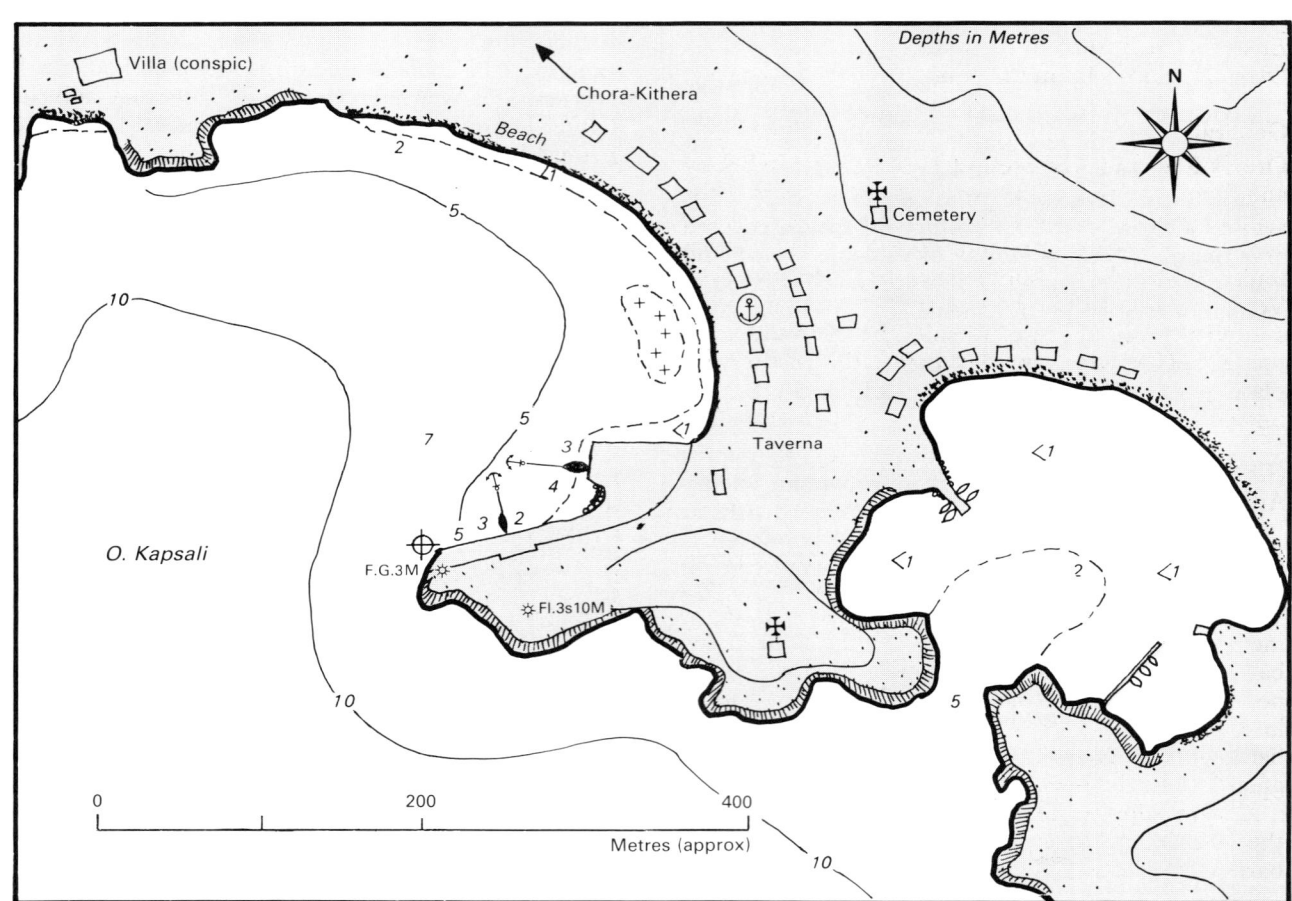

ORMOS KAPSALI
36°08'·2N 23°00'·2E (F.G.3M)

ORMOS KAPSALI (Kithera)
Admiralty chart no. 712

Approach

Conspicuous From the distance Vrak. Avgo (Ovo Island) which means Egg Island – it is roughly egg-shaped – is conspicuous. From the S and E a

windmill on Ak Grosso and the fort above the *chora* are conspicuous. From the W the fort can be seen as you near Ak Trakhilos. Once into the large bay, two large white villas to the W of the harbour and the lighthouse on the bluff above the harbour are conspicuous.

By night Use the light on the bluff (Fl.3s10M) and the light on the end of the quay (F.G.3M).

146

Dangers With strong westerlies there are gusts off the high land and a considerable swell around the coast.

Mooring

Only the W cove is deep enough for a yacht. The E cove is shallow and rock-bound. Moor stern-to or alongside the outer half of the quay if there is not a swell. The bottom is sand, rock and weed, reasonable holding once the anchor is in.

Shelter Whatever the wind direction I have invariably encountered a swell in the harbour making it uncomfortable. With strong S winds the harbour is untenable.

Note It is reported that it is prohibited to anchor in the harbour without permission from the port police. A yacht can be fined for contravening this regulation.

Authorities Port police and customs.

Facilities

Water Local sources only.
Provisions Limited provisions at the harbour, better shopping in the *chora*.
Eating out Tavernas on the waterfront.
Other PO and OTE in the *chora*.

General

Ormos Kapsali is picturesque as are the walled *chora* and fort, a steep climb above. The walled *chora* is the capital of Kithera although nowadays Potamos is the commercial centre. The fort, on what looks like an impregnable rocky bluff, was first built by the Venetians in 1316 to protect their new trade route around the Peloponnese. Despite the poor shelter in the harbour it is well worth a visit to this picturesque place – most of the time in the summer it is tenable if uncomfortable.

ORMOS POTAMOU (Andikithera)

Admiralty chart no. 712

At the northern end of Andikithera the natural harbour of Ormos Potamou is a narrow inlet running southwards and open to the N. Anchor in 6–12 metres at the S end of the inlet. At the head of the bay there are above- and below-water rocks. The bottom is sand and rock. There is invariably a swell in the bay and with even moderate N winds the harbour is untenable. With SW–W winds there are gusts into the harbour.

Meagre supplies can be obtained ashore. Despite the unsafe anchorage the island is attractive in a barren desolate sort of way.

The quay at Kapsali looking W. *Nigel Patten.*

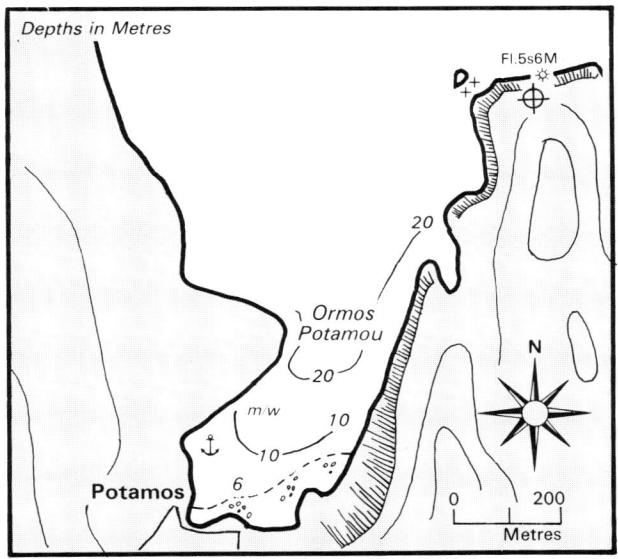

ORMOS POTAMOU
35°53'·5N 23°17'·7N (Fl.5s6M)

III. The Gulf of Patras and the Gulf of Corinth

(Patriakos Kolpos and Korinthiakos Kolpos)

Approaching the Gulf of Patras from the west, the coast is low-lying although backed by high land. Much of this coast is shallow salt marsh and shoal water extends some distance offshore particularly on the north side of the gulf. Approaching the narrow entrance to the Gulf of Corinth, the coast rises abruptly to high mountains. The sides of the Gulf of Corinth are flanked by two high mountain ranges scarred by winter torrents and split by deep gorges. On the south coast Mt Killini (Zyria) rises to 2377 metres (7800ft) and on the north coast Mt Parnassos reaches 2454 metres (8051ft). Well into late spring these mountains are capped with snow.

The Gulf of Corinth is 60 miles long from the Straits of Rion and Andirrion (once known as the 'little Dardanelles') to the Corinth Canal. Surrounded by high mountains, the gulf is much like a large lake and indeed the scenery resembles that of an Alpine lake. The narrow alluvial plain on the south coast is extensively cultivated with vineyards and fringed by attractive beaches. On the north coast the mountains are for a large part bare of vegetation although in places, particularly Navpaktos and Itea, there are patches of green contrasting with the barren mountains behind.

The history of the gulfs has largely revolved around the fortunes of Corinth. Using the Corinth Canal saves a distance of approximately 150 miles between the Ionian Sea and Athens. In antiquity, vessels were transported across the isthmus on rollers on a road called the *diolkos* and Corinth controlled this passage between the Ionian and the Aegean. From the Archaic period right up to the end of Roman rule the city flourished and grew fat on its

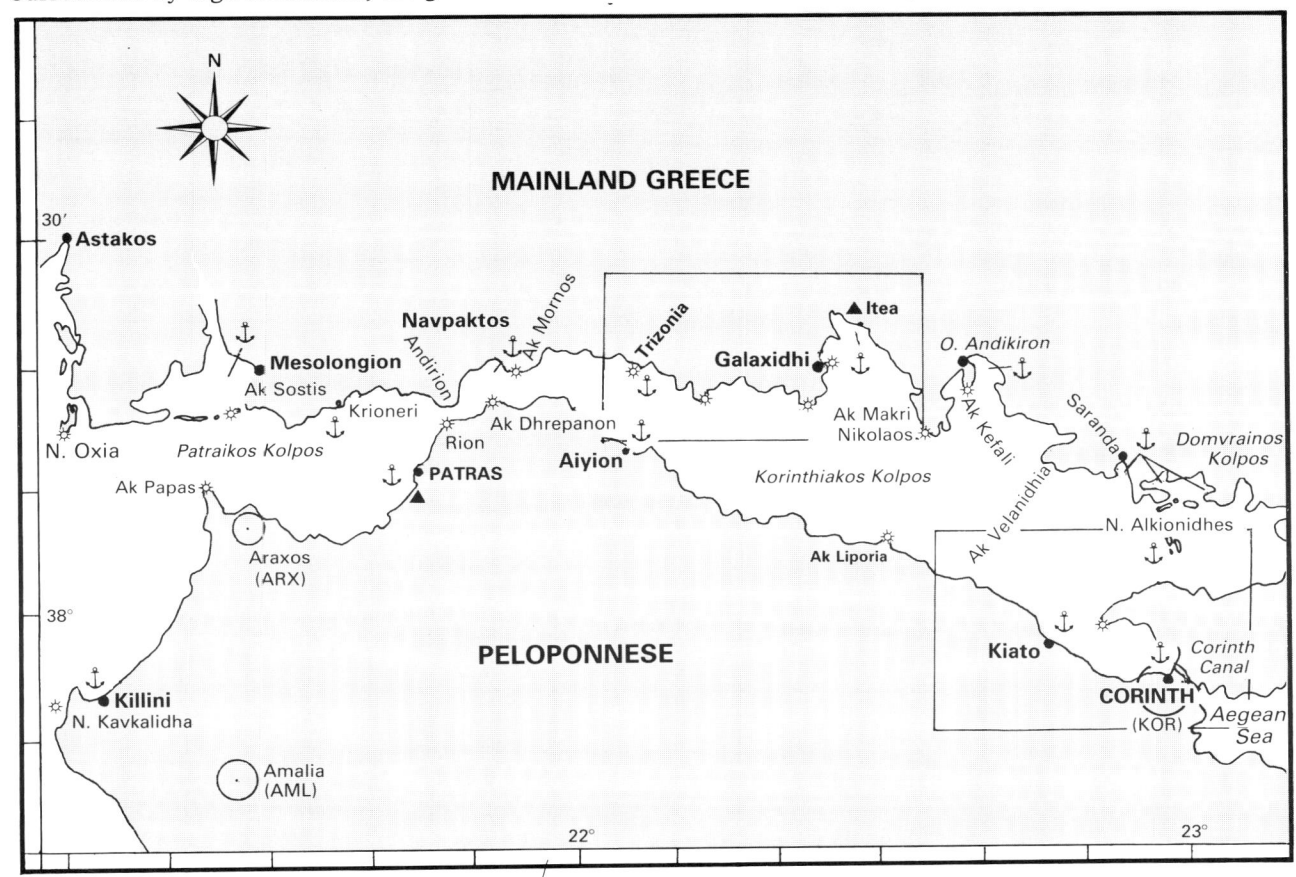

149

income from the *diolkos*. In 522 and 551 earthquakes destroyed the city and it never regained its former prosperity.

The city and control of the gulf passed through successive invaders: the Normans sacked it in 1147; Villhardouin captured it in 1212; the Turks in 1458; the Knights of Malta in 1612; the Venetians in 1687; and, in 1715, the Turks acquired it yet again until it finally became a part of Greece at the beginning of the War of Independence. Today Corinth has little to exercise the perceptions, but its former feats and glories have passed into our language and culture.

At the entrance to the Gulf of Patras two maritime incidents took place – one of historical note and the other just a footnote to history.

Proceeding down the channel between Oxia Island and Scrofa the coast becomes low-lying for some 25 miles before the town of Mesolongion appears hovering over the salt marsh. In and around the channel off Oxia the Battle of Lepanto took place. The Turks prepared their fleet in Navpaktos, then known as Lepanto, and engaged the combined Christian fleet under Don John of Austria in this desolate spot. The Christian fleet with galleys from Venice, Genoa, the Papal States, Spain, Sicily and Naples defeated the Turks, sinking and capturing some 250 galleys and freeing 15,000 galley slaves. This was the last major sea battle fought with galleys rowed by slaves and effectively demolished Turkish control of the sea. It is recorded that Cervantes, the author of Don Quixote, lost the use of his left hand here. The late Peter Throckmorton attempted to locate some of the galleys lost in this action but uncovered nothing from the thick silt that covers the bottom.

It was also here under the lee of Scrofa that a small ship Byron was on put in to evade a Turkish brig-of-war on New Year's Eve in 1823. En route to Mesolongion from Cephalonia his Ionian skipper elected to anchor until the Turks passed. Apparently feeling unsafe they later went further north to Astakos, then called Dragomestre. Eventually three ships from Mesolongion found Byron's ship and escorted it safely into the marshy fortress. Although Byron liked the sea and ships he knew very little about them and his companions were even more ignorant of matters nautical. David Howarth records this amusing episode on the trip to Mesolongion in his *The Greek Adventure*:

'The passengers in this boat were a land-lubberly lot, except perhaps Tita the gondolier, and the crew seems not to have been much better. Fletcher the valet had caught a cold and had to lie down on the only mattress on board, Dr Bruno was prone to wring his hands and weep at any threat of disaster, and Loukas could not swim. Byron himself liked boats, but had never learned much about them. And as they returned through the Oxia channel, the boat missed stays and ran aground in a squall. Two thirds of the crew climbed out on the bowsprit and jumped ashore, Byron told Loukas he would save him, and Dr Bruno stripped to his flannel waistcoat and running about like a rat (it was Byron's description) shouted 'Save him indeed! By God, save me rather – I'll be the first if I can.' Thereupon, after striking twice, the boat blew off again. The crew was

removed from the rocks by one of the escort ships, and that evening, without any more alarms, Byron reached the entrance of Missalonghi.'

Byron accomplished little in Mesolongion. The guerrilla chiefs assembled around him for the money he had brought. The collection of Philhellenes gathered in Mesolongion for the most part grumbled and argued amongst themselves and with the Greeks. Byron was appointed a 'commander' but could do little to organise the ill-assorted groups around him. It was more his death of fever on 19 April 1824 that inspired the world and focussed attention on the Greek struggle than his presence – as he lay dying he is reported to have said: 'I do not lament for to terminate my wearisome existence I came to Greece. My wealth, my abilities, I devoted to her cause. Well, there is my life to her.'

Many yachts pass through the Gulf of Patras and the Gulf of Corinth – most are using it simply as a short cut to the Aegean saving 150 miles on the trip around the Peloponnese. For the yachtsman who is not in a hurry to reach the Aegean the two gulfs, more particularly the Gulf of Corinth, are good cruising areas with a lot of attractive harbours and anchorages. In the Gulf of Corinth the south coast is relatively straight and offers few secure anchorages, but the north coast is much indented with many attractive and safe anchorages separated by short distances.

Weather patterns in the Gulf of Patras and the Gulf of Corinth

The prevailing winds in the summer are from the W. Across the low salt marsh on the N of the Gulf of Patras the wind is from the NW to WNW. In the Gulf of Corinth the high mountains funnel the wind so it comes from the W. It normally blows from midday until well into the evening and may reach Force 5–6 in July or August. The wind may also blow from the NE at Corinth and sometimes blows right down to the Gulf of Patras. Again it is funnelled into an E wind in the two gulfs. In Krissaios Kolpos (Gulf of Krissa) and Ormos Andikiron (Antikyrra) there is frequently no wind even when it is blowing strongly in the middle of the gulf.

In the spring and autumn the winds vary between W and E – depending largely on the winds in the Ionian and the Aegean. In the Gulf of Patras there are frequently violent thunderstorms which may last for some time in the spring and autumn. Waterspouts are fairly frequent here in unsettled weather and believe me, you don't need to see a big waterspout in action.

Although gusts off the high mountains could be expected, in my experience they have been little stronger than the winds in the middle of the two gulfs. The mountains appear to funnel the wind (W or E) for the length of the gulf rather than act as obstacles off which gusts might blow. Only at the Corinth end is this not the case with NE winds where gusts blow off the high land with some violence.

Data

PORTS OF ENTRY
Patras
Itea

PROHIBITED AREAS
A small harbour on the E side of Ormos Andikiron and the area immediately surrounding it.

MAJOR LIGHTS
Ak Oxia Fl(2)15s17M
Nisis Kavikalidha (Cape Killini) LFl.WR.20s12/9M
Ak Pappas LFl(2)30s10M
Ak Ay Sostis Fl.WR.5s17/14M
Rion Fl.G.6s4M
Andirrion Fl.R.6s4M
Ak Mornos Fl(3)15s6M
Ak Dhrepanon Fl.10s22M
Nisis Trizonia Fl.4s4M
Ak Psaromita Fl(2)15s21M
Ak Andromakhi Fl(3)15s6M
Nisis Apsifia (Galaxidhi) Fl.7s5M
Ak Makri-Nikolaos Fl.4·5s5M
Ak Likoporia Fl(2)16s10M
Ak Kefali Fl.3s4M
Ak Melangavi Fl.10s17M

Quick reference guide

	Shelter	Mooring	Fuel	Water	Provisioning	Tavernas	Plan
Killini	B	A	B	A	B	B	●
Mesolongion	A	ABC	B	A	B	B	●
Krioneri	O	C	O	O	O	C	
Patras Yacht Harbour	A	A	B	A	A	B	●
Patras	B	A	A	A	A	A	●
Navpaktos	B	A	A	A	B	B	●
Nisis Trizonia	A	C	O	B	C	C	●
Aiyion	C	AC	B	B	B	A	●
Kallithea	B	C	O	B	C	C	●
Erateini	C	C	B	B	C	O	●
Panormos	C	C	O	O	O	O	
Vidhavis	C	C	O	O	O	C	
Anemokambi	B	O	O	O	O	C	●
Galaxidhi	A	A	B	B	B	A	●
Itea	C	A	B	B	B	C	●
Andikiron	B	C	B	B	C	C	●
Ay Saranda	B	C	O	B	C	C	
Gulf of Domvraina	B	C	O	O	O	O	
Nisidhes Alkonidhes	C	C	O	O	O	O	●
Agriliou	O	C	O	O	O	O	
Loutraki	O	C	B	B	B	B	
Corinth	A	AB	B	B	A	B	●
Corinth Canal	O	O	O	O	O	O	●
Kiato	B	A	B	A	A	B	●

Gulf of Patras
(Patriakos Kolpos)

KILLINI (Kyllini, Glarenza)
Admiralty chart no. 2404

Approach
The harbour actually lies outside the Gulf of Patras 20 miles SW of the entrance. Castel Tornese on a hill inland of Killini is conspicuous from some distance away. The lighthouse on Nisis Kavikalidha is also conspicuous. Closer in the buildings of Killini and the harbour mole will be seen against the low-lying coast.
By night Use the light on Nisis Kavikalidha LFl.WR.20s12/9M (red sector 059°-092°) and the light on the buoy at the entrance (Fl.G).
Dangers
1. A reef runs out from the headland immediately NW of the harbour and it should be given a good offing as it can be difficult to see. Make the immediate approach to the harbour from the NE.

Mooring
Berth stern or bows-to the mole on the W side where shown taking care of the ballasting which extends underwater in places. The bottom is mud, good holding.
Shelter Good shelter from the prevailing NW–W winds. Open to the E.
Authorities Port police and customs.

Facilities
Water On the quay.
Fuel In the village.
Provisions Most provisions can be obtained.
Eating out Tavernas along the waterfront.
Other PO. OTE. Exchange. Bus and train to Patras. Ferry to Zakinthos.

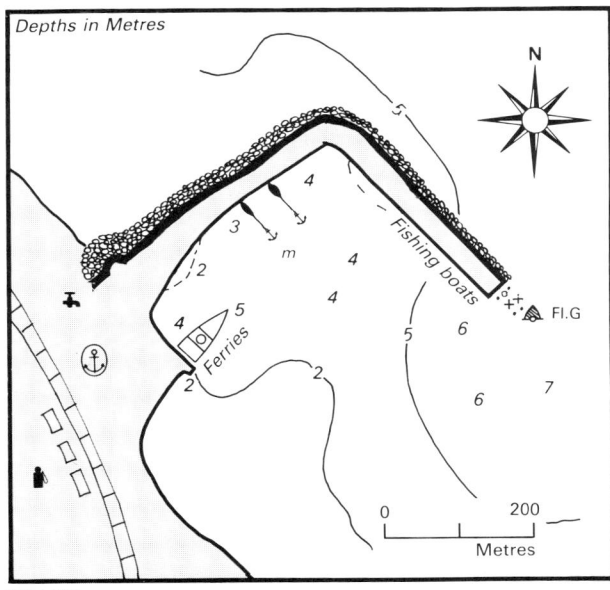

KILLINI
37°56'·5N 21°09'E

General

Known in Venetian times as Glarenza, the port was once an important link in the trade route around the Peloponnese. It is difficult to think of this dusty little place, now the ferry terminal for Zakinthos, being a thriving cosmopolitan place full of the sights and sounds of foreign sailors and merchants en route to or from the Orient.

The castle on the heights to the S was built in 1220 by Geoffrey Villehardouin and later passed to the Venetians who named it Castel Tornese. It was taken by the Turks during their occupation of the Peloponnese and finally partially destroyed by Ibrahim Pasha in 1825. It is now being restored and is worth a visit – it commands superb views over the surrounding countryside and the approaches to the Gulf of Patras.

MESOLONGION (Missolonghi)

Admiralty chart no. 1676
Imray-Tetra chart G13

Approach

Conspicuous The white lighthouse on Nisis Ay Sostis and the group of houses at the entrance to the canal will be seen first. The red and green buoys marking the entrance to the dredged channel are difficult to pick out from the distance and in bad visibility it can be quite a job finding them until close to. Once the buoys are located the canal is marked out by four pairs of beacons.

By night Use the light on Nisis Ay Sostis (Fl.WR.5s17/14M red sector 010°-059°) and the lights on the outer buoys (Fl.R.4·5s and Fl.G.4·5s). The channel beacons are lit (all Q.R and Q.G.2M). The lights on the buoys at the seaward end can be very difficult to locate and the lights of the beacons marking the channel are not easily seen against the lights of the town.

Note The canal was dredged to a least depth of 6 metres in 1986. In parts there are depths of 8 metres. At the entrance to the basin don't cut the corner but head for the middle of the basin to clear the shallows on the E.

Mooring

Stern or bows-to or alongside the N quay. Most yachts elect to go alongside. Some yachts prefer to anchor off the W side of the basin. The bottom is mud, good holding.

Shelter Excellent shelter from all winds although the prevailing wind pushes a chop across the large basin into the NE corner.

Authorities Port police and customs.

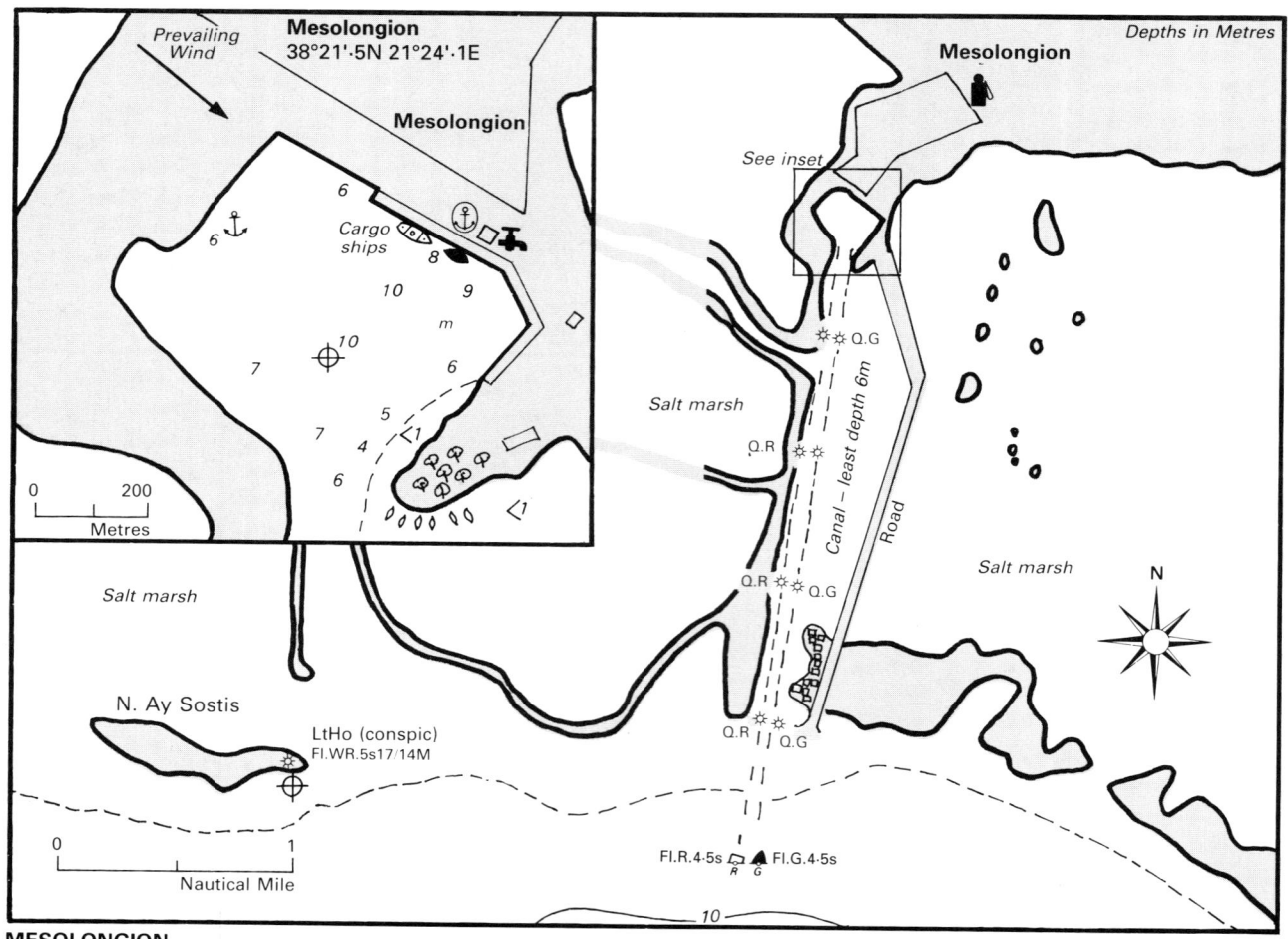

MESOLONGION
38°19'·3N 21°22'·4E (N. Ay Sostis light)

Stilt houses at the entrance to Mesolongion canal.

Facilities

Water On the quay. Showers in the hotel SE of basin.
Fuel In the town a considerable distance (30 minutes' walk) away.
Repairs Some mechanical repairs. Hardware shops.
Provisions Good shopping for all provisions. Ice available.
Eating out Hardly a good taverna for a town of this size. Avoid any in the town that are labelled 'Self Service Cafeteria'. The taverna at the harbour is as good as any. However the cafés around the central square are pleasant enough.
Other PO. OTE. Bank. Bus to Athens.

General

Neither the harbour nor the town of Mesolongion has much charm, but the locals are friendly and somehow Mesolongion grows on you. The entrance to the canal has some interesting fishermen's houses standing on stilts in the shallow water looking like something out of SE Asia. The picture is reinforced by locals up to their knees in the salt marsh pushing rakes through the mud to collect shellfish, mostly the enormous golden-shelled fan mussel. The surrounding salt marsh supports a variety of water birds.

Those visiting Mesolongion for its associations with Byron will be disappointed for there is little to see and little to remind us that Byron died here. There is a statue of the poet and a small museum houses a few relics from the War of Independence, but just as it had never been heard of before Byron died here, so it seems to have slipped back into an anonymity fostered by the featureless salt marsh all around it.

KRIONERI

Situated under the steep slopes of Mt Varasavon (922 metres) the open bay offers limited protection from the prevailing winds. There are 2–5 metre depths in the middle section of the short pier off the village where some shelter from E winds can be gained. The

extremity and E side of the pier is shallow. Taverna on the waterfront.

Caution The shoal water off Ak Evinos between Mesolongion and Krioneri is marked at its extremity by a S cardinal lightbuoy (Q(6)+LFl.15s).

LIMIN PATRON (Patras, Patrai)

Admiralty chart no. 2404
Imray-Tetra chart no. G13

Approach

Conspicuous The buildings of the city are easily identified from some distance off. The dome of Ay Andreas church is conspicuous close to the S entrance to the harbour. A chimney is conspicuous just inland from the N entrance. The outer breakwater is quite low and it can be difficult to identify until closer in, but the cargo ships and ferries within the harbour show up well.
By night The S entrance is lit: Q.G.2M on the inner breakwater/Q. on the buoy off the breakwater. The N entrance is lit: Fl.G.5s8M and Fl.R on the buoy off the yacht 'marina'. The elbow of the detached

S entrance to Patras harbour.

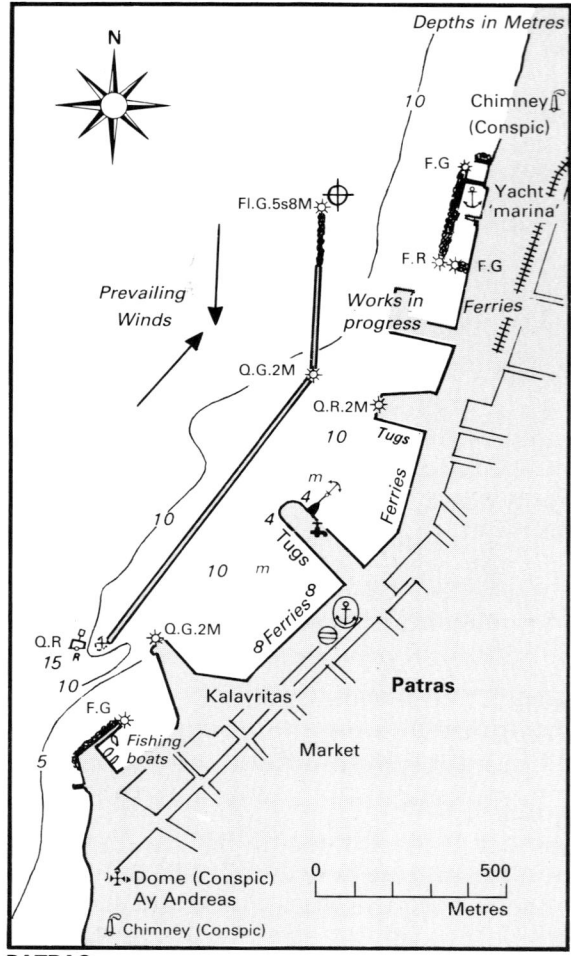

PATRAS
38°15′·6N 21°44′E (Fl.G.5s8M)

breakwater is lit (Q.G.2M) and the head of the pier opposite it (Q.R.2M). The harbour lights are difficult to distinguish against the lights of the city until 1–2 miles off. On calm nights there are numerous fishing boats with bright lamps outside the harbour whose bright lights bobbing up and down in the swell give the appearance of navigation lights. The aero beacon (Fl.R) on Profitis (6½ miles SE of Ak Pappas) shows up well.

Dangers

1. With the brisk prevailing breeze from the W there can be a confused sea off the breakwater, bothersome rather than dangerous.
2. Large ferries are constantly coming and going from the port and a good lookout must be kept in the approaches and the harbour itself.

Mooring

Go stern or bows-to or alongside the S or N side of the central mole. The bottom is mud, good holding.

Shelter There is nearly always some surge in the harbour with all strong winds – uncomfortable but not normally dangerous. The tugs and workboats entering and leaving the harbour also cause a lot of wash.

Authorities A port of entry. Port police, customs and immigration close to the quay.

Facilities

Water On the quay when the 'water man' turns up.
Fuel Near the quay. A mini-tanker can deliver to the quay.
Repairs A yard near the yacht 'marina' can haul yachts. Most mechanical repairs. Engineering and electrical work possible. Good hardware shops and a chandlers.
Provisions Good shopping for all provisions.
Eating out Numerous tavernas of all types including some good fish tavernas out of the immediate quayside area.
Other PO. OTE. Banks. Greek gas and *Camping Gaz*. Hire cars and motorbikes. Regular buses to Athens, around a 2½ hour trip. Ferries to Ithaca, Corfu, and Italy.

General

Patras is the largest city in the Peloponnese and the third largest in Greece. The city and the harbour are noisy and grubby but lively. You enter Patras thinking you will dislike it and slowly you end up quite liking it. The carnival (in late February and early March – traditionally ten days before Lent) is celebrated with as much gusto as Easter in Patras. The first time I entered Patras it was one in the morning in early March and it was a rather odd experience to be handed sweets and hit on the head by masked strangers after a gruelling slog to windward. What do you do. Buy your own plastic club and mask and walk around hitting other strangers on the head? For this appeared to be the proper thing to do during the carnival.

Historically the city has always been important as a commercial centre and the western gateway to Greece. The city was celebrated during the War of Independence when the Bishop of Patras first raised the Greek flag here. This patriotism was remembered all over Greece for many years and was the subject of countless illustrations which can be seen in many of the museums. The Turks retaliated by razing the town and the present city was laid out on a grid system.

The wine from the region is excellent including the ubiquitous *demestica* – a visit to the Achaia-Klauss wine factory that makes this and other wines is well worth while.

PATRAS YACHT HARBOUR

In the old caique basin at the N end of the harbour there is a yacht harbour/club. Entry is from the S keeping close to the outer breakwater where there are 4 metre depths in the entrance. There are 1–4 metre depths inside. The basin is crowded with local yachts and there is no guarantee you will find a berth here. Inside there is all-round protection. Water and electricity. Showers (cold) and toilets. Yachts are craned ashore onto the hard. Supermarket about 500m going towards Patras.

Guardian Llanos Vasilli ☎ (061) 429130

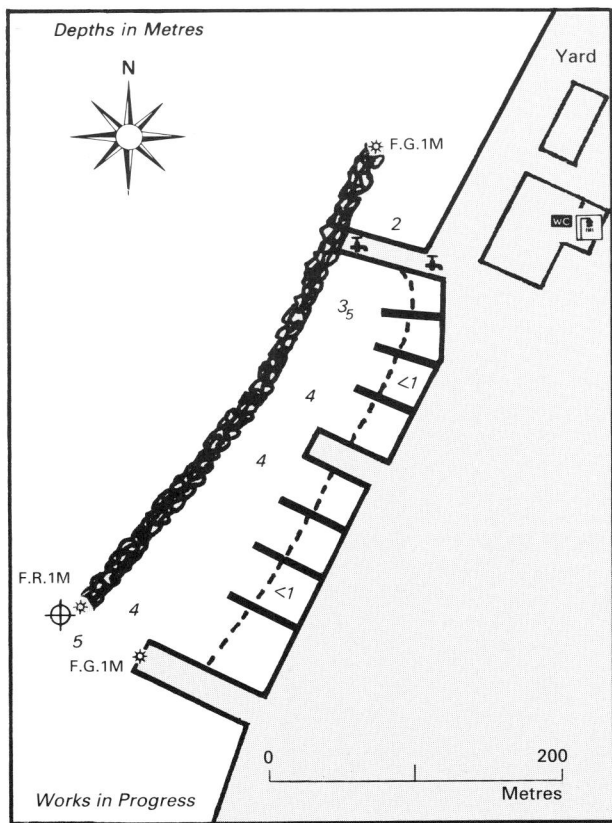

PATRAS YACHT HARBOUR
38°15'·7N 21°44'·3E (F.R.1M)

DHIAVOLOS RION AND ANDIRRION
(Strait of Rhion and Anti-Rhion)

This narrow strait, only one mile wide, is the western entrance to the Gulf of Corinth. A Venetian fort stands on Rion (conspicuous) and another on Andirrion. A current of up to 2 knots has been reported to flow either way through this strait depending on the wind direction, though in my experience there is normally a W–going current despite the prevailing W winds. If the wind is against the current it is easily seen as a small patch of troubled water. Care needs to be taken of the numerous car ferries plying between Rion and Andirrion.

The strait is lit on either side: Rion Fl.G.6s4M and Andirrion Fl.R.6s4M.

Gulf of Corinth
(**Korinthiakos Kolpos**)

NAVPAKTOS (Lepanto)

Approach
Conspicuous From the distance the castle walls on the hill above the town and the buildings of the town are conspicuous. Closing the town, the castellated walls of the harbour will be seen.
By night The entrance is lit Fl.G.1·5s3M.
Note The medieval harbour is very small so a yacht should have everything ready for berthing before entering. A large yacht should not attempt to get in here as there simply isn't room.

Mooring
Go stern or bows-to on the S side of the harbour or off the fuel jetty wherever there is room. Beware of floating lines from the local fishing boats. The bottom is soft mud, not always the best holding. The small harbour gets very crowded in July and August so you may not be able to find a berth – after all it doesn't take too many yachts to fill a harbour of this size. Crossed anchors are also something you can do little about given the difficulties of manoeuvring once inside and the lack of space. Large yachts should anchor off the beach to the W of the harbour in settled weather or go to Patras or Nisis Trizonia in unsettled weather.
Shelter Reasonable shelter from the prevailing wind although a prolonged westerly sets up a surge. Winds from the SW and SE funnelling into the bay cause a surge though in the summer this is more uncomfortable than dangerous.

Andirrion on the N side of the narrow division between Patraikos Kolpos and Korinthiakos Kolpos.

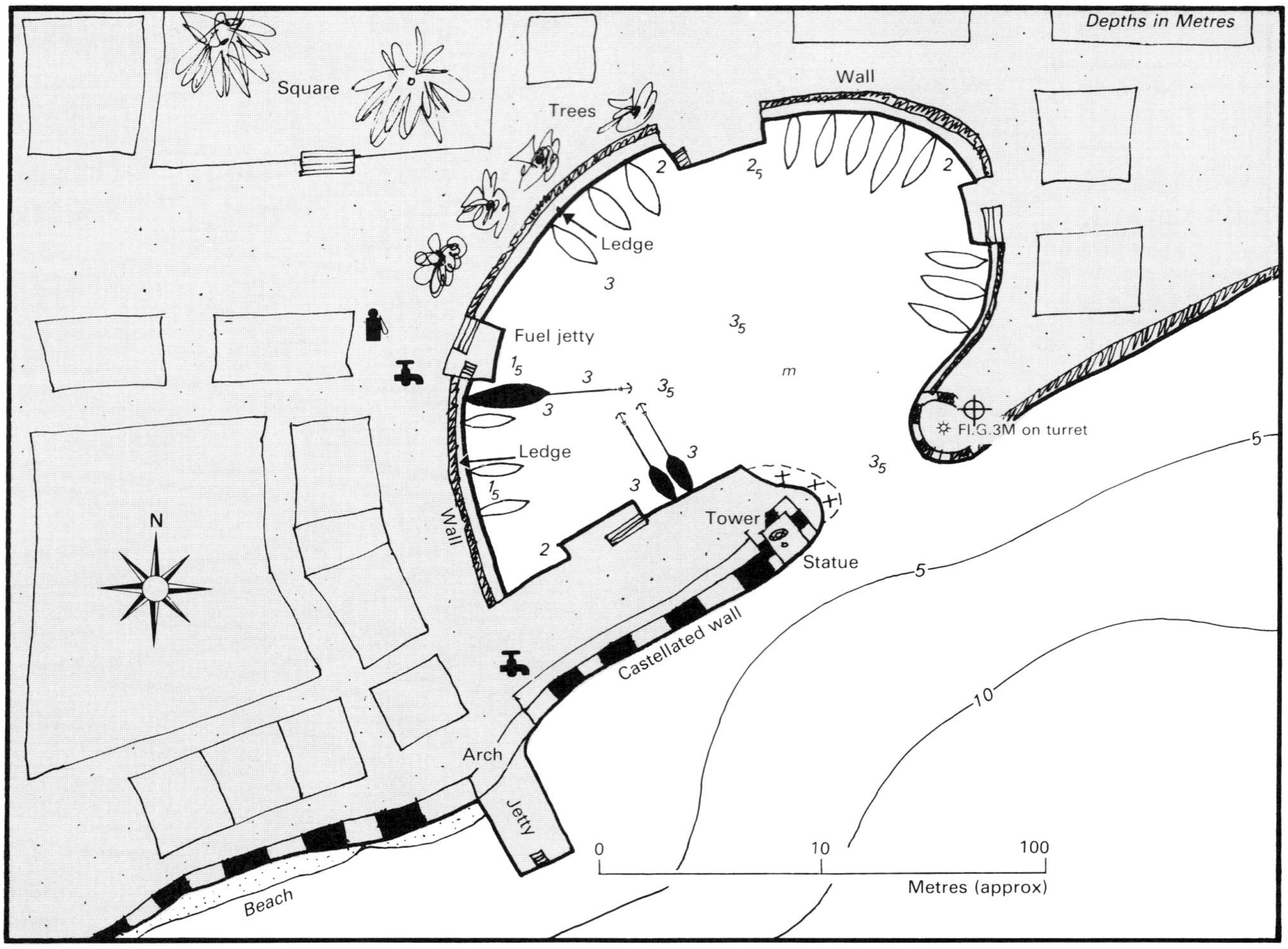

NAVPAKTOS
38°23'·5N 21°49'·7E (Fl.G.3M)

Facilities

Water On the quay.

Fuel Close to the quay – a hose can be led down to the fuel quay.

Repairs Minor mechanical repairs. Hardware shops.

Provisions Good shopping for all provisions. Ice available.

Eating out Numerous tavernas in the town.

Other PO. OTE. Bank. Greek gas and *Camping Gaz*. Bus to Andirrion where you can get a ferry across to Rion and catch the bus to Athens or Patras.

General

The minute medieval harbour bordered by old plane trees and under the shadow of the Venetian castle (now a park) is a captivating place. It is a pity the same cannot be said for the reinforced concrete sprawl on either side of the old town. Nor is the harbour a quiet place – traffic rumbles and buzzes around the road by the harbour, the locals are an animated lot and all the animation goes on in the square by the harbour, and at night the bar on the W side plays loud music of the mind-numbing type for local and aging adolescents alike. Yet despite these irritations the place is a gem.

Navpaktos harbour E side.

It is well worth a walk up to the castle to escape the hubbub. Navpaktos is well watered and in the summer heat it is strange to hear water bubbling away when not so far away it is scarce. The town was

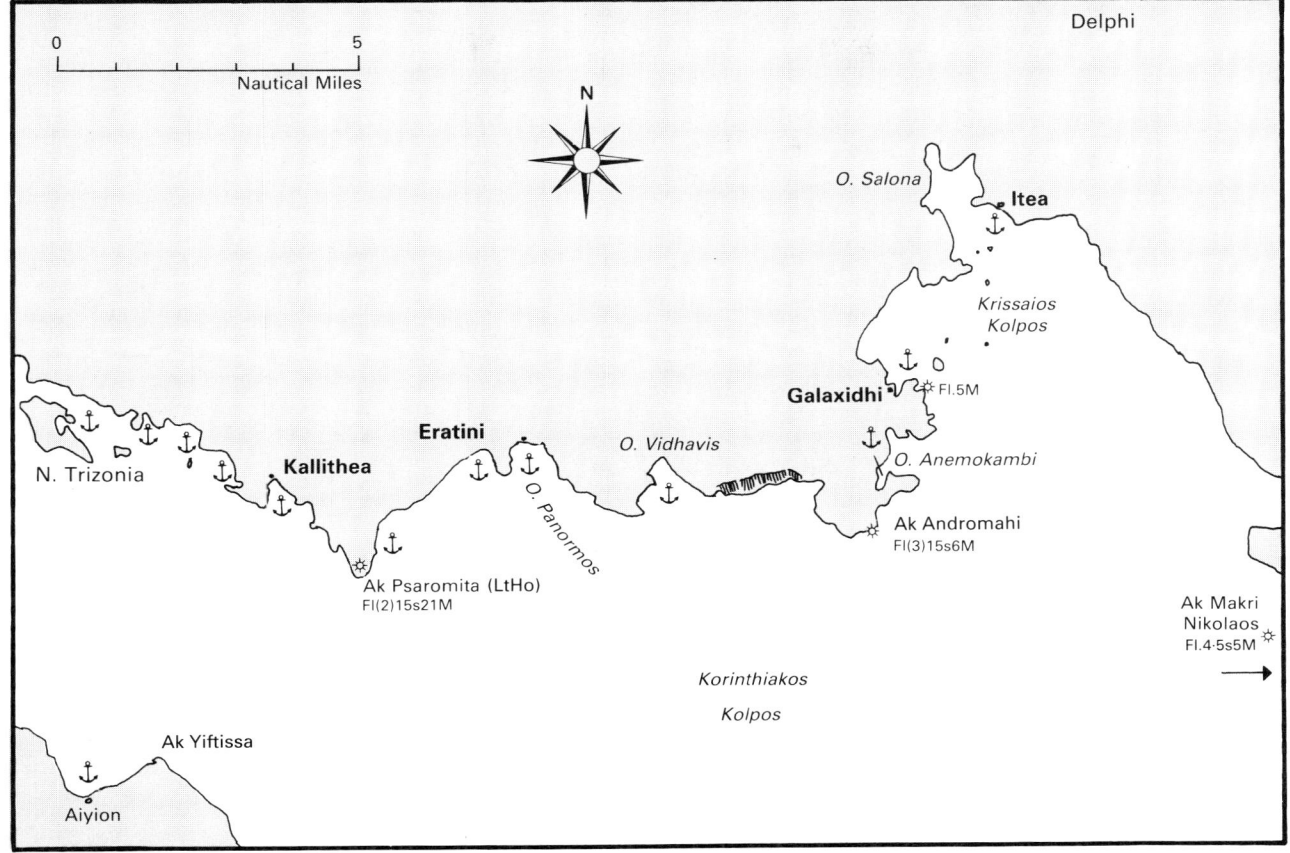

Delphi

0 ——— 5
Nautical Miles

N

O. Salona   **Itea**

Krissaios Kolpos

Galaxidhi   ☆ Fl.5M

O. Anemokambi

O. Vidhavis

Eratini

O. Panormos

Kallithea

N. Trizonia

Ak Psaromita (LtHo)
Fl(2)15s21M

Ak Andromahi
Fl(3)15s6M

Ak Makri
Nikolaos
Fl.4·5s5M
→

Korinthiakos

Kolpos

Ak Yiftissa

Aiyion

KORINTHIAKOS KOLPOS

known in medieval times as Lepanto and it was here that the Turks refitted before the disastrous (for them) Battle of Lepanto. The medieval harbour is one of the best examples of its type in the Mediterranean and should not be missed.

Navpaktos harbour – the most perfectly preserved little medieval harbour in Greece.

NISIS TRIZONIA

Approach
From the distance the island is difficult to make out against the nearby hills of the mainland. From the W a villa on the saddle of Nisis Trizonia stands out well and from the E an escarpment on Nisis Ay Ioannis is conspicuous. Closer in the village on the mainland opposite the island will be seen, but the small hamlet on the island and the entrance to the bay are not visible until you are near the anchorage.

Mooring
Anchor where convenient in the bay. The bottom is mud and weed – good holding once the anchor has cut through the weed, but getting through the weed cover can be difficult in places. Just keep persisting. Good all-round shelter but with NW–W winds there are gusts down into the bay.

Note Work is in progress to create a yacht harbour on the N side of Trizonia bay. A short breakwater has been built out from the N entrance point and two concrete piers built out from the W and N sides. The N side has been quayed and partially dredged. Yachts have been using those bits of the harbour where work is not in progress. Care is needed until work is complete.

157

Facilities

Water in the small square in the hamlet. Most provisions can be found. Tavernas in the village – one of these with tables by the small port has excellent fish and other fare. The hotel and restaurant on the NW side of the bay has been recommended and can offer telephone and fax facilities. *Caïque* ferry to the village on the mainland.

General

The land around the bay is green and lush – mostly vines and olives. The small fishing hamlet has changed little over the years despite the number of yachts using the sheltered bay. Even if you do not eat ashore it is well worth your while to go ashore for an *ouzo* or brandy and coffee – sitting around the little square overlooking the small harbour you'll easily lose an evening.

AIYION (Aigion, Vostitsa)

Admiralty chart no. 2404
Imray-Tetra chart no. G13

Opposite Nisis Trizonia on the S side of the Gulf of Corinth, the open bay of Aiyion is the terminus for the ferry from Kallithea. Anchor in the bay or go stern-to the jetty (7 metre depths off). The bay is not secure with strong W and E winds and is open to the N. Good shopping for provisions and good tavernas ashore.

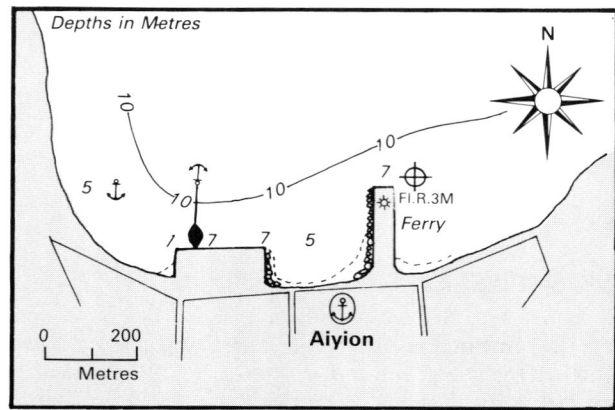

AIYION
38°15'·2N 22°04'·7E (Fl.R.3M)

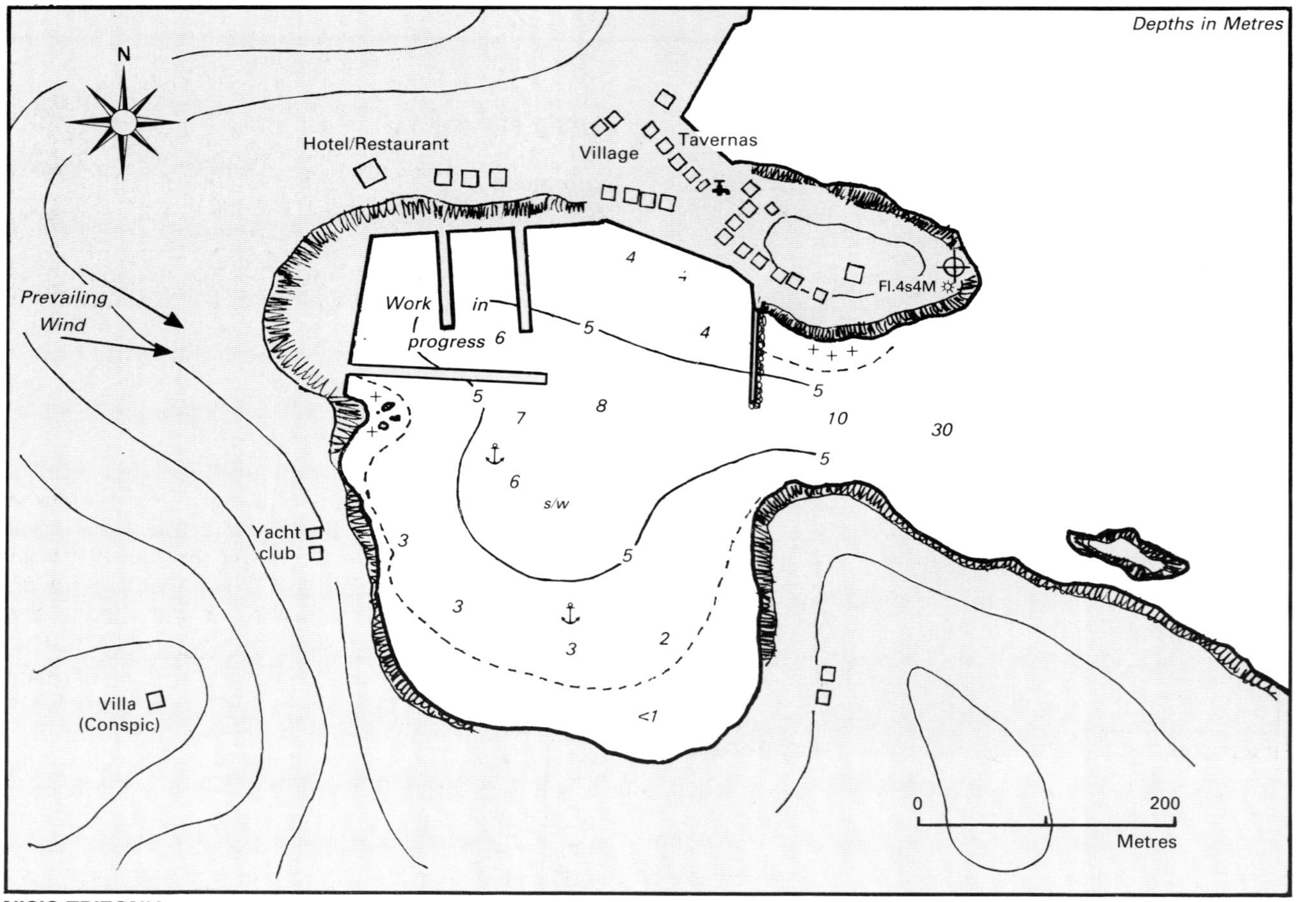

NISIS TRIZONIA
38°22'N 22°04'·7E (Fl.4s4M)

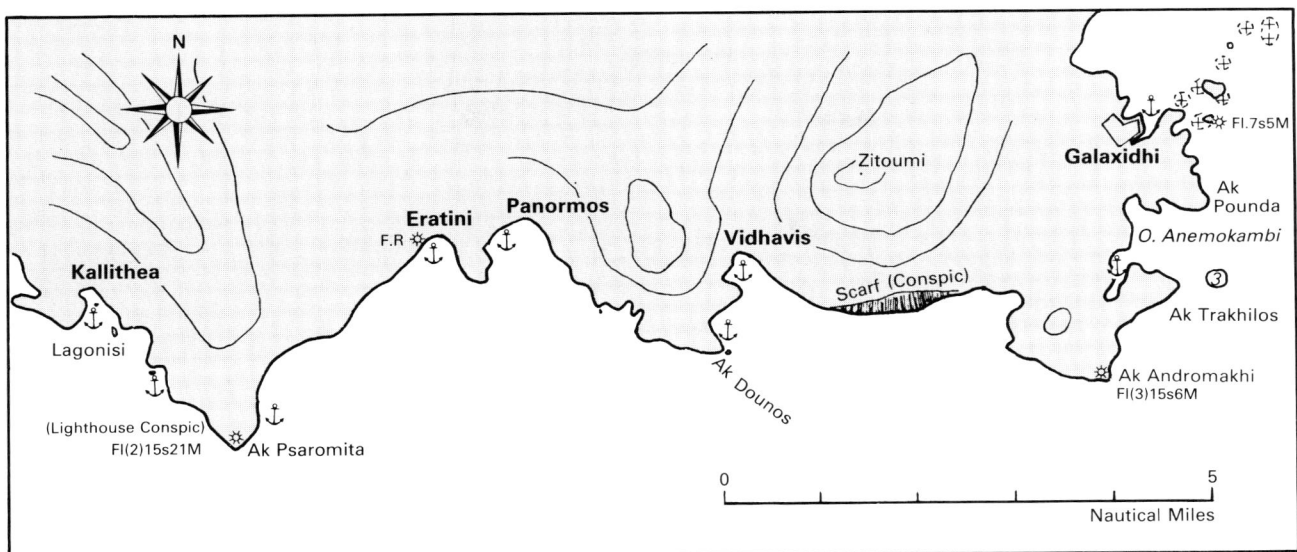

KALLITHEA TO GALAXIDHI

SKALA KALLITHEA

Situated 4 miles SE of Nisis Trizonia. On the E side of the entrance is the small islet of Lagonisi and further into the bay there is another small islet with a chapel on it. The bay hooks NW to give good shelter from W winds although E winds send in some swell. Open to the S. Anchor in 3–6 metres just N of the islet with the chapel. The bottom is sand – good holding.

Some provisions ashore. Tavernas. Ferry to Aiyion. The anchorage is pleasant enough although the proximity of the new coast road around the bay detracts from its charms.

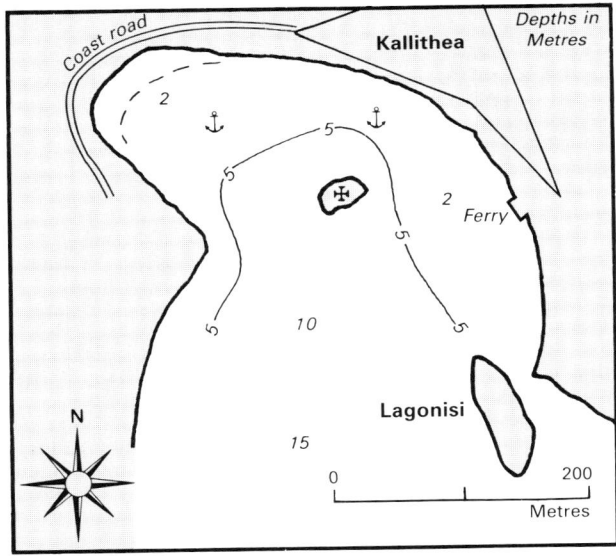

KALLITHEA
38°21′N 22°09′·5E

AK PSAROMITA

About ½ a mile N of the lighthouse on the cape there is a tiny creek where shelter from W winds is reported to be good.

Ak Psaromita and lighthouse looking E.

ERATINI

Situated 3 miles NE of Ak Psaromita (the lighthouse on the cape is conspicuous). A large white hotel behind the beach to the W of Eratini is conspicuous and closer in a church in the village stands out well. The bay affords reasonable shelter from the prevailing winds though some swell rolls into it. It is not a secure spot in unsettled weather. Anchor in 5–12 metres off the village. A small pier has 3 metre depths at its extremity and a yacht can go bows-to if there is room.

Most provisions can be found and tavernas open in the summer. PO. OTE.

Note A small harbour has recently been built on the E side of the bay. Local fishing boats are kept here and depths look adequate for small yachts. Shelter inside looks good. The sketch plan should be treated with caution.

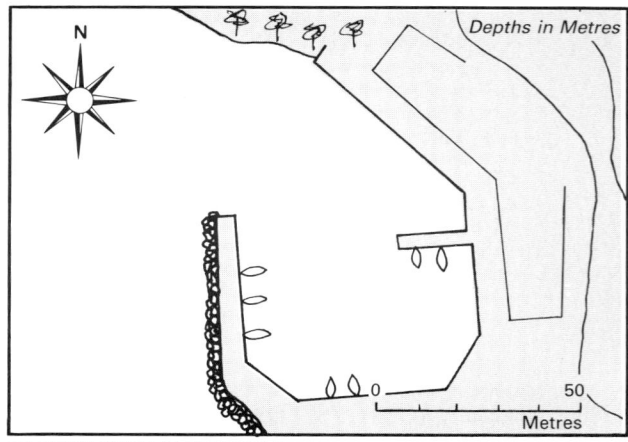

ERATINI CAIQUE HARBOUR

ORMOS PANORMOS

Situated over the headland immediately E of Eratini. Shelter as for Eratini. Care needs to be taken of shallows extending some distance out from the head of the bay – easily seen in calm weather. Tavernas open in the summer and limited provisions are available.

ORMOS VIDHAVIS (Ay Pandes)

Lying 2 miles to the E of Panormos on the E side of Ak Dounos. The islet of Xeronisi off the cape is easily identified. Vidhavis affords good shelter from W winds but E winds send in some swell. Open to the S. Anchor in 3–6 metres at the head of the bay. Tavernas ashore.

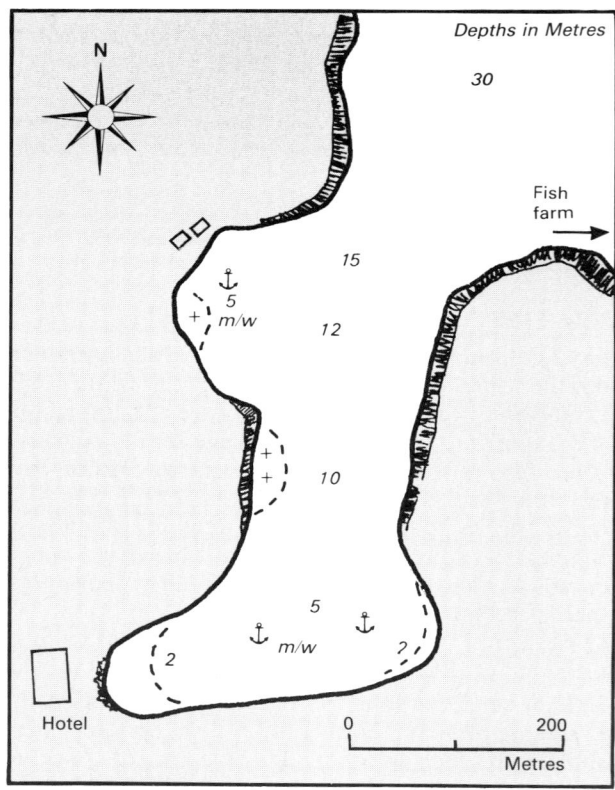

ORMOS ANEMOKAMBI
38°21′N 22°23′E

Ak Andromakhi looking E. The light structure is difficult to make out until close to.

The bay is marred by the awful road scar right around it but otherwise is an attractive place. In calm weather there is a pleasant anchorage in the bay just N of Xeronisi.

ORMOS ANEMOKAMBI (Andromaki)

An almost landlocked bay lying just N of Ak Andromaki. The light structure on the cape is difficult to see until close to. In the approaches Ifalos Trakhilou lying 0·4 miles E of Ak Trakhilou, the S entrance point of Anemokambi Bay, has 3 metre depths over it. It is easily seen in calm weather. In the bight before Anemokambi inlet and on the N side of the bay there are now fish farms. Large buoys mark the limits of the fish farms and by day entry to the bay is straightforward, but at night care is needed.

Anchor where convenient in 3–12 metres. The bottom is mud and weed, good holding. Good shelter. There is a hotel at the head of the inlet with a restaurant. The new road around the bay has brought the hotel and campers in the summer, but it is still an attractive place worth a look.

GALAXIDHI
Imray-Tetra chart no. G13

Approach

The approach to the harbour should be made between Nisis Apsifia and Nisis Ay Yeoryios until past the stone beacon on the reef E of the entrance and then into the harbour as shown on the plan.

Conspicuous Once up to Ak Pounda, Nisis Apsifia and Nisis Ay Yeoryios can be distinguished. Apsifia has a single tree on it and a white shed next to the light structure. Ay Yeoryios has a church on the S end and another on the NW end. On the headland sheltering Galaxidhi the buildings of the naval college are conspicuous. The beacon (roughly rectangular) marking the reef off the entrance to Galaxidhi is easily identified. Once up to Ay Yeoryios the buildings of Galaxidhi (the cathedral is conspicuous) will be seen.

By night There is a light on Nisis Apsifia (Fl.7s5M) and a light off the W side of the entrance to the harbour (Q.RG.2M 080°-R-216°/216°-G-347°). A night entry is not recommended.

N. Apsifia   N. Ay Yeoryios

Nisis Apsifia (with a solitary tree and a hut) and Nisis Ay Yeoryios (chapel just visible) in the approaches to Galaxidhi.

Beacon

Approach to Galaxidhi harbour looking SW. The rectangular beacon marking the reef and the cathedral in the town are easily identified.

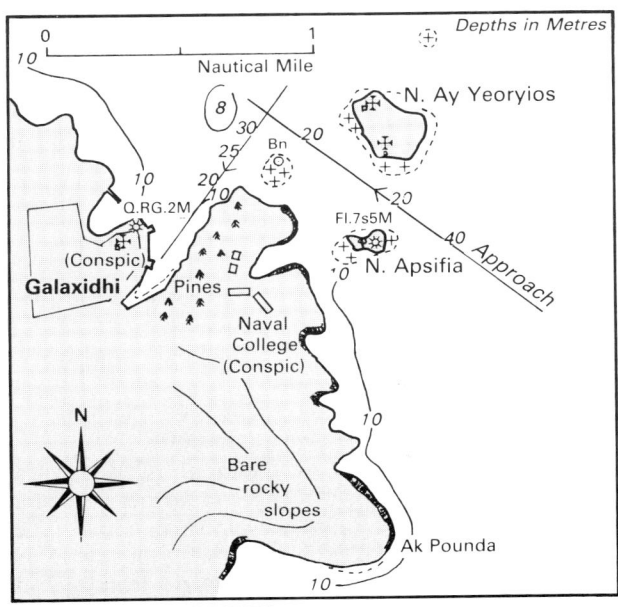

GALAXIDHI APPROACHES

Dangers

1. Care needs to be taken of the reefs fringing Nisis Apsifia and Nisis Ay Yeoryios – see plan.
2. Care needs to be taken of the reef off the E side of the entrance marked by a stone beacon. Although local boats pass between this reef and the coast, this passage is not recommended even with local knowledge.

Mooring

Go stern or bows-to the quay on the W. It is better to go bows-to as ballasting extends some distance under the water. The bottom is mud and weed, good holding.

Shelter Good all-round shelter. NE winds send some swell in – more uncomfortable than dangerous. It has been reported that there can be a tidal surge similar to the *marrobio* experienced in some harbours on the S of Sicily, but I have yet to encounter any reliable reports of its occurrence here.

Authorities Port police.

Facilities

Water On the quay.
Fuel Can be delivered by mini-tanker.
Repairs Limited mechanical repairs. Hardware shop.
Provisions Good shopping for most provisions.
Eating out Tavernas around the waterfront and others in the village.
Other PO. OTE. Exchange. Greek gas. Bus to Itea and then on to Delphi. Taxi to Delphi.

General

From the distance the rocky islets and stony hills hide the tranquil narrow inlet of Galaxidhi harbour. Hemmed in by a pine-studded peninsula to the E and the town hunched on a rocky mound to the W, this harbour is one of the most pleasing in the Gulf of Corinth. In the 18th and early 19th centuries it was a prosperous port until the Turks occupied the area and captured the fleet. Near the harbour there is an interesting small museum displaying curios including

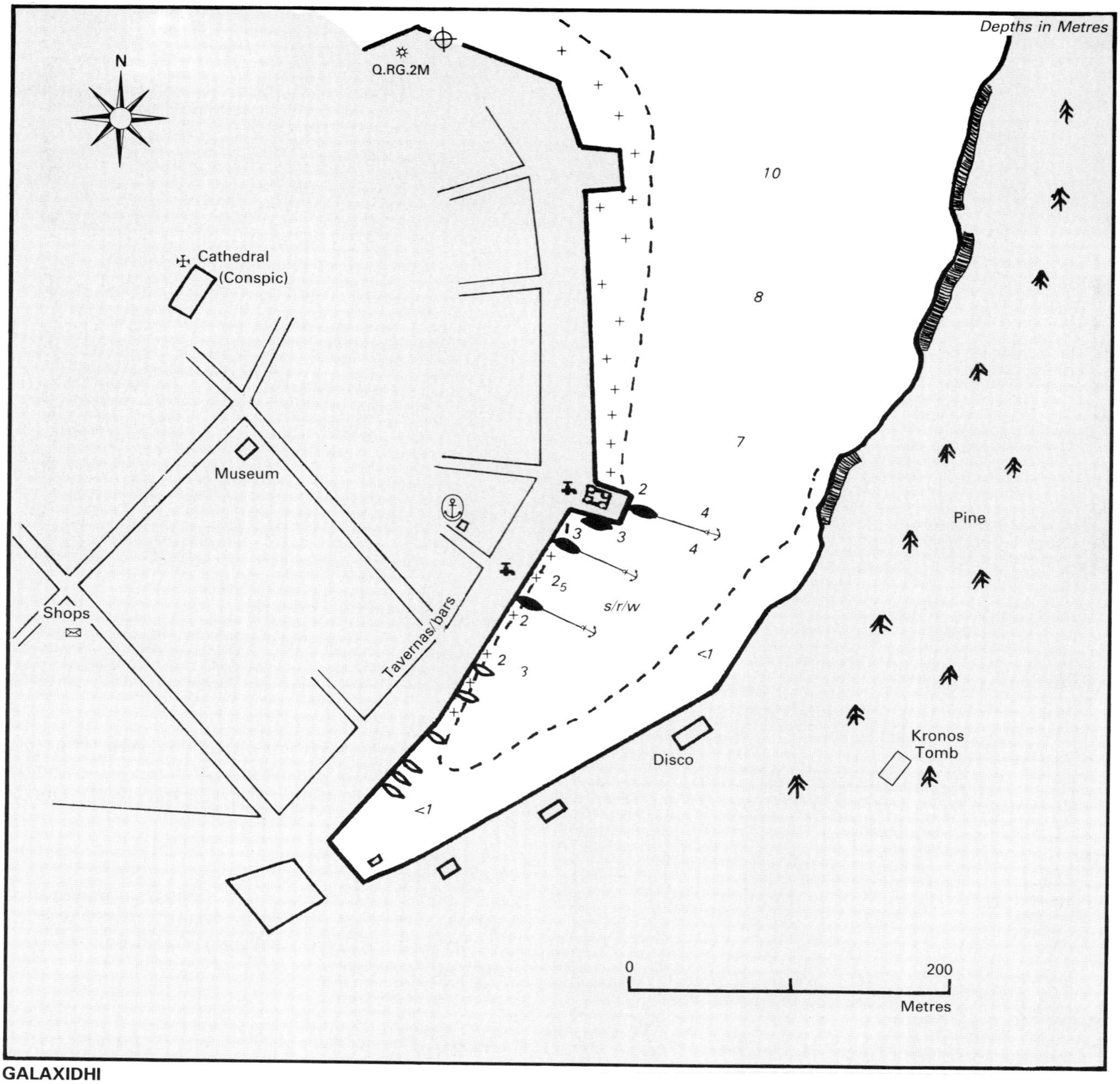

N

Depths in Metres

Q.RG.2M

Cathedral
(Conspic)

Museum

Shops

Tavernas/bars

10

8

7

2

3 3

3

4

4

2 5

s/r/w

2

2 3

<1

<1

Pine

Kronos
Tomb

Disco

0   200

Metres

GALAXIDHI
38°22'·8N 22°23'·2E (Q.RG.2M)

some fine figureheads from its heyday as a thriving shipping town.

Today it lies as quietly as it has done for over a century and offers shelter only to yachts. It has a modest amount of tourism and some fairly sophisticated restaurants and gift shops with sophisticated prices will be found on the waterfront. This is the nearest safe harbour to Delphi which can be reached by the local bus or taxi.

Galaxihi looking from the E side of the inlet.

Itea pier looking S from the town quay.

ITEA
Imray-Tetra chart no. G13

Approach
The buildings of the small town of Itea are conspicuous from the distance. Care is needed to keep well clear of Molimenos and Stafidha, the islets in the approaches to Itea. Reefs and shoal water surround Stafidha for some distance. The pier head is lit: Fl.RG.3s4M.

Mooring
Go stern or bows-to or alongside off the W or the E side of the pier depending on the wind direction. The W side is generally best. The shelter is only adequate although often the prevailing breeze peters out before it gets up into Krissaios Kolpos. Open entirely to the S.

Authorities Itea is a port of entry. Port police, customs and immigration.

Facilities
Fuel in the town. PO. OTE. Good shopping for provisions. A number of fairly ordinary tavernas. Bus to Athens which stops at Delphi.

General
The waterfront is pleasant enough, but the rest of the town is a grubby little place which, when contrasted with the charm of Galaxidhi, offers little to the yachtsman. It is more convenient than Galaxidhi for Delphi and the back streets have interesting workshops servicing the agricultural hinterland, but that is about it for Itea. The surrounding countryside is fertile and much of the plain and the slopes is planted with olive trees where it is not scarred by opencast mining.

Note On the W side of the town there is a fishing harbour affording good all-round protection. However there are only 1–1·5 metre depths in the entrance and along the outer breakwater. Most of the harbour is very shallow. Small craft drawing less than 1 metre could get in here with care. Good all-round shelter inside.

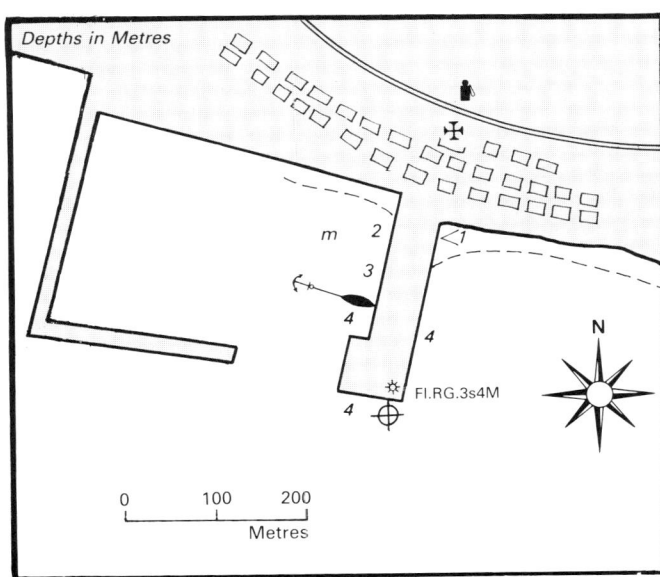

ITEA
38°25'·8N 22°25'·5E (Fl.RG.4M)

DELPHI

Ancient Delphi is easily visited from Galaxidhi or Itea and although acknowledged as one of the most spectacular and beautiful classical sites in Greece, it is for my taste, at least in summer, also spectacularly overcrowded. There are frequently twenty to thirty coaches lining the road in the summer and it is best visited in spring.

Delphi was regarded by the ancients as the centre of the world. Its spectacular site amidst ravines, rocky bluffs and sheer cliffs on the side of Mt Parnassos contributes for a large part to its air of mystery. It takes its name from Apollo Elphinos when the god was worshipped in the shape of a dolphin. As well as Apollo other gods were associated with Delphi, notably Dionysus and Athena. The Delphic oracle was famous throughout Greece – it is interesting to note that the interpretations were vague and often obscene but had the reputation of being more truthful than elsewhere. Its fame diminished during the Roman times.

The French school began excavating the site in 1892 and have continued to do much of the work. A museum houses most of the important finds.

ORMOS SALONA (Krissa)

Imray-Tetra chart no. G13

Lying at the NW extremity of Krissaios Kolpos, there are a number of sheltered coves bordering the bay, but the opencast mines on the coast hideously scar it and with any wind a haematite red stains the sea and the surrounding land. Recently fish farms have been built in some of the coves so there is really little point in heading up into the bay.

It was in this bay that Frank Abney Hastings proved the worth of a steam-powered ship in more ways than one. With a small escort he steamed into the bay and destroyed a much bigger Turkish fleet. Not only could he manoeuvre under power but his iron hull was less susceptible to damage. According to H. M. Denham he used hot shot (heated in the boilers) because he feared solid shot would simply go straight through an enemy ship without doing any real damage. It is somewhat ironic that the place where an iron ship was first used for combat in Greece is now a mass of mines extracting iron ore.

ORMOS ANDIKIRON (Antikyrra)

Imray-Tetra chart no. G13

This large bay to the E of Ak Makri-Nikolaos has a number of anchorages around it that can be used by a yacht depending on wind and sea.

Ormos Veresses Lies immediately NW of Ak Trakhilos. Affords good shelter with W winds. Untenable with NE–E winds. Anchor in 3–10 metres.

Ormos Isidhorou Lies on the S side of Kefali, the high headland on the W side of Andikiron proper. Good shelter from W and NE–E winds, although westerlies may creep around Ak Pangalos and up

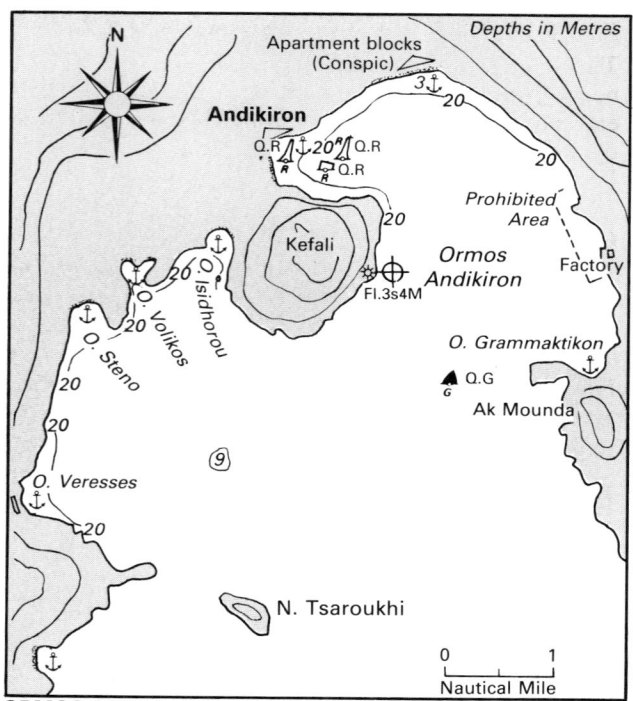

ORMOS ANDIKIRON
38°21'·6N 22°38'·8E (Fl.4M)

into here. Anchor in 5–10 metres. Care needs to be taken of large concrete mooring blocks on the bottom off the beach by the café. Café ashore.

Immediately W of Isidhorou are two other bays worth exploring.

Andikiron The large bay entered between Kefali on the W and Ak Mounda on the E. The town of Andikiron (Aspra Spitia) around the head of the bay and the factory 'suburb' on the NE (tower blocks conspicuous) is easily identified. On the W side of the bay there is a military base and on the SW side two large red and white mooring buoys (lit: Q.R). A yacht can go bows-to the quay off the town or off a quay at the E end of the town. Alternatively anchor off although it is quite deep – 8–12 metres. Reasonable shelter although NE–E winds make the western end of the bay uncomfortable and possibly untenable. Water on the town quay. Good shopping for provisions and tavernas ashore. PO. OTE.

Note The W side of the bay houses a military base.

Ormos Grammatikon The bay in the SE of Andikiron. The bay is designated as a military zone and although a yacht may anchor here, photographs of the area are forbidden.

ORMOS AY SARANDA (Saranti)

The bay lying 6 miles E of Ak Velanidhia, Ay Saranda offers good shelter from the prevailing winds. It is very deep and you will need to anchor in 15–20 metres and take a line ashore if necessary. Open S. Tavernas ashore.

KOLPOS DOMVRAINIS (Dobrena)

The much-indented gulf lying E of Ak Tambourlo. A number of small islands are peppered across the entrance. The anchorage off the village of Aliki at the E end has been recommended as an anchorage. Poor holding reported in places. Tavernas ashore.

ORMOS LIVADHOSTROU

A large bay immediately E of Kolpos Domvrainis. There are several bays and coves which look worth exploring.

NISOI ALKONIDHES (Kala Nisia)

A group of three small islands lying to the S of Kolpos Domvrainis in Kolpos Alkionidhon. With W or E winds shelter can be found anchored between Dhaskalio and Zoodhokos. A bar with depths of 1 metre or less connects the southernmost tip of Dhaskalio to the middle of Zoodhokos. Anchor in the cove to the S of the bar off the monastery on Zoodhokos (sheltered from the E and NE) or on the N side of the bar between Dhaskalio and Zoodhokos (sheltered from the W). The bottom is sand – good holding.

Once the islands supported a prosperous monastery, the buildings of which still stand on these lonely islands.

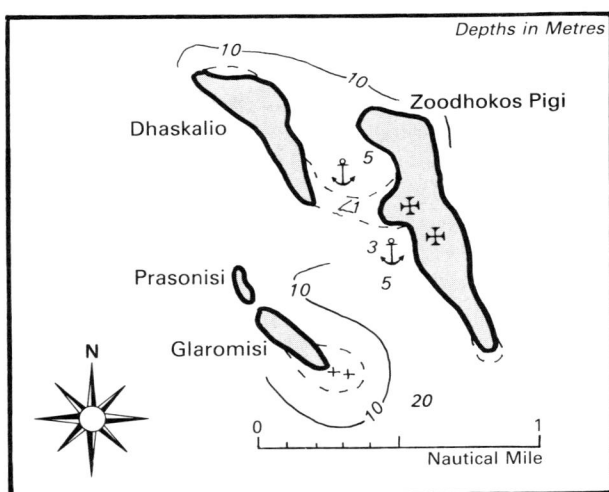

ALKIONIDHES NISOI
28°07'N 22°59'E

ORMOS AGRILIOU

A shallow bight lying 3 miles E of Ak Melangavi (the lighthouse on the cape is conspicuous from the distance), this open anchorage has been used by some yachts waiting to go through the canal. It offers some shelter from the NE but is open to all other directions.

ORMOS LOUTRAKIOU

Admiralty chart no. 2404
Imray-Tetra chart no. G13

The open bay lying N of the Corinth Canal. Used by some yachts while waiting to go through the Corinth Canal. Large hotels conspicuous from the distance line the edge of the bay. It offers shelter from the NE but is open to the W and S. Anchor where convenient in 3–6 metres. The bottom is sand and weed with some rocks – the holding is uncertain in places.

Corinth Canal
(Dhiorix Korinthou)
Admiralty chart no. 1600
Imray-Tetra chart no. G13

The canal is 3·2 miles long, 25 metres (81ft) wide, the maximum permitted draught is 7 metres (23ft) and the limestone from which it is cut rises to 76 metres (250ft) above sea level at the highest point. The canal is closed on Tuesdays to repair the crumbling limestone sides and for dredging.

From the Gulf of Corinth the breakwaters protecting the NW end of the canal (Posidhonia) are difficult to see from seaward. Iso.R.2s and Iso.G.2s lights are exhibited on the ends of the breakwaters with a stated range of 10 miles although the actual range seems much less. Although there is room for a yacht to anchor behind the NW end under the S breakwater, the holding here is bad and the authorities do not like you doing so – I don't recommend it. Go to Corinth or just chug around outside.

From the Aegean the canal zone offices and the signal mast on the S bank of the canal are conspicuous. A mole protects this end of the canal. An Iso.G.2s10M is exhibited at the extremity of the mole and an Iso.R.2s10M on the S side of the canal.

A current of 1–3 knots is stated to flow either way in the canal depending on the wind direction. Certainly the last time I went through when strong westerlies had been blowing for several days there was at least a 2 knot current. If you happen to get stuck behind a large ship in the canal further complications can ensue from the wash produced by its propellers which create a washing machine effect behind it.

There are mobile hydraulic lifting road bridges at either end which raise a section to let yachts pass or move to the side for larger craft. The following signals concerning entry into the canal are displayed on a signal mast at either end of the canal.

By day	By night	Signal
Blue flag	One white light	Entry permitted
Red flag	Two vertical white lights	Entry prohibited

The canal zone authorities use VHF channel 11.

A yacht may have to wait up to three hours before entering the canal. The paperwork and canal fees are done at Isthmia at the Aegean end of the canal. Moor

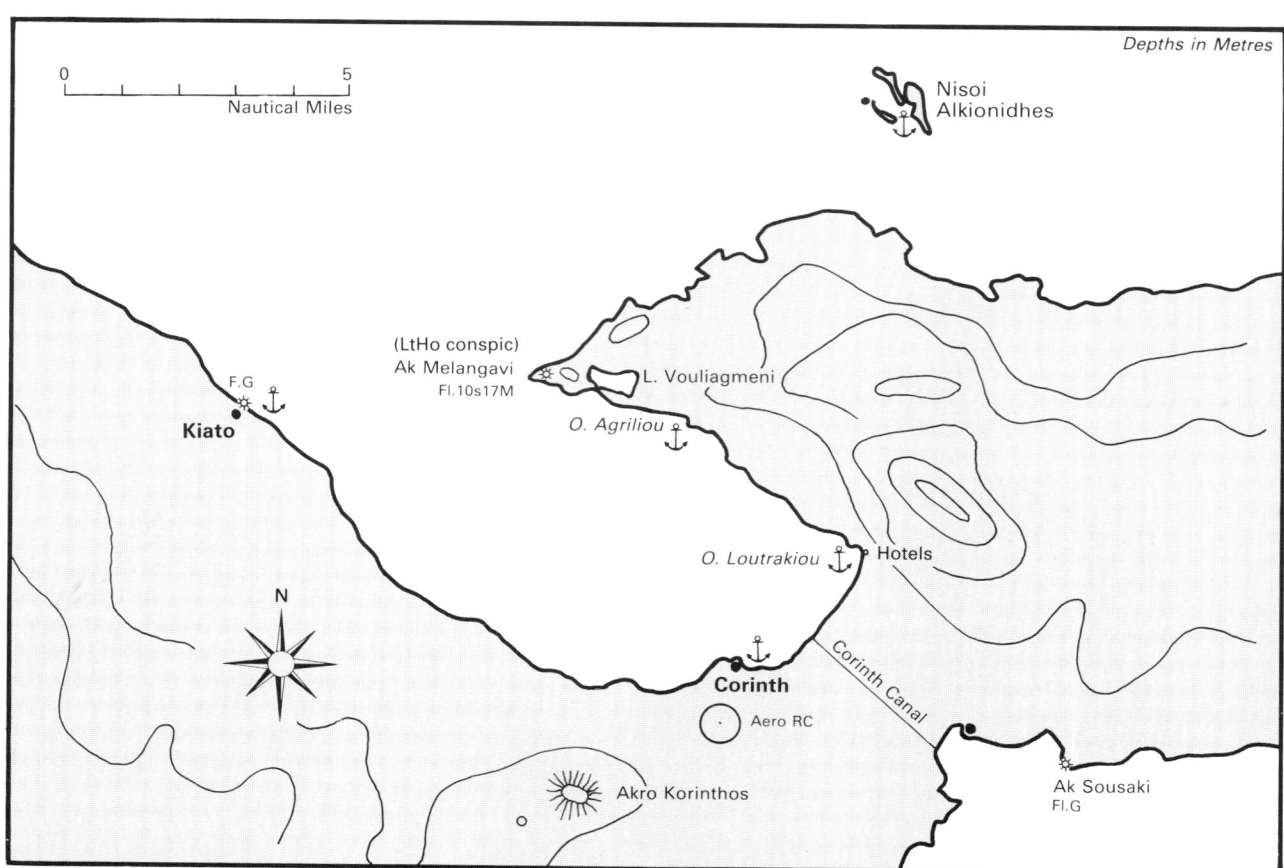

APPROACHES TO CORINTH CANAL

Corinth Canal looking SE. *Aerofilms*

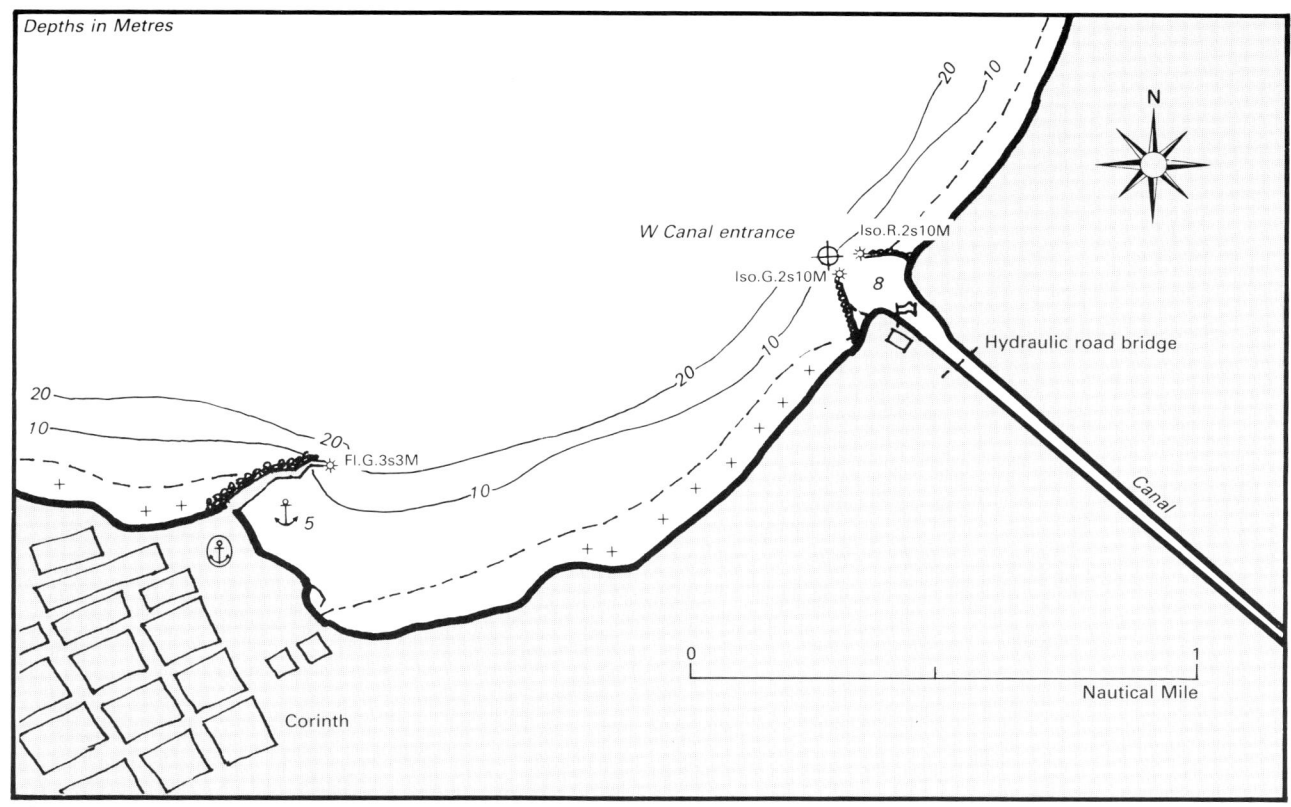

CORINTH CANAL – WEST ENTRANCE
37°57'·2N 22°57'·5E (Iso.G.2s10M)

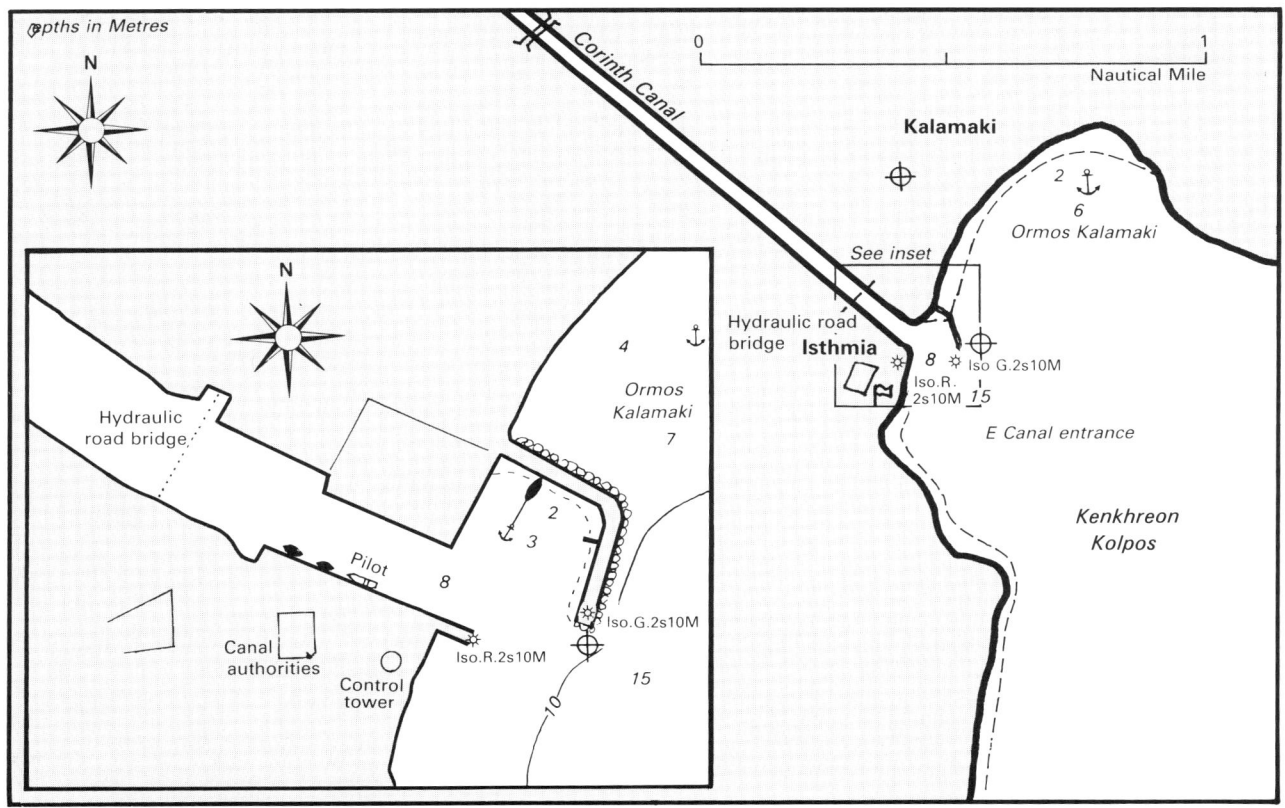

CORINTH CANAL – EASTERN ENTRANCE
37°54'·9N 23°00'·6E (Iso.G.2s10M

alongside the quay on the S side of the canal taking care of the rough concrete and reinforcing iron protruding in places. About one half of the quay has been repaired and rubber fendering placed alongside. Large yachts may pay the pilot outside the canal – he will come alongside in a launch.

The Corinth Canal is probably one of the most expensive canals per mile in the world. Costs in 1993 were around the drachma equivalent of £40 for yachts of 0–10 tons and £80 for 10–20 tons. On Sundays and holidays 30% is added and for night passages 25% is added. Yachts which attempt to alter their certificates or present photocopies will find themselves charged at a higher rate which may explain some of the letters I get from irate owners complaining about the charges. It is difficult to predict what costs will be in advance due to fluctuations in the exchange rate and variations in the percentage increase of canal fees by the authorities.

The ancients used to drag ships across the isthmus on a paved road (the *dhiolkos*), parts of which can still be seen on the N side. Octavian in pursuit of Antony after the Battle of Actium had his ships dragged across here. At various times the Greek and Roman rulers worked out schemes for a canal but Nero was the only one to start digging. Using 6000 Jews, he didn't even get to the rock before insurrection in Gaul diverted his energies. The present canal was started by a French company and finished by the Greeks in 1893. It was enlarged after damage suffered in the Second World War. Two bridges, a railway bridge and a road bridge, cross it at the maximum height of the cut.

Caution Severe gusts blow off the surrounding high land at either end of the canal. They are particularly bad at the Aegean end with NE winds.

CORINTH HARBOUR
Admiralty chart no. 1600
Imray-Tetra chart no. G13

Approach

Conspicuous The harbour is difficult to locate from the distance. The high-rise buildings of Corinth city are easily identified and the harbour lies immediately NE of the cluster of buildings. The harbour mole will be seen closer in.

By night Use the light on Ak Melangavi (Fl.10s17M) and the lights at the entrance to the Corinth Canal (Iso.R.2s10M and Iso.G.2s10M) although the range of the canal lights appears less. The harbour mole is lit on the extremity (Fl.G.3s3M) although it is difficult to pick up against the loom of the town lights. There are four large floodlights along the quay. The yacht harbour is lit F.R and F.G, though these should not be relied on.

Dangers
1. With strong NE winds there can be severe gusts down into this end of the Gulf of Corinth.
2. With strong westerlies a swell piles up at this end of the gulf although once behind the mole you are out of it.

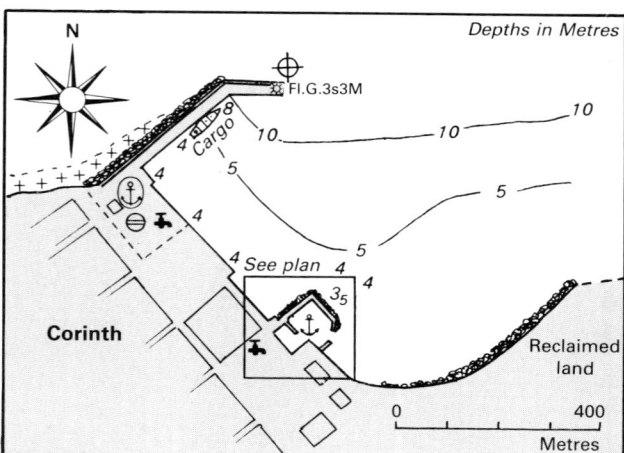

CORINTH
37°56'·7N 22°55'·9E (Fl.G.3M)

Mooring

Yachts up to 20 metres or so can go stern or bows-to in the yacht harbour. Depths appear to be irregular in places off the outside of the mole and yachts drawing 2·5–3 metres should proceed with caution, although once inside the harbour there are 4 metre depths nearly everywhere. The bottom is mud, good holding. Very large yachts should berth alongside in the commercial port where possible.

Shelter Good all-round shelter in the new yacht harbour. The outer harbour is considered dangerous in strong NE winds.

Authorities Port police and customs.

Facilities

Water In the square by the yacht harbour and on the quay in the commercial harbour once the 'waterman' is located.
Fuel In the town. A mini-tanker can be arranged to deliver fuel to the quay.

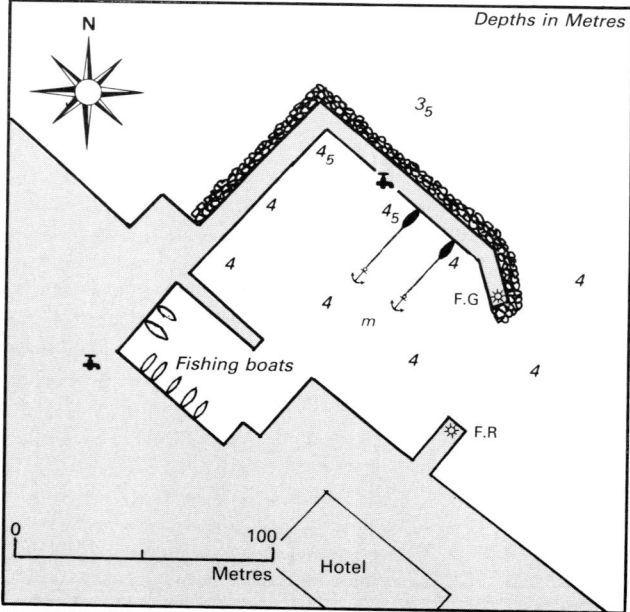

CORINTH YACHT HARBOUR

The new yacht harbour at Corinth looking E from inside it.

Repairs Mechanical and engineering repairs possible. Good hardware shops in the town.

Provisioning Good shopping for all provisions. Several large supermarkets in the town and a small fruit and vegetable market at the N end several streets in from the quay.

Eating out Tavernas in the town.

Other PO. OTE. Banks. Greek gas and *Camping Gaz*. Hire cars and motorbikes. Bus to Patras and Athens.

General

Corinth is a bustling modern and thoroughly nondescript city – just the sort of place you would expect of a city that has been hastily erected after a series of earthquakes demolished previous cities here. It seems to be more of a crossroads for people going elsewhere than a centre.

The same could not be said about ancient Corinth sitting on a plateau behind modern Corinth and the ruins of this infamous city deserve a visit. The ancient city commanded the passage of trade between the mainland and the Peloponnese and across the isthmus between the Ionian and the Aegean. Consequently it was an important and rich city. The Corinthians were fine seamen and possessed a large fleet with which they founded and protected colonies in Corfu and Syracuse. Some believe the first trireme was built here. They paid particular attention to the gods of the sea – to Poseidon and to Palaimon. The latter was the protector of harbours and myth has it that he was originally Melikertes who was transported to Corinth on a dolphin.

The hard-living Corinthians were evidently hard-working as well. Their pottery was esteemed throughout the Mediterranean and from the 5th century BC the Corinthian style of architecture embodied in the Corinthian column became one of the most popular styles – continuing on through Byzantium and to the present day. From the 4th to the 2nd centuries BC Corinth earned a reputation for itself of a fast-living city where in an age of loose living the inhabitants were notorious for their vices. From this hedonistic age we get the term Corinthian, used in the early 19th century to describe a hard-living sportsman devoted to pugilism, horse racing and yachting! The term survives today as the name of various yacht clubs and football teams.

KIATO

Imray-Tetra chart no. G13

Approach

Conspicuous The town of Kiato can be seen from the distance and closer in the high retaining wall of the harbour mole is easily identified. A cathedral with a red tile cupola and belfry is conspicuous behind the harbour.

By night The F.G on the end of the breakwater is difficult to pick up against the lights of the town. A green neon light to the E of the harbour has a good range!

Mooring

Go stern or bows-to or alongside the mole wherever there is sufficient room. The harbour is 15 metres deep near the extremity of the mole so if possible go alongside.

Shelter Good protection from W winds although some swell works its way around the end of the mole. Open to the E and dangerous with winds from that direction. With strong N winds it has been suggested yachts go under the high part of the sea wall rather than the low part near the root of the mole as sheets of spray come over the low part drenching any yacht berthed there.

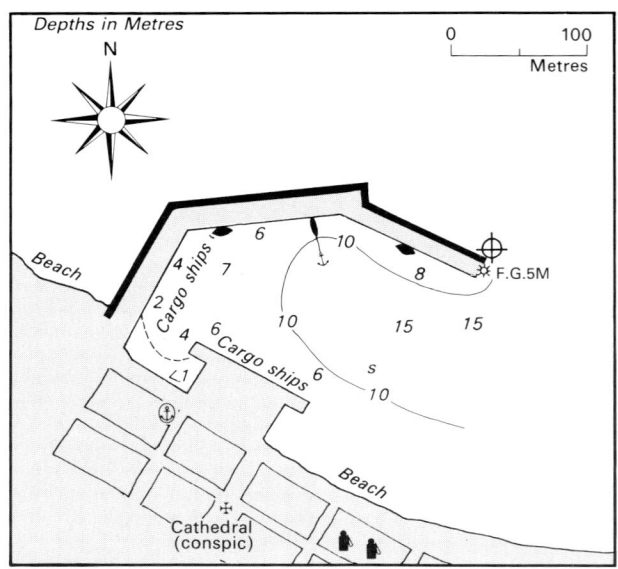

KIATO
38°00°·9N 22°45′·3E (F.G)

Corinth Canal looking E.

Authorities Port police and customs.

Note The small harbour immediately E of the main harbour is always crowded with local boats. Depths in it are uneven with a few shallow spots.

Facilities

Water Close to the quay.

Fuel In the town. A mini-tanker can be arranged to deliver to the harbour.

Provisions Good shopping for all provisions in the town.

Eating out Tavernas near the waterfront.

Other PO. OTE. Bank. Greek gas and *Camping Gaz.* Hire cars. Bus to Athens.

General

Although principally a town based on the busy commercial harbour, Kiato is developing into a popular tourist resort based on the good bathing beaches nearby. The surrounding land is intensively cultivated in citrus and the vine.

IV. The Saronic and Eastern Peloponnese

The Aegean Sea is entered from the west around Ak Maleas or through the Corinth Canal, the southwesternmost and northwesternmost limits of the sea area covered in this chapter.

The Aegean takes its name from Aegeus, the father of Theseus, who flung himself into the sea when he believed his son to have been killed in Crete. Theseus had gone to Crete as part of the annual tribute of young Athenian men and women to the Minotaur, but with the help of Ariadne slew the monster and escaped. Ariadne was unceremoniously dumped on Naxos and perhaps the gods clouded his memory for his foul deed because he forgot the prearranged signal to his father to tell him that all was well. If his ship carried a black sail then Aegeus would know his son had perished, a white sail would mean he was alive. Aegeus, seeing the black sail on the approaching ship, was overcome with grief and leapt to his death.

The Aegean geographically divides Europe from Asia although the islands in the sea form a bridge between the two continents. Between the islands, without compass or sextant, the merchants of ancient times could cross the Aegean and be out of sight of land for only a few hours. Almost as important as the island bridge across the sea were the regular summer winds blowing from the north. These winds, now called by the Turkish name, the *meltemi*, were then called the etesian winds from the Greek *etos*, a year, because they blow regularly every year. Traders could sail across the Aegean with this wind and return in the spring or autumn when the northerlies are light and southerlies sometimes blow. The winter winds can be fierce and some ancient states forbade traders to cross the sea in the winter months.

The area covered in this chapter encompasses three significant historical centres. Mycenae at the head of the Argolic Gulf was the centre of the Mycenaean period which succeeded the Minoans and provided the material for Homer's epics. Athens was of course the centre of Classical Greece, although it is all too easy to attribute too much to this ancient city and forget the contributions to art, oratory, science, and commerce from other city-states all over Greece. Lastly, the fleets of Idhra (Hydra) and Spetsai were of key importance in determining the outcome of the War of Independence and both Navplion and Aigina were at different times the capitals of the newly liberated Greece.

In the Saronic Gulf the yachtsman will come upon the greatest concentration of yachts in Greece. Most of these are based at the marinas along the Attic coast from where a considerable number of charter companies operate. Many charter yachts follow the Saronic trail to Aigina, Poros, Idhra and Spetsai and to nearby harbours and anchorages, so if you wish to avoid the crowds in the summer stay away from the charter yacht milk run and head for the eastern coast of the Peloponnese where there are unspoilt harbours and anchorages.

Weather patterns in the Saronic and Eastern Peloponnese

The normal summer wind differs radically depending on where you are in this area. Along the mainland coast from the Corinth Canal to Ak Sounion and the sea area between the mainland coast and Methana, the *meltemi* is the normal wind. It blows from the NNE to NE at about Force 4–6, although it may be stronger around Ak Sounion. Around the Methana peninsula and Poros it is usually less. The *meltemi* starts blowing in July and dies in October. If the *meltemi* does not blow, (and it is not as regular here as in the Cyclades or the Dodecanese), the wind in this sea area is generally from the south, usually getting up about midday, blowing Force 2–4, and dying off about sunset.

Moving south and east, in Kolpos Idhras (Gulf of Hydra) and Argolikos Kolpos (Argolic Gulf), the prevailing wind is from the SE. It gets up about midday, blows Force 3–5, occasionally more, and dies down at night. In Argolikos Kolpos this wind can be relied upon in the summer for 90% of the time. Down the eastern Peloponnese the wind may be a weak *meltemi* from the NE or a southerly from the SE or SW. In the spring and autumn the wind is predominantly from the S over the whole area and is generally weak.

In general there are few weather problems in the area. When the *meltemi* is blowing there are strong gusts off the high land near the entrance to the Corinth Canal and around Ak Sounion. Along the eastern coast of the Peloponnese there may be a katabatic wind at night. Astrous is particularly notorious for this wind which arrives without warning and often reaches Force 6–7 where

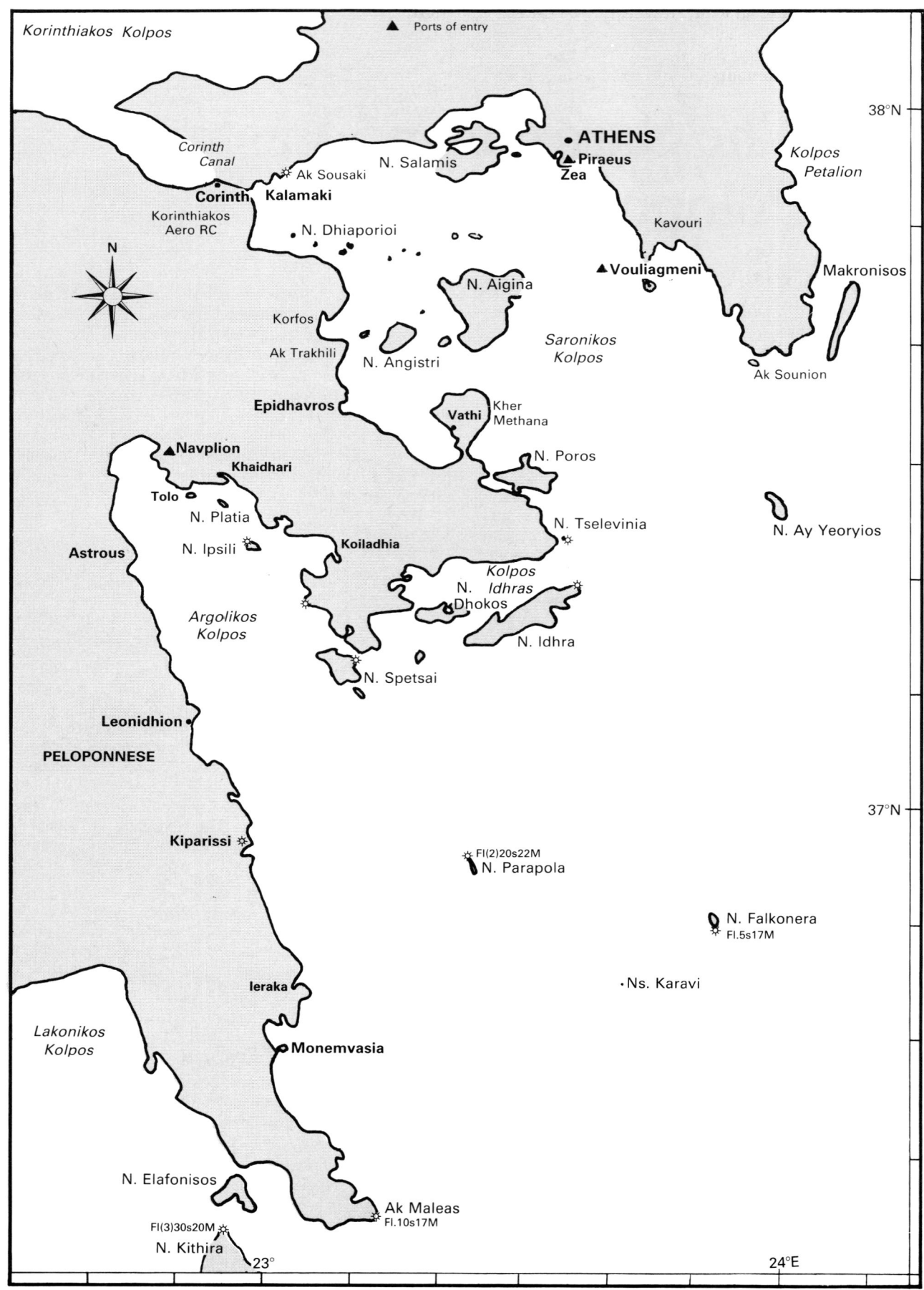

Korinthiakos Kolpos

▲ Ports of entry

38°N

Corinth Canal

N. Salamis

ATHENS
▲ **Piraeus**
Zea

Kolpos Petalion

☼ Ak Sousaki
Corinth **Kalamaki**

Korinthiakos Aero RC

Kavouri

● N. Dhiaporioi

N **N. Aigina**

▲ **Vouliagmeni**

Makronisos

Korfos

Saronikos Kolpos

Ak Trakhili

N. Angistri

Ak Sounion

Epidhavros

Vathi Kher Methana

● N.
Dhokos

N. Poros

▲ **Navplion**
Khaidhari

Tolo

N. Platia

N. Ipsili ☼

Koiladhia

N. Tselevinia ☼

N. Ay Yeoryios

Kolpos Idhras
N.
Dhokos ☼

Astrous

Argolikos Kolpos

☼

N. Idhra

☼ N. Spetsai

Leonidhion ●

PELOPONNESE

37°N

Kiparissi ☼

☼ Fl(2)20s22M
◗ N. Parapola

◗ N. Falkonera
☼ Fl.5s17M

● Ns. Karavi

Ieraka

Lakonikos Kolpos

Monemvasia

N. Elafonisos

Ak Maleas
☼ Fl.10s17M

Fl(3)30s20M ☼
N. Kithira   23°

24°E

previously there was no wind. It usually lasts for 4–6 hours. In the spring and autumn there may be thunderstorms accompanied by a squall, but these last only one or two hours on average. In the winter the Saronic and Argolic Gulfs have a mild sunny climate making them popular places for yachts in the winter.

Data

PORTS OF ENTRY
Zea Marina
Vouliagmeni
Navplion

PROHIBITED AREAS
1. It is prohibited to navigate in Ormos Salamis in an area half a mile off the southern shore between a point one mile and a point two miles E of Ak Petritis.
2. It is prohibited to enter an area NE of Ormos Elevsinos, one mile E of Limin Elevsis.
3. It is prohibited to navigate between Salamis and the NE side of the mainland except in a narrow channel in the fairway. It is prohibited to navigate in this channel at night.
4. It is prohibited to anchor outside the channel mentioned above.
5. It is prohibited to navigate and anchor in the northern part of the bay immediately N of Poros town where there is a naval college.
6. Nisis Ipsili is used for target practice by the Greek Navy.
7. Although not listed as such, Nisidhes Karavi (36°46′N 23°36′E), three barren islets lying off the eastern Peloponnese, are used for target practice by the Greek air force.

MAJOR LIGHTS
Corinth Canal (W side) Iso.R.2s10M
Corinth Canal (mole head) Iso.G.2s10M
Ormos Sofikou (Korfos) Fl.4s5M
Ak Kalamaki Fl.2s5M

Mainland coast
Ak Sousaki Fl.G.10s12M
Ak Karas Fl.WR.4s8/6M
Ak Konkhi Fl.3s9M
Nisis Psittalia Fl(2)15s25M
Limin Irakleous (E breakwater) Fl(2)G.4s9M
Ak Filatouri Fl(2)14s5M
Poros Themistokleous LFl.G.6s13M
Piraeus Harbour LFl.R.6s13M
Zea Marina (S mole) Fl(2)R.6s7M
Mounikhias (N mole) Iso.G.2s6M
Mounikhias (S mole) Iso.R.2s8M
Ellinikon (aero beacon) AlFl.WG.6s15M
Nisis Fleves Fl(3)10s8M
Vouliagmeni (mole head) Fl(3)R.12s7M

Aigina
Ak Plakakia Fl(2)15s7M
Ak Tourlos Fl.3·6s5M
Nisis Moni Fl(2)WRG.10s7-4M
Nisis Lagousa LFl.7·5s5M

Poros
Ak Dana (N entrance) Fl.WR.4s8/5M
Ak Stavros S Point Fl.RG.3s4/4M

Idhra
Ak Zourva Fl(3)20s17M
Nisis Dhokos (SE point) Fl(2)WR.12s6/4M

Nisis Ay Yeoryios (SE end) Fl(2)15s17M

Spetsai
Ak Fanari (Baltiza) Fl.WR.5s18/14M
Ak Mavrokavos Fl.WR.2s5/3M
Nisis Petrokaravo Fl(2)9s7M

Argolikos Kolpos
Ak Korakas Fl.7s5M
Nisis Ipsili (SW point) Fl.5s9M
Limin Khaidhari (E point) Fl(3)WR.15s5/3M
Ak Skala (Nisis Tolo) Fl(2)WR.10s5/3M
Ak Panayitsa (Navplion) Fl.1·5s5M
Ak Astrous Fl.3s5M
Ak Sambateki LFl.7·5s4M

E Peloponnese
Nisis Parapola Fl(2)20s22M
Nisis Falkonera (S end) Fl.5s17M
Nisis Monemvasia Fl.5s6M
Ak Maleas Fl.10s17M

Quick reference guide

	Shelter	Mooring	Fuel	Water	Provisioning	Tavernas	Plan
Attic Coast							
Ormos Kalamaki	C	C	B	B	C	C	
Salamis	B	AC	B	A	B	B	•
Zea Marina	A	AB	A	A	A	A	•
Mounikhias	A	A	B	A	A	A	•
Faliron	B	A	B	A	A	A	•
Kalamaki (Alimos)	A	A	A	A	A	A	•
Glifadha 4	A	A	B	A	B	A	•
Glifadha 1, 2, 3	A	A	A	A	B	A	•
Voula	B	AB	A	B	B	B	
Vouliagmeni	A	A	A	A	C	B	•
Varkiza	B	A	B	A	B	B	•
Ormos Anavisou	B	C	B	B	C	B	•
Sounion	C	C	O	O	O	B	•
Peloponnese and off-lying islands to Poros							
Ormos Linari	C	C	O	O	O	O	
Frangolimani	C	C	O	O	O	O	
Ormos Dimani	C	C	O	O	O	O	
Korfos	A	AC	B	A	B	B	•
Ormos Selondas	B	C	O	O	O	O	
Nea Epidhavros	O	C	O	B	O	C	
Epidhavros	B	AC	B	A	B	B	•
Vathi (Methana)	A	AC	O	O	O	C	•
Limin Aigina	A	A	B	A	A	A	•
Perdika	B	AC	O	B	B	B	•
Ay Marina	O	C	O	O	O	B	•

	Shelter	*Mooring*	*Fuel*	*Water*	*Provisioning*	*Tavernas*	*Plan*
Souvalas	C	A	O	O	C	C	●
Angistri	C	A	O	B	C	C	●
Dhoroussa	B	C	O	O	O	C	
Methana	A	A	B	A	A	B	●
Poros	A	ABC	A	A	A	A	●
Nisis Soupia	C	C	O	O	O	O	

Kolpos Idhras and Argolikos Kolpos

Ermioni	A	AC	B	A	A	B	●
Limin Idhras	B	A	O	A	A	A	●
Mandraki (Idhra)	C	C	O	O	O	C	●
Ormos Skindos (Dhokos)	B	C	O	O	O	C	●
Baltiza (Spetsai)	A	AC	A	A	A	A	●
Dapia (Spetsai)	C	A	B	B	A	A	●
Ormos Zoyioryia (Spetsai)	B	C	O	O	O	C	
Porto Kheli	A	AC	B	B	A	B	●
Koiladhia	A	AC	O	B	B	C	●
Khaidhari	A	C	O	B	B	B	●
Tolo	C	AC	B	B	A	A	●
Navplion	A	AB	B	A	A	A	●
Astrous	A	A	B	A	B	B	●
Tilos	B	A	B	B	B	C	
Leonidhion	C	A	O	A	C	B	●
Poulithra	C	A	O	O	C	C	●
Fokianos	C	C	O	O	O	O	

Peloponnese

Kiparissi	B	AC	B	B	C	B	●
Ieraka	A	AC	O	O	C	B	●
Monemvasia	B	AC	B	B	A	A	●
Palaio Monemvasia	B	C	O	O	O	O	●

Athens and the mainland Attic coast

This section from the Corinth Canal to Ak Sounion is mostly mountainous barren terrain. Around Athens there is the large flat Attic Plain much of which is covered by Athens and Piraeus and their outlying suburbs. There are a considerable number of industrial installations along the coast: the large petrochemical refinery near the canal (the gaseous by-products burning off are conspicuous at night); the shipyards and naval base near Perama and on Salamis; and numerous factories and mills between Perama and Piraeus – in fact some 60% or more of Greek industry surrounds the capital. Between Piraeus and Glifadha the coast is lined by high-rise apartment blocks. A motorway and railway run parallel to the coast between Athens and the canal.

Athens is a comparatively modern city whose modern architecture compares badly with the ancient monuments in the centre. It has grown rapidly as the young from the islands and rural mainland have arrived here by the thousands looking for work.

Consequently the outlying suburbs have been built to house these migrants with little planning or thought and are particularly unattractive. The geographical situation is similar to that of Los Angeles so Athens has a smog problem that is often worse than that of the smog capital of the USA – at times you will see the green-grey cloud of the dreaded *nefos* hanging over the city as you approach from seawards. It is not surprising that many have voted Athens the worst capital city in Europe. The city's population is some three million plus, about one third of the total population of Greece.

Although the natives of a particular island or region will always run down the natives of another island or region ('they are liars/cheats/thieves/etc.'), between the natives of Athens and the rest of the population there is a very real enmity. There are effectively two races in Greece: those Greeks who live in Athens and the others. I well remember being introduced to an Athenian on Spetsai with the admonition that he was an Athenian, but a 'good person' despite that handicap.

Athens, partly because of its position and communications and partly because much of the wealth is concentrated here, is the Greek equivalent of the Hamble or the French Riviera. Along the coast there are six marinas out of a total of nine marinas in the whole of Greece. The marinas are all crowded and although many of the yachts are owned by Greeks, still a very small percentage of the overall population takes to the water purely for pleasure. Most of the bareboat charter companies and the skippered yachts for charter are based at Zea or Kalamaki. A yacht entering the Aegean will inevitably home in on Athens and its string of marinas for the facilities and availability of spares and nautical items which will only be found there. Apart from that there is little point in going there as the surrounding sea is dirty and polluted and the scenery quite unrepresentative of the rest of Greece. You will have seen Athens but not Greece.

CORINTH CANAL See Chapter III Gulf of Corinth

ORMOS KALAMAKI
While waiting to proceed through the canal or after coming through from the Gulf of Corinth, a yacht can anchor in Ormos Kalamaki immediately N of the canal entrance. Good shelter from the *meltemi* although there are strong gusts off the high land above. The bottom is sand and weed – only mediocre holding. Tavernas on the shore. Fishing boats are kept moored here all year round.

Salamis
(**Nisos Salamina**)

An arid rocky island devoid of vegetation. It is much indented, but there are few anchorages available to yachts because of the extensive naval installations around the coast near which anchorage is prohibited. This is no great loss as the water is very polluted (a

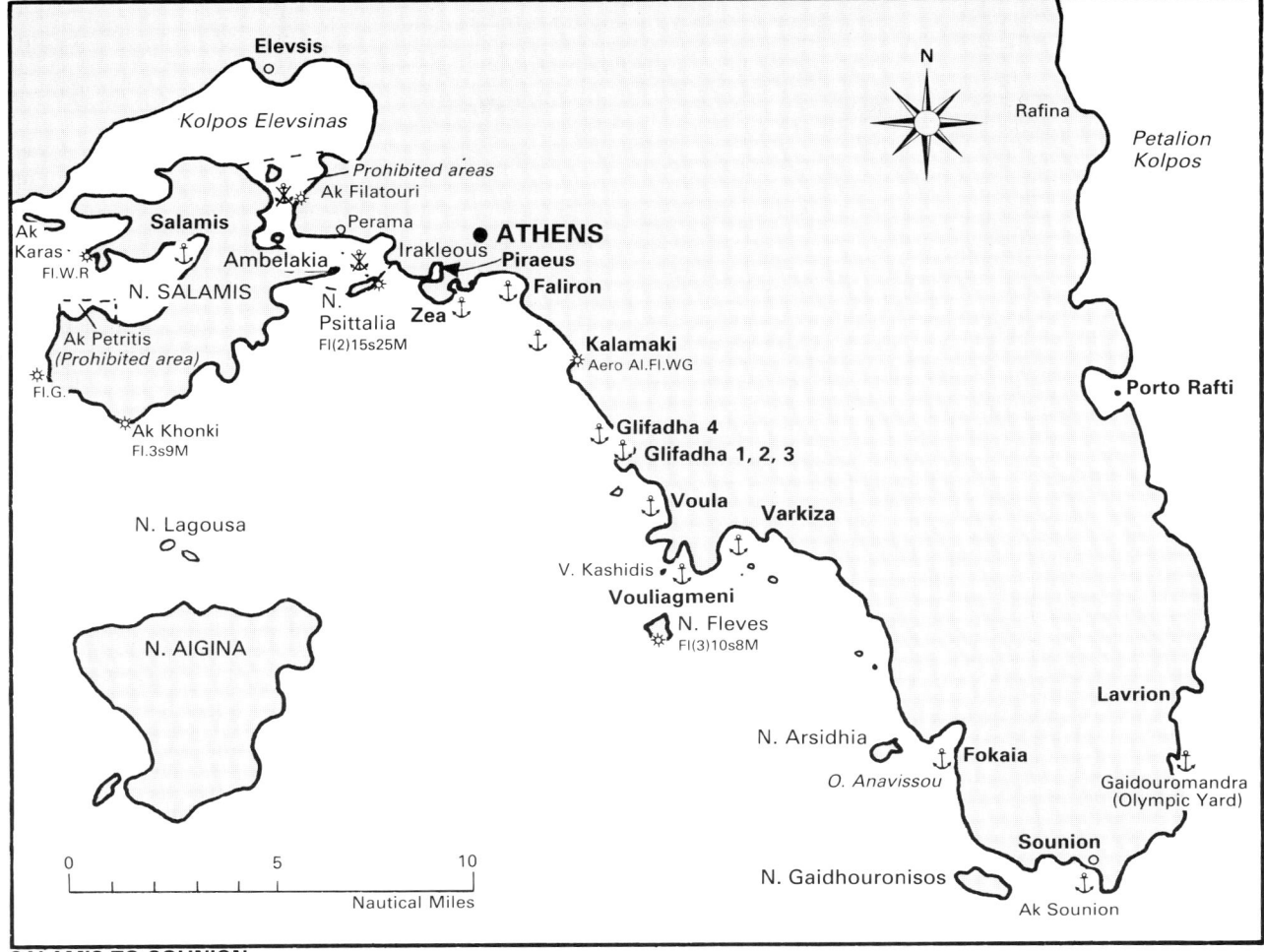

SALAMIS TO SOUNION

dirty oily brown colour with all sorts of objectionable flotsam) and the nearby coast is an industrial wasteland.

Caution For about 6 miles E of the Corinth Canal in Kolpos Kenkhreon (Gulf of Kenkhreo) there are strong gusts off the mountains on the N side of the gulf when the *meltemi* is blowing. The gusts become less fierce the further E and S you go.

NAVY PRACTICE AREA
The sea area between the Corinth Canal and Salamis is often used by the navy for exercises. Nisis Ipsili in this area is used for target practice.

ORMOS SALAMIS (Salaminos)

Prohibited Areas
1. In Ormos Salamis navigation is prohibited within half a mile of the shore between one and two miles E of Ak Petritis (the southern entrance of the bay).
2. Navigation is prohibited in an area around Elevsis in the Kolpos Elevsinos.
3. Except for a narrow channel in the fairway, navigation is prohibited between the NE side of Salamis and the mainland coast opposite. Navigation at night is prohibited. Large ships are

not permitted to navigate (without special permission) in the area enclosed by Nisis Psittalia, Salamis and the mainland (Ormos Keratsiniou). Anchorage is prohibited in the area.

SALAMIS (Salamina)

Approach
Salamis village lies at the head of Ormos Salamis. The boatyard on the N side of the bay and the houses of the village are easily identified.

By night Use the light on Ak Karas (Fl.WR.4s8/6M) and the light on the pier head at Salamis (2F.R(vert)3M).

Mooring
Anchor off in 2–4 metres or go stern-to the inside of the inner mole (2 metre depths) or the short pier (2–3 metres) if there is room. The mole and the pier are usually crowded with fishing boats. The bottom is sand and weed – good holding.

Shelter Good shelter from the *meltemi*. Southerlies whip up a short chop across the large bay.

Facilities
Water At the root of the mole.
Fuel In the town.

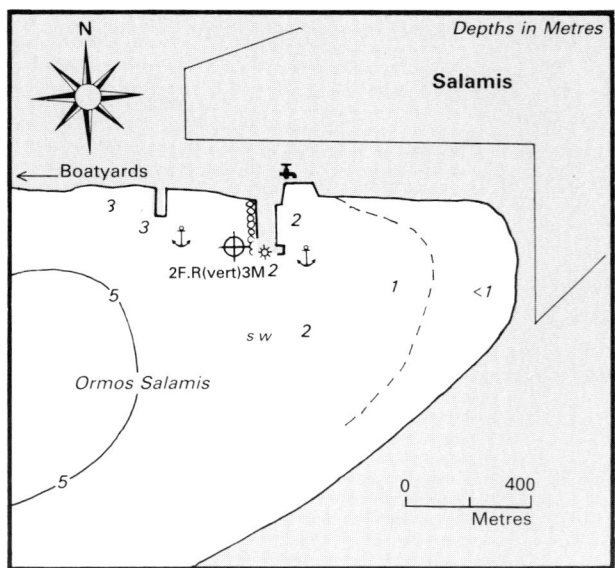

SALAMIS
37°57'·7N 23°29'·6E (2F.R.3M)

Provisions Good shopping for provisions.
Eating out Tavernas.
Other PO. OTE. Bus to Paloukia and ferries to the mainland (Perama and Piraeus).

General

The village has a run-down appearance, but the locals are friendly and it is a convivial enough place if you are hauled out at the boatyard.

BOATYARDS

To the W of the village there are a number of yards which can haul out yachts up to 40 tons. They can carry out general repairs including some engine repairs and welding and machining jobs. Anchor off the boatyard where there is reasonable shelter from all but strong SW winds.

AMBELAKIA

At Ambelakia, on the E side of Salamis, in the bay immediately opposite Perama a new boatyard has opened. The yard is located in the SW corner of the bay with a quayed area and short pier where yachts can berth. The yard has a 100 ton travel hoist and hard standing ashore. All manner of repairs including steel and stainless steel fabrication, wood and GRP repairs, mechanical and general engineering repairs are undertaken and other work can be arranged in Piraeus. Contact Theo Bekris, Bekris & Co Ltd, 18902 Ambelakia, Salamis ☎ (office) 412 5111 (yard) 467 1588/467 4120 *Fax* 453 2858 Telex 213072 THEO GR.

Battle of Salamis

Around 22 September 480 BC in the narrow winding channel between the NE side of Salamis and the mainland opposite (the same area where navigation is restricted), the Battle of Salamis was fought between the Greeks and the invading Persians under Xerxes. The Greek battle plan was worked out by Themistocles in considerable detail (as was discovered only recently with the recovery of the Troezein Stone in the Trikeri Channel) and ranks as one of the great strategic victories in the history of naval warfare.

The Persians were based at Faliron and intended to take the Greeks in a pincer movement between their fleet and a land force marching along the coast. A conventional battle between the two forces would probably have meant a resounding defeat for the numerically inferior Greek force. Themistocles devised a trap. He leaked information to the Persians that the Greek force was going to withdraw and Xerxes immediately dispatched his ships to bottle the Greeks up in Salamis. Two hundred Egyptian ships blockaded the western entrance while the remainder of Xerxes' fleet was arrayed across the eastern entrance. Xerxes had a silver throne set up on the mainland to view the defeat of the Greeks.

The Greek fleet emerged and then retired, apparently in confusion, to a position behind a promontory where they again formed up in battle order. The enemy fleet advanced and were totally surprised to find the Greek fleet waiting for them. The more handy Greek *triremes* caused chaos in the narrow channel and the Persian fleet became hopelessly confused, so much so that it was recorded they accidentally sank some of their own ships. This battle effectively destroyed the Persian fleet and with it the Persian threat in the Aegean.

BOATYARDS

At Perama on the mainland coast about 3 miles W of Piraeus there are a number of yards which will haul out yachts up to 200 tons. A large travel hoist is reported to be able to haul craft up to 100 tons out. All mechanical and engineering repairs carried out. Wood and GRP repairs arranged. Electrical and electronic work.

Make arrangements from Zea as there are no suitable anchorages close by and navigation is restricted to this area.

PIRAEUS COMMERCIAL HARBOUR

This large harbour is for ferries and commercial cargo ships only. A yacht should not attempt to enter or berth here.

ZEA MARINA

Admiralty chart no. 1520
Imray-Tetra chart no. G14

Approach

The roadstead between the coast of Salamis and Piraeus is crowded with ships (cargo and ferries) at anchor and under way. Care is needed when navigating through this maze, especially at night.

Conspicuous The multi-storey apartment blocks of Piraeus and the outlying suburbs of Athens are spread along the coast making it difficult to identify exactly where Piraeus and Zea Marina are. A tall chimney with red and white bands is conspicuous W

Zea Marina

Approaches to Zea Marina looking NW.

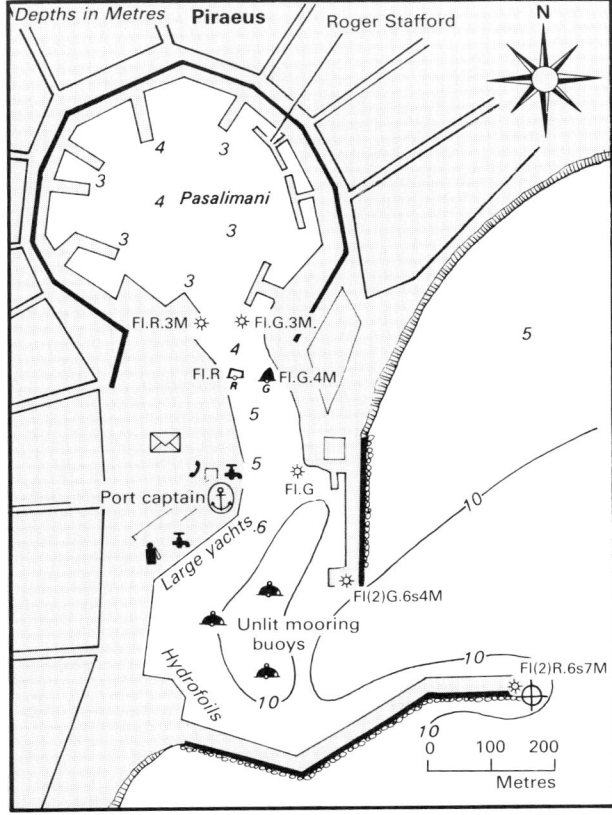

ZEA MARINA
37°56′N 23°39′·2E (Fl(2)R.7M)

of Piraeus and the stadium at Faliron is easily identified. Between Piraeus and Zea there is a rocky bluff covered in apartments. Closer in, Piraeus Commercial Harbour (there are always ferries coming and going) and the outer mole of Zea can be identified.

By night The lights which stand out are: Ak Khonki light on the SE tip of Salamis (Fl.3s9M); the light on Nisis Psittalia (Fl(2)15s25M); the lights at Piraeus Commercial Harbour (LFl.R.6s13M); the light on the extremity of the outer mole of Zea (Fl(2)R.6s7M); the aero beacon at the airport (AlFl.WG.6s15M); and the light on Nisis Fleves (Fl(3)10s8M). The lights are not always easy to pick up against the loom of the lights of Athens and Piraeus. The entrance to Zea is lit: Fl(2)R.6s7M and Fl(2)G.6s4M. The channel into Pasalimani is lit: Fl.G.1·5s4M and Fl.R.1·5s3M.

Dangers

1. Care is needed of the large amount of shipping coming and going from Piraeus and the anchorage off it. Some of the new ferries and the hydrofoils approach at considerable speed (25–30 knots) so keep a good lookout aft. There are traffic separation zones for ships coming and going from the Aegean, but do not count on shipping sticking to the correct zone.
2. With the *meltemi* there can be gusts in the approaches.

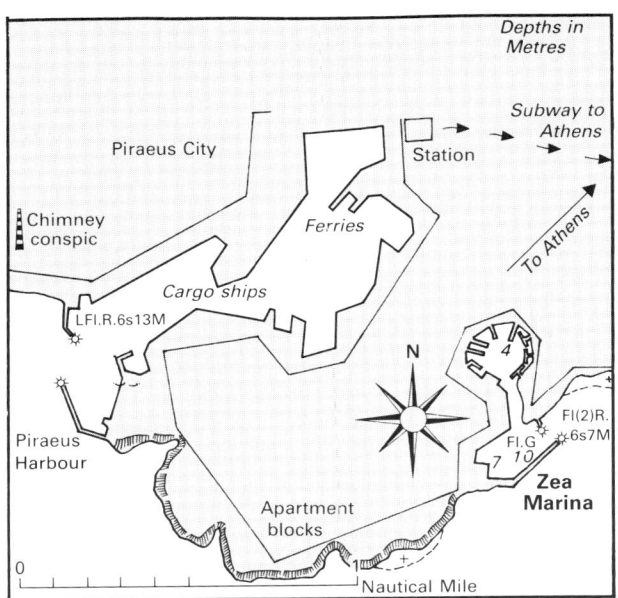

PIRAEUS – COMMERCIAL HARBOUR, ZEA AND TURKOLIMANI

Mooring

A marina attendant will direct you to a berth, probably alongside the outer end of the outer mole if you are only staying for a short period. The inner harbour (Pasalimani) is generally full as most of the berths are permanently occupied by Athens-based yachts.

Shelter Pasalimani has excellent all-round shelter. The outer harbour can be uncomfortable in strong southerlies when a reflected swell causes a surge to develop.

Authorities A port of entry: port police, customs, and immigration. Port captain and marina staff. Marina charges are made.

Facilities

Services Water and electricity (220v) can be connected to all berths. Showers and toilets.
Fuel On the quay.
Repairs Mechanical repairs. All types of engineering work possible. Wood and GRP repairs. Electrical and

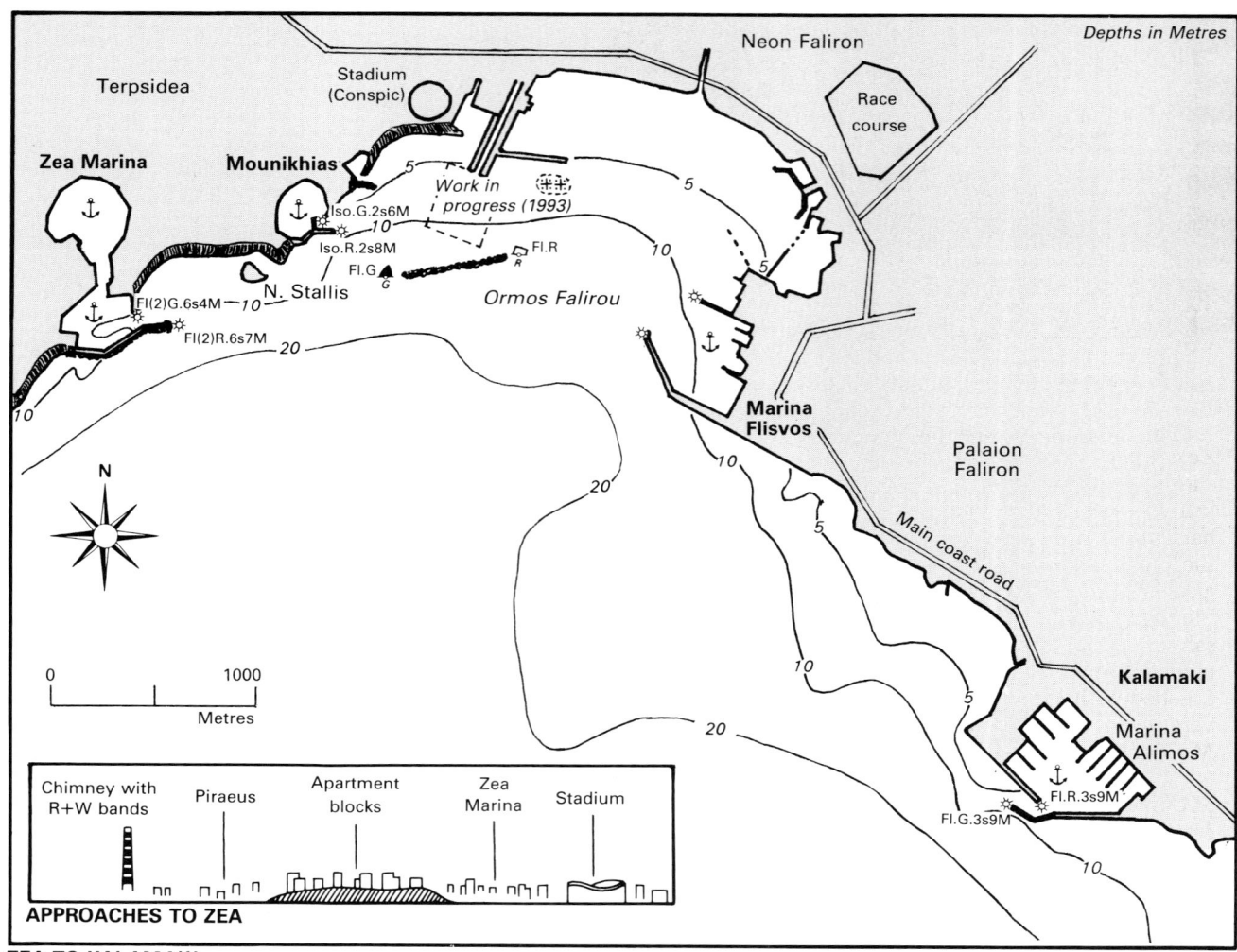

APPROACHES TO ZEA

ZEA TO KALAMAKI

electronic repairs. Most spares for marine engines and boat gear can be found or ordered. All repairs can be carried out including specialist marine diesel repairs, GRP work and electrical and electronic work. Marine grade stainless steel can be purchased and work carried out. Most types of exotic hardwood can be found. Galvanizing work. Propellers can be made to order. Masts and rigging can be made and repaired. Sailmakers. Good chandlers near the marina. Most charts and relevant nautical publications can be obtained. Greek charts are available from an office beneath the naval hospital near the marina. Excellent hardware and tool shops. If repair work cannot be carried out or organised from here it is unlikely it can be done elsewhere in Greece. Yachts are not generally hauled out at Zea although a few occasionally are.

Roger Stafford runs a pier in Pasalimani and can organise repairs and wintering. Contact Roger Stafford, 29 Grigoriou E' Street, Kastella, 185 34, Piraeus. ☎ (01) 41 36 416 (off), (01) 41 34 469 (quay). Telex 241623 STAF GR. *Fax* (01) 422 1557.
Provisions Excellent shopping for all provisions. Several markets nearby. Ice can be ordered.
Eating out All types of tavernas and restaurants nearby.

Other PO and OTE at the marina. Banks nearby. Consular offices in Athens for all European and most overseas countries. Greek gas and *Camping Gaz*. Hire cars and motor bikes. Bus to Athens and from there to all over Greece. Underground to Athens. Ferries to most destinations in the Aegean. Hydrofoils to the islands in the Saronic Gulf and to ports on the eastern Peloponnese. Internal flights to all destinations in Greece. International flights all over the world.
Enquiries Zea Marina ☎ 451 1480/ 451 3944/ 451 3623

General

Zea is a dirty, noisy, crowded harbour and if you don't have a headache after arriving from some comparatively peaceful island you will be one of the lucky few. Yet Piraeus city grows on you. It has many amenities not found elsewhere in Greece: movie theatres with the latest films from the West End; a choice of restaurants (Chinese, Indian, steak houses, French, Italian); bars and nightclubs; English magazines and newspapers only a day old; and shop windows crammed with all the consumer goods you don't need (especially on a boat), but like to look at.

The inner basin (Pasalimani) at Zea Marina.

Near the commercial harbour over the hill from Zea the markets and a warren of alleys with tiny shops stocked with a miscellany of wares are intriguing places to wander around. In the outer harbour of Zea the luxury yachts of the very rich line the quay outside the marina offices – the brass gleams, the brightwork is immaculate despite the blistering sun, and the flower arrangements on the saloon table would probably pay for a week's mooring of a small yacht. And when you have finished with Piraeus then a trip into Athens – at the very least to visit the Acropolis and the National Museum – must be made now that you are here.

MOUNIKHIAS (Turkolimani, Mikrolimani)
Imray-Tetra chart no. G14

The almost circular harbour immediately east of Zea. The harbour is administered by the Royal Hellenic Yacht Club and foreign yachts are not always welcome here. The best policy is to go to Zea and then check with the authorities at Mounikhias to see if there is a berth available.

Approach
The entrance is straightforward. It is lit by a light on either side of the entrance (Iso.G.2s6M and Iso.R.2s8M).

Mooring
Moor where directed by the marina attendant. There are laid moorings to all berths. A lot of yachts are kept on fore and aft moorings in the middle of the harbour. Good all-round shelter.

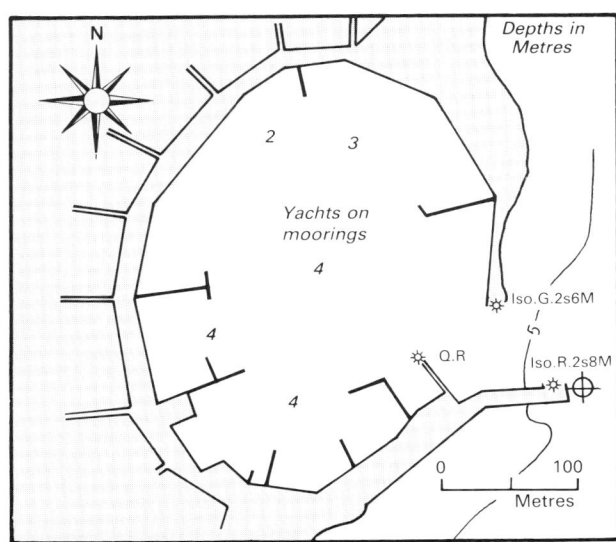

MOUNIKHIAS
37°56'·3N 23°39'·7E (Iso.R.8M)

Facilities
Around the marina are numerous, mostly expensive, restaurants (specialising in sea food) and cafés. Provisions nearby. Yacht club.

FALIRON (Flisvos)
Imray-Tetra chart no. G14

Approach
The harbour on the E side of Ormos Falirou. The outer breakwater is easily identified.
By night The outer breakwater is lit on the extremity (Fl.G.4s7M) and the N breakwater is lit on the extremity (F.R.2M).

Mooring
Go stern-to or bows-to where directed or where convenient. Large yachts berth along the outer mole on the S. There are few berths for visiting yachts and most prefer to go to Zea or Kalamaki.
Shelter The harbour is open to the W and with strong W winds it can get very choppy in the harbour.

Mounikhias looking ESE.

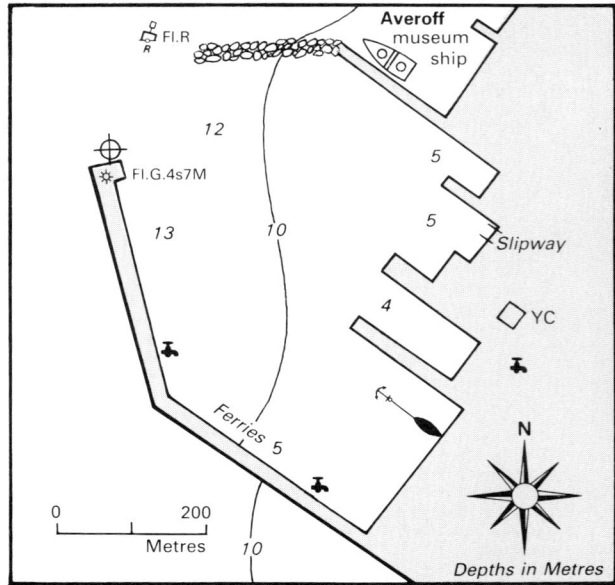

FALIRON
37°56'N 23°40'·8E (Fl.G.7M)

Facilities

Services Water and electricity can be connected to most berths.
Fuel Can be delivered to the quay.
Provisions Good shopping for provisions in Faliron.
Eating out Tavernas in Faliron.
Enquiries ☎ 982 9218/982 8537.

KALAMAKI (Alimos Marina)
Imray-Tetra chart no. G14

Approach

The marina lies about 2¼ miles to the SE of Mounikhias.

Conspicuous A large blue hangar at the airport to the SE is conspicuous. Following the coast, the outer moles and masts of yachts moored within will soon be seen. Immediately W of the marina a green lawn in a cemetery with a conspicuous white cross can be identified. The entrance is not apparent until you are right up to the marina.

By night The entrance is lit: Fl.G.3s9M and Fl.R.3s9M. Despite the range of the lights they can be difficult to see against the bright flashing lights along the waterfront.

Dangers
1. Care must be taken of the reef running SW from Ak Ay Kosmas about 1 mile S of the Marina. A light tower stands towards the end of the reef: light Q(9)15s5M.

Mooring

Go stern-to or bows-to under the W mole wherever you can. There are laid moorings tailed to a buoy or to the quay. The visitors' quay is theoretically along the inner W mole (berths A–E), but it is so congested here with permanent berth holders that it can be an exasperating time trying to find a berth. Asking at the office normally doesn't help at all.

Kalamaki (Alimos) Marina.

Shelter Excellent all-round shelter.

Authorities Port police and customs. Port captain and marina staff. Marina charges are made – the fees will sometimes be asked for in foreign currency, though this is technically illegal in an EC country.

Note The marina has little security and a number of yachtsmen have asked me to mention that a 'minder' is virtually mandatory. Lone females should be wary of wandering around at night.

Facilities

Services Water and electricity (220v) near every berth. Showers and toilets near the office.
Fuel On the quay.
Repairs Most mechanical repairs. Light engineering work including stainless steel work can be arranged. Wood and GRP repairs. Electrical and electronic repairs. Sailmaker. Chandlers along the main coast road. Yachts can be craned onto the hard in the marina if there is room.
Provisions Good shopping for provisions nearby. Ice available.
Eating out A few tavernas and restaurants along the coast road, but nothing special.
Other PO, OTE, and banks in Faliron. Greek gas and *Camping Gaz.* Hire cars and motorbikes. Regular buses into Athens and Piraeus from outside the marina.
Enquiries ☎ 982 8642/981 3315/982 1850.

General

Kalamaki is one of the newest marinas and has quickly filled up with yachts. The surrounding suburbs are drab apartment blocks and the marina is not much better. Moreover it is directly underneath the path of aircraft taking off from the nearby airport and this feature together with the dreary surroundings does little to endear Kalamaki to anyone. At night a disco within the marina blasts out enough decibels to shiver your GRP. If you get the impression I don't much like the place you are right and neither, for that matter, do most people who visit here.

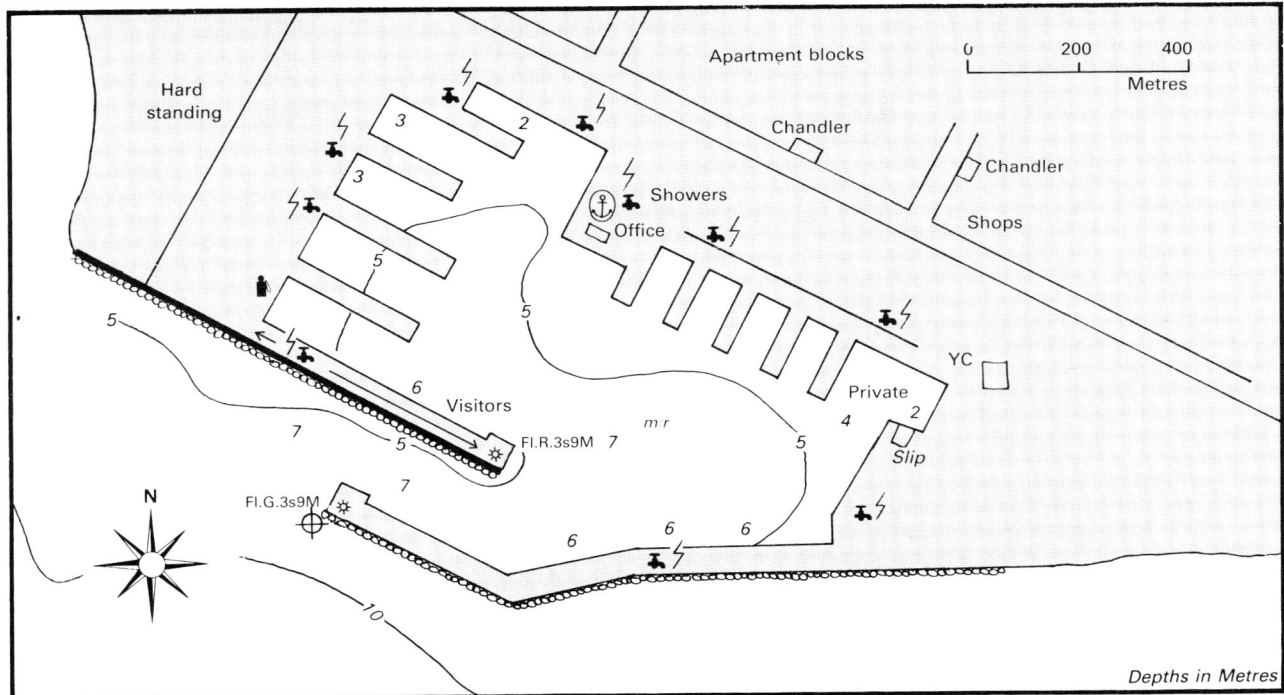

KALAMAKI
37°54'·8N 23°42'·1E (Fl.G.9M)

GLIFADHA MARINA 4 (Glyphada)

Although called 'Marina 4', this is in fact the first of the Glifadha marinas to be encountered when bound down the coast from Athens.

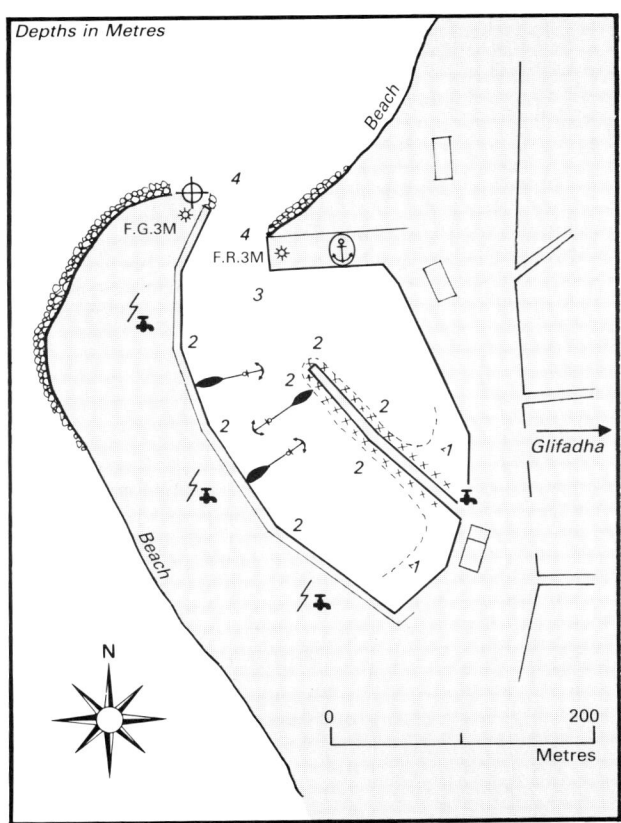

GLIFADHA MARINA 4
37°52'·3N 23°44E (F.G.3m)

Approach

The harbour lies approximately 3 miles SE of Kalamaki. Care must be taken of the reef running SW of Ak Ay Kosmas.
By night The entrance is lit: F.G.3M and F.R.3M.

Mooring

Go stern-to or bows-to where directed. There are laid moorings tailed to the quay. The harbour is normally very crowded and you will be lucky to find a berth.
Shelter Good all-round shelter.
Authorities Port police and a port captain. Marina charges are made.

Facilities

Services Water and electricity at every berth.
Fuel A mini-tanker can deliver to the quay.
Repairs Most repairs can be arranged.
Provisions Good shopping for provisions in Glifadha.
Eating out Tavernas and restaurants in Glifadha.
Other PO. OTE. Banks. Hire cars and motorbikes.
Enquiries ☎ 894 1967/894 7979.

General

If you can arrange a berth here this is one of the more agreeable marinas near Athens. However it is directly under the flight path of aircraft landing at Athens airport and consequently not a quiet place to be.

GLIFADHA MARINA (1, 2, 3) (Glyphada)

Approach

Conspicuous The large hotels around Ormiskos Glifadha and a church with a blue cupola behind the harbour are conspicuous. Closer in, the masts of

181

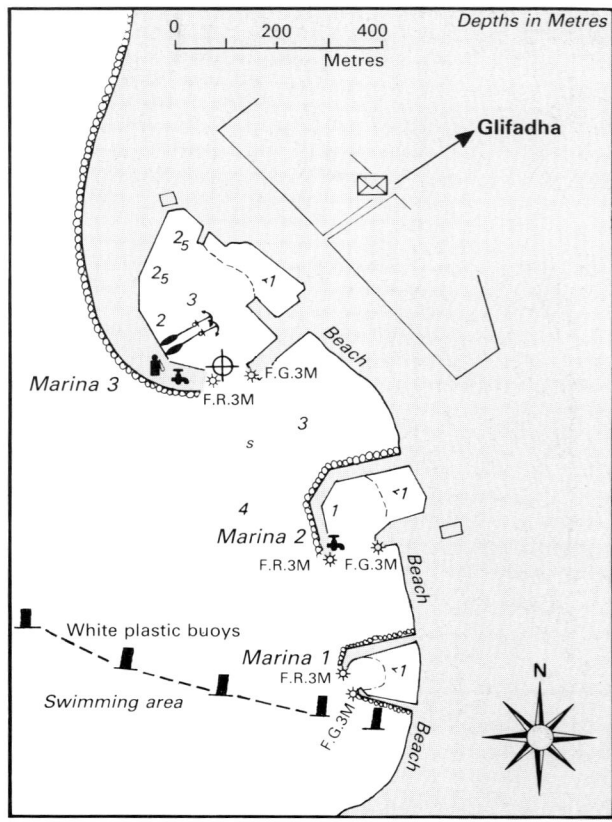

GLIFADHA MARINA (1, 2, 3)
37°51'·8N 23°44'·6E (Marina 3: F.R)

yachts in the marina and a hoarding on the extremity of the mole of Marina 3 are conspicuous.

By night The entrances to all three marinas are lit F.G.3M and F.R.3M which could conceivably lead to confusion. The loom of the lights behind makes identification of the lights difficult anyway.

Mooring

Go stern-to or bows-to where directed in Marina 3. There are laid moorings tailed to the quay. The marina is small, crowded, and you will be lucky to find a berth here.

Shelter Good shelter although strong southerlies send in an uncomfortable swell.

Authorities Port police and port captain. Marina charges are made.

Facilities

Services Water and electricity at or near every berth.
Fuel On the quay.
Repairs Some mechanical repairs. Chandlers.
Provisions Good shopping for provisions in the town.
Eating out Tavernas in Glifadha. Buses to Piraeus and Athens. Athens airport is close by.

General

The marinas are essentially private with few places for visitors. They are, in any case, altogether disagreeable since they are directly under the flight path of aircraft landing at the nearby airport. On average there will be a jet about 100–200 metres overhead every 10 minutes making such a deafening noise that it hurts the eardrums.

Note For some time it has been planned to redevelop Glifadha Marinas 1, 2, 3 and 4 and incorporate them into a large complex with a total capacity of 1800 berths. A development ashore is intended to complement the 'super-marina'. At the time of writing work has not started and it is now some eight years since the project was first publicized.

VOULA

A small harbour S of Glifadha. A mole running S from the coast and curving around to the E has 2–4 metre depths behind it. A small buoy marks the limit of the channel into the entrance. The harbour is full of local yachts and it can be difficult to find a berth. Tavernas and shopping nearby.

VOULIAGMENI

Approach

Conspicuous A large white hotel on the hill above the marina is conspicuous. Once into Ormos Vouliagmenos the marina will be seen on the W side of the bay.

By night Use the light on Nisis Fleves (Fl(3)10s8M) and the lights at the entrance: Fl(3)R.12s7M, Fl.R.1·5s2M, Fl.G.1·5s2M and Fl.G.1·5s2M.

Dangers

1. Care must be taken of Vrak Kasidhis, the reef lying approximately 350 metres S of the W entrance to Ormos Vouliagmeni. There is an inside passage but the prudent course is to pass to seaward of the rock.

Mooring

Berth stern-to or bows-to where directed. There are laid moorings tailed to the quay or a small buoy. The marina is usually fully booked although for a short stay there may be a vacant berth.

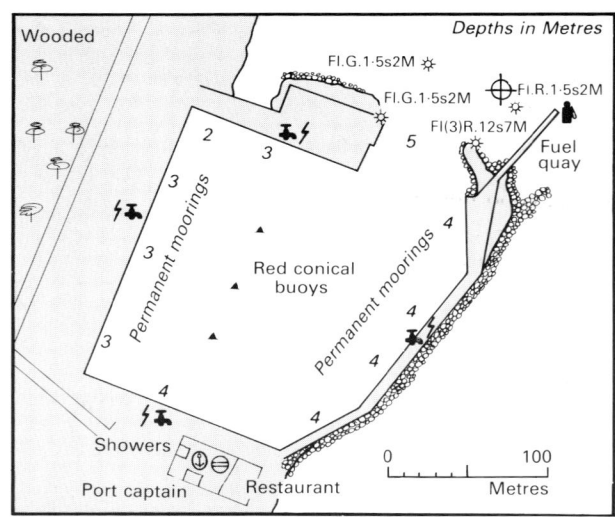

VOULIAGMENI
37°48'·3N 23°46'·6E (Fl.R.2M)

Vouliagmeni Marina looking WNW from near Ak Zostir.

Shelter Good shelter although strong southerlies cause a reflected swell that makes it uncomfortable inside.

Authorities A port of entry: port police, customs, and immigration. Port captain and marina staff. Marina charges are made which tend to be higher than for the other marinas.

Facilities

Services Water and electricity at or near every berth. Shower and toilet block.
Fuel On the quay.
Repairs Most repairs can be arranged.
Provisions Most provisions can be obtained. Ice available.
Eating out Tavernas nearby.
Other Taxis available at the marina.
Enquiries ☎ 896 0012/896 0415.

General

Vouliagmeni was the first marina to be built in Greece and the developers chose a wonderful site in the bay away from the hustle and bustle of Athens and Piraeus. The peninsula on the W side of the bay is an up-market suburb with very expensive bits of real estate discreetly scattered around the wooded slopes. Likewise the marina is an up-market place full of millions of dollars' worth of little ships.

VARKIZA (Varkilas)

Approach

A small harbour in the NW corner of the large bay immediately E of Ormos Vouliagmenos.
By night The entrance is lit: F.R.3M.

Mooring

Berth stern-to or bows-to the outer mole or inside the basin if there is room. The bottom is sand, rocks and weed, good holding.
Shelter Good shelter in the basin. Mediocre shelter from the *meltemi* on the mole.

Facilities

Water On the quay.
Fuel A mini-tanker can deliver to the quay.
Provisions Most provisions can be found nearby.
Eating out Tavernas nearby.

General

The small harbour is crowded with local boats, but a small yacht may find a berth here. Varkiza is an

Varkiza looking ESE.

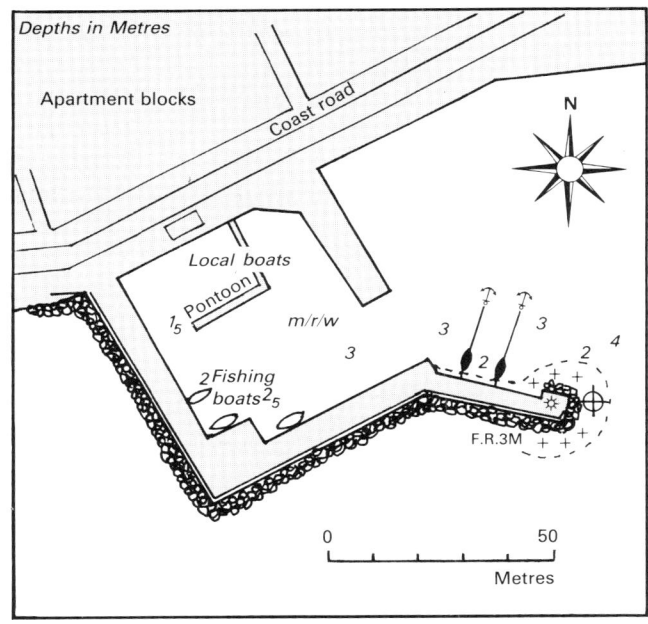

VARKIZA
37°49'·1N 23°48'·3E (F.R.3M)

outer suburb of Athens, mostly bland apartment blocks and the wide coast road to whisk commuters in and out of Athens.

ORMOS ANAVISSOU

The large bay with Nisis Arsidha lying off the entrance. There are a number of anchorages around the bay.

1. On the W side. Open to the *meltemi*.
2. In the NW corner where a number of boats are

183

Anchorage on the W side of Ormos Anavissou. Some yachts are kept here on permanent moorings through the summer.

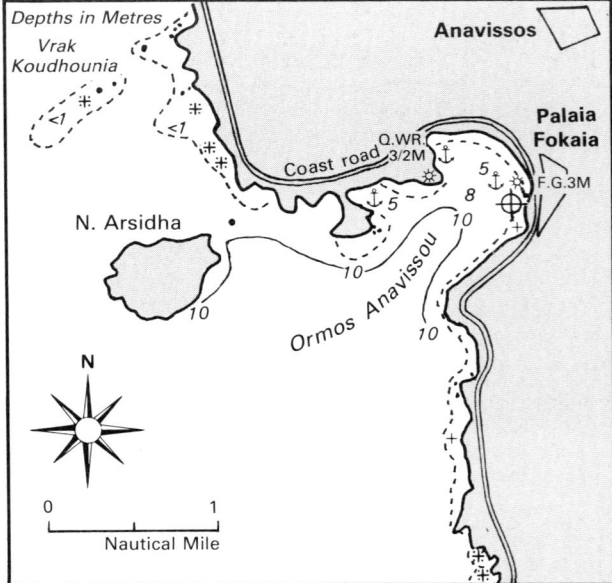

ORMOS ANAVISSOU
37°43'·2N 23°56'·7E (F.G.3M)

kept on permanent moorings. Reasonable shelter from the *meltemi*.

3. Off Palaia Fokaia. The small harbour here is mostly shallow and a yacht should not attempt to berth in here. Anchor off the harbour in 3–5 metres. Care must be taken of patches of coral-like rock that can foul an anchor. Good shelter from the *meltemi* although there are gusts into the bay. Fuel in the town. Water at the root of the mole. Good shopping for provisions and tavernas in the village.

NISIS GAIDHOURONISOS (Patroklou)

The humpbacked islet lying close off the coast S of Ak Katafiyi. It is lit on the NE side: LFl.14s5M. It is possible to pass inside the islet though care must be taken of the reef just under the water lying near to the middle of the fairway at the eastern end.

There is a useful anchorage on the NE end if W-SW winds are blowing. There is a fish farm in here but still room for a number of yachts to anchor.

SOUNION

The bay under Ak Sounion is often used by yachts waiting for the *meltemi* to die before proceeding into Kolpos Petalion or returning to Athens.

The temple on the cape is conspicuous from the distance. Anchor where convenient. The bottom is sand and weed – bad holding. In the N of the bay

there is reported to be a 3·5 metre patch of sand which is good holding. Make sure your anchor is well in and holding as the gusts into the bay have caused numerous yachts to drag anchors here. Good shelter from the *meltemi* although there are strong gusts into the bay. Tavernas on the shore.

The temple of Poseidon on the cape is easily reached after a short walk from the shore. It was built around 444 BC, probably to a design by Hephaisteion of Athens. Visit it in the morning as in the afternoon and evening it is overrun by day-trippers from Athens. The young Byron is supposed to have carved his name on one of the columns. Afterwards he penned a few lines on his visit:
'Sunium's marbled steep
Where nothing save the waves and I
May hear our mutual murmurs sweep.'

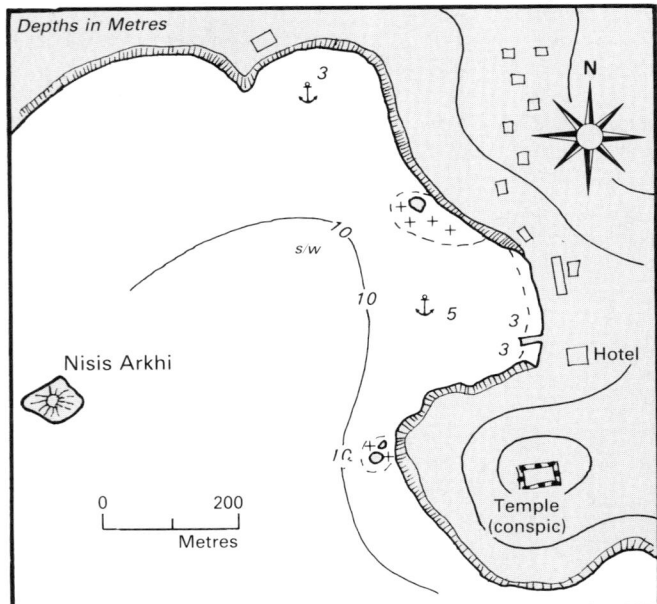

SOUNION
37°39'N 24°01'·5E

Ak Sounion and the anchorage under it looking E.

The anchorage under Ak Sounion looking SW. *Nigel Patten.*

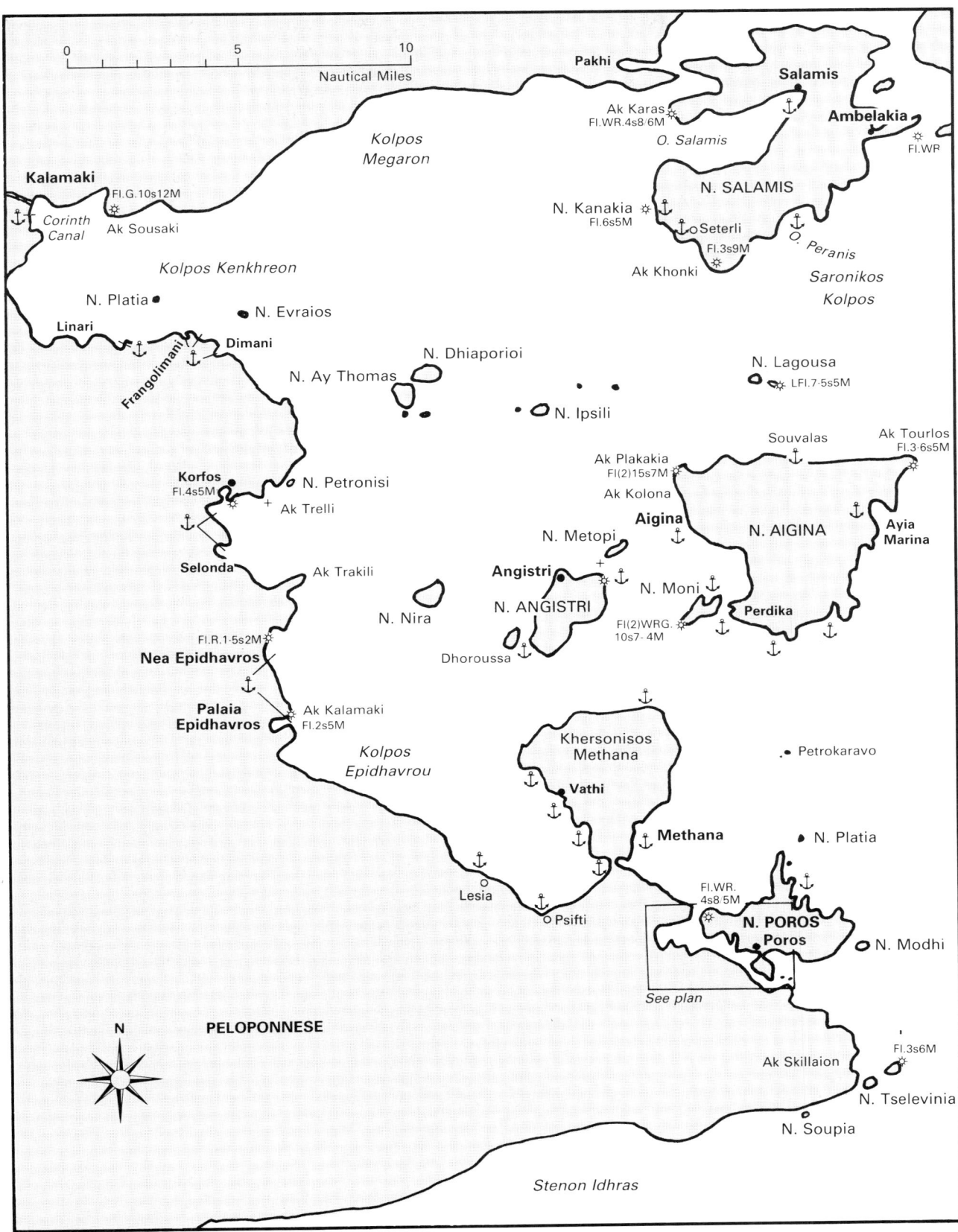

CORINTH CANAL TO POROS

The Saronic Islands and the adjacent Peloponnese coast

The coast

This section covers the coast from the Corinth Canal down to Ak Skillaion and around the corner to Ak Mouzaki opposite the NW tip of Nisos Dhokos. It is mostly mountainous with a ridge running along the coast between 600 and 900 metres (2000–3000ft) high reaching the summit at Ortholithi (112 metres/3625ft) opposite Methana peninsula. The upper slopes are rocky and devoid of vegetation, but the lower slopes along the coast are densely wooded in pine. Methana peninsula, properly Khersonisos Methanon (almost an island but for a narrow isthmus), is an extinct volcano.

ORMOS LINARI

Lies on the S shore of Kolpos Kenkhreon 5 miles SE of the canal. Poor shelter as a swell enters with strong northerlies. Open to the NW–W. No facilities.

FRANGOLIMANI

A landlocked bay 3½ miles E of Linari. It is steep-to until close to the shore. A beach around the SW side. You will have to drop your anchor in 15–20 metres and take a line ashore. The bottom is hard sand and weed – bad holding. A swell enters with strong northerlies and shelter is not as good as it looks. The slopes above are being developed for summer villas.

ORMOS DIMANI

Lies about one mile SE of Frangolmani. Open to the NE only. In settled weather it is an attractive anchorage. No facilities. Like those at Frangolimani the slopes above it have been developed for villas.

NISOI DHIAPORIOI

A group of uninhabited islands lying to the E of Ak Spiri. The channel between the two largest islands, Ay Thomas and Ay Ioannis, does not have the depths shown on chart 1657. A reef joins the two islands with the deepest part (3–4 metres) nearest to Nisis Ay Ioannis.

NISIS IPSILI

Lies to the ESE of Nisoi Dhiaporioi and is used for target practice by the Greek navy.

KORFOS (Limin Sofikou)

Approach

A nearly landlocked bay 1½ miles W of Ak Trelli. The islet of Petronisi with fish farms around it is easily identified in the approaches. The houses of the village will not be seen until into the bay.

By night The E side of the entrance is lit: Fl.4s5M. With care a night entry is possible.

Dangers

1. Care must be taken of the reef running out from Ak Trelli for nearly 400 metres. With any chop on the water it can be difficult to see and because Ak Trelli is low-lying it is difficult to determine where the reef starts and finishes.
2. With W–NW winds there are fierce gusts off the land.

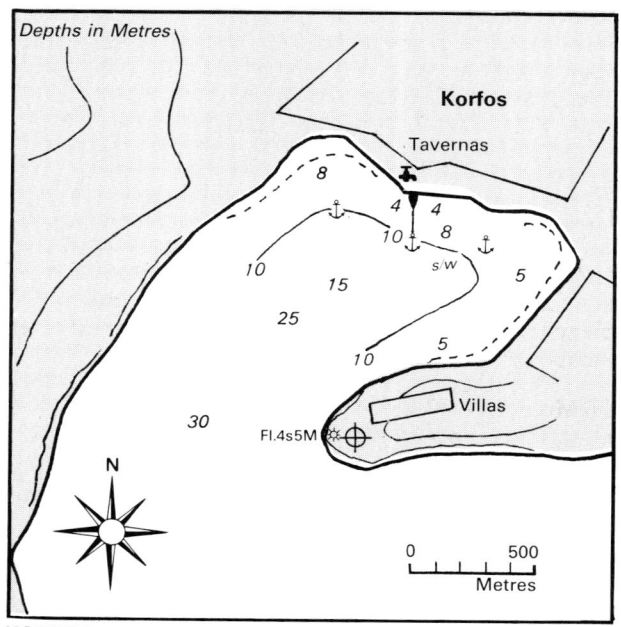

KORFOS
37°45'·5N 23°07'·7E (Fl.4s5M)

Approach to Korfos looking N from just outside the entrance.

Korfos waterfront looking N from the anchorage.

Palaia Epidhavros. The town quay looking W.

Mooring

Anchor in the bay in 10–12 metres or go stern or bows-to off the quayed area on the N side just off several tavernas here. There are mostly 3–4 metre depths off the new quay although care is needed at the ends. The bottom is mud and weed, poor holding in places, so make sure your anchor is well in.

Shelter Good all-round shelter although there are strong gusts with westerlies.

Facilities

Water On the quay.
Fuel A mini-tanker can deliver to the quay.
Provisions Good shopping for all provisions in the village.
Eating out Good tavernas along the waterfront.
Other PO. OTE. Infrequent bus to Athens.

General

The bay is attractive enough, but the same cannot be said for the awful concrete villas that have been thrown up around the slopes. The best part of Korfos is a taverna on the waterfront where the locals are a friendly lot. John at *The Crab* taverna is helpful to yachties ☎ (0741) 95216/85325.

ORMOS SELONDA

A deep inlet 2 miles S of Korfos. It is now largely obstructed by several fish farms, but it is possible to get through them and anchor. It is mostly very deep for anchoring. Even with the fish farms here it is a tranquil pleasant spot. Open to the E–SE only.

NEA EPIDHAVROS

Lies about 3 miles N of Palaia (Old) Epidavros. It is open N–E–S and should only be used in calm weather. There is a short pier but the depths off it are insufficient for a yacht (1–1·5 metres) and the ballasting extends some distance underwater. A light (Fl.R.1·5s2M) is exhibited on the extremity of the pier. In calm weather anchor off in 4–8 metres. Taverna ashore.

EPIDHAVROS (Old (Palaia) Epidavros, Epidhavro, Epidauros)

Approach

Conspicuous The entrance to Ormos Palaia Epidhavrou is difficult to see from seaward. A road scar on the hill on the S side of the bay is conspicuous. Closer in, the light structure and a church on the N side of the bay will be seen. The village of Palaia Epidhavros at the head of the bay will not be seen until you are in the entrance. Once into the bay proceed between the two beacons marking the channel to the quay.

By night Use the light on the N side of the entrance (Ak Kalamaki Fl.2s5M), on the two beacons (Q.G.2M, Q.R.2M) and on the pierhead (Fl.R.3s3M).

Mooring

Go stern-to or bows-to the pier or the quay or anchor in the bay. The bottom is mud and weed, reasonable holding.

Shelter Good shelter. Although the bay is open E, winds from the E rarely blow in the summer with any force.

Authorities Port police.

Facilities

Water On the quay.
Fuel In the town.
Provisions Good shopping for most provisions.
Eating out Tavernas on the waterfront and in the town.
Other PO. OTE. Exchange facilities. Greek gas. Hire motorbikes. Taxis can be hired to go to Epidhavros Theatre.

General

Set at the base of steep wooded slopes, Palaia Epidhavros is an attractive small village. However the real attraction is Epidhavros Theatre about 30 minutes away by taxi – the easiest way of getting there.

The theatre is accepted to be the best preserved of all Greek theatres and one of the finest pieces of classical architecture in existence. Some sensible restoration has been carried out, but the theatre is mostly original. The acoustics of the theatre are perfect: a piece of paper rustled on the stage or a coin dropped on the floor can be clearly heard from any one of the 14,000 seats. There is a festival of ancient Greek drama in the summer and seats and transport can be booked at Palaia Epidhavros.

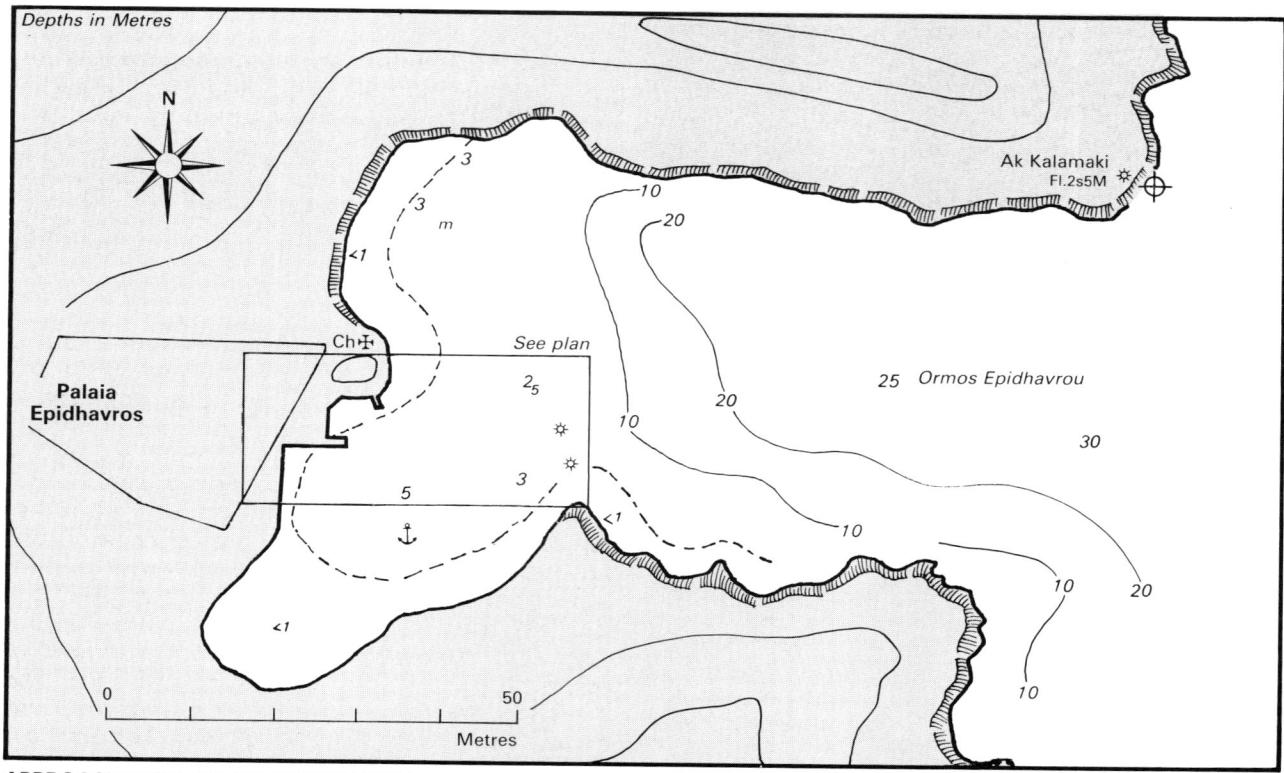

APPROACHES TO PALAIA EPIDHAVROU
37°38'·5N 23°10'·2E (Ak Kalamaki light)

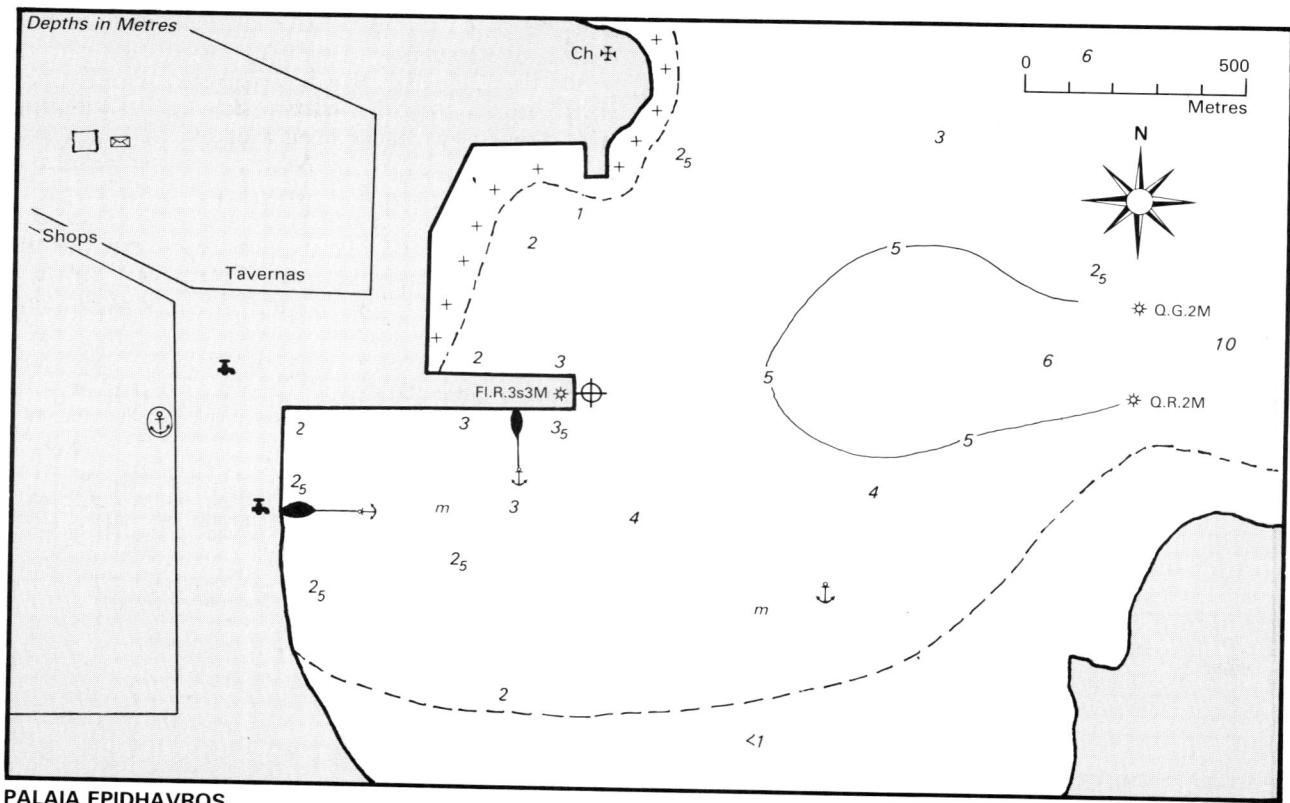

PALAIA EPIDHAVROS
37°38'·3N 23°09'·5E (Fl.R. on pier)

The site was renowned in ancient times not for its theatre but as a sanctuary of the Askeplion: a religious centre for curing the sick and infirm. Extensive temples, hospitals, sanatoriums and the bath-houses covered a site comparable to Delphi. Little remains of the buildings today but the site on the pine-clad slopes has a certain feeling of quiet and calm about it. A museum on the site houses local finds.

VATHI (Methana)

Approach

Vathi is a small fishing harbour on the W coast of the Methana peninsula. The rough stone breakwater and houses of the village will not be seen until close to in the approach from the N.

By night A F.R.3M is exhibited on the N side of the entrance.

Mooring

Go stern or bows-to the quay off the tavernas on the S side. Alternatively anchor and take a long line ashore to the rough stone breakwater. The bottom is mud and weed, mostly good holding, although a bit soft in places.

Shelter Good shelter, although strong N-NE winds gust into the harbour, more bothersome than troubling.

Facilities

Several café/tavernas ashore. Infrequent bus to Methana town.

General

The hamlet is a delightful spot and well off the Saronic charter milk run. On the black basalt slopes a short distance N there is an old caldera betraying the peninsula's recent volcanic origins.

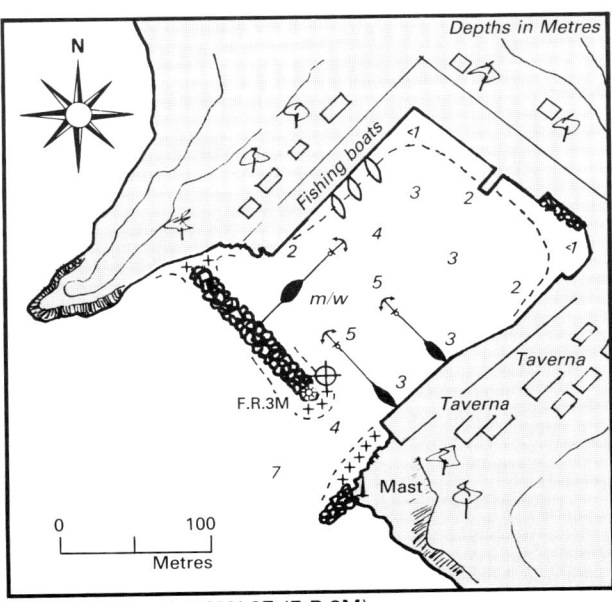

VATHI 37°35′·7N 23°20′·3E (F.R.3M)

Note

To the S of Vathi there are several deserted bays that can be used in calm weather. A yacht can also anchor off on the SW side of Kolpos Epidhavrou in calm weather.

Aigina

(Aiyina, Aegina, Egina)

Aigina is the roughly triangular island lying some 12 miles SW of Zea Marina. The summit of Aigina, Oros (534 metres/1745ft), is near the southern end of the island. The island is mostly rocky and barren, but there are a few wooded areas around the coast.

The position of Aigina guarding the northwestern approaches to the Aegean has meant that it was important from the very early days of trade. It was occupied by a Neolithic people who were in turn supplanted by a Bronze Age people around 2000 BC. The Mycenaeans occupied it about 1400 BC, but appear to have abandoned it after a couple of centuries. Later it was recolonized and the inhabitants began to build up their own merchant marine fleet. In the Battle of Salamis the fleet from Aigina was said by Herodotus to have distinguished itself above all others. The growth of the maritime fleet aroused the envy of the Athenians to the extent that Aristotle remarked that the island was 'the eyesore of Piraeus'.

At the beginning of the Peloponnesian War the island opted for the Spartan side (its relationship with Athens had never been a happy one), and was subsequently subdued by Athens. It never recovered and thereafter endured the usual succession of invaders: the Romans, Byzantium, the Saracens, Venetians and Turks. From 1826–28 the city was the capital of the newly liberated Greece and the first modern Greek coins were minted here and the new Greek national flag flown.

The island is very popular with tourists and Athenians alike. By hydrofoil from Zea it is only 20 minutes away and is a popular excursion for the smog-bound Athenians. Tourists visiting Athens often come on a day trip here. Consequently the strip of water between Aigina and Athens is constantly churned up with ferries and hydrofoils hurrying back and forth and at the weekends with Athens-based pleasure boats scurrying to get out or back to the capital.

AIGINA (Aegina, Egina)

Admiralty chart no. 1657
Imray-Tetra chart no. G14

Approach

Conspicuous The town of Aigina is conspicuous from the distance. Closer in a Doric column on Ak Kolona immediately NW of the town and a white chapel near the outer end of the W mole are conspicuous. A red conical buoy marks a rock with 3m over it.

Aigina. Ak Plakakia looking NE.

Entrance to Aigina harbour looking NE.

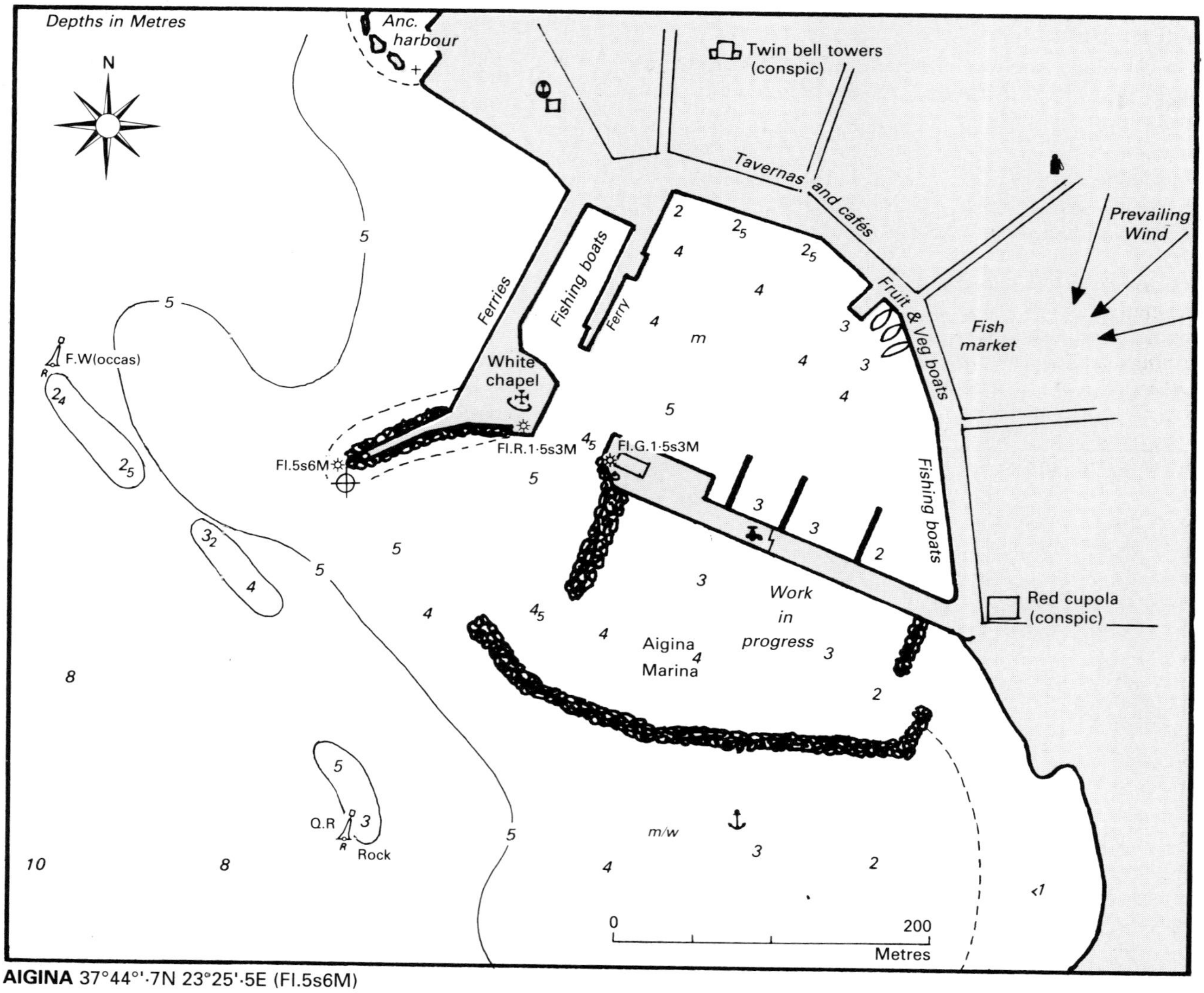

Depths in Metres

N

Anc. harbour

Twin bell towers (conspic)

Tavernas and cafés

Prevailing Wind

Fish market

5

5

F.W(occas)

2₄

2₅

Ferries

Fishing boats

Ferry

White chapel

3₂

4

5

Fl.5s6M

Fl.R.1·5s3M

Fl.G.1·5s3M

2

2₅

4

2₅

4

m

3

3

3

4

5

4₅

5

5

4

4₅

3

Aigina Marina

Work in progress

3

3

3

2

Fruit & Veg boats

Fishing boats

Red cupola (conspic)

8

4

2

5

Q.R

3

Rock

10

8

5

4

m/w

3

2

<1

0   200

Metres

AIGINA 37°44°'·7N 23°25'·5E (Fl.5s6M)

190

By night Use the light on Ak Plakakia (Fl(2)15s7M), Nisis Moni (Ak Kostis Fl(2)WRG.10s7-4M; the white sector 296°-322° covers the safe passage across the shoal water between Aigina and Angistri), and the lights at the entrance (Fl.5s6M, Fl.R.1·5s3M and Fl.G.1·5s3M).

Dangers

1. Care should be taken when making an approach from the S as shoal water extends E from Nisis Metopi across to Aigina. There are least depths of 8–9 metres through the fairway of the channel.
2. Care is needed at the entrance to the harbour as numerous ferries and hydrofoils use it and they enter and leave at speed. A good lookout is needed.

Mooring

Go stern-to or bows-to the town quay. The S mole is taken up with private and charter company berths. The harbour gets very crowded with yachts in the summer months.

Shelter Good all-round shelter although strong southerlies send in an uncomfortable swell. The bottom is mud with some rocks – poor holding in places. Several yachts have wintered afloat here.

Authorities Port police and customs.

Facilities

Water Can be delivered by mini-tanker to the harbour.
Fuel Near the harbour. A mini-tanker can deliver to the quay.
Repairs Limited mechanical repairs. Hardware shops.
Provisions Good shopping for provisions. Fruit and vegetables can be bought from *caïques* moored on the town quay. Ice available.
Eating out Good tavernas around the waterfront.
Other PO. OTE. Banks. Greek gas and *Camping Gaz*. Hire motorbikes and bicycles. Buses to the other villages on the island. Ferries to Piraeus and to the other islands in the Saronic Gulf.

General

The small town around the harbour is a pleasant homely sort of place despite the large numbers of tourists deposited here in the summer months. It has the distinction of being the first place in Greece where the Greek flag was raised at the end of the Greek War of Independence. This flag differed from the present-day one, being red and gold in colour. The single column on Ak Kolona is all that remains of the Temple of Aphrodite that formerly stood on the cape.

AIGINA MARINA

A marina has been constructed just outside the S breakwater. A detached breakwater provides protection from the S. At the time of publication work seemed to have slowed down and no facilities are in place. When complete the marina will provide much

needed additional berths for the crowded old harbour. Water and electricity will be installed.

PERDIKA

Approach

The small bay on the SW end of Aigina. The small village on the N side of the bay is easily identified from seaward.

By night Use the light on Nisis Moni (Fl(2)WRG.10s7-4M) and the light on the end of the outer mole (Fl.R.1·5s2M).

Mooring

Anchor in the bay in 3–4 metres. The short pier has 3 metre depths off the W side where a yacht can go stern-to or bows-to if there is room. A new mole has been built to the W of the pier and there may be room to go bows-to off the end. The quay between the two moles has 1·5–1·8 metre depths off it and care is needed if going on here. The bottom is mud and weed – good holding.

Shelter Good shelter from the normal summer winds. The bay is open to the W and with fresh to strong NW-W winds the outer part of the harbour is very uncomfortable and may become untenable.

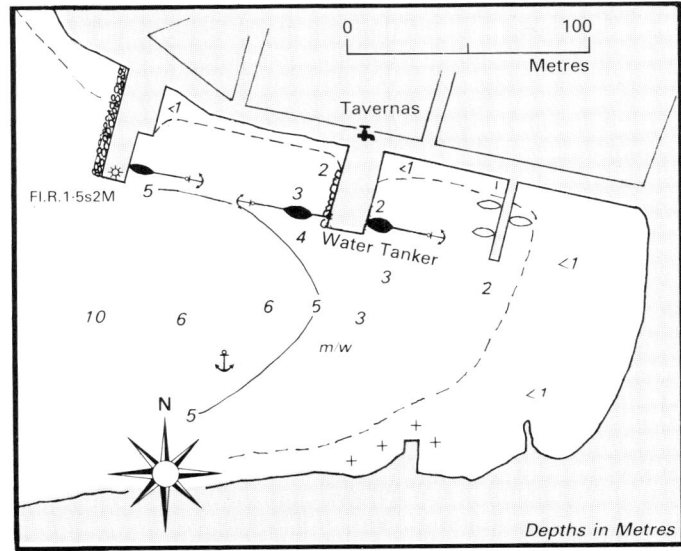

PERDIKA
37°41′N 23°27′E

Perdika looking E from the entrance.

Facilities

Water on the quay. Fuel 500m out of the village. A grocery shop. Good tavernas on the waterfront, some of which specialise in seafood.

General

The bay is an attractive place, but fills up quickly in the summer with visiting yachts. Get here early and wander around the village.

NISIS MONI

In calm weather a yacht can anchor in the bay on the N side of the island. Anchor in 8–10 metres. A taverna opens in the summer. The S side of the island is bare weathered rock, but on the N side it is partially wooded.

AYIA MARINA

An open bay near the NE corner of the island. A large hotel on the waterfront is conspicuous. In calm weather anchor near the NW corner of the bay in 4–6 metres. Sand and weed bottom. A small quay in the NW corner is reserved for *caïque* ferries bringing tourists to see the Temple of Aphaia. It would be prudent to leave someone on board the yacht while visiting the temple in case there is a sudden change in the weather.

The Temple of Aphaia (5–6 BC) on the NE corner of the island has been called the most perfectly developed classical temple in Greece. Cruise ships anchor in Ayia Marina to disembark passengers wishing to view it. In calm weather this is the nearest anchorage to the temple for a yacht – alternatively buses run from Aigina town to Ayia Marina.

SOUVALAS

A small harbour situated midway along the N coast. A short mole (50 metres long) runs W from the E side of the coast and has 2 metre depths just inside.

If there is room moor bows-to the mole. Care must be taken as the depths inside are uneven and there is little room for manoeuvring. Taverna ashore.

BOATYARD

To the W of Souvalas there is a boatyard which can haul yachts on a cradle and slip. Some mechanical repairs possible. Enquire at the yacht club in Aigina town for details.

Angistri

(Aykistri)

Angistri is the small island lying 4 miles to the west of Aigina and connected to it by a strip of shoal water (8–9 metres least depth through the channel near to Aigina). Angistri is hilly with the summit on the eastern side (296 metres/965ft). It is covered for the most part in pine and supports a small population.

ANGISTRI (Megalohorio, Saint Georgis)

Approach

A small harbour on the NW corner of Angistri. Care must be taken when approaching the harbour from the E because of the reefs and shoal water between Angistri and Nisis Metopi. The end of the breakwater is lit: Fl.G.

Mooring

Go stern-to or bows-to the short pier inside the breakwater or bows-to the quay to the N of the pier. Alternatively anchor off clear of the approaches to the quay. Local ferries spend the night on the quay taking up most of the room available. Good shelter except for strong NE–E winds when it is untenable.

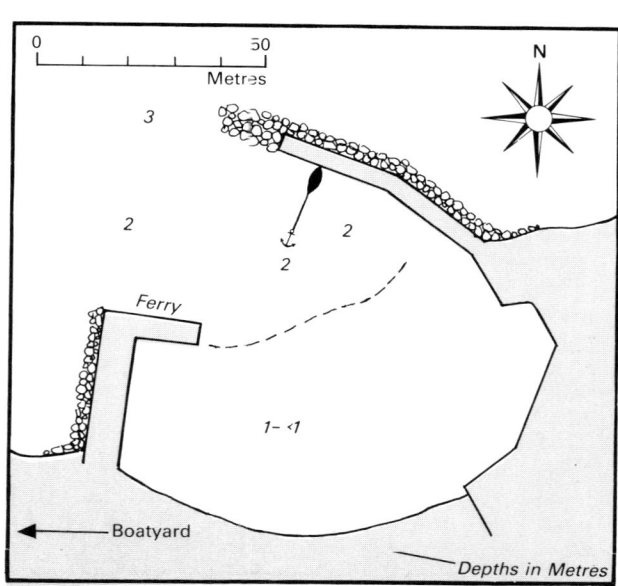

SOUVALAS

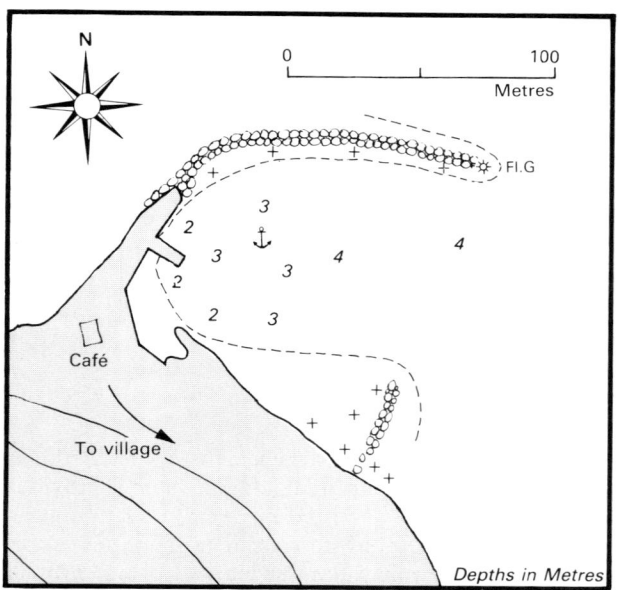

ANGISTRI
37°43′N 23°21′E

Facilities
Tavernas and cafés at the harbour. Provisions available in Angistri village.

General
Tripper boats run across to here from Aigina in the summer, but the island retains a simplicity and charm of its own. Recently a number of villas have been built on the slopes around the harbour.

NISIS DHOROUSSA ANCHORAGES

Nisis Dhoroussa lies off the SW tip of Angistri. The narrow channel between the two islands is deep and clear of dangers. Opposite Nisis Dhoroussa there are a number of small bays offering good shelter from the normal summer winds (SE or NE) in attractive surroundings. Anchor where convenient. A delightful wooded little corner. A taverna opens in the summer.

METHANA

Approach
Conspicuous The town of Methana is easily identified from some distance off. The marina lies near the S end of the town.

By night Use the light on the headland (Fl.G.3s3M) and the lights at the narrow entrance (Q.G.3M and Q.R.3M) – care needed.

Dangers Care is needed negotiating the narrow entrance into the harbour.

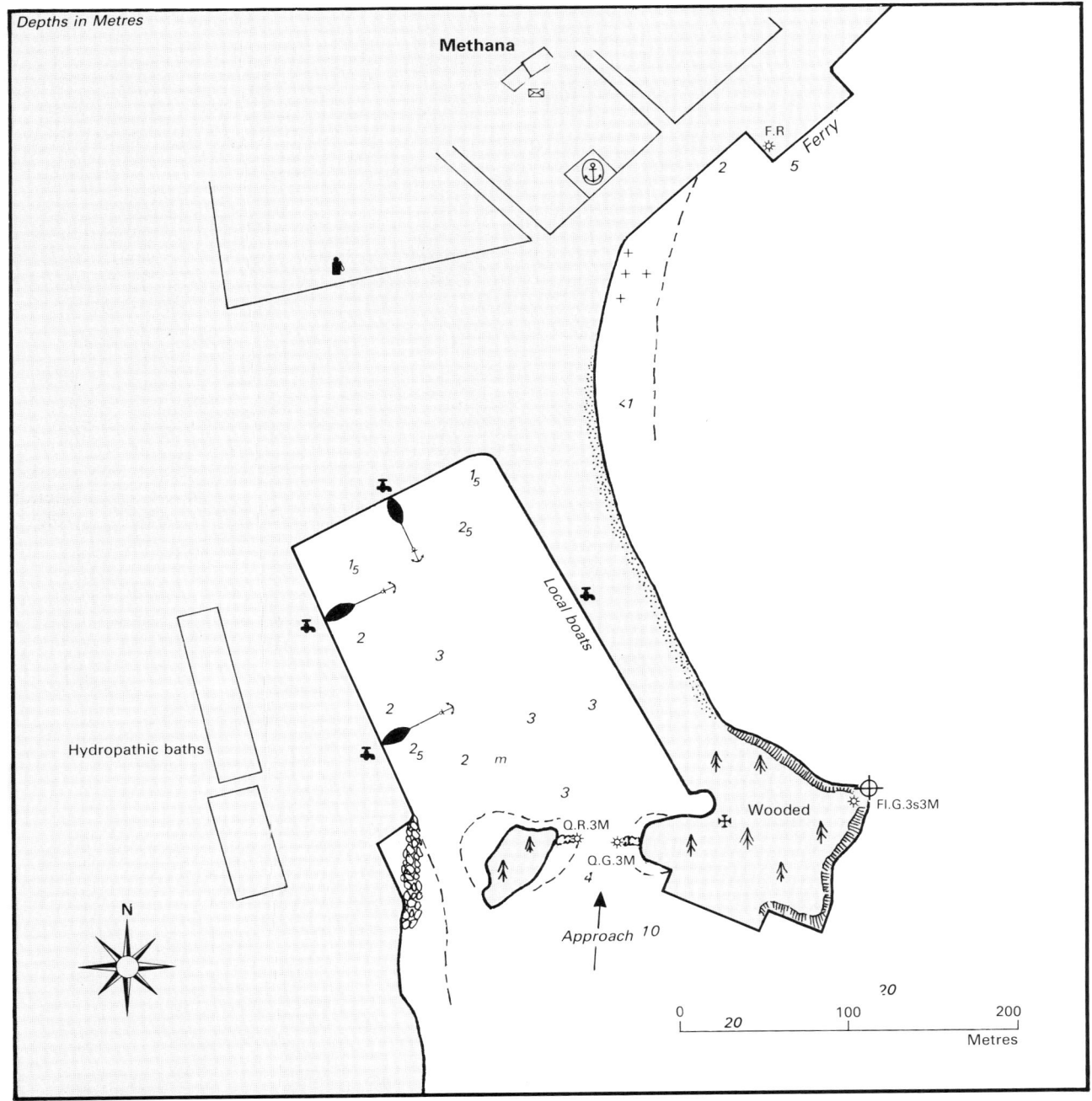

METHANA
37°34′·6N 23°23′·5E (Fl.G.3s3M)

The entrance to Methana harbour looking NW.

Mooring

Go stern-to or bows-to the quay on the W or N. Depths off the quay are variable, between 1·5–2·5 metres, but if you touch bottom it is all mud. The bottom of sticky black mud is excellent holding, but messy when you haul the anchor up again.

Shelter Good all-round shelter. A number of yachts are wintered afloat here.

Authorities Port police and customs. Methana is classified as a marina.

Facilities

Water On the quay.

Fuel Near the quay. A mini-tanker can deliver to the quay.

Repairs Some mechanical repairs. Hardware shops.

Provisions Good shopping for provisions. Ice available.

Eating out Tavernas in the town.

Other PO. OTE. Bank. Greek gas and *Camping Gaz*. Ferries to Piraeus and to the islands in the Saronic Gulf.

Enquiries ☎ (0298) 92324 (town hall) or 92279 (port police).

General

The lasting impression of Methana is not visual, but olfactory. The characteristic rotten-egg smell of the sulphuretted hydrogen bubbling up into the harbour is so pungent that the village above Methana is called Vromolimani or 'stinking shore'. The buildings on the west side of the harbour house sulphur baths to which people suffering from rheumatic diseases come. You can have a free bath in the harbour if you fancy it. Boats moored here are said not to have fouling problems as the sulphur in the water kills off weed and barnacles.

PETROKARAVO

The group of jagged rocks (the highest is 15m/49ft), lying 3½ miles S of the southern tip of Aiyina. There are considerable depths close to the rocks. They are covered by one of the red sectors of the light on Nisis Moni (Fl(2)WRG.10s7-4M) and the red sector of the light on the W tip of Poros (Ak Dana Fl.WR.4s8/5M).

NISIS PLATIA

The small island (7m/23ft high) approximately 1½ miles NE of the northern tip of Poros. It is surrounded by a reef and is unlit.

Nisos Poros

The Rorschach-blob island of the Saronic. It lies close to the coast of the Peloponnese separated from it by a narrow and in places very shallow channel. The island is extensively wooded (mostly pine but also olive and citrus groves) and is cultivated in places. Most of the population live in Poros town.

In ancient times the island was known as Kaularia and was the centre of the Kaularian league, a maritime confederacy of the 7th century BC amongst whose members were Athens, Aiyina, Epidhavros, Troezein, Ermioni, Navplion, Praisiai and Poros. Its patron was Poseidon and a few remains of a temple to Poseidon (about 6 BC but built on an earlier site) can be found on a picturesque site on the east coast of the island.

In 1831 at the end of the Greek War of Independence the islanders opposed the first Greek government and formed a constitutional committee to replace it which had widespread support from the surrounding islands. The Greek ships *Hellas* and *Hydra* were blown up in the harbour by Admiral Miaoulis in defiance of the new government when it sent forces to crush the rebellion. A Greek naval establishment and naval cadet school are situated immediately north of Poros town, perhaps to ensure that there are no further insurrections on the island.

POROS

Admiralty chart no. 1599
Imray-Tetra chart no. G14

Approach

Conspicuous From the N the narrow channel leading into the large landlocked bay is difficult to see from the distance. The numerous ferries plying this stretch of water will seem to disappear or appear from nowhere. Closer in the lighthouse on the E side of the entrance will be seen. Once in the large bay, the town of Poros will be clearly seen. A light blue clock-tower is conspicuous.

From the S the buildings on the low-lying isthmus can be seen but it is difficult to see the entrance to the narrow channel. Keep close to the Poros side of the channel and keep a good lookout for the numerous ferries which come rocketing out of the narrow channel.

By night From the N use the two lights on the E side of the entrance (Ak Dana Fl.WR.4s8/5M and Ak Nedha Fl.R.2s2M). From the S a night entrance is difficult because of the unlit islands in the approaches. The red sector of the light on the S Point of Poros covers the islands (Ak Stavros Fl.RG.3s4M: 284°-R-309°).

Dangers
1. Care is needed of the shallows on the Peloponnese side of the channel through Poros town. Stick close to the Poros side. Local *caïques* make a good

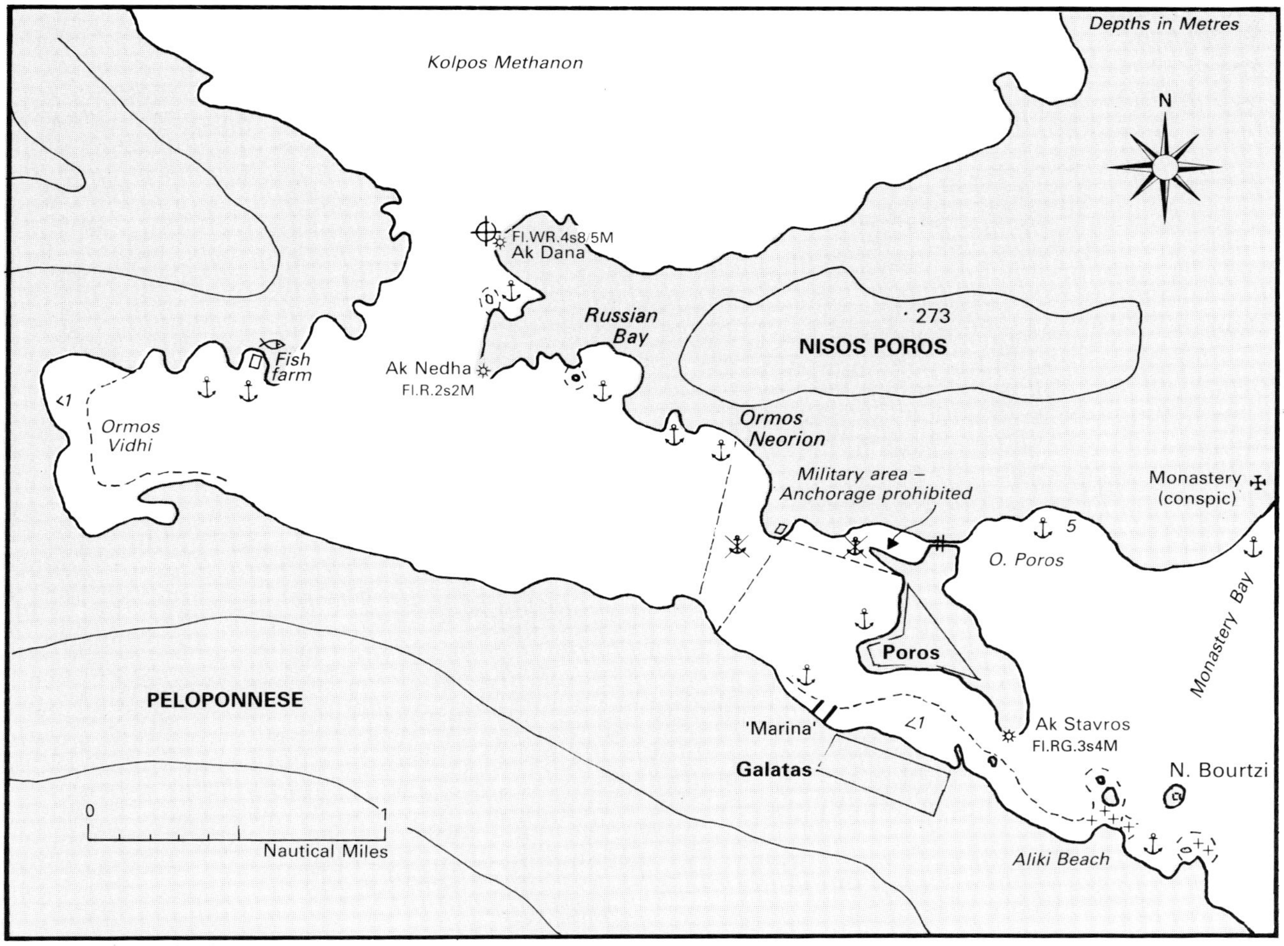

Depths in Metres

Kolpos Methanon

Fl.WR.4s8.5M
Ak Dana

Russian
Bay

NISOS POROS

· 273

Fish
farm

Ak Nedha
Fl.R.2s2M

Ormos
Neorion

Ormos
Vidhi

Military area –
Anchorage prohibited

Monastery
(conspic)

O. Poros

5

Monastery Bay

PELOPONNESE

Poros

'Marina'

Galatas

Ak Stavros
Fl.RG.3s4M

N. Bourtzi

Aliki Beach

0

1

Nautical Miles

APPROACHES TO POROS
37°31'·7N 23°25'·6E (Ak Dana light)

Ak Dana and lighthouse at the W entrance to Poros channel
looking E.

living pulling inattentive yachtsmen off the sticky
mud.
2. Care is needed of the ferries and hydrofoils
entering and leaving at speed.

Mooring

Go stern-to or bows-to the quay on the N or
alongside or stern-to the quay on the S in the narrow
channel. The quay is very low so care is needed with
your fenders. The wash from ferries, particularly the
hydrofoil, can be uncomfortable and you must pay
attention to your warps and fenders when alongside.
The holding off the N quay is patchy. The bottom in
the channel is mud – excellent holding.

The light structure on the 'corner' of the W entrance (Ak Nedha)
to Poros channel looking E.

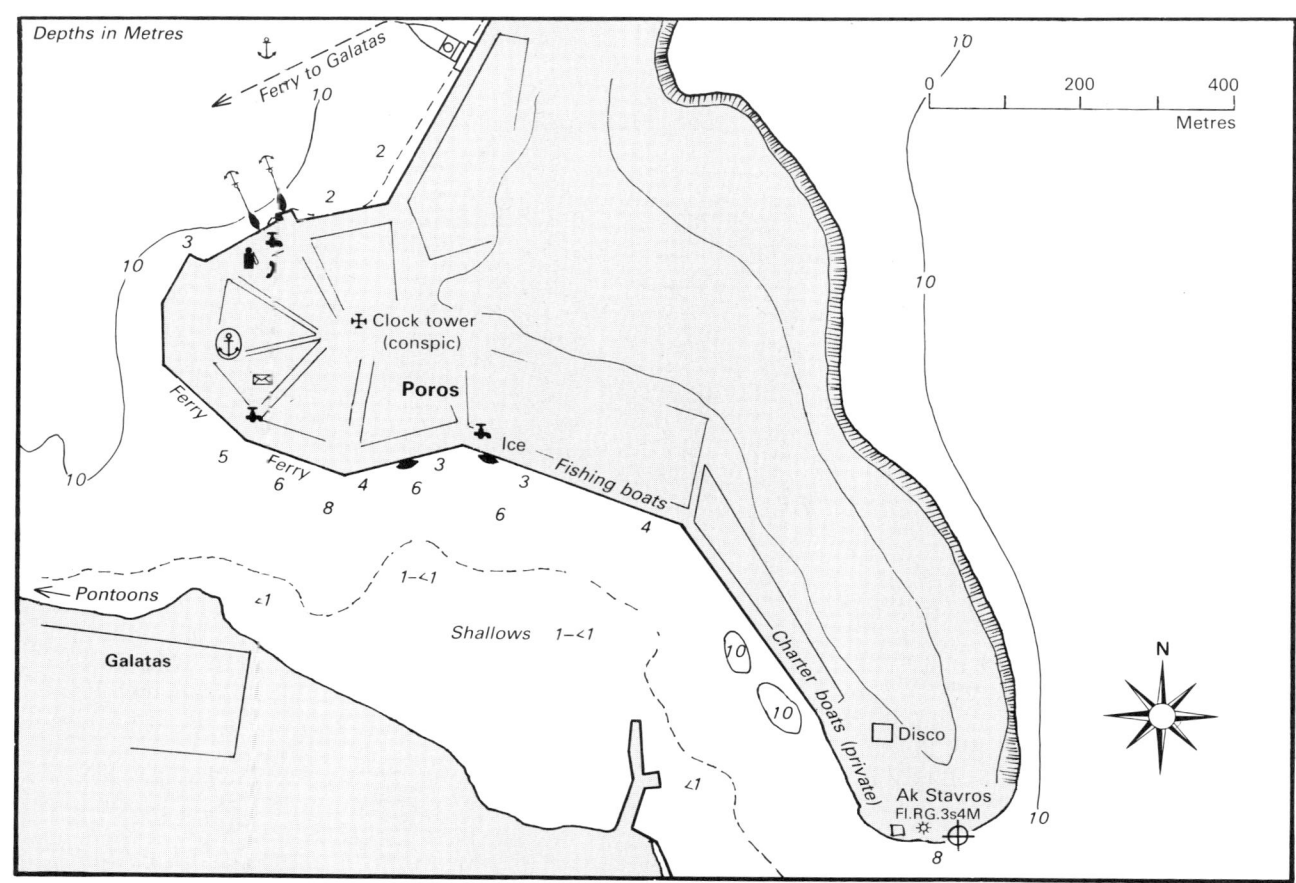

POROS
37°29'·7N 23°27'·8E (Ak Stravros light)

Shelter Good all-round shelter although strong westerlies cause some slop on the N quay. There are strong gusts off the hills of the Peloponnese with strong southerlies. A number of yachts winter afloat here.

Authorities Port police and customs.

Approach to Poros town looking ESE.

Facilities

Water On the quay. Showers available in several of the bars on the waterfront.

Fuel A mini-tanker delivers to the quay.

Repairs Some mechanical repairs. Hardware shops. Two chandlers.

Provisions Good shopping for all provisions. Ice available.

Eating out Numerous tavernas on the waterfront and behind. Also tavernas at Galatas across the strait.

Poros looking W from the ridge above the town. *Nigel Patten*.

Yorgiou at the *Café Remetzo* on the waterfront serves a good breakfast or a cool beer in the evening.

Other PO. OTE. Banks. Greek gas and *Camping Gaz*. Laundrette close to the N quay. Hire cars, motorbikes and bicycles. *Caïque* ferries across to Galatas. Ferries to Piraeus and the other islands in the Saronic Gulf.

General

The small volcanic peninsula on which Poros town is built was known in ancient times as Sphaeria. Poros means a 'strait' or 'ferry' and is a later name. The town built on the rocky slopes is attractive and the approach by sea one of the most beautiful in Greece. Poros is a popular tourist spot as well as being popular with day-trippers from Athens. In the season they pour into Poros, yet it somehow manages to stand up to it all and remains a likable place.

If you are berthed on the S quay it can get smelly at the height of the season from the sewerage emptying into the harbour. If the smell doesn't prevent you from sleeping, the latest in popular music will assail your eardrums from the numerous bars along the waterfront.

Note A mini-marina is under construction just W of Galatas. This basically consists of a number of pontoons out from the shore. Shelter here is reasonable although not perfect and is still affected by the wash from ferries and hydrofoils. Water and electricity are expected to be laid on to the pontoon berths.

ANCHORAGES NEAR POROS

1. *Ormos Vidhi* Anchor in the bay or any of the coves on the N side. The water here is a bit murky. Taverna on the beach at the head of the bay.
2. *Ak Dana* Anchor in the cove tucked under the cape. Good shelter from the prevailing winds and clear water.
3. *Russian Bay* Nisis Dhaskalia under Ak Nedha is easily recognised by the conspicuous white chapel on it. Anchor in the bay under the island. The bottom is mud and weed, good holding once through the weed. Good shelter from the prevailing winds.
4. *Ormos Neorion* In the bay SE of Dhaskalia where a number of charter yachts have permanent moorings there is good shelter.
5. *Aliki* A reef connects the small islets to the SE of Poros Channel to the mainland. Pass between the islets and Nisis Bourtzi. Good shelter. Sandy bottom. Taverna on the beach.
6. *Ormos Porou* Is quite deep until a short distance off. Poor holding. Taverna on the beach.
7. *Monastery Bay* As for Ormos Porou.

NISIDHES TSELEVINIA

These two islands, Spathi and Skilli, lie to the S of Poros just before you 'turn the corner' to head into Kolpos Idhras (the Hydra Gulf). The passage between the two islands is deep and clear of dangers in the fairway. However great care is needed of the numerous ferries and hydrofoils which charge through the narrow channel at full speed (the ferries come through at 15–20 knots, the hydrofoil at around 30 knots).

The passage between Nisis Spathi and the Peloponnese is obstructed by a reef just below the water. Off the SW tip of Spathi there is a small islet and behind it a secluded anchorage.

NISIS SOUPIA

An islet lying close off the coast about 1½ miles W of Nisis Spathi. The islet looks like a crouching frog when viewed from the E. Anchor behind the islet where convenient. Good shelter in settled weather. The bottom is covered in thick weed and is poor holding in parts. Mulberry trees around the shore and a small farm ashore.

HYDRA BEACH HOTEL

This large hotel complex lies approximately 8½ miles W of Nisis Spathi. It is easily identified from seaward. There is a small boat harbour attached to the complex (2 metre depths just inside), but it is usually crowded with *caïque* ferries.

ERMIONI (Hermioni, Kastri)

Approach

Conspicuous The village of Ermioni saddling the headland is easily identified from seaward. The end of the headland is wooded (mostly conifers).

By night Use the light on Ak Kastri (Fl.1·5s5M) and on the molehead (F.R.2M). The new breakwater head is lit Fl.G.2s3M.

Dangers Care needs to be taken of the remains of the ancient mole on the N side of the headland.

Mooring

Go stern-to or bows-to behind the outer mole if there is room. Larger yachts can anchor in the bay. The harbour can get crowded in the summer. The bottom is mud and weed with some rocks – poor holding in patches.

Shelter Good all-round shelter behind the mole. One or two yachts have wintered afloat here. The new stone breakwater running out from the shore on the W provides additional shelter from northerlies though not from northeasterlies which can blow fiercely off the hills.

Authorities Port police.

Note On the S side of the peninsula there is a protruding quayed area with 2–5 metre depths off it. The bottom drops off quickly to 10 metres and more. The rest of the quayed area is bordered by underwater rubble. The S quay is entirely open to southerlies and easterlies so does not provide all-round shelter. However with offshore winds it is a delightful spot and comparatively peaceful in the summer compared to the other side of the headland.

Facilities

Water On the quay.
Fuel In the town.
Repairs Limited mechanical repairs. Hardware shop.
Provisions Good shopping for most provisions. Ice available.

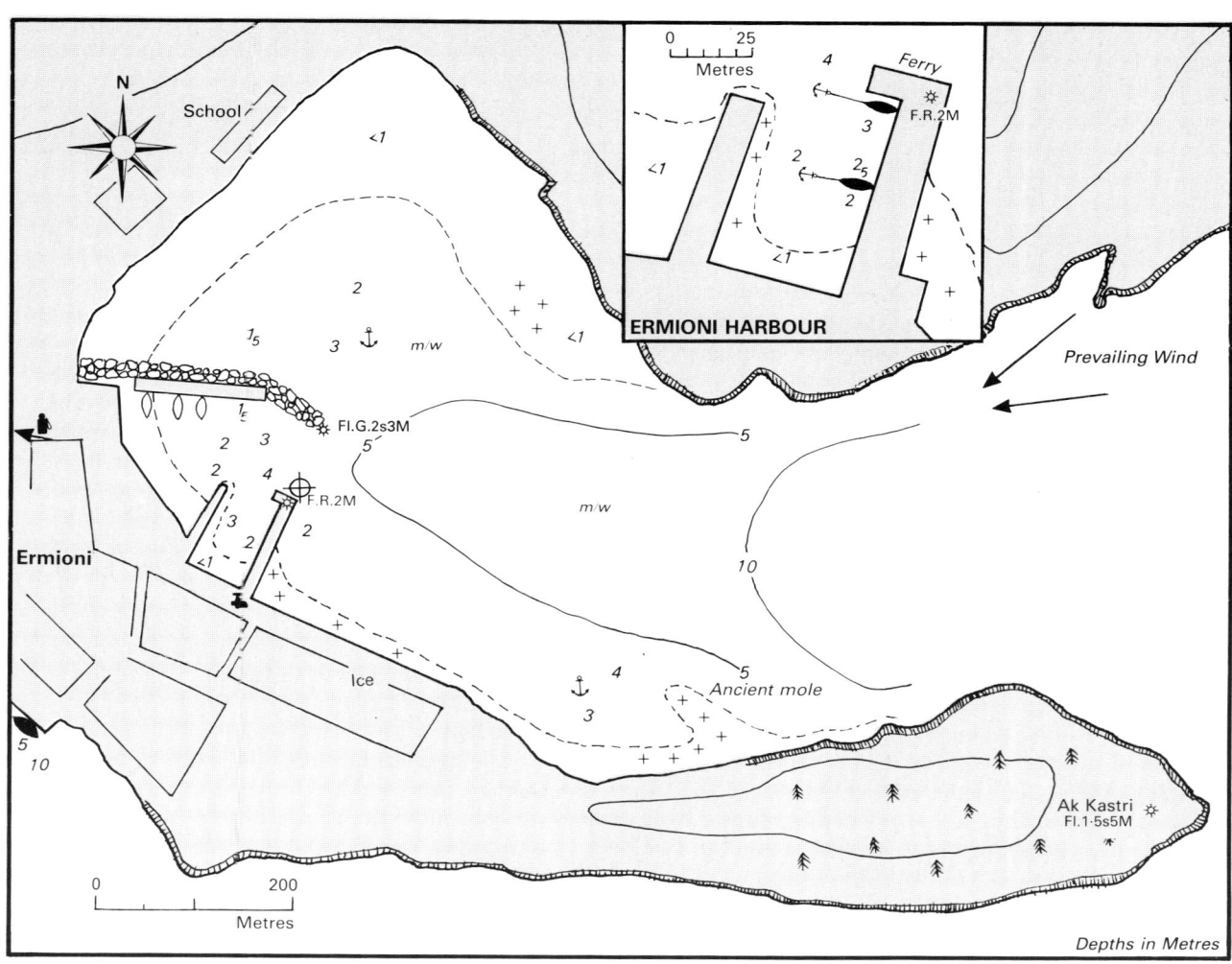

ERMIONI
37°23'·2N 23°15'E (F.R.2M)

Eating out Tavernas on the waterfront and on the S side of the headland.

Other PO. OTE. Bank. Greek gas. Car and motorbike hire. Ferries to Piraeus and the islands in the Saronic Gulf.

General

The village has been relatively untouched by tourism although there are now several small hotels of what has been called the 'pour and fill' variety. Walk over the saddle of the town to the S side of the headland where things are peaceful and you can sit in a bar on the waterfront with wonderful views over the water.

In ancient times Ermioni was of some importance. The remains of an ancient mole and parts of a wall can be seen on the N side of Ak Kastri. Pausanias records that a festival in honour of Poseidon was held here and depending on your interpretation of the ancient Greek, either swimming or boat races were held – it is possible Ermioni was the site of the first small boat regatta in recorded history.

ORMOS KAPARI

The large bay immediately S of Ermioni. In the SW corner there is good shelter from the normal summer winds. Anchor in 2–5 metres. The bottom is sand and weed – good holding. Care must be taken of Vrak Kapari, an islet and rocks lying to the E of the southern entrance point. Some of the rocks are only just above water and are difficult to see.

Idhra
(Hydra)

The long narrow island lying parallel to the Peloponnese coast and bordering the south side of Kolpos Idhras. It is mountainous throughout rising to the summit, Mt Eros (590 metres/1935ft), near the centre. It is everywhere arid and sterile and devoid of vegetation.

Idhra appears not to have been of any importance in ancient times. It was during the centuries of Turkish rule that it prospered and built up a large mercantile marine fleet. It paid no taxes but supplied sailors for the Turkish fleet. In 1821 it was the first of the islands to pledge its sizeable fleet (some 150 ships) to the Greek cause. Admiral Miaoulis, admiral of the Greek fleet, was an Hydriot as were many of the other captains and sailors who distinguished themselves against the Turks. It has been said that but for the Hydriot fleet and sailors, the War of Independence would not have been won.

The Hydriot fleet never recovered from the war effort and Idhra declined in importance to become a backwater of the Saronic until it was discovered by discerning travellers. It became a fashionable resort, and in the early days of tourism the rich and famous holidayed in Idhra, though now it is visited by larger numbers ferried in daily from Piraeus.

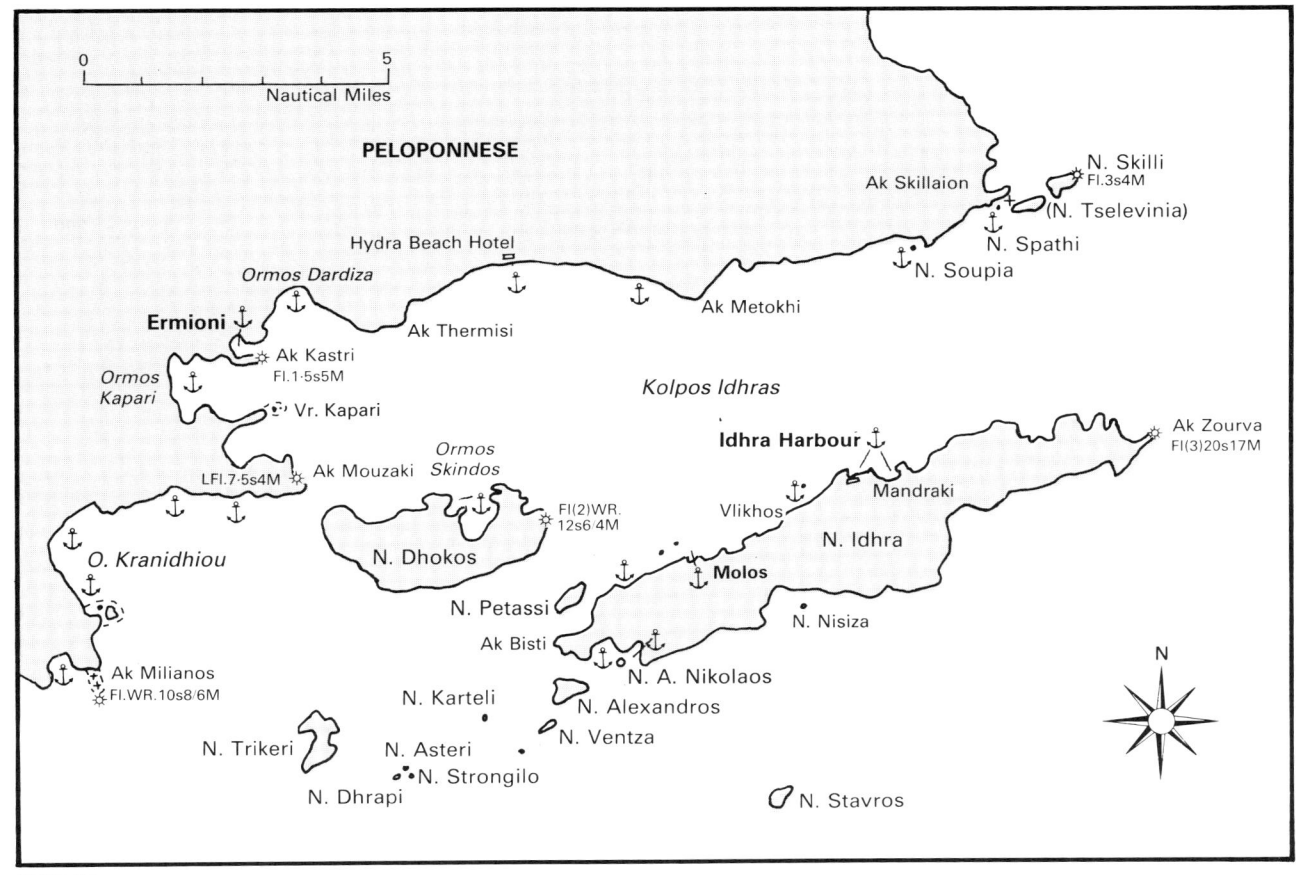

IDHRAS

LIMIN IDHRAS (Hydra, Ydra)

Approach

Conspicuous A white monastery on the hill above the harbour is conspicuous from some distance off. Closer in the small town of Idhra built around the natural amphitheatre above the harbour will be seen.

By night Use the light on the E side (Fl.R.1·5s3M) and the lights at the entrance (F.R.2M and F.G.2M).

Dangers Care is needed of the numerous craft, ferries and hydrofoils and pleasure craft, entering and leaving the narrow entrance, often at speed.

Mooring

Go stern-to or bows-to the town quay or the N mole. The latter has underwater ballasting projecting a short distance out in places so care is needed when berthing there. If possible go on the N mole in case N–NW winds blow. In the summer the harbour is very crowded and it is not unusual for yachts to be berthed three out from the quay. Crossed anchors are a fact of life here and there is little you can do about it. The bottom is mud and weed with some rocks – poor holding in places.

Shelter With strong N–NW winds a dangerous surge develops and the only safe place is on the N mole.

Authorities Port police and customs.

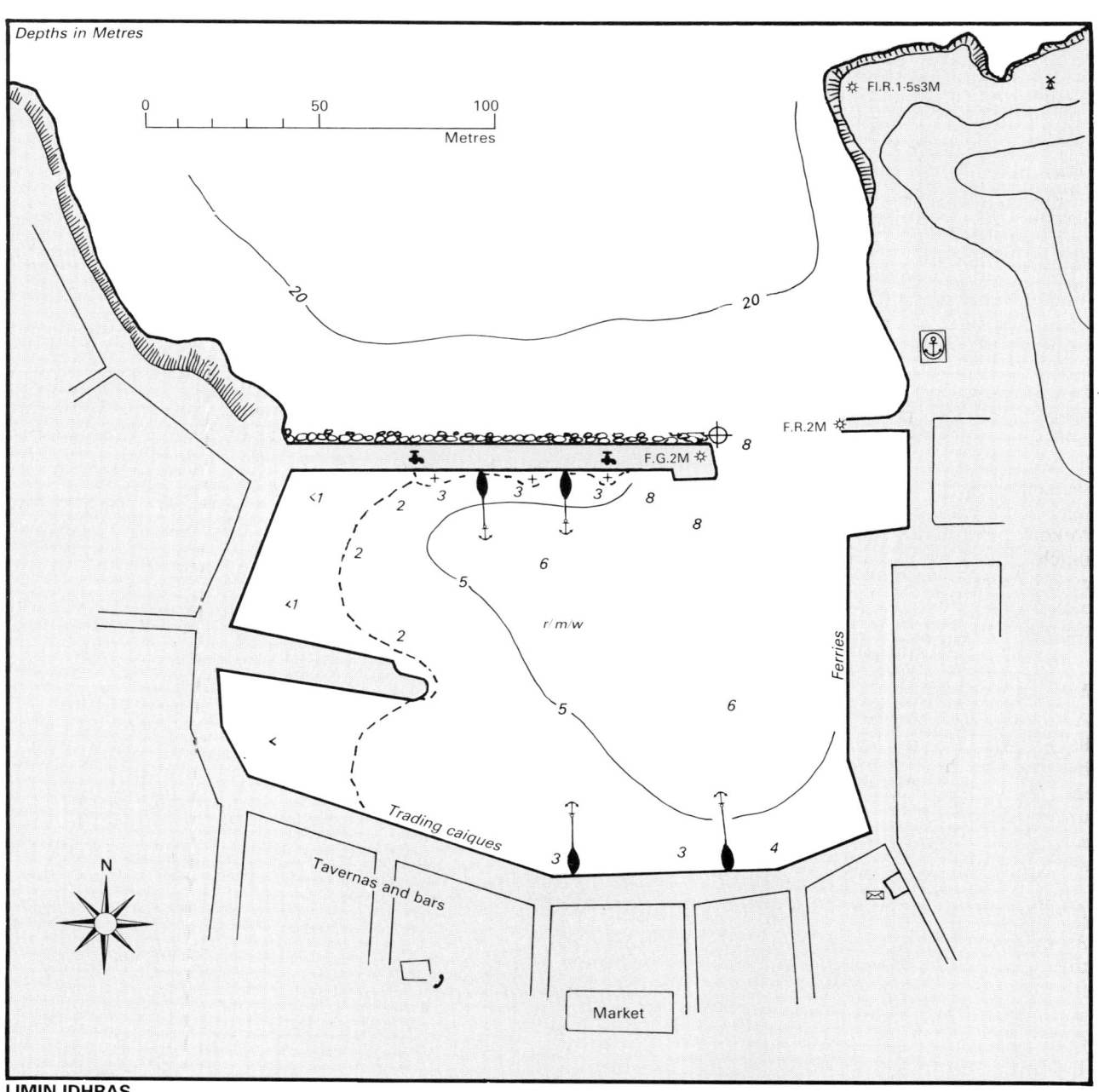

LIMIN IDHRAS
37°21′·1N 23°28′E (F.G.2M)

Idhra harbour looking ESE. *Nigel Patten.*

Facilities
Water On the quay.
Provisions Good shopping for most provisions. Ice from the market.
Eating out Tavernas on the waterfront and in the town. I suggest you go into the town away from the overpriced tavernas and bars on the waterfront.
Other PO. OTE. Bank. Greek gas and *Camping Gaz.* Ferries to Piraeus and the other islands in the Saronic Gulf.

General
Among the buildings of the town there are many large stately houses built in the time when Idhra was a prosperous town and possessed a large mercantile fleet. In the 1950s and 60s Idhra became a fashionable artists' colony attracting, amongst others, songwriter and performer Leonard Cohen, the champion of depressive and suicidal ballads. He still has a house here.

Later it became a popular tourist island, but it has not experienced the extensive development of Mikonos or Rhodes and remains architecturally very much of the 18th and 19th centuries. In the summer months there are about 10 ferries a day and perhaps one or two cruise ships anchored off or berthed in the tiny harbour.

MANDRAKI
A bay about ¾ of a mile E of Hydra. A hotel at the head of the bay is conspicuous. Sheltered from the S but open to the N. Good shelter in settled weather though northerlies, even light ones, make it uncomfortable. Anchor in 3–6 metres. The bottom is sand, mud and weed – good holding. Tavernas ashore. Water taxi to Idhra.

ANCHORAGES SW OF LIMIN IDHRAS
Along the northern side and at the SW end of Idhra there are several anchorages affording some shelter from the prevailing SE wind. At times there may be gusts off Idhra though they vary in strength and duration.
1. *Vlikhos* Anchor off the hamlet. Taverna ashore.
2. *Ormos Molos* A small bay opposite Nisis Kivolos. Taverna ashore.

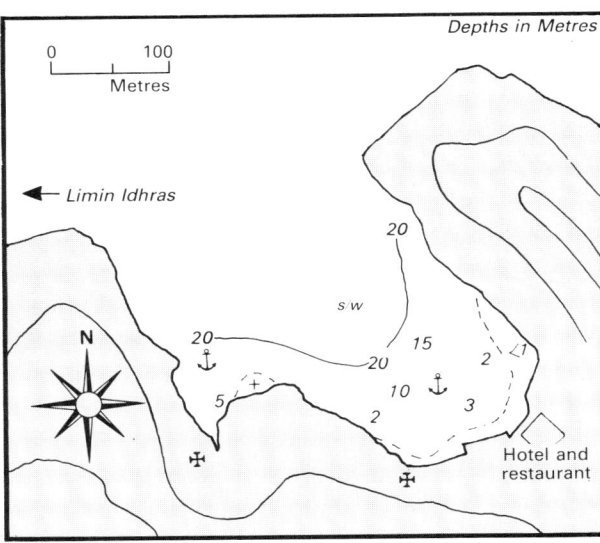

MANDRAKI
37°21′N 23°29′E

3. *Petassi* Opposite the NE end of Nisis Petassi there are several small coves that can be used.
4. *Bisti* Under Ak Bisti there is a bay that can be used though it is quite deep.
5. *Ay Nikolaos* NE of Nisis Ay Nikolaos there is a large bay that can be used in calm weather. Marvellous surroundings and clear water. When the prevailing wind gets up a swell is pushed in here.

NISIS DHOKOS
The bluff barren island off the SW end of Idhra. Stenon Petassi, the channel between Idhra and Dhokos, is deep and clear of dangers. The winds in this channel are variable and often die away altogether so it is best to motor through until they pick up again. One or two families live in Ormos Skindos on the north side of the island.

ORMOS SKINDOS
A large bay with a number of coves around the edges providing good shelter from the normal summer winds.

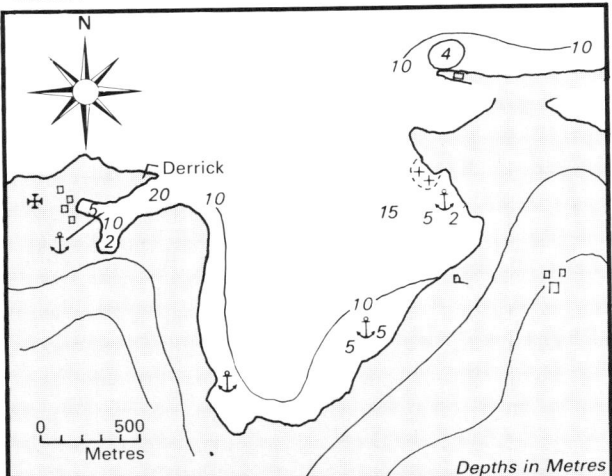

ORMOS SKINDOS
37°20′·5N 23°20′E

Nisis Dhokos. Anchorage in the W cove of Ormos Skindos.

Anchorages

1. On the E side where possible. Anchor in 2-5 metres with a line ashore if necessary. Yachts also anchor SW of this anchorage. Reasonable shelter from the prevailing wind although at times it can be uncomfortable. The bay is popular as a lunch stop but is often deserted at night. Open W across the bay and NW.

2. In the NW corner a small inlet with a number of houses around the shore provides good shelter. Anchor in 7–10 metres. Sand and weed bottom. The large buoy formerly in here has been moved but its substantial mooring chain is still on the bottom.

NISIS TRIKERI

The islet midway between Idhra and Spetsai. Fishing boats will often be seen around it. Between Trikeri and Idhra there is a chain of islets and islands: Asteri, Dhrapi, Strongilo, Dhisakki, Tagari, Karteli, Ventza and Alexandros. The red sector of the light on the E side of Baltiza Creek (Ak Fanari Fl.WR.5s18/14M red sector covers 254°-278°) covers these islands and rocks as well as Ifalos Trikeri (least depth 5 metres) and Ifalos Milianos (least depth 7 metres) lying between Nisis Trikeri and Spetsai.

Argolikos Kolpos
(Argolic Gulf) and the eastern Peloponnese

Argolikos Kolpos reaches back up to the north from the more southerly Saronic Islands of Spetsai and Idhra. It is surrounded by high mountains except at the head of the gulf where there is the flat plain of Argos. The mountains on the western side of the gulf are the first of the Parnon range which continues right down the eastern side of the Peloponnese to Ak Maleas. The mountains are rugged and barren and the shore inhospitable. Generally there are good depths close off the coast as the mountains drop sheer into the sea. The highest peaks are covered with snow in the winter and often well into the spring.

AK MILIANOS (Ay Amilianos)

A reef partly under the water on which the sea breaks extends about ¼ of a mile S of the cape. A white church on the cape is conspicuous. A small light structure marks the extremity of the reef (chart.Fl.WR.10s8/6M red sector covers 314°-357° over Ifalos Milianos and Ifalos Trikeri).

In the bay immediately W of Ak Milianos there are several attractive calm-weather anchorages.

Spetsai

The roughly oval island lying in the eastern approaches to Argolikos Kolpos. It has a gentler aspect than either Idhra or Dhokos and the climate is described by the Admiralty *Pilot* as 'exceedingly healthy'. Much of the island is covered by pine trees planted in an inspired afforestation programme implemented in the early part of this century. Most of the population lives in Spetsai town on the northern coast (conspicuous from the east).

Spetsai has the distinction of being the first island (with Idhra) to revolt against the Turks and commit her merchant fleet to the Greek cause. The local heroine was Boubalina (many of the local boats are named after her) who commanded the Spetsai fleet – her most daring deed was the destruction of part of the Turkish fleet at Navplion with fire ships. The deed is commemorated by a regatta in September when a small *caïque* rigged out as an old trader is set on fire in the harbour accompanied by a noisy fireworks display and much merriment. Like that of Idhra the mercantile power of Spetsai declined after the War of Independence.

Spetsai town is more akin to the Italian Riviera than a Greek town although recent architectural additions have reduced the effect. Of late a number of large hotels have been built in the town to cater for the large numbers of tourists who descend on the island in the summer.

Just outside the town the large public school, the Anarghyrios and Korghialenios School of Spetsai, is modelled on an English public school. John Fowles taught at the school for a time and his novel *The Magus* is set on the island – most of the places in the novel can be easily identified including the Villa Yasemia on the west coast where most of the action in the novel takes place.

SPETSAI (BALTIZA CREEK) (Spetses, Balza, Palaio Limani)
Admiralty chart no. 1518 (Spetsai Channel)
Imray-Tetra chart no. G14

Approach

Conspicuous From the distance the houses of Spetsai town around the northern shores and on the gentle slopes are easily seen. Closer in, the lighthouse on Ak Fanari, the headland forming the E side of the harbour, and a number of whitewashed windmill towers (now converted to houses) are conspicuous.

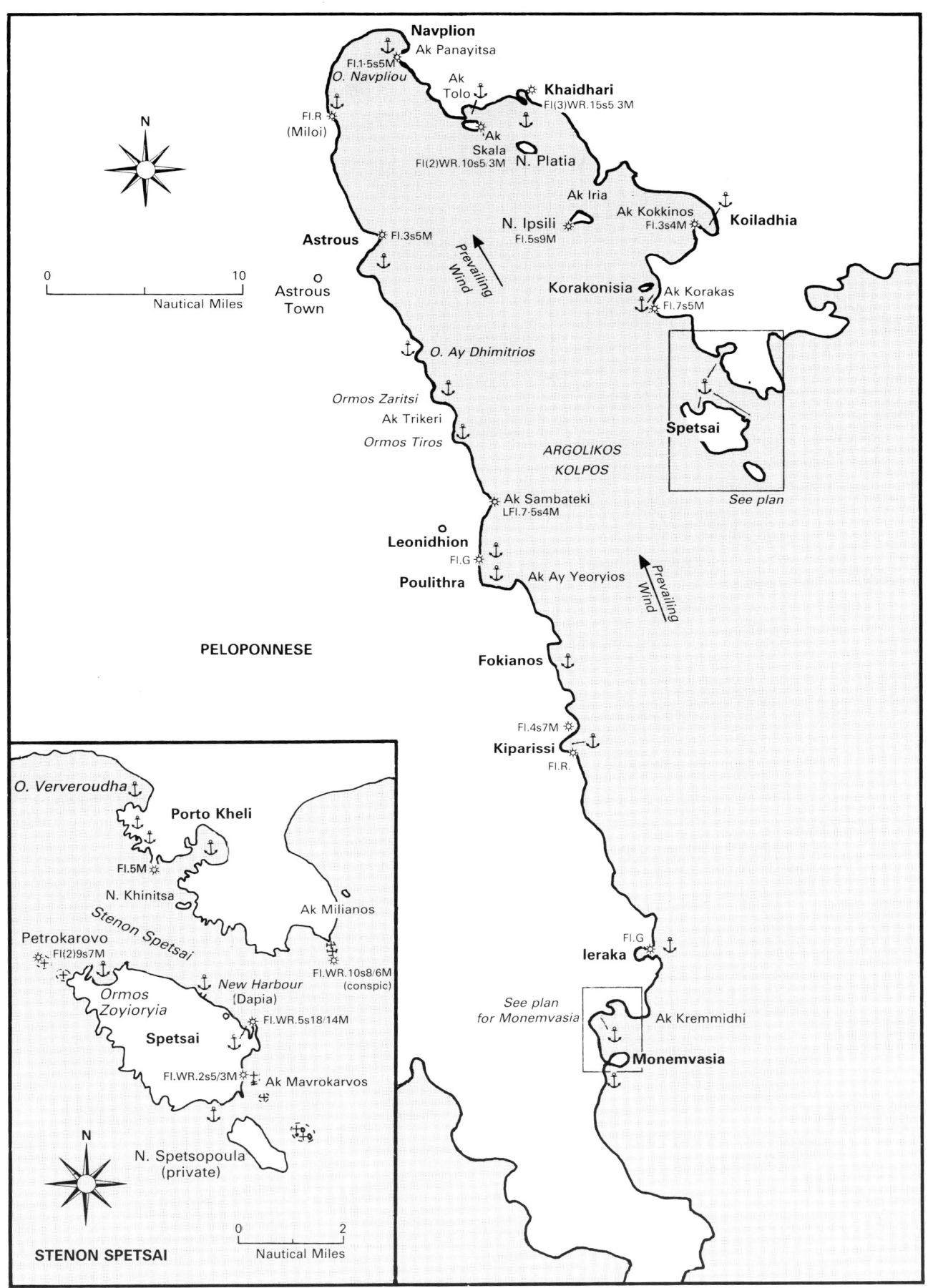

Navplion
Ak Panayitsa
Fl.1·5s5M
O. Navpliou
Ak Tolo
Khaidhari
Fl(3)WR.15s5·3M
Ak Skala
Fl(2)WR.10s5·3M
N. Platia
Ak Iria
N. Ipsili
Fl.5s9M
Ak Kokkinos
Fl.3s4M
Koiladhia
Astrous
Fl.3s5M
Astrous
Town
Korakonisia
Ak Korakas
Fl.7s5M
O. Ay Dhimitrios
Spetsai
See plan
Ormos Zaritsi
Ak Trikeri
Ormos Tiros
ARGOLIKOS
KOLPOS
Ak Sambateki
LFl.7·5s4M
Leonidhion
Fl.G
Poulithra
Ak Ay Yeoryios
Prevailing Wind
Fokianos
Fl.4s7M
Kiparissi
Fl.R.
PELOPONNESE
Fl.G
Ieraka
See plan for Monemvasia
Ak Kremmidhi
Monemvasia

STENON SPETSAI

O. Ververoudha
Porto Kheli
Fl.5M
N. Khinitsa
Ak Milianos
Petrokarovo
Fl(2)9s7M
Ormos Zoyioryia
New Harbour (Dapia)
Fl.WR.10s8/6M (conspic)
Spetsai
Fl.WR.5s18/14M
Fl.WR.2s5/3M Ak Mavrokarvos
N. Spetsopoula (private)

N

0   2
Nautical Miles

N

0   10
Nautical Miles

ARGOLIKOS KOLPOS AND THE EASTERN PELOPONNESES

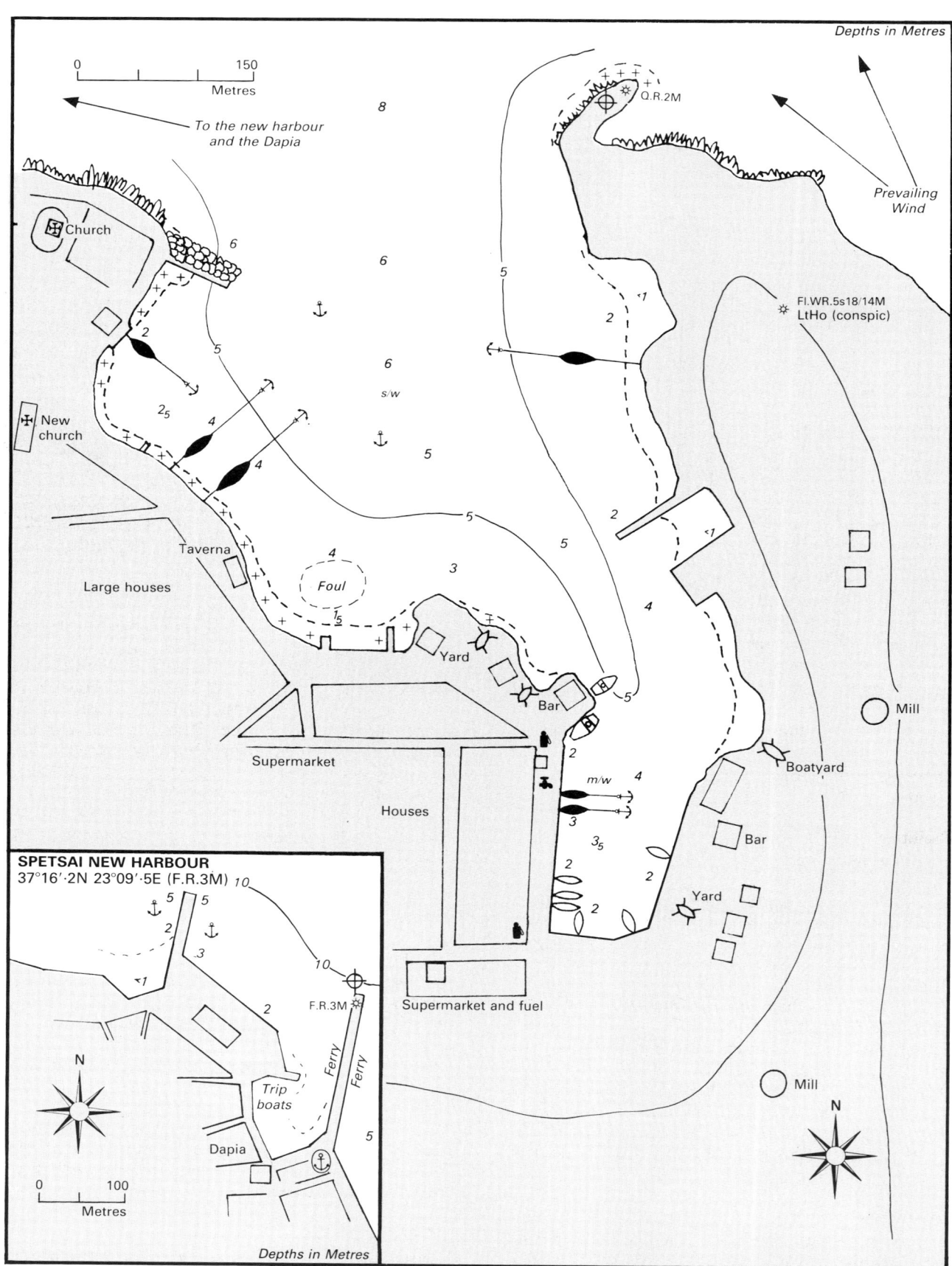

Depths in Metres

0 ——— 150
Metres

To the new harbour
and the Dapia

8

Q.R.2M

Prevailing
Wind

Church

6

6

5

Fl.WR.5s18/14M
LtHo (conspic)

6

New
church

s/w

2₅

4

4

5

4

5

Taverna

Large houses

4

Foul

3

1₅

5

4

Mill

Yard

Bar

5

Boatyard

Supermarket

2

m/w

4

Bar

Houses

3

3₅

Yard

SPETSAI NEW HARBOUR
37°16'·2N 23°09'·5E (F.R.3M)

10

2

2

2

5   5

2

.3

10

1

F.R.3M

2

N

Ferry
Ferry

Trip
boats

Supermarket and fuel

Dapia

5

Mill

N

0 ——— 100
Metres

Depths in Metres

SPETSAI – BALTIZA CREEK
37°16N 23°10'E (Q.R.2M)

Approach to Baltiza Creek looking SE. *Rosie Rigby*.

By night Use the light on Ak Fanari (Fl.WR.5s18/14M) and the light on the extremity of the headland (Q.R.2M).

Dangers
1. Care should be taken rounding the extremity of the headland where there are some above-water rocks and a short reef.
2. There is often a confused swell at the entrance with S winds.

Mooring

Anchor in the bay with a long line ashore or stern-to or bows-to in the inner harbour if there is room. Baltiza Creek is a popular destination for yachts in the season and the inner harbour will usually be full to bursting and the outer harbour too crowded for you to swing at anchor. In the outer harbour the bottom is sand and weed (poor holding in patches) and in the SW corner there is a large permanent mooring chain fouling the bottom. In the inner harbour the bottom is mud – excellent holding.

Shelter With strong NW winds the outer harbour is uncomfortable and possibly dangerous for small yachts. The inner harbour has excellent all-round protection and a number of yachts are wintered afloat here.

Authorities Port police and customs in the new harbour.

Facilities

Water On the quay.
Fuel On the quay.
Repairs Yachts are hauled out in any one of the three yards around the harbour, though you will need to book early to get a place. Some mechanical repairs. Old-fashioned wood repairs. Small chandlers. Hardware shops.
Provisions Good shopping for provisions near the harbour and in town. Ice available.
Eating out Good tavernas near the harbour and others in town.
Other PO. OTE. Banks. Greek gas and *Camping Gaz*. Hire motorbikes and bicycles. Horse drawn gharries. Car ferry to Kosta across Spetsai Strait and ferries and hydrofoils to Piraeus and the other islands in the Saronic Gulf.

General

Spetsai is an attractive town popular with tourists and Athenians alike. For some unknown reason tourists rarely stray from the town into the Old Harbour. Spetsai restaurants often have an excellent dish peculiar to the island, fish à la Spetsiosa, a

Baltiza Creek looking N from the head of the inlet.

casserole of fish, tomatoes and green peppers covered in cheese – which is well worth sampling.

Spetsai old harbour and environs is a wonderful place to wander around. There are several yards building *caïques* and Spetsiot boats are said to be among the best in Greece. Tim Severin had his replica galley built here for his voyages tracing the routes of Jason and the Argonauts and Odysseus wandering home from the Trojan War.

Around the harbour are many grand old houses built in the prosperous era of the 18th and 19th centuries when Spetsiot ships traded all over the eastern Mediterranean and because no cars are allowed on the island (motorbikes unfortunately are) walking around the old quarter is a delight.

SPETSAI NEW HARBOUR

Off the Dapia at Spetsai town there is a mole and a small boat harbour. The mole is reserved for ferries and the small boat harbour for local *caïque* ferries. A yacht will be turned away by the port police.

On the W side of the ferry mole and boat harbour there is a short mole and a quay. There are underwater rocks off the quay, but on the W side of the mole there are 2–5 metre depths. Go stern-to where convenient. There is usually an uncomfortable swell with the normal summer winds and it is untenable with northerlies.

ORMOS ZOYIORYIA

A large bay on the NW corner. Anchor in the bay in 5–8 metres. On the W side of the bay there is a small cove offering good shelter from all but NE–E winds. The bottom is sand with some rock – good holding.

Sometimes at night a katabatic wind will blow out of Argolikos Kolpos from the NW making the bay uncomfortable and sometimes untenable. The cove on the W affords shelter from this wind.

The surroundings here are attractive with a wooded foreshore and clear water. A taverna on the shore.

NISIS PETROKARAVO

The islet off the NW tip of Spetsai. It is lit: Fl(2)9s7M. Between the islet and Spetsai there is a reef which has a deep passage through it nearer to Spetsai than Petrokaravo. The prudent course is to go around the outside of Petrokaravo.

SPETSOPOULA

The small island lying off the SE tip of Spetsai. It is the private property of Stavros Niarchos (the ship owner whose fleet rivals that of the late Onassis) and landing is prohibited on it. There is a private harbour on the N end of the island where Niarchos' large yacht is sometimes moored. Care must be taken when navigating between Spetsai and Spetsopoula as there are a number of reefs in the general vicinity.

PORTO KHELI (Heli)
Admiralty chart no. 1518 (Spetsai Strait)
Imray-Tetra chart no. G14

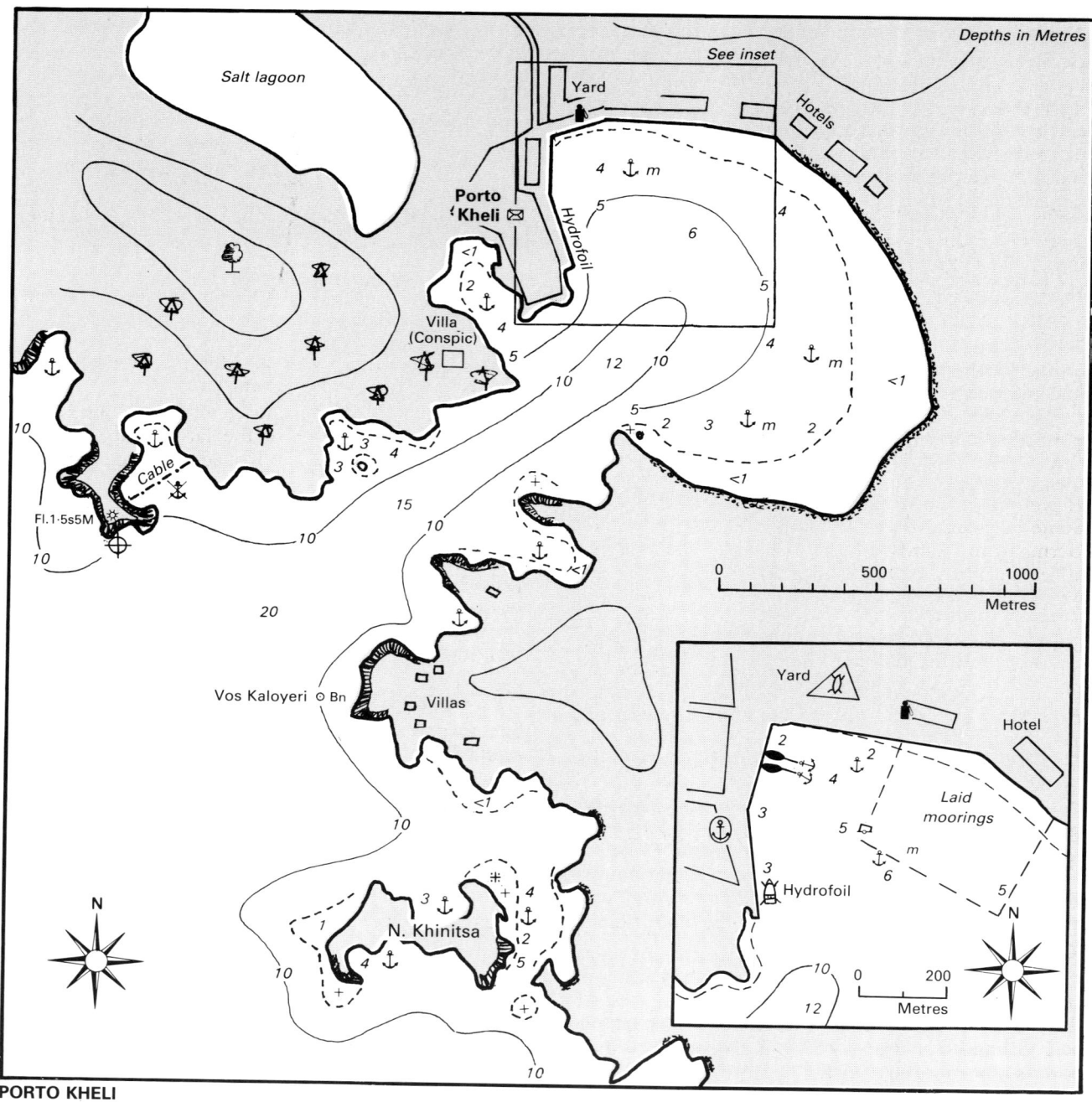

PORTO KHELI
37°18'·9N 23°07'·7E (Fl.1·5s5M)

Approach

Conspicuous A large white hotel on the SE side of the entrance and a number of large villas on the E side of the channel are conspicuous from the W. From the E Nisis Khinitsa is easily identified. Closer in the light structure on the W side and the beacon marking the reef off the E side of the entrance will be seen.

By night A night approach can be difficult as there is only the one light on the W side (Fl.1·5s5M).

Caution The channel between Nisis Khinitsa S of the entrance and the mainland has 2 metres' depth in the fairway, but the bottom is uneven and extreme caution is needed when navigating through the channel. The prudent course is to keep to seaward of the island.

Mooring

Go stern-to or bows-to the quay or anchor off. The bottom is sticky mud – excellent holding.

Shelter Excellent all-round shelter. However with the regular SE day breeze the berths on the quay can be uncomfortable with the slop that is kicked up across the bay. Numbers of yachts are wintered afloat here.

Authorities Port police and customs.

Anchorages On either side of the entrance channel into Porto Kheli there are numerous coves where a yacht can anchor depending on the wind direction (see plan). Shelter in the coves is generally good enough to overnight in most of them.

Facilities

Water Local water is brackish. Drinking water is delivered by tanker.

Fuel Near the quay. A mini-tanker delivers to the quay.

Repairs Yachts are hauled at the boatyard here. Some mechanical repairs. Frank's Yacht Station is a German-run company that will look after yachts afloat (on moorings) or ashore. Wintering and repair work can be carried out. Most mechanical and light engineering work can be arranged. Life raft servicing can be arranged. Yachts up to 7 tons can be craned out. Contact Frank's Yacht Service, Frank Wenzloff, Odos Costa 2, Porto Kheli.

Provisions Good shopping for provisions. Ice available.

Eating out Good tavernas around the waterfront and in the village.

Other PO. OTE. Bank. Greek gas, *Camping Gaz*. Bus to Athens. Ferry (hydrofoil) to Piraeus and the islands in the Saronic Gulf.

General

The long quay was built in the 1960s when Porto Kheli was zoned as a NATO base. The plan was eventually shelved and the unfinished harbour and airstrip nearby, used today by small planes, are all that remain of the scheme. Over the years trees have been planted and roads laid so that what was a dust bowl is now more convivial.

Kheli or *heli* means eel in Greek, probably referring to the numbers of eels which once lived here,

especially in the landlocked saltwater lagoon on the W side. The landlocked bay is not unattractive and is custom-made for water sports, so it is not surprising that a number of hotels have been built – in the summer the bay is choked with sailboards, dinghy sailors, paragliding, jet skis, water skiers, and a few swimmers taking their chances amongst the flotsam of skimming plastic and whirling propellers.

NISIS KORAKONISIA

A small island lying immediately N of Ak Korakas (light: Fl.7s5M). On the coast just N of the island there is a small bay sheltered from the normal summer wind. Anchor where convenient. The bottom is sand and rock – good holding. A few houses around the shore. You can also anchor in the cove on the E side of the island. Wonderful surroundings.

AK AY SPIRIDHION

Just N of this headland with a white church on it there is a bay affording reasonable shelter from the prevailing wind. Anchor in 4–5 metres off the beach. Taverna ashore in the summer.

In calm weather there are several other anchorages off sandy beaches in the vicinity.

KOILADHIA (Koilas, Kilas)

Approach

The large bay in the easternmost part of the gulf with the islet of Koiladhia in the entrance.

Conspicuous The white church on Ak Kokkinos is conspicuous and closer in the large church in the village will be seen. Nisis Koiladhia in the entrance is easily identified.

By night A night entrance should be made with care. Use the light on Ak Kokkinos (Fl.3s4M) and the light on the pierhead (2F.G(vert)3M).

Dangers Care must be taken of the reefs bordering the channel off Ak Kokkinos and Nisis Koiladhia.

Mooring

Anchor off the village in 2–3 metres. The short pier off the village is usually crowded with fishing boats, but there may be spaces available. The bottom is mud – excellent holding.

Shelter Good all-round shelter in the bay. Boats are left on moorings here all year round.

Note Nisis Koiladhia is privately owned by a ship owner and the small harbour on the SE side is private.

Facilities

Water On the quay.

Fuel Out of town.

Provisions Most provisions can be found. Ice available.

Eating out Several tavernas on the waterfront which often have good fresh fish.

Other PO. OTE. Greek gas. Taxis.

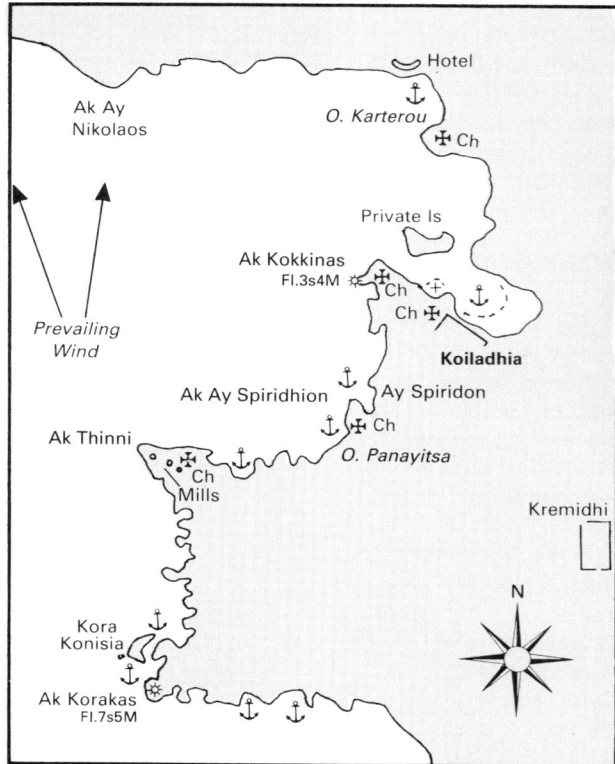

AK KORAKAS TO AK AY NIKOLAOS

The church (conspic) in Koiladhia.

NISIS IPSILI AND NISIS PLATIA

On the NE side of the gulf there are two islands. Nisis Ipsili, the southern of the two, is a bold crescent-shaped island. Nisis Platia to the N is of lower aspect.

There are no anchorages around Ipsili as the depths are considerable right up to the edge. On Platia there is an anchorage on the N side sheltered from the afternoon breeze blowing up the gulf but fish farms now obstruct much of the anchorage.

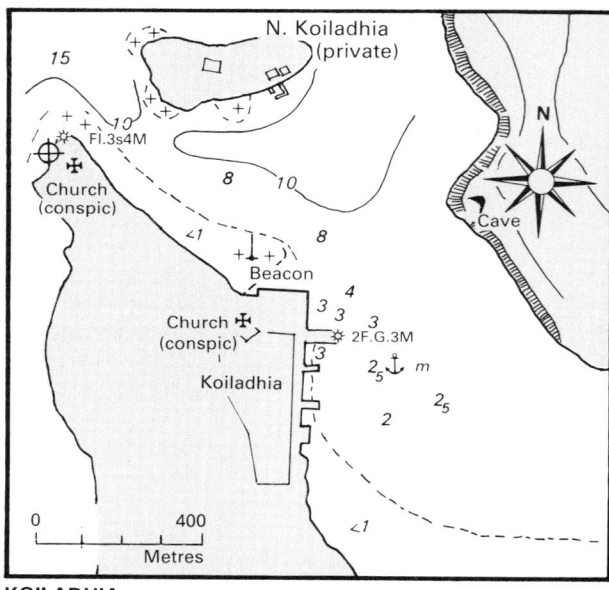

KOILADHIA
37°25'·4N 23°06'·8E (Fl.3s4M)

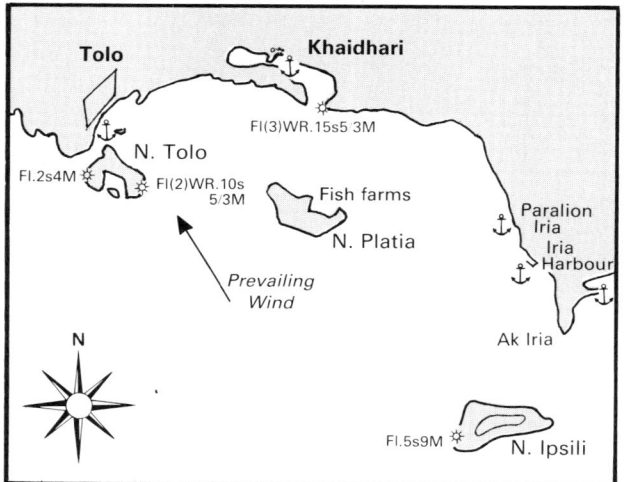

AK IRIA TO TOLO

OTHER ANCHORAGES

On the E side of Ak Iria there is a solitary anchorage in a cove worth exploring. In settled weather a yacht can anchor off the long sandy beach by the hamlet of Kantia. The anchorage is exposed to the afternoon breeze so be prepared to move off when it gets up. Taverna ashore.

KHAIDHARI (Drepano. Vivari)

The entrance to this deep inlet is difficult to see from seaward. The ruins on the W side and the light structure on the E side (Fl(3)WR.15s5/3M) will be seen when closer in. Anchor at the head of the inlet in 3–8 metres or go bows-to the mole on the NW.

General

Koiladhia is very much a proper working and fishing village with a large resident fleet. The look-alike reinforced concrete houses are not the image you may have of a Greek village, but the place grows on you and the locals are a friendly bunch.

In the Franchthi Cave prominent on the E side of the anchorage numerous prehistoric remains have been found, including a skeleton from the Mesolithic period, the oldest found in Greece.

The bottom is mud and weed – good holding. Good all-round shelter. A number of yachts have wintered afloat here. Tavernas and cafés ashore.

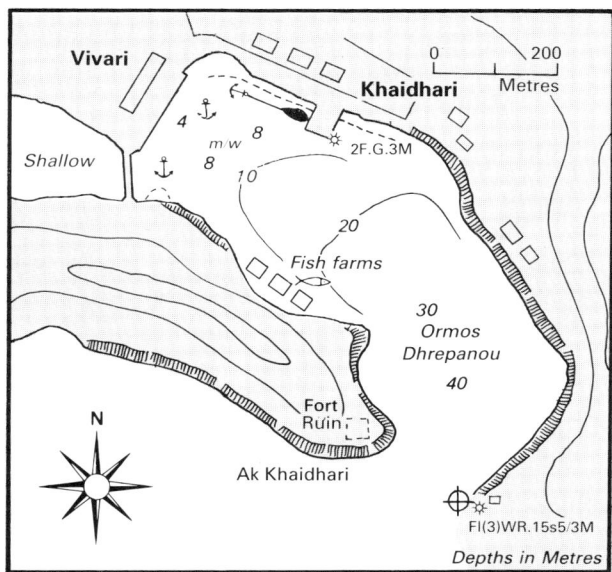

KHAIDHARI
37°31'·4N 22°56'·1E (Fl(3)WR.5/3M)

TOLO (Tolon)

Approach

Conspicuous Nisis Platia and Nisis Tolo lying close off the coast are easily identified. A white chapel on a conical peak behind Tolo village is conspicuous. The small harbour lies in Stenon Tolo at the SW end of the village.

By night Use the light on the S end of Nisis Tolo (Ak Skala Fl(2)WR.10s5/3M), on Ak Khaidhari (Fl(3)WR.15s5/3M) and on Ak Megali (Fl.2s4M). The end of the mole is lit: 2F.R(vert)3M.

Dangers Ifalos Tolo is a reef approximately ¾ of a mile SE of Ak Skala, the SE extremity of Nisis Tolo. The reef has 3·5 metres least depth over it and is covered by the red sectors of the light on Ak Skala (315°-343°) and on Ak Khaidhari (046°-058°).

The small harbour at Tolo looking SE across to Nisis Tolo.

Mooring

Anchor off the village or go alongside or stern-to or bows-to the outside of the S mole. Inside the little harbour is usually crowded with fishing boats whose owners take exception to visiting yachts taking their spaces. The bottom is sand, good holding.

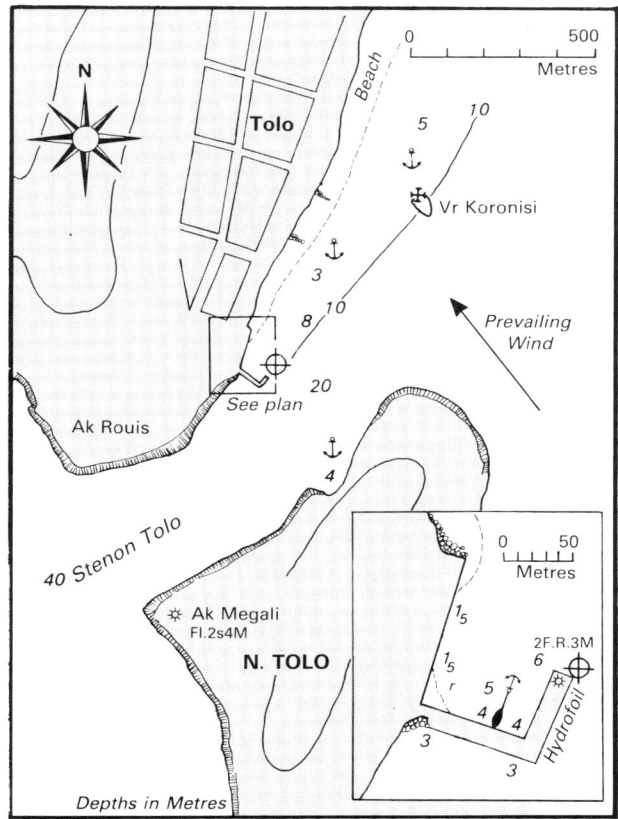

TOLO
37°30'·9N 22°51'·5W (2F.R.3M)

Shelter Off the village it can get bumpy with the afternoon breeze, but the holding on sand is good. Alongside the outside of the mole you are protected from the afternoon breeze, but completely exposed to westerlies.

Facilities
Water Limited from private sources.
Fuel In the town.
Provisions Good shopping for provisions.
Eating out Numerous tavernas on the waterfront, several of which often have fresh fish.
Other PO. OTE. Bank. Greek gas and *Camping Gaz*. Hire cars. Bus to Navplion. *Caïque* ferry to Spetsai. Hydrofoil to Piraeus.

General

Tolo was a small fishing village that has developed into a tourist resort on the strength of its sandy beach. Of late it has become very crowded with tourists on package holidays and little remains to remind you that fish, and not people, was once the principal industry here.

ORMOS KARATHONA

The large bay between Tolo and Navplion. A yacht can anchor at the southern end of the bay where there is some protection from the prevailing southerlies blowing up the gulf. A breakwater provides additional shelter if you can get under it and take a long line to it. Taverna ashore.

NAVPLION (Nauplion, Nauplia)

Admiralty chart no. 1518

Approach

Conspicuous The large town will not be seen until around Akronavplia. A chapel on Ak Khondros and a hotel on Akronavplia will be seen. The fortress of

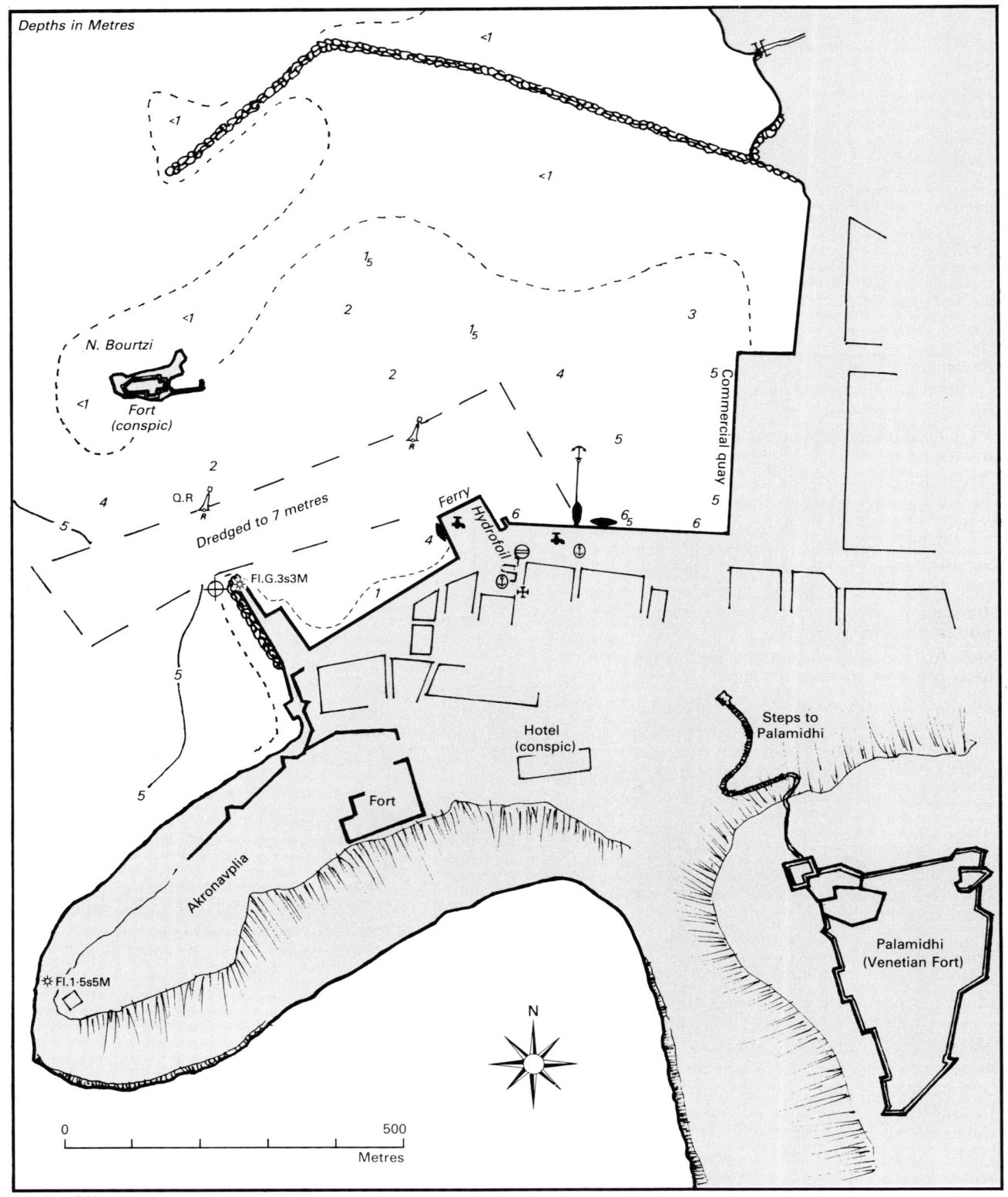

Depths in Metres

N. Bourtzi

Fort (conspic)

Dredged to 7 metres

Q.R

Fl.G.3s3M

Ferry

Hydrofoil T.

Commercial quay

Steps to Palamidhi

Hotel (conspic)

Fort

Akronavplia

Fl.1·5s5M

Palamidhi (Venetian Fort)

N

0   500
Metres

NAVPLION
37°34'·1N 22°47'·6E (Fl.G.3M)

Palamidi will also be seen. Once close to the point the small fort on Nisis Bourtzi will be seen.

By night Use the light on Ak Panayitsa (Fl.1·5s5M) and the lights at the entrance (light buoy Q.R and Fl.G.3s3M).

Mooring

Go alongside or stern-to or bows-to the quay in the large inner basin. The bottom is gooey mud which plough anchors will sometimes pull through.

Shelter Good shelter although strong NW winds cause an uncomfortable slop. If the swell becomes dangerous anchor off.

Authorities A port of entry: port police, customs, and immigration.

Note Sewerage empties into the harbour and with the summer heat it can get very smelly.

Facilities

Water On the quay when you can find the waterman.

Fuel In the town.

Repairs Some mechanical repairs. Good hardware shops.

Provisions Excellent shopping for provisions. Ice available.

Eating out Numerous tavernas in the town including some quite sophisticated places in and around the old streets.

Other PO. OTE. Banks. Greek gas and *Camping Gaz*. Hire cars and motorbikes. Buses to Athens. Ferry (hydrofoil) to Piraeus.

General

The large town of mostly 18th- and 19th-century buildings, mainly two- or three-storeyed and shuttered and balconied, is a gem. The stone houses seem to be engulfed in vegetation as they vie with each other to grow the biggest swathe of bougain-villea or clematis. The narrow cobbled streets wind in and out of modest mansions and less modest public buildings, many of them built in golden sandstone that seems to absorb colour from the sun. Shops and tavernas are tucked away in streets everywhere. It is the sort of place you could willingly live in and has always been the most important city of the Argolid. At the beginning of the fledgling Greek Republic after the War of Independence Navplion was briefly capital before Athens was chosen.

In the square the museum is the large building originally built by the Venetians as a naval arsenal. It has a number of interesting exhibits including a suit of Mycenaean armour, a reminder that this whole area was the heartland of the Mycenaeans and in fact Navplion may have been a Mycenaean naval base at one time. Navplion is also thought to be the birthplace of Palamedes who is credited with the invention of lighthouses, the art of navigation, and the games of dice and knucklebones.

The Venetian citadel, Palamidi, is reached by a winding track of about 1000 steps. The hot climb is worthwhile, not only to view the most finely-preserved piece of Venetian military architecture in existence, but also for the view over the Argolic Gulf. Alas, the vast structure was militarily out of date not long after it was completed. The citadel is open 0800–1845.

Mycenae
(Mikinai)

This ancient city situated some nine miles from the head of Argolikos Kolpos was the centre of a great Helladic civilization between about 1650 and 1100 BC. Despite scholarly conjecture it is widely accepted that the period dominated by Mycenae (and therefore called the Mycenaean period) fits in with the Achaeans of Homer's *Odyssey* and *Iliad*, although he probably telescoped events occurring over five centuries into a smaller timescale.

The site was occupied very early on, but not until 1700–1650 BC did it become important. Its position guards the approaches to the Argolic Gulf and the natural land route through the mountains to Corinth. The Mycenaeans were a militant race that quickly came to dominate Greece: their domain covered the whole of the Peloponnese, the Aegean Islands, the Greek mainland and Crete.

Their cultural influence spread even further, to Asia Minor, Cyprus, Egypt and the Ionian Islands. The wealth of Mycenae was legendary and the dead were buried with lavish amounts of treasure, much of which was lost to grave robbers in later centuries. Particularly notable are the gold death masks of which the mask of Agamemnon found by Heinrich Schliemann is the most famous. The Mycenaean period came to an abrupt end around 1000 BC and scholars are still at a loss to explain just what it was that stopped a great civilization in its tracks and put the clock back for four centuries in the Greek 'Dark Ages'.

The site can be conveniently visited from Navplion (by taxi or bus) and there is enough for the layman to see to make it a worthwhile excursion. The site on a virtually treeless hill can be unbearably hot in the summer and it is recommended you go early in the morning and take a hat and water.

KIVERION

A bight on the Peloponnese coast opposite Ormos Karathona. It is really only suitable in calm weather before the afternoon wind gets up. Tavernas ashore.

ASTROUS (Astros, Paralion Astros)

Approach

Conspicuous The rocky headland, connected by a low isthmus (on which the village is built) to the Peloponnese, looks like an island from the distance. Closer in, the castle and some houses on the headland and the lighthouse are conspicuous. From the N and E the village will not be seen until you are around the headland.

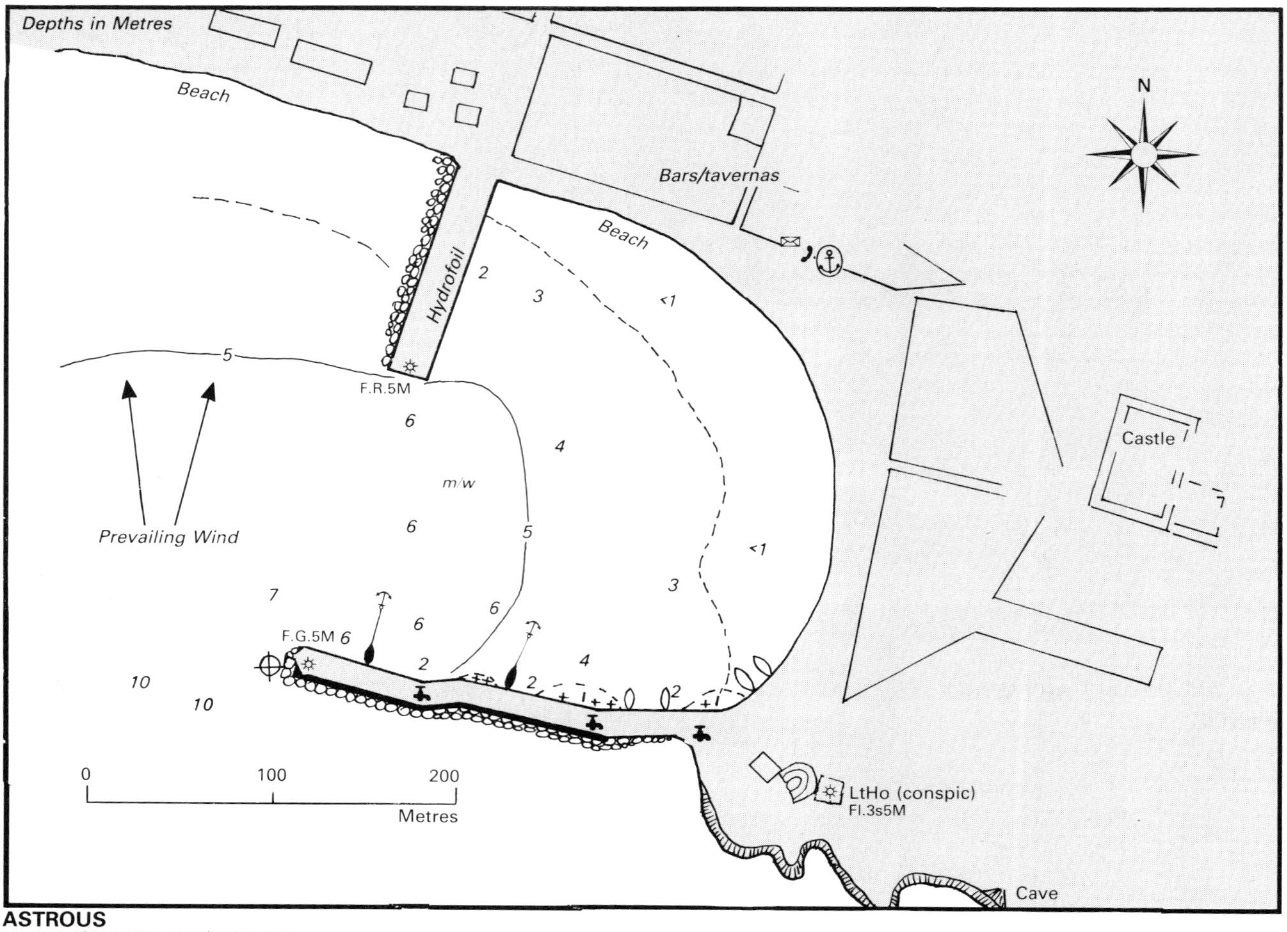

ASTROUS
37°24'·9N 22°46'·1E (F.G.5M)

Astrous harbour looking W from near the castle.

Ak Astrous and lighthouse looking NE.

By night Use the light on Ak Astrous (Fl.3s5M) and the lights at the entrance (F.R.5M and F.G.5M).

Mooring

Go stern-to or bows-to either mole where convenient. Along the S mole the ballasting projects some distance underwater in places. The bottom is mud and weed – poor holding in places.

Shelter Good shelter from the prevailing southerlies. Care is needed at night as Astrous is notorious for katabatic winds which can blow off the mountains in the evening – it is generally over in 3–4 hours.

Authorities Port police.

Facilities

Water At the root of the S mole.

Fuel On the outskirts of the village.

Provisions Most provisions can be obtained. Ice available. Better shopping in Astrous town about 2½ miles away.

Eating out Good tavernas on the waterfront and in the village.

Other PO. OTE. Irregular bus service to Astrous town and Tripolis. Hydrofoil to Navplion and Piraeus.

General

Astrous is a bustling fishing village and tourist resort. The village is built around the slopes above the harbour with the new development along the long sandy beach around the bay. The harbour is one of my favourite places in the gulf and even with its tourism remains a likable and very Greek village.

The medieval castle on the top of the hill is in reasonable condition and well worth the short walk up to it for the views over the gulf. Local folklore tells of a subterranean passage leading from the castle to the cave at sea level on the S side of the headland, but I haven't been able to find any trace of it. On the tip of the headland are the ruins of a large classical building.

The village around the harbour is properly called Paralion Astrous and the main village of Astrous is some 2½ miles inland. It is a down-to-earth agricultural town in the middle of a region which is noted for its orchards and particularly for its peaches. Also nearby is Moni Loukous, a large monastery approximately 2½ miles from the village, which is worth a visit.

ANCHORAGES BETWEEN ASTROUS AND TIROS

Along the steep-to coast between Astrous and Leonidhion are several anchorages suitable as lunch stops in calm weather.

1. *Ay Dhimitrios* The bay under Ak Ay Dhimitrios. Tucked into the cove on the S you can overnight with care although any northerlies will mean you must leave.
2. *Ormos Krioneri* Anchor in the SW corner. Really only a lunch stop.
3. *Ormos Zaritsi* Anchor off the beach in the SW.

TIROS

A small harbour in Ormos Tiros offering good shelter from the prevailing SE wind. Three windmills are conspicuous on the ridge. There are 2–6 metre depths behind the short mole although care is needed of a rocky patch about one third up from the root of the mole. Go stern or bows-to the short mole leaving the end free for the hydrofoil. Care needed of floating mooring lines. Good shelter.

Water from local sources. Fuel can be delivered. Most provisions and tavernas in the village. Hydrofoil to Piraeus.

LEONIDHION (Leonideon, Plaka)

Approach

Conspicuous The harbour is difficult to locate from the distance. A mill converted to a house on the beach to the N of the harbour and a white church behind the harbour can be identified closer in. The hotel in the village will also be seen. Only a small part of the mole is visible as most of it is behind a continuation of the beach.

By night Use the light on Ak Sambateki (LFl.7·5s4M) and the light on the extremity of the mole (Fl.G.1·5s3M).

Leonidhion looking W. The beach extends along much of the mole.

The mole at Leonidhion looking S.

Dangers With the normal southerly sea breeze there is a confused swell in the entrance.

Mooring

Go stern-to or bows-to the mole. The bottom is hard sand with some rocks – poor holding in patches.

Shelter With the regular SE day breeze there is an uncomfortable surge in the harbour. With southerly gales it could be untenable in here.

Authorities Port police.

Facilities

Water On the quay.

Provisions Good shopping in Leonidhion town about 2½ miles away.

Eating out Good tavernas on the waterfront.

Other Bank in Leonidhion town. Taxis. Hydrofoil to Piraeus.

General

The small hamlet under the towering cliffs is a pleasant, mostly unspoilt spot. The fertile valley (citrus, olives, figs and market gardening) winds between the high mountains to Leonidhion town – a modest place untouched by tourism. About 30 minutes away by taxi is the small monastery of Elonas, on a spectacular cliffside site reminiscent of those at Meteori. It is well worth visiting. The surrounding Parnon range is rugged and steep-to with cliffs dropping sheer for 600–700 metres (2000–2300ft).

In the region around Leonidhion a dialect known as 'Tsakonika' used to be spoken by the older inhabitants and is considered to be a link between ancient (Doric) and modern (Demotic) Greek.

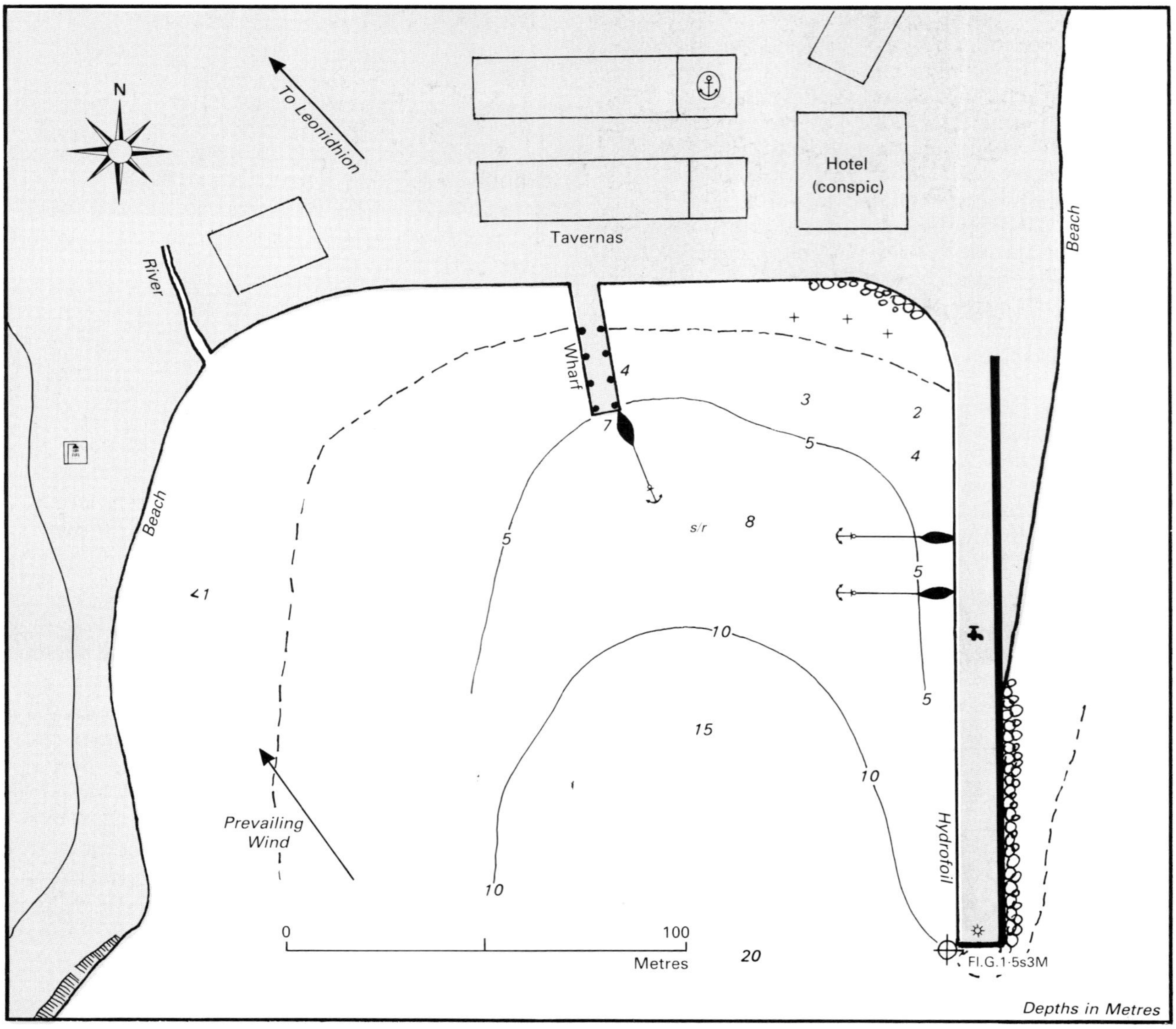

LEONIDHION
37°08′·8N 22°53′·6E (Fl.G.3M)

POULITHRA

A small fishing harbour 2 miles S of Leonidhion. A white church near the harbour is conspicuous. Go stern-to or bows-to the short mole. Good shelter from the normal summer southerlies. With northerlies a swell works into the harbour. Tavernas ashore. The hamlet of Poulithra is about ¾ of a mile away.

FOKIANOS (Phokianos)

A bay lying just S of Ak Turkoviglia. With the normal summer wind from the SE it is untenable but it affords good shelter from the northerlies. A cove in the NE corner has reasonable shelter. Care is needed of large permanent moorings on the bottom which may foul an anchor. Permanent bottom nets have also been reported. A beach runs around the head of the bay under the steep slopes behind – wonderful wild surroundings.

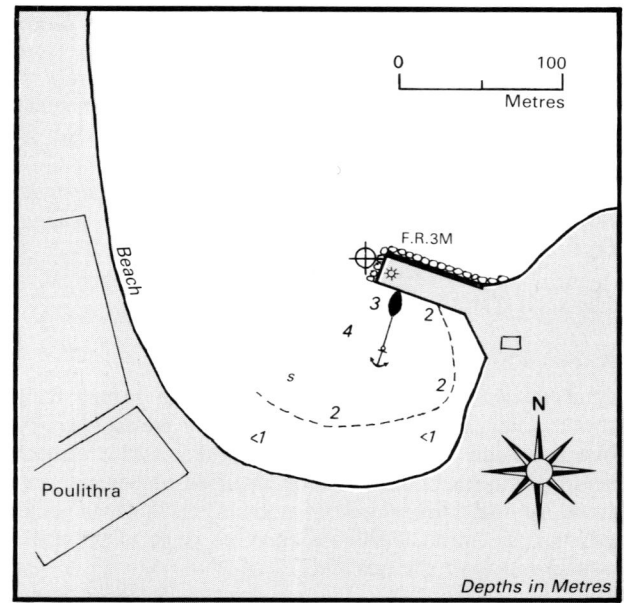

POULITHRA
37°07′N 22°54′·2E (F.R.4M)

Kiparissi and the pier off the village looking SSE. *Nigel Patten.*

Kiparissi. Anchorage off the village. *Nigel Patten.*

KIPARISSI (Kyparissi)

Approach

This large bay lies about 5 miles S of Fokianos. The houses of the hamlet cannot be seen until you are in the entrance to the bay and it can be difficult to identify just where it is from the distance.

By night There are lights on either side of the entrance: N side (Ak Kortia) Fl.4s7M and S side (Ak Nisaki) Fl.R.1·5s3M.

Mooring

There are several places a yacht can go.

1. Kiparissi. Anchor off the village or go alongside the ferry pier off the village. Reasonable shelter although a swell tends to enter with the SE wind making it very uncomfortable. With winds from the N the anchorage can be untenable.
2. Go stern or bows-to the quay in the SE corner. It is very deep a short distance off (15-20 metres). Good shelter although there may be a little swell with northerlies. A tranquil spot with just a chapel ashore.
3. There is some shelter from NE winds in the cove on the N side of the bay.
4. N pier. A short pier on the N side of the bay was used by the hydrofoil and may still be used if the S pier becomes untenable. Go stern-to or bows-to or alongside the mole. Some shelter from SE winds and good shelter from NE winds. It is about 3 kilometres to the village, but taxis are available.

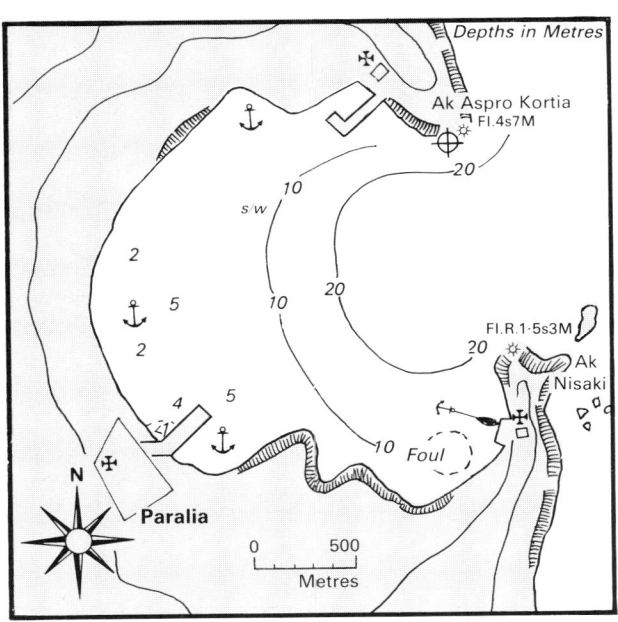

KIPARISSI
36°59'·1N 23°00'·3E (Ak Kortia light)

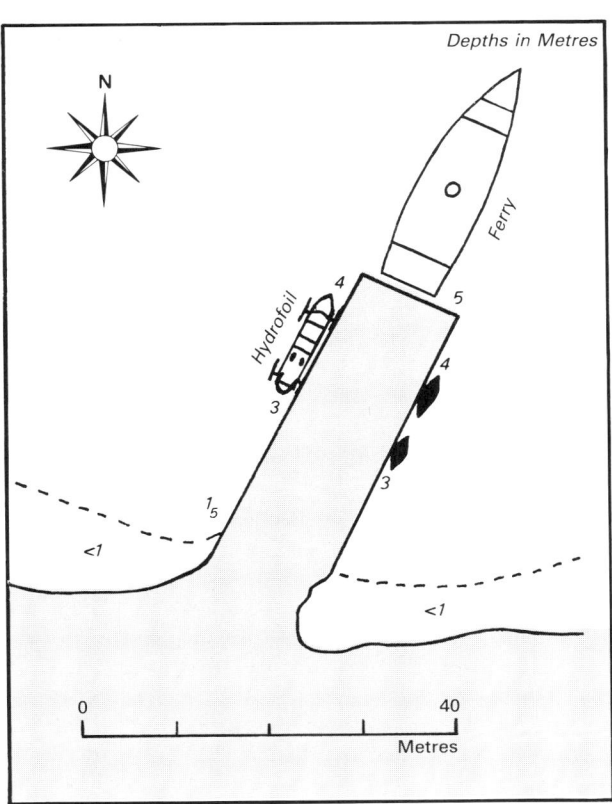

KIPARISSI TOWN QUAY

Note The bottom is mostly sand and thick weed, not everywhere good holding.

Facilities

Provisions and tavernas in the village. PO. OTE. Hydrofoil and ferry to Piraeus and Monemvasia.

General

The small village is quite unspoilt and the bay, surrounded by mountains, a spectacular spot.

IERAKA (Yerakas)

Admiralty chart no. 712

Approach

The narrow entrance between the high cliffs is difficult to locate even quite close in.

Conspicuous From the N a church on a knoll about one mile NW of Ak Vathi is conspicuous. The light structure will only be seen from a short distance off when approaching from the N.

By night The approach is difficult as the light at the entrance (Ak Kastro Fl.G.1·5s3M) is obscured except between 240°-200°.

Ieraka looking W from Ak Kastro.

Dangers With strong northerlies there is a confused reflected swell in the approaches and in the entrance.

Mooring

Go bows-to the quay. Some care needs to be taken as the depths are uneven and underwater rocks litter the bottom off the quay. Shallow-draught craft can go through the bottleneck and anchor at the entrance to the lagoon. The bottom is mud with some rocks and weed, reasonable holding.

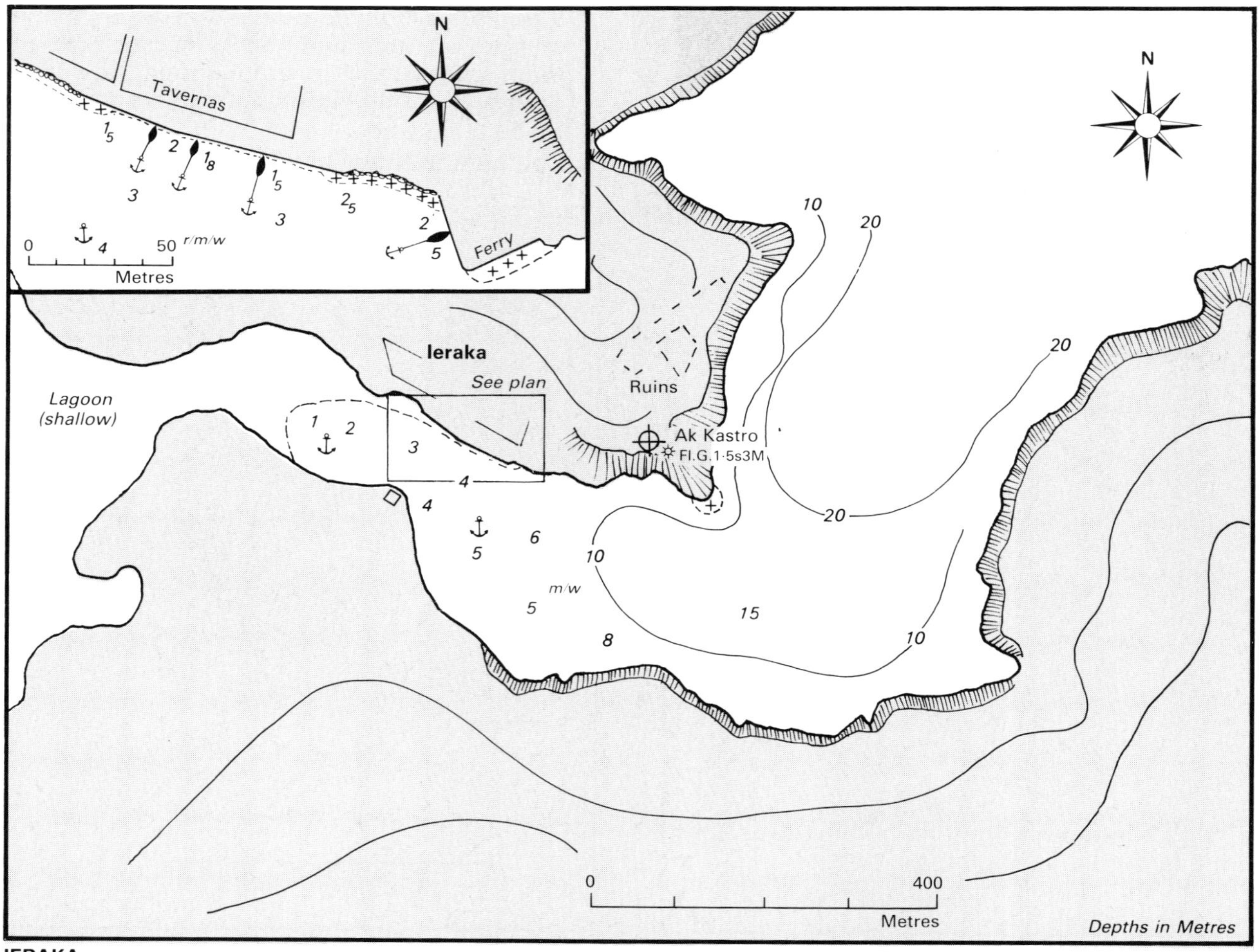

IERAKA
36°47'·2N 23°05'·3E (Ak Kastro light)

Monemvasia old town looking down from the citadel. p.217

Above. Chapel on Methana peninsula. p.189
Right. Leonidhion. p.213

Above. Idhra town quay. p.200
Below left. Entrance to a Byzantine church in Adhamas on Milos. p.272
Below. Phaeton on Spetsai. Cars are prohibited on the island though sadly motorbikes are not. p.207

Above. The yacht pier at Adhamas looking S. p.272
Below. Thira. Looking from Skala across to Nea Kammeni. *Nigel Patten.* p.284

Above. Monastery of the *Virgin of the Presentation* on Amorgos. **p.269**

Thira. Finikia looking down from the village. *Nigel Patten*. **p.283**

Trading *caïque*. Palon on Nisiros. **p.418**

Above. Katapola on Amorgos. p.266

Khalkis N harbour looking NNE. p.302
Below. Set-net to the east of Volos. p.313

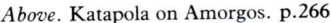

Poros looking E. p.194

Below. Fisherman. Volos. p.313
Below right. Bronze model of the *Argos* on the waterfront at Volos. p.315

Sigriou on Lesvos – the bay on the south side of the hamlet. p.372

Lesvos. Mithimna castle and town looking up from the harbour. p.369

Porto Koufo.

Nisis Dhiaporos looking E from the mainland. p.343

Below. Samos. Pithagorion inner basin looking southwest. p.391

Shelter Good all-round shelter, although a surge develops with strong northerlies – uncomfortable, but not normally dangerous. If you are on the quay the surge causes a yacht to roll considerably making things uncomfortable – go ashore for a meal!

Facilities

Tavernas and a café ashore. The tavernas have limited fare and you will probably be asked whether you want pork chops or fish. Some provisions from a little shop. Ferry to Piraeus.

General

The small hamlet surrounded by the hostile mountains of the Parnon is hardly touched by outside influences. In the hot afternoon sun out of the cooling touch of the *meltemi* the whole hamlet snoozes until the cool of evening when things come to life again. On the summit of the entrance is an extensive ruined acropolis, probably of Mycenaean origin.

MONEMVASIA (Monemvassi)
Admiralty chart no. 712

Approach

Conspicuous The humpbacked island of Monemvasia (likened to a little Gibraltar) connected to the Peloponnese by a causeway is easily identified from the distance. Closer in the village of Monemvasia on the mainland, and from the S the old village on the island, will be seen.

By night Use the light on the end of Nisis Monemvasia (Fl.5s6M) and the light on the end of the mole (F.R.3M).

Dangers With the *meltemi* there are fierce gusts in the approaches to the bay.

Mooring

Go stern-to or bows-to the mole or anchor off on the S side of the headland off the small fishing village.

Nisis Monemvasia and the old town looking NW.

Ayia Sofia on the summit of Nisis Monemvasia.

Care is needed towards the root of the mole where the bottom is uneven and depths decrease over the rocky bottom. Take care to keep clear of the ferry and hydrofoil berth on the end of the mole. The bottom is sand, rocks and weed – poor holding in patches.

Shelter Shelter is good on the mole although the *meltemi* sends a swell into the bay and this causes a surge behind the mole which sets boats rolling. At times this can be most uncomfortable and you should ensure you have plenty of fenders out. Shelter in the anchorage on the S side of Nisis Monemvasia is just adequate from the *meltemi* although you will roll around depending on the strength of the wind. It is open S.

Authorities Port police and customs.

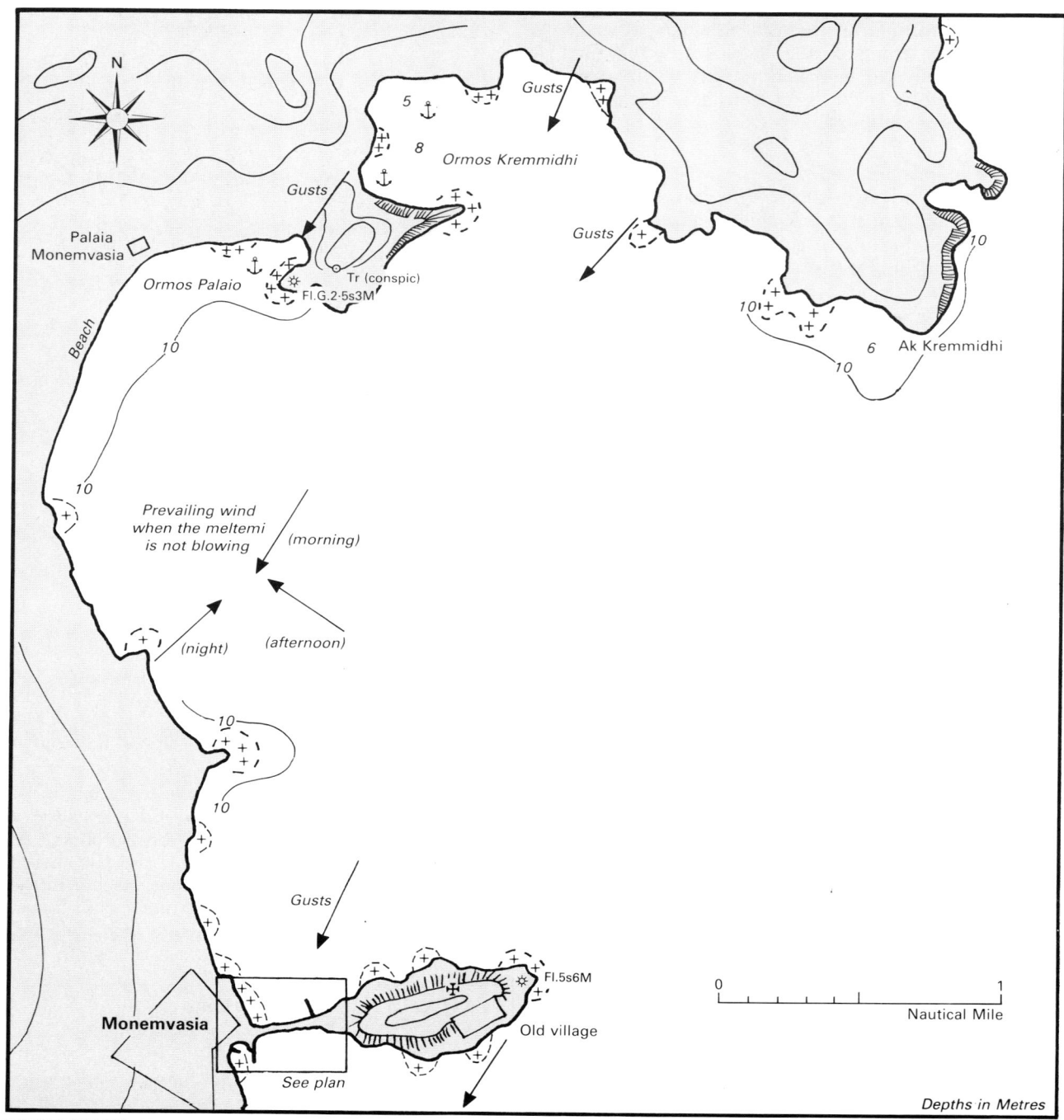

MONEMVASIA APPROACHES

MONEMVASIA MARINA

A new marina is under construction on the coast immediately S of Yefira. At the time of publication part of the outer breakwater was complete and a jetty and two pontoons installed. There are berths for around 40 yachts up to around 15m LOA. Facilities have yet to be installed.

Facilities

Water A mini-tanker can deliver.
Fuel Near the root of the mole. A mini-tanker can deliver.
Repairs Minor mechanical repairs. Hardware shop.

Provisions Good shopping for all provisions. Ice available.
Eating out Good tavernas. In the old village on the island there are a number of excellent tavernas in a romantic setting between the steep slopes and the sea. Good *ouzeries* with octopus mezes around the fishing harbour.
Other PO. OTE. Bank. Greek gas and *Camping Gaz*. Ferry (hydrofoil and regular ferry) to Piraeus.

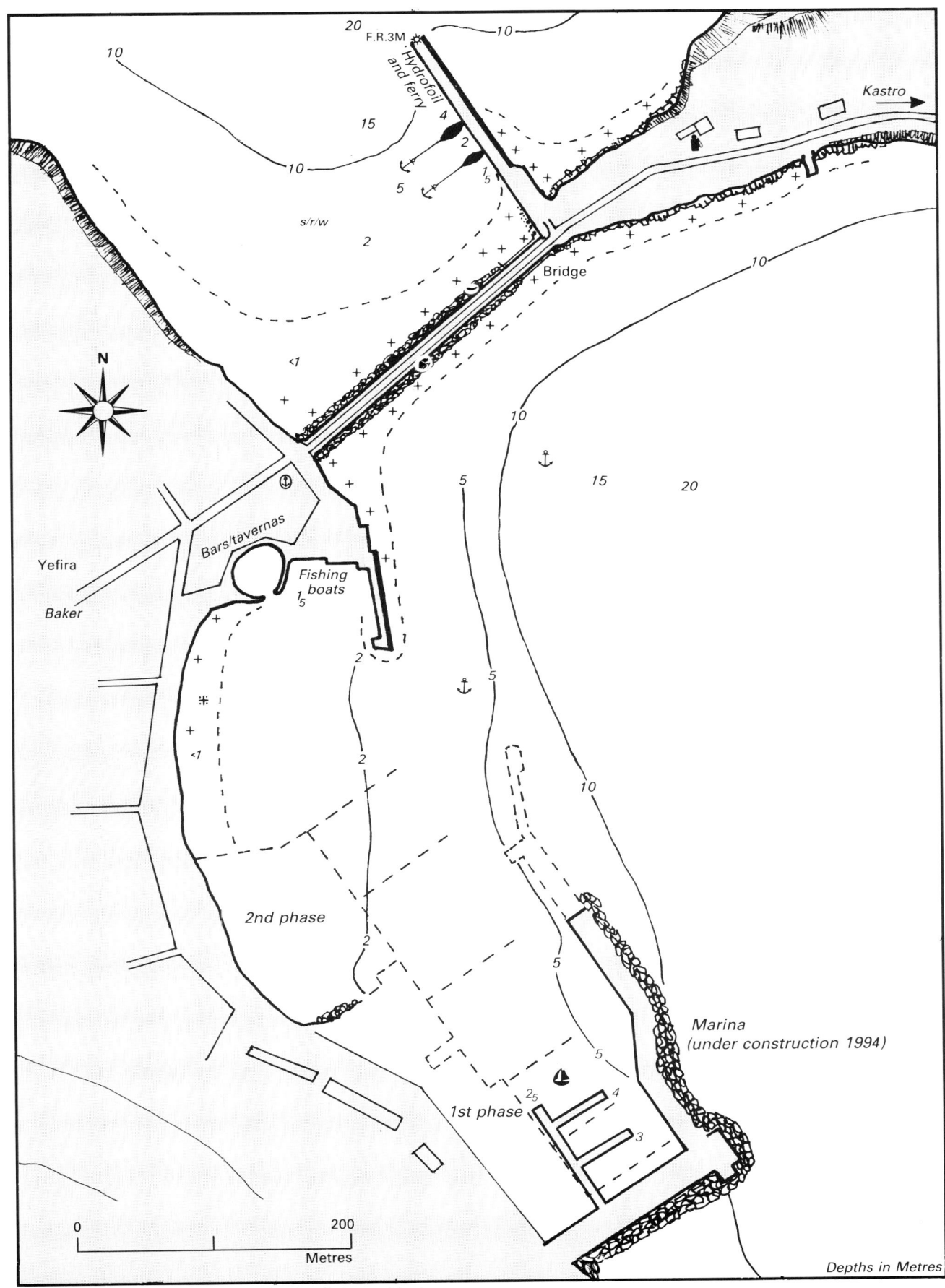

20 F.R.3M

Hydrofoil and ferry

Kastro

10

10

10

10

15

4

2

5

1 5

s/r/w

2

10

Bridge

10

<1

10

10

15

20

N

5

Yefira

Bars/tavernas

Fishing boats

1 5

Baker

2

5

2

<1

2nd phase

2

10

5

1st phase

Marina
(under construction 1994)

5

5

2 5

4

3

0   200

Metres

Depths in Metres

MONEMVASIA 36°41′·4N 23°02′·5E (F.R light position)

General

Monemvasia Island was called Minoa in ancient times suggesting a Cretan influence. Until the 20th century it was an important port, the last port of call before setting off around Cape Malea. The old fortified village is of Byzantine origin although the Venetians rebuilt much of it.

You should not miss an opportunity to visit the old village which is slowly coming to life again in a sympathetic way. The gift shops and restaurants do not detract from its character if you squint your eyes and don't dally too long. There are a number of interesting churches in the village, but to get to the best of them, Ayia Sofia, you will have to climb up the zig-zag path behind the village to the summit. The fortified path and tunnel into the fort with its iron gates still intact is as impressive as the fortifications at the top, and if you run out of breath on the way up it is a good excuse to sit down and enjoy the superb views down onto the roofs of the old village and out over the sea.

Ayia Sofia stands on the very edge of a sheer cliff on the N side with what the *Blue Guide* quaintly describes as a 'view of wild grandeur at sunset'. The church has interesting frescoes and its situation on the edge of the cliff affords a view of the wild hinterland of the Peloponnese and the grand sweep of Ormos Monemvasia.

In the past Monemvasia was called Malmsey or Malvoise by the French, hence the name of the famous red and white wines shipped (but not necessarily grown in the region as many writers have erroneously inferred) from the port in its heyday. The strong sweet red wine was known to travel well and hence was much in demand on the extended voyages in the age of sail – and from this we should learn the lesson that a small yacht is not the place for good wine, especially delicate whites and some of the more fragile reds, so drink up before any of that good wine you have on board goes off.

ANCHORAGES IN ORMOS MONEMVASIA

1. *Ormos Palaio* In the NW corner of Ormos Monemvasia this small bay offers good shelter from all but W–SW winds. Care must be taken of the reef off the southern entrance. The S entrance is lit: Fl.G.2·5s3M. Anchor in 6–8 metres on a sandy bottom. From about the 6 metre line into the head of the bay large permanent moorings foul the bottom. There are a few villas and fishermen's houses around the bay.

2. *Ormos Kremmidhi* Lies just around the cape from Ormos Palaio. Open to the S–SE. Anchor in 5–8 metres on a sandy bottom. The severe gusts into the bay with the *meltemi* make this an inferior anchorage to Palaio.

Islands lying off the Peloponnese

Between the Peloponnese coast and Milos and Sifnos there are several small and uninhabited islets.

Nisis Parapola (Belopoula) (light 36°55'·8N 23°53·5'E)
An islet lying approximately 21 miles off the coast from a point midway between Kiparissi and Ieraka. It is quite high at 227 metres (745ft) and easily seen by day. It is lit on the N: Fl(2)20s22M. It is reported that the bay on the SW side affords some shelter from NE winds.

Nisidhes Karavi (36°46'N 23°36'E)
A group of three small islets that look like one from the distance. Although the maximum height is only 33 metres (110ft) they are easily identified by day. Care is needed to give the islets a wide berth as they are sometimes used by the Greek air force for target practice and I would suggest, having been one mile off while live rockets were used, that a yacht keep at least 3 and preferably more miles off the islets. (There is no mention in the relevant publications of the fact that it is a prohibited zone.)

Nisis Falkonera (36°50'N 23°53'E)
The high bold islet lying approximately midway between Parapola and Milos. It is easily identified by day and is lit on the S end (Fl.5s17M). It is reported that a bay on the SW side affords shelter from N winds, but as with other islands in the vicinity, there are likely to be fierce gusts off the lee side.

V. The Cyclades

(Kikladhes Nisoi)

This is the central group of islands in the Aegean so named because they more or less surround Delos, the ancient centre of trade and worship (*kukloi* – rings). I will not attempt to describe the islands here, but describe each separately when I come to them. To impose some order on the scattered islands they are broken down into three sections: northern, middle and southern Cyclades.

Northern Cyclades Kea, Kithnos, Siros, Andros, Tinos, Mikonos, Delos, and Rinia.

Middle Cyclades Serifos, Sifnos, Andiparos, Paros, Naxos, Dhenoussa, Iraklia, Skhinoussa, Koufonisia, Amorgos, and Levitha.

Southern Cyclades Milos, Kimolos, Folegandros, Sikonos, Ios, Thira, and Anafi.

Weather patterns in the Cyclades

The prevailing wind in the summer is the infamous *meltemi* blowing from the N–NW. The *meltemi* begins to blow fitfully at first in June, blows strongest in July, August and early September, and dies during late September and October. In July and August the *meltemi* blows at Force 5–6 and may reach Force 7–8 on occasions. It may blow for 1–3 days or it may sometimes blow for 2 weeks at a time. There is no way of knowing for just how long it will blow. It has a thermal component in that it loses some strength at night and increases again in the day.

In June and again in late September the wind strength is considerably less at about Force 3–4 and there may be wind from other directions. The direction of the *meltemi* varies down through the Cyclades. In the northern Cyclades it blows from the NE, curving to blow from the N in the middle Cyclades and curving again to blow from the

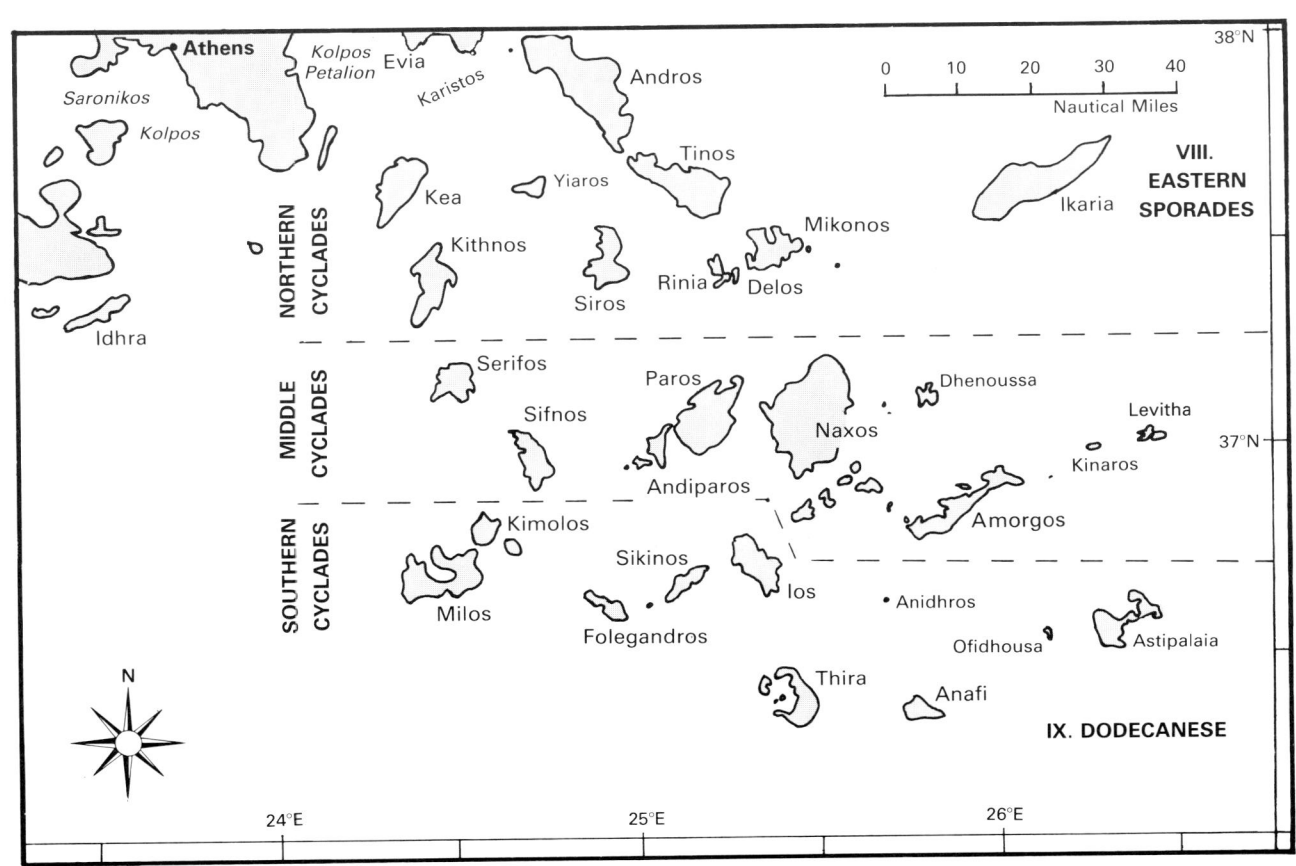

NW–WNW in the southern Cyclades. In the SW islands of the Cyclades the wind is marginally less strong than in the northern and eastern islands.

Route planning with the *meltemi* is essential if you are not to spend an uncomfortable time beating to windward in a strong breeze with short seas stopping your progress. Also remember that the gusts off the lee sides of the islands cause additional problems going to windward and may at times stop all progress.

How to get back to windward through the Cyclades is a much debated point. I favour going S in a great semicircle around the southern Cyclades where the wind is less strong and you can make to the N through the Saronic islands. From Kos or Kalimnos head for Astipalaia, Anafi, Thira, Ios, Folegandros, Kimolos and Milos. At times the *meltemi* can be just as strong around Ios/Folegandros/Milos as elsewhere, so you may need to keep going to the Peloponnese! Others maintain that you should go N in the eastern Cyclades or the Dodecanese and then W through the northern Cyclades. One thing is clear – going E through the Cyclades is infinitely preferable to going W when the *meltemi* is blowing.

In the spring and autumn the wind is predominantly from the N although there are also winds from the S. Gales are commonly from the N or the SE.

Note Care must be taken of violent gusts off the high land on the lee side of the islands when the *meltemi* is blowing. These gusts may be considerably stronger than the wind strength on the open sea – gusts of Force 7–8 may be experienced when the wind on the open sea is Force 5–6. At times small whirlwinds may accompany the gusts which strike with great force very quickly. Places noted for these squalls are the Doro Channel between Evia and Andros, the south coasts of Andros and Tinos, Yiaros, the Kea Channel, Mikonos, Naxos and the islands S of it, the S coast of Amorgos, Kimolos, Folegandros, and the S side of Ios.

In the summer months the Cyclades are hot and temperatures average 25°–26°C (79°F) and often reach 33°–35°C (95°F). In the summer there is very little if any rain and many of the islands run short of water towards the end of the season. Snow will only fall on the peaks of Andros and occasionally Tinos in the winter.

Data

PORTS OF ENTRY
Ermoupolis (Siros)

PROHIBITED AREAS
2M offshore around Yiaros Island.
Nisidhes Karavi is sometimes used for target practice by the air force.

MAJOR LIGHTS
Kea
Ay Nikolaos Fl(2)10s15M
Ak Tamelos Fl(2)15s17M

Kithnos
Ak Kefalos Fl.4s9M
Ak Ay Dhimitrios Fl.15s7M
Ak Merikha Fl.WR.1·5s5/3M

Siros
Nisis Gaidharos Fl.6s12M
Ermoupolis Fl.G.3s6M
Ak Trimeson Fl(2)14s12M
Ak Velostasi Fl(3)12s6M

Andros
Ak Fassa Fl.10s25M
Ak Kastri Fl.6s8M
Ak Kolona Fl.3s5M
Ormos Kastrou Fl(2)15s6M
Ak Gria Fl.20s25M

Vrakhoi Kaloyeroi (Kaloyeri Reef) Fl(2)15s17M

Tinos
Nisis Dhisvaton Fl.10s16M
Ak Livadha Fl.15s7M
Limin Tinou Fl.R.3s7M

Mikonos
Ak Armenistis Fl.10s22M
Nisidhes Prasonisia Fl.3s6M

Nisis Nata Fl.3s6M

Serifos
Ak Spathi Fl(3)30s19M
Ak Kiklops Fl(2)14s9M

Sifnos
Ak Filippos Fl.5s9M
Ak Kokkala Fl(3)12s9M

Andiparos
Ak Korakas LFl.12s14M

Paros
Ifalos Paroikia Q.WRG.3-2M
Ak Kratzi Fl(3)WG.15s6/4M

Naxos
Limin Naxou Fl.WR.3s6/4M
Ak Stavros Fl(2)16s13M
Vrakhoi Amaridhes Fl.WR.4s5/3M
Vrakhonisos Kopria Fl(2)12s10M

Dhenoussa
Ak Kalota Fl(3)15s10M

Iraklia
Nisis Mikro Avelos Fl(3)10s6M

Skhinoussa
Mirsini Fl.4s6M

Amorgos
Ak Gonia Fl.8s11M
Ormos Katapola/Ak Ay Ilias Fl(2)16s6M
Ay Annas/Ak Langadhia Fl.5s8M
Nisidhes Liadhi (N) Fl(2)20s9M

Levitha
Ak Spano LFl.16s10M

Milos
Nisidhes Akradhia Fl.10s10M
Ak Bombardha Fl.4·4s6M
Andimilos Fl.2s8M

Nisis Paximadhi Fl(2)15s8M
Nisis Ananes Fl(3)12s9M

Poliagos
Ak Maskoula Fl.5s19M

Folegandros
Ak Aspropounda Fl(3)30s17M

Sikonos
Ormos Skala Fl.1·5s5M

Ios
Ak Fanari Fl.1·5s5M

Thira
Ak Akrotiri Fl.10s24M
Epanomeria Fl.4s7M

Nisidhes Khristiana
Fl(3)9s10M

Anafi
Ak Petradhia Fl.4s5M

Quick reference guide

	Shelter	Mooring	Fuel	Water	Provisioning	Tavernas	Plan
Kea							
Ay Nikolaos	B	AC	B	B	B	B	●
Ormos Pisa	C	C	O	O	O	O	
Ormos Kavia	B	C	B	B	C	C	●
Khalidhoniki	B	C	O	O	O	O	●
Ormos Polais	O	C	O	O	O	O	●
Kithnos							
Ormos Fikiadha	B	C	O	O	O	O	●
Ormos Kolona	B	C	O	O	O	O	●
Merikha	B	AC	B	B	C	C	●
Loutra	C	AC	O	B	C	C	●
Ay Stefanos	B	C	O	B	O	O	●
Kanala	O	C	O	O	O	O	
Siros							
Ermoupolis	B	AB	B	B	A	A	●
Nisis Gaidharos	B	C	O	O	O	O	
Ormos Varis	B	C	O	O	C	C	●
Finikas	B	AC	B	B	C	B	●
Ormos Galissas	C	C	O	B	C	C	
Ormos Kini	C	C	O	B	C	C	
Ormos Delfino	B	C	O	O	O	O	●
Ormos Grammata	C	C	O	O	O	O	●

	Shelter	Mooring	Fuel	Water	Provisioning	Tavernas	Plan
Andros							
Gavrion	B	AC	B	B	B	B	●
Batsi	B	AC	B	A	B	B	●
Palaioupolis	O	C	O	O	O	C	
Kastro	C	AC	B	B	B	B	●
Korthion	O	C	O	B	C	C	
Tinos							
Tinos	A	A	B	A	A	B	●
Ormos Panormos	C	C	O	B	C	C	
Mikonos							
Mikonos	C	A	B	B	A	A	●
Ormos Ornos	B	C	O	O	O	C	●
Ormos Plati Yialos	B	C	O	O	O	C	
Ormos Ay Annas	B	C	O	O	O	C	
Rinia							
Ormos Skhino	C	C	O	O	O	O	●
South Bay	B	C	O	B	O	O	●
Ormos Miso	B	C	O	O	O	O	●
Serifos							
Livadhi	B	AC	B	A	B	B	●
Ormos Koutala	C	C	O	O	O	O	●
Sifnos							
Ay Yeoryios	B	C	O	O	O	C	●
Kamares	C	AC	O	A	B	B	●
Ormos Vathi	B	C	O	O	O	C	●
Ormos Fikiadha	C	C	O	O	O	O	●
Ormos Plati Yialos	C	C	O	O	O	C	●
Faros	B	C	O	B	C	C	●
Kastro	O	C	O	B	B	C	●
Andiparos							
Ormos Dhespotico	B	C	O	O	O	O	●
Andiparos	C	C	O	O	B	C	●
Paros							
Paroikia	B	AC	B	B	A	A	●
Ormos Naousis	A	C	O	O	O	O	●
Naoussa	B	AC	B	A	B	B	●
Piso Livadhi	B	AC	O	A	C	B	●
Aliki	C	C	O	O	O	C	
Naxos							
Naxos	B	ABC	B	A	A	A	●
Ormos Prokopis	C	C	O	O	O	O	
Ormos Kouroupa	C	C	O	O	O	O	
Ormos Kalando	C	C	O	O	O	O	●
Apollonia	O	C	O	B	C	C	●
Dhenoussa							
Ormos Roussa	C	C	O	O	O	O	●
Ormos Dhendhro and Stavros	B	C	O	O	C	C	●
Iraklia							
Ayios Yeoryios	C	C	O	O	C	C	●
Ormos Pigadhi	C	C	O	O	O	O	

	Shelter	Mooring	Fuel	Water	Provisioning	Tavernas	Plan
Skhinoussa							
Ormos Mirsini	B	C	O	O	O	C	•
Agrilos	C	C	O	O	O	O	
Koufonisia							
S Cove	C	C	O	B	C	C	
Parianos	B	AC	O	O	O	O	•
Drima and							
Andikaros	C	C	O	O	O	O	•
Amorgos							
Katapola	B	AC	O	A	B	B	•
Ormos Kolofana	C	C	O	O	O	C	
Kalotiri	C	C	O	O	O	O	•
Ormos Ay Annas	C	AC	O	B	C	C	•
Levitha							
Ormos Levitha	A	C	O	O	O	O	•
Ormos Pnigo	B	C	O	O	O	O	
Milos							
Adhamas	B	AC	B	A	B	B	•
Apollonia	B	AC	O	B	C	C	•
Voudhia	C	C	O	O	O	O	•
Kimolos							
Sikia	C	C	O	O	O	O	•
Pirgonisi	B	C	O	O	O	O	•
Psathi	C	AC	O	O	C	C	•
Semina	B	C	O	O	O	O	
Prasonisi	O	C	O	O	O	O	
Poliagos							
Nisis Manolisi	C	C	O	O	O	O	•
Folegandros							
Karavostasi	B	ABC	O	O	C	B	•
Vathi	C	C	O	O	O	O	•
Sikonos							
Skala	C	C	O	B	C	C	
Ios							
Ios	A	A	O	B	B	B	•
Ormos Koumbaras	C	C	O	O	O	O	
Ormos Milopotamou	C	C	O	O	O	O	•
Ormos Manganari	B	C	O	O	O	C	•
Ormos Tris Klises	B	C	O	O	O	O	•
Thira							
Ay Nikolaos	C	C	O	O	C	C	
Finikia	C	C	O	O	C	C	
Skala Thira	C	A	O	O	A	A	•
Nea Kameni							
(SE cove)	B	AB	O	O	O	O	•
Monolithos	C	A	O	B	O	C	•
Anafi							
S Coast	C	C	O	O	O	C	
Skala	C	C	O	O	C	C	

Northern Cyclades

Nisos Kea
(Zea, Tzia)

A craggy and mountainous island lying a little over 12 miles east of Ak Sounion in the approaches to the Kolpos Petalion. A high mountain ridge runs down the east coast with the summit, Mt. Ayias Ilias (561 metres/1840ft), near the east coast 4 miles south of the northern extremity of Kea. Most of the inhabitants live in the *chora* (Kea) or at Ay Nikolaos. The island is mostly barren although there are patches of cultivated and wooded ground near the coast.

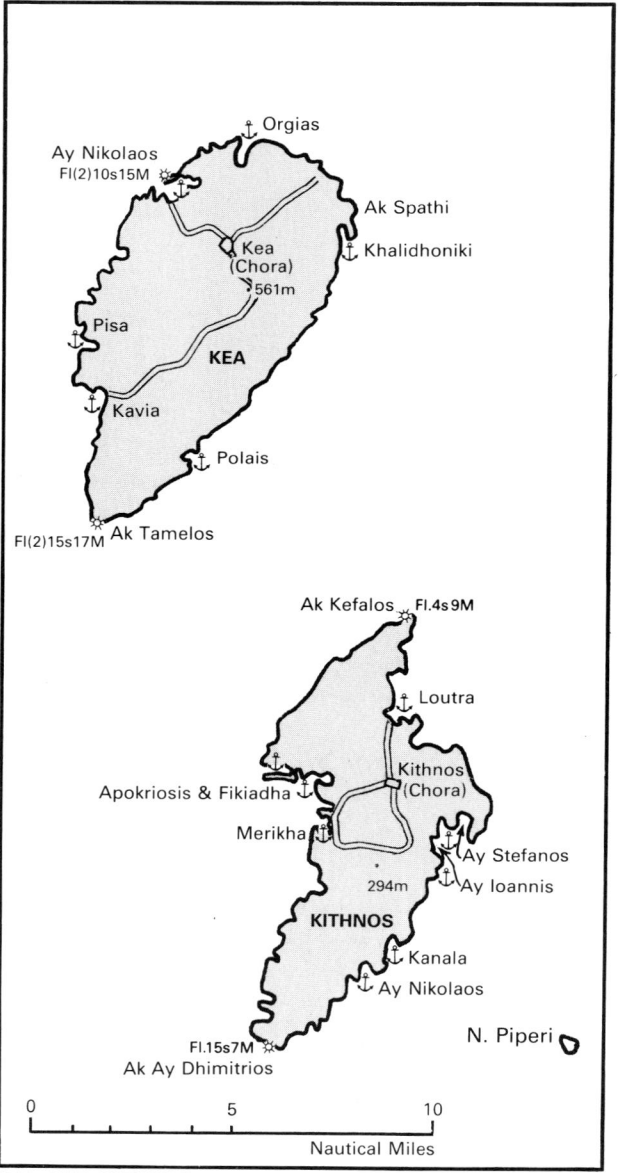

KEA AND KITHNOS

In ancient times the island was considerably more important than it is now. It had four cities and produced the lyric poets Simonides and Bacchlides and the physician Erasistratos. A few ruins of the cities remain and there is a large lion with a face like a big pussy cat carved out of a rock face (about 6 metres/20ft long) to the east of the *chora*. The ancient Keans were apparently noted for their modesty and temperance. Today the population is much diminished (about 2000), as the young leave the island to find work in Athens.

LIMIN AYIOS NIKOLAOU

(Aghiou Nicolaou, Livadhi, Vourkari)
Admiralty chart no. 1833
Imray-Tetra chart no. G31

Approach

Conspicuous The village or *chora* (Kea) on the hill behind the harbour is visible from the N. The entrance is not easy to spot from the distance but the general location on the NW end of the island is obvious. Closer in the chapel on the N side of the entrance and a church on the S side are conspicuous.

By night Use the lights on either side of the entrance (N side: Fl(2)10s15M; S side: Fl.1·5s3M). The mole

at Korissia is lit: Fl.G.3s3M.

Note With the *meltemi* there are strong gusts off the high land in the vicinity of the harbour.

Mooring

There are three possibilities:

1. *Ormos Livadhi* The S arm of the bay. Moor stern-to or bows-to the quay at Korissia keeping clear of the ferry berth behind the mole. Reasonable shelter from the *meltemi*. Alternatively anchor off in the bay in calm weather. The bottom is mud and weed, not everywhere good holding.

2. *Vourkari* The NE arm of the bay. Anchor in the bay or go stern-to or bows-to the quay in the space indicated between the hatched lines on the plan. The bottom comes up quickly just before the quay and consequently it is best to go bows-to if possible. On either side of this space it is too shallow off the quay. The bottom drops off quickly here (over 10 metre depths 30 metres out from the quay) so make sure you have an adequate length of chain or line to let go. The bottom is mud and weed and not everywhere good holding. As the *meltemi* blows straight on to the quay ensure your anchor is holding before tying up to

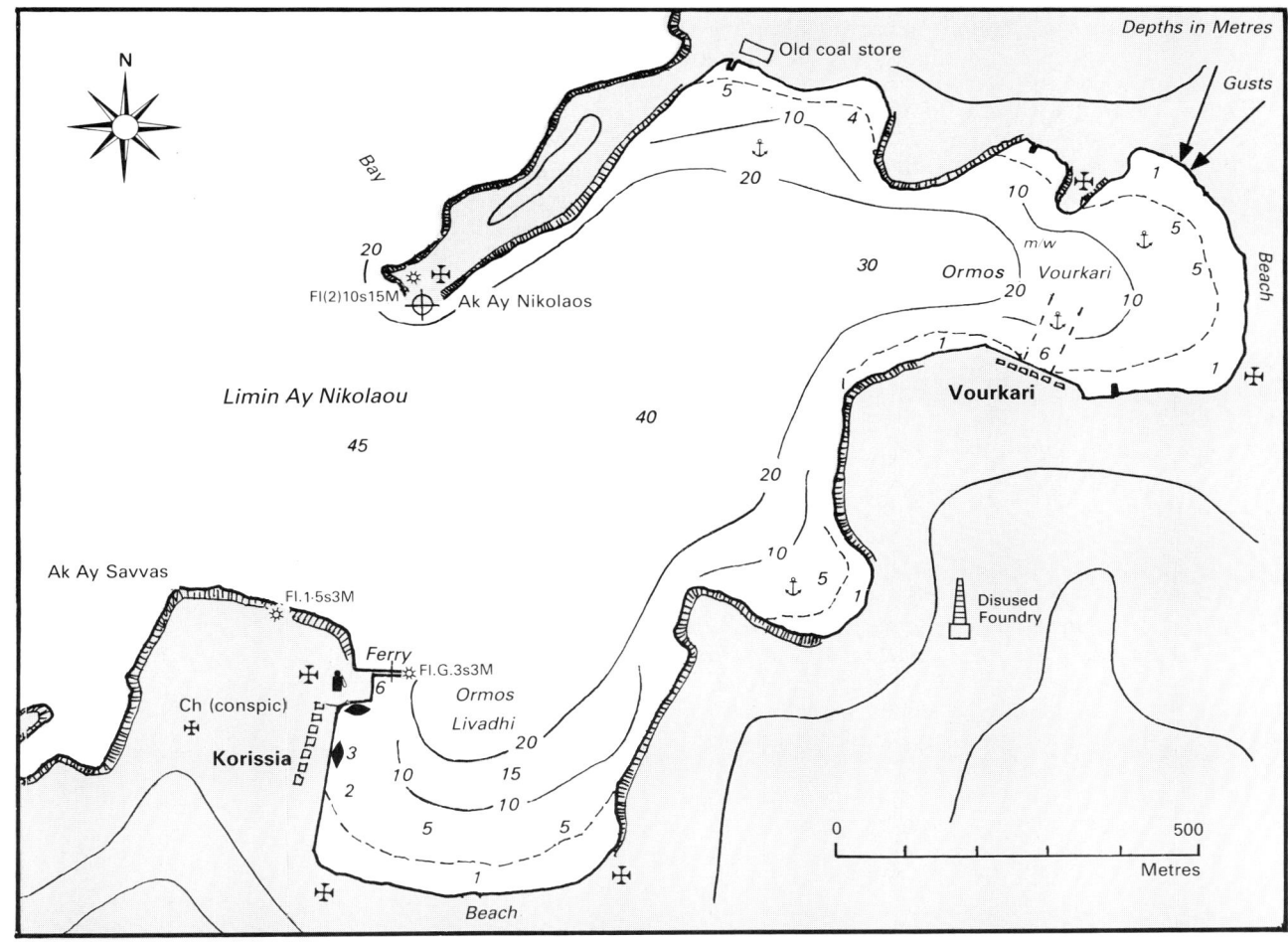

AYIOS NIKOLAOU
37°40'·1N 24°18'·8E (Ak Ay Nikolaos light)

the quay. In the summer there are a lot of yachts using this bay.

3. Anchor off the old coal bunkering depot in the N arm of the bay. Good shelter from N winds. The bottom is mud and weed, indifferent holding.

Authorities Port police at Korissia.

Facilities

Water Near the quay at Vourkari though it is often rationed in the summer.

Fuel Near the quay at Korissia. A mini-tanker can deliver to the quay (☎ 24-100).

Provisions Some provisions available at Vourkari and Korissia.

Eating out Tavernas at Vourkari and Korissia.

Other Telephone. Irregular bus to the *chora*. Ferry to Lavrion.

General

Ayios Nikolaos is more often than not crowded in the summer with Athens-based yachts, the picturesque hamlet of Vourkari being the most popular. The bay was once important as a coaling station for steamers plying between Black Sea ports and western Europe. Recent excavations on the N side of the bay by the American school have unearthed an important Bronze Age settlement inhabited from around 2000 BC to 1400 BC. Pottery, domestic and ornamental, and the classic Cycladic figurines have been unearthed amongst the buildings, many of which are now just under the sea.

The *chora* on the hill, a huddle of glaring white houses, is picturesque and well worth a visit – enquire about the bus to get there and walk back downhill. About 20 minutes' walk to the E of the village is the large lion (the pussy cat) carved from the rock face and attributed to an Ionian sculptor from around 600 BC.

ORMOS PISA

A small bay on the W coast about 1½ miles N of Ak Makropoundha. Open to the W and S. With the *meltemi* some swell creeps into the bay making it uncomfortable. Anchor in 4–8 metres near the head of the bay. Sandy bottom. No facilities.

There is a cove immediately N of Ormos Pisa that looks good, but it is very deep even close in.

ORMOS KAVIA (Koundouros)

A small bay lying approximately one mile to the E of Ak Makropounda. Care must be taken of a reef lying about one third of a mile SSW of Makropoundha. A number of windmills on the slopes around the bay are conspicuous as well as a large building on the N side of the entrance to the bay.

Anchor in 3–6 metres on a sandy bottom. Good shelter from the *meltemi* and open only to the S.

The bay is being developed with new hotels and houses, but sympathetically so. Manos runs a taverna here and can arrange for provisions, gas, ice, water, fuel, showers, indeed anything it is possible to procure on Kea; he boasts not only English but French, Italian, Arabic and a little German!

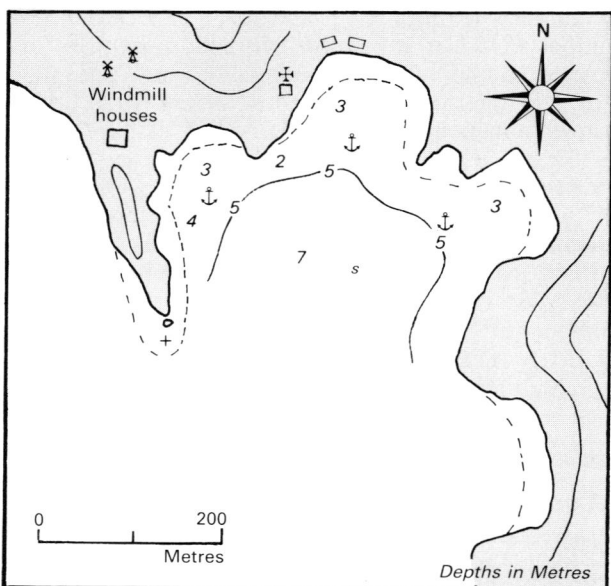

ORMOS KAVIA
37°34'·5N 24°16'·5E

ORGIAS

A small cove on the N side of Kea suitable in calm weather only. Anchor in 4–5 metres near the head of the inlet. There are a few houses around the slopes.

Note A rock above water has been reported 0·4NM E of the entrance to Orgias.

KHALIDHONIKI

A small cove on the NE corner of the island under Ak Spathi. Anchor near the head of the cove in 3–5 metres on a sandy bottom. Good shelter from the *meltemi*. There are a few houses around the bay but little else.

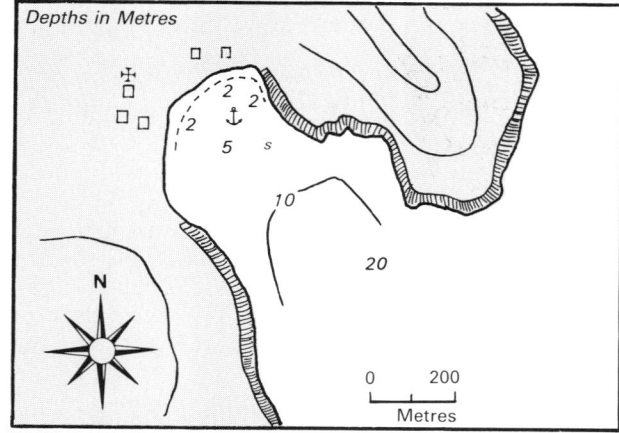

KHALIDHONIKI
37°38'·7N 24°24'·2E

ORMOS POLAIS

An open bay on the SE coast of Kea 3 miles NE of Ak Tamelos. In the middle of the bay there is a small islet joined by a reef to the shore. Anchor to the E of the islet and the reef in 3–4 metres. The bottom is

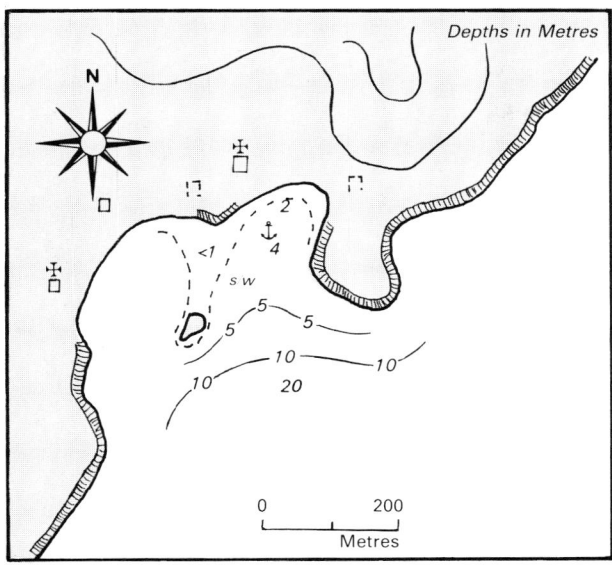

POLAIS
37°33′·5N 24°20′E

sand and weed with some rock and not everywhere good holding. Reasonable shelter from the *meltemi*.

There are a few ancient ruins ashore including the remains of a temple.

Nisos Kithnos

(Kythnos, Thermia)

A barren rocky island lying a little over 6 miles SE of Kea. The hump of the island is highest in the middle where the summit reaches a modest 294 metres (965ft). The population mostly lives in the *chora* (Kithnos) on the hill above Ormos Apokriosis and in Merikha. The island has a modest tourist trade in the summer, but on the whole is little touched by tourism.

APOKRIOSIS AND FIKIADHA

Admiralty chart no. 1825

Approach

These two bays are situated one mile to the N of Merikha where the huddle of houses around the harbour is conspicuous. Care should be taken of the underwater rocks on the S side of the entrance to Ormos Apokriosis and on the NE side of the entrance to Fikiadha.

By night There are no lights.

Dangers With the *meltemi* there are strong gusts into the approaches and the bays.

Mooring

Anchor at the E end of Apokriosis or in the middle of Fikiadha. The bottom is sand and weed – good holding once the anchor has cut through the weed. Good shelter from N winds and nearly all-round shelter in Fikiadha.

Facilities

None.

General

Both bays provide good shelter in pleasant surroundings. There are a few houses and new villas and good white sand beaches.

ORMOS KOLONA (Sand Bar Bay)

Immediately W of Fikiadha on the other side of the sand bar is a long bay which also provides good shelter from the *meltemi*. Anchor in 3–5 metres in the cove on the N side or at the head of the bay on the W side of the sand bar. The bottom is sand, good holding. Good shelter from the *meltemi*. Open W.

There are wonderful white sand beaches around the bay and virtually deserted surroundings.

KITHNOS. ORMOS KOLONA TO MERIKHA

Kithnos. The anchorage at Fikiadha looking W across the sand bar to Ormos Kolona.

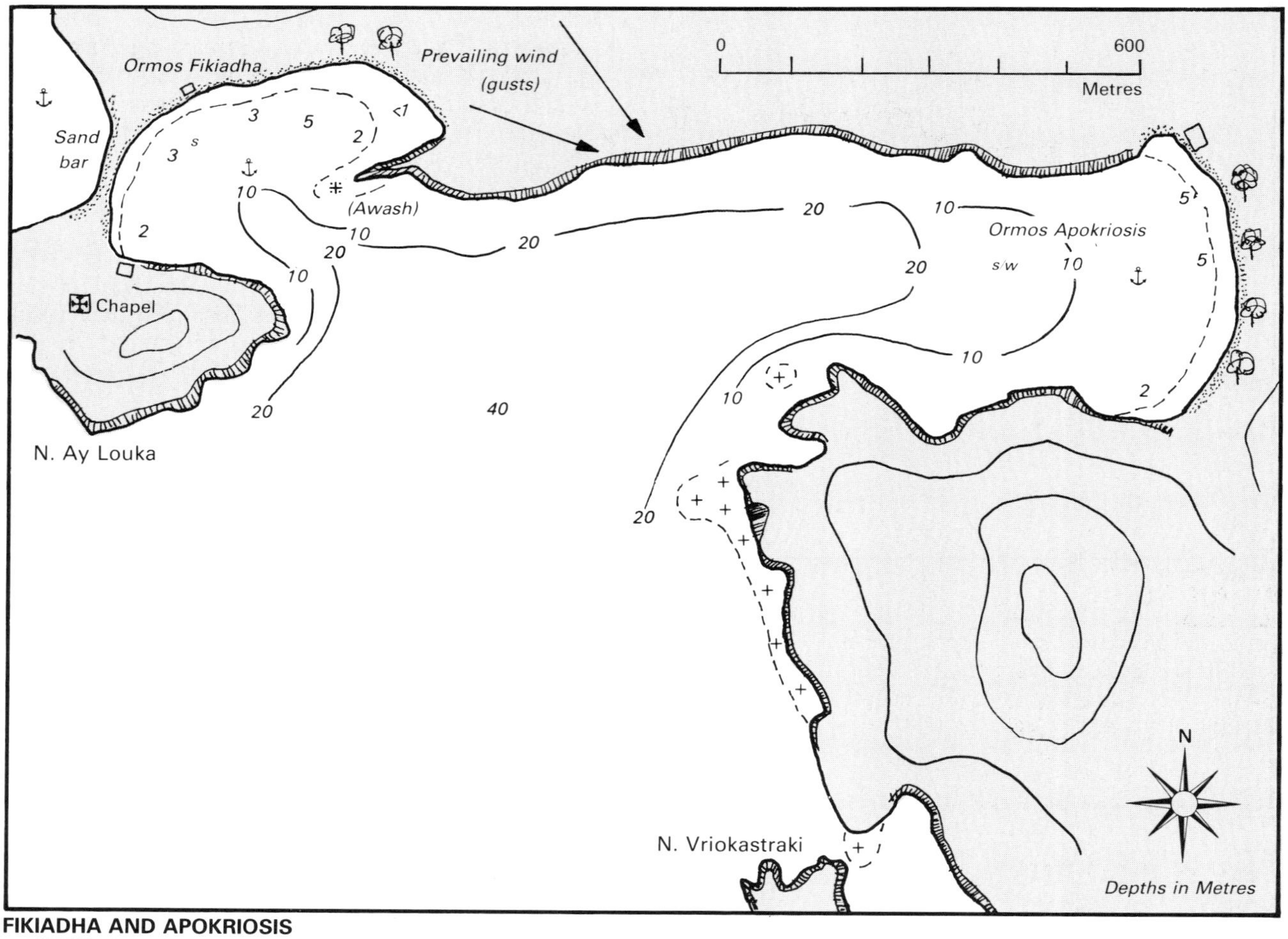

FIKIADHA AND APOKRIOSIS
37°25′N 24°23′E

EPISKOPIS
Admiralty chart no. 1825

Lies in between Merikha and Ormos Apokriosis.
With the *meltemi* swell enters the bay. In calm
weather or with SE–E winds anchor in 3–10 metres
where convenient. Open to the W.

MERIKHA (Merikhas)
Admiralty chart no. 1825

Approach
A small harbour on the W coast and the ferry port of
Kithnos. The buildings of the town are conspicuous
from seaward.

By night Use the light on Ak Merikha
(Fl.WR.1·5s5/3M): the red sector covers Nisis
Merikha on the S side of the entrance (340°-R-030°).

Mooring
Go stern-to or bows-to the inner moles wherever
there is room or anchor off with a long line ashore S
of the ferry quay. It is too shallow to berth off the
village quay.

Shelter Reasonable shelter from the *meltemi* although
there are strong gusts into the bay that can be most
uncomfortable.

Authorities Port police and customs.

Kithnos. Merikha looking ESE. *Nigel Patten.*

Facilities
Fuel Sometimes available.
Provisions Most provisions can be found although
supplies are much dependent on the ferry.
Eating out Tavernas on the waterfront.
Other Telephone. Greek gas. Bus to the *chora*. Ferry
to Lavrion.

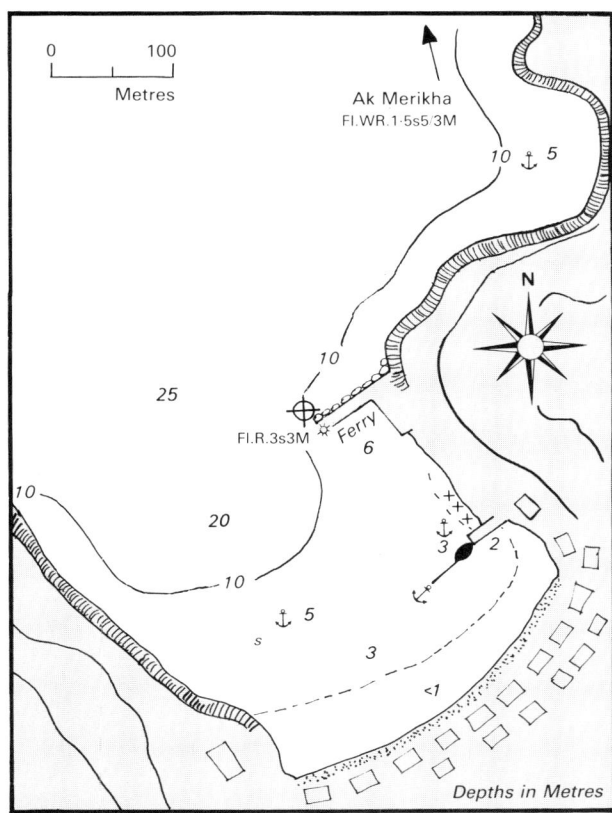

MERIKHA
37°23'·5N 24°23'·8E (Fl.R.3M)

General

Merikha is a comparative newcomer of a village, really built to service the ferry port. Just N of it are traces of the ancient city of Vriokastro.

LOUTRA (Loutron, Port Irene)
Admiralty chart no. 1825

Approach

Straightforward by day and night. The light structure on the S side of the entrance is conspicuous.

By night Use the light on Ak Kefalos (Fl.4s9M) and the light on the S side of the entrance (Fl.1·5s3M).

Kithnos. Loutra looking N. *Nigel Patten.*

Mooring

Go stern or bows-to the quay off the village or anchor in the SE cove off Ay Irini. The normal procedure in Ay Irini is to anchor and take a line ashore to the NE side. Care is needed of a large chain in the middle lying approximately NW-SE which can foul an anchor. Off Loutra part of the quay is reserved for yachts and a short mole provides some shelter from the *meltemi*. The bottom is sand, mud and weed and not everywhere good holding.

Shelter On the quay at Loutra and at Ay Irini there is some shelter from the *meltemi* although it can be uncomfortable from the swell reflected in.

Facilities

Water Close to the quay at Loutra.
Fuel Sometimes available.
Provisions Limited provisions.
Eating out Several tavernas and cafés.
Other PO. Telephone.

General

The hot mineral springs have been esteemed throughout history except for the present age when spa resorts have become unfashionable. The ancient Greeks and Romans used them and King Otto, Greece's first king, built the institute now standing. The hot springs still run though no visitors come to the spa any more. Near Ak Kefalos (about two hours' walk) are the ruins of a medieval citadel and town, though few buildings remain intact.

AYIOS STEFANOS AND AYIOS IOANNIS
Admiralty chart no. 1825

Two bays on the E coast of Kithnos affording good shelter from the *meltemi*. There are gusts off the high land at the entrance. Care should be taken of the reef lying 100 metres SE of the headland separating the two bays.

Anchor near the head of either bay and take a line ashore to a tree or a rock. The bottom is sand and weed – bad holding in places.

Limited water ashore, otherwise no facilities. There is a small hamlet at Ayios Stefanos. Although there is little here and despite the gusts from the *meltemi*, the bays are well worth a visit.

ORMOS KANALA AND
ORMOS AY NIKOLAOS

Lie respectively 4½ and 6¼ miles SW of Ak Ay Ioannou, the easternmost tip of Kithnos. They offer indifferent shelter from the *meltemi*, but can be visited in calm weather. Both are open to the S and E. No facilities.

Near Kanala is the monastery of the Panayia Kanala, the Virgin of the Canal, because reputedly the icon of the virgin in the monastery was

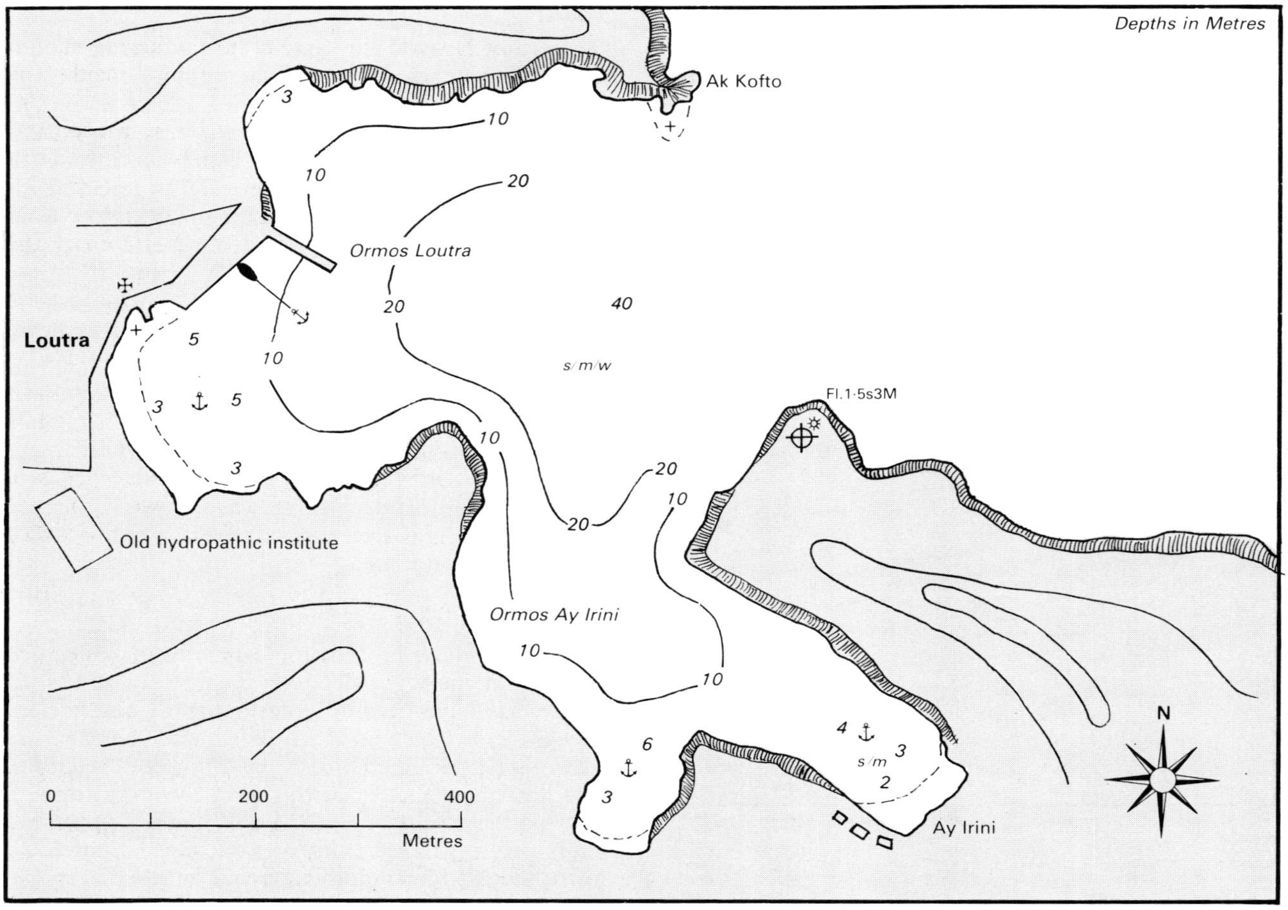

Depths in Metres

Ak Kofto

10

3

10

20

Ormos Loutra

20

40

s/m/w

Loutra

5

10

3 ⚓ 5

Fl.1·5s3M

3

10

20

10

Old hydropathic institute

20

20

Ormos Ay Irini

10

10

4 ⚓ 3

s/m

2

6

⚓

3

Ay Irini

N

0   200   400

Metres

LOUTRA
37°26'·6N 24°26'E (Fl.1·5s3M)

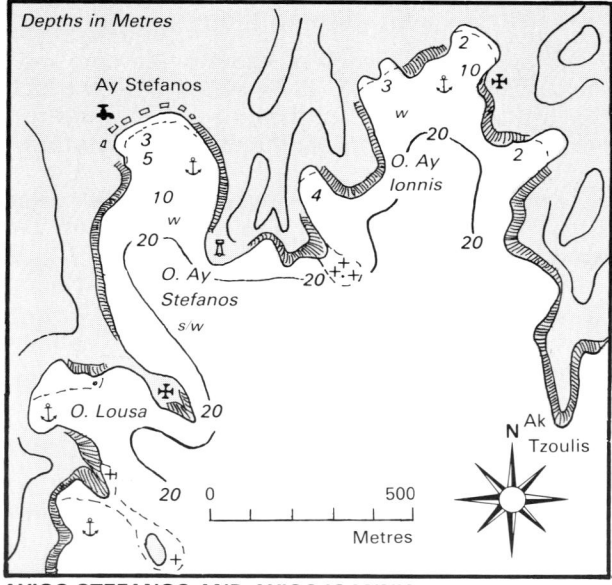

Depths in Metres

Ay Stefanos

2

3 ⚓ 10

w

3

20

O. Ay
Ionnis

2

10

w

4

20

20

O. Ay
Stefanos

s/w

⚓ O. Lousa 20

N Ak
Tzoulis

20   0   500

Metres

AYIOS STEFANOS AND AYIOS IOANNIS
37°24'N 24°27'·5E

discovered in a canal, though exactly where is uncertain. Her feast days are 15 August and 8 September when large numbers of pilgrims are said to come here.

Siros
(Syros, Syra)

A hilly, mostly barren island. The north is rugged and mostly uninhabited while the south has gentler slopes and is cultivated near the coast. Most of the population live in Ermoupolis, the port and also the nominal capital of all the Cyclades.

Nothing much remains of ancient Siros which was sited where Ermoupolis now stands. In the Middle Ages the inhabitants moved inland until the Venetians, ever mindful of the potential of the harbour and the strategic position of Siros along the Aegean trade route, occupied the island and restored its prosperity. In the 17th century the island came under the protection of the French and so escaped Turkish occupation. Siros took no part in the Greek War of Independence, but did take refugees from Psara and Khios.

In the steam age Siros became the principal port in the Aegean and a major coal-bunkering station for ships on passage through the Cyclades. Its importance declined when oil replaced coal and ships could do longer passages without the need to refuel.

The twin villages on the two hills behind the harbour reflect the island's history. Old Siros became the Venetian and Genoese Roman Catholic village

SIROS

1. Care needs to be taken of an oil-bunkering station on the S side of the harbour just inside the entrance.
2. Care is needed of Ifalos Karfomeni, a reef and shoal water on the S side of the harbour. It is marked by a light buoy (occas).

If a yacht keeps close to the end of the N breakwater where there are good depths, the bunkering station and reef are easily avoided.

Mooring

Go stern-to or bows-to the quay on the N or W side of the harbour. The bottom is mud – good holding.

Shelter Good shelter from the *meltemi* although there are gusts and a surge develops making it uncomfortable. The wash from ferries also makes it uncomfortable. With SE winds a swell rolls in making the harbour very uncomfortable and possibly dangerous for small yachts.

Note The harbour is very smelly in places from sewerage emptying into it.

Authorities A port of entry: customs, port police and immigration authorities.

Facilities

Water On the quay. Reported non-potable. A tanker can supply drinking water.

Fuel Near the W quay. ☎ (0281) 23784 or call on VHF Ch 8 for a minitanker.

and the descendants remain predominantly Roman Catholic. The Psariote and Khiot refugees established Ermoupolis (Hermoupolis: named after Hermes, the god of traders) which is the Greek Orthodox quarter. Ermoupolis has spilled over from its original site and now spreads around the waterfront. The port is still a mercantile centre and a major ferry port. The island is also famous for the production of *loukoumi* or Turkish Delight which here is excellent and not to be confused with some of the sickly-sweet imitations made elsewhere.

ERMOUPOLIS (Port Siros)

Admiralty chart no. 1833
Imray-Tetra chart no. G31

Approach

Conspicuous The twin villages on the hill above the harbour are easily seen from the distance. From the N and S, Nisis Gaidharos and Nisis Strongilo, immediately ESE of the harbour, are easily identified. Closer in a large cathedral on the slopes behind the town and the breakwaters are conspicuous.

By night Use the light on Nisis Aspronisi (Fl(2)12s5M) and Nisis Gaidharos (Fl.6s12M). The entrance to the harbour is lit: Ak Kondoyiannis Fl.3s4M; the N breakwater head Fl.G.3s6M and S breakwater Fl.R.3s6M. Ifalos Karfomeni is marked by a light buoy Q.R though it is not to be relied upon.

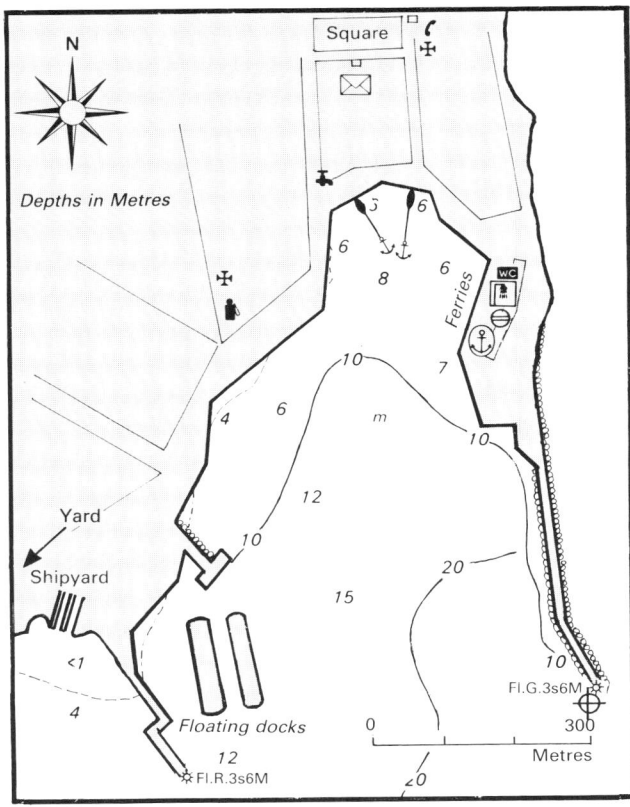

ERMOUPOLIS
37°26'·2N 24°56'·8E (Fl.G.6M)

Repairs A boatyard in the SE hauls yachts. Most yacht repairs can be carried out including mechanical, engineering, and GRP repairs. Mechanical and general engineering repairs. General hardware shops. Sail repairs can be carried out – go to the cheese shop at Chiou 28! Yachts can be hauled out for emergency repairs.

Shopping Good shopping for all provisions nearby.

Eating out Good tavernas around the waterfront and others in the town.

Other PO (open until 2400). OTE. Banks. WC and showers near the port police. Greek gas and *Camping Gaz*. Hospital. Hire cars and motorbikes. Buses to the principal villages. Ferries to Piraeus, nearby Cyclades, Crete, and Samos.

General

Although still the capital of the Cyclades, Siros is no longer the commercial and cultural centre. The buildings around the harbour reflect the past power and glory: an 18th-century square paved with marble and shaded by trees and complete with bandstand; impressive public buildings; an opera house modelled on La Scala; elegant 19th-century mansions with wrought iron balconies; and an extra large Catholic cathedral. Today the town no longer bustles as it must have done in the 19th and early 20th centuries – around the harbour the trading *caïques*, coasters and ferries go about their business, but there is not the boom of a big town. A museum near the square houses finds from nearby islands and a few finds from Siros.

PROHIBITED ANCHORAGE

It is prohibited to anchor in an area ½ a mile N and S of Nisis Aspronisi and between Aspronisi and Siros. It is permitted to sail in this area.

Caution A reef (Tripita Reef) with 2·7 metres least depth over it lies one mile W of Nisis Aspronisi. Aspronisis is also fringed by reefs.

NISIS GAIDHAROS

The island lying close off the coast opposite Ak Kondoyiannis at the entrance to Ermoupolis.

On the SE corner of the island there is a small cove that provides good shelter from the *meltemi*. Approximately halfway into the cove there is a bar with 2·5 metre depths over it. On the W side of the bar near the coast there is a sunken obstruction. Once over the bar anchor in 3 metres on a sand and weed bottom. No facilities.

ORMOS VARIS

A deeply indented bay on the SE side of Siros immediately W of Ak Khondra. Anchor near the head of the bay in 3–5 metres or in the cove on the W side in 3–5 metres. The bottom is sand and good holding. Good shelter from the *meltemi* although there are gusts.

Several tavernas around the waterfront and a hotel at the head of the bay. Fuel about 800 metres away on the road to Ermoupolis.

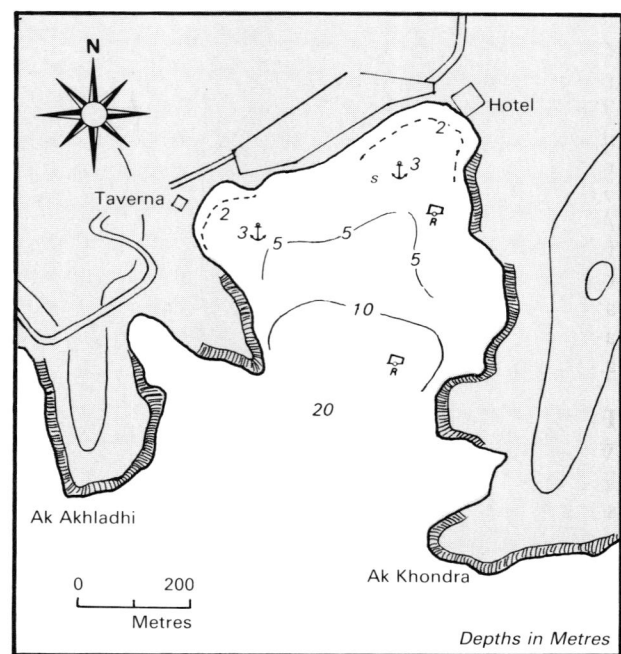

ORMOS VARIS
37°23'·4N 24°56'·7E

FINIKAS (Foinikas)
Admiralty chart no. 1825

A sheltered bay on the SW coast of Siros.

Approach

Nisis Psathonisi and the village of Finikas are conspicuous in the approaches.

By night Use the light on Psathonisi (Fl.2s4M) and the light on Vrak. Dhimitra (Fl.R.1·5s3M vis. only over 198°-085°).

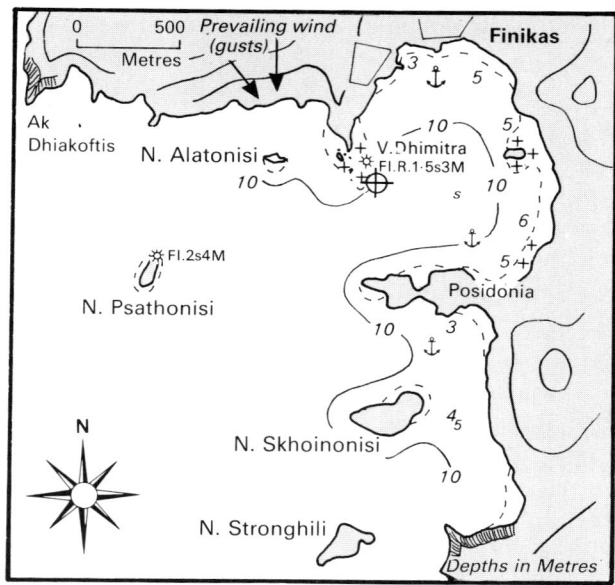

FINIKAS
37°23'·6N 24°52'·5E (V. Dhimitra)

Mooring

Go stern or bows-to the pier in the NW corner. With the *meltemi* blowing the S side of the pier is best. There are generally 3–4 metre depths although care is needed towards the root of the pier where large rocks obstruct berthing. The bottom is sand and weed with some rocks, generally good holding. Alternatively anchor off in 3–5 metres. Good shelter from the *meltemi* although there are gusts into the bay. The harbour in the SE corner (Posidonia) appears to be a military area and a yacht should not attempt to berth here without first inquiring if it is all right to do so.

Facilities

Water on the pier. Electricity to be installed. WC and showers at the root of the pier. A mobile repair service that can also supply diesel. Several tavernas and hotels around the shore. Some provisions in the village.

General

The bay and the beach are most attractive so it is not surprising that a number of hotels have been built around the bay. Nearly everyone who visits here likes the place and it is well worth stopping here with the bonus in the *meltemi* season of excellent shelter.

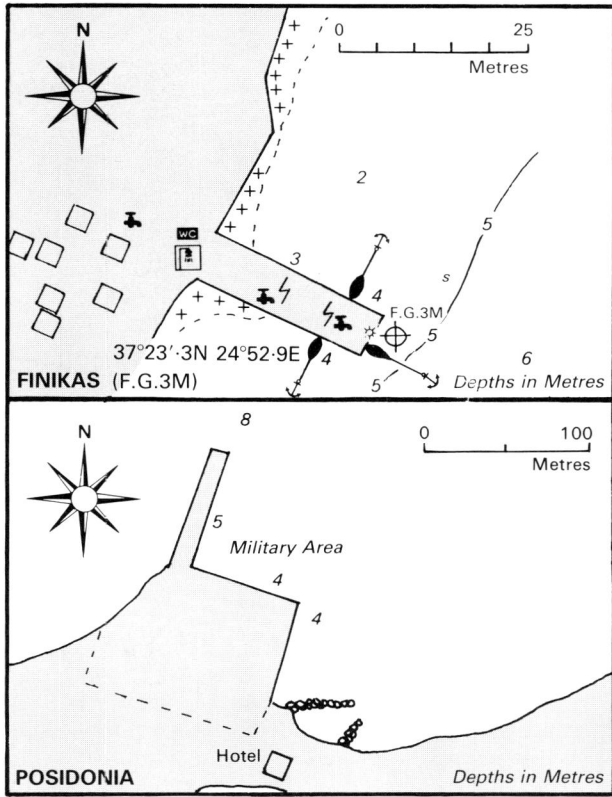

FINIKAS (F.G.3M)
37°23′·3N 24°52′·9E

POSIDONIA

ORMOS GALISSAS

A small bay lying immediately S of Ak Katakefalos. Anchor in 4–5 metres at the head of the bay. There are 3 metre depths about 50 metres off the beach.

The bottom is sand and good holding. Reasonable shelter from the *meltemi* although some swell penetrates into the bay. A taverna ashore and some provisions can be obtained in the village.

ORMOS KINI

A small bay on the W coast of Siros immediately opposite Ermoupolis on the E coast. Care must be taken of the reef lying just over half a mile off the coast WNW of the bay. Care must also be taken of a sand bar just under the water that extends from the S side of the bay to halfway across it. Anchor in 3–5 metres in the NE corner. Reasonable shelter from the *meltemi*. A taverna ashore and limited provisions can be obtained.

ORMOS DELFINO

A small bay approximately one mile N of Kini. It can be recognised when close in by the small islet in the middle. Anchor in 3–4 metres behind the islet. Reasonable shelter from the *meltemi* although there are gusts off the high land. No facilities.

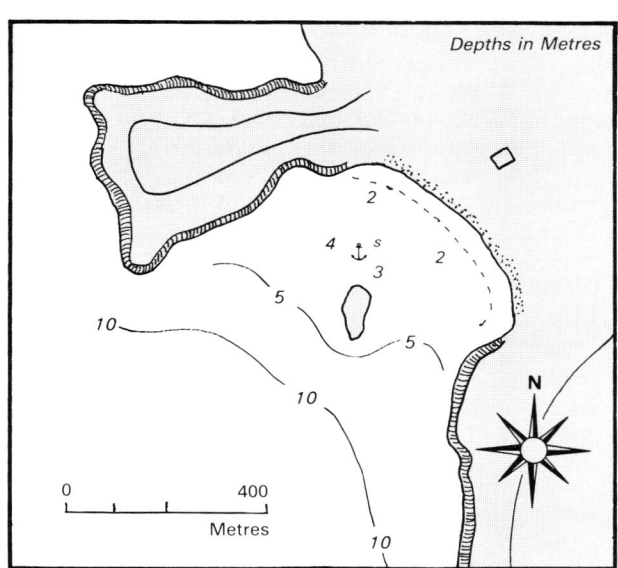

ORMOS DELFINO
37°27′·5N 24°53′·8E

AETOU

A tiny inlet about one mile N of Delfino. Anchor in the N cove in 4–5 metres. Gusts.

ORMOS GRAMMATA (Megas Lakkos)

Lies at the N end of Ormos Megas on the NW of Siros. Ak Grammata, a bell-shaped light yellow rocky bluff conspicuous from seaward, forms the western side of the bay. Anchor on the W or E side of the bay in 4–5m. Although the bottom is sandy it does not appear to be good holding. With the *meltemi* there are severe gusts off the high land and it is prudent to take a long line ashore. No facilities.

Ak Grammata is covered with the names and dates of seafarers who have sheltered here over the

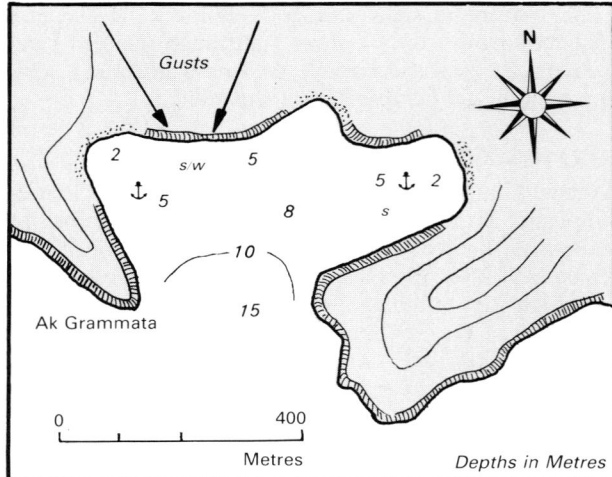

ORMOS GRAMMATA
37°30′N 24°53′·3E

centuries waiting for the infernal *meltemi* to die down and no doubt many readers of this book will likewise add their names to the list.

NISOS YIAROS (Yioura)

The island nearly midway between Kea and Tinos about 8 miles NW of Siros. It is a barren uninhabited lump of rock with no anchorages. It is in any case prohibited to anchor off or land on the island. When the *meltemi* is blowing there are strong gusts off the south coast and a yacht should keep a prudent distance off.

DORO STRAIT (Stenon Kafirevs/ Kafireos)

This strait lies between the N end of Andros and the S end of Evia. The strait is 6 miles across at its narrowest part. A current runs through the strait in a SW direction at 2–4 knots but the Admiralty Pilot reports that a southerly current of 7 knots was recorded with a strong northerly gale. The *meltemi* is funnelled through the strait and accompanying it are steep confused seas. With gales from the N small yachts should exercise considerable caution in the vicinity of the strait. I have seen large ships anchor in the roadstead off Karistos rather than proceed through the strait and during a Force 10 gale which lasted several days I counted over twenty ships anchored off waiting for the gale to abate. Even after the *meltemi* dies down a confused sea will remain for some time. In the event of strong northerly winds a yacht can shelter at Karistos on Evia or the bays to the E of it (see Chapter VI).

Andros

The northernmost and second largest of the Cyclades. It is mountainous throughout with the summit in the middle of the island, Mt Kouvarion, rising to 1134 metres (3721ft), with another peak, Mt Petalon, about a mile to the NE, rising to 944 metres (3097ft). These peaks are snowcapped in the winter and in early spring. It is well wooded and cultivated in places.

The island is named after Andreus, a general from Crete. During the Persian invasions Andros sided with the invaders which cost it dearly after the Athenian sea victory off Salamis. During the Peloponnesian War it sided with Sparta – it must have had some longstanding grudge against Athens. The ancient capital was at Palaioupolis on the west coast, but few ruins remain. It passed in turn to the Romans and to Byzantium and eventually to the Venetians in 1207 who built many of the fortified towers and the distinctive dovecotes dotted around it. It was occupied by the Turks in 1556 and became Greek after the War of Independence.

Today Andros is popular with Greek holidaymakers although a few foreign tourists are discovering it. The *chora* at Kastro is well worth a visit by land if you decide not to take on the *meltemi* and sail around in the summer.

GAVRION

Admiralty chart no. 1833
Imray-Tetra chart no. G31

Approach

Conspicuous The entrance to Ormos Gavrion is difficult to see from the distance. The group of islands to the S of the entrance (Plati, Gaidharos, Akamatis, Prasso, and Megalo) are easily identified and closer in the light structure on the W entrance point and the buildings of the village will be seen. Once at the entrance to the bay things are straightforward.

By night Use the lights on either side of the entrance to the bay: Ak Kastri (Fl.1·5s5M) and Ak Marmara (Fl.RG.2s3M, the red sector covers If Vouvi and the islands described above over 248°-005°). The breakwater is lit on the extremity Q.G.3M. The reefs and the unlit islands lying to the S of the entrance make a night approach from the S difficult and possibly dangerous. (See *Dangers* below.)

Dangers

1. Care must be taken of Ifalos Vouvi, a reef and shoal water approximately half a mile SE of the entrance.
2. Shoal water extends some distance off the islets in the approach from the S, especially Nisis Akamatis and Nisis Plati.
3. If coasting towards Gavrion from Batsi care is needed of Vrak Rosa, an above-water rock and reef approximately 200 metres ESE of Ak Marmara.
4. With the *meltemi* there are strong gusts down into Gavrion. Although there is good shelter inside, the gusts can make manoeuvring difficult off the quay.

Note The ferries using Gavrion enter and leave at speed. A good lookout should be kept for them in the vicinity of the bay.

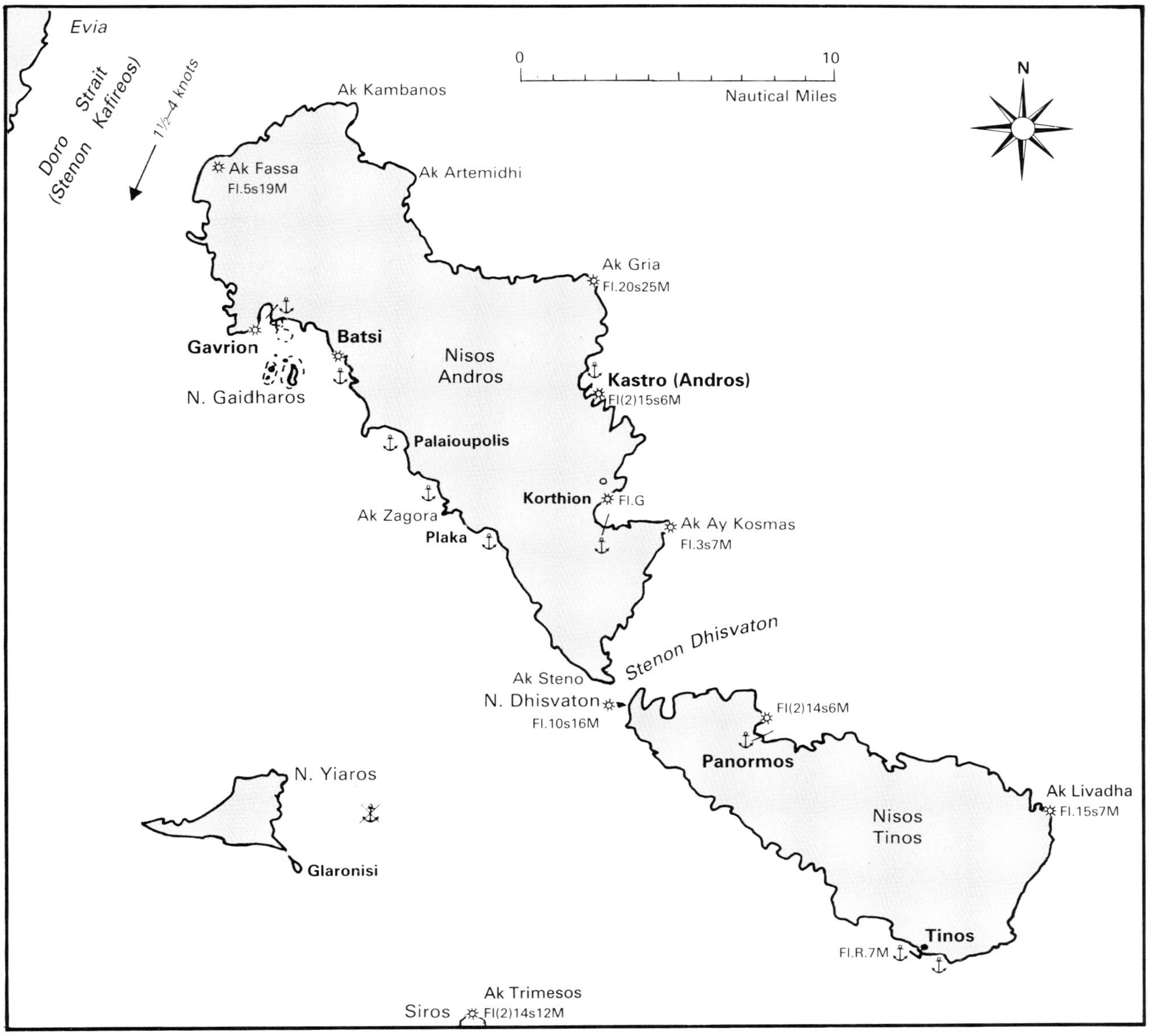

Map labels (top map):

Evia

Doro Strait (Stenon Kafireos)

1½–4 knots

0   10
Nautical Miles

N

Ak Kambanos

☼ Ak Fassa
Fl.5s19M

Ak Artemidhi

Ak Gria
Fl.20s25M

Gavrion

Batsi

N. Gaidharos

Nisos
Andros

⚓ **Kastro (Andros)**
Fl(2)15s6M

⚓ **Palaioupolis**

Korthion ☼ Fl.G

☼ Ak Ay Kosmas
Fl.3s7M

Ak Zagora
Plaka

Ak Steno
N. Dhisvaton ☼
Fl.10s16M

Stenon Dhisvaton

Fl(2)14s6M

⚓ **Panormos**

N. Yiaros

⚓

Nisos
Tinos

Ak Livadha
☼ Fl.15s7M

Glaronisi

Fl.R.7M ⚓ **Tinos**

Ak Trimesos
Siros ☼ Fl(2)14s12M

ANDROS AND TINOS

Mooring

Anchor at the head of the bay or go stern-to or bows-to or alongside the quay S of the ferry pier. It is also possible to tuck into the E corner of the ferry pier though one of the ferries often spends the night here and will take a line across to the quay effectively blocking yachts in until it leaves. When anchoring tuck as far into the NW corner as you can to ensure you leave sufficient room for the large ferries to manoeuvre. The sight of one of these maritime juggernauts steaming towards you before dropping its anchor and going hard astern towards the ferry quay takes a bit of getting used to. The bottom is mud and weed, mostly good holding once through the weed.

Shelter Good shelter from the *meltemi* although there are strong gusts off the land.

Authorities Port police.

Note In the summer there are numerous ferries thundering in and out of Gavrion and they have little concern for yachts manoeuvring in the bay. Keep well out of their way when berthing or anchoring.

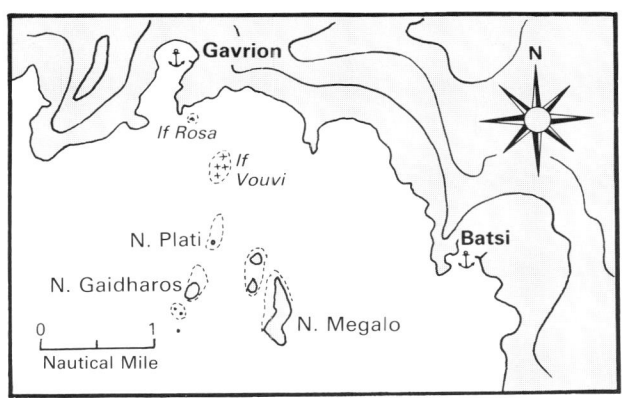

⚓ **Gavrion**

N

If Rosa

If Vouvi

N. Plati

N. Gaidharos

N. Megalo

Batsi ⚓

0   1
Nautical Mile

APPROACHES TO GAVRION AND BATSI

Gusts

N

0   300

Metres

<1

2

3

5

4

m w

8

Gavrion

Ferries

7

3

5   3

10   Q.G.3M

5

3

<1

4

<1

5

15

Mill

10

5

10

5

3

Ak Marmara

FI.RG.2s3M

7

Red sector covers Ifalos Vouvi

11

20

19

Vr. Rosa

10

17

FI.1·5s5M

5

10

5

Ak Kastri

Depths in Metres

GAVRION
37°52′·9N 24°43′·5E (Q.G.3M)

236

Facilities

Water In the village about 50 metres from the quay though it can be in short supply in the summer.
Fuel Near the quay.
Provisions Good shopping for most provisions. Ice near the quay.
Eating out Tavernas in the village and around the beach.
Other PO. OTE. Hire cars and motorbikes. Bus to Kastro. Ferry to Rafina and Piraeus.

General

The natural harbour of Gavrion offers the best shelter on Andros. The village is a modest uninspired little place, but not unpleasant. It is the ferry port for Andros and the ferries come and go frequently in the summer, bringing Athenians getting away from the smog of Athens to the clear air of the islands and every year more tourists getting away from more crowded islands. Gavrion is a safe enough place to leave your boat (put out a second anchor for security) and explore inland.

BATSI
Admiralty chart no. 1833

Approach

A small harbour 2¾ miles SE of Gavrion. Batsi village is conspicuous from seaward. By night use the light on Ak Kolona (Fl.3s5M) and the light on the extremity of the mole (Fl.G.2s3M). With the *meltemi* there are strong gusts down into the bay and approaches.

Mooring

Anchor in the bay or go alongside the mole if there is room (it is usually crowded). Good shelter from the *meltemi* although the gusts off the land from the E can make it uncomfortable. With strong southerlies a surge develops.

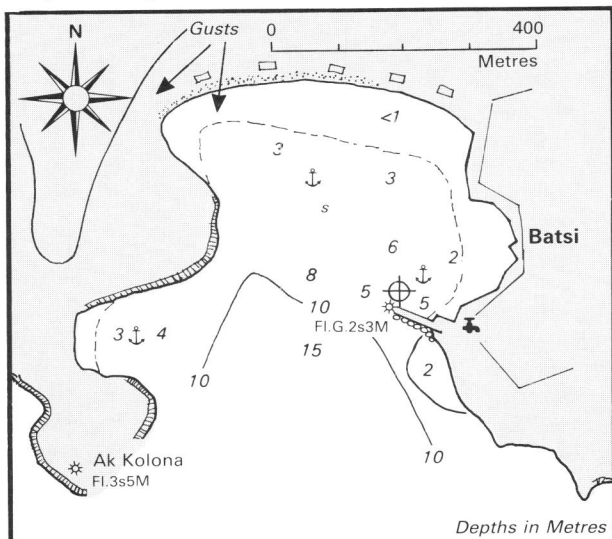

BATSI
37°51'·2N 24°46'·7E (Fl.G.2s3M)

Facilities

Water On the quay.
Fuel In the village.
Provisions Most provisions can be found.
Eating out Tavernas on the beach and in the village, and bars around the waterfront.
Other PO. OTE. Bus to Gavrion and Kastro.

General

Batsi is a pleasant enough little place if somewhat overwhelmed by tourists. The locals who aren't cashing in on the tourism with bars and boutiques seem mesmerized by the parade of foreigners through their village who apparently come here to do little else than lie in the sun and drink in the bars.

ORMOS PALAIOUPOLIS

An open bay 4 miles SE of Gavrion. Anchor at the N end of the bay under Ak Thiakion where there is reasonable shelter from the *meltemi* although some swell penetrates. There have been reports that the holding is suspect. Clear water and delightful surroundings. In calm weather it is possible to anchor off the small fishing hamlet built near the ruins of ancient Palaioupolis.

There are few ruins remaining (part of an ancient breakwater can be seen on the sea bottom), but the site is enchanting and a good lunch stop in calm weather.

ORMOS PLAKA

A small bay under Ak Zagora. Anchor in 2–4 metres on a sandy bottom. The bay is subject to strong gusts off the high land with the *meltemi*.

KASTRO (Kastron, Port Andros)
Admiralty chart no. 1833

Approach

The harbour faces directly into the *meltemi* and the approach is difficult. The reef running out from the headland can be identified by the seas breaking on it and the spume over it. Stick close to the N side where there are good depths off the end of the mole.

Mooring

Go stern-to or bows-to behind the mole. The bottom is rock and weed, poor holding, but there is usually a laid mooring free behind the mole. Care must be taken of ballasting along the quay in places. With the *meltemi* there is a surge in the harbour and it is best to pull well off and go ashore by dinghy.

Facilities

Water From local sources nearby.
Fuel On the outskirts of the village.
Provisions Good shopping in the village.
Eating out A taverna and bar near the harbour and others around the waterfront and in the village.
Other PO. OTE. Bank. Irregular bus to Batsi and Gavrion.

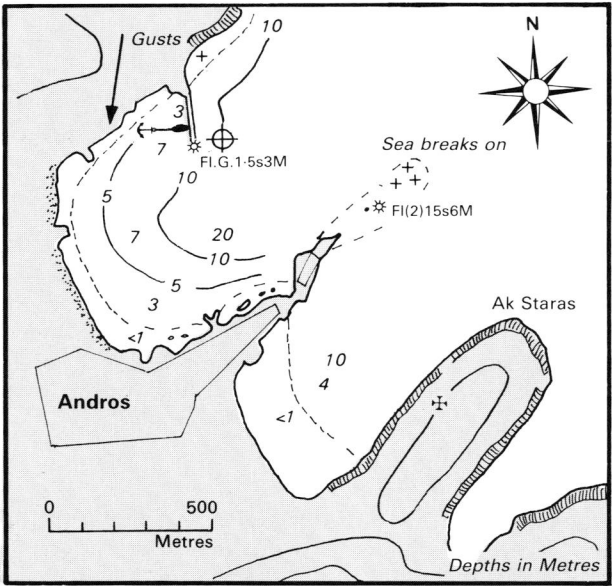

KASTRO
37°50'·6N 24°56'·2E (Fl.G.3M)

General

Kastro, or more properly Andros, is the capital of the island. It is a long hot walk around the bay to the village which straggles out along the rocky tongue forming the S side of the harbour, but it is well worth the effort to visit it. The town sits hunched over its rocky headland with the houses looking out over brown rock and the wind-tossed waters of the bay. On the end of the headland there is a small maritime museum and in the central square an archaeological museum and a museum of modern art.

KORTHION
Admiralty chart no. 1833

An open bay on the E coast 6 miles S of Kastro. The village of Korthion lies on the W side of the bay. On Ak Ay Aikaterina, the N side of the bay, there is a light (Fl.1·5s4M) and on the extremity of the breakwater a F.R.3M is exhibited. Anchor in the bay in 2–4 metres. With the *meltemi* a considerable swell rolls in making the anchorage uncomfortable and possibly untenable. Ashore limited provisions are available and there are several taverna/cafés.

STENO STRAIT (Stenon Dhisvaton)

This strait separates the S end of Andros and the N end of Tinos. Two islands, Nisis Dhisvaton and Nisis Kaloyeri, lie off the NW tip of Tinos. The strait is a little over half a mile across at its narrowest part. A current setting towards the SW runs through the strait, but not with the strength of the current in the Doro Strait. With the *meltemi* there are strong gusts through the channel.

Tinos

A mountainous rugged island lying immediately south of Andros across a narrow strait. The summit, Korifi Tsiknias (713 metres/2340ft), lies at the SE end of the island and Polemos Kambos in the centre of the island rises to 637 metres (2090ft). The island is wooded and the slopes are extensively terraced and cultivated. There are a large number of villages (there are said to be 64) peppered around the island and many Venetian dovecotes and towers. The main port and capital is Tinos.

The ancient name of the island was Ophiousa, referring to the large number of snakes to be found here in ancient times. The name Tenos, corrupted to Tinos, may be derived from the Phoenician word, *tenok*, for snake. Poseidon was credited with ridding Tinos of snakes by sending storks to devour them. The Venetians occupied the island and held it for 500 years until the Turks took it in 1714.

The long Venetian occupation established Catholicism on Tinos and today Catholic convents, schools and churches are scattered around the island. In 1822 the discovery of the miracle-working icon of the Virgin ironically transformed this very Catholic island to a place of pilgrimage for those of the Orthodox faith.

Tinos produces some reasonable *retsina* (from the barrel) and an average red and white wine. Tiniot water is said to be the purest in Greece although this claim is also made by a number of other places.

TINOS
Admiralty chart no. 1833

Approach

Conspicuous The large town of Tinos is clearly visible from the distance. Above the town the church of the *Panayia* is conspicuous. Closer in the harbour breakwater and the entrance are easily identified.

By night Use the lights on the extremities of the breakwaters, Fl.R.3s7M, Fl.G.2s3M and the light on the inner mole (Fl.R.2s3M).

Dangers

1. With the *meltemi* there are strong gusts off the high land in the vicinity of the harbour.
2. Care is needed of the reef and shoal water extending S from Ak Akrotiri, the cape in the S approaches to Tinos. The extremity is reported to be marked by a yellow buoy.

Mooring

Proceed into the inner harbour and go stern-to or bows-to the N quay between the cargo mole and the ferry quay or immediately E of the ferry quay. Care should be taken of the ledge protruding a short distance underwater from the quay. The bottom is mud, good holding.

Shelter Good all-round shelter although strong southerlies are said to cause a surge. Wash from the ferries can also be uncomfortable.

Authorities Port police and customs.

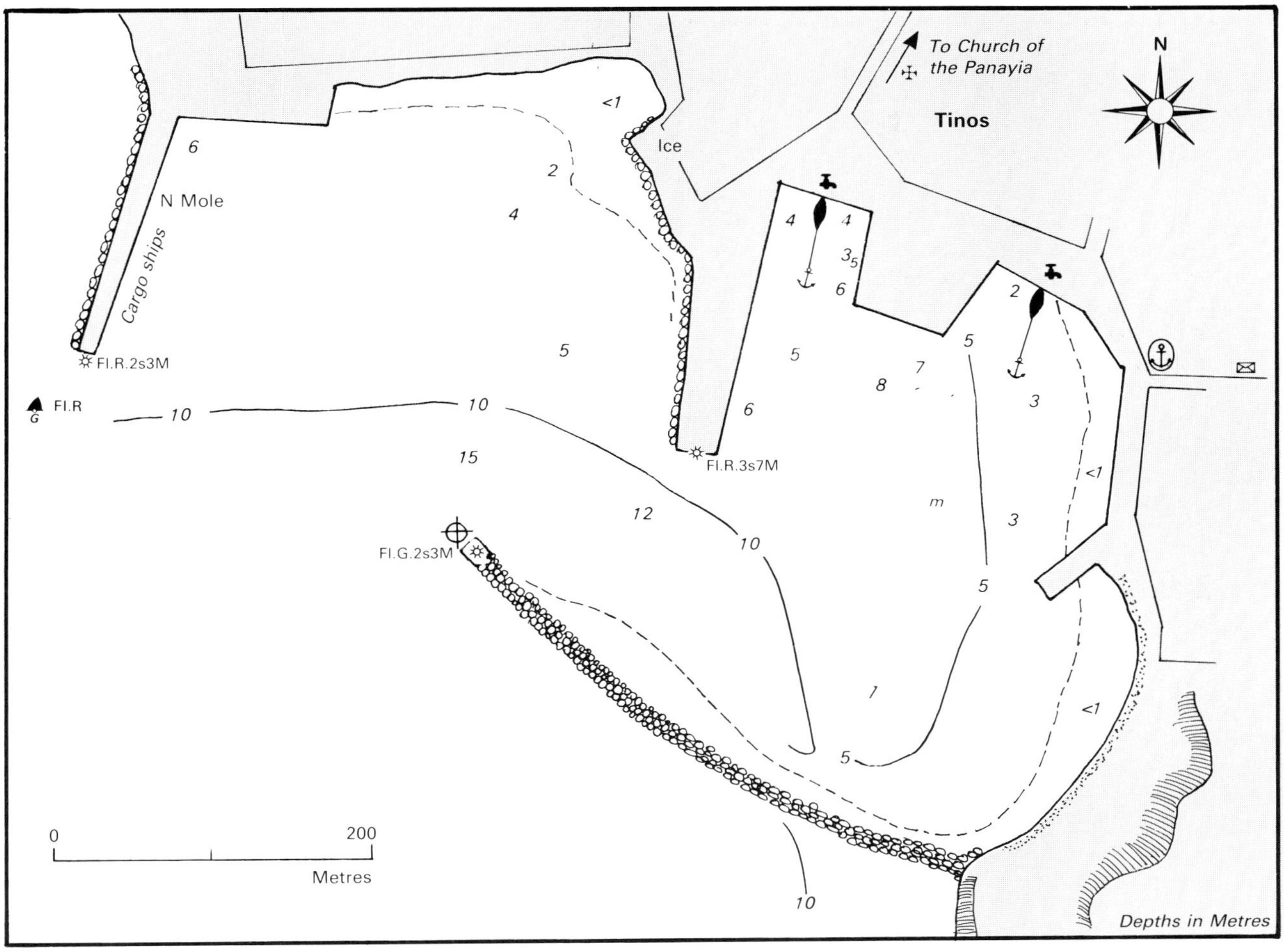

TINOS
37°32′·2N 25°09′·5E (Fl.G.2s3M)

Tinos harbour looking N from the harbour to the church of the Panayia. *Neville Bulpitt.*

Facilities

Water On the quay (reputed to be the purest in Greece!).
Fuel In the town. A mini-tanker can deliver to the quay.

Repairs Some mechanical repairs and light engineering. Hardware shops.
Provisions Good shopping for all provisions close by. Ice available near the quay.
Eating out Tavernas nearby.
Other PO. OTE. Banks. Greek gas and *Camping Gaz.* Hire motorbikes. Buses to the principal villages. Ferries to Piraeus.

General

Despite a sizeable Catholic population, Tinos is a centre of the Orthodox faith and the Church of the *Panayia* (the Virgin Mary/Our Lady – also called *Tiniotissa* and *Evangelistria*) is the focus of this faith. The modern church is sited above the town and is devoted to the miracle-working icon of *Our Lady of Good Tidings* discovered in 1822. Twice a year, on 25 March and 15 August, thousands of sick and crippled pilgrims come to Tinos seeking a cure. This Greek Orthodox 'Lourdes' has apparently cured many if the innumerable gold and silver votive offerings adorning the already ornate interior are anything to go by.

The church also contains a shrine commemorating the sinking of the Greek cruiser *Helle* (*Elli*). On 15 August 1940 the cruiser was anchored outside the port attending the celebrations. An unknown submarine, probably Italian, torpedoed the ship, sinking her and killing many of the crew. Greece was not at war at this stage and the atrocity caused an uproar all over Greece. Just below the church a museum contains some interesting finds including a sundial from the first century BC.

PANORMOS

A bay on the NE side of Tinos providing some protection from the *meltemi*. Nisis Planitis, with a light structure (Fl(2)14s6M) on it and connected by a narrow isthmus to Tinos, forms the N side of the bay and is easily identified. A beacon on the N side of the bay marks a reef.

The W inlet of the bay is used for shipping marble from the hinterland. There are two piers, the larger of which has 5–6 metre depths at its extremity. The smaller pier has 2 metre depths at its extremity. The anchorage can be dangerous with a strong *meltemi* when a swell works its way around into the bay.

Mikonos

(Mykonos)

A rocky barren island which is mostly low-lying. Mt Ay Ilias rises to 364 metres (1194ft) in the NW and Mt Anomeritis rises to 351 metres (1152ft) in the SE. The population mostly lives in Port Mikonos or in Tourliani in the middle of the island. The town of Mikonos, the tourist Mecca of Greece, is the real attraction because, apart from fine sandy beaches, the island has scenically little else.

Note Between Naxos and Mikonos a strong southerly current has been reported after a prolonged *meltemi*.

MIKONOS (Mykonos)

Admiralty chart no. 1833
Imray-Tetra chart no. G31

Approach

Conspicuous The white cluster of the buildings of Mikonos town is conspicuous from the distance. Closer in a line of windmills on a low ridge behind the harbour is conspicuous and the harbour breakwaters will be seen.

By night Use the light on Ak Armenistis (Fl.10s22M) and closer in the lights on the extremities of the breakwaters (Fl.G.2s3M and Fl.R.3s3M).

Dangers This is a very windy corner of the Aegean when the *meltemi* is blowing and there can be severe gusts in the vicinity of the harbour and a confused swell at the entrance. Yachts have been known to stay for weeks in Mikonos rather than venture out into the howling *meltemi*.

Mooring

Berth stern-to or bows-to the quay running SE from the N mole. Care must be taken of underwater rocks which extend a short distance from this quay. The bottom in the harbour has a thick weed cover and plough-type anchors do not always cut through at

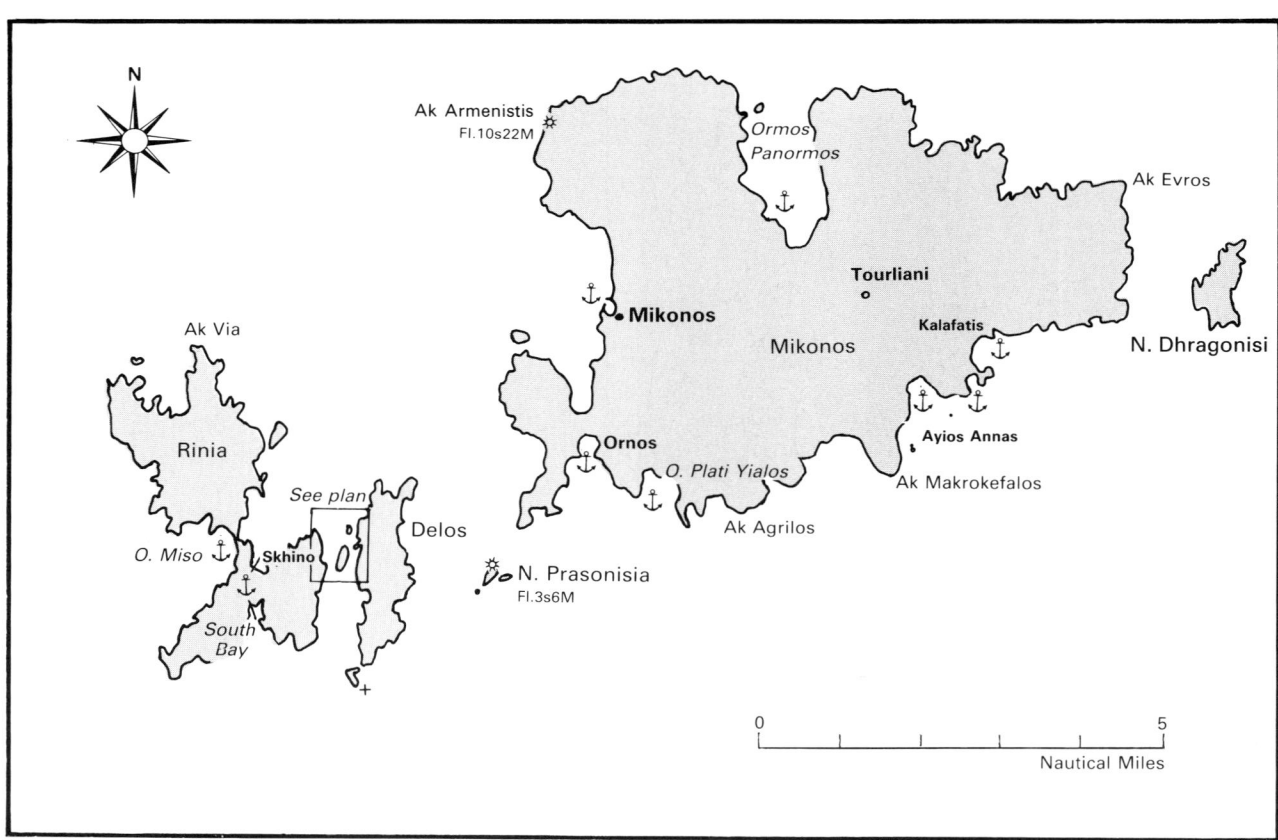

MIKONOS, DELOS AND RINIA

first. A second anchor is sometimes required. All of the N quay is now used by ferries so do not attempt to berth there.

Note If a port policeman whistles and shouts at you from the quay, he is directing you to a berth. You can communicate on VHF channel 12 as he normally carries a portable VHF to give you directions for berthing.

Shelter Protection from the *meltemi* can only be described as adequate and indeed some consider the harbour dangerous. Wash from the ferries and particularly from their bow-thrusters can cause problems. However most problems emerge from inexperienced sailors pulling other people's anchors up and not from the physical characteristics of the harbour. Open to the W–SW.

Authorities Port police and customs.

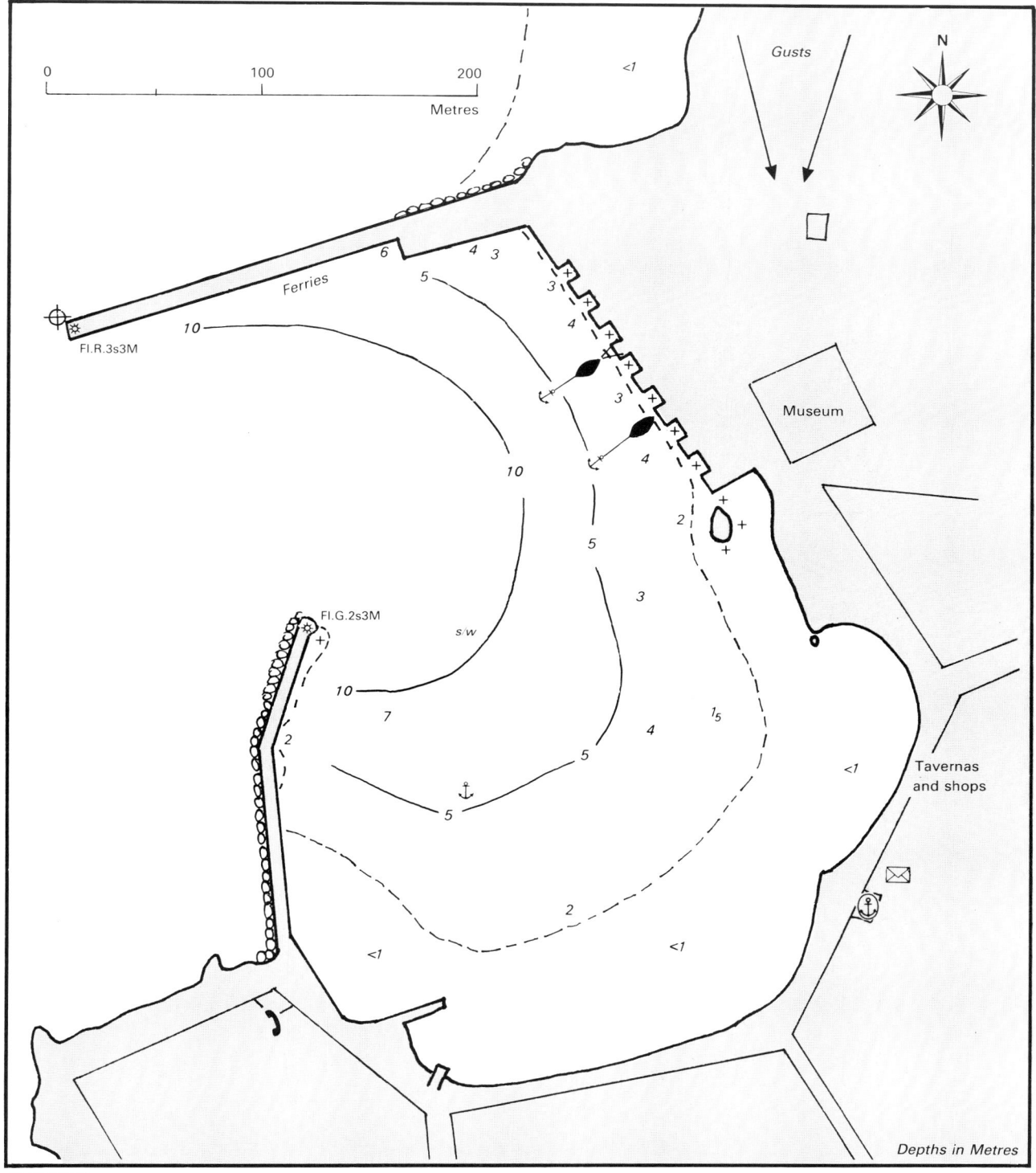

MIKONOS
37°27'·1N 25°19'·6E (Fl.R.3s3M)

Facilities

Water Can be delivered by mini-tanker. Reported to be expensive.

Fuel In the town. A mini-tanker can deliver to the quay.

Repairs Limited mechanical repairs.

Provisions Good shopping for provisions nearby. Ice available near the harbour.

Eating out Tavernas of all types ranging from cheap and fairly awful to good and expensive, in some cases very expensive.

Other PO. OTE. Banks. Greek gas and *Camping Gaz.* Hire cars, motorbikes, and bicycles. Ferries to Rhodes and Piraeus. Internal flights to Athens, international flights to some European airports.

General

Mikonos has almost passed into the English language to describe a certain type of touristy island in the way that Benidorm describes the most shabby of resorts. To 'mikonos' means to take the most wonderful place and completely change the values and worth of the community so that while physically little appears to have changed, the place is soulless and possesses little that was valuable in the old community. So it is that in the summer the locals rub shoulders with the yacht set, the jet set, backpackers, artists – real and pseudo, nudists and recently the gay set as well as plain ordinary holidaymakers. Mikonos is bright and breezy by day and by night the hum of the bars and throb of discos into the wee hours is all part of the scene.

The town is a dazzling white cluster of cubes stacked around a natural amphitheatre above the harbour. Mikonos epitomizes the Greek flair for choosing a superb site and tailoring a natural architecture to it. The houses, the churches (there are said to be 365 of them, a bit of an exaggeration), and the narrow winding alleys appear to be a naturally evolved form sculpted from the rocks of the island itself. There may be hordes of tourists from all over the world, and more photographs of Mikonos than of any other town in Greece, films and documentaries may have featured it, yet Mikonos retains that wonderful appearance and certain architectural something that so many flock to see. For the yachtsman the cosmopolitan flavour of Mikonos may be a refreshing contrast to the simpler pleasures of the other islands.

Note There are plans for a new marina to be built to the N of Mikonos harbour. As yet no formal plans have been published and work is yet to start.

ORMOS ORNOS

The bay on the S side of Mikonos immediately E of Ak Alogomandra. Anchor in 5–10 metres at the head of the bay. The bottom is sand and weed – poor holding in places. Good shelter from the *meltemi* although there are strong gusts into the bay. Open to the S.

There is a hotel on the beach and several tavernas. It is two miles to Mikonos town, buses every hour.

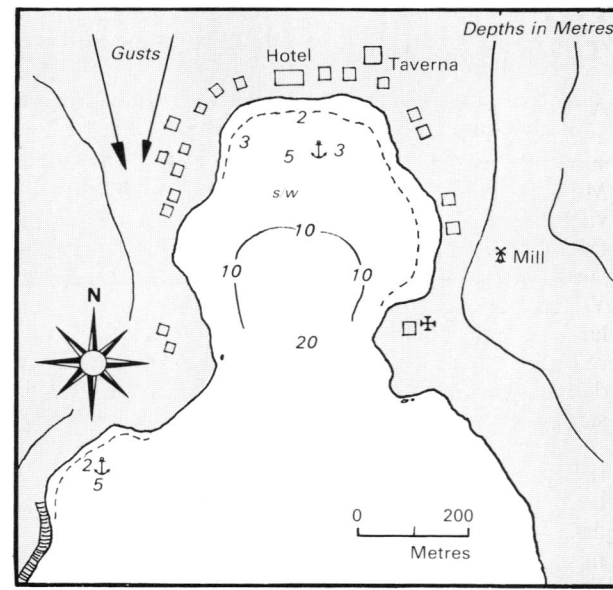

ORMOS ORNOS
37°25'·3N 25°19'·5E

Just to the E of Ornos there are a number of small bays sheltered from the *meltemi*. They have sandy beaches and tavernas nearby.

ORMOS AYIOS ANNAS (Baraga)

Lies immediately E of Ak Makrokefalos. Anchor in 3–6 metres. The bottom is sand and weed. Good shelter from the *meltemi*. Open S. Close eastwards there is a cove also offering shelter from the *meltemi*.

Some of these beaches are unofficially 'no clothes' beaches and some are the preserve of men only who gambol about and indulge in their particular practices.

Note Between Ayios Annas and the cove to the E of it there is a gravel-loading facility with three large unlit mooring buoys off the loading gantry.

KALAFATIS

A bight offering reasonable protection from the *meltemi* although completely open to the S and E. It lies immediately E of Ormos Ay Annas and Ak Tarsanas. Care must be taken of a reef on the W side of the bight. Anchor off the N end of the beach in 3–4 metres off the hotel complex. Taverna and café ashore.

PANORMOS

The large bay on the N side of Mikonos. It can only be used outside the *meltemi* season as it blows straight into here. On the W side of the bay there is an attractive cove with suitable depths for anchoring and a taverna ashore.

Delos

(Dhilos, Mikro Delos)

A small low barren island with the extensive ruins of ancient Delos on the west coast. Every day in the summer tripper boats ferry sightseers over from Mikonos to see these ruins. It is now prohibited for a yacht to berth or anchor at Delos so you will have to take a ferry over if you wish to visit the ruins. A large notice at the small harbour says simply 'No Yachts' and in Ormos Fourni a notice prohibits landing and anchoring overnight. Recently it was reported that yachts could anchor off, but must depart before 1500 hours. Other yachts have reported staying overnight.

Delos was once the political and religious centre of the ancient world. Legend has it that Apollo was born here and Artemis on nearby Rinia. The Delos oracle was consulted before major decisions and its fame was second only to that of Delphi. How did Delos become the centre of the ancient world? The most succinct answer is provided by Ernle Bradford:

'Delos, the hub around which the Cyclades (Kukloi – rings) radiate, was formed by nature to be the focal point of a seaman's world. If one is tempted to ask why so small an island, without any natural resources, ever became what it did, then the answer can be given by any sailor. Delos is the last, and best, anchorage between Europe and Asia. To the east it is shielded by Mykonos, to the north by Tinos, and to the west by Rheneia. Looking at a chart, it is easy to see how the direct sea route between the Gulf of Nauplia (with Argos at its head) flows straight across the latitude of 37°10′ north of Patmos and Samos. Exactly in the centre of this trading route lies Delos. At the same time, it is almost in the centre of the trading route between the Dardanelles and Crete. Religious centres may sometimes, as at Rome or Lourdes, attract trade and commerce. But more often one will find that where the trade is, there are also temples. Merchants, then as now, are eager to purchase security in both worlds.'

Ernle Bradford *The Greek Islands*

In those days the ancient harbour was larger and better protected than it is today. The breakwater was some 165 metres long and the harbour extended south for half a mile and was divided by moles into five basins. Yet despite Ernle Bradford's praise for the natural attributes of Delos, I cannot help thinking there are other better natural harbours nearby. Ormos Naoussa on Paros or Ormos Dhespotico, for instance, are better protected and more accessible than Delos. In any case for whatever reasons the ancients settled on Delos and transformed this rocky little island into the centre of the world.

In 700 BC the island was under the protection of Naxos and the centre of the Ionian League of islands. Athens soon entered the league and before long was commanding Delian affairs. It was purified in 543 BC by Peristratos and thereafter the island was not to be defiled by human birth or death. The dying and any women nearing childbirth were taken across to nearby Rinia. The island was subsequently purified

on several other occasions, presumably because someone had a heart attack or some similar fairly instant demise and died before they could be whisked off to Rinia.

After the defeat of the Persians the first great period of prosperity for Delos began. In Macedonian times it enjoyed privileges akin to those of a 'free port' and its wealth and power were immense. By 200 BC the first Romans came to Delos and although the Athenians remained, the power soon shifted to the Romans. Around 80 BC it was sacked and although it was rebuilt, its power was on the wane. A wall was built around it but by 3 AD the island was finished. In that year it was put up for sale, but there were no takers.

The remaining ruins and the site should not be missed. The site has been likened to Pompeii, not for any architectural similarity, but for the completeness of the picture of ancient life that can be gleaned from it. Many of the ruins have been vandalised by past invaders and collectors of antiquities and of course by the Greeks themselves who have carted off the conveniently-hewn stone to build their houses on Mikonos, but much remains: the five lean lions guarding the sacred lake; the temple of Apollo in the great square of Apollo; the theatre; the bright mosaics of dolphins, panthers, birds, fruit and flowers; and the remains of what was the busiest harbour in antiquity.

DELOS CHANNEL (Stenon Dhilos)

A yacht transiting the channel must exercise caution when the *meltemi* is blowing. The channel between Delos and Rinia and the Nisidhes Remmatia is fringed by reefs. When the *meltemi* is blowing it is funnelled into the channel and may blow at Force 7

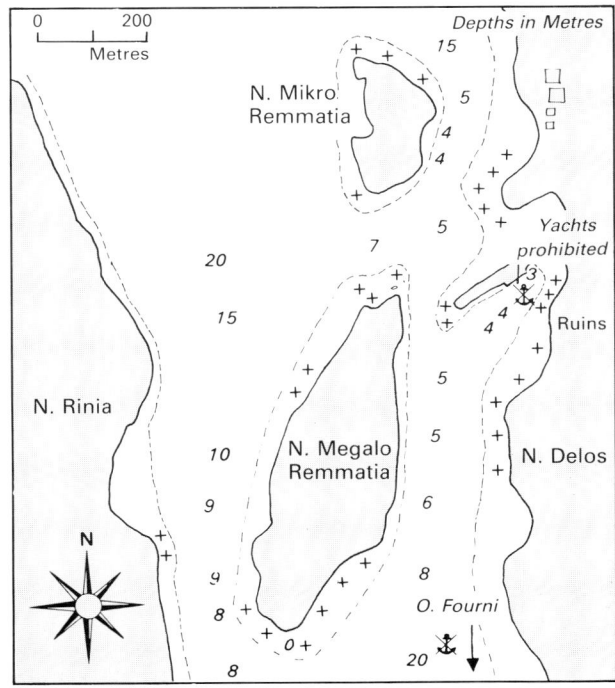

DELOS CHANNEL

Ancient Delos.

or more on occasions. The combination of a narrow shallow channel fringed by reefs and strong winds and short seas can make navigation a tricky business – care is needed.

Rinia
(Rhenea, Megalo Delos)

The barren rocky island separated from Delos by the narrow Delos Strait. The island is nearly divided into two by a narrow isthmus. The northern half is the higher of the two (149 metres/490ft). There are several sizeable farms on the island and even a herd of cows as well as sheep and goats.

ORMOS SKHINO

This anchorage is not suitable with the *meltemi*. It offers good shelter in southerlies. Anchor in 3–5 metres on a sandy bottom.

Rinia. S Bay looking S. *Nigel Patten.*

SOUTH BAY

On the S side of Rinia affords good shelter from the *meltemi*. Anchor near the head of the bay in 3–5 metres on a sandy bottom. No facilities. Water from a well in the field nearby.

ORMOS MISO

A large bay on the W side sheltered from the *meltemi*. Anchor in one of the two coves at the northern end where shown on a sandy bottom. No facilities.

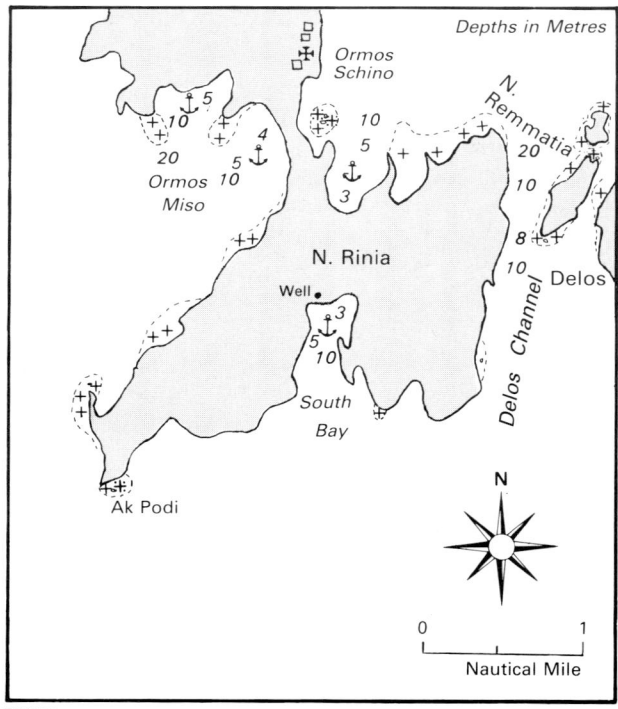

RINIA

244

Middle Cyclades

Serifos
(Seriphos)

A dome-like island with the white houses of the *chora* on a conical hill SE of the summit of Mt Troullos (585 metres/1919ft). The island appears barren from seaward but at Livadhi it is green and wooded around the shore and inland from the *chora* there are several green valleys in startling contrast to the burnt brown mountain sides. There are a number of iron ore mines at Megalo Khorio on the west coast of the island and at Koutala on the south, but there is little active mining today. Livadhi has a modest tourist trade in the summer, but for the most part the island is populated by the old (particularly noticeable in the *chora*) as the young have deserted the island for Athens.

LIVADHI (Livadhiou)
Admiralty chart no. 1833
Imray-Tetra chart no. G33

Approach

Conspicuous Coasting around the S coast the lighthouse on Ak Spathi is conspicuous. From the N and E Nisis Vous can be recognised and closer in the

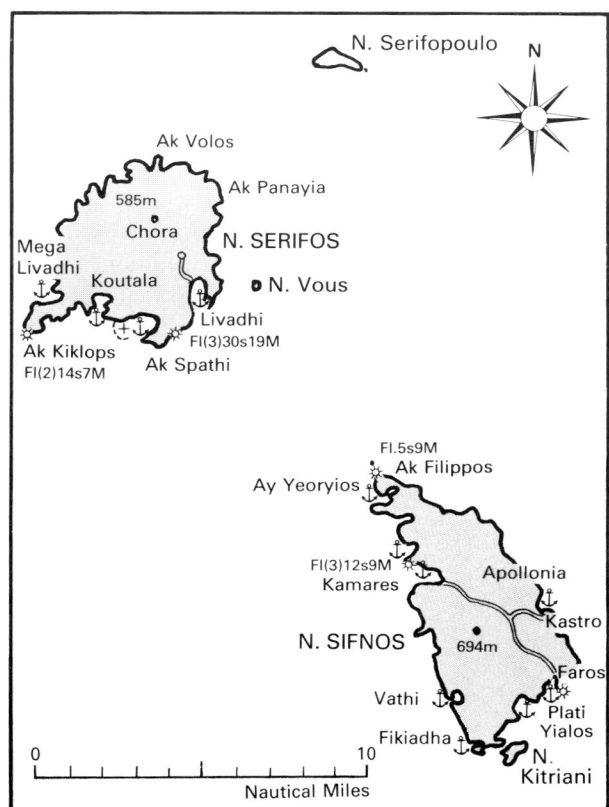

SERIFOS and SIFNOS

white houses of the *chora* on the hill above the harbour are easily seen. Once at the entrance to Ormos Livadhiou the approach is straightforward.

By night From the S use the light on Ak Kiklops (Fl(2)14s9M) and Ak Spathi (Fl(3)30s19M). The extremity of the breakwater is lit (Fl.R.1·5s3M). From the N a night approach can be difficult, especially if visibility is not good. There are no useful lights and Nisis Vous is not lit – if coming from the Saronic a S approach is safer even if slightly longer.

Dangers With the *meltemi* there can be strong gusts off the lee side of the island and in the immediate approaches to Livadhi.

Serifos. Livadhi looking S from below the *chora*.

Mooring

Anchor in the bay or go stern-to or bows-to the small jetty off the village on the S side of the bay. The bottom is sand and weed – mostly good holding although there have been reports of bad holding in places. When the ferry is not due yachts also go alongside or stern-to the ferry quay.

Shelter Good shelter from the *meltemi* although there are gusts into the bay. With strong SE winds a swell works around into the bay although it is still tenable. In the summer the harbour is often crowded with yachts.

Authorities Port police.

Facilities

Water On the jetty.
Fuel A mini-tanker can deliver to the quay.
Provisions Most provisions can be obtained at Livadhi.
Eating out Good tavernas in the village and around the beach.
Other PO and OTE at the *chora*. Exchange facilities. Greek gas. Bus to the *chora*. Hire motorbikes. Ferry to Milos and Piraeus.

General

The nearly landlocked bay fringed by trees providing welcome shade from the sun and the white houses of the *chora* on the hill above like icing on a bun are like

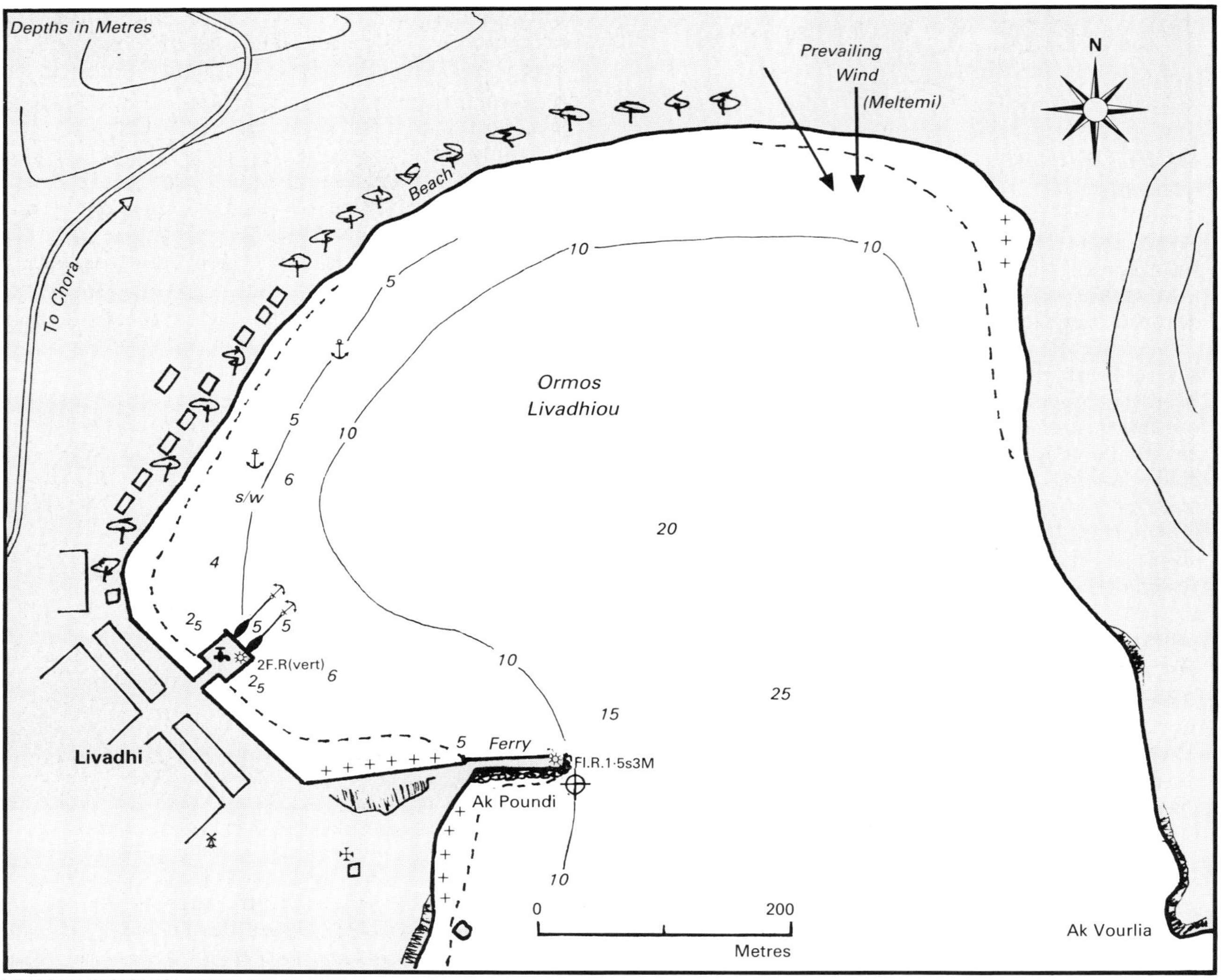

Depths in Metres

To Chora

Beach

Prevailing
Wind
(Meltemi)

N

10

10

*Ormos
Livadhiou*

5

5

10

s/w

6

20

4

2₅ 5 5

2F.R(vert)

2₅ 6

25

10

15

Livadhi

5 Ferry

Fl.R.1·5s3M

Ak Poundi

10

0   200

Metres

Ak Vourlia

LIVADHI 37°08′·6N 24°30′·9N (Fl.R.3M)

a cliché of received ideas of the Cyclades. The view from the *chora* down onto the bay and over the sea and islands beyond is worth the trip, even the hot walk up if you miss the bus. The *chora* remains much as it always was, but the settlement around the bay has acquired the usual trappings for the summer tourist trade including highly amplified disco music which, in this otherwise tranquil spot, pierces the night-time air with an unnatural cacophony.

ORMOS KOUTALA

An open bay on the S side of Serifos offering good shelter from the *meltemi*. Anchor in either of the two coves at the head of the bay. In the NE cove anchor in 3–5 metres on a sandy bottom. In the NW cove care must be taken of a foul area where large mooring chains have been laid. Anchor where shown in 6–10 metres on a sandy bottom. Good shelter from the *meltemi* although there are strong gusts into the bay.

On either side of the bay are the remains of iron ore mines and jetties and the concentration of ore is reported to cause local magnetic anomalies. A number of villas have been built around the shores.

Serifos. Livadhi looking SE from the *chora. Nigel Patten.*

246

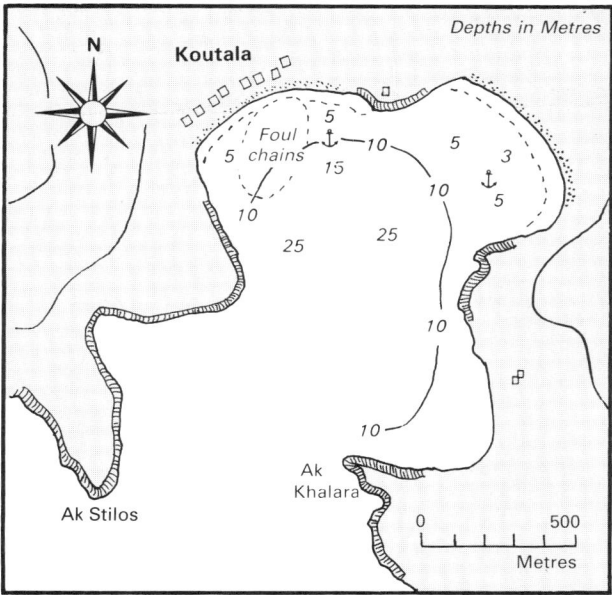

KOUTALA
37°08′N 24°27′·5E

MEGA LIVADHI

An inlet NE of Ak Kiklops. It is reported to offer good shelter from the *meltemi*.

NISIS SERIFOPOULA

A barren uninhabited island lying 4½ miles NE of Serifos.

Sifnos

(Siphnos)

The high bold island lying 7 miles SE of Serifos across the often windy Sifnos Channel. The island is hilly throughout rising near the centre to Mt Ayios Ilias (694 metres/2277ft). The west coast is barren and burnt rock, but on the east side of the island, where most of the population live, it is greener and cultivated in places. Most of the population live in the capital, Apollonia, on a hill inland.

In ancient times the inhabitants were vilified for their greed and deceit. On one occasion the Sifniotes offered a gilt egg at Delphi instead of the customary gold one and Apollo in revenge destroyed the gold mines which had formerly earned a great deal of revenue for the island. On the east coast the decaying medieval village of Kastro is a delightful place surrounded by a wall into which two- and three-storey houses have been built. The village and former capital looks down onto Ormos Kastro and across to Andiparos and Paros.

Today the beaches on the SE coast of the island are popular and a number of small hotels have been built around the coast.

Sifnos. Ayios Yeoryios.

AYIOS YEORYIOS

A narrow inlet on the NW tip of the island. It provides good shelter from the *meltemi* and indeed from all but W winds. There is room for one or two small yachts at the head of the bay. Anchor fore and aft as there is no swinging room, or moor bows-to the outer end of the S quay taking care of the underwater rocks projecting some distance out. There are 8–10 metre depths at the dogleg and 3–4 metres in the middle of the inlet with 2 metre depths until quite close to the edges. The head of the inlet is shallow.

Two tavernas and two ceramic workshops ashore. At one time the last hand-formed giant amphora-like pots were made here.

NORTH BAY

Just N of Kamares there is a small bay affording shelter from the *meltemi*. Cliffs surround the bay except where two deep gullies descend into the bay. Anchor in 4–5 metres between the gullies. The bottom is sand and weed, not everywhere good holding. No facilities.

Note Vourlitha, which lies between this bay and Ayios Yeoryios, has been recommended as an anchorage, but I find it a bleak desolate spot affording little shelter, certainly not as good as that offered by nearby anchorages.

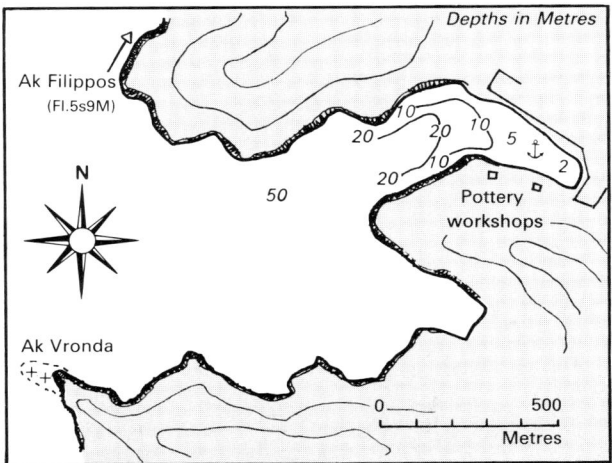

AY YEORYIOS 37°02′N 24°38′E

KAMARES
Admiralty chart no. 1833

Approach
Conspicuous It is difficult to see where the entrance is to the bay – vessels appear to pop out of a slit in the cliffs. Once near the entrance the buildings of the town and the outer mole can be seen.

By night Use the light on Ak Kokkala (Fl(3)12s9M) and on the S side of the entrance (Fl.3s6M). The breakwater is lit on its extremity: Fl.G.1·5s3M.

Dangers It is advisable to take down your sails before entering the bay as with the *meltemi* there are strong gusts from all directions at the entrance and inside the bay.

Mooring
Berth stern-to or bows-to the quay between the two moles or anchor at the head of the bay. The bottom is hard sand and weed with some rocks – fair holding only.

Shelter Good shelter from the *meltemi* although there are gusts. With W winds a swell rolls into the bay.

Authorities Port police and customs.

Facilities
Water On the quay.

Sifnos. Kamares looking NE.

Fuel None locally although you may be able to get some delivered to the quay. Enquire ashore.

Provisions Most provisions although supplies are much dependent on the ferries.

Eating out Good tavernas nearby.

Other A regular bus runs to Apollonia, the island capital, where there are a PO and OTE and better

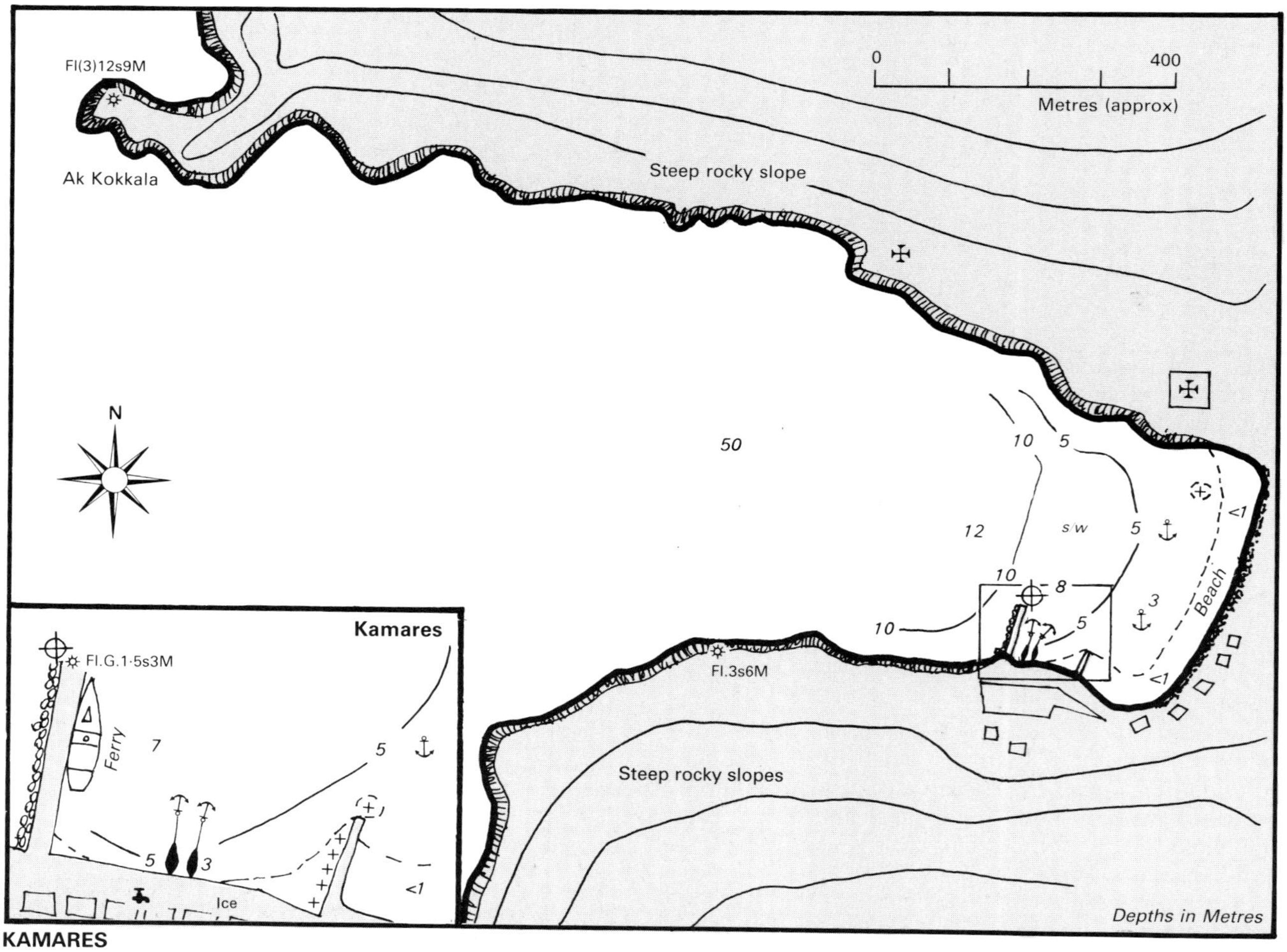

KAMARES
36°59'·5N 24°40'·5E (Fl.G.3M)

shopping for provisions. Ferries to Milos and Piraeus.

General

Kamares is the ferry port for Sifnos and while the setting between the high cliffs and hills is spectacular, the village lacks that certain something. However I recommend a trip to Apollonia and Kastro from here.

Sifnos. Kamares looking WNW from the slopes behind the bay. *Nigel Patten.*

ORMOS VATHI
Admiralty chart no. 1825

A landlocked bay affording the best all-round shelter on Sifnos. The entrance is somewhat difficult to identify. There is a light structure on the S side of the entrance (Fl.2s7M). Anchor in the N of the bay in 3–4 metres on the gently shelving bottom – sand and weed, good holding. Depending on draught (not much over a metre) small yachts may be able to go

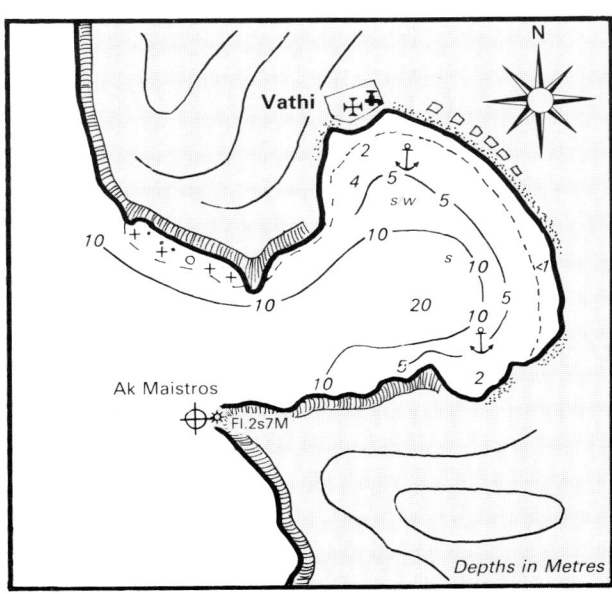

ORMOS VATHI
36°55'·5N 24°41'·1E (Fl.2s7M)

bows-to the quay. There are a number of coves on the S side where a yacht can also anchor. There are strong gusts from the *meltemi* into the bay, but the holding is good and no sea enters.

Water near the church. Tavernas ashore. The surroundings here are wonderful, the water a translucent turquoise, and there are several tavernas on the beach for a run ashore.

FIKIADHA
Admiralty chart no. 1825

A deserted inlet immediately S of Vathi which offers reasonable shelter from winds N through E to S. Open to the W only. Anchor in the inlet with a long line ashore or go bows-to the short pier below the chapel (1·5 metre depths at the extremity). The bottom is sand and mud with some rock, not everywhere good holding. Apart from the chapel the inlet is quite deserted, magnificently so.

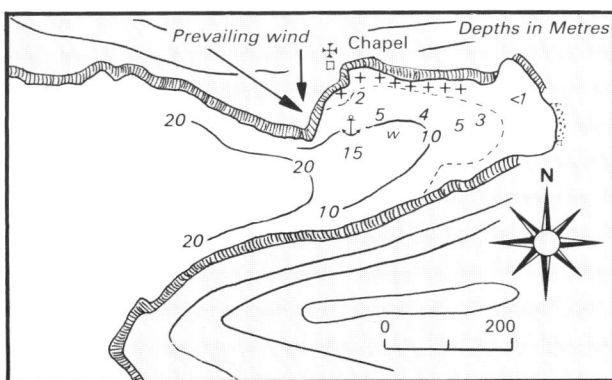

FIKIADHA
36°54'·3N 24°42'·3E

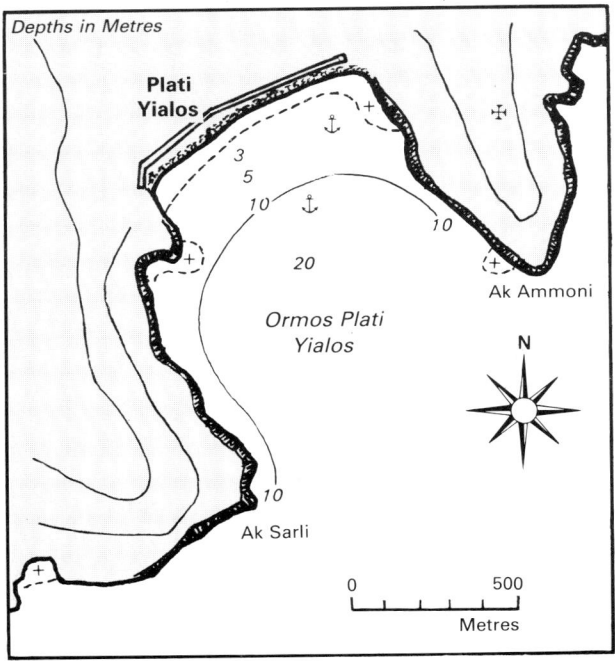

ORMOS PLATI YIALOS
36°55'·5N 24°44'E

PLATI YIALOS
Admiralty chart no. 1825

A U-shaped bay on the SE coast. Good shelter from the *meltemi* although there are strong gusts into the bay. Anchor off the NE corner in 5–7 metres. There are 2 metre depths approximately 80 metres off the beach. The bottom is sand and rock, not everywhere good holding. Tavernas and hotels on the beach.

FAROS (Pharos)
Admiralty chart no. 1825

An inlet near the SE tip of Sifnos providing good shelter from the *meltemi*. Open only to the S. The church on Ak Petalos, on the W side of the entrance, and the light structure on Ak Stavros, on the E side of the entrance, are conspicuous. Anchor off the village in 3–12 metres. There is a short quay in the NE corner of the bay where a few yachts may be able to go bows-to. Alternatively anchor in the coves on the W and E side of the entrance. The bottom is sand and weed – good holding once through the weed. Good shelter from the *meltemi* although there are strong gusts into the bay.

Tavernas at the head of the bay and limited provisions. A number of villas and small hotels have been built around the adjacent coastline – mostly frequented by the young. The bay, hemmed in by high land, is a wonderful place with good swimming in the clear water and good snorkelling around the adjacent coast.

Sifnos. Faros looking NE.

KASTRO

An open cove under the medieval village on the slopes above. The cove lying immediately N of Ak Miti is suitable only in calm weather, being entirely open to the prevailing summer northerlies. Anchor in 3–4 metres off the tiny beach and take a long line ashore. The bottom is sand and weed, mostly adequate holding.

There is a hamlet by the beach and a track leading up to the fascinating huddle of medieval houses perched on the steep slopes. If the weather does not permit a visit by yacht then take a bus or taxi from Kamares to Apollonia and from there to Kastro.

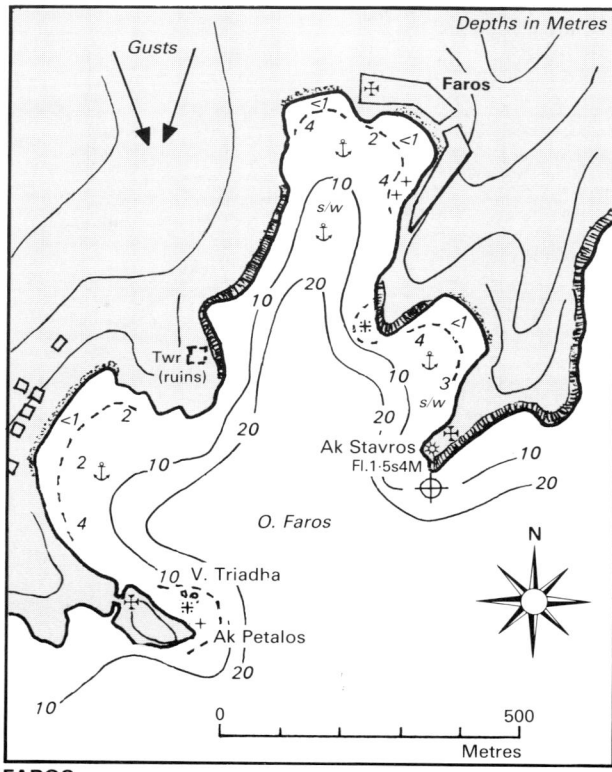

FAROS
36°56′·3N 24°45′·4E (Ak Stavros light)

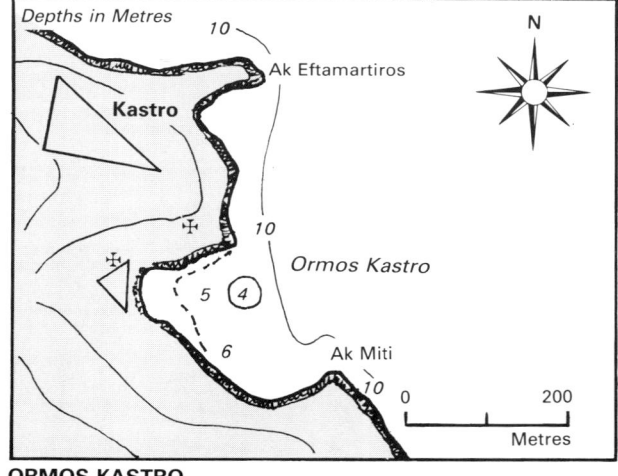

ORMOS KASTRO
36°58′·3N 24°45′·1E

Andiparos

(Anti-Paros)

The island of Andiparos lies close off the SW side of Paros, separated by a narrow shallow channel. It is low-lying (299 metres/981ft at the summit in the middle) and barren. The village of Andiparos lies on the east coast near the narrowest part of the channel. Near the south end of the channel there is a deep cave containing a small chapel and spectacular stalactites and stalagmites. Excursions from Andiparos village and Paroikia by tripper boat.

The two islands to the south of Andiparos, Nisis Dhespotico and Nisis Strongilo, are barren and uninhabited.

NISIS DHESPOTICO

On the S side of this island there is a deserted bay offering good shelter from the *meltemi*. Open only to the S.

ORMOS DHESPOTICO

The large bay between Nisis Dhespotico and Andiparos. It is protected on the N and E by Andiparos and on the S and W by Nisis Dhespotico and the islet of Tsimindri in the NW. The channel on the N side of Nisis Tsimindri has less than one metre depths. The channel on the S side of

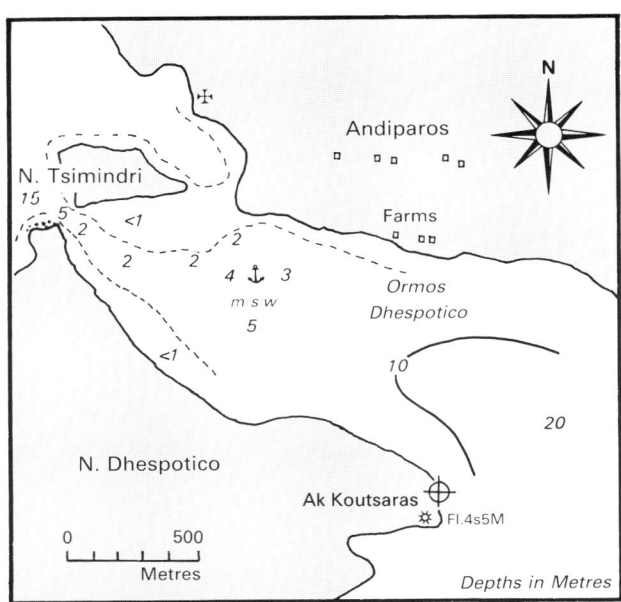

ORMOS DHESPOTICO 36°57'·5N 25°02'E (Ak Koutsaras light)

Tsimindri has 2 metre depths in the fairway. It should be attempted in calm weather only with someone up front conning you through.

Anchor in 2–4 metres where convenient on the N side. The bottom is sand and weed – good holding. In the 16th and 17th centuries the bay was a laying-

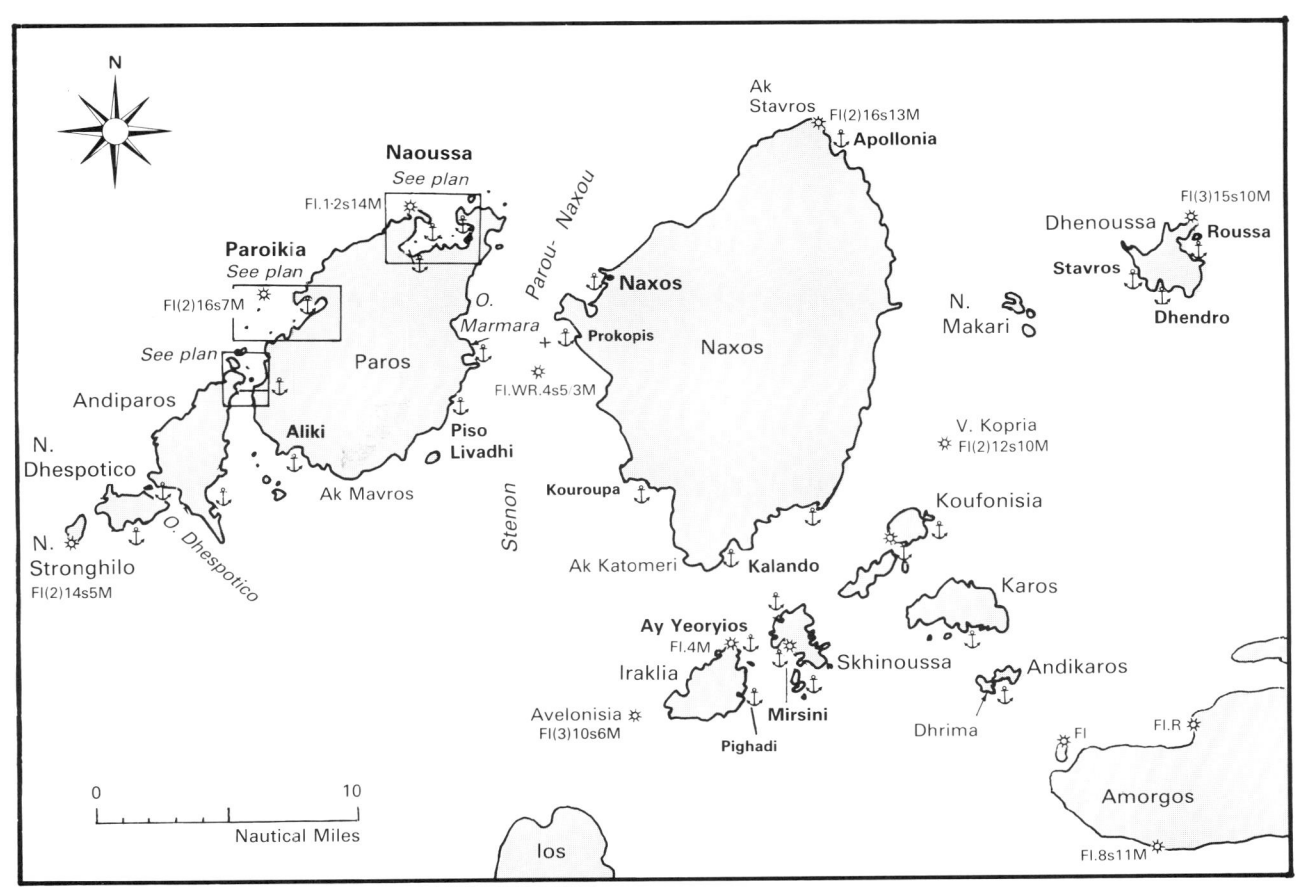

ANDIPAROS, PAROS, NAXOS AND ADJACENT ISLANDS

up port for pirate galleys. Now there are only a few houses and farms on the Andiparos side and a few tripper boats which come here in summer. Out of season it is a wonderful deserted place, attractive in a bleak sort of way.

STENON ANDIPAROU (Anti-Paros Channel)
Admiralty chart no. 1832
Imray-Tetra chart no. G33

The narrow channel between Nisos Andiparos and Nisos Paros running approximately N to S.

Yachts normally use the passage on the E side of Remmatonisi known as the '14-foot passage' from the original survey by Commander Graves in 1842. The channel should only be attempted by day with due care and attention. Remmatonisi and the coast of Paros are fringed with above- and below-water rocks and with the *meltemi* there are strong gusts down the channel raising a short disturbed sea. A deep-draught yacht should not attempt the channel and small to medium-sized yachts should do so with someone up front conning you through and one eye on the depth-sounder. A yacht attempting the passage for the first time should do so in calm weather if possible when the reefs fringing the passage are easily seen. With the *meltemi*, identifying the green of the safe passage and the brown of rocks in the underwater mosaic becomes more difficult.

The channel on the W side of Remmatonisi can also be used by shallow-draught yachts with due care and attention although there are less depths than on the E side.

Note Recent charts show the deeper passage to be on the W side of Remmatonisi, but in my experience the passage on the E side is better. If anyone out there wants to survey either passage again in calm weather, please let me know the results.

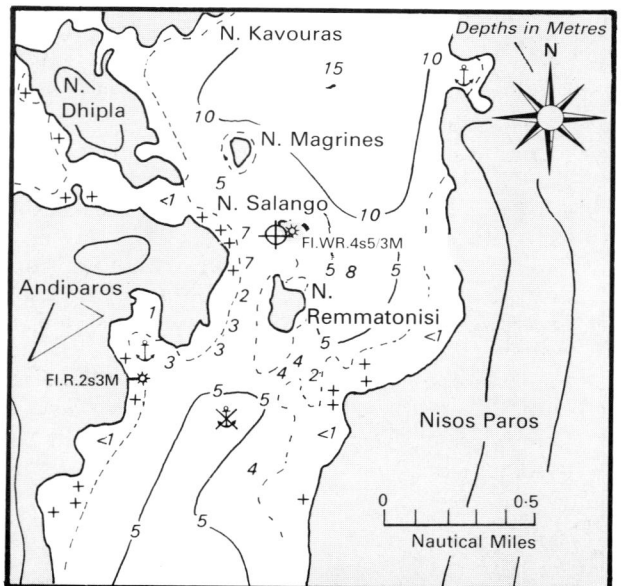

STENON ANDIPAROU (ANDIPAROS CHANNEL)
('14 foot passage') 37°02'·9N 25°05'·3E (N. Salango light)

ANDIPAROS

In the cove off the village on the W side of Andiparos channel a yacht can find some shelter from the *meltemi*. Anchor in 2–3 metres on a sandy bottom. There are 2 metre depths at the extremity of the short pier but this is used by the local ferry and fishing boats. Several tavernas on the waterfront and limited provisions can be found in the village.

Around the southern end of the channel there are numerous enchanting coves to be explored in calm weather. The shallow water and sandy bottom produce those wonderful blues and greens so often reproduced on postcards.

Paros

A large oval island which is essentially one mountain with two peaks: Mt Ayios Ilias (771 metres/2530ft) to the NW and Mt Karamboli (747 metres/2450ft) to the SE. The land slopes down evenly from the two peaks to the sea. The land is mostly barren and burnt rock with few trees. The port and capital is Paroikia on the NW coast.

The island was colonised early on by the Ionians from Asia Minor. In the 7th century BC the new Parians sent a party to colonise Thasos. Archilochus, the lyric satirist credited with inventing Iambic verse, was born on Paros and accompanied the colonizing party to Thasos. Ernle Bradford relates some amusing details about the poet: he was thrown out of Sparta for his 'cowardice and licentious character' and when fighting the Thracians admitted on one occasion to throwing away his shield and running away. Unfortunately this likable muse was killed whilst fighting the neighbouring Naxians. During the Persian invasions Paros sided with the Persians and with their defeat was consequently subdued. and became subject to Athens. In the Middle Ages the island was colonised by the Venetians until falling to the Turks in 1537.

In ancient times Parian marble was famous. The marble was called *Lychnites* – won by lamplight – as it was mined underground in tunnels. Because the marble was difficult to mine, the mines were abandoned after classical times and were last used in 1844 when marble was required for Napoleon's tomb. The mines and tunnels can still be seen today. Parian wine was also famous in antiquity and today the red wine made on the island is passably palatable. Paros is a popular tourist island, Paroikia fairly bulges at the seams in summer, and consequently facilities are well developed.

Ak Ay Fokas (light structure and church conspicuous), the N entrance point to Ormos Paroikia looking NW.

Ormos Paroikia looking SW. *Nigel Patten.*

PAROIKIA
Admiralty chart no. 1832

Approach

Conspicuous In the approaches to Paroikia there are a number of islands and reefs encircling the bay. From the N these are: Portes, two in number and looking like a pair of bookends; Petrokaravo, an almost submerged rock difficult to identify in rough seas; Vouves, low with a reef off the NE end and a reef with 3 metres over it 0·2 miles to the SW; Nisidhes Ay Spiridhonos, high and jagged (with a white chapel on one) except for the easternmost islet which is low; and Mavro Tourlos off the N end of Nisis Kavouras, high and jagged. Further into the bay, Kaki Skala and Peponas are low and the reef approximately in the middle of the bay is conspicuous with a prominent light structure on it. The white houses of Paroikia are easily seen once into the bay. A white church with a blue cupola is conspicuous on Ak Ay Fokas. The harbour off Paroikia is easily identified when close in.

By night Use the light on Portes (Fl(2)16s7M), on Ak Ay Fokas (Fl.3s6M) and on Ifalos Paroikias, the reef in the middle of Ormos Paroikias (Q.WRG.3-2M red sector covers 090°-124°/green sector covers 026°-056°). Street lights illuminate the ferry quay.

Dangers

1. Care is needed of the reef and above-water rock just N of Nisidhes Ay Spiridhonos and of the shoal water just N of Vouves in the approaches to Ormos Paroikias.
2. Care must be taken of the reef and shoal water extending out from Ak Ay Fokas. There are depths of 3 metres or less some 300 metres S of the cape.
3. Care is needed of a reef running out from the coast on the S side of the entrance to Ormos Paroikias.
4. Care is needed of underwater debris lying off the headland opposite the harbour at Paroikia.

Mooring

Berth stern-to or bows-to in the inner harbour or in calm weather off the outside of the mole. The bottom is mud and weed, mostly good holding.

253

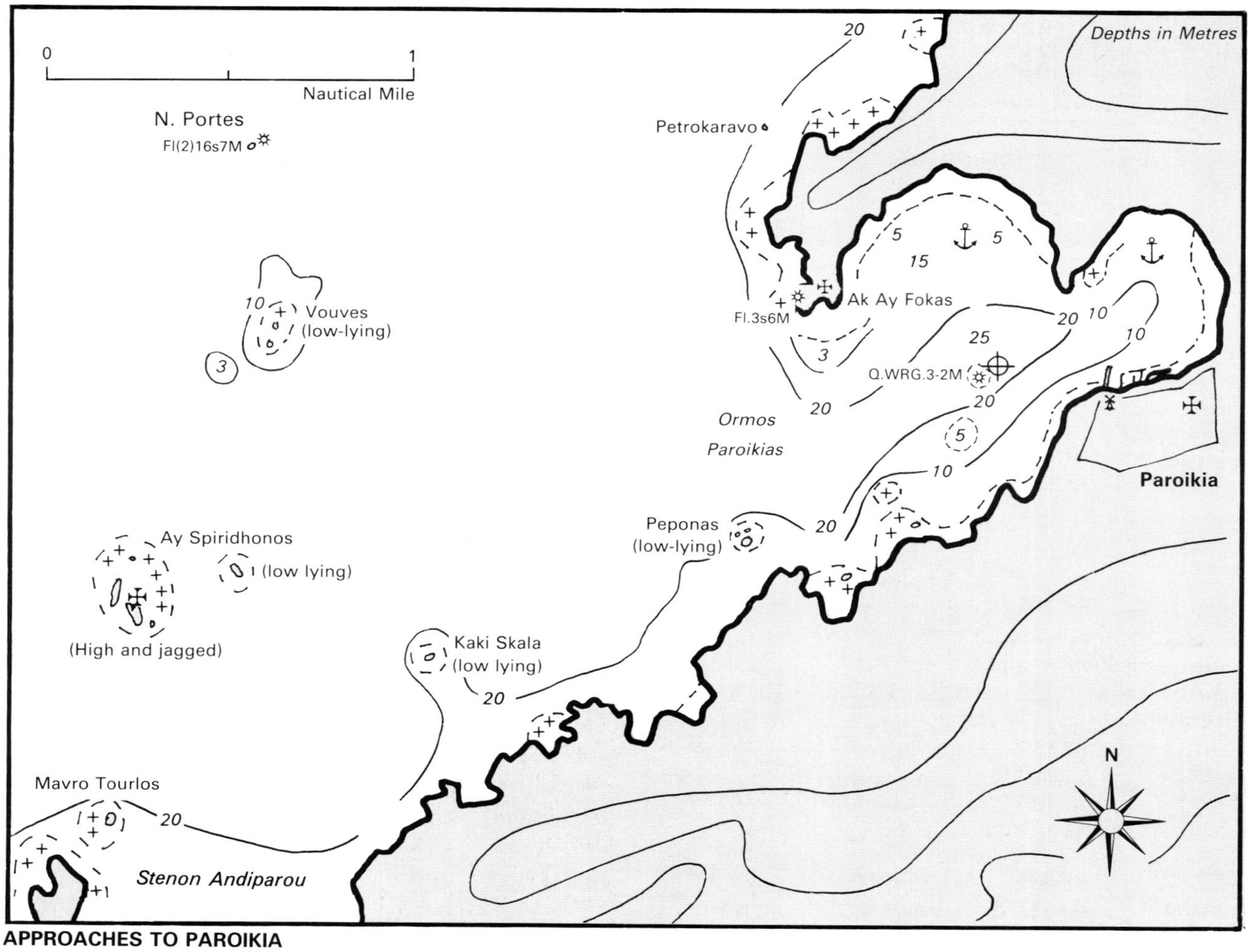

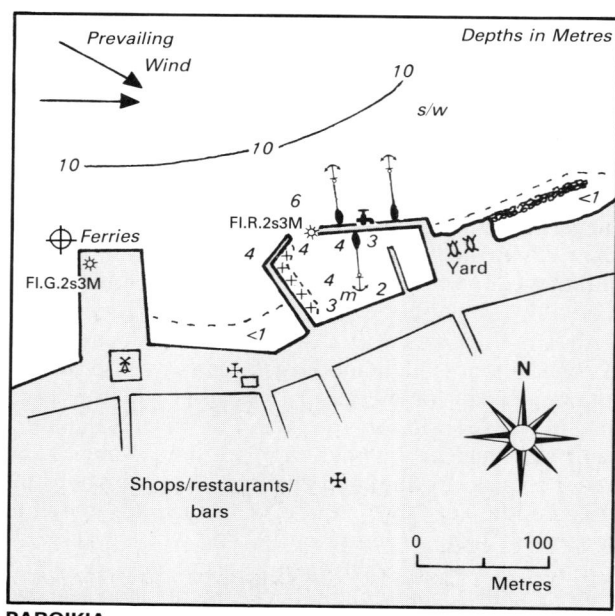

APPROACHES TO PAROIKIA
37°05'·3N 25°09'·1E (Ifalos Paroikia)

Shelter Excellent shelter inside the harbour. If the inner harbour is crowded and the *meltemi* makes berthing on the outside of the moles impossible, it is best to anchor in one of the bays to the N of the harbour. The NE bay is best.

Authorities Port police and customs.

Anchorage A yacht can anchor in either of the two bays on the N side of Ormos Paroikias. The bay in the NE affords the best shelter from the *meltemi*. Anchor in 4–6 metres on sand, mud and weed, good holding once through the weed.

Facilities

Water On the quay once the 'water man' is located.
Fuel On the outskirts of town. A mini-tanker can deliver to the harbour.
Repairs Some mechanical repairs possible. General hardware.
Provisions Good shopping for all provisions in the town. Ice available.
Eating out Good tavernas of all types. I favour some of the local tavernas in the streets behind the harbour, but there are all sorts of other tavernas in town, even a Vietnamese restaurant.
Other PO. OTE. Banks. Greek gas and *Camping Gaz*. Hire cars, motorbikes and bicycles. Buses to the

other villages on the island. Ferries to Piraeus, Rhodes, Iraklion and nearby Cyclades islands.

PAROIKIA
37°05'·3N 25°09'·1E (Fl.G.2s3M)

Paroikia harbour looking NE from the town quay.

General

Built on a gentle slope beside the sea with steep slopes behind, Paroikia is typically Cycladic – houses, shops, churches are dazzling white cubes with bougainvillea and wisteria providing splashes of natural colour. The old quarter around the 13th-century *Kastro* is an intriguing place full of narrow winding alleys and archways, stone houses and shops with wooden balconies.

Paroikia possesses the finest church in the Aegean, the Katapoliani (Ekatontepiliani). The name is said to mean 'the church of the 100 doors', but more probably means simply 'below the town'. The church is in fact three churches under one roof and it is well worth a visit for the beautiful interior – a mixture of the original and some recent renovation in neo-Byzantine style. On 15 August pilgrims converge on the church although the celebrations cannot compete with the Tiniot festival. Near the church the archaeological museum houses some interesting finds including a slab of the Parian Chronicle recording Greek history from pre-Homeric times and some sculptures in Parian marble.

The harbour is busy in the summer with ferries constantly coming and going bringing throngs of holidaymakers to the main port. The town resounds to the babble of different languages, the entreaties of waiters wanting your custom, and the click of camera shutters, and no wonder – some of the streets ending literally at the sea on the W of the town rival those in Mikonos for wonderful Cycladic architecture.

NAOUSA
Admiralty chart no. 1832

Approach

This large much-indented bay lies on the N end of Paros between Ak Korakas and the islet of Gaidhouronisi.

Conspicuous The white lighthouse on Ak Korakos is conspicuous and from the entrance to the bay the factory buildings on the S side of Ormos Langeri, the

Cycladic windmill at Paroikia.

Ak Korakas and lighthouse on the W side of the entrance to Ormos Naousis looking SW.

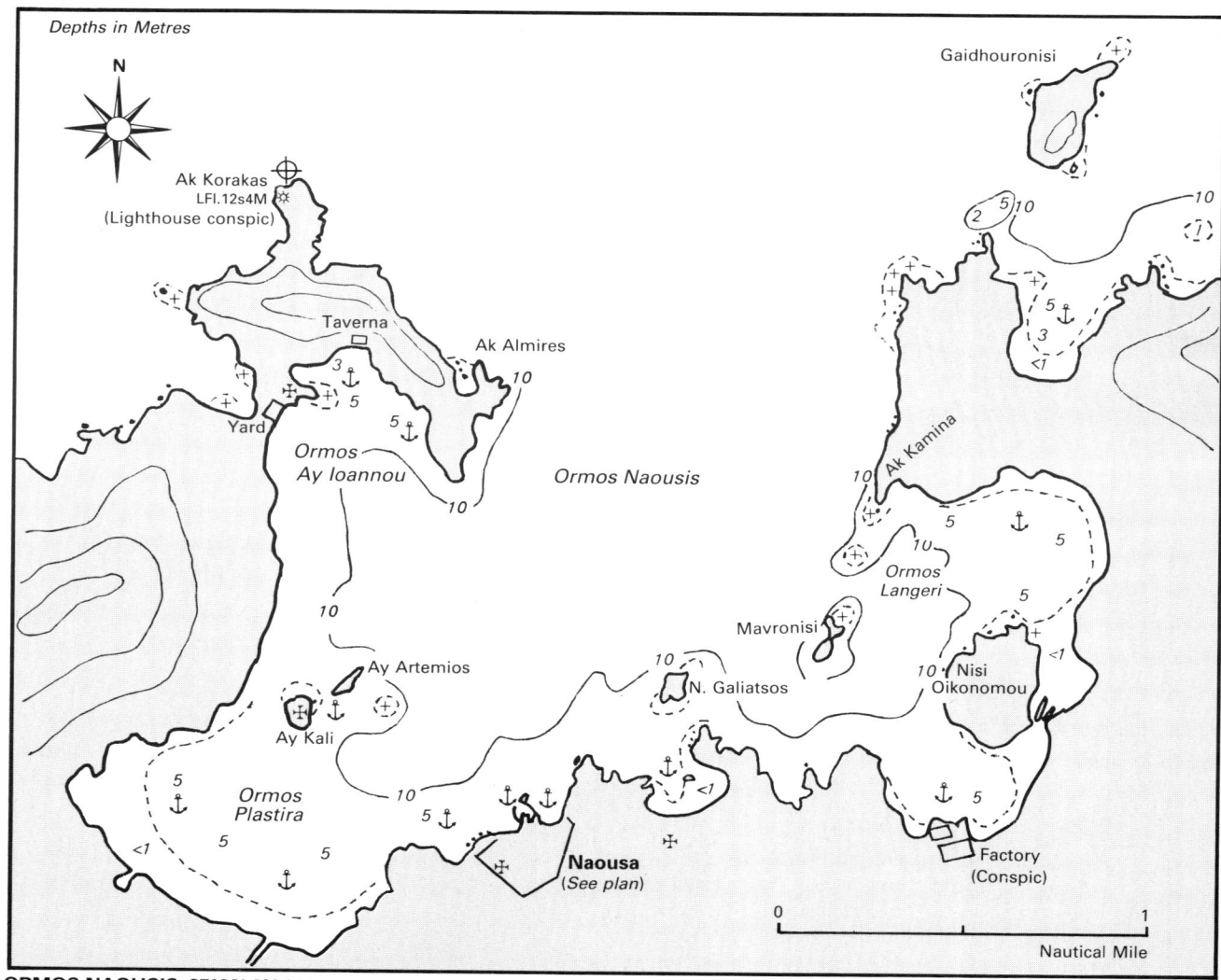

ORMOS NAOUSIS 37°09'·3N 25°13'·5E (Ak Korakas)

white houses of Naousa, and a large church with a red cupola behind the village, are conspicuous.

By night A night approach is not recommended. In good visibility use the light on Ak Korakos (LFl.12s14M) and the lights at the entrance to Naoussa harbour (Fl.R.1·5s3M and Fl.G.1·5s3M).

Dangers Care is needed of the above- and below-water rocks fringing the islets and shores of the large bay.

Mooring

There are numerous anchorages around the bay.

1. *Ormos Langeri* Care is needed of the reef in the N entrance to the bay midway between Mavronisi and Ak Kamina. Anchor at the N end where convenient in 4–10 metres on mud, sand, and weed, good holding. Good shelter from the *meltemi* tucked into the N end. Yachts can also anchor at the S end of the bay in calm weather or southerlies. The S end is somewhat spoiled now by the large factory buildings there.

2. *Ormos Ay Ioannou* Anchor where convenient at the N end in 3–10 metres. The bottom is mud, sand and weed, good holding. Good shelter from

the *meltemi*. A small chapel in the NW corner of the bay is conspicuous and nearby there is a small boatyard. This anchorage is idyllic: sun-baked rock eroded into wonderful shapes, clear turquoise water, a small white chapel perched on the rock near the water, even the boatyard with bright *caïques* hauled out fits into the scene, so consequently it is popular in the summer. A taverna opens in the summer.

3. *Ormos Plastira* In calm weather anchor where convenient. With the *meltemi* some shelter can be found anchored in 3–4 metres under Nisis Ay Kali.

4. *Naousa* Most of the space in the harbour is taken up with local boats and tripper boats. A few yachts can go stern-to or bows-to the W breakwater with a long line ashore. The bay immediately E of the Venetian fort is reported to be a good anchorage close to the facilities at Naoussa. Yachts also anchor off just W of the harbour in 4–10 metres on sand and weed, good holding. The *meltemi* doesn't normally blow home here although then again it can at times.

Authorities Port police at Naousa.

Entrance to Naousa harbour looking SE.

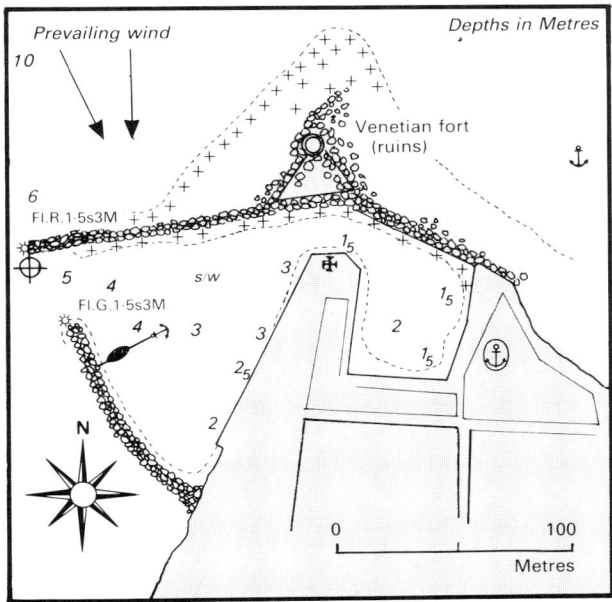

NAOUSA
37°07'·6N 25°14'·2E (Fl.R.3M)

Facilities

Water Water Limited amounts locally.
Fuel Can be delivered by mini-tanker to the harbour.
Repairs Minor repairs at Naousa. A yacht may be able to be hauled at the yard in Ormos Ay Ioannou.
Provisions Most provisions can be found at Naousa.
Eating out Good tavernas at Naousa.
Other PO. OTE. Bank. Greek gas. Hire motorbikes and bicycles. Bus to Paroikia.

General

The bay is a much indented amoeboid shape of sun-baked rock enclosing clear blue and turquoise water. Much of the rock has been sculpted into weird and wonderful shapes that give the bay a desolate feel. Although popular in the summer, there is nearly always somewhere to tuck yourself into away from the others. Out of season it is positively lonely.

Naousa was a small fishing village that has grown into an attractive tourist resort. The tavernas and bars clustered around the edge of the inner basin provide a pleasant spot to while away an evening. A windsurfing school operates from a hotel on the E side of the bay.

ORMOS MARMARA

A large bay on the E coast. Although it looks as if there should be good shelter here, the *meltemi* blowing down the strait between Paros and Naxos sends a swell in. Anchor in the NW corner in light N winds or calm weather.

PISO LIVADHI (Marpissa, Tsipidho Bay)

Approach

A small harbour approximately 1½ miles SSW of Ormos Marmara.

Conspicuous A peak with a conspicuous white building on the summit immediately N of Piso Livadhi is easily identified. Closer in a cluster of villas and small hotels around the coast will be seen. The breakwater is easily identified once up to the bay.

By night There are no lights and a night approach is not recommended (see Dangers below).

Dangers A reef and shoal water extends E from the breakwater for about 250 metres. Keep well off and approach the bay from the SE.

Mooring

Go stern-to or bows-to the breakwater with a long line to it. Some care is needed of permanent moorings fouling the bottom. The bottom is sand and weed, good holding. When the ferry is not due in (it normally arrives in the morning and early evening, but does not stay for long) small yachts can go bows-to the short pier where there are 1·5–2 metre depths.

Shelter Reasonable shelter from the *meltemi* although with a prolonged blow there can be a surge in here.

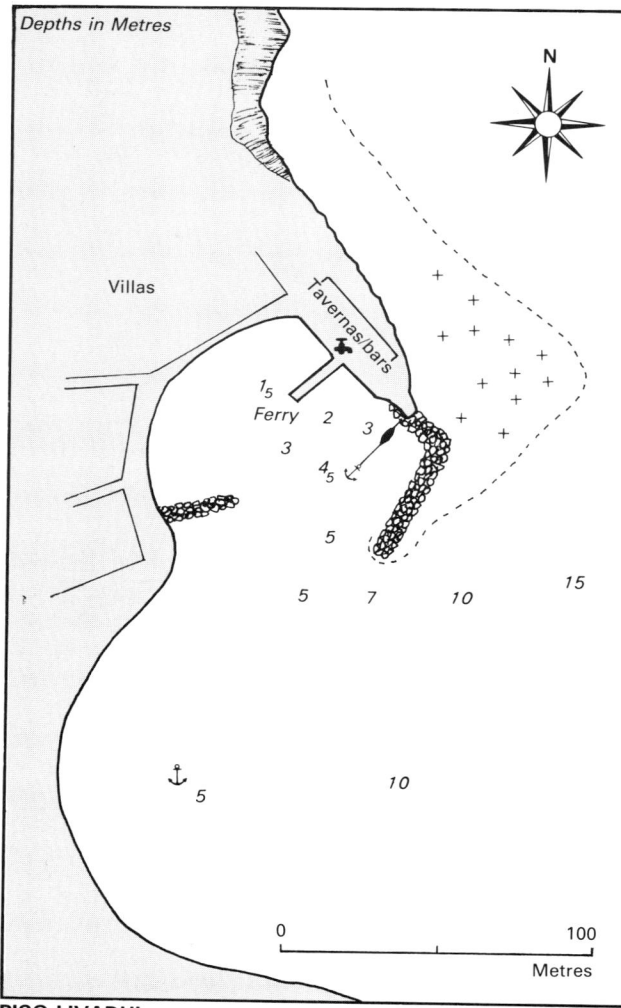

Depths in Metres

Villas

Tavernas/bars

1·5
Ferry 2 3
3
4·5
5

5 7 10 15

5 10

0   100
Metres

PISO LIVADHI
37°02′N 25°15′·5E

Open to the SE when it is uncomfortable and can become untenable.

Anchorage In calm weather a yacht can anchor in the S part of the bay.

Note Yachts should not anchor in the vicinity of the entrance where the ferry needs room to manoeuvre.

Facilities

Water At the root of the mole.
Provisions Some provisions available in the village.
Eating out Several tavernas around the waterfront with wonderful views over the harbour and the strait.
Other Ferry to Naxos and Amorgos.

General

The small village has a modest amount of tourism in the summer and is a convivial place much removed from the hustle and bustle of Paroikia. The setting is wonderful under the slopes of Paros on the edge of Stenon Parou-Naxou. The anchorage in the S part of the bay makes a good lunch stop in calm weather.

ALIKI

A bay on the SW coast of Paros lying 2 miles NW of Ak Mavros. Anchor in 2–3 metre depths in the bay. Sandy bottom. There are a number of piers on the E side of the bay, but there are insufficient depths off them. (The middle pier has 1·5 metre depths at the extremity, but the others have less than one metre.) A hotel and a taverna ashore.

STENON PAROU-NAXOU (Paros-Naxos Strait)

This strait separating Paros and Naxos is fringed by rocks and reefs. There are also two reefs in the fairway: Ifalos Kalipso (Vrakhoi Tsamban), and Vrakhoi Amaridhes, which has a conspicuous light structure on it (Fl.WR.4s5/3M red sector covers 185°-015°) and a wreck at its S extremity, though the latter has now all but disappeared underwater. With the *meltemi* a current sets to the S at about ½–1½ knots, although with southerlies there is a N-going current. These currents also affect the group of islands to the S of Naxos, but are much modified by the channels between the islands and it is difficult to determine precise directions and rates.

Naxos

The largest and most fertile of the Cyclades. From seaward the west coast appears rocky and bare but inland the island is wooded and cultivated. The island is mountainous throughout with two high peaks: the summit Mt Zeus lies just to the south of the middle of the island and is 1084 metres (3308ft) high, and 6 miles to the north Mt Korna is 1065 metres (3250ft) high. In the interior valleys the slopes are terraced and olives, citrus orchards and cypresses grow. The lower plains are cultivated with figs, vines and market gardens.

Naxos is the island where Theseus abandoned Ariadne on his way back to Athens from Crete. It was with Ariadne's help that Theseus penetrated the labyrinth and slew Ariadne's half-brother the Minotaur. Ariadne, in love with Theseus and he apparently in love with her, sailed away from Crete and the first place they landed at was Naxos. Just why Theseus abandoned her has always puzzled classical scholars, but it at least provided the material for one of Catullus' best long poems:

'...Here are the never silent sands of Naxos
here Theseus vanishes towards the north,
a woman watches from the empty beach
unflagging grief in her heart

Ariadne doesn't yet believe, quite,
she is witnessing what her eyes see –
she's only just woken from a trap
(of sleep)
found herself alone on the island...'

Catullus transl. by Peter Whigham

Luckily Dionysus landed on the island and they fell in love at first sight. They appear to have been happy together and Ariadne bore the god many

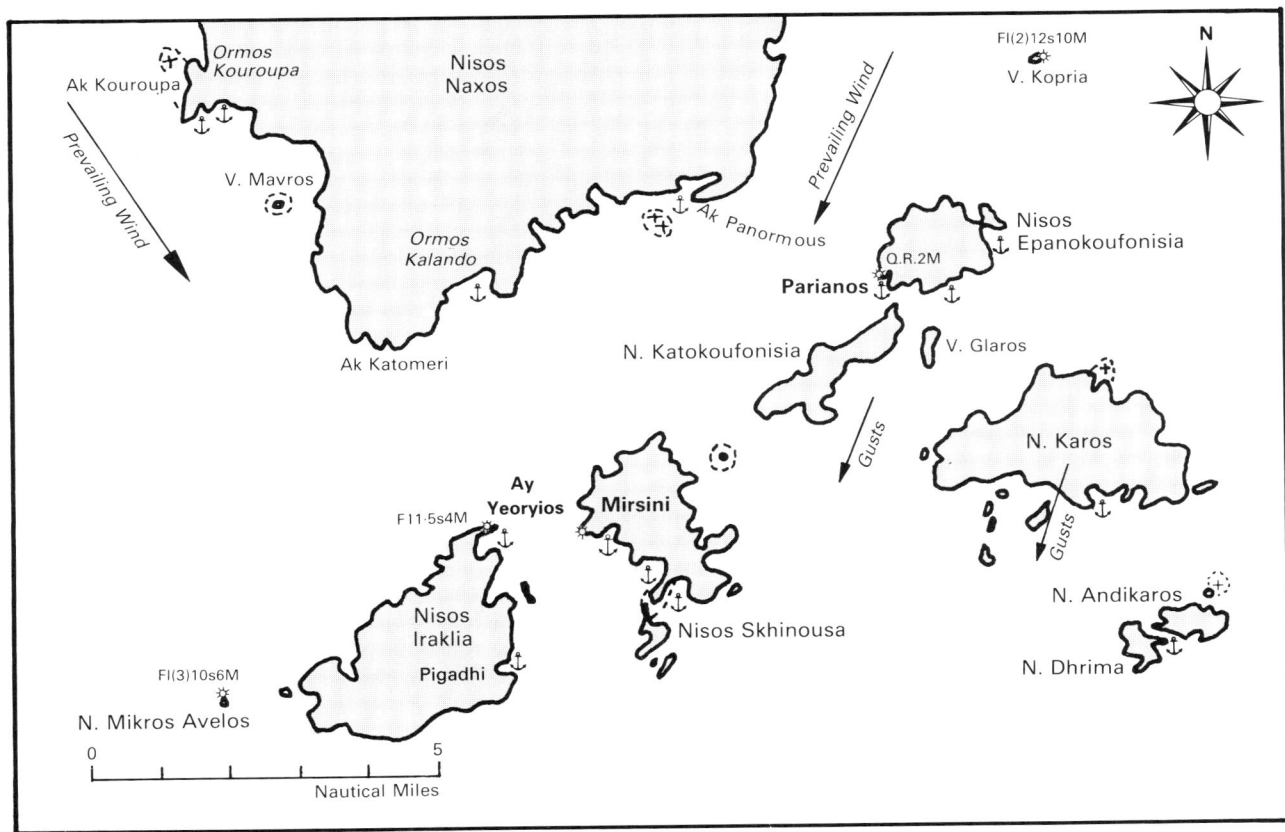

Map labels:
Ak Kouroupa — Ormos Kouroupa — Nisos Naxos — Fl(2)12s10M — V. Kopria — N
V. Mavros — Prevailing Wind — Prevailing Wind
Ormos Kalando — Ak Panormous — Q.R.2M — Nisos Epanokoufonisia — Parianos
Ak Katomeri — N. Katokoufonisia — V. Glaros
Gusts — N. Karos
Ay Yeoryios — Mirsini — Gusts
F11·5s4M — N. Andikaros
Nisos Iraklia — Nisos Skhinousa — N. Dhrima
Fl(3)10s6M — Pigadhi
N. Mikros Avelos
0 — 5
Nautical Miles

NAXOS AND ADJACENT ISLANDS

children. Dionysus, the god of the vine, appears to have been a gentler, less raucous god than his Roman namesake, Bacchus, and he blessed Naxos with great fertility and good wine. Today Naxian white wine is still quite palatable, though perhaps not good enough for Dionysus if he is around.

Naxos was sacked by the Persians in 490 BC and thereafter the island steadfastly aided the Athenians. In 1207 the Venetian adventurer Marco Sanudo occupied the island and it remained a Venetian duchy for 300 years. The succeeding dynasty of Sanudo, the Crispi, ruled over most the Cyclades until Naxos fell to the Turks in 1566. It became Greek in 1832.

If you decide to leave your yacht at Naxos town, the only really safe harbour on the island, then the magnificent interior is well worth visiting. The young Byron on visiting Naxos wanted to buy the island and return here to retire. In Apollonia a large unfinished marble statue some 10·5 metres high lies in the marble bed it was carved from. It was intended for Delos, but probably it was decided that the marble was of poor quality. There are also a number of Byzantine churches with good frescoes.

NAXOS
Admiralty chart no. 1832
Imray-Tetra chart no. G33

Approach

Conspicuous Ak Moungri to the SW of the town has a conspicuous conical peak on it. Closer in the hump of white buildings of Naxos town and a marble arch on Nisis Vakkhos (joined by a causeway to Naxos) will be seen. The breakwater and harbour are easily identified and there is usually a ferry or two in the harbour or coming or going to aid identification.

By night The extremity of the breakwater is lit: Fl.WR.3s6/4M red sector covers 223°-139°.

Dangers
1. Care must be taken of Vrakhos Frouros, the reef lying approximately 1¼ miles WSW of the harbour and 0·3 miles N of Ak Moungri, the S extremity of Ormos Naxou. By day the reef, two rocks just above water surrounded by underwater rocks and shoal water, is easily identified in calm weather and there are no problems in passing between it and the cape. With any sea running the above-water rocks are more difficult to locate and it is prudent to go well outside them.
2. With the *meltemi* there are gusts and some swell at the entrance to the harbour.
3. A good lookout must be kept in the approaches to the harbour for the numerous ferries coming and going, often at considerable speed until right up to the harbour.

259

Approaches to Naxos harbour looking SE.

Mooring

There are several places a yacht can go depending on the wind direction and strength.

1. Anchor under the breakwater in the NE corner. There are convenient depths of 4–7 metres; take care to avoid the 2 metre shoal shown on the plan. The bottom is sand, rock, and weed, good holding once the anchor bites properly. Good shelter from the *meltemi*. Southerlies send a swell in. The only disadvantage with this anchorage is the noisy disco on Vakkhos.
2. There may be a berth for small yachts in the old basin though normally it is crowded with local boats. Good shelter from the *meltemi*.
3. Go stern-to or bows-to in the new basin immediately S of the old basin. The bottom is uneven towards the shore, but in the rest of the basin there are mostly 2·5–3·5 metre depths. Shelter from the *meltemi* although there is a surge. In addition, the wash from the ferries and tripper boats penetrates into the basin so ensure you are pulled well off the quay. The bottom is sand and rock, not everywhere good holding.
4. Anchor and take a long line ashore on the NE side of the isthmus joining Nisis Vakkhos to Naxos. The bottom is sand, rock, and weed, good holding once the anchor is in. Open to the *meltemi* but sheltered from southerlies.

Shelter The best shelter from the *meltemi* is anchored under the outer breakwater. The *meltemi* causes a surge in the new S basin which makes it uncomfortable although tenable. In strong southerlies a yacht would be advised to anchor on the NE side of the isthmus.

Authorities Port police and customs.

Note The anchorage under the breakwater and in the new basin are much affected by the wash from the ferries and tripper boats.

Facilities

Water On the main ferry mole. and near the cafe/bar on Vakkhos. Showers and WC near the new basin.

Fuel Close to the root of the mole. A mini-tanker can deliver to the harbour.

Repairs Some mechanical repairs can be carried out. Hardware shops.

Provisions Good shopping for provisions in the town. Wine from the barrel. Ice available.

Eating out Good tavernas in the town.

Other PO. OTE. Banks. Greek gas and *Camping Gaz*. Hire cars, motorbikes and bicycles. Buses to the main villages on the island. Ferries to Piraeus, Rhodes, Iraklion and nearby Cyclades islands.

General

The town, built on a low hummock by the water, is a typically whitewashed Cycladic place with a smattering of Venetian here and there. I have been reprimanded for calling it 'somewhat scruffy' in earlier editions, but it has been cleaned up since then. The warren of alleys, arches and tunnels around the Venetian castle on the summit of the hill is the most fascinating part of the town. It was the up-market end of town and many of the entrances sport coats of arms from the time when Naxos ruled over the surrounding islands.

The marble arch on Nisis Vakkhos (or Bacchus) is part of a temple begun about 530 BC and never finished. The archaeological museum in the town houses early Cycladic finds, Mycenaean pottery and gold jewellery and classical finds. The museum was once a schoolhouse where the writer Nikos Kazantakis (best known for *Zorba the Greek*) taught for 12 years before returning to his native Crete.

Naxos town looking SE from the anchorage under the breakwater.

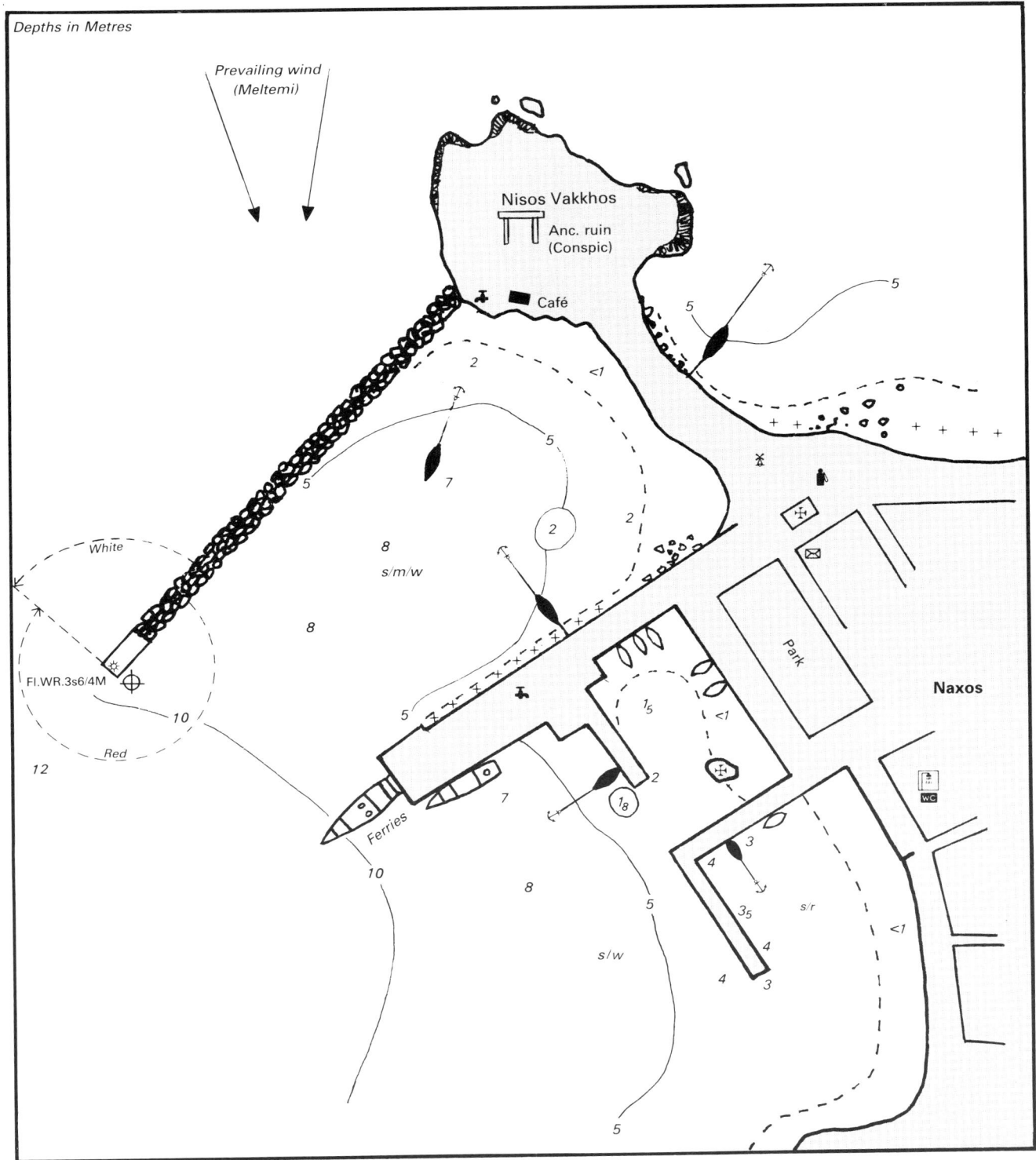

Depths in Metres

Prevailing wind
(Meltemi)

Nisos Vakkhos

Anc. ruin
(Conspic)

Café

Naxos

Park

White

Fl.WR.3s6/4M

Red

Ferries

s/m/w

s/r

s/w

NAXOS 37°06′·5N 25°22′·1E (Fl.WR.6/4M)

ORMOS AYIOS PROKOPIOU

Lies under the lee of Ak Prokopis about 3 miles S of Naxos. Anchor off in 6 metres. Sandy bottom. There is shelter from the *meltemi* but nearly always some swell in the bay.

Caution

1. Care must be taken of Ifalos Kalipso (Vrakhoi Tsamban) lying approximately 0·8 miles SW of Ak Prokopis.

2. Care must be taken of the reef lying 0·4 miles off Ay Nikolaos in the S of Ormos Prokopis.
3. Care must be taken of Vrakhoi Amaridhes already mentioned.
4. From a position roughly parallel to Vrakhoi Amaridhes and extending down to Ak Parthenos, above- and below-water rocks fringe the coast of Naxos up to just over a mile off.

The solitary arch of the temple remaining on Nisis Vakkhos.

ORMOS KOUROUPA (Ay Ioannis)

An open bay under Ak Kouroupa. A large unfinished hotel complex on Ak Kouroupa is conspicuous from seaward. Anchor off in 4–6 metres. There is a short pier, but it is rock-bound. The bottom is sand with some rocks – good holding. The *meltemi* is funnelled down the Paros-Naxos Strait and pushes a swell around the cape making it very uncomfortable.

ORMOS KALANDO

A bay on the SE coast about 1½ miles NE of Ak Katomeri. Anchor near the head of the bay in 3–6 metres. Sandy bottom. Good shelter from the *meltemi* although there are gusts into the bay. No facilities.

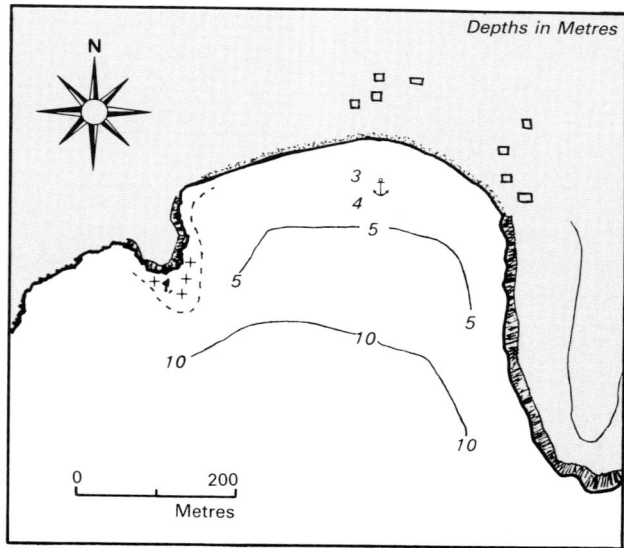

ORMOS KALANDO
36°56′N 25°28′·5E

APOLLONIA

A bight near the NE tip of Naxos. A short breakwater provides some protection from the *meltemi* although some swell is pushed around the end of it. Go bows-to the outer part of the breakwater with a long line to it. Reasonable protection from the *meltemi*.

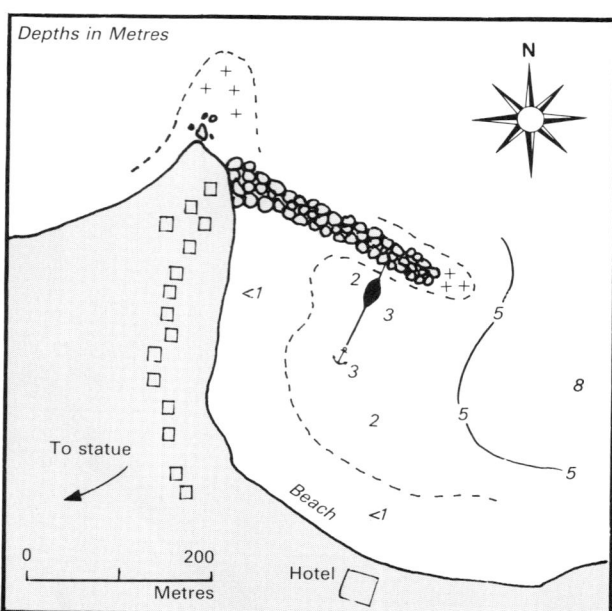

APOLLONIA
37°11′N 25°33′·3E

A small village ashore with several tavernas and a hotel. The unfinished statue of Apollo lies a short distance directly inland from the village.

Dhenoussa
(Dhonoussa)

A small high island (489 metres/1064ft) lying nine miles off the east coast of Naxos. There are three anchorages: Ormos Roussa on the NE corner, Ormos Dhendro on the south, and in calm weather off the village of Stavros.

ORMOS ROUSSA

A bay on the E coast of Dhenoussa partially sheltered by Nisis Skilonisi (Trigono). Although there is a narrow channel between Skilonisi and Dhenoussa with good depths, the prudent course is to enter the bay from the SE. The cove in the northern corner (5–6 metres) affords the best shelter from the *meltemi*, but the holding on a rocky bottom is not the best. It may be better to anchor on the W side of the bay in 3–5 metres where the holding is better. The anchorage is safe enough when the *meltemi* is blowing but gets very uncomfortable with the swell that rolls in.

Meagre provisions can sometimes be obtained from a 'shop' in a house near the shore.

ORMOS DHENDRO (Khendro)

A bay on the S coast of Dhenoussa lying immediately E of Ak Dhendro. A chapel is conspicuous on the cape. Care must be taken of the reef lying off the cape. Anchor near the head of the bay in 5–6 metres. Further into the bay (in 3–4 metres) lies a wreck. Good shelter from the *meltemi* although there are gusts into the bay.

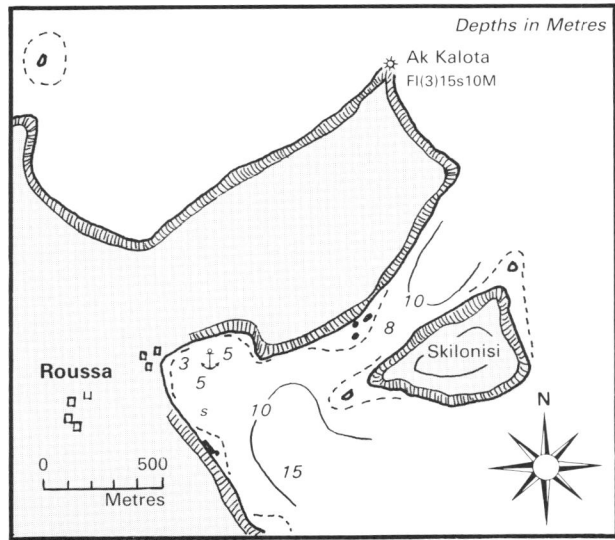

ORMOS ROUSSA
37°07'·4N 25°49'·8E

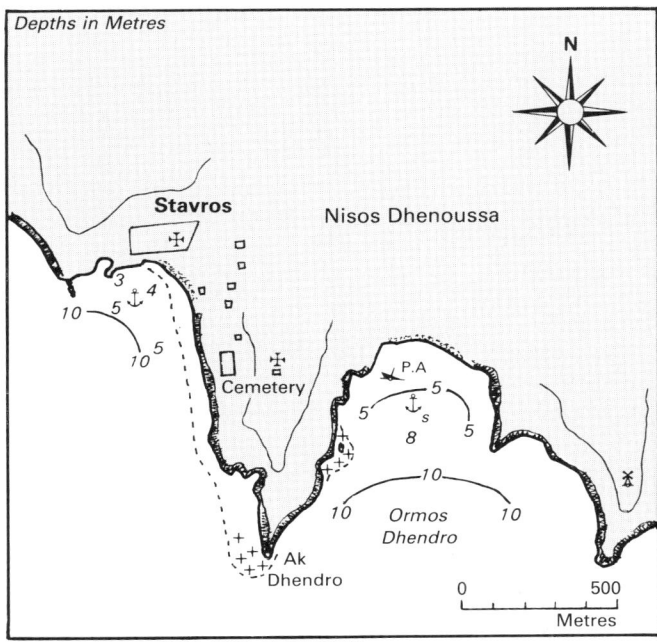

ORMOS DHENDRO AND STAVROS
37°05'·5N 25°48'·5E

STAVROS

A small village on the western side of Ak Dhendro. Anchor off the village in 4–5 metres. If there is room you can go bows-to the quay where there are 1·5 metre depths in the middle. Shelter here is not as good as in Ormos Dhendro, but is useful in calm weather or light northerlies. A taverna and café ashore. Limited provisions can be found, but the islanders are much dependent upon the ferry from Naxos for most things.

Iraklia

A small barren island lying 3 miles SSE of Ak Katomeri. There is a small hamlet at Ayios Yeoryios.

AYIOS YEORYIOS (Iraklia)

A deep inlet on the NE tip of Iraklia. The entrance is somewhat difficult to see from the N. The houses at the head of the bay can be seen from the entrance. Although open to the NE the *meltemi* does not always blow home although on other occasions it will do so. Anchor in 3–6 metres. There is just room for a small yacht to go bows-to inside the short mole. The bottom is sand with some rocks – good holding.

Taverna ashore. The small hamlet in the rocky bay is most attractive.

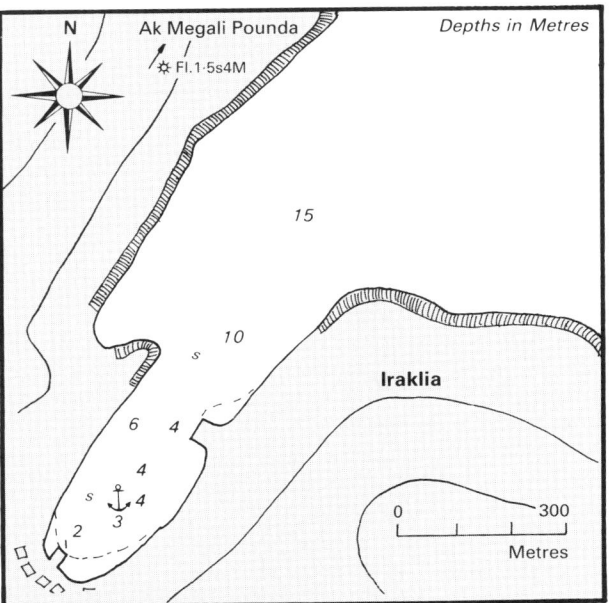

AYIOS YEORYIOS
36°52'·3N 25°28'·5E (Ak Megali Pounda light)

Ay Yeoryios on Nisis Iraklia looking NNE. *Nigel Patten.*

PIGADHI (Pegadi)

A deep inlet near the SE tip of Iraklia. Open to the ENE and consequently a swell rolls in with the *meltemi*. In calm weather it is an attractive fjord to visit. Anchor in 6–10 metres near the head of the bay. The bottom is sand with some rocks – reasonable holding.

Skhinousa

A small island one mile to the NE of Iraklia. There are a few houses at Mirsini and a small *chora* on the hill above. There are a number of attractive deserted coves around the island, their shelter depending on the wind direction. Nisis Agrilos lies off the SW side of Skhinoussa, but the passage between Agrilos and Skhinoussa is shallow and rock-bound.

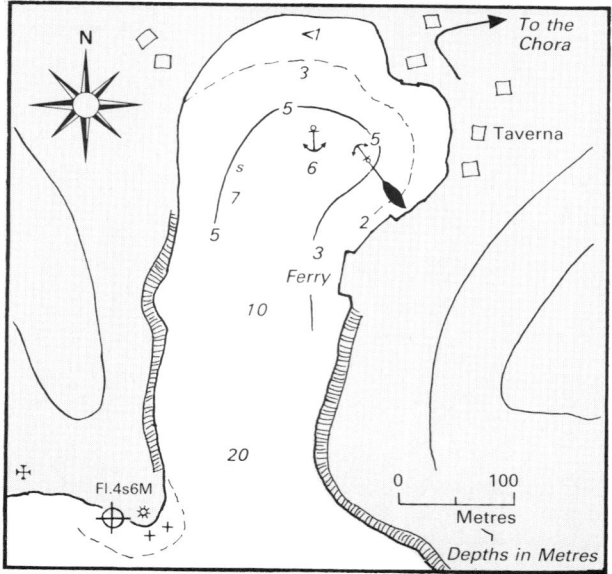

MIRSINI
36°51′·3N 25°30′·5E (Fl.4s6M)

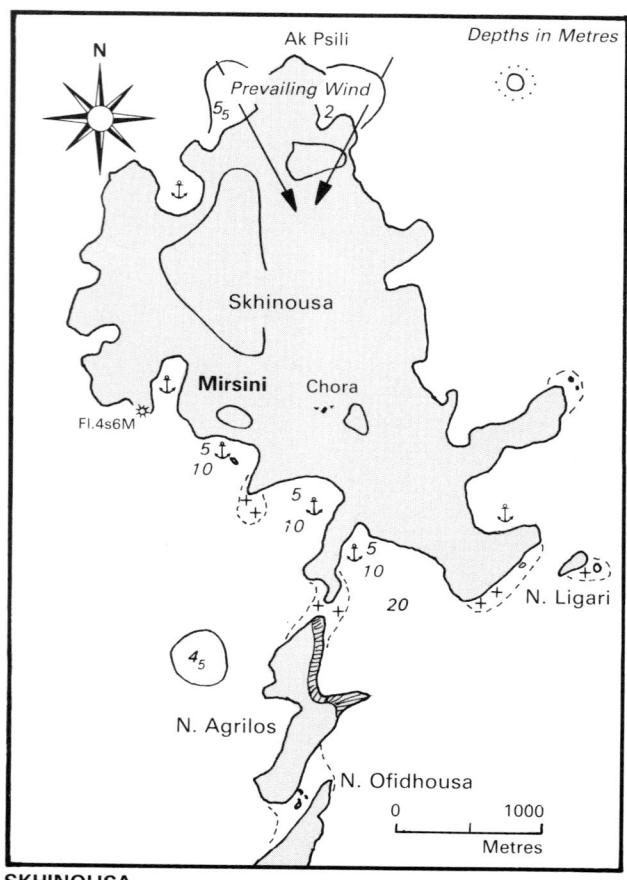

SKHINOUSA

MIRSINI (Myrseni)

Approach

A narrow inlet on the W side of Skhinousa, almost directly opposite Ayios Yeoryios on Iraklia. The entrance is difficult to locate until the small white chapel with a blue roof immediately due W of the entrance and the light structure are spotted. The entrance is lit Fl.4s6M, but a night approach needs care.

Skhinousa. The entrance to Mirsini looking NNW.

Mooring

Anchor in the bay in 5–8 metres. The bottom is sand and weed, not everywhere good holding. Small yachts can squeeze in bows-to just N of the ferry quay. Good shelter from the *meltemi* although there are gusts into the bay.

Facilities

Several tavernas on the shore. Ferry to Naxos and Amorgos.

General

A few tourists arrive here in the summer on the ferry, but most visitors arrive by yacht. The unspoiled *chora* on the hill above is quite untouched and a delight to visit. You will also find a few

Skhinousa. Mirsini looking ESE. *Nigel Patten.*

provisions there and a good old fashioned *cafeneion* where the loudest noise is the clack of counters from the old men playing backgammon.

ANCHORAGES S OF MIRSINI

To the SE of Mirsini are two bays offering some shelter from the *meltemi* although they are better visited in calm weather.

NISIS AGRILOS

The skinny islet running S from Skhinousa approximately a mile SSE of Mirsini. There is not a passage around the N end of the islet as stated in the Admiralty Pilot. The bay under the headland opposite the islet affords reasonable shelter from the *meltemi* in rugged but attractive surroundings.

KOUFONISIA

Two islands about one mile NE of Skhinousa: Lower (Kato) Koufonisia is the southwestern island while Upper (Epano) Koufonisia lies to the NE. There are three anchorages on Upper Koufonisia:

1. A bay on the NE tip of the island provides some shelter from the *meltemi* although a swell rolls in. Open to the E. Anchor in 3–5 metres. Sandy bottom. Deserted.
2. Off Koufonisia village. Anchor in the bay in 3-5 metres on a sandy bottom. Reasonable shelter from the *meltemi* but there is always a residual swell with the *meltemi* which causes yachts at anchor to roll horribly. A breakwater and quay have been built on the W side of the bay for the ferry. When the ferry is not in here a yacht can go stern or bows-to, but the swell causes awful snatching at the shore lines and it is not a comfortable place to be. Open S and E. Some provisions and tavernas ashore. A quaint OTE in the bottom of a village house.

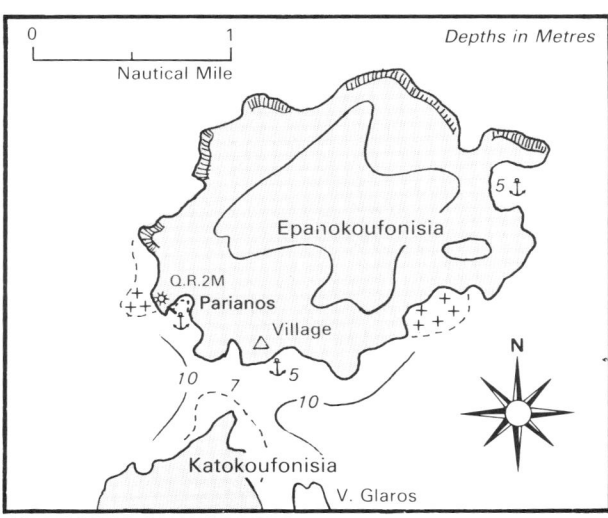

KOUFONISIA ANCHORAGES

3. *Parianos* A small harbour on the SW side of Epanokoufonisia. A mole closes off part of the inlet with 5–6 metre depths in the entrance and 3 metre depths in the middle. The end of the mole is lit Q.R.2M. A number of fishing boats are kept here on permanent moorings and the bottom is littered with permanent moorings. Anchor with a trip-line and you may also be able to pick up a mooring if one is free. It is possible to go bows-to the quay in a few places, but care is needed of rock ballasting along the quay and permanent moorings off it. Good shelter from the *meltemi* although there are gusts. The bay is a pleasant 20 minute stroll from the village. The fishing harbour has a bleak but beautiful aspect to it – and the water is clean enough to swim in.

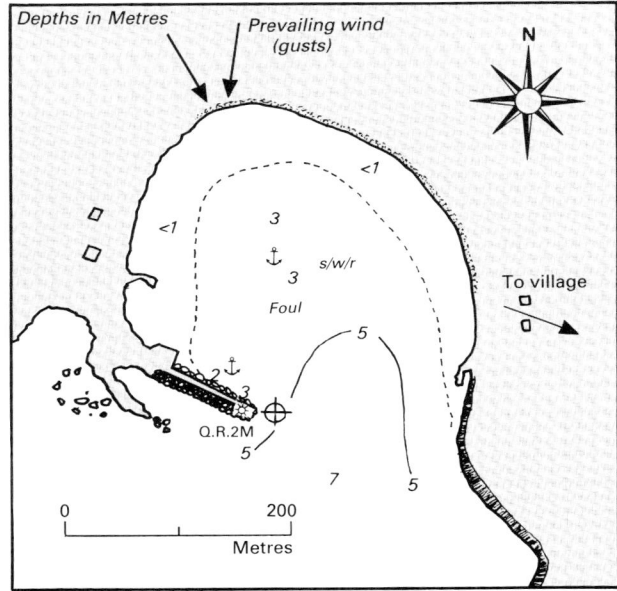

PARIANOS (KOUFONISIA)
36°56′·1N 25°35′·5E (Q.R.2M)

Koufonisia. Parianos harbour looking W. *Nigel Patten*.

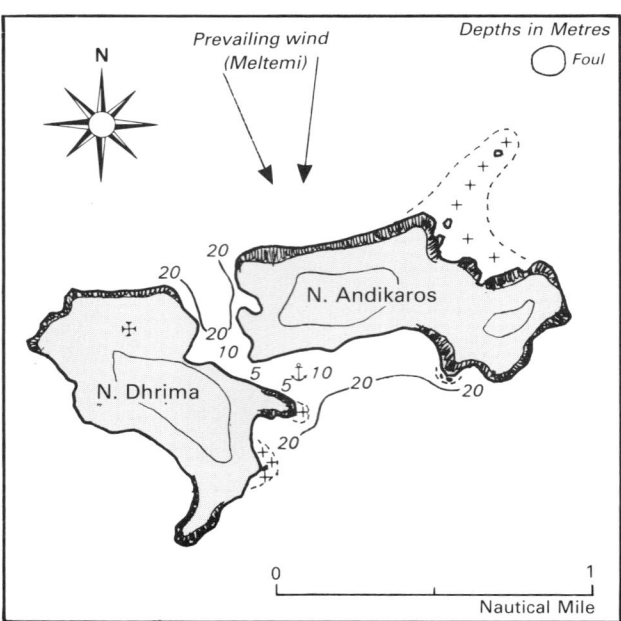

NISOI DHRIMA AND ANDIKAROS

Karos and Andikaros
(Keros)

The southeasternmost of this group of islands off the south coast of Naxos. The SW tip of Amorgos lies 3 miles to the SE of Andikaros. On the S side of Karos there is a tiny cove about halfway along, but there are severe gusts into here with the *meltemi*. Anchor in 4–5 metres near the head. The bottom is sand and rock and not everywhere good holding. The surroundings are bleak and inhospitable on this sun-baked barren island.

Andikaros consists of two islands: Nisis Dhrima to the SW and Andikaros to the NE. The narrow channel between them has 4 metres least depth. In calm weather a yacht can anchor at the SE end of the channel where there is reasonable shelter from the *meltemi* although there are severe gusts.

Note There is an above-water rock approximately ¼ of a mile N of the E end of Andikaros. The rock sits on a shelf with least depths of 10 metres which extends approximately ½ a mile N of the E end of Andikaros. The above-water rock is normally easily spotted, but with the *meltemi* it can be difficult to see until close to. In 1992 I spotted what I thought was a shallow area at the extremity of the shelf, but a Force 7 *meltemi* made investigation a little difficult.

Caution In the vicinity of Koufonisia, Karos and Andikaros there can be severe gusts off the lee side of the islands with the *meltemi*. Care is needed with a strong *meltemi* when there can be extremely fierce gusts when on passage from Stenon Parou-Naxou to Amorgos.

Amorgos

The easternmost of the Cyclades apart from the small islands of Kinaros and Levithia. It is mountainous throughout dropping sheer into the sea in many places. Mt Krikelos is 821 metres (2693ft) high at the NE end; Mt Ayios Ilias is 698 metres (2290ft) high in the middle; and Mt Korax (Raven) is 607 metres (1991ft) high at the SW end. The cliffs are spectacular, especially at the NE end and on the south coast where they drop straight down into the sea for 300 metres or so, giving you the impression that the island was simply sliced off here like so much cheese. Most of the island is burnt barren rock though inland the valleys are cultivated in places.

In the past the islanders had a reputation as wreckers and pirates. The island was colonised in classical times but appears to have been of minor importance. The poet Simonedes settled here and became known as Simonedes of Amorgos. The island is off the main tourist route and mostly visited by backpackers. There is exccllent underwater fishing around the coast and a school of dolphins will often be seen in the vicinity of the island.

Note When the *meltemi* is blowing there are severe gusts off the S side of Amorgos and big seas on both the NW and SE sides.

KATAPOLA (Vathi)

Approach

Conspicuous The *chora* and a line of windmills on the hill above the harbour are conspicuous from seaward. Houses straggle around the head of the bay with a monastery and church with a blue cupola conspicuous in the middle. Katapola lies in the SE corner of the bay.

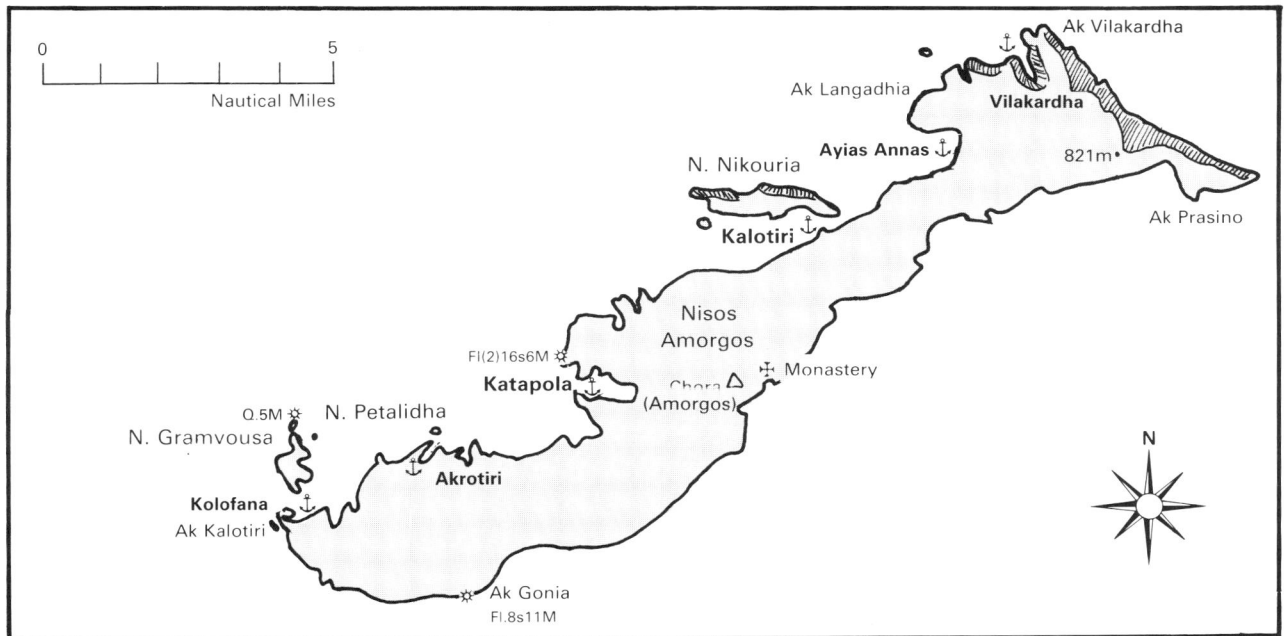

AMORGOS

By night Use the light on Ak Ayios Ilias: Fl(2)16s6M. Apart from this light there are no others, but with good visibility it is possible to make a night entrance.

Dangers With the *meltemi* there are strong gusts into the bay though these lift at Katapola.

Mooring

Go stern-to or bows-to the quay under the lee of the ferry quay. The bottom is mostly sand and weed with some rocks – good holding once the anchor bites.

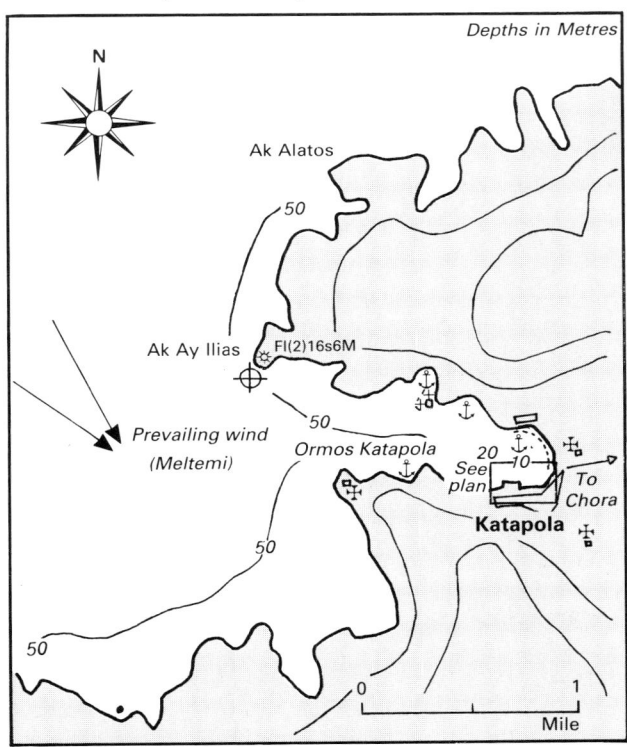

APPROACHES TO ORMOS KATAPOLA
36°50'·3N 25°50'·4E (Ak Ay Ilias light)

Ormos Katapola looking W from the slopes above the bay.

Shelter The shelter under the lee of the ferry quay is better than it appears even with the *meltemi* funnelling in.

Note Sewerage emptying into the harbour makes it smelly in the summer heat.

Authorities Port police.

Anchorage A yacht can anchor in several places in the bay.

1. In the cove immediately W of Katapola. Shelter in here is better than it looks as there is something of a lee from W–NW winds.
2. In calm weather anchor off the hamlet in the NE corner of the bay. Care needs to be taken of laid moorings on the bottom. Good tavernas ashore.
3. In the cove W of the NE hamlet. Shelter from the *meltemi* is not the best here.

Facilities

Water On the quay.

267

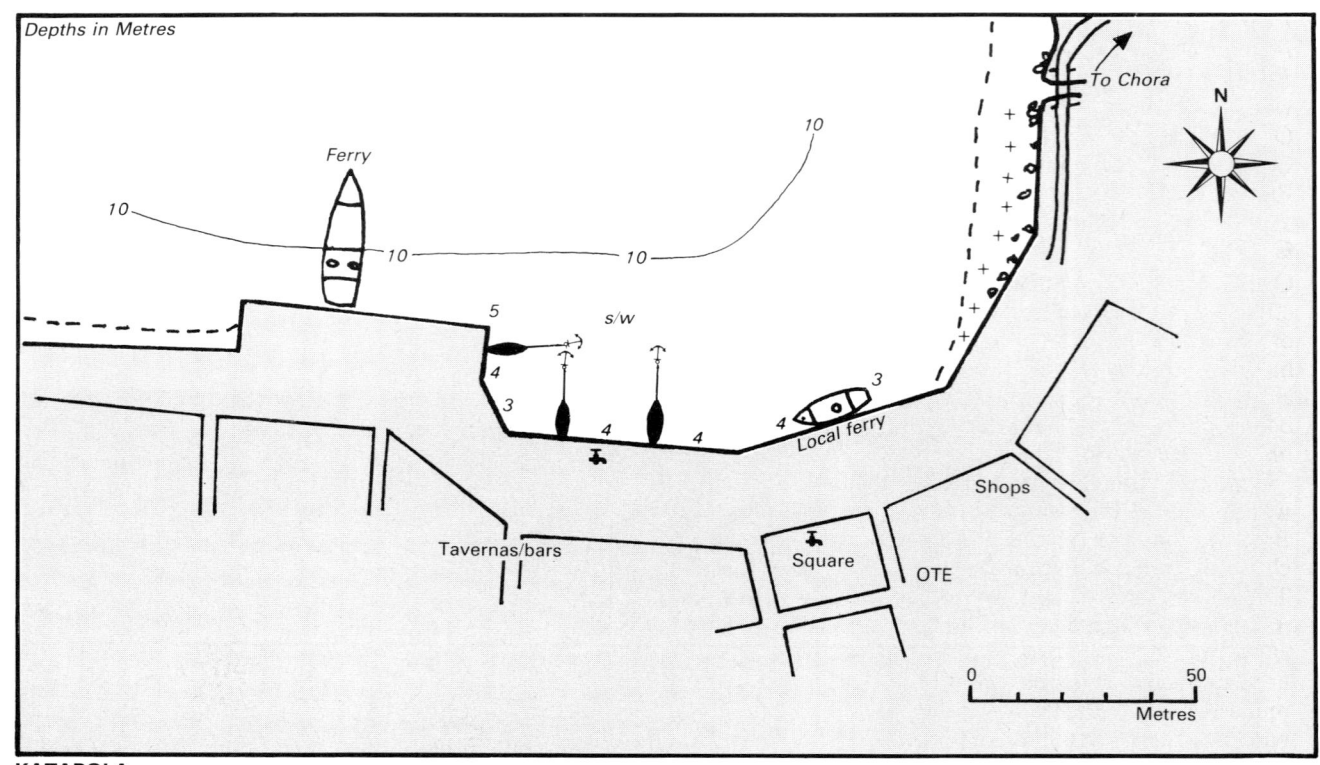

KATAPOLA
36°49'·5N 25°52'E

Katapola looking SW from the slopes above the bay.

Fuel Small quantities sometimes available.
Provisions Most provisions can be obtained.
Eating out Pleasant tavernas and bars on the waterfront.
Other PO. OTE. Exchange office. Bank in the *chora*. Greek gas. Hire motorbikes. Ferries to Naxos, Piraeus and Rhodes.

General

Ormos Katapola is a magnificent deep bay with steep cliffs dropping sheer into the sea. The small village of Katapola is a pleasant relaxed spot and the harbour quite secure. Few tourists come here although recently there has been an influx of backpackers who have not helped the foreigner's image in Amorgos.

The *chora* above is typically Cycladic. It is on the way to the monastery of the Panayia of the Presentation which occupies a spectacular site on a cliff suspended between the sky and the sea below. The best way to get there is either to hire a motorbike or alternatively to get the local bus to the *chora* and then on to a stop nearby – the driver is used to dropping people off at the nearest stop to the monastery. It is then a hot steep climb (remember to take a bottle of water) to the monastery itself which, even in this secular age, manages to instill a feeling of reverence and monastic quiet into the most hardened of sceptics.

ORMOS KOLOFANA

A small bay about ½ a mile S of the southern tip of Nisis Gramvousa. Anchor in 3–4 metres at the head of the bay on a sandy bottom. With the *meltemi* a swell rolls in.

ORMOS AKROTIRI

A bay midway between Kolofana and Katapola. An islet, Nisis Petalidha, lies off the entrance. Open to the NE. There is a pier in the bay with 2 metre depths at the extremity.

ORMOS KALOTIRI

Lies on the SE side of Nisis Nikouria. Anchor on the NW side of the bay in 4–5 metres. Sandy bottom. With the *meltemi* there are strong gusts into the bay. Nisis Nikouria is connected to Amorgos by shoal water. The narrow passage, Stenon Kakoperator, is reported to have 2·5–4 metre depths in the fairway. Keep closer to the N side than the S side where a reef and shoal water extend out into the channel.

ORMOS AYIOS ANNAS (Aghios Ioanna, Yialis, Aigiali)

Approach

The small harbour lies off the village of Yialis in the SE of Ormos Ay Annas. From the W the houses of the village are easily identified. From the E the houses will not be seen until into the bay, but the

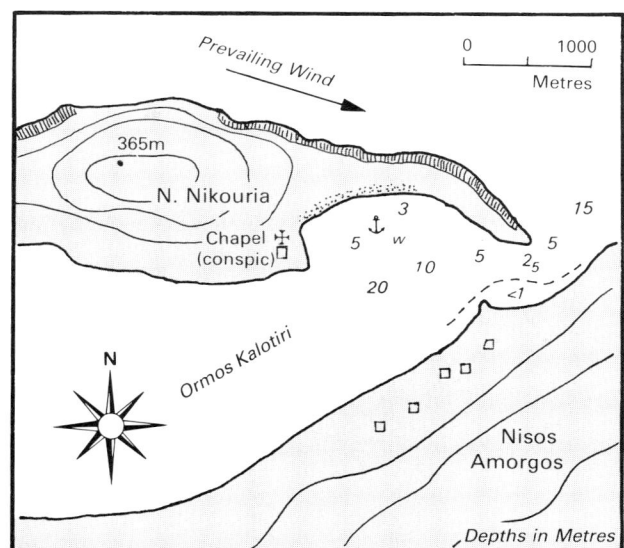

KALOTIRI
36°35'N 25°55'·5E

Massive steep-to cliffs, 'sliced off like so much cheese', at the NE end of Amorgos.

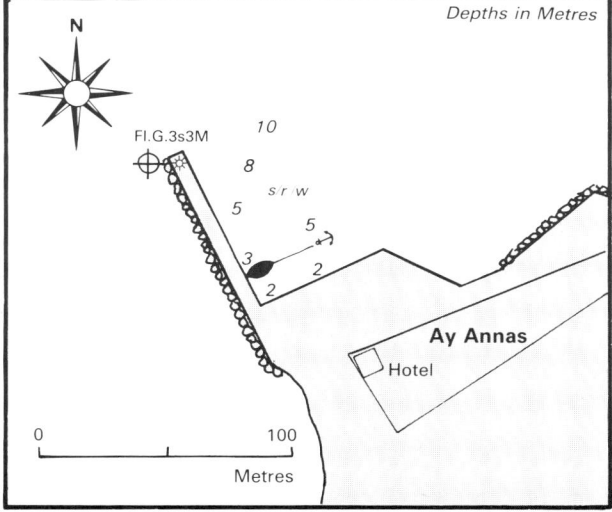

AYIAS ANNAS
36°54'·2N 25°58'·5E (Fl.G.3M)

269

Amorgos. Ayios Annas looking NE. *Nigel Patten.*

small islet N of Ak Langadhia is easily identified. Closer in the mole off the village is easily identified.

By night Use the light on Ak Langadhia (Fl.W.5s8M) and on the molehead (Fl.G.3s3M).

Dangers With the *meltemi* there are strong gusts into the bay and big seas in the vicinity.

Mooring

Go stern-to or bows-to the mole or the quay clear of the ferry berth. The bottom is mostly rock and not good holding – make sure your anchor is well in.

Shelter The bay is open to the W–NW and with the *meltemi* some swell rolls into the bay. There are also strong gusts into the bay.

Facilities

Water Available nearby.
Provisions Some provisions available in the village.
Eating out Tavernas on the waterfront.

General

The small bay has a modest tourist income, but is relatively untouched. The hinterland supports a few small villages, though how they survive is difficult to know in this barren baked landscape. For the visitor the steep-sided bay with small villages around the slopes is a wonderful spot well worth a visit despite the *meltemi*.

ORMOS VILAKARDHA

On the NE tip of Amorgos there is a magnificent fjord-like inlet which can be used in calm weather. With the *meltemi* a swell is pushed straight into it. Anchor near the head of the inlet where convenient – though depths are considerable. At the head of the inlet a ravine cuts through the high cliffs. Around Ak Vilakardha on the NE end of Amorgos are spectacular cliffs rising sheer to some 700 metres (2275ft) in places.

Kinaros and Levitha

Kinaros is a barren jagged island 11 miles ENE of Amorgos. It is inhabited only occasionally by a solitary shepherd and his flock. Levitha, lower in aspect than Kinaros, lies 5 miles to the east. The deep bay on the south coast affords good shelter and two families live at the head of the bay. A tale, probably anecdotal, relates that a member of one of the families here was suddenly taken ill while a large yacht belonging to a Greek minister was anchored off. He ordered up a helicopter to take the patient to hospital and, concerned by the lonely situation of the island, had a radio installed so that if help was needed again the inhabitants needed only to call for it and it would come – on his special authorisation.

Note A strong SE current is reported to flow in the vicinity of the islands and between the islands and Amorgos.

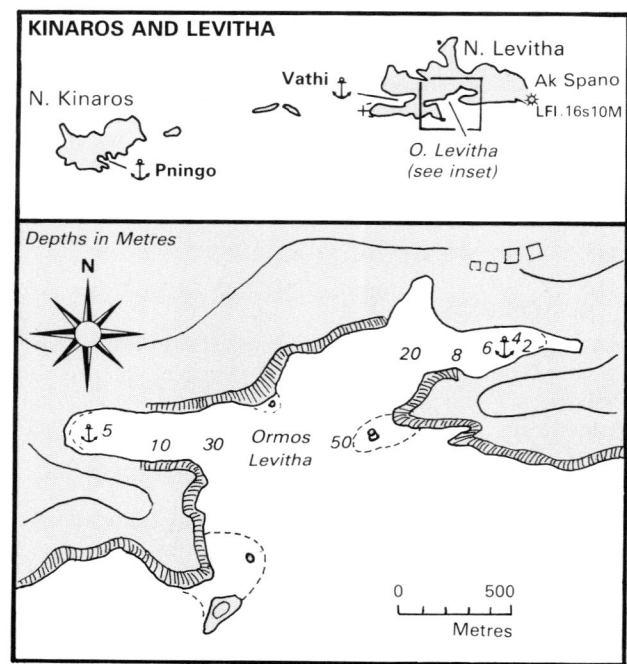

ORMOS LEVITHA
37°00′N 26°27′·5E

ORMOS LEVITHA

A landlocked bay on the S coast. The entrance to the bay is located in the saddle between the higher ends of the island. There is a large conspicuous rock immediately W of the entrance.

The E arm of the bay offers the best shelter. Anchor in 4–5 metres near the head with a long line to bollards ashore. The bottom is mud with some rocks – good holding. Good all-round shelter.

Only a lighthouse keeper and a few fishermen inhabit the island. There is a small taverna in a farmhouse about 15 minutes' walk up the hill from the quay. Good fresh fish is served in pleasant surroundings. Remember to take a torch for the return trip.

Southern Cyclades

Levitha. E side of the bay looking SE. *Nigel Patten.*

You can also anchor in the W creek on Levitha in 4–5 metre depths with a long line ashore.

ORMOS VATHI

On the W side of Levitha there is a deep bay offering some shelter from the *meltemi* although some swell penetrates into here. Anchor in 4–5 metres near the head of the bay. The bottom is sand and rock, not everywhere good holding.

ORMISKOS PNINGO (Kinaros)

On the S side of Kinaros there is a long narrow inlet affording nearly all-round shelter. Anchor near the head of the inlet in 4–5 metres. The bottom is rock and not the best holding – it is prudent to get a line ashore if possible. Good shelter from the *meltemi*. Closed in by the inlet you feel closed off from the world in here. It is a lonely spot – wonderfully so.

Milos
(Melos)

The southwesternmost of the Cyclades, Milos is an ancient volcano which, like Thira, long ago erupted and scooped out the giant bay. The circular mountain ridge enclosing the bay is mostly barren and sterile. The summit at the SW end is Mt Profitis Ilias, rising to 751 metres (2464ft). Alum, sulphur (hot sulphur springs still exist), barium and kaolin are mined and the open cast mines around the slopes of the island are easily identified from seaward.

Milos was the centre of a pre-Minoan Bronze Age civilization and finds on the island of the distinctive 'harpy' sculptures have added much to our knowledge of this early Cycladic civilization. No doubt these early settlers used the island as a stepping stone during their island by island colonization of the Aegean. Later it came under the Minoans and later still passed to the Mycenaeans.

Milos opted for the Spartan side during the Peloponnesian War, thereby angering the Athenians to such an extent that they carried out the infamous massacre recorded by Thucydides. The Athenians besieged Milos which, after some months, surrendered unconditionally, whereupon all able males were slaughtered and the women and children enslaved.

The Franks and later the Turks colonized the island, but it enjoyed considerable freedom and prospered. A large part of the income of the island during this time was derived from pirate fleets who used the remote anchorages around the islands and sold their booty at Milos from where it was resold to merchants. In the First World War the large natural harbour was a British naval base.

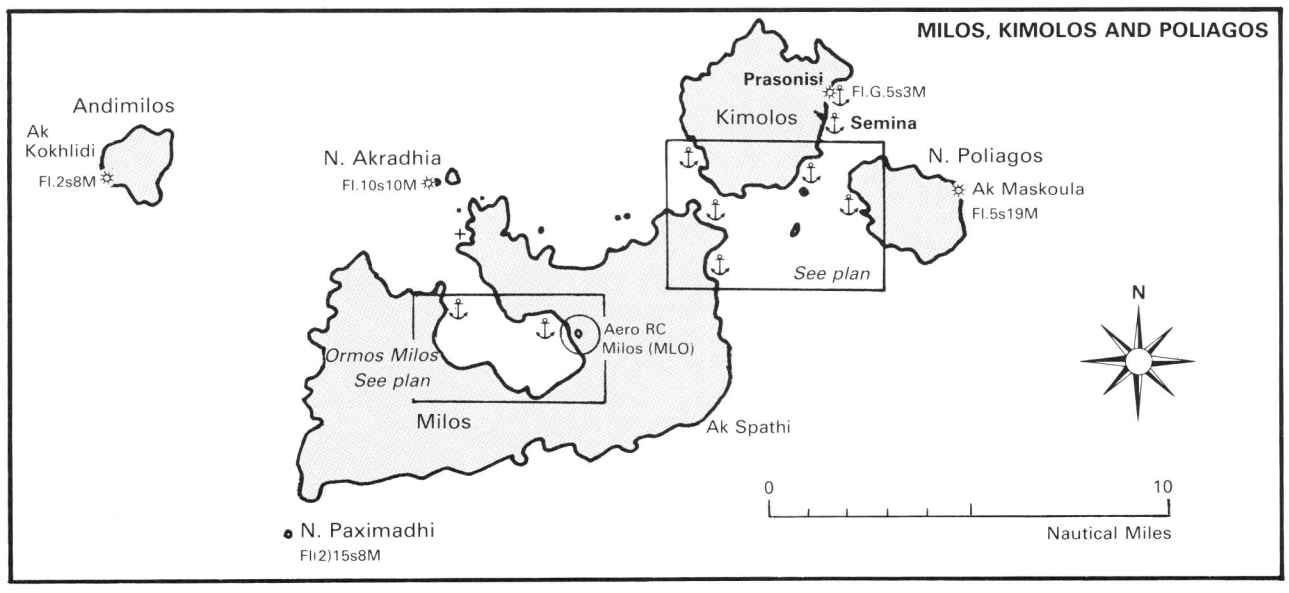

It was during the Hellenistic period that the Venus de Milo properly, the Aphrodite of Milos, was sculpted, and though it is probably one of the best-known pieces of ancient Greek sculpture, reproduced thousands of times in history and art history books, its source and the island it comes from are little known. The statue was found in the late 19th century by a farmer collecting old Greek stones for fieldwalls. He removed the top half (the statue is carved from two pieces of marble) and negotiated to sell it to the French consul who took it to his house for safekeeping. The French ship sent to collect it arrived to find that the Sultan's governor had forcibly taken the statue and put it aboard a ship bound for Istanbul. Captain de Marcellus decided to retake the statue and landed an armed party which after a brief skirmish got it back and aboard the French ship. It is said that it was during this skirmish that the Venus de Milo lost her arms which were spirited away by a local. Despite reports of the arms being rediscovered at various times, the Venus still hasn't acquired them and probably shouldn't lest it change our accepted perception of the armless beauty art historians are so familiar with.

ADHAMAS (Port Milos)
Admiralty chart no. 1832

Approach

Conspicuous Approaching the entrance to Ormos Milos the lighthouse on Nisidhes Akradhia and the village of Milos (the *chora*) on the peak on the E side of the entrance are conspicuous. Rounding Ak Bombardha the village of Adhamas will be seen.

By night Use the light on Nisidhes Akradhia (Fl.10s10M) and Ak Bombardha (Fl.4·4s6M). The jetties off the opencast mine on the E side of Ormos Milou are lit: 2F.R.3M and F.R.3M.

Dangers

1. With the *meltemi* there are heavy confused seas off the entrance to Ormos Milou. Special care must be taken between Voi Kounidhi and Nisidhes Akradhia where the waves rebound off the N side of Milos and cause a heavy sea up to a mile off.

2. Care must be taken of rocks and reefs bordering the E side of the entrance to Ormos Milou. Vos Monopodhro is a square rock easily identified. Off Ak Fourkovouni there are several detached above-water rocks eroded into fantastic wind-sculpted shapes.

3. At times the *meltemi* can gust down off the high land in the vicinity of Ak Bombardha.

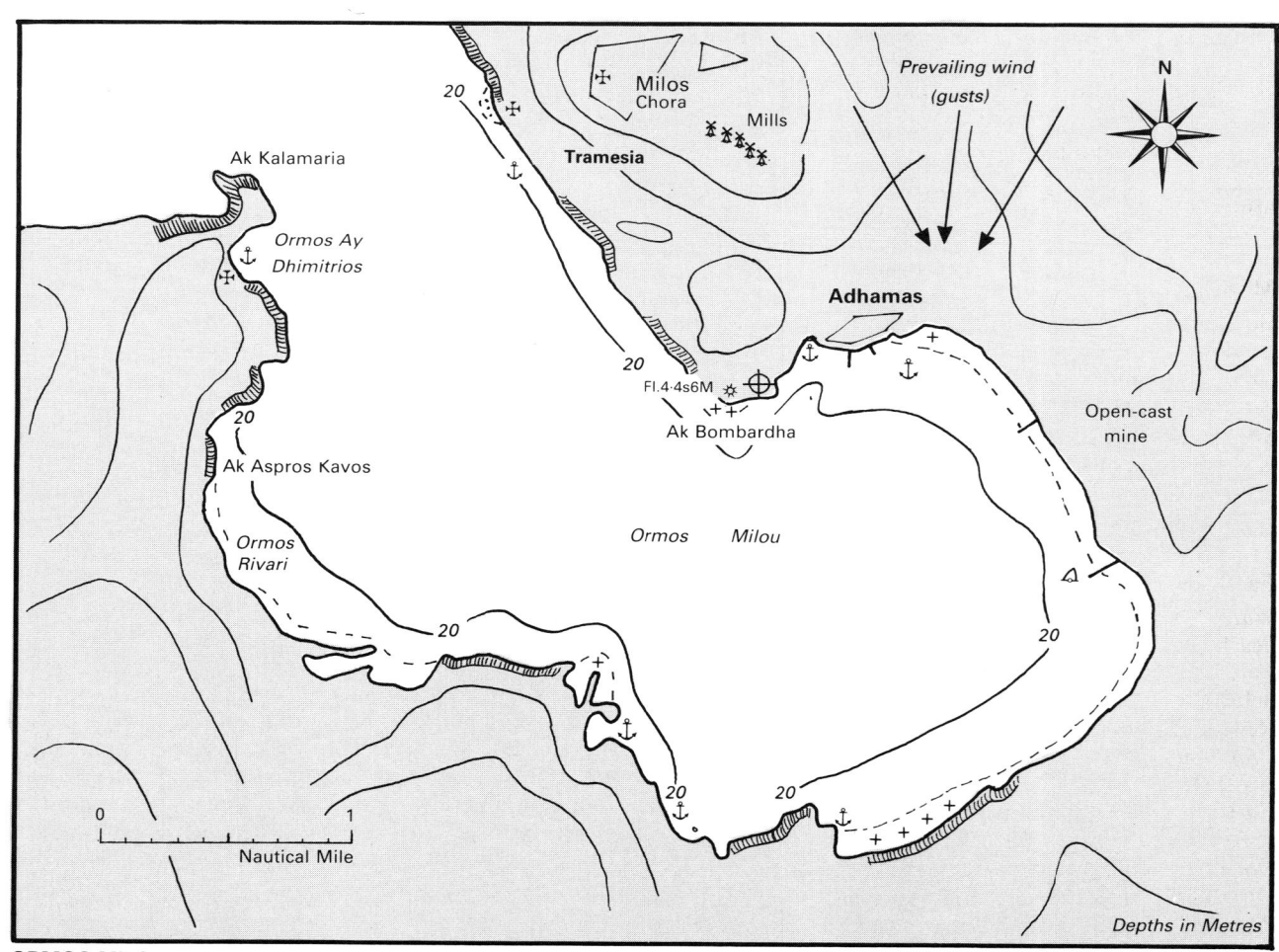

ORMOS MILOU 36°43′·3N 24°26′·0E (Ak Bombardha light)

Nisis Akradhia and lighthouse in the approaches to Ormos Milou looking N.

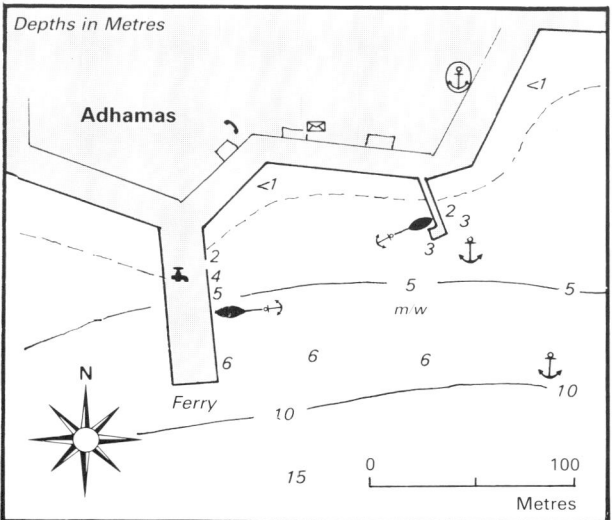

ADHAMAS
36°43′·5N 24°27′E

Mooring

Go stern-to or bows-to the E side of the ferry pier or. bows-to the short pier to the E of it. Alternatively anchor off the village E of the short pier. The bottom is mud, rocks and weed – poor holding in places.

Shelter Good shelter from the *meltemi* although there is some residual swell. With strong S winds Adhamas is dangerous from the long fetch across the bay.

Authorities Port police and customs.

Facilities

Water On the ferry pier. Apply to the tourist office nearby.
Fuel On the outskirts of town. A mini-tanker can deliver.
Repairs Limited mechanical repairs. Hardware shop.
Provisions Good shopping for most provisions. Ice available.
Eating out Only mediocre tavernas in my experience at Adhamas.
Other PO. OTE. Bank. Greek gas and *Camping Gaz*. Hire cars, motorbikes and bicycles. Ferries to Piraeus, Thira and Soudha. Internal flights to Athens.

General

The huge natural harbour is impressive to look at but the yachtsman is liable to curse this very size for the sea that can be raised inside in strong winds. I have always found Adhamas an indifferent sort of place – perhaps a few too many reinforced concrete buildings to be classified as attractive and a few too many tourists for the size of the place.

The *chora* (Milos) on the hill above is attractive and the view over the bay superb. As at Thira, the eye sees the volcanic crater that is now the bay, but the mind finds it difficult to compute the size of explosion that produced it.

OTHER ANCHORAGES IN ORMOS MILOU

1. An unnamed bay on the S side of Ormos Milou approximately SSW of Ak Bombardha. It looks to offer reasonable shelter from the *meltemi* and small yachts could creep in under the headland. Open to the E.
2. Ormos Ay Dhimitrios on the W side of the entrance to Ormos Milou. Open to the NE–E and not really a good place to be in the *meltemi*.

ANDIMILOS (Anti-Milos)

A high steep-to island lying 5 miles WNW of Milos. It rises to 686 metres (2250ft). With the *meltemi* there are severe gusts off the SW side of it, such that small whirlwinds are created. Keep well off! On the W side there is a light on Ak Kokhlidi: Fl.2s8M.

KIMOLOS

A low barren island lying immediately NE of Milos from which it is separated by a narrow channel. The small population lives in the *chora* or at Psathi. Formerly it was called Echinousa on account of the sea urchins found here (Pliny) and Argentiera on account of its silver mines. In the Middle Ages it was an infamous pirate haunt.

STENON KIMOLOU (Kimolos Channel)
Admiralty chart no. 1832
Imray-Tetra chart no. G33

The area enclosed by Milos, Kimolos and Poliagos islands is an attractive mini-cruising area with a number of well-sheltered anchorages. In one or other of the anchorages shelter can be found from winds from any direction. Care must be taken of the reefs and shoals which fringe the islands and islets. In the plan these cannot be shown in great detail.
Caution With the *meltemi* there are severe gusts off the SW side of Nisos Poliagos, down through Stenon Kimolou-Poliagos (the channel between Kimolos and Poliagos) and off the S side of Nisos Kimolos. Although there is not a big sea in the lee of the islands, the wind can be very strong indeed.
1. *Ormos Sikia* On the SW side of Kimolos. Open to the W–NW and unsuitable when the *meltemi* is blowing. With light northerlies and easterlies there is adequate protection in here. Anchor in

273

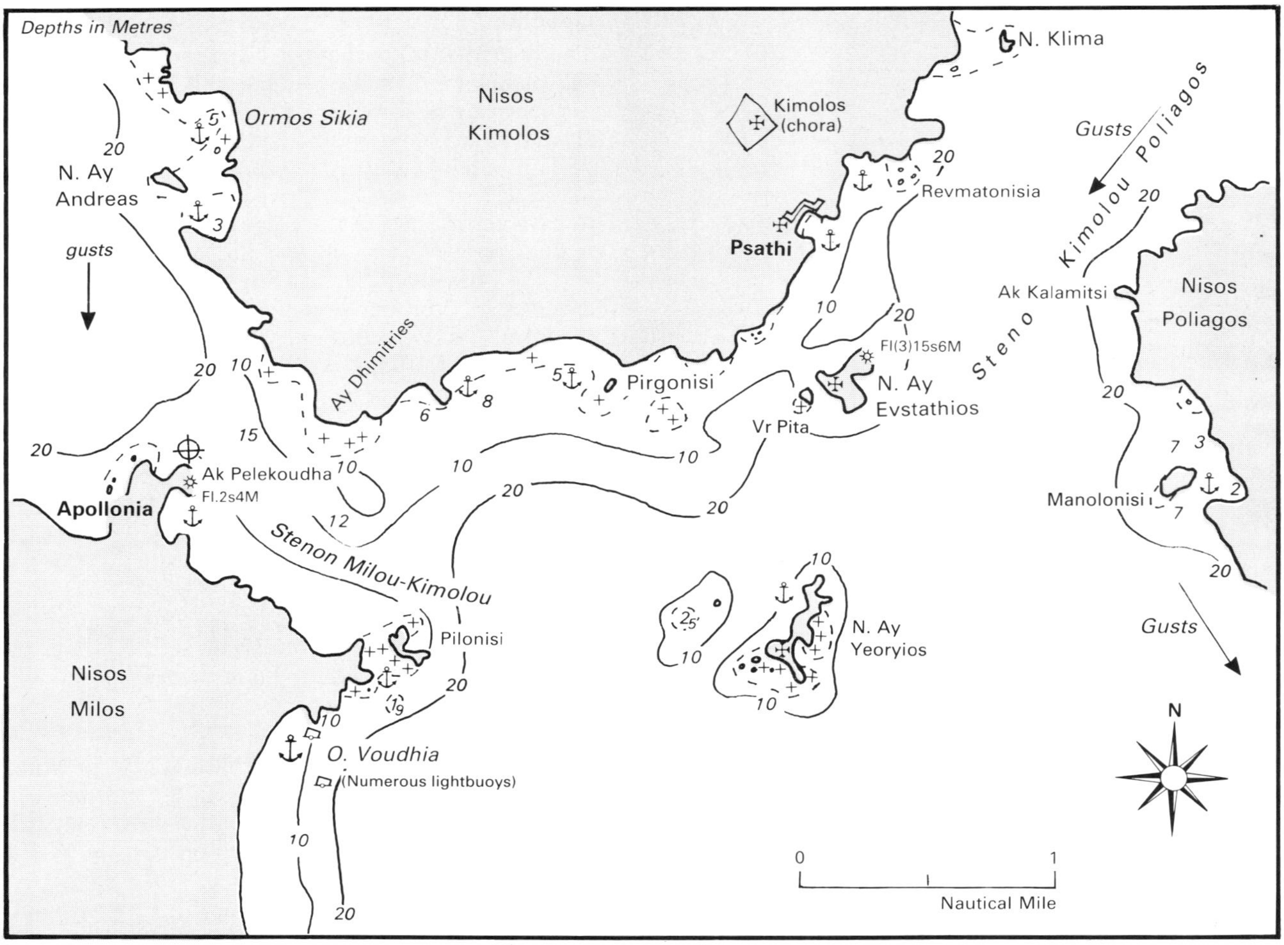

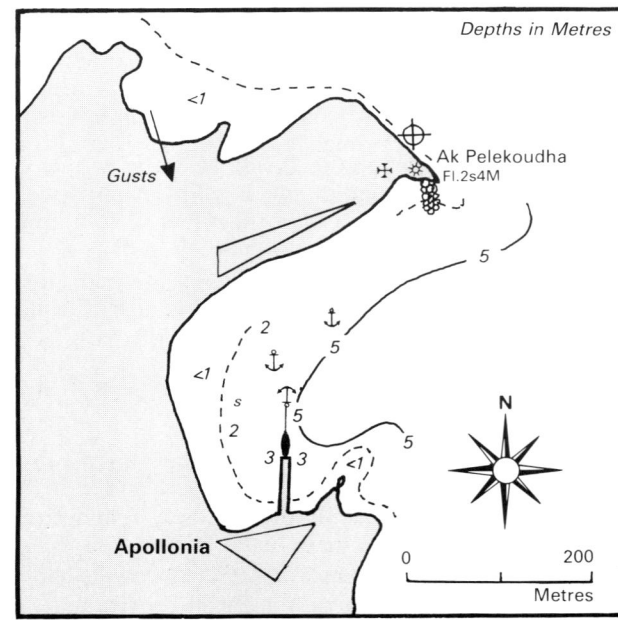

STENON MILOU-KIMOLOU 36°46′·2N 24°31′·7E (Ak Pelekoudha light)

3–4 metres on the S side of the islet (Ay Andreas) in the middle of the bay. Care must be taken of the reef connecting Ay Andreas to Kimolos. A yacht can also anchor to the N of the islet in 3–5 metres.

2. *Apollonia* A bay on the S side of Stenon Milou-Kimolou directly under Ak Pelekoudha. Anchor in 2–4 metres on the E side of the bay off the beach or off the hamlet on the S side. Alternatively go stern-to or bows-to the pier which has 3 metre depths at the extremity. Good holding on a sandy bottom. The shelter from the *meltemi* is better than it might appear on the plan although there are still strong gusts into the bay. It is completely open to the E. Several tavernas and a mini-market ashore.

3. *Ormos Voudhia* A bay lying about one mile SE of Apollonia. A 1·9 metre patch lies 0·2 miles S of Pilonisi (connected to Milos by a causeway). Anchor in 5–8 metres in the N corner of the bay. Good shelter from the *meltemi*. There are opencast mines ashore and a wharf and ore-carrier on the waterfront, so the bay is not really the most attractive place to bring up for the night.

4. *Pirgonisi anchorage* A long sandy beach extends nearly right around the S side of Kimolos. A yacht can anchor anywhere off the beach and obtain excellent shelter from the *meltemi*. At the E end of the beach a low rocky islet, Pirgonisi, is connected

APOLLONIA
36°46′·2N 24°31′·7E (Ak Pelekoudha light)

to the shore by a reef. A yacht can tuck under Pirgonisi off the beach in attractive surroundings. The bottom comes up gradually to the beach and is sand and weed, good holding. A few villas have been built around the shoreline.

Approaches to Apollonia looking W.

5. *Psathi* A cathedral in the *chora* above and 4 windmills on a ridge are conspicuous. Closer in, the houses around Psathi Bay are conspicuous. A ferry uses the quay on the N side. Anchor in the bay or with care go bows-to the quay on the S side. The bay is not well sheltered from the *meltemi* and should only really be used in calm weather. Open to the S–SE. Limited provisions and two taverna/cafés ashore. *Caïque* ferry to Milos.

6. *Semina Creek* A fjord-like bay approximately 1¼ miles N of Psathi. The N side of the entrance is lit (Fl.G.5s3M) although the operation of the light is reported to be intermittent. There is a short mole which the fishing boats use. Anchor in the bay in 4–6 metres. Poor shelter from the *meltemi* which is funnelled straight down Stenon Kimolou-Poliagos.

7. *Prasonisi anchorage* Under the NE tip of the island (Ak Anatoli) is a small cove with an islet in the middle. Anchor in 3–4 metres on either side of the islet and take a line ashore. Care should be taken of the reef connecting the islet to Kimolos. Poor shelter from the *meltemi*.

8. *Manolisi* On the W side of Poliagos a yacht can anchor behind Manolisi Island in 2–3 metres. Sandy bottom. Shelter from the *meltemi*. The islet is connected to Poliagos by a sand bar with 1–1·5 metre depths over it. A delightful utterly secluded spot.

POLIAGOS (Poliagaios, Polino)

A barren island close SE of Kimolos. Apart from Manolisi anchorage mentioned above, in calm weather yachts can also anchor off in several of the coves along the S side.

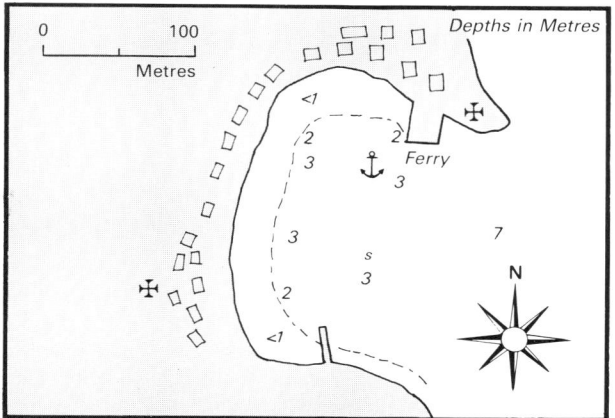

PSATHI
36°47′N 24°34′·5E

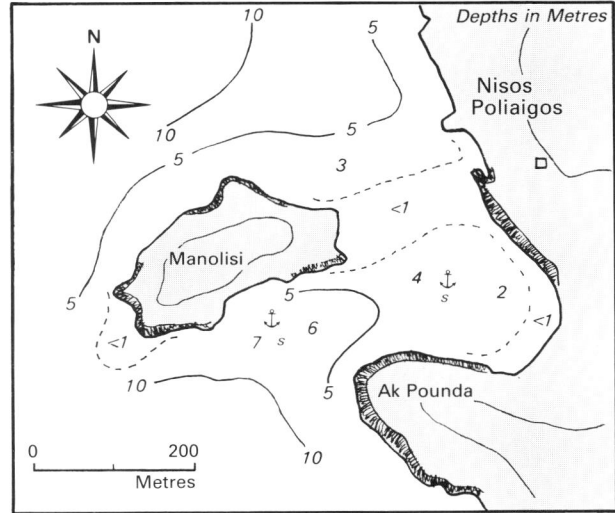

MANOLISI
36°46′N 24°36′·5E

Psathi on Kimolos. *Nigel Patten.*

KARAVOSTASI
Admiralty chart no. 1832

Approach
Conspicuous Nisidhes Adhelfia, the jagged islets lying E of Karavostasi and SW of Nisis Kardhiotissa, are easily recognised. Closer in Dhio Adhelfia, the small islet in the middle of the entrance to Karavostasi,

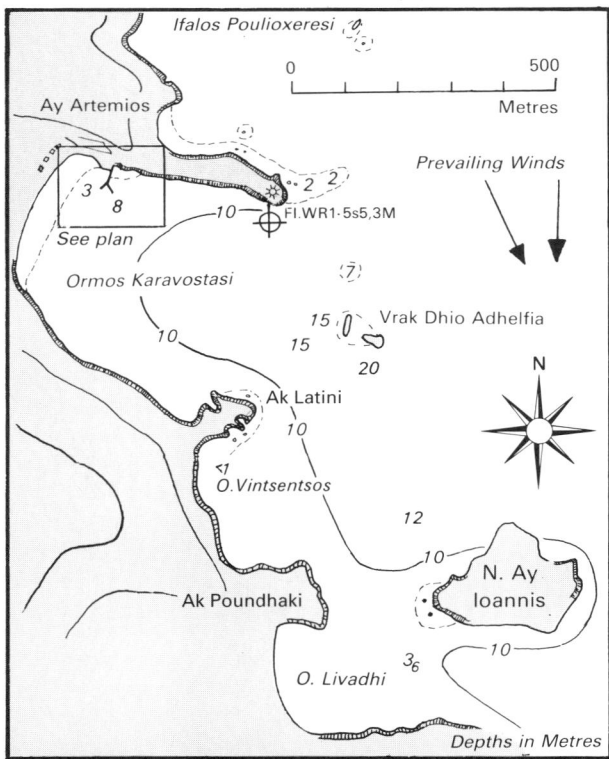

KARAVOSTASI APPROACHES
36°37′N 24°57′·2E (Fl.WR.3/5M)

Folegandros
(Pholegandhros, Polikandros)

A barren rocky island lying 14 miles east of Milos. It is steep-to with some impressive cliffs on the south side. At the NW end the island is 311 metres (1020ft) high and at the SE end Mt Elevtherios is 415 metres (1361ft) high. The small *chora* sits on the edge of the cliff on the NE side and is a delightful oasis of green trees and shrubs in the otherwise barren island.

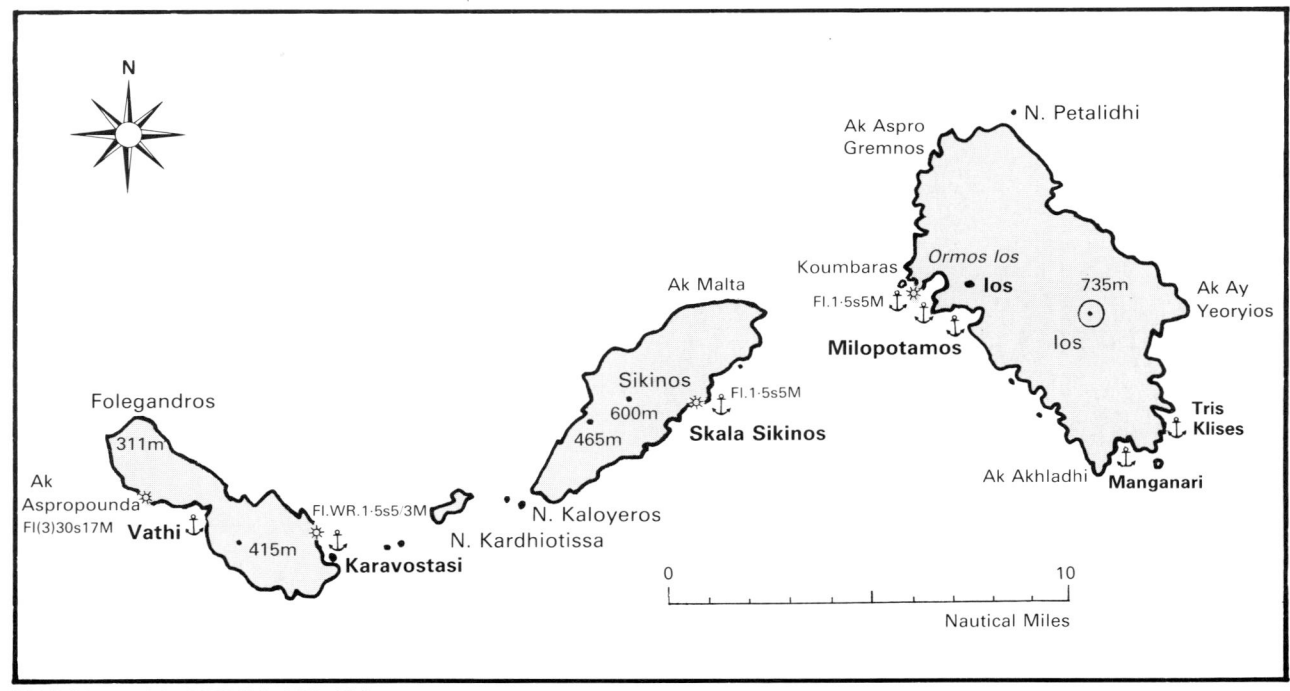

FOLEGANDROS, SIKINOS AND IOS

will be seen. The white houses around the bay and a church on a low hill behind are also conspicuous.

By night A night approach is not recommended. Use the light on the N side of the entrance (Fl.WR.1·5s5/3M red sector covers 202°-248° and 344°-096° over Ifalos Poulioxeres) and the light on the end of the new mole (Q.G.3M occas).

Dangers

1. Care is needed of Ifalos Poulioxeres to the NNE of the entrance and the reef running NE from the N entrance point to Karavostasi.
2. With the *meltemi* there are strong gusts and a disturbed swell at the entrance to the bay.

Mooring

Go stern-to or bows-to the mole where shown. When the W side of the ferry mole is not in use a yacht can go alongside here overnight. When the harbour is packed you may be able to squeeze in somewhere in

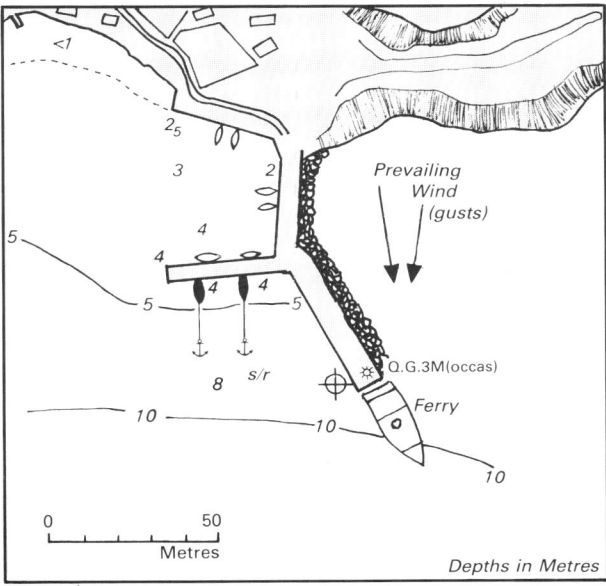

KARAVOSTASI
36°36'·9N 24°57'E (Q.G.3M)

Karavostasi looking SE from above the hamlet.

Karavostasi.

the fishing boat area though berths here are jealously guarded. The bottom is sand and rock – poor holding in places.

Shelter Reasonable shelter from the *meltemi* although a prolonged blow sets up a surge in the bay which makes things uncomfortable though still tenable. Open SE–E.

Facilities

Limited. Some provisions can be obtained although supplies are much dependent on the ferry. Several tavernas and bars. Bus to the *chora*. Ferry to Ios and Milos.

General

The bay with its jagged headland and small islets in the approaches is attractive in a parched sun-baked way. A few backpackers come here in the summer. It is about an hour's walk (or much shorter bus ride) to the *chora* sited on the edge of a cliff and something of an oasis with trees and greenery contrasting with the otherwise barren island. There are a few tavernas and limited supplies here.

Karavostasi literally means a 'ship-stop'. Before the new ferry mole was built the ferry would anchor in the bay and passengers and cargo were brought ashore in small boats. Even a strong *meltemi* could not stop the ferry and it literally roared into the bay, unloading and loading again as quickly as possible, before steaming off to some more secure port.

ORMOS VATHI

A large bay on the W side of Folegandros to the E of Ak Aspropounda. With the *meltemi* there are very strong gusts into the bay and a swell works its way in. In calm weather anchor off in 4–5 metres. The bottom is sand and weed, poor holding in places.

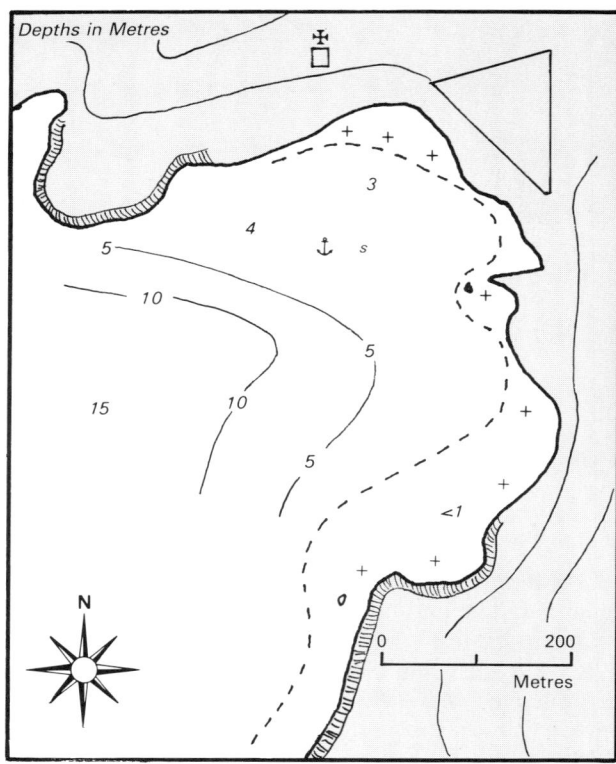

PORT VATHI
36°37'·8N 24°53'·6E

Vrakhonisidhes Adhelfia in Steno Folegandrou-Sikonou, looking N.

Ios

Lies to the east of Sikinos across a narrow (3½ miles) strait. The island is mountainous and barren but in the words of the Admiralty *Pilot* '...it has a softer and more genial aspect than either Folegandros or Sikinos.' Mt Pirgos in the middle of the island rises to 790 metres (2410ft).

Ios is claimed to be the burial place of Homer. On a voyage from Samos to Athens the old blind bard died. His body was thrown overboard and washed up on Ios where the sea buried him on the beach. His body is now said to be buried on the northern slopes of Mt Pirgos. An apocryphal story, but then you never know.

Today the island is extremely popular with young sun-lovers. Nude bathing is tolerated here (although it is still technically illegal in Greece) and the beaches around the island are packed with red and in some cases lobster-red bodies.

Sikinos

A barren dry island to the E of Folegandros. It was once called the wine island because of the excellence of its wine, but I cannot attest to this fact today. The small *chora* lies inland under a ruined fortified monastery.

ORMOS SKALA

The only harbour on Sikinos, situated 3 miles SW of Ak Malta. The buildings around the bay are conspicuous from the S, but not from the E. There is a light on the E side of the bay (Fl.1·5s5M) and the short mole is lit (Fl.R.2s3M).

Anchor in the bay in 2–3 metres. Care must be taken of underwater rocks and rubble on the W side of the bay. The bottom is sand – reasonable holding. There is a short mole on the W side of the bay, but it is always crowded with *caïques*. Good shelter from the *meltemi* although there are strong gusts. Open to the S. Some provisions available and tavernas ashore. The small village around the bay is most attractive and popular with Greek tourists.

Ormos Iou looking SW from the *chora*. Nigel Patten.

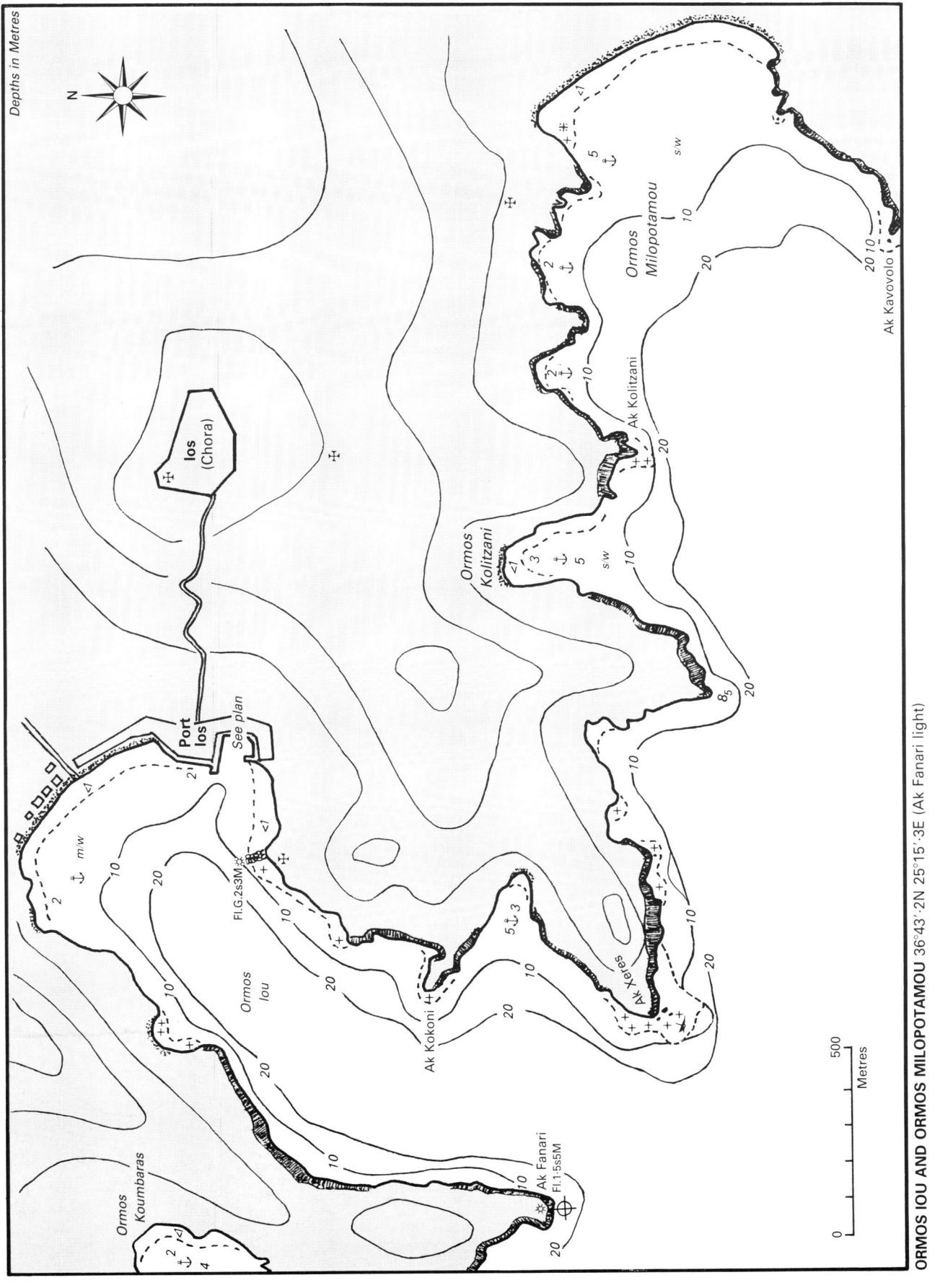

ORMOS IOU AND ORMOS MILOPOTAMOU 36°43'·2N 25°15'·3E (Ak Fanari light)

Ios harbour looking N.

PORT IOS
Admiralty chart no. 1832

Approach
Conspicuous The *chora* of Ios on the hill above the harbour and two windmills on the hill below the village are conspicuous from seaward. Nisis Dhiakofto NW of the entrance to Ormos Iou stands out clearly. Once up to the entrance the light structure on Ak Fanari can be distinguished and a few buildings around the beach will be seen. The buildings around the harbour cannot be seen until you are into the bay.

By night Use the light on Ak Fanari (Fl.1·5s5M) and the light on the end of the rough stone breakwater (Fl.G.2s3M).

Dangers
1. Care should be taken of the reef that runs S for about 100 metres from Ak Xeres.
2. With the *meltemi* there are strong gusts into the bay.

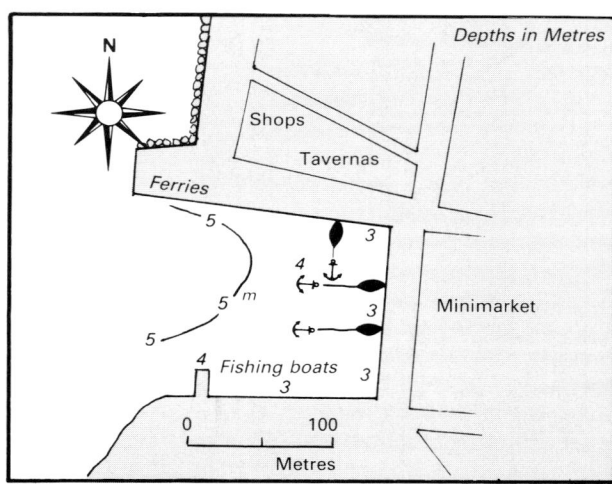

IOS HARBOUR
36°43'·4N 25°16'·4E

Mooring
Go stern-to or bows-to in the basin. The bottom is mud – excellent holding.

Shelter All-round shelter out of the gusts from the *meltemi*.

Authorities Port police and customs.

Anchorage Yachts can anchor on the N side of the bay in 2–8 metres on mud and weed, good holding. Good shelter here from the *meltemi*.

Facilities
Water Public fountain in the square.
Fuel A mini-tanker can deliver to the basin.
Provisions Most provisions can be found near the harbour. Ice from the NE corner of the harbour.
Eating out Tavernas and bars around the harbour.
Other PO and OTE in the *chora*. Exchange facilities. Greek gas. *Camping Gaz* in the *chora*. Hire motorbikes. Bus to the *chora*. Ferries to Piraeus, Thira and Iraklion.

General
By night the waterfront throbs to the sound of music from bars and discos as young bodies weave their way from bar to bar to disco. Ios is the centre for the young backpackers sleeping rough on the nearby beaches. By day nudism rules (a sign painted on a cliff proclaims: 'Clothes are prohibited') and the nearby beaches are packed with the young of all nationalities complying with this sign. The *chora* above is a maze of streets packed with bars, boutiques and backpackers.

ORMOS KOUMBARAS
Admiralty chart no. 1832

The bay immediately N of Port Ios. Anchor in 3–4 metres. Indifferent shelter from the *meltemi*.

ORMOS MILOPOTAMOU
Admiralty chart no. 1832

The large bay immediately S of Port Ios. On the N side of the bay there are four coves where a yacht can anchor. The two easternmost coves are the better sheltered. Anchor where convenient. The bottom is sand – good holding. Good shelter from the *meltemi* although there are strong gusts into the bay and some swell may enter in a prolonged blow. Open to the W and S. There are a number of hotels and tavernas on the beach. Much frequented by nudists.

ORMOS MANGANARI
A large bay on the S coast of Ios. In the NE corner of the bay there is a rocky islet. Anchor near the head of the bay in 3–8 metres or in the W or E of the bay. The bottom is sand, excellent holding. You can tuck into the cove on the W with a long line ashore to the N side. Open only to the S. Good shelter from the *meltemi* although there are gusts into the bay. A small

hotel and tavernas ashore. A *caïque* brings the nature-lovers (topless and bottomless) daily from Ios.

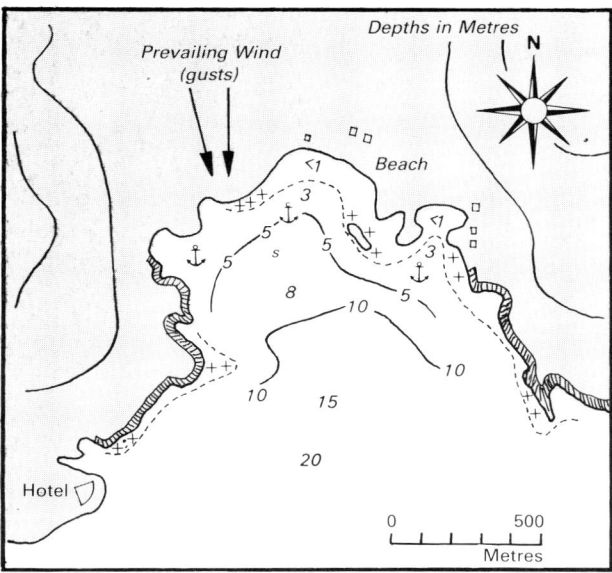

ORMOS MANGANARI
36°39′·4N 25°22′·1E

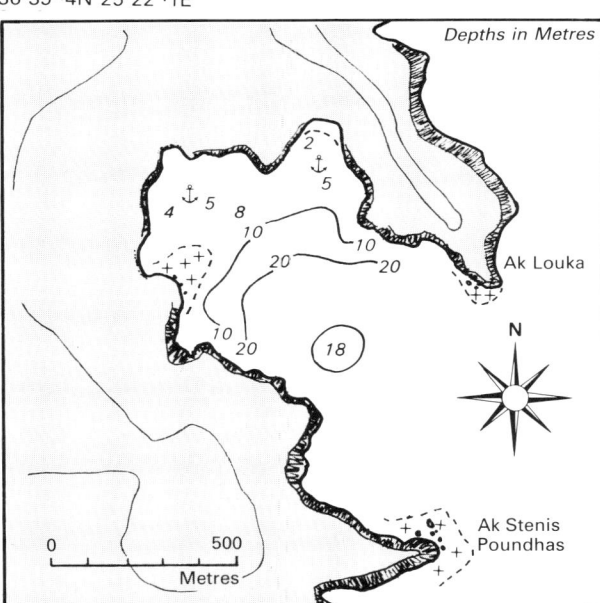

ORMOS TRIS KLISES
36′40′N 25°23′·5E

ORMOS TRIS KLISES

A bay on the S coast about 1½ miles NE of Manganari. Anchor in either of the two coves in 3–5 metres on a sandy bottom. Good shelter from the *meltemi* although there are strong gusts into the bay. No facilities.

Care must be taken of a reef on the W side of the bay and of a shallow patch near the head of the E cove.

Thira
(Thera, Psira, Santorini)

Like Milos, Thira is a giant volcano. The principal island is Thira, shaped like a new moon encircling the rim of the crater now filled with water. To the NW Thirasia forms another part of the rim and in the middle a black mass of cinder and lava (Kammeni and Nea Kammeni) is the volcanic plug. Thira is steep-to on the west coast: variegated pumice cliffs in pastel shades of red, brown, grey, green and slate blue drop sheer into the sea from 150–300 metres and keep going down for another 300 metres. The east coast is low-lying, sloping evenly up to a hilly ridge running along the island. The summit of Thira, Mt Ayios Ilias, is a conical peak in the SE of the island with a white monastery and a cluster of communication towers on top which are conspicuous from seaward. The white domed houses of the capital, Thira (Fira), extend along the cliff top on the west coast about 213 metres (700ft) above the tiny harbour and present a remarkable (and much photographed) sight from seaward.

Legend has it that Thira originated from a lump of earth presented to Jason and the Argonauts by Triton (a local African god) which was later dropped into the sea where Thira (or *Kalliste* – the most beautiful – as it was called then) is now. The island was an important Minoan settlement until it blew itself to pieces in c.1440–1450 BC and destroyed the Minoan civilization as well (see 'Thira and the Atlantis Legend'). It was later subject to Athens and the Egyptian Ptolemys made it into a naval base. In the Middle Ages it was part of the duchy of Naxos. In the early 20th century it was a place of exile for political prisoners.

Thira is unlike anywhere else in the world. The volcanic crater is some six miles long by four miles wide and viewing it from Thira town, the mind cannot comprehend the sort of massive explosion that moved so much solid material to scoop out this deep bay. It may give you pause for thought to remember that the volcano is still active and that your yacht is moored in the crater.

The strange landscape breeds strange tales. Vampires are said to exist on the island and the inhabitants report that ghostly apparitions haunt the countryside at night. The volcanic soil is especially fertile and like the land around Mt Etna and Vesuvius the soil produces fine grapes for wine. Of the bottled wines Atlantis white or red and Nikteri white are quite palatable. Local wine can also be obtained from the barrel.

Thira is unique and consequently it is one of the places in the Aegean that must be visited. In the summer as many as four cruise ships may be anchored in the bay beneath Thira town disembarking thousands of sightseers. The yachtsman is lucky in so far as he can visit Thira town and then retire to the peace of another anchorage around the crater.

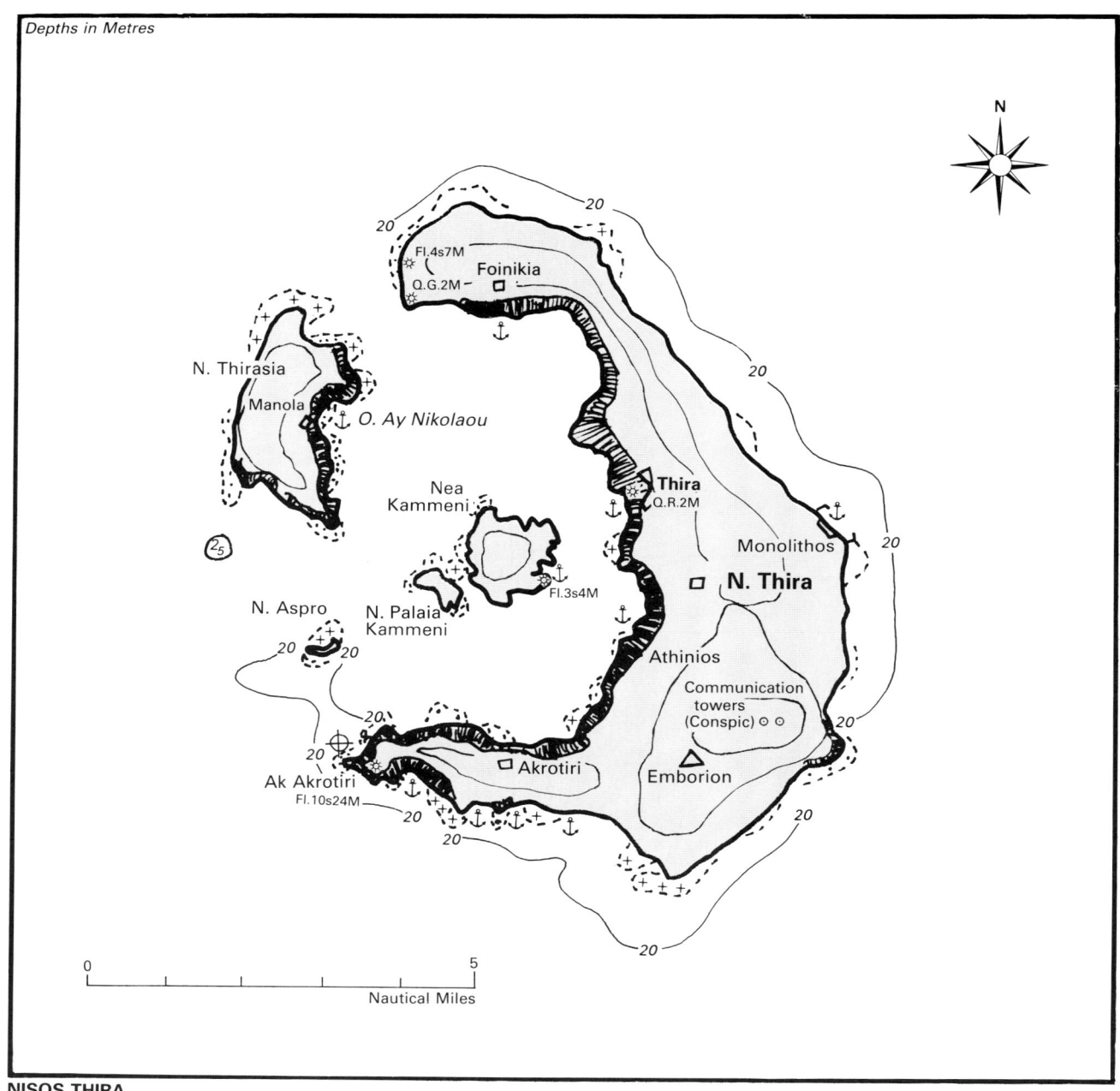

Depths in Metres

N. Thirasia
Manola
⚓ *O. Ay Nikolaou*

Fl.4s7M
Q.G.2M
Foinikia
⚓

Nea Kammeni

N. Aspro
N. Palaia Kammeni
Fl.3s4M

Thira
Q.R.2M
Monolithos
□ **N. Thira**

Athinios
Communication towers (Conspic) ⊙ ⊙

Ak Akrotiri
Fl.10s24M
□ Akrotiri
△ Emborion

0 ———————— 5
Nautical Miles

NISOS THIRA
36°21'·5N 25°21'·4E (Ak Akrotiri light)

Thira and the Atlantis legend

Plato first recorded the Atlantis legend that has baffled historians to the present. His description of an ancient island civilization which vanished as the result of a great natural catastrophe has been variously fixed in the Antilles, America, an island somewhere on the continental shelf off the Mediterranean, Malta – and most often in Plato's imagination. In the last thirty years the location of Atlantis has moved to Greece and many eminent authorities now believe that Thira was in fact the fabled island.

We know that Thira was populated before 2000 BC and that in the period before the catastrophic eruption an advanced and inventive Minoan civilization existed on Thira and Crete. Although the excavations at Akrotiri on Thira are interesting, the range of technological and artistic achievements of the Minoans is best seen at Iraklion and the Palace of Knossus. This civilization ended abruptly around 1400 BC and for some time it was hypothesized that a Mycenaean invasion had simply swept it away. Yet Thira erupted at about the same time and the hypothesis of Professor Marinatos and others is that this mega-explosion not only destroyed Thira but also caused a *tsunami* or seismic sea wave which destroyed the Cretan-based Minoans.

Thira is the largest known active caldera in the world. It is about five times the size of Krakatoa near Java and the eruption of Thira is estimated have been about three times greater than that of Krakatoa in 1883. Here is a description of that recent eruption:

'In the course of two days, 26–27 August 1883, 23 sq. km of Krakatoa disappeared as a result of a series of violent explosions. The biggest explosion at 10 a.m. on the 27th, was heard from Alice Springs in Australia to Martinique, and from Ceylon to Northern Malaya. Atmospheric shock waves from it travelled three and a half times round the globe. The blast caused serious damage to houses up to 160 km away. Tidal waves were associated with the explosions and that associated with the biggest explosion was reliably reported as 17 metres high at Vlakke Hoek lighthouse 88 km away from Krakatoa. The waves destroyed nearly 300 towns and villages on the surrounding coasts of Java and Sumatra, and a large proportion of the coast population, amounting to over 36,000 people, was drowned.'

J. V. Luce *The End of Atlantis*

From this it may be inferred that the earlier Thira explosion could effectively destroy life on Crete only 60 miles away. The blast would destroy buildings and tidal waves perhaps 60–100 metres high moving at 160 km per hour would swamp nearby islands. Crete would have been covered in a layer of acidic ash between 10–75cm thick (10cm effectively destroys the soil for 2 years or more). And so in the end we come back to Plato's words: 'But afterwards there occurred violent earthquakes and floods; and in a single day and night of misfortune the island of Atlantis disappeared in the depths of the sea.'

The excavation of Akrotiri on the south of Thira has revealed a prosperous city with three-storey mansions and wall paintings of quite exquisite beauty. However the excavations have added to the puzzle of Thira as not a single inhabitant has been found buried in the ash and pumice. Excavations on Crete and other islands in the vicinity reveal previous eruptions and it is likely that Thira was abandoned before the final catastrophic eruption that engulfed Akrotiri.

Since the great eruption of about 1400 BC the volcano of Thira has remained active. In 236 BC it erupted again and separated Thirasia from the NW end of Thira. In 196 BC Old Kameni (Hiera) appeared. In 1570 AD the south coast of Thira collapsed into the sea. Three years later Small (Mikra) Kammeni appeared and in 1711–12 Nea Kammeni appeared. In 1866 a violent eruption began and lasted two years. At the end in 1868 an islet, Afotessa, appeared and then disappeared again. In 1925–26 another eruption joined Small Kammeni to Nea Kammeni. In July 1956 a massive earthquake caused much damage destroying many of the buildings at Finikia and Thira. The epicentre of this earthquake was off the north coast of Amorgos and it produced *tsunamis* up to 17 metres high.

NISIS THIRASIA

The westernmost island. The only anchorage is in Ormos Ayios Nikolaos. Anchor off the small hamlet at the foot of the cliffs. The short pier has 3 metre depths at its extremity but it is used by *caïque*-ferries from Thira and Finikia. Good shelter from the *meltemi* although there is invariably some swell in the bay. Open to the S and E. Tavernas ashore. A zig-zag track leads up the cliffs to the village above where some provisions can be obtained.

NISIS NEA KAMMENI

The once hot lump of ash and cinders in the middle of the crater. There are a number of very small inlets around the island where a yacht can anchor. The anchor must have a trip line as the bottom consists of very large rocks which easily snag an anchor.

The best anchorage on Nea Kammeni is in a cove on the SE corner. There is a light structure on the S side of the entrance (Fl.3s4M). Unfortunately most of the quayed area here is used by the local tripper boats and there is little room for even small yachts. Squeeze in where you can. Care must be taken of a foul area off the W side of the cove. There is a small chapel ashore. Open only to the E.

A yacht can also anchor immediately N of the entrance to the cove with a long line ashore. There is reasonable shelter from the *meltemi* here. Several coves N of this anchorage can also be used with care.

Caution Nea Kammeni is infested with very big and bold rats who will not hesitate to come aboard.

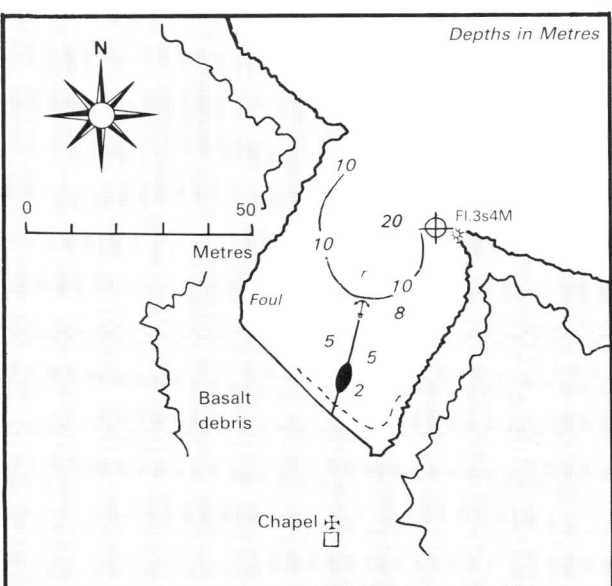

NEA KAMMENI (SOUTHEAST COVE)
36°24'·1N 25°24'·3E (Fl.3s4M)

Thira

The principal island. There are a number of anchorages around the island:

1. *Finikia (Epanomeria)* Lies on the N end of Thira under Ak Epanomeria. There is a short pier with 6 metre depths at the extremity, but it is usually crowded with fishing boats and *caïque*-ferries. Anchor to the W of the mole in 10–20 metres. The bottom is rocky and the anchor should have a trip line. Some shelter from the *meltemi* although there is always some ground swell here. Completely open to the S.

   Two tavernas on the waterfront. A track leads up the cliff to the village of Finikia above.

Thira. Finikia looking NE.

2. *Skala Thira* The harbour for the capital of Thira (Fira) on the steep slopes above. The harbour here, really just a quay cut into the base of the cliff, is very open and you should not leave a yacht unattended. Go stern-to or bows-to with a line to the large mooring buoy off the quay. There is invariably considerable confusion when a yacht on the inside wants to leave. All the yachts on one side or the other must drop their lines or pass them around the yacht leaving, an exercise which leaves ample scope for confusion. Getting out from the spider's web of lines is further complicated by the wash from tripper boats, ferries, and boats carrying passengers to and fro from the cruise ships anchored off. It is recommended you do not leave a yacht unattended on the quay.

Berths on the quay have a lee from the *meltemi* although there is a slop onto the quay. However the wash from other craft passing nearby, especially ferries and cruise ships, is significantly worse than any slop generated by the wind. The small harbour is for local craft.

Water on the quay. There are several taverna/cafés by the harbour. A donkey can be hired for the climb up to the town above or you

can take the recently installed funicular. At Thira town there is good shopping for provisions and excellent restaurants and bars. The view from the *chora* is simply stupendous.

Note The buoy is not always in place. Winter storms or more likely galvanic corrosion in the sulphurous waters corrodes the mooring chain and it can take some time before the authorities replace it. If it is not in place there are few alternatives. You can drop an anchor and go stern or bows-to, but it shelves very steeply off the quay to 20 plus metres. In addition the bottom is foul with large boulders and a trip-line on the anchor is essential.

Looking down onto the yacht quay from Skala Thira.

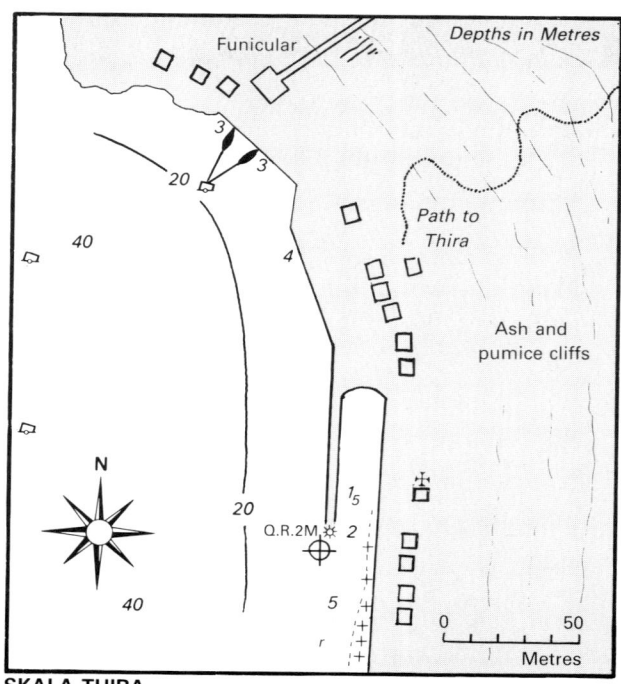

Thira. Skala yacht quay looking ENE. The new funicular is on the left of the photograph.

SKALA THIRA
36°25'·1N 25°25'·7E (Q.R.2M)

The cove under Ak Akrotiri used by local fishermen.

Ak Akrotiri and lighthouse looking NNW.

3. *Athinios* A small harbour 4 miles ENE of Ak Akrotiri used for loading pumice from nearby quarries. It is usually crowded with coasters loading or waiting to be loaded. The village of Megalo Khorion stands atop the cliff behind. If you are going to berth here care must be taken of a submerged mole and debris immediately W of the short pier. There are mostly 6 metre depths off the quay. Go and reconnoitre by dinghy before attempting to berth.

4. *Ak Akrotiri* On the S side of Ak Akrotri there are a number of anchorages sheltered from the *meltemi*.

Directly under the cape there is a deserted bay used by a few local fishing boats on permanent moorings. Anchor in 4–6 metres on a boulder-strewn bottom – use a trip line. A light breeze blows around the W point of the bay and holds you into the ground swell making for a comfortable night's sleep.

Approximately 1½ miles to the E there is a bight with a few houses and a taverna on the shore. Anchor in 4–5 metres. A further 1½ miles to the ESE there is another bight used by local fishing boats. The bottom off the S coast is coarse sand – good holding. These latter anchorages get some ground swell which causes yachts here to roll awfully.

5. *Monolithos* A small harbour approximately halfway along the E coast. A rough breakwater extends for 150 metres in an easterly direction with 2–3 metre depths inside the outer end. The western half of the harbour is shallow. Go bows-to with a long line ashore to the breakwater near its extremity. With the *meltemi* some swell works its way into the harbour. Ashore there are a taverna and showers.

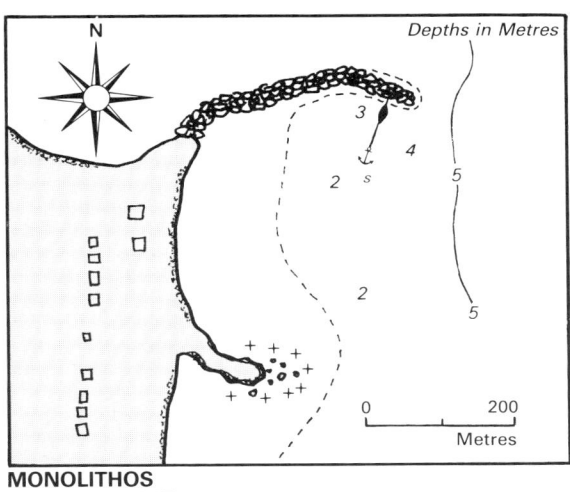

MONOLITHOS
36°24'·5N 29'·2E

NISIDHES KHRISTIANA

A group of jagged rocks lying about 9 miles SW of Ak Akrotiri on Thira. There are no anchorages and they are uninhabited.

Anafi
(Anaphe)

The southeasternmost of the Cyclades. A barren burnt lump of an island with a small *chora* and an exposed anchorage on the south coast. Legend has it that Apollo raised the island from the sea to provide refuge for Jason and the Argonauts during a storm – a myth probably connected to the Thira eruption. A few backpackers are attracted to the island's long sandy beaches.

Skala on Anafi. *Nigel Patten.*

Immediately W of the hamlet a broken-down breakwater running S provides some shelter from westerlies. Anchor in 3–6 metres and with the *meltemi* try to tuck yourself under the breakwater with a long line to it. There is a small pier, but it is always crowded with *caïques*. The bottom is sand – good holding. With the *meltemi* there are gusts and a ground swell making the anchorage very uncomfortable – yachts at anchor roll around awfully. Open to the SW–S–E. Limited provisions and tavernas in the hamlet.

About 3 miles to the E an open bay with a long sandy beach can be used in calm weather.

SKALA ANAFI

A bight on the S coast. The *chora* on the hill and the hamlet around the landing place are conspicuous. There is a light at Skala: Fl.4s5M. The eastern end of the island is a high precipitous peak separated by flat land from the rest of the island and looks like a separate island from the distance. A white chapel on the summit of the peak is conspicuous. Care must be taken of the low-lying Voi Rokana, a rock lying 1¼ miles E of the hamlet and approximately ¼ of a mile offshore.

The eastern end of Anafi looking NW. Note the conspicuous chapel perched precariously on the summit.

VI. Evia and the Northern Sporades

This chapter covers the island of Evia lying parallel to mainland Greece (Locris, Boeotia, Attica), the mainland coast itself from Ak Sounion to the Trikeri peninsula, and the northern Sporades. The inner route up the narrow gulf between Evia and the mainland is the more often travelled, there being sheltered waters and many safe harbours and anchorages. Along the east coast of Evia there are few safe anchorages sheltered from the prevailing wind. Nonetheless in the days of sail, *caïques* bound for the north would take the open water route making for Skiros and then slanting NW to Thessaloniki. The return trip was generally down the inner route.

In classical and Venetian times Evia and Skiros were important intermediate ports along the northern Aegean trade route between Athens and what is now northern Turkey. The trip from west to east was a gruelling slog (with a lot of rowing) against the prevailing winds.

The agricultural and mineral wealth of Evia ensured its own early development into a powerful state with a large fleet of its own, but it was later subdued by Athens. When the Venetians occupied it they considered it important enough to rank it as a kingdom and the standard of Negroponte (as Evia was called under the Venetians) was one of the three flown in St Mark's Square in Venice. Today, despite its proximity to Athens, Evia remains for the most part a wild and unspoiled island.

In ancient times an enemy of Athens wishing to invade the city-state would follow a fairly standard route from the north down through Evia and the adjacent mainland to southern Greece. The Pass of Thermopylae and the Plain of Marathon are probably the two best-known classical battle sites. The land force would be landed or supported from the sea and consequently this stretch of sea resounded to sea battles of which the Athenian harassment of Xerxes' fleet in the Trikeri Channel is possibly best known. Not only the Persian invaders under Xerxes, but also the Macedonians, the Romans (under Glabrio and Cato), and the Turks, used this passage to get to southern and western Greece. In 1941 the British force (with the Australians and New Zealanders), retreating from the Germans in Macedonia came down through here and were evacuated from beaches in Evia and the Saronic Gulf.

Kolpos Petalion and the southern part of Evia are regularly cruised by Athens-based yachts, but further N there are fewer yachts to be seen except around the northern Sporades where a number of flotillas are based.

Weather patterns in Evia and the Northern Sporades

The prevailing wind in the summer is the *meltemi* blowing from the NE. As in the Cyclades the *meltemi* begins fitfully in June, blows strongest in July and August, and dies at the end of September and October. In July and August it blows at Force 4–6 and may reach Force 7 on occasion. In the spring and autumn the wind is again predominantly from the N (NE–NW) but there are regular winds from the S as well.

There are a number of local variations to the overall weather pattern. In the Trikeri and Orei Channels (Stenon Trikeri and Stenon Oreon) the wind is funnelled into the channel so that it blows from the E–ENE. In the gulf of Volos (Pagasitikos Kolpos), a NW wind, Force 2–5, often blows down the valley at the head of the gulf in the spring and autumn. There may also be southerlies which can also blow in the summer months.

In the winter, gales are more often than not from the NE and can be exceptionally harsh. In early December (1980) a gale from the NE reached Force 10 and snow covered most parts of Evia down to sea level. In the mountains, up to a metre of snow fell and transport, telecommunications and electricity facilities were knocked out for three days. Snow on the decks is not what most people associate with Greece.

As in the Cyclades care must be taken of gusts off high land when the *meltemi* is blowing. Places noted for these squalls are the Evia coast in Kolpos Petalion, the Evia coast N of Khalkis, and the E coast of Skiros.

In the summer the temperatures are high averaging 25°–26°C. Thessaly has the reputation of being the hottest place in Europe and certainly Volos is very hot in the summer (average temperature 27°C). In the spring and autumn there may be rain showers and thunderstorms. The latter may be accompanied by squalls, but they are normally short-lived affairs, usually over in 2 hours or so. The winters are harsher than those in more southern climes with colder temperatures and substantial snowfalls.

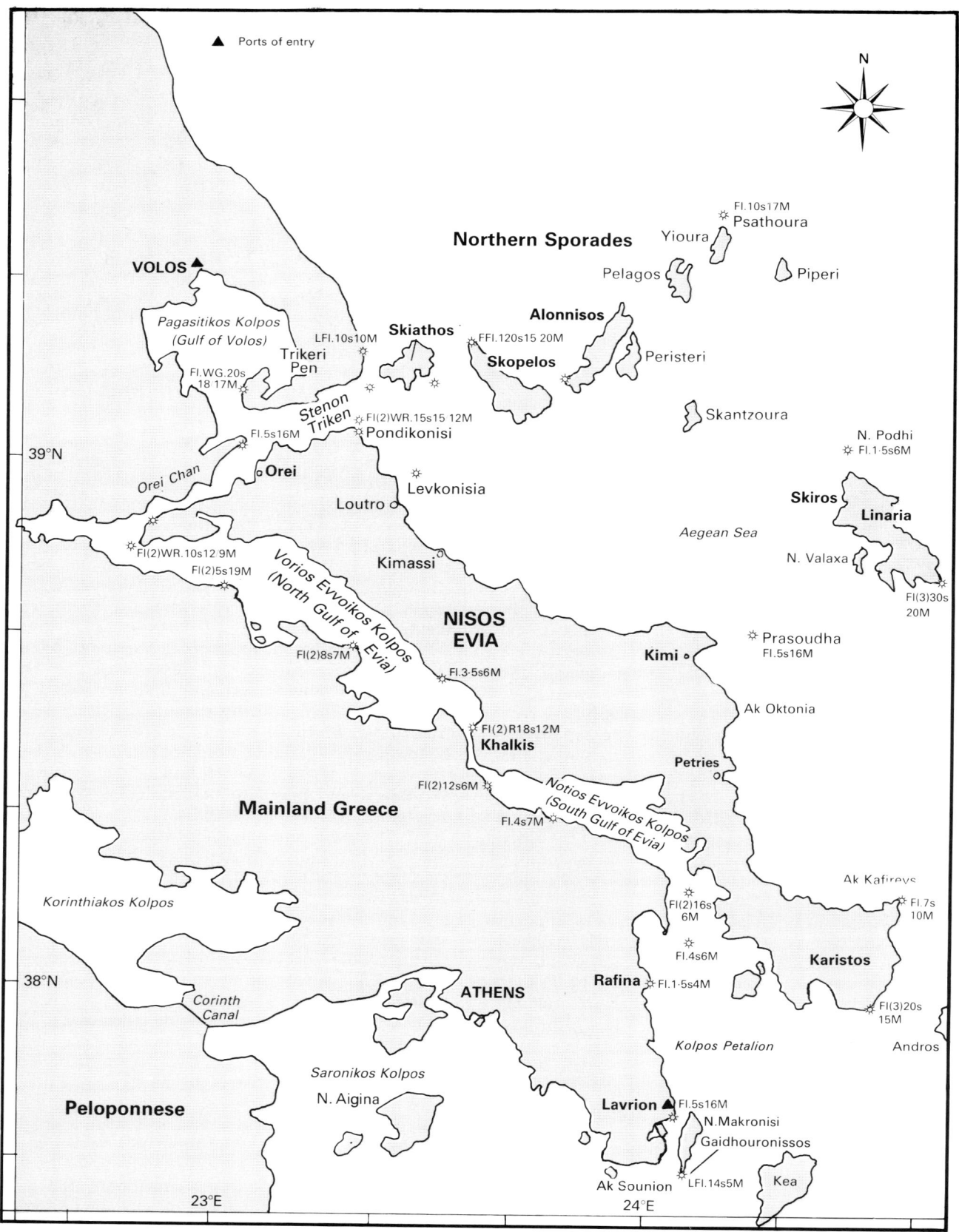

▲ Ports of entry

N

Northern Sporades

Fl.10s17M
Psathoura
Yioura
Pelagos
Piperi

VOLOS ▲

Pagasitikos Kolpos
(Gulf of Volos)

Skiathos
LFl.10s10M
Alonnisos
FFl.120s15 20M
Trikeri Pen
Skopelos
Peristeri
Fl.WG.20s
18 17M
Stenon Triken
Fl(2)WR.15s15 12M
Pondikonisi
Skantzoura
Fl.5s16M
39°N
Orei Chan
Orei
Levkonisia
N. Podhi
Fl.1·5s6M
Loutro
Aegean Sea
Skiros
Linaria
Fl(2)WR.10s12·9M
Kimassi
N. Valaxa
Fl(2)5s19M
Vorios Evvoikos Kolpos
(North Gulf of Evia)
NISOS
EVIA
Prasoudha
Fl.5s16M
Fl(3)30s
20M
Fl(2)8s7M
Fl.3·5s6M
Kimi
Ak Oktonia
Fl(2)R18s12M
Khalkis
Petries
Fl(2)12s6M
Mainland Greece
Notios Evvoikos Kolpos
(South Gulf of Evia)
Fl.4s7M
Ak Kafireys
Fl.7s
10M
Fl(2)16s
6M
Korinthiakos Kolpos
Fl.4s6M
Karistos
38°N
Rafina
Fl.1·5s4M
Corinth
Canal
Fl(3)20s
15M
Kolpos Petalion
Andros
Saronikos Kolpos
N. Aigina
Lavrion ▲
Fl.5s16M
N.Makronisi
Peloponnese
Gaidhouronissos
Ak Sounion
LFl.14s5M
Kea
23°E
24°E

Data

PORTS OF ENTRY
Lavrion
Volos

PROHIBITED AREAS
1. Anchoring is prohibited in the northern part of Ormos Marathon and at Ormos Ayios Marina.
2. Landing is prohibited in the vicinity of Ormos Ayios Marina and on the nearby islands of Stira, Verdhouyi and Kavaliani.
3. Landing is prohibited on Nisos Yiouri in the Northern Sporades.

MAJOR LIGHTS
Nisis Patroklou (Gaidhouronissos) LFl.14s5M
Ak Vrisaki Fl.5s16M
Nisis Mandhili (Doro Channel) Fl(3)20s15M
Ak Velani Fl.1·5s4M
Vrakhinisis Dhipsa Fl.4s6M
Nisidhes Verdhouyi (Nisis Ligia) Fl(2)16s6M
Ormos Oropou (SE point) Fl.4s7M
Ak Avlis (Dhiavlos Avlidhos) Fl(2)12s6M
Ak Kakokefali Fl(2)R.18s12M
Ak Mnima Fl.3·5s6M
Ak Stalamata Fl(2)8s7M
Ak Arkitsa Fl(2)5s19M
Nisis Strongili (S islet) Fl(2)WR.10s12/9M
Ak Vasilina Oc.WG.5s14/11M
Ifalos Panagitsa (Orei Reef) Fl(2)12s9M
Aryioronisos (E end) Fl.5s16M
Ak Trikeri AlFl.WWG.20s18/17M
Volos - Cement Factory W jetty Fl(2)10s12M
Pondikonisi Fl(2)WR.15s15/12M
Ifalos Levtheris Fl(2)8s8M
Ak Sepia LFl.10s10M
Nisis Repi (Skiathos) Fl(2)WR.10s6/9M
Ak Gourouni (Skopelos) Fl(3)30s20M
Ak Telion (Alonissos) Fl(3)12s7M
Nisis Psathoura Fl.10s17M
Ak Lithari (Skiros) Fl(3)30s16M
Nisis Arapis (Ak Kafirevs) Fl(2)15s10M
Nisis Prasoudha (Kimi) Fl.5s16M
Levkonisia (NE Evia) Fl(3)15s6M

Quick reference guide

	Shelter	Mooring	Fuel	Water	Provisioning	Tavernas	Plan
Evia and adjacent coast							
Gaidhouromandra	B	AC	B	A	O	C	●
Lavrion	B	A	B	A	A	B	●
Ormos Ayios Nikolaos	B	C	O	O	O	O	
Tourkolimani	C	C	O	O	O	O	
Porto Rafti	B	AC	B	B	B	B	●
Rafina	C	A	B	B	B	B	●
Ayios Andreas	C	A	O	O	O	O	
Nea Makri	C	A	B	B	B	C	
Ormos Marathonas	O	C	O	O	O	O	
Ormos Oropos	O	C	B	B	B	C	
Ormos Kastri	B	C	O	O	O	O	

	Shelter	Mooring	Fuel	Water	Provisioning	Tavernas	Plan
Karistos	A	A	B	A	A	A	●
Nisidhes Petaloi	C	C	O	O	O	O	●
Nea Marmari	C	AC	B	A	B	B	●
Nea Stira	C	C	O	B	C	C	
Almiropotamos	B	C	O	O	O	O	
Voufalo	A	C	O	O	O	C	●
Aliverion	A	A	O	A	B	B	●
Amarinthos	O	C	B	B	B	B	
Eretria	B	C	B	B	A	B	●
Khalkis	B	AB	A	A	A	A	●
Larimna	C	C	B	A	B	C	●
Ormos Atlantis	B	C	O	O	C	C	●
Ayios Konstandinos	O	AB	O	B	B	B	
Nea Artaki	B	C	B	B	A	B	
Limni	O	C	B	B	B	C	
Loutra Adhipsou	O	C	B	B	A	B	

	Shelter	Mooring	Fuel	Water	Provisioning	Tavernas	Plan
Northern Evia Channels and the Gulf of Volos							
Limin Stilidhos	B	AB	B	B	A	C	●
Karavomilos	C	C	O	B	C	C	
Rahes	C	C	O	B	C	B	
Ormos Vathikelon	A	C	O	O	O	O	
Ormos Glifas	C	C	B	A	B	B	
Orei	A	A	B	A	B	B	●
Ormos Pteleou	B	C	O	B	C	B	
Ay Kiriaki	C	C	O	B	C	C	
Nisis Palaio Trikeri	C	C	O	O	C	C	
Skala Trikeri	O	C	O	O	O	O	
Limin Vathoudhi	A	C	O	B	O	C	●
Petraki	B	C	O	O	O	O	
Amalioupolis	C	AC	B	A	B	B	●
Fearless Cove	B	C	O	O	O	O	●
Nea Ankhialos	C	A	B	B	C	B	
Ay Yeoryios	A	AC	O	B	C	C	
Volos	B	A	A	A	A	A	●
Ormos Andriami	C	C	O	O	O	O	
Platania	C	C	B	B	B	B	
Pondikonisi	C	C	O	O	O	O	
Skiathos							
Koukounaries	A	A	O	B	O	C	●
Skiathos	B	ABC	B	A	A	A	●
Skopelos							
Glossa	B	AC	O	A	C	B	●
Ormos Panormos	B	C	O	O	O	C	●
Ormos Agnondas	B	AC	O	O	O	C	●
Ormos Stafilos	C	C	O	O	O	O	
Limin Skopelon	B	A	B	A	A	B	●
Alonissos							
Ormos Mourtia	O	C	O	O	O	O	
Patitiri	B	A	A	A	B	B	●
Votsi	B	C	O	B	O	C	●
Ormos Tzorti	B	C	O	O	O	O	
Steni Vala	B	C	O	O	O	C	
Ormos Firakos	O	C	O	O	O	O	
Peristeri							
Ormos Xero Bay	B	C	O	O	O	O	
Ormos Vasiliko	A	C	O	O	O	O	

	Shelter	Mooring	Fuel	Water	Provisioning	Tavernas	Plan
Pelagos							
Ormos Kira Panayia	C	C	O	O	O	O	●
Limin Planitis	A	C	O	O	O	O	●
Skantzoura							
Ormos Paurassa	C	C	O	O	O	O	
Ormos Skantzoura	C	C	O	O	O	O	
Skiros							
Av Fokas	C	C	O	O	O	O	
Linaria Cove	B	C	O	O	O	C	
Limin Linaria	B	A	B	A	B	C	●
Ormos Akladhi	B	C	O	O	O	O	
Ormos Tribuki	O	C	O	O	O	O	
Ormos Renes	C	C	O	O	O	O	
Ormos Glifadha	B	C	O	O	O	O	
East Coast of Evia							
Ormos Petries	B	AC	O	B	C	C	●
Kimi	B	A	A	A	C	C	●
Ormos Loutro	C	C	O	O	O	O	

West coast of Evia and adjacent mainland coast

This section covers the stretch of water hemmed in between the island of Evia and the adjacent mainland coast. The section is split into a further two sub-sections covering the sea area S of Khalkis (Kolpos Petalion and Notios Evvoikos Kolpos/the S Gulf of Evia) and N of Khalkis (Vorios Evvoikos Kolpos/the N Gulf of Evia).

Evia (also Evoia, Euboea, or Euripos after the narrow channel at Khalkis) or Negroponte, the Venetian name, is the long mountainous island lying parallel in a NW/SE direction to the mainland coast. After Crete it is the largest Greek island. The irregular mountain range is geographically the continuation of the Pilion range running down the east side of the Gulf of Volos. Mt Dhirfis (Dhelfi), 45 miles NW of Ak Kafirevs, is the summit of the island at 1874 metres (5718ft). Ten miles further NW, Mt Pixaria is 1445 metres (4406ft) high, and at the southern end of the island Mt Okhi is 1398 metres (4586ft) high. Between these considerable peaks the island is rugged and steep-to with little flat land except on the W coast. The peaks are covered in snow in the winter and often far into the spring. On the lower slopes the mountains are densely wooded in pine, plane, holm oak and olive trees. The coastal plains on the west are fertile and intensively cultivated in corn, vines, figs and market gardens. Lignite and magnesite are mined and marble quarried – Evian *cipollino* was prized above all others by the Romans.

The mainland coast opposite is also mountainous, although it is not in the league of the Evian mountains. Mt Knimis, standing inland from the cape of the same name in the N, is 946 metres (3077ft) high, a peak opposite Khalkis with a conspicuous white patch near the summit rises to 1030 metres (3350ft), and Mt Pendelikon near Athens rises to 1119 metres (3638ft). For the most part the mainland mountains are barren or covered in *maquis*, but the coastal plain is wooded or cultivated. From a point opposite Khalkis the motorway north mostly follows the coastline.

In antiquity Evia was divided between seven city-states of which Khalkis and Eretria were the two most important. These two cities were rivals for the fertile Lelantine Plain lying between them with Khalkis finally winning by default when Eretria was razed by the invading Persians. After the Persian wars Evia came under the sway of Athens. It passed on to Rome and to Byzantium without too many hiccups.

When the Venetians took Evia they renamed the island, calling it Negroponte, meaning 'black bridge' – a corruption of the name of the bridge spanning the Euripos Channel. Under the Venetians it ranked as a kingdom. In 1470 the island was occupied by the Turks and remained under Turkish rule until it became Greek in 1830.

The proximity of the mainland coast to Athens (Rafina is only 18½ miles away) has raised this area to the dubious status of a summer commuter belt. Large villas line much of the coast between Lavrion and Khalkis and land development is beginning north of Khalkis. Athenians have also started to go to Evia, but the poor roads and sheer size of the island ensure that most parts of it remain virtually untouched.

i. Coasts south of Khalkis

GAIDHOUROMANDRA (Gaidaromandri)

Approach

Conspicuous From the S the boatyard cannot be seen until you have rounded Ak Fonias. Once around the cape the boatyard, the masts of the yachts on the hard and the large main building are conspicuous. From the N the two tall chimneys at Ay Nikolaos and the buildings of Lavrion will be seen before the boatyard.

By night Use the light on Ak Fonias (Fl.2·4s6M). A night approach is not recommended because of the unlit mooring buoys and the yachts on them in the bay, and the various foul areas which are difficult to identify at night.

Note In the approach keep to the S side of the bay to avoid the wreck (see below).

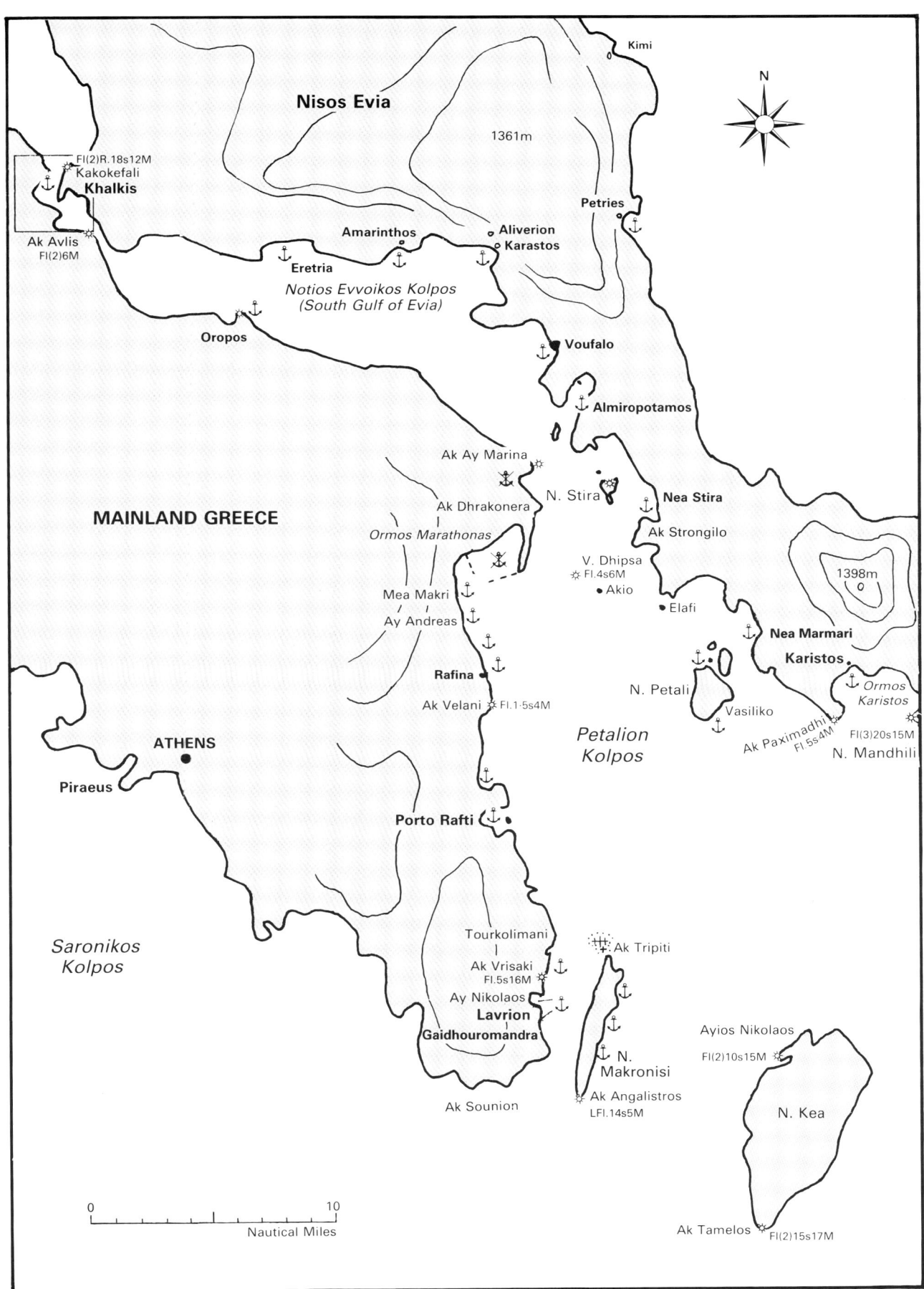

Nisos Evia

Kimi

1361m

Fl(2)R.18s12M
Kakokefali
Khalkis

Petries

Ak Avlis
Fl(2)6M

Amarinthos   **Aliverion**
                 Karastos

Eretria

Notios Evvoikos Kolpos
(South Gulf of Evia)

Oropos

Voufalo

Almiropotamos

Ak Ay Marina

Ak Dhrakonera   N. Stira   **Nea Stira**

Ormos Marathonas   Ak Strongilo

MAINLAND GREECE   V. Dhipsa
                                 Fl.4s6M
                                 Akio   1398m
Mea Makri   Elafi
Ay Andreas   **Nea Marmari**

Rafina   **Karistos**

Ak Velani   Fl.1·5s4M   N. Petali   *Ormos*
                                 Vasiliko   *Karistos*
ATHENS   *Petalion*   Ak Paximadhi   Fl(3)20s15M
                            Kolpos   Fl.5s4M
Piraeus   **N. Mandhili**

Porto Rafti

Saronikos
Kolpos   Tourkolimani
                             |
                        Ak Vrisaki   Ak Tripiti
                        Fl.5s16M
                        Ay Nikolaos   Ayios Nikolaos
                        Lavrion   Fl(2)10s15M
Gaidhouromandra
                                    N.
                                 Makronisi   N. Kea
                        Ak Sounion
                             Ak Angalistros
                             LFl.14s5M

0   10
Nautical Miles   Ak Tamelos   Fl(2)15s17M

PETALION KOLPOS AND SOUTH GULF OF EVIA

Olympic quay and yard at Gaidhouromandra looking NW from
the S side of the bay.

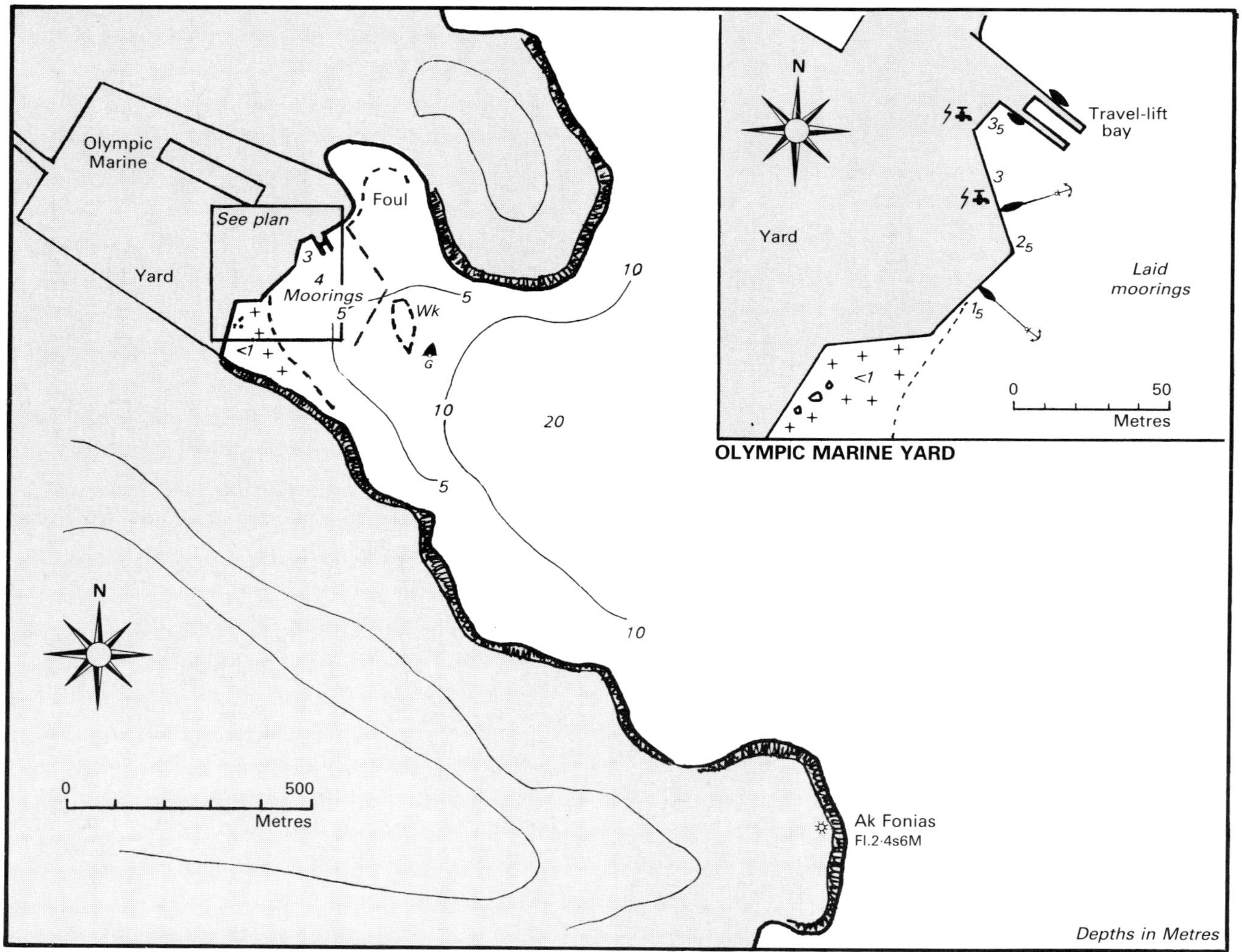

OLYMPIC MARINE YARD

Travel-lift
bay

Yard

Laid
moorings

N

0   50
Metres

Olympic
Marine

Foul

See plan

Yard

3

4
Moorings

5

5

Wk

G

<1

10

10

20

5

10

N

0   500
Metres

Ak Fonias
Fl.2·4s6M

Depths in Metres

GAIDHOUROMANDRA (OLYMPIC MARINE)
37°41'·8N 24°03'·7E

292

Dangers

1. Care must be taken of a wreck just under the water in the bay marked by a small green conical buoy. The small buoy is not always in place and care must therefore be taken when navigating in the bay. Some anger has been expressed at Olympic Marine for not clearly marking this obstruction, though to no avail.
2. Care is also needed of debris in the cove on the N side of Gaidhouromandra.

VHF Ch 12

Mooring

Go stern or bows-to the quayed area where there are sufficient depths or pick up a buoy. Care must be taken not to approach the SW part of the quayed area which is shallow and rock-bound. It is not recommended you anchor because of the foul bottom.

Shelter Although open to the E and SE, the protection in the bay is better than it looks. Reasonable protection from the *meltemi* although it can be a bit bumpy at times. Moderate winds from the E and SE do not blow home.

Authorities Olympic Marine staff. VHF channel 12. A charge is made to go on the quay or on a mooring buoy.

Facilities

Services Water and electricity on the quay. Shower and toilet block.

Fuel Can be delivered by mini-tanker.

Repairs Yachts up to 40 tons can be lifted out by a travel-hoist. Hard standing for around 600 yachts. The yard will undertake all types of work including marine engine repairs, woodwork, and specialist GRP repairs. (The latter include repairs to yachts suffering from osmosis.) Life rafts and fire extinguishers can be serviced. General *gardiennage* including winter lay-up and commissioning. For information on services and charges contact Olympic Marine S.A. Lavrion, Attica, Greece. ☎ 0292 25782/4. Telex 21-5522 OLYA-GR. Fax (0292) 22569.

Provisions Nearby in Lavrion. There is a market on Thursday.

Eating out Foti's taverna at the yard offers good food at good prices. Otherwise tavernas in Lavrion.

Other Telephone, telex, and fax services available. Infrequent bus service to Athens.

General

At one time Olympic Yachts built Carter 33s, 37s, and 39s, and Olympic 45s here, which accounts for the comparatively large numbers of these yachts in Greek waters. Now patrol boats are built. With the demise of yacht building Olympic Marine turned to laying up yachts and after a few hiccups has evolved into a competent and well-run yard. There have been plans to build a marina here for some time and every now and again the project surfaces again, but at the time of writing nothing has been started.

If Olympic Marine has any drawbacks it is that it is in the middle of nowhere. Sleepy Lavrion is nearby, (a bicycle is a good idea or it is about half an hour's brisk walk), but to get into Athens and back on the bus takes up a day.

LAVRION
Admiralty chart no. 1833

Approach

Conspicuous The harbour lies immediately N of Gaidhouromandra and from the S the buildings of the town are easily identified. From the N the two tall chimneys at Ay Nikolaos in the bay N of Lavrion (Ormos Thorikou) will be seen.

By night Use the lights on Ak Fonias (Fl.2.4s6M) and Ak Ergastiria (Fl.1.5s4M). The two chimneys at Ay Nikolaos are lit by fixed red lights with a good range.

Mooring

Go stern or bows-to or alongside the L-shaped pier on the N leaving the ferry berth clear. The bottom is mud, good holding.

Shelter Good shelter tucked in behind the pier. As with Gaidhouromandra, moderate winds from the E–SE do not blow home.

Authorities A port of entry: port police, customs and immigration.

Facilities

Water On the pier on the W.

Fuel Can be delivered by mini-tanker.

Repairs Most mechanical repairs.

Provisions Good shopping for provisions nearby.

Eating out Tavernas in the town.

Other PO. OTE. Bank. Greek gas and *Camping Gaz*. Infrequent bus to Athens. Ferry to Kea and Kithnos.

N pier at Lavrion looking WSW from the slag heap.

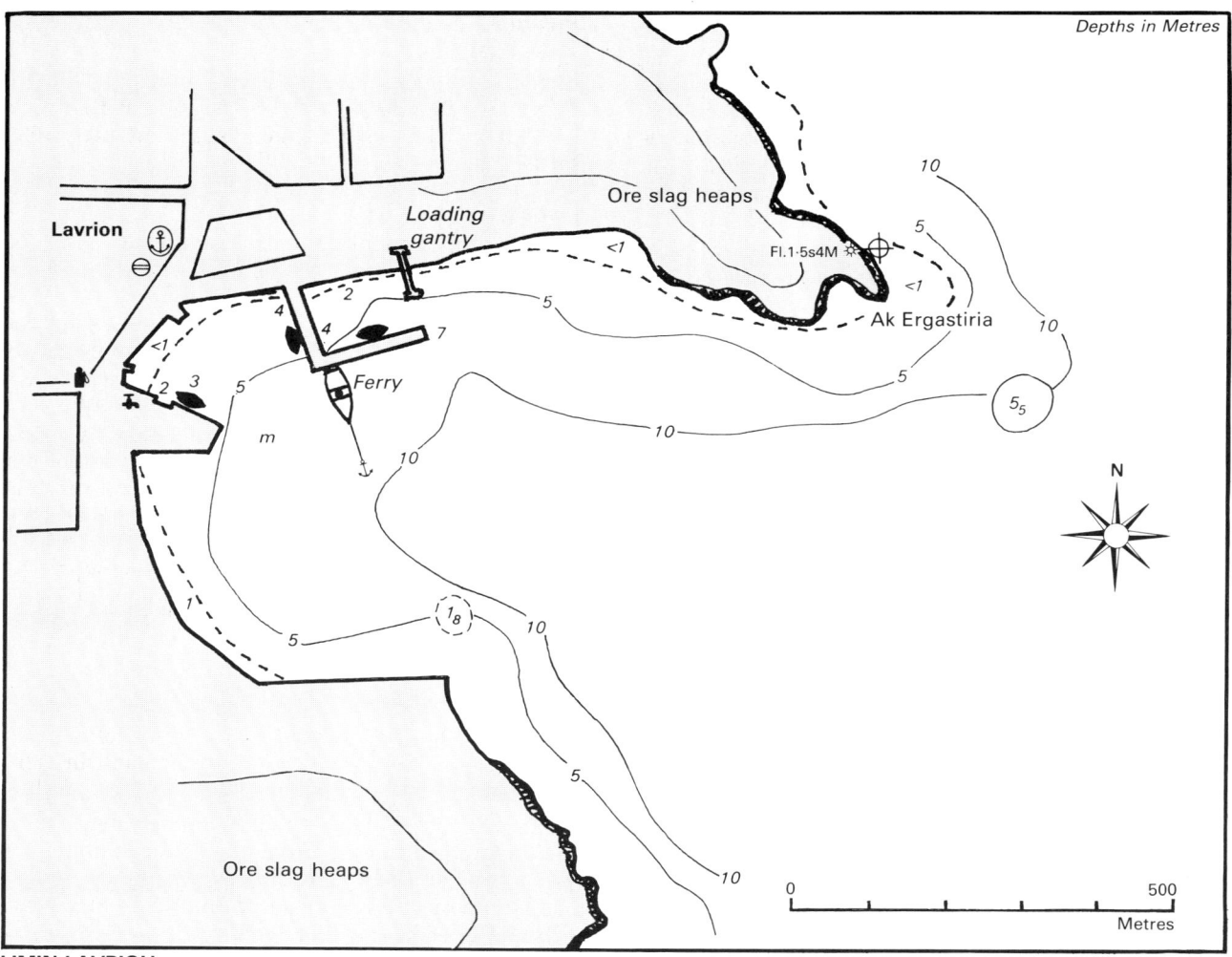

LIMIN LAVRIOU
37°42'·9N 24°04'E (Ak Ergastira light)

General

Lavrion was once an important port shipping cadmium and manganese and small amounts of lead from the reworking of the ancient mine tailings. The mines were probably worked as early as 1000 BC and in classical times large amounts of silver were extracted from the Lavrion mines whose wealth boosted Athens' commercial power.

Today Lavrion is a grubby 'has-been' port with piles of slag and ore littered around the coast. Yet it has its own charm, a sort of faded dignity and glimpses of old-world wealth in the slums, and most of those who spend some time here while working on a boat in the Olympic yard have a certain fondness for the place that is not readily apparent on a first visit.

ORMOS AYIOS NIKOLAOS (Vrisaki, Frangolimani)

This bay lies immediately S of Ak Vrisaki and is the site of a large power station and several other factories. Two very tall chimneys (red and white bands) are conspicuous from a considerable distance off. There are a substantial pier and quayed sections, but these are for cargo ships only. Anchor in the bay. Good shelter from the *meltemi*. Open only to the E.

TOURKOLIMANI

Half a mile N of Ak Vrisaki this bay offers reasonable shelter from the *meltemi*. Anchor in the N cove. Open to the SE.

MAKRONISI (Nisos Eleni)

The long thin island lying parallel to the Attica coast between Ak Sounion and Nisos Kea. It is a rugged hilly island rising to 274m (899ft) at the N end. The E coast of the island has numerous bays and coves along it that can be used according to the wind direction. Most of them are open to the *meltemi* blowing down from the NE although Ormos Angalistros at the S end and Ormos Yerolimonias about a third of the way up on the E side look as if they would give some shelter from the *meltemi*. Care is needed of Ifalos Angalistros, the reef lying 0.15 miles S of the entrance to Ormos Angalistros.

Note When passing through Stenon Makronisou, the channel between Makronisos and the mainland coast, care must be taken of Ifalos Tripiti, a reef just awash, lying half a mile NW of Ak Tripiti, the N extremity of Makronisos. The remains of a wrecked coaster that formerly marked the reef have all but disappeared.

PORTO RAFTI (Ormos Markopoulo, Raptis, Mesoyaias)

Approach

Conspicuous Nisis Raftis with a large statue atop is conspicuous from seaward. Closer in the cluster of villas and apartment blocks skirting the shore will be seen.

By night Use the light on Nisis Raftis: Fl.2s9M. A night approach should be made with caution.

Dangers

1. Caution must be exercised in the vicinity of the anchorage on account of the permanent mooring floats on the surface.
2. Care must be taken of a foul area off the N side of Limin Mesoyaias.

Mooring

Anchor in the NW corner in 4–10 metres. Alternatively go stern or bows-to the quay in the cove on the N side of Ak Pounda. The bottom is mud or sand – good holding.

Shelter Good shelter from the *meltemi*. Although the bay is open to the E and SE these winds do not blow home and the islands in the entrance break up the swell. A number of yachts are regularly wintered here.

Authorities Port police.

Facilities

Water At Raftis.
Fuel A mini-tanker can deliver to Raftis.
Provisions Most provisions can be found at Raftis. A supermarket although it is a fair distance from Raftis.
Eating out Tavernas at Raftis and others around the shore.
Other PO. OTE. Infrequent bus to Athens.

General

Around the shores of this fine natural harbour the Athenians have built their summer villas and apartments transforming what was a simple fishing community into a prospering summer commuter belt. Incredibly the inhabitants have taken the worst of instant reinforced concrete non-architecture found around Athens and transplanted it here – the result is simply awful and were it not for the remarkable beauty of the bay, it would look like Athens itself.

The statue on Rafti Island probably dates from the Roman occupation and is known locally as the tailor – whence the modern name of the harbour (*rafti* = tailor).

ORMOS VRAONAS

A large bay just over 2 miles N of Porto Rafti. Local boats are kept on permanent moorings and in calm weather a yacht can anchor here. It is partially sheltered from the NE by a small islet on the N side.

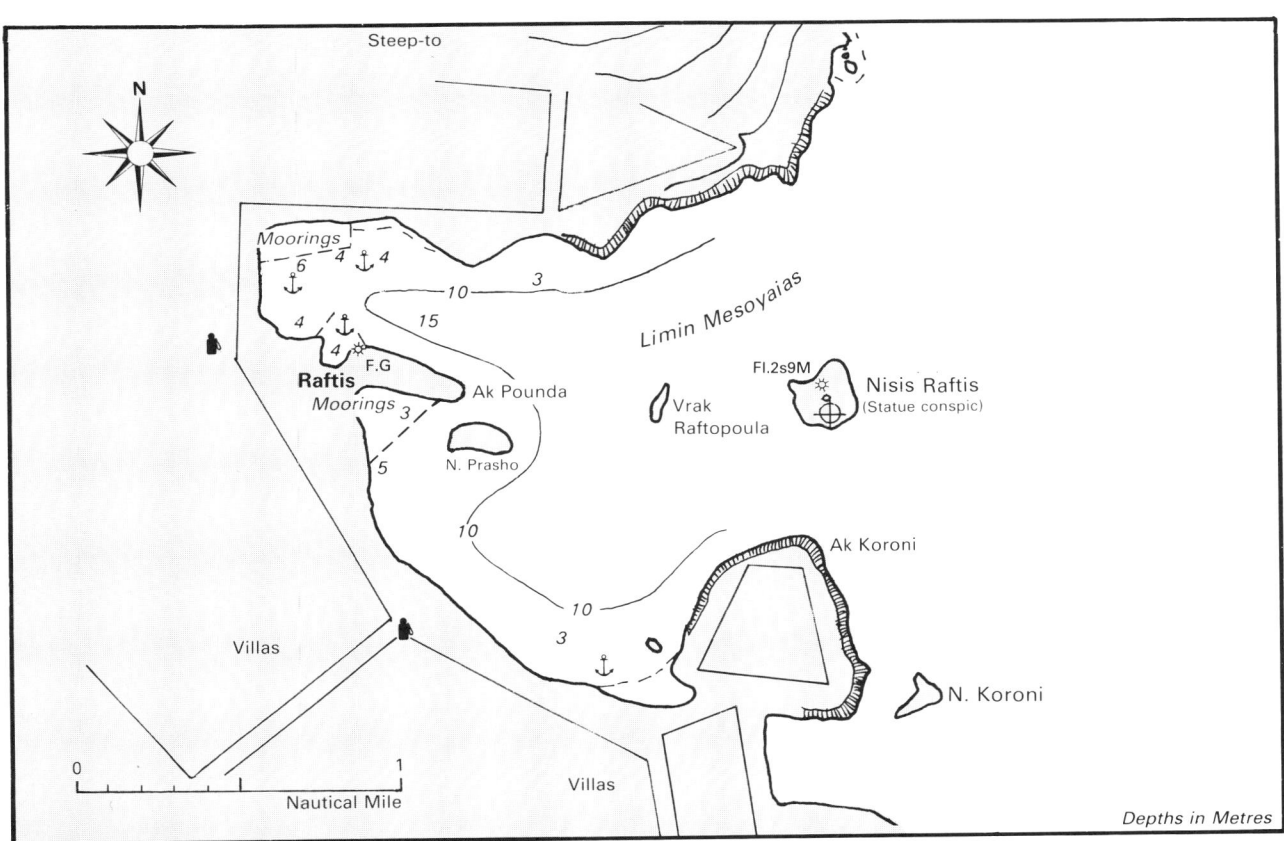

PORTO RAFTI
37°53′N 24°07′·7E (N. Raftis light)

ARTIMEDOS YACHT CLUB

Along the coast between Ormos Vraonas and Rafina, the coast is lined by villas and apartment blocks which stretch in an almost unbroken line along the coast. The effect is not attractive. At Loutra there is a small private yacht harbour, the Artimedos Yacht Club, where small yachts may find a berth. Good shelter inside the harbour. Provisions and tavernas nearby.

RAFINA

Approach

A ferry harbour 7 miles N of Porto Rafti. The cluster of buildings on a knoll above the harbour and the slopes behind is easily identified. Closer in the new mole will be seen. The harbour is lit: Fl.G.1·5s3M, F.G.3M and Q.G on the buoy off the new mole.

Mooring

Go stern or bows-to in the inner basin. The harbour is nearly always uncomfortable. With N and S winds there is a surge in the basin which could be dangerous in strong S winds.

Facilities

Water on the quay. Fuel nearby. Provisions and tavernas in the town. PO. OTE. Ferries to Evia and the northern Cyclades. Bus to Athens.

General

The town is a pleasant enough place, but the uncomfortable harbour means that most yachtsmen's memories of it are less than favourable. Unless it is flat calm outside the surge in the harbour is simply awful, though when the new mole is finished shelter may be improved.

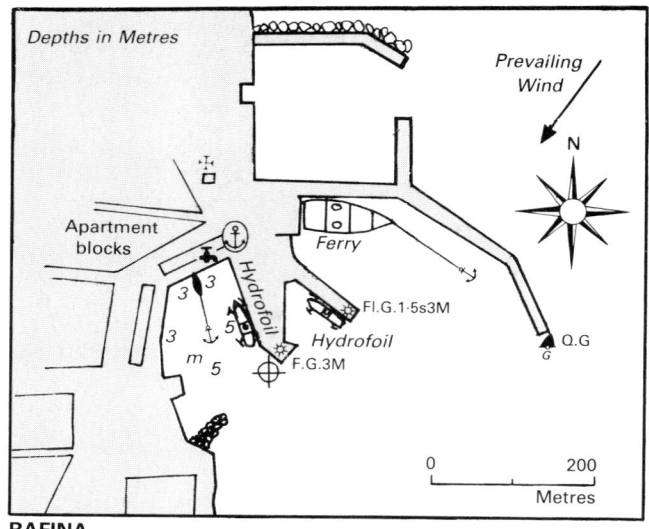

RAFINA
38°01′·4N 24°00′·6E (F.G.3M)

NAOMA

About ¾ of a mile N of Rafina there is a small boat harbour affording protection from the *meltemi*. There are 2 metre depths reported close inside. Open to the S. There are a number of large hotels nearby.

AYIOS ANDREAS

About 2½ miles N of Rafina a curved mole forms a small boat harbour.

NEA MAKRI

About 3¾ miles N of Rafina an 'L' shaped mole forms a small harbour offering shelter from the *meltemi*. There are reported to be 2 metre depths close inside the extremity of the mole.

Rafina looking ENE.

ORMOS MARATHONAS

In calm weather a yacht can anchor on the W side of the bay. If the *meltemi* is blowing a considerable swell sets into the bay and it is unwise to anchor off this lee shore.

The Battle of Marathon

The Battle of Marathon in which the Athenians defeated the Persians has come down through history as the battle *par excellence* where the valiant few triumphed over superior forces. Of it Dr Johnson said: 'That man is little to be envied whose patriotism would not gain force upon the Plain of Marathon.' For the layman there is little to see but the site of the battle and the grave mounds.

The Persian invasion of Greece reached the Plain of Marathon without hindrance. The Athenians commanding the only road to Athens numbered 10,000 while the Persian force numbered at least 24,000. (Estimates of the Persian force vary between an impossible 5¼ million and 24,000). The Persians delayed attacking the strong Greek position and eventually decided to take Athens from the sea. Some time around mid-August 490 BC the Persians began to embark for the sea invasion whereupon the Greeks launched a surprise attack. The Persians were not properly drawn up for battle and the surprise attack confused their forces. In the rush to put to sea 6,400 Persians were killed while the Athenians lost 192.

This battle proved that the Persians, once thought to be invincible, could be defeated. During the battle the ghostly figures of Pan and Theseus are said to have appeared to assist the Athenians and to this day the plain is said to resound to the cries of battle and the clash of arms. Contrary to normal practice the bodies of the dead were buried where they fell in honour of their valour. Excavations of the grave mounds confirmed this ancient tradition associated with battle.

PROHIBITED ANCHORAGE AND LANDING

1. Anchoring is prohibited in the area enclosed by an imaginary line running 2¼ miles SW of Ak Marathonas and then 1½ miles NW (the N half of the bay). A floating target lies in this area.
2. Landing is prohibited between Ak Dhrakonera and a point 2 miles NW of Ak Ay Marina.
3. It is prohibited to enter the harbour enclosed by a mole under Ak Ay Marina.

These areas and the harbour at Ay Marina belong to the Greek army and are mostly used for recreational purposes.

ORMOS OROPOS

An open bay directly S of Eretria, it is the mainland ferry terminal for Eretria. Local craft are kept here in the summer on permanent moorings. Reasonable shelter. Provisions and tavernas in Nea Palatea.

Evia coast south of Khalkis

ORMOS KASTRI

Lying 2 miles NE of Nisis Mandhili on the SE coast of Evia, this bay affords good shelter to a yacht waiting for the wind and sea to moderate in the Doro Strait. Anchor at the head of the bay in 4–6 metres. The bottom is sand – good holding. There is another unnamed bay 1¼ miles NE of Kastri which also provides good shelter from the *meltemi*. No facilities.

DORO STRAIT (Stenon Kafirevs/Kafireos) See Andros in Chapter V.

KARISTOS (Karysto)

Approach

Conspicuous The town of Karistos at the foot of the high mountain range is easily seen from seaward. Nisis Ay Pelayia with a chapel on it lies a mile SW of the harbour and a fort immediately E of the harbour is conspicuous.

By night Use the lights on Nisis Paximadhi (Fl.5s4M) and Nisis Mandhili (Fl(3)20s15M) and once into Ormos Karistou the lights at the entrance to the harbour: Fl.G.1·5s3M and 2F.R(vert)3M.

Dangers With strong N winds there are violent gusts into Ormos Karistou off the surrounding mountains. Care must be taken if sailing into the bay. The Admiralty *Pilot* states that light cloud around the summit of Oros Okhi, the peak inland of Karistos, heralds N winds.

Mooring

Berth stern or bows-to the town quay in the inner basin. It is often very crowded in here with fishing boats – if you can't find a berth go stern or bows-to the quay W of the ferry pier. The bottom is mud – good holding.

Karistos looking E.

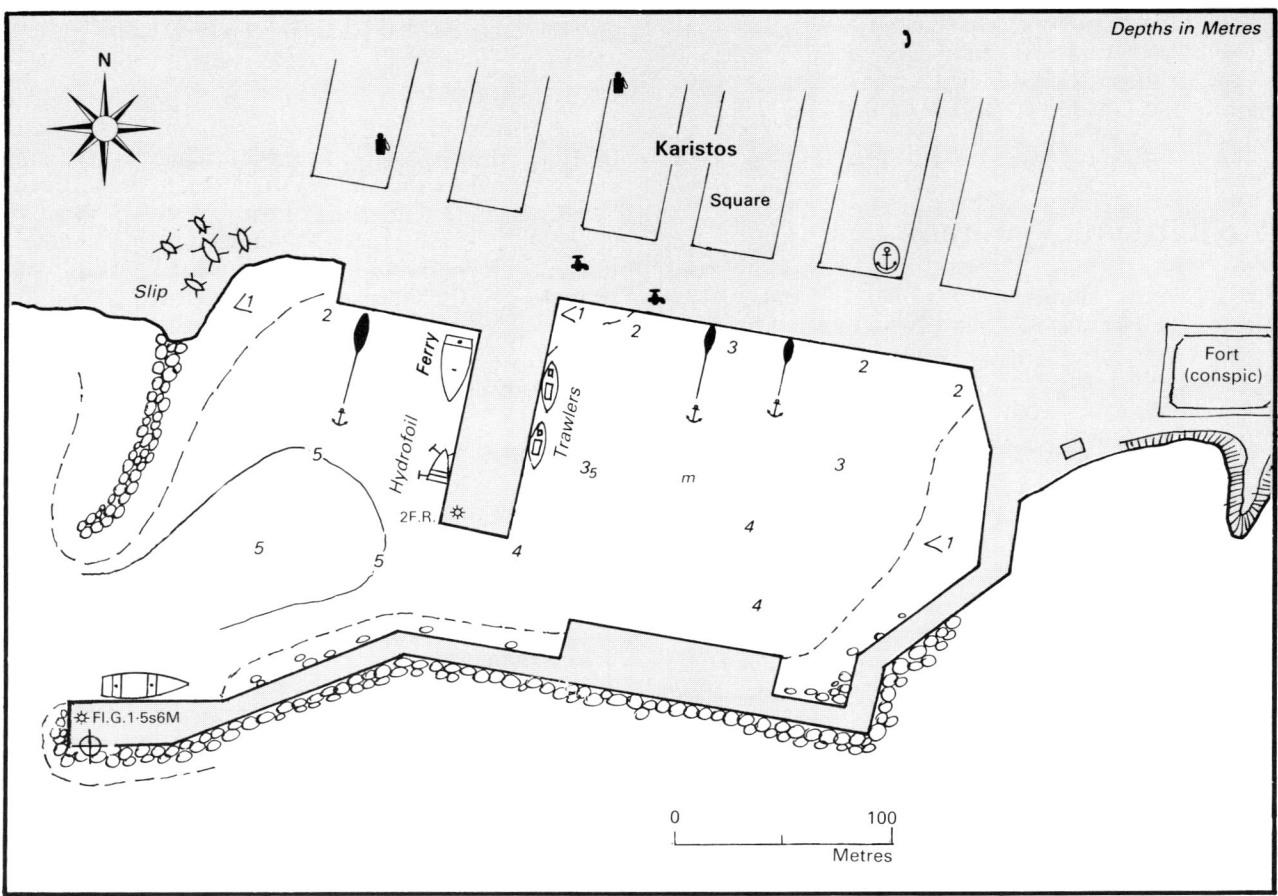

KARISTOS
38°00'·5N 24°25'E (Fl.G.6M)

Shelter Good all-round shelter.
Authorities Port police and customs.

Facilities

Water Nearby in the square.
Fuel In the town. A mini-tanker can deliver to the quay.
Repairs Minor mechanical repairs.
Provisions Good shopping for provisions nearby in the town.
Eating out Good tavernas and bars around the waterfront.
Other PO. OTE. Bank. Greek gas and *Camping Gaz.* Infrequent bus to Khalkis. Ferry and hydrofoil to Rafina.

General

Karistos is a growing tourist resort situated on a narrow strip of land at the foot of a magnificent mountain range. In places the range drops sheer to the sea for 500 metres or more and if the seafarer is daring or foolhardy he can take a bus trip along the road cut into the mountainside. The rugged interior is well worth an excursion and there is good trekking in the hills behind.

Nisidhes Petaloi

This group of islands lies off the SW coast of Evia a short distance to the NW of Nisis Paximadhi. The two largest islands are Megalo Petali and Xero.

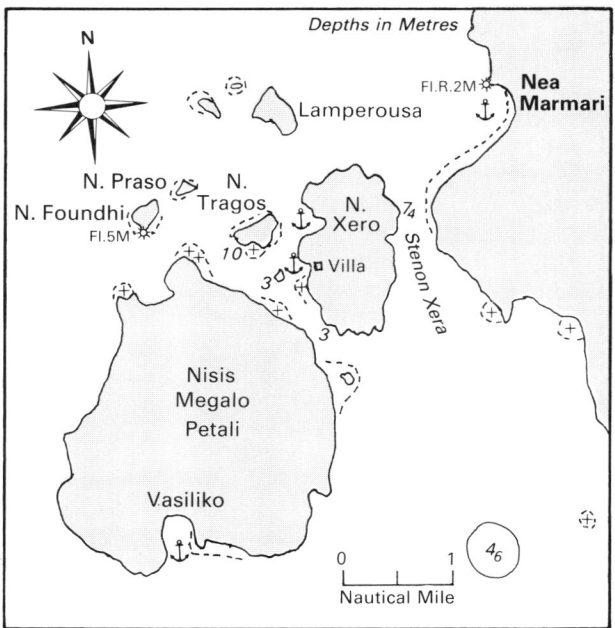

NISIDHES PETALOI

Ormos Nea Marmari and Nisidhes Petaloi looking SW.

There are numerous anchorages between them and it is possible to find shelter from just about all winds:

1. *Vasiliko* On the S side of Nisis Megalo Petali, this bay offers reasonable shelter from the *meltemi*. Anchor in 4–6 metres at the head of the bay. Sandy bottom. Open only to the S.
2. *Nisis Xero* A cove on the SW corner of the island off a large villa affords some shelter from the *meltemi*. Care needs to be taken in the approach of a reef off the SE corner of Nisis Tragos which is sometimes marked by a stake. There are now fish farms in here though it is still possible to get in.
3. *Nisis Tragos* On the S side there is a large villa with a small harbour, but this is strictly private.

Caution In Ormos Marmari between Evia and Nisidhes Petaloi there are strong gusts off the high land on Evia with the *meltemi*.

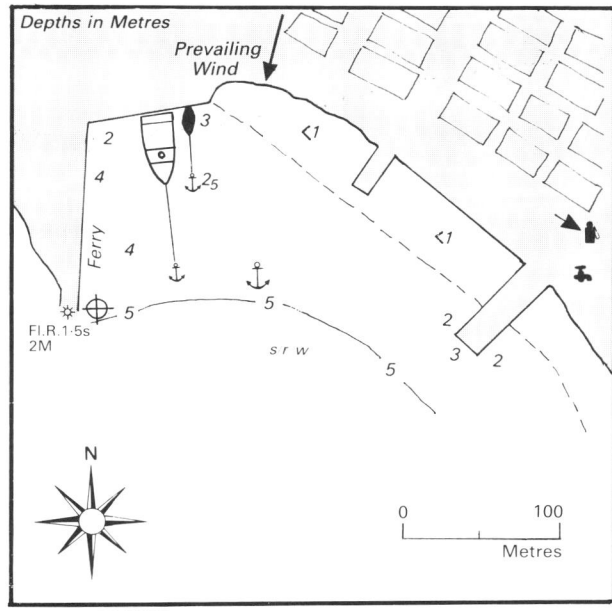

NEA MARMARI
38°03′N 24°19′E (Fl.R.2M)

NEA MARMARI

Ormos Marmari is the bay opposite the northernmost of the Nisidhes Petaloi. Nea Marmari is in the SE corner of the bay. The village can be seen from seaward. Moor stern-to the quay or the pier, or anchor off. The depths are uneven in the area enclosed by the mole and the quay – there are some 2 metre patches so care must be taken. There are 2·3 metre depths off the extremity of the pier. The bottom is sand and weed with some rocks. Good shelter from the *meltemi* although there are strong gusts. Open to the W–SW, but the fishing boats and several yachts remain afloat for the summer.

Port police. Water on the waterfront. Fuel in the town. Good shopping for provisions. Tavernas on the waterfront. Ferry to Rafina.

NEA STIRA

Three miles NE of Ak Strongilo lies the village of Nea Stira. The natural camber of the coast provides some protection from the *meltemi* although there are strong gusts into the bay. Tavernas and limited provisions ashore.

Prohibited landing

It is prohibited to land on Nisis Stira, the adjacent islets and Nisidhes Verdhouyi (Berdugi) and Nisis Kavaliani.

ALMIROPOTAMOS (Almyro Potamo)

A long attractive bay with steep-to mountains above. There are strong gusts into the bay with the *meltemi*. The bottom is mostly sand and weed, good holding once you find a patch of sand. There are a number of anchorages:

1. At the entrance there is a cove on the W side though it is reported to be blocked by a fish farm.
2. In the cove NW of the islet.

3. In the cove on the NE side. A bus runs twice a day to Khalkis from the village above. The bottom is mostly sand and weed, good holding once you find a patch of sand. There are a number of anchorages:

VOUFALO (Bouphalo)

An almost landlocked bay lying approximately 4 miles N of Nisis Kavaliani. The houses of the tiny hamlet in the inlet can be seen from seaward. On the W of the N entrance there is an islet with a fish farm on the E side.

A sand spit with concrete blocks along it extends from the E side and partially protects the anchorage. Anchor in 5–6 metres behind the sand spit. A very small yacht can go bows-to the short pier (1 metre depths). The holding has been reported to be poor. Virtually all-round shelter tucked behind the sand spit. Simple tavernas ashore.

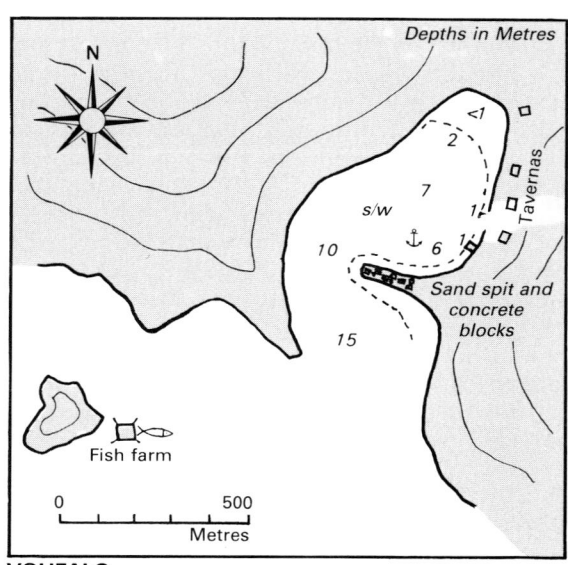

VOUFALO
38°18′N 24°07′·5E

ALIVERION (Karastos)

Approach

Conspicuous The two tall chimneys of Pirgos power station are visible from a considerable distance off. Closer in a small chimney and the harbour breakwaters are conspicuous.

By night Use the lights at the entrance to the harbour: Fl.G.4s7M and Fl.R.1·5s3M. The power station is lit up with bright lights at night.

Mooring

Go stern or bows-to behind the mole or on the town quay. A small cargo ship occasionally uses the long section of the town quay. The bottom is mud – excellent holding.

Shelter Good all-round shelter although strong S winds produce some surge and spray comes over the mole. Strong N winds do not blow home.

Authorities Port police.

Facilities

Water On the town quay and N side of harbour.
Fuel None available locally.
Provisions Limited provisions locally.
Eating out Several tavernas around the harbour with good local fare.
Other PO, OTE and bank in Aliverion town about 30 minutes away.

General

The harbour is properly called Karastos and the town a short distance away is Aliverion. It is a captivating and friendly place that has mostly been bypassed by tourism. The giant power station of Pirgos on the opposite side of the bay is soon accepted as a part of the scenery and not the blot on the landscape it might first appear to be.

AMARINTHOS

Between Aliverion and Eretria a yacht can anchor off Amarinthos. A small fishing harbour is usually packed solid with fishing boats. The *meltemi* does not blow with any strength here. Fuel, good provisions and tavernas in the village.

ERETRIA (Nea Psara)

Approach

The bay lying approximately 5 miles W of Amarinthos. The approaches are surrounded by above- and below-water rocks and a yacht should make the approach to the bay from the S. The light structure on the W side of the entrance (char. Fl.WR.1·5s5/3M red sector covers 061°-342°) is at the extremity of a sunken ancient mole running out from the coast.

Mooring

Anchor in the NE corner in 3–10 metres. There is a small *caïque* harbour on 'Dream' Island, but it is too small and mostly too shallow for even a small yacht. At the quay in the NW corner where the car ferries berth the depths are insufficient for a yacht. Good shelter from the *meltemi*. Open to the W and S.

Facilities

Port police and customs. Fuel in the town. Good shopping for provisions and good tavernas on the waterfront. Bus to Khalkis and ferry to Oropos.

General

Eretria is also called Nea Psara. In 1822 the Turks massacred the population of Khios and nearby Psara after a rebellion and the survivors of Psara fled to Evia where they were given land at Eretria/Nea Psara. It is a growing tourist resort, hence the inevitable renaming of the island on the E side of the bay as 'Dream' Island.

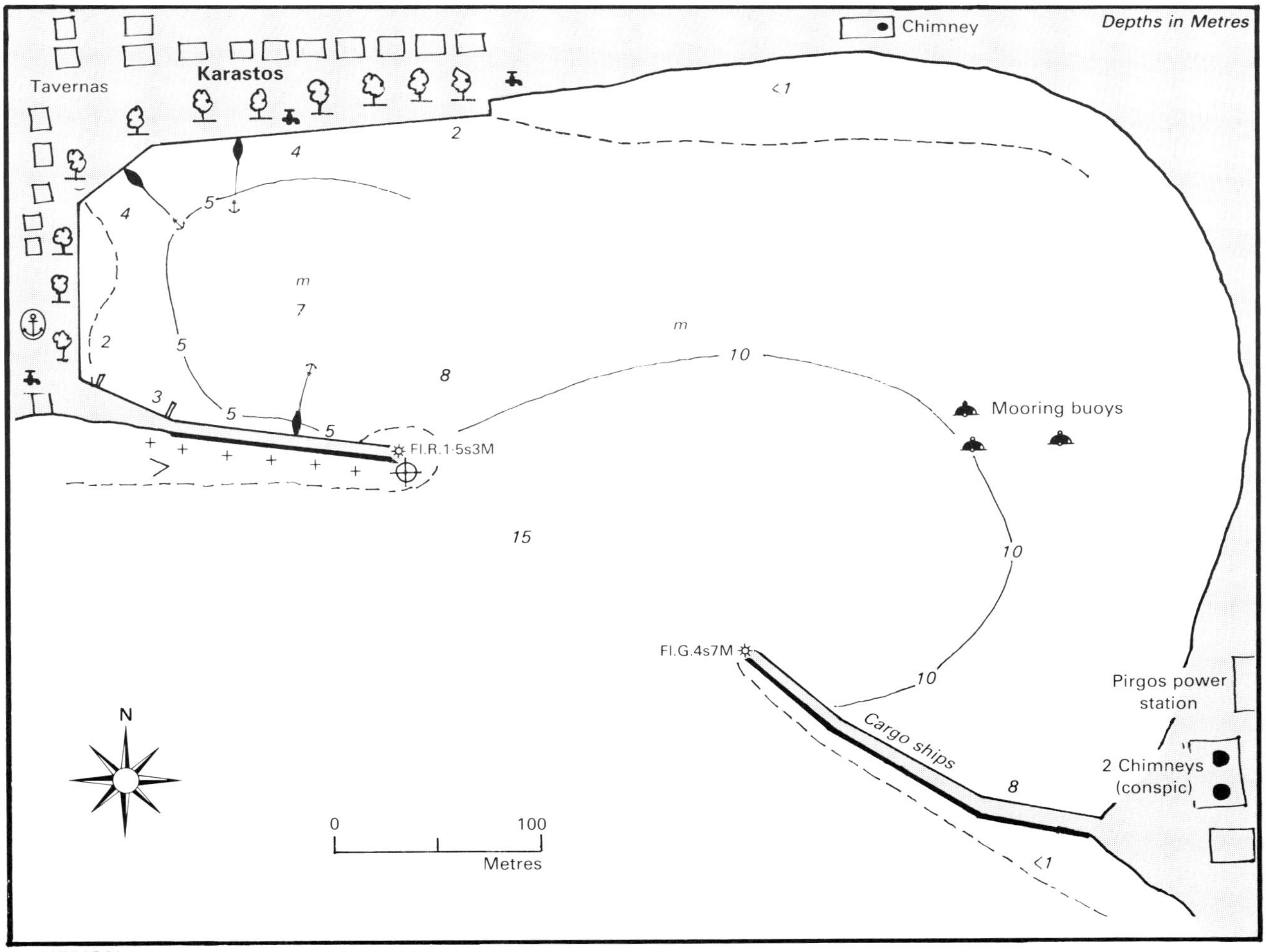

Depths in Metres

Chimney

Karastos

Tavernas

< 1

4

2

5

4

m
7

m

2

5

8

10

3

5

5

Mooring buoys

Fl.R.1·5s3M

10

15

10

Fl.G.4s7M

10

Cargo ships

Pirgos power
station

8

2 Chimneys
(conspic)

N

0   100
Metres

< 1

ALIVERION
38°23′·5N 24°02′·4E (Fl.R.3M)

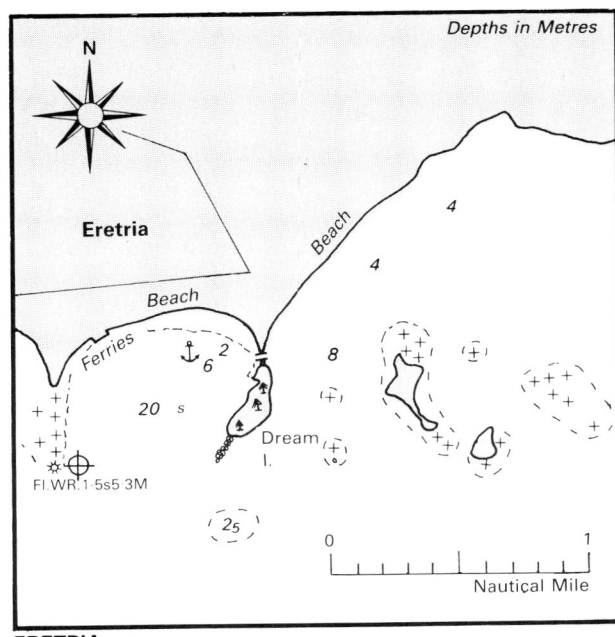

Depths in Metres

N

Eretria

Beach

4

Beach

4

Ferries

2

6

8

20 s

Dream
I.

25

Fl.WR.1·5s5 3M

0   1
Nautical Mile

ERETRIA
38°22′·9N 23°47′·4E (Fl.WR.5/3M)

DHIAVLOS EVIRIPOU (Approaches to Khalkis)
Admiralty chart no. 2802
Imray-Tetra chart no. G2

S approach
Conspicuous The huge cement factory complex on
the W side of the entrance to the S harbour is
conspicuous from a considerable distance off. There
are always a number of ships anchored off the
entrance to Ormos Mikro Vathi. The narrow buoyed
entrance to the S harbour is easily negotiated.

By night Use the light on Ak Avlis (Fl(2)12s6M) and
the light buoys: Q.G and Fl.G.2s. Further in use the
light on Vrak Passandassi (Fl.3s5M) and in the
approaches to the bridge the lights on the S side
(Fl.R.2s4M and 2F.R.3M) and the light buoys
(Q.G).

Note A new high road bridge has been built over the
narrows N of the cement factory. Air height under
the bridge is 32 metres.

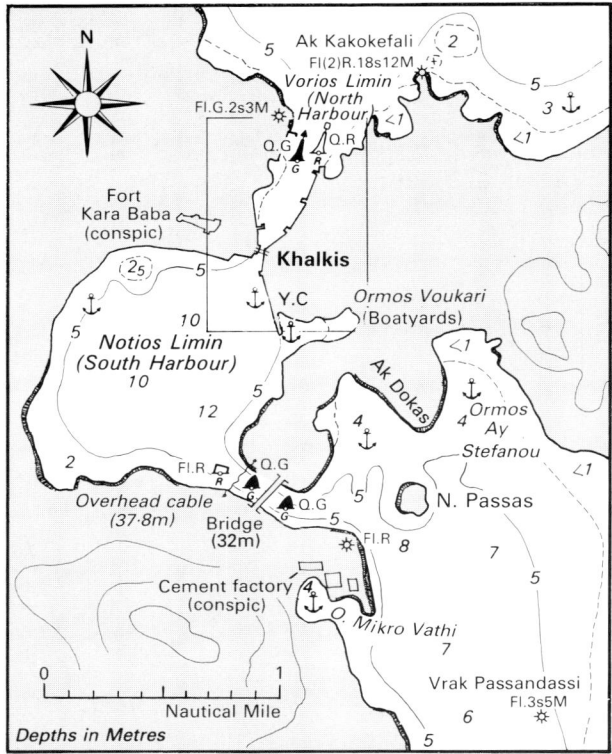

APPROACHES TO KHALKIS (SOUTH HARBOUR)

N approach

Conspicuous The large modern buildings of Khalkis are visible from the distance. Ak Kakokefali is conspicuous as a rocky promontory without buildings on it.

By night Use the light on Ak Kakokefali (Fl(2)R.18s12M), on the W bank (Fl.G.2s3M), and the light buoys marking the channel: Q.G/Q.R.

Mooring

S harbour In the S harbour anchor on the N side of the basin or go stern or bows-to or alongside on the E quay in Voukari. In both places a yacht is completely out of the current.

Note In the NW corner of Ormos Vourkari is Khalkis Yacht Club. It may be possible to find a berth here. Yachts normally berth bows-to because ballasting extends a short distance out from the quay. Depths are variable with 1-2 metres off the quay. Water and electricity. Showers and toilets. Yachts are craned onto the hard.

Khalkis bridge viewed from the S.

N harbour Go stern or bows-to or alongside the town quay where indicated on the E side of the harbour or stern or bows-to the short mole extending from the W side where a few local yachts are kept. On the town quay a yacht is completely out of the current but on the W mole the weak current could make manoeuvring difficult. There is no good shelter from the *meltemi* in the N harbour. A very large yacht should anchor off in the bay to the E of Ak Kakokefali.

Signals These signals are displayed on the signal mast on the W side of the bridge platform.

By day	By night	Meaning
Three vertical black balls	Green, white, red vertical lights	Bridge closed
	White fixed light in the middle of the bridge.	Bridge closed at night.
Two black cones points together above a cone point down	Green, white, green vertical lights.	Bridge open to S-bound vessels.
Two black balls separated by a black cone point up	Red, white, red vertical lights.	Bridge open to N-bound vessels.

A siren sounds and a flashing light warns boat traffic that the bridge is opening.

Tidal streams In the N harbour the spring range is about 0·8 metres (2·5ft) and the neap range about 0·2 metres (0·5ft). This must be borne in mind when mooring up or you may take the ground and miss the bridge. In the S harbour the spring and neap ranges are small. All depths given in the harbour plans are at mean low water springs. High water occurs in the N harbour approximately 1 hour 12 minutes after high water in the S harbour. The difference in time and range produces strong tidal streams which may reach 6–7 knots at springs. However this is only in the very narrow section spanned by the bridge and a short distance N and S of the bridge the stream is considerably less. When the bridge is opened the current may still be running at 2–3 knots but there is no difficulty negotiating the narrows. Sailing through is prohibited.

KHALKIS BRIDGE

The bridge spans the narrow gap between Evia and the mainland. The gap is 39·3 metres (129ft) wide and the bridge slides back into a recess under the road. The bridge is opened at slack water for a very short time only, usually at night. As it is impossible to predict the times of slack water with any accuracy, the skipper of a yacht should go to the port police as soon as possible to find at what time the bridge is going to open and to pay the bridge fees. The bridge is rarely opened during the day because of the

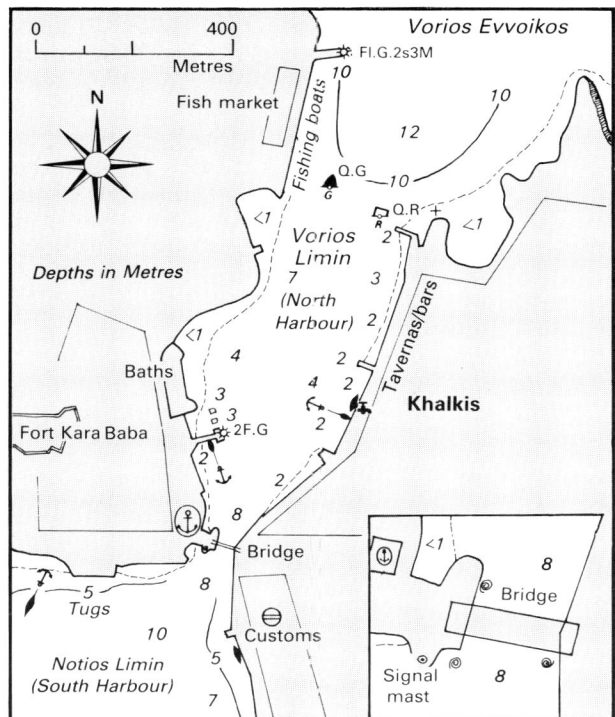

KHALKIS
38°28'N 23°35'E

The dangerous currents in the channel are mentioned by ancient sources: Livy, Cicero, Pliny and Strabo commented on them and tradition has it that Aristotle flung himself into the channel because of his inability to explain the phenomenon. The channel was first spanned as early as 411 BC. Under Justinian the fixed bridge was replaced by a movable wooden bridge. Under the Venetians the island took its name of Negroponte, the 'black bridge', from the bridge across to the mainland from Khalkis. In 1896 a Belgian company built an iron swing bridge that remained until 1962 when the existing bridge was built.

disruption to road traffic. Yachts have been kept waiting for up to 30 hours so it is wise to anticipate long delays here. The following is an extract from one yachtsman's experience:

'The reliability of the bridge openers is awful and the first night we were trying to get north, they overslept and missed the slack-water period. On the second night, just as we were about to suffer a repeat performance, an irate German yachtsman woke the officials and we just got through before the tide was too strong.'

The bridge officials use VHF channel 12, though this should not be relied upon for getting the word to proceed through the channel. A charge is made (3000Dx in 1993).

Facilities

Services Water and fuel on the quay in the N harbour (☎ 22609/22280 for fuel; ☎ 22213/29770 for water).

Repairs Some mechanical repairs. Yachts are hauled out in the boatyards in Voukari. Hardware shops.

Provisions Good shopping for all provisions. Ice at the fish market.

Eating out Numerous good tavernas nearby.

Other PO. OTE. Banks. Greek gas and *Camping Gaz*. Hire cars, motorbikes and bicycles. Buses and trains to Athens.

General

Khalkis is the modern capital of Evia and the centre of communications for the island. Ancient Khalkis was similarly a prosperous city-state controlling the passage of commerce in the Evia channel.

ii. Coasts north of Khalkis

LARIMNA (Larmes)
Admiralty chart no. 2802

The very tall chimney belching smoke at the cupronickel refinery is conspicuous from a considerable distance off. The chimney is painted in red and white bands and lit at night with red lights. Anchor off or go bows-to the short pier. The bottom is mud and shells – excellent holding. Fuel in town. Water near the pier. Most provisions available. Poor tavernas.

The village is grimy and blackened from the fumes of the refinery. These fumes deposit an oily unpleasant grime over a yacht. The only reason for a visit here is to see the ancient harbour which is in good condition although parts of it have been wantonly destroyed in recent years.

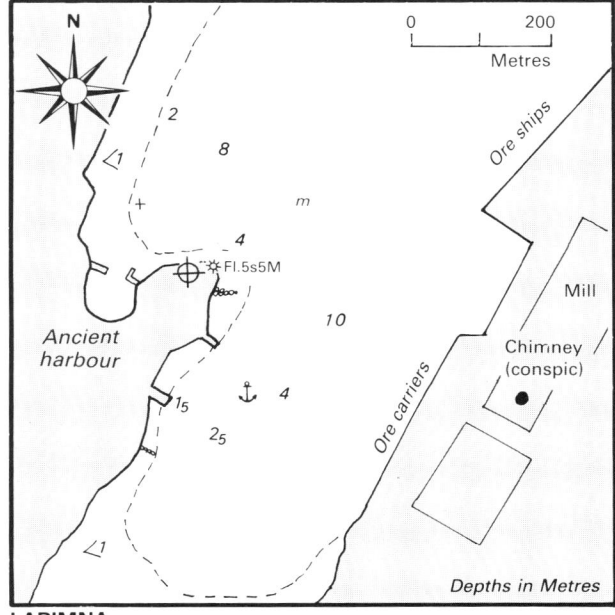

LARIMNA
38°34'·3N 23°17'·3E (Fl.5s5M)

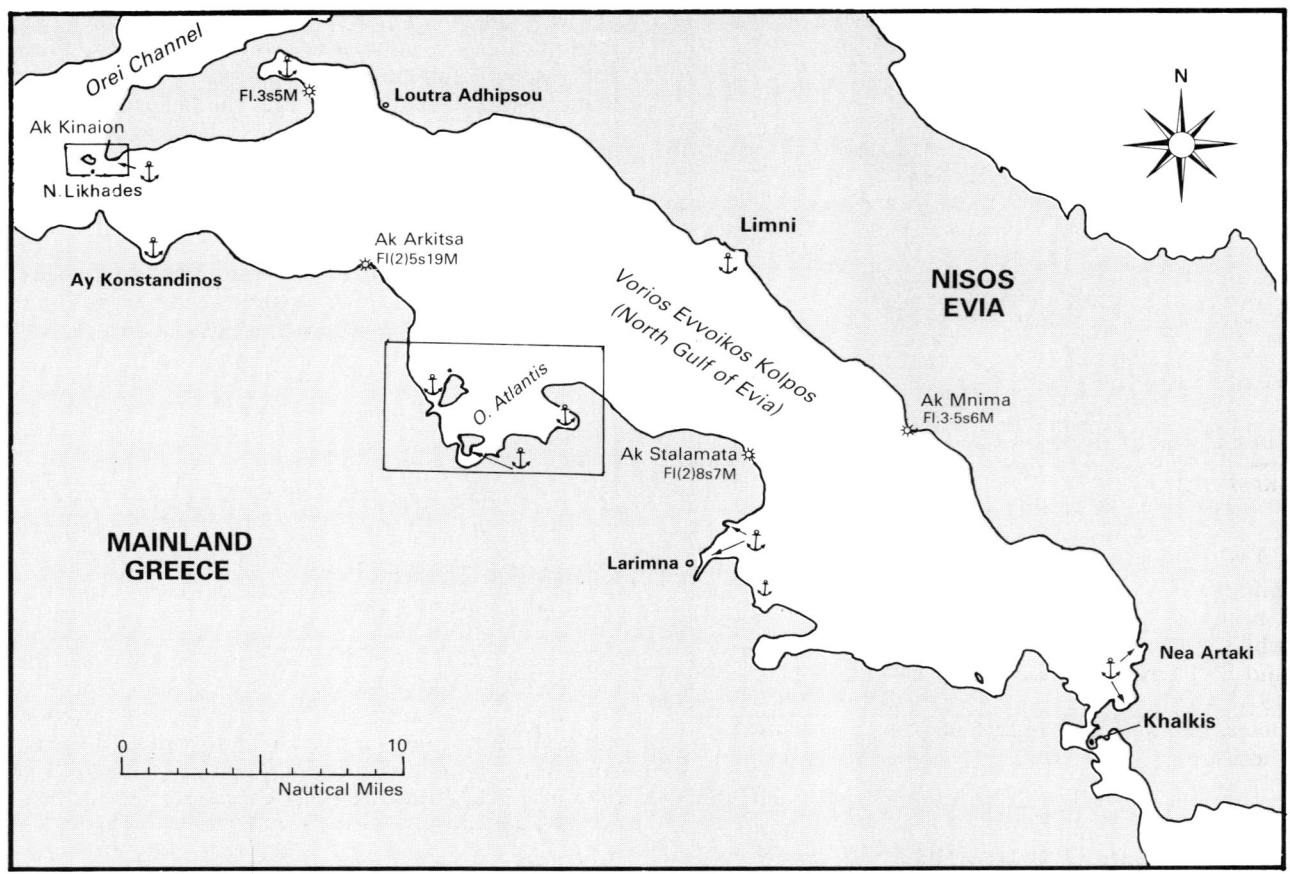

NORTH GULF OF EVIA (Vorios Evvoikos Kolpos)

UNNAMED BAY

About 2 miles SW of Ak Larmes there is a bay offering good shelter from the *meltemi*. The SW side of the bay is a low lying islet connected to the land by a reef just below water. Much of the bay is now obstructed with fish farms, but there is room for several yachts to anchor in here. Anchor in 10 metres on sticky red clay, excellent holding.

ORMOS ATLANTIS (Atlandi, Atalante, Opuntius)

In this large bay on the W side of the gulf there are a number of anchorages affording shelter from the *meltemi*.

1. *Ormos Ay Ioannis Theologos* Anchor at the head of the bay. Open to the W. Provisions and tavernas ashore.
2. *Ormos Amirou (Almyro)* In the S corner of Ormos Atlantis under the lee of Nisis Gaidharos. In the middle of the entrance care must be taken of a below-water rock. There is now a fish farm and a mussel farm in the bay, but yachts can anchor to the W of them. All-round shelter can be found in this bay although there are strong gusts into it with W winds. The motorway N runs past the head of the bay.
3. *Nisis Atlantis* Anchor in a cove on the SW side of the island. There are now fish farms here.

4. *Skala Atlantis* (see harbour plan). A small fishing harbour opposite the cove on Nisis Atlantis. Moor stern or bows-to the outer end of the mole. Care must be taken entering the harbour as the entrance silts. Taverna and café at the root of the mole. Good shopping for provisions in Atlantis village on the low hill to the NNW of the harbour.

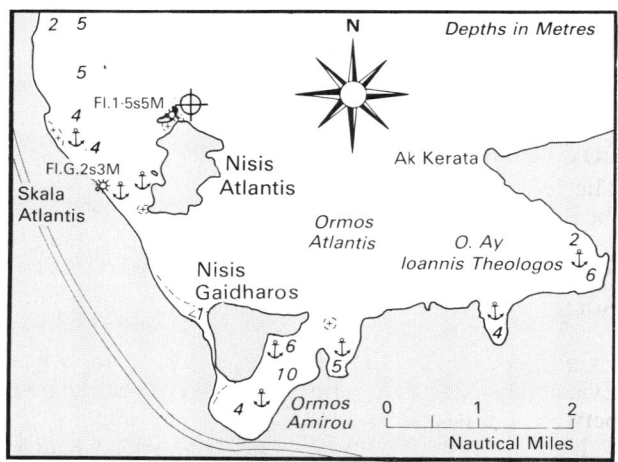

ORMOS ATLANTIS
38°41'·1N 23°05'·5E (Nisis Atlantis light)

304

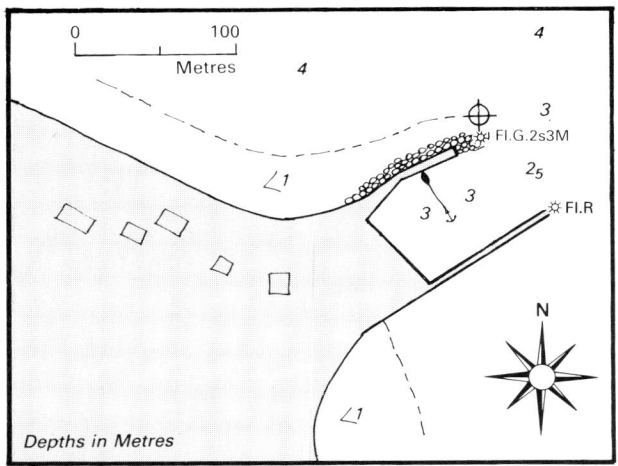

SKALA ATALANTI
38°40'·4N 23°04'·6E (Fl.G.3M)

AYIOS KONSTANDINOS

The mainland ferry terminal for Skiathos. There is a long quayed section with 7 metre depths (a part of which is used by the ferry). Entirely open to the N and E. There is a small fishing harbour (50 metres by 15 metres!) but this is always crowded with fishing boats. Ashore most provisions can be obtained and there are good tavernas.

Evia side of the channel

NEA ARTAKI (Vatondas)

Three miles NNE of Khalkis this open bay provides some shelter from the *meltemi*. Open to the W and to the S for a short distance. Anchor off in the bay. A large number of fishing boats and a few yachts are moored here so the overall shelter must be better than it appears. There are strong gusts down into the bay with the *meltemi*. Ashore there are provisions and tavernas.

LIMNI

Anchor off the SW side of the village. The depths are considerable. There are quayed sections off the village. Strong gusts with the *meltemi*. Open to the S and W.

LOUTRON ADHIPSOU

The ferry terminal for the car ferry from Arkitsa on the mainland.

NISOI LIKHADES (Likada)
Admiralty chart no. 1196

Lying close off Ak Kinaion, the westernmost point of Evia, there is a narrow but easily navigable channel between the islands and the cape. A current of up to 2 knots may run through the channel in either direction depending on the wind direction. With the *meltemi* there is a S going current, generally less than 2 knots. Keeping close to Ak Kinaion there are good depths in the channel except for a 4 metre patch

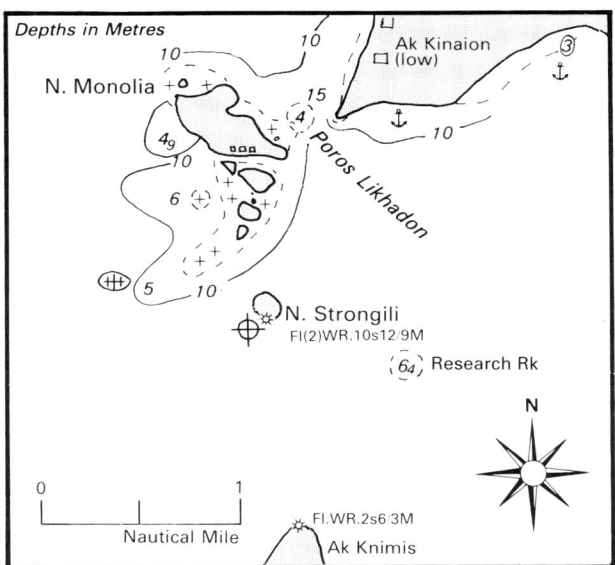

NISOI LIKHADHES
38°48'·4N 22°49'·2E (N. Strongili light)

extending 500 metres in a NNE direction from the SE tip of Nisis Monolia.

A yacht can anchor on the S side of Ak Kinaion where there is a good lee from N winds. Fishing boats anchor on the S side of Nisis Monolia (open only to the E), but care must be taken of the above- and below-water rocks surrounding this anchorage.

North Evia channels and the Gulf of Volos
(Maliakos Kolpos, Dhiavlos Oreon, Dhiavlos Trikeri, Gulf of Volos or Pagasitikos Kolpos)

MALIAKOS KOLPOS

A shallow gulf bulging westwards from the W extremity of Evia. The coast is predominantly low-lying. The northbound motorway skirts the head of the gulf. The Pass of Thermopylae lies near the corner of the gulf.

STILIDHOS (Stilis, Stylis)
Admiralty chart no. 1196

Situated on the N side of Maliakos Kolpos, Stilidhos is the port for the town of Lamia. It is surrounded by shoal water and a dredged channel leads into it. The channel is marked at the outer end by a pair of light buoys (Q.G and Q.R) and the beacon (Fl.R.2s2M) on Nisis Kaloyiros, a low sandy islet, and a beacon (Fl.G.2s2M) off the low shore on the other side.

Moor stern-to or bows-to or alongside the central pier. The bottom is mud – good holding. Good shelter from the *meltemi*. Open to the S. Port police. Fuel in the town. Small yachts can be craned onto the quay. Good shopping for provisions. Tavernas in the town. Buses to Athens and Volos.

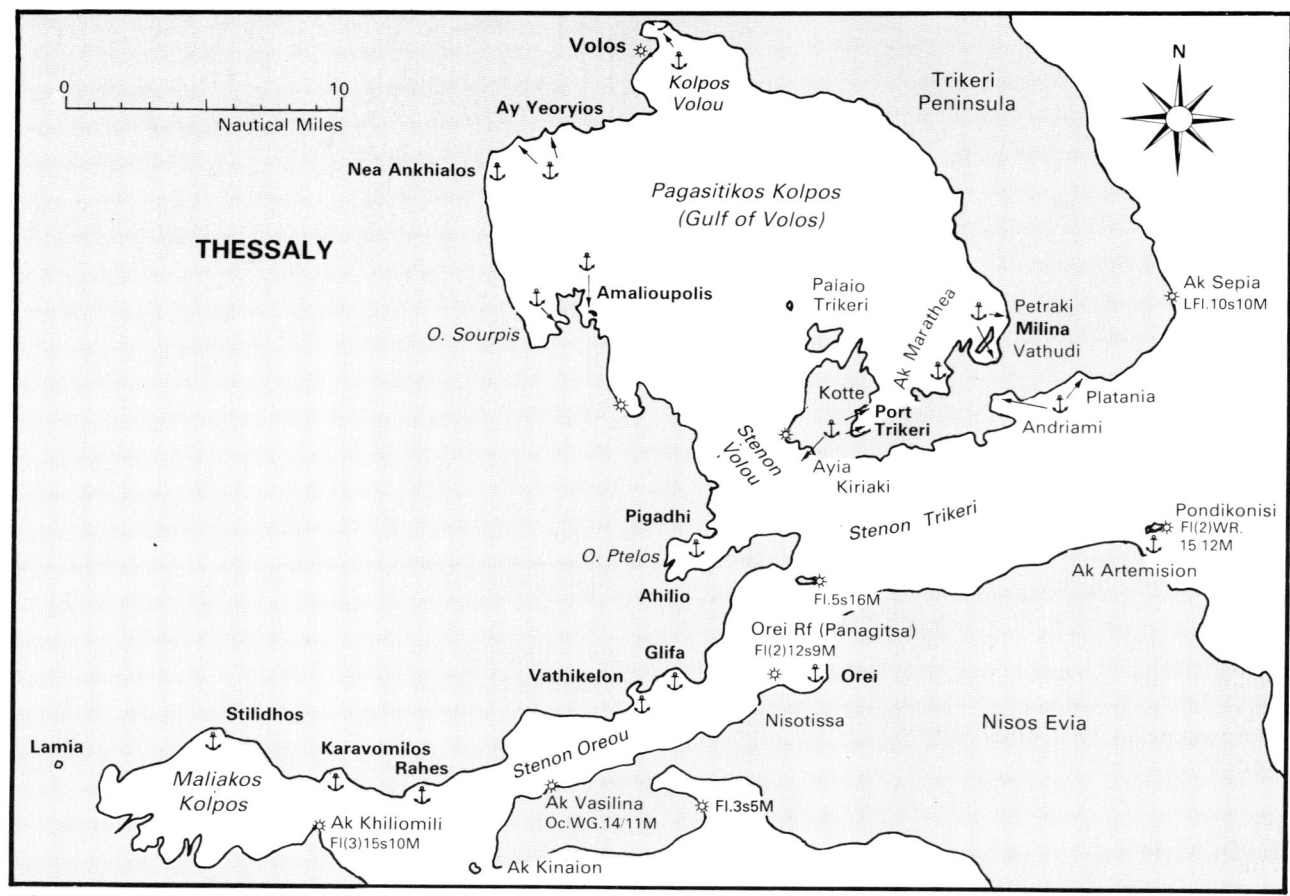

NORTHERN EVIA CHANNELS AND THE GULF OF VOLOS

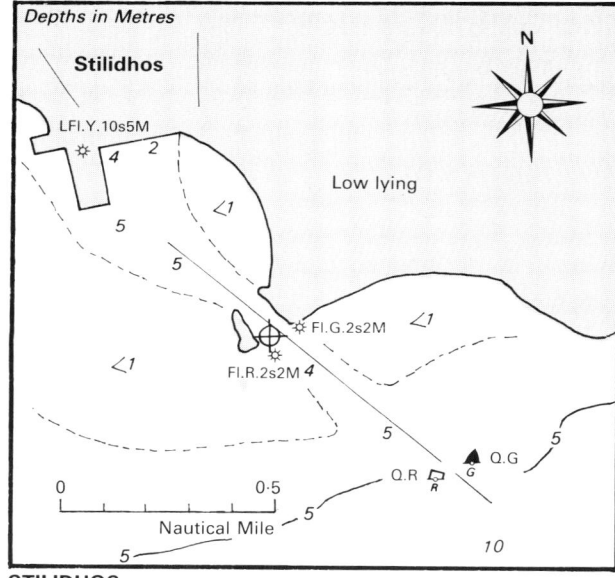

STILIDHOS
38°54'·2N 22°37'·3E (Fl.R.2M)

KARAVOMILOS

Karavomilos is a large bay about 4½ miles SE of Stilidhos and opposite Ak Khiliomili. Local fishing boats are kept on moorings in the summer. Protection from the *meltemi* appears to be good. Provisions and tavernas ashore.

RAHES

Immediately E of Ak Dhrepanon is Rahes where local fishing boats and a few yachts are kept on moorings through the summer. A large cement factory and quayed area are conspicuous just E of Rahes. The shelter in the bight is better than it looks on the chart. Provisions and tavernas ashore.

Rahes.

Stenon Oreou
(Orei Channel)

This channel separates Evia from the Thessaly coast. The channel is very narrow – in places it is little more than a mile across and there can be currents of up to 2½ knots in places. The tidal range at springs is 0·8 metres (2·5ft) at Orei, the highest tidal range in the eastern Mediterranean. The coast is mostly mountainous and wooded although there is a narrow low-lying strip of land bordering the mountains along the Evia coast.

ORMOS VATHIKELON (Vathykelos)

Lying 1½ miles W of Glifa, this almost landlocked bay offers good all-round shelter. An islet off the W entrance point with a white church on it is easily identified. The bay is very deep for anchoring – mostly 10–20 metres around the NE side. The E side of the bay, where there are better depths for anchoring, is used to leave the car ferries from Glifa for the night. The bottom is mud and weed – good holding once through the weed. There are no facilities, just a few villas around the olive-clad slopes. Care is needed of the dangerous rock lying approximately 20 metres off the E side of the entrance.

GLIFA (Glypha)

The ferry terminal for the car ferry running to Nisiotissa on Evia. The short pier is used by the car ferry. With the *meltemi* some swell works its way into the bay. Anchor off the village or in the cove to the E. Fuel in the village and water on the quay. Most provisions available and several tavernas.

Ormos Vathikelon.

OREI (Oreon, Oreios)

Approach

Conspicuous This part of the coast is low-lying and wooded and it can be difficult to identify features. The hut and metal tower on Ifalos Oreon or Panagitsa lying ½ a mile off the coast is easily identified – there are good depths in the fairway between the reef and the coast. Just N of the harbour a factory is conspicuous. Closer in the buildings of Orei and the mole and the light structure will be seen.

By night Use the light on Panagitsa (Fl(2)12s9M) and at Orei (Fl.R.1·5s3M).

Mooring

Go stern-to or bows-to the mole or the iron wharf. The hydrofoil uses the outer part of the mole. The bottom is sand and weed – good holding.

Shelter Good all-round protection. The *meltemi* does not blow home here.

Authorities Police.

Glifa looking WSW.

The marble bull hauled from the sea at Orei. *Conrad Jenkin.*

Note It should be remembered that the tidal range at Orei is 0·8 metres (2·5ft) at springs and allowance should be made for this. Some, like myself, lulled into a false sense of security in the virtually tideless Mediterranean, have found themselves stuck on the bottom here.

Facilities

Water At the root of the mole.
Fuel Near the wharf.
Provisions Good shopping for provisions.
Eating out Pleasant tavernas on the waterfront.
Other PO. OTE. Irregular bus to Khalkis. Hydrofoil to the Volos and the Northern Sporades.

General

In ancient times Orei was an important maritime city. Above the harbour the remains of the Acropolis which guarded the harbour can be seen. In 1965 a Hellenistic marble bull was dredged from the sea by fishermen and placed in the town square. Today it remains a pleasant place with a modest summer tourist trade and the few yachts which venture into Dhiavlos Oreon.

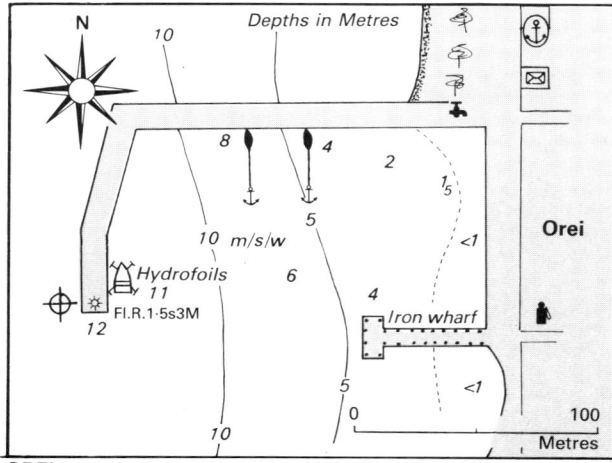

OREI
38°56'·9N 23°05'·0E (Fl.R.3M)

308

Gulf of Volos
(Pagasitikos Kolpos)

This gulf opens up to the north from Stenon Volou. The coast is mountainous except for the west coast which is low and marshy between Amalioupolis and Volos. The Trikeri peninsula beginning at Mt Pilion (1548 metres) is rugged and densely wooded. Mt Pilion is covered with snow in the winter and much of the spring – a ski lift operates in the winter. The gulf has a number of attractive anchorages and it is well worthwhile detouring from the northern channels to explore it.

Note The prevailing winds in the summer are from the NE or SE.

ORMOS PTELEOU

The large bay on the W side of the entrance to Stenon Volou entered between Ak Pigadhi and Ak Khondhros. The bay has now been much developed on the N side with clusters of villas around the slopes. There are several anchorages around the bay.

1. *Ahilio* The village in the SW corner. The anchorage off the village is exposed to the *meltemi* which pushes a swell in. Good shelter with SE winds. Provisions and tavernas ashore.
2. *Ormiskos Loutro* The large bay in the NW corner bordered by low marshland. A ruined tower, called Achilles Tower, sits on the headland E of the bay. Anchor in the N where there is something of a lee from the *meltemi*. Open SE across the bay.
3. *Ormiskos Pigadhi* The bay immediately E of Loutro. Anchor in the cove on the E side of the bay in 6 metres. Good shelter from the *meltemi*. Open SE across the bay. The tower on the W side of the bay is locally called Achilles' Tower and Pigadhi is said to be the bay from which Achilles set sail for Troy.
4. Immediately N of Ak Alkini there is a cove with a settlement around it. There is a quayed area used by local fishing boats and there appears to be something of a lee from the *meltemi* here. Provisions and tavernas ashore.

AYIA KIRIAKI (Trikeri Bay)

An open bay on the E side of the entrance to the Gulf of Volos. The village of Ayia Kiriaki on the hill above is conspicuous from seaward.

The bay is very deep. Anchor off the boatyard or in the SE corner of the bay, though the latter is very crowded with fishing boats. Just to the E of the boatyard a new quay has been built. There are 2–3 metre depths off the quay but the bottom drops away quickly. Some 20 metres off the quay there are 20 metre depths and 25 metres off there are 30 metre depths. The bay is sheltered from the *meltemi*, but open to the W and S. There is another cove immediately W of the fishing hamlet where a yacht can anchor.

A large fleet of fishing boats is based at Ayia Kiriaki. Limited provisions and taverna/cafés ashore.

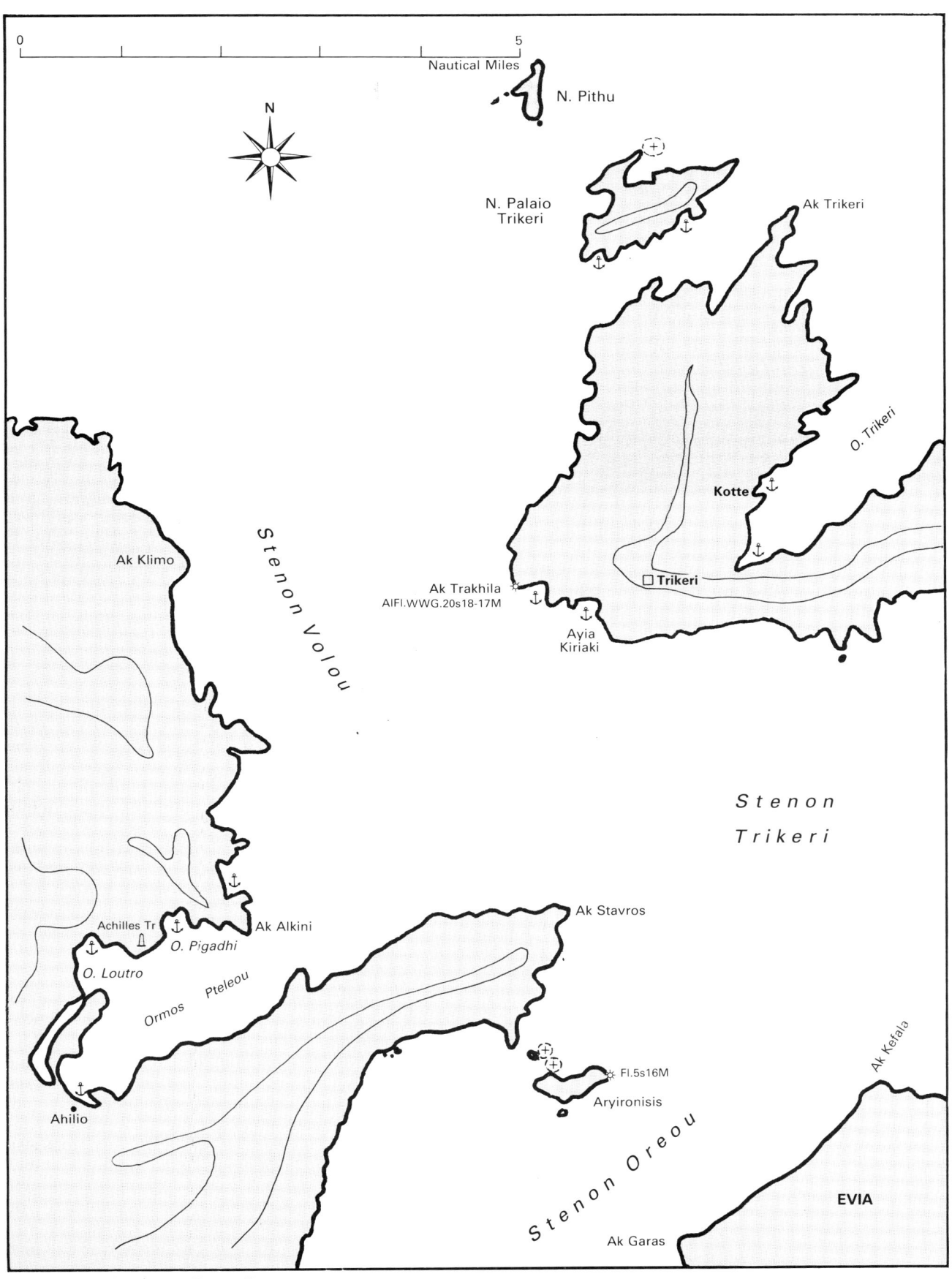

0   5
Nautical Miles

N

N. Pithu

N. Palaio Trikeri

Ak Trikeri

O. Trikeri

Ak Klimo

Stenon Volou

Kotte

Ak Trakhila
AlFl.WWG.20s18-17M

☐ **Trikeri**

Ayia
Kiriaki

Stenon Trikeri

Ak Stavros

Achilles Tr

Ak Alkini

O. Pigadhi

O. Loutro

Ormos Pteleou

Ahilio

Aryironisis

Fl.5s16M

Stenon Oreou

Ak Kefala

EVIA

Ak Garas

STENON VOLOU (Volos Channel)

Ormiskos Pigadhi on the N side of Ormos Pteleou.

Ayia Kiriaki (Ormos Trikeri) at the entrance to the Gulf of Volos looking S.

The boatyard in the bay hauls out yachts. The village of Ayia Kiriaki above the bay used to be dependent on the ferry from Volos until the rough road from Milina was built.

There is now a rough stone mole here that provides some protection from the S but is mostly occupied by *caïques*.

NISIS PALAIO TRIKERI (Palaeo Trikiri)
On the S side of this island there is the small village of Palaio Trikeri which is conspicuous from the S. Anchor in the bay off the village. Good shelter from the *meltemi*. Limited provisions available ashore.

PORT TRIKERI
The deep bay running SW into the Trikeri peninsula. In calm weather anchor off the small fishing village of Kortis (Kotte) (open to the NE–E) or at the head of the bay (open E). Spectacular scenery under the steep slopes above.

AVRA ANCHORAGE
To the E of Ak Marathea there is an idyllic anchorage for a small yacht in a cove with a white house at the head.

ORMOS VATHOUDHI (Vathudi)
Situated in the SE corner of the Gulf of Volos (Pagasitikos Kolpos), this anchorage is protected by Nisis Alatas on the W and the Trikeri peninsula on the E. The anchorage is entered from the N and there are good depths right into the bay. Anchor in 5–10 metres in the NE corner of the bay. A short jetty extends from the shore with 1–2 metre depths off the end. The bottom is mud and sand – good holding. Good all-round shelter.

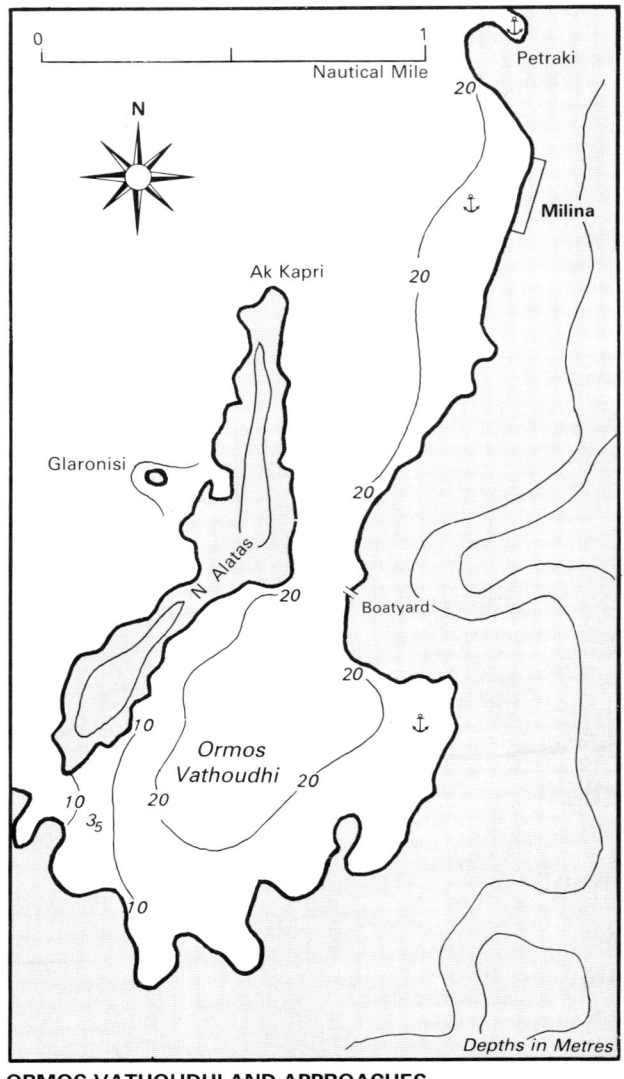

ORMOS VATHOUDHI AND APPROACHES
39°09′N 23°12′·5E

Avra anchorage.

Ormos Vathoudhi sheltered by Nisis Alatas looking NW.

Kòrtis (Kotte) Ayia Kiriaki.

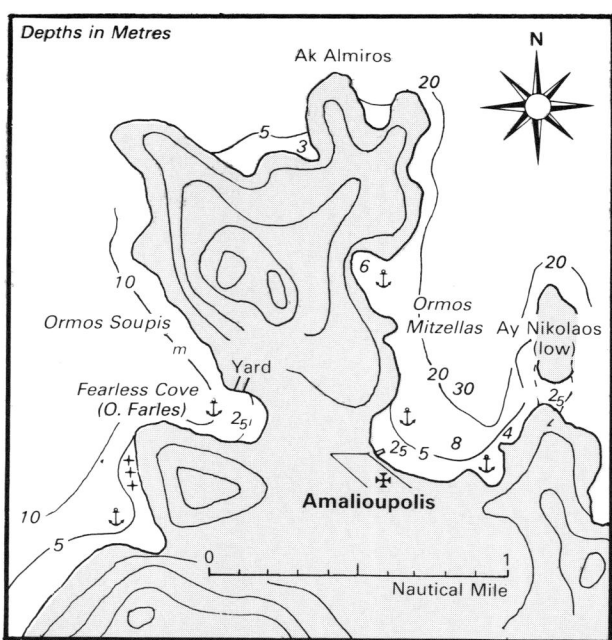

AMALIOUPOLIS
39°10'N 22°53'·5E

A number of yachts are wintered afloat here and it has been reported to be almost impossible to find a space to swing in the NE corner on account of the numerous permanently moored yachts there. Yachts are hauled out at the boatyard on the E side of the entrance.

Tavernas and cafés ashore. Water tap at the root of the jetty. Provisions and tavernas at Milina, the village about 3 kilometres N. A number of summer villas have been built around the shores of the bay.

Caution Although there are 3 metre depths in the fairway of the S passage between Nisis Alatas and the peninsula, care must be taken of underwater rocks fringing the passage. A yacht was reported to have been lost on the rocks here in 1980.

PETRAKI

Half a mile N of Milina, Petrakia cove offers good shelter from the *meltemi*. Open to the NW.

W side of the Gulf of Volos

AMALIOUPOLIS AND NEARBY ANCHORAGES (Ormos Mitzellas, Ormos Soupis)
Admiralty chart no. 1196

On the W side of the entrance to the Gulf of Volos a steep-to headland juts out from the coast ending in Ak Periklis and Ak Almiros. The headland is indented with a number of bays and on the E side is the village of Amalioupolis at the head of Ormos Mitzellas.

Note Navigation is prohibited within a 5 mile radius of the military area at 39°13'·3N 22°48'·5E. However, in practice local yachts do not observe the prohibition and anchor at Amalioupolis and nearby anchorages.

1. *Amalioupolis* The village is conspicuous from seaward. Anchor off the town or go stern-to the short pier (2·5 metre depths at the extremity). The bottom is sand – good holding. The small fishing harbour here is usually full of local boats. With the *meltemi* some swell rolls into the anchorage. Good shelter from SE winds. Port police. Water near the pier. Good shopping for provisions. Tavernas and cafés.

2. Half a mile N of Amalioupolis there is an unnamed cove providing some shelter from the *meltemi*. Anchor near the head of the bay in 2–4 metres.

3. *Loutraki Amalioupolis* (Fearless Cove) A sheltered cove in Ormos Soupis on the W side of the headland. Anchor near the head of the cove in 3–6 metres. The bottom is mud, excellent holding.

Amalioupolis looking NW.

Good all-round shelter. Although the cove is open to the W for 1½ miles the wind does not blow home from that direction. A boatyard on the N side of the bay hauls yachts.

4. *Ay Ioannis Bay* Lies just to the S of Loutraki Amalioupolis. Anchor in 2–5 metres. Much of the bay is shallow towards the head. Good shelter from the *meltemi* and the SE.

Note On the W side of Ormos Soupis there is a large factory complex with storage tanks, gantries and several long jetties.

NEA ANKHIALOS (Nea Aghialos)

About 7 miles N of the factory complex in Ormos Soupis and tucked into the W corner of the gulf is Nea Ankhialos. Here there is a small circular fishing harbour entered by a narrow channel protected by a short mole. There is room for a couple of yachts alongside the outer end of the mole where there are 1·5–2·5 metre depths. Shallow-draught craft may be able to find a berth inside.

Provisions and tavernas nearby. The little harbour is a gem despite the busy road along the shore. Just across the road from the harbour are the ruins of ancient Pyrasos.

AYIOS YEORYIOS

An almost totally enclosed bay between Nea Ankhialos and Ak Angistri. Local fishing boats are kept on permanent moorings or go stern-to the quay on the W side. Provisions and on the S side. Anchor off tavernas ashore.

The small harbour at Nea Ankhialos looking out to the entrance.

VOLOS
Admiralty chart no. 1196

Approach

Conspicuous The large city and a cement factory one mile to the E of the city are easily seen from the distance. The commercial docks, a large grey silo behind the docks and the church of Ayios Konstandinos (especially the clock tower) immediately behind the small yacht harbour are conspicuous. The harbour is generally full of cargo ships.

By night Use the light on Ak Seskoulo (Fl.1·5s6M) and at the cement factory (Fl(2)10s12M). The end of the breakwater is lit (Fl.G.1·5s3M), as is the extremity of the commercial pier (F.R at each corner).

Ay Yeoryios looking SSW.

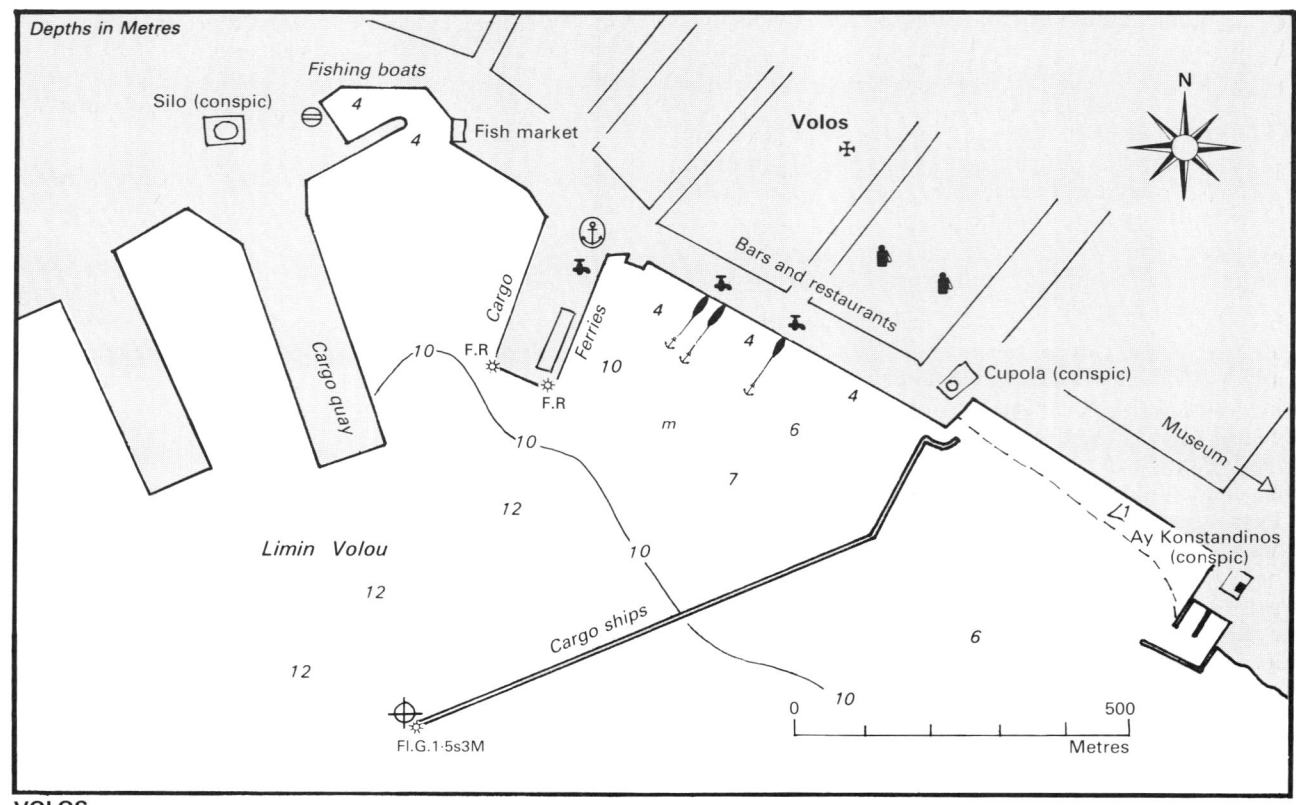

VOLOS
39°21′·2N 22°56′·6E (Fl.G.3M)

Mooring

Go stern-to or bows-to the town quay in the commercial harbour where there are a number of laid moorings for the yachts kept there permanently. The bottom is very soft mud and even plough-type anchors drag through it a number of times before holding properly. Occasionally there is a mooring buoy free but check first before picking a mooring up.

Shelter Good shelter although there is a fetch of 1 mile across the bay with S winds.

Authorities A port of entry: port police, customs and immigration.

Note To the E of the commercial harbour a small yacht harbour has been constructed. Local boats are kept here.

Facilities

Water On the quay.

Fuel Near the quay. A mini-tanker can deliver.

Repairs Most mechanical repairs. General light engineering including stainless steel welding and machining work can be carried out. General electrical work. Yachts are hauled out in the bay S of the commercial harbour. Good chandlers. Excellent hardware and tool shops.

Provisions Excellent shopping for all provisions. Good SPAR supermarket in the W of the town. Wine from the barrel. Ice from the fish market.

Eating out The tavernas and bars fronting the quay are fairly flashy and of varying quality. Good Italian restaurant amongst them. Towards the fishing harbour and further along to the SE are more convivial tavernas.

Other PO. OTE. Hospital. Banks. Hire cars, motorbikes and bicycles. Buses and trains to Thessaloniki and Athens. Ferries to the northern Sporades and Syria. Internal flights to Athens.

Note Volos is a good base from which to visit the spectacular monasteries at Meteori – buses and trains run regularly.

Volos town quay looking WNW.

General

Volos is one of the most important commercial harbours in Greece, handling most of the Thessalian exports: cereals, silk, cotton, olive oil, sugar and soap. Until the disastrous earthquakes of 1954 and 1955 Volos rivalled Piraeus in commercial power. After the earthquakes which flattened a large part of the city it was rapidly rebuilt and once again it is prospering.

The present harbour was built in 1912 but Volos has always been an important maritime town. Jason and the Argonauts set sail from Volos (then Iolkos) – a fact commemorated by a bronze model of the Argo in a square by the harbour. The local wine is also called, appropriately enough, Argo.

The museum (towards the SE end of the city) contains an excellent collection of artifacts from Iolkos and Pagasai-Demetrias (across the bay S of Volos). Its collection of painted *stelai* is one of the best in the world and I recommend a visit. The faded paintings on the *stelai* show touching scenes from everyday life in ancient Greece – Protos, a muscular-looking man walking his dog, Metrophanes holding out his hands to his child, Hediste lying wan in bed – scenes far removed from the friezes of warriors and chariots and wounded lions we commonly think of as ancient funereal art.

Trikeri Channel

(Stenon Trikeri)

This channel separates Evia from the Trikeri peninsula (Khersonisos Trikeri). Although it is wider than Stenon Oreou, there can still be appreciable currents of up to 1½ knots, usually setting towards the SW. The coast is mountainous on both sides. The mountains of the Trikeri peninsula drop sheer into the sea – they are scarred and scoured and mostly devoid of vegetation and habitation.

Off the mouth of the gulf, Athenian *triremes* had their first brush with the invading Persians under Xerxes. This was a delaying tactic by the Athenians rather than an attempt to hold the invaders. The tactic had an unforeseen success as soon afterwards a NE gale wrecked many of the Persian craft. Herodotus relates the story:

'The Persian fleet...made the Magnesian coast between Casthanea and Cape Sepias and on its arrival the leading ships made fast to the land, while the remainder, as there was not much room on the short stretch of beach, came to anchor and lay off-shore in lines, eight deep. In this position they remained during the night; but at dawn next day the weather, which was clear and calm, suddenly changed, and the fleet was caught in a heavy blow from the east – a 'Hellespontian' as the people there call it – which raised a confused sea like a pot on the boil. Those who realised in time that the blow was coming, and all who happened to be lying in a convenient position, managed to beach their vessels and to get them clear of the water before

they were damaged, and thus saved their own lives as well; but the ships which were caught well off-shore were all lost...'
Trans. Aubrey de Selincourt (quoted in Ernle Bradford *The Greek Islands*)

The modern yachtsman can only wonder why the Persian fleet did not choose the nearby natural harbour of Skiathos.

ORMOS ADRIAMI

A large bay on the N side of the channel. Anchor in a cove on the N side in 5–8 metres. Reasonable shelter from the *meltemi* although some swell works around into the cove. Open S. No facilities.

PLATANIA

An open bay 2½ miles E of Andriami affording some shelter from the *meltemi*. There is invariably some swell in the bay. The village of Platania at the bottom of a valley is conspicuous from seaward. There are 1·5 metre depths off the extremity of a short jetty at the E end of the bay. There is a water tap at the root of the jetty. The bay shelves gently to the shore with a mud and sand bottom – good holding. Good shopping for provisions and numerous tavernas open in the summer. The new quay is used exclusively by the fishing fleet and *caïques*.

PONDIKONISI

Lies on the S side of Stenon Trikeri NE of Ak Artemision on Evia. A cove on the SW corner of the island gives good shelter from the *meltemi*.

Northern Sporades

The Sporades ('Sporades' means scattered or sown) are divided into two groups: the northern Sporades described here and the southern or eastern Sporades lying along the coast of Asia Minor. The latter group is today commonly known as the Dodecanese (the islands stretching from Karpathos to Patmos) and the eastern Sporades (those islands north of Patmos to Limnos). The eastern Sporades are less visited than the northern Sporades and consequently the name 'the Sporades' invariably refers to the northern group described here.

The main group of islands curves in a sickle shape from the southern corner of the Trikeri peninsula northwards to the tiny sea-washed rock of Psathoura. Forty miles north of here Mt Athos rises out of the sea at the bottom of the Khalkidhiki. Skiros lies to the SE of the main group and although it belongs geographically and politically to these islands, it has tended to develop independently.

Lying out of the mainstream of history the islands have few archaeological remains. Recently indications of Minoan occupation have been unearthed at Stafilos on Skopelos. The islands were subject-allies of Athens and later of Macedonia and Rome. Skiros has always been of more importance

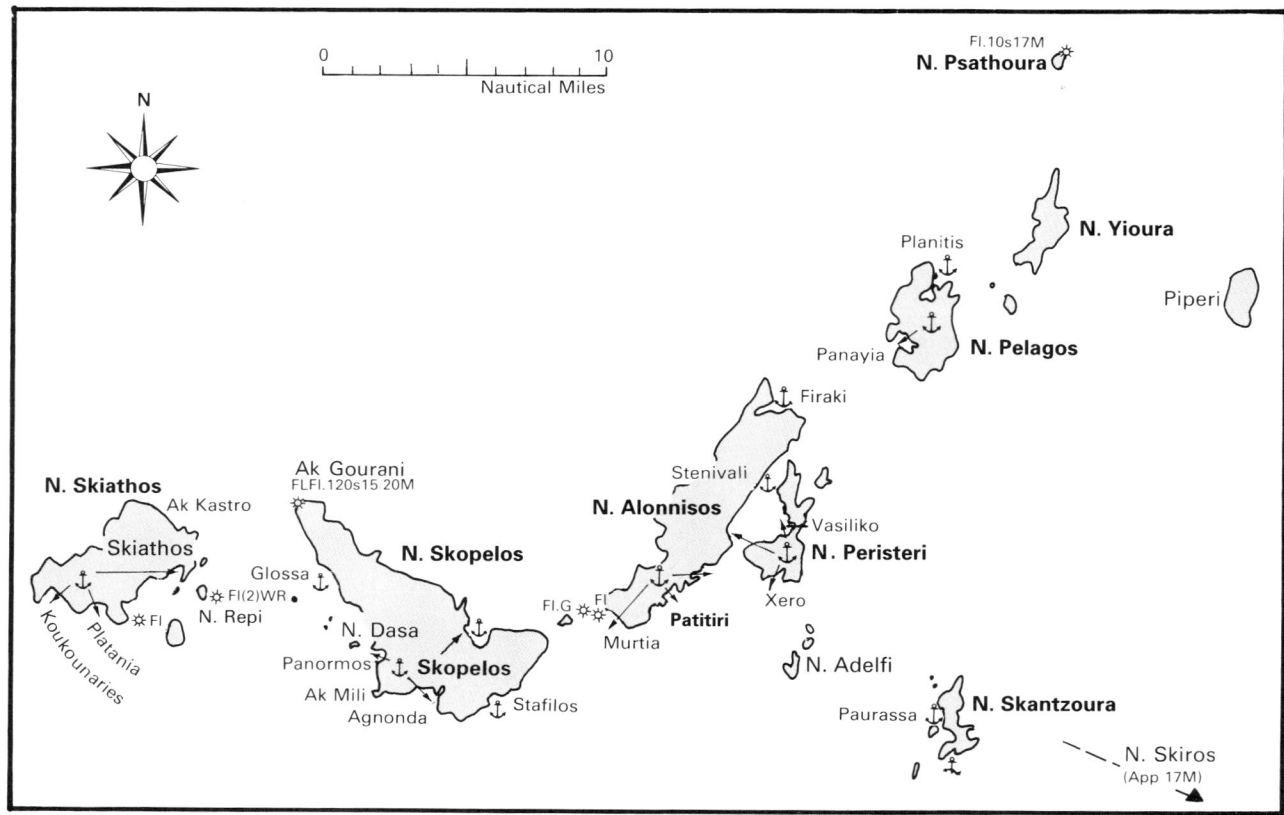

NORTHERN SPORADES

than the other islands, situated as it is on the trade route between Athens and Asia Minor.

During the Middle Ages the islands were easy prey for pirates. The inhabitants moved inland to fortified villages and not until the late 19th century did they begin to return to coastal villages. Consequently, most of the towns around the coast are of comparatively recent origin.

The popular architecture of the group is distinctive – the houses are washed in white, blue and pink and have gabled roofs with grey or red slates. Today the beautiful scenery and fine sandy beaches have been attracting growing numbers of tourists to the more accessible islands of the group.

Weather patterns in the Northern Sporades

The *meltemi* does not blow as strongly down through the Northern Sporades as it does further S. It blows from the NNE, but the direction is much altered by the islands and channels between them. The islands stop most of the sea on the S side except around Pelagos which gets the whole fetch of the sea from northern Greece. The combination of the *meltemi* and the flat seas on the lee side of the islands makes for some exhilarating sailing and not surprisingly the area is popular for flotilla holidays.

Skiathos

The nearest of the islands to the mainland coast. With good ferry services and an airport it attracts more visitors than the other islands. From 1538 until 1830 the inhabitants moved to an almost inaccessible rocky spur on the northern end of the island. The Kastro, as it was called, was connected to the island by a drawbridge which could be raised in times of siege. Today it is deserted and almost the entire population lives in Skiathos town.

STENON SKIATHOU (Skiathos Channel)

This narrow channel separates Skiathos from the mainland. Ifalos Levtheris (Lephtari Rock) lies in the channel 1¾ miles E of Ak Arapis. It is marked by a light structure (conspic): char. Fl(2)8s8M. A variable current sets either N or S through the channel at ½–1½ knots.

KOUKOUNARIES

Approach

A small harbour in the NE corner of Ormos Koukounaries on the SW corner of Skiathos. The large Skiathos Palace Hotel at the E end of the bay is conspicuous and the small harbour is immediately below it.

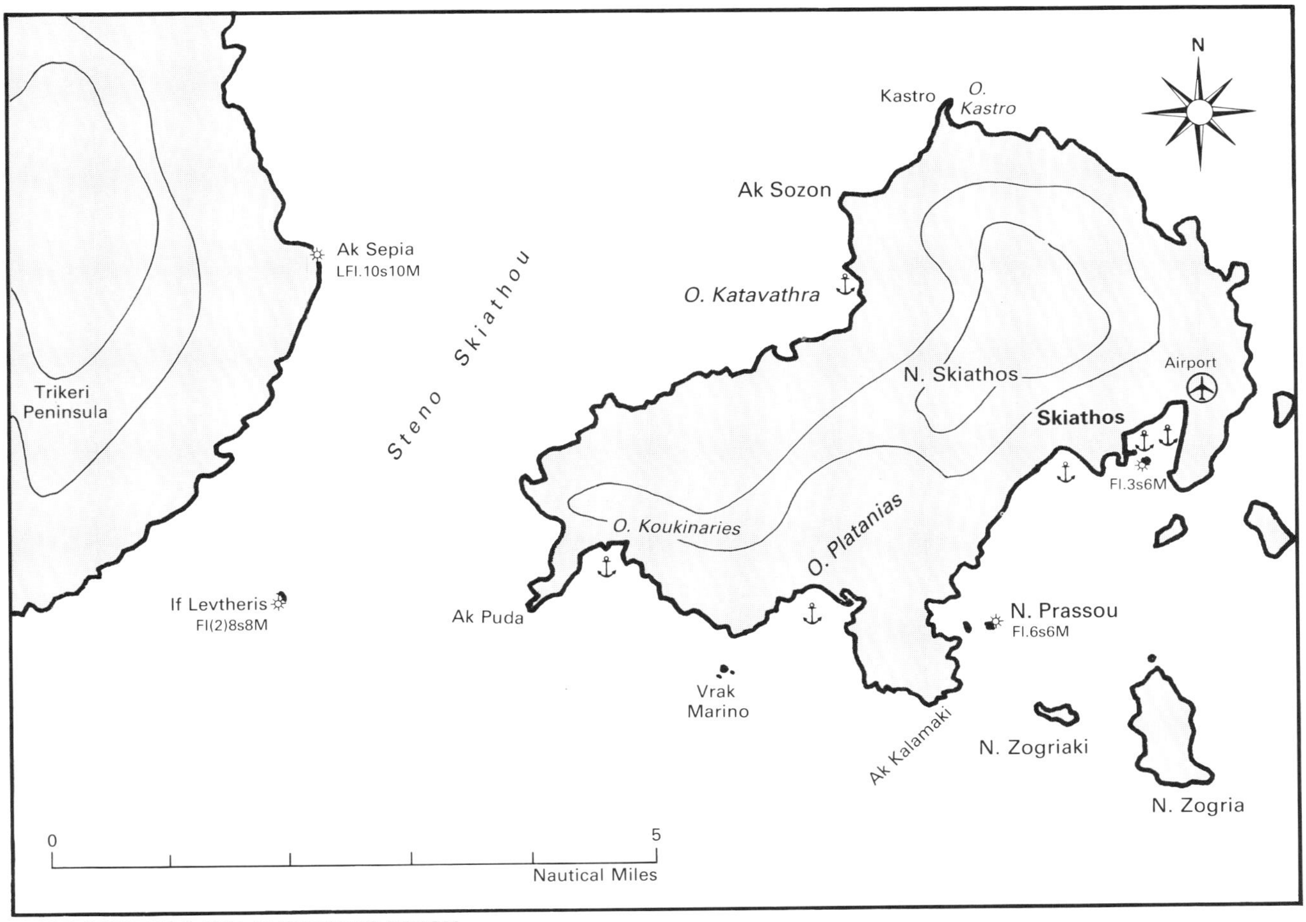

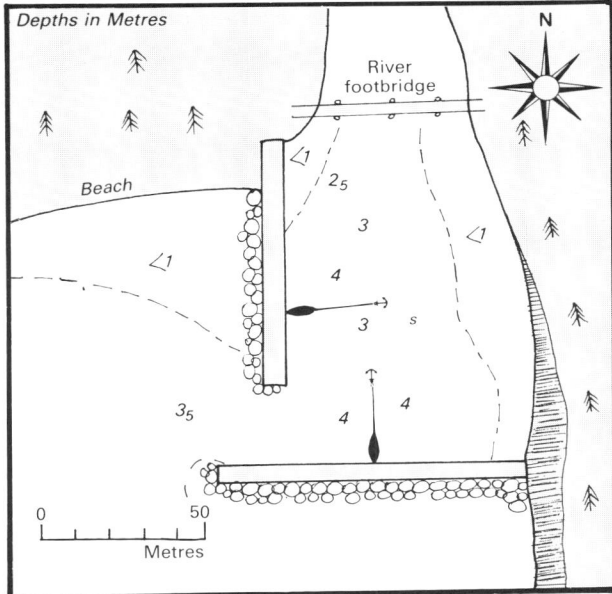

NISOS SKIATHOS AND STENON SKIATHOU

Mooring

Go stern-to or bows-to either mole. Excellent shelter. A number of boats are wintered afloat here. If the small harbour is full, anchor off the beach where there is good shelter from the *meltemi*.

Facilities

Several tavernas nearby.

Approach to Koukounaries looking N. Note conspicuous hotel above the harbour.

KOUKOUNARIES
39°09'N 23°24'·5E

General

Koukounaries is often said to be the best beach in the Aegean. It is a fine beach with the pines providing a wonderful aspect, but is not the best beach in the region in my opinion (see Khalkidhiki section).

317

ORMOS PLATANIA

A large bay to the E of Koukounaries with several hotels on the beach. Good shelter from the *meltemi*.

SKIATHOS

Admiralty chart no. 1196

Approach

Conspicuous The cluster of islands surrounding Skiathos harbour is easily identified. The lighthouse on Nisis Repi is conspicuous from the S and E. The buildings of Skiathos around the harbour, particularly a large building on the headland forming the E side of the old harbour and a church with a conspicuous clock tower on high ground to the N of the old harbour, are conspicuous.

By night Use the lights on Nisis Prassou (Fl.6s6M), Nisis Repi (Fl(2)WR.10s9/6M red sector covers 261°-313°), and Dhaskalonisi in the immediate approaches (Fl.3s6M). The end of the mole is lit: Fl.R.1·5s3M.

Mooring

Go stern-to or bows-to the northern part of the quay in the new harbour. The bottom is mud and weed, good holding. The old harbour on the S side is reserved for excursion boats though there may be a few berths here for small yachts.

Shelter Good shelter from the *meltemi* in the new E harbour, but the wind does blow beam on so make sure your anchor is well in. With southerlies a swell rolls in and unless you are tucked right under the mole, it is very uncomfortable.

Authorities Port police and customs.

Anchorage It is also possible to anchor at the head of the bay and a number of yachts are wintered afloat here. Keep well clear of the area where anchoring is prohibited under the flight path of the airport. The bottom is mud, sand and weed – good holding.

Facilities

Water On the quay though you need to find the 'waterman' to unlock the tap. Showers.

Fuel Can be delivered to the harbour by mini-tanker – contact the port police or ☎ 42921.

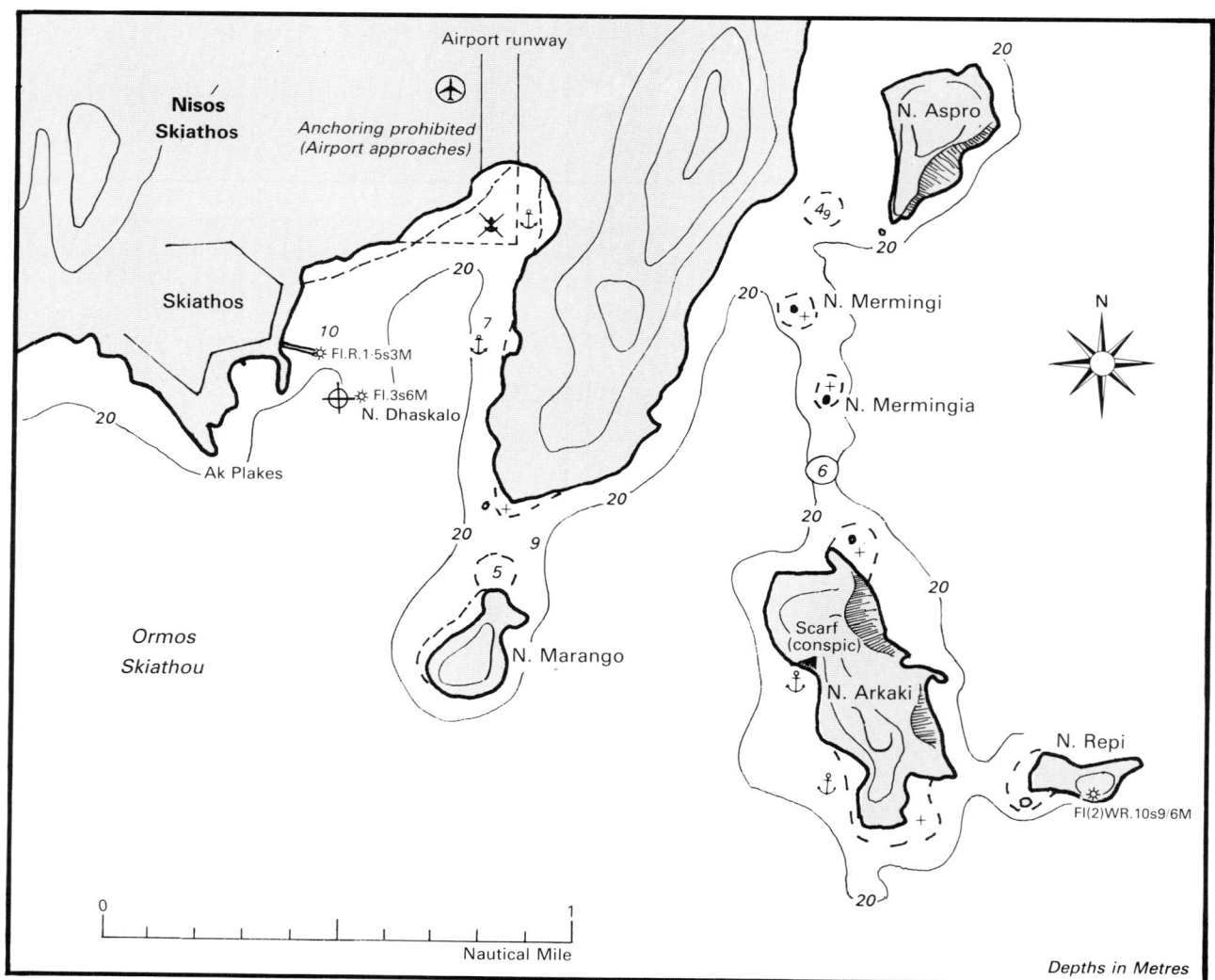

APPROACHES TO SKIATHOS 39°09'·7N 23°29'·7E (N. Dhaskalo)

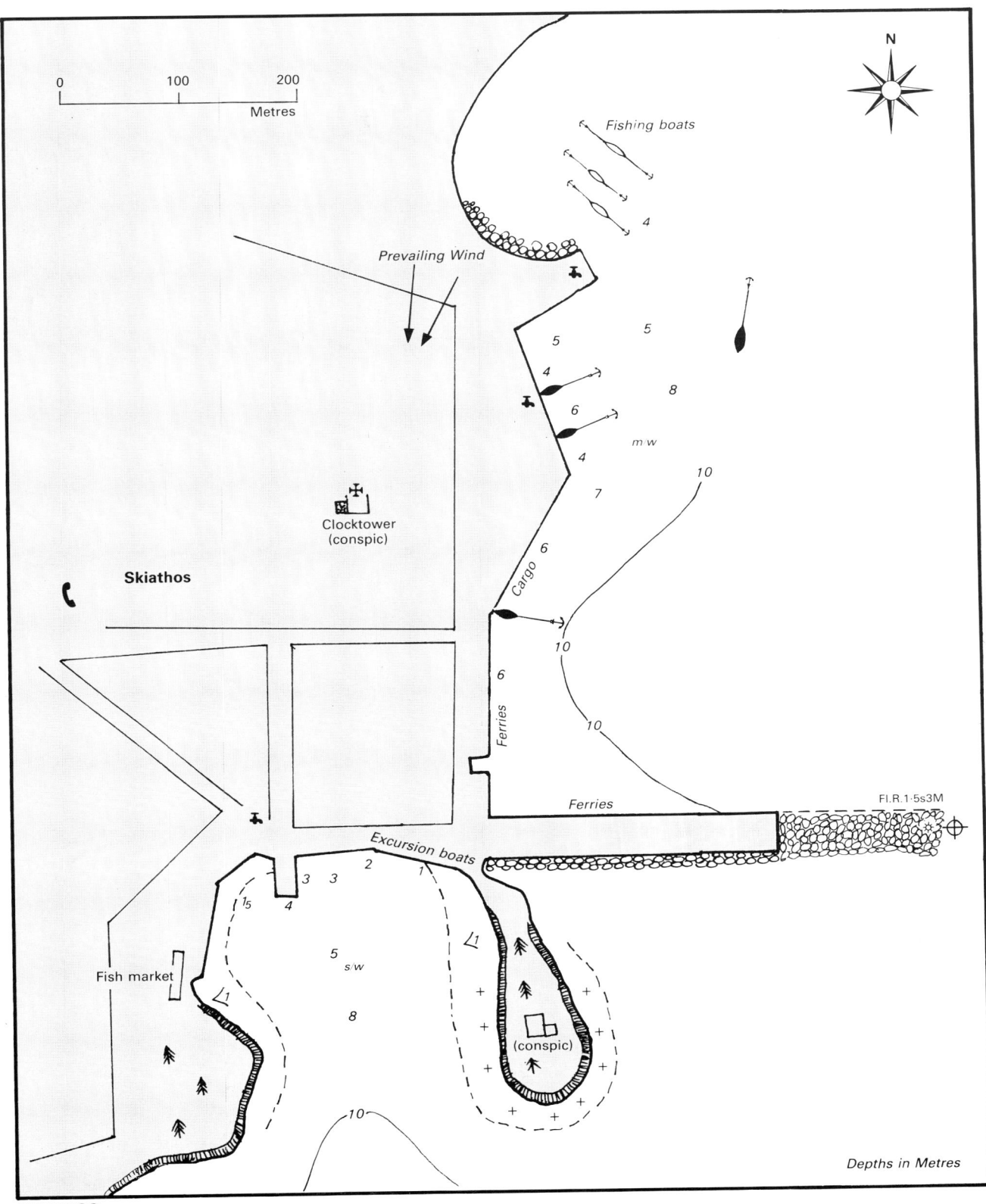

Fishing boats

Prevailing Wind

Clocktower
(conspic)

Skiathos

Cargo

m w

Ferries

Ferries

Fl.R.1·5s3M

Excursion boats

Fish market

s/w

(conspic)

Depths in Metres

SKIATHOS
39°09′·8N 23°29′·6E (Fl.R.3M)

Repairs Some mechanical repairs. Yachts are hauled out at the yard at the head of the bay. Limited chandlery. Good hardware shops.

Provisions Good shopping for all provisions. Ice can be ordered.

Eating out Good tavernas in the town.

Other PO. OTE. Banks. Greek gas and *Camping Gaz.* Hire cars, motorbikes and bicycles. Ferries to Volos, Ayios Konstandinos and Skopelos. European charter flights. Internal flights to Athens and Thessaloniki.

General

The small town of Skiathos has grown in recent years to become a sort of junior league Mikonos with discos, bars and good restaurants livening up the night. In the summer the town is packed with tourists attracted to the sandy beaches, yet it remains a pleasant easy-going town and most of the locals are still friendly enough. But a quiet place it is not and those seeking less noise and fewer people are advised to head E.

Skopelos

Skopelos (ancient Peparethos), like Skiathos, is densely wooded in pine over its slopes. It is also very fertile – vines, olives, almonds, pears, citrus fruit and plums for which the island is famous are grown. It is more intensively cultivated than Skiathos and the inhabitants (perhaps because they are farmers and not seafarers risking their lives at sea) are said to be more conservative.

The capital is Skopelos (*chora*-Skopelou) on the east side of the island. The island has long been considered a remote place – dissident Byzantines were exiled here far from the pleasures of Constantinople. In 1538 Barbarossa slaughtered the entire population of the island so presumably all the present inhabitants are immigrants who arrived in the 16th century. The island still has a remote feel to it in places and in the winter you can feel positively isolated on it. Today the islanders are an industrious and prosperous lot who seem quite happy to see tourists coming to their island, yet make few concessions to them outside Skopelos and Glossa.

GLOSSA (Loutraki)

Approach

Conspicuous The village on the hill above the harbour is easily seen from a considerable distance off. A large brown church in the middle of the village is conspicuous and below the small settlement behind the harbour will be seen.

By night The entrance is lit: Fl.G.2s3M and Fl.R.2s2M.

Glossa looking SSW.

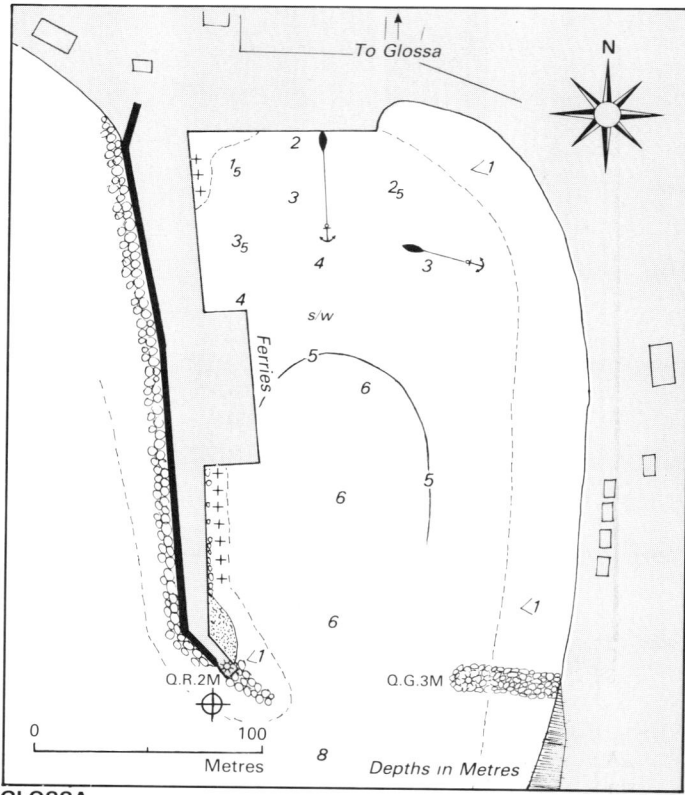

GLOSSA
39°10'·1N 23°36'·9E (Q.R.2M)

Mooring

Go stern-to or bows-to the quay on the N or on the mole if there is room. The bottom is sand and weed – good holding.

Shelter Good shelter from the *meltemi*. Open to the S although the local fishing boats are moored here all year round.

Facilities

Most provisions are available – better shopping in the village on the hill above. Good tavernas on the waterfront. Bus to Skopelos. Ferry to Skiathos.

General

Glossa has grown into a modest tourist resort and the once sleepy village is now invaded every day by visitors from Skiathos who come for its splendid beaches to the SE of the harbour. It is an arduous walk in the hot sun to the village of Loutraki above, but worth it for the magnificent views over to Skiathos and Evia.

ORMOS PANORMOU

Approach

The bay lies half a mile SE of Nisis Dhasa which is easily identified. The entrance to Panormos is difficult to make out (particularly from the S), but a new 3-storey hotel at the head of the bay is conspicuous when approaching from the W.

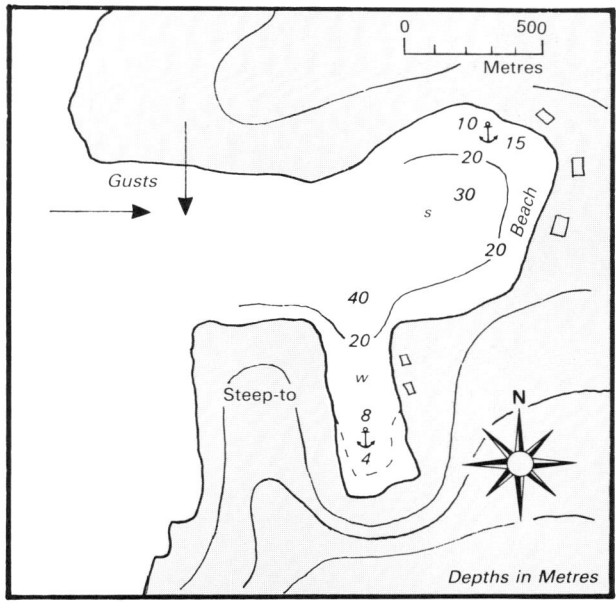

ORMOS PANORMOS
39°06'·5N 23°40'E

Mooring

The large bay is very deep even close to the beach (anchor in the NE corner in 10–15 metres). The inlet running S from the bay has better shelter. Anchor in the S corner in 4–8 metres and take a line ashore. There can be strong gusts from the N and NW into the bay so make sure your anchor is well in.

Facilities

Several tavernas on the beach of the large bay.

General

The secluded inlet on the S features in Michael Carroll's *Gates of the Wind*. Anyone who has read this book will immediately recognise his house on the E side of the inlet. Those who have not read it should obtain a copy (it is published in paperback by a Greek publisher) for the descriptions of the islands and particularly of Skopelos and Panormos just before the outside world learnt of these enchanted places.

AGNONDA

An enclosed bay 2½ miles E of Ak Miti. When strong N winds make the approach to Limin Skopelos dangerous the ferry calls here and a bus connects to Skopelos. The light structures on either side of the entrance are conspicuous: (Fl.R.2s3M and Fl.G.2s3M).

Anchor in the bay and take a line ashore or go stern-to or alongside the quay. Good shelter from the *meltemi*, but with southerlies a swell rolls in.

Taverna/bars ashore. The pine-clad inlet is a popular spot with Skopelites in the summer.

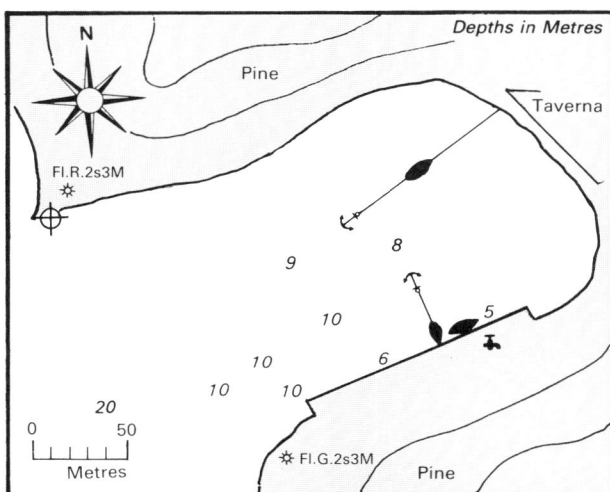

AGNONDA
39°05'·4N 23°42'·1E (Fl.R.3M)

STAFILOS (Staphylos)

An open bay on the S coast affording good shelter from the *meltemi*. The craggy headland joined by a low isthmus to Skopelos is easily identified. Care must be taken of the reef immediately S of the islet on the W side of the bay. Anchor in 3–4 metres in the NE corner. Open to the S.

A few summer villas have been built around the slopes. The bay is named after a Minoan prince (Staphylos), and recently archaeologists discovered evidence of a Cretan settlement, including a gold-plated sword handle and a gold diadem. This makes Stafilos the most northerly Minoan settlement so far unearthed.

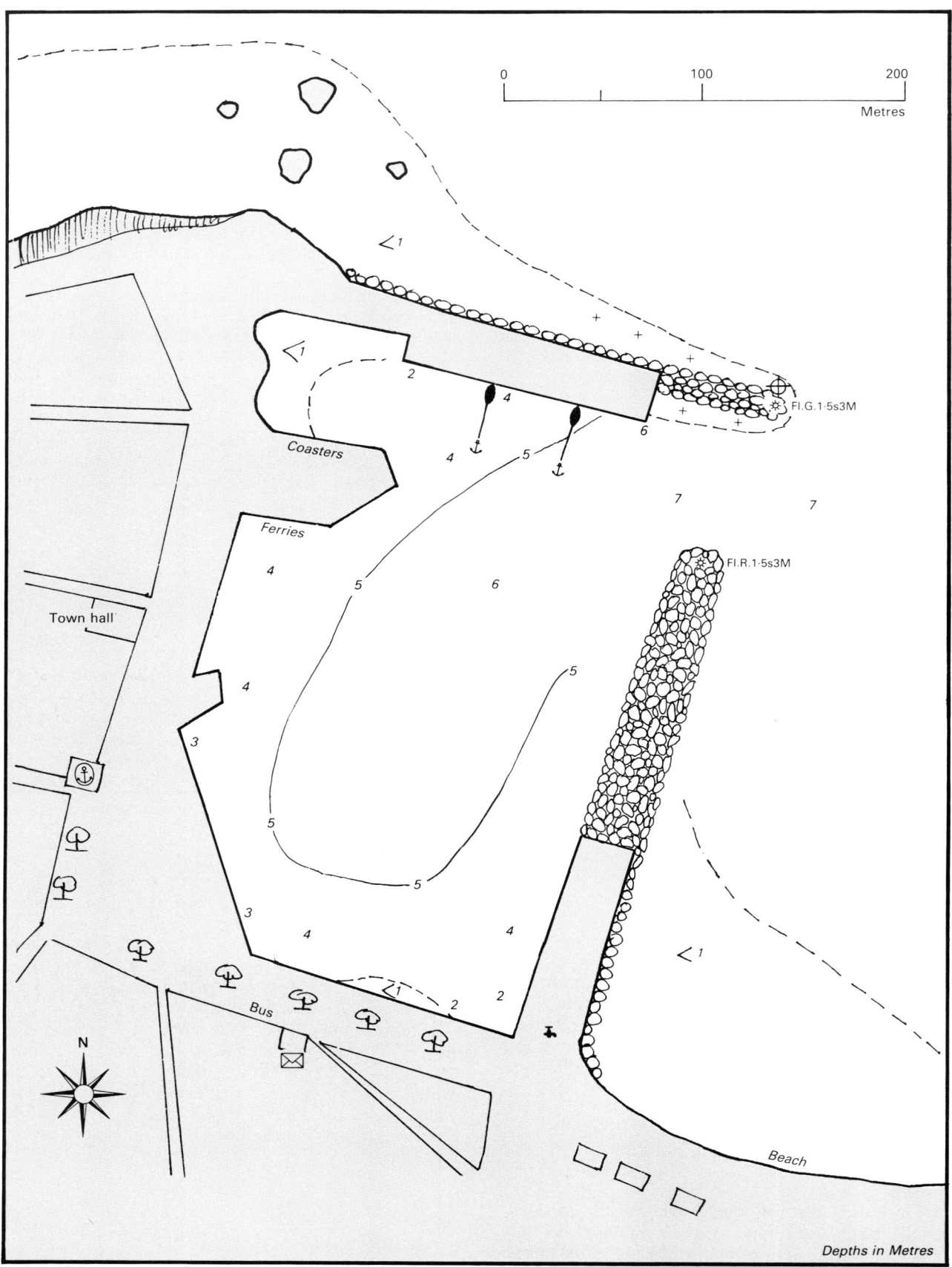

0   100   200

Metres

< 1

< 1

2

4

Coasters

4   5

4

Ferries

4   5   6

Town hall

4   5

3

5

5

5

3

4   4

Bus   < 1   2   2

N

Beach

7   7

Fl.G.1·5s3M

Fl.R.1·5s3M

< 1

Depths in Metres

SKOPELOS
39°07'·2N 23°44'·1E (Fl.G.3M)

LIMIN SKOPELOU

Approach

Conspicuous From the E the town of Skopelos will not be seen until you enter Ormos Skopelou. Once you are in the bay the cluster of houses above the harbour stand out in dazzling white. The harbour moles are easily identified.

By night Use the light on Nisis Mikro (Fl.4s6M) and the lights at the entrance (Fl.G.1·5s3M and Fl.R.1·5s3M).

Dangers With strong NE winds (including a prolonged *meltemi*) a steep and dangerous sea builds up over the shoal water in the approaches to the harbour. In these conditions it is difficult and sometimes dangerous to enter or leave the harbour. In this weather the ferry goes to Agnonda on the W coast of Skopelos.

Mooring

Go stern-to or bows-to the N quay. The bottom is mud – excellent holding.

Shelter With a strong *meltemi* it can get very uncomfortable in the harbour. Ease off the warps and keep the yacht some distance off the quay. The wash from the numerous ferries and hydrofoils using the harbour is also bothersome. Otherwise shelter is good.

Authorities Port police and customs.

Facilities

Water On the quay.

Fuel Can be delivered by mini-tanker from the FINA agent.

Repairs Limited mechanical repairs. Hardware shops.

Provisions Good shopping for all provisions. Wine and brandy from the barrel. Ice available.

Eating out Good tavernas on the waterfront and in the town.

Other PO. OTE. Bank. Hire motorbikes and bicycles. Bus to Glossa. Ferries to Patitiri and Volos.

General

The houses and churches (there are said to be 120) of the town are piled one upon another around a rock amphitheatre above the harbour. The houses are jammed together along narrow curving alleys that restrict access to pedestrians, donkeys and the occasional suicidal motorcyclist. An altogether delightful and relaxing place that has altered little (apart from acquiring some more tavernas and bars) despite the growing numbers of tourists discovering it.

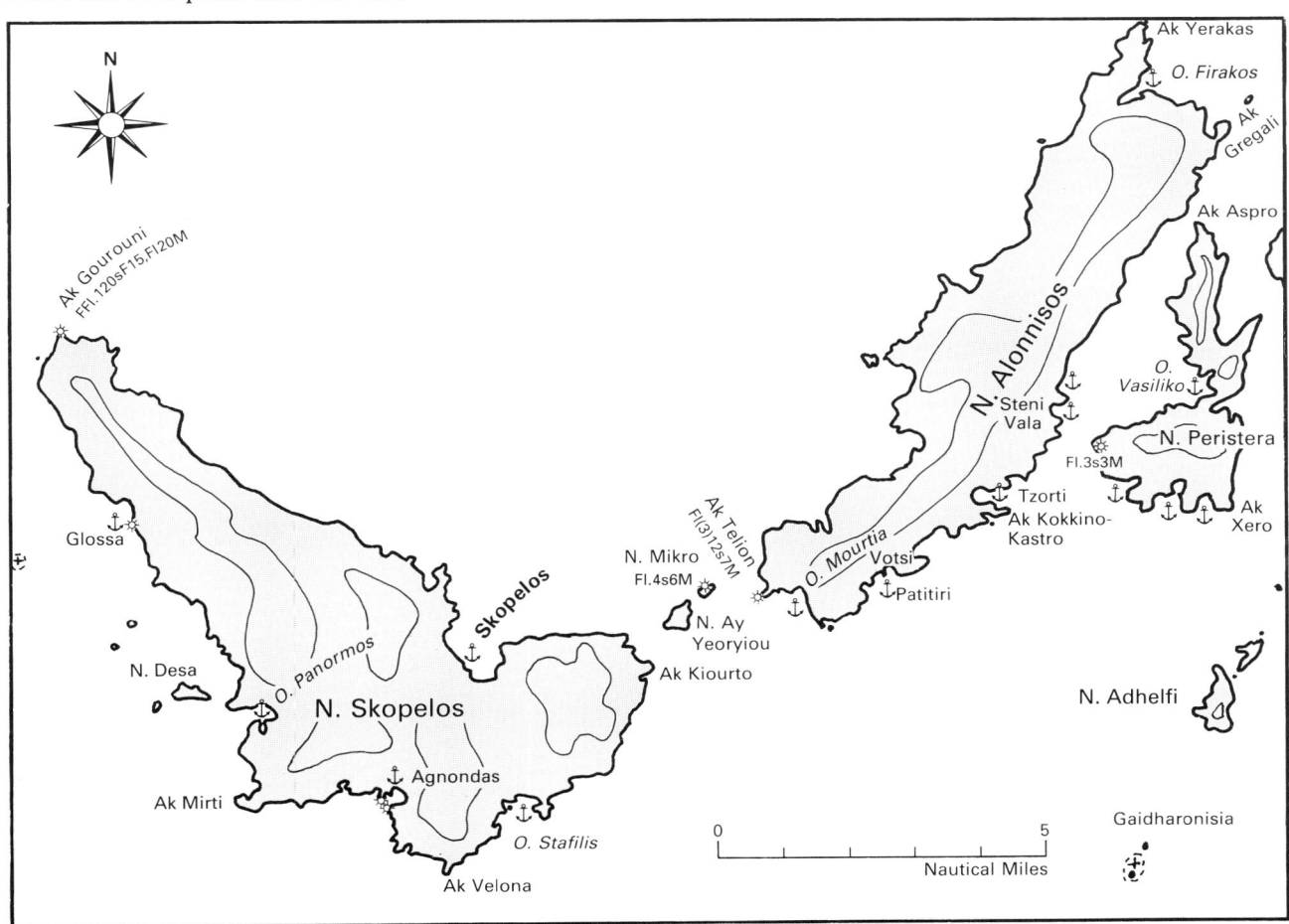

NISOI SKOPELOS AND ALONNISOS

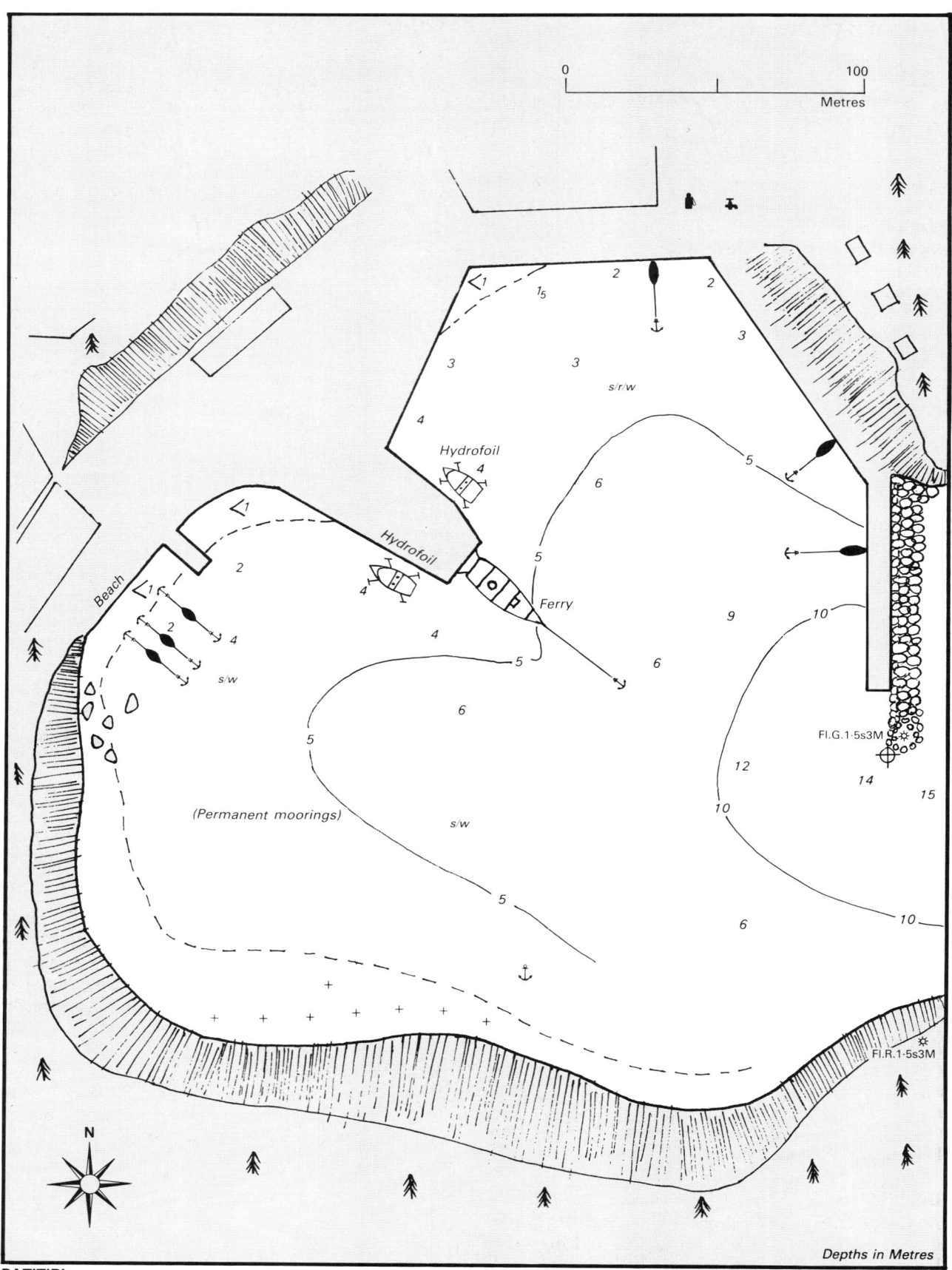

PATITIRI
39°08′·7N 23°52′E (Fl.G.3M)

Alonnisos
(Khelidromi)

In ancient times called Ilkos, this hilly wooded island relies on the donkey and the *caïque* as much as on motor vehicles. The old capital of Alonnisos, on a hill in the south of the island, was largely deserted after a severe earthquake in 1965. The islanders moved to Patitiri and Votsi, but recently rebuilding has started in the old hill village. At Ormos Tzorti evidence of Neolithic and other ancient habitation has been discovered. Whether this was also the site of ancient Halonessos, a city that ancient commentators say disappeared into the sea during a catastrophic earthquake, is uncertain as some authorities believe Psathoura, the northernmost island, to be the site.

ORMOS MOURTIA (Mourtias)
An open bay on the SW of Alonnisos offering some shelter from the *meltemi*. Open to the S. Anchor in 4–6 metres in the bay. The village of Alonnisos on the hill above is 30 minutes' steep climb up a donkey track. In unsettled weather Patitiri is a safer harbour to leave a yacht in if you want to visit the hill village.

PATITIRI

Approach
Conspicuous The old village of Alonnisos on the hill behind is visible from seaward. The village and harbour of Patitiri are not easily seen from the N or S until you are close to.
By night The entrance is lit: Fl.R.1·5s3M and Fl.G.1·5s3M.

Mooring
Go stern-to or bows-to the NE quay or anchor fore and aft off the beach on the W side where shown. The bottom is sand and weed – good holding.
Shelter Good shelter from the *meltemi*, although some swell tends to creep around into the harbour making it a bit rolly at times. Partially open to the E and SE.
Authorities Port police.

Facilities
Water Near the quay.
Fuel Near the quay.
Provisions Most provisions can be obtained. Ice available.
Eating out Tavernas and bars on the waterfront.
Other PO. Exchange facilities. Ferries to Skiathos. Hydrofoil to Volos.

General
As has recently happened on the other islands in the group, the capital of the island has moved from the hill village down to the harbour. Patitiri is a lovely spot surrounded by the cliffs on the S and pine-clad slopes behind, so inevitably it has attracted a growing number of tourists, but remains a pleasant spot still.

VOTSI
A cove immediately N of Patitiri which a number of fishing boats use in preference to Patitiri. A short breakwater extends from the E side of the cove and a 'snoot' of a breakwater on the W. Anchor in the NE corner in 6–10 metres and take a line ashore to a tree. Alternatively go on the new quay reported to have been recently built on the E side. Good shelter from the *meltemi* and open only to the SW for a short distance. Towards the head of the bay the bottom shelves gently.

Tavernas ashore. It is a short walk over the saddle to Patitiri.

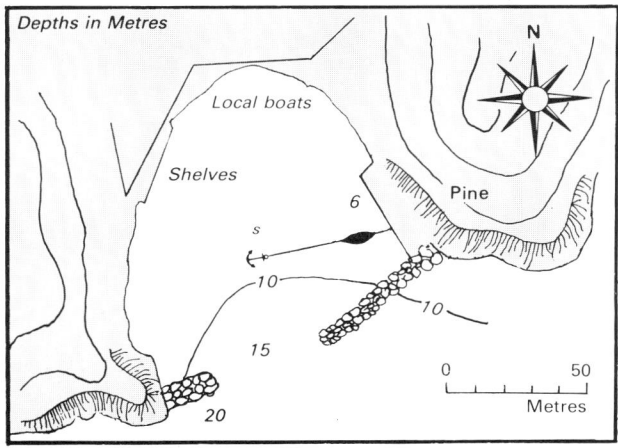

VOTSI
39°08'·9N 23°52'·4E

AK KOKKINOKASTRO
Kokkinokastro is the red cliffy cape 2½ miles N of Patitiri (*kokkino* means 'red'). Kokkinokastro is thought to be the site of ancient Ilkos (about the fifth century BC).

ORMOS TZORTI
A cove close N of Ak Kokkinokastro with good shelter from the *meltemi*. Anchor where convenient and if necessary take a long line ashore. Sandy beach and pine-clad slopes.

STENI VALA
A small cove on Alonnisos opposite the S end of Peristeri Island. Sheltered from the *meltemi*, but open to the SW. There is a quay with 1 metre depths off it. Tavernas on the shore.

ORMOS FIRAKI (Port Eiraka)
A bay on the N end of the island. The bay is very exposed and is untenable with the *meltemi*, but in calm weather makes a good lunch stop.

Nisos Peristeri

(Xero)

The island lying roughly parallel to and just to the E of Alonnisos. There are two anchorages sheltered from the *meltemi*.

ORMOS XERO

On the S coast of Peristeri lying immediately W of Ak Xero. Open to the S. Uninhabited.

ORMOS VASILIKO

The bay at the N end of the large bay on the W coast. Two white houses on the hill above are conspicuous. Care must be taken of the reef on the W side of the entrance. Anchor in 4–8 metres in the bay. Nearly all-round shelter. A number of fishing boats are permanently moored here and there is a small hamlet ashore.

Note The 3 fathom patch shown on Admiralty charts Nos. 1085 and 1087 extending across the northern passage between Alonnisos and Peristeri is in fact a smallish patch off the end of Peristeri. There are considerable depths in the fairway.

Nisos Pelagos

Lies 4 miles to the NE of Alonnisos. It is deserted except for large herds of goats. A number of sunken Byzantine ships have been discovered off the coast and in 1970 a quantity of pottery was recovered.

Note It is reported that the Greek government has declared Pelagos Island a nature reserve. At one time there was talk of banning yachts from the island, but this does not seem to have happened and yachts continue to visit the island. Yachtsmen should take care not to disturb wildlife around the island or they may find they are banned from here.

MONASTERY COVE

A small cove on the E side of the island where a yacht can moor in settled weather to visit the monastery. On Admiralty chart no. 2072 it is the bay immediately S of the bay showing 8 and 2 fathoms. The monastery itself is on a small headland at the S end of that bay. Anchor in 5 metres and take a line ashore. The cove is protected only from W winds and should be visited in calm weather only.

Steps are cut in the rock to climb to the monastery several hundred feet above. It is a lonely and haunted place and now that the last monk has died it stands as a lonely unmanned sentinel for Mt Athos – visitors should take care not to desecrate the spot whether believers or not.

KIRA PANAYIA (Ayios Petros)

A large bay on the SW corner of Pelagos. Nisis Pelerissa and the high plateau on the SE side of the bay are easily distinguished. There is deep water N and S of Nisis Pelerissa.

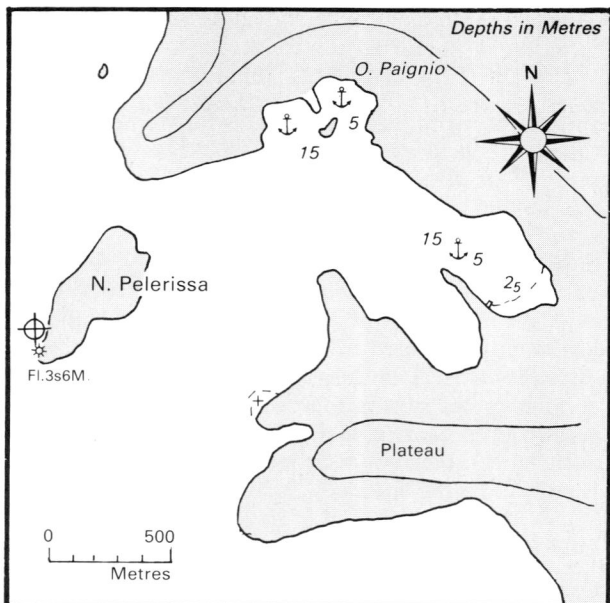

KIRA PANAYIA
39°18'·8N 24°02'·3E (Pelerissa light)

Good shelter from the *meltemi* can be found in Ormos Paignio, although with northerlies there are vicious gusts into the bay. Anchor in the cove on the NW side or behind the islet in the middle of the bay and take a line ashore. The bottom is sand – good holding.

A yacht can also anchor in the cove on the E side in 2–4 metres. The bottom is sand and thick weed – poor holding.

ORMOS PLANITIS (Planidhi)

A large landlocked bay on the N side of Nisos Pelagos. Nisis Sphika lies close to the W side of the narrow entrance which is difficult to see until you are close in. With strong N winds a considerable sea piles up at the entrance to Planitis and it is a frightening experience being pushed by the wind and

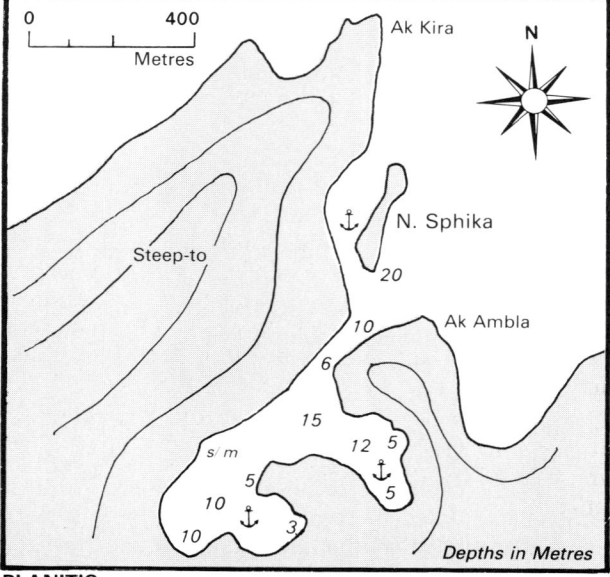

PLANITIS
39°21'N 24°04'·5E

sea towards the entrance which is only 82 metres (270ft) wide. Conversely with strong N winds it can be difficult to leave the bay. There is a least depth of 6 metres over the bar at the entrance. Inside the bay the water is always smooth.

Anchor in either of the two forks of the bay. A favourite place is in 3 metres in the NE corner of the southernmost part of the bay. Excellent all-round shelter. The bottom is sand and mud with some weed – good holding. It is deserted apart from a large herd of goats, and the crackle of several million cicadas.

There is a shallow passage between the S end of Nisis Sphika and Pelagos which in settled weather makes an attractive lunch stop. Explore with caution.

NISIS YIOURA

A precipitous jagged island with no sheltered anchorages. A herd of the European wild goat, the now rare ibex, lives on the island and every year an armada of *caïques* sets out to cull the herd under the supervision of an official. Michael Carroll gives a lively description of the cullers and the culling in his *Gates of the Wind*.

NISIS PIPERI

The Pepperpot. There are no anchorages on it.

Nisis Psathoura

The northernmost of the northern Sporades, it is very low (0·6 metres/2ft), but the lighthouse (40 metres/131ft) is conspicuous. An extensive submerged city, possibly ancient Halonnesos, is reported to lie off the N end of the island.

Currents Around Psathoura Island and also to the N of it the current sets strongly towards the SW. On passage between Porto Koufo and Pelagos in November, I estimated the current to be about 1½ knots to the SW. Quite possibly it is stronger at other times of the year. With strong winds from the N and S the seas in the vicinity of Psathoura can be exceptionally disturbed and steep.

NISIS SKANTZOURA

Lies about 15 miles E of the S end of Skopelos. A number of small islands and shoals lie off the coast. On the W coast of the island a yacht can anchor in Ormos Paurassa opposite Nisis Paurassou in 5 metres or in Ormos Skantzoura to the S in 3–4 metres. Limited shelter from the *meltemi*. Open to the W–SW. The bottom is sand and weed. Excellent underwater fishing in the vicinity of the island.

Caution Nisis Skantzoura and the islets surrounding it are comparatively low-lying and are unlit. Care must be taken in the vicinity of the island, especially at night.

Skiros
(Skyros)

The most easterly and the largest of the northern Sporades. It is nearly divided into two by a narrow isthmus in the middle. The summit of the island lies in the rugged southern half where Mt Kokhilas rises to 792 metres (2600ft). The lower slopes of the high ground are wooded in pine and *maquis*. The northern half of the island is fertile and cultivated in parts.

The capital, Skiro' or Khorio, is more like a Cycladic village than the villages on Skiathos or Skopelos. The white cubist houses with flat roofs are built on a steep slope with a Venetian castle on the summit. In the village there is an unusual amount of carved wood – doors, shutters, chairs and stools. Skiros embroidery is also much in evidence. Some of the best island folk art is contained in the Faltaitz Museum near the castle – one of the best of its kind in Greece.

Ancient Skiros was ruled by King Lykomedes. It was he who treacherously killed Theseus, king of Athens, by hurling him over a cliff into the sea. His body was recovered and forty years later taken to Athens for a burial befitting his rank. Later Achilles was sent here by his mother to keep him away from the Trojan Wars in which it had been prophesied he would die. The wily Odysseus, en route to the wars, discovered his identity and lured him away to his prophesied death.

The island has always been important because of its position on the trade route across the northern Aegean. The Athenians colonised it and the Venetians held it for some considerable time. The Venetian castle overlooking Khorio has ancient masonry incorporated in its construction and was the likely site of the ancient acropolis.

The inhabitants of the island have been little touched by tourism although the 'younger set' are beginning to discover it. Some of the old men wear linen blouses and black pantaloons and boots and most sport big bushy moustaches. A herd of wild ponies, descendants of the ancient breed called Pikermic and akin to Shetland ponies, roam the island. Despite the rough seas and strong winds around the island it is well worth a visit; the islanders are very friendly and the scenery is grand and wild.

SKIROS ((Skyros)
Admiralty chart no. 2048
Imray-Tetra chart no. G25

On this island battered by both wind and sea (its ancient name was Anemosa meaning 'windy') the anchorages are all on the SW coast. From the N these are:

Ormos Ay Fokas and Ormos Pevko Lie N of Nisis Valaxa. These two bays offer shelter from the *meltemi* but there is invariably some swell in the bays. They are both deserted.

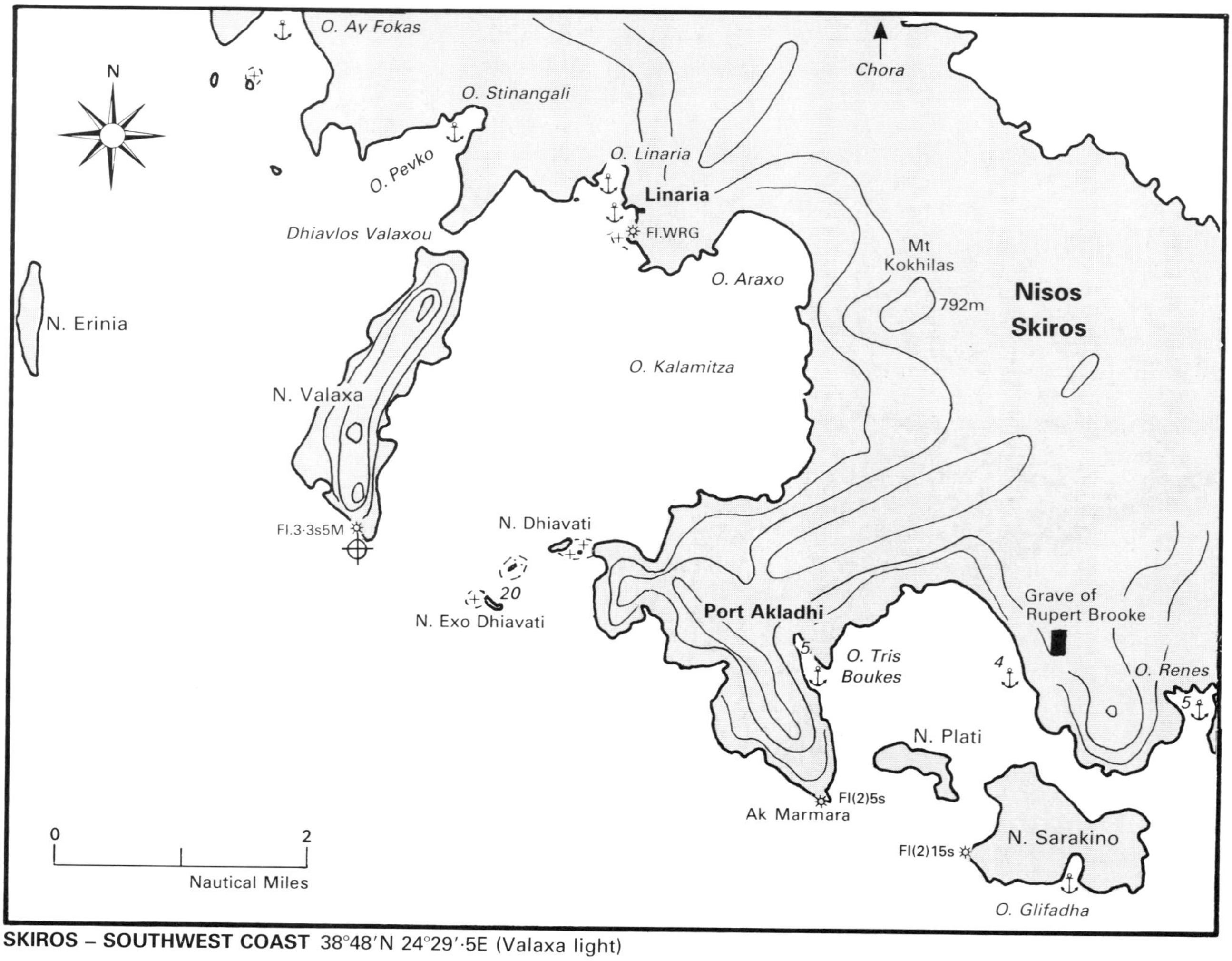

SKIROS – SOUTHWEST COAST 38°48′N 24°29′·5E (Valaxa light)

Dhiavlos Valaxou There are depths of 2–5 metres in this passage keeping close to the N end of Nisis Valaxa. On the Skiros side of the channel there are least depths of 5 metres. The ferry between Linaria and Kimi often uses this passage.

Ormiskos Linaria Lies further to the N from the ferry port of Linaria. Good shelter from the *meltemi*. The bottom is mud – good holding. Taverna on the beach.

LIMIN LINARIA
Imray-Tetra chart no. G25

Approach
Once past Nisis Valaxa some of the buildings around the harbour will be seen. The harbour proper will not be seen until you are right up to it when approaching from the S.

By night Use the light on the S end of Nisis Valaxa (Ak Valaxa Fl.3·3s5M) and the light on the end of the mole at Linaria (Fl.WRG.2·5s6-4M red sector 353°-021°/white sector 021°-120°/green sector 120°-300°).

Dangers With the *meltemi* there are strong gusts off the high land and confused seas in the approaches to the harbour.

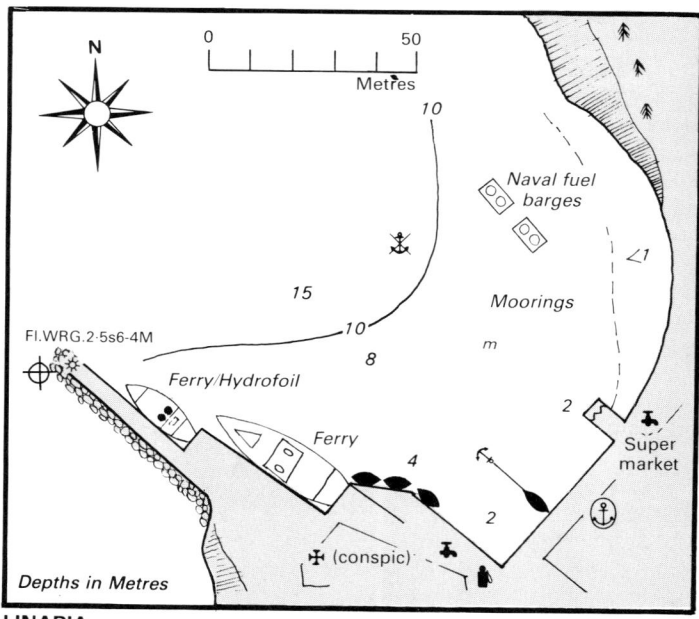

LINARIA
38°50′·6N 24°32′·2E (Fl.WRG.6-4M)

Above. Nisis Trizonia bay looking ESE. *Claude Mauge*. p.157

Right. The *chora* at Serifos looking up from the anchorage in Livadhi. p.245

Below. Simi harbour. p.419

Above. Taverna. Leonidhion. p.213
Below. Plomarion on Lesvos. p.374

Naxos. Looking towards Vakkhos from the new S basin. p.259

Approach to Ermioni looking W. p.198

Pirgadikia looking NE. p.344

Thunderstorm forming over the E Peloponnese. It is difficult to tell if it will cause a squall over the sea although the odds are it will.

Simi harbour looking east from the head. p.419
Below. The *chora* and castle on the summit of the south ridge at Skala, Astipalaia. p.437

Skiros. Linaria looking NE.

Mooring

Moor alongside the quay in the S. The harbour was dredged to 3–5 metres recently. Keep well clear of the ferry quay and do not anchor N of it as the ferry turns in this area before berthing.

Shelter Good shelter from the *meltemi*. Open to the NW–W.

Authorities Port police.

Facilities

Water On the quay.
Fuel On the quay.
Provisions Some provisions available at Linaria. Better shopping in the *chora*.
Eating out Several tavernas nearby and others in the *chora*.
Other PO and OTE in the *chora*. Irregular bus to the *chora*. Ferries to Kimi and Volos and a hydrofoil to Skiathos.

General

Linaria is the place most yachts make for and the small amount of quay space can be cluttered in the high season. It is more of a staging post for passengers on the ferry to get to the *chora* than a village as such, but is a pleasant enough place and really the only place from which to visit the *chora*.

Anchorages S of Linaria

Ormos Akladhi Lying on the W side of Ormos Trebuki, this bay offers good shelter from the *meltemi*. Anchor in 5 metres near the head of the bay. The bottom is sand and weed.

Ormos Trebuki If you want to visit the grave of Rupert Brooke anchor off the river mouth on the E side of Ormos Trebuki in 4–8 metres. (In calm weather only.) The bottom is sand and weed. To get to the grave follow the river bed for about 20 minutes and the grave will be found in an olive grove on the W side. I am not much of a fan of Rupert Brooke's poetry, more a fan of the man, but there are few of us who do not know the last lines of *The Old Vicarage*:

'And after, ere the night is born,
Do hares come out about the corn?
Oh, is the water sweet and cool,
Gentle and brown above the pool?
And laughs the immortal river still
Under the mill, under the mill?
Say, is there Beauty yet to find?
And Certainty? and Quiet kind?
Deep meadows yet, for to forget
The lies, and truths, and pain? ...oh! yet
Stands the Church clock at ten to three?
And is there honey still for tea?'

Ormos Renes Anchor in a cove in the NW or NE corner. It is fairly deep for anchoring. The bottom is sand and weed.

Ormiskos Glifadha Lies on the S side of Nisis Sarakino. Anchor at the head of the creek in 4–6 metres. The bottom is sand and weed. Good shelter from the *meltemi*. Open only to the S.

Caution With a strong *meltemi* blowing there are violent gusts down onto the SW coast off the high mountains. These are especially fierce in Ormos Trebuki. Caution must be exercised on the lee side of the island on account both of the gusts and of the considerable seas raised by the *meltemi*.

East coast of Evia

For the most part this coast is rugged and precipitous with little shelter for yachts. The prevailing NE winds push considerable seas across the northern Aegean until they crash onto this coast. The coast is only sparsely populated and the scenery spectacular and wild. The only harbour of any size is Kimi approximately halfway along the coast, but there are a number of other anchorages offering some shelter from the prevailing winds.

ORMOS PETRIES (Ay Apostoli)

Lies 23½ miles NW of Ak Kafirevs and directly opposite Aliverion on the other coast.

Approach

The entrance is difficult to identify from the N. Closer in the light structure (Fl.5s4M) will be seen and once into the bay the hamlet and breakwater are easily located. With the *meltemi* there is some swell at the entrance, but once into the bay the water is flat.

Caution Just N of the head of the breakwater lies the sunken wreck of a coaster or large trawler. Some of the superstructure is 2 metres or less under the surface and could rip out the bottom of an unsuspecting yacht. In calm weather it can be seen under the water.

Mooring

Anchor in 5 metres in the bay or go bows-to the breakwater with a long line ashore. The bottom is sand and weed with scattered rocks, good holding as long as you choose your spot to drop anchor. There

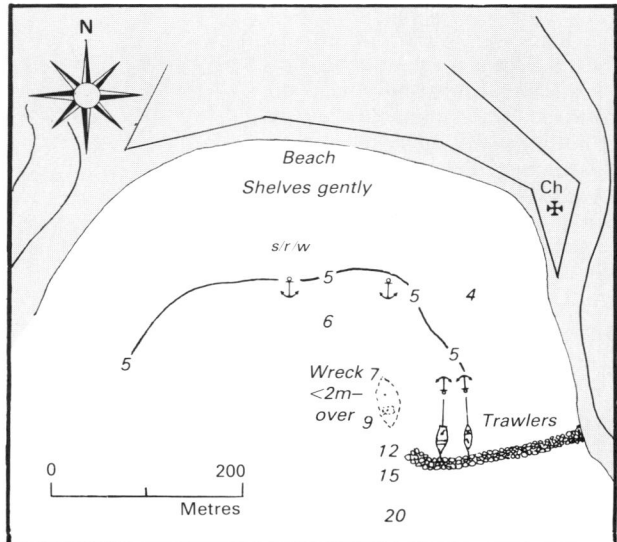

PETRIES
38°24′·3N 24°12′E

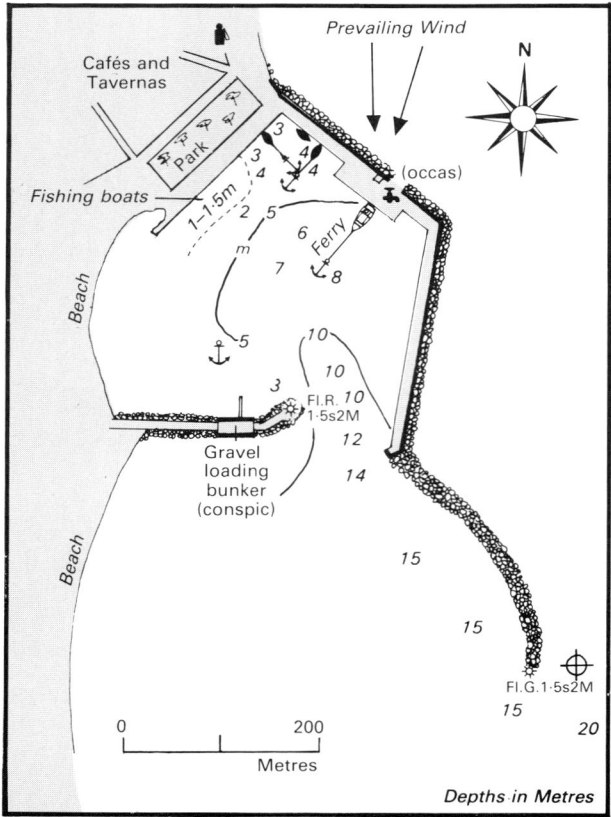

KIMI
38°37′·6N 24°07′·6E (Fl.G.2M)

are numerous permanent moorings around the bay so beware of floating lines. Good shelter from the *meltemi*.

Facilities

Several tavernas on the beach in the summer. Limited provisions.

General

The setting in the large bay is spectacular, but the hamlet is a sorry collection of reinforced concrete houses mostly thrown up in the last few years. Nonetheless it is well worth a visit and the harbour is conveniently placed to break a voyage on the outside of Evia.

KIMI (Kymi, Paralia)

Approach

Conspicuous From the S and E the village of Kimi above the harbour is visible from seaward. From the north Nisis Prasoudha and the lighthouse on it are easily identified and closer in a communication tower and dish on the ridge above the harbour are conspicuous. The harbour breakwater and entrance are easily identified.

By night Use the lights on Nisis Prasoudha (Fl.5s16M) and at the harbour entrance (Fl.R.1·5s2M and Fl.G.1·5s2M).

Dangers With the *meltemi* blowing a heavy sea rolls onto the Evia coast. There is invariably a confused swell around Ak Kimi and at the entrance to the harbour.

Mooring

Go stern-to or bows-to the N mole or the N end of the W quay taking care to avoid the shallow patch. The harbour is often crowded with fishing boats and it can be difficult to find a berth. Care is needed of

permanent moorings fouling the bottom. The bottom is mud – excellent holding.

Shelter Good shelter from the *meltemi* although there can be a surge in here.

Authorities Port police and customs.

Facilities

Water On the quay or in the town.
Fuel Near the quay.
Provisions Some provisions available. Better shopping in Kimi 30 minutes' walk up the hill. Ice available.
Eating out Several tavernas near the harbour.
Other Bus to Khalkis. Ferry to Skiros.

General

The grubby harbour and the hamlet around it (properly Paralia, Kimi being the village on the hill above) are unprepossessing, but the setting is magnificent; the high mountains severed by deep gorges are densely wooded and drop down to long sandy beaches battered by the angry seas that crash onto this coast. It is a pleasant if steep walk up to Kimi along the wooded road and the view from the village across the sea to Skiros is spectacular.

ORMOS LOUTRO

Lies 9 miles SE of Ak Artemision. A reef runs from the NE side of the entrance in a SE direction for approximately 350 metres. Enter the bay from the S. Anchor in 3–4 metres in the bay. Sheltered from the *meltemi*. Open to the E and S.

VII. Northern Greece

This section covers the sea area from Thermaikos Kolpos eastwards to Alexandroupolis in the northeast corner of Greece. It is a sea seldom cruised by yachtsmen yet it offers some of the grandest scenery and without doubt the finest sandy beaches in Greece. Describe northern Greece to a yachtsman who has cruised solely in southern Greece, in the Saronic, Cyclades, Crete or the Dodecanese, and he will be inclined to think you are describing a country geographically removed from the Mediterranean.

The climate is Balkan rather than Mediterranean with extreme differences between the summer and winter. The winters are harsh and cold with a high average rainfall and occasionally snow even at sea-level – no place for a yacht to spend the winter. The summers are hot and often described as languid. The terrain is mountainous and densely wooded. Pine, chestnut, plane, oak and poplar are common down to the water's edge. The coastal plains, deposited by the large rivers flowing through the region, are fertile and cultivated in maize, tobacco, rice, beans, sugar-beet, sunflowers and of course the vine. The fauna is prolific and said to include the jackal, wild cat, boar, roe deer and, in the remote areas, wolves. By the lakes and marshes bird life abounds: vultures, sea eagles, storks, herons, cormorants, pelicans, waders and ducks can be seen in large numbers. Flatfish, mussels and scallops are found in the shallows off the large rivers.

Just as the climate is Balkan rather than Mediterranean, so the peoples of this area are partly of Balkan origin. In ancient times the mountain-dwelling folk were regarded as wild and barbaric by the civilization centred around Athens. Around the coast the Greeks intermarried with the indigenous population and have always been regarded with suspicion by Greeks from the south. The move for an independent Macedonia only heightens suspicion towards the inhabitants of Greece's Balkan inheritance.

The region reached its zenith when Alexander the Great toppled the Athenians and made Macedonia

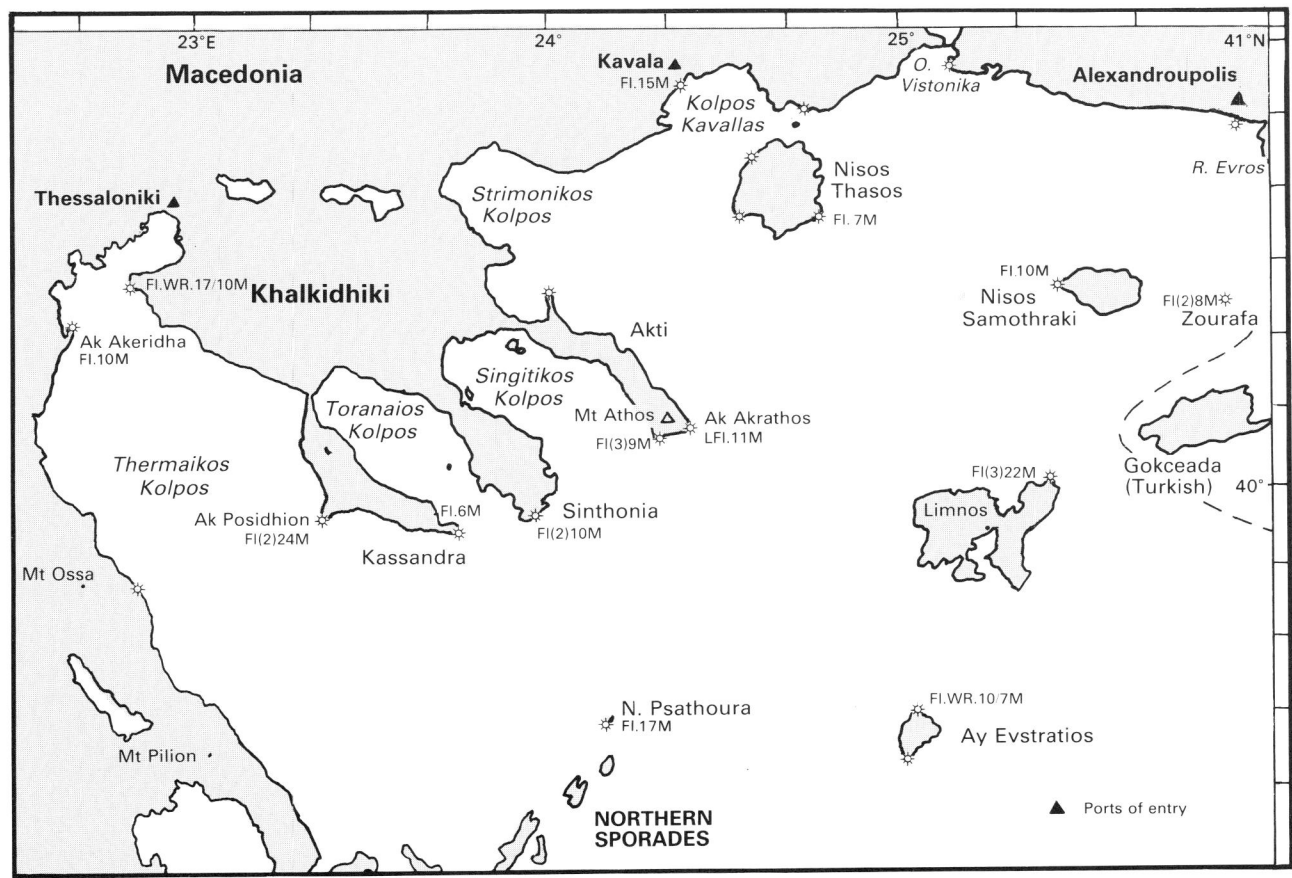

the centre of his empire. Not that things changed very much as the young Alexander was a great admirer of the Greeks and their civilization. After his death the power slipped away in the internecine struggles which went on for nearly two centuries. The usual succession of invaders followed the collapse of power, taking a harsher toll than in other regions since this was the first part of Greece they encountered after a long and hungry march over the mountains. The Goths, Huns, Ostrogoths, Bulgars, Slavs and Saracens laid waste to the region. By 1444 the Turks had secured the region and it remained under Turkish rule until 1913. At the beginning of the Second World War a combined Greek, English, Australian and New Zealand force was smashed by the German army and what had been an attempt to hold the German invasion turned into a frantic retreat to the southern beaches. The allied troops were evacuated from beaches on Evia and in the Saronic.

Until recently these northern provinces were little known to outsiders and indeed even Greeks from the southern regions viewed northerners with some suspicion. Today, tourism has opened up the area, especially around Kavala and on Thasos. Yet much of the coast remains virtually inaccessible except by sea, and for the yachtsman who desires solitude and magnificent scenery it would be difficult to find places to match those in northern Greece.

Weather patterns

Because there is no outstanding weather pattern for the whole region the weather patterns are described in each section.

Data

PORTS OF ENTRY
Thessaloniki
Kavala
Alexandroupolis

PROHIBITED AREAS
Off the mouth of the Evros river near the Greek/Turkey border. (Yet the local fishing boats frequent the area and sometimes anchor off here whilst fishing.)

MAJOR LIGHTS
Ak Sepia LFl.10s10M
Ak Dhermatas Fl(2)10s11M
Ak Atheridha Fl.5s10M
Thessaloniki (Nisis Kavoura. Axios) Fl(2)WRG.12s7-5M
Thessaloniki (Yacht Club) DirIso.WRG.10s10M
Thessaloniki Airport Aero Al.WG.6s13M
Ak Mikro Emvolon Fl(3)G.15s5M
Ak Megalo Emvolon Fl.WR.10s17/10M
Ak Epanomi Fl(3)18s6M
Ak Posidhion Fl(2)15s24M
Ak Psevdhokavos Fl(2)10s10M
Ak Pinnes Fl(3)15s9M
Ak Akrathos LFl.10s11M
Nisidhes Stiliaria N islet Fl.2·5s6M

Nisis Kavkanas Fl(3)18s6M
Ak Kara Orman Fl.5s15M
Ak Ammodhis Fl(2)10s6M
Ak Keramotis Fl.WR.4s6/4M
Ak Prinos (Thasos) Fl.5s7M
Ak Atspas (Thasos) Fl(2)10s6M
Ak Boumbouras (Thasos) Fl.3s7M
Ak Fanari Fl.8s6M
Alexandroupolis Fl(3)15s24M
Ak Akrotiri (Samothraki) Fl.5s10M
Nisis Zourafa (Samothraki) Fl(2)10s8M

Quick reference guide

	Shelter	Mooring	Fuel	Water	Provisioning	Tavernas	Plan
Damoukhari	C	C	O	O	O	O	
Stomion	O	C	B	B	B	B	
Limeniskos Pierias	A	C	O	O	O	O	
Methoni	C	C	O	B	C	C	
Thessaloniki Marina (Aretsou)	A	A	B	A	A	A	•
Kerasia	B	AB	B	B	B	B	
Ak Epanomi	O	C	O	O	O	O	
Nea Kallikratia	O	C	B	B	B	C	
Nea Moudhania	B	AB	B	B	B	B	
Potidhaias (Portas)	A	A	B	B	B	B	
Nea Fokea	C	C	B	B	B	B	
Paliourion	C	C	B	B	B	B	
Nea Marmara	B	A	B	A	A	A	•
Porto Carras	A	A	B	A	C	A	•
Porto Koufo	A	ABC	B	A	B	B	•
Ormos Sikias	B	AC	O	B	O	C	•
Ormos Sarti	C	C	B	B	C	C	
Ahlada	C	C	O	O	O	O	
Nisis Dhiaporos	A	C	O	O	O	O	•
Pirgadikia	C	C	B	B	C	C	
Panayia	B	AC	B	B	B	B	•
Ammouliani	B	C	B	B	C	B	•
Ammouliani caïque harbour	B	AC	B	B	C	C	•
Ouranopolis	O	C	B	B	B	B	
Ormos Plati	A	C	O	O	O	O	•
Nea Rodha	B	AC	B	B	C	C	
Ierissos	B	AC	B	B	B	C	•
Stratonion	C	C	O	B	C	C	
O. Olimbiadhos	C	C	B	B	B	C	
Stavros	B	AC	B	A	B	B	
Ormos Elevtheron	A	A	B	B	B	B	•
Kavala	B	A	A	A	A	A	•
Keramotis	B	AB	B	B	B	B	•
Thasos							
Limin Thasou	A	A	B	A	A	A	•
Limenaria	B	C	B	B	A	B	
Limin Lagos	A	AB	B	A	B	C	•
Alexandroupolis	A	AB	B	A	A	B	•
Samothraki							
Kamariotissa	A	AB	B	A	B	B	•

Thermaikos Kolpos and Thessaloniki

Thermaikos Kolpos, the Gulf of Thermai, is enclosed by the northern Sporades in the south, by the high mountain range beginning at the Pilion range and extending north to towering Mt Olympus on the west, and by the relatively low-lying Kassandra Peninsula on the east. The gulf terminates in the small Kolpos Thessalonikis in the north.

The dominating feature of the gulf is without doubt the massive mountain range on the west side stretching from Thessaly to Macedonia. In the south

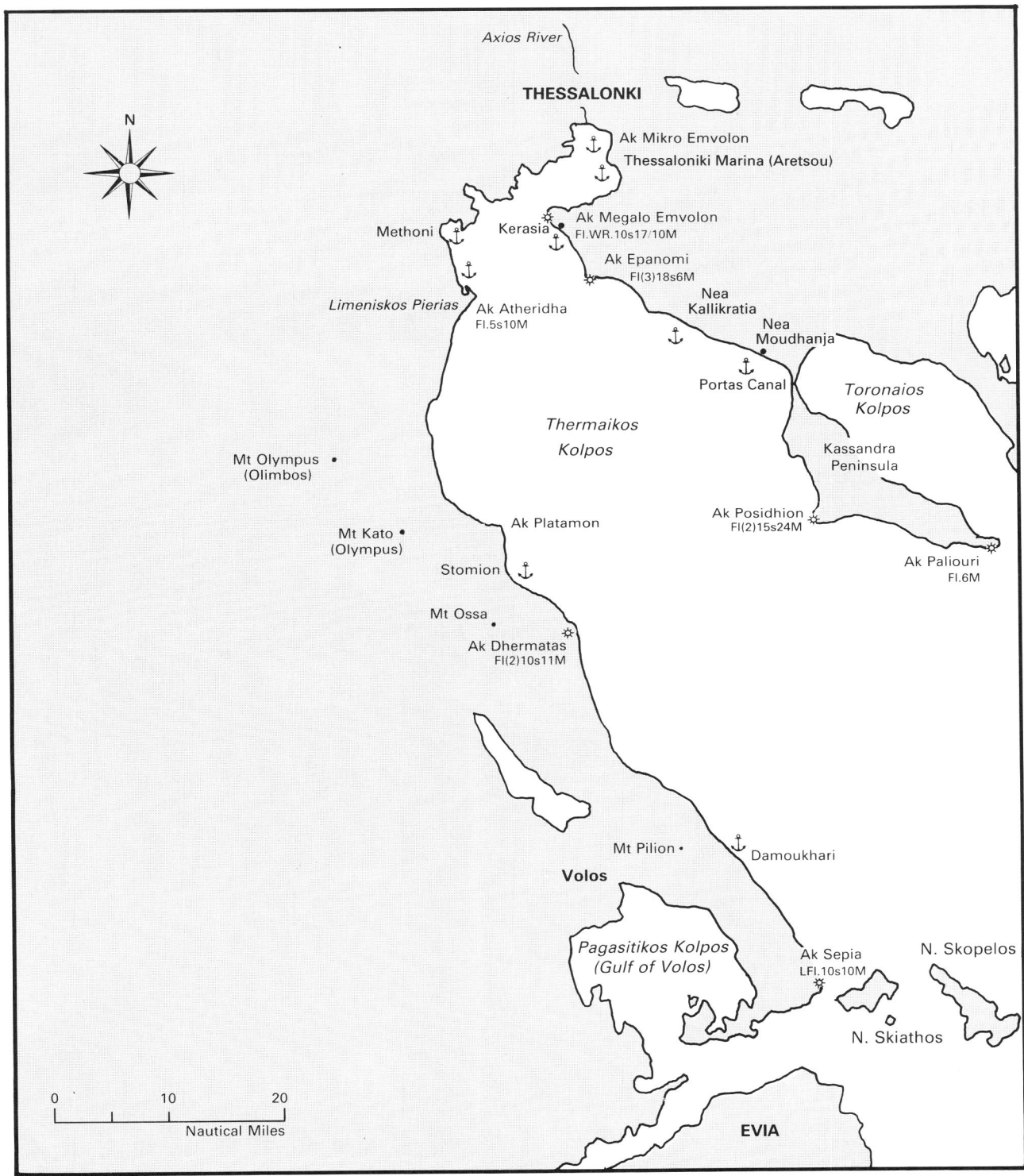

THERMAIKOS KOLPOS

Mt Pilion at 1545 metres (5079ft) is the highest of the Pilion range. Thirty miles further north the first peak of the Olympus range, Mt Ossa (Kissavos), climbs to 1978 metres (6489ft). To the northwest of Mt Ossa the towering peaks of the Olympus Range proper begin: Mt Kato Olimbos (Low Olympus) at 1587 metres (5205ft) stands to the south of Pano Olimbos (High Olympus), the massif being topped by Mitikas (the needle) at 2911 metres (9550ft) and Stefani (the Throne of Zeus) at 2909 metres (9545ft). Surrounding the highest peak are nine other peaks standing over 2680 metres (8800ft). The range is the highest in Greece and peaks are covered in snow from autumn through to late spring.

Although there are other mountain ranges in Greece, also called Olympus, this is the one famous for its association with the gods. Here Zeus ruled and the gods dined, played, drank and argued in what the mortals down below believed was the ultimate in the good life. The first recorded ascent of Mitikas by mortals was as late as 1910 and the range was not properly mapped until 1921. Today the ascent is described as arduous rather than difficult and in fact the major part can be made by four wheel drive and donkeys.

Weather patterns in Thermaikos Kolpos

In the summer months the *meltemi* blows in the gulf from the NE, but not with any consistency. In the S of the gulf it is more regular, normally blowing Force 3–5 although it may blow Force 6–7 on occasions, raising a short steep sea. Although the *meltemi* is not a regular occurrence in the N of the gulf, when it does blow it can be with considerable strength and it has on occasions reached Force 8.

The regular wind in the N half of the gulf, and in the S if the *meltemi* is not blowing, is from the W–SW. This seabreeze gets up about mid-morning, blows Force 2–4, and dies down at night. A light northerly may blow at night.

In the spring and autumn the wind is predominantly from the N although S winds may also occur. In the winter, spring and the autumn a NW wind, locally called the *vardaris* and similar to the *mistral* that blows down the Rhône, may blow down the Axios river at Force 6–8 and may last from a day to a week.

Current

In March and April a strong current is reported to set out of the gulf, owing to the melting of snow in the mountains increasing the flow of fresh water into the sea.

ORMOS DAMOUKHARI

Lying immediately S of Ak Damoukhari, this narrow inlet is open only to the E–SE. With the *meltemi* blowing a yacht could expect to find reasonable shelter in the bay.

LIMENISKOS LITOHOROU

There is a small and very shallow fishing harbour here. Taverna ashore.

ORMOS STOMION

Lying 7 miles NW of Kavo Dhermatas, this open bay is exposed to the N through to E. In calm weather anchor off the village.

LIMENISKOS PIERIAS

Lying 1¾ NW of Ak Atheridha, this small-craft basin affords good shelter from all winds. The approach channel is reported to be dredged to 1·8 metres and the inner basin reported to have depths of 5 metres. Approach from the NE and anchor in convenient depths.

ORMOS METHONI

Lying 6½ miles NW of Ak Atheridha is the open bay of Methoni which is used by fishing boats. Anchor in the SW corner. Care is needed as shallows run a considerable distance out from the coast. Tavernas ashore.

THESSALONIKI (Salonika)
Admiralty chart no. 2070

Approach

Conspicuous The large built-up city is visible from a considerable distance off. Large cargo ships anchored in the bay and the commercial docks are

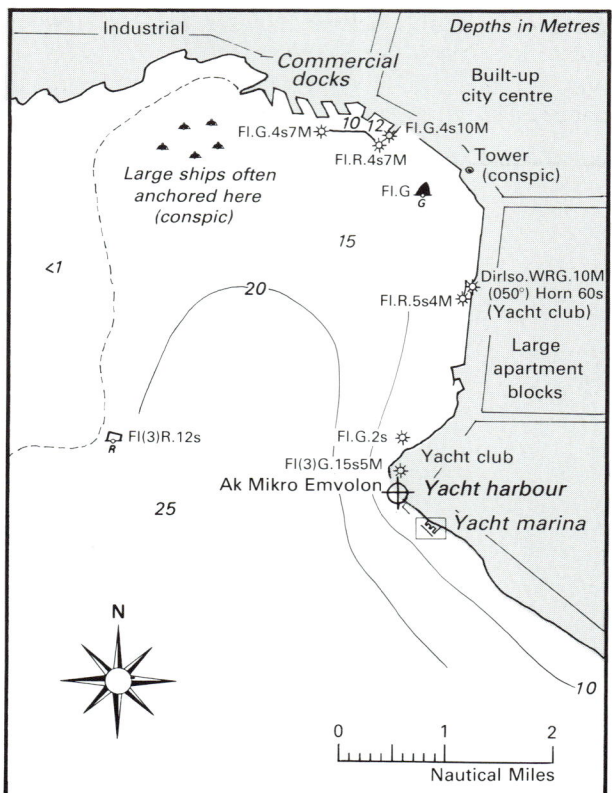

THESSALONIKI
40°35'·2N 22°56'·2E (Ak Mikro Emvolon light)

Yacht harbour under Ak Mikro Emvolon and just W of Aretsou marina.

conspicuous. A yacht should always go to the yacht marina at Aretsou on the S side of Ak Mikro Emvolon. A church on the hill and a radio mast behind the marina are conspicuous. Closer in, the outer breakwater and the yachts in the marina can be easily seen.

By night Use the lights on Ak Megalo Emvolon (Fl.WR.10s17/10M red sector covers 335°-025°), Ak Mikro Emvolon (Fl(3)G.15s5M) and at the entrance to the marina (Fl.G.2s5M and Fl.R.2s5M). The radio mast behind the marina is lit with fixed red lights.

Dangers With the *meltemi* blowing there are strong gusts into Ormos Thessalonikis.

Note A yacht is not welcome at the congested commercial harbour. In any case the water is very polluted and it is not a pleasant place to be. The best place to make for is the marina on the S side of Ak Mikro Emvolon. On the N side of Ak Mikro Emvolon there is a private yacht harbour. A further 1½ miles N there is another private yacht harbour and club, but the depths are insufficient for even very small yachts.

AK MIKRO EMVOLON YACHT HARBOUR

Directly under Ak Mikro Emvolon is a yacht harbour (formerly a fishing harbour) that appears to offer good shelter. The harbour is difficult to spot from the distance as the outer breakwater is covered in grass and blends in with the slopes behind. A small white chapel on the end of the inner breakwater will be seen when closer in. There are several pontoons inside.

THESSALONIKI MARINA (Aretsou)

Mooring

A marina attendant will direct you to a berth. Moorings are laid and you pick up one of the small plastic buoys floating on the surface.

Shelter Excellent all-round shelter although W–SW winds cause an uncomfortable slop inside. Yachts are wintered afloat in the marina.

Authorities Port police and marina staff at the marina. A charge is made. The commercial harbour is a port of entry and the relevant officials are stationed there.

Facilities

Services Water and electricity on the quay. Showers and toilets.

Fuel On the quay.

Repairs A crane can be arranged to haul yachts out

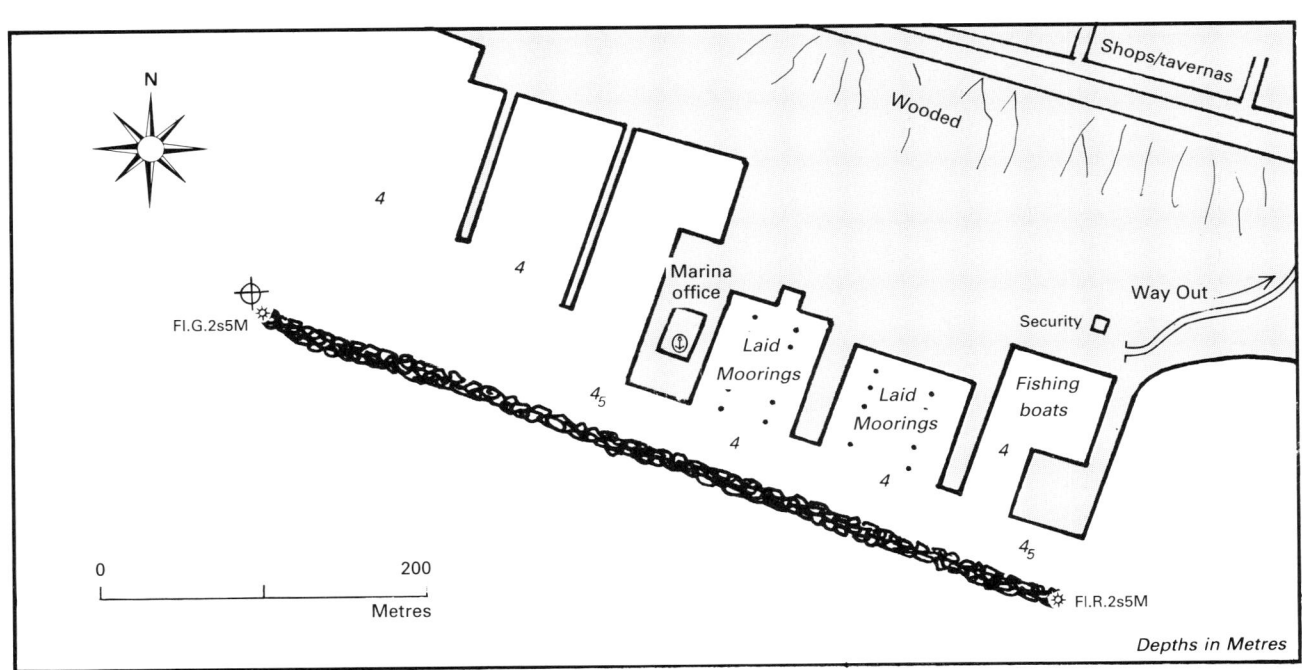

THESSALONIKI MARINA (ARETSOU)
40°34'·6N 22°56'·5E (Fl.G .2s5M)

onto the hard by the marina. Most mechanical repairs. Electrical repairs. Chandlers and hardware shops in the city.

Provisions Most provisions can be found in the vicinity of the marina. Better shopping in the city. Ice can be ordered.

Eating out Numerous tavernas nearby.

Other PO and OTE in the city. Banks. Greek gas and *Camping Gaz*. A gas filling station on the outskirts of the city. Hire cars and motorbikes. A regular bus runs every 15 minutes from just above the marina into the city. Buses to Kavala and Athens. Ferries to Limnos, Lesvos and Khios. Internal flights to Ioannina, Limnos and Athens. International flights to some European countries.

General

Thessaloniki, or Salonika as it is still known to many, is the second largest city in Greece. Although it has an ancient pedigree, the modern office buildings and apartment blocks radiating from the centre effectively shroud this past. I must confess to an instant dislike of Thessaloniki – it is a noisy industrial city where the industry has covered the waters of the bay in a black oily scum and poisoned the fish. As in Athens it is wise in any fish restaurant to enquire as to whether the fish is local. If it is don't touch it.

The marina is sited outside the badly polluted bay in the green and wooded suburb of Aretsou. In the city the Archaeological Museum houses important finds from Neolithic to Byzantine times from all over northern Greece.

KERASIA (NEA MIKHANIONA)
40°28′·3N 22°50′·8E

A fishing harbour in the large bay under Ak Megalo Emvolon. A breakwater is connected to the shore by a piled jetty. Another jetty extends out from the shore under the breakwater. The pierheads are lit: F.G.3M/F.R.3M. The harbour is always crowded with fishing boats but a yacht will be able to find a berth alongside the jetty or the inside quayed area of the breakwater. Shelter appears to be good although strong southerlies would probably send a swell in.

Ashore there is a village. Provisions and tavernas.

Just to the S there is a small yard which hauls yachts.

AKRA EPANOMI

The termination of a low-lying neck of land approximately 8½ miles SE of Ak Megalo Emvolon. The cape is marked by a light structure (Fl(3)18s6M) and a light buoy Fl.G) at the outer end of the shoals extending from the cape. Anchor on either side of the cape according to the wind direction. Open to the W.

NEA KALLIKRATIA

Lying 10 miles SE of Ak Epanomi is the small town of Nea Kallikratia at the head of an open bight. There is a small harbour here.

NEA MOUDHANIA
40°14′·2N 23°16′·6E

A village lying approximately 5 miles NW of Portas Canal. A new harbour is under construction off the village with all the basic elements in place. Two L-shaped breakwaters enclose a basin with the breakwaters running out from the shore extending further out to provide additional protection. Two light structures are in place at the entrance but at present only a Fl.R.3s5M is exhibited. A few local pleasure craft berth alongside on the S side but as work progresses more quay space will become available. Shelter appears to be good.

Ashore there is a small resort village. PO. Bank. Provisions and tavernas.

Khalkidhiki
(Halkidiki, Chalcidice)

The Khalkidhiki peninsula (Khalkidhiki Khersonisos) is the most prominent geographical feature of Macedonia. It is like a hand reaching down into the northern Aegean with three small peninsulas forming the fingers: Kassandra, Sinthonia, and Akti or Mt Athos. On the east side the Khalkidhiki is low-lying with the highest point on the Kassandra peninsula rising to a miserly 353 metres (1158ft). The rest of the Khalkidhiki is mountainous with Mt Athos rising sheer from the sea to 2033 metres (6670ft) at the southern end of the Akti peninsula. The countryside is densely wooded – mostly with pine, but also with olive, hazel, oak and poplar. In many places the pine and poplar grow down to the water's edge and shade what are, in my opinion, the finest sandy beaches in Greece.

The Khalkidhiki received its name from the colonies established there from Khalkis in Evia around 800 BC. The most important city to emerge from the colonisation was Olynthos, situated at the head of Toronaios Kolpos (also called Kolpos Kassandras and the Gulf of Sinthonia). It reached its zenith in the fifth and fourth centuries BC. In 480 BC Xerxes gathered his troops and ships here for the assault on Thessaly and Attica. Prior to this he had a canal cut across the narrow neck of land connecting the Akti peninsula to the rest of the Khalkidhiki to avoid the terrible storms encountered around Mt Athos. A few earth scars are all that remains of the canal-cut today.

The Akti Peninsula
(Khersonisos Akti, Ayios Oros)

This rugged peninsula has for over 10 centuries existed as a world unto itself. Divorced from the modern world, the holy community has no roads or electricity and few telephones. The medieval monasteries occupy spectacular sites on rocky bluffs and precipitous cliff-sides and have been likened to

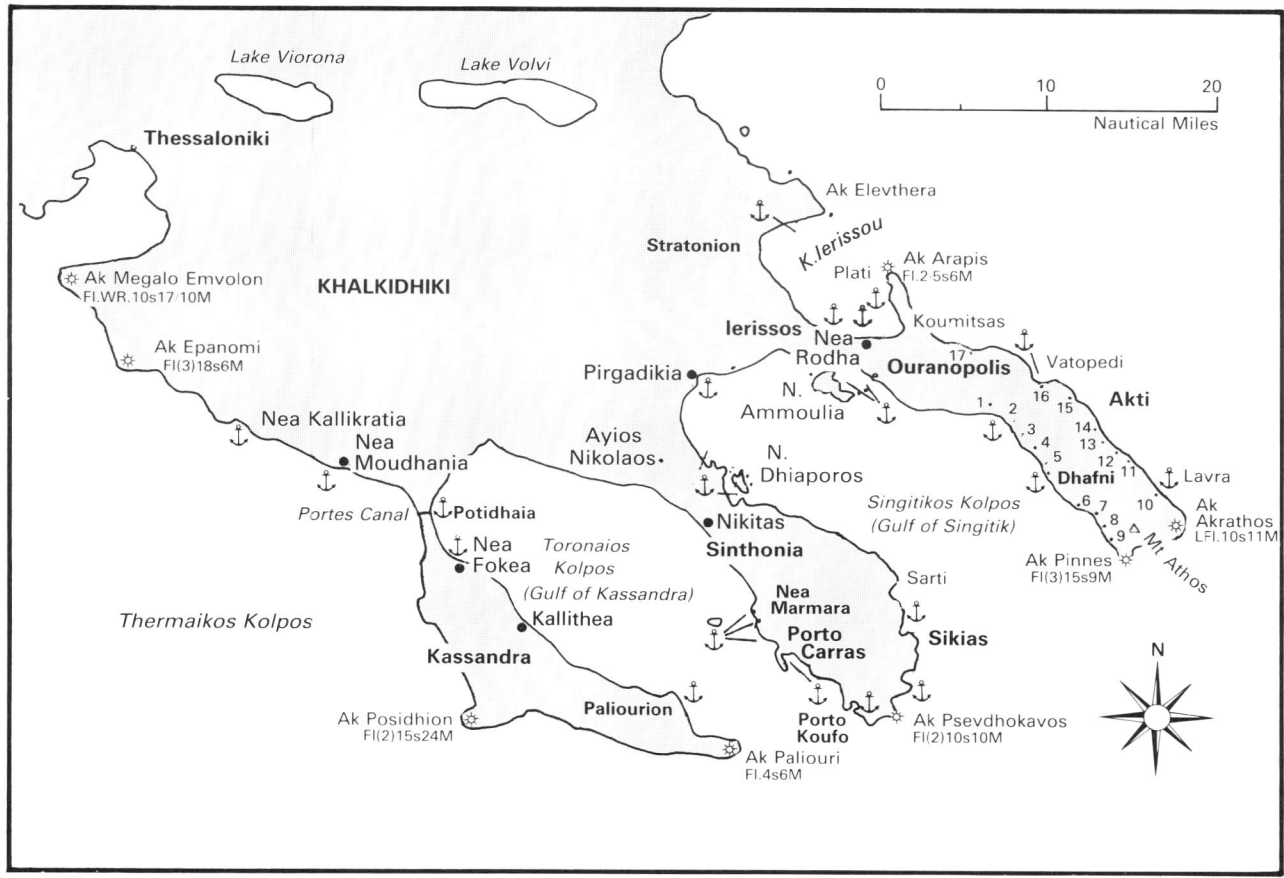

KHALKIDHIKI

Tibetan monasteries such as the Potala of Lhasa. Time is still reckoned by the Julian calendar (13 days behind the Roman calendar) and the day is ruled by the Byzantine clock with hours of variable length.

Females are not allowed to set foot in the monasteries and a yacht with women on board is not allowed to approach closer than 500 metres from the shores of the peninsula. In former times the rule was stricter, formulated by Constantine Monomachus in 1060: access was denied to 'every woman, every female animal, every child, and smooth-faced person'. Although officially the rule is still in force, female animals can now be found in the community and visitors do not have to be bearded.

The monasteries are divided into coenobite and idiorrhythmic communities. Coenobite monasteries are communal and the members are clothed alike and live from a common pool of resources. In the idiorrhythmic monasteries the members live apart and provide the clothes and food from their own resources. As well as 20 monasteries there are hermits (*Anchorites*) who live by themselves in what often seem to be inaccessible cells (particularly on the southern slopes of Mt Athos), the hermitage of two or three hermits (*Sarabaites*) and vagabond monks (*Gyrovakes*).

Although the peninsula is geographically and politically a part of Greece, it has administrative autonomy which includes financial and judicial authority. Monks of any race are accepted (apart

from Greeks, the community includes Russians, Bulgarians, Serbs and Romanians) and on entering the holy community they become Greek subjects.

Without doubt the best way to see the Akti is from the sea. The medieval monasteries clinging to the cliffs at the edge of the wild interior (jackals are reported to be common) belong to a world that was bypassed by our modern age a long time ago. To visit the interior it is easiest to go on a conducted tour, although a more sedate visit to a single monastery captures more of the spirit of the place and is more convenient for a yacht on this desolate shore. Permits are issued by the Greek Ministry of Foreign Affairs (2 Zalokosta St, Athens) or by the Ministry of Northern Greece (48, Eleftheriou Venizelou St, Thessaloniki).

The procedure is as follows: go first to your Consulate, which must vouch for you; then to the Ministry of Foreign Affairs, for a permit; then to the immigration police. At Dhafni the immigration police will check your papers and you are free to go to Karyes where, after a police inspection, you are free to tour the Akti peninsula. In 1988 only a limited number of permits (about ten a day) were being issued so you may have to wait in line until you can get one. A permit is not necessary to sail around the peninsula, but you cannot of course land. Ierissos is the safest place to leave a yacht if taking the local ferry to the community.

Mount Athos. *Conrad Jenkin.*

Weather patterns around the Khalkidhiki

In the summer the *meltemi* blows with considerably less force than it does further south. Normally it will blow from the NE–E at Force 2–4, but often it does not blow for days and even weeks on end. In spring and early summer there will often be SE winds but these rarely blow more than Force 3–4.

With strong winds from any direction, caution must be exercised in the vicinity of the Akti peninsula where there will be strong gusts off the high mountains. Around Mt Athos particular care must be taken as the gusts can be violent and the seas disturbed around Ak Pinnes and Ak Akrathos, although Xerxes was being over-cautious digging a canal to get his ships safely into Singitikos Kolpos.

PORTAS CANAL (Dhiorix Neas Potidhaias)

40°11′·9N 23°19′·3E (W entrance)

This shallow canal cuts the Kassandra peninsula off from the mainland. It is over ½ mile long and has a minimum width of 36 metres. A bridge spans the canal with a vertical clearance of 18 metres. The canal is dredged to 2·5 metres minimum depth, but is subject to silting particularly at the W entrance and at the edges. The W entrance is lit: Fl.R.3s3M/Fl.G.2s3M. The E entrance is lit: Fl.G.2s3M/Fl.R.2s3M.

At the W end there is a short quay usually occupied by local fishing boats and a small basin too shallow for most craft. At the E end there is a small basin in the canal where a small yacht might find a berth. It is shallow around the edges. The village of Portas or Potidhaia is on the S side of the canal. Fuel station nearby. Provisions and tavernas.

NEA FOKEA

A small resort about 8 miles SE of Portas Canal. A square stone tower on the bluff above the bight is conspicuous. Local fishing boats are kept on moorings in the bight on the N side of the bluff with the tower. There is a short jetty off the village. Provisions and tavernas ashore.

The setting is attractive although it is a pity about some of the new non-architecture ashore.

KALLITHEA

A small resort. You can anchor off in calm weather. PO. Bank. Provisions and tavernas.

PALIOURION (Kannavitsa Bay)

The only good anchorage on the W side of the Toronaios Kolpos. Open to all sectors E. Anchor at the head of the bay or off a pier which is reported to have 2·5 metre depths at its extremity. Fuel in the town and some provisions available.

NIKITAS

A small resort village in the NE corner of Toronaios Kolpos (Gulf of Kassandra). In settled weather a yacht can anchor off. Open S and W. Provisions and tavernas ashore.

NEA MARMARA

Approach

The harbour lies under the S side of Ak Nea Marmara. The buildings of the town 3 miles NE of Nisis Kelifos (Khelona Island) are easily identified. A church on the waterfront is conspicuous.

By night The entrance is lit: Fl.R.1·5s3M and Fl.G.1·5s3M.

Mooring

A yacht can go bows-to the quay behind the W mole in 1·5–2 metres or alongside the W side of the central pier. Alternatively anchor off the beach on the N side staying well clear of the pier used by the local ferry.

Shelter Good shelter from northerlies.

Authorities Port police.

Facilities

Water On the quay.

Fuel Near the quay.

Provisions Good shopping for all provisions.

Eating out Good tavernas including good fish restaurants around the waterfront.

Other PO. OTE. Bank. Greek gas and *Camping Gaz.* Hire cars and motorbikes. Bus to Thessaloniki. Hydrofoil to the Northern Sporades.

General

There was probably a settlement here in ancient times pre-dating the Byzantine settlement that no doubt made use of the natural harbour. Greeks from Turkey were resettled here in 1922 in one of the exchanges of populations and the new village christened Nea Marmaras. It has developed into a large resort town and the original village around the natural harbour now climbs up and over the steep-to hummock behind the harbour.

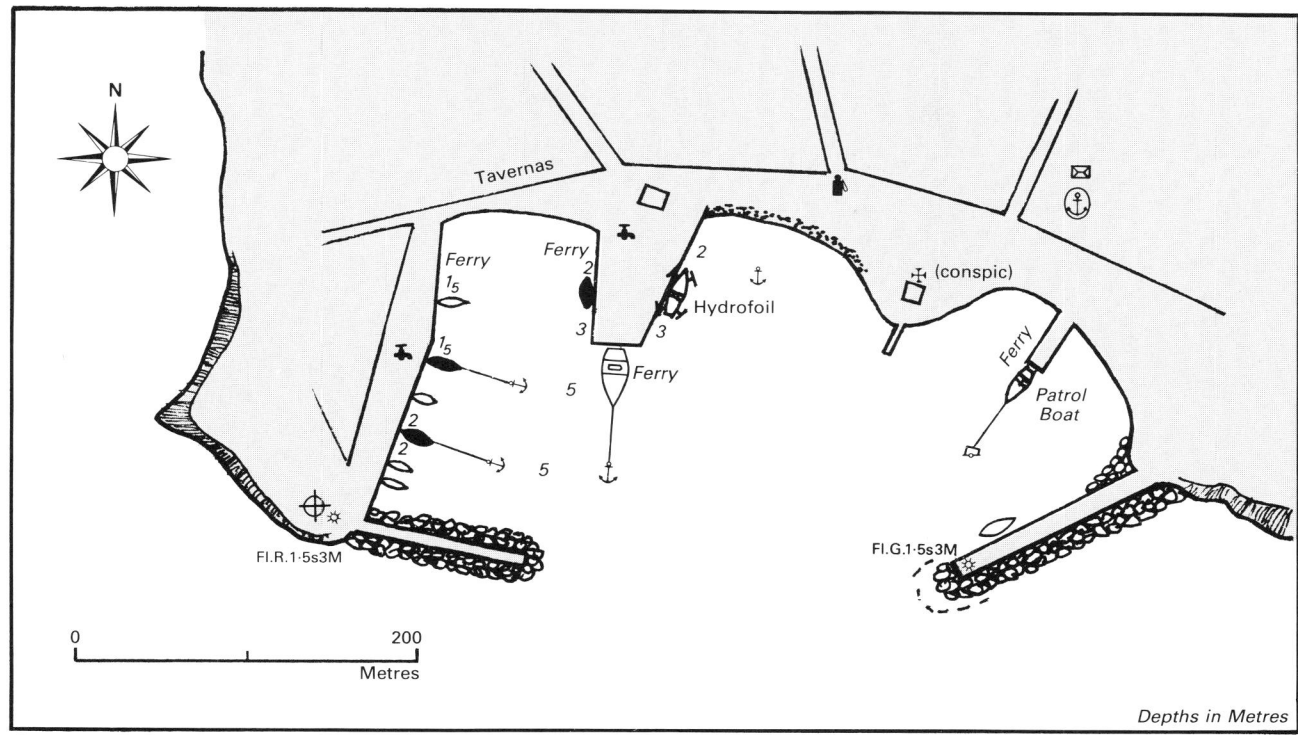

NEA MARMARA 40°05'·8N 23°46'·8E (FI.R.1·5s3M)

PORTO CARRAS MARINA (Porto Karra)

Approach

Conspicuous From the N and W the two hyper-hotels and the buildings of the marina complex can be easily distinguished from the town of Nea Marmara. From the S only the town of Nea Marmara will be seen until you are into the bay.

By night The entrance is lit: F.R.3M and F.G.3M. There are leading lights through the entrance: front F.Y.3M and rear F.Y.3M.

Dangers With strong NW–W–SW winds there is a disturbed swell at the entrance but it is quiet inside.

Note The entrance channel is usually marked by 4 pairs of small red plastic buoys which are not lit.

Mooring

Go stern-to or bows-to where directed. There are laid moorings tailed to the quay or a buoy. Do not use your own anchor.

Shelter Good all-round shelter.

Authorities Port police and marina staff. A charge is made.

Note The harbour is mostly dredged to a least depth of 5 metres.

Facilities

Services Water. Electricity (220V). Showers and toilets. Laundry service.
Fuel A mini-tanker can deliver.
Repairs Travel-hoist. Covered workshops. Some yacht repairs can be carried out including mechanical and engineering repairs.

Provisions Limited. Go to Nea Marmara.
Eating out Numerous restaurants and tavernas around the harbour.
Other PO. Exchange at the hotel. Bank in Nea Marmara. Medical centre. Golf course. Tennis. Horse riding centre. Telephone and fax service. Hire cars and bikes. Taxis. *Caique* ferry to Nea Marmara.

Contact Porto Carras, Sithonia, 63081 Khalkidhiki. ☎ (0375) 71381 *Fax* (0375) 71229.

General

Porto Carras marina was developed along the lines of the Languedoc–Roussillon marinas in the S of France by the Greek shipping magnate John Carras – hence the name. As well as two hyper-hotels, the marina complex houses squash and tennis courts, a swimming pool, theatre, conference centre, casino, restaurants, bars and an array of boutiques and other shops.

The marina was recently taken over by the Vernicos Group and there are plans to improve facilities here.

When Porto Carras was built, a model farm was developed nearby and improved wine-making facilities were imported. The wines produced here with improved techniques are now excellent and the reds and whites bottled under the appellation *Porto Carras Domaine* are well worth sampling.

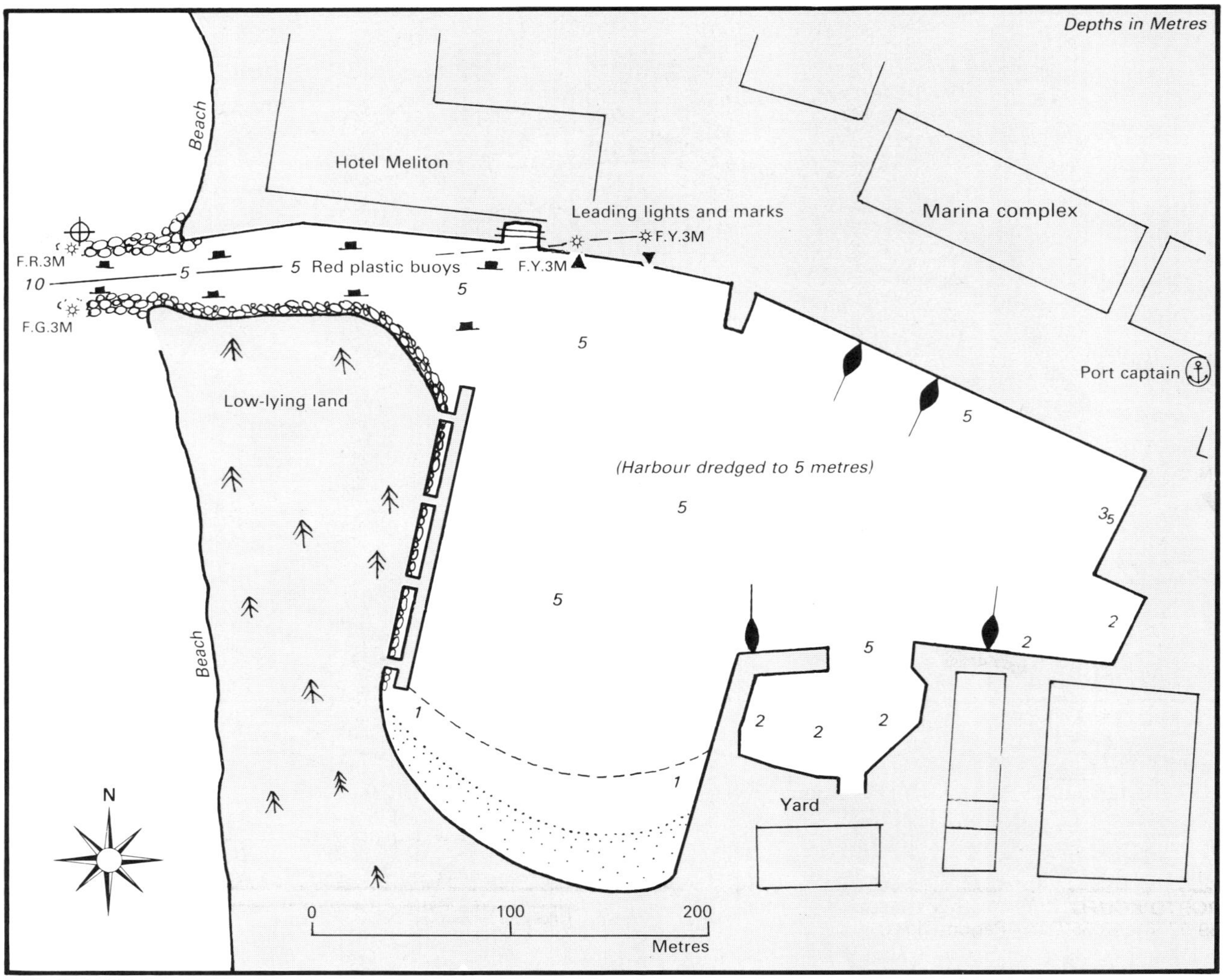

Depths in Metres

Beach

Hotel Meliton

Leading lights and marks

Marina complex

F.Y.3M

F.R.3M

10

5

5 Red plastic buoys

F.Y.3M

F.G.3M

5

5

Low-lying land

Port captain

5

(Harbour dredged to 5 metres)

5

3 5

Beach

5

5

3 5

N

1

5

2

1

2

2

2

Yard

0   100   200

Metres

PORTO CARRAS
40°04'·8N 23°47'·8E (F.R.3M)

Porto Carras looking NNW.

UNNAMED COVES S OF PORTO CARRAS

Less than a mile S of Porto Carras are two small coves with sandy beaches at the head. Open only to the W, they offer sufficient protection for an overnight stay in the summer. The more southerly of the two has a short quay where a small yacht can moor stern-to.

LIMIN TORONIS

Limin Toronis is an inlet at the head of Ormos Toronis, the bay on the S side of Ak Papadhia. Good shelter from northerlies in the bay which is open only S.

PORTO KOUFO

Admiralty chart no. 1679

Approach

Conspicuous From the distance the entrance to the landlocked bay is difficult to make out. A white hut on Ak Laimos (½ mile S of Ak Pagona) and Peristeronisi are conspicuous and closer in the wooded plain and a house on the E side of the bay can be seen.

By night Use the lights on Ak Pagona (Fl.G.2·5s3M) and Ak Spilia (Fl.R.2·5s2M).

Dangers With strong offshore winds there are severe gusts off the high land in the approaches to Porto Koufo.

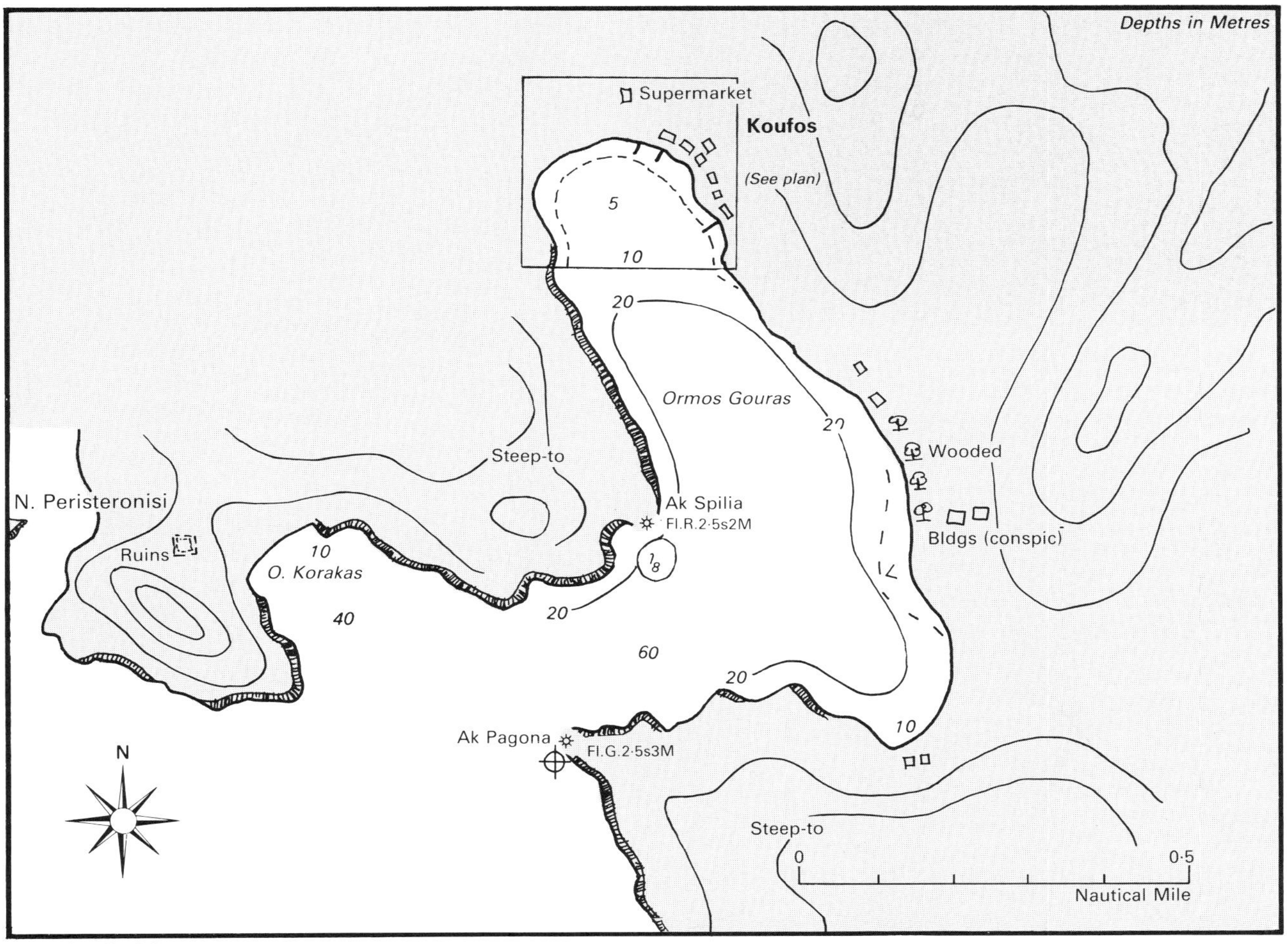

Depths in Metres

☐ Supermarket

Koufos

(See plan)

5

10

20

Ormos Gouras

Steep-to

20

☐ Wooded

N. Peristeronisi

Ak Spilia
Fl.R.2·5s2M

Ruins

10

O. Korakas

40

20

20

60

Bldgs (conspic)

N

Ak Pagona
Fl.G.2·5s3M

10

20

10

Steep-to

0   0·5

Nautical Mile

PORTO KOUFO
39°57'·6N 23°55'E (Ak Pagona light)

Mooring

Anchor in the bay in 7–10 metres. Alternatively go bows-to the quay just S of the E pier where there are 2.5 metres about 10 metres off and 1–2 metres about 2 metres off the quay. Care is needed of ballasting extending out from the quay. Care is also needed in selecting a spot – reconnoitre first. Larger yachts may be able to negotiate a berth on the N pier which is used by a charter company. The bottom is mud and weed – good holding once the anchor is through the weed.

Shelter Good shelter although there can be violent gusts with strong S winds.

Facilities

Water Near the pier though it is reported not to be potable.
Fuel On the road out to Nea Marmara. A mini-tanker can deliver.
Provisions Supermarket near the quay and another on the road out of town. Wine from the barrel at the 'far' supermarket. Ice available.
Eating out Tavernas ashore, several with good fresh fish.
Other Metered telephone. Greek gas and *Camping Gaz.* Bus to Nea Marmara and Thessaloniki.

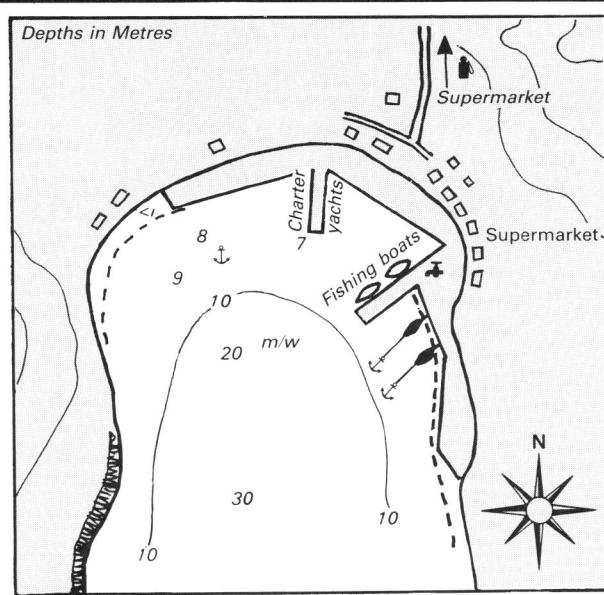

Depths in Metres

Supermarket

Charter yachts

8

9

10

7

Fishing boats

Supermarket

20   m/w

30

10

10

N

PORTO KOUFO

General

Porto Koufo must be one of the most magnificent natural harbours in the Mediterranean. Sheer red cliffs at the entrance open up to the large landlocked bay bordered by poplars and cultivated fields. What was a small fishing hamlet now caters for a few tourists in the summer. In the winter the harbour is a

Porto Koufo looking S from the head.

base for tunny fishing boats working around the Khalkidhiki.

Singitikos Kolpos

ORMOS KARTALI

Two miles N of Ak Psevdhokavos is an open bay with a number of above-water rocks in the entrance. Open to the S and E it offers good shelter from N winds.

ORMOS SIKIAS

Admiralty chart no. 1679

Approach

Six miles N of Ak Psevdhokavos lies the large bay of Ormos Sikias. The rocks of Ifaloi Kepes (Kepes Reef) lying off the S entrance point can be identified and closer in the windmills and a house at the head of the bay are conspicuous.

By night The S entrance point, Ak Adholo, is lit (Fl.1·5s4M), as is the end of the breakwater at Skala Sikias (Fl.R.3s3M), but a night entrance is not really recommended.

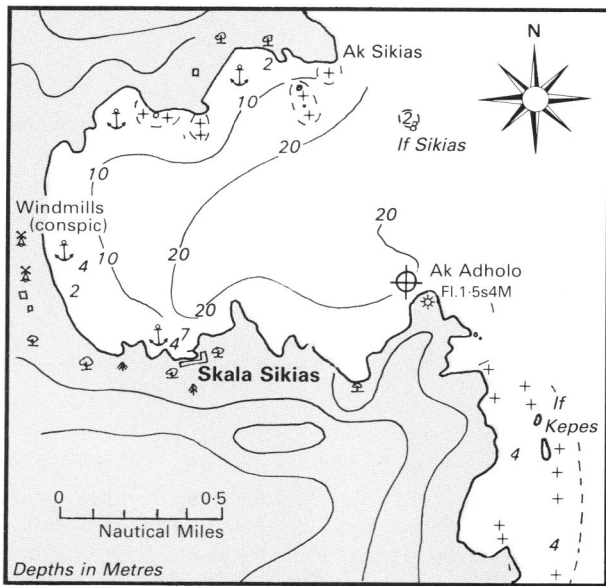

ORMOS SIKIAS
40°02'·5N 24°00'·8E (Ak Adholo light)

342

Dangers

1. Ifaloi Kepes. An above-water islet and reef borders the coast off the S entrance point for up to 700 metres off the coast.
2. Ifalos Sikias. A reef with 2·8 metres over it lying about 600 metres SE of Ak Sikias, the N entrance point. There is also an islet with a reef extending SSE for 250 metres from it closer to the N coast and a reef off Ak Sikias itself.

Mooring

1. Anchor in either of the two coves on the N side of the bay. The bottom is sand, good holding. Reasonable shelter from northerlies but open to the E–SE.
2. Anchor at the head of the bay off the wonderful sandy beach around the head of the bay. Open NE–E.
3. *Skala Sikias* Anchor in the cove off the village in 3–5 metres or go bows-to the short mole if there is room. There are 3 metre depths at the extremity of the mole. Good shelter behind the mole from most winds.

Shelter The bay suffers from an uncomfortable swell rolling in after NE winds except if you are tucked in behind the mole at Skala Sikias.

Facilities

Water and several tavernas at Skala Sikias.

General

The beaches around the bay are composed of wonderful fine golden sand shaded by pine and poplar, the stuff tour operators' dreams are made of. The new road has opened up Sikias to land-based tourism and though it has now lost its remoteness, it remains a wonderful place.

ORMOS SARTI

An open bay that affords some protection from N winds in the NW corner off the village. Care is needed of above water rocks and a reef just NW of the bay. Provisions and tavernas ashore. Fuel on the main road to the N.

Skala Sikias looking N into Ormos Sikias.

AHLADA

A cove immediately N of Sarti. There is a small fishing harbour here and small yachts may find room to go bows-to behind the mole. Explore with care. Alternatively anchor off in the cove. A swell rolls in with the prevailing SE wind.

NISIS DHIAPOROS AND ADJACENT ANCHORAGES (Dhimitri Island)

Approach

S Passage This leads into Ormos Mesopanayia between Ak Xifaras and Ak Plaka, the SE extremity of Nisis Dhiaporos on about 240°. A reef extends N from Ak Xifaras with Petronisi and Kalamonisia islets marking the extremity of the reef. A reef extends S and E from Ak Plaka with an above-water rock near the outer end. The S Passage lies between the last-mentioned rock and the Kalamonisia islets, all of which are clearly visible by day. There is 4 metres least depth in the fairway.

N Passage Leads into Ormos Dhimitri between Nisis Ambelitsi and Nisis Peristeri. A reef extends E and S from Peristeri with the SE edge of the reef marked by an above-water rock. A narrow rocky reef fringes Ak Zavos, the NW extremity of Nisis Dhiaporos, and the N Passage is between this reef and the reef surrounding Peristeri.

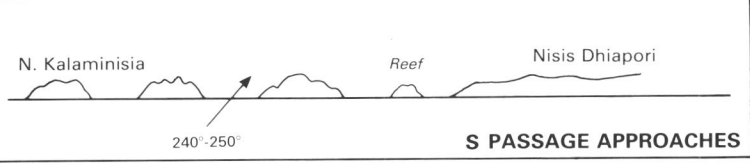

Caution On the accompanying plan it is impossible to show the reefs and above-water rocks in great detail. A yacht should proceed with caution and not attempt an approach by night. By day the reefs and above-water rocks are clearly visible and the approaches are in practice more straightforward than the accompanying notes might appear to indicate.

Mooring

There are numerous anchorages around Nisis Dhiaporos and the adjacent coast. The bottom is mostly mud or sand – good holding.

1. *Ormos Mesopanayia* Anchor on the N side under Nisis Dhiaporos. The S side of the bay is mostly shallow and a yacht should keep close to Nisis Dhiaporos when passing through Ormos Mesopanayia.
2. *Ormos Koumaroudhes* Anchor off the bight on Nisis Dhiaporos.

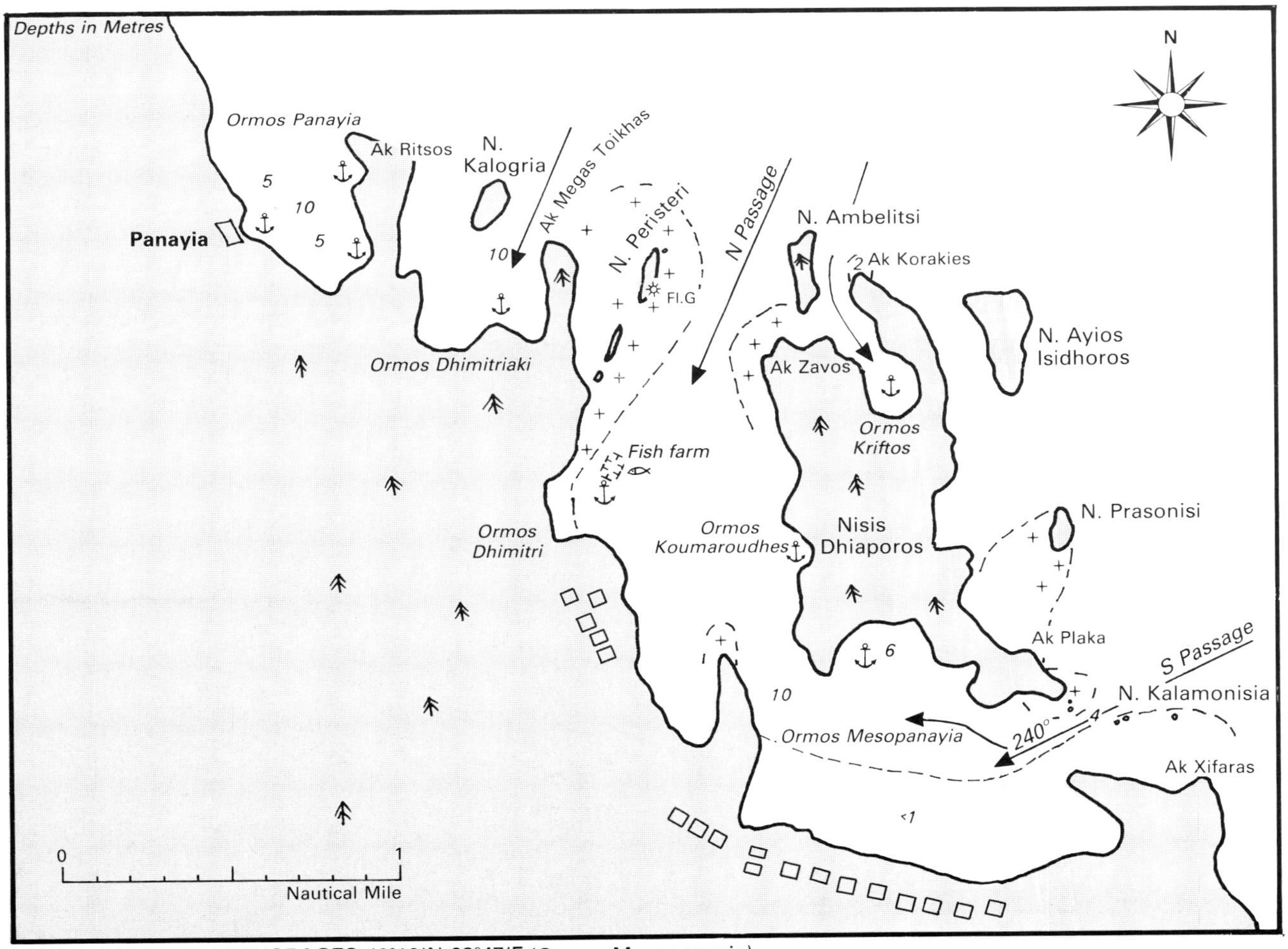

NISIS DHIAPOROS ANCHORAGES 40°12′N 23°47′E (Ormos Mesopanayia)

3. *Ormos Kriftos* The bay on the N side of Nisis Dhiaporos. Enter the bay on the E side of Nisis Ambelitsi.

4. *Ormos Dhimitriaki* Enter the bay between Nisis Kalogria and Ak Megas Toikhas. A yacht can also anchor in Ormos Dhimitri to the S. There is a fish farm in here but still room to anchor.

5. *Panayia* Straightforward with good depths throughout. The best shelter is in the NE corner of the bay, but some care must be exercised as the bottom is foul with laid moorings. In the W of the bay there is a pier used by a ferry that makes daily trips to the Akti peninsula. It can be used when the ferry is not in – 3 metre depths off the end.

Facilities

None except at Panayia: Water on the pier. Fuel in the town. Most provisions can be obtained – mini-market near the pier. Ice available. Several tavernas and cafés. The village of Ayios Nikolaos about 2½km inland has additional facilities.

General

Behind the island the water is a little murky from the river draining into it, but everywhere else the water is clear, a wonderful turquoise over sand and rock. Numerous villas and a few small hotels have been built around the coastal flat at Mesopanayia but apart from that the coast is little built up. It is well worth spending a few days pottering around the island and nearby coves.

PIRGADIKIA
40°20′·2N 23°43′E (Q.R.2M)

A small village at the head of the gulf in the NW corner. There is a small pier off the village with a light on the extremity (char. Q.R.2M). Fishing boats and a few small pleasure craft are kept on permanent moorings in the cove on the W side of the hummock the village is built on. Shelter is better than it looks

KOLPOS IERISSOU AND NISIS AMMOULIANI

although the anchorage should not be used in unsettled weather. Provisions and tavernas ashore. The little village is a gem of a place and well worth the effort to get up to.

NISIS AMMOULIANI
Admiralty chart no. 1679

Lying in the NE corner of Singitikos Kolpos this island offers a number of good anchorages according

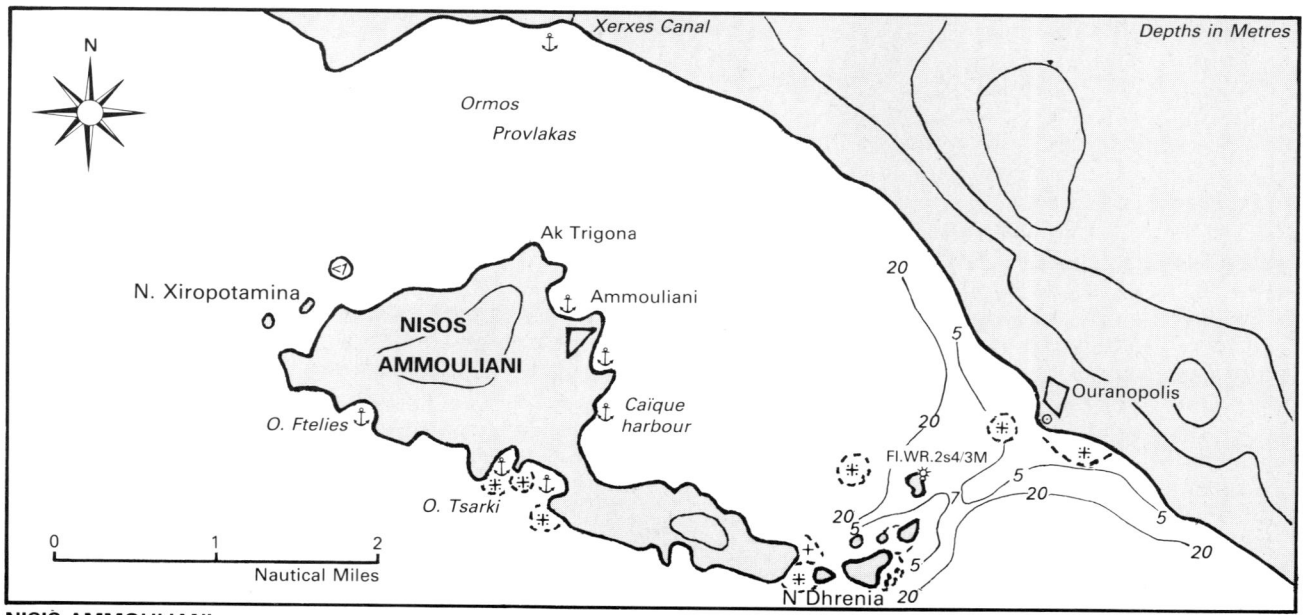

NISIS AMMOULIANI

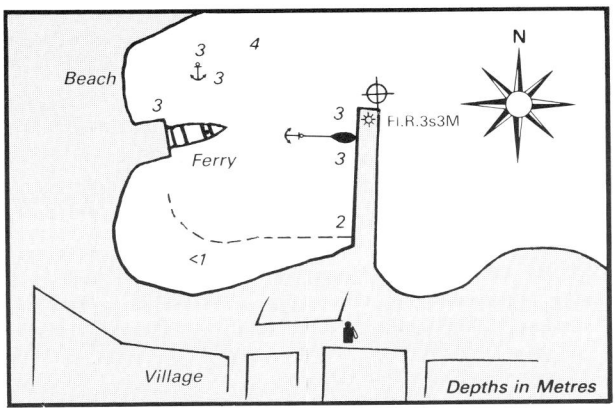

AMMOULIANI VILLAGE 40°20'·2N 23°55'·3E (Fl.R.3M)

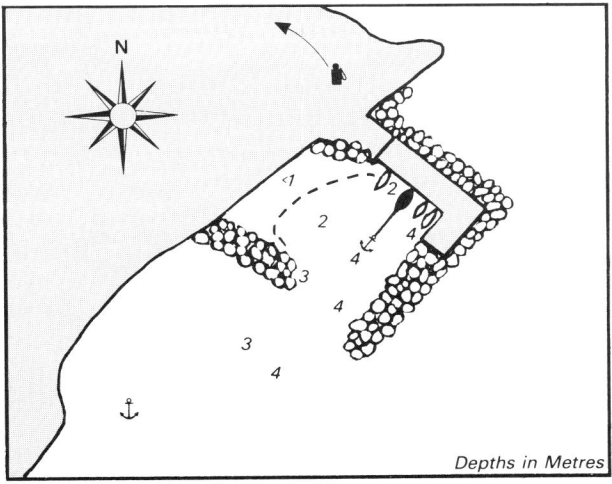

NISIS AMMOULIANI – NEW CAIQUE HARBOUR

to the wind direction. Off the NW extremity of the island lie the islets Nisidhes Xiropotamina and off the SE extremity the islets Nisidhes Dhrenia. In the channel between the easternmost of the Nisidhes Dhrenia and the Akti peninsula there are least depths of 4–7 metres in the fairway. Anchorages around the island are as follows:

1. On the W side of Nisis Ammouliani anchor in Ormos Ftelies (open to the W) or in Ormos Tsarki (open to the S). In both bays the holding is uncertain so make sure the anchor is well dug in and holding. Care is needed of the reefs on either side of Ormos Tsarki.

2. *Ammouliani village* On the NE corner of the island. A Fl.R.3s3M on the end of the mole. Go stern-to or bows-to the outer half of the mole. The central quay on the W is used by ferries. Alternatively anchor off N of the ferry quay in 3 metres. Provisions and tavernas ashore. Fuel from the supermarket near the root of the mole or on the outskirts of the village.

3. The bay immediately S of Ammouliani village. Anchor in 4–6 metres off the short mole. Indifferent shelter.

4. *Caïque* harbour. On the N of the large bay below Ammouliani village a small *caïque* harbour has been constructed. Small yachts may find a berth inside. There are 4 metre depths in the entrance

and 2 metre depths off the quay. Alternatively anchor off to the SW of the harbour.

OURANOPOLIS

In fine weather a yacht can anchor off Ouranopolis in Ormos Provlakas. The square Prosforion Tower (24 metres high) is conspicuous on Ak Pirgos. Care must be taken of shoal water sometimes marked by a pole about 100 metres SW of the mole at Ouranopolis. The anchorage of Ouranopolis is not a secure one and in unsettled weather it is wise to return to one of the anchorages on Ammouliani Island. Most provisions and fuel can be obtained at Ouranopolis.

DHAFNI

The control port for the Akti peninsula. A yacht must clear in here before landing anywhere on the Akti peninsula.

Dhafni is situated about ½ mile N of Ak Kastanias in an open bay. There is limited shelter from N–NE winds from the natural camber of the coast but it is open from NW through W to S. The seabed rises abruptly making anchoring difficult. A short stone pier has 2 metre depths at its extremity and a yacht can go stern-to the pier. The bay is not safe in unsettled weather when the prevailing summer wind is funnelled in from the NW–W setting up an uncomfortable slop. A large mooring buoy in the bay is for ships.

The monasteries
(see plan on page 336)

1. *Moni Konstamonitou. Coenobite* Founded in the 11th century. Most of the buildings in the deep defile are of the 19th century. A yacht can anchor off in the bay in calm weather .

2. *Dhoheiariou (Dohiariou). Idiorrhythmic* Founded in the 10th century. The central church, the Katholikon, is said to be one of the finest on Mt Athos.

3. *Xenofondos. Coenobite* Founded in the 10th century by the monk Xenofon.

4. *Moni Ayiou Paneleimonos. Coenobite* Founded in 1169, it once supported 1500 Russian monks. It was badly damaged by fire in 1968 but it is still spectacular. There is a very small harbour nearby.

5. *Xiropotamou. Idiorrhythmic* First mentioned in the 10th century, most of the buildings date from the 18th century.

6. *Simonopetra. Coenobite* Founded in 1257 by St Simon, this is one of the most spectacular of the monasteries. The monastery is built on a rocky bluff connected to the cliff by a bridge. Heavy beams overhang the rock sides so that the parts of the monastery built on the beams literally hang in space above the sea and rocks below.

7. *Gregoriou. Coenobite* Founded c. 1395.

8. *Dionysiou. Coenobite* Founded in 1375, it stands on a spectacular precipitous rock.

9. *Ayiou Pavlou. Coenobite* Founded in the 11th century, it occupies a spectacular site on a cliff overlooking a gorge below.

Around the southern end of the Akti peninsula live scattered colonies of monks and hermits in almost inaccessible (or so it seems, looking up at them) huts clinging to the mountainside. The important colonies are one at St Anne's on the SW corner and a colony of painters and woodcarvers at Kerassia on the SE corner. A yacht can anchor close under Ak Dhiapori at Voulevtiria or at a small cove one mile ENE of Ak Pinnes in calm weather only. A yacht should not be left unattended and must be prepared to leave with the slightest hint of a change in the weather.

Caution Violent gusts blow off Mt Athos with strong winds from any direction. In calm weather it is interesting to stand inshore to see the monasteries. With strong winds the violent gusts and the considerable seas raised around the bottom of the Akti peninsula make it prudent for a yacht to keep some distance off.

10. *Grand Lavra. Idiorrhythmic* Situated under the massive height of Mt Athos, this is the largest of the monasteries. Apparently it alone has never suffered from the fires which have badly damaged the other monasteries.

LAVRA HARBOUR (Mandraki)

A minuscule harbour carved out of rock lying 2 miles N of Ak Akrathos. The fort by the harbour and the monastery above are conspicuous. The entrance to the harbour is immediately S of the fort. There are reported to be 1·8 metre depths inside, but with any sort of swell running it would be dangerous for even a very small yacht to attempt to enter.

11. *Karakallou. Coenobite* Founded in the 15th century.
12. *Filotheou. Idorrhythmic* First mentioned in the 12th century. The monks employ themselves woodcarving.
13. *Iviron. Idiorrhythmic* Founded in 979. There is a pier here with 2 metre depths at its extremity. In calm weather it is possible to anchor off in 4–9 metres.
14. *Stavronikita. Idiorrhythmic* Founded in 1542.
15. *Pantokrator. Idorrhythmic* Built in the 14th century on a sea-washed rock in a small cove. It appears to be possible to anchor off the monastery in calm weather.
16. *Vatopedi. Idiorrhythmic* Founded in the 10th century, this is the most modern monastery with electricity, telephone and regular communication by ferry with Ierissos. Anchor off the monastery in 5–8 metres. Open to all sectors N.
17. *Esphigmenou. Coenobite* First mentioned in 1034. The most northerly of the monasteries. A yacht can anchor off in calm weather.

ORMOS PLATI

Admiralty chart no. 1679

Lying on the W side of Ak Arapis, this bay offers good shelter from the prevailing winds. It is open only to the SW. Anchor in 5–8 metre depths in either of the two coves in Ormos Plati or in Ormos Frangou immediately N of Ormos Plati. The bottom is sand and weed – good holding.

Both bays are deserted although fishing boats from Ierissos and Koumitas occasionally shelter here.

Note This area is a part of the Akti peninsula and as such it is off-limits to yachts. In 1989 a yacht was requested to leave by a police patrol boat.

Caution The passage between Nisidhes Stiliaria and Ak Arapis has less depth than that shown on chart 1679 and also appears more rock-bound than shown. Pass to seaward of the outermost of Nisidhes Stiliaria.

KOUMITSAS

A small village in the SE corner of the Gulf of Ierissos. Local fishermen report that there is a small fishing harbour with 'about 2 metre depths'.

NEA RODHA

A village between Koumitsas and Ierissos. There is a short mole on the W side of the bay. A chapel on the bluff above the miniature harbour is conspicuous. A light is exhibited at the end of the mole: Fl.R.2s3M. A small yacht may be able to go bows-to the end of the mole where there are 2–3 metre depths although it is usually crowded with fishing boats. The inner half of the mole is shallow (less than a metre). Provisions and tavernas in the village a dusty 20 minute walk away.

IERISSOS

Approach

A small fishing harbour lying about ½ mile to the SE of Ierissos village. The large hotel behind it is

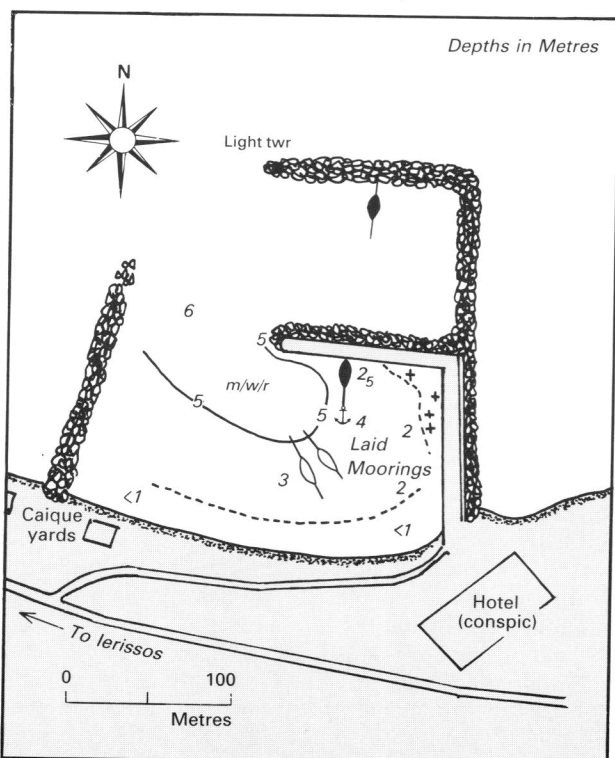

IERISSOS
40°24'N 23°52'·5E

conspicuous. A night entry is not recommended as there are no lights and numerous unlit moorings in the harbour.

Mooring

Go stern-to or bows-to with a long line to the breakwater in the outer half of the harbour or in the inner basin. Alternatively anchor inside the inner or outer parts of the harbour. The inner harbour is crowded with local fishing boats. Care must be taken of the very large mooring chains on the bottom and of the numerous mooring buoys and lines on the surface.

Facilities

Tavernas at the harbour. Ierissos village is about one mile away from the harbour and here there is fuel and most provisions can be obtained. Also PO and OTE, and several tavernas and cafés. A bus runs to Kavala. There are several yards building wooden fishing caiques along the beach from the harbour.

General

There are good beaches of coarse sand on either side of the harbour and the hinterland is pleasantly wooded with poplar, pine and olive trees. Ierissos has developed into a dusty ramshackle resort on the strength of the sandy beach nearby. The harbour is the nearest safe harbour to the site of Xerxes Canal 2 miles to the SE although you are likely to be disappointed – there is little to see of the famous canal today.

STRATONION

Lies at the head of Ormos Stratonion in the NW corner of Kolpos Ierissou. Anchor off the village. There are two piers extending from the shore for loading ore from the nearby manganese mines. Limited provisions and fuel ashore. The bay is open to the E and S.

Between Stratonion and Ak Elevthera there are a number of coves offering good shelter from N winds, but open to the S. The cove nearest to Ak Elevthera offers the best shelter in beautiful surroundings. Open to the S and W.

The mainland coast

This section covers the mainland coast of Northern Greece from Strimonikos Kolpos to Alexandroupolis including the nearby island of Thasos. The region is mountainous although not spectacularly so and much of the high land is bordered by low-lying plains and marshes deposited by the four large rivers emptying into the sea along the coast: the Strimon, the Nestos, the Akmar and the Evros. The river Nestor is the boundary between Macedonia and Thrace and the river Evros is the border between Greece and Turkey. The countryside is for the most part densely wooded in pine and olive. The coastal plains are well-watered and fertile, producing large crops of grain and tobacco.

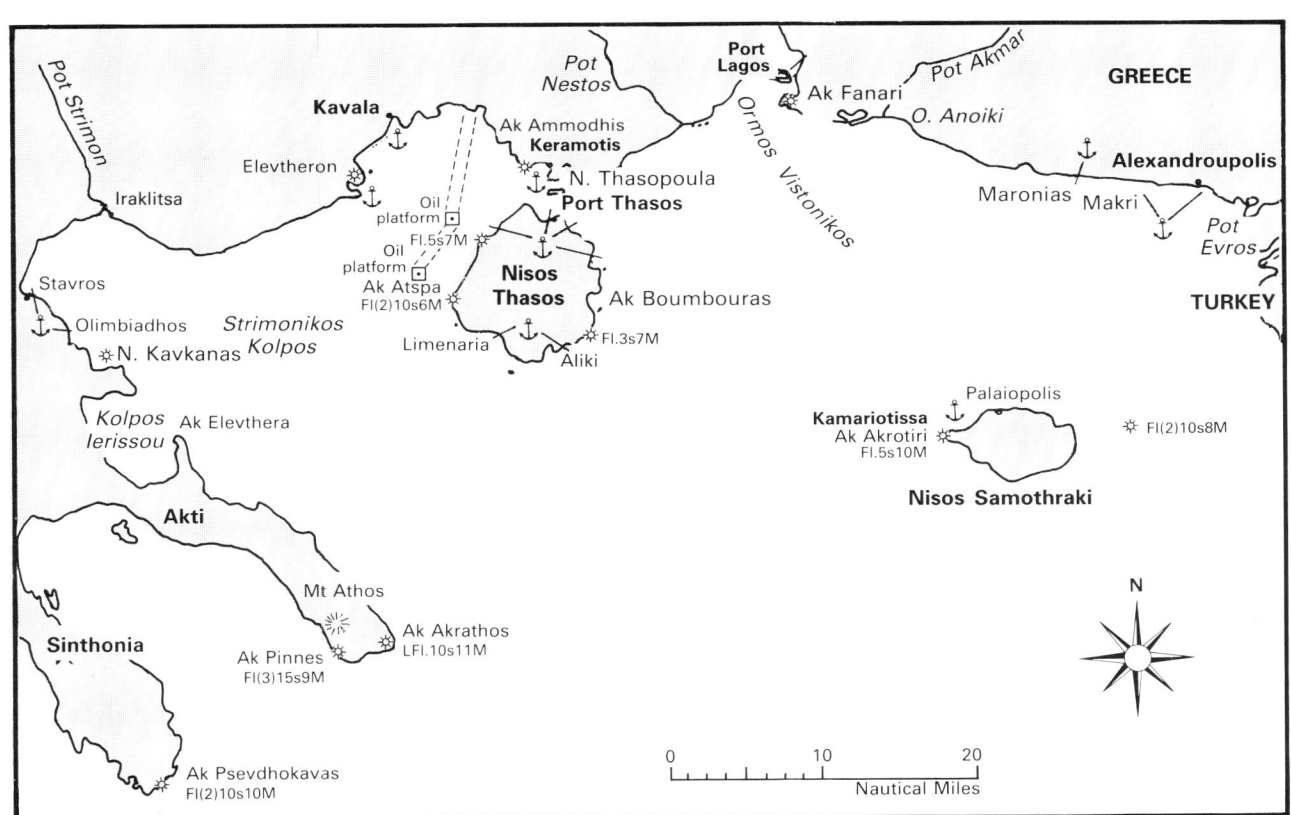

STRIMONIKOS KOLPOS TO ALEXANDROUPOLIS

Weather patterns in Northern Greece

(These weather patterns also apply to Samothraki.)

In the summer months the *meltemi* blows only fitfully in this area. Normally the *meltemi* blows from the NE at Force 2–5, but on many days there will be little or no wind at all. If the *meltemi* does not blow a SW sea breeze will often set in about midday and blow at Force 2–4. In the winter, spring and autumn the wind is again from the NE or the S, but severe gales are most often from the NE.

In the comparatively shallow waters off this coast, particularly in Stenon Thasou, Ormos Vistonikos, Ormos Anoiko and the shallows off Alexandroupolis, a very short steep sea is kicked up with strong winds from the S. These seas can be aggravated by the W-going current setting along the coast which can vary from ½ to 1½ knots. (In Stenon Thasou the current is E-going.)

With S winds the sea level can increase by as much as 0·5 metres and conversely with N winds the sea level can decrease.

ORMOS OLIMBIADHOS

Lies 6½ miles to the NW of Ak Elevthera. In the S corner of the bay there are two coves of which the cove to the E has 2–4 metre depths and offers some shelter from NE winds. Open to the N–NW. A short mole provides some protection and a small yacht may be able to go bows-to the end.

In the village there are provisions and tavernas. The setting on a coastal plain with mixed deciduous and pine all hemmed in by steep-to mountains is spectacular. The village is a sleepy little place that sees some tourism but not a lot.

STAVROS

Admiralty chart no 1679

A large bay in the SW corner of Strimonikos Kolpos. There is a short pier off the village and at the time of writing works were underway in the vicinity. As far as could be determined an additional mole was being built to form a small harbour enclosed by a L-shaped mole. A light is exhibited on the end of the pier (F.R.1M) but this may be moved when the works are finished.

Fishing boats use the pier and are kept on permanent moorings off the village so shelter is probably better than it appears. Water on the quay. Fuel by mini-tanker.

The village has developed into a thriving resort with hotels, bars and cafes dotted around the shore. PO. Bank. Provisions and tavernas.

ORMOS TSAYEZI (Iraklitsa)

In the N corner of Strimonikos Kolpos at the mouth of the river Strimon there is a shallow basin which was formerly Amfipoleos harbour. However the entrance is reported to have silted to depths of less than 1 metre.

Caution At the mouth of the river Strimon the shoals are reported to extend further than indicated on the chart. A current of about 2 knots is also said to set to the S because of the considerable flow of fresh water from the river.

ELEVTHERON (Dhevtro)

Admiralty chart no. 1679

Approach

This large bay lies 6 miles to the S of Kavala. A number of large hotels around the beach on the W side of the bay and a large silo at the root of the oil wharf are conspicuous.

By night Use the lights on the N entrance point (Fl.3s4M), on the pier at Elevtheron (2F.R(vert)3M), and at Nea Iraklitsa (2F.G.3M and F.R.3M).

Mooring

In settled weather anchor off Nea Peramos or in the SW corner of the bay. In unsettled weather go stern-to or bows-to or alongside the N side of the large cargo pier in the NE corner of the bay at Nea Iraklitsa. There are 7 metre depths along the outer end of the pier. The surroundings are not attractive but the shelter is nearly all-round. In strong S winds many of the fishing boats normally based in Kavala shelter here.

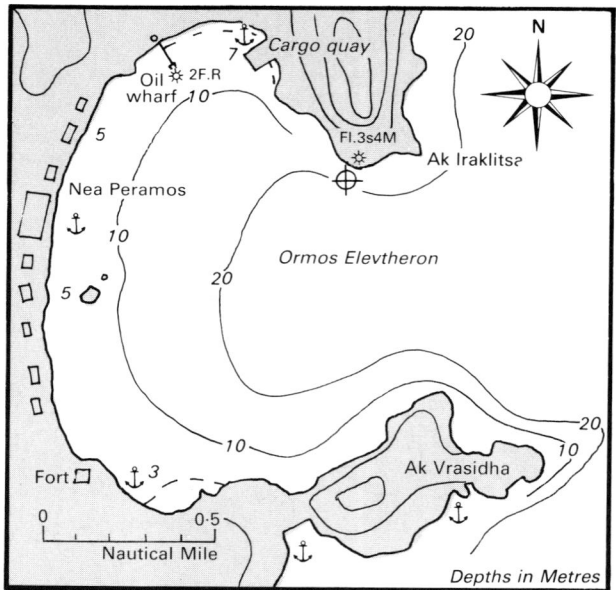

ELEVTHERON
40°50'·6N 24°19'·7E (Fl.3s4M)

Facilities

In Nea Peramos most provisions can be obtained and there are several tavernas and cafés.

General

In settled weather the large bay has attractive anchorages on the S and W sides off long sandy beaches. The fort on the S side begs to be explored.

KAVALA
Admiralty chart no. 1679

Approach

Conspicuous The large city on the rocky bluff and sprawled over the hills behind is conspicuous from the distance. Closer in, a fort and a church with a red cupola on the rocky bluff are conspicuous. The harbour moles are easily identified.

By night Use the light on Ak Kara Orman (Fl.5s15M) and the lights at the entrance (Fl.G.1·5s3M and Fl.R.1·5s3M). A light buoy (Q.G) marks a wreck halfway along the inside of the S mole.

Mooring

Moor stern-to the N quay in the outer harbour if you can find room. The yacht club is strictly private with no facilities for visitors and, it is reported, few manners. The quay in the outer harbour is very high and you will have difficulty getting ashore unless you are near a ladder. The inner basin is usually crowded with fishing boats. You may be able to find a berth in the inner basin, but do enquire if it is OK to berth there – yachts which muscle into fishing boat berths should not be surprised to be unceremoniously evicted when boats return. The bottom is mud – excellent holding.

Shelter With strong S winds an uncomfortable surge develops and many of the fishing boats shelter at Elevtheron. However a number of yachts are moored all year round off the N mole and quay. Strong S winds are rare in the summer.

Authorities A port of entry: port police, customs and immigration authorities.

Facilities

Water On the N quay and in the inner basin.
Fuel Can be delivered to the N quay and near the quay in the inner basin.
Repairs Most mechanical and general engineering repairs. Chandlers. Excellent hardware and tool shops.
Provisions Excellent shopping for all provisions. The best shopping area is immediately behind the fish market. Ice from the fish market.
Eating out Excellent tavernas including several fish tavernas near the fish market with delicacies such as sole, scallops and some of the best prawns in Greece.
Other PO. OTE. Banks. Greek gas and *Camping Gaz*. A gas filling station some distance out of the city. Hire cars and motorbikes. Buses to Thessaloniki and Alexandroupolis. Ferries to Thasos. Internal flights to Athens.

General

Kavala is an important commercial port and first impressions of the city from a harbour churned up by ferries, tugs and workboats commuting to the oil rig are not likely to be favourable. Yet stay a day here and you begin to like this busy friendly city.

Kavala outer harbour looking WNW.

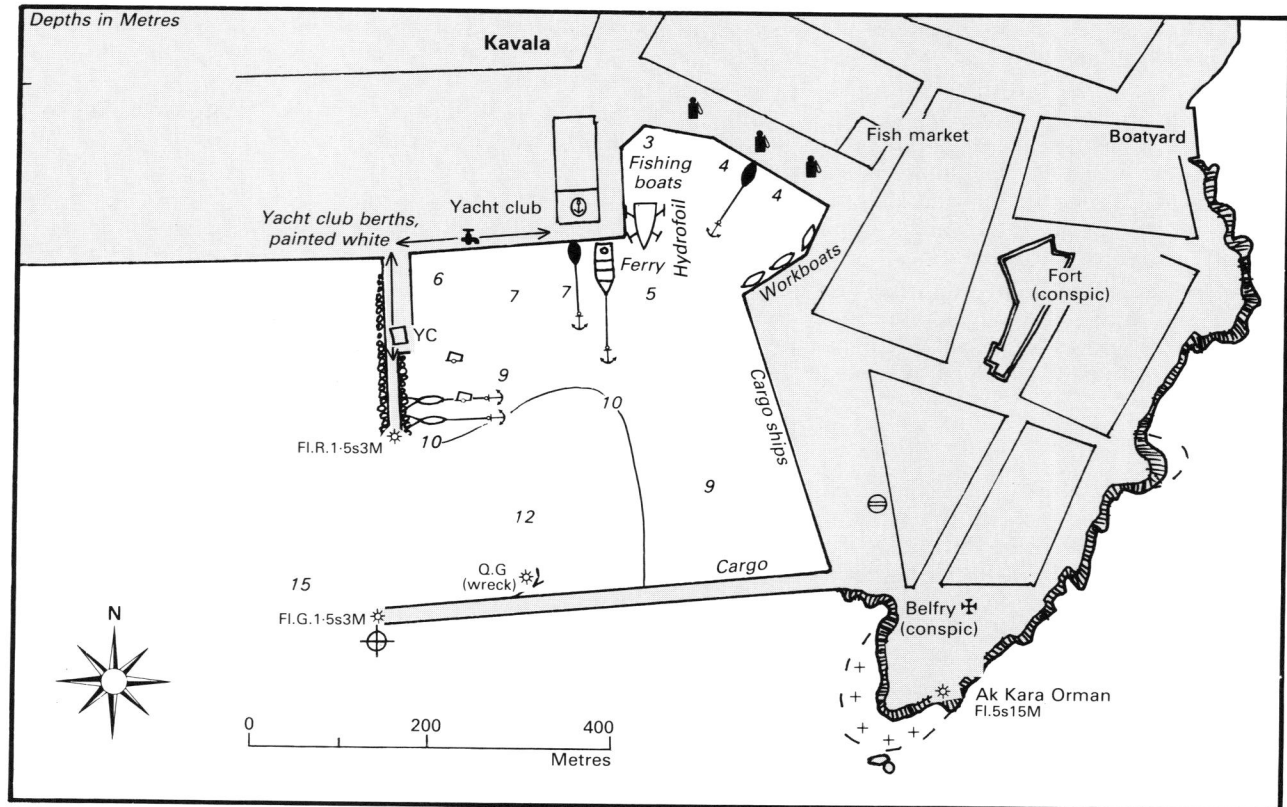

KAVALA
40°55'·9N 24°24'·3E (Fl.G.3M)

In the city an aqueduct (based on Roman design but built by the Turks in the 16th century) is prominent. On the rocky bluff the house of Mehmet Ali, a rich merchant of Kavala in the 18th century, who effectively ruled the city, has been preserved and is now a folklore museum. The archaeological museum near the harbour houses classical finds from the area.

NOTE On the E side of Ak Kara Orman there is a fishing harbour where a small yacht may find a berth. Fuel nearby. A small boatyard close by hauls yachts. Provisions and tavernas ashore.

KAVALA WEST HARBOUR

On the W side of Ormos Kavala there is a dogleg breakwater extending NE for approximately 300 metres which protects a quayed area. This is a commercial port and not for yachts.

KAVALA COMMERCIAL HARBOUR

Approximately 2 miles E of Kavala a large commercial harbour is under construction. Grandly titled the 'Phillip II of Macedonia' harbour, it is unlikely to offer much in the way of facilities for yachts. At the time of publication the silos and hoppers for the cement works supplying the contractors was conspicuous behind the harbour works themselves.

KERAMOTIS
Admiralty chart no. 1679

Approach

Keramotis is the principal ferry port connecting Thasos to the mainland. On the low-lying sand spit terminating in Ak Keramotis a few houses and the light structure will be seen before the sand spit itself.

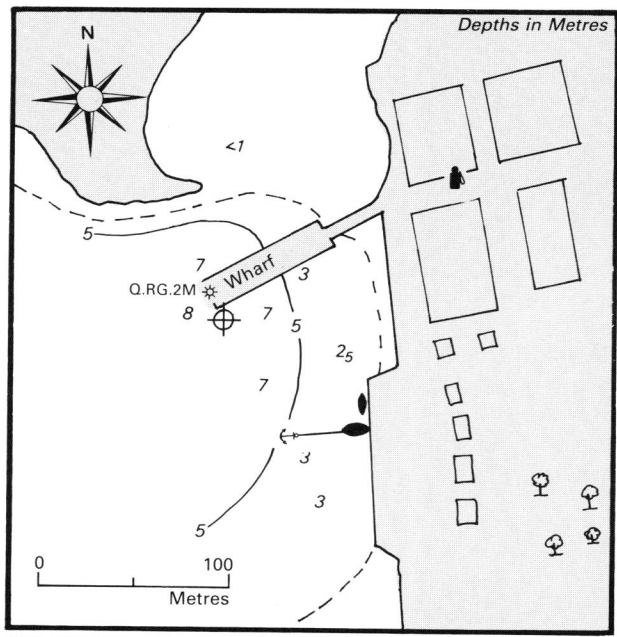

KERAMOTIS
40°51'·6N 24°42'·2E (Q.RG.2M)

Once into the lagoon behind the sand spit, the village of Keramotis and the harbour are easily identified.

By night Use the lights on Ak Keramotis (Fl.WR.4s6/4M) and on the pier head (Q.RG.2M).

Mooring

Go stern-to or bows-to or alongside the quay. The wharf is usually crowded with coasters and fishing boats.

Shelter Is better than it looks. W winds cause a limited swell.

Authorities Port police and customs.

Facilities

Fuel near the quay. Good shopping for provisions. PO. OTE. A number of tavernas and cafés. Buses to Alexandroupolis and Kavala. Car ferry to Thasos.

Note On the N side of the lagoon a number of mooring buoys (red and white vertical stripes) probably belong to the Greek navy. It would be prudent not to anchor in this area.

OIL RIG PLATFORM

Lying 3½ miles NW of Ak Prinos on Thasos and 9½ miles SSE of Kavala is an oil rig platform which is conspicuous by day and night. Recently another platform was erected approximately 5 miles SSW of the original platform. Workboats regularly ply between the platform and Kavala. At night the platforms are lit by a battery of white lights (they could be mistaken for large ocean liners) and a Mo(V)15s10m.

AK AMMODHIS

A rock just under the water is reported to lie ½ mile SSW of Ak Ammodhis.

RIVER NESTOS

Shoaling is reported to extend as much as ½ mile further than indicated around the mouth of this river. I have noticed discoloured water as far as 1 mile off the coast, but a check on the depth showed no disparity with charted depths. Nonetheless it would be prudent to keep some distance off the river mouth. The land in the vicinity of the river mouth is very low-lying and it is often difficult to establish the limits of the coastal plain around it. A cluster of communication towers approximately ½ mile inland on the coastal plain (Pedhias Khrisoupoleos) is conspicuous.

STENON THASOU (Thasos Strait)

In the comparatively shallow water in the strait and in Ormos Vistonikos a short steep sea is quickly raised with strong winds. In Stenon Thasou a current sometimes sets to the E at a rate of ½–1½ knots.

Nisos Thasos

This round lump of marble separated from the mainland by a shallow sea strait enjoyed some power and prosperity in ancient times. Its position allowed it to be easily defended and moreover it was and still is an enchanting and beautiful island.

The early colonists were the Parians who soon prospered from the Thasian gold mines. Despite being a well defended and powerful city-state, Thasos meekly submitted to the invading Persians.

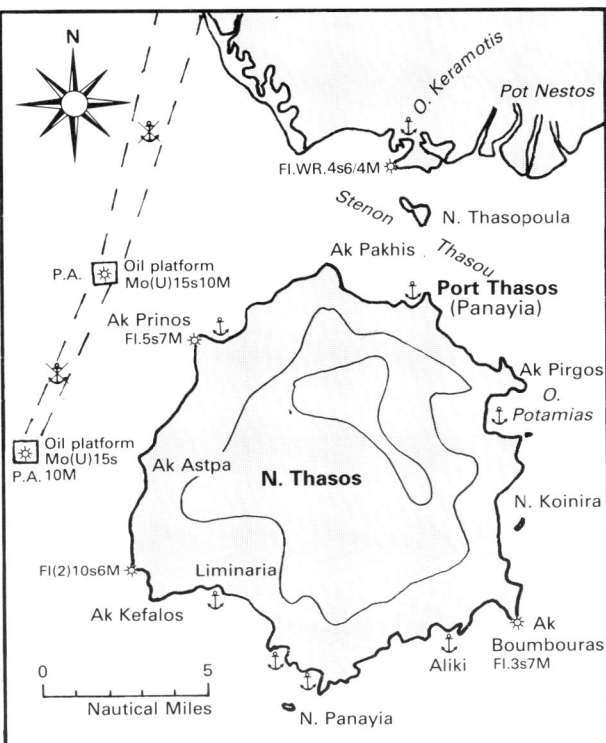

NISOS THASOS

After Xerxes was defeated at Salamis the island had its ups and downs with Athens, but its merchants prospered on its mineral wealth (including Thasian marble which was renowned throughout the ancient world) and its famous black wine. In medieval times it suffered from pirate attacks until the Genoese Gattelusis and later the Turks occupied the island and restored order.

Today its prosperity is based on the natural beauty of the island: its sandy beaches, pine-clad hills, running streams (even in summer) and ancient monuments attract a growing number of tourists each year.

PORT THASOS (Limin Panayia)
Admiralty chart no. 1679

Approach

Conspicuous The buildings of the town in the natural amphitheatre at the foot of the hills can be seen from the distance, but the harbour moles are very low and difficult to see. The two white light structures on the

Thasos harbour looking NW from the ruins of the ancient city
behind the harbour.

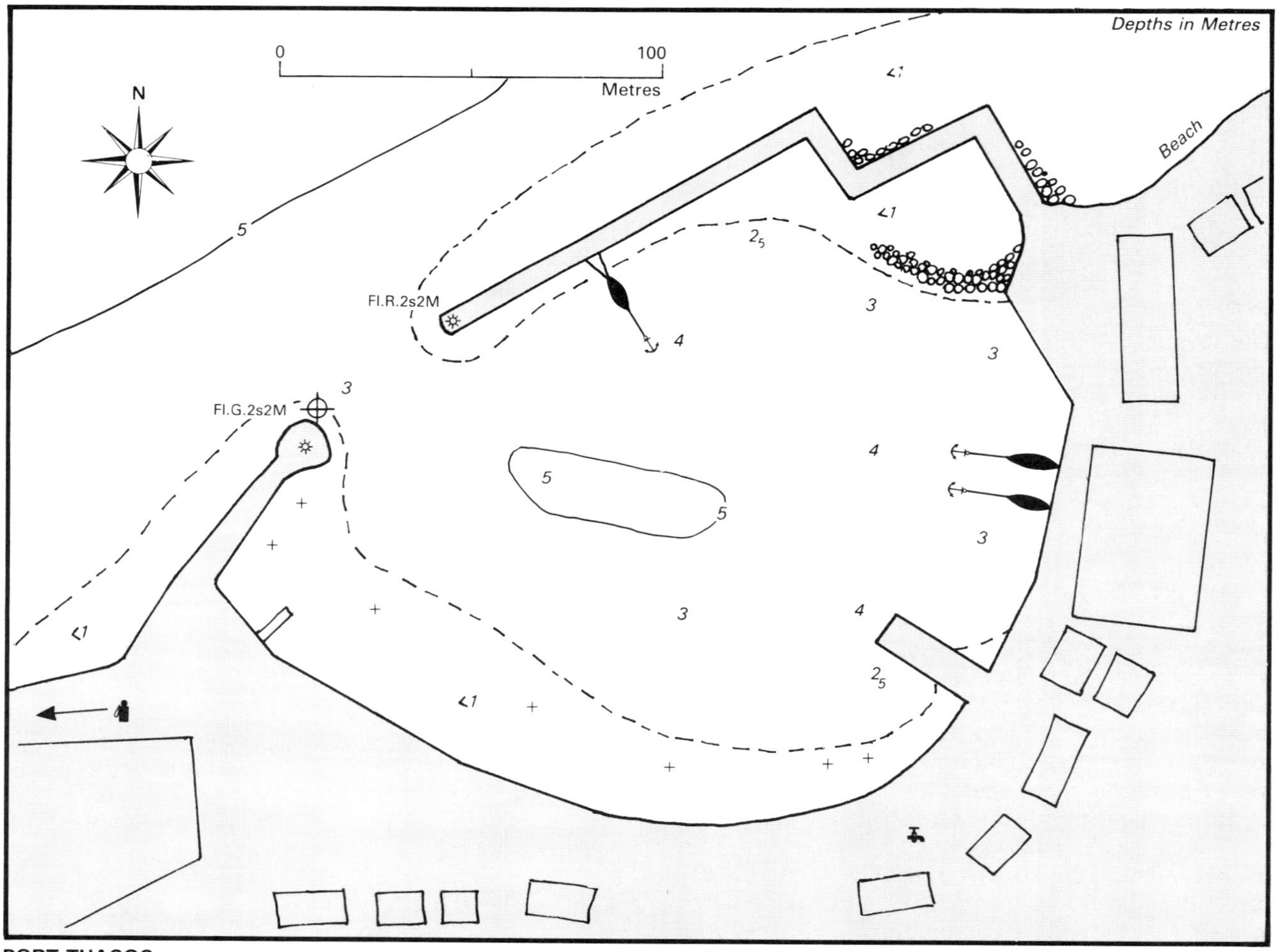

Depths in Metres

0   100
Metres

N

5

Beach

Fl.R.2s2M

2₅

Fl.G.2s2M   3

5   5

PORT THASOS
40°47′N 24°42′·7E (Fl.G.2M)

extremities of the moles will be seen before the moles.

By night Use the light on the SE of Nisis Thasopoula (Fl.WR.4·5s6/4M) and the lights at the entrance (Fl.G.2s2M and Fl.R.2s2M).

Dangers Care should be taken of the remains of an ancient mole, mostly submerged, approximately 300 metres to the NE of the harbour. Approach the harbour from the N or NW.

Mooring

Go stern-to or bows-to the quay in the SE corner of the harbour. If it is crowded here go bows-to the E mole although you will not be able to get close to the mole and you will have to use a dinghy to get ashore. The bottom of the harbour was said to be originally constructed of marble, but I found only mud and shingle – good holding.

Shelter Excellent all-round shelter. The occasional yacht has wintered afloat here.

Authorities Port police and customs (by the ferry quay).

Facilities

Water On the quay.

Fuel On the waterfront to the W of the harbour. A mini-tanker can be arranged to deliver to the harbour.

Repairs Limited mechanical repairs. *Caïques* are hauled out and built to the E of the harbour.

Provisions Excellent shopping for all provisions. Wine from the barrel.

Eating out Excellent tavernas on the waterfront.

Other PO. OTE. Bank. Greek gas and *Camping Gaz.* Hire cars and motorbikes. Buses around the perimeter of the island. Ferries to Keramotis and Kavala.

General

The town of Thasos is built on the same site as the ancient capital and wandering around the town you experience an architectural *pot-pourri* of the old and the new. Most of the new town is within the 2½ miles of walls and towers that surrounded the ancient city. Thasos possessed two fine harbours. The surviving oval harbour was the ancient naval harbour. The ancient commercial harbour to the E is now mostly destroyed.

Close by this latter harbour is one of the most charming spots in the town – shaded by trees and close to the ruins of the *agora*, it is a short but steep walk up the hill behind to the ancient theatre and the *acropolis* that look out over Thasos. More than any of the other classic sites I have visited in Greece, Thasos conveys in both its substance and its atmosphere what an ancient Greek city was like. The museum houses most of the valuable finds from the site.

Thasos black wine, for which it was famed in ancient times, is widely available, but in my experience the modern brew is of mediocre quality, though I have been told that much of it is now produced not on Thasos but on the mainland opposite.

Anchorages around Thasos

ORMOS PRINOS

On the N side of Ak Prinos, this open bay affords some shelter from the prevailing NE winds by means of the natural camber of the bay. Off the village of Prinos there is a wharf and a short pier but the latter is used by the car ferry to Kavala. Anchor in the bay. Some provisions available ashore and a number of good tavernas.

ORMOS LIMENARIA

On the SW corner of Thasos, Ormos Limenaria offers good shelter from N winds. Open to the S. Anchor in the bay. There are two short jetties with 2 metre depths at the extremities. In the small harbour there are 2 metre depths if you keep to starboard and mostly 3 metre depths on the S quay. It may be possible for a small yacht to find a berth in here where there is good shelter. Although shelter from northerlies is reasonable in the bay, there is usually some ground swell which can at times be uncomfortable.

Fuel and water on the waterfront. Good shopping for all provisions. Excellent tavernas and bars on the waterfront. Limenaria was originally built to house workers from the nearby mines. In recent years it has developed into a large tourist resort.

PEFKARI AND POTOS

Along the coast to the SE of Limenaria are Pefkari and Potos where a yacht can anchor off in settled weather. Open to the S.

ALIKI

On the SE corner of Thasos 2 miles to the W of Ak Babouras (Stravros) there are a number of small coves offering good shelter from N winds. Open only to the S. Aliki is the easternmost of the coves and there is a taverna on the beach.

ORMOS POTAMIAS

A large bay on the E coast of Thasos on the S side of Ak Pirgos. Anchor at the N end of the bay where there is reasonable shelter from NE winds. The bottom is sand and shelves gently to the shore. At the S end of the bay at Skala Potamias there is a rough stone breakwater, but the depths around it are insufficient even for a small yacht.

MAKRIAMMOS

On the NE corner of Thasos there is the open bay of Makriammos. In the N corner of the bay there is a short mole which provides some protection from NE winds. Moor bows-to near the extremity where there are 2 metre depths.

Approach to Port Lagos looking NNE.

PORT LAGOS (Ormos Vistonikos)
Admiralty chart no. 1679

Approach

Ormos Lagos lies in the NE corner of Ormos Vistonikos. It is a natural lagoon connected to the sea by a dredged channel. A hotel on Ak Fanari and a large factory and silo on the E side of the entrance to the harbour are conspicuous. The green conical buoy marking the outer edge of the shallows off Ak Fanari is difficult to see from seaward. Once inside Ormos Vistonikos, the buoys marking the dredged channel are easily identified and entry into the harbour is straightforward. The channel and the harbour are kept dredged to 6 metres.

By night Use the light on Ak Fanari (Fl.8s6M), the light buoy off the cape (Fl.G), the light buoys marking the channel (Q.G.2M and Q.R.2M), and the lights at the entrance (Fl.R.3s2M and Q.G.2M). There are leading lights: on 023° F.Y and F.Y.3M.

Mooring

Go stern-to or bows-to on the W quay. Excellent all-round shelter.
Authorities Port police and customs.

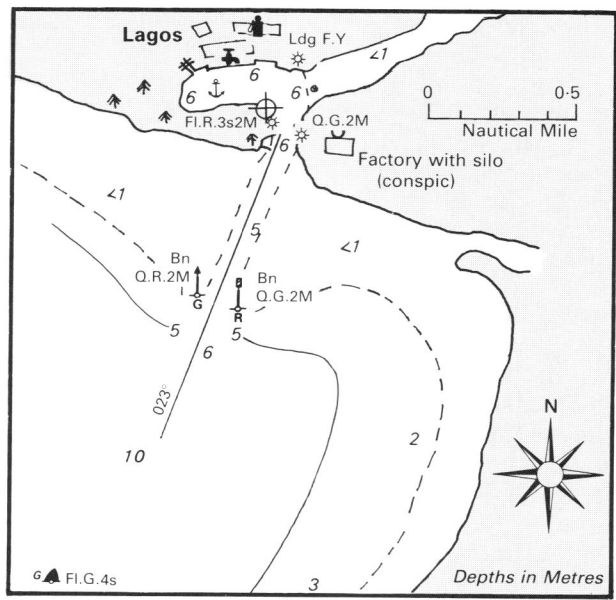

PORT LAGOS
41°00'·2N 25°07'·6E (Fl.R.2M)

Facilities
Water On the quay.
Fuel About 500 metres away.
Provisions Some provisions can be obtained. Ice available.
Eating out Tavernas.
Repairs Yachts are craned onto the hard in the SW corner.

General

Lagos is an important port for the shipment of grain from the hinterland. Although it is a commercial port, the approach to and setting of Port Lagos are attractive. The surrounding marshes are a haven for all types of waterbirds rarely seen in other parts of Greece. The surrounding area is now a protected bird reserve and a walk through the lagoons is recommended. Just E of Lagos on the main road there is a delightful monastery built on an islet in the middle of one of the lagoons.

AK MARONIAS

One mile to the W of Ak Maronias a rough stone L-shaped breakwater extends W and then N from the coast. A small yacht could use this harbour in fine weather.

MAKRI

Seven miles to the W of Alexandroupolis lies a small *caïque* harbour serving the village of Makri on the hill above. At the entrance there are less than 2 metre depths and it is rock-bound. Inside there would be excellent shelter. The entrance is lit F.G/F.R.3M. It deserves further exploration in settled weather.

ALEXANDROUPOLIS
Admiralty chart no. 1679

Approach

Conspicuous The buildings of the large town are visible from the distance. The white lighthouse on the promenade and three red storage tanks behind the harbour are conspicuous. The outer mole of the harbour and the entrance are easily identified.

By night Use the main light (Fl(3)15s24M) and the lights at the entrance (Fl.R.1·5s2M and Fl.G.1·5s 3M).

Dangers With strong S winds there is usually a lumpy sea over the shallow bank extending some miles off the coast in the approaches to the harbour.

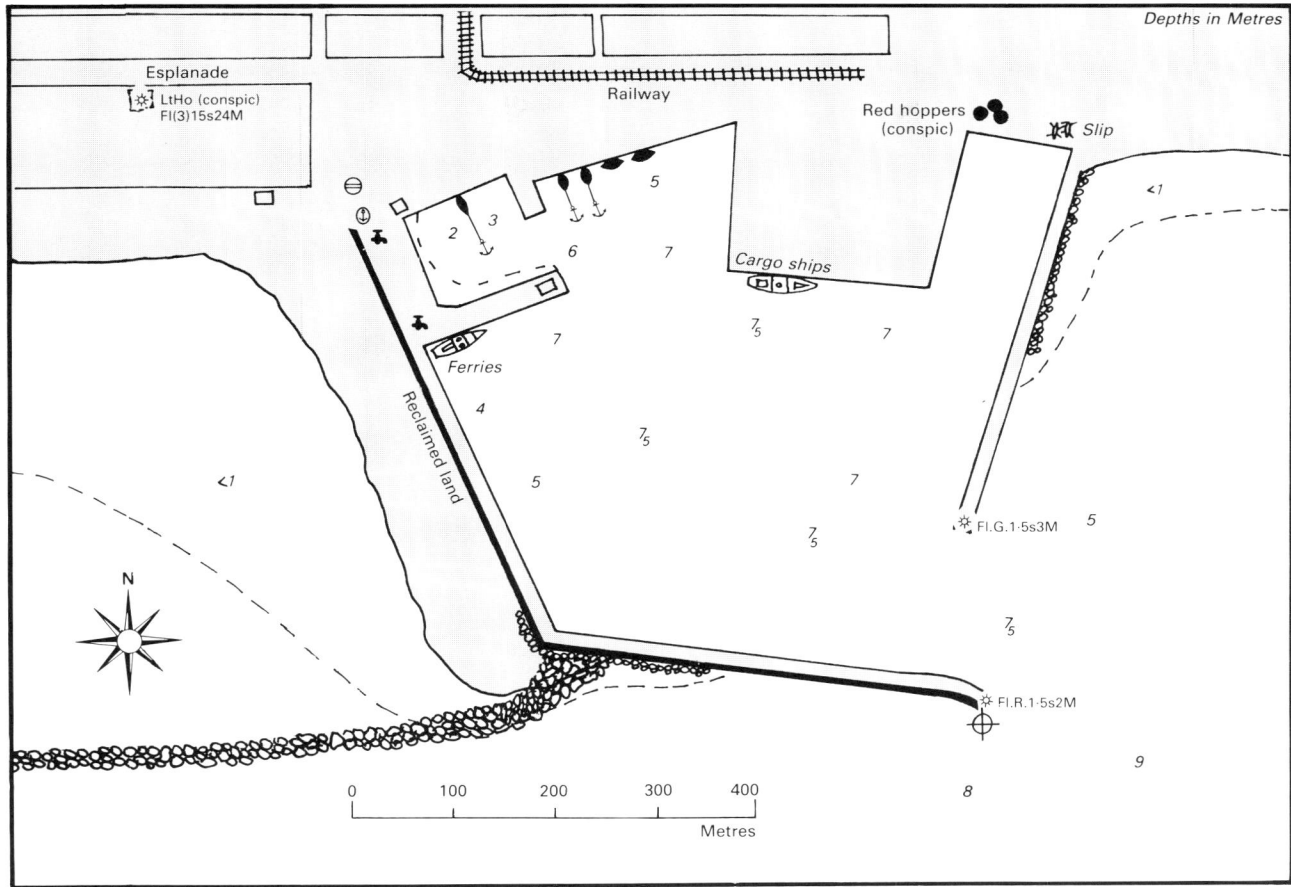

ALEXANDROUPOLIS
40°50′·4N 25°53′·3E (Fl.R.2M)

Mooring

Go stern-to or bows-to or alongside the N quay near the entrance to the inner harbour or in the inner harbour itself. The bottom is sticky mud – excellent holding.

Shelter Good shelter although strong S winds send in some swell – uncomfortable but not dangerous.

Authorities A port of entry: port police, customs and immigration authorities.

Facilities

Water On the quay in the inner harbour.
Fuel Near the quay.
Repairs Most mechanical and light engineering repairs. Excellent hardware shops.
Provisions Excellent shopping for all provisions. Ice from a fish shop near the waterfront.
Eating out Good tavernas in the town.
Other PO. OTE. Banks. Greek gas and *Camping Gaz.* Hire cars and motorbikes. Buses to Kavala and Istanbul. Train to Thessaloniki and Istanbul. Ferry to Samothraki. Internal flights to Athens.

General

Alexandroupolis, named after King Alexander (born 1893) and not Alexander the Great, is a modern bustling city and port. It is important as the major road and rail link with Turkey and also for the shipment of grain and tobacco from the hinterland. In the shallows 8 miles to the SE of the harbour where the Evros river flows into the sea, the local fishing boats net flatfish, mostly sole, and though most of it finds its way to Thessaloniki and Athens, some can be found in the tavernas at Alexandroupolis.

Samothraki
(Samothrace)

Until recently Samothraki has not had a secure harbour and for this reason has remained a solitary island shrouded in mystery. It is a forbidding-looking place, a gigantic lump of marble rising up to 1600 metres (5200ft) at the summit of Mt Fengari. On the west, Ak Akrotiri forms a shallow bay in which the harbour of Kamariotissa nestles.

The mysterious ancient inhabitants of the island, the Kabeiri (Cabeiri), were of pre-Greek origin, possibly of Phoenician or Phrygian stock, and worshipped the Great Earth Mother rather than the male gods which dominated classical times. The strength of the Kabeiri was such that Samothraki was regarded as a sacred island and a sanctuary for initiates of the cult, although this may have been a spin-off from the inaccessibility of the island.

They had a soft spot for seafarers and initiation into their rites was deemed to be good luck and a safeguard against shipwreck. The power of the Kabeiri throughout the ancient world ensured Samothraki an independent existence throughout the Greek struggles until late into the Roman period.

The ruins of the ancient temple-city lie on a rocky ridge amongst wild olives and maquis. The American school of archaeologists have mostly been responsible for clearing the site and organising the small museum housing most of the finds that were not spirited away by early explorers. Of these the best known is the *Winged Victory of Samothrace* removed by the French in 1863 and now in the Louvre in Paris. The splendid site looking across to the mainland is well worth a visit. Above, in a craggy pocket, is the principal village (*chora*) of Samothraki.

KAMARIOTISSA

Approach

Conspicuous From the N and W a tower on the NW corner of the island and the small village of Kamariotissa are conspicuous. From the S the low-lying sand spit terminating in Ak Akrotiri is not visible until you are very near it, but the light structure on the extremity is visible from some distance off. Closer in the cluster of buildings at Kamariotissa and the harbour mole are easily identified.

By night Use the light on Ak Akrotiri (Fl.5s10M) and the light on the extremity of the mole (Fl.R.3s3M).

Dangers By day or night caution must be exercised whilst navigating in the vicinity of the low-lying Ak Akrotiri when relative distances between the cape and the high mountains behind can be confused.

Mooring

Go stern-to or bows-to or alongside the mole or the quay wherever there is room. The bottom is sand and shingle – good holding. The harbour is usually crowded with fishing boats and it can be difficult to find a berth. You may have to go alongside a fishing boat and then move when it leaves.

Shelter Good all-round shelter although a strong SW wind might make the harbour uncomfortable.

Kamariotissa harbour on Samothraki looking S.

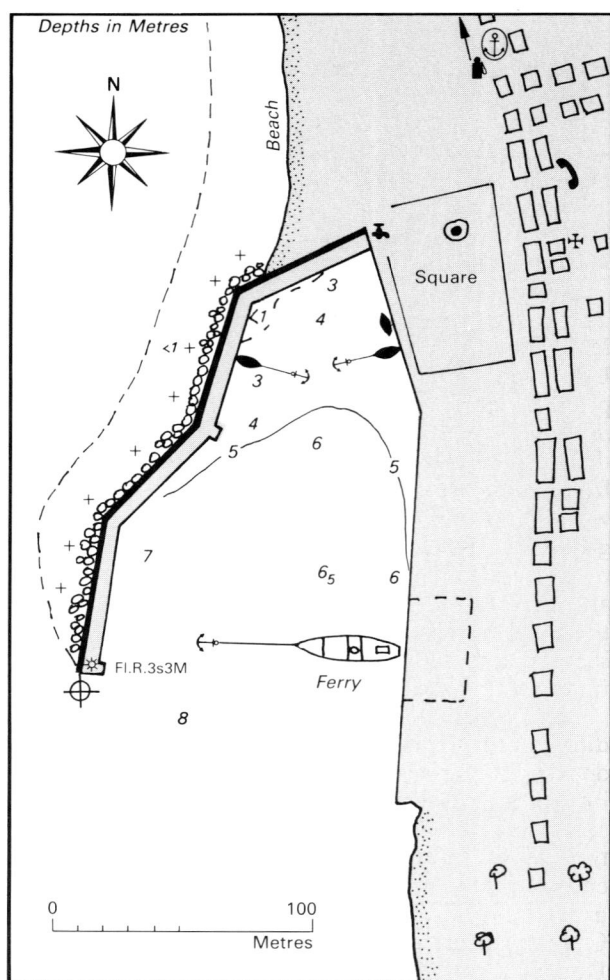

KAMARIOTISSA
40°28'·6N 25°28'·2E (Fl.R.3M)

Authorities Port police.

Facilities

Water At the root of the mole.
Fuel On the waterfront. A mini-tanker can deliver.
Provisions Most provisions can be obtained.
Eating out Good tavernas on the waterfront.
Other PO. OTE. Bus to the *chora*. Ferry to Alexandroupolis.

General

Kamariotissa is essentially a small fishing hamlet and the ferry port for Samothraki. The inhabitants are very friendly towards visiting yachtsmen as they rarely see a great number of yachts here. It is a safe place to leave a yacht when visiting the archaeological site on the N side of the island.

To get there take a taxi inland to Palaeopolis and then enquire at the hotel for admittance. It is a short walk to the site itself where there are remains of several of the initiation buildings including the Arsinion which was the largest circular building in ancient Greece. A small museum nearby houses finds from the site. While you are there it is worth going on to the *chora* which is not far away.

VIII. The Eastern Sporades

The eastern Sporades stretch down the coast of Asia Minor linking northern Greece to the Dodecanese. Like the other islands in the Aegean, they are the peaks of mountains that once stood on the plain of the Aegean. Geographically Samothraki belongs to this group of islands, but politically it is administered from Alexandroupolis and its communications are with the north. Limnos, the most northerly of the group described here, hovers in its own limbo in the middle of the northern Aegean. Generally the islands are more fertile and greener than the Cyclades and the Dodecanese. Lesvos and Samos in particular will surprise the visiting yachtsman with their well-watered, cultivated plains and extensive pine forests.

The history of the group of islands is patchy and difficult to summarise as a whole – the historical detail for each island can be found in the introduction to each one. Very early on Limnos was an important link between Europe and the islands to the south. It had a highly developed Bronze Age culture of a Minoan-Mycenaean type and metalworking probably filtered into the Cyclades and Crete from there. With the decline of Limnos, the Dorians and Ionians moved in. The Ionic Confederacy was centred around Khios and Samos and the adjacent mainland coast. The confederacy prospered and for some time rivalled Athens in its high life and appreciation of the arts. The chief cities of the group – Khios, Ephesus, Smyrna and Miletus – endured as important centres long after the decline of the confederacy.

Lesvos existed outside the confederacy in a somewhat chaotic state until the beginning of the 6th century BC when Pittacus calmed the island and earned for himself a place as one of the Seven Sages of Greece. Soon afterwards, around 540BC, Polykrates of Samos achieved his meteoric rise to fame and fortune and control of the group revolved around this tyrannical genius and the Persians pushing up from Asia Minor.

The decisive Battle of Salamis ousted the Persians and ushered in the usual succession of invaders: the Romans, the Saracens, Byzantine rulers, the Venetians and the Genoese, and the Turks. Looking at the islands today (with the exception of Psara), it is hard to believe that they were often entirely abandoned by the native inhabitants as successive waves of invaders swept down on them and corsairs mopped up whatever was left. Indeed it is unlikely that the present populations of the islands are descended from the original inhabitants at all. The group became part of Greece in 1912 after the Balkan Wars.

Today the eastern Sporades are considered to be important military outposts and soldiers are stationed on all of the islands. Photographs of many of the harbours, much of the coastline and some of the interior are forbidden. A sign in Greek and English or of the pictorial type (a camera with a cross on it) will usually be found prohibiting photographs. It should be observed, or all your film may be confiscated and exposed!

With the exception of Samos, the islands are to a large extent off the tourist track. Consequently many facilities are underdeveloped. Yacht equipment and servicing beyond the basic fisherman's needs is unobtainable. Tavernas are mostly of the local type and the comparatively sophisticated (such as it is) fare of Corfu, Mikonos or Rhodes will not be found. However the friendliness of the locals more than makes up for these small deficiencies and prices on the whole are cheaper than elsewhere. The basics are there – good harbours, good centres for provisions and communications – but not the gloss. For many including myself that is a blessing.

Weather patterns in the eastern Sporades

The prevailing wind in the summer is the *meltemi*. It blows fitfully at first in June getting up to full strength in July, August and September and dies in October. In July and August it blows strongly, about Force 4–6, and may reach Force 7 on occasions. In the more southerly islands of the group it blows from the N–NNW but in Limnos it blows from the NE. Around much of the group the *meltemi* is funnelled by the land including the adjacent Turkish coast so in places it can be blowing from the W. In the spring and autumn there are often S winds, but they rarely exceed Force 4–5.

In the winter strong winds may be from the SE or the NE. In the more northerly islands strong winds are most often from the NE and strong S winds can be expected to become strong NE winds which may often blow for several days. In the winter exceptionally severe storms can strike the group. (In December 1980 Force 10 was reported in Lesvos.)

In common with the other islands in the Aegean there are gusts off the high land on the lee side of an island. With the *meltemi* these gusts are especially severe off Samos and Ikaria and parts of Lesvos. With prolonged strong winds from the N the seas surrounding Limnos can become especially confused and it is prudent to wait a day after the wind has died to let the sea subside.

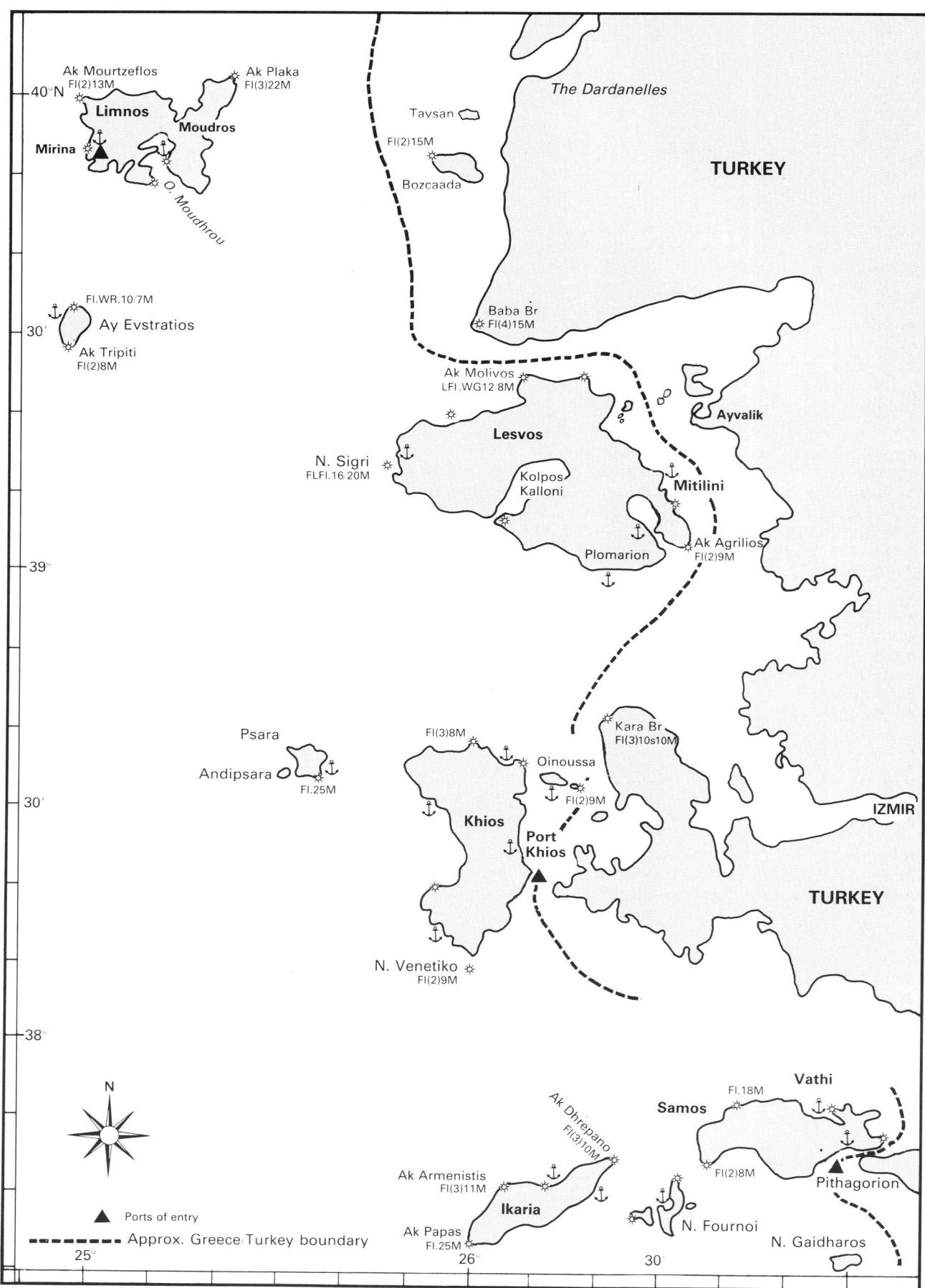

Ak Mourtzeflos
Fl(2)13M
Ak Plaka
Fl(3)22M

40°N

Limnos

Moudros

Mirina

O. Moudhrou

The Dardanelles

TURKEY

Tavsan

Fl(2)15M

Bozcaada

Fl.WR.10/7M

30'
Ay Evstratios

Ak Tripiti
Fl(2)8M

Baba Br
Fl(4)15M

Ak Molivos
LFl.WG12/8M

Ayvalik

N. Sigri
FLFl.16/20M

Lesvos

Kolpos
Kalloni

Mitilini

39'

Plomarion

Ak Agrilios
Fl(2)9M

Psara

Fl(3)8M

Oinoussa

Kara Br
Fl(3)10s10M

Andipsara
Fl.25M

30'

Khios

Fl(2)9M

IZMIR

**Port
Khios**

TURKEY

N. Venetiko
Fl(2)9M

38°

N

Vathi

Fl.18M

Ak Dhrepano
Fl(3)10M

Samos

Ak Armenistis
Fl(3)11M

Fl(2)8M

Pithagorion

▲ Ports of entry

Ikaria

N. Fournoi

Ak Papas
Fl.25M

N. Gaidharos

▬ ▬ ▬ Approx. Greece/Turkey boundary

25°

26°

30°

Data

PORTS OF ENTRY
Mirina (Limnos)
Mitilini (Lesvos)
Limin Khios
Pithagorion (Samos)

PROHIBITED AREAS
Khios It is prohibited to enter or anchor in the N cove at Laghana.

Photographs of many of the harbours and parts of the coastline of Limnos, Lesvos, Khios and Samos are prohibited.

MAJOR LIGHTS
Ay Evstratios
Ak Tripiti Fl(2)10s8M
Nisis Ay Apostoloi Fl.WR.5s10/7M

Limnos
Ak Plaka Fl(3)30s22M
Ak Mourtzeflos Fl(2)14s13M
Ak Kastron Fl.3s7M
Vrak.Kombi (Ak Lena) Q(2)6s10M
Ak Kavos (Sagradha) Fl.3s5M

Lesvos
Ak Korakas Fl.WR.5s10/7M
Ak Molivos LFl.WG.10s12/8M
Nisis Sigri FLFl.30s16/20M
Nisis Garbia Fl.3s6M
Ak Agrilios Fl(2)12s9M
Mitilini Fl(3)13·5s6M
Nisidha Panayia Fl.10s7M

Psara
Ak Ayios Yeoryios Fl.10s25M

Khios
Ak Anapomera Fl(3)12s8M
Vrak Strovilo Fl.5s10M
Ormiskos Mesta Fl.3s6M
Nisis Pasha Fl(2)30s9M

Ikaria
Ak Pappas Fl.20s25M
Ak Armenistis Fl(3)12s11M
Vrak Evdhilos Fl.7·5s6M
Ak Dhrepanon Fl(3)24s10M

Samos
Ak Kotsikas Fl(2)16s6M
Ak Gatos Fl(3)14s6M
Ak Ayios Dhomenikos Fl.3·6s5M
Ak Pangozi (Karlovasi) Fl.5s8M

Fourni
Ak Trakhili Fl(2)15s7M
Ak Saita (Malaki) Fl(2)12s8M

Quick reference guide

	Shelter	Mooring	Fuel	Water	Provisioning	Tavernas	Plan
Limnos							
Mirina	A	AB	B	B	A	B	•
Ormos Plati	B	C	O	O	O	O	•
Ormos Thanos	B	C	O	O	O	C	•
Ormos Ay Pavlou	C	C	O	O	O	O	
Ormos Kondia	B	C	O	O	O	C	•
Ormos Moudhrou	A	AC	B	B	B	C	•
Ormos Plakas	C	A	O	O	O	O	
Ormos Hefaistia	C	C	O	O	O	O	
Ayios Evstratios	B	AB	O	A	C	C	•
Lesvos							
Mitilini	A	AB	B	A	A	A	•
Skala Mistengnon	B	AC	O	B	O	C	•
Ormos Makri							
Yialos	O	C	O	O	O	O	
Skala Sikaminias	O	A	O	B	C	C	
Mithimna	A	A	A	A	A	A	•
Petra	B	A	O	O	C	C	•
Ghavdholos	B	AB	O	B	C	C	•
Sigri	B	C	O	B	B	C	•
Erresos	B	AC	O	B	B	B	•
Kolpos Kalloni	A	C	O	B	C	C	•
Plomarion	B	AC	B	A	A	B	•
Ormos Mersinia	B	C	O	O	O	C	•
Kolpos Yeras	A	C	O	O	C	C	•
Psara	A	A	O	O	C	C	•
Oinoussa							
Mandraki	A	AC	O	A	C	C	•
Nisis Pasha	B	C	O	O	O	O	•
Khios							
Limin Khios	A	AB	B	A	A	B	•
Vrondados	B	A	O	A	C	C	•
Volissos (Limnia)	B	A	B	B	C	C	•
Marmara	B	AB	B	B	C	C	•
Ormos Kolokithia	C	C	O	B	C	C	
SW corner	B	C	O	O	O	O	
Ormiskos Mesta	C	C	O	O	O	O	
Emborios	B	C	O	B	C	C	
Ikaria							
Evdhilos	C	A	O	B	B	C	•
Ayios Kiristos	O	AC	B	A	A	B	•
Samos							
Karlovasi	B	A	B	A	B	B	•
Vathi	O	AB	B	B	A	A	•
Pithagorion	A	A	A	A	A	A	•
Ormos							
Possidonion	B	C	O	O	O	O	
Nisis Samopoula	O	C	O	O	O	C	
Marathakambou	O	C	O	B	C	C	
Ormos Limnionas	C	C	O	O	O	O	
Fourni							
Ormos Korseon	C	C	B	B	C	C	•
Fourni anchorages	B	C	O	O	O	O	•

Limnos

(Lemnos)

Although it geographically belongs to the eastern Sporades, Limnos, situated as it is in the middle of the northern Aegean, is isolated from the other islands of the group. Few tourists go there and ships no longer call on the way to the Dardanelles – even the soldiers stationed there act as if the strategic significance of the island has been somehow overrated by the top brass and really they should be somewhere else. In ancient times none of this was true when Limnos was an important island with one of the most advanced Bronze Age civilizations in Greece.

There were two main reasons for its importance. Lying halfway across the wind-tossed Aegean, it was the logical stepping stone between Europe and Asia Minor. It is likely that Troy was founded from Limnos and there was contact with Lesvos and northern Greece. As a stepping stone, Limnos possessed an abundance of well-sheltered natural harbours including the great Bay of Moudhros. Today, although the island is only partially wooded and cultivated on the east coast, it is easy to see how once, when the soft contours (there are no very high peaks) were covered in green woods, this was one of the finest islands in the northern Aegean.

The name Limnos is possibly derived from a cult of the Minoan mother-goddess, but the principal gods of the island were Hephaestus and the Kabeiri based on Samothraki. Hephaestus is supposed to have berated Zeus one day about his treatment of Hera whereupon he was thrown out of Olympus and fell onto Limnos – breaking both legs. Not until he had fashioned special leg-braces of gold could he

walk. The myth probably derives from the volcanic nature of the island and also the tradition of metalworking that existed from early times when these skills spread from the north down to the Greek archipelago.

In classical times the island acquired ill repute from the so-called 'Limnian deeds'. The women of the island refused to serve Aphrodite who was making poor old Hephaestus miserable with her numerous affairs with other gods and mortals. Aphrodite responded by afflicting the unfortunate women with evil smells (Ernle Bradford suggests 'body odour and halitosis' in the euphemistic jargon of advertising) causing their husbands to ignore them. The incensed women of Limnos went on the rampage and murdered all males on the island. Jason and the Argonauts on their adventures discovered the island full of frustrated women and not surprisingly dallied two years repopulating it.

The site of the principal Bronze Age city is at Hephaestia on the east of the island. The Italians have excavated the site and also conducted underwater exploration of Charos Reef (Ifalos Keros) lying 7 miles off the east coast. The discovery of marble blocks gives some substance to the identification of the reef with ancient Chryseis. It is thought this was the site of the ancient city until, as Herodotus recorded, it was engulfed by the sea after an earthquake.

Limnos achieved some prominence again when Moudhros Bay was the base for the Gallipoli campaign. Almost as if the failure of that campaign affected the island, ever since its importance has

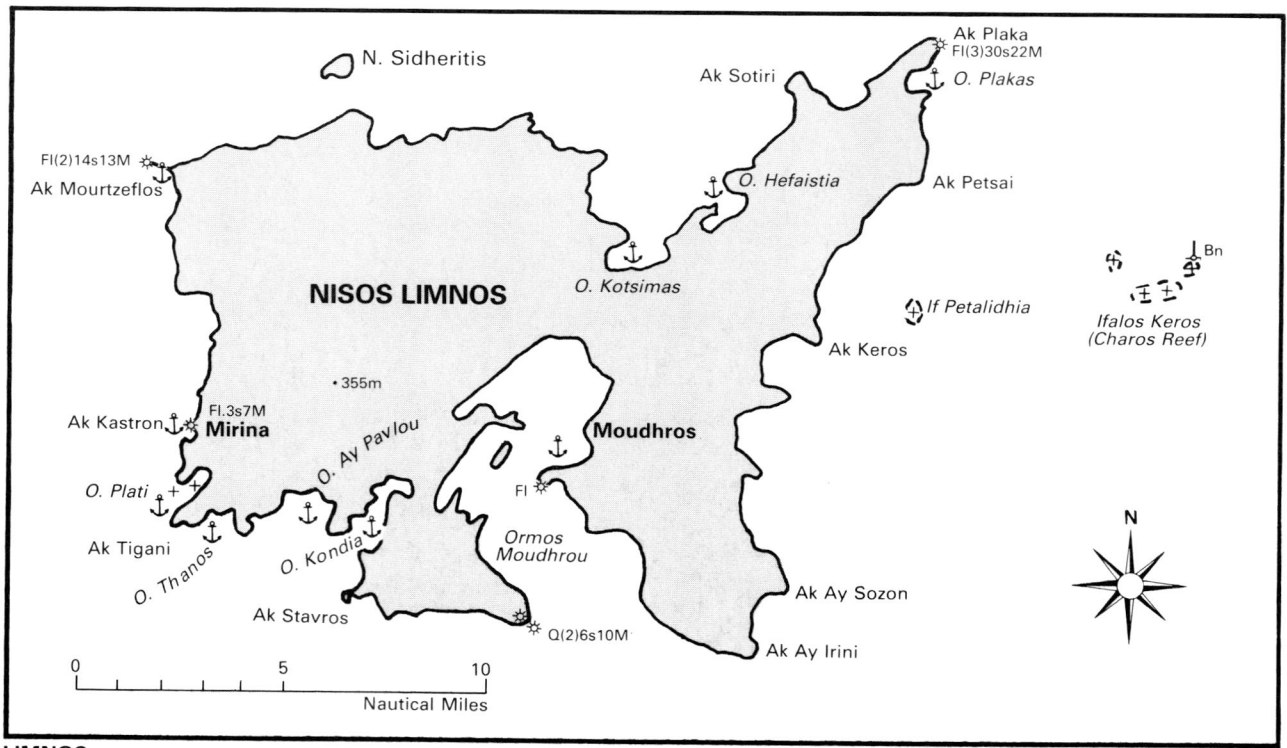

declined and even the tourist boom has not touched the island. A local asked me when I was there: 'We have fine beaches, clear water, good harbours, friendly people, but no tourists – why?' I couldn't really tell him that I liked Limnos as it is in its splendid isolation.

MIRINA (Myrinas, Merini, Kastro)
Admiralty chart no. 1661

Approach
Conspicuous The castle on the rocky bluff on the N side of the entrance and a white church on a rocky bluff at the root of the outer breakwater are conspicuous. The buildings of the town can be seen from the N and W but not from the S until you are into the bay. The S breakwater is easily identified.

By night Use the light on the castle (Fl.3s7M) and the lights at the entrance (Q.R.3M and Q.G.2M). The inner basin is lit: F.R.2M.

Mooring
Go stern-to or bows-to or alongside the N mole or the quay. The bottom is mud – good holding.

Shelter Good shelter from the prevailing NE winds. Southerlies may cause a surge.

Authorities A port of entry: port police, customs and immigration. The most convenient port for clearing out to the Dardanelles.

Note The inner harbour is normally crowded with fishing boats. Because the inner harbour is so narrow anchor lines are weighted – a yacht wishing to moor here should enquire for a place and also ensure its anchor line is weighted. Under normal conditions the outer harbour affords good shelter so there is little to be gained by going into the inner harbour.

Facilities
Water A tap at the root of the N mole.
Fuel On the far side of the town.
Repairs Some mechanical repairs and light engineering work. Good hardware and tool shops.
Provisions Good shopping for all provisions. Ice available nearby.
Eating out Several good tavernas near the inner harbour and on the beach.
Other PO. OTE. Banks. Greek gas. Helpful tourist office. Buses to the principal villages. Ferries to Lesvos, Piraeus and Kavala. Internal flights to Thessaloniki and Athens.

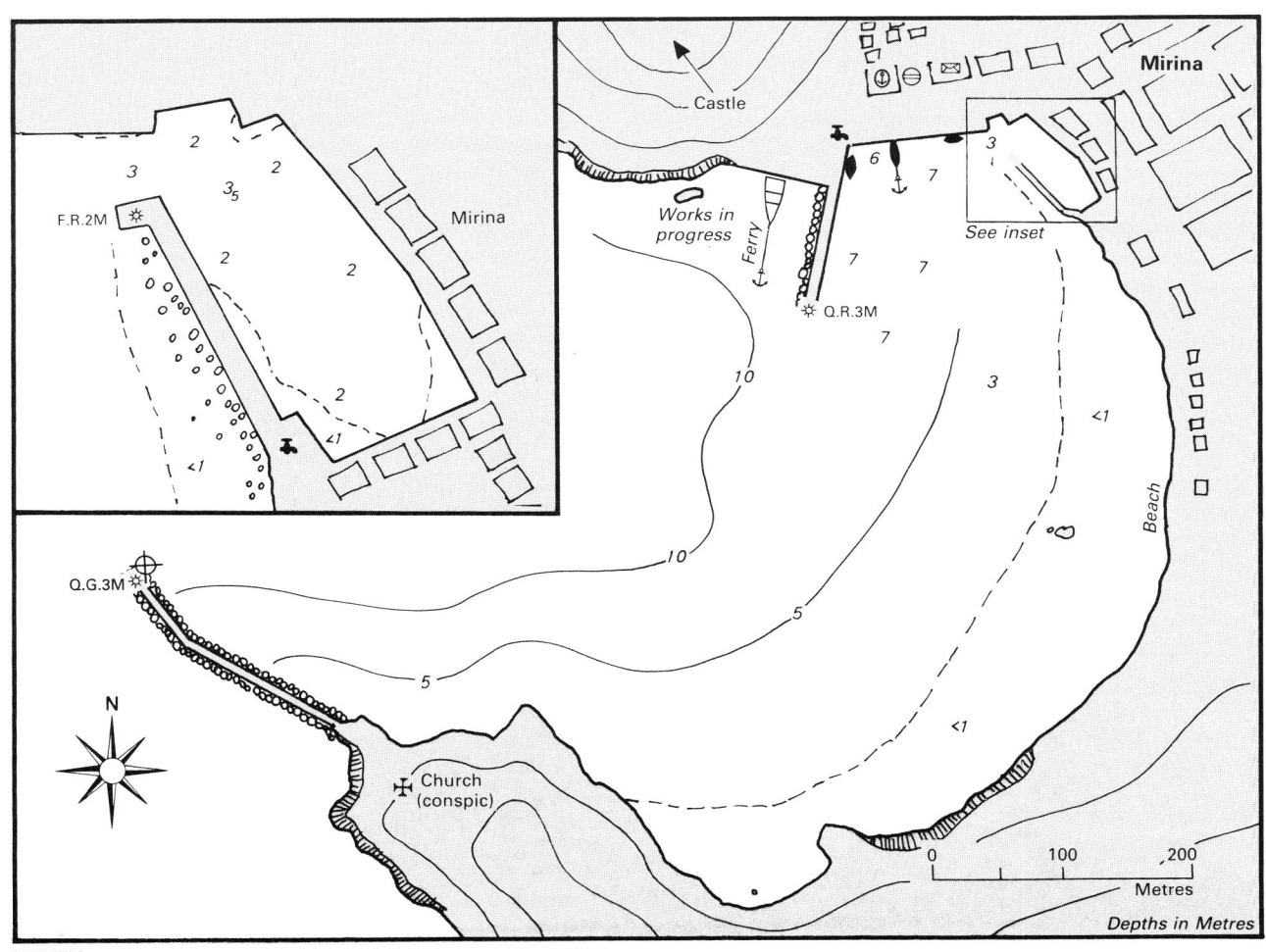

MIRINA
39°52'·3N 25°03'·2E (Q.G.3M)

Mirina (Limin Limnos) looking NE from the S side of the bay.

General

Built near the site of the ancient capital, Mirina has only recently readopted its ancient name. Formerly it was called Kastro after the Genoese castle dominating the town. The castle is worth a visit as much for the site as for the castle itself – photographs are prohibited.

Few yachts visit Mirina and those which do use it primarily as the most convenient port for clearing for the Dardanelles. Yet it is a friendly place and a convenient base for visiting other anchorages around the island.

ORMOS PLATI

Lies N of Ak Tigani and provides good shelter from N winds. Open to the SW. Care should be taken of the reef extending SE from the N side of the entrance and a reef on the SE side of the bay. Anchor in 4–8 metres on sand. Taverna on the beach.

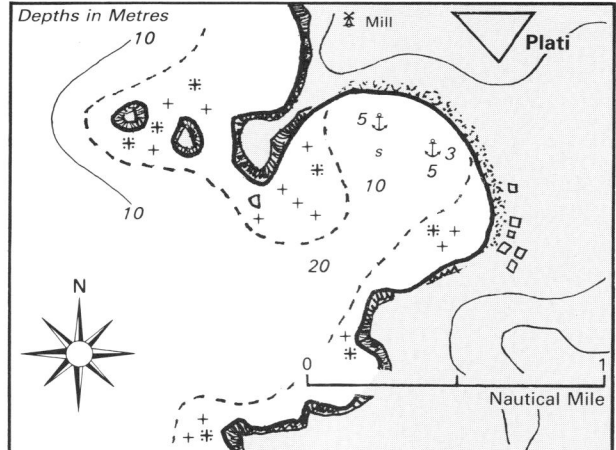

ORMOS PLATI
39°51'·4N 25°04'·3E

ORMOS THANOS

The double-headed bay lying just E of Ak Tigani. Care is needed of the reef and shoal water extending for half a mile SSW of Ak Tigani. Vrakhonsis Tigani, a rock which occasionally dries, lies approximately 0·2 of a mile SSW of Nisis Tigani.

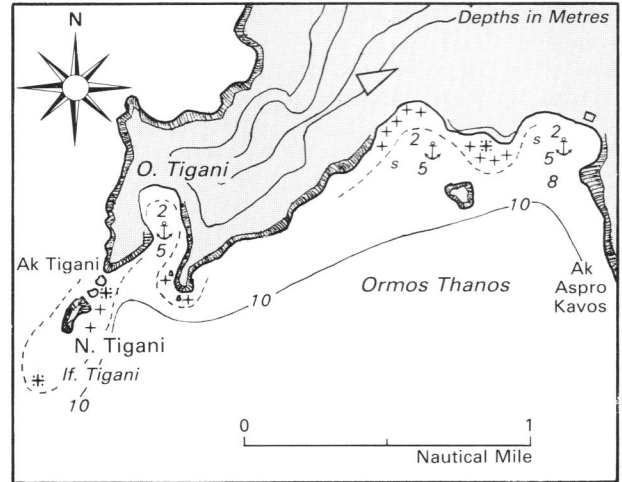

ORMOS THANOS
39°50'N 25°03'E (Ak Tigani)

There is reported to be a passage between Ifalos Tigani and Nisis Tigani with 7 metre depths, but this is not recommended. A yacht must keep well off the cape before making the approach to the bay. There are several places a yacht can anchor.

1. Immediately under Ak Tigani there is a cove where a yacht can anchor with a long line to the shore. Anchor in 4–8 metres.
2. On the W side of the islet in Ormos Thanos a yacht can anchor in 4–8 metres on sand. The head of this cove is rock-bound.
3. On the E side of the bay and the islet. This is the best anchorage. Anchor off the beach in 4–8 metres on sand. Taverna ashore. Good shelter from the *meltemi*.

ORMOS AY PAVLOU
Admiralty Chart No. 1661

The large bay lying E of Ormos Thanos. Care is needed of the reef in the middle of the bay. It is easily identified in calm weather. There are a number of places a yacht can anchor around the large bay.

1. In the SW corner. The head and sides of the cove are obstructed by reefs and shoal water. Anchor in 4–5 metres in the middle of the cove. Mediocre shelter from the *meltemi*.

2. In the NW corner. The N side of the cove is obstructed by reefs and shoal water. Anchor in the SW of the cove in 4–5 metres on sand and weed. Mediocre shelter from the *meltemi*.

3. At the head of the bay off the long beach. Anchor in 4–6 metres on sand and shingle. Reasonable shelter from the *meltemi*.

4. In the cove on the E side. Anchor in 3–6 metres on sand. Good shelter from the *meltemi*.

ORMOS KONDIA
Admiralty chart no. 1661

The large bay E of Ormos Ay Pavlou and N of Ak Stavros. There are several places a yacht can anchor around the large bay.

1. On the W side of the bay there are several coves where a yacht can anchor. Mostly 3–8 metres on sand. Reasonable shelter can be found from the *meltemi*.

2. *Dhiapori* At the NE head of the bay is Dhiapori. Anchor in 4–7 metres off the hamlet on mud. Good shelter from the *meltemi*. Taverna ashore.

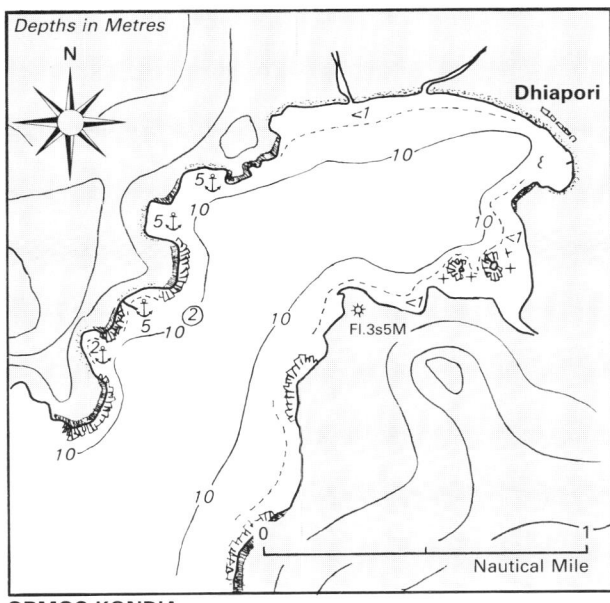

ORMOS KONDIA
39°51′N 25°10′E

ORMOS MOUDHROU (Moudra)
Admiralty chart no. 1661

Approach
Conspicuous The entrance to the large bay is easily identified. Nisis Kombi and the light tower on it are conspicuous. Once through the channel between Ak Kavos and Pondikonisia, the village of Moudhros and a cathedral in it are easily identified.

By night Use the lights on Nisis Kombi (Q(2)6s10M) and Ak Kavos (Fl.3s5M), the light buoy opposite (Fl.R), and the lights at Moudhros (F.R, Q.G and Q.R, but not to be relied upon).

Dangers
1. Care must be taken of the reef extending for half a mile SW from Ak Velanidha, the E entrance point.

2. Once up to Ak Kavos care is needed of the extensive reefs and shoal water bordering the coast and islets in the bay. The plan can only show these approximately and it is recommended you use Admiralty chart no. 1661 if you intend to explore the bay in detail.

Mooring
Once into the bay there is a choice of anchorages or a yacht can proceed to the town of Moudhros on the E side of the bay.

At Moudhros there are 3–4 metre depths off the outer half of the pier. Go alongside as far towards the root of the pier as possible to leave room for local coasters to berth. The S side is recommended as giving better shelter from the *meltemi*. A small harbour with the entrance on the S side is mostly shallow but with care a small yacht can use it.

Shelter Good shelter from the *meltemi*.

Authorities Port police at Moudhros.

Anchorages There are numerous anchorages around the large bay.

1. *Blenheim Cove* Open NE–E.
2. N of Nisis Alogo under the headland ending in Ak Kaloyeraki.
3. *Ormos Vourlidhia* Open NE.
4. *Fuller Cove* Open NE.
5. *Tarrant Cove* Open NE.
6. *Ormos Kavos* Under Ak Kavos. Open S.

Facilities
(At Moudhros village)
Water On the quay.
Fuel In the town.
Provisions Most provisions can be obtained in the village.
Eating out Several tavernas.
Other PO. OTE. Bus to Mirina. The airport is near the head of the bay.

General
Ormos Moudhros is one of the finest fleet anchorages in the northern Aegean and it was from here, the ill-fated Gallipoli campaign was launched. North of Moudhros village lies Australian pier and the remains of Egyptian pier. I find it difficult to conjure up what it must have been like when the bay was packed full of battleships, cruisers, destroyers and transport ships when looking at the forgotten and deserted bay today.

In the plan of Moudhros Bay I have identified Yam, Yrroc, Eb and Denmad Hills which when read from right to left, as H. M. Denham points out, tells us what the British surveyors thought of their captain who was alleged to have worked them too hard and stopped their leave. Photographs are prohibited of some sites around the bay.

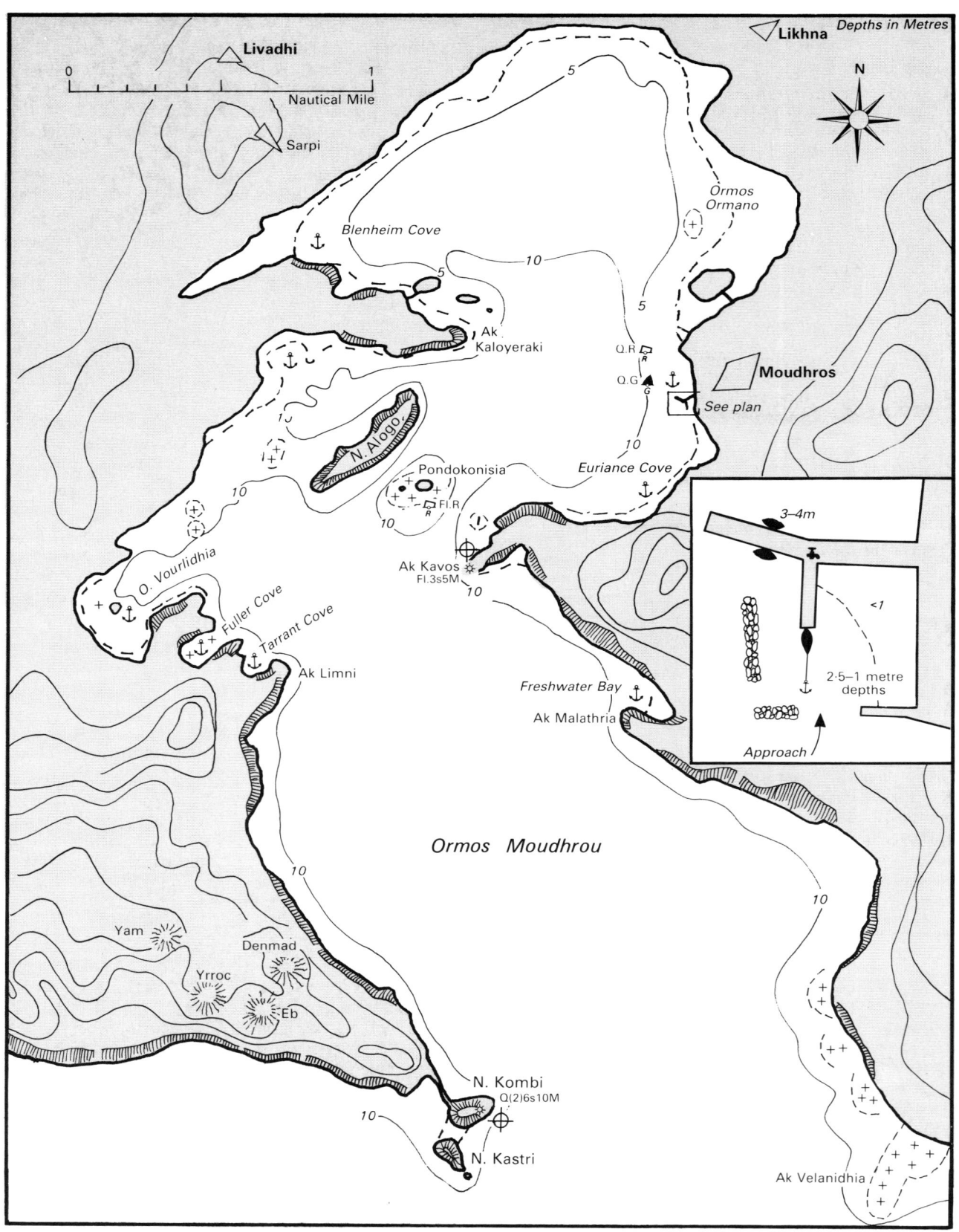

MOUDHROS – HARBOUR AND ANCHORAGES
49°47′·9N 25°14′·2E (Kombi light) 39°51′·1N 25°14′·2E (Ak Kavos light)

East coast

On the E coast there are several large bays that can be used in calm weather. Care must be taken of Ifalos Petalidhia and Ifalos Keros (Charos Reef) lying off the E coast.

ORMOS PLAKAS

On the SE side of Ak Plaka there is a large bay with a short breakwater at the N end. There are 2–4 metre depths on the outer end of the quay where a yacht can go bows-to with care. Alternatively anchor in 3–5 metres in the lee of the breakwater.

ORMOS HEFAISTIA

The large bay of Ormos Pournias lies on the W side of Ak Plaka. On the E side of this bay is Ormos Hefaistia where some shelter can be found from the *meltemi*. Anchor in 5–8 metres on mud or sand.

ORMOS KOTSINAS

The bay on the SW side of Ormos Pournias. Some shelter from the *meltemi* tucked under the N side of the bay. Anchor in 5–8 metres. Military post ashore. Taverna on the S side of the bay.

Nisos Ayios Evstratios

AYIOS EVSTRATIOS
Admiralty chart no. 1659

Approach

Conspicuous The harbour lies 1½ miles SSW of Ak Kalamaki, beneath a small hill with a conspicuous whitewashed cemetery on the top.

By night The end of the mole is lit: Fl.R.2s3M.

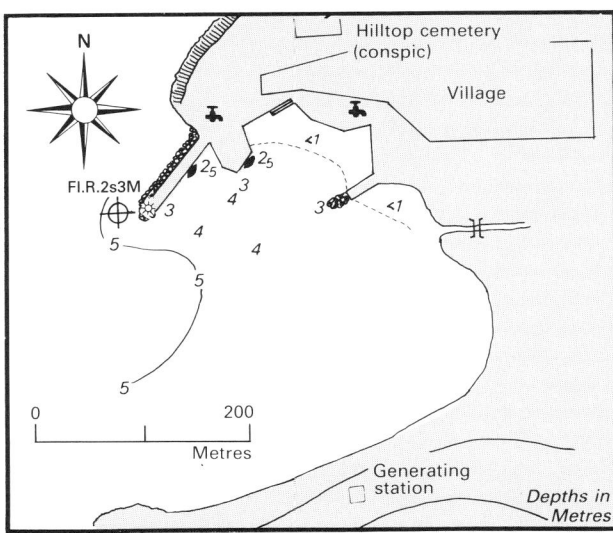

AYIOS EVSTRATIOS
39°32'·4N 24°59'·2E (Fl.R.2s3M)

Mooring

There are 3 metre depths along most of the length of the new quay and yachts can berth alongside or stern-to or bows-to. A sandy bottom with scattered rocks gives fair holding.

Shelter Reasonable shelter from the *meltemi* although a surge develops with prolonged NE winds. Open SW.

Facilities

Water On the quay.
Provisions Basic provisions only.
Eating out One taverna.
Other PO. Metered telephone at the taverna. Infrequent ferries in summer to Evia and Limnos.

General

Since the 1968 earthquake which destroyed many of the buildings the population has dwindled to about 300, almost all of whom live in the one fishing village. The new breakwater and quay were only finished at the end of 1986 and as yet there is plenty of room for visitors and no commercialism, but very little of interest to see either.

The harbour is a useful stopover between the northern Sporades and Lesvos. The rest of the island is rocky and barren, but there are some pleasant beaches and caves under the cliffs. Until recently political offenders were deported to the island.

Lesvos
(Lesbos, Mitilini, Mytilene)

One of the largest islands in the Aegean after Crete and Evia and the largest of the eastern Sporades, Lesvos is the jewel of the group. It is grander, greener and more fertile than any of the other islands. A prosperity founded on agriculture and local industry provides an economic balance rarely seen in the Greek islands and tourism simply provides the icing on the cake.

The island is roughly oval in shape with two deep landlocked gulfs on the southern side. It is mountainous throughout rising from Mt Ordhimos (512 metres, 1680ft) in the west to the twin peaks of Mt Olympus in the southeast and Mt Lebetimnos in the northeast (by coincidence they are both 958 metres or 3176ft). In the west the island is mostly barren and rocky, but the interior and the east are forested with olives, chestnuts, oak, pine and poplar, though sadly in 1992 a forest fire razed a large area. The flat land is cultivated with market gardens and fields of tobacco. The olives of Lesvos have long been celebrated and today the plump olives and Lesvos olive oil are among the best in Greece.

Just as the spacious and wooded island is pleasing to the eye, so the ancient associations are memorable ones of the gentle arts of music and philosophy. Greatest of all is the poetess Sappho who was born on Lesvos about 612BC, although it is uncertain exactly where she was born – perhaps Eressos or Mitilini.

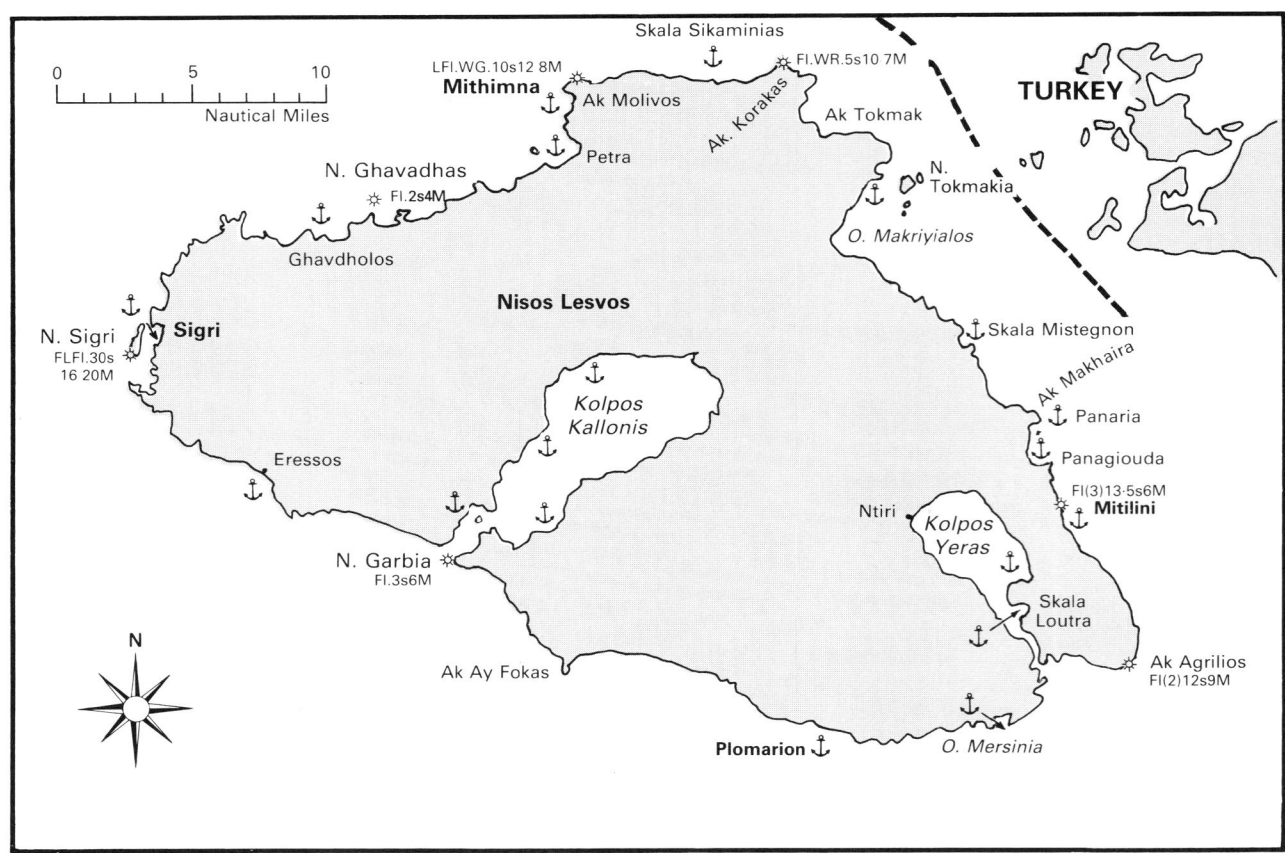

NISOS LESVOS

Allegations that Sappho was a lover of her own sex gave the word Lesbian to the world although this is based on just a few lines of her poetry (on Atthis – 'I was in love with you once Atthis, long ago...') and appears to have been contrived to cast a slur on her character and poetry after the 7th century AD. Today allegations of homosexuality matter less and we are only just beginning to uncover fragments of her poetry. For nearly 1000 years Sappho was regarded almost as a goddess, Plato called her the tenth muse and later only Catullus and Horace came close to her flowing and sensual poetry. These lines are a direct translation by Catullus:

'Godlike the man who
sits at her side, who
watches and catches
that laughter
which (softly) tears me
to tatters: nothing is
left of me, each time
I see her,
...tongue numbed; arms, legs
melting, on fire; drum
drumming in ears; head–
lights gone black.'

Sappho is said to have died in true poetic style, jumping off the cliffs on the southwest corner of Levkas when rejected by her lover Phaon – though in fact there is no real evidence that she ever visited Levkas. Still, it's an appropriately tragic story, and she was, after all, getting on for romping around with lovers.

Sappho did not emerge from a cultural vacuum. The names associated with Lesvos are a rollcall of gentle artists and wise sages: Terpander the father of Greek music; Arion the dolphin-loving poet; Alcaeus, a contemporary of Sappho; Pitticus, who united the cities of the island and whose wise rule won him a place among the Seven Sages of Greece; Epicurus, whose benign humanitarian philosophy was forgotten after Christianity and only later rediscovered; Aristotle, who resided for some time here; and Aesop who wrote many of his fables on Lesvos. Indeed it is difficult to find anybody who was nasty living on Lesvos in ancient times though I'm sure they were lurking about in the background.

The geographical position of Lesvos and its sheltered natural harbours meant that from ancient times the island was an important trade link between Asia and Greece. Mitilini is still reminiscent of the Levant and the old trading days, but the division between Greece and Turkey severed communications and destroyed the island's role as a commercial intermediary. After prosperity in ancient Greek and Roman times the island suffered from Saracen invasions and Byzantine expulsions of the invaders and not surprisingly the local inhabitants moved away from the sea to the hills. Not until the 14th century, when Lesvos was given to that remarkable Genoese adventurer Francesco Gattelusio, did the island again enjoy some measure of calm and prosperity. For a century the island was once more a trading centre. In 1462 the Turks occupied Lesvos and it effectively remained under Turkish occupation until 1912.

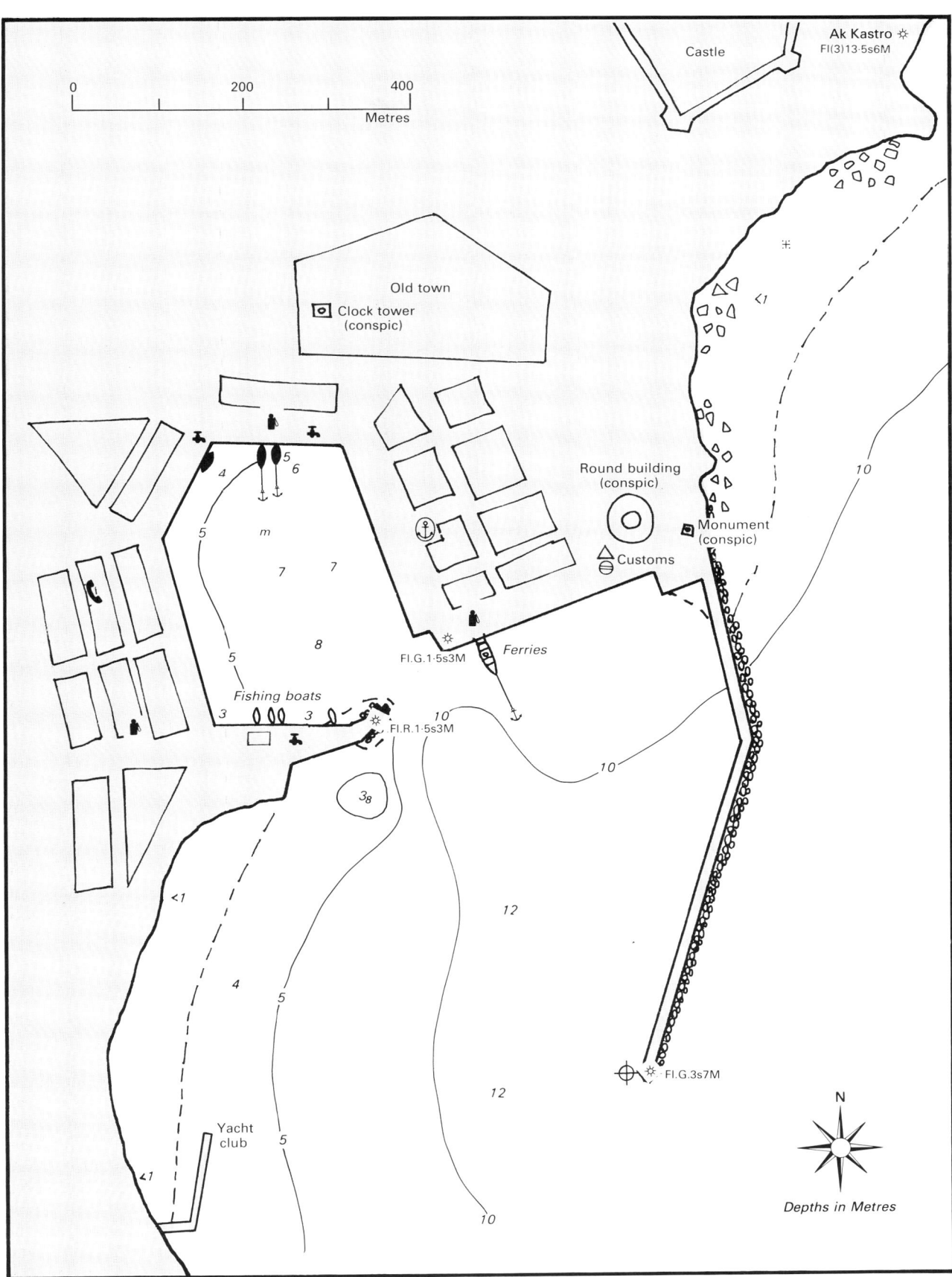

Castle

Ak Kastro ☼
Fl(3)13·5s6M

0   200   400
Metres

Old town
⬛ Clock tower
(conspic)

Round building
(conspic)

⬛ Monument
(conspic)

△ Customs
⊖

4   5
6

5

m

7   7

8

5

Fishing boats

3   3

Fl.G.1·5s3M

Ferries

Fl.R.1·5s3M

10

10

3₈

<1

12

4

5

Fl.G.3s7M

12

5

Yacht
club

<1

10

N

Depths in Metres

MITILINI
39°06′N 26°33′·8E (Fl.G.7M)

The heritage of the island is largely literary and cultural and its archaeological remains are few and undistinguished. It was Sappho who said that poets attain immortality and long after hewn stones have gone, her poetry and her loves will be remembered.

MITILINI (Mytilene)
Admiralty chart no. 1664

Approach
Conspicuous The buildings of the town and the castle on the headland are conspicuous from some distance off. Closer in, a large circular building and a monument in front of it are conspicuous. The outer breakwater and harbour entrance are easily identified.

By night Use the lights on the castle headland (Fl(3)13·5s6M), on the outer breakwater (Fl.G.3s7M), and at the entrance to the inner basin (Fl.G.1·5s3M and Fl.R.1·5s3M). The Fl.G at the entrance to the inner basin is weak and cannot be confused with the Fl.G on the outer breakwater.

Mooring
Proceed into the inner harbour and moor alongside or stern-to or bows-to at the N end. The bottom is soft mud and some plough-type anchors will drag through it. The harbour can be smelly at times from sewerage emptying into it.

Shelter Good all-round shelter although the harbour can be uncomfortable with strong S winds. Moor in the SW corner of the inner harbour during these winds.

Authorities A port of entry: port police, customs and immigration authorities.

Note The harbour on the N side of the peninsula is not well protected and is used only by a few coastal trading *caïques* and fishing boats in fine weather.

Facilities
Water On the quay by arrangement with the resident 'water man'.

Fuel Near the quay. A mini-tanker can deliver.

Repairs General mechanical repairs and light engineering work. A yard on the N side of the castle can haul yachts. Good hardware and tool shops. Limited chandlery.

Provisions Excellent shopping for all provisions. Ouzo and brandy from the barrel. Ice available out of town.

Eating out Good tavernas including some good fish tavernas on the S mole.

Other PO. OTE. Banks. Greek gas and *Camping Gaz*. Hire cars and motorbikes. Buses to the principal towns and villages. Ferries to Piraeus and Ayvalik in Turkey. Internal flights to Athens.

General
Mitilini is the commercial heart of the island. Coasters, trading *caïques* and large fishing craft clutter the harbour. The town hums with local

Mitilini – its architecture and atmosphere still very much a part of the Levant.

industry. In the old town the narrow winding streets are lined with market stalls and local craft shops – the atmosphere is redolent of an Oriental bazaar. The whole combines into a likable Levantine mixture and the city, at first noisy and grubby, in the end charms the visitor.

On the waterfront and scattered around the outskirts of Mitilini are some grand old baronial houses dating from the prosperous mercantile era of the harbour. The archaeological museum houses finds from the classical period and some wonderful mosaics from a Roman villa showing figures from Menander's comedies.

PANAGIOUDA
The small harbour of Panagioudia lies close NW of Ak Asfali (Kara tepe), the prominent cape 1¾ miles N of Mitilini. There is little room for a yacht but with care a small yacht can go bows-to the quay off the village where there are depths of 1·5–1·75 metres. There are 2·5 metres in the entrance but care is needed not to stray to either side on the W or NE where it is shallow. Good shelter from the *meltemi*. Provisions and tavernas ashore.

PANARIA
Lying close under Ak Makhaira there is an attractive bay sheltered from the *meltemi*. Anchor at the head of the bay N of the islet in 4–6 metres. Taverna ashore.

SKALA MISTEGNON
Lying 7 miles NW of Mitilini, this is the small harbour for the village of Mistegnon on the hill above. The harbour is open to the SE for a limited

Mitilini. The entrance to the inner harbour.

sector. Moor bows-to the outer end of the mole taking care of the ballasting which extends underwater. The mole is usually crowded with local fishing boats so you will probably have to anchor in the more exposed S half of the bay. The bottom is mostly sand and weed with some rock patches.

Tavernas ashore and most supplies can be obtained in the village above.

Ancient Thermis is about 3 miles S. The hot mineral springs still exist and a hotel has been built nearby. The springs were famous in the ancient world and a temple to Artemis and a complex of baths were excavated by the British School of Archaeology in the early 1930s.

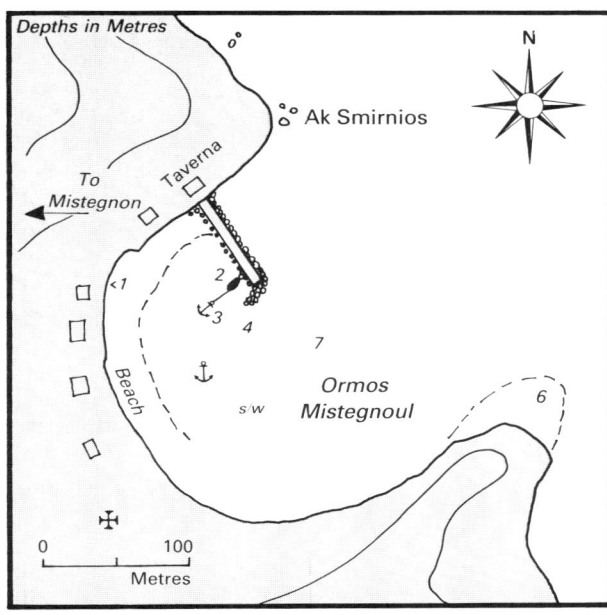

SKALA MISTEGNON
39°13′N 26°29′E

ORMOS MAKRI YIALOS

In the large bay of Makri Yialos SW of Ak Tokmak there are a number of coves on the N side providing some shelter from the *meltemi*.

Caution Ormos Makri Yialos and Tokmakia Nisoi in the bay are fringed by above- and below-water rocks. Caution must be exercised in this area. Approximately one mile S of Ak Tokmak a reef extends for some 400 metres in a NE direction from the shore. In the S part of Ormos Makri Yialos there is an islet known as Praselogos or Erimonisi which is fringed by underwater rocks. Special care must be taken of these as they are not well marked on the chart.

SKALA SIKAMINIAS

One and a half miles SW of Ak Korakas lies the miniature fishing harbour of Skala Sikaminias in which there is room for 1 or 2 small yachts drawing no more than 1·5 metres. Moor bows-to the extremity of the mole. Good shelter with N winds but in strong NE winds the harbour could be dangerous. A taverna and limited provisions available in the fishing hamlet.

MITHIMNA (Methymna, Molivos)

Approach

Conspicuous The castle on the hill above the town is conspicuous from some distance off. Closer in, the town and the huddle of buildings around the small harbour at the foot of the hill can be seen.

By night Care needed. Use the light on Ak Molivos (LFl.WG.10s12/8M green sector covers 219°-239° only) and the light at Mithimna (F.R.3M).

Dangers

1. Above- and below-water rocks fringe Ak Molivos and the harbour mole for some distance. The harbour should be entered from the SE.

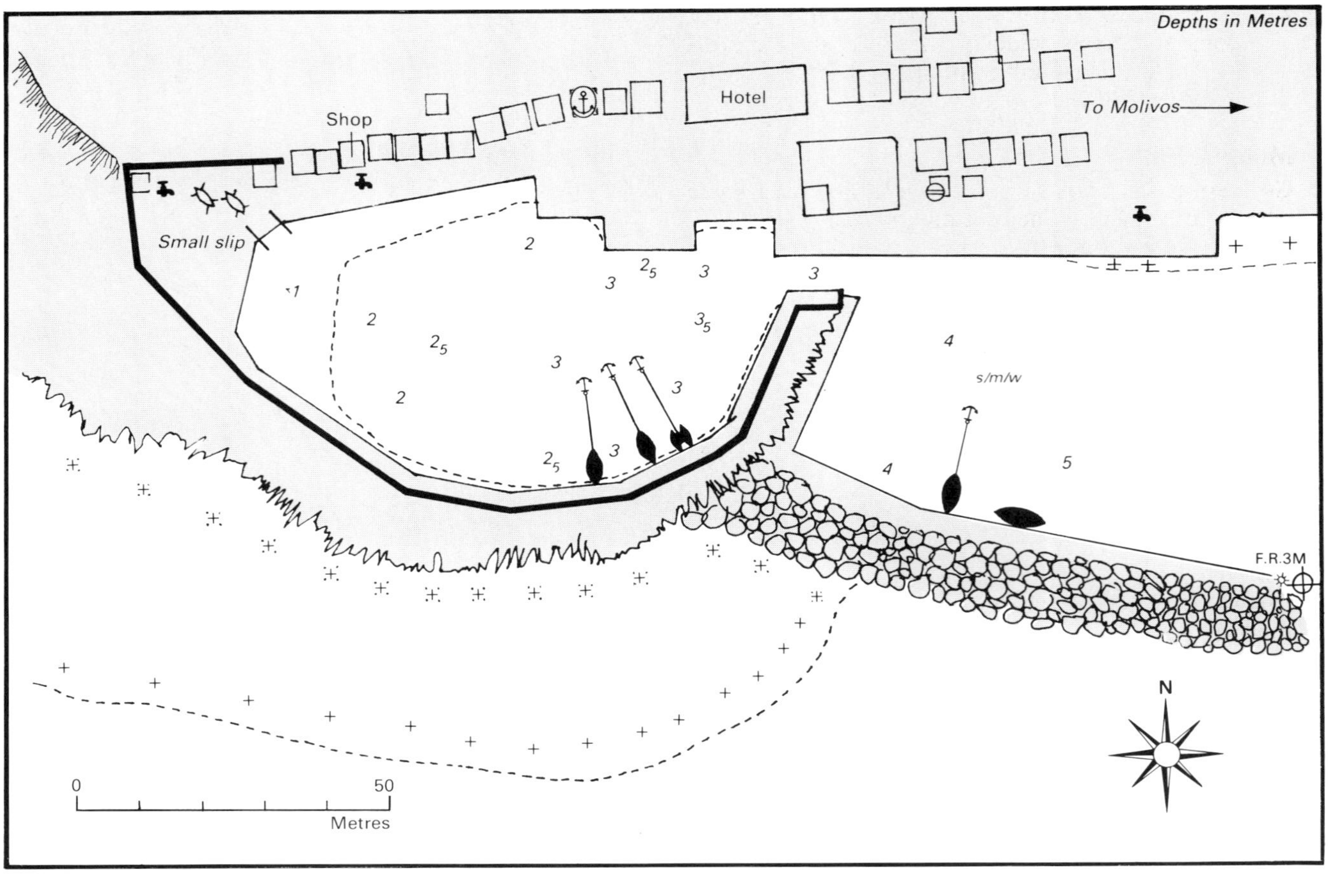

MITHIMNA
39°21'·8N 26°10'·2E (F.R.3M)

Mithimna harbour looking W from the road to the town. The new quayed area is here still under construction.

2. The entrance to the inner basin is very narrow (about 10 metres wide but free of obstructions) and small yachts only will be able to enter the harbour which is crowded with fishing boats.

Mooring

Go stern-to or bows-to or alongside the outer mole where convenient. The bottom is mud, sand and weed, good holding. In the inner basin there is little room amongst the fishing boats. The bottom in the inner basin is thin mud over rock, bad holding.

Shelter Good shelter in the outer part of the harbour and excellent shelter in the inner basin.

Authorities Port police and customs.

Anchorage In calm weather a yacht can anchor in the bay, but a swell sets in with the *meltemi* and the holding is uncertain.

Facilities

Water On the quay.

Provisions Good shopping for all provisions in the town. Ice on the quay.

Eating out Good tavernas in the town and around the harbour.

Other PO. OTE. Bank. Hire bikes. Bus to Mitilini.

General

Arion, the lyric poet (625BC), who was saved from drowning by a music-loving dolphin, was born here. Presumably his spirit survives as the town has developed into something of an artists' resort as well as a tourist resort.

The town is a maze of cobbled streets and passages winding in and out of medieval fortifications and a historical preservation order will hopefully keep it that way. The stone and timber houses, many with small timber balconies, look over the cliffs to the bay beneath. A growing number of tourists come to Mithimna as not only is the town pleasant and near to good bathing beaches, but the locals are welcoming – the clink of glasses will often be heard late into the night.

PETRA (Kavaki)

A small village off a sandy beach under Ak Kavaki. There is a small harbour N of Petra village on the S side of Ak Kavaki. Anchor off the village in 5–10 metres on sand and weed. Poor shelter from the *meltemi* here. Under the mole on the N side of the bay there is reasonable shelter from the *meltemi*. Go stern-to or bows-to the outer end of the mole. A few fishing boats are kept here but otherwise it is deserted.

The village of Petra is a sleepy place with some modest tourism in the summer. Some provisions can be obtained and there are tavernas. The bay and the village are a delight being wooded and well-watered. In the village the church of Panayia Glykofiloussa built on a rocky bluff near the beach stands out from seaward.

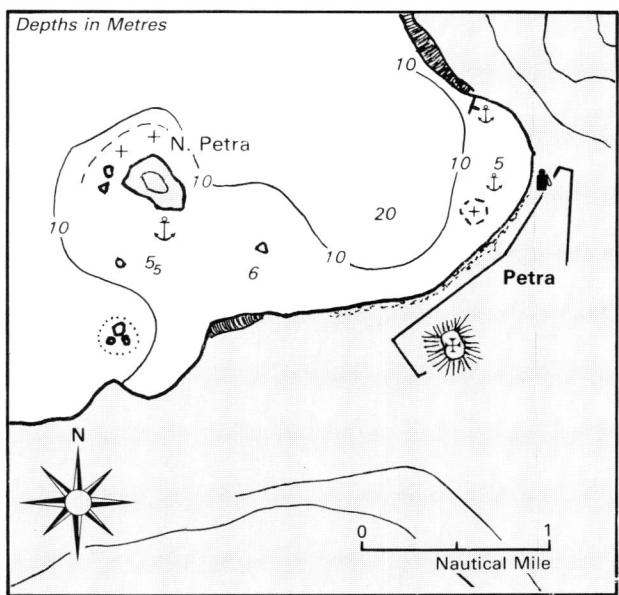

PETRA

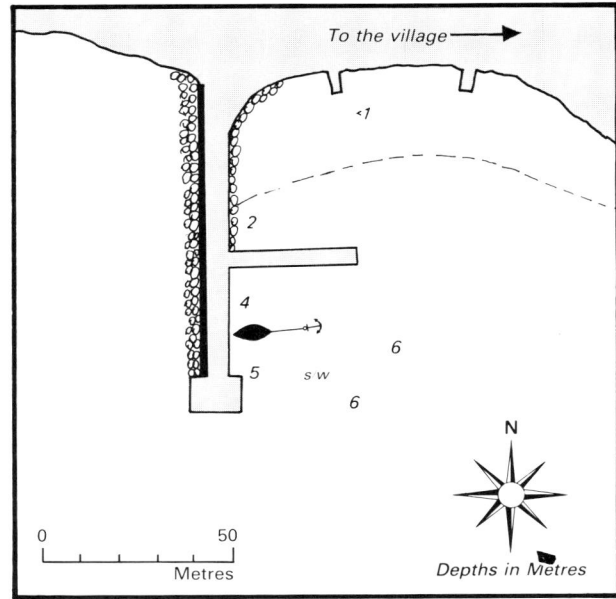

PETRA
39°20'·5N 26°10'·5E

Caution Care is needed of the reef in the bay off the village. A stick sometimes marks the reef but is not to be relied upon. In calm weather it is possible to anchor under the islet to the W – care is needed in the vicinity of the islet and the above- and below-water rocks around it.

GHAVDHOLOS

Approach

The islet to the E of the harbour and the church and bell-tower on the headland are conspicuous. Once around the island the mole and harbour entrance are easily identified.

Mooring

Go stern-to or bows-to or alongside the mole where there is room. The bottom is mud and weed, good holding. Good shelter from the *meltemi*.

Dangers You will have to turn sharply to starboard to avoid the shallows on the W side of the harbour.

Facilities

Water near the quay. Some provisions in the village and a taverna.

General

The little village is a friendly place where the locals eke out a living fishing or cultivating the fertile land around the head of the bay. There are reported to be hot springs here, but although I got whiffs of sulphuretted hydrogen from the shore by the village, I couldn't find them.

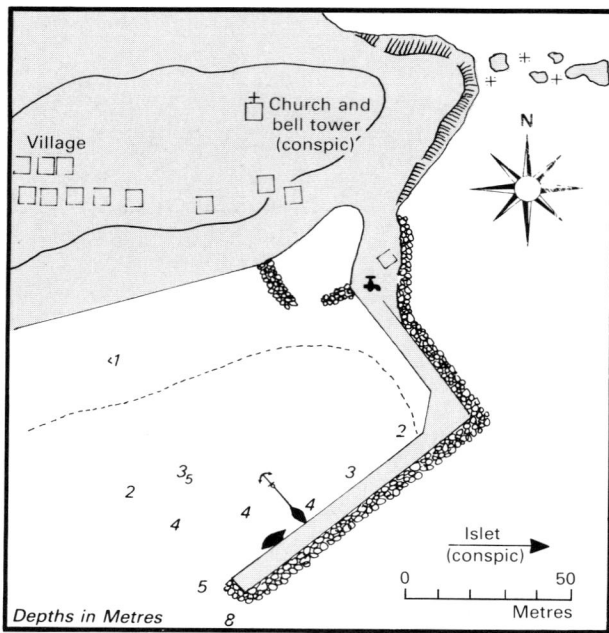

GHAVDHOLOS 39°17′N 25°58′·5E

Ghavdholos looking SE from the hamlet.

LIMIN SIGRIOU (Sigri)
Admiralty chart no. 1668

Approach

From the N the narrow N channel between Nisos Sigri and Lesvos can be used by day. The reef extending NE from Nisos Sigri is marked by breakers. In the S channel between Nisis Sedhousa and Lesvos there are considerable depths.

Conspicuous From the S, Nisis Sedhousa, the lighthouse on Nisos Sigri and Sigri village are conspicuous.

By night Use the light on Nisos Sigri (FFl.30sF16,Fl20M) and the light on Ak Saratsina (Fl.WR.3s5/3M red sector covers 122°-160° and 219°-239°). Care is needed in a night approach from the S. The N channel should not be attempted at night under any circumstances. The NW corner of the quay is lit Fl.2s3M.

Dangers Care is needed in the N channel when a heavy sea is running and breakers heap up over the shoal water in the vicinity and the channel itself.

Mooring

Anchor in the cove on the S side of Sigri village or go alongside the quay tucked as far as possible into the

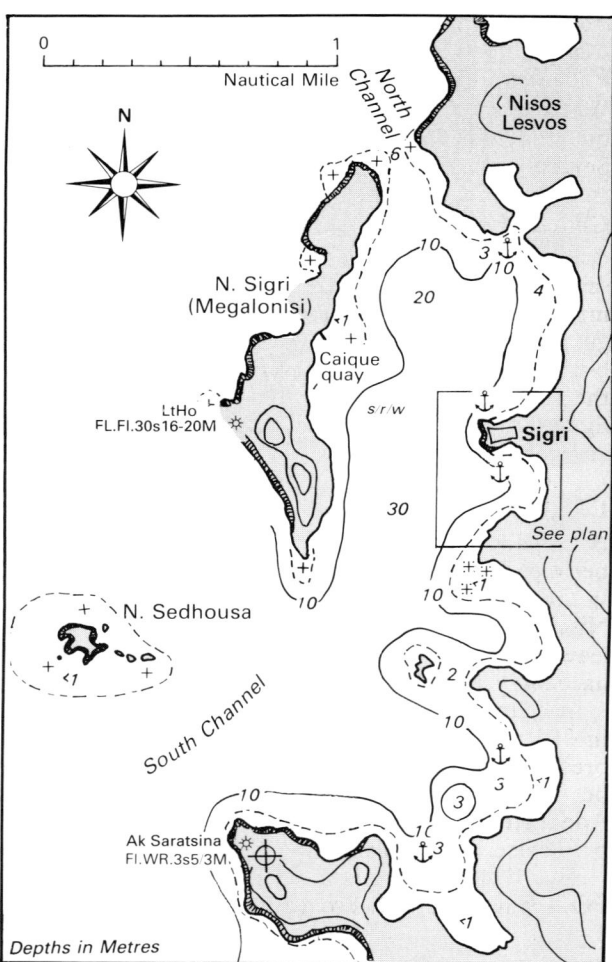

APPROACHES TO SIGRI
39°11′·4N 25°50′E (Ak Saratsina light)

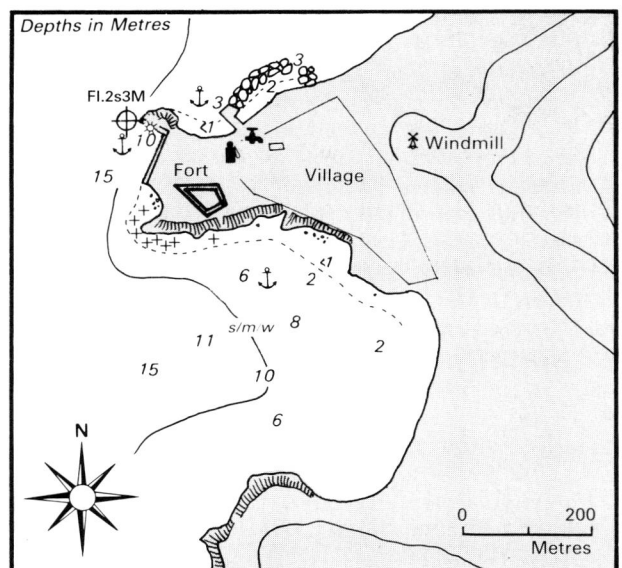

PORT SIGRI
39°12'·7N 25°50'·8E (Fl.2s3M)

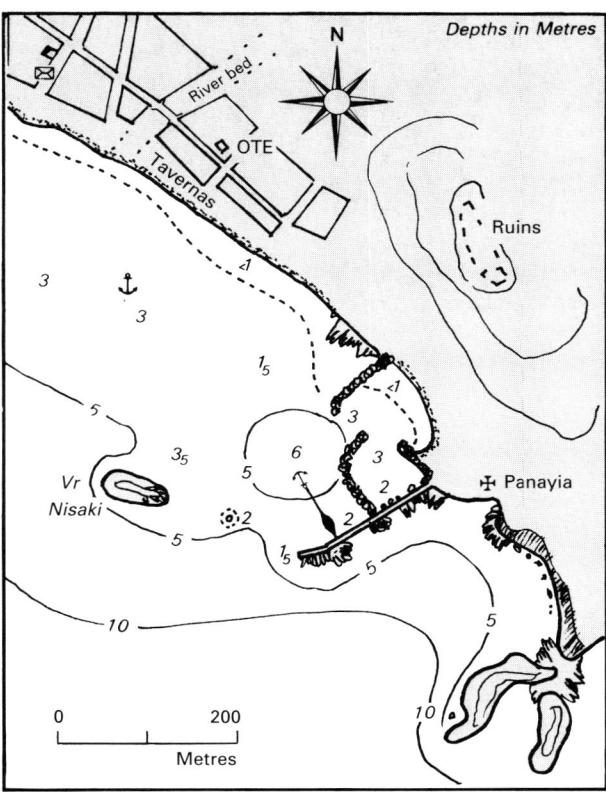

ERRESOS

NE corner. The bottom is sand, weed and rock and is poor holding in patches.

Shelter It can get a little bumpy on the quay, but not dangerous unless the wind turns to the W or S in which case anchor N of the promontory.

Authorities Customs.

Facilities

Water near the *caïque* harbour. Fuel near the new quay. PO. OTE. Most provisions can be obtained. Several tavernas and cafés. Bus to Mitilini.

General

A few tourists visit this fishing village for the nearby sandy beaches, but for the most part life carries on much as it has always done. Sigri is noted in most guide books for its petrified forest on the W coast, but most visitors are not impressed by the sight. For the yachtsman the petrified remains near the lighthouse on Nisis Sigri (Megalonisi) are more accessible.

ERRESOS

A small fishing harbour approximately midway between Sigriou and Kolpos Kalloni. Care is needed in the approaches of a rock just awash between Vrak. Nisaki and the end of the breakwater. A yacht should leave Nisaki to starboard in the approaches to the harbour.

In calm weather a yacht can anchor off the beach in 2–4 metres or go stern or bows-to the end of the breakwater if there is room. Small yachts may find a berth inside the small basin with local boats. Adequate shelter from the prevailing winds on the breakwater. Open S and W.

The village ashore is a small and amicable resort. PO. Exchange office. Provisions and tavernas. Taxis.

KOLPOS KALLONI
Admiralty chart no. 1668

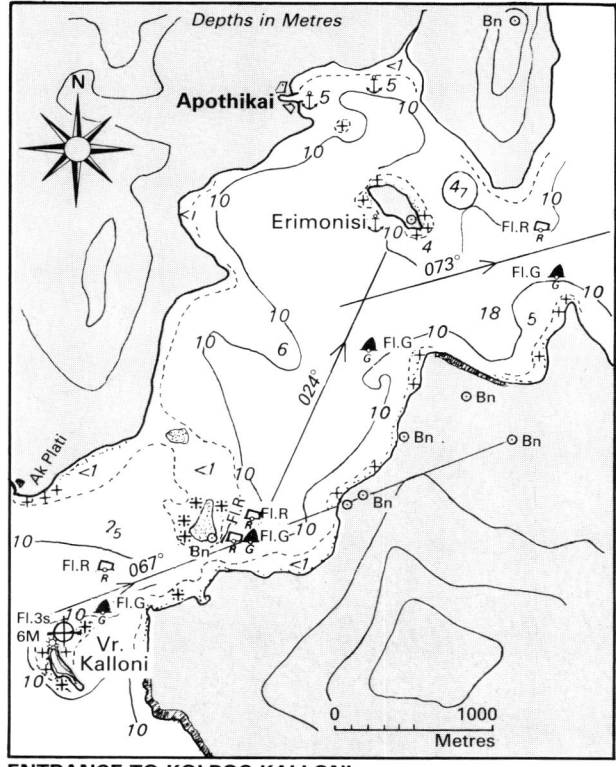

ENTRANCE TO KOLPOS KALLONI
39°04'·7N 26°04'·7E (Vr. Kalloni light)

Approach and entrance

The narrow mountainous entrance to this large landlocked gulf is easily negotiated by day. Proceed on the N side of Nisis Garbia taking care of the reef marked by buoys and by a beacon on the extremity extending 0·15 miles NE of it. The channel is of the shoal water extending from the NW side of the entrance.

By night Not recommended despite the lights available. Use the light on Nisis Garbia (Fl.3s6M) and the light·buoys marking the channel (Fl.R and Fl.G).

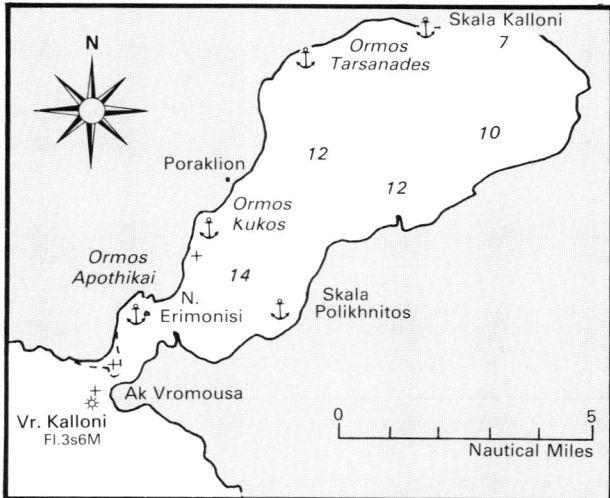

KOLPOS KALLONI

Anchorages in the gulf

1. *Ormiskos Apothikai* This bay on the N side of the entrance affords the best shelter in the gulf. Care must be taken of the reefs and shoal water around Erimonisi and the isolated reef just off the W entrance to the bay. Anchor in the bay in 5–10 metres or go bows-to the short pier where there are 3 metre depths off the end, though care must be taken of rock ballasting. A number of fishermen and their families inhabit the hamlet and in a simple taverna at the root of the pier simple fare is served.

Ormos Apothikai looking SE.

2. *Ormos Kukos* A bay approximately 2½ miles N of the entrance to the gulf. Anchor in 8–10 metres. Some shelter from the *meltemi*.
3. *Parakilon* A bight just above Kukos. Anchor in 4–6 metres off a small breakwater. Poor shelter from the *meltemi*.
4. *Ormos Tarsanades* A bight in the NW corner of the gulf. Poor shelter from the *meltemi*.
5. *Skala Kalloni* An L-shaped mole protects a small harbour at the head of the gulf. There are 1·5–2 metre depths along the outer end of the mole. Go alongside if possible. Further inside it gets shallow. Alternatively anchor off the beach. Provisions and tavernas ashore. PO.
6. *Skala Polikhnitos* A small harbour just E of the entrance to the gulf. The harbour has 2 metre depths in the entrance and 2 metre depths off the short E mole. There are 2–3 metre depths in the middle of the harbour and 2·5 or better depths under the outer W mole. Go bows-to (there is some underwater ballasting) either mole. Good protection from the *meltemi*.

Water on the quay and fuel nearby. Some provisions and tavernas ashore.

Note With the *meltemi* there are fierce gusts into Kolpos Kalloni and a considerable sea can be raised despite the limited fetch.

PLOMARION (Plomari)
Admiralty chart no. 1664

Approach

Conspicuous The town is conspicuous from some distance off. A cathedral with belfry behind the harbour is conspicuous. The harbour moles and light structures are easily identified.

By night Use the lights at the entrance: F.G.2M and F.R.2M.

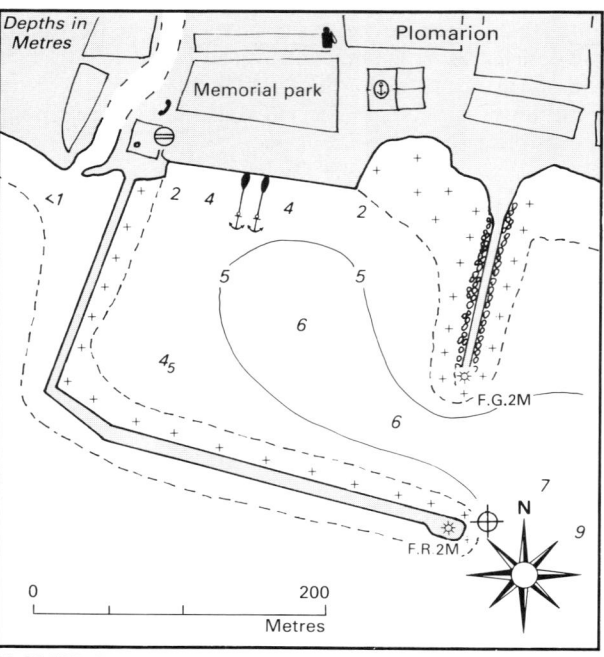

PLOMARION
38°58'·4N 26°22'·2E (F.R.2M)

Plomarion harbour looking SE from the town.

Mooring

Go stern-to or bows-to or alongside the projecting quay. The bottom is sand with some rocks.

Shelter Good shelter from the *meltemi* although somehow a surge can develop making it uncomfortable. With S winds a swell enters the harbour. Nonetheless the fishing boats are kept here in the winter in the SW corner of the harbour.

Authorities Port police and customs.

Facilities

Water On the quay.
Fuel In the town.
Repairs Some mechanical repairs possible. General hardware shops.
Provisions Excellent shopping for provisions. Wine and *ouzo* can be bought from the barrel.
Eating out Good local tavernas in the town.
Other PO. OTE. Bank. Hire bikes. Bus to Mitilini.

General

Plomarion was established in the 19th century (as Bilmar) when the islanders moved down to the shores after piracy had been suppressed. Narrow cobbled streets and passages wind in and out of the stone and timber houses built in a Turkish style with wooden balconies. Behind the town the countryside is covered in olive groves and thick chestnut and pine forest so that the town, sandwiched between the sea and the mountains, is a wonderful place. Plomarion is also famous for its ouzo, marketed as *Barbajanis Ouzo*, which is praised by connoisseurs of the aniseed-flavoured brew all over the northern Aegean.

ORMOS MERSINIA

A large bay lying 3 miles SW of the entrance to Kolpos Yeras. It is a double-headed bay. Anchor at the head of the W cove in 4–10 metres. The bottom is sand and weed – good holding. Good shelter from the *meltemi*. Taverna ashore. Alternatively anchor in the E cove in 5–10 metres.

The bay sits under heavily wooded slopes and is a delightful place. There is also a good anchorage in Ormos Tarti immediately W.

KOLPOS YERAS
Admiralty chart no. 1664

Approach and entrance

This second landlocked gulf lies about 25 miles E of Kolpos Kalloni. The approach is straightforward by day but should not be attempted at night. Keeping well clear of Ak Kavourolimni which has a reef running N of it, pass between the cape and Vrak Kaloyeros, a reef marked by a beacon. Leave the beacon about 150 metres to starboard and proceed up the channel leaving Reef Rock (Vromonisi) and Square Rock (Ay Vasilios) to port.

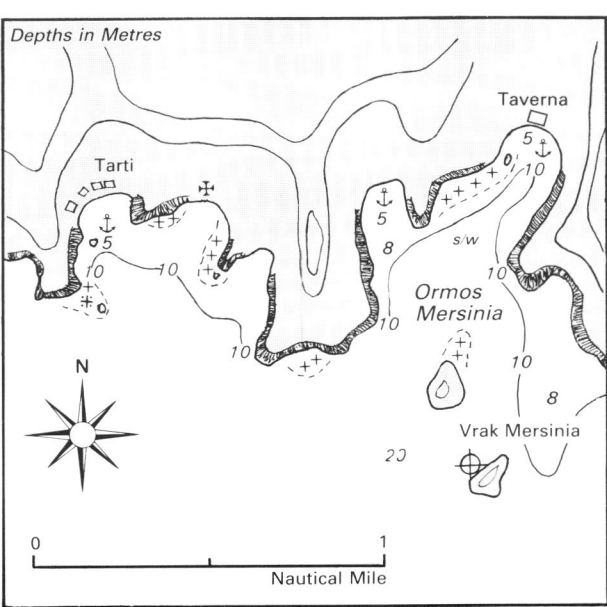

ORMOS MERSINIA 38°58'N 26°30'.8E (Vrak Mersinia)

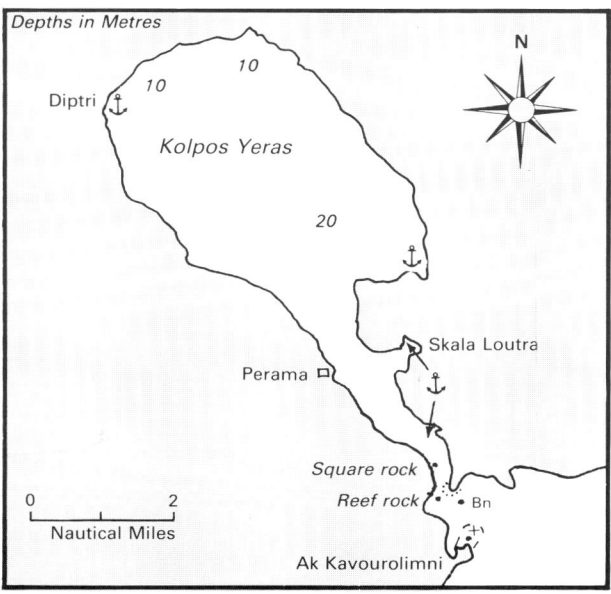

KOLPOS YERAS

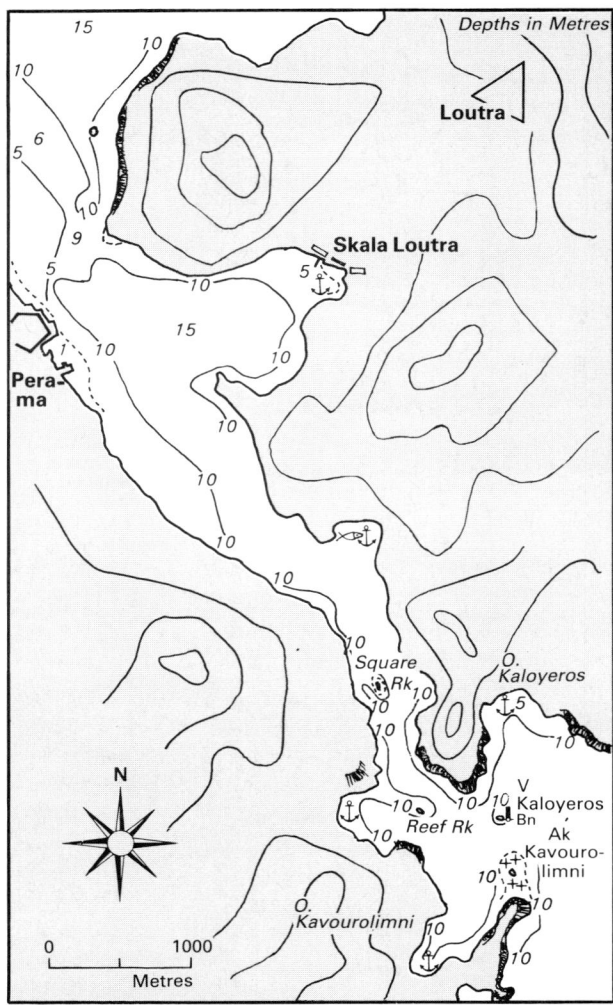

ENTRANCE TO KOLPOS YERAS

Anchorages in the gulf

1. *Skala Loutra* The bay on the E side of the entrance channel. Anchor in 5–10 metres on mud. There are 2–4 metre depths off most of the short pier. Water ashore. Several café/tavernas. A yard on the E side of the bay.

2. In the cove in the entrance channel S of Loutra. There is now a fish farm here, but there is still room to anchor.

3. *Diptri (Nipti)* In the NW corner of the gulf. There are 5 metre depths off the extremity of the mole and a taverna ashore.

4. SE corner. In settled weather there is a delightful cove in the SE corner of the gulf.

5. *Perama* On the W side of the entrance channel. In calm weather a yacht can go bows-to the end of the pier where there are reported to be 2·5 metre depths. It is a shabby place and the water is polluted by the nearby tannery. Port police.

6. *Ormiskos Kavourolimni* The bay tucked under the W entrance point to the gulf. Also just N of Kavourolimni on the W side there is an attractive bay.

7. *Ormos Kaloyeras* The bay tucked under the E entrance point looks to offer good shelter from the *meltemi*.

Skala Loutra in Kolpos Yeras.

Note With the *meltemi* blowing the gusts into the gulf are not as fierce as those blowing into Kolpos Kalloni.

Khios and adjacent islands

Psara

Psara is a small barren island lying 10 miles west of the north of Khios. Together with Spetsai and Hydra, Psara was one of the first islands to revolt against the Turks. Its ships harried Turkish shipping along the coast scoring some notable successes. On a number of occasions the Turks mounted expeditions to squash the small island community, but were unable to land because of bad weather until June 1824. In that year Hosref Pasha landed a large force and massacred the population. A few survivors established Nea Psara (Eretria) on Evia. The island has never recovered.

Psara harbour looking NE.

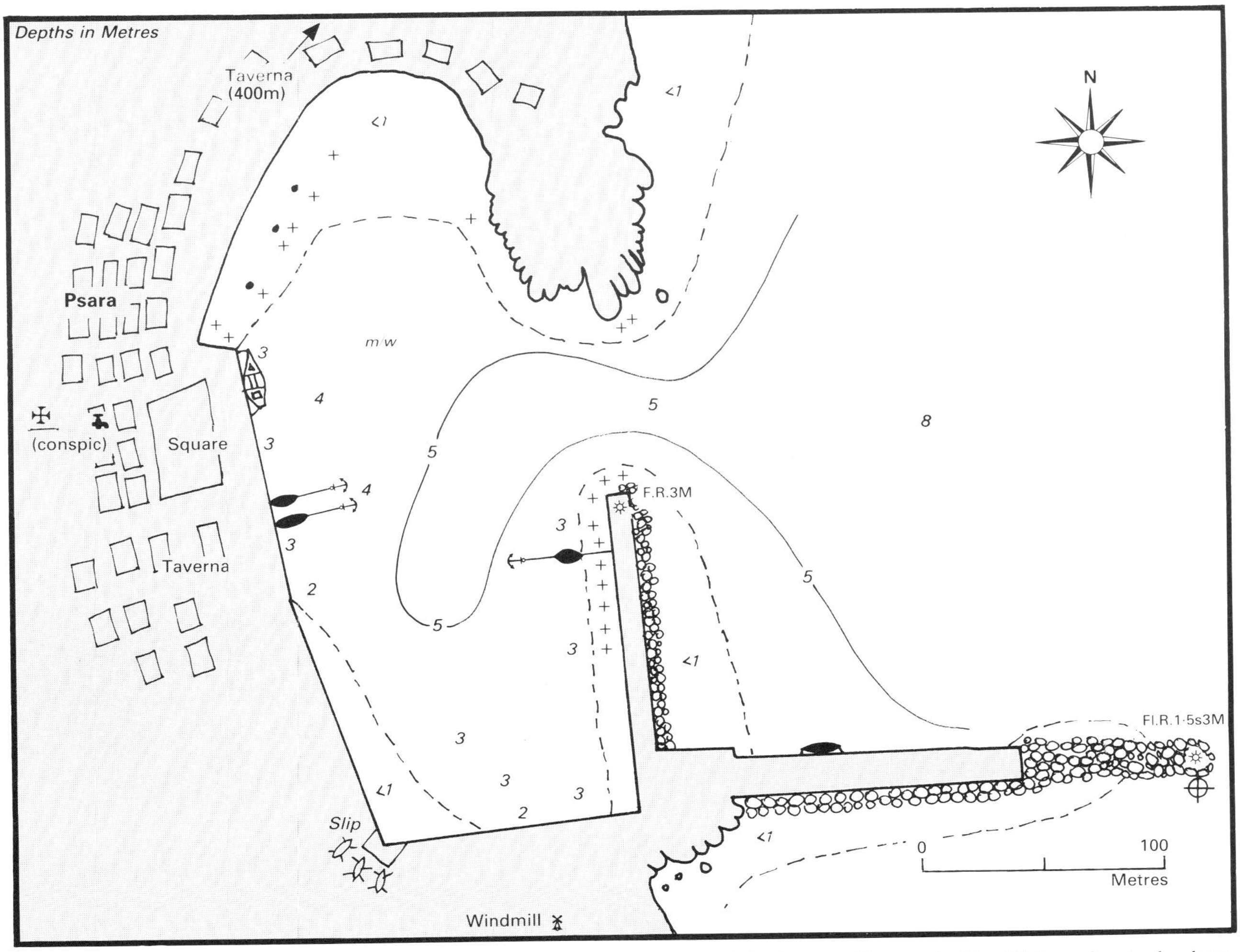

Depths in Metres

Taverna
(400m)

N

Psara

(conspic)   Square

Taverna

m w

F.R.3M

F.R.1·5s3M

Slip

0   100

Metres

Windmill

PSARA
38°32'·4N 25°34'·1E (Fl.R.3M)

Mandraki harbour on Oinoussa looking W from close to the short
N mole.

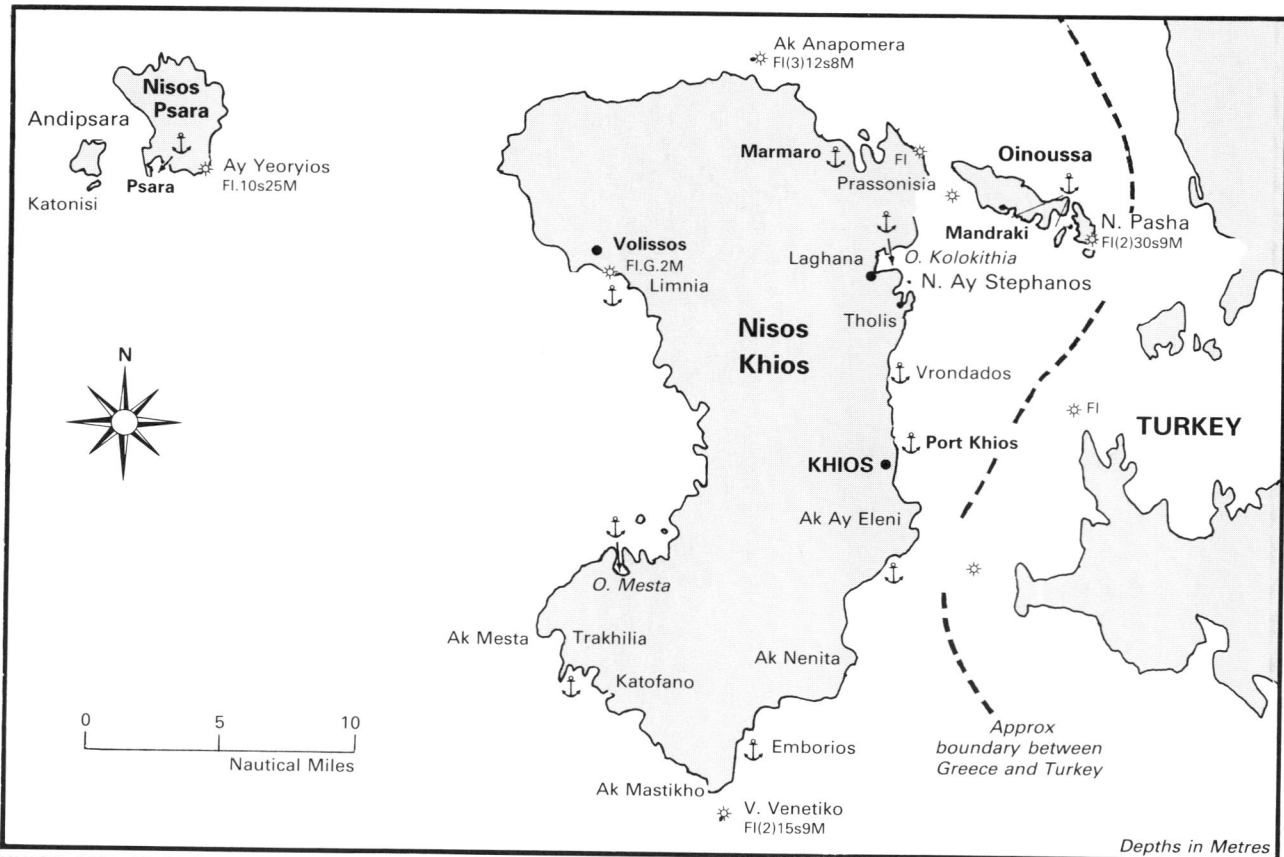

KHIOS AND ADJACENT ISLANDS

PSARA
Admiralty chart no. 1568

Approach
Conspicuous The small village on the low ridge of Ak Trifilli is easily seen from the distance. Two large churches in the village are conspicuous from the E and S. The mole will not be seen until close to.

By night Use the light on Ak Ay Yeoryios (Fl.10s25M) and the light at the entrance (Fl.R.1·5s3M). The inner mole is lit: F.R.3M. The harbour lights are not always to be relied on.

Dangers When approaching from the W care should be taken of the reefs fringing Nisis Andipsara and Vrakhonisis Katonisi. These islands and rocks are not lit at night making a night approach from the W difficult.

Mooring
Go stern-to or bows-to where convenient. The bottom is mud and weed with some rocks – good holding.

Shelter Good all-round shelter although strong NE winds may make it uncomfortable.

Authorities Port police.

Facilities
Water Limited supplies on the island.
Provisions Limited provisions available but the villagers are dependent on the ferry from Khios for many things
Eating out Café/taverna.
Other PO. Local ferry to Khios.

General
There is little left of what was a prosperous town: a few crumbling houses and warehouses, windmills on the ridges and the large natural harbour. Inland amongst the scorched rock of the island (there is little good earth for cultivation) is a Mycenaean necropolis though it has not been systematically excavated to date. Homer mentioned the island; he called it Psyrie, but said nothing about it, and apart from the brief age when it possessed a fine merchant fleet and lost it all against the Turks, to most people including Greeks the name Psara means little or nothing to this day.

Oinoussa

This barren island lies just over a mile to the east of the north of Khios. At one time it supported a prosperous seafaring community, but today the population is much diminished.

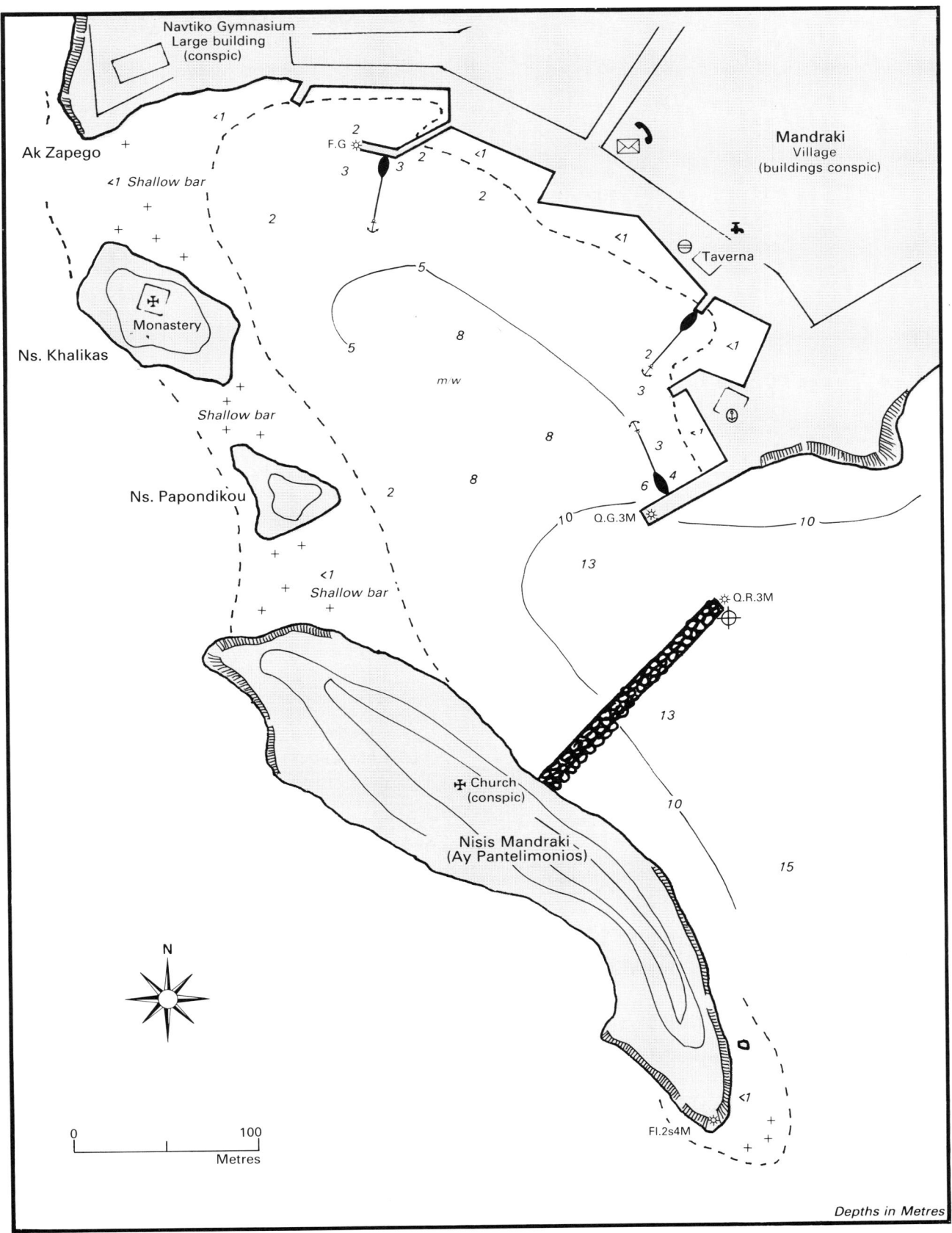

Navtiko Gymnasium
Large building
(conspic)

Ak Zapego

<1 *Shallow bar*

F.G

Monastery

Ns. Khalikas

Shallow bar

Ns. Papondikou

<1 *Shallow bar*

Mandraki
Village
(buildings conspic)

Taverna

Q.G.3M

Q.R.3M

Church
(conspic)

Nisis Mandraki
(Ay Pantelimonios)

Fl.2s4M

N

0   100
Metres

Depths in Metres

MANDRAKI (Oinoussa)
38°30′·6N 26°13′·2E (Q.R.3M)

379

MANDRAKI (Oinoussa)

Approach

Conspicuous From the S the village is conspicuous from the distance. From the N Vrak. Prassonisia and the light structure on it are easily identified. Closer in the church and light structure on Nisis Mandraki (Ay Pantelimonios) are easily seen and rounding Mandraki the harbour mole will be seen.

By night Use the light on Prassonisia (Fl(2)10s5M), on Nisis Mandraki (Fl.2s4M), and the lights at the entrance (Q.G.3M and Q.R.3M). The pier inside is lit: F.G.3M.

Caution The island of Oinoussa is fringed by reefs. Care should be taken of the reef lying approximately half a mile SE of Prassonisia – it usually has breaking water over it. There are 10 metre depths in the fairway between this reef and Nisis Oinoussa. The three islets protecting Mandraki harbour are joined to one another by shallow rock-bound bars and there is no entrance between them.

Mooring

Moor stern-to or bows-to where convenient or anchor off. The bottom is mud and weed – good holding.

Shelter Good all-round shelter: a yacht can always find somewhere secure to moor in the harbour, even with strong SE winds which do not blow home.

Authorities Port police and customs.

Facilities

Water A tap near the quay.

Provisions Some provisions can be obtained but the villagers are largely dependent on the local ferry from Khios.

Eating out A few tavernas – fresh fish is sometimes available.

Other PO. Local ferry to Khios.

General

Closing the harbour, one gains the impression that Oinoussa is a large and prosperous village, but on closer inspection many of the large and once elegant houses are shuttered and in need of a lick of paint. That is because the island's ship owners no longer live here, but in New York, London, Paris, Athens, or wherever the high life and big business come together. This apparently insignificant little island has produced the richest ship-owning families of Greece including the richest of them all, Costa Lemos. Contrary to popular belief the biggest and richest Greek shipping magnate is not Niarchos or the late Onassis, but this private man whose name means nothing to most people. Apparently Greek ship owners control some 70 million tons of shipping, the same tonnage as all the EC countries put together.

NISIS PASHA AND CHANNEL (Pasha)
Admiralty chart no. 1568

Nisis Pasha lies off the E end of Nisos Oinoussa separated by a narrow channel with 3·5 metres least depth in the fairway. The W coast of Nisis Pasha is indented with several bays and coves which offer good shelter from the *meltemi*. A bay on the E coast of Nisos Oinoussa also offers good shelter. The bottom is mostly sand with some weed – reported to be indifferent holding.

Recently a number of fish farms have sprung up in several of the bays and coves restricting the amount of space available around the island, though there is still room enough to find shelter here.

Caution The coasts of Oinoussa, Nisis Pasha and the islets in this area are fringed by reefs. By day these are readily picked out but care must be taken as the sketch plan can only show these reefs crudely.

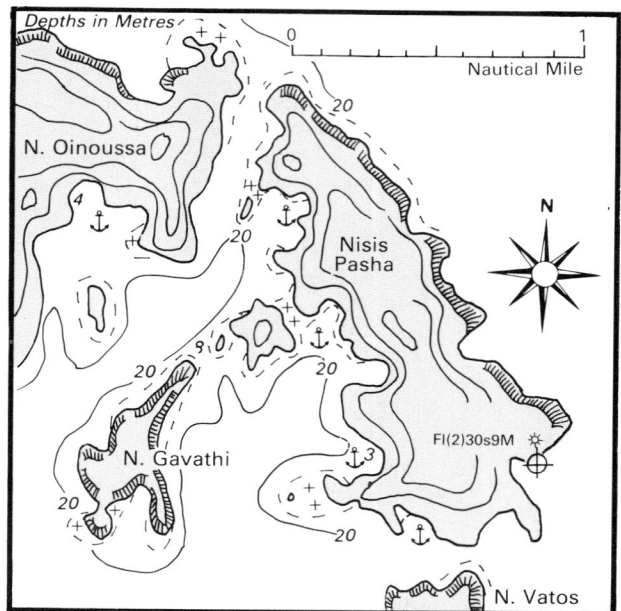

NISIS PASHA
38°30'·1N 26°17'·7E (Pasha light)

Khios
(Chios, Hios)

Many islands claim to be the birthplace of Homer, but Khios seems to be the most likely. Homer called the island 'craggy' and the epithet is deserved. Much of Khios, especially the high mountain ridge running from Mt Profitis Ilias (1297 metres, 4255ft) in the north and terminating in low-lying Ak Mastikho in the south, is a lunar landscape of parched and pitted rock. Only on the northwest coast where thick pine forest covers the lower slopes and on the fertile plains in the south does the island bear any resemblance to ancient descriptions praising its fertility. In fact both the geography and history of Khos are like a pattern that has been broken so many times that the original concept has been forgotten. Fertile plains rise up to barren rock, a severe plateau descends to a wooded valley, and the valley ends in a rocky bay scarred and broken by the sea.

The ancient history of Khios was illustrious enough but it has been somewhat overwhelmed by the tragedy of contemporary history. The name of the island was possibly derived from a word of Phoenician origin meaning 'mastic'. Along with Samos and Smyrna (Izmir), Khios became part of the Ionic Confederacy and enjoyed a considerable measure of affluence in which the arts prospered. Homer, that 'blind old man of rocky Khios', Thales of Miletus, and later the tragic poet Ion were of the era. The Romans sacked it and thereafter the island sank into obscurity, being invaded by the Saracens and later becoming a pirate stronghold. With the Gattelusio family in control of Lesvos, the Genoese Giustianni family established control of Khios in the early 14th century and it again became prosperous.

The Turks took it in 1566 and occupied the island until 1912. The Greek war of independence began in 1821 and in 1822 the Khians joined the revolt. The Turks took a terrible revenge that reverberated around the world. The towns of Khios were razed, 25,000 Khians were massacred and 47,000 enslaved (in Nea Mon there is a bizarre chamber full of the bones of a few of those massacred). Delacroix commemorated the event in his famous picture and Victor Hugo was inspired to write his *The Child of Khios*. The Greek Admiral Kanaris achieved a small revenge in the same year when he destroyed the Turkish flagship and its commander, but the real effect of the massacre was to awaken the world to the Greek struggle.

Those Khians who managed to escape were scattered all over Europe. Many later became prosperous merchants and ship owners (the Rallis brothers of London were from Khios). Khios had barely recovered when the great earthquake of 1881 shattered the island and killed 3,500. Yet the island has recovered and modern Khios bustles and chatters still with the sounds of the Levant.

If there is one pattern to Khios it is the cultivation of the mastic tree (*Pistacia lentiscus*) for its resin. Polunin and Huxley in their *Flowers of the Mediterranean* have this to say about the shrub:

'A resin is obtained from the punctured stems which is the mastic used in medicine and varnish-making; it is cultivated in the island of Chios for this purpose. Mastic has been used since classical times as a chewing-gum for preserving the gums and sweetening the breath. The Arabs produce an oil from the berries which is edible and used for illumination; it makes a popular sweet meat called masticha, and a liqueur known as 'mastiche'. Probably the balm of Genesis and the mastic tree of Susannah.'

I might add that Sultans' ladies also believed it to be an aphrodisiac, ensuring its cultivation under Turkish occupation; today it is used mainly to make *mastika*, which is a potent liqueur, and in that strange concoction the Submarine. The latter is a spoonful of sickly sweet mastic jam in a glass of water and just how you properly consume this treat without getting it all over yourself and the table I have yet to discover.

Khios harbour looking N from the town quay.

LIMIN KHIOU (Khios, Hios)
Admiralty chart no. 1568

Approach
Conspicuous The tall buildings of the city are visible from some distance off. A communications tower festooned with discs is conspicuous to the S of the city. A cathedral with a blue cupola is conspicuous in the city. The harbour moles and harbour entrance are readily identified.

By night Use the lights at the entrance: Fl.G.3s4M and Fl.R.3s6M. The N mole exhibits a 2F.Y(vert)5M 290 metres from the head. The jetty off the S breakwater has a 2F.R(vert)3M on the end. The harbour lights are difficult to see against the lights of the city.

Dangers With the *meltemi* there is a disproportionately lumpy sea in the Khios Channel and the approaches to Khios harbour with the prevailing northerlies blowing against the north-going current. This can make the passage up the channel from the S an uncomfortable and prolonged affair.

Mooring
Go stern-to or bows-to or alongside on the W quay or on the pier off the S mole. The bottom is sticky mud – excellent holding.

Shelter The S and W quay can be uncomfortable with the slop set up across the large harbour (nearly half a mile) by the *meltemi*.

Authorities A port of entry: port police, customs and immigration authorities.

Note
1. Work is in progress in the SE corner of the harbour. Care must be taken of underwater obstructions until the work is complete.
2. Sewers emptying into the harbour make it smelly in the summer when the sewerage has stewed a bit.

Facilities
Water On the quay.
Fuel In the town. A mini-tanker can deliver to the quay.

381

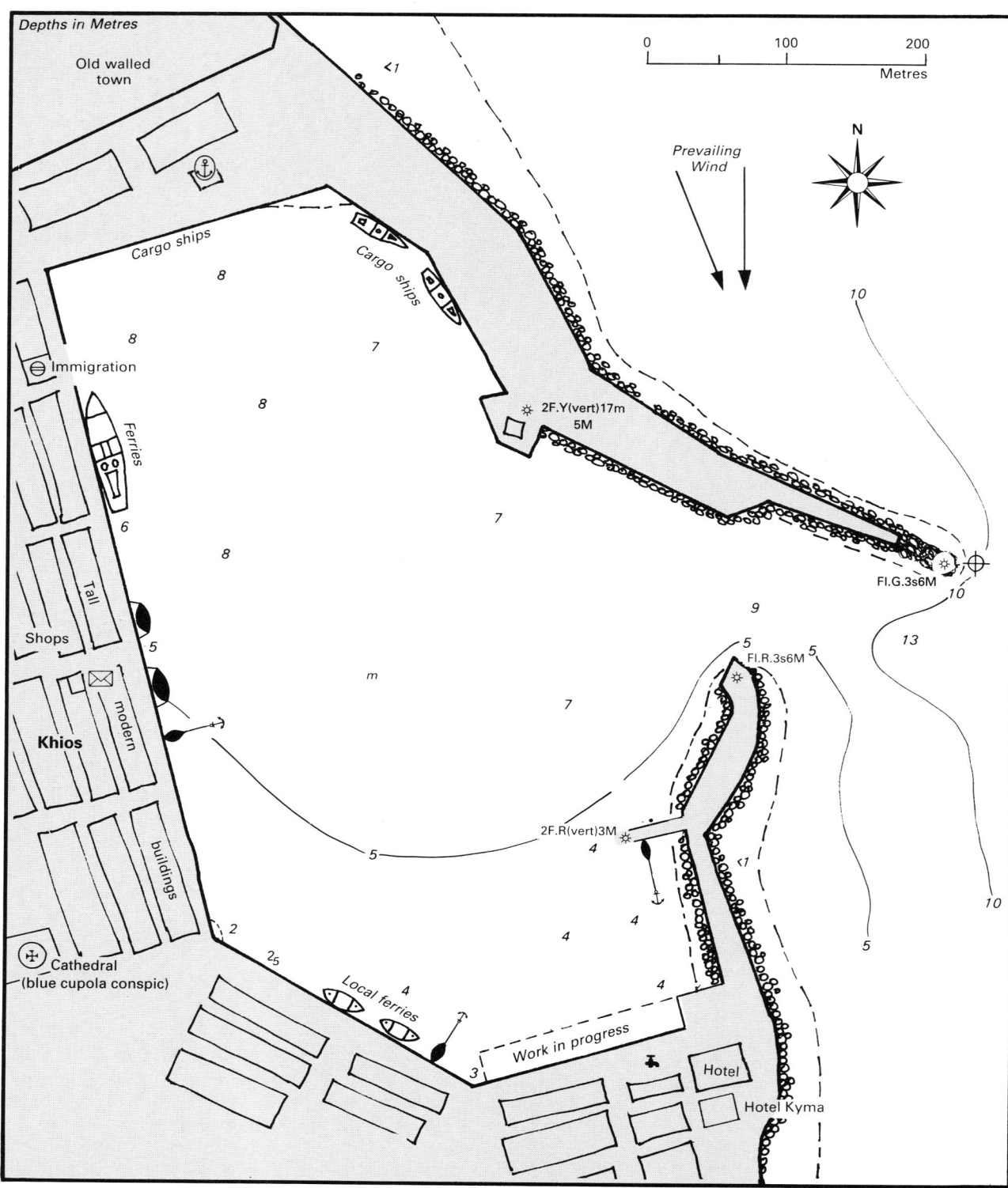

PORT KHIOS
38°22'·3N 26°08'·7E (Fl.G.6M)

Repairs Most mechanical repairs. Light engineering work possible. Excellent hardware and tool shops.
Provisions Excellent shopping for provisions. Wine can be bought from the barrel. A sort of permanent market will be found in the area behind the W quay. Ice available.

Eating out Tavernas in the town though I have discovered no really good ones.
Other PO. OTE. Banks. Greek gas and *Camping Gaz*. Hospital. Hire cars and motorbikes. Buses to the major villages. Ferries to Piraeus and Volos. Local ferries to Samos, Oinoussa, Psara and Ceşme in Turkey. Internal flights to Athens.

General

Khios is a noisy bustling harbour with an atmosphere closer to the Levant than to the islands to the W. Two-stroke three-wheelers buzz about, local ferries charge in and out, cranes creak unloading coasters – the only noise which penetrates the hubbub is the toot of the inter-island ferry.

The city largely dates from the 1881 earthquake which devastated the island and although a few of the old buildings survive they are overshadowed by the newer buildings. Even being generous, the city cannot be described as architecturally distinguished. The town makes few concessions to tourism although an optimistically large hotel has been built near the SE corner of the harbour. A small museum in a converted mosque houses a few ancient finds. The dull white lumps of mastic are for sale everywhere.

VRONDADOS

A miniature fishing harbour lying 2½ miles N of Limin Khiou. It offers good shelter for a small yacht, but is normally very crowded and you will have problems finding a berth. Care must be taken entering and berthing as the bottom is uneven and there is very little room for manoeuvring.

Water near the quay. Cafés and tavernas. The area now has mushrooming hotels and not inconsiderable numbers of tourists.

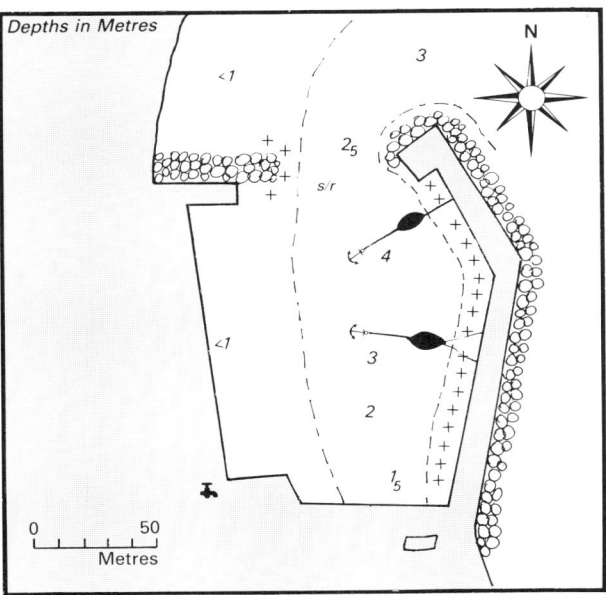

VRONDADOS

AYIOS IOANNIS THOLIS

This narrow inlet lies immediately W of Ak Pakhis. At the head of the inlet there is a large yard which hauls out very big *caïques* and yachts. The owner states he can haul vessels out up to 1000 tons – this figure should be taken with the proverbial grain of salt, but there were 200–300-ton *caïques* and a 25-ton displacement motorboat hauled out in the yard when I was there. Apart from the yard the inlet is deserted.

ORMOS KOLOKITHIA

This large bay lies just N of Nisis Ayios Stefanos with the hamlet of Laghana in the SW corner. The bay in the SW corner is very deep for anchoring with 20–25 metre depths a short distance off the quay on the N side. On the S side there are 10–20 metre depths where a yacht can anchor and take a line ashore. Provisions and tavernas in the village.

Note The cove in the NW corner is a naval establishment and it is prohibited to enter it or navigate in the vicinity.

MARMARO (Kardhamila)

Approach

Conspicuous The village cannot be seen until you are into the bay. A windmill on a rocky spur and the village and a cemetery above it are easily identified once you are in the entrance.

By night Use the lights on Vrak Margariti at the entrance to the bay (Fl.3s5M) and on the end of the mole (Fl.G.2s3M).

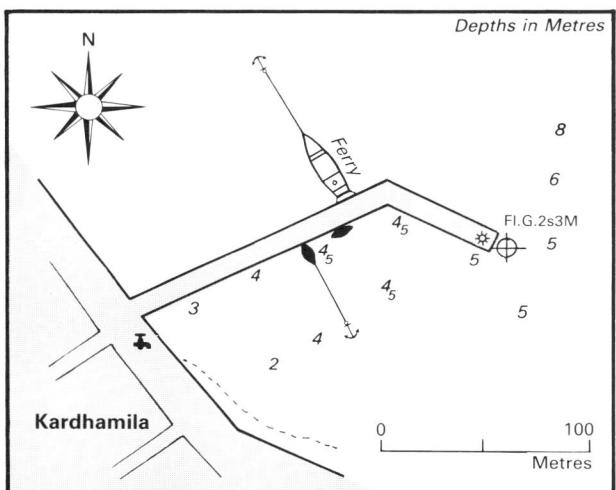

MARMARO
38°32′·7N 26°06′·6E (Fl.G.3M)

Mooring

Go stern-to or bows-to or alongside the inside of the mole. The bottom is mud and weed, patchy holding, so it is better to go alongside if possible.

Shelter Good shelter from the *meltemi*.
Authorities Port police and customs.

Facilities

Water At the root of the mole.
Fuel In the town.
Provisions Most provisions can be found. Ice available.
Eating out Tavernas on the waterfront.
Other PO. OTE. Bank. Buses and a ferry to Psara and Khios.

Approach to Marmaro on Khios looking S. Note windmill on
rocky spur.

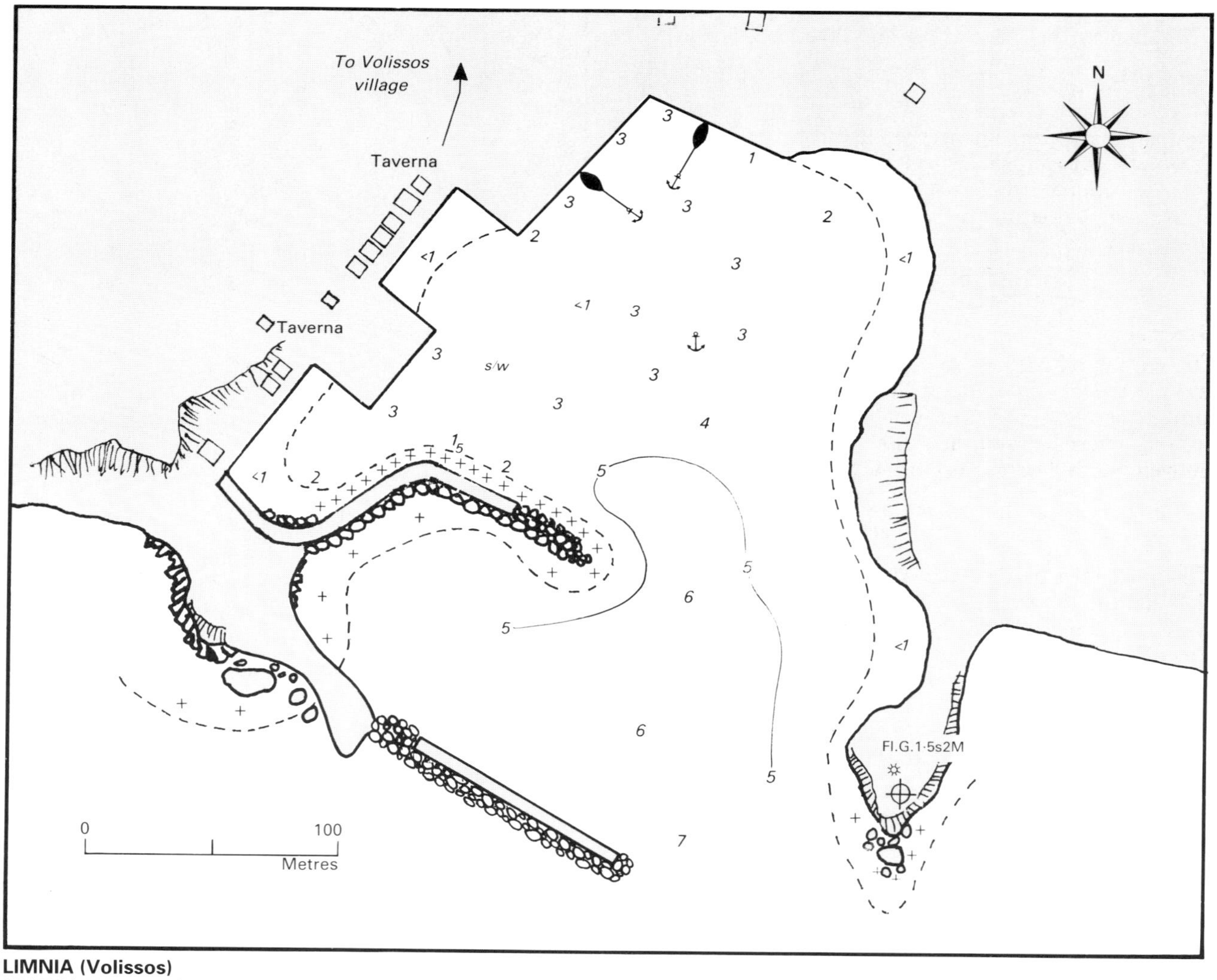

LIMNIA (Volissos)
38°28'N 25°55'·5E (FI.G.2M)

General

The village of Kardhamila is a delightful spot at the foot of a rough gorge cutting down through the mountains. A stream keeps everything watered and green through the summer in contrast to the parched and almost lunar mountains above the village.

LIMNIA (Volissos)

Approach

Conspicuous The village of Volissos and the castle above are visible from some distance off. Closer in the light structure on the SE side of the entrance can be seen.
By night Not recommended. Use the light on the E entrance point: Fl.G.1·5s2M.
Dangers Care should be taken of the above- and below-water rocks fringing the coast in the approaches to the harbour.

Mooring

Go stern or bows-to the quay in the NW corner. The bottom is sand and weed, good holding.
Shelter Good all-round shelter although SW winds make it a bit uncomfortable.

Facilities

Water From the taverna.
Fuel In Volissos village up the hill.
Provisions Most provisions can be obtained in Volissos about 1½ miles up the hill.
Eating out Tavernas by the harbour and several others in Volissos.
Other Bus to Khios from Volissos village.

General

The harbour is a quiet little place occupied only by a few fishermen. The village above is crumbling and ruinous but engaging. There is little tourism here but nothing overwhelming and the village and harbour are well worth a detour up the W coast of Khios.

MESTA

This long inlet on the W coast affords only mediocre shelter from the *meltemi*. Care must be taken of a reef lying 300 metres N of the eastern entrance point. Proceed into the inlet and go stern-to or bows-to the short pier or alongside the quay on the NE side. There are 7–8 metre depths alongside the quay and 3–5 metre depths off the pier. The bottom is mud and weed but the holding is not reliable. With a strong *meltemi* there are gusts and some swell creeps around into the inlet. Good shelter from southerlies.

Water from a tap near the root of the pier. Limited provisions and tavernas ashore.

Southwest Khios
Trakhilia, Angelia and Katofano

On the S side of the SW corner of Khios under Ak Mesta there are several bays affording good shelter from the *meltemi*. They are all open to the S and in the event of southerlies a yacht should make for Ormos Mesta or proceed up the Khios Channel to Khios.

Anchor where shown in any of the bays on the plan. The bottom is mostly sand with some weed and is good holding. Camping ground in Katofano. Small development at Angelia. Apart from a few olive groves and dwellings ashore nothing else disturbs this peaceful and quite enchanting corner of the island.

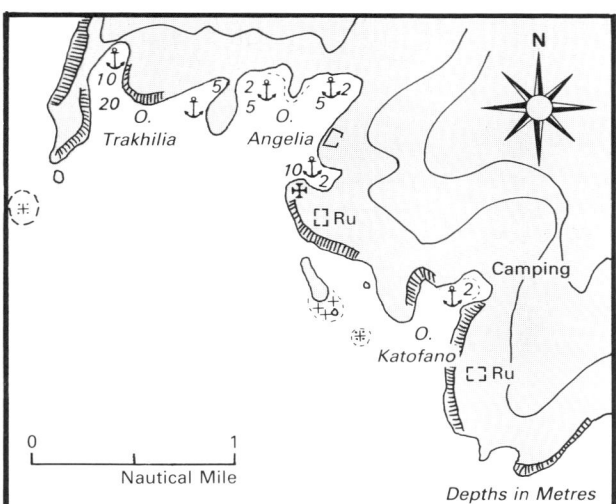

TRAKHILIA, ANGELIA AND O. KATOFANO

ORMISKOS EMBORIOS

Lying 3 miles NNE of Ak Mastikho this small cove provides good shelter from the *meltemi*. A ruined monastery on a hilltop immediately N is conspicuous. It is open to the SE. Anchor where convenient. The bottom is sand – good holding. Tavernas and hotels ashore.

Ikaria
(Nicaria)

Ikaria is a huge precipitous slab of rock wedged into the sea to the west of Samos. The island has green wooded and cultivated valleys in the north, but the high slopes and the south coast are mostly barren. The name probably derived from the Phoenician word *ikor* referring to an abundance of fish and there are still considerable fleets working the waters here and around the nearby Nisidhes Fournoi. The alternative and mythological origin of the name is derived from the legend of Daedalus and Icarus who contrived to escape from Crete by fabricating wings from feathers and wax. Icarus flew too high and the sun melted the wax so that he fell into the sea near Ikaria.

Evdhilos on Ikaria looking NE from the village.

EVDHILOS

Approach

Conspicuous Vrakhonisis Evdhilos with the light structure on it is conspicuous. From the E the village and the harbour mole are easily seen.

By night Use the light on Vrak Evdhilos (Fl.7·5s6M) and the light on the end of the mole (Fl.G.2s3M).

Mooring

Go stern-to or bows-to the mole or the pier in the S or anchor off. Much of the quay and parts of the mole have underwater ballasting extending out from them so it is best to go bows-to. The mole quay is also quite high and there are few places to secure warps to.

Evdhilos on Ikaria looking NW from the SE side of the bay.
Neville Bulpitt.

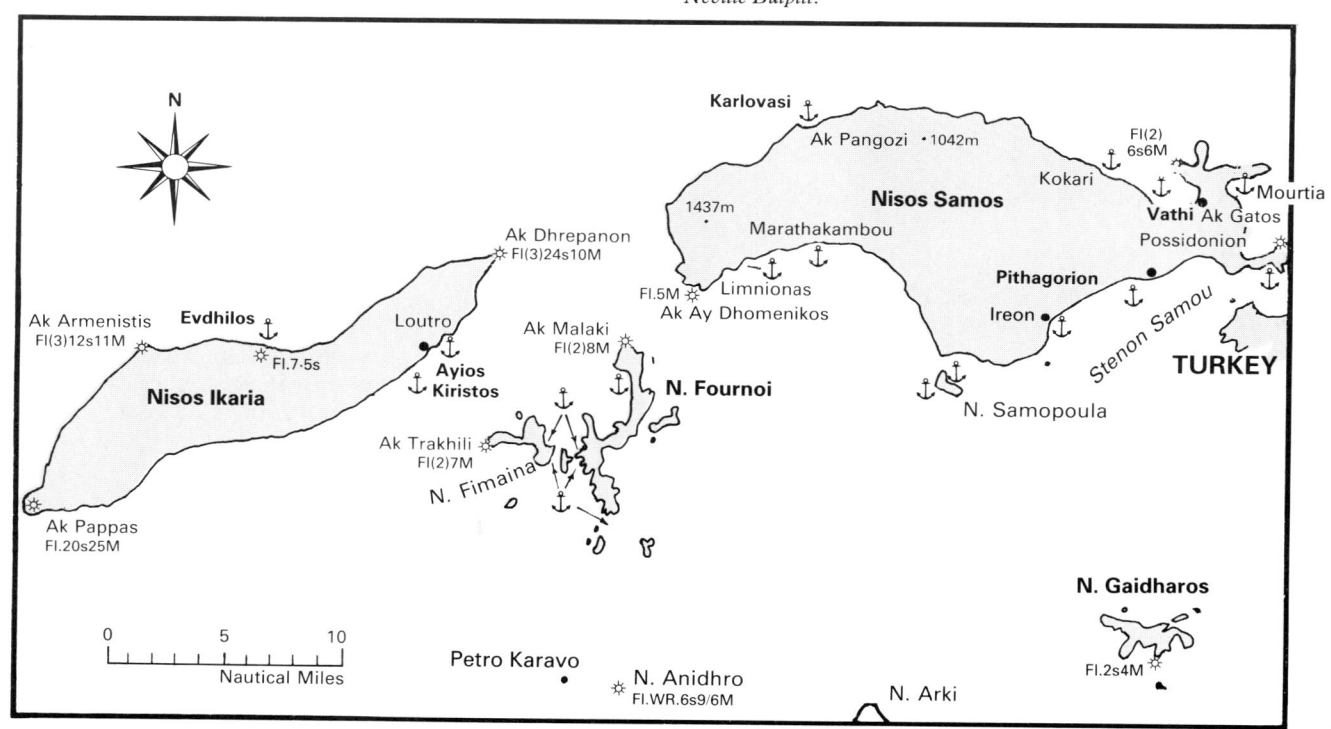

IKARIA TO SAMOS

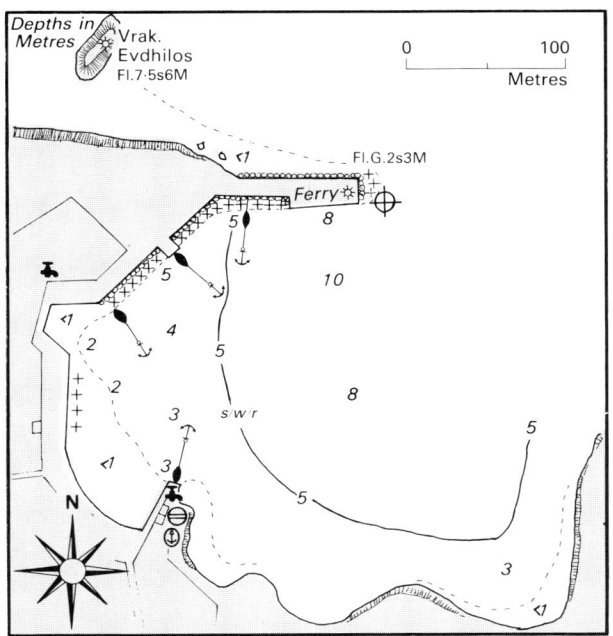

EVDHILOS
37°38′N 26°10′·9E (Fl.G.3M)

Shelter With a strong *meltemi* some swell creeps around the end of the mole. With strong NE winds the harbour is untenable.

Authorities Port police and customs.

Facilities

Water A tap near the quay.
Provisions Some provisions in the village.
Eating out Several tavernas and a number of cafés.
Other PO. Bus to Ayios Kiristos. Ferries to Samos and Piraeus.

General

The tiny village sandwiched between a rocky bluff and high mountains is attractive and friendly. Ikaria doesn't get a lot of tourism compared to nearby Samos although the new ferry service is changing that. Good underwater fishing along the precipitous coast that drops sheer into the sea in the vicinity.

CAUTION

Along the S coast of Ikaria severe gusts sweep down off the high mountains.

AYIOS KIRISTOS (Agios Kirykos)
Imray-Tetra chart no. G32

Approach

The capital and ferry port of Ikaria lies on the SE side of the island.

Conspicuous The town and the harbour mole are easily identified from the distance.

By night Use the light on the end of the mole: Fl.R.3s3M.

Dangers With N winds there are severe gusts into the harbour and off the high land in the approaches – some caution is advised with the *meltemi*.

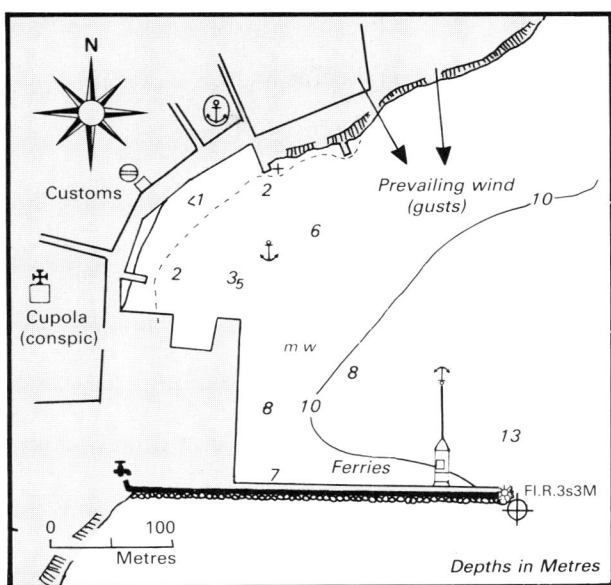

AYIOS KIRISTOS
37°36′·8N 26°17′·9E (Fl.R.3M)

Mooring

Anchor off or moor alongside the mole.

Shelter With N winds there are severe gusts into the harbour and with S winds a swell works its way around the end of the mole so the harbour is really only tenable in calm weather.

Authorities Port police and customs.

Facilities

Water Near the mole.
Fuel In the town (about ¼ of a mile).
Provisions Good shopping for provisions.
Eating out Good tavernas.
Other PO. OTE. Bank. Hire motorbikes. Ferry to Piraeus.

General

The town is an attractive straggle of buildings up the steep slopes from the harbour and the locals are friendly – but the uncomfortable harbour detracts from the attractions of Ayios Kiristos.

ORMOS LOUTRO (Thermia)

Just over half a mile NE of Ay Kiristos is the bay of Loutro which affords reasonable shelter from the *meltemi*. Anchor in the bay, or small yachts can go on the quay off the old hydropathic institute. The former name of the place was Thermia describing the hot springs utilised by the hydropathic institute.

AKRA DHREPANON

Immediately S of the cape there is an open bay partially protected from the *meltemi* which in calm weather could be used for visiting the ancient ruins of Drakanon. The ancient circular tower is conspicuous from seaward.

Loutro (Thermia) on Ikaria looking NE. *Nigel Patten*.

Samos

While Lesvos is the jewel of the eastern Sporades, Samos is the rough-cut diamond. The high mountain ridge running the length of the island is an extension of Mt Mykale in Turkey – from the southeast corner of the island it is a single sea mile across to Cape Mykale making Samos the closest of the Greek islands to Turkey. In the west the range rises sheer from the sea to Mt Kertetevs (1437 metres, nearly 5000ft) and runs to the east to the Ambelos range (1041 metres, 3730ft). Deep gullies score the mountainsides and peaks and bluffs assume shapes which even the restrained language of the Admiralty *Pilot* describes as 'fantastic'. Thick pine forest covers most of the lower slopes and villages perch precariously on small plateaus. There is a grandeur and grace to Samos unequalled elsewhere.

In ancient times Samos was lavishly praised: it was known as Parthenoarroussa for its beauty: Dryoussa for its oaks, Anthemis for its flowers, and Hydrele for its abundant springs. The name Samos is probably derived from a Phoenician word meaning 'high'. As part of the Ionic Confederacy it prospered, but it was under the ambitious Polykrates that the island rose to the height of its prosperity in the 6th century BC.

Polykrates was equal parts tyrant and aesthete – a sort of latter-day Odysseus. He rose swiftly to power, conquering nearby islands and assembling a large fleet and army. To Samos he invited poets and artists and under his patronage three of the greatest engineering feats in the ancient Greek world were achieved: the harbour at Pithagorion, the underground conduit and tunnel behind Pithagorion, and the temple to Hera on Ak Kolonna. The temple has gone, but the remains of the harbour and the tunnel are still there. Polykrates was finally lured to the mainland coast and crucified (literally) by the Persians.

Samos then passed from Sparta to Athens and thence to the Romans. Anthony sacked it before the Battle of Actium. Aided by Cleopatra he gave a mammoth feast on the island to which all the civilized world was invited and which went on for months. This was his way of starting a war and the only question men had was, what would the victory feast be like? As we know there was no victory feast, only defeat and hopeless suicide.

After the Roman occupation the island fell into obscurity and was the lair of pirates, apart from a brief period of Byzantine rule. The inhabitants fled to Khios and Lesvos leaving the island open for the Turks to occupy in 1566. It became part of Greece in 1912.

You might expect an island ravaged and pillaged by corsairs for so long to be run down and poor in spirit. Not a bit of it, Samos leaves you with the feeling of a happy island populated by friendly people. The scenery is superb from the extensive pine forests on the mountain slopes (Samian pine is considered to be the best for *caïque* building) to the cultivated plains. Sadly forest fires have destroyed much of the pine forest on the S coast. Apart from the sweet white Samos muscat wine, the excellent *Saimaina white sec* is available in Vathi, Karlovasi and Pithagorion. A sweet red *moschata* is also produced.

KARLOVASI
Admiralty chart no. 1568
Imray-Tetra chart no. G32

Approach
Conspicuous From the distance the buildings of the town are easily identified. A church with a blue cupola on a precipitous rock bluff and two large churches with blue cupolas in the town are conspicuous. The harbour is to the W of the town and the harbour moles are easily identified.

By night Use the light on Ak Pangozi (Fl.5s8M) and the lights at the entrance (Fl.G.4·5s3M and Fl.R.4·5s3M).

Dangers With the *meltemi* there can be a confused sea off the coast around the harbour and at the entrance.

Karlovasi harbour looking ENE.

Mooring
Go stern-to or bows-to in the SE corner. The bottom is sand, mud and weed, good holding.

Shelter Good shelter, but with the *meltemi* some swell creeps around the end of the outer mole – uncomfortable but not dangerous. With strong S winds there are gusts off the high mountains behind.

Authorities Port police and customs.

Note Photographs of the harbour and the coast to the W are prohibited.

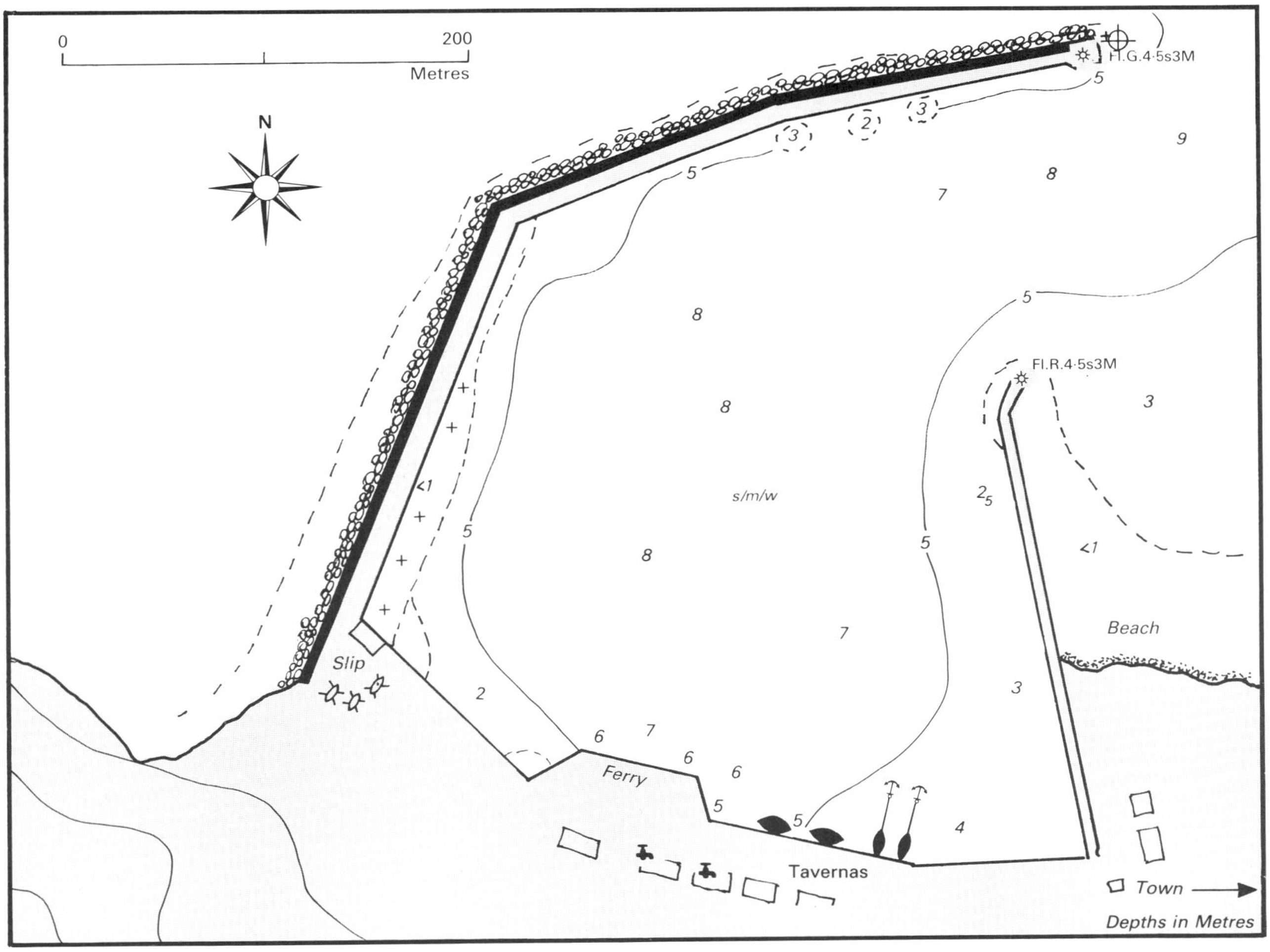

KARLOVASI
37°47'·9N 26°40'·9E (Fl.G.3M)

389

Facilities

Water On the quay.
Fuel In the town about 2 miles away.
Repairs Limited mechanical repairs. The yard in the SW corner of the harbour hauls out yachts.
Provisions Some provisions at the harbour. Good shopping for provisions in Karlovasi village.
Eating out Tavernas on the waterfront.
Other PO and OTE in Karlovasi village. Bus to Vathi.

General

The harbour is a sleepy little spot that seems to have seen more prosperous times. In recent years a little tourism has arrived to brighten up the harbour front. Inland, Karlovasi proper is a straggling market village serving the agricultural needs of the hinterland. The centre is most attractive – all stone houses and cobbled streets.

KOKARI

A bay lying approximately 3½ miles W of Ak Kotsikas. In calm weather or light westerlies anchor off the village in 7–10 metres on sand and weed. Taverna ashore.

VATHI (Samos)

Approach

The capital and principal ferry port of Samos lies in a large bay on the NE corner of the island.
Conspicuous The buildings of the town straggling around the bay and up the slopes behind are easily identified.
By night Use the light on Ak Kotsikas (Fl(2)16s6M) and the light on the end of the mole (Fl.R.3s4M).
Dangers Ormos Vathi is completely open to the N–NW and consequently the *meltemi* sends a heavy confused swell into the bay. There are also strong gusts off the high land in the vicinity.

Mooring

In the SE corner a small yacht harbour has been built. There are mostly 3m depths inside. Berth stern or bows-to in a vacant spot or where directed. There are laid moorings tailed to a small buoy.
Shelter Sheltered from the *meltemi* although a surge is set up – more uncomfortable than dangerous. A charge is made.
Authorities Port police and customs.

Vathi looking NE.

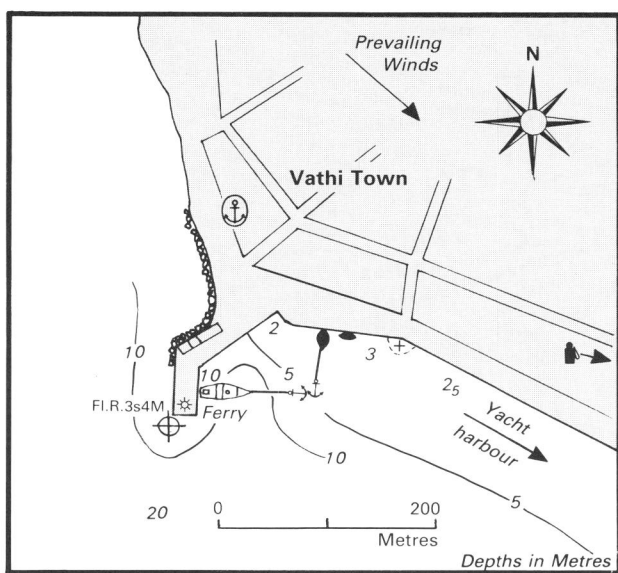

VATHI
37°45'·4N 26°58'·2E (Fl.R.4M)

Facilities

Water On the quay.
Fuel On the waterfront to the E.
Provisions Good shopping for all provisions nearby.
Eating out Good tavernas nearby.
Other PO. OTE. Banks. Greek gas and *Camping Gaz.* Hire cars and motorbikes. Buses to the principal villages. Ferry to Piraeus, Kavala, Khios and Kuşadasi in Turkey.

General

The waterfront is an ugly huddle of modern buildings on the dusty main street. The large bay is attractive towards the head and the old town (Samos) on the hill behind is a more sympathetic place.

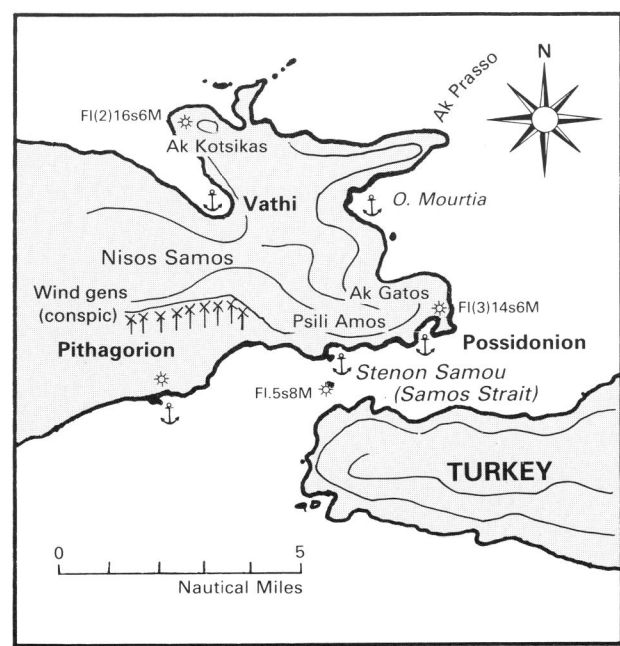

STENON SAMOU (SAMOS STRAIT)

Stenon Samou
(Samos Strait)
Imray-Tetra chart no. G32

The narrow strait between the E end of Samos and mainland Turkey. (The Turks call the strait Dilek Boğazi.) At its most narrow the strait is less than a mile across. In the strait there is the small rocky islet of Bayrak Adasi (Turkish) with a light structure on it (Fl.5s8M). A yacht can pass either N or S of the islet. On the N side there is a rocky shoal with a least depth of 9m in the fairway. On the S side there are greater depths.

The narrow strait channels the fairly weak N-going current into a strong current with overfalls. The current sets to the E and may attain a rate of 3–4 knots in the narrow section of the strait although it is normally less, around 1–2 knots. The overfalls are usually worse on the N side than the S side. The overfalls combined with strong gusts off the high land of Samos with the *meltemi* can make the passage very uncomfortable at times and care is needed.

ORMOS MOURTIA

The large bay on the E end of Samos. A monastery on the slopes is easily identified. Anchor in the cove at the head of the bay in 5 metres on a sandy bottom. Some shelter from the *meltemi* although a swell normally enters. Open to the S and E.

POSSIDONION

A small bay lying on the S side of Ak Gatos, the SE tip of Samos. The light structure on the cape (Fl(3)14s6M) is easily identified from the N. Anchor in 5–10 metres on a sandy bottom. Good shelter from the *meltemi* although there are strong gusts down into the bay and channel. Ashore there are a few houses and several tavernas in attractive surroundings. About 2 miles to the W at Psili Amos there is an anchorage behind an islet. A few houses and a simple taverna ashore.

PITHAGORION (Pythagoreon, Tigani)
Admiralty chart no. 1568
Imray-Tetra chart no. G32

Approach

Conspicuous A line of 9 wind generators on the ridge E of Pithagorion are conspicuous and the buildings of the town are visible from some distance off. A large red-roofed hotel to the W of the town and Metamorfosis, a fortified stone monastery on the waterfront, are conspicuous. Closer in, the outer mole is easily identified.
By night Use the light on Ak Fonias (Fl.2s4M) and the lights at the entrance (Fl.R.1·5s2M and Fl.G.1·5s2M). From the W the lights at the entrance cannot be seen until close in. Care is needed of the beacon at the entrance to the inner harbour which is unlit.
Dangers With the *meltemi* there are strong gusts off the high land in the approaches to the harbour.

Pithagorion looking WNW from the harbour entrance. Note conspicuous monastery on the extreme left of the photo.

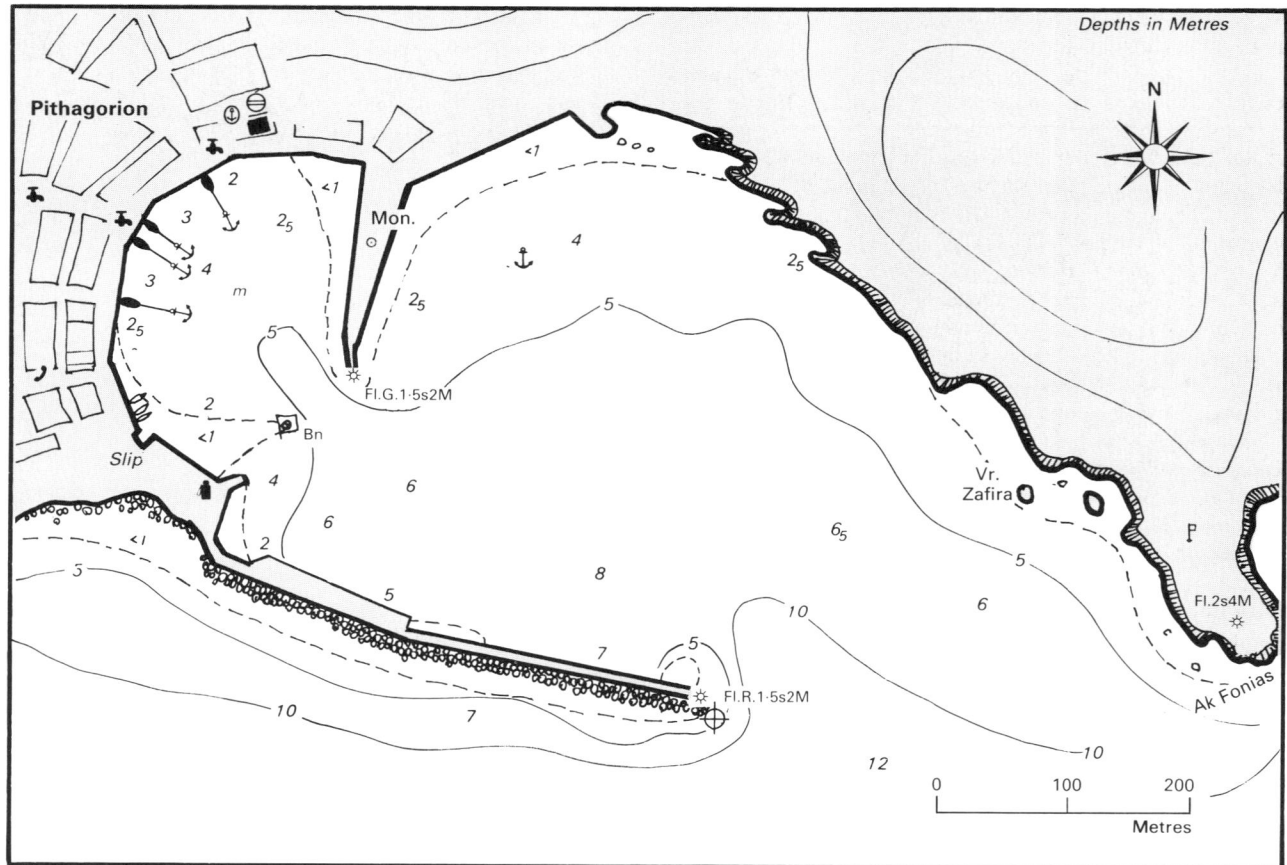

PITHAGORION
37°41'·3N 26°57'·2E (Fl.R.2M)

Note Once inside the outer mole the beacon marking the limit of the shallows on the S side of the entrance to the inner basin is easily identified. There are 4 metres' least depth in the fairway between the beacon and the inner mole.

Mooring

Go stern-to or bows-to the W quay. The bottom is mud – excellent holding.

Shelter Good shelter in the inner basin although the *meltemi* causes an uncomfortable slop in the harbour. Yachts sometimes anchor outside the inner harbour off the shore in 3–5 metres where there is good shelter and it is more comfortable.

Authorities A port of entry: port police, customs, and immigration.

Facilities

Water On the quay. Showers and toilets.
Fuel About 3km out of town. A mini-tanker can deliver to the quay. There is a fuel quay at the entrance to the harbour but hours are somewhat unpredictable.
Repairs Some mechanical repairs. Hardware shops and limited chandlery.
Provisions Good shopping for provisions nearby. Ice available.
Eating out Good tavernas on the waterfront and in town.

Other PO. OTE. Bank. Greek gas and *Camping Gaz*. Hire cars, motorbikes and bicycles. Regular bus to Vathi. Ferries to Patmos and Kuşadasi in Turkey. Internal flights to Athens.

Note The authorities are doing their best to help yachtsmen stopping here and are normally helpful with formalities and any minor problems.

General

Set at the foot of pine-covered hills and looking over to the Turkish mountains, the town of Pithagorion is becoming increasingly popular as a tourist resort and justifiably so. It is a thoroughly agreeable place, set in magnificent surroundings with high wooded mountains behind and looking across the Samos Strait, and just big enough to have good facilities and small enough to be intimate.

The town was named Pithagorion comparatively recently, in 1955, in honour of Pythagoras. Formerly it was called Tigani meaning 'frying pan' – a name which is self explanatory once you have seen the shape of the harbour. Pithagorion is situated on the site of the ancient city of Samos which rose to prominence under Polykrates the tyrant. During Polykrates' swift rise to power, what Herodotus described as three of the greatest engineering feats in the Greek world were achieved.

The first was the mole which protected the harbour and which survives in part today as part of the quay and the root of the outer mole.

The second was the temple of Hera built on Ak Kolonna. In its day bigger and better than any other – today only a single column remains standing amongst the ruins. A small museum in Pithagorion houses some of the finds from the temple site.

The third was the tunnel hewn through the mountain to bring water to the city and also probably as an escape route. It still exists today although the middle section has collapsed. The original was a mile long and 2·4 metres (8ft) square and for its day an extraordinary engineering feat. The entrance is immediately behind Pithagorion and a part of the tunnel can be explored by those who don't suffer from claustrophobia, though considerable care is needed. It is open six times a week on three days – enquire at the tourist office.

NOTE

There is a new harbour under construction immediately E of Pithagorion. There are conflicting reports over whether it is to be a commercial, yacht or a military harbour.

IREON

At the W end of the large bay running around to Pithagorion is the village and small fishing harbour at Ireon. A short breakwater provides some shelter. Anchor off in 3-4 metres. The *meltemi* does not gust into his corner.

Provisions and tavernas ashore.

NISIS SAMOPOULA (Samioupoula)

A *caïque* from Pithagorion runs tourists out to the island in the summer and anchors in a cove on the E side of the island. Ashore there is a small hamlet with a taverna.

MARATHAKAMBOU

A fishing harbour on the SW of Samos. An outer breakwater runs E from a natural bight with a short inner breakwater extending S from the coast. There are 3-4m depths in the entrance and outer part of the harbour. Anchor in the outer part or go bows-to the short pier running out from the shore. There are 2 metres depths at the extremity of the pier. With the *meltemi* there are strong gusts off the land so ensure your anchor is holding well.

Provisions and tavernas ashore. The surroundings are spectacular with precipitous cliffs and hills rising abruptly from the shore. Sadly much of the pine has been burnt in recent forest fires.

NOTE

This is a military area although now opened up for a little tourism. Photographs are prohibited.

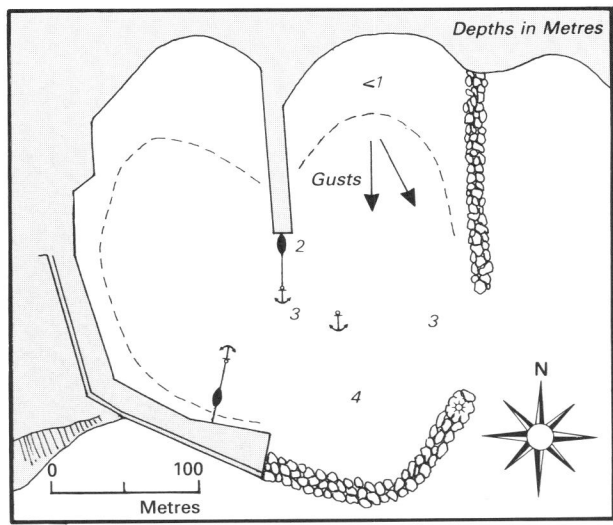

MARATHOKAMBOU

ORMOS LIMNIONAS

Lying close N of Ak Khrondos Kavos, this bay offers shelter from N winds, but is subject to fierce gusts off the mountains above. It is open to the S.

Caution On the W and S sides of Samos severe gusts sweep down off the high mountains with the *meltemi*. Unless a yacht is proceeding to Limnionas or Marathakambou it is a good policy to keep at least 2–3 miles off the S coast.

Nisidhes Fournoi
(Phournoi)

FOURNOI (Ormos Korseon, Kampos)
Admiralty chart no. 1568

Approach

The steep-to high islands (of Fourni and Fimaina) are visible from many miles away (Nisis Fournoi is 515 metres, 1686ft high).

Conspicuous From the N the village of Fournoi (Korseon) and 2 windmills on the ridge to the SW of the village are conspicuous. From the S the village cannot be seen but the windmills are conspicuous.

By night Not recommended. There is only the light on Ak Svistokaminos (S side of Ormos Korseon): Fl.WR.2s4/3M (red sector covers 034°-138° and 172°-243°).

Dangers With the *meltemi* there are strong gusts off the high land and through the channel between Nisis Dhiapori and Nisis Fimaina. The current sets to the N and causes a confused sea.

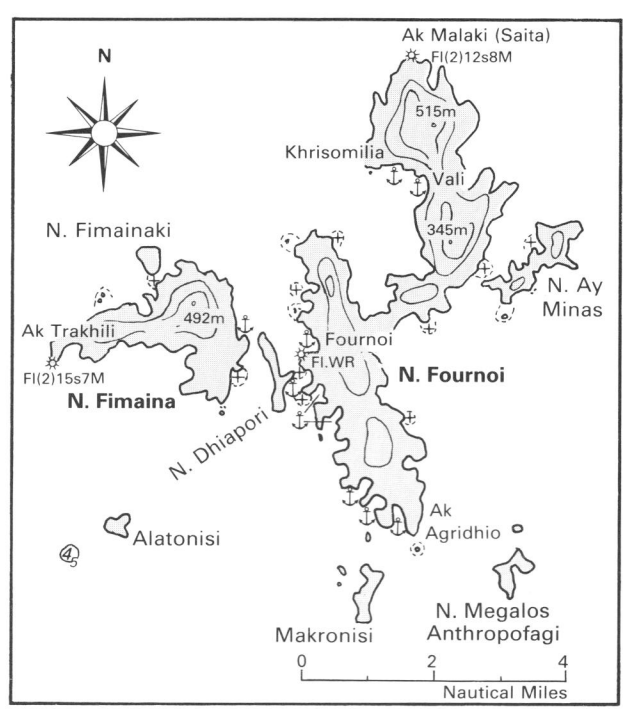

NISIDHES FOURNOI

Fournoi or Kampos looking N.

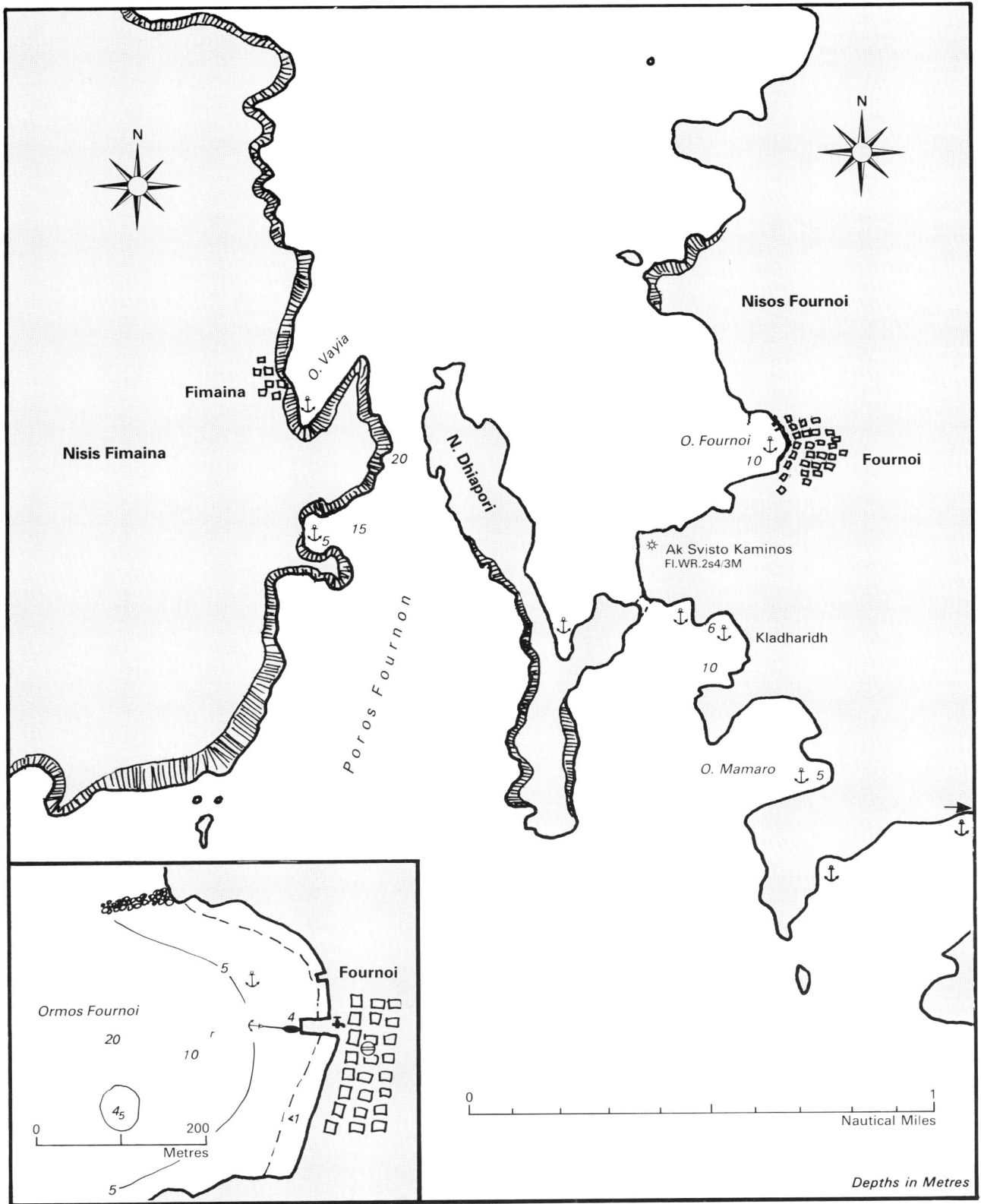

ORMOS FOURNOI
37°34′·5N 26°29′E

Mooring

Anchor off Fourni village where convenient. The bottom here is a thin layer of mud over rock and it is difficult to find a patch where the anchor will hold.

Shelter Reasonable shelter from the *meltemi* although the poor holding means it is not a secure place to be.

Authorities Port police and customs.

Facilities

Water Tap near the quay.

Fuel Small quantities may be available.

Provisions Some provisions can be obtained but the villagers are largely dependent on the *caïque* ferry from Ikaria for supplies. Ice available.

Eating out Several tavernas – fresh fish is often available.

Other PO. Metered telephone. Local ferry to Ayios Kiristos.

General

Fournoi (Korseon, Kambos) is the only major village on the island and the population and facilities are concentrated here. A large fishing fleet is based here and the locals are friendly to visiting yachts. The coves S of the village are mostly deserted and the surrounding jagged coastline offers good underwater fishing.

ANCHORAGES AROUND THE ISLANDS

1. *Fimaina (Ormos Vayia)* The bay on Nisis Fimaina opposite Ormos Korseon. Poor shelter from the *meltemi*. Taverna ashore.
2. *Nisis Dhiapori* In the bay on the E side immediately SW of Ak Svistokaminos.
3. *Cliff Bay* The cove on Nisis Fimaina on the W side of the narrow channel between Fimaina and Dhiapori. Some shelter from the *meltemi*.
4. *Kladharidhi* Anchor in the bay sheltered on the W by Nisis Dhiaporoi. Reasonable protection from the *meltemi*.
5. *Ormos Marmaro* Anchor at the N end of the bay with a long line ashore. Depths are considerable. Good protection from the *meltemi*.
6. In the large bay immediately S of Marmaro there is reported to be good shelter from the *meltemi*. Anchor at the head of the bay in 5-8 metres, good holding once the anchor is in. Ashore there is an ancient marble quarry with unfinished columns and other bits and pieces lying around.
7. At the S end of Nisis Fourni there is a large bay immediately W of Ak Agridhio that looks as though it would offer good shelter from the *meltemi*. There is also another inlet NW of it.
8. *Ormos Khrisomilia* On the N end of Fournoi on the W side there is the large bay of Khrisomilia. A yacht can anchor off here in calm weather though depths are considerable. To the E there is the small cove of Vali which is said to afford some shelter from the *meltemi* though again depths are considerable.

CAUTION

With the *meltemi* there are severe gusts off the high land of the islands and in the strait between Fimaina and Fournoi (Poros Fournon) considerable confused seas are pushed down. Care is needed when navigating in the vicinity of the islands which in the *meltemi* season are very windy places indeed.

IX. The Dodecanese

The Dodecanese, the Twelve Islands, lie in a crescent chain down the Asiatic Turkish coast curving west towards Crete. The name 'Dodecanese' is of comparatively recent origin. It came into use in 1908 when twelve islands of this group excluding Lipso, Kos and Rhodes but including an outsider, Ikaria, protested about their deprivation of the special privileges and tax exemptions they had been granted in the 16th century by the Turks. Since then the name has come to include Lipso, Kos and Rhodes, but to exclude Ikaria. The group is also known as the Southern Sporades.

Like most of the Greek Islands, the Dodecanese are the tops of mountains that stood on the plain of the Aegean long since flooded. The islands are for the most part bare of vegetation although not to such an extent as the Cyclades. Several of the islands with abundant natural springs, notably Kos and Rhodes, are relatively green and wooded.

The history of the Dodecanese has largely revolved around the fortunes of Rhodes which dominated trade in this corner of the Aegean from ancient times until the 19th century. Today Rhodes dominates the new trade in tourists in the Dodecanese. In the early Middle Ages the Knights of St John, based in their fortress in Rhodes, stamped the area with their military signatures. Most of the military architecture is not the ubiquitous Venetian and Genoese architecture so prevalent in other parts of Greece, but that of the Knights. The occupation of the Knights nonetheless ensured the Venetians access to the trade in this part of the world. When the Knights finally capitulated to the Turks in 1522, the Dodecanese were to remain under Turkish rule until 1912.

Despite such a long period of unbroken occupation the islands have remained intrinsically Greek and there is as little here to remind you of the long years under Turkish rule as elsewhere in Greece. After the Italo-Turkish war (1911–12) the islands were awarded to Italy although they were to be passed on in due course to Greece. This promise was later conveniently forgotten and the Dodecanese remained under the Italians until the Second World War. Finally in 1947 they officially became part of Greece. For those not familiar with modern Greek history it comes as quite a shock to learn that these islands have been a part of Greece for such a short time when visually and culturally they appear to be as much a part of Greece as any of the other islands.

The special tax exemptions the islands enjoyed under Turkish rule exist to this day. Special exemptions from customs duties mean that alcohol and cigarettes are cheap – in some cases less than the duty-free prices. Theoretically a yacht should clear customs when leaving the Dodecanese even if bound for somewhere else in Greece but in practice it is rarely enforced.

Weather patterns in the Dodecanese

In the summer the prevailing wind is the *meltemi* blowing from the NW–W. It starts fitfully in June, blows strongly in July through to September and again fitfully in October. In the summer months it regularly blows Force 4–6 and may on occasion reach Force 7. It does not blow every day, but may blow without a break for 5–10 days.

In the spring and autumn the wind frequently blows from the SE, about Force 2–4, although it may be stronger on occasion. In the winter the wind is predominantly from the SE although gales may come from the N or S.

When the *meltemi* is blowing at full strength in July and August the gusts off the lee side of an island can be considerably stronger than the wind strength in the open sea. Gusts are particularly strong off Patmos, Kalimnos, Kos, Niseros, Tilos, Karpathos and Astipalaia. In the comparatively open stretch of sea between Astipalaia and Karpathos a large and disturbed sea is set up when the *meltemi* blows for days on end. Although it is possible to go N when the *meltemi* is blowing, it makes better sense to plan to be heading S in July and August. The typical short seas it sets up make sailing or motoring to windward arduous and tiring.

In the summer months it is very hot in the Dodecanese although the *meltemi* provides some relief. Temperatures may reach 35°C although the average temperature is less. In the winter the climate is mild. The overall climate is similar to that in Crete or Sicily.

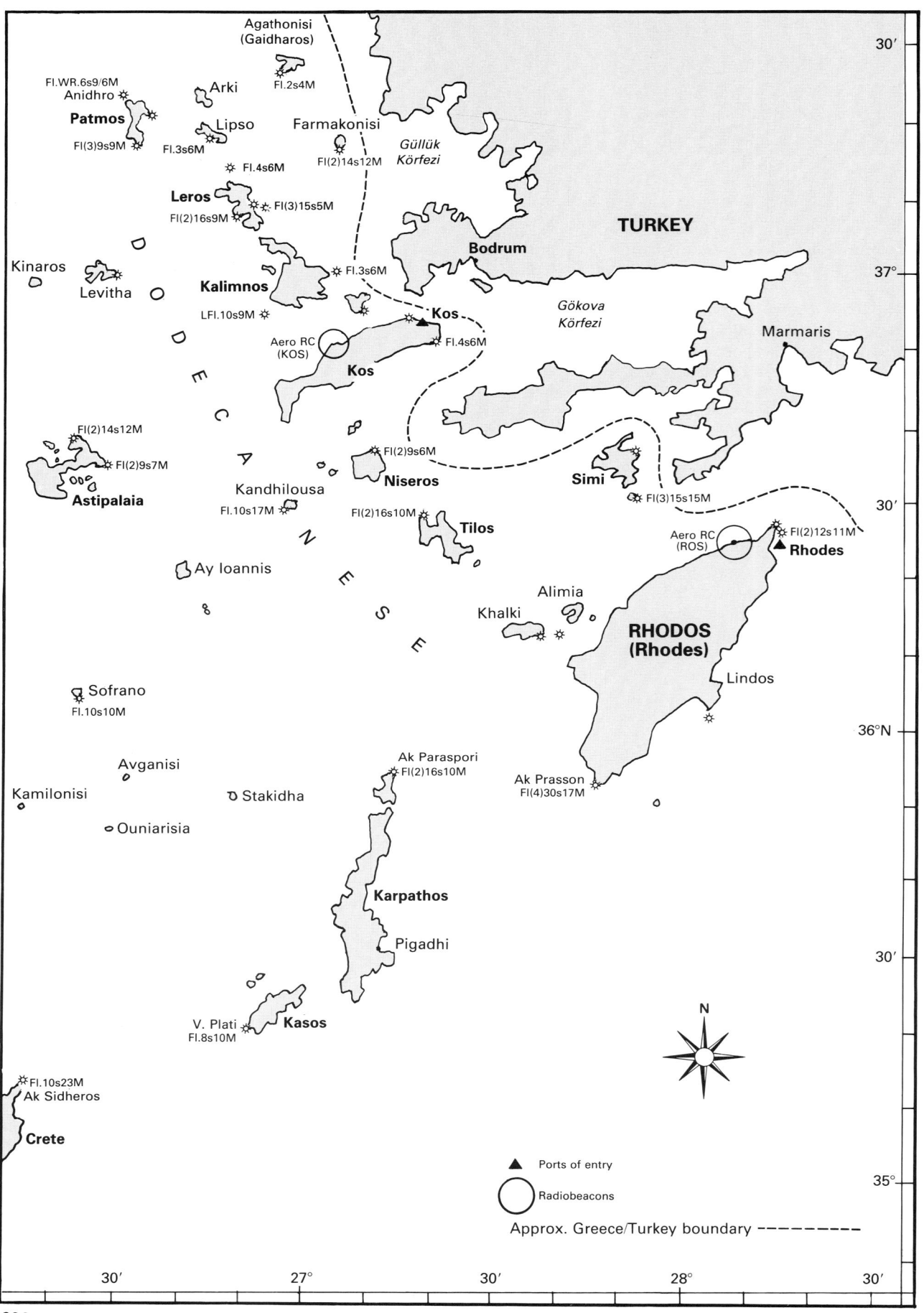

30'

Agathonisi
(Gaidharos)

Fl.WR.6s9/6M
Anidhro ✦
Patmos   Arki

Fl.2s4M

Lipso   Farmakonisi   *Güllük*
                                   Körfezi
Fl(3)9s9M   Fl.3s6M   Fl(2)14s12M

☀ Fl.4s6M

Leros   **TURKEY**
Fl(2)16s9M ✦ Fl(3)15s5M

Kinaros   37°
         ✦ Fl.3s6M   **Bodrum**
Levitha **Kalimnos**

         LFl.10s9M ☀   **Kos**   *Gökova*
                                           Körfezi
Aero RC   ▲
(KOS)   **Kos**   Fl.4s6M   Marmaris

Fl(2)14s12M
       ✦ Fl(2)9s7M
Astipalaia   ☀ Fl(2)9s6M
                  Kandhilousa **Niseros**   **Simi**
       Fl.10s17M   ☀ Fl(3)15s15M
               Fl(2)16s10M ☀   30'
                         Tilos   Aero RC   ☀ Fl(2)12s11M
                                          (ROS)
     ✦ Ay Ioannis   ▲ **Rhodes**
                                        Alimia
                         Khalki   ☀
                              ☀   **RHODOS**
                                          (Rhodes)
     ♘ Sofrano   Lindos
     Fl.10s10M
                                                      ☀
                                     36°N
     Avganisi   Ak Paraspori ☀
                   ☀ Fl(2)16s10M   Ak Prasson ☀
Kamilonisi ⚬ Stakidha   Fl(4)30s17M
     ⚬
   ⚬ Ouniarisia
                                                      ⚬

                         Karpathos

                         Pigadhi

                                                      30'
            ⚬⚬
     V. Plati ☀ **Kasos**
     Fl.8s10M

☀ Fl.10s23M
Ak Sidheros   N
                                       ⊛
Crete

                   ▲ Ports of entry   35°

                   ◯ Radiobeacons

                   Approx. Greece/Turkey boundary --------

   30'   27°   30'   28°   30'

Data

PORTS OF ENTRY
Kos
Rhodos

PROHIBITED AREAS
1. *Leros* It is prohibited to navigate and land on the S and SW side of Ormos Partheni.
2. *Leros* It is prohibited to navigate and land on the S side of Ormos Lakki in the vicinity of the naval buildings.

MAJOR LIGHTS
Nisis Anidhro Fl.WR.6s9/6M

Patmos
Ak Yeranos Fl.3s7M
Ak Ilias Fl(3)9s9M

Lipso
Ak Gatos Fl.3s6M
Nisis Kalapodhia Fl.4s6M
Vrak Saraki Fl(2)8s6M

Nisis Gaidharos Fl.2s4M
Nisis Farmakonisi (S summit) Fl(2)14s12M

Leros
Ormos Alindas Fl.3s5M
Vrak Ay Kiriaki Fl(3)15s5M
Ormos Lakki (Ak Lakki) Fl(2)16s9M
Nisis Glaros Fl.1·5s4M

Kalimnos
Nisis Kalolimnos Fl.3s6M
Limin Kalimnou Fl.R.2s4M
Vrak Safonidhi LFl.10s9M

Pserimos
Ak Rousa Fl(2)WR.10s12/9M
Vrak Nekrothikes Fl.WR.5s6/4M

Kos
Ak Ammoglossa Fl.R.4s4M
Ak Louros Fl(3)WR.15s6M
Ak Fouka Fl.4s6M

Nisis Yiali (Ay Andonios) Fl.2s4M
Niseros (Ak Palos) Fl(2)9s6M
Nisis Kandheliousa Fl.10s17M
Tilos (Vrak Gaidharos) Fl(2)16s10M

Simi
Nisis Marmaras Fl.3s5M
Nisis Khondros Fl.1·5s5M
Ak Koutsoumba Fl.3s5M
Vrak Kouloundros (Troumbeta Rock) Fl(3)15s15M

Nisis Khalki (Skala) Fl.WR.6s8/6M

Rhodes
Nisis Tragusa Fl(2)WR.14s8/6M
Kamiros Skala Fl.3s5M
Ak Milon (Zonari) Fl.WR.4s6/4M
Limin Rodhou (Ay Nikolaos) Fl(2)12s11M
Vrak Paximadha Fl.WR.4s9/6M
Ak Prasson Fl(4)30s17M

Karpathos
Ak Kastellos Fl.WR.3s7/4M
Nisidha Dhespotiko Fl.5s6M
Ak Paraspori (Saria) Fl(2)16s12M

Nisis Stakidha Fl.3s8M
Ounianisia Fl(2)16s7M
Nisis Megalo Sofrano Fl.10s10M
Vrak Strongili Fl(2)WR.10s7/5M

Kasos
Vrak Plati Fl.8s10M

Astipalaia
Ak Floudha Fl(2)14s12M
Ak Exopetra Fl(2)9s7M

Quick reference guide

	Shelter	Mooring	Fuel	Water	Provisioning	Tavernas	Plan
Patmos and adjacent islands							
Skala Patmos	B	AC	A	A	B	A	•
Anchorages near							
Skala Patmos	BC	C	O	O	O	C	•
Nisis Arki	A	AC	O	B	C	C	•
(Port Augusta)							
Lipso							
Ormos Lipso	B	AC	B	A	C	B	•
Lera Lipso	B	C	O	O	O	C	•
Nisis Gaidharos	B	AC	O	C	C	C	•
Nisis Farmakonisi	C	C	O	O	O	O	•
Leros							
Ormos Lakki	B	AB	B	A	B	B	•
Ormos Partheni	A	C	O	O	O	C	•
Ormos Plakouti	C	C	O	O	O	O	
Xerocambo	B	C	O	O	O	O	
Ormos Alindas	C	AC	B	A	B	B	•
Pandeli	B	AC	B	B	C	B	•
Kalimnos							
Limin Kalimnou	A	A	B	A	A	B	•
Vathi	B	A	O	B	C	C	•
Ormos Akti	O	C	O	O	O	O	
Baia Isolavecchia	O	C	O	O	O	O	
Baia de Sicati	O	C	O	O	O	O	
Ormiskos Vorio	B	C	O	O	C	C	
Telendhos	O	C	O	O	O	C	
Ormos Linaria	O	C	O	O	O	C	
Vlikathia	B	C	O	O	O	C	
Pserimos	C	C	O	O	C	B	•
Kos							
Mastihari	B	AB	O	B	C	B	•
Limin Kos	B	A	B	A	A	A	•
Kardamena	B	AC	O	B	C	B	•
Ormos Kamares	B	BC	O	A	O	C	•
Nisis Yiali	C	C	O	O	O	O	

	Shelter	Mooring	Fuel	Water	Provisioning	Tavernas	Plan
Niseros							
Mandraki	C	AB	B	A	B	B	•
Palon	B	A	O	B	C	B	•
Livadhi (Tilos)	C	BC	B	A	B	C	•
Simi							
Simi	B	A	B	A	A	A	•
Panormittis	A	C	O	O	C	C	•
Pethi	B	AC	O	B	C	C	•
Ormos Marathouda	C	C	O	O	O	O	
Ormos Faneromeni	C	C	O	O	O	O	
Ay Emilianos	C	AC	O	O	O	O	•
Nisis Seskli	C	C	O	O	O	O	
Rhodes							
Mandraki	A	A	A	A	A	A	•
Ormos Trianda	O	C	O	O	O	O	
Lindos	B	C	O	B	C	A	•
Ay Apostoli	C	C	O	O	O	O	
Ormos Lardhos	O	C	O	O	O	C	
Istros/Vigli	O	C	O	O	O	O	
Ormos Langonia	O	C	B	B	B	C	
Khalki	B	ABC	O	B	C	C	•
Potamos	B	C	O	O	O	O	
Alimia	B	C	O	O	O	O	•
Karpathos							
Limin Karpathou	C	AB	B	B	A	B	•
Ormos Makri Yialo	C	C	O	O	O	O	
Ormos Amorfos	C	C	O	O	O	O	
Finiki	C	A	O	A	C	C	•
Tristoma	C	C	O	O	O	O	•
Kasos							
Limin Kasou	C	A	B	B	C	C	•
Ormos Khelatronas	C	C	O	O	O	O	
Nisidhes Kaso	O	C	O	O	O	O	
Astipalaia							
Skala	B	ABC	B	A	B	B	•
Maltezana	B	BC	O	O	C	C	•
Vathi	A	C	O	O	O	C	•
Ormos Agrilithi	B	C	O	O	O	O	•
Ormos Livadhi	C	C	O	O	O	O	

Patmos

The northernmost of the Dodecanese. The island is composed of three barren volcanic lumps joined to one another by narrow isthmuses. The natural harbour of Skala lies on the central isthmus and above it is the focal point of the island – the *chora* of Patmos crowned by the monastery of St John the Divine. The chora, like that of Astipalaia, belongs more to the Cyclades than to the Dodecanese. The glaring white squat houses and courtyards contrast vividly with the grey stone monastery above.

Patmos belongs to the Christian age rather than to antiquity. St John the Divine was banished to Patmos by the Emperor Domitian. Here he dictated the wild poetry of the Apocalypse, found in the book of Revelations, to his disciple Prochorus. Halfway up the road between Skala and the *chora* is the Church of the Apocalypse and the Cave of St Anne where St John transmitted the fiery words of god to his disciple – at least so legend says, as we have no real proof that St John did actually write the Apocalypse whilst on Patmos.

For centuries the island was the home of Saracen pirates until 1088 when St Christodoulos was granted permission to establish a monastery in honour of St John. The continued presence of the pirates dictated the fortified walls surrounding the monastery. The monastery prospered and its library became one of the largest in Greece outside Mt Athos. Many of the manuscripts have since been dispersed (many of them to England), but the valuable *Codex Porphyrius* written on purple vellum in silver and gold and some excellent Byzantine illuminations remain. The Treasury has a number of valuable icons and stoles. Special arrangements have to be made to see items not on display

Patmos is the spiritual centre of the Greek Orthodox Church after Mt Athos. Near the Church of the Apocalypse stands the new theological college attended by students from all over Greece. At Easter the celebrations are carried out with considerable pomp and later much gusto.

SKALA PATMOS
Admiralty chart no. 1669
Imray-Tetra chart no. G32

Approach
Conspicuous In the approaches to Skala Patmos there are a number of rocks and islets which are easily identified by day. Patmos *chora* and the fortress-like monastery on the crown of the hill S of Skala Patmos are conspicuous from some distance off. Skala Patmos lies almost in the middle of the island at the lowest point. The white houses of Skala Patmos are easy to see as you enter the bay.

By night Use the light on Ak Ilias (Fl(3)9s9M), Vrak Kavouronisia (Tragos Rock: Fl(2)WR.16s5/3M red sector covers 087°-232° over the reef N of the islet), Ak Aspri (Fl.WR.2s5/3M red sector covers 272°-320° over Ifalos Khelia, Nisis Khelia and Skopeloi Sklavaki), and the light at Skala Patmos (Fl.R.1·5s2M).

Dangers
1. Care should be taken of the numerous reefs associated with the rocks and islets in the approaches; Skopeloi Tragos lies 0·1 mile N of Vrak Kavouronisia (Tragos Rock). Ifalos Khelia lies 0·6 miles S of Nisis Khelia. Ifalos Sklavaki lies 0·2 miles SW of the more westerly of the two Sklavaki islets.
Note Ifalos Khelia is at the limit of the red sector of Ak Aspri light.

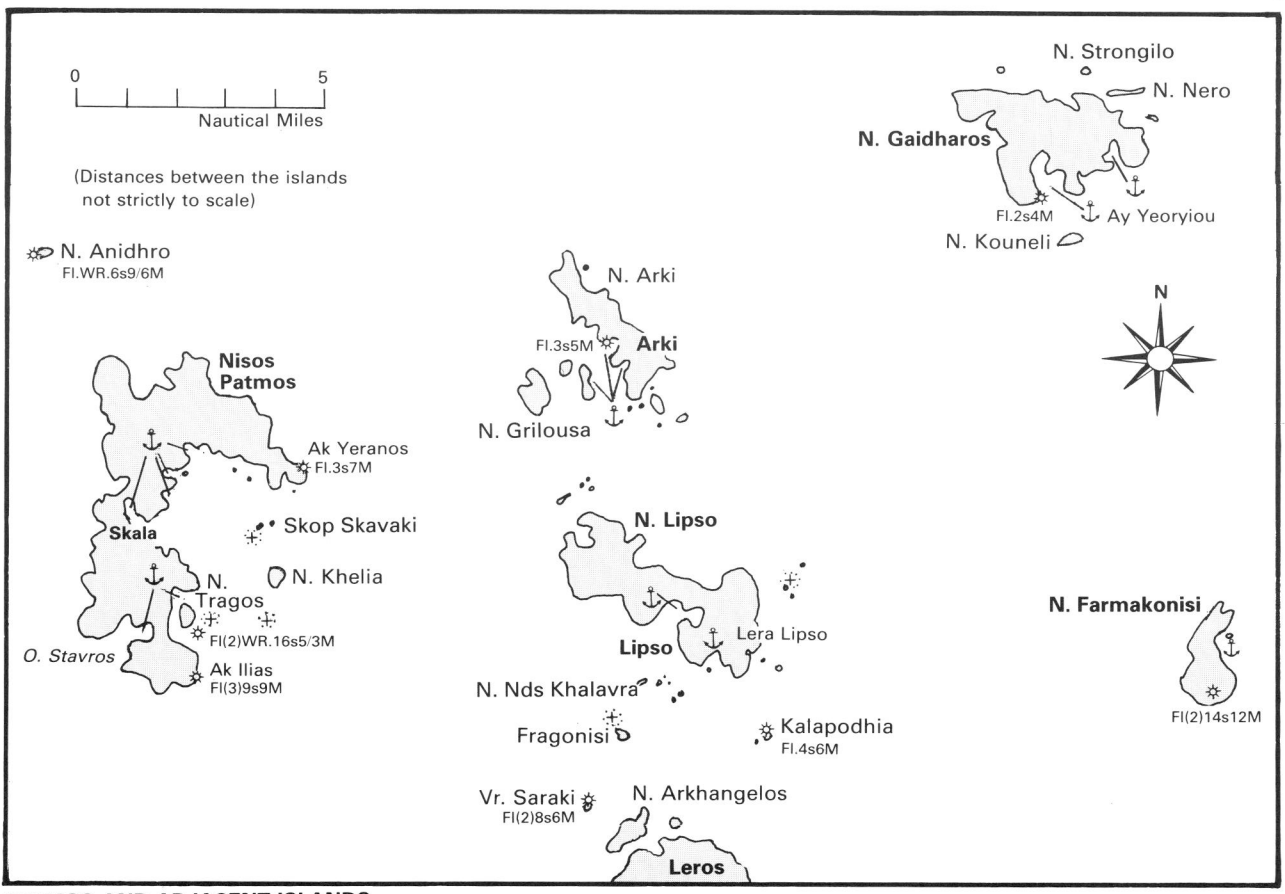

PATMOS AND ADJACENT ISLANDS

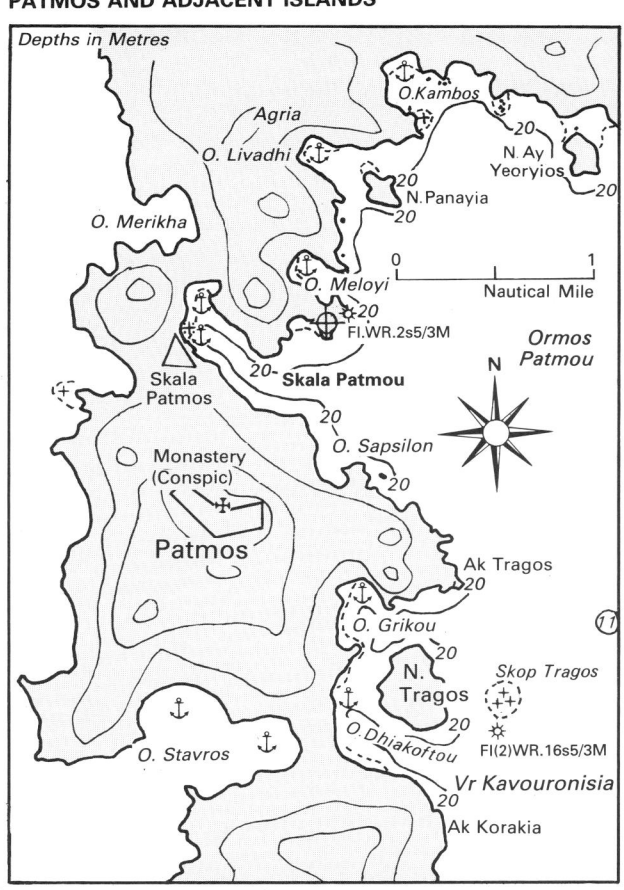

APPROACHES TO SKALA PATMOU
37°19'·7N 26°33'·9E (Ak Aspri Fl.WR)

miles S of Nisis Khelia. Skopeloi Sklavaki lies 0·2 miles SW of the more westerly of the two Sklavaki islets.

2. With the *meltemi*, strong gusts blow into the bay off the surrounding high land.

Mooring

Go stern-to or bows-to the quay immediately NW of the ferry quay. The bottom is sand and weed – good holding.

Shelter Shelter from the *meltemi* is better than it looks on the plan. The bay is open SE and with moderate SE winds it is uncomfortable – with strong SE winds probably untenable.

Authorities Port police and customs.

Anchorage Yachts can anchor near the head of the bay in 6–10 metres. Good shelter from the *meltemi*.

Facilities

Water On the quay. Enquire to the 'water man' at the Skala Hotel.

Fuel Can be obtained from a station at the head of the bay. There is a jetty near the fuel station with 2–3 metre depths at its extremity. A mini-tanker will deliver to the quay at Skala Patmos.

Repairs A slip at the head of the bay hauls out local *caïques*. Some mechanical repairs can be carried out at Skala Patmos. Good general hardware shops.

Provisions Good shopping for provisions at Skala.

Eating out Good tavernas on the waterfront.

401

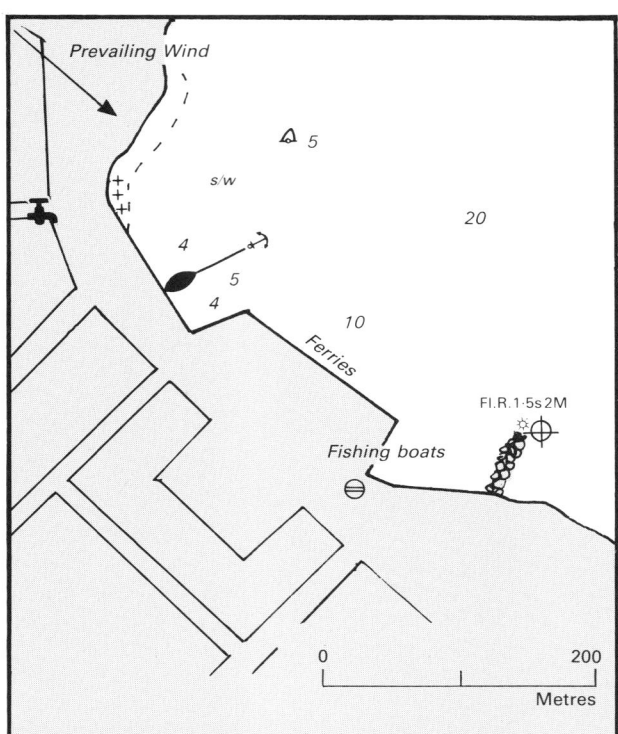

SKALA PATMOU
37°19'·2N 26°32'·8E (Fl.R.2M)

Other PO. OTE. Bank. Greek gas and *Camping Gaz.* Hire motorbikes and bicycles. Bus to the monastery. Daily ferry to Piraeus and Rhodes and local ferry to Kos and Samos.

General
Skala Patmos has largely grown up to meet the needs of cruise ships and the daily ferry bringing people to see the monastery of St John. Most of the buildings around the harbour date from the Italian occupation and unlike many of the towns that grow up around a busy ferry port, Skala is a pleasant town in itself. Remember when visiting the monastery to dress appropriately – bikinis and even shorts are inappropriate.

OTHER ANCHORAGES NEAR SKALA PATMOS
Imray-Tetra chart no. G32

1. *Ormos Meloyi* The first bay to the NE of Skala Patmos. Anchor at the head of the bay. The bottom is sand and weed. Open to the SE. Taverna ashore.
2. *Ormos Livadhi* Immediately N of Ormos Meloyi. An islet, Nisis Panayia, in the entrance to the bay is easily recognised. Anchor at the head of the bay. Holding and shelter as for Meloyi.
3. *Ormos Kambos* Immediately NE of Livadhi. Anchor where convenient. Holding as for Meloyi, but open to the S as well as the SE. There are a number of villas around the bay, a taverna, and a shop where basic provisions can be obtained.
4. *Ormos Grikou* Lies 2 miles to the SE of Skala. Anchor in 8–10 metres off the hamlet at the head of the bay. A jetty on the N side is reported to have 2 metre depths alongside. The bottom is thick weed – difficult to get through so make sure your anchor is well dug in. Open to the SE although Nisis Tragos provides some protection from this direction. Taverna ashore. Bus to Skala in the summer.

ORMOS STAVROS
On the W coast of Patmos almost opposite Ormos Griko. With the *meltemi* there is usually some swell in this bay. Open to the SW.

Islands adjacent to Patmos

To the E of Patmos lies a group of four small islands surrounded for the most part by islets and rocky spurs. They are mostly barren and the inhabitants scrape a living from fishing and a little agriculture and latterly some tourism.

Patmos looking W. The fortress-like monastery on the summit is conspicuous.

ARKI

A much indented island lying six miles ENE of Ak Yeranos on Patmos. About halfway along the W coast lies Port Augusta and Port Stretto, protected by a number of small off-lying islands.

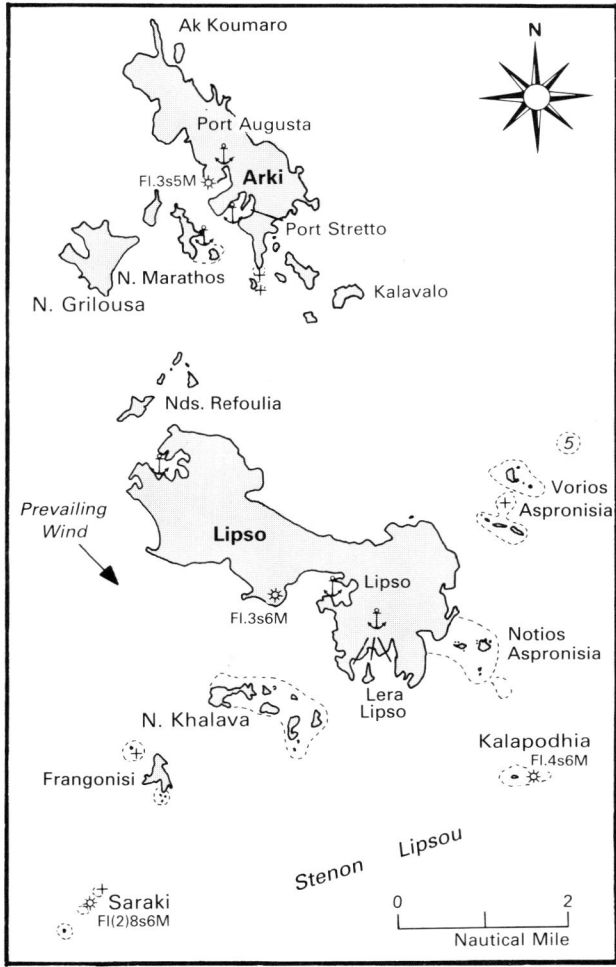

ARKI AND LIPSO

PORT AUGUSTA

Approach

The dogleg inlet on the W side of Arki. The islets in the approach are easily recognised. The light structure is conspicuous. A light (Fl.3s5M) is exhibited on the N side of the entrance but a night entrance is not advised. Care is needed of the reef running out for approximately 15m from the N entrance point.

Mooring

The inlet is very narrow once around the dogleg. In the middle of the inlet there are 4–5 metre depths shelving gradually to the sides. Go stern-to or bows-to the quay at the head of the inlet where there are mostly 2–4 metre depths. The bottom is mud and weed with a few rocks, good holding. Good all-round shelter in attractive surroundings.

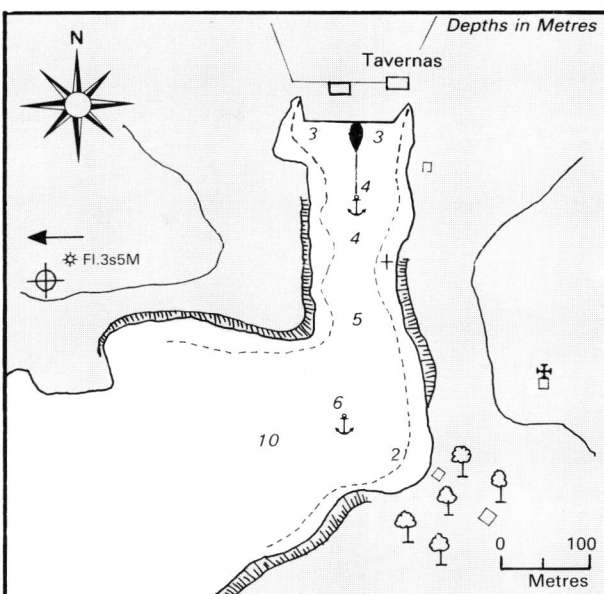

PORT AUGUSTA 37°22'·9N 26°43'·8E (Fl.3s5M)

Facilities

Two tavernas on the waterfront.

PORT STRETTO

Two inlets lying immediately S of Port Augusta. Anchor in 4–5 metres in the W inlet and in 10–12 metres in the E inlet. The bottom is sand and weed – good holding. Good shelter from the *meltemi* but open S.

NISIS MARATHO

The island lying in the approaches to Port Augusta and Port Stretto. On the SE side of the island there is an attractive anchorage sheltered from the *meltemi*. Anchor in 5 metres on a sandy bottom and take a line ashore. Taverna ashore.

Nisos Lipso
(Lipsa)

The island lying two miles S of Arki. It supports a small population in the village of Lipso (Sokoro) on the S side of the island. There is a harbour here in a dogleg bay, and there are a number of small bays under the SW tip of the island.

ORMOS LIPSO

Approach

Conspicuous Nisidhes Khalavra, the islets off the SW corner of Lipso, are easily identified from the distance. Closer in, a white church on the S side of the entrance and the light structure on the N side of the entrance will be seen until the bay opens up and the houses of Lipso become visible.

By night Use the light on Ak Gatos (Fl.3s6M) and on the quay in the bay (F.R.3M).

Lipso looking W. *Nigel Patten.*

Caution With the *meltemi* there are fierce gusts into the bay.

Mooring

Go stern-to or bows-to the quay on the W side. Alternatively anchor off in the bay. The bottom is sand, mud and weed – good holding once through the weed.

Shelter Good shelter from the *meltemi* although there are strong gusts. In the event of strong southerlies anchor in 4–5 metres at the southern end of the bay.

Authorities Customs and port police.

Facilities

Water On the quay.
Fuel On the E quay.

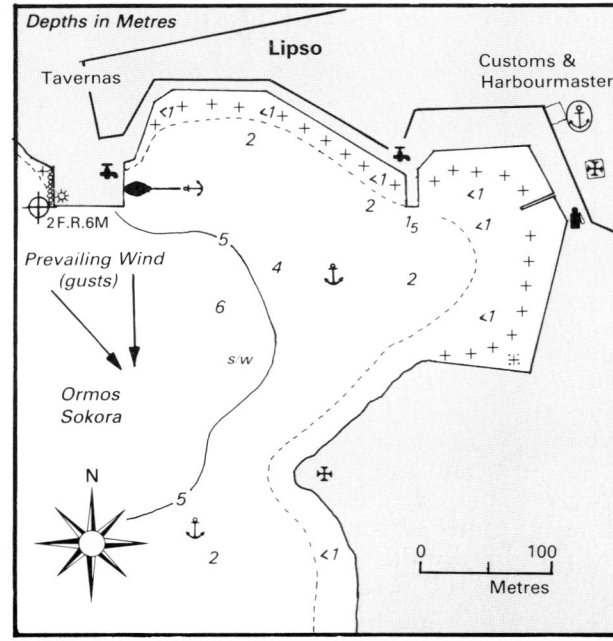

LIPSO
37°17'·8N 26°45'·8E (F.R.3M)

Provisions Most provisions can be obtained in the village.
Eating out A number of good tavernas near the waterfront, some with good fresh fish.
Other PO. Exchange. Ferry to Patmos.

General

The small village is attractive in a higgledy-piggledy sort of way. A few tourists come here but mostly the villagers derive a living from fishing and agriculture.

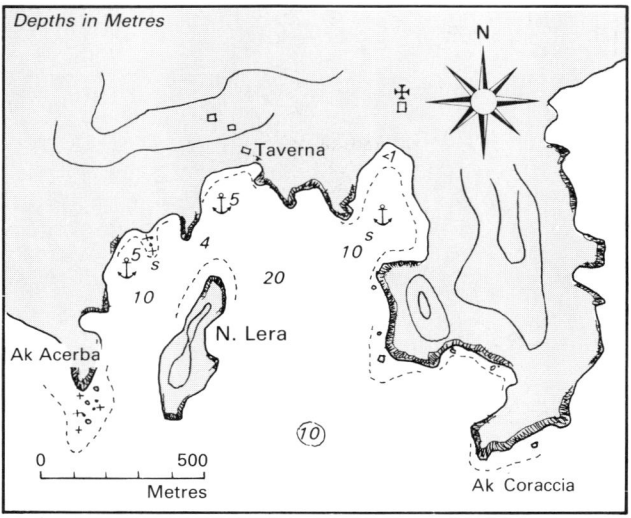

LERA LIPSO
37°16'·5N 26°46'·5E

LERA LIPSO

On the S side of Lipso in the bay situated between Ak Acerba and Ak Coraccia there are several coves affording good shelter from the *meltemi*.

Care must be taken of a reef extending S from Ak Acerba. Proceed around either side of the islet (Lera) in the bay and anchor where convenient in any of the coves around the N side. The bottom is sand and weed and good holding. Good shelter from the *meltemi* but completely open to the S. There is a small taverna on the beach in the centre cove but otherwise there are no facilities.

Nisis Gaidharos
(**Agathonisi**)

The much-indented island lying 10 miles NE of Arki and 8 miles W of the Turkish coast. It is easily identified from the distance. I am not sure whether the island is technically part of the Dodecanese or the eastern Sporades, but include it here for convenience.

On the S coast there are two deep bays. At the head of the westernmost of the two (Ay Yeoryios) there is a small fishing hamlet and it is here that a yacht should make for. The western entrance point of the bay is lit: Fl.2s4M.

Go stern or bows-to the N part of the ferry quay off

the hamlet. The bottom is mud, sand and weed, good holding. Good shelter from the *meltemi*.

Water, but it is reported not to be potable. Some provisions are available and there are three tavernas. Ferry to Pithagorion.

Ashore there is a small hamlet mostly inhabited by fishermen and their families who often go across to Turkish waters to poach the richer fishing grounds there. They are a hardy and friendly lot.

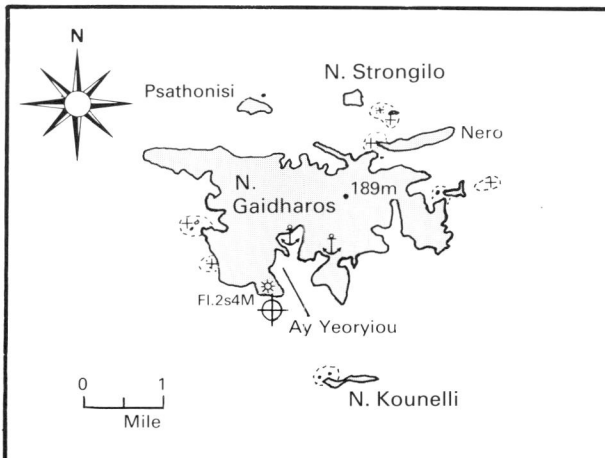

GAIDHAROS
37°26'·8N 26°57'·6E (light on SW end)

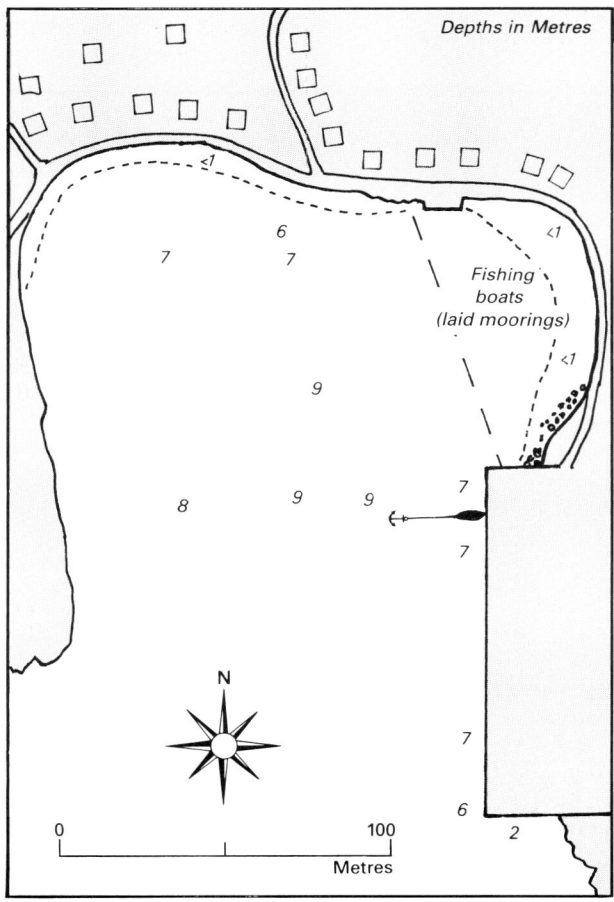

AY YEORYIOU

Gaidharos. Ay Yeoryiou looking SE. *Nigel Patten.*

Nisis Farmakonisi
(Pharmako Island)

The small island lying 14 miles E of Lipso just off the Turkish coast. On the E side of the island there is a small cove offering some shelter from the *meltemi* but completely open to the S and E. The cove can be recognised by four arches near the shore, the remains of a Roman villa.

Ashore there are a few ruins dating from the Romans and a small Byzantine church. It is here that Julius Caesar was captured by pirates and held to ransom for 38 days. H. M. Denham relates that he kept in good spirits and exercised and jested with his captors. Once released after the ransom was paid, he gathered an expedition together and in turn captured the pirates who were sentenced to death by crucifixion.

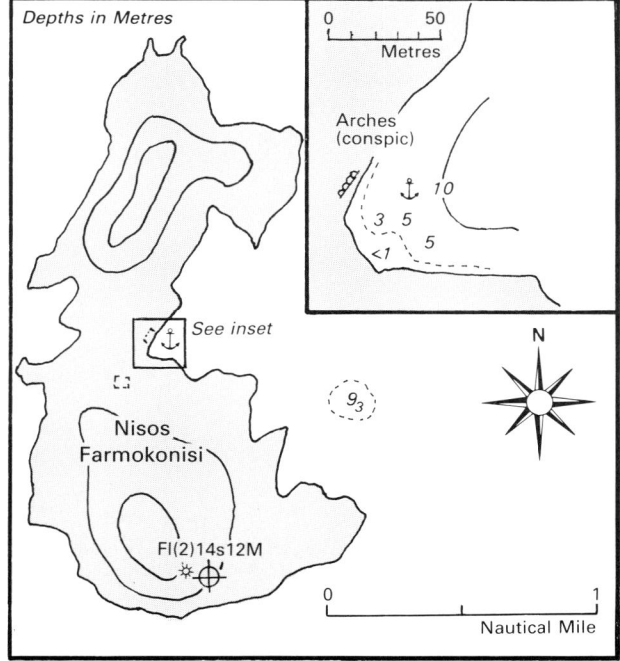

FARMAKONISI 37°16'·9N 27°05'·3E (light on S end)

Leros

Leros lies close north of Kalimnos and the two islands were referred to as one in antiquity – the Kalydnian Isles of Lero-Kalimno. Leros means 'dirty' or 'grubby' in Greek and the inhabitants have a reputation for being dour and given to lying and thieving. In my experience the islanders are nothing like this: Leros is a handsome island peopled with friendly and generous islanders. On my first visit the local fishermen in Ormos Partheni gave me a large mackerel and wished me luck on my trip.

Leros is less harsh than its sister island Kalimnos. The hills are rounded and sloped and the countryside around Ormos Lakki and Platanos is wooded and green. Platanos itself is a jumble of hibiscus, jasmine, bougainvillea and oleander. It is a thoroughly likable island capital with friendly inhabitants and a fine view over Ormos Alindas and Panali.

The island was associated in antiquity with the cult of Artemis. The worship of the mother-goddess when most of the civilized world had switched to the worship of the father-god may have contributed to the Lerians' bad reputation among the surrounding islanders. During the carnival (in February or March) satirical verses are composed which the children recite at parties given in the houses of newly-weds. Stuart Rossiter in the *Blue Guide to Greece* considers these customs to derive from ceremonies associated with Dionysus of Eleusis. Whatever the mythopoeic origins everyone has a good time.

ORMOS LAKKI (Porto Lago)
Admiralty chart. 1669

Approach
Conspicuous From the W the Kalaboshi peninsula has a distinctive white appearance. The group of rocks NW of the entrance and the light structures on either side of the entrance can be seen closer in. At the entrance to the bay the fort and 4 windmills at Alinda will be seen, but they are obscured by a hill as you proceed further into the bay. The buildings of Lakki and the mole are conspicuous once inside the bay.

By night Use the lights on either side of the entrance to Ormos Lakki (Ak Lakki Fl(2)16s9M and Ak Angistro Fl.2·5s5M) and the light on the end of the mole at Lakki (Fl.R.3s3M).

Dangers
1. With the *meltemi* there are strong gusts off the high land in the approaches and in the bay. There is also a confused sea at the entrance to the bay.
2. With strong southerlies there are gusts and a confused sea in the entrance to the bay and a considerable swell penetrates right into the bay itself.

Note It is prohibited to approach within 200 metres of the naval establishment on the S side of Ormos Lakki. The buildings of the naval establishment are clearly visible once inside the bay.

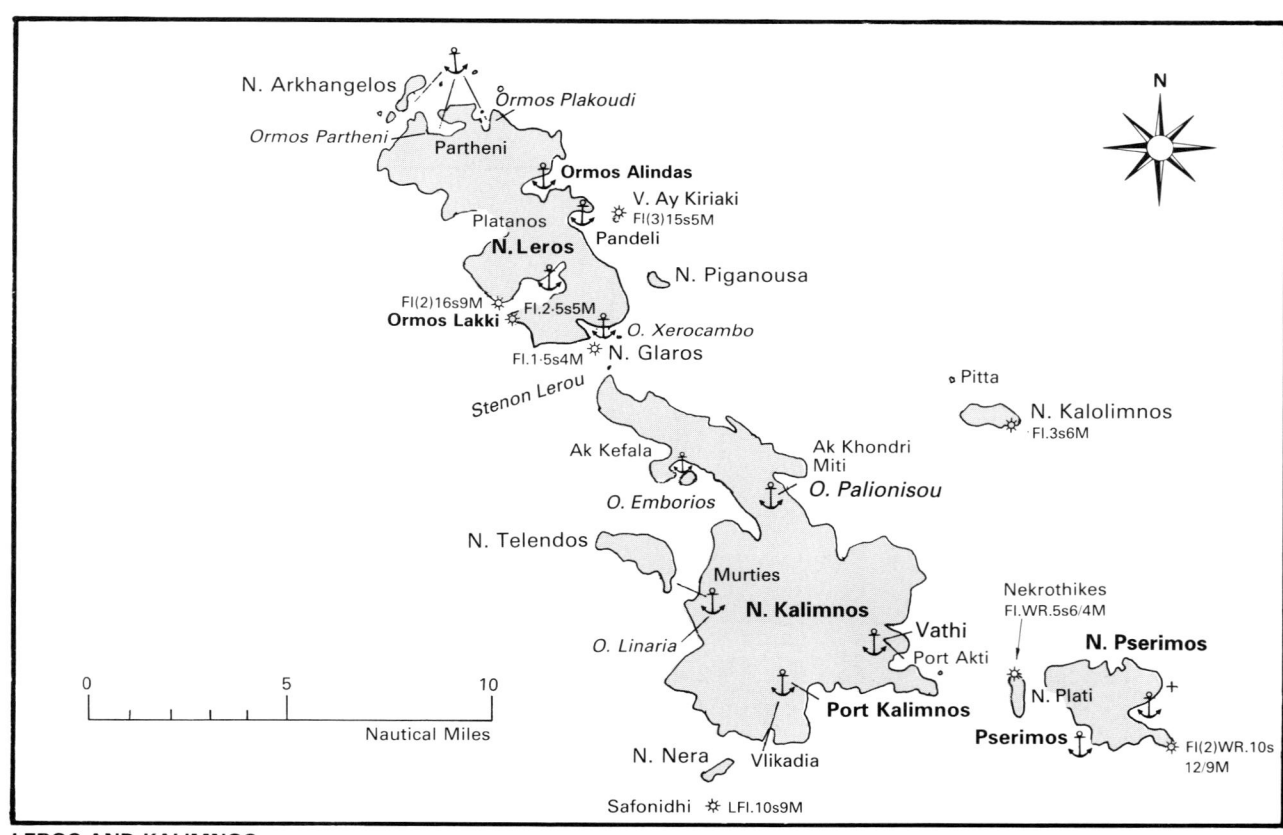

LEROS AND KALIMNOS

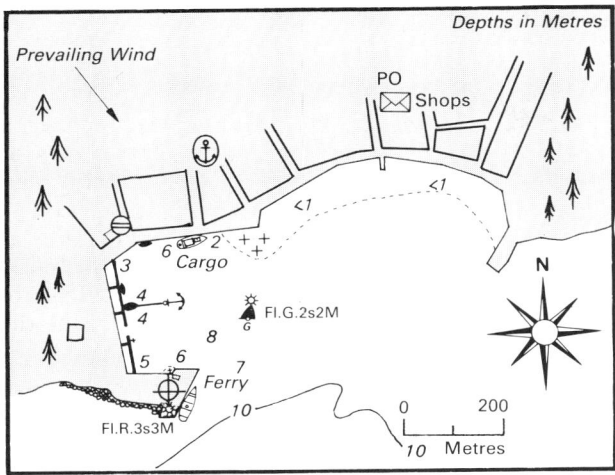

PORT LAKKI
37°07'·7N 26°51'E (Fl.R.3M)

Leros. Lakki looking N from the mole.

Mooring

Go stern-to or bows-to or alongside the wharf or the quay. Beware of a steel rod projecting underwater on the S section of the wharf.

Shelter With the *meltemi* there are gusts off the hills into the harbour and a yacht is blown off the quay. With strong SW and W winds the harbour is dangerous. Strong gusts blow down into the bay from the surrounding hills and a surge develops at the head of the bay and in the harbour. The ferry goes to Ormos Alindas in this weather.

Authorities Port police and customs.

Note The harbour can be smelly in the summer from the sewerage emptying into it.

Facilities

Water On the quay – reported not potable.
Fuel In the town.
Repairs Boatyard at the head of the bay. 50-ton travel-hoist. Mechanical, some engineering, wood and GRP repairs possible. Showers and toilets. Contact Evros Boatyard. Constantin N Kalantzopoulos. ☎ (Leros) (0247) 23921/24733 *Fax* (0247) 23947 ☎ (Athens) (01) 363 2570 *Fax* (01) 362 7005

Provisions Good shopping for most provisions. Ice can be delivered from a factory outside the village.
Eating out Tavernas nearby.
Other PO. OTE. Hire motorbikes and bicycles. Bus to Platanos, the island's capital near Ormos Alindas. Ferries to Piraeus and Rhodes.

General

The large buildings surrounding Ormos Lakki all date from the Italian occupation when the bay was the Italian naval base. Many of the buildings have been used as hospitals – there are three mental hospitals, two children's hospitals and a general hospital.

The mental hospitals have recently been under scrutiny from the European media with Leros described as a 'Devil's Island'. The condition of the inmates, many of whom have been here since they were children, is appalling – they have been shown crawling naked on dirty floors with few if any amenities and few trained staff to look after them. The conditions are not far short of those depicted in lithographs of 19th-century care of the mentally ill. The Greek government has promised to clean up its act, but little has been done to date.

ORMOS PARTHENI
Admiralty chart no 1669

A large dogleg bay offering good all-round protection on the N side of Leros. The prohibited area at the entrance is marked by three large red and white can buoys. The S and SW side of the bay including the concrete wharf are also military areas and yachts are prohibited from navigating in the vicinity. Anchor in 3–8 metres at the head of the bay in the E known as

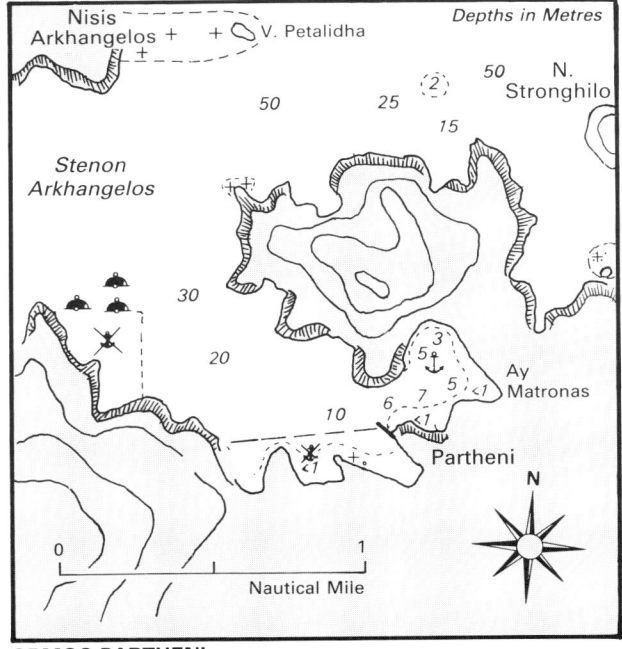

ORMOS PARTHENI
37°11'·5N 26°48'E

Ayias Matronas. The bottom is mud and weed – good holding.

A few fishermen use the bay. A café/taverna. Photographing any part of the bay is forbidden.

NISIS ARKHANGELOS

On the S side of the island opposite the entrance of Ormos Partheni there is a small cove sheltered from the *meltemi*. Good underwater fishing around the nearby rocks.

ORMOS PLAKOUDI

On the NE coast of Leros, Ormos Plakoudi offers good shelter in all except NE–E winds. In the middle of the entrance to the bay the group of above-water rocks can be left to either side (5 metre depths and over on both sides). Anchor off the small fishing hamlet.

ORMOS ALINDAS
Admiralty chart no. 1669

Approach

This deep bay situated on the E coast of Leros is the alternative ferry port in strong W–SW winds.

Conspicuous The Venetian castle on the rocky summit of Ak Kastello and four windmills on the saddle of a hill above the town are conspicuous from some distance off.

By night Use the light W of Ak Kastello (Fl.3s5M) and the light on the pier in the bay (F.R.3M).

Dangers With the *meltemi* there are strong gusts into the bay.

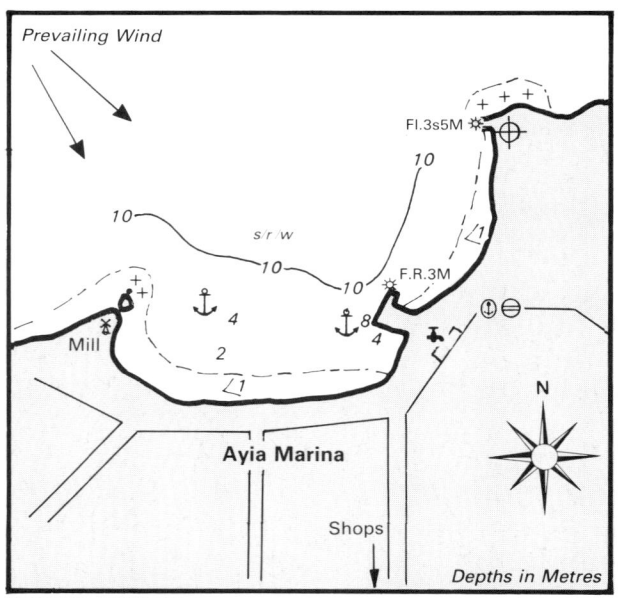

ORMOS ALINDAS
37°09'·7N 26°51'·5N (Fl.3s5M)

Leros. Ormos Alindas and quay looking W from Platanos. *Nigel Patten.*

Mooring

Anchor close W of the short mole in 4–6 metre depths or go alongside the mole in calm weather. The bottom is hard sand and rock – bad holding.

When the *meltemi* is blowing strongly the best palce to be is in the NW corner of the bay. Anchor in 3-6m.

Shelter The *meltemi* gusts into the bay from W–NW setting up an uncomfortable choppy sea. With a strong *meltemi* the anchorage off Ay Marina is untenable. Anchor in the NW corner or go to Pandeli.

Facilities

Water Near the quay.
Fuel In the village.
Repairs Agmar in Ayia Marina can organise most repairs including mechanical repairs.
Provisions Most provisions can be found nearby.
Eating out Tavernas on the waterfront.
Other PO. OTE. Bank.

General

The village of Ayia Marina is the village near the water while on the saddle of the hill above the bay, about fifteen minutes' walk away, is Lero or Platanos, the main town of the island. Both Ayia Marina and Lero are thoroughly pleasant places with an abundance of bougainvillea and clematis adorning the houses.

PANDELI (Panali)

Approach

On the S side of Ak Kastello and Ak Pandelis lies a large bay and in the NW corner is Pandeli with a small harbour off the beach.

Mooring

Go alongside stern or bows-to the outer part of the mole or anchor off the beach in 4–8 metre depths. The bottom is sand and weed – good holding. Good protection from the *meltemi*. A small cove immediately W can also be used. Open S and E.

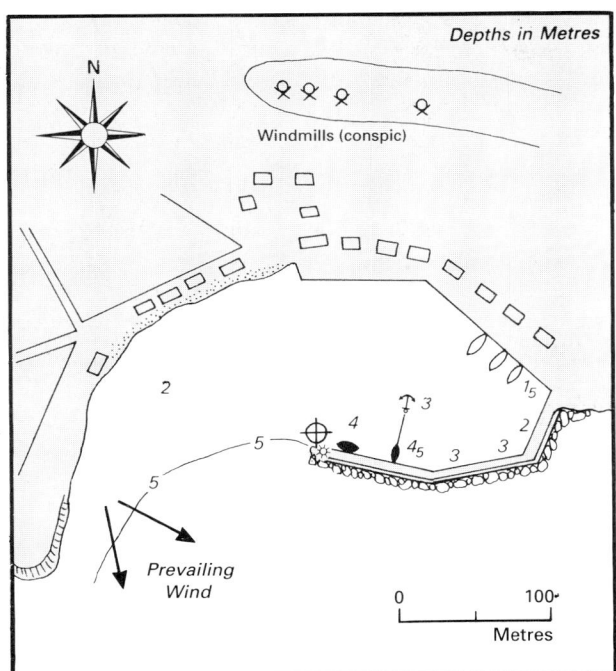

PANDELI
37°08'·99N 26°51'·82E

Facilities
Some provisions ashore. Tavernas on the waterfront.

General
The setting is wonderful with a few houses around the beach and the local fishing boats drawn up close to the beach. Oleander, bougainvillea and tamarisk grow profusely in the village with fishing nets strung up to dry along the beach. Platamos is about a fifteen minute walk up the hill.

Pandeli harbour looking NE. *Neville Bulpitt.*

ORMOS XEROKAMBOS
On the S side of Leros this large bay offers good shelter from the *meltemi* being open only to the S. Anchor at the head of the bay off the small hamlet. Taverna ashore.

Kalimnos

The sister island of Leros lying immediately S of it separated by Stenon Lerou. This great craggy lump of rock is for the most part steep-to and bare of vegetation. Kalimnos imparts a feeling of prehistoric permanence – long after the human race has disappeared, you get the feeling, Kalimnos will remain much as it is today. It is not so much the height of the mountain range (Mt Profitis Ilias or Parasivia is a scant 679m) but the sheer bulk of it which is impressive from seaward.

In ancient and medieval times the island followed the fortunes of Kos. The Italian occupation in 1912 was actively opposed by the Kalimniots who painted the Greek national colours everywhere to annoy their masters. During the Second World War many of the islanders, faced with starvation when their livelihood of sponge-fishing was denied them, emigrated all over the world. You will meet many American and Australian Greeks in the capital who have returned home to have a look at their island.

The grubby sprawling capital of Pothia (Port Kalimnos) is the centre of sponge-fishing in Greece. In ancient times the sponge was used much as we use artificial sponges today – for washing and cleaning up the after-dinner mess. It also had other uses:

'The servants in the 'Odyssey' swabbed tables with it, while it was in great demand with artisans, who used it to apply paint, and with soldiers who had no drinking vessels to hand. In the Middle Ages, burned sponge was reputed to cure various illnesses. Together with olive oil it has been used from time immemorial as a contraceptive pessary by the oldest professionals – who oblivious of the fact that they figure in the pages of Athenaeos, still flourish in Plaka today – using roughly the same sort of slang, in which the word 'sponge' finds many a picturesque use.'

Lawrence Durrell *The Greek Islands*

Artificial sponges have replaced many of the uses of this little animal and most of the natural sponges being washed out in Kalimnos harbour are sold to tourists.

LIMIN KALIMNOU (Kalymnos, Pothia)
Admiralty chart no. 1669
Imray-Tetra chart no. G34

Approach
Conspicuous From the distance the buildings of Kalimnos town around the bay and a number of white oil storage tanks to the E of the town are conspicuous. Closer in, the monastery on the hill above the town, the silver cupola of the cathedral on the waterfront and the outer mole are easily identified.

By night Use the lights at the entrance: Fl.R.2s5M and Fl.G.2s3M. The paucity of lights in the approaches to the harbour means care must be taken. Even in the bay the harbour lights are difficult to make out against the loom of the town lights. A large floodlit cross on the hill SE of the town shows up well.

Dangers With the *meltemi* blowing there are strong gusts off the high land down into the approaches and in Ormos Kalimnou itself.

Mooring

Go stern-to or bows-to the quay in the SW. The bottom is mud and weed and the holding uncertain if an anchor cannot cut through the weed cover. Yachts can also go stern-to or bows-to at the SW end of the outer commercial basin with a long line ashore.

Shelter Good shelter – the gusts from the *meltemi* are not troublesome in the harbour. With strong southerlies an uncomfortable swell enters the harbour but it is not dangerous.

Authorities Port police and customs.

Facilities

Water On the quay. Contact Kalimnos Yachting near the quay or the sponge factory.

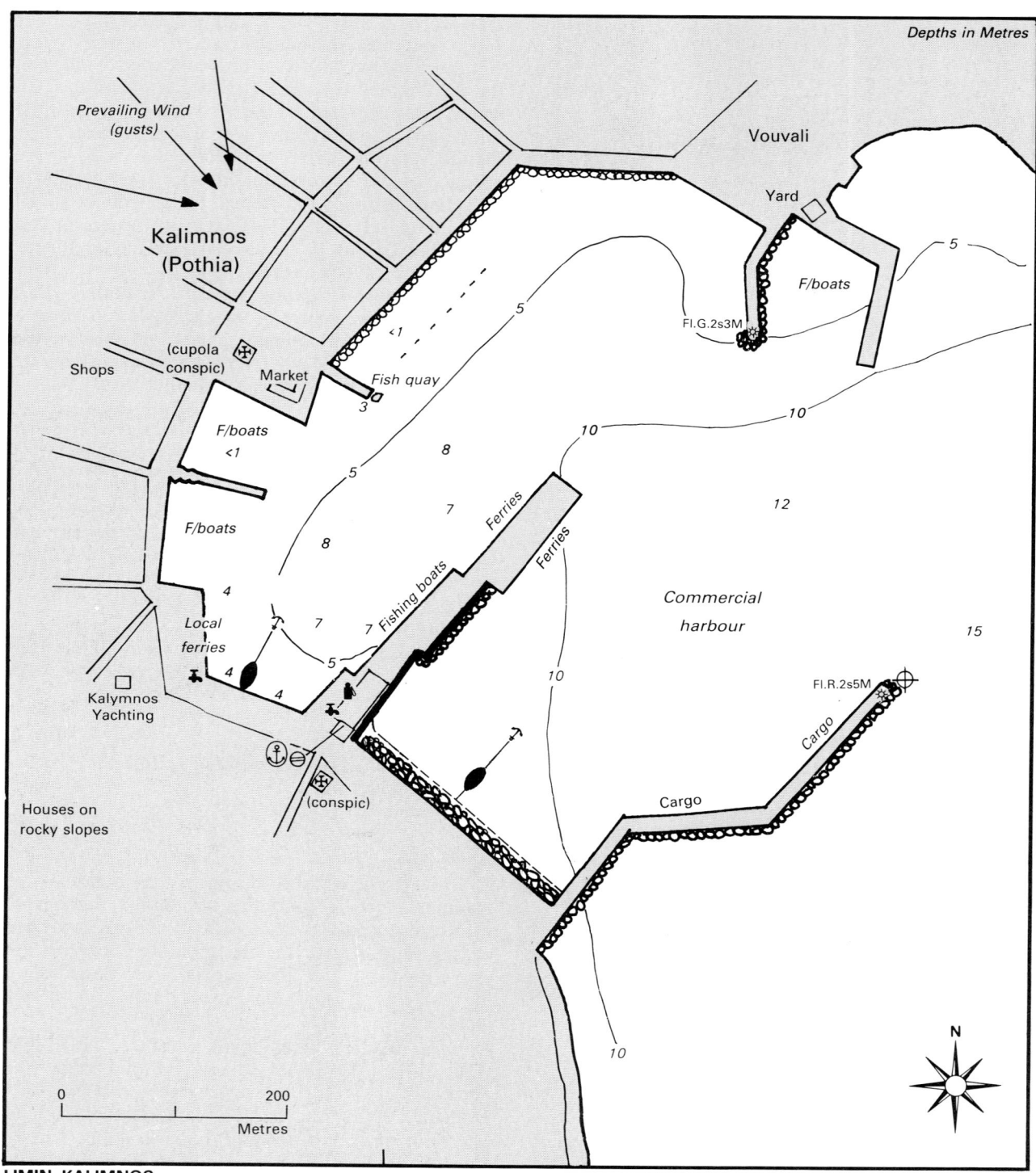

LIMIN KALIMNOS
36°56'·9N 26°59'·5E (Fl.R.5M)

compressor is used and deeper waters off Africa and Cyprus are fished. A museum could be filled with the ancient patched gear still being used.

The town of Kalimnos is attractive from the distance. Many of the houses are washed in various shades of blue – a practice continued from the days of the Italian occupation when the blue houses reminded their Italian masters of the Greek colours. On closer inspection the town is rather dusty and grubby with the hustle and bustle of tripper boats and fishing boats loading and unloading their cargoes and trucks, cars, vans, motorbikes, three-wheeler mini-trucks and vans buzzing along the waterfront. Sponges are of course for sale everywhere.

ORMOS AKTI (Ati, Katsouni)
Immediately NW of Ak Kahli, the SE extremity of Kalimnos, lies Ormos Akti. Much of the bay is now obstructed by fish farms though there is still room to anchor. With a strong *meltemi* a swell enters the bay and there are gusts off the surrounding hills.

Yacht quay in Kalimnos harbour looking NE.

Fuel In the town. A mini-tanker can deliver to the quay.

Repairs Most mechanical repairs can be carried out. Some light engineering work. A boatyard to the E of the town hauls out large *caïques* and a few yachts. The Kalimnos sponge-boats are also built here. Good hardware and tool-shops. Basic chandlery can be obtained from a number of shops near the fish quay.

Provisions Good shopping for all provisions. Ice available.

Eating out Tavernas on the waterfront and in the town. Noisy bars on the waterfront.

Other PO. OTE. Banks. Greek gas and *Camping Gaz*. There is a gas filling factory just outside the town. Hire cars, motorbikes and bicycles. Intermittent bus service to the other villages on the island. Daily ferries to Piraeus and Rhodes.

General
Kalimnos is the home of the Kalimniot sponge-divers – the sponge-boats, most of the *trehandiri* type and about 10–12 metres in length, are built in the boatyard immediately E of the town. Originally the sponge-divers fished in shallow waters, jumping overboard with a heavy stone slab and scooping the sponges off the bottom into a net. Nowadays a

Kalimnos town looking from the yacht quay.

VATHI

One mile N of Ormos Akti lies the deep fjord of Vathi. From the E the deep slit in the hills can be seen from the distance. Moor stern-to or bows-to the NW side of the short mole (the end is used by tripper boats). Alternatively anchor further into the inlet with a long line to the shore off the village. The bottom is sand and weed – good holding. Good shelter from the *meltemi* although there are strong gusts off the surrounding hills.

In the small hamlet at the shallow head of the inlet, limited provisions can be obtained and there are several tavernas. Near the mole there is a 'yacht club' which can supply water, showers, ice, and of course food and drink.

The valley inland from Vathi is extremely attractive – orange and lemon groves and lush market gardens contrast with the steep red rock hills in this, one of the few lush parts of Kalimnos.

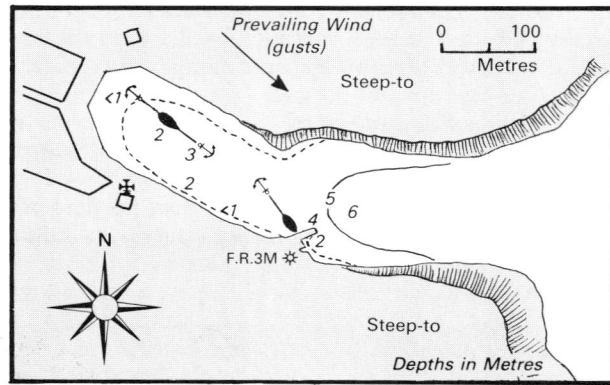

VATHI – KALIMNOS
36°58'·5N 27°02'E

ORMOS PALIONISOU (Baia Isolavecchia)

A bay on the S side of Ak Poundha. Although this bay appears suitable, the holding (rock covered by a thin layer of sand and weed) is bad. Near the shore there are several iron stakes to take a line ashore, but the bay should only really be used in calm weather.

EMBORIOS (Vorio Bay)

A bay lying on the SE side of Ak Kefala. The islet of Kalavros lying in the entrance can be identified and closer in, the hamlet at the head of the bay will be seen. Off the hamlet there is a T-pier but this is usually occupied by fishing boats. Anchor in the bay in 6–10 metres and take a line ashore. The bottom is mud and sand with thick weed over it. Unless the anchor manages to get through the weed the holding is uncertain – use a fisherman. Reasonable shelter from the *meltemi*.

Ashore there is a convivial taverna.

MIRTIES

A small village in Stenon Telendhos. There is a small harbour here used by local *caiques* and tripper boats running to Nisos Telendhos. There may be room for a small yacht or anchor off in calm weather . Water on the quay. Provisions and tavernas ashore.

NISIS TELENDHOS

In calm weather anchor off the small hamlet on the E coast. It is quite well sheltered from the *meltemi* here. The craggy lump of Telendhos conveys a prehistoric permanence – always has been there and always will be – and indeed has been inhabited since prehistoric

Kalimnos. Vathi looking W from near the entrance to the inlet. *Nigel Patten*

times as well as by the Greeks, Romans and later in the Middle Ages. The island was joined to Kalimnos up to the 15th century when an earthquake rearranged the topography and submerged the land-bridge.

ORMOS LINARIAS

Is virtually untenable except in calm weather. It is open to all sectors westward and subject to strong gusts off the hills in southerly winds.

ORMOS VLIKADIA (Vlikhadhia)

On the S coast of Kalimnos, one mile W of Ak Ayios, Yeoryios is open only to the S. It provides good shelter from the *meltemi* although there are gusts off the surrounding hills. Summer villas and a taverna ashore.

Pserimos

PSERIMOS

Situated on the SW side of Nisis Pserimos, the entrance to the bay is difficult to see except from the SW. Once at the entrance the houses of the hamlet and the rough stone mole are easily seen. Go stern or bows-to the E end of the quay if there is room. You may have to wait until the tripper boats from Kos return at night before you get a berth here. The bottom is sand and weed with some rocky ledges – good holding on the sand. With a *meltemi* blowing a swell enters the bay but if a yacht can manage to tuck itself into the NW corner behind the mole it is not unduly uncomfortable.

Tavernas on the beach. The hamlet of gleaming whitewashed houses is a holiday place for the locals from Kos and Kalimnos.

Caution Care must be taken to avoid the reef just N of Ak Sphuri off the island. The outer rocks are awash and easily spotted.

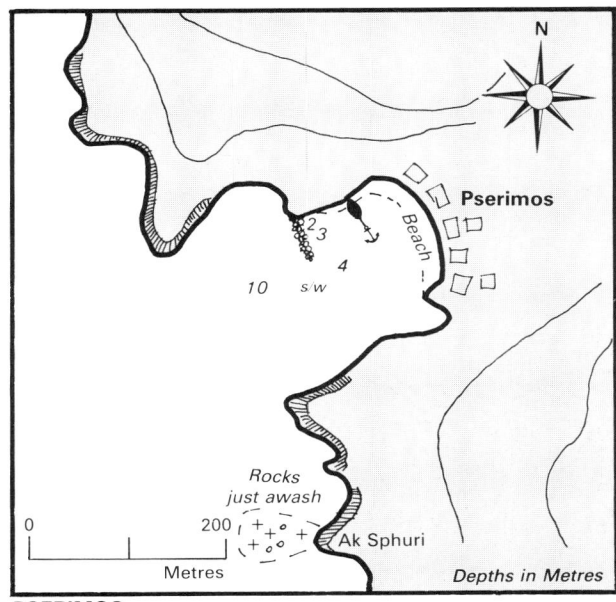

PSERIMOS
36°55'·5N 27°08'E

Kos
(Stanko, Istanköy)

Kos lies tucked into the Gulf of Kos (the ancient Ceramic Gulf, Turkish Gokova Korfezi) between the Myndus peninsula to the north and the Dorian promontory to the south. The fingers of Turkey reach out to touch the island enclosing the ancient triangle of trading power that vied with Rhodes to dominate the southwestern Aegean. Kos was probably not an important partner in the power hexapolis and not until the city of Kos was founded in 366 BC on the present site of the modern capital did it prosper and become an important maritime power. Today the harbour is probably much as it was when Kos was a powerful city.

The island has always been much praised for its fertility. A mountain ridge runs its length (the summit attains a height of 845 metres near the NE end) and on the eastern side it is precipitous and barren. It is the western side which is well-watered and fertile. Sandy beaches fringe the cultivated plain which produces fine vegetables, melons and grapes. The Kos variety of lettuce was introduced to England from here. Perhaps the mulberry trees on which the silkworm feeds also covered these slopes in antiquity. Kos was once famous for its silk and in particular the *Coae vestes*, the diaphanous flowing silk dresses prized by Roman women – sadly no longer made or worn.

Ancient Kos had many famous citizens but above them all stands Hippocrates, the great physician of antiquity and the father of modern medicine. We know little of the old healing methods but we do know that for the Hippocratic school the site of the sanatorium was as important as the methods. (The tranquillity of Epidavros, of mysteries earlier than Hippocrates, is proof enough.) The Aesculapion (Ascelepion) is just outside Kos town and should not be missed. The three terraces lie in a peaceful setting near to medicinal springs on a limestone hill overlooking the Gulf of Kos. The Italians rebuilt much of the Aesculapion to the original plan without destroying the calm of the place. It is the appropriate place to remember the Hippocratic Oath:

'I shall look upon him who shall have taught me this art even as one of my parents. I will share my substance with him and relieve his need should he be in want. His children shall be as my own kin, and I will teach them the art, if they so wish, without fee or covenant...The regimen I adopt shall be for the benefit of my patients according to my ability and judgement, and not for their hurt or for any wrong. I will give no deadly drug to any, though it be asked of me, nor will I counsel such, and especially I will not aid a woman to procure abortion. Whatsoever house I enter, there I will go for the benefit of the sick refraining from all wrong doing or corruption, and especially from any act of seduction, of male or female, of bond or free. Whatever things I may hear concerning the life of men during my attendance of the sick, or even apart from them, which should be kept secret, I will keep my own counsel upon, deeming such things as sacred secrets.'

Recently more tourists have been discovering Kos and several large hotels have been built around the

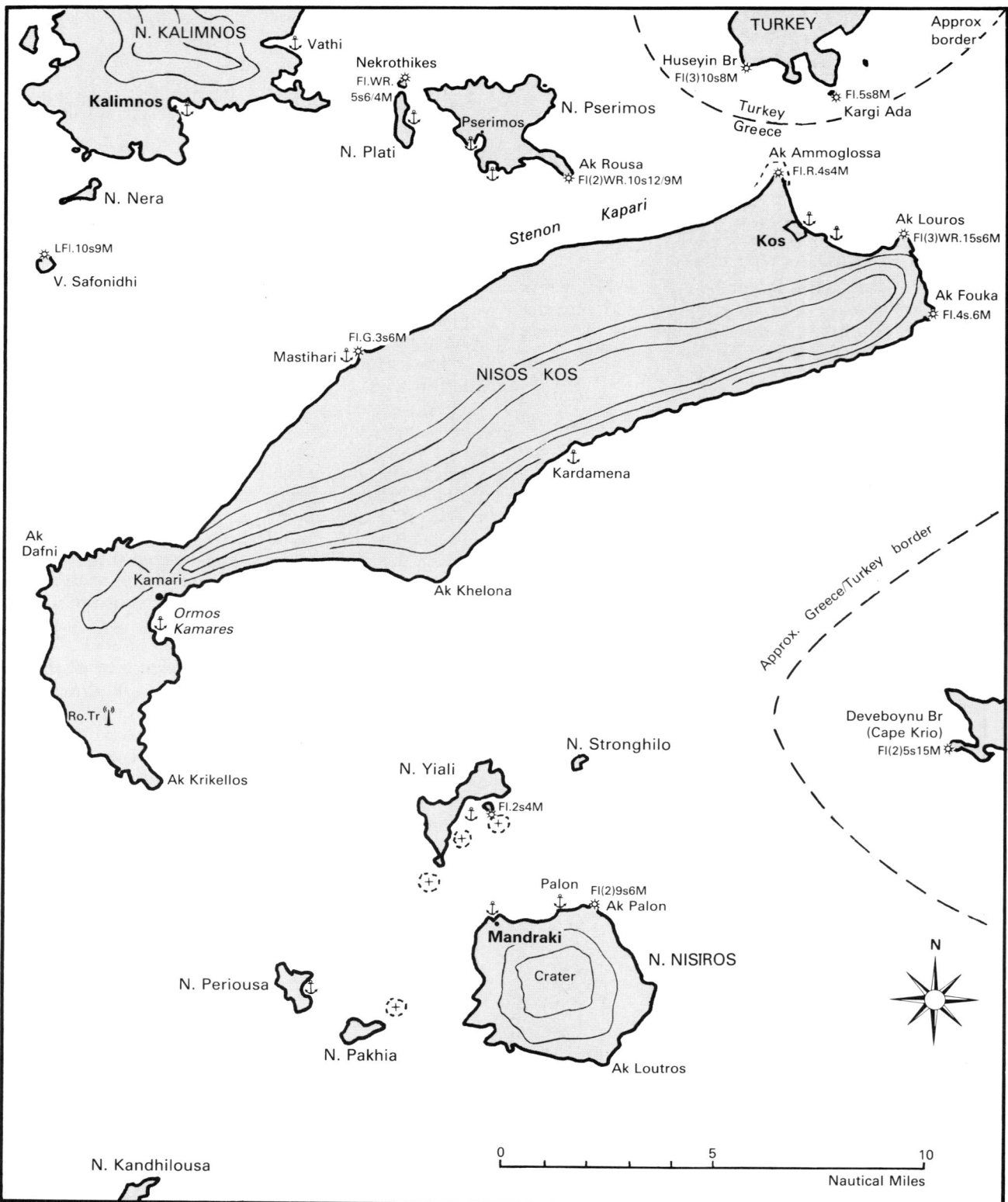

KALIMNOS TO NISIROS

sandy beaches. In many ways it resembles Rhodes –
the green slopes, large hotels, the bustling harbour
under the castle of the Knights – and like Rhodes it
wants to have an ever larger slice of the tourist pie
whatever the cost.

KOS (Ko, Stanko)
Admiralty chart no. 1616
Imray-Tetra chart no. 35

Approach
Conspicuous From the E the fort on the S side of the entrance, the palace, a chimney near the entrance and a minaret in the town are conspicuous. From the N and W a large brown hotel on the spit ending in Ak Ammoglossa is conspicuous from some distance off. Rounding the point the entrance to the harbour is easily seen.

By night Use the lights on Ak Ammoglossa (Fl.R.4s4M), Ak Fouka (Fl.4s6M), and Ak Louros (Fl(3)WR.15s6M, and the lights at the entrance (Fl.G.3s3M and F.R).

Dangers The shoals extending from Ak Ammoglossa should be given a good offing. With a strong *meltemi* blowing there are often confused seas off Ammoglossa, but once around it the sea is comparatively flat.

Mooring
Go stern-to or bows-to the town quay or on the new quay on the E side. The bottom is mud – excellent holding.

Shelter With a strong *meltemi* there is often an uncomfortable surge in the harbour.

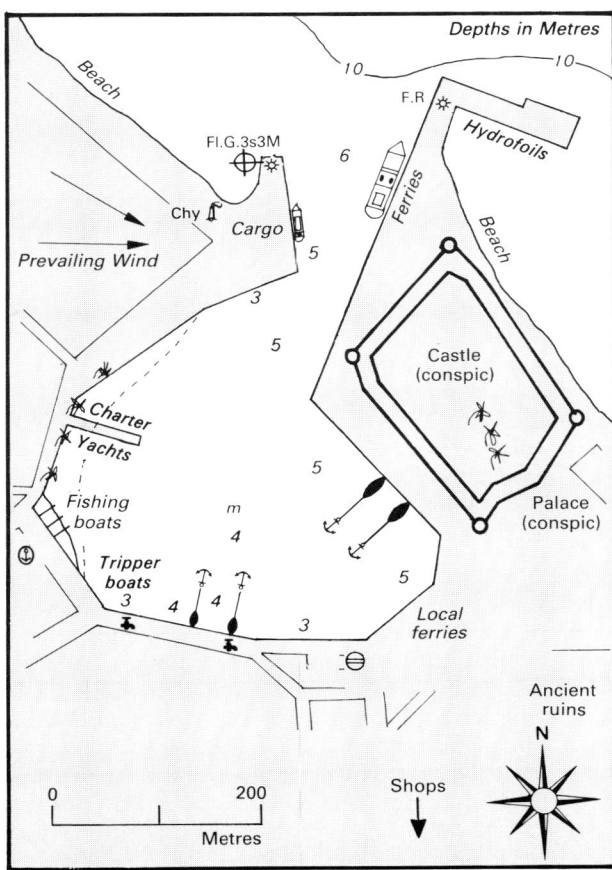

KOS
36°53'·9N 27°17'·3E (Fl.G.3M)

Authorities A port of entry: port police, customs, health and immigration authorities.

Anchorage Large yachts can anchor off the beach S of the entrance in settled weather.

Note The harbour is dirty and smelly with overburdened sewers running into it.

Facilities
Water On the town quay.

Fuel In the town. A mini-tanker can deliver to the quay.

Repairs Some mechanical repairs. Hardware shops and some chandlery available.

Provisions Excellent shopping for provisions and a good market just up from the harbour. Ice from a factory on the outskirts of town.

Eating out Excellent tavernas in the town.

Other PO. OTE. Banks. Greek gas and *Camping Gaz.* Hire cars, motorbikes and bicycles. Intermittent bus service to the other villages on the islands. Daily ferries to Piraeus and Rhodes and to Bodrum in Turkey. International and internal flights to Kos airport.

General
Kos is a likable mixture of medieval Frankish and Turkish architecture with a few contributions of Italian monumental. Oleander, bougainvillea, jasmine and hibiscus grow in profusion and classical remains from the era of Greek prosperity are used in novel ways – a sarcophagus forms the basin for a fountain, fragments of ancient marble prop up the branch of a tree, part of a marble column forms the base for a flower box, huge hewn blocks of stone line the path in a park. The fort and the adjacent park, shaded by old spreading plane trees (one of which is reputed to be that which Hippocrates taught under, although it is only 400–500 years old – a nice tradition anyway) and cooled by the *meltemi*, is quite one of the most pleasant places to be on a hot summer's day. A small museum in the town houses Greek and Roman finds from the excavations.

In recent years Kos has attracted growing numbers of tourists and it seems as if the city of Kos is set to revive ancient rivalries and challenge Rhodes for the valuable annual cargo of bodies craving sun and sand. The town has changed to accommodate this new trade and though I think it retains much of its character, you may, like some others, think it has become 'all fast food and discos'.

KOS MARINA
Just under a mile SE of the old harbour a new marina is under construction. The outer breakwater, inner breakwater, and quayed areas are in place at the time of writing. The marina is expected to be complete in 1996-97.

It will provide approximately 300 plus yacht berths and a large area of hard standing ashore.

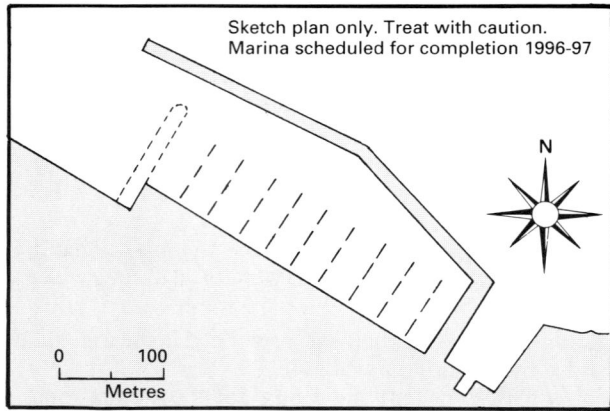

Sketch plan only. Treat with caution.
Marina scheduled for completion 1996-97

N

0   100
Metres

KOS MARINA

MASTIHARI

A large new harbour about halfway along the NW coast of Kos. An L-shaped breakwater provides good protection from the *meltemi*. The entrance is lit (Fl.G.3s6M) though the light is not to be relied upon. The harbour is used by inter-island ferries, local ferries, and coasters.

The harbour appears to have silted since it was built and care is needed over depths. Go stern or bows-to the N quay close to the 'square' quay in the corner. The W quay has mostly less than 1 metre off it.

Provisions and tavernas ashore. Ferry to Kalimnos.

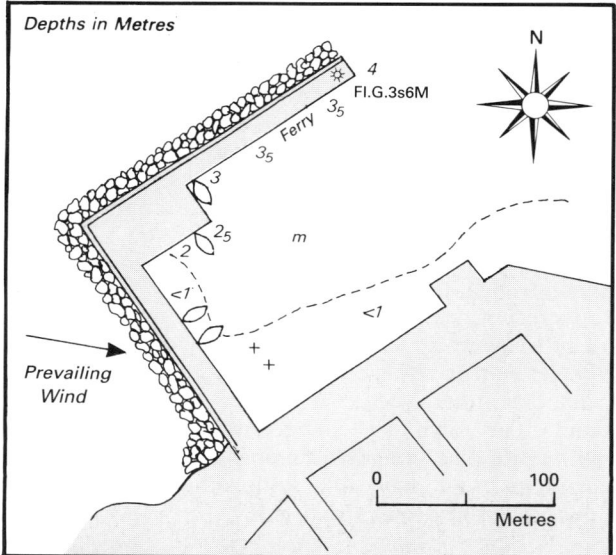

Depths in Metres

N

4
Fl.G.3s6M

Ferry 3₅
3₅
3₅
3
2₅   m
2
<1   <1
+
+

Prevailing Wind

0   100
Metres

MASTIKHARI
36°51'·2N 27°04'·6E

NOTE

Off the SE coast of Kos fierce gusts blow down off the surrounding hills when a strong *meltemi* is blowing. The worst spots seem to be off the three prominent capes, Krikellos, Khelona, and Fouka. Around Cape Krio on mainland Turkey there are also fierce gusts and disturbed seas.

KARDAMENA

Approach

The small harbour lies almost exactly halfway along the SE coast of Kos. The long sprawl of hotels and bars and tavernas along the coast is easily identified. Care needs to be taken of two swimming platforms lying off the harbour (lit: F.R).

Caution With the *meltemi* there are fierce gusts off the high land of Kos and care is needed.

Mooring

Go stern-to or bows-to off the pier running out from the beach, checking first to see you are not taking a local's berth. The bottom is sand and weed, good holding.

Shelter Good shelter from the *meltemi* which gusts off the land. Open S.

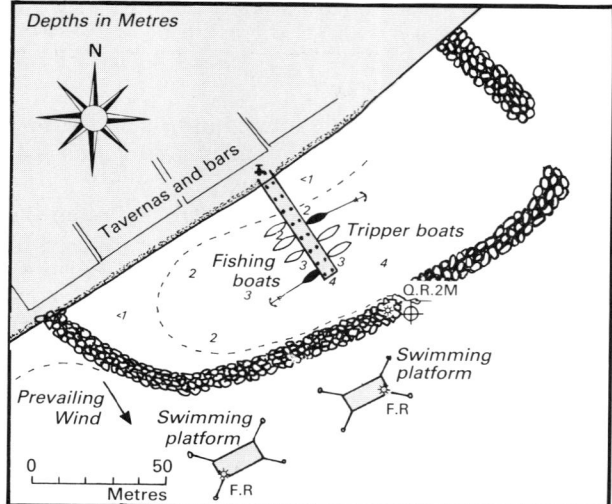

Depths in Metres

N

Tavernas and bars

<1
2
Tripper boats
Fishing boats 3 3
2   4   4
Q.R.2M
<1
2

Prevailing Wind

Swimming platform
Swimming platform
F.R
F.R

0   50
Metres

KARDAMENA 36°46'·8N 27°09'E (Q.R.2M)

Facilities

Water At the root of the pier.
Fuel About 200 metres away in the village.
Provisions Good shopping for provisions.
Eating out Numerous tavernas and bars nearby.
Other PO. OTE. Exchange. Hire cars and motorbikes. Internal and international flights from the airport about 5 km away.

General

Once a small fishing village, Kardamena is now a sprawl of a resort catering to package holidaymakers who want little to do with things Greek and frequent any establishment that remotely resembles the 'local' at home. The resort is only 5 kilometres from the airport so getting the hordes to and from Kardamena is simplified. The prize of the resort is the wonderful long sandy beach often described as the best in the Dodecanese. At night the resort fairly pulsates to the sound of over-amplified music of all descriptions, so don't bank on getting a lot of sleep.

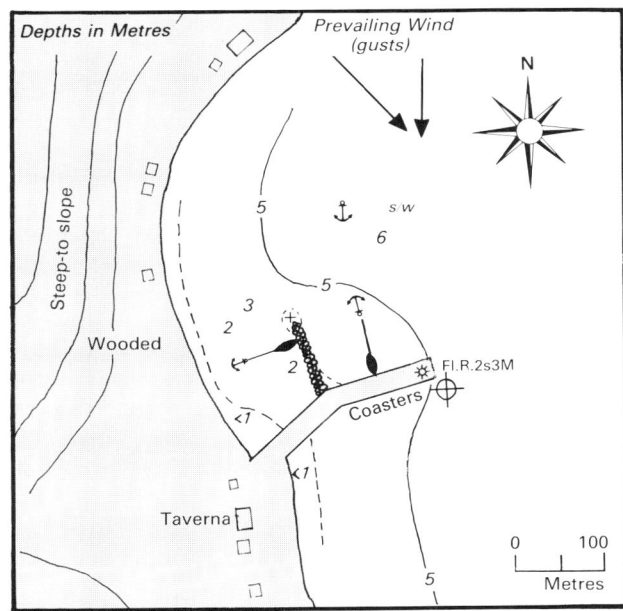

KAMARES
36°44'·2N 26°58'·3E (Fl.R.3M)

ORMOS KAMARES (Kamara, Palaeokastro)

Situated on the S end of Kos, this bay and the small harbour offer good shelter from the *meltemi*. A large white hotel on the N side of the bay is conspicuous from some distance off and the small harbour is on the W side of the bay. Anchor in the bay in 4–6 metres or go stern-to or bows-to or alongside the outer end of the mole. There is also room in the small fishing harbour for a few yachts. The bottom is sand and weed – good holding. With the *meltemi* blowing the gusts into the bay are not strong or prolonged.

Water at the root of the mole. Also a taverna at the root of the mole and a disco further round the beach.

Note Work is in progress enlarging the quay for coasters which load ore mined near here.

NISIS YIALI (Yali)

Three miles NW of Niseros an open bay on the S coast of Nisis Yiali offers some lee from the *meltemi*. The island is scarred by extensive quarries and in the bay a large loading chute extends into the sea. The sea is usually discoloured by dust from the quarry. A yacht seeking shelter here should anchor in 5–6 metres to the NE of the loading chute. The bottom is sand and good holding. Care must be taken of a reef 350 metres S of the islet (Ay Antonios) off the E end of Yiali and of numerous large mooring buoys in the vicinity of the quarry.

Caution About half a mile off the SW tip of Yiali lies a reef just under water which is not easily seen, especially when the *meltemi* is blowing.

Nisiros

Almost square, Nisiros is an extinct volcanic crater poking out of the sea SW of Deveboynu Burun (Cape Krio) in Turkey. The rich soil on the slopes of the cone is terraced and cultivated with olives and citrus trees. Until recently the hot sulphurous springs were renowned for their medicinal properties, but the hydropathic institute looks abandoned today. If the weather allows, it is a thoroughly pleasant excursion to the crater (2½ miles across) where there is a spectacular view of the surrounding sea and islands. If Mandraki harbour is untenable tuck into Palon where there is better shelter.

LIMIN MANDRAKI

Approach

The buildings around the harbour and the harbour mole on the NW corner of the island are easily identified from the N. The harbour actually lies a short distance E of Mandraki village.

By night A Q.G.2M is exhibited on the end of the mole.

Mooring

Go alongside or stern-to the mole or the quay. With a strong *meltemi* a swell creeps around the end of the mole making the harbour uncomfortable and possibly dangerous. With a strong N–NE wind the harbour is untenable. Port police.

Nisiros. Mandraki looking WSW.

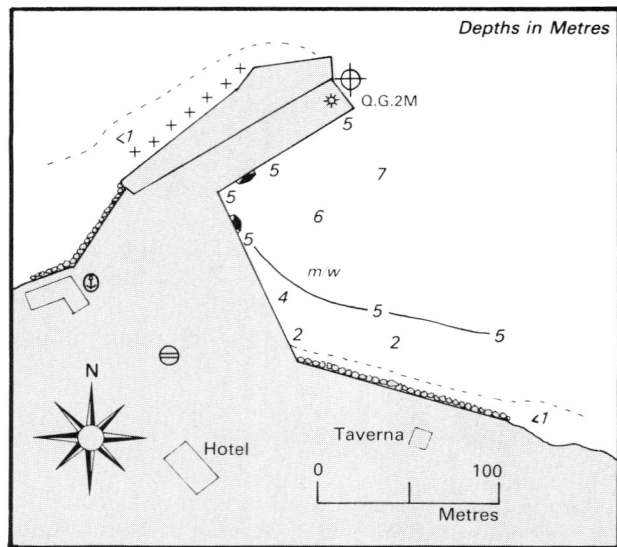

MANDRAKI
36°36'·8N 27°08'·3E (Q.G.2M)

Note Care is needed of the ferry calling here, which does not normally anchor, but holds itself off with its propeller causing a lot of wash for yachts berthed nearby.

Facilities

Good shopping in the nearby village. Good tavernas. PO. OTE. Daily ferry to Kos.

General

The village on the terraced slopes is most attractive and in settled weather the harbour is well worth a visit. A bus runs from Mandraki (there is one at 1000 hours) to the crater and it is an excursion which shouldn't be missed.

PALON (Palos)

Approach

This small *caïque* harbour lies 2 miles to the E of Mandraki harbour.

Conspicuous From the E the buildings of the abandoned hydropathic institute, a cluster of large stone buildings with red roofs immediately E of Palon, are conspicuous. From the W the harbour will not be seen until you are around the rocky headland sheltering it, but a gantry and a cluster of buildings on the coast immediately W of the headland will be seen. Closer in a church in the village and the harbour breakwaters are easily identified.

By night The entrance is lit: Fl.G.3s3M/Fl.R.2s3M.

Dangers

1. Care needs to be taken of the reef running N for about 100 metres from Ak Ammodes. The final approaches to the harbour should be made on a course due S towards the entrance.
2. With the *meltemi* there are fierce gusts and a wicked short sea off the N side of Nisiros.

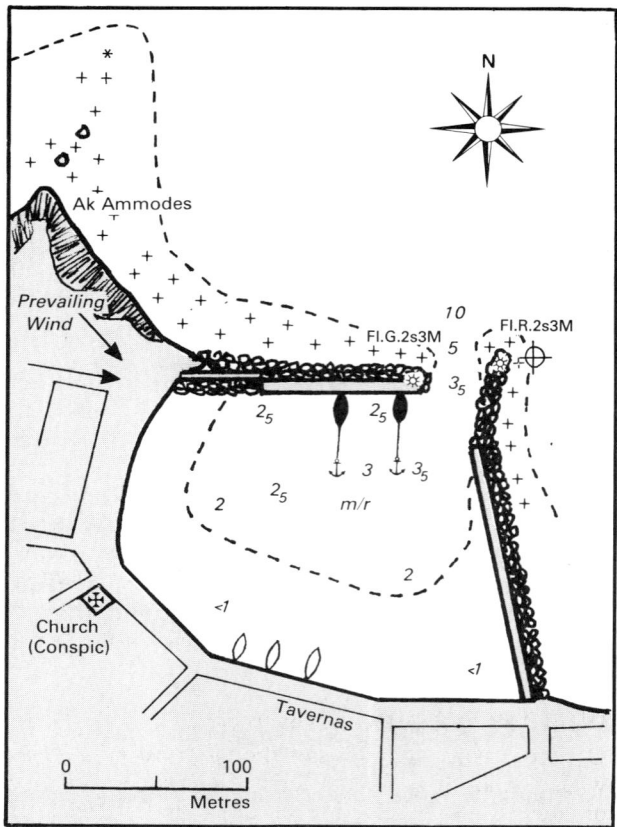

PALON
36°37'·3N 27°10'·7E (Fl.R.3M)

Mooring

Go stern-to or bows-to the N mole. The bottom is mud, sand, and rocks, good holding.

Shelter Good shelter from the *meltemi* although there may be some surge with a prolonged blow.

Facilities

A mini-market and several tavernas in the village. Good fish sometimes available. Irregular bus to Mandraki.

General

The little harbour and the village are wonderful. You can swim in the harbour. The hinterland is green and wooded. The tavernas sit on the edge of the harbour and you can spend most of the day in one sipping

Niseros. Palon harbour looking E from the ridge above.

cold beer and watch the locals watching you. Around Palon there is good if steep walking, or you can wander along the coast to the old hydropathic institute.

NISIS PERIOUSA

Approximately 4½ miles WSW of Mandraki is Nisis Perigousa. Local fishing boats sometimes shelter in the bay on the E coast where there is some shelter from the *meltemi*.

Tilos

Situated between Nisiros and Khalki this long thin island is seldom visited by tourists or yachts. It was known in medieval times as Episcopi, a name that probably referred to its watchtowers from which it could signal to Rhodes of an approaching enemy. The Italians revived the name calling it Piscopi. Today, as in many of the small islands off the tourist track, many of the young leave for the big cities of Rhodes or Athens.

ORMOS LIVADHIOU (Livadia)

On the E coast of Tilos lies the large bay of Livadhi with a small quay for the ferry. Go bows-to the quay or alongside the left side of the quay amongst the local *caïques*. With a strong *meltemi* blowing there are gusts off the surrounding hills and a swell works its way around into the bay so it can become very uncomfortable in here. The quay and the anchorage are open from NE through to SE. Port police. Water tap near the quay. Most provisions can be obtained and there are a number of tavernas. In settled weather it is an attractive and friendly place to visit.

Note In the SE corner of the bay there is a very small fishing harbour which has 2 metre depths in the entrance and off the N breakwater. A small yacht

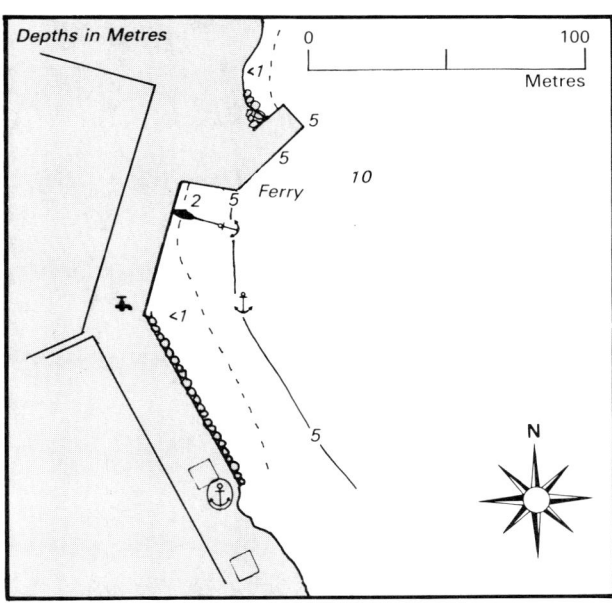

ORMOS LIVADHIOU
36°25′N 27°26′E

may be able to squeeze in here with care. The entrance is lit: Fl.R.3s3M.

Simi

Simi lies in the entrance to the Gulf of Doris (Turkish – Hisarönü Körfezi) looking like a giant Rorschach ink blob. From seaward it is a barren precipitous island, but inland there are patches of pine forest. The indentations in the coastline provide numerous anchorages and in fact the principal harbour is an entirely natural feature.

Simi was once famous for shipbuilding and sponge-diving. Simiot shipwrights built many of the fast galleys for the Knights of St John and later for their Turkish masters. Even today Simiot *caïques* seem to be better cared for than in many of the other islands. Simiot divers were once known as the best in the Aegean although Kalimniot divers would contest that claim. Today few Simiots risk the dangers of sponge-fishing and Kalimnos is the undisputed centre.

LIMIN SIMIS (Symi, Syme)
Admiralty chart no. 1669
Imray-Tetra chart no. G35

Approach

Conspicuous From the N the houses of Simi on the ridge above the town are conspicuous. From the S and E the harbour will not be seen until you are right into the bay. From the S it is easy to confuse the entrance to Pethi, the large bay immediately SE, with that of Simi. Entering Ormos Simis the houses of Simi town are immediately conspicuous. A white church on the N quay is also conspicuous.

Tilos. Livadhiou looking SE. *Nigel Patten.*

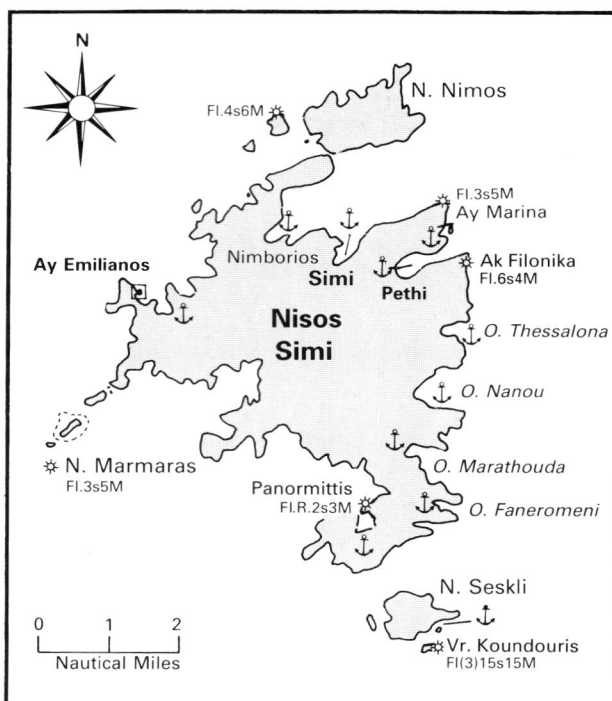

NISOS SIMI

By night Use the light on Ak Koutsoumba (Fl.3s5M) and the light on the quay (Q.G.2M).

Mooring

Go stern-to or bows-to the quay on the N side of the harbour taking care to leave the part of the quay allotted to the ferries clear. Most of the western quay is reserved for local trip boats and the local ferry. The depths in the harbour drop off rapidly and you should be prepared to let go your anchor in 12–20 metres. The bottom is mud and rock – poor holding in places.

Shelter Good shelter from the *meltemi*. With strong S winds there is a considerable surge in the harbour which can become dangerous with prolonged southerlies. The ferries (five or more in the summer) create a considerable wash when they arrive about mid-morning.

Authorities Port police and customs. A charge is made for berthing and rubbish disposal.

Facilities

Water On the quay.
Fuel Small amounts locally.

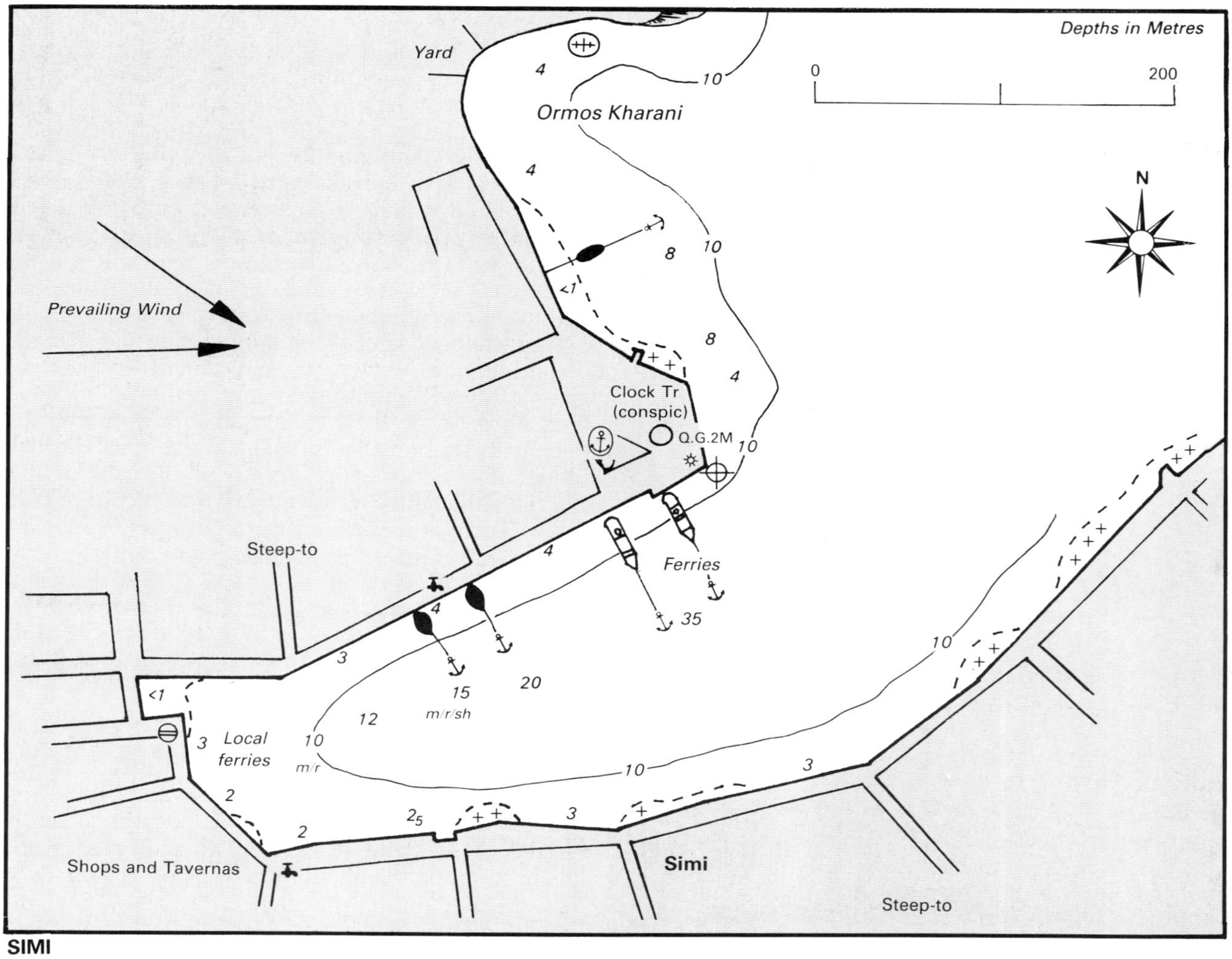

SIMI
36°37'·2N 27°50'·6E (Q.G light)

Simi harbour looking W. *Nigel Patten.*

Repairs Limited mechanical repairs. A boatyard hauls out large *caïques* and the occasional yacht in the cove N of the harbour.

Provisions Good shopping for provisions.

Eating out Excellent tavernas in some delightful locations in the town.

Other PO. OTE. Banks. Greek gas and *Camping Gaz.* Hire motorbikes. Daily ferries to Rhodes.

General

Discovering Simi is like discovering an exotic plant in the desert. The muted blue, amber, cream and rose-hued houses have been built one upon the other up the steep sides of the inlet like a child's building block version of a town. On the S side of the harbour a staircase leads up the hill to the houses on the top and though this heart-thumping climb takes it out of you in the summer, it is worth the effort both for the views from the top and for the fine old houses built on rocky projections and inclines on the way. The people of Simi remain detached from the daily

Simi.

The clock tower on the N side of the entrance to Simi harbour.

onslaught of tourists from Rhodes and you can almost hear an audible sigh when the ferry departs.

Simi was once famous for its sponge-divers – Simiot divers were often used to recover antiquities from the sea bottom – but today its fleet is much diminished. Some of the craft and the antiquated equipment are there, but fewer and fewer young Simiots take up the profession.

PETHI (Pedhi)

Over the hill to the SE of Simi lies the deep inlet of Pethi. The S entrance is lit: Ak Filonika Fl.6s4M. Care needs to be taken of an above-water rock in the middle of the entrance – it is easily seen by day.

At the head of the inlet is a pier with 5–7 metres at the outer end. Go alongside where convenient. Part of the pier is taken up at times with the water tanker which berths here to pump water to Simi. Alternatively anchor in 6–10 metre depths to the N of the pier. The bottom is sand and weed, good holding once through the weed. Good shelter from the *meltemi* although there are gusts off the surrounding hills.

Tavernas on the waterfront. It is a long hike over the steep ridge to Simi town.

421

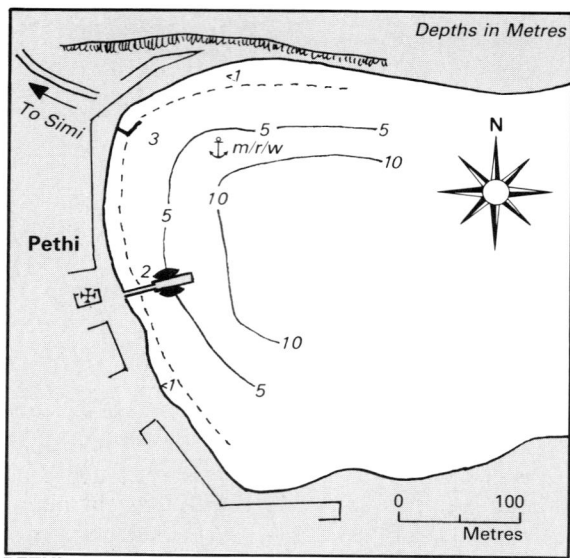

PETHI
36°36′N 27°51′·5E

AY MARINA

Immediately N of the entrance to Pethi there is an attractive anchorage behind the islet of Ay Marina. A reef connects the islet to the coast on the N so the approach must be made from the S. Anchor in 4–5 metres on a sandy bottom. There is a lee from the *meltemi* here remarkable for its calm. A good bathing beach ashore under an elaborate stone wall and beautiful clear water. Taverna ashore.

ORMOS THESSALONA

Lies just over half a mile S of Ak Filonika. Magnificent precipitous cliffs drop straight into the sea at the head of the bay. Anchor where convenient. Some protection from the *meltemi* although a swell will sometimes roll in depending on the strength of the *meltemi*.

ORMOS NANOU

A large bay just S of Thessalona. A good lunch stop with wild steep-to scenery and clear water.

ORMOS MARATHOUDA

Three miles S of Pethi lies Ormos Marathouda open only to the E. Anchor in 4–8 metres at the head of the bay. Subject to gusts off the hills.

ORMOS FANEROMENI

One mile S of Marathouda lies the deep inlet of Ormos Faneromeni open only to the E. Anchor at the head of the bay. Also subject to gusts off the hills.

NISIS SESKLI ANCHORAGE

Nisis Seskli lies off the S end of Simi separated by a deep channel (Stenon Seskli). On the SE side of Nisis Seskli lies Ormos Skomisa, immediately N of Vrakhonisis Koundouris (Troumbeta). A small islet, Artikonisi, partially protects the cove from the W–SW. The cove should be approached from the E. Anchor in the middle of the cove in 5–6 metres on a sandy bottom. Good shelter from the *meltemi* in attractive deserted surroundings.

PANORMITTIS

Approach

An enclosed bay on the SW corner of Simi. A white windmill on the E side of the entrance and the large white buildings of the monastery are conspicuous.

By night Use the light on Nisis Marmaras (Fl.3s5M) and the light on the NE side of the entrance (Fl.R.2s3M). Care is needed of yachts at anchor which may not be carrying anchor lights.

Dangers With the *meltemi* there can be gusts and confused seas off the entrance.

Mooring

Anchor in 3–6 metres in the NE side of the bay. There is sometimes room on the pier in the S corner although most of the space is taken up by local ferries and tripper boats. The bottom is sand and weed with some rocks – good holding once the anchor has cut through the weed.

Shelter Good all-round shelter.

Facilities

Limited provisions and a small taverna ashore. Bread available at the monastery.

General

The bay is attractive in a sparse sort of way and the monastery on the SE side complements it, being a sparse sort of place itself. When the ferries and tripper boats arrive the bay is transformed into a noisy crowded place for a few hours, but outside that it is a peaceful spot.

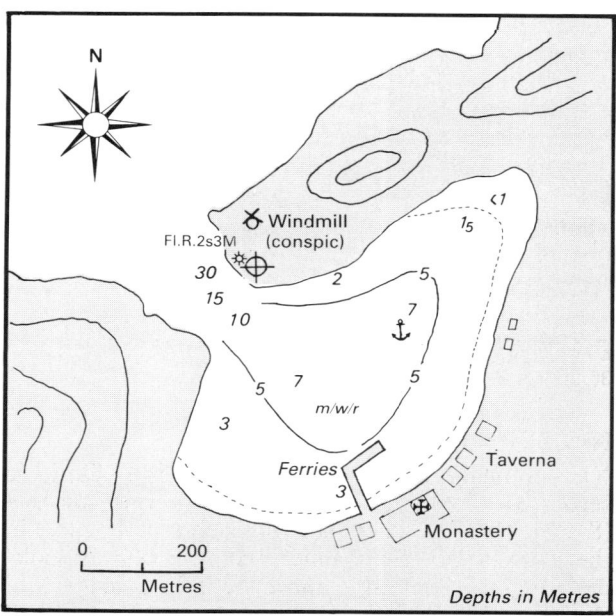

PANORMITTIS
36°33′·2N 27°50′·6E (Fl.R.2s3M)

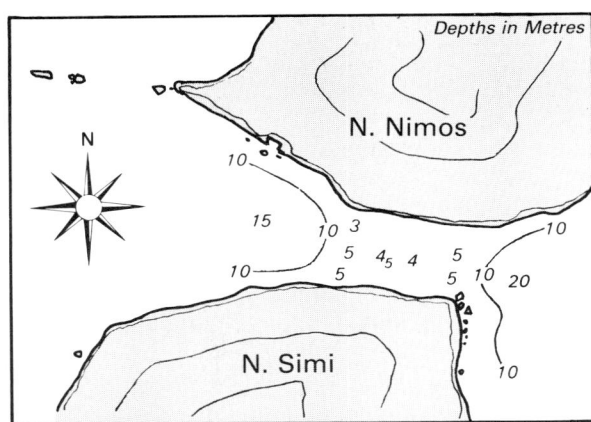

NIMOS PASSAGE (Stenon Nimou)

Simi. Panormittis looking SW.

AY EMILIANOS

On the W coast of Simi some shelter from the *meltemi* can be found under a short headland on the E side of Ak Kefala. From the N the monastery of Ay Emilianos on the headland and another monastery on the slopes inland are easily identified. Anchor in 8–10 metres on the S side of the headland. There is only the monastery ashore.

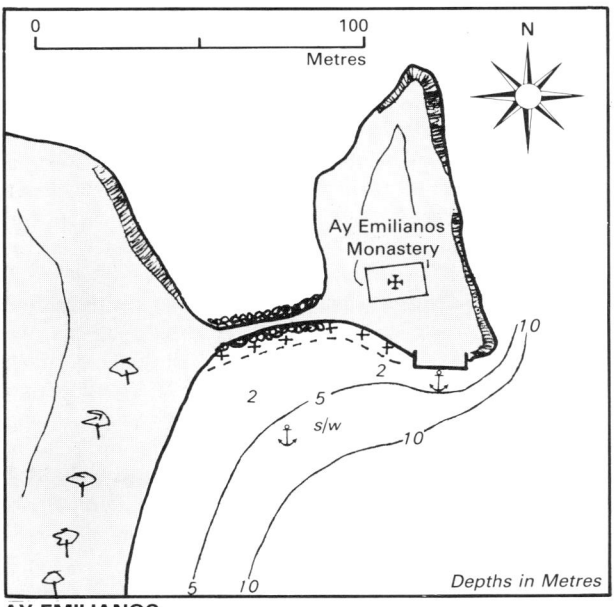

AY EMILIANOS
36°36′·4N 27°46′·5E

NISIS NIMOS (Nemos)

Nisis Nimos, immediately N of Nisos Simi, is separated from the latter by a narrow channel (Stenon Nimou). There is a least depth of 4 metres in the fairway of the channel and although it looks daunting the first time through, it is a convenient short cut that avoids circumnavigating Nimos. With a strong *meltemi* blowing into the channel the depth

at the trough of any swell may reduce the depth by about one metre at most. Just look straight ahead and not at the variegated sea bottom passing under the keel.

Rhodes
(Rodhos)

The largest island of the Dodecanese, Rhodes lies at the southern end of the chain of islands stretching down the west coast of Asiatic Turkey. Its name is of uncertain origin but possibly comes from the Greek word for the rock-rose which grows all over the island. In antiquity it had many names: Stadia, referring to its ellipsoid shape; Ophioussa, from the many snakes on the island; Poeissia, referring to its fertility; Olyessa, because it is earthquake prone; and Makaria, calling it simply the blessed isle.

As the ancient name, Stadia, states, the island is roughly ellipsoid or diamond-shaped. A mountain range runs from N to S with the highest peak, Mt Ataviros (1215 metres), situated in the middle of the west coast. Unlike many of the other islands of the group, Rhodes is fertile not only in the valleys and on the plains but also on the high hills. Pine, olive, orange and lemon, fig and pear trees grow well. *Maquis* and wildflowers (including the rock-rose) grow in the countryside, while hibiscus, bougainvillea and jasmine run riot over village houses. Butterflies seem to be everywhere – so much so that Rhodes has been called the butterfly island. In addition to butterflies, the fauna is said to include deer, foxes, hares, badgers, partridges, vultures, jackdaws, jays and the Rhodes dragon – a lizard growing as long as 50cm (14in) – though you are unlikely to find any of these around the crowded north end of the island.

This garden island with its dry hot summers and mild winters (the climate resembles that of Sicily) has been popular throughout history: smiled upon by the sun-god Helios; extravagantly praised by Strabo; beloved by Tiberius who deserted Capri for a time, bringing his entire retinue with him; the Knights of St John were reluctant to leave their castle even when surrounded by hostile neighbours; and the Italians

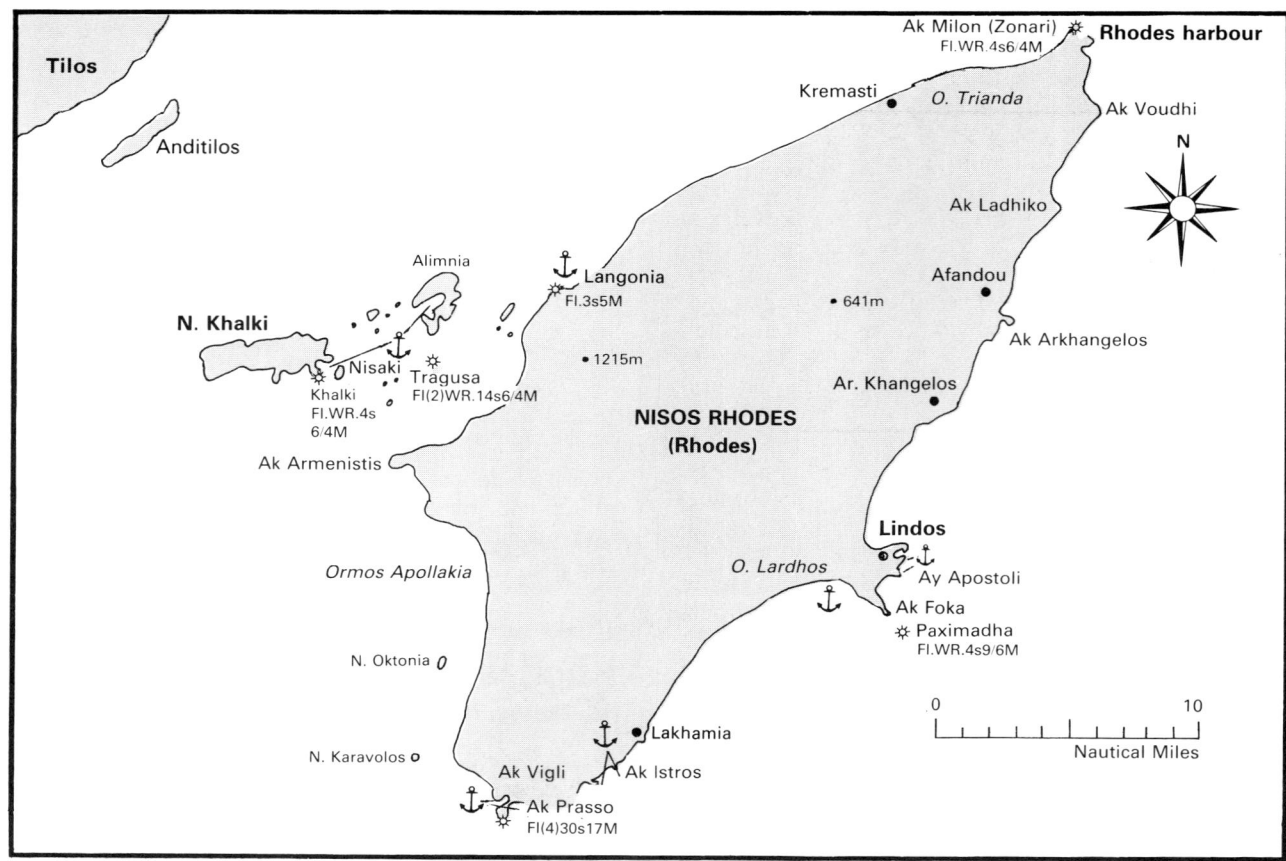

RHODOS, ALMANIA AND KHALKI

who occupied Rhodes in 1912 intent on creating another Capri. Today Rhodes is without doubt the most popular tourist island in Greece. Hotels stretch along the east and west coasts from Rhodes city where sun and sandy beaches create an irresistible lure for sun-starved northerners.

The significant history of Rhodes is neatly compacted into two periods: the story-book times of ancient Greece and the violent period of the Knights of St John. Moreover, such has been the influence of Rhodes on the surrounding islands that its history can to a large extent be read as the history of most of the Dodecanese.

The island has always been important as a trading centre between Asia and Africa and Greece and Italy. Homer mentions three cities on Rhodes: Lindos, with its natural harbour on the east; Ialysos, in the northwest; and Kamiros, about 20 miles down the west coast from Ak Milon (Zonari). Rhodes along with Kos, Knidos and Halicarnassus monopolised trade in this southwest corner of the Aegean.

In 408BC the three cities mentioned by Homer decided to pool their resources and found the city of Rhodes on its present site. Hippodamus of Miletus designed the new city and built a series of harbours on the eastern side of the low-lying peninsula on which the city was built. The new city and its splendid harbour complex swiftly eclipsed the other three cities to become the most important city and trading centre in the southwestern Aegean. The Rhodians built up their own fleet of merchant vessels

to become a major sea power. And they managed all this without upsetting the major warring powers around them – in effect a little Switzerland growing ever more prosperous.

The Rhodians managed successfully to evade being caught up in the international politics of the time until the death of Alexander the Great, when the Mediterranean was plunged into chaos. Rhodes refused to help Antigonus invade Egypt (which was after all its major trading partner). Demetrius Polioketes, a would-be Alexander, enters the history books at this point. To teach the Rhodians a sharp lesson he assembled a large force and the gargantuan siege machine for which he is famous – the Helepolis. The contraption was estimated to be nine storeys high, weighed perhaps 125 tons and rolled up to the city walls on giant oak wheels. It sprouted huge catapults, drawbridges which could be dropped down to release troops, a nest on top for archers, and was shielded against enemy arrows.

Around Rhodes today, piled in heaps or lying about the castle walls, you can see the heavy stone balls believed to be the missiles Demetrius flung at the city. He did a lot of damage but at the end of a year he had still not beaten the stubborn Rhodians. He signed a treaty with them and ordered all his siege machinery to be sold and the money donated to the Rhodians for a statue to commemorate the great siege. Thus the statue of the sun-god Helios was born. Chares began the statue in 302BC and twelve years later the Colossus of Rhodes was complete.

Perhaps it did stand astride Mandraki harbour as commentators say and perhaps not. Wherever the precise site of the 35 metre high statue was it became a landmark for all ships nearing the island until it was toppled by the earthquake of 227BC.

Rhodes endured as an important economic and sea power until 43BC when Cassius sacked the city and destroyed it. Rhodian marine law was universally admired, parts were absorbed into the Venetian sea code and its spirit is with us today. For centuries the city attracted artisans and artists. In Roman times Caesar, Brutus, Anthony, Cicero and Tiberius all studied in Rhodes. Pliny counted over 2000 statues when he was there and yet today a mere handful remain, so complete was Cassius' sacking of the city.

Until 1309 Rhodes drifted with the mainstream of history: ruled by Byzantium; sacked by the Saracens; ruled by the Venetians and later by the Genoese who in 1306 gave shelter to the Knights of St John. In 1309 the refugees became the masters of Rhodes. They built the huge fortified castle that dominates the town today and acquired a fleet of fast galleys which harried Turkish merchant vessels up and down the coast. They expanded from Rhodes to Khalki and Alimia, Simi and Tilos, Kos and Kalimnos. In all of these places the castles or the remains of castles built by the Knights can be seen today.

The huge fortifications of Rhodes withstood two great sieges – in 1444 from Egypt and in 1480 from the Turks. In 1522 Suleiman I assembled a force reckoned to number over 100,000 men against 650 Knights and 1200 supporters. The defence of the Knights against such a force is one of history's great battles. They held out for five months before the Grand Master, Villiers de l'Isle Adam, capitulated on honorable terms. It is said that Suleiman watching the Grand Master leave remarked, 'It is not without some regret that I oblige this old Christian to leave his home.'

Rhodes remained under Ottoman rule until the Italians occupied it in 1912. Intent on recreating the glory of Rhodes, they set about restoring and tidying up the castle and the town. They have been much criticized for their restoration work, but I do not think it is overdone and most of it gives a good feeling of what medieval fortifications were like. For the student of military warfare, Rhodes has probably the best preserved medieval fortifications in Greece. During the Second World War the island was occupied by the Germans and in 1947 it became Greek along with the rest of the Dodecanese.

LIMIN RHODOU – MANDRAKI
Admiralty chart no. 1666
Imray-Tetra chart no. G3, G35

Approach
Conspicuous From the W and N the city of Rhodes on a low-lying spit of land can be identified from a long way off. Large hotels line the beach on the W. From the S and E a chimney S of the town and the E mole of Ormos Akandia are conspicuous. The large

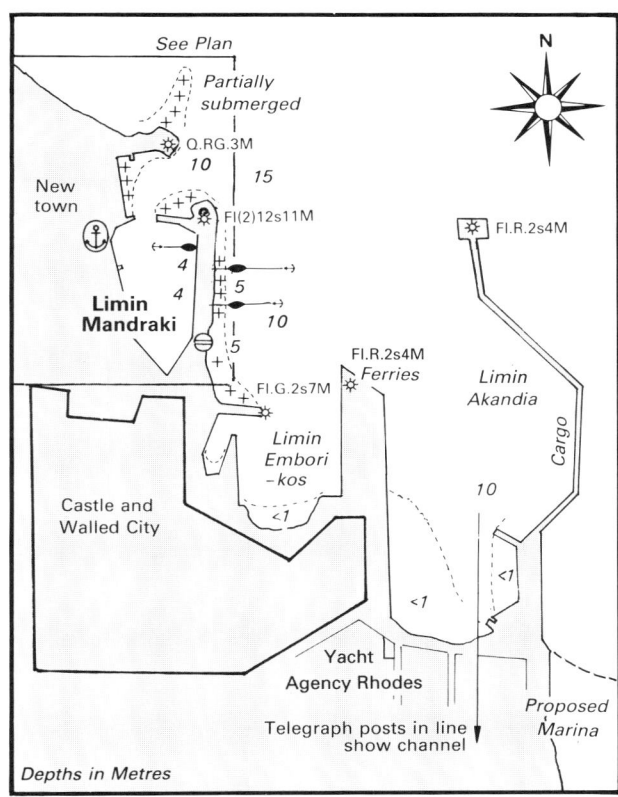

LIMIN RHODOU

ferries in Limin Emborikos also show up well. Mandraki basin, where a yacht should make for, is easily identified by the small fort with the lighthouse (Ayios Nikolaos), a cupola, the belfry, the market and the three windmills on the mole forming the E side of Mandraki. On either side of the entrance to Mandraki there is a tower with a bronze deer on top.

By night Use the light on Ak Milon (Zonari Fl.WR.4s6/4M red sector covers Ifalos Kolona over 286°-314°), Ay Nikolaos (Fl(2)12s11M), the W breakwater head (Fl.G.2s4M), Limin Emborikos (Fl.R.2s4M), and the lights at the entrance to Mandraki (Q.RG.3M, F.R and F.G.2M). Some of the lights are difficult to identify against the loom of the city lights. Approaching from the W the light at Rhodes airport (AlFl.WG) some 10 miles S of the city is easily picked up.

Dangers
1. Keep well off Ak Milon (Zonari) and the shoal water running N from it and the reef (Ifalos Kolona) extending N from the outer mole protecting the entrance to Mandraki.
2. Care should be taken when strong southerlies are blowing as there is a disturbed swell at the entrance to Mandraki, although once inside the basin there are no problems.

Mooring
Berth where directed or where convenient. The harbour is hopelessly crowded in the summer with yachts often two or three out from the quay. Mandraki is now designated as a marina although as

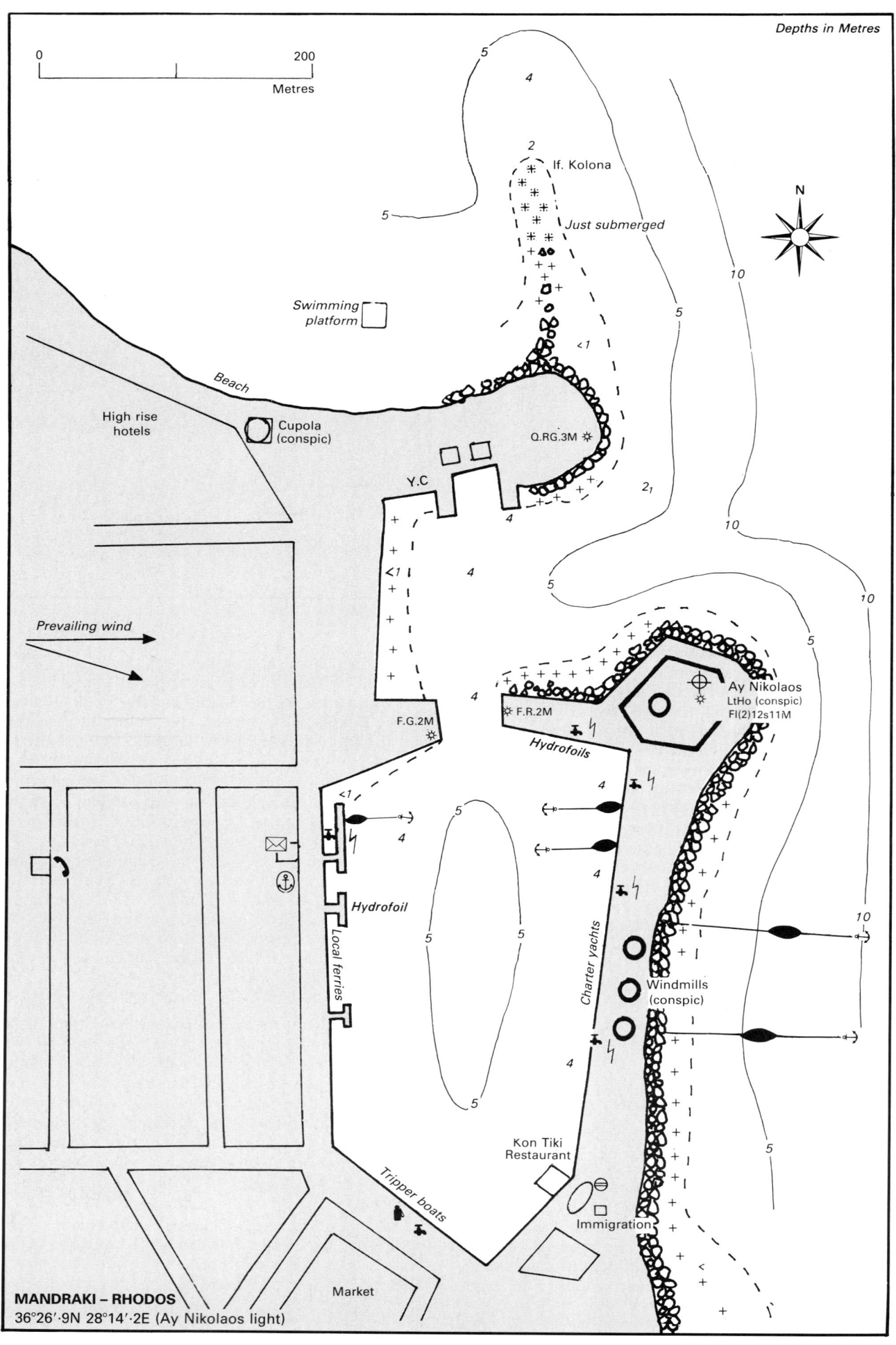

Depths in Metres

5

4

2 If. Kolona

* *
* *
* *
* *
* *
+ △○
+ +
+ □ +
+ +

Just submerged

N

10

5

5

Swimming platform □

5

10

Beach

High rise hotels

Cupola (conspic)

<1

Q.RG.3M ☀

10

10

Y.C

2₁

4

<1

4

Prevailing wind

5

4

5

5

4

Ay Nikolaos LtHo (conspic) Fl(2)12s11M

☀ F.R.2M

Hydrofoils

4

F.G.2M ☀

<1

5

4

4

Windmills (conspic)

10

Hydrofoil

✉

⚓

5

5

Local ferries

Charter yachts

5

4

5

Kon Tiki Restaurant

Tripper boats

Immigration

Market

MANDRAKI – RHODOS
36°26'·9N 28°14'·2E (Ay Nikolaos light)

yet few additional facilities have been introduced. Hopefully moorings will be laid so that the crossed anchors and frayed tempers of the past are avoided.

Shelter Good all-round shelter in the harbour. Numerous boats winter afloat here.

Note Fouled anchors are a common occurrence simply because there are so many yachts. A large mooring chain lying approximately 30 metres out from the quay is also easily fouled. Many yachts choose to avoid the chaos in the summer and anchor on the E side of Mandraki in 10 metres with a long line ashore to a rock. With the *meltemi* a swell works its way around and hits yachts beam on here causing them to roll around awfully and the wash from the numerous ferries entering and leaving Rhodes also makes a berth here most uncomfortable.

Authorities A port of entry: port police, customs and immigration authorities. Customs and immigration are at the root of the E mole in Mandraki and the port police are on the W side. Marina charges are made in Mandraki.

Note There are plans to build a marina on the E side of Akandia where shown on the plan of Rhodes Harbour. The first phase will provide 500 berths for craft up to 35 metres LOA. At the time of publication the feasibility study had been completed but work had yet to start on the marina.

Facilities

Services Water and electricity on the quay. Showers and toilets.

Fuel A mini-tanker delivers to the quay.

Repairs Yachts up to 40 tons, but limited by the depths prevailing in the approach channel, can be hauled by travel hoist at Akandia. The channel to the hoist basin is normally dredged to 2–2·5 metres, but is prone to silting to as little as 1·5 metres. Go first to the boatyard where the leading marks for the channel will be described. The telegraph poles in a street directly behind the hoist basin must be kept in line to show the channel. Care is needed as the boatyard has a bad reputation for theft although attempts are being made to correct this. All mechanical repairs. Most engine spares can be obtained within a few days from Piraeus. Wood and GRP repairs. Light engineering work including stainless steel work carried out. Electrical and some electronic repairs. Sail repairs. Life raft service. Good hardware and tool shops. Several chandlers.

Yacht Agency Rhodes A long-established company in Rhodes who have a well-stocked chandlery, including many imported items and a good stock of books and charts. They are also brokers and charter agents. The staff are knowledgeable and helpful and can usually obtain most bits of gear. Mail can be sent to them and will be held for collection. Yacht Agency Rhodes, PO Box 393, Byronos 1 and Kanada St, GR85100 Rhodes (on the waterfront between Nereus boatyard and the commercial port). ☎ (0241) 22927 *Fax* (0241) 23393 Telex (0292) 253 NCLR GR. VHF channel 73 is monitored. Call sign C & N.

Provisions Good shopping in the new town around the harbour and in the white octagonal market. Near the market local white wine can be bought from the barrel. Bulk white and red wine and brandy, *ouzo* and gin are available from the CAIR bottling plant in the industrial estate behind the boatyard. Ice available.

Eating out Good tavernas – ask around for recommendations. Most of those in the old town are overpriced with poor food and should be avoided.

Other PO. OTE. Banks. Greek gas and *Camping Gaz*. Turkish baths in the old town. Hire cars, motorbikes and bicycles. Bus service to the important villages. Organised excursions to Lindos, the Valley of the Butterflies, Kamiros etc. Daily ferries to Piraeus via Crete or the northern Cyclades. Daily ferries to Marmaris in Turkey in the summer. International and internal flights.

Approach to Mandraki looking SW.

General

Rhodes city – you either love it or hate it. After the sleepy peace of many of the other islands in this area, Rhodes town fairly hums and bustles as only the most important tourist town in Greece can. But it is not overpowering and once you are accustomed to the fact that you are back in a busy city the place does grow on you.

Rhodes city consists of two distinct parts: the old city surrounded by the walls built by the Knights and the new town largely built by the Italians during their occupation of the island. Much of the old city was restored by the Italians and although they have been criticized for producing 'Hollywood' castles and towers, with the passing of time the reconstruction has weathered and blended into the original medieval stonework. In the new town the buildings lining the waterfront were also largely built by the Italians in a monumental style to designs by Florestano di Fausto. The other notable buildings mostly date from the Turkish occupation.

Mandraki was probably the harbour used by the Knights to keep their swift galleys in, although some believe the basin now called Emborikos was the galley harbour and Mandraki was occupied only by small boatbuilders. The word Mandraki is the diminutive of *mandra* meaning 'a sheep fold' and is used in many other places to describe a small enclosed harbour.

Here in ancient times the Colossus of Rhodes may have stood – the bronze statue of Helios the sun-god, one of the seven wonders of the world despite the postcards which show him looking more like a rather ridiculous jolly green giant. Although the popular opinion is that the statue did not stand astride the harbour entrance, I agree with Ernle Bradford that there is no reason why this should not have been so: 'My opinion is that, as is so often the case, the ancient story is true; the statue of the Sun God literally be-straddled the narrow entrance to the galley harbour. It is a small boat harbour, and one must bear in mind that the ships of the ancients were, by modern standards, only small boats. Most of them, no doubt, lowered their masts when entering harbour under oars – just as the galleys often did in the time of the knights. In any case, a statue with a total height of 105 feet would have given plenty of clearance between its legs even if their masts were raised.'

Ernle Bradford *The Greek Islands*

The statue was destroyed by an earthquake in 227BC and 80 years later sold as scrap.

Beyond the old and new city stand the blank reinforced concrete hotels and suburbs of the holiday town relieved only by the abundance of oleander, bougainvillea and hibiscus. On Ak Zonari stands the Hydrobiological Institute housing an interesting collection of preserved and live marine animals caught in local waters.

Note When on passage between Rhodes and Lindos there are fierce gusts off the high land when the *meltemi* is blowing strongly. If you are heading to Rhodes from Lindos it is best to leave very early in the morning when the *meltemi* sometimes dies off for a while.

Between Rhodes city and Lindos there are several bays and coves that can be used in settled weather.

LINDOS (Limin, Lindhou)

Approach

The castle and the town are conspicuous. By night there are no lights although on a clear night entry is possible with care.

Mooring

Anchor where convenient. The bottom is sand with some rock – good holding. The bay is open to the E and southerlies send in a swell. With the *meltemi*

Lindos looking NE. *Nigel Patten.*

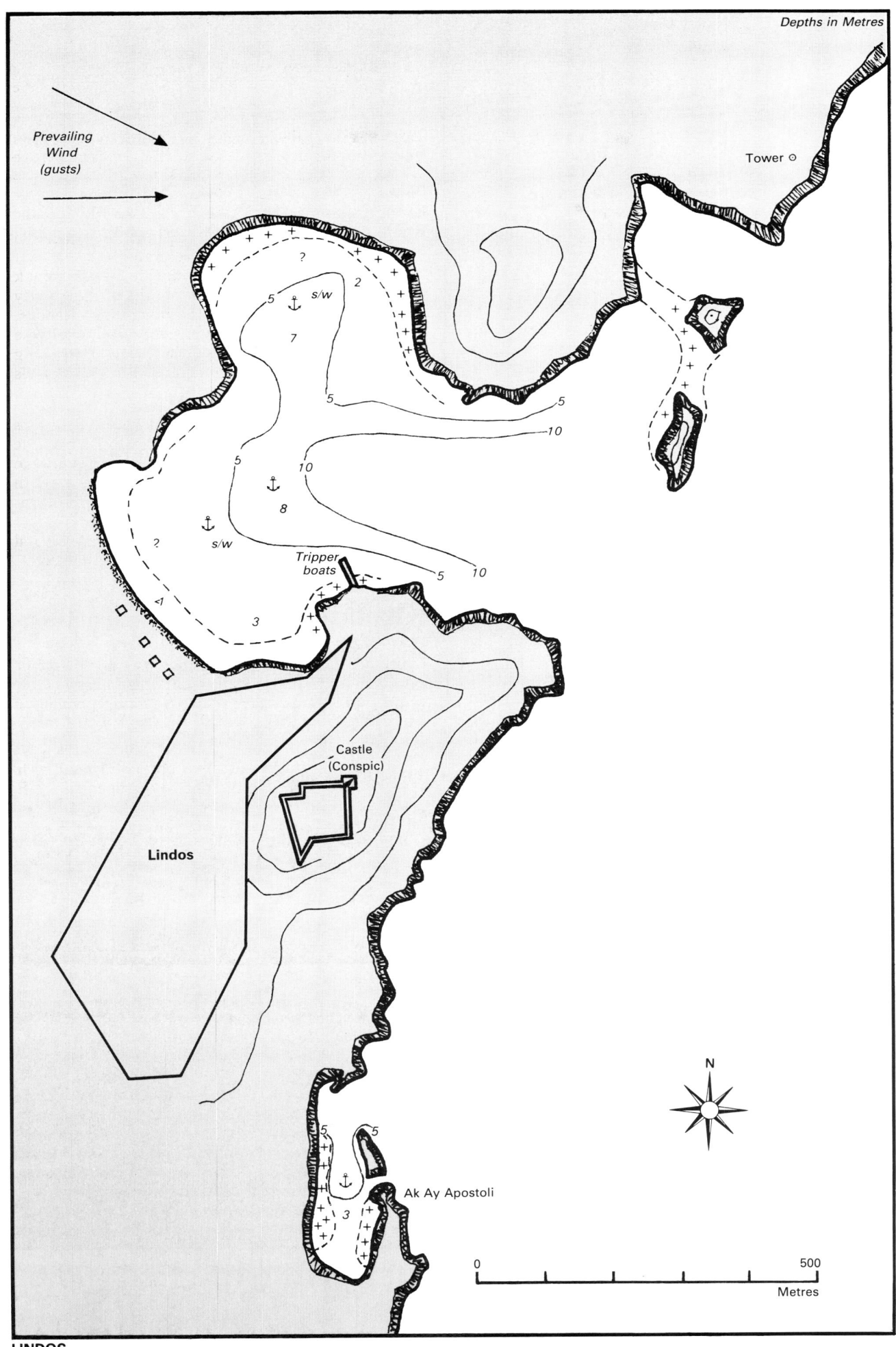

Depths in Metres

Prevailing Wind (gusts)

Tower ⊙

?

s/w 5 ⚓ 2

7

5 5

10

5 ⚓ 10

⚓ 8

2 s/w

Tripper boats

2 ⚓ 5 10

3

Castle (Conspic)

Lindos

N

5 5 ⚓

Ak Ay Apostoli

3

0   500

Metres

LINDOS
36°05'·7N 28°05'·4E

there are fierce gusts down into the bay so make sure your anchor is well in before leaving a yacht unattended.

Facilities

Water Limited from local sources.
Provisions Most provisions can be found.
Eating out Numerous excellent if somewhat expensive tavernas.
Other PO. OTE. Banks. Hire cars, motorbikes and bicycles. Buses to Rhodes.

General

Early in the morning or late in the afternoon, Lindos, with its small winding streets between medieval houses and the toy castle perched on a rock summit as if about to topple into the bay, is uniquely beautiful. In the heat of the day coaches and ferries transport hundreds of tourists from Rhodes – the narrow streets are packed tight and the beach resembles something from Cannes or Nice.

Lindos, commanding the superb natural harbour, was the principal city of the island before the foundation of Rhodes in about 408BC. The acropolis within the medieval castle affords an all-round view over land and sea – before 1000 hours or after 1600 hours there are few people about. In the village the old houses with black and white pebble mosaic courtyards and staircases are a legacy from the prosperous Middle Ages.

AY APOSTOLI

Situated immediately S of Ormos Lindou. It is possible to anchor here – take a line ashore as there is limited swinging room. The enclosed inlet appears to offer good shelter, but any swell rebounds around the bay making it uncomfortable.

ORMOS LARDHOS

To the S of Lindos under the rocky Ak Foka lies the wide bay of Lardhos. In settled weather anchor off the small hamlet at the E end of the bay. There is a friendly taverna ashore. The gusts off the hills here are often less bothersome than in Lindos.

AK ISTROS

The cape 6 miles NE of Ak Prasso which is the southernmost tip of Rhodes. There is an anchorage off a small hamlet on the SW side of the cape.

AK VIGLI

Lies 1 mile SW of Ak Istros. It can be easily distinguished by a tower on the extremity of the cape. There is an anchorage on the N side of the cape in 3–6 metres giving some shelter from the *meltemi*.

AK PRASSO

The southernmost tip of Rhodes. It is connected to Rhodes by a low neck of land and from the distance looks like an island. The cape and the lighthouse on it are conspicuous from some distance off. On the N

side of the cape there is good shelter from S winds in 2–4 metre depths. On the S side of the cape there is good shelter from the *meltemi* in a small cove in 2–4 metre depths. The bottom in both anchorages is sand and good holding.

NOTE

When on passage along the E coast of Rhodes, the Khina Rocks lying 4 miles SE off Ak Vigli are low-lying and difficult to pick out.

ORMOS LANGONIA (Kamiros Skala)

On the W coast of Rhodes one mile to the E of Ak Kopria lies Langonia. It offers only limited shelter from the W and some shelter from the S. There is a quay where the *caïque* ferry from Khalki berths. Fuel and water ashore.

ORMOS TRIANDA

Situated on the NE tip of Rhodes Island, this open bay offers shelter from the S and SE only. It is untenable with the *meltemi*. Anchor in 4–8 metres off the beach which is lined with large hotels. The bottom is sand and good holding.

Khalki and Alimia

Lying off the W coast of Rhodes, these two islands have always been dependent on their large neighbour. Khalki has a small dwindling population – nearly all of it living around the harbour. Alimia is deserted.

KHALKI (Halkia, Skala, Emborios)

Approach

Conspicuous The three windmills on top of the ridge behind the village are conspicuous from a long distance off. The harbour proper will not be seen until you are into the bay.

By night A night approach is not recommended because of the numerous unlit rocks and reefs in the approaches. Use the light on Nisaki Fl.WR.6s.8/6M (232°-R-244° and 280°-R-297°) and on the N entrance

Khalki looking ENE out into the bay.

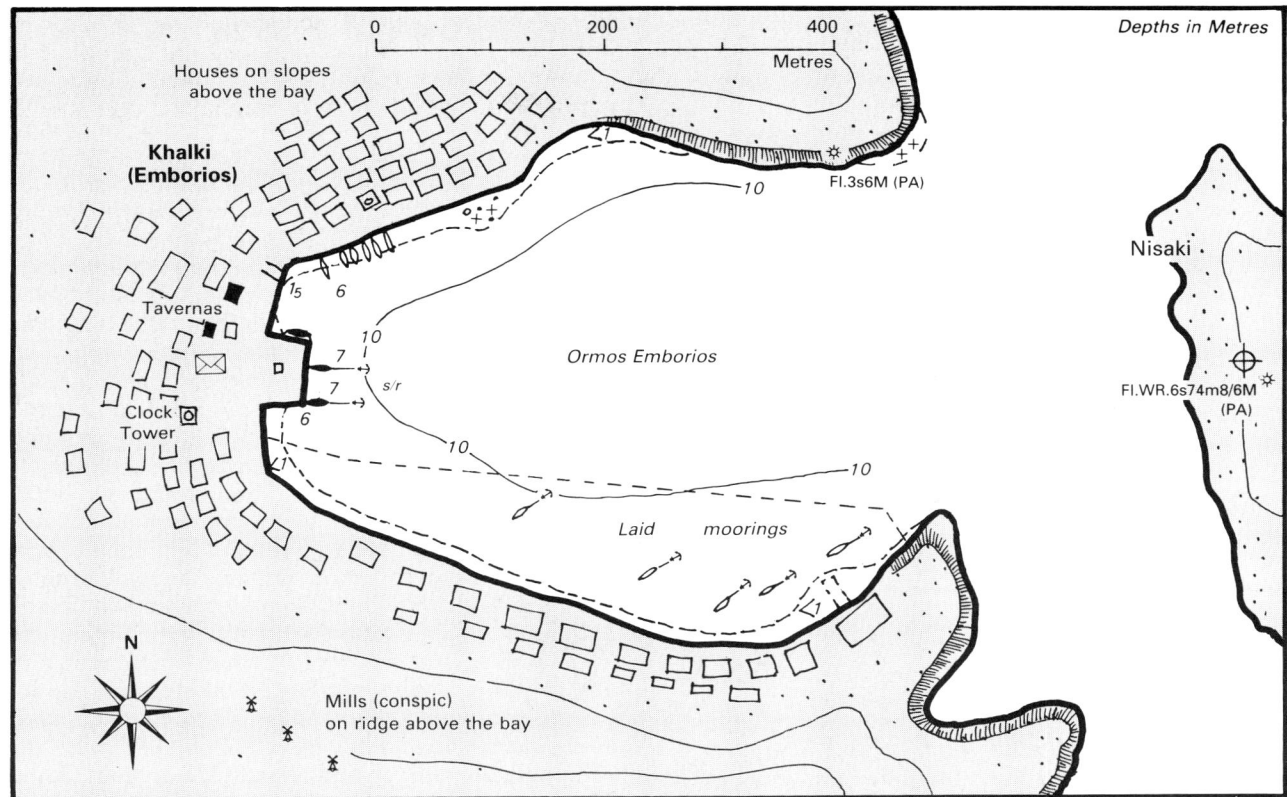

ORMOS EMBORIOS
36°13'·2N 27°37'E (Fl.WR.8/6M)

Dangers Care must be taken of the numerous above- and below-water rocks in the approaches and the strait between Khalki and Alimia. Xera rock although above water is difficult to see and the reef immediately due W of Nisaki is only just awash and difficult to spot. Most of the other rocks and islets can be identified by day even off a comparatively small scale chart, though care is needed.

Mooring

Go stern-to or bows-to or alongside the ferry berth or anchor off. If you are on the ferry berth on one of the days the ferry is due the port police will ask you to move off for the 30 minutes or so which it stays. The bottom is sand and rock – the holding uncertain in places.

Shelter Good shelter from the *meltemi* although there are gusts into the bay. With strong S winds a considerable swell enters the harbour.

Authorities Port police.

Facilities

Water Limited supplies locally.

Provisions Most provisions can be found although the island is dependent on the ferry for most things.

Eating out Several convivial tavernas. Fresh fish sometimes available.

Other PO. OTE. Ferry to Skala Kamiros on Rhodes.

General

Although many of the houses are in ruins the village on the slopes around the bay is attractive. In many ways it reminds me of Simi town on a smaller and poorer scale. The fort on the precipitous rock behind the village (cone-shaped and 670 metres high), like the fort on Alimia, was a watchtower for Rhodes. Inside is the small church of Ay Nikolaos.

ORMOS POTAMOS

The bay on the S of Khalki immediately W of Khalki harbour. Good shelter from the *meltemi*. Anchor at the head of the bay where convenient. The bottom is sand and rocks, reasonable holding.

ORMOS ALIMIA

Approach

The large bay on the S of Nisis Alimia. From the N and S the ruined fort above the bay is conspicuous. A few white houses and a small church are conspicuous once you are at the entrance to the bay.

By night Not recommended. There are no lights and the unlit rocks and reefs in the approaches make it dangerous.

Dangers Care must be taken of the numerous above- and below-water rocks in the approaches and the strait between Khalki and Alimia. See notes for Khalki.

Mooring

Anchor in either of the two bays. The S bay is mostly quite deep compared to the N bay. The bottom is sand and weed – good holding.

Alimia looking SW from the castle.

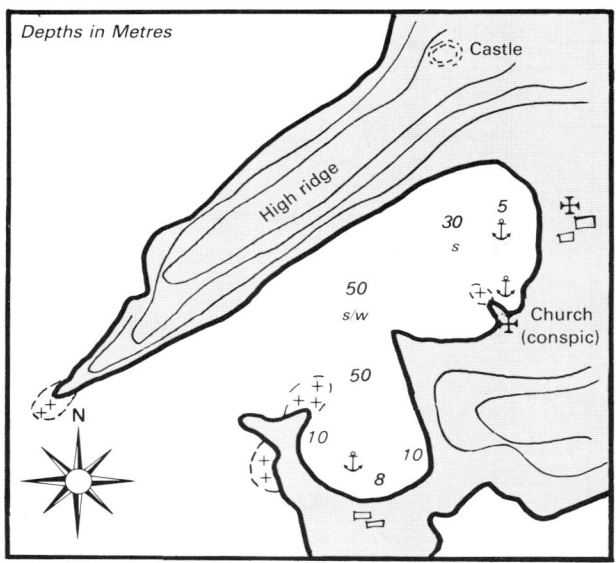

ALIMIA
36°16′N 27°44′E

Shelter The S bay offers good shelter from the *meltemi* although there are gusts. The N bay may get some swell pushed in by a strong *meltemi* although there is some shelter tucked in behind the spit the church is built on.

Facilities
None.

General
Nobody lives on Alimia although a few fishermen from Khalki have houses there. The fort above the E bay is a long hot walk up the rocky hill – from the summit there is a commanding view over Khalki and Rhodes. In the S bay there are a number of deserted buildings left over from the Second World War. In one of these nostalgic German soldiers drew a series of cartoons depicting what life was like back home and what life might have been like on some distant tropical island if there had been no war.

Karpathos and Kasos

These two sea-swept islands are the most southerly of the Dodecanese. Lying between Crete and Rhodes in a stretch of angry sea, the islands seem to have been bypassed by history. Today a few tourists visit them and, of the islanders themselves, it is said that more Karpathiots live in Athens than in Karpathos.

Kasos is ellipsoid in shape and steep-to on all sides. Very little vegetation is to be seen on the island even around the major village of Fri. In 1824 the Egyptians ravaged the island and from all appearances Kasos never recovered. (The Kasiots remember it as the Holocaust.) When I entered Ormos Khelatronas for the first time there appeared to be people lining the cliffs surrounding the bay – on closer inspection these were scarecrows. Yet nothing is grown in the vicinity of the bay and my imagination ran wild speculating that these scarecrows were a device, perhaps an old custom, designed to let any invading Egyptians know the Kasiots were ready and waiting this time.

Karpathos (also known by its medieval name of Scarpanto) is also mountainous and steep-to, but by comparison with Kasos is a green and fertile island. A mountain ridge runs from NE to SW with Mt Kalolimni (Lástra) at 1200 metres the highest in the centre of the island. The W coast is mostly barren except in the valleys, but the E coast is covered in pine. On the S coast there are fertile valleys and plains planted in olives, citrus and fruit trees. Most of the population lives in the southern part of the island and there are many small and attractive villages in this region. It is well worth making an excursion inland from Pigadhia if the weather permits you to leave your yacht there safely.

PORT KARPATHOS (Pigadhia)

Approach
Conspicuous The town, the mole and the small islands immediately S of the harbour are conspicuous.

By night Use the light on Nisidha Dhespotika in Ormos Pigadhia (Fl.5s6M) and the light on the end of the mole (Q.R.1M). A fixed red light is also exhibited on a television repeater just W of the town.

Dangers With the *meltemi* there are fierce gusts in the approaches.

Mooring
Go alongside or stern-to or bows-to the new mole in the SW corner. It may be possible for small yachts to squeeze in under the mole although most berths are occupied by local boats – care is needed of the depths under the mole and it would be best to reconnoitre first.

Shelter With the *meltemi* there are strong gusts into the harbour making it most uncomfortable. The harbour is open to the NE and there is a surge with strong S winds.

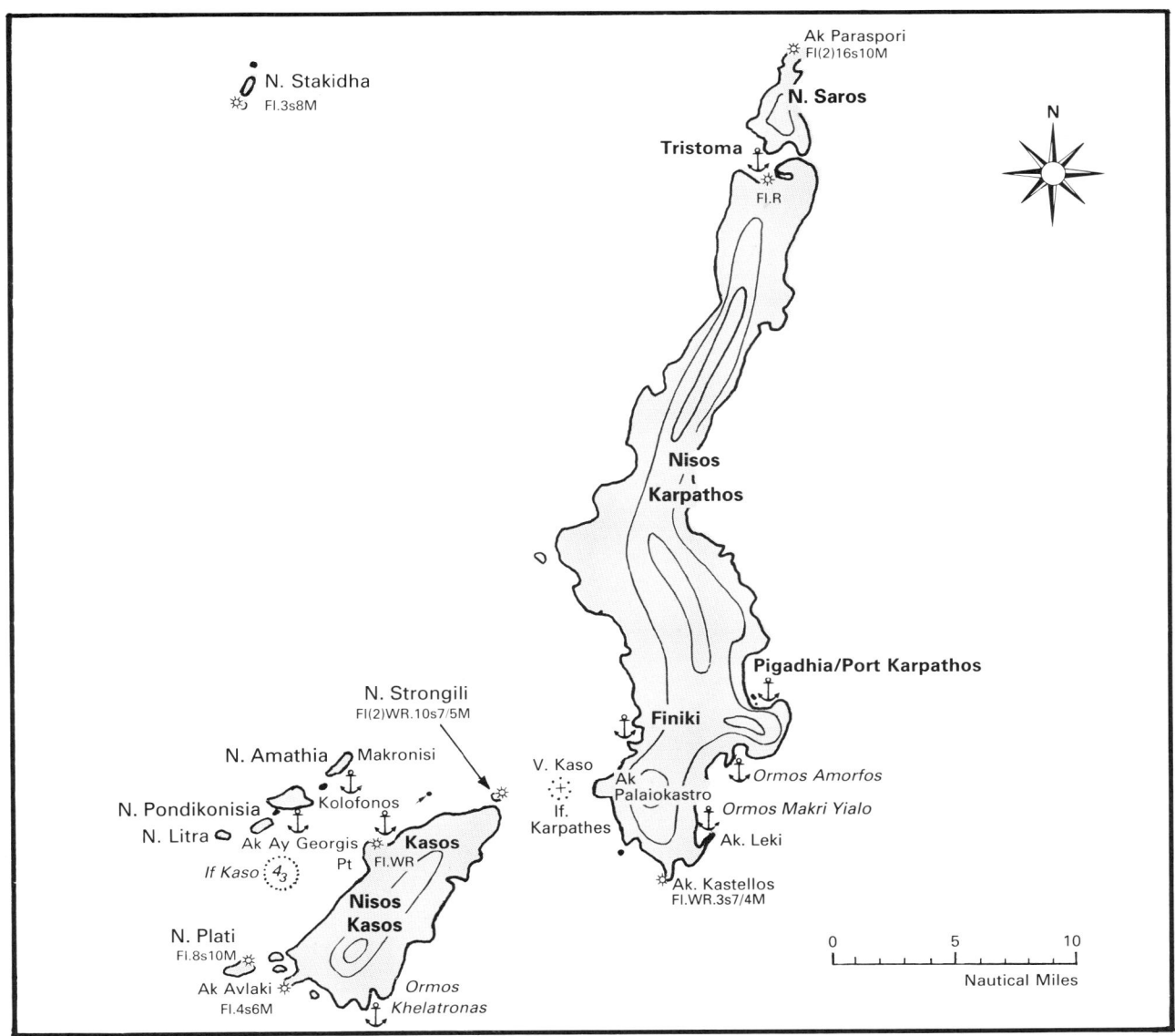

KARPATHOS AND KASOS

Authorities Port police and customs.

Facilities
Water Local sources.
Fuel In the town. It may be possible to get deliveries to the quay.
Provisions Good shopping for provisions in the village.
Eating out Good tavernas in the town.
Other PO. OTE. Bank. Greek gas. Hire motorbikes. Ferry to Piraeus and Rhodes.

General
The small town of Pigadhia more than makes up for the uncomfortable harbour – fringed by green trees and gardens, it is both attractive and friendly. In recent years travellers getting off the beaten track have come here and the place has acquired a modest tourist trade, though not an overpowering one. It is the best place to use as a base for exploring the island.

ORMOS AMORFOS (Amphorphi Bay)
The large bay under Ak Volokas. Anchor in the N corner of the bay. The bottom is sand with some rocks, good holding. This bay has been reported to be less subject to gusts off the hills than Makri Yialo to the S. Open to the S and SE.

ORMOS MAKRI YIALO (Makris Yialos)
A deserted bay lying near the S end of the island close northward of Ak Lingi. Anchor in 4–8 metres near the head of the bay. The bottom is sand – good holding. The bay offers good shelter from the *meltemi* although the bay is subject to strong gusts. Open to the E.

FINIKI (Foiniki)

Approach
The small harbour lies on the N side of the bay close N of Ak Palaiokastro. The houses around the bay will be seen closer in.

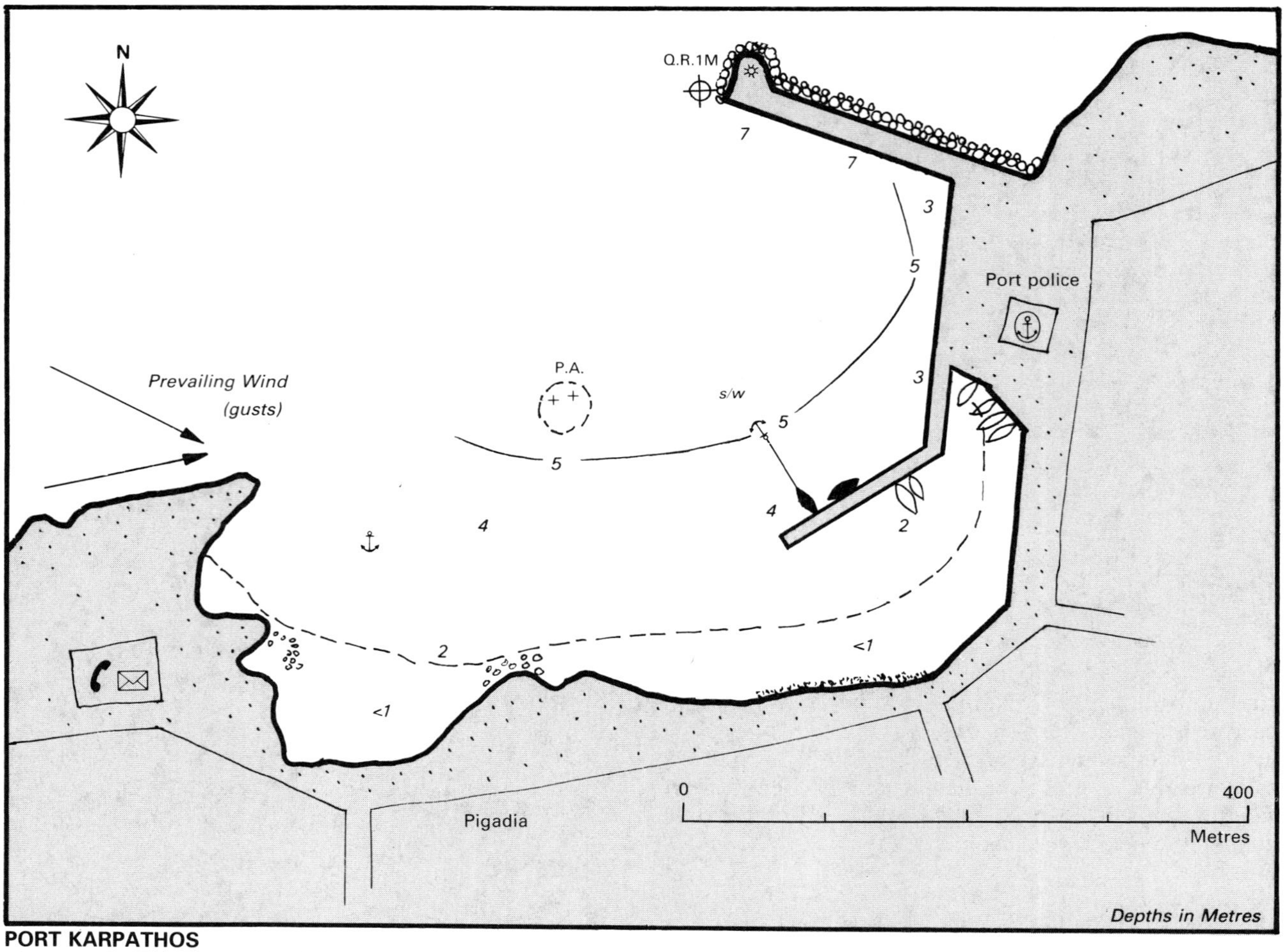

PORT KARPATHOS
35°30'·7N 27°12'·9E (Q.R light)

Dangers Care must be taken of a reef lying approximately 60 metres SE from the extremity of the breakwater. Keep close to the end of the rough stone breakwater.

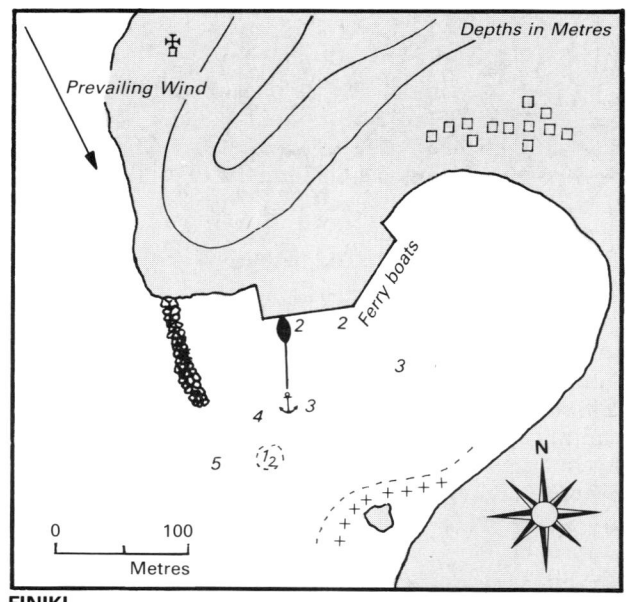

FINIKI
35°29'·5N 27°08'·5E

Mooring

Go stern-to or bows-to the quay where there are 2–2·5 metre depths off. The N and E sides of the bay are shallow.

Shelter Adequate shelter from the *meltemi* but open to the S. With southerly winds dangerous gusts are reported to blow off the high land and a swell enters the harbour.

Facilities

Ashore in the small fishing hamlet there is a café/taverna but little else.

TRISTOMA
Admiralty chart no. 1666

This long sheltered inlet on the NW corner of Karpathos appears on the chart to offer the best shelter on the island. However with a strong *meltemi* blowing heavy seas pile up at the entrance and there are fierce gusts off the hills. With strong southerlies there are also gusts off the surrounding hills. Entry is by the southernmost passage. Anchor at the head of the inlet or in the cove on the NE side.

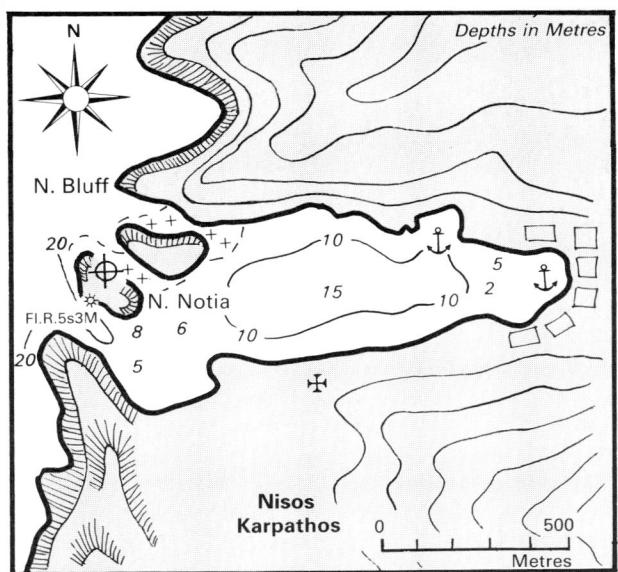

TRISTOMA
35°49'·3N 27°12'·3E (Notia light)

Limin Kasou looking NE.

NISIS SARIA (Saros)

Lies immediately N of Karpathos separated only by a narrow channel. The channel has been reported to have 3–4 metre depths and to be easily navigated in calm weather. (I have not navigated the channel and cannot confirm these depths.) With strong winds gusts blow out of the channel according to the wind direction.

IFALOS KARPATHOS (Karpathos Rock)

A reef in the channel between Kasos and Karpathos near the SW end of Karpathos. The reef has less than 2 metre depths over it and can be difficult to spot with any swell running. Unless a yacht is proceeding along the W coast of Karpathos it is no danger to yachts crossing between Kasos and Karpathos.

CAUTION

During the *meltemi* season strong gusts blow off the S and E sides of Kasos and Karpathos. Large and disturbed seas will be encountered in Stenon Kasou (Kasos Strait) between Kasos and Crete and especially in Stenon Karpathou (Karpathos Strait) near the southern tip of Rhodes. In the latter sea area the bottom comes up quickly from 600–700 metres to 100–200 metres causing a wicked cross-sea.

LIMIN KASOU (Port Kasos, Emborio, Ophris, Ofris, Fri)

Approach

Conspicuous From the W the town of Fri to the W of the harbour and a pink-roofed church fronted by palms near the harbour are conspicuous. From the E a white church on the headland to the E of the harbour and the mole are also conspicuous.

By night The end of the mole is lit: Fl.G.1·5s3M. On Ak Ay Yeoryios a light is exhibited: Fl.WR.2·4s

The miniature harbour at Ophris. *Nigel Patten.*

5/3M red sector covers 083°-175° and 241°-251°). Care must be taken not to head for the Q.R.2M exhibited in the shallow and rock-bound *caïque* harbour off the village of Fri.

Dangers With the *meltemi* there are gusts and a confused sea in the approaches to the harbour.

Mooring

Go stern-to or bows-to the mole. The bottom is rock and sand.

Shelter Reasonable shelter from the *meltemi* although there is a surge in the harbour with a prolonged blow. Open to the NE. With strong winds from the S there are gusts off the high hills behind. With southerlies the fishermen either move elsewhere or anchor on the S side of the harbour with a warp ashore.

Authorities Port police and customs.

Facilities

Water Tap on the beach.
Fuel Limited amounts in the town.

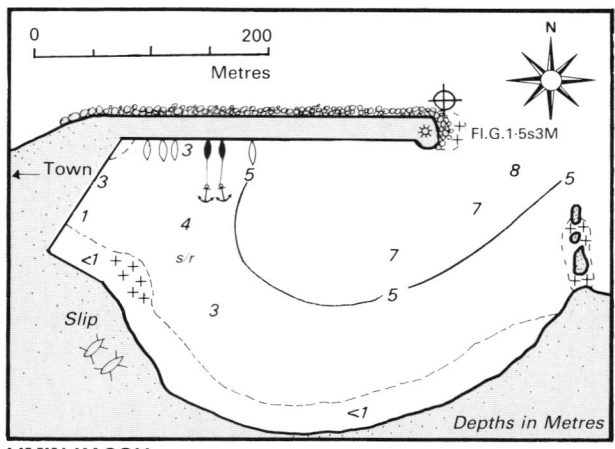

LIMIN KASOU
35°25'·3N 26°57'·4E (Fl.G.3M)

Provisions Most provisions can be found in Fri.
Eating out Several tavernas in Fri.
Other PO. OTE. Bank. Greek gas. Ferry to Piraeus and Rhodes.

General

Fri, situated just W of the harbour, is a tatty town with a run-down charm. In many ways it seems like something out of North Africa. The small *caïque* harbour surrounded by houses is a pleasant spot and the friendly locals make up for its neglected appearance.

KASONISIA (Kaso Islets)

Shelter from the *meltemi* can be obtained in a number of small coves on the S side of these islands – sponge-boats fishing the area often use the low-lying Makronisi or Armathia (the largest of the group) where some shelter from N winds can be obtained. The bottom is sand and reported to be good holding.

IFALOS KASOU (Kasos Rock)

Lies in the channel between Kasos and Kasonisia. It is no real danger to sailing yachts since the least depth over it is 4·5 metres. A transit of Ak Ay Yeoryios and Nisis Kolofonos clears it.

ORMOS KHELATRONAS

At the S end of Kasos this deserted bay offers good shelter from the *meltemi*. Anchor in 4–8 metres at the head of the bay. The bottom is sand with not a patch of weed in sight – excellent holding. The *meltemi* gusts down off the hills and a swell invariably works its way around into the bay making it a little rolly, but you are safe enough. Idyllic and sometimes spooky surroundings.

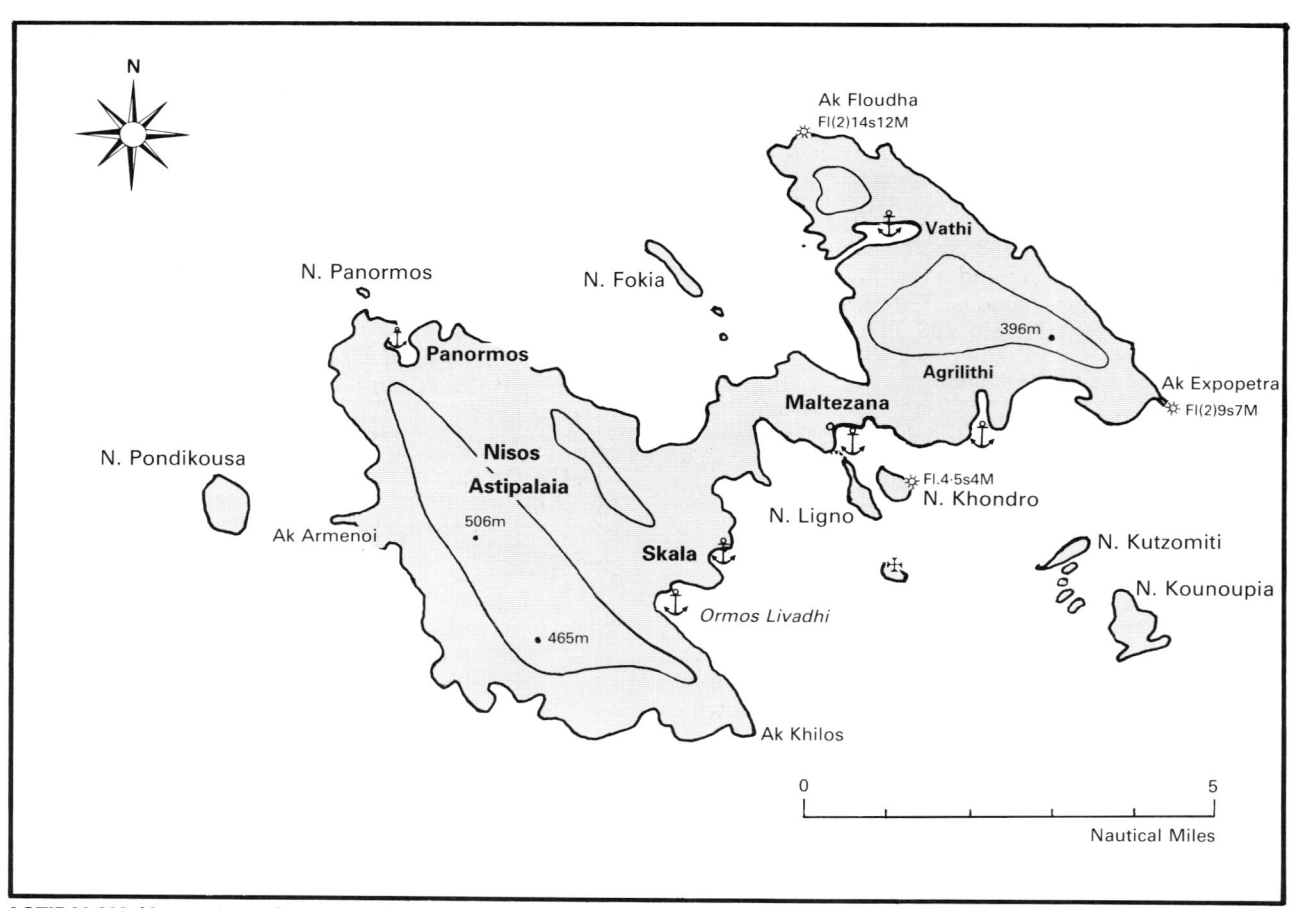

ASTIPALAIA (Astypalaea, Stampalaia)

Astipalaia

(Astypalaea, Stampalia)

Lying like an almost forgotten part of the Dodecanese, 35 miles west of Nisiros, Astipalaia (also called Stampalia in the Middle Ages and again during the Italian occupation) consists of two mountain ranges joined by a long slender isthmus. When approaching from the north or south it appears to be two islands. The coastline is much indented and offers a number of safe anchorages – until the Romans and later the English suppressed piracy in the Aegean, the island was a natural lair for pirates with good shelter and a strategic position to pounce on merchant shipping.

In antiquity the island was famed for its seafood and its fertility. Pliny praised its mussels and the surrounding seabed was supposed to have the best sponges in the Aegean. Today little of this is evident – the land is mostly barren or scrubby, the mussels nonexistent, and the sponge-divers go to the African coast. However crayfish often appear on taverna menus. In the Middle Ages the Venetian family Quirini ruled the island. In 1912 it was the first of the Dodecanese to be occupied by the Italians. These last occupants built little and the character of the island is more like that of the Cyclades than that of the Dodecanese.

CAUTION

From Ak Exopetra (Poulari) across the S coast of Astipalaia to Ak Khilos there are strong gusts off the land when the *meltemi* is blowing.

SKALA ASTIPALAIA (Periyialo)

Approach

Conspicuous The castle with two white churches inside is conspicuous from some distance off. The white houses of the *chora* and a line of 4 windmills on the hills are also conspicuous. Entering the bay, the houses along the waterfront and the quay are easily seen.

By night Use the light on the N side of the bay (Fl.WR.1·3s4/2M red sector covers 261°-293°) and the two lights on the quay (3F.R.3M and 3F.G.3M in an inverted triangle configuration).

Dangers With the *meltemi* there can be strong gusts off the high land in the approaches.

Mooring

Moor alongside the ferry quay although you may have to move off for a short time if the ferry is due. Alternatively anchor in the bay. With care a couple of yachts can go bows-to the short pier off the town. The bottom is sand and weed, reasonable holding.

Shelter With the *meltemi* there are gusts into the bay which can make a berth on the quay uncomfortable.

Skala (Astipalaia) looking W from the slopes above the village.

The bay is completely open to the SE and in the event of such a wind the local fishermen go to Maltezana.

Authorities Port police and customs.

Facilities

Water Near the quay.

Fuel On the N side of the bay. A mini-tanker can deliver to the quay.

Provisions Most provisions can be obtained in the village, but the island is largely dependent on the ferry for supplies and there may be a shortage of some items (particularly fruit and vegetables).

Eating out Good tavernas around the waterfront, several with superb views over the bay.

Other PO. OTE. A bank's representative. Hire motorbikes. Ferry to Piraeus and Rhodes.

General

The harbour and the *chora* above, which virtually form one town straggling from the bay to the summit, are most attractive from seaward although a little dilapidated on closer inspection. The castle dominating the *chora* (variously named Astipalaia or Stampalia or Kastello after the castle) was built in the 13th century by John Quirini. Legend has it that the castle was successfully defended on one occasion by the defenders throwing beehives onto the attackers. From the castle there is a magnificent view across to Maltezana to the NE and Ormos Livadhi to the SW.

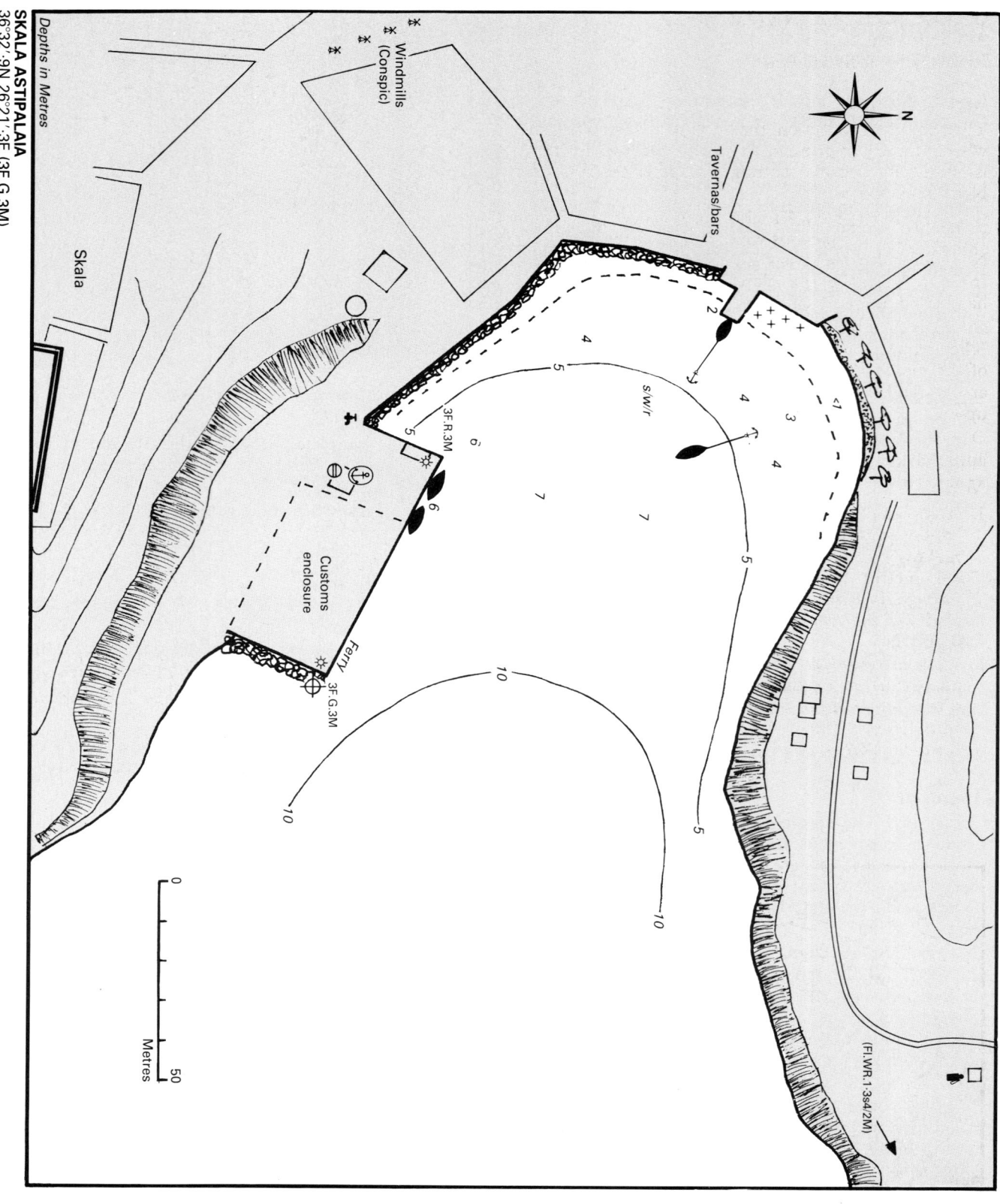

SKALA ASTIPALAIA
36°32'·9N 26°21'·3E (3F.G.3M)

Depths in Metres

Windmills
(Conspic)

Skala

Tavernas/bars

N

2

4

5

s/w/r

4

3

<1

4

4

7

5

5

5

6

3F.R.3M

6

7

10

10

10

5

Customs
enclosure

Ferry 3F.G.3M

3F.R.3M

(Fl.WR.1·3s4/2M)

0

50

Metres

ORMOS MALTEZANA (Analipsis)
Admiralty chart no. 1666
Imray-Tetra chart no. G34

Approach
This bay is situated on the middle of the S coast where the island is almost divided into two by the isthmus. The normal entrance is on either side of Nisis Khondro.

Conspicuous Nisis Ay Kiriaki, the low islet just S of Ligno, has a conspicuous white chapel in the middle. Nisis Khondro and Nisis Ligno are easily identified from the distance and closer in the mole and the hamlet behind it are easily seen.

By night Not recommended. Use the light on Nisis Khondro (Fl.4·5s4M) and the light on the extremity of the mole (Fl.G.3s3M). The fuel barge and buoys are marked by a F.W but this is not to be relied upon.

Dangers With the *meltemi* there are gusts in the approaches.

Note
1. It is possible to enter and leave Ormos Maltezana by the passage between the islet connected by a reef to Nisis Ligno and the islet N of it. There are 4·3 metres least depths in the fairway. The passage is easily negotiated by day though the clarity of the water makes it look shallower than it really is.
2. Care is needed of the fuel barge moored approximately on the 10 metre line in the middle of the bay. On the S and E sides of the barge are three orange buoys – presumably mooring buoys for the tanker.

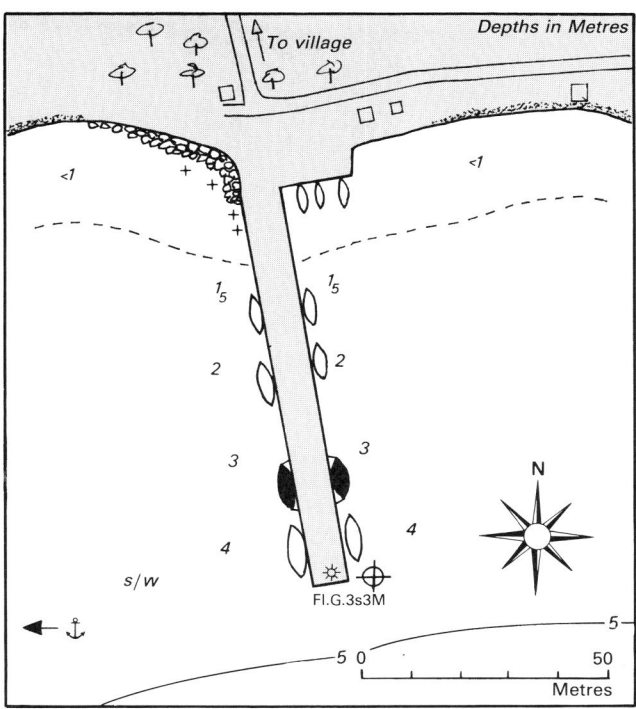

MALTEZANA
36°34'·6N 26°23'·3E (Fl.G.3M)

Mooring
Anchor in the bay or go alongside the pier if there is room. Do not take berths belonging to local fishing boats on the pier. The bottom is sand and weed, good holding.

Shelter Good shelter from the *meltemi* with few gusts. Although partially open to the SE the wind does not blow home and little swell enters the bay.

Facilities
Some provisions in the hamlet. Several tavernas and cafés ashore.

General
The bay is attractive with an anomalous (for Astipalaia) green foreshore under the barren burnt slopes behind and clear water in the bay. The good lee from the *meltemi* also comes as a blessed relief. On the slopes NW of the hamlet there is an airstrip.

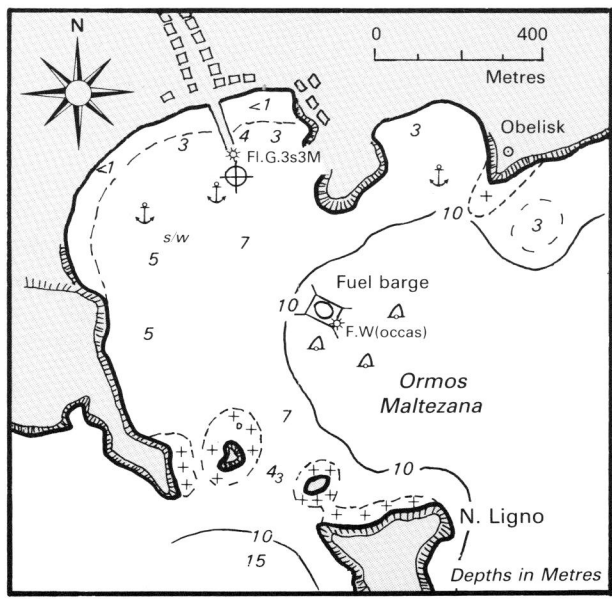

MALTEZANA
36°34'·6N 26°23'·3E (Fl.G.3M)

ORMOS AGRILITHI

A deserted inlet lying approximately 1 mile NE of Nisis Khondro. Good shelter from the *meltemi* although there are gusts off the slopes. Anchor where convenient and take a long line ashore. The bottom is sand – good holding. The deserted bay is a wonderful wild spot which, with the *meltemi* howling outside, can feel like your own private paradise.

Note The shoal patch (Ifalos Baraka) (4·5 metres/2½ fathoms) lying approximately half a mile SE of the E entrance point to Agrilithi is visible in calm weather but is difficult to spot with the *meltemi* kicking up a chop.

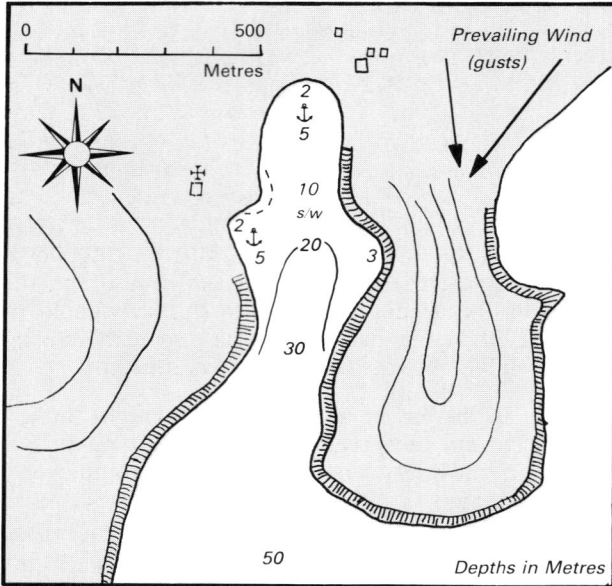

AGRILITHI
36°35′N 26°25′·4E

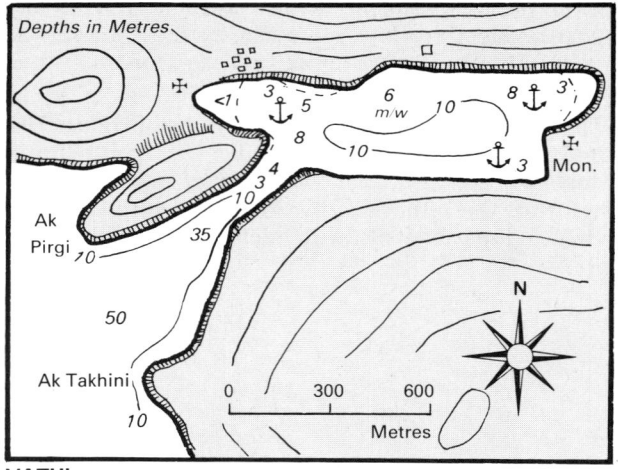

VATHI
36°37′N 26°25′E

VATHI

Admiralty chart no. 1666

This landlocked inlet on the NE tip of the island offers good all-round shelter. The entrance is somewhat difficult to pick out from the cliffs. Anchor off the small hamlet in the W corner in 3–5 metre depths. There is thick weed on the bottom, but find a clear patch to drop the anchor in and the holding is good. Mild gusts with the *meltemi*. A few large trawlers are usually moored off the fishing hamlet. A café/taverna.

PANORMOS

In the bay at the NW tip of Astipalaia shelter from the *meltemi* can be found in a cove on the W side of the bay. Anchor in 4–5 metres on a sandy bottom. No facilities but peaceful surroundings.

ORMOS LIVADHI

On the S side of the *chora* (Astipalaia) is the large bay of Livadhi with a pleasant anchorage at the head of the beach. The bottom is sand and the gusts from the *meltemi* are not too bad here.

NISIS AY IOANNIS (Nisis Sirina)

A high domed island lying approximately 19 miles SE of Astipalaia. Nisidhes Adelfia, a group of high jagged islands approximately 4 miles NW of Sirina, are conspicuous and the bold outline of Ay Ioannis is easily identified. A light is exhibited on Nisis Plakidha (Fl.WR.3s9/6M), the largest island of Nisidhes Trianisia to the SE of Ay Ioannis but navigating in the vicinity of these islands and rocks at night should be avoided.

On the S of Ay Ioannis there is a large bay which local fishermen use. It is reported that most of the bay is quite deep with a rock-strewn bottom, but in the NE corner there is a patch of sand suitable for anchoring in. The fishermen have a permanent mooring here and don't seem to mind visitors using it when they leave at night to fish around Nisidhes Trianisia. Good shelter from the *meltemi*. The bay is only open S.

Ashore there is little except two chapels and a herd of goats.

X. Crete
(Kriti)

Crete is the largest and most important island in the Aegean. Lying across the mouth of the southern Aegean, it both commands the southern approaches to Greece and forms the link between the Peloponnese and Asia Minor through Kasos, Karpathos, and Rhodes. While it is politically and geographically a part of Greece, its inhabitants have always thought of themselves as being Cretans first and Greeks second.

Crete is dominated by the high mountain backbone which runs throughout its length. Approaching from seaward the peaks of the mountains, snow-capped in the winter and well into the spring, can be seen from a considerable distance off. On the western end of the island the Levka Ori (White Mountains) are a mountain range reaching 2469 metres (8100ft); in the middle of the island the Idhi Ori (Ida) are three conspicuous peaks with the highest peak (Oros Psiloriti or Mt Ida) reaching 2456 metres (8060ft); and at the eastern end the Oros Dhikti (Lasithi Mountains) attain 2133 metres (7000ft).

For the most part the island is rocky and barren except for the plains on the north coast which are cultivated and the high Lasithi Plateau, a fertile bowl in the mountains. On the south coast the land drops away abruptly to the sea except around Ierapetra. The favourable climate enables a wide variety of fruit and vegetables to be grown: olives, grapes, carob beans, bananas, peaches, oranges (said to be the best in Greece), melons, tomatoes (early season tomatoes for Greece are grown at Ierapetra), and a wide variety of other fruits and vegetables. The flora of Crete is varied with some 140 indigenous species including many varieties of the orchid family.

The history of Crete, both ancient and modern, has often been turbulent. It was inhabited in Neolithic times and again during the Cycladic period, but to most people Crete is known as the centre of the Minoan civilization which ruled over the eastern Mediterranean from 2000–1450BC (middle and late Minoan). Perhaps one of the more gentle civilizations to exist, it gave us the beautifully decorated pottery which can be seen in the museum at Iraklion and the graceful palaces that Sir Arthur Evans lovingly excavated and recreated. The palace of Knossus is the best known, but the palaces at Phaistos on the south coast and Kato Zakros on the east coast, though there is less to see, are worth visiting for both the superb sites and the peace away from the crowds at Knossus. The Minoan civilization disappeared almost overnight around 1450BC with the eruption of Thira when it is thought tidal waves, earthquakes and ash obliterated the palaces, the fleet, and the land.

By about 800BC the Dorians had established themselves on Crete and in the classical period small city-states were scattered around the island. There was an orderly progression through the Roman occupation into the Byzantine period. Many beautiful frescoes still exist from the Byzantine era in churches on Crete and a Cretan school of fresco painting flourished – so much so that Cretan artists were in demand all over Greece. Towards the end of the Byzantine period the Saracens occupied Crete and remained for over a century. The island was retaken for Byzantium by the Emperor Nikephoros who employed the bizarre device of catapulting the heads of captured prisoners into the stronghold of Iraklion (then Kandak or Kandia), so demoralizing the defenders that they eventually capitulated.

After the Fourth Crusade the island was ruled by the Genoese until the 13th century when it was sold to Venice. The Venetians occupied the island until 1669 and most of the castles and forts still standing date from this era. The harbours on the northern coast were of vital importance in the Venetian trade route from the Peloponnese to Asia Minor and they fought long and hard to stop the Turks taking Crete. The Turks won through in 1669 and were to hold Crete until 1898. For the Cretans it was a time of much hardship and poverty and there were many insurrections bloodily put down by the Turks. The spirit and the independence of the Cretans in their battle against the Turks is immortalised in the prose of Nikos Kazantakis. Crete became a part of Greece in 1913.

The Cretans, battered by the misfortune of history, but never beaten, have today recovered some degree of prosperity through tourism. However much you despise the reinforced concrete dormitories lining the beaches, you cannot at the same time deny the rise in living standards they have brought with them. Crete is a booming tourist island and the yachtsman is lucky enough to be able to explore its more remote parts and so sample something of the island that is denied to most. The Cretan has a certain reserve that can be mistaken for hostility, but once this has been overcome the visitor will find he is welcome and will be treated as a privileged visitor.

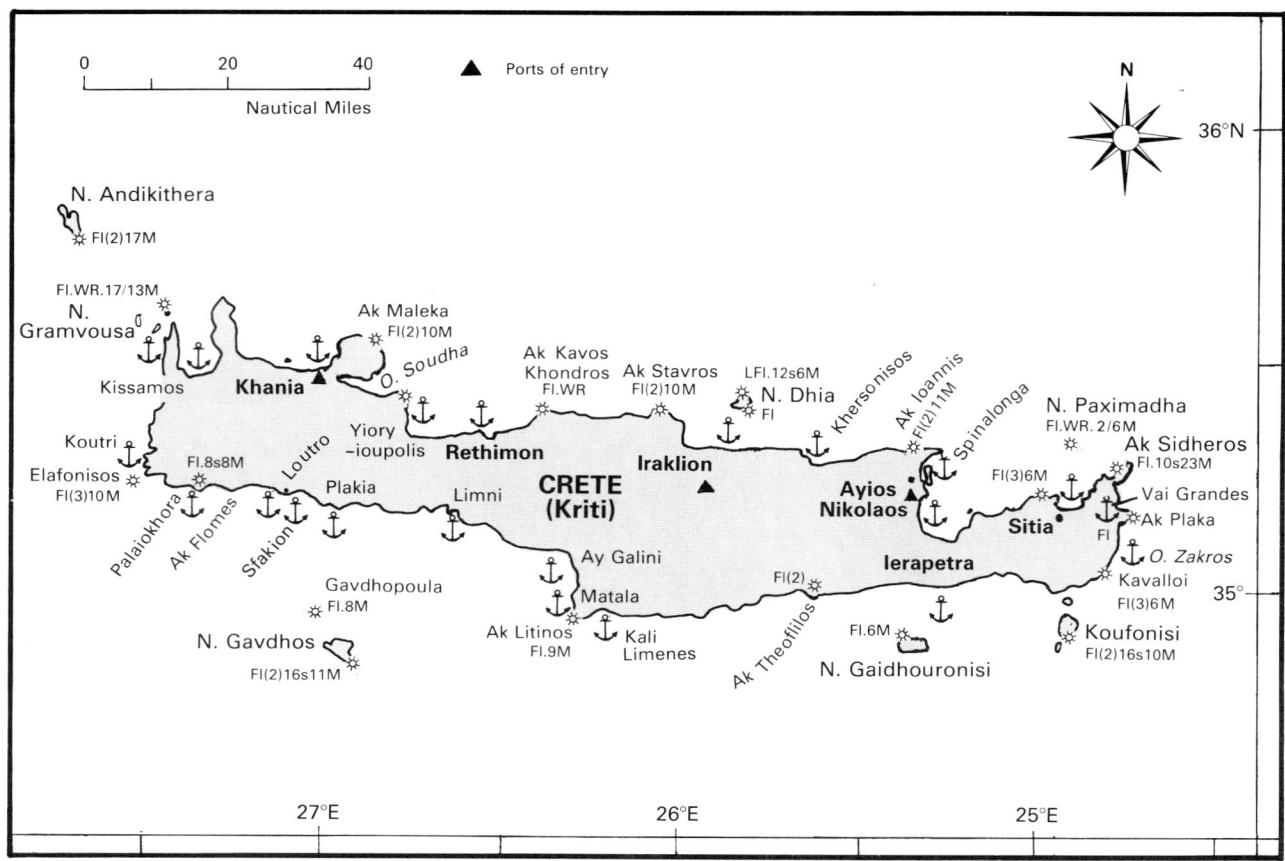

Weather patterns in Crete

In the summer the prevailing wind is the *meltemi* blowing from the NW–WNW. In common with the rest of the Aegean it blows strongest in July and August. It does not usually blow more than Force 5–6 off the northern coast and is more often Force 3–4. In the spring and autumn the wind is predominantly from the S, about Force 2–4.

The southern coast is notorious for the squalls that blow off the high mountains with the prevailing summer winds. The Admiralty *Pilot* tersely warns that: 'Strong squalls blow down from the mountains during northerly winds. These squalls often begin suddenly, and they may be violent close inshore.'

In the summer months Crete is very hot: the average temperatures often get to 35°–36°C in July and August and can reach 40° at times. In the winter the mountains are covered in snow down to the lower slopes, but the coastal plains have a mild winter climate and the coastal towns are agreeable places to winter afloat.

Data

PORTS OF ENTRY
Khania
Iraklion
Ayios Nikolaos

PROHIBITED AREAS
1. Navigation is prohibited in an area extending 500 metres N, NE and E of Ak Maleka.
2. Navigation and anchorage are prohibited in Ormos Soudhas except for the channel running up the middle of the bay (not marked) and at Limin Soudhas. It is prohibited to enter at night.
3. It is prohibited to anchor in an area extending ¾ mile E and SE of Ak Soudha.
4. Navigation and anchorage are prohibited in the areas shown around Ak Sidheros.

MAJOR LIGHTS
Nisis Gramvousa (NW point) Fl.WR.10s17/13M
Ak Maleka Fl(2)12s10M
Ak Dhrepanon Fl(3)30s20M
Nisis Soudha Fl.G.4·8s5M
Ak Khondros Kavos Fl.WR.6s12/8M
Ak Stavros Fl(2)14s10M
Irakliou (N mole head) Oc.G.3s9M
Iraklion (Pier head) Oc.R.3s7M
Nisis Dhia (N point) LFl.12s9M
Nisis Dhia (Ak Stavros) Fl.6s12M
Ak Ay Ioannis Fl(2)12·8s11M
Ormos Ay Nikolaos (Mikronisos) Fl.WR.3s6/4M
Ak Vamvakia Fl(3)18s6M
Nisis Paximadha Fl.WR.6s8/6M
Ak Sidheros Fl.10s23M
Nisidhes Kavalloi Fl(3)12s6M
Koufonisi Fl(2)16s10M
Gaidhouronisi Fl.7·5s6M
Ak Theofilos Fl(2)12s6M
Megalonisi Fl(3)24s11M
Ak Litinos Fl.7s9M

Gavdhopoula (NW point) Fl.8s8M
Nisos Gavdhos (S point) Fl(2)16s12M
Nisis Loutro LFl.10s5M
Nisis Skhisto Fl.8s8M
Nisis Elafonisos Fl(3)24s10M

Quick reference guide

	Shelter	Mooring	Fuel	Water	Provisioning	Tavernas	Plan
North Coast							
Kissamos	B	ABC	O	O	O	C	●
Khania	A	A	B	A	A	A	●
Soudha	A	ABC	B	B	B	B	●
Yioryioupolis	B	BC	B	B	B	B	●
Rethimon	B	AB	B	A	A	A	●
Ormos Bali	B	C	O	O	O	C	
Iraklion	A	A	B	A	A	A	●
Khersonisos	B	AC	B	B	B	A	●
Spinalonga	A	C	B	B	B	B	●
Ayios Nikolaos	B	AB	A	A	A	A	●
Ay Nikolaos Marina	A	A	O	A	B	B	●
Pahia Ammos	C	A	B	B	B	B	
Sitia	B	A	A	A	A	A	●
Ak Sidhero	B	C	O	O	O	O	●
South Coast							
Nisis Gramvousa	B	C	O	B	O	O	●
Koutri	O	C	O	O	O	O	
Palaiokhora	B	ABC	B	B	B	B	●
Loutro	B	C	O	B	C	C	●
Sfakia	O	C	B	B	B	B	
Plakia	O	C	B	B	B	B	
Limni	O	C	O	O	O	O	
Ay Galini	B	A	B	A	B	B	●
Matala	C	C	B	B	B	B	
Kali Limenes	B	C	B	B	C	C	●
Ierepetra	B	A	B	B	B	B	●
Ormos Zakros	C	C	O	O	O	C	
Ormos Grandes	C	C	O	O	C	C	

Northern coast of Crete

KISSAMOS (Kavonisi, Kastelli)

Approach

The harbour lies in the SW corner of Kolpos Kissamos to the E of a rocky spur. The town of Kastelli and the harbour mole are easily identified.

By night The entrance is lit: Fl.G.2s3M and Fl.R.3s3M.

Mooring

Moor alongside or anchor off inside the mole.

Shelter Good shelter from the W and NW although there is often some surge inside. Open to the E and SE.

Authorities Port police.

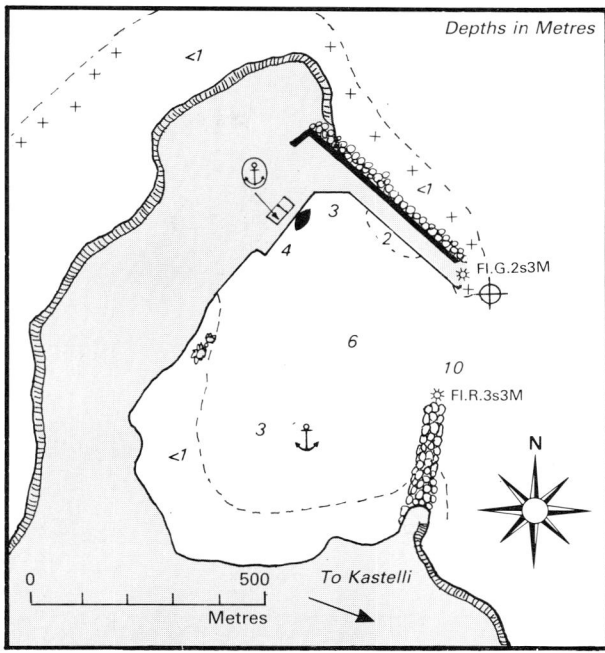

KISSAMOS
35°31′ 23°38′·4E (Fl.G.3M)

Facilities

A taverna/café and a telephone at the harbour. In Kastelli fuel and provisions can be obtained.

General

Kissamos is the harbour for Kastelli town about one mile to the E. The harbour is used by a few fishing boats and coasters and a ferry.

KHANIA (Hania)

Admiralty chart no. 1658

Approach

Conspicuous The town is visible from some distance off. Closer in a white mosque on the waterfront, the lighthouse on the E side of the entrance, and a number of chimneys in the town are conspicuous.

By night Use the light on the E side of the entrance (Fl.R.2·5s7M) and the lights on either side of the entrance to the inner harbour (F.G.3M and F.R.3M). The buoy off the detached breakwater is lit Q(3)15s.

DANGERS

The approach is difficult with strong onshore winds. A dangerous sea heaps up on the shoal water at the entrance and care is needed in the immediate approaches. The new detached breakwater improves matters, but it is still difficult with onshore winds.

Note The new detached breakwater is marked at the E end by an E cardinal buoy and lit Q(3)15s.

Mooring

Go stern-to or bows-to the S quay immediately inside the inner harbour. The bottom is soft mud and rock

Khania harbour looking N to the entrance.

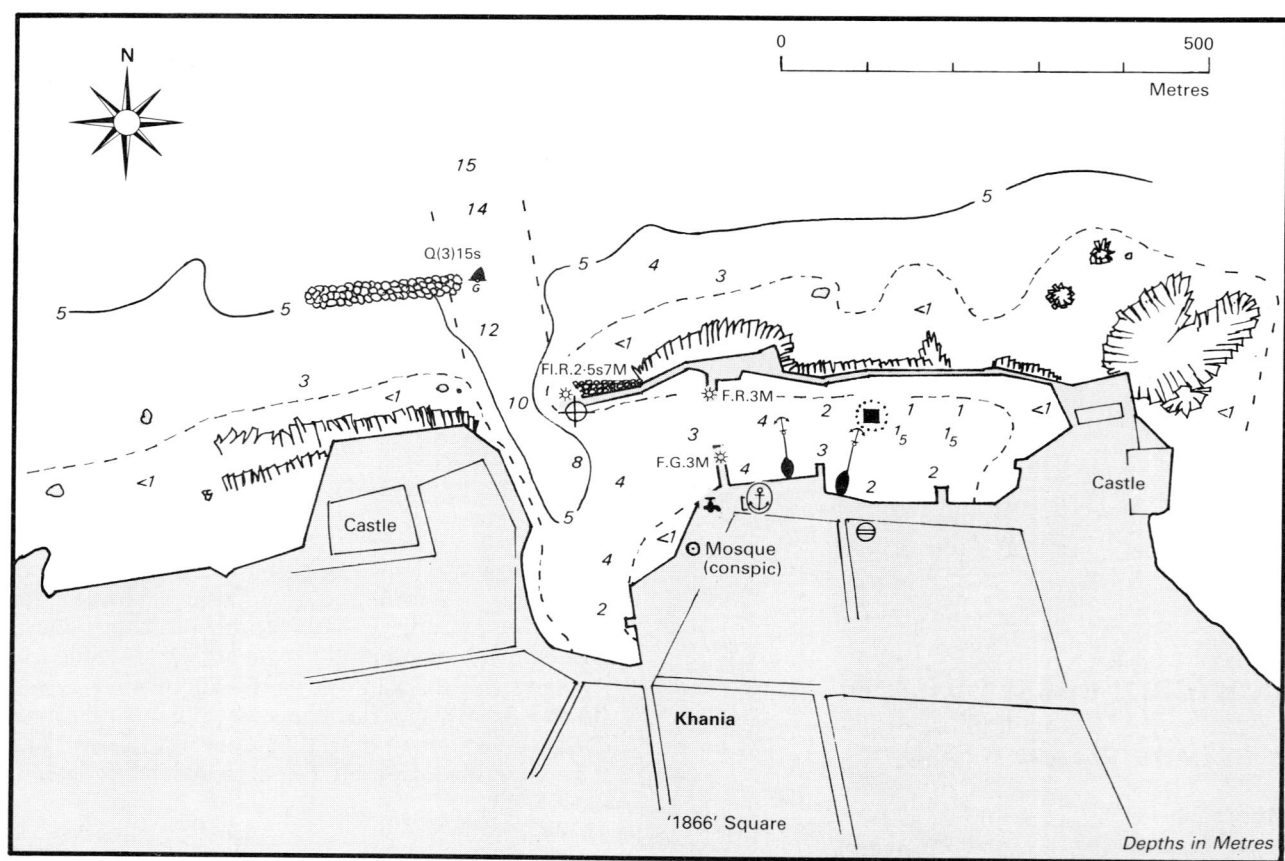

KHANIA
35°31'·2N 24°01'E (Fl.R.7M)

and it is wise to lay two anchors out as the holding is not good.

Shelter Good all-round shelter although strong northerlies cause a surge in the harbour and spray comes over the outer mole. A number of yachts have wintered afloat here, but in bad northerly gales they take a line across to the other side of the harbour.

Authorities Port of entry: port police, customs, and immigration.

Facilities

Water On the quay.

Fuel In the town. A mini-tanker can deliver to the quay.

Repairs Mechanical repairs. Some light engineering work. Good hardware and tool shops. Chandlers at Skrydlof 26 near 1866 Square.

Provisions Excellent shopping for all provisions. Ice available.

444

Eating out Good tavernas near the waterfront and in the town.

Other PO. OTE. Banks. Greek gas and *Camping Gaz* in 1866 Square. Hire cars, motorbikes and bicycles. Buses to Iraklion. Ferries from Soudha. Internal flights to Athens.

General

Khania was for centuries the capital of Crete and was only recently demoted in favour of Iraklion. The Venetian city around the harbour is a fascinating place – cobbled streets, imposing Venetian houses, mosques and minarets, and the market. The lighthouse on the mole is of Venetian-Turkish origin. None of this has been tarted up and turned into a toy town – the city exists with modern additions and crumbling edges and a bustling, busy life to it. In recent years it has become popular with tourists, but the harbour provides a sanctuary from the hurly-burly if you need it.

Everyone who has wintered here has recommended it even though the harbour can be uncomfortable at times. The town has a buzz to it that is there even when the tourists have departed and, unlike many other tourist spots, doesn't die in the winter.

ORMOS SOUDHAS
Admiralty chart no. 1658

Note It is reported that the authorities have turned some yachts away from here, not allowing them to enter even after a long passage. Alternative safe ports are Khania to the W or Rethimon to the E.

Approach

Conspicuous The high plateau of Akrotiri peninsula is easily recognised from the distance. Atop the peninsula are a number of high towers with military scanners. Nisis Soudhas, with a fort and naval buildings, is conspicuous. The narrow entrance to the channel free for navigation is marked by two light buoys (Fl.R/Fl.G) which are difficult to pick out. On either side of the light buoys and extending to the shore are large black mooring buoys holding the anti-submarine net. The channel free for navigation which runs down the middle of the bay is unmarked. A large flour mill near the harbour is conspicuous. Proceed to the harbour taking care to avoid the restricted area around the naval dockyard.

By night It is prohibited to enter Ormos Soudhas at night.

Caution Ormos Soudhas is the Greek navy's southern base and care must be taken to avoid the prohibited area to the N and E of the Akrotiri peninsula (extending out approximately 0·75 to 1 mile from the

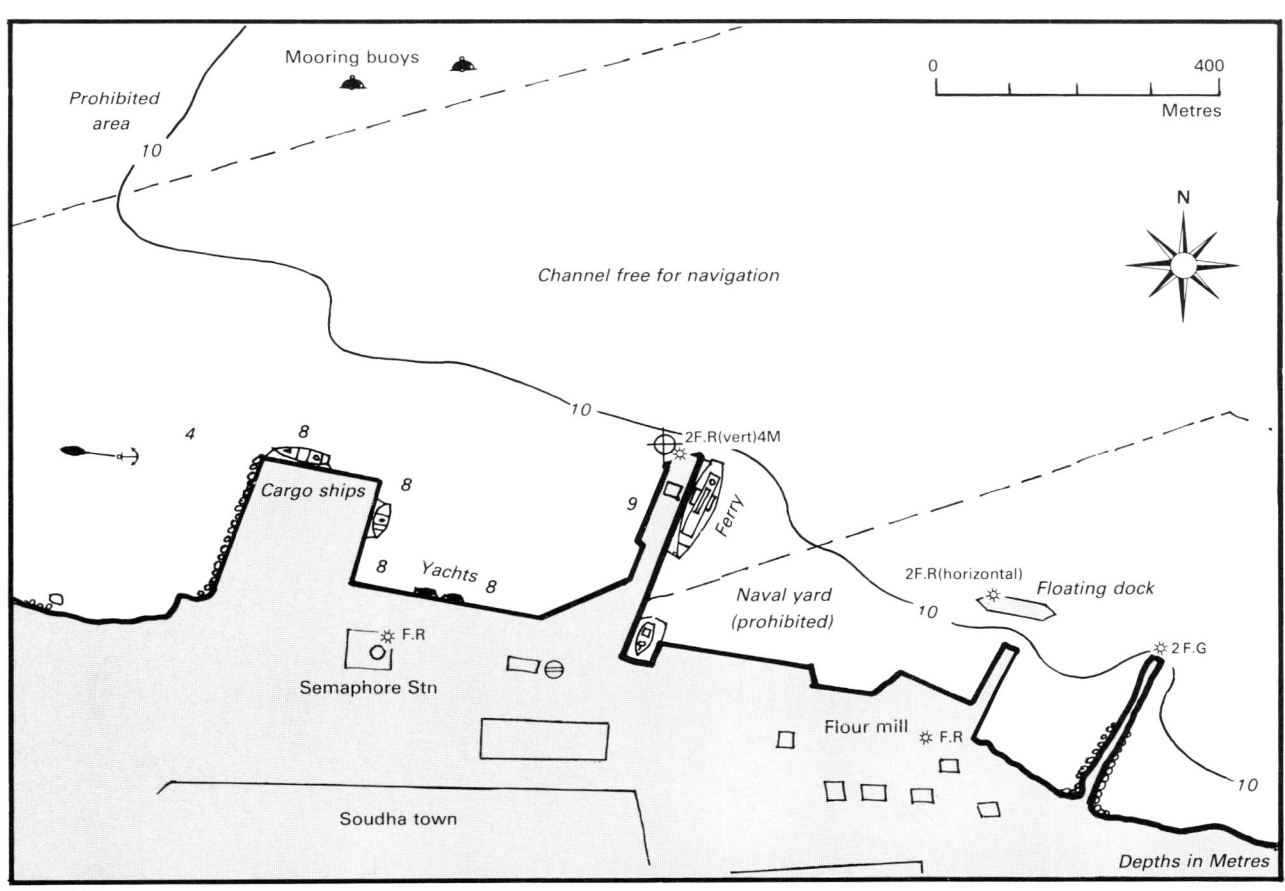

SOUDHA
35°29'·5N 24°04'·7E (2F.R(vert)4M)

coast) and the prohibited area N and S of the channel free for navigation in Ormos Soudhas (the channel runs 283° true from the buoys at the entrance and is 0·2 miles wide).

Mooring

Go alongside or stern-to or bows-to on the S quay.

Shelter Good shelter – so much so that the wind in Ormos Soudhas is generally no indication of conditions outside.

Authorities Port police, customs.

Facilities

Water On the ferry mole.
Fuel In the town. A fuel tanker can be arranged.
Provisions Good shopping for provisions. Ice available.
Eating out Tavernas ashore.
Other PO. OTE. Bank. Greek gas. Ferry to Piraeus – this is the ferry port for Khania. Regular bus service (every ten minutes) to Khania.

General

Although an excellent harbour, Soudha is about as dull and uninteresting as only a restricted naval base could be.

YIORYIOUPOLIS (Yeorgioupoleos)
Admiralty chart no. 1658

A small harbour at the mouth of the Almiros river. From seaward the church on the small island connected by a causeway to the land and a hotel on the beach are conspicuous. Care must be taken in the approach because of the shoal water and underwater rocks in the bay. In the mouth of the river keep close to the quay as it is shallow on the opposite side of the river. Moor alongside. Good shelter except from strong N–NE winds.

Water in the town. Most provisions can be obtained and there are several tavernas in the village. Buses to Khania and Iraklion. An attractive friendly little place well worth visiting.

RETHIMON (Rethymno)
Admiralty chart no. 1658

Approach

Conspicuous From the W the fort on the headland and the buildings of the town are conspicuous. From the E a white church on a hill to the E of the town and two minarets in the town stand out clearly. Closer in the breakwater is easily identified.

By night Use the lights at the entrance: F.G.3M and Fl.R.3s4M. The mole sheltering the inner harbour is lit on the extremity: F.G.3M.

Dangers There is often a rolling swell at the entrance.

Mooring

Go stern-to or bows-to the inside of the jetty on the E side or alongside the quay on the N. If your yacht draws 1·5 metres or less it is possible to moor in the small Venetian harbour. Caution must be exercised when entering, as the depths are uneven and the entrance is subject to silting. Inside the small harbour moor stern-to the S quay. It is very crowded with fishing boats – room for 2 or 3 boats.

Shelter Good shelter from the *meltemi* tucked under the jetty on the E. Excellent all-round shelter in the inner harbour.

Authorities Port police and customs.

YIORYIOUPOLIS 35°22′N 24°16′E

Rethimon. The old Venetian harbour.

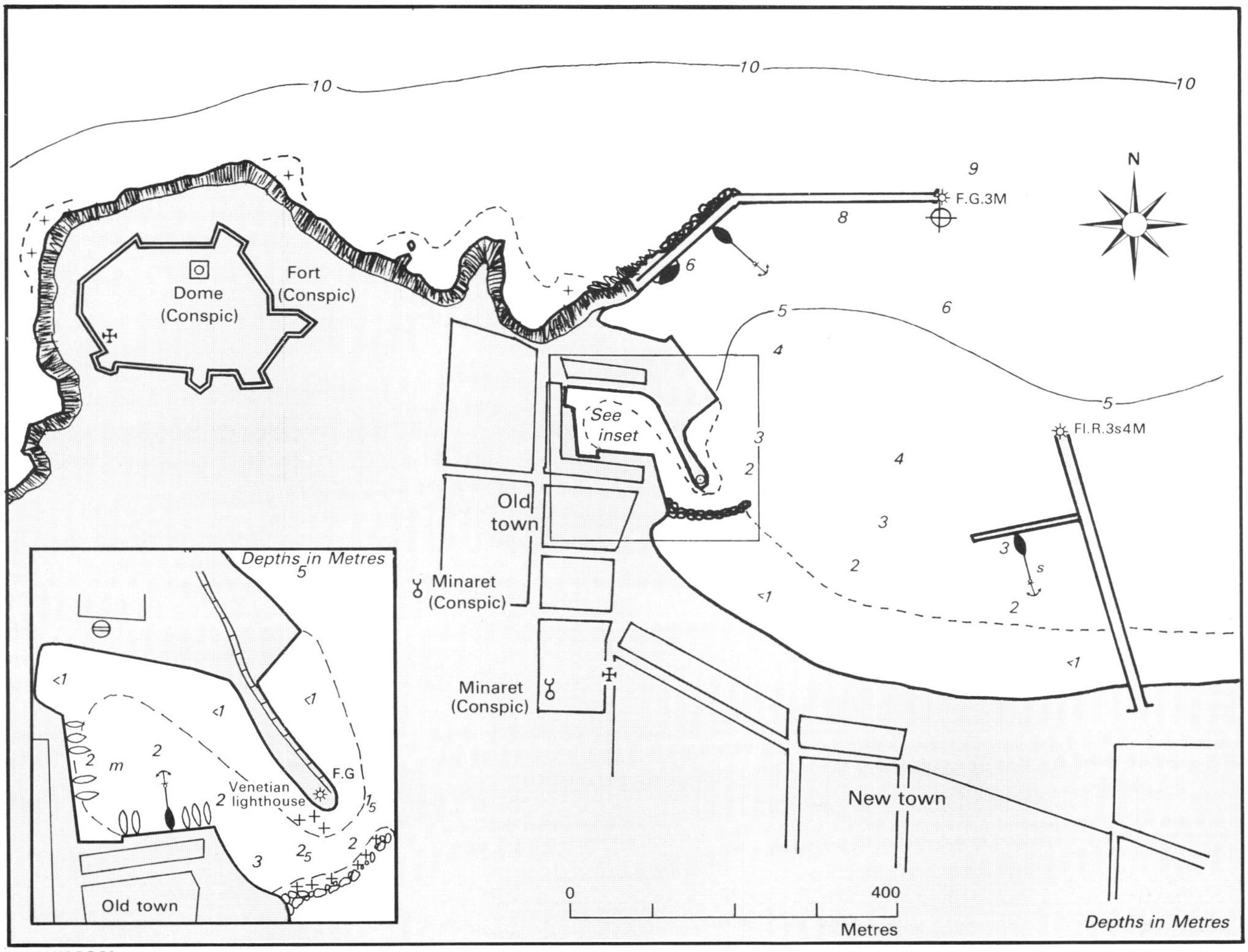

RETHIMON
35°22'·5N 24°29'·E (F.G.3M)

Rethimon harbour looking E from near the castle.

Facilities

Water On the quay.
Fuel In the town, but a mini-tanker can be arranged.
Repairs Some mechanical repairs. Hardware shops.
Provisions Good shopping for all provisions. Ice available.
Eating out Excellent tavernas including several good fish restaurants around the Venetian harbour.
Other PO. OTE. Banks. Greek gas and *Camping Gaz*. Hire cars, motorbikes and bicycles. Buses to Khania and Iraklion.

General

The old Venetian town and harbour is one of the most attractive spots on Crete. If you can squeeze into the inner Venetian harbour you will be moored an arm's length from a taverna or café in the old town. The town also shows signs of the Turkish occupation with wooden balconies on some of the houses and two well-preserved minarets. In the last week of July the Cretan wine festival is held here.

ORMOS BALI

A large bay approximately 16 miles E of Rethimon. Care is needed of the rocks extending out from the W entrance to the bay. The two coves on the W side of the bay are reported to afford good shelter from the prevailing winds. The more northerly of the coves has a short breakwater providing additional shelter. Taverna ashore.

IRAKLION (Herakleion, Candia)
Admiralty chart no. 1658

Approach

Conspicuous From the NW the town and the long N mole (over a mile long) are easily distinguished. The fort at the entrance to the inner harbour and the ferries in the outer harbour are conspicuous. From the E a large brown building at the airport to the E of the city and the white oil storage tanks in the SE corner of the harbour are also conspicuous. The gantries of cranes in the harbour are also conspicuous.

By night Use the lights at the entrance (Oc.G.3s9M and Oc.R.3s7M) and the entrance to the inner

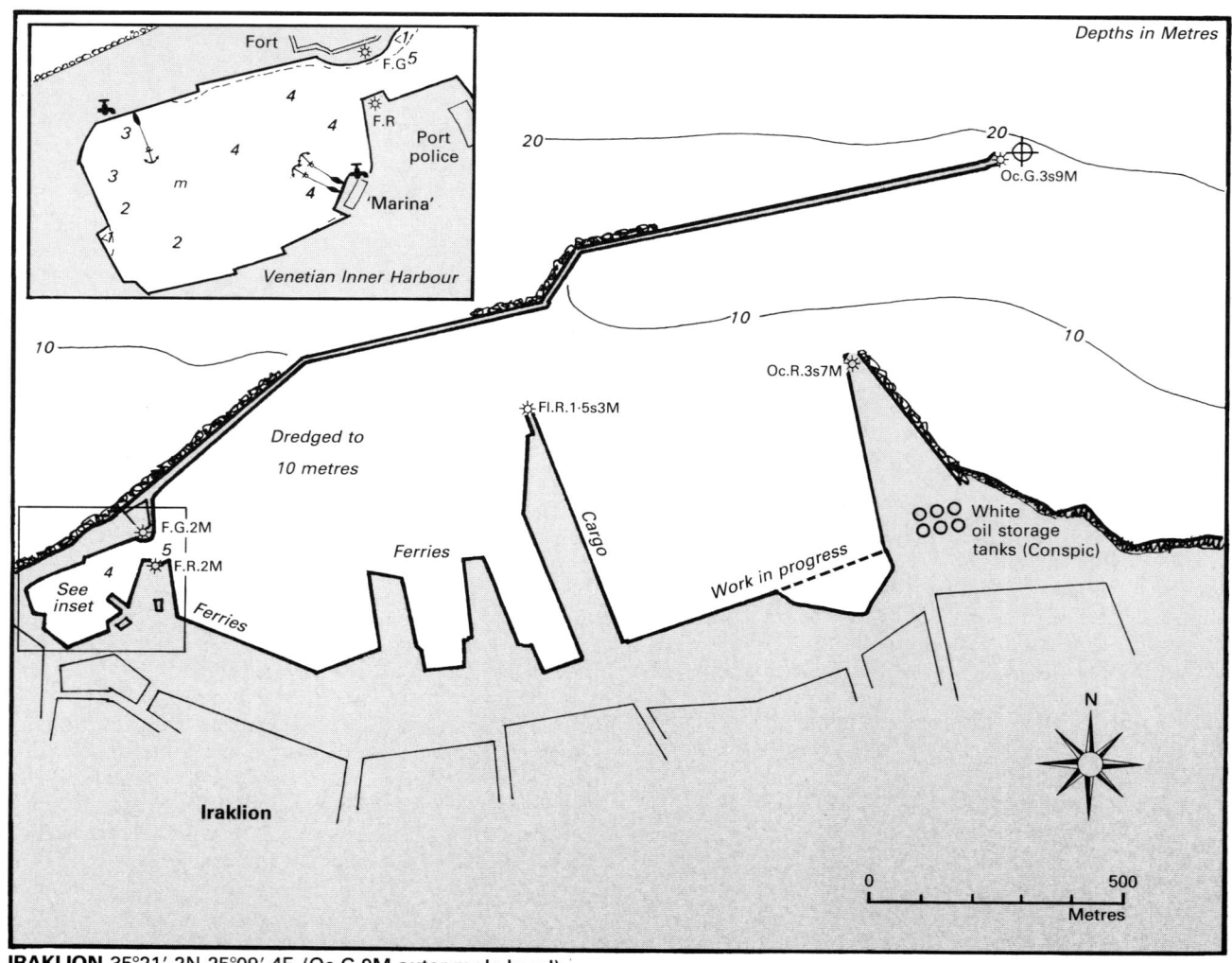

IRAKLION 35°21′·2N 25°09′·4E (Oc.G.9M outer mole head)

Iraklion. The inner harbour looking E.

harbour (F.G.2M and F.R.2M). The commercial pier is lit Fl.R.1·5s3M. There is also a light at the airport to the E of the harbour: Aero Al.WG.4s15M.

Dangers

1. With the *meltemi* there can be a confused swell at the entrance, but inside it is quiet.
2. Care is needed of the numerous ferries coming and going from the harbour.

Mooring

Proceed to the inner Venetian harbour and berth stern-to or bows-to at the so-called marina on the E or on the quay on the N where there are sufficient depths. Good holding in mud. The inner harbour is often full of fishing boats and it can be difficult to find a place to berth.

Shelter Excellent shelter although there is an uncomfortable surge with strong NE winds. The occasional boat winters here.

Authorities A port of entry: port police, customs and immigration.

Facilities

Water On the quay.

Fuel In the town, but a mini-tanker can deliver to the quay.

Repairs Some mechanical repairs. Light engineering work possible. Small yachts can be hauled out in the 'marina'. Large *caïques* are hauled out at the slip in the SE corner of the harbour. Hardware shops.

Provisions Excellent shopping for provisions. Ice available. Fish is often for sale on the SW corner of the inner harbour.

Eating out Excellent tavernas including several good fish tavernas. Some good tavernas around the market in the centre of town.

Other PO. OTE. Banks. Greek gas and *Camping Gaz.* There is a factory to the W of the city where gas bottles can be filled. Laundromat nearby. Hire cars, motorbikes and bicycles. Buses to most parts of the island. Daily ferry service to Piraeus; less regularly to Rhodes. Regular air service to Athens and less regularly to Khania and Rhodes. International flights from many of the major European airports.

General

Iraklion is the fifth largest city in Greece and appears to be a city composed almost entirely of travel agents and car-hire agencies:

'On the first day, one knows beyond contradiction that Iraklion is one of the least pleasant cities of the Mediterranean and nothing to do with that splendid imagined Crete of mountains and mountaineers, ancient palaces and tiny churches rich in paintings.'

Hopkins *Crete: Its past and people*

Adam Hopkins goes on to say that for some people…'It becomes possible to like Iraklion…only people born there actually love it' (*ibid*) but for the yachtsman there is little attractive to find about the city in the short time he is likely to be there. The attraction lies outside the city at Knossus and later in the museum at Iraklion where you can mull over the Minoan world that was.

Knossus

Situated a short distance outside Iraklion (about a 2½ mile walk, or buses leave regularly from the town centre) are the remains of Knossus. In common with other well-known archaeological sites in Greece, Knossus is crowded in the summer and the bustling noisy tour parties detract somewhat from the architectural merits of the place. Nonetheless it is well worth a visit and in the early morning or late afternoon when most of the tourists have left, something of the atmosphere of Knossus can be felt. Knossus was not the only Minoan palace in Crete, but it is considered to be the archetype of such palaces and reconstruction by Sir Arthur Evans makes it easier for the layman to visualize what Minoan architecture was like compared to say Phaistos or Zakros.

The existing palace lovingly excavated by Sir Arthur Evans from 1900 and later by the British School in Athens was built around 1700BC. The heart of Knossus was the central court where business was conducted and the locals idled away the day discussing matters great and small. Around the central court were placed the archives, the storerooms, devotional areas and some living quarters – forming a whole unit that was light and airy and architecturally pleasing. The palace was not only a pleasant place to live in, but also boasted amenities such as running water and a proper drainage system. Some criticism has been levelled at Sir Arthur Evans' reconstruction of Knossus, but without his work there would be little for the layman to see.

The eruption of Thira probably destroyed Knossus and the other Minoan palaces in Crete, indeed it effectively destroyed the Minoan civilization, and reduced to rubble a structure that outstrips much contemporary architecture.

KHERSONISOS (Limin Khersonisou)
Admiralty chart no. 1677

Approach
Conspicuous From the W a white church and a mill on Ak Khersonisos are conspicuous. Rounding the headland behind which the harbour lies a number of large white hotels to the E of the harbour are conspicuous. From the E the hotels lining the foreshore are conspicuous.

By night There are no lights and a night approach would be dangerous because of the numerous reefs fringing the harbour.

DANGERS
1. There are numerous reefs fringing the coast and harbour. Care should be taken of the reef off Ak Khersonisos, the reef around the square rock between the cape and the harbour, and the reef that projects N and E of the headland and the harbour.
2. On entering the harbour, care must be taken to avoid the submerged mole which has only a few rocks just above water, and to avoid the shoal patch immediately W of the head of the built-up mole. (See plan).

Mooring
Go bows-to the built-up mole or anchor off. Care must be taken in the harbour where the depths are uneven – reconnoitre first in a dinghy. The bottom is sand and rock, poor holding.

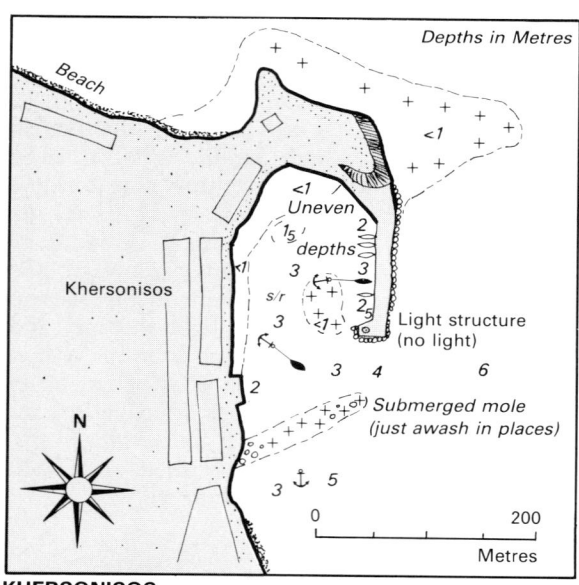

KHERSONISOS
35°19'·3N 25°23'·6E

Khersonisos looking S.

Shelter Good shelter from the *meltemi* and open only to the SE.

Anchorage It is possible to anchor off in the bay immediately S of Ak Khersonisos although there is usually some swell in here.

Facilities
Water In the town though care is needed as it is not all potable. Enquire first.
Fuel In the town.
Provisions Good shopping for provisions in the town.
Eating out A wide choice of tavernas of all types.
Other PO. OTE. Bank. Hire cars, motorbikes and bicycles.

General
Khersonisos is built on the ancient town of Chersonesos though there is little left to see amid the concrete wilderness that has engulfed the site and spread out all along the coast. The resort has become something of a by-word for the sort of tasteless development akin to that in Benidorm where those who come on holiday are looking only for the proverbial sun, sand and sex. If you can find your way through the lager louts of assorted nationalities thronging the streets there is a Venetian mosaic fountain in one of the hotels.

SISSI-MILITUS
Note It is reported that approximately 10 miles E of Khersonisos there is a small harbour with 2–3 metre depths inside and a quay where a yacht can go stern-to or bows-to. Caution advised.

NISIS DHIA (Standia)
A barren rocky island lying 6 miles NNE of Iraklion. On the S coast Ormos Mesarios offers some shelter from northerly winds.

Leper Island at the entrance to Spinalonga lagoon looking N from the lagoon.

SPINALONGA LAGOON

Approach

Conspicuous From the W and E Nisis Spinalonga with a Venetian fort on top is conspicuous.

Entrance There are 3–4 metre depths over the sand bar between Nisis Spinalonga and the W shore of Crete. In the lagoon the depths vary between 3–6 metres.

Dangers There are usually strong gusts off the high land between Ak Ayios Ioannis and Nisis Spinalonga with the *meltemi*. Once in the lagoon the gusts are less severe and not so frequent.

Mooring

Anchor where convenient in the lagoon. A reasonable lee can be found under Nisis Spinalonga. There is a

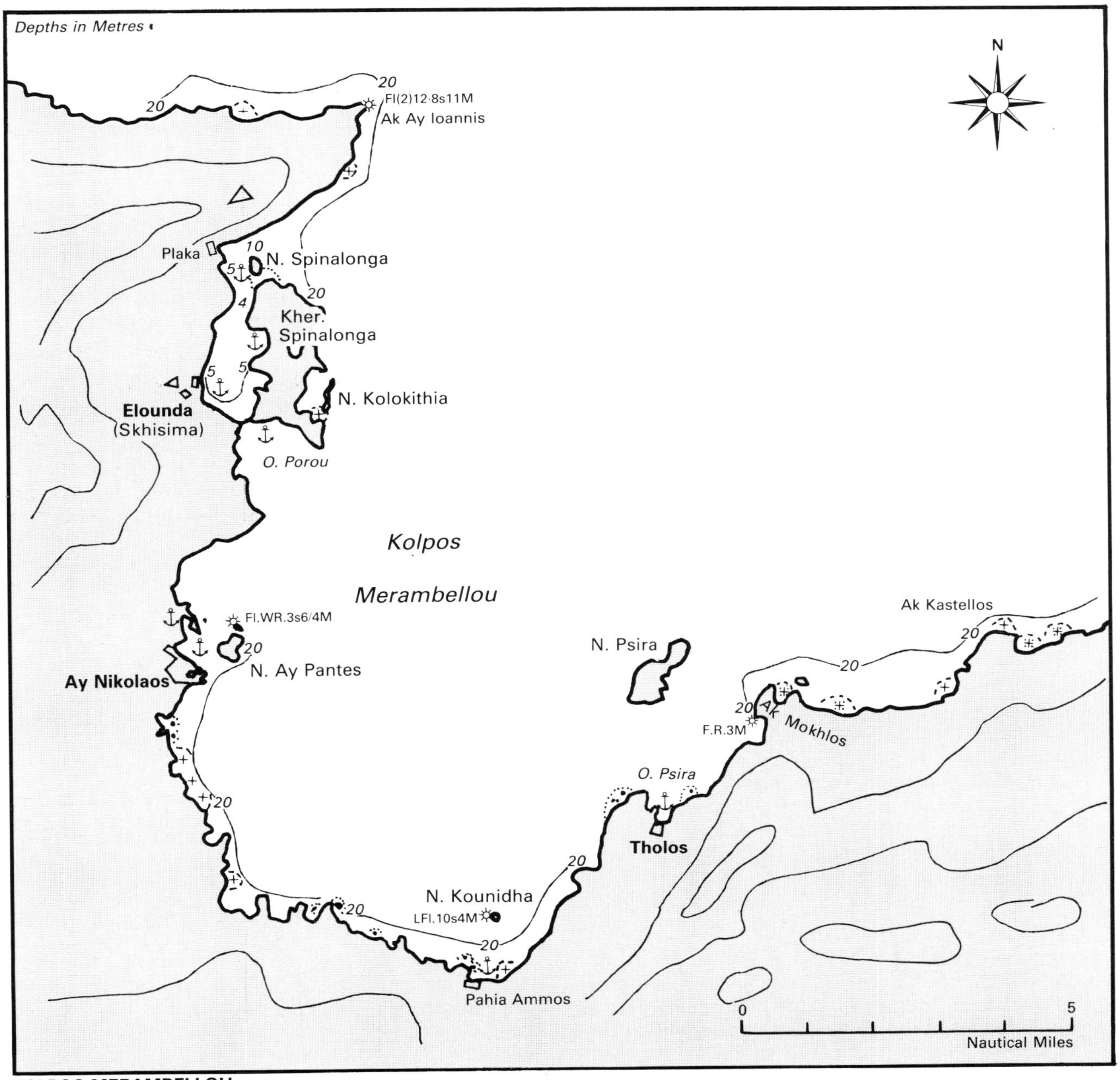

Depths in Metres

N

20
20
Fl(2)12·8s11M
Ak Ay Ioannis

Plaka
10
N. Spinalonga
5
20
4
Kher.
Spinalonga
5
5
N. Kolokithia
Elounda
(Skhisima)
O. Porou

Kolpos

Merambellou

Ak Kastellos
20
Fl.WR.3s6/4M
N. Psira
20
20
20
N. Ay Pantes
20
F.R.3M
Mokhlos
Ay Nikolaos

O. Psira

Tholos

20
N. Kounidha
20
LFl.10s4M
20
Pahia Ammos

0   5
Nautical Miles

KOLPOS MERAMBELLOU

The old leper settlement on Leper Island.

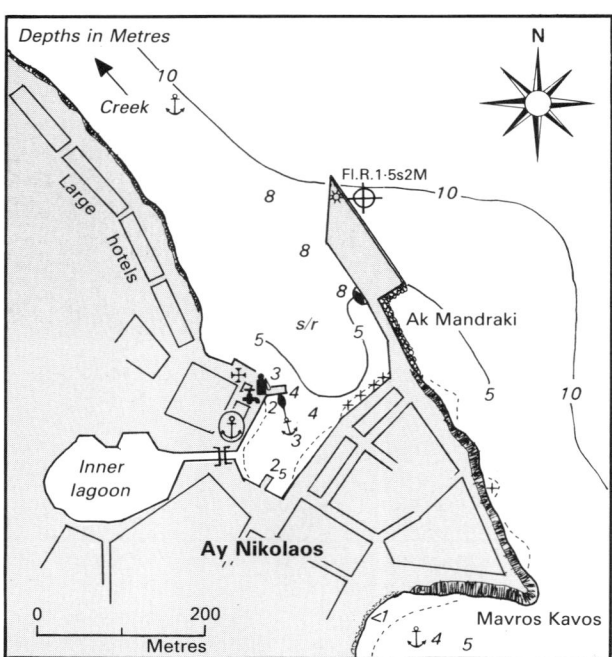

AY NIKOLAOS
35°11′·6N 25°43′·3E (Fl.R.2M)

good shelter with few gusts at Elounda (Skhisma). Here there is a short pier with 1·5–2·5 metre depths off it though it is invariably crowded with tripper boats.

Facilities

At Elounda: Most provisions can be obtained. Excellent tavernas including several good fish tavernas. PO. OTE. Hire cars, motorbikes and bicycles.

General

It is fascinating to sail in the enclosed lagoon watching the sea bottom slip past a few metres under the keel. At one time the flat waters of the lagoon were a seaplane base.

Do not miss Nisis Spinalonga. Beneath the Venetian fort there is a small deserted settlement which was once a leper colony. The settlement and the fort surrounded by the shallow waters of the lagoon are most picturesque. Nisis Spinalonga makes a good lunch-stop before going on to Ayios Nikolaos.

AYIOS NIKOLAOS (Limin Ayiou Nikolaou)
Admiralty chart no. 1677

Approach

Conspicuous From the N and E, Nisis Ay Pantes with a white church on its summit is conspicuous. The buildings of the town including many large hotels along the foreshore are also conspicuous.

Ayios Nikolaos looking NW.

By night Use the light on Nisis Mikronisos (Fl.WR.3s6/4M; the red sector covers 036°-200°) and the light on the extremity of the mole (Fl.R.1·5s2M).

Dangers Ifalos Nikolos, the reef approximately in the middle of Ormos Ay Nikolaou, has 5 metres least depth over it.

Mooring

Go alongside the mole or stern-to the short jetty on the W. All the space in the inner harbour is taken by day-trip boats and you will be told to move if you take one of these places. The bottom is sand, rocks and weed, reasonable holding.

Shelter With the *meltemi* a small amount of swell works its way around the end of the mole, uncomfortable rather than dangerous.

Anchorage The creek N of the harbour offers good shelter from the *meltemi*, but it is full of local boats on permanent moorings and the bottom is foul with these moorings.

Authorities A port of entry: port police, customs, and immigration.

Facilities

Water On the pier on the W.

Fuel At the pier on the W. A mini-tanker can deliver to the N quay.

Repairs Minor mechanical repairs. Hardware shops.

Provisions Good shopping for provisions. Ice available.

Eating out Numerous tavernas nearby.

Other PO. OTE. Banks. Greek gas and *Camping Gas*. Hire cars, motorbikes and bicycles. Buses to Iraklion and Sitia.

General

Ayios Nikolaos may once have been a small fishing village – now it is a booming tourist resort festooned with large hotels. Some people like the place, but personally I find the heart and soul of the town have been gutted to cater for the large numbers of tourists descending on it every summer.

AYIOS NIKOLAOS MARINA

A new marina has been built at Ayios Nikolaos and at present all the basic structure including the breakwaters and piers are in place. Shelter appears to be good. Water and electricity points are installed but no other facilities are ready yet. Provision has been made for operating a travel hoist and providing repair facilities. The marina is expected to be open for business with limited facilities in 1995.

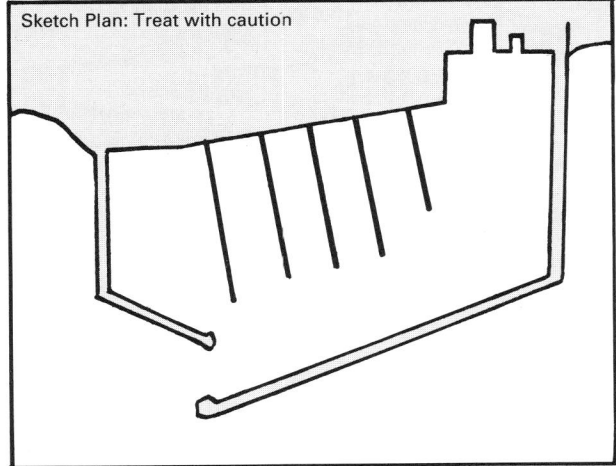

Sketch Plan: Treat with caution

AY NIKOLAOS MARINA

PAHIA AMMOS (Pakhias Ammou)

Admiralty chart no. 1677

A small harbour in the SW corner of Kolpos Merambellou. Care must be taken of the reefs around the two small islets 100 metres and 400 metres NNW of the harbour. Approach from the NE. There are 2–3 metre depths at the extremity of the mole. Sometimes a small coaster is moored stern-to the extremity of the mole and a warp is taken right across to the pier on the opposite side of the harbour effectively stopping any yacht entering. With the normal NW wind a swell works its way around the mole making the harbour uncomfortable. Open to the NE–E.

Some provisions can be obtained and there are several tavernas and cafés in the small village ashore.

SITIA

Admiralty chart no. 1677

Approach

Conspicuous From the W the white light structure on Ak Vamvakia is conspicuous. The buildings of Sitia and the outer (N) mole are conspicuous once the cape has been rounded. From the E the buildings of the town and the fort on the hill are conspicuous.

By night Use the light on Ak Vamvakia (Fl(3)18s6M), the light on the N mole (Fl.G.1·5s3M) and the lights at the entrance (F.G and F.R).

Mooring

Go stern-to or bows-to the inner N mole. The bottom is sand and weed with some rock.

Shelter With the *meltemi* there is a gentle surge of no consequence in the harbour. Open to the NE.

Authorities Port police and customs.

Facilities

Water On the quay.

Fuel On the outer N mole and in the town near the harbour.

Repairs Limited mechanical repairs. Hardware shops.

Provisions Good shopping for provisions. Ice available.

Eating out Excellent tavernas including several good fish restaurants, some in wonderful locations at the edge of the harbour.

Other PO. OTE. Bank. Greek gas and *Camping Gas*. Hire cars, motorbikes and bicycles. Buses to Ayios Nikolaos, Iraklion and Ierapetra.

General

Approaching from the sea, Sitia appears as a huddle of houses on a bare rocky hillside. Once in the inner harbour the tree-lined esplanade fronting the harbour comes as an unexpected surprise. Here you can sit in

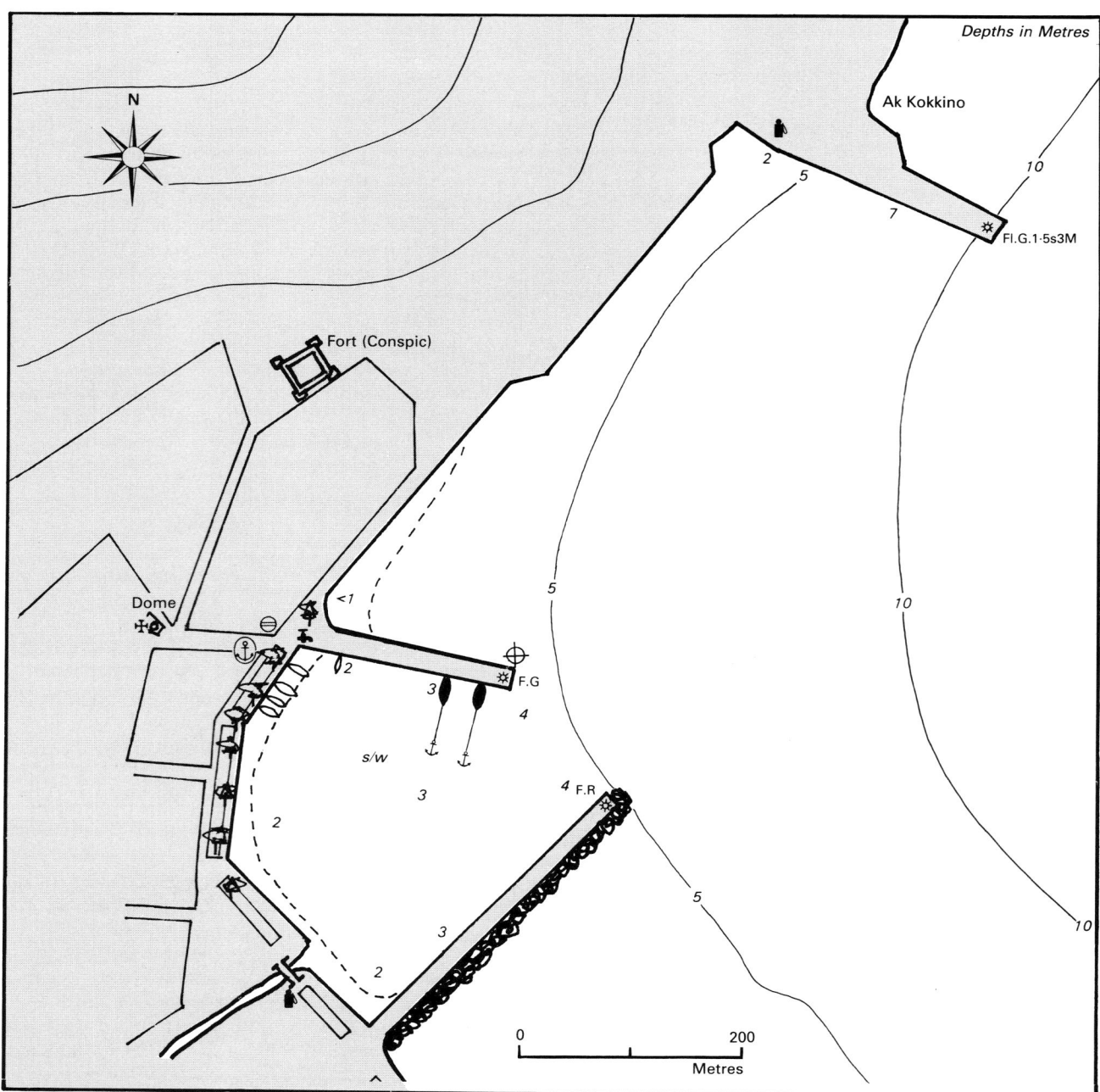

SITIA 35°12′·7N 26°06′·5E (F.G)

a friendly taverna over a good meal and watch dusk fall over the bay. Further inland is a green fertile plain mainly planted with vines. Sitia was formerly called La Sitia from whence the name of the province – Lasithi.

AK SIDHERO
Admiralty chart no. 1677

Approach
The lighthouse on the cape is easily identified. Approach the cape with caution because of the above- and below-water rocks fringing it. A night approach would be dangerous because of these rocks and reefs.

Dangers
1. *Ifalos Spitfaiar (Spitfire)* A detached reef lying 3 miles W of Ak Sidheros. It is difficult to see with any swell running.
2. *Vrakhoi Pinakl (Pinnacle)* Above and below-water rocks lying close off the coast just over a mile W of Ak Sidheros. The above-water rocks are easily identified.
3. *Nisis Sidhero* The islet half a mile W of Ak Sidheros. Approximately 200 metres N of the islet there is an isolated reef.
4. *Skopeloi Sidheros* The above and below-water rocks NNE of Ak Sidhero. The above-water rocks are easily identified.

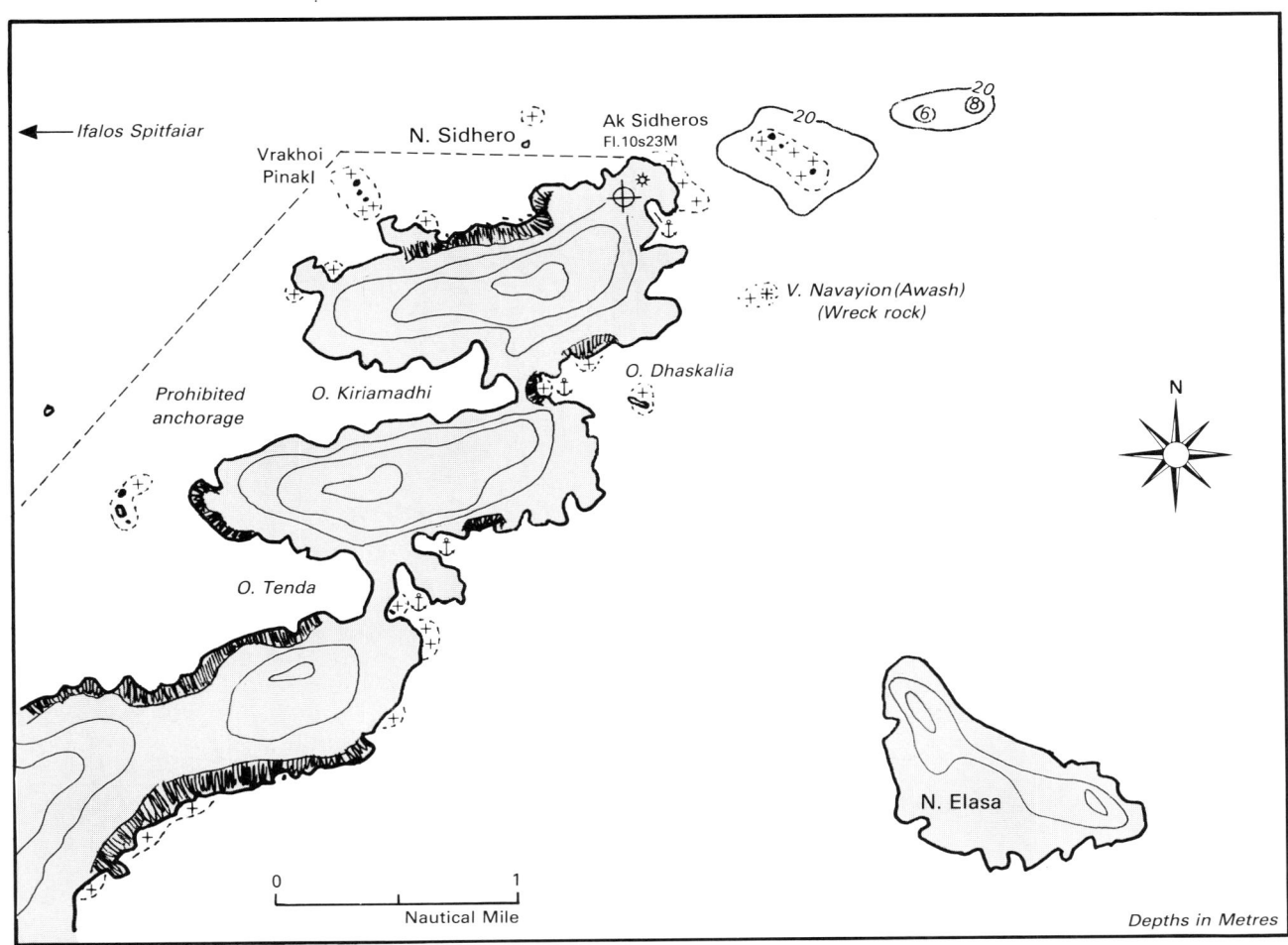

AK SIDHEROS 35°19′N 26°18′·7E (Ak Sidheros light)

5. *Vrakhoi Navayion* A reef just awash SE of Ak Sidheros.
6. Off the E side of Ak Sidheros a reef fringes the coast. It is just awash in places.

Mooring

By day anchor in any of the bays and coves shown on the plan. In the small cove immediately S of Ak Sidheros it is necessary to anchor fore and aft or take a long line ashore. The bottom is mostly sand, rock and weed.

Note It is prohibited to use the anchorages on the W side of Ak Sidheros which are designated as a military zone.

Facilities

None.

General

There are no inhabitants here, bar the lighthouse keeper and a few fishermen. The scenery is on a grand scale here and the isolation, the utter quiet and the razorback reefs surrounding the coast, can instill a sense of dread as the sun goes down.

Southern coast of Crete

NISIS GRAMVOUSA (Grambusa)

On the SE side of this island there is a bay sheltered from northerly winds (NW–NE). Anchor in the bay on the S side of Nisis Gramvousa in 3–6 metres. In southerlies anchor under the isthmus formed by Khersonisos Tigani. On Gramvousa there is a quay with reasonable depths where a yacht can go bows-to with care.

Water from a well by the chapel. No facilities. At one time the island was a notorious pirate stronghold until an Anglo-French expedition flushed the pirates out in 1828.

ORMOS KOUTRIS (anc. Phalasarna)

An indifferent anchorage off the ancient city and harbour of Phalasarna – suitable only in settled weather. The ancient harbour hewn from solid rock now lies some 6 metres above the present sea level.

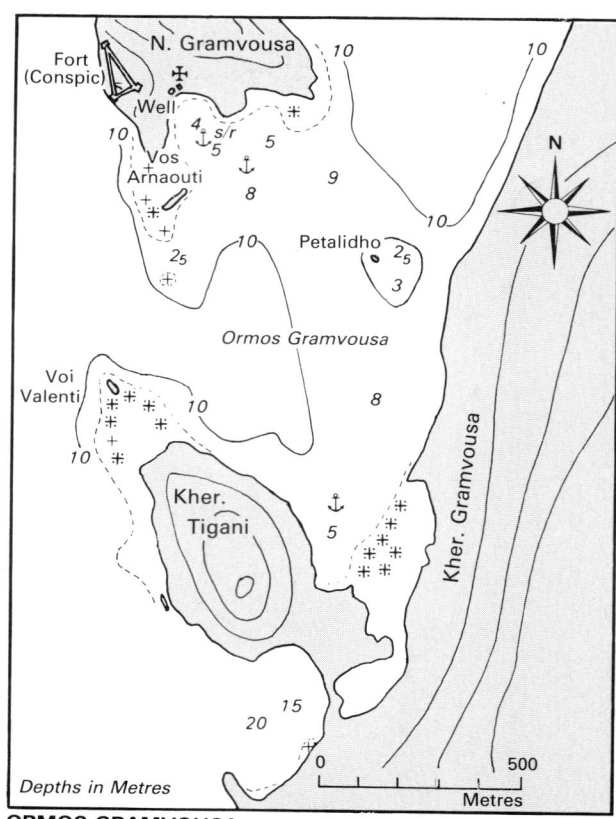

ORMOS GRAMVOUSA
35°36′N 23°35′E

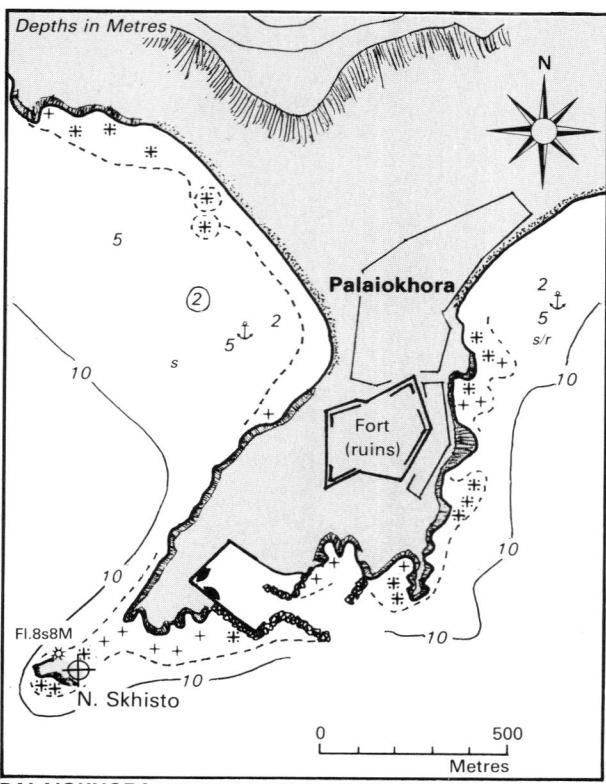

PALAIOKHORA 35°13′·3N 23°40′·3E (N. Skhisto light)
NOTE The harbour details should be used with caution
– reconnoitre first.

CAUTION

All along the S coast there are severe gusts off the high mountains with westerly and northerly winds. Care must be taken under these conditions as the squalls can be of exceptional violence. If a yacht is making a longish passage along the coast it is worthwhile standing off about 5 miles, as suggested by the Admiralty *Pilot*.

PALAIOKHORA (Palaeohora)
Admiralty chart no. 1633

An anchorage lying near the SW tip of Crete. A prominent headland with a fort on it is easily recognised. Go alongside or stern-to or bows-to in the new harbour on the E side of the rocky headland. Alternatively anchor on either side of the headland according to the wind direction.

Note the plan of the harbour must be interpreted with extreme caution. Reconnoitre first by dinghy. Work is in progress (1991) on the harbour. When complete it will offer good protection.

Palaiokhora. The new harbour looking S. *Nigel Patten*.

Loutro looking SW. *Nigel Patten.*

Water and fuel in the village. Good shopping for all provisions. Good tavernas. Bus to Khania. Palaiokhora has recently expanded into a prosperous tourist resort and a number of hotels have been built around the shores.

ORMOS FOINIKIAS AND ORMOS LOUTRO
Admiralty chart no. 1633

On either side of Ak Mouros shelter can be found depending on the wind direction. On the W side there is Ormos Foinikias sheltered from NE–E. On the E side there is Ormos Loutro offering better shelter from N–W–SW. In Ormos Loutro anchor in 4–10 metres off the village. The bottom is sand, good holding. Both bays are open to the S.

A few tavernas and limited provisions available ashore. Loutro is the ancient Phoenix described by St Luke in *Acts (27:12)* and was much used in those days by Alexandrian shipping.

SFAKION
An anchorage off the village of Sfakia suitable in calm weather. The once small village has become a booming tourist resort in recent years. Good tavernas and good shopping for all provisions. Daily buses to Khania.

NISOS GAVDHOS (anc. Claudia)
The island lying about 20 miles S of Ak Mouros. There is a small quay inside the SE tip that the *caïque* ferry from Palaiokhora uses. Two tavernas.

The population has dwindled over the years from some 350 families in 1945 to around 70 individuals today. The island is the most southerly point of Europe if you allow islands into the geographical framework. It is about a 40-minute walk to the village on the summit.

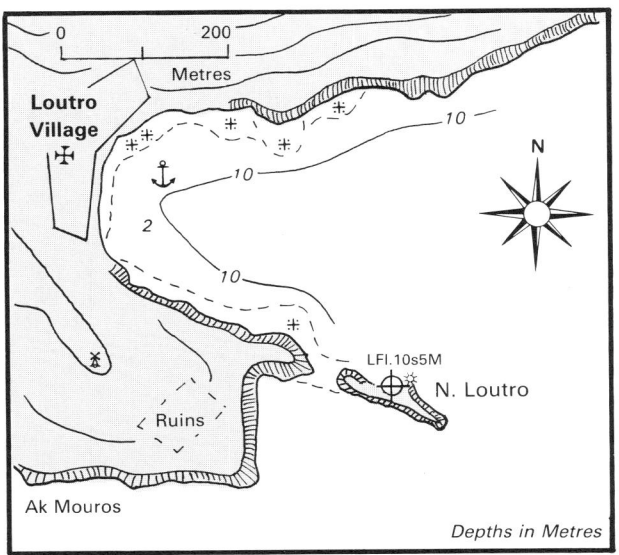

ORMOS LOUTRO
35°11'·8N 24°05'E (N. Loutro light)

FRANGOKASTELLI
An anchorage about 6 miles E of Sfakia. A deserted Venetian castle (hence the name 'Frank's castle') stands on the cape.

ORMOS PALKIA
Lies 8 miles E of Kakomouri headland. Suitable only in settled weather.

LIMNI
A cove at the foot of a ravine 5 miles E of Plakia. During the Second World War it was used to evacuate British, Australian and New Zealand troops from Crete to Egypt.

457

AY GALINI (Erimoupolis)
Admiralty chart no. 1633

Approach
From seaward the village and the mole are conspicuous. The end of the mole is lit: FR6M.

Mooring
Go stern-to or bows-to or alongside the quay. The bottom is sand – good holding. Good shelter from the prevailing summer winds, but dangerous in strong southerlies. Port police and customs.

Facilities
Water on the quay. Fuel in the town. Good shopping for all provisions. Good tavernas. PO. OTE. Buses to Iraklion and Rethimon.

General
At one time an important port for shipping produce from the hinterland, its importance declined when lorries began taking the produce to Iraklion for shipment. Recently it has become a popular tourist spot and a number of hotels have been built around the shore.

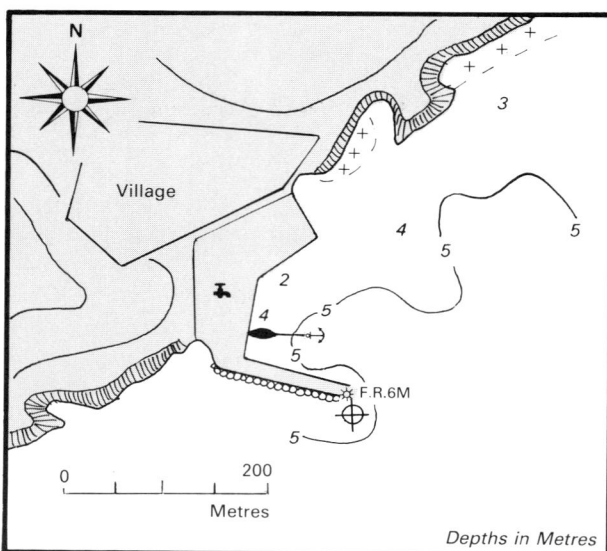

AY GALINI
35°05′·7N 24°41′·4E (F.R.6M)

MATALA
Admiralty chart no. 1633

A horseshoe-shaped bay on the W side of Ak Litinos. Suitable only in calm weather as the prevailing wind causes a swell to roll in. Good shopping for provisions and good tavernas ashore. Daily buses to Iraklion.

Matala is mentioned in the *Odyssey* as the place where Menelaus' ships were wrecked when returning from Troy. It was known to be an important Roman port and was used at least up until Byzantine times.

KALI LIMENES (Kalon Limenon)
Admiralty chart no. 1633

Approach
A small bay on the E side of Ak Litinos. A church on the S side of the bay and the oil storage tanks on Nisis Ay Pavlos are conspicuous. There is a light on Megalonisi: Fl(3)24s11M.

Mooring
Anchor in the bay in 3–6 metres. Good shelter from the N and W, but open to the E and S. It is also possible to anchor under Nisis Trafos to the E where some shelter from easterlies can be found. Port police and customs.

Facilities
Limited provisions and tavernas in the village.

General
Nisis Ay Pavlos is a bunkering station and the 'T' piers on the island are used by large ships. Kali Limenes (Fair Haven or Good Harbour) was visited by St Paul in AD59 when he was en route from Myra to Rome in a Roman corn ship. Bad weather had forced the ship to go south of Crete and it being late in the year, they considered wintering in Kali Limenes. Eventually a decision was made to leave and the ship was later wrecked in Malta.

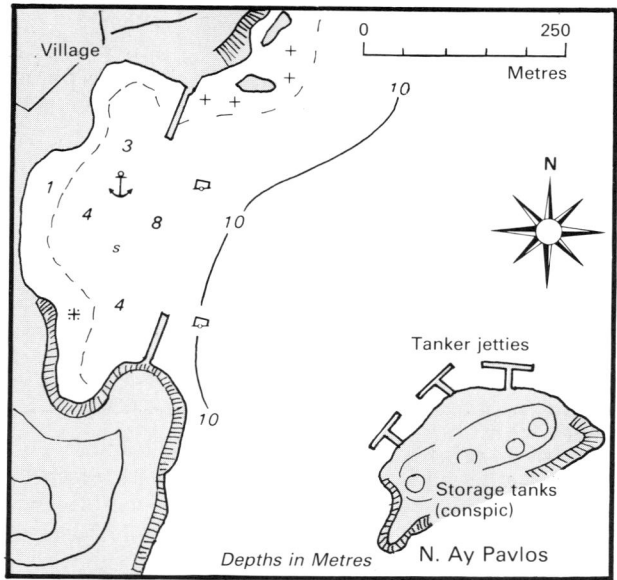

KALI LIMENES
34°56′N 24°48′E

NISOS GAIDHAROS (Donkey Island)
During strong southerlies a yacht can find a useful lee under the northern shores of the island. A *caique* ferry from Ierepetra runs tourists to the island in the summer. A taverna on the island.

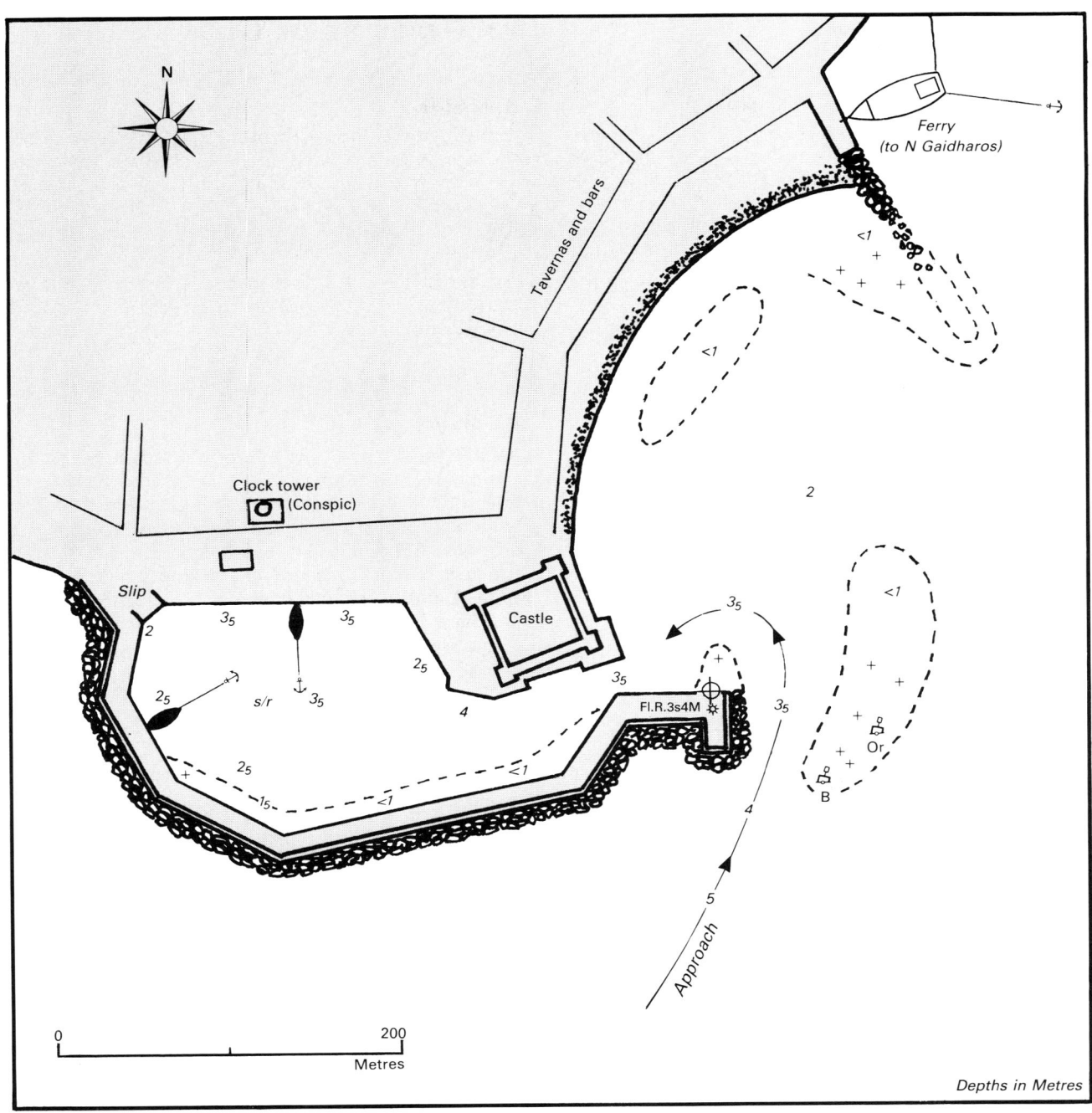

IEREPETRA
35°00′·3N 25°44′·4E (Fl.R.4M)

IEREPETRA
Admiralty chart no. 1633

Approach
Conspicuous The town at the foot of a plain is conspicuous from the distance. Closer in, a chimney in the town and the fort and a clock tower behind the harbour are conspicuous.

By night The entrance is lit (Fl.R.3s4M), but a night approach is hazardous because of the reefs and shoal water in the immediate approach.

Dangers
1. Care must be taken of the reef lying close off the entrance. In 1992 it was marked by two buoys, one with a black topmark and the other with an orange topmark. The entrance to the harbour is between the two buoys and the end of the breakwater. Care is needed as the violent winter storms in this area seem to rearrange the sea bottom.
2. With strong southerlies there is a confused swell off the entrance which makes the entry through the narrow entrance difficult.

Ierepetra looking SW.

Mooring

Go stern-to or bows-to the N or W side. The bottom is mud and rocks.

Shelter Good shelter except in strong southerlies when seas may come over the breakwater. In past winters the harbour wall has been repeatedly destroyed or partially destroyed.

Authorities Port police and customs.

Note For a number of years there have been plans to extend the outer mole, but it seems likely that for the present further work will be confined to repairing storm damage to the existing harbour.

Facilities

Water Near the quay.
Fuel In the town.
Repairs Some mechanical repairs. Hardware shops.
Provisions Good shopping for all provisions.
Eating out Good tavernas on the waterfront.
Other PO. OTE. Banks. Greek gas and *Camping Gaz*. Hire cars and motorbikes. Bus to Iraklion and Sitia. Ferry to Gaidharos.

General

Ierepetra (pronounced 'Erepetra') was an important town in Minoan and again in Roman times although few architectural remains are to be found today. Its importance now lies in its mild summer and winter climate: the nearby market gardens grow early produce for the European market and of late an increasing number of tourists have been attracted here. Several large hotels have been built around the shores of the bay to cater for the latter trade.

KOUFONISI (Kuphu Island)

These islands lie off the SE tip of Crete. They are uninhabited today, but Minoan and Roman ruins on the largest island indicate they were inhabited in earlier times.

KATO ZAKROS

A large sandy bay at the foot of a dramatic gorge. In settled weather anchor in the N of the bay. Care must be taken of a reef running out from the middle of the bay and of other rocks around the shore. Two tavernas on the shore.

At the foot of the gorge on an exquisite site are the ruins of a Minoan summer palace.

Kato Zakros. *Nigel Patten.*

ORMOS GRANDES

Admiralty chart no. 1677

The large bay on the N side of Ak Plaka. The best anchorage is at Kouremenos in the N of the bay where there is good shelter from the prevailing winds. Two miles to the N of Kouremenos is Vai where a yacht can anchor off. The sandy beach is easily identified by the extensive groves of palm trees along the foreshore. A yacht reported being anchored off Vai for two weeks in June and experiencing only the normal summer winds blowing off the land.

A hotel and tavernas ashore. 'Vai' is probably an old word for palms and the place is named on modern Greek charts as Finikodasos (palm grove).

Appendix

I. USEFUL ADDRESSES
National Tourist Organisation of Greece (NTOG)
United Kingdom
National Tourist Organisation of Greece, 4 Conduit Street, LONDON W1R DOJ. ☎ 0171-734-5997

United States
National Tourist Organisation of Greece, 645 Fifth Avenue, Olympic Tower, NEW YORK 10022. ☎ 421 5777

France
Office National Héllènique du Tourisme, 3 Avenue de l'Opéra, PARIS 75001. ☎ 1 42 60 65 75

Netherlands
Griekse Nationale Organisatie voor Tourisme, Leidsestraat 13, NS1017 AMSTERDAM. ☎ 25 42 12

Germany
Griechische Zentrale für Fremdenverkehr, Neue Mainzerstrasse 22, 6 FRANKFURT/MAIN. ☎ 236 562

Greece
National Tourist Organisation of Greece, 2 Amerikis Street, ATHENS. ☎ 01 3223 111

Consular offices in Greece
United Kingdom
Athens 1 Ploutarchou Street, 106 75 Athens ☎ (1) 7236211 *Fax* (1) 7241872

Corfu 2 Alexandras Avenue, 491 00 Corfu ☎ 661 30 055 *Fax* 661 37 995

Crete 16 Papa-Alexandrou St, 71202 Heraklion ☎ 81 224 012 *Fax* 81 243 935

Patras 2 Votsi Street, 262 21 Patras ☎ (61) 277 329 *Fax* (61) 225 344

Thessaloniki 8 Venizelou Street, Eleftheria Square, PO Box 10322, 541 10 Salonika ☎ 31 278 006 269 984

Syros 8 Akti P Ralli Hermoupolis, Syros 841 00 ☎ 281 22232/28922 Fax 281 23 293

Rhodes 11 Merikas St, 85100 Rhodes ☎ 24127 *Fax* 241 2205

United States
Leoforos Vas, Sofias 29, ATHENS. ☎ 712-951

Germany
Odos Karoli Kai, Dimitriou 3, ATHENS. ☎ 724-801

Yacht clubs
Hellenic Yachting Federation, 7 Akti Navarchou Kountourioti, 185 34 Piraeus ☎ 4137 351

Hellenic Open Sea Sailing Club, 4 Papadiamandi Street, Mikrolimani, PIRAEUS. ☎ 4123-537

Hellenic Yacht Club, Mikrolimani, PIRAEUS. ☎ 4127-575

Hellenic Yacht Club, 4 Metamorfosseos Street, KALAMAKI. ☎ 9829-948

Compressed air service stations
Hellenic Federation of Submarine Activities, ☎ 9819-961

Barracuda Club, Corfu

Corfu Naval Club. ☎ 30-470

Naval Athletic Club of Kalamaria, Thessaloniki. ☎ 412-068

Liami School, Piraeus

Aga-Chropi Co., 8 Markou Botsam Street, Drapetsona, Piraeus. ☎ 4615-260

III. USEFUL BOOKS AND CHARTS
Admiralty publications
Mediterranean Pilot Volume III (NP 47)
Covers the Ionian Sea.
Mediterranean Pilot Volume IV (NP 48)
Covers the Aegean Sea.
List of Lights Volume E (NP 78)
Mediterranean, Black and Red Seas.

Yachtsman's pilots
Imray Mediterranean Almanac editor Rod Heikell. Imray. A biennial publication with light lists, radio, astro ephemeris and the other associated information found in an Almanac.

The Ionian Islands to the Anatolian Coast: a sea-guide H. M. Denham. John Murray.

The Aegean: a sea-guide to its coasts and islands H. M. Denham. John Murray. Classic yachtsman's guides although no longer revised and kept up to date. Contain much interesting information particularly on naval history.

Saronic Rod Heikell. Tetra Publications Ltd. Covers the Saronic Gulf and eastern Peloponnese in detail.

Ionian Rod Heikell. Tetra Publications Ltd. Covers the Ionian only, in detail.

Hafenhandbuch Mittelmeer Teil V. Ostliches Mittelmeer. DSV – Verlag GmbH. Covers the Eastern Mediterranean from Albania to Cyprus. The extent of the area covered means that many harbours and anchorages are not mentioned at all. In German.

Hafen und Ankerplatze in Griechenland Gerd Radspieler. Covers the Ionian, Saronic Gulf and Eastern Peloponnese only. In German.

Guide Pratique de Grèce et Turquie Jacques Angles. Editions du Pen Duick. Covers the Dodecanese. In French.

Other guides

The Blue Guide to Greece Edited by Stuart Rossiter. A. and C. Black. The usual excellent quality of this series.

The Greek Islands Lawrence Durrell. Faber. Lots of glossy photographs and Durrell's own inimitable description of the islands.

The Greek Islands Ernle Bradford. Collins Companion Guide. An excellent background guide from an author who has sailed his own yacht around Greece.

Dumont Guide to the Greek Islands Edited by Evi Melas and translated by Russell Stockman. Stewart Tabori & Chang, NY; or Webb & Bower, UK. Good guide with glossy photos.

The Rough Guide to Greece Ellingham, Jansz and Fisher. Routledge and Kegan Paul. Down-to-earth guide.

The Mediterranean Greenpeace.

Berlitz Guides to Athens/Corfu/Crete/Greek Islands/ Peloponnese/Rhodes/Salonica and Northern Greece. Good, compact, and necessarily brief, guides.

The Peloponnese E. Karpodini-Dimitriadi. Ekdotike Athenon.

Prospero's Cell: a guide to the landscape and manners of the island of Corcyra Lawrence Durrell. Penguin. On Corfu.

Reflections on a Marine Venus: a companion to the landscape of Rhodes Lawrence Durrell. Penguin. On Rhodes.

Bitter Lemons Lawrence Durrell. Faber. On Cyprus.

Crete: Its Past, Present and People Adam Hopkins. Faber. Excellent general introduction to Crete.

Crete John Freely. Weidenfeld & Nicolson. Good guide.

Pausanias Guide to Greece Volumes I & II Translated by Peter Levi. Penguin. Pausanias was a doctor who spent twenty years travelling around Greece in the reign of Hadrian recording details of Greek cities, customs and beliefs. Interesting and useful to this day.

Herodotus The Histories (Historiai).

Greek Society Antony Andrewes. Pelican.

The World of Odysseus M. I. Finley. Penguin. Life in Homeric times.

The Penguin Atlas of Ancient History Colin McEvedy.

Fortresses and Castles of Greece Volumes I & II and *Fortresses and Castles of Greek Islands* Alexander Paradissis. Translated by S. A. Paradissis, Efstathiadis Brothers. The most detailed descriptive work on all Greek forts and castles. Published and readily available in Greece.

The Venetian Empire Jan Morris. Penguin. Very readable account of the Venetian maritime empire that touched so many Greek islands and coastal harbours, leaving its forts and castles everywhere. Recommended.

The Greek Adventure David Howarth. Collins. Excellent and very readable account of the Greek War of Independence.

The End of Atlantis J. V. Luce. Paladin. Good account of the Thira eruptions.

General

The Colossus of Maroussi Henry Miller. Penguin. A 'must' to read even if you are not going to Greece.

Zorba the Greek Nikos Kazantzakis. Faber.

Freedom and Death Nikos Kazantzakis.

Cavafy: a critical biography Robert Liddell. Duckworth. The biography of the forgotten poet of Alexandria.

The Alexandrian Quartet Lawrence Durrell.

The Poems of Catullus Translated by Peter Whigham. University of California Press.

Mani: travels in the Southern Peloponnese and *Roumeli: travels in Northern Greece* Patrick Leigh Fermor. Penguin. Contain much interesting and esoteric information on Greece and the Greeks in general as well as on the areas covered.

Eleni Nicholas Gage. Fontana. Easy read on the Civil War in Greece.

Hellas – A Portrait of Greece Nicholas Gage. Collins Harvill. Contains some interesting information not found in other 'portraits'.

A Literary Companion to Travel in Greece Edited by Richard Stoneman. Penguin.

Sappho to Shelley. Greek Literature: An Anthology. Edited by Michael Grant. Penguin.

The Jason Voyage: the quest for the Golden Fleece and *The Ulysses Voyage: sea search for the Odyssey* Tim Severin. Arrow Books (*Jason*) and Hutchinson (*Ulysses*). The conventional and unconventional interpretations of two ancient voyages after retracing the routes in a replica galley.

Gates of the Wind Michael Carroll. John Murray. Interesting account of the Northern Sporades.

Flora

Flowers of Greece and the Aegean Anthony Huxley and William Taylor. Chatto & Windus.

Flowers of the Mediterranean Anthony Huxley and Oleg Polunin. Chatto & Windus.

Both the above have excellent colour photographs and line drawings for identification.

Herbs of Greece Alta Niebuhr.

Trees and Bushes of Britain and Europe Oleg Polunin. Paladin. Excellent guide with colour photographs for identification.

Trees and Shrubs of Greece George Sfikas.

Marine life

Hamlyn Guide to the Seashore and Flora and Fauna of the Mediterranean A. C. Campbell. Comprehensive guide to Mediterranean marine life.

The Yachtsman's Naturalist M. Drummond and P. Rodhouse. Angus & Robertson. About Britain and northern Europe, but many species are common to the Mediterranean.

British Whales, Dolphins and Porpoises F. C. Fraser. As above.

Mediterranean Wildlife The Rough Guide. Peter Raine. Harrap-Columbus. Patchy guide that includes a chapter on Greece.

Fishes of Greece Published by the Efstathidis Group and available in Greece. A poor guide.

Dangerous Marine Animals B. W. Halstead, P. S. Auerbach and D. R. Campbell. Wolfe Medical. The standard reference work.

Food

Greek Cooking Robin Howe.

Food of Greece Vilma Chantiles.

The Best of Greek Cooking Chrissa Paradissis.

Food in History Reay Tannahill. Paladin. Contains some interesting details on Greek food as part of a general history.

British Admiralty charts

Chart	Title	Scale
176	Cap Bon to Ra's At Tin	1,175,000
180	Aegean sea	1,100,000
183	Ra's At Tin to Iskenderun	1,100,000
188	Entrance to the Adriatic sea	
	including Nisos Kerkira	300,000
189	West coast Nisos Sapientza to Nisos Paxoi	300,000
203	Nisos Zakinthos to Nisos Paxoi	150,000
206	Nisos Kerkira and approaches	150,000
	Vorion Stenon Kerkiras	25,000
224	Marmara Denizi	300,000
236	Hisaronu korfezi to Taslik burnu, including	
	Rodhos	300,000
682	Gulf of Kalamata (Kalamai)	74,300
720	Harbours and anchorages in the Ionian islands	
	Limin Ayias Evfimias	5,000
	Ormos Fiskardho: Limin Samis	7,500
	Ormos Ay Andreou: Ormos Pis'aetou:	
	Ormos Kioni: Ormos Polis: Ormos Vasilikis	10,000
	Ormos Pera Pigadhi	12,500
	Ormos Porou: Ormos Frikon	15,000
872	Kalimno to Rhodes, including the Gulfs of	
	Kos, Doris and Symi	220,000
1030	Southwest entrance channels to	
	the Aegean Sea	150,000
1031	Akra Yerakas to Nisos Kea	150,000
1037	N. Falkonera to N. Ios	150,000
1038	Steno Sifnou to Steno Kafirea	150,000
1040	Nisos Ios to Vrakhonisidhia Kondheliousso	150,000
1055	Rhodes Channel and Gokova Korfezi	150,000
1062	Nisos Vorioi, Nisos Sporadhes	150,000
1085	Kolpos Petalion to Strimonikos kolpos	
	including Thermaikos kolpos	300,000
1086	Strimonikos kolpos to Edremit korfezi	300,000
1087	Kolpos Petalion to Edremit korfezi	300,000
1091	Nisos Kitri	300,000
1196	Ports and anchorages on the east coast of	
	Greece:	
	Likhadhes nisoi	37,500
	Limin Stilidhos, Ormos Sourpis and Ormos	
	Mitzellas, Approaches to Limin Volou.	
	Ormos Skiathou	25,000
	Limin Volou	12,000
1439	Sicily to Kriti	1,100,000
1440	Adriatic sea	1,100,000
1513	Kolpos Elevsinas	25,000
1530	Samos strait	50,000
1537	Nisidhes Fournoi with the straits between	
	Nisos Samos and Nisos Ikaria	75,000
1541	Plans in the southern Kikladhes and	
	Nisos Astipaalaia	
	Nisos Thira	60,000
	Nisos Ios, Ormos Iou	15,000
	Nisos Astipalaia, Ormos Analipsis	15,000
	Nisos Amorgorgos, Ormos Katapola	10,000
	Nisos Folegandros, Ormos Karavostasi	10,000
	Nisos Ios, Ormos Manganari	10,000
	Nisos Astipalaia, Ormiskos Skala	7,500
	Nisos Thira, Ormos Thiras	5,000
	Nisos Thira, Ormos Athinios	5,000
1546	Samos strait to Güllük korfezi	103,300
	Kus Adasi roads	12,500
1554	Vorias Evvoikos Kolpos and approaches	
	to Volos	110,000
	Cont of Maliakos Kolpos	160,000

Chart	Title	Scale
1556	Vorios Evvoikos Kolpos and approaches	
	to Volos	110,000
	Cont of Maliakos Kolpos	110,000
1557	Port Argostoli	19,800
1568	Ports and anchorages in the eastern	
	Aegean sea:	
	Limin Karlovasi	5,000
	Limin Pithagoriou	10,000
	Ormos Psaron, Limin Khiou	12,000
	Poros Fournon: Ormos Bogazi and	
	Ormos Pasha	25,000
1596	Piraievs	12,500
1597	Petali gulf and the eastern part of the Euripo	
	(Evripos) channel	116,000
1598	Poros Megaron Ayios Theodhoroi and Elevsis	
	Elevsis	7,500
	Ayois Theodhoroi (oil terminal)	10,000
	Poros Megaron	12,500
1599	Ormos Falirou and Limenas Porou	
	Ormos Falirou	12,500
	Limenas Porou and approaches	15,000
1600	Akra Psaromita to Akra Ay Theodhoroi	100,000
	Ishmos Korinthou	25,000
1616	Kos anchorage	12,000
1631	Anchorages on the north coast of Kriti	
	Angirovolion Kastelliou	10,000
	Stenon Ay Theodhoron	12,500
	Ormos Gramvousa	15,000
	Ormos Koutris: Angirovolion Kolimvariou	75,000
1645	Nisos Khios and Izmir Korfezi	150,000
1647	Nisos Tinos to Nisos Ikaria	100,000
1657	Saronikos Kolpos	100,000
	Aiyina	10,000
1658	Plans on the north coast of Kriti:	
	Khania	6,000
	Limin Soudhas: Angirovolion Yeoryioupoleos	7,500
	Iraklion	18,000
	Rethimnon	18,000
	Ormos Soudhas	25,000
1665	Nisos Lesvos and Candarli korfezi to	
	Baba burnu	150,000
1666	Harbours and anchorages in the	
	Dhodhekanisos	
	Ormos Tristoma: Ormos Lindhou:	
	Limin Rodhou	10,000
	Ormos Vathi: Ormos Analipsis	12,000
	Limin Kastellorizou	18,000
	Ormos Lardhos: Approaches to Nisos Meyisti	
	(Nisos Kastellorizon)	50,000
1667	Rhodes island	98,400
1669	Harbours and anchorages in the	
	Dodecanese islands:	
	Limin Kalimnou	7,500
	Ormos Lakki: Ormos Alinda	10,000
	Limin Simis	12,500
	Ormos Partheni and approaches	20,000
	Approaches to Limin Skala	25,000
1671	Anchorages on the south coast of Nisos Dhia	10,000
1675	Nisos Lesvos, Mitilini	7,500
	Nisos Lesvos. Ormos Sigri	20,000
	Nisos Lesvos, entrance to	
	Kolpos Kallonis	20,000
	Nisos Lesvos, entrance to	
	Kolpos Yeras	25,000
	Turkey. Approaches to Ayvalik	50,000

1676	Prokolpos Patron to entrance of Korinthiakos Kolpos	100,000
1677	Anchorages on the north coast of Kriti: Ormos Pakhias Ammou; Ormos Erimoupolis:	
	Akra Sidheros: Ormos Ay Nikolaou	10,000
	Ormos Sitias	15,000
	Ormos Poru	18,000
	Ormos Grandes	24,000
	Akra Sidheros	40,000
1683	Harbours and anchorages on the southeast coast of Greece	
	Yithion	10,000
	Steno Spetson	25,000
	Kolpos Monemvasias	25,000
	Ormos Methonis	15,000
	Koroni	10,000
	Spetsai	7,500
	Navplion	7,500
	Limin Monenvasias	5,000
1685	Nisis Venetico to Nisos Spetsai including the channels between Akra Maleas and Kiriti	251,000
1687	Port and anchorages in the Aegean Sea	
	Kavalas	12,500
	Kolpos Kavalas and approaches	75,000
	Nea Karvali	20,000
	Stratonion	12,500
	Thasos	6,000
	Keramotis	20,000
	Porto Koufo	18,000
	Ormos Elevtheron	20,000
1707	Harbours and anchorages in Nisos Kriti	
	Ormoi Palaiokhoras	12,500
	Ormos Kaloi Limenes	12,500
	Ierapetra	10,000
	Ayios Nikolaos	10,000
	Iraklion	10,000
	Rethimnon	7,500
	Ormos Matala	7,500
	Sitia	7,500
	Khania	5,000
	Ay Galini	5,000
1825	Plans in Kikladhes	
	Ormos Kastro	7,500
	Ormos Fikiadha: Ormos Vathi: Ormos Faros: Ormos Merikha: Ormos Loutron	10,000
	Ormos Espiskopis and Ormos Apokriosis	15,000
	Ormos Platis Yialos: Ormos Foinikes: Ormos Ay Stefanou	20,000
1832	Plans in the Kikladhes	
	Ormos Milou: Stena Kimolou	37,500
	Angirovolion Karavostasi: Ormos Iou	12,000
	Limin Paroikias and Stenon Andiparou: Ormos Naousis	25,000
	Ormos Naxou	18,000
1833	Plans in the Kikladhes:	
	Limin Tinou	10,000
	Ormos Kamares: Ormos Koutala: Ormos Livadhiou: Limin Sirou: Ormos Ay Nikolaou: Limin Lavriou	12,000
	Ormos Korthiou	20,000
	Ormos Kastrou: Ormos Mikonou: Ormos Gavriou	25,000
	Approaches to Limin Sirou	37,500
1898	Islands of Kos, Niseros and Piskopi	114,000
2070	Approaches to Thessaloniki:	60,000
	Limenas Thessalonikis	10,000
	Ormos Thessalonikis	20,000
2404	Ports in south-western Greece:	
	Limenas Patron: Limenas Kalamatas	10,000
	Limin Killinis	12,500
	Ormos Zakinthou: Limenas Katakolou	15,000
	Ormos Navarinou	17,500
	Ormos Aiyiou	20,000
	Ormos Loutrakiou	20,000
2405	Ports in western Greece:	
	Dhioriga Levkadhos	15,000
	Preveza	20,000
	Krissaios Kolpos	25,000
	Approaches to Dhioriga Levkadhos and Preveza; Kolpos Andikiron	50,000
2406	Kerkira and Igoumenitsa with approaches	
	Igoumenitsa; Kerkira (Corfu)	7,500
	Approaches to Kerkira; approaches to Igoumenitsa	25,000
2682	Kolpos Petalion to Nisos Nisiros	300,000
2824	Scarpanto and Kaso islands (ancient Carpathos and Kassos)	73,000
2836A	Grecian Archipelago – southern sheet	600,000
2836B	Grecian Archipelago – northern sheet	600,000
3485	Port Plateali (Platea)	4,280
3496	Skrofa point to Cape Kamilafka	150,000
3678	Kriti – north coast. Rethimnon to Kolpos Merambellou	150,000
3679	Nisos Kriti to Nisos Karpathos	150,000
3680	Kriti – southern coast. O. Loutro to Ierapetra	150,000
3681	Kriti – western part	150,000
3923	Niseros and adjacent islands	45,000
3926	Lero island and approaches	45,000
3927	Patmos, Arki and Lipso	45,000

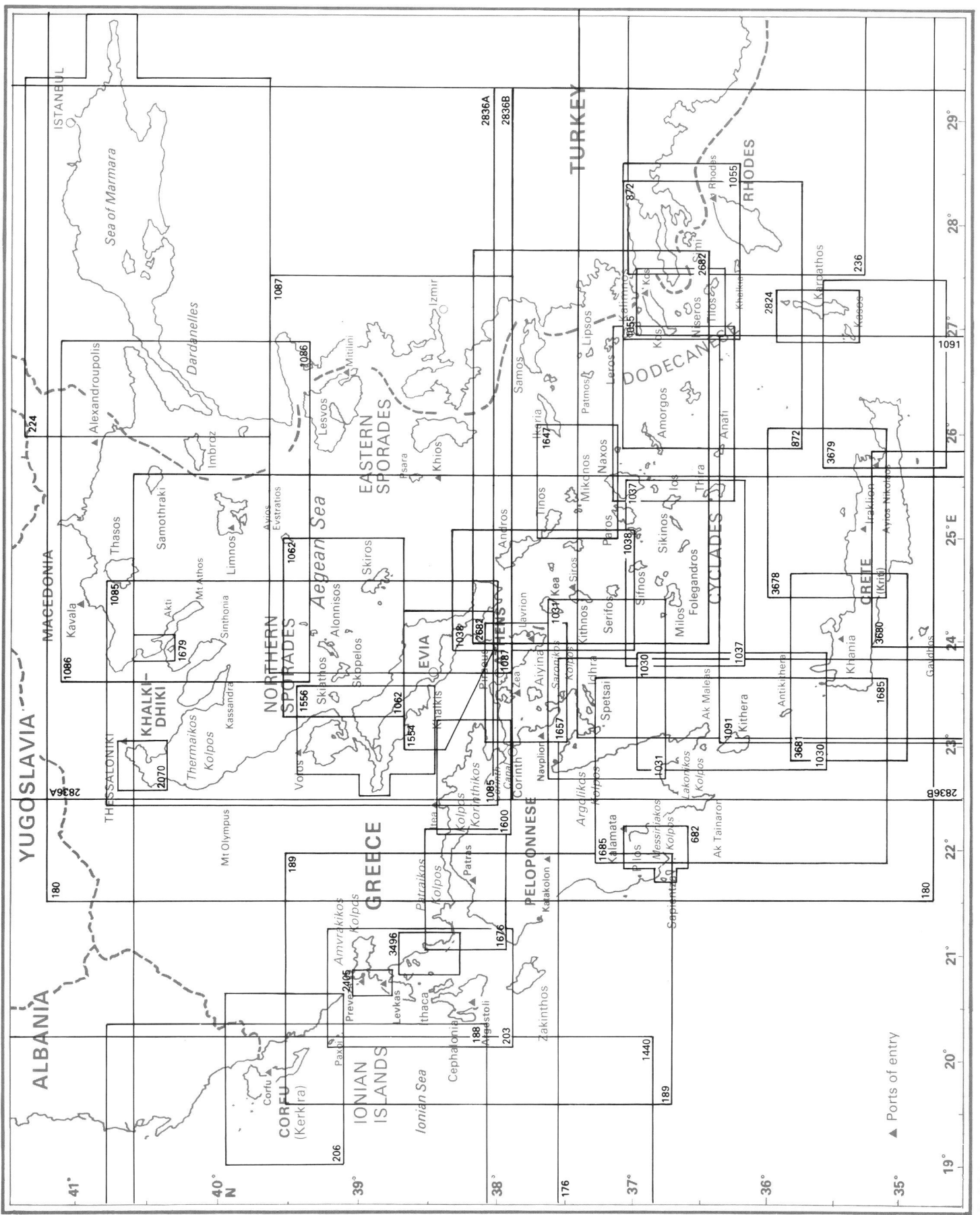

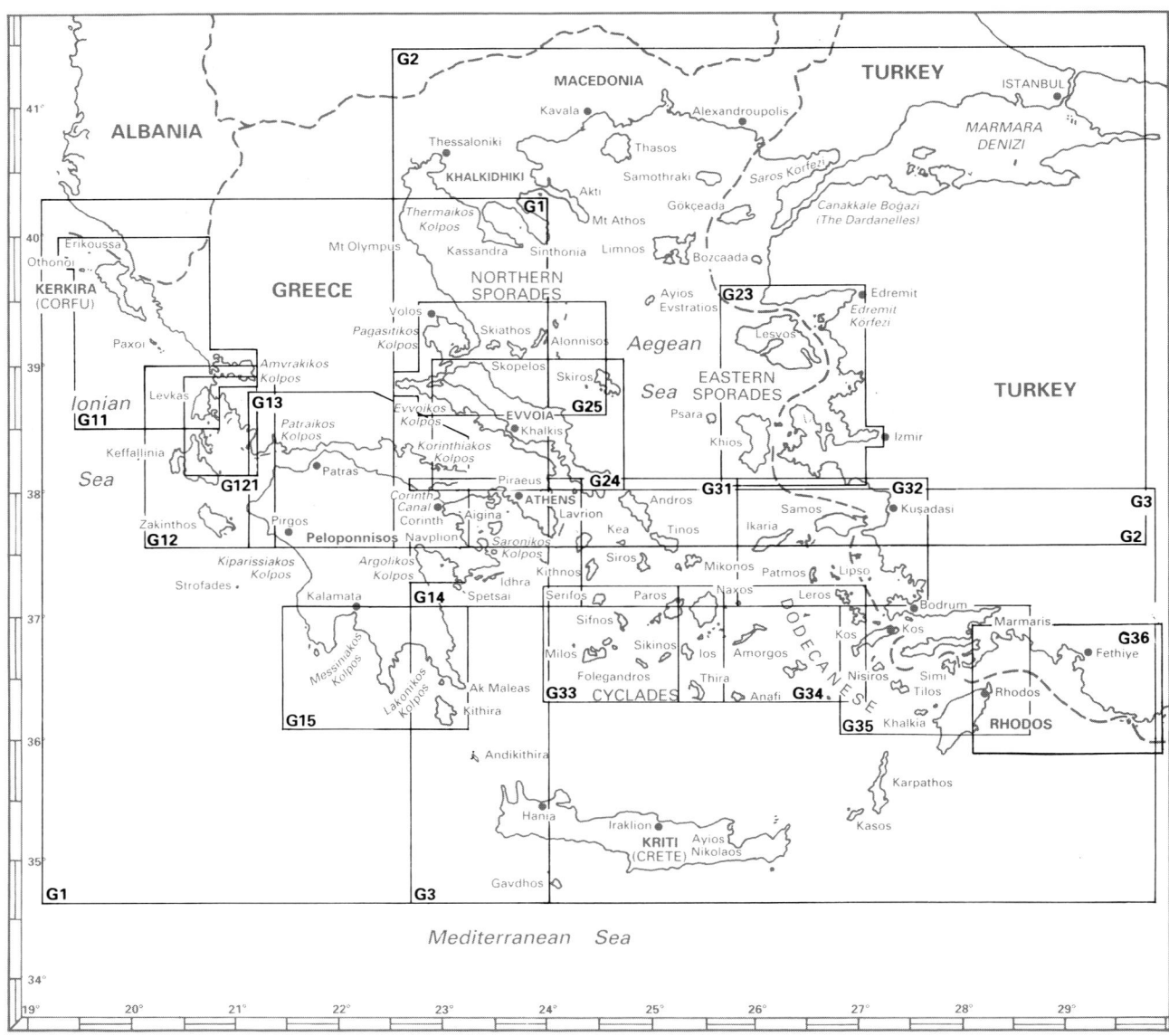

Imray-Tetra charts for the Mediterranean

Chart	Title	Scale
G1	Mainland Greece and the Peloponnisos Passage Chart	1:729,000
	Plans Approaches to Piraeus and Ormos Falirou	
G11	North Ionian Islands – Nisos Kerkira to Nisos Levkas	1:182,400
	Plans Ormos Gouvion (N. Kerkira), Vorion Stenou Kerkiras (N. Kerkira), Limin Kerkiras	
	Insets Amvrakikos Kolpos, Nisos Othonai	
G12	South Ionian Islands. Nisos Levkas to Nisos Zakinthos	1:188,200
	Plans Kolpos Aetou (N. Ithaki), Dhioriga Levkadhos (Levkas Canal), Ormos Argostoliou (N. Keffalinia), Ormos Zakinthou (N. Zakinthos)	

Chart	Title	Scale
G121	Inland Sea. Nisos Levkas to Nisos Kefallinia	1:93,400
	Plans Dhioriga Levkadhos (Levkas Canal), Ormos Vasilikas (N. Levkas), Ormos Fiskardho (N. Kefallinia), Ormos Ayias Eufimias (N. Kefallinia), Ormos Frikon (N. Ithaki)	
G13	Gulfs of Patras and Corinth	1:218,800
	Plans Mesolongi, Ormos Loutrakiou, Kiato, Patrai, Ormos Andikirou, Ormos Aiyiou, Krissaios Kolpos, Dhiorix Korinthou (Corinth Canal)	
G14	Saronic and Argolic Gulf	1:189,000
	Plans Marina Alimos, Ormos Falirou, Limin Porou (N. Poros), Steno Spetson (N. Spetsai), Limin Aigina (N. Aigina)	

466

G15	Southern Peloponnisos	1:189,700

G15 Southern Peloponnisos   1:189,700
Ormos Navarinou to Nisos Kithira
Plans Kalamata, Ormos Navarinou, Yithion,
Yefina (Monemvasia), Methoni Koroni

G2 Aegean Sea (North Part) Passage Chart 1:720,500
Plans Canakkale Bogazi (The Dardanelles)

G23 Eastern Sporades *In preparation*

G24 Nisos Evvoia *In preparation*

G25 Northern Sporades and North Nisos
Evvoia   1:183,800
Plans Linaria (Skiros), Ormos Skiathou
(N. Skiathos)

G3 Southern Aegean   1:758,800
Plan Limin Rhodos

G31 Northern Cyclades   1:189,700
Plans Ormos Mikonou (N. Mikonos),
Ormos Gavriou (N. Andros),
Limin A. Nikolaou (N. Kea),

G32 Southern Sporades and Coast of Turkey 1:189,700
Plans Kusadasi Liman (Turkey),
Limin Karlovasi (N. Samos),
Limin A. Kirikou (N. Ikaria), Steno
Samou (N. Samos), Limin Pithagoriou
(N. Samos), Ormos Patmou (N. Patmos)

G33 Southern Cyclades (Sheet 1 – West) 1:190,000
Plans Steno Kimolou (N. Kimolos),
Ormos Livadhiou (N. Serifos),
Steno Andiparou (N. Paros),
Ormos Naxou (N. Naxos),

G34 Southern Cyclades (Sheet 2 – East) 1:190,000
Plans Ormos Kalimnou (N. Kalimnos),
Ormos Maltezana (N. Astipalaia)

G35 Dodecanese and Coast of Turkey 1:190,000
Plans Bodrum, Rhodos, Kos, Marmaris
& Simi

G36 South Coast of Turkey   1:190,000
Marmaris to Kastellorizon
Plans Marmaris, Rhodos, Kastellorizon,
Approaches to Kastellorizon, Fethiye, Gocek

II. GLOSSARIES
USEFUL GREEK WORDS

IN THE TAVERNA

Greek salad *horiatiki salata*
yoghurt starter *tzatziki*
cod roe starter *taramasalata*
green salad *marouli salata*
cheese pie *tiropita*
stuffed vine leaves *dolmades*
stuffed tomatoes *dhomates yemistes*
stuffed green peppers *piperies yemistes*
cooked aubergine and tomato salad *melitzanes imam*
moussaka *moussaka*
beans *fassolia*
soup *soupa*
lamb *arni, arinaki*
beef chop *brizola mouskhari*
pork chop *brizola khirino*
kebab *souvlaki*
lamb in lemon sauce *arni avglolimoni*
meatballs *keftedes*
beef and onion stew *mouskhari stifado*
beef in tomato sauce *mouskhari kokinisto*
red mullet *barbouni*
tuna *tonna*
swordfish *xsfia*
mackerel *kolious*
sole *glossa*
baby squid *kalamares, kalamarakia*
octopus *octipothi*
prawns *garides*
crayfish *astakos*
fish soup with vegetables *psarossoupa*

SHOPPING

apples *mila*
apricots *verikoka*
aubergines *melitzanes*
baker *fourno*
beans *fassolia*
beef *mouskhari*
biscuits *biscottes*
bread *psomi*
butcher *hassapiko*
butter *voutiro*
carrots *carrotta*
cheese *tiri*
chicken *kotopoulo*
chocolate *socolata*
coffee *café*
cucumber *angouri*
eggs *avga*
fish shop *psaropolion*
flour *alevri*
garlic *scordo*
green pepper *piperes*
grocer *bakaliko*
ham *zambon*
honey *meli*

jam *marmelada*
lamb *arinaki*
lemon *limoni*
margarine *margarini*
meat *kreas*
melon (watermelon) *karpouzi*
milk *gala*
mutton *arni*
oil *lathi*
onions *kremidia*
oranges *portokalia*
parsley *maidano*
peach *rodakina*
pepper *piperi*
pork *khirino*
potatoes *patatas*
rice *rizi*
salt *alati*
sugar *zahari*
tea *tsai*
tomatoes *dhomates*
water *nero*
wine *crassi*
yoghurt *yaourti*

GENERAL

Yes *ne*
no *khi*
please *parakalo*
thank you *efharisto*
OK *endaksi*
hot *zeste*
cold *krio*
here *etho*
there *eki*
hello *herete*
goodbye *adio*
good morning *kalamera*
good evening *kalaspera*
good night *kalanikta*
good *kalo*
bad *kako*
today *simera*
tomorrow *avrio*
later *meta*
now *tora*
I want *ego thelo*
where is *pou inai*
big *megala*
small *mikro*
one *ena*
two *thio*
three *tria*
four *teissera*
five *pende*
six *hexa*
seven *epta*
eight *octo*
nine *eneia*
ten *theca*

GREEK NAMES AND TERMS FOUND ON CHARTS

Agios see Ayios
Akra (Ay) cape
Akrotirion promontory, cape
Aliki salt pan

Almira Salt marsh
Ammos sand
Anatoli east.
Anatolikos eastern
Andi- (Anti-) opposite
Angali bight
Angirovolion anchorage
Apano (Pano) up, upper
Aspro white
Avathi shallows
Avlax channel
Ayios (Ay) saint

Dhiavlos strait
Dhiorix canal
Dhitikos (Ditikos) western
Dhromos road

Elos marshy
Epinion small port
Eripion ruin
Evripos tidal channel
Exo outer
Fabrica factory
Faros lighthouse
Frourion four

Glossa tongue
Gremmos cliff

Ifalmiros brackish
Ifalos (If) reef
Ipsilos high
Isthmos isthmus

Kambos plain
Kastron castle
Kato lower
Kavos cape
Kefala head
Khersonisos (Kher) peninsula
Khoiradhodhis shoal
Kluara (Chora) main town or village of an island
Koilas natural hollow, valley
Kolpos (K.) gulf
Kolposis wide bay
Korifi, Kerfi peak, summit

Lakka large pit, watercourse
Levkos white
Limeniskos small harbour
Limin (L.) harbour
Limni lake, marsh
Livadhi meadow, pasture
Lofos hill
Longos wood, grove
Loutra baths, spa

Makriopounda salient point
Mandraki small sheep-fold
Mavros black
Megalos/Megas big
Mikros small
Milion mile
Miti cape
Molos breakwater, mole
Moni monastery

Neos new
Nero water
Nisis/Nisaki islet
Nisos/Nisia (N.) island
Notios southern

Ormos (O.) bay
Oros mountain
Palaios old
Pralia coast
Pelagos sea
Perama ferry
Petra rock
Pirgos tower
Platis broad
Polis city, town
Poros strait, ford
Porto small harbour
Potamos (Pot) river
Pounda cape, point

Revma current, stream

Simandir buoy
Skala quay, stairway, small port
Skopelos (Skop) reef
Stavros cross
Stenon strait

Telonion customs house
Thalassa sea

Vassilikos royal
Vathi deep
Vorios northern
Vrakhonisis (Vrak) rocky islet
Vrakhos rock

GREEK NAUTICAL TERMS

Albouro mast
Aristera port, left
Axion propeller shaft
Dexia starboard, right
Flokos jib
Hellico propeller
Karina keel
Ksilino wood
Kouverta deck
Lagouthera tiller
Lasca pay out, slacken
Matsa boom
Mezzana mizzen
Mihani motor
Pani sail, mainsail
Plastico plastic, GRP
Plori bow
Primi stern
Skini rope
Timoni tiller, helm
Vira haul in, tighten

IV. CONVERSION TABLES

metres–feet

m	ft/m	ft
0·3	1	3·3
0·6	2	6·6
0·9	3	9·8
1·2	4	13·1
1·5	5	16·4
1·8	6	19·7
2·1	7	23·0
2·4	8	26·2
2·7	9	29·5
3·0	10	32·8
6·1	20	65·6
9·1	30	98·4
12·2	40	131·2
15·2	50	164·0
30·5	100	328·1

centimetres–inches

cm	in/cm	in
2·5	1	0·4
5·1	2	0·8
7·6	3	1·2
10·2	4	1·6
12·7	5	2·0
15·2	6	2·4
17·8	7	2·8
20·3	8	3·1
22·9	9	3·5
25·4	10	3·9
50·8	20	7·9
76·2	30	11·8
101·6	40	15·7
127·0	50	19·7
254·0	100	39·4

metres–fathoms–feet

m	fathoms	ft
0·9	0·5	3
1·8	1	6
3·7	2	12
5·5	3	18
7·3	4	24
9·1	5	30
11·0	6	36
12·8	7	42
14·6	8	48
16·5	9	54
18·3	10	60
36·6	20	120
54·9	30	180
73·2	40	240
91·4	50	300

kilometres–statute miles

km	M/km	M
1·6	1	0·6
3·2	2	1·2
4·8	3	1·9
6·4	4	2·5
8·0	5	3·1
9·7	6	3·7
11·3	7	4·3
12·9	8	5·0
14·5	9	5·6
16·1	10	6·2
32·2	20	12·4
48·3	30	18·6
64·4	40	24·9
80·5	50	31·1
120·7	75	46·6
160·9	100	62·1
402·3	250	155·3
804·7	500	310·7
1609·3	1000	621·4

kilograms–pounds

kg	lb/kg	lb
0·5	1	2·2
0·9	2	4·4
1·4	3	6·6
1·8	4	8·8
2·3	5	11·0
2·7	6	13·2
3·2	7	15·4
3·6	8	17·6
4·1	9	19·8
4·5	10	22·0
9·1	20	44·1
13·6	30	66·1
18·1	40	88·2
22·7	50	110·2
34·0	75	165·3
45·4	100	220·5
113·4	250	551·2
226·8	500	1102·3
453·6	1000	2204·6

litres–gallons

l	gal/l	gal
4·5	1	0·2
9·1	2	0·4
13·6	3	0·7
18·2	4	0·9
22·7	5	1·1
27·3	6	1·3
31·8	7	1·5
36·4	8	1·8
40·9	9	2·0
45·5	10	2·2
90·9	20	4·4
136·4	30	6·6
181·8	40	8·8
227·3	50	11·0
341·0	75	16·5
454·6	100	22·0
1136·5	250	55·0
2273·0	500	110·0
4546·1	1000	220·0

Useful conversions

1 inch = 2.54 centimetres (roughly 4in = 10cm)
1 centimetre = 0.394 inches
1 foot = 0.305 metres (roughly 3ft = 10 metres)
1 metre = 3.281 feet
1 pound = 0.454 kilograms (roughly 10lbs = 4.5 kgms)
1 kilogram = 2.205 pounds
1 mile = 1.609 kilometres (roughly 10 miles = 16 km)
1 kilometre = 0.621 miles
1 nautical mile = 1.1515 miles
1 mile = 0.8684 nautical miles
1 acre = 0.405 hectares (roughly 10 acres = 4 hectares)
1 hectare = 2.471 acres
1 gallon = 4.546 litres (roughly 1 gallon = 4.5 litres)
1 litre = 0.220 gallons

Temperature scale

t°F to t°C is 5/9 (t°F − 32) = t°C
t°C to t°F is 9/5 (t°C + 32) = t°F

So		
70°F = 21.1°C	20°C = 68°F
80°F = 26.7°C	30°C = 86°F
90°F = 32.2°C	40°C = 104°F

V. COMMUNICATIONS

ISTANBUL

Sea of Marmara

TURKEY

Dardanelles

Izmir

Imbroz

RHODES

Rhodes

Simi

Karpathos

Kasos

Tilos

Niseros

Kos

Kalimnos

Leros

Lipsos

Patmos

DODECANESE

Samos

Ikaria

Khios

Psara

Lesvos

Mitilini

Ayios Evstratios

EASTERN SPORADES

Aegean Sea

Amorgos

Anafi

Naxos

Ios

Thira

Sikinos

Folegandros

Mikonos

Tinos

Andros

Paros

Siros

Kea

Kithnos

Sifnos

Serifos

Milos

CYCLADES

Iraklion

Ayios Nikolaos

CRETE (Kriti)

Khania

Gavdhos

Antikithira

Alexandroupolis

MACEDONIA

Kavala

Keramoti

Thasos

Samothraki

Limnos

Mirina

Mt Athos

Akti

Sinthonia

Kassandra

THALKI-DHIKI

Thermaikos Kolpos

Thessaloniki

YUGOSLAVIA

ALBANIA

Ioannina

Mt Olympus

Larissa

Volos

NORTHERN SPORADES

Skiros

Alonnisos

Skopelos

Sitos

EVIA

Khalkis

GREECE

Patraikos Kolpos

Itea

Kolpos Korinthikos

Patras

Corinth Canal

Corinth

Navplion

Amvrakikos Kolpos

Preveza

Levkas

Ithaca

Paxoi

Cephalonia

Argostoli

Zakinthos

Killini

Katakolon

Pilos

Sapienza

Kalamata

Messiniakos Kolpos

Tripoli

PELOPONNESE

Spetsai

Idhra

Ak Maleas

Lakonikos Kolpos

Ak Tainaron

Kithira

Athens

Piraeus

Saronikos Kolpos

Aiyina

KERKIRA CORFU (Kerkira)

IONIAN ISLANDS

Ionian Sea

470

Greece – Airports and ferry routes

Index